# Management Information Systems

*Solving Business Problems with Information Technology*

**Second Edition**

**GERALD V. POST**
*University of the Pacific*

**DAVID L. ANDERSON**
*DePaul University*

Irwin
McGraw-Hill

Boston • Burr Ridge, IL • Dubuque, IA • Madison, WI • New York
San Francisco • St. Louis • Bangkok • Bogotá • Caracas • Lisbon
London • Madrid • Mexico City • Milan • New Delhi • Seoul
Singapore • Sydney • Taipei • Toronto

***McGraw-Hill Higher Education***

*A Division of The **McGraw-Hill** Companies*

MANAGEMENT INFORMATION SYSTEMS
SOLVING BUSINESS PROBLEMS WITH INFORMATION TECHNOLOGY
Copyright © 2000, xxxx by The McGraw-Hill Companies, Inc. All rights reserved.
Printed in the United States of America. Except as permitted under the United States
Copyright Act of 1976, no part of this publication may be reproduced or distributed in
any form or by any means, or stored in a data base or retrieval system, without the prior
written permission of the publisher.

This book is printed on acid-free paper.

domestic       1 2 3 4 5 6 7 8 9 0 DOW/DOW 9 0 9 8 7 6 5 4 3 2 1 0 9
international   1 2 3 4 5 6 7 8 9 0 DOW/DOW 9 0 9 8 7 6 5 4 3 2 1 0 9

ISBN 0-07-229756-5        3 2280 00679 5108

Publisher: *David Brake*
Senior sponsoring editor: *Rick Williamson*
Developmental editor: *Christine Wright*
Senior marketing manager: *Jodi McPherson*
Project manager: *Margaret Rathke Bogovich*
Production supervisor: *Michael R. McCormick*
Designer: *Jennifer McQueen Hollingsworth*
Cover illustrator: *Wendy Grossman*
Photo research coordinator: *Sharon Miller*
Supplement coordinator: *Mark Sienicki*
Compositor: *Shepherd Incorporated*
Typeface: *10/12 Times Roman*
Printer: *R. R. Donnelley & Sons Company*

**Library of Congress Cataloging-in-Publication Data**

Post, Gerald V.
    Management information systems : solving business problems with
information technology / Gerald V. Post, David L. Anderson. — 2nd
ed.
        p.    cm.
    Includes bibliographical references and index.
    ISBN 0-07-229756-5
    1. Management information systems.  I. Anderson, David L. (David
Lee), 1953–   . II. Title.
HD30.213.P67 2000
658.4'038—dc21                                                99–16364

INTERNATIONAL EDITION ISBN 0-07-116978-4
Copyright © 2000. Exclusive rights by The McGraw-Hill Companies, Inc. for
manufacture and export. This book cannot be re-exported from the country to which it is
consigned by McGraw-Hill. The International Edition is not available in North America.

www.mhhe.com

*To my parents,*
*for emphasizing the value of education,*
*and the joy of a good book.*

Jerry

*To my father and mother,*
*sister and brother-in-law,*
*for their support and encouragement*
*throughout the education and writing process.*

David

At McGraw-Hill Higher Education, we publish instructional materials targeted at the higher education market. In an effort to expand the tools of higher learning, we publish texts, lab manuals, study guides, testing materials, software, and multimedia products.

At Irwin/McGraw-Hill (a division of McGraw-Hill Higher Education), we realize technology will continue to create new mediums for professors and students to manage resources and communicate information with one another. We strive to provide the most flexible and complete teaching and learning tools available and offer solutions to the changing world of teaching and learning.

# Irwin/McGraw-Hill is dedicated to providing the tools necessary for today's instructors and students to navigate the world of Information Technology successfully.

Seminar Series - Irwin/McGraw-Hill's Technology Connection seminar series offered across the country every year, demonstrates the latest technology products and encourages collaboration among teaching professionals.

Osborne/McGraw-Hill - A division of the McGraw-Hill Companies known for its best-selling Internet titles *Harley Hahn's Internet & Web Yellow Pages* and the *Internet Complete Reference,* offers an additional resource for certification and has strategic publishing relationships with corporations such as Corel Corporation and America Online. For more information, visit Osborne at *www.osborne.com.*

Digital Solutions - Irwin/McGraw-Hill is committed to publishing Digital Solutions. Taking your course online doesn't have to be a solitary venture. Nor does it have to be a difficult one. We offer several solutions, which will let you enjoy all the benefits of having course material online. For more information, visit *www.mhhe.com/solutions/index.mhtml.*

Packaging Options - For more about our discount options, contact your local Irwin/McGraw-Hill Sales representative at 1-800-338-3987, or visit our web site at *www.mhhe.com/it.*

# *Preface*

## A TALE OF TWO CAREERS

Jack Lewis had it made. Or so he thought. A number of well-timed promotions at his Midwest publishing firm, W.C. Green, Inc., had landed him comfortably in the role of marketing director of the educational book division. Unlike many of his colleagues, Jack tried to keep up with the latest changes in information technology. He entered data into spreadsheets to create color graphs for budgets and expenses. His reports were created with professionally designed word-processing templates. The dark mahogany desk, the 180-degree view of the duck pond, and the $30,000 of computer hardware and software in his office were testament to his success. Then it happened. A competitor developed an information system that used advanced technology to deliver custom books to students on demand over the Internet. Caught without a competitive marketing strategy, W.C. Green saw sales drop dramatically. Driving home after losing his job, Jack still could not figure out what went wrong.

Julie Nilar just wouldn't quit. She too had a marketing degree like Jack, but decided not to pursue a traditional career right out of college. A nationally ranked bicycle racer, on graduating she chose to develop her cycling skills in international competition, and dreamed of being chosen for the U.S. Women's Olympic Road Team in the year 2000. To pay the bills she got a part-time job as a marketing representative for Rolling Thunder bicycles, a small Colorado mail-order service providing custom-made bicycles to a national customer base. Because international competition kept Julie away for long periods of time, she always took her laptop with her to stay in touch with the office. No stranger to information technology, one project she developed during these long absences was a powerful database that kept track of Rolling Thunder's suppliers, customers, and their orders. This application became a powerful tool for Rolling Thunder and one which led to greatly increased productivity for the company.

## MANAGERS AND INFORMATION TECHNOLOGY

As these two contrasting scenarios demonstrate, continual improvements and advances in information technology (IT) are encouraging even more changes to business and society. Managers and business professionals who use IT not only to present and deliver information but also to solve their business problems will reap the rewards while those who do not will be left behind to ponder what went wrong.

The last few years brought exciting changes to managers, and the future promises even more. Increased competition forces organizations to cut costs and operate with fewer managers. The growth of small businesses encourages entrepreneurs to run their own businesses and consulting firms. Continual performance improvements, expanded storage capacity, increased capabilities of software, and the Internet affect all aspects of management.

The exponential growth of the Internet is exceeding all forecasts. The Internet holds the potential to revolutionize virtually all aspects of business. Consumers are presented with more choices and more data. Companies have more ways to track customer actions and preferences. Investors have instant access to data around the world. Managers have more ways to communicate and share ideas.

Continuous changes in IT present two challenges: learning to use it and finding new opportunities to improve management. Most students have taken a hands-on course that teaches them how to use a computer and application software. Many expect the introductory MIS course to be more of the same—hands-on computer usage tied to specific needs. However, there are more complex and interesting problems to be solved. Managers need to apply their knowledge of IT tools to solve management problems and find new opportunities to improve their organizations. The focus of this book is to investigate the more complex question: How can we use IT to improve our performance in the business environment?

## Features that Focus on Solving Problems

**ABOUT THE BOOK**    Each chapter contains several unique features to assist in understanding the material and in applying it to analyze and solve business problems.

- **What You Will Learn in This Chapter.** A series of questions that highlight the chapter's key issues.
- **Lead Case.** An introductory, real-world case illustrates the problems explored in the chapter.
- **Overview.** A brief summary of the chapter's goal and outline.
- **Trends.** Sidebar boxes that present major changes, brief histories, or trends that affect the topics in the chapter.
- **Reality Bytes.** Brief applications, mini-cases, and discussions that emphasize a specific point, highlight international issues, business trends, or ethics. They also illustrate problems and solutions in the real world. The following is an example of a Reality Bytes box from Chapter 1.

---

### Reality Bytes      1–5    Making Money on the Internet

For years, much of the content on the Internet has been offered free to users. Yet, it costs money to create and maintain web sites, and someone has to bear this cost. The two basic choices are (1) charge users for the content, or (2) sell advertising space. Increasingly, web sites are turning to advertising revenue. In 1998, marketers spent slightly over $2 billion on Internet advertising. Experts were predicting substantial increases in advertising. Only a few elite companies like *The Wall Street Journal* have been able to make any money through subscriptions. With the expansion of the Internet, even more exciting possibilities exist. For example, many vendors have discussed embedding Internet access into everyday appliances. One expert, Mr. Cutler of Net.Genesis, suggests the possibility of companies providing free Internet-enabled toasters, where the toaster would burn a new ad into your toast each morning. He suggests: "You see that ad impression while you are buttering your toast. In exchange for your time, you get a free toaster. How badly would Procter & Gamble love to be able to target you at that key moment?"

- **Chapter Summary.** A list of the chapter topics.
- **A Manager's View.** A short summary of how the chapter relates to managers and to the overall question of how information technology can improve management.
- **Key Words.** A list of words introduced in that chapter. A full glossary is provided at the end of the text.
- **Review Questions.** Designed as a study guide for students.
- **Exercises.** Problems that apply the knowledge learned in the chapter. Many utilize common application software for solving the problem.
- **Additional Reading.** References for more detailed investigation of the topics.
- **Industry-Specific Cases.** In-depth discussion of the lead case and several other companies. Each chapter highlights a specific industry and compares different approaches to the problems faced by the firms.

| CHAPTER | INDUSTRY |
|---------|----------|
| 1 | Fast Food |
| 2 | Entrepreneurial Business |
| 3 | Specialty Retail |
| 4 | Retail Sales |
| 5 | Airlines |
| 6 | Wholesale Trade |
| 7 | Automobiles |
| 8 | Computer Hardware |
| 9 | Package Delivery |
| 10 | Franchises |
| 11 | Travel |
| 12 | Government Agencies |
| 13 | Financial Services |
| 14 | Health Care |

- **Discussion Issue.** A brief dialogue between managers to highlight a specific topic. Most emphasize ethical issues. The discussion and related questions form a starting point for class discussions.
- **Appendix.** Hands-on application and demonstration of various tools to help managers solve common business problems.

## Goals and Philosophy

- All of the chapters emphasize the goal of understanding how information technology can be used to improve management. The focus is on understanding the benefits and costs of technology and its application.
- The role and importance of *objects* in understanding information technology is emphasized. The object approach is bringing major changes to the application development and the use of technology. A firm grasp of the concepts makes it easier to use new applications, analyze business situations, and communicate with IT developers. The use and managerial importance of object-oriented technology are highlighted throughout the text.

- An emphasis on the importance of database management systems. Increasingly, managers need to retrieve data and utilize a DBMS to investigate, analyze, and communicate.

- An emphasis on the importance of communication and integration of data. Understanding information technology requires more than knowledge of basic application packages. Students need to use and understand the applications of technologies like OLE, Notes, and the Internet.

- Students increasingly want to know how technology is used to solve problems in their chosen major/functional area. Several current applications, including hands-on exercises, are highlighted in Chapter 9. The applications can be expanded to even more detail depending on the background of the students.

- In-depth, industry-specific cases that illustrate the use of technology. By focusing each chapter on a specific industry, students can understand and evaluate a variety of approaches. Many cases illustrate companies varying over time, so students can see the changes occurring in business, and understand the evolving role and importance of information technology.

- Rolling Thunder Database. A medium-sized, detailed database application of a small business is available on CD-ROM with each copy of the text. Specific Rolling Thunder exercises are highlighted in each chapter with an icon. The database, in Microsoft Access format, contains data and applications suitable for operating a small (fictional) firm. Students can practice finding and organizing data, creating tables, generating reports, and examining many aspects of a complete database application, including the code that drives the application. It also contains data generation routines so instructors can create their own scenarios. More information on how to utilize this application in your course is included in the Instructor Resources.

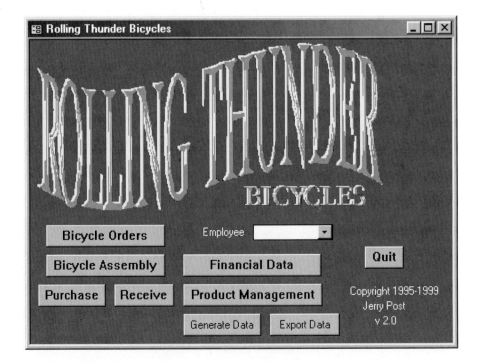

## Changes to the Second Edition

Some exciting changes have arisen in information systems and in education. This edition was written in response to the continued growth of the Internet, the expansion of enterprise software, and the student demand for applications. Changes to this edition directly reflect reviewer feedback on important topics and features. Each chapter has been updated and revised, but significant updates include:

- **The Internet and Electronic Commerce.** The Chapter 6 coverage of networks and the Internet has been expanded and updated. However, the Internet and electronic commerce are discussed throughout the text and in most of the cases. Although the Internet is a major change factor in business and society, the concepts behind the Internet (networks, transactions, decision support, and so on) are the same as they have always been in MIS. So, it is easier to discuss their applications with each chapter.

- **Enterprise Resource Planning and Integration.** Chapter 7 on Integration has been completely rewritten to highlight the capabilities and importance of ERP products. The emphasis is on the business need to integrate data. The chapter begins with the business issues and then shows how ERP products support managers.

- **Workgroups and Teamwork.** Chapter 7 includes a more detailed explanation of the software tools available to support workgroups, joint authorship, and shared documents.

- **New Industry-Specific Cases and Reality Bytes.** All of the chapter cases and most of the Reality Bytes examples have been replaced or rewritten. To make room for the appendices, there are now fewer cases in the text. However, all of the cases and Reality Bytes from the first edition are on the web site for the book (www.mhhe.com/ business/mis/post).

- **Rolling Thunder Bicycle Company.** This database application has been integrated into more chapters, and exercises have been added to every chapter. In particular, note the object-oriented description in Chapter 3 that serves as a good introduction to the details of the company.

- **Application Appendix.** Every chapter has an application appendix that examines a hands-on topic. These appendices provide a new level of instruction, enabling the instructor to focus on hands-on applications that are relevant to the specific chapters. Each appendix has sample applications and a set of Exercises that illustrate the topic. The Exercises can also be combined with the Rolling Thunder Bicycle case—providing a small but realistic illustration of decision making and management in a real-world environment. The topics can be covered in class, in a lab, or given as assignments. PowerPoint slides and the sample application files are all available on the Instructor CD-ROM.

| CHAPTER | APPENDIX TOPIC |
|:---:|:---|
| 1 | Finding Information (Web search strategies) |
| 2 | Displaying Data (Chart options) |
| 3 | Creating Web Pages (Basic HTML) |
| 4 | Accounting Review (Accounting summary definitions) |
| 5 | Data Normalization (Designing databases) |
| 6 | Network Technical Definitions (ISO model and more) |
| 7 | Interactive Online Meetings (Net Meeting) |
| 8 | Forecasting (Introductory statistics in Excel) |
| 9 | Financial Definitions (Ratio definitions and analysis) |
| 10 | Optimization (Mathematical programming in Excel) |
| 11 | Presentations (Creating PowerPoint slide shows) |
| 12 | Visual Basic (Introduction to programming and macros) |
| 13 | Project Management (Introduction to Microsoft Project) |
| 14 | Computer-Related Laws (Summary and reference to legal environment) |

## Organization of the Text

The text is organized into four parts to explore answers to the question of how information technology can improve management.

| ORGANIZATION |
|:---|
| Chapter 1:　　　Introduction |
| Part 1:　　Personal Productivity and Business Operations |
| Chapter 2:　　　Personal Productivity |
| Chapter 3:　　　Solving Problems |
| Chapter 4:　　　Operations and Transactions |
| Chapter 5:　　　Database Management |
| Part 2:　　Business Integration |
| Chapter 6:　　　Networks and Telecommunications |
| Chapter 7:　　　Integration of Information |
| Part 3:　　Decisions and Models |
| Chapter 8:　　　Models and Decision Support |
| Chapter 9:　　　Decisions in Business Areas |
| Chapter 10:　　Complex Decisions and Artificial Intelligence |
| Chapter 11:　　Strategic Analysis |
| Part 4:　　Designing and Managing Information Systems |
| Chapter 12:　　Systems Development |
| Chapter 13:　　Organizing Information System Resources |
| Chapter 14:　　Information Management and Society |

- **Part 1.** Information technology is used to improve business transactions and operations.
- **Part 2.** IT is fundamental in the communication and integration of data across an organization.
- **Part 3.** IT plays a crucial role in building models, analyzing situations, and making decisions.
- **Part 4.** How information systems are developed and organized.

The organization of the text is based on two features. First, each chapter emphasizes the goal of the text: applying information technology to improve management and organizations. Second, the text is organized so that it begins with concepts familiar to the students and builds on them.

Each chapter is organized in a common format: (1) the introduction ties to the goal and raises questions specific to that chapter; (2) the main discussion emphasizes the application of technology and the strengths and weaknesses of various approaches; and (3) the application of the technology in various real-world organizations with end-of-chapter cases.

**Chapter 1 (Introduction)** examines the changing nature of IT, business, and society. These changes highlight the need for business managers to understand how IT can be used to improve decisions, jobs, and the entire organization.

**Part 1, Chapter 2 (Personal Productivity)** presents a review of hardware and software that shows how managers use IT for personal tasks. Instead of simply describing technology and defining terms, the chapter focuses on advantages, disadvantages, and appropriate uses of the various hardware and software tools.

**Chapter 3 (Solving Problems)** discusses how to analyze and solve business problems, emphasizing the systems approach to give students experience with the subjective side of managing IT. The chapter also introduces students to business object-oriented design.

**Chapter 4 (Operations and Transactions)** emphasizes the importance of transaction-processing systems. It presents common problems and demonstrates how IT is used to collect, process, and store quality data.

Most systems rely on databases for transaction processing, so **Chapter 5 (Database Management)** concludes this section. It includes hands-on applications that illustrate the use and management of databases, focusing on the importance of managers' understanding of database queries. The appendix illustrates the basic techniques of data normalization and database design.

**Part 2** covers a crucial component of MIS that is often ignored or treated lightly in other texts: communication and integration of information. Today's managers work in teams and rely on information systems to capture, transmit, and analyze information from diverse locations and in various formats.

**Chapter 6 (Networks and Telecommunications)** focuses on the various choices, relative merits, and costs of networks and telecommunications systems, as well as the physical connection of computers to share data. A separate appendix explains the technical details in more depth.

**Chapter 7 (Integration of Information)** shows that businesses can make substantial gains through using technology to integrate the data across the company. Integration and technology can change the way businesses operate and improve decision making. The chapter also discusses the challenge of combining various forms of data (text, images, sound, and video) into information that can be used to make business decisions.

**Part 3** focuses on making decisions. It emphasizes the importance of models in management. Beginning with basic uses of models, the section examines the various IT tools available to help managers examine various aspects of making decisions.

**Chapter 8 (Models and Decision Support)** introduces models and highlights their importance in making tactical-level decisions. The chapter discusses the common uses of models in making decisions. It concludes by examining enterprisewide models and the use of enterprise information systems to examine problems across the entire organization.

**Chapter 9 (Decisions in Business Areas)** integrates MIS with courses in other disciplines by examining common problems in accounting, marketing, finance, human resources management, production, and design. Basic problems are introduced in each area with the appropriate model. A hands-on version of the problem is developed using common IT tools. The application exercises encourage students to explore the models and tools in more depth. A technical appendix reviews the basic financial ratios and computations used to analyze companies. Students are encouraged to analyze the financial aspects of the cases in each chapter.

**Chapter 10 (Complex Decisions and Artificial Intelligence)** emphasizes the issues and problems involved in more complex decisions, which are decisions that involve more complex analysis, greater accuracy, or faster responses. The text then shows how basic AI techniques, including Expert Systems, can be used by managers to reach better decisions.

**Chapter 11 (Strategic Analysis)** examines difficult decisions, which are unstructured problems involving strategy. The chapter focuses on common problems in strategy (utilizing Porter's five-forces model). It explores the ways in which IT is used to sharpen an organization's competitive advantage.

**Part 4** discusses how information systems are designed and created. Again, the focus is on the role of managers in the development process.

**Chapter 12 (Systems Development)** examines basic issues in developing and implementing systems. The text emphasizes the role played by managers in helping design new systems. It examines the various development methodologies in terms of their strengths and weaknesses so managers can help determine which method should be used to develop systems they need. The chapter also emphasizes the increasing role of end-user participation in all of the development methodologies.

**Chapter 13 (Organizing Information System Resources)** examines the various methods of organizing MIS resources. It focuses on the fundamental issues of centralization and decentralization. By emphasizing the strengths and weaknesses of various IT organizational schemes, managers can learn to solve organization problems and determine how to align MIS to fit their needs.

**Chapter 14 (Information Management and Society)** examines the ways in which IT is changing society. It also encourages managers to think about the effects of their choices on members of society, both inside and outside the organization. Basic issues include privacy, security, and ethical issues in IT related to managers, programmers, and organizations. Common methods used to provide information security are also presented.

*The Case Appendix in the Instructor's Manual* has seven longer cases that can be assigned as comprehensive projects. The appendix begins with a brief discussion of how to approach business cases. Students are encouraged to review Chapter 3 (Solving Problems), which includes more ideas on business analysis and case organization. Except for one, all of the cases involve real-world organizations. Students are encouraged to use the library and computerized search tools to obtain additional information on the organization, competitors, and the industry.

**INSTRUCTOR RESOURCES**

*A presentation managers Instructor CD-ROM* is available to adopters and offers the following resources for course presentation and management. All the instructor supplements were created by the authors, except the testbank:

- *Instructor's Manual* includes answers to all end-of-chapter review questions, exercises, and teaching notes for the industry-specific cases. Teaching tips and ties to the PowerPoint slides are included for each chapter.
- A printed test bank contains true/false, multiple choice, and short answer questions, as well as mini-cases.
- Computerized/Network Testing with Brownstone Diploma software is fully networkable for LAN test administration, but tests can also be printed for standard paper delivery or posted to a web site for student access.
- Lecture notes and overheads are available as slide shows in Microsoft PowerPoint format. The slides contain all of the figures along with additional notes. The slides are organized into lectures and can be rearranged to suit individual preferences.
- Several additional databases and exercises are available. The instructor can add new data, modify the exercises, or use them to expand on the discussion in the text.
- The Rolling Thunder database application is available in Microsoft Access format. It is a self-contained application that illustrates many of the concepts and enables students to examine any facet of operating a small company. The *Instructor's Manual* includes further guidance on how to incorporate this innovative tool into your course.
- Video clips are available that highlight how specific companies apply and use information technology.

The Irwin/McGraw-Hill Information Systems Video Library contains fourteen 10 to 12 minute videos on numerous companies demonstrating the use of a variety of IT facets, such as intranets, multimedia, computer-based training systems, and concepts like client-server computing and business process reengineering. It is available free to adopters.

## Digital Solutions

- web site/OLC—The book's web site at *http://www.mhhe.com/business/mis/post* provides resources for instructors and students using the text. The Online Learning Center (OLC) builds on the book's pedagogy and features with self-assessment quizzes, key words, and glossary of terms, additional PowerPoint slides, and web links.
- Pageout/Pageout Lite—Our Course web site Development Center. Pageout offers a syllabus page, web site address, online Learning Center content, online quizzing, gradebook, discussion forum, and student web page creation. Pageout Lite, a scaled-down version of Pageout, offers three templates for posting your own material online and instantly converts it to HTML.

## Packaging Options

Irwin/McGraw-Hill has a huge selection of IT products that can be packaged with this text to meet the needs of your course—three different application software series of manuals and CDs on the Microsoft Office suite, Internet Explorer and Netscape products, programming languages, and Internet literacy. For more about our discount options, contact your local Irwin/McGraw-Hill sales representative or visit our web site at www.mhhe.com/it.

**ACKNOWLEDGMENTS**   Like any large project, producing a book is a team effort. In developing this book, we have had the privilege of working with dedicated professionals. The contributions of many people have resulted in an improved book, and made the process enjoyable.

First, we thank our students over the years who encouraged us to explore new technologies and to focus on how IT can benefit students, managers, and organizations. We are indebted to the reviewers listed below who offered many improvements and suggestions. Their ideas and direction substantially improved the book.

David Bateman, Saint Mary's University

Linda J. Behrens, University of Central Oklahoma

Michael K. Bourke, Houston Baptist University

John Bradley, East Carolina University

Kevin Brennan, University of Rochester

Jane M. Carey, Arizona State University—West

Chuleeporn Changchit, University of Iowa

Drew S. Cobb, Johns Hopkins University

Jack Cook, State University of New York—Geneseo

Virginia R. Gibson, University of Maine

Mark R. Gruskin, University of Michigan—Dearborn

William L. Harrison, Oregon State University

Thomas Hilton, Utah State University

Betsy Hoppe, Wake Forest University

Kevin Kelly, Portland State University

James E. LaBarre, University of Wisconsin—Eau Claire

Louis A. LeBlanc, University of Arkansas—Little Rock

Yvonne Lederer-Antonucci, Widener University

William E. Leigh, Jr., University of Central Florida

Douglas C. Lund, University of Minnesota

Jane Mackay, Texas Christian University

Murli Nagasundaram, Boise State University

Fred Niederman, University of Baltimore

John E. Powell, University of South Dakota

Dick Ricketts, Lane Community College

Robert Dowd Wilson, California State University—San Bernardino

This text has been substantially improved through the dedication and professionalism of the editors and staff at Irwin/McGraw-Hill. It is a pleasure to work with people like Christine Wright, Rick Williamson, Jodi McPherson, and Maggie Rathke Bogovich whose guidance, support, ideas, and answers to innumerable questions were invaluable to the project.

**Jerry Post**

**David Anderson**

# Brief Contents

# Contents

# Introduction

McDonald's uses a considerable amount of information technology to maintain consistency, monitor employees, and track sales.

## MCDONALD'S

Since 1955, McDonald's Corporation has sold more than 100 billion hamburgers. From a single drive-in in Des Plaines, Illinois, to today's system of nearly 25,000 restaurants across 115 countries, McDonald's has become synonymous with a quality product at a reasonable price. Equally important, it has been marketed as more than a place to get a hamburger. Ronald McDonald, the clean restaurants, and each new product or promotional theme adds to the fun that keeps 40 million customers a day of all ages coming back around the world.

Eighty percent of worldwide McDonald's are franchised. Each restaurant meets strict requirements to make it the same as all others. This ensures that each time you drive or walk into a McDonald's, no matter where you are, the Big Mac that you order will always be the same taste, size, weight, and quality. It will also be competitively priced.

Legal contracts, quality standards, and performance specifications help to ensure that individual restaurants and food orders will be the same. What most individuals do not think about when they walk or drive into McDonald's is that McDonald's management information system (MIS) plays an important role in ensuring the quality and consistency of each Big Mac. McDonald's has a strict requirement that food be fresh and not stored more than a certain amount of time. Management information systems assist managers to order and track inventory. Because restaurants are not consistently busy throughout the day, management information systems also help the manager to maximize the scheduling of individuals to cook and serve the food. Management information systems further help track restaurant cash flow and guard against inaccuracy and waste. As McDonald's adds new products and addresses increasingly specific market segments, the manager must make more complex decisions about the best mix of products to serve at each meal and throughout the day. McDonald's new Made For You production system in the United States and Canada uses a point of sale system to register each customer's "Made For You" order. Special promotions and community events add additional factors to the equation that can be addressed more realistically through management information systems.

OVERVIEW    Welcome to the information age. Going shopping? As a consumer, you have instant access to millions of pieces of data. With a few clicks of the mouse button, you can find anything from current stock prices to video clips of current movies. You can get product descriptions, pictures, and prices from thousands of companies across the United States and around the world. Trying to sell services and products? You can purchase demographic, economic, consumer-buying-pattern, and market-analysis data. Your firm will have internal financial, marketing, production, and employee data for past years. This tremendous amount of data provides opportunities to managers and consumers who know how to obtain it and analyze it to make better decisions.

There is no question that the use of computers in business is increasing. Walk into your local bank, grocery store, or fast food restaurant and you will see that the operations depend on computers. Go into management offices and you will find computers used to analyze marketing alternatives, make financial decisions, and coordinate team members around the world.

The expanding role of technology raises some interesting questions. What exactly are computers being used for? Who decided to install them? Do computers increase productivity or are they just expensive paperweights? Are there new uses that you should be considering? Are there some tasks that should be performed by humans instead of computers? How can you deal with the flood of data that you face every day?

THE EXPANDING
ROLE OF
INFORMATION
TECHNOLOGY

Technology is changing society, business, and jobs. The next few years will be exciting for managers. You will have the opportunity to use new technologies to solve problems, expand your knowledge, change society, and make money in the process. The Internet is an important component of information systems.

This text illustrates how people use computers to make decisions. These decisions and the use of computers increasingly affect all our lives. As prices drop and capabilities increase, computers are used in increasingly diverse fields. Musicians use computers to create music scores, generate new sounds, and play passages that no human could ever play. Artists use computers to create new techniques and design or modify their work. Computer artwork has become a crucial part of business presentations, especially in marketing campaigns.

Researchers in history, philosophy, and political science use computers to track documents, search for data, or look for correlations among various events. Computer software also assists in language translation. The software makes the initial translation; human interpreters work on the complicated passages and idioms to clean up the result. Existing computer translators supply fairly rigid substitutions and do not evaluate the semantic content of the documents, so humans still must polish the result.

## Reality Bytes    1–1   Too Much Data, Too Little Information

With hundreds of millions of pages on the Web, when you perform a search you often end up with hundreds of thousands of matches. Some are relevant, some are helpful, but many are useless. Several search engines have been developed to try and interpret your question to provide better matches. However, with hundreds of millions of pages, it is increasingly difficult for a machine algorithm to narrow down the search. Researchers at IBM's Almaden Research Center have developed a new system called Clever that uses a different approach. Essentially, it searches for key sites on a topic that tend to be generated by experts in the field. It finds these key nodes by examining links to the site and the description of those links. In the end, the searcher is provided with a list of the authority sites and primary hubs.

It is hard to imagine health care delivery without the use of computers. Computers track patients, treatments, pharmaceuticals, and appointments. Computers control machines such as x-rays, radiation therapy, and magnetic resonance imaging (MRI) scanners. Computer image-enhancement techniques provide clearer pictures and 3-D images. Computers are even being used to treat medical problems. Computers are wired to muscles to provide exercise and control for injured or paralyzed patients. Other techniques such as virtual reality are used to provide surgeons 3-D visualizations of complex body components to help guide laser and gamma "knives."

Even though it will not dwell on the thousands of specialized uses of computers, this book presents techniques that are valuable for anyone who wants to learn to evaluate situations and find useful applications of information systems. The ability to analyze situations and solve problems is needed by everyone, regardless of specialty.

An effect of changing technology is that it alters the way businesses operate, which changes the jobs that people perform, leisure activities, politics, crime, and society in general. Whereas many of the changes will be beneficial, some can have deleterious side effects. As a manager, you have an obligation to examine the potential side effects of your decisions. In particular, you need to consider how the use of technology affects customers, employees, and society at large. You must consider the effects computers have on privacy and understand the ethical problems that arise. These issues are explored in-depth in Chapter 14 but also arise in cases throughout the book.

Computers are everywhere. In 1999, about 50 percent of U.S. households possessed at least one personal computer. In business, almost all employees who work at desks (in the industrialized nations) are using computers in their jobs. In 1990, the Gartner Group reported that 76 percent of all desk workers were using computers. In larger corporations, the number was 84 percent. In total, 26 percent of the 113 million U.S. employees were using computers in their jobs. Figure 1.1 presents the average usage figures by industry for 1993 (the most recent figures available). Even among manufacturing and industrial firms (which have thousands of production workers), the use of computers exceeded 60 percent.

All of this technology is not cheap. Information technology costs (computers, associated equipment, and software) constitute a major expense for most businesses. Figure 1.2 displays the average spending on information technology by industry in 1993 (most recent year's figures available). Comparing the number to other business costs, note that

**FIGURE 1.1**

Regardless of the industry, most employees can expect to use computers to help with their jobs. These percentages reported by *Computerworld* include all employees, including line workers. For management jobs, the percentages are much closer to 100 percent.

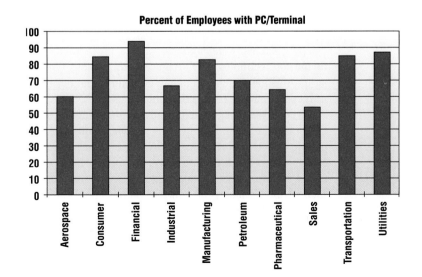

**FIGURE 1.2**

As reported by *Computerworld,* firms in different industries use information systems in different amounts. However, even a medium-sized firm with $100 million in revenue can easily spend $1 million a year on information systems.

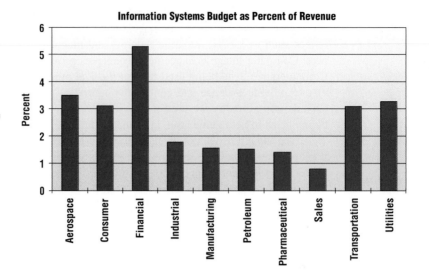

spending on information resources accounted for 14 percent of the total U.S. capital investment by businesses in 1992. In some industries, the figure is as high as 50 percent. By 2000, between the costs of resolving the year-2000 (Y2K) problem and building an Internet presence, all of these numbers increased.

Why do firms spend so much money on information systems? Are these investments profitable? The short answer to these questions is that spending money on computer hardware and software does not guarantee success. For this investment to pay off, managers need to learn how to use the technology. Knowing how to operate various hardware and software packages is only one step. The key to building and using effective information systems is that managers need to know how to apply technology to solve problems and make decisions. Hence, you need to understand the role of managers and the decisions they make. Before examining the roles of managers, this chapter will first clarify the definition of information systems.

**WHAT IS MIS?**    The first step in learning how to apply information technology to solve problems is to get a broader picture of what is meant by the term *management information system.* You probably have some experience with using computers and various software packages. Yet, computers are only one component of a management information system. A **management information system (MIS)** or *computer information system (CIS)* consists of five related components: hardware, software, people, procedures, and collections of data. The term **information technology (IT)** represents the various types of hardware and software used in an information system, including computers and networking equipment. The goal of MIS is to enable managers to make better decisions by providing quality information.

The physical equipment used in computing is called **hardware.** The set of instructions that controls the hardware is known as **software.** In the early days of computers, the **people** directly involved in MIS tended to be programmers, design analysts, and a few external users. Today, almost everyone in the firm is involved with the information system. **Procedures** are instructions that help people use the systems. They include items such as user manuals, documentation, and procedures to ensure that backups are made regularly. **Databases** are collections of related data that can be retrieved easily and processed by the computers. As you will see in the cases throughout the book, all of these components are vital to creating an effective information system.

So what is information? One answer to that question is to examine the use of information technology on three levels: (1) data management, (2) information systems, and

## Data, Information, Knowledge, and Wisdom

Consider the case of a retail store that is trying to increase sales. Some of the data available includes sales levels for the last 36 months, advertising expenses, and customer comments from surveys.

By itself, this data may be interesting, but it must be organized and analyzed to be useful in making a decision. For example, a manager might use economic and marketing models to forecast patterns and determine relationships among various advertising expenses and sales. The resulting information (presented in equations, charts, and tables) would clarify relationships among the data and would be used to decide how to proceed.

Determining how to analyze data and make decisions requires knowledge. Education and experience create knowledge in humans. A manager learns which data to collect, the proper models to apply, and ways to analyze results for making better decisions. In some cases, this knowledge can be transferred to specialized computer programs (expert systems).

Wisdom is more difficult to define but represents the ability to learn from experience and adapt to changing conditions. In this example, wisdom would enable a manager to spot trends, identify potential problems, and develop new techniques to analyze the data.

(3) knowledge bases. **Data** consists of factual elements (or opinions or comments) that describe some object or event. Data can be thought of as raw numbers or text. Data management systems focus on data collection and providing basic reports. **Information** represents data that has been processed, organized, and integrated to provide more insight. Information systems are designed to help managers analyze data and make decisions. From a decision-maker's standpoint, the challenge is that you might not know ahead of time which information you need, so it is hard to determine what data you need to collect. **Knowledge** represents a higher level of understanding, including rules, patterns, and decisions. Knowledge-based systems are built to automatically analyze data, identify patterns, and recommend decisions. Humans are also capable of **wisdom,** where they put knowledge, experience, and analytical skills to work to create new knowledge and adapt to changing situations. To date no computer system has attained the properties of wisdom.

To create an effective information system, you need to do more than simply purchase the various components. Quality is an important issue in business today, particularly as it relates to information systems. The quality of an information system is measured by its ability to provide exactly the information needed by managers in a timely manner. The information must be accurate and up-to-date. Users should be able to receive the information in a variety of formats: tables of data, graphs, summary statistics, or even pictures or sound. Users have different perspectives and different requirements, and a good information system must have the flexibility to present information in diverse forms for each user.

### Collecting, Analyzing, and Sharing Data

**WHY INFORMATION TECHNOLOGY IS IMPORTANT**

An enormous amount of data is available to managers—generated internally and externally. It is impossible to deal with this volume of data without information technology. But the power of information technology extends beyond these basic tasks. As a manager, you will face a rapidly changing world. The people and firms that can rapidly respond to these changes will profit. The best managers will understand the business, their role in it, and the ways that changes in the world affect the firm.

It is tempting to believe that once you learn how to use a word processor, a spreadsheet program, and a database management system, you have all the computer knowledge needed to solve business problems. In fact, these are powerful tools that will help you solve business problems that arise at a personal level. But businesses have many more levels of problems,

In 1997, Fortuna Alliance set up a web site, in which it claimed to be a new company. Essentially, however, it was a chain letter pyramid scheme. Customers were asked to "invest" between $250 and $1,750 a month. In return they were supposed to receive $5,250 a month. The Bellingham, Washington, company received at least $5 million before the FTC shut it down. It was a typical fraud story, except the perpetrators simply moved to Antigua and set up a new web site. They did not even bother to change the name of the company. Susan Grant, director of the National Consumers League Internet Fraud Watch observes: "One thing is true about Web scammers—they are so arrogant. Fortuna just put up a new web site recently and went back in business. There will always be plenty of people who don't check with us (http://www.fraud.org) or the FTC (http://www.ftc.gov) to see whether there are lawsuits against an investment site." Paul Luehr, chairman of the FTC Internet Coordinating committee, notes that the international character of the Internet makes it difficult to stop the scams: "We're out there and making headway, but a global community where scams can pop up today and disappear tomorrow is a big job."

such as data collection, departmental teamwork, information shared throughout the corporation, and uses of IT that help the business gain a competitive advantage.

To create and use information systems to their full advantage, it helps to have a basic knowledge of the technology. All hardware and software has limitations, advantages, and disadvantages. The first step toward successful use of any technology is to choose the correct tool for each job or problem. For example, after being introduced to spreadsheets, many people automatically try to generate a spreadsheet to solve every problem when there might be better tools available. By understanding the advantages and limitations of each tool you will be able to choose wisely.

## Analyzing and Building Systems

Managers are also responsible for improving their jobs and extending their company's influence. Information technology will play a key role in any organization. Successful managers will continuously evaluate current operations and explore new alternatives.

The scientific approach is a method that is useful for analyzing systems, identifying problems, and generating possible solutions. The scientific approach has been refined over thousands of years. **Systems analysis and design** is a refinement of these methods, and represents a field of study closely associated with information systems. Analysis and design techniques used by MIS professionals are useful to any business manager or student who needs to understand and solve complex problems. Even if you do not intend to become an MIS professional, these techniques will help you solve problems in any business discipline.

Similarly, you need to recognize what types of problems can be solved by users (such as yourself) and which are so complex that they require the support of a trained MIS staff. Attempting to solve problems that are too complex can lead to costly mistakes. Calling in expensive MIS professionals for simple projects that you can do yourself is equally a waste of time and money. Along the same lines, the more you know about MIS, the easier it is to communicate with MIS professionals. This communication is essential to developing systems that meet your needs.

## Traditional Management and Observations

**WHAT DO MANAGERS DO?** To create useful information systems, it is helpful to examine the various roles of management. Traditional concepts of management focus on organizing, planning, and control. However, when observed at their jobs, managers appear to spend most of their time in

Managers and professionals spend considerable time in meetings. Providing support for teamwork and group decisions is an important issue in MIS.

meetings, talking on the phone, reading or preparing reports, discussing projects with their colleagues, explaining procedures, and other activities that are difficult to fit into the traditional framework.

Henry Mintzberg, a psychologist who studies management, classifies managerial tasks in three categories: (1) interpersonal, (2) informational, and (3) decisional. Interpersonal roles refer to teaching and leading employees. Informational tasks are based on the transfer of information throughout the organization, such as relaying information to subordinates or summarizing information for executives. Decisions involve evaluating alternatives and choosing directions that benefit the firm.

Other researchers have studied managers and developed alternative classifications. Fred Luthans uses three classifications of management activities. He indicates that approximately 50 percent of a manager's time is spent on traditional management activities (planning, organizing, etc.), 30 percent in formal communications, and 20 percent in informal networking. Formal communications include attending meetings and creating reports and memos. Informal networking consists of contacts with colleagues and workers that tend to be social in nature but often involve discussions regarding business and jobs.

## Making Decisions

In many ways managers expend a lot of their effort in making decisions or contributing information so others can make decisions. When you look at courses offered for future managers, you will find a focus on administration, human behavior, quantitative modeling and problem solving, decision theory, and elements of business ethics and globalization. Typically, these courses are designed to help managers solve problems and make decisions. However, if you ask managers how much time they spend making decisions, they are likely to say that they seldom make decisions. That seems like a contradiction. If managers and executives do not make decisions, who does?

In many organizations, day-to-day decisions are embodied in the methodology, rules, or philosophy of the company. Managers are encouraged to collect data and follow the decisions that have resulted from experience. In this situation and in many others, the managers are directly involved in the decision process, even though they may not think they are making the final choice.

The broader **decision process** involves collecting data, identifying problems, and making choices. One more step is often involved: persuading others to accept a decision and implement a solution. With this broader definition, many of the tasks performed by managers are actually steps in the decision process. Meetings, phone calls, and discussions with colleagues are used to collect data, identify problems, and persuade others to choose a course of action. Each of these steps may be so gradual that the participants do not think they are actually making decisions.

Because of the subtlety of the process and the complexity of the decisions, it is often difficult to determine what information will be needed. Decisions often require creativity. Because data generally need to be collected *before* problems arise, it is challenging to design information systems to support managers and benefit the organization. One important job of management is to examine the need for information and how it can be used to solve future problems.

## BUSINESS AND TECHNOLOGY TRENDS

Several important trends are affecting the role of managers and the organization of business. To understand the current state and future prospects of management information systems, it is helpful to examine how technology, business, and management have changed over time. Two important concepts stand out in information systems. First, there is still much that we do not know. Second, technology changes rapidly. You have probably experienced the fact that software and hardware you studied in earlier courses have already become obsolete.

Businesses and management have been changing as well. Difficult economic times provide even more incentive to change. To be better managers and to understand the role of technology in business, you must be aware of how this environment is changing. Success in business comes from identifying patterns and being the first to take advantage of them.

As described in Figure 1.3, the primary focus will be on six basic trends: (1) specialization, (2) management by methodology, (3) decentralization and small business, (4) reliance on temporary workers, (5) internationalization, and (6) the increasing importance of service-oriented businesses. These trends will be discussed throughout the text to illustrate how they affect the use of information systems and how managers can use information systems to take advantage of these trends. Tightening job markets also means that managers must continually work on self-improvement. To survive, you must provide value to the organization.

### Specialization

The basic advantages of specialization and division of labor in manufacturing were discussed by Adam Smith more than 200 years ago. The concepts are now being applied to managers. As functional areas (such as marketing or finance) become more complex, they also become more specialized. Area managers are expected to understand and use increasingly sophisticated models and tools to analyze events and make decisions. As a result, the demand for managers with specific technical skills is increasing, while the demand for general business managers is declining. This trend is reflected in MIS by the large number of specialized tools being created and the increased communication demands for sharing information among the specialists.

### Management by Methodology and Franchises

An important result of specialization is the reduction of management tasks to smaller problems. Using specialization coupled with technology, firms have reduced many management problems to a set of rules or standard operating procedures. Day-to-day prob-

## Management Trends

For thousands of years, there was little need for management in firms. Business primarily consisted of small firms in agriculture, retail, or various trades. Workers were typically hired based on their specific skills. Unskilled workers were hired on a temporary basis for simple manual labor.

The spread of mass production techniques in the early 1900s encouraged firms to expand in size to take advantage of economies of scale. Firms then needed huge numbers of low-skilled workers on a permanent basis. The production process had to be efficiently organized and supervisors were needed to control and manage the workers. Managers were also needed to coordinate the huge flow of raw materials and inventories needed to keep the production lines moving. Frederick Taylor devised his *Principles of Scientific Management* (1911) to make production as efficient as possible. Partly in response to this rigid doctrine, in the 1930s several researchers explored the psychology of work and employee motivation.

Mass production requires mass marketing and mass consumption, which means that firms needed retail outlets to carry their products and distribution channels to deliver the products. Improved communication enabled firms to create regional and national advertising campaigns. All of these tasks required more middle-level managers to make decisions and control the process. As organizations grew in size and complexity, financial and accounting controls became increasingly important—hence the need for more managers and more information. Alfred Sloan, head of General Motors, devised a centralized organizational structure to help him run his enormously complex corporation. He relied on layers of middle managers in a hierarchical chain-of-command to solve ordinary problems and collect and summarize data for upper management.

Some of the nationwide firms in the retail sector (e.g., Sears, Kmart, and Woolworth), were organized in a similar fashion. The hierarchical system allowed central management to set overall strategies, purchase products in bulk, and store large quantities in warehouses. However, individual store managers made their own decisions about which products to stock, how to arrange merchandise, and how to market products at the local level. Adapting concepts developed in World War II, and with the advent of computers, the field of operations management was formed to create and analyze quantitative models.

In the 1950s, Ray Kroc, founder of McDonald's, chose a different approach and relied on the franchise model to build and control his company. With the franchise approach, typical operating decisions are reduced to a set of rules and procedures. Control and decisions are centralized, and local managers simply carry out standard instructions. Management theory began concentrating on systems analysis, with special attention on dynamic systems, feedback, and control.

As Leavitt and Whisler pointed out in 1958, increased use of computers enables firms to decrease the number of midlevel managers and increase centralized control. Although it took several years for technology to progress far enough to support these changes and for managers to take advantage of the technology, several companies have begun to emphasize this approach. For example, Wal-Mart, Mrs. Fields Cookies, and Service-Master have relied on technology and management by methodology to provide efficient centralized control.

lems can be addressed with a standard methodology. For example, the manager's guidebook at Wal-Mart or at Mrs. Fields Cookies explains how to solve or prevent many common problems. These rules were created by analyzing the business setting, building models of the business, and then creating rules by anticipating decisions and problems. This approach gives less flexibility to the lower-level managers but encourages a standardized product, consistent quality, and adherence to the corporate philosophy.

Management by methodology also allows firms to reduce their number of middle managers. By anticipating common problems and decisions, there is no need to call on

**FIGURE 1.3**

Changes occurring in the business world affect the use of information technology. These trends and their implications are discussed throughout the book. Managers who understand these trends and the relationship with technology will make better decisions.

| BUSINESS TREND | IMPLICATIONS FOR TECHNOLOGY |
|---|---|
| Specialization | • Increased demand for technical skills<br>• Specialized MIS tools<br>• Increased communication |
| Methodology & Franchises | • Reduction of middle management<br>• Increased data sharing<br>• Increased analysis by top management<br>• Computer support for rules<br>• Re-engineering |
| Decentralization & Small Business | • Communication needs<br>• Lower cost of management tasks<br>• Low-maintenance technology |
| Temporary Workers | • Managing through rules<br>• Finding and evaluating workers<br>• Coordination and control<br>• Personal advancement through technology<br>• Security |
| Internationalization | • Communication<br>• Product design<br>• System development and programming<br>• Sales and marketing |
| Service Orientation | • Management jobs are information jobs<br>• Customer service requires better information<br>• Speed |

trained managers to solve the daily problems. Franchises like McDonald's or Mrs. Fields Cookies carry this technique one level further by making the franchisee responsible for the financial performance of individual units. The common management tasks, however, are defined by the central corporation.

As companies have changed, so have the jobs of managers. College graduates 20 years ago often looked forward to lifelong careers with large companies. The goal was to start at some lower level in the firm, work diligently, and progress up the ladder to higher levels of management. Although only a few people would ever make it to the level of vice-president or chief executive officer (CEO), there was always the hope of becoming a regional or district level manager. Figure 1.4 illustrates this traditional hierarchy and highlights the typical middle management roles of data collection and analysis performed for this type of organization.

Today, companies are making major changes. Figure 1.5 shows a company divided into smaller, decentralized teams. Individual teams follow predefined procedures and are responsible for the performance of their team. Technology is used to facilitate communication and share data between the teams. Individual managers succeed as their team succeeds. Although some talented managers may eventually be promoted to higher-level teams, most workers will remain within the lower-team levels. Many of these workers could become part-time or contract employees who work with a team at one company to solve a specific problem, then move on to a new assignment with another company. As emphasized by Hammer and Champy, in this environment, an individual's skills become crucial to getting and keeping job assignments.

**FIGURE 1.4**

In a traditional organizational structure, lower-level managers deal with customers and collect basic data. Middle-level managers analyze the data, create reports, and make suggestions to upper-level managers. The higher-level managers make decisions and set rules to guide the other managers.

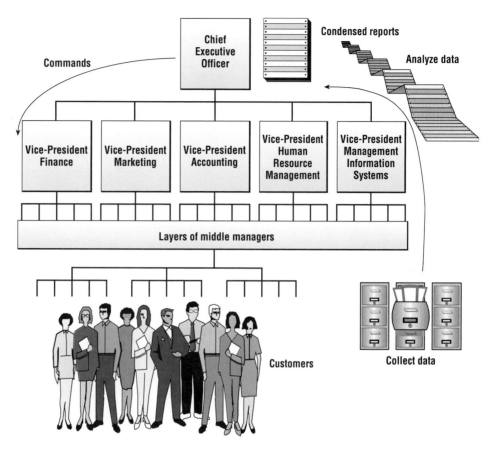

Reality Bytes    1-3    **Re-engineering Management Roles**

Traditional management of companies often created layers of bureaucracy—middle-level managers who spent their careers overseeing lower-level managers, creating reports, and interpreting commands from higher-level managers. A fundamental purpose of re-engineering is to use technology to eliminate these jobs.

In an interview in *The Wall Street Journal,* Michael Hammer and James Champy, leading proponents of re-engineering, commented on the future roles of managers. Hammer observes:

> I think there are a lot of people who will never find a job again. The market is over for bureaucrats. If you can't design or sell products, if you can't do real work, I'd get real nervous . . . A successful career will no longer be

about promotion. It'll be about mastery. What is a successful career for a lawyer? Very few people want to be managing partner; it's about being the best tax attorney you can be.

Champy notes that future workers need to thoroughly understand the entire business:

> We want workers to make decisions, and they can't do that without a knowledge about the business context. You also have to [learn] more behavioral things. Now that we've given you more control, how do you behave and make decisions—from how do you deal with a worker who isn't functioning, to what do you do when a customer asks for something that isn't in the rule book?

**FIGURE 1.5**
In the last few years, many companies have moved toward a more decentralized form of management. They have removed the middle layers of management and replaced them with smaller teams. Franchises and smaller teams have become the primary service contact with customers. Information sharing becomes crucial in this environment. Teams communicate directly and share data across the company.

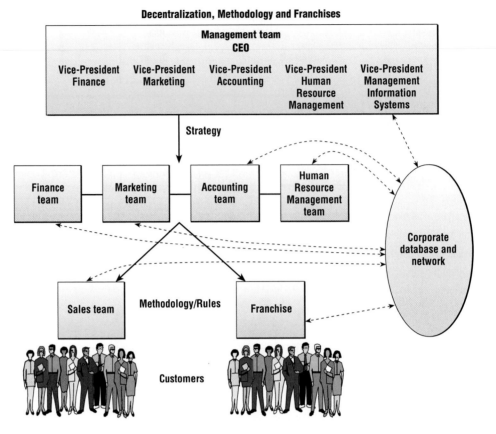

## Merger Mania

Up to the late 1800s and early 1900s, most businesses were small, having markets limited to small geographic regions. A brief history of industrial organization reveals four waves of mergers in the United States: (1) the horizontal mergers of the late 1800s epitomized by the oil and banking industries; (2) the vertical integration of the early half of the twentieth century, illustrated by the oil, steel, and automobile companies; (3) conglomerate mergers of the 1950s and 1960s, in which firms like IT&T (an international telecommunications giant) acquired subsidiaries in many different industries (including a bakery!); and (4) giant horizontal mergers of the late 1990s. All of these mergers arose to take advantage of economic power, but technology made them possible. Without communication (telegraph and telephones earlier, computer networks later), firms could not grow beyond a certain size because managers could not monitor and control lower-level workers.

The mergers in the mid- to late 1990s were impressive in terms of the size of the firms and the sectors involved. The banking industry was one of the first to begin consolidation. Relaxation of federal restrictions quickly led to large regional and national banks. The telecommunications industry also experienced several changes, such as the ABC-Disney merger between telecommunications and entertainment industries. Telephone, Internet, and cable companies also were fertile ground for mergers, such as MCI and WorldCom or AT&T and TCI. The horizontal mergers in the petroleum, food production, automobile, and grocery industries represented major consolidations of operations as

**Reality Bytes    1–4    Who Are You?**

One of the nagging problems in electronic commerce is verifying the identity of the participants. For example, how do you know that the web site offering to sell you a product is legitimate? How does the vendor know that you are who you claim to be and that you will actually pay the price? In many cases, these questions can be handled with traditional credit cards. The credit card company assumes the risk from both sides. In exchange for a payment from vendors, the credit card company guarantees payment for the product, and generally helps consumers if the vendor does not supply the promised goods. However, with online commerce, the vendor gets hit with the costs for invalid or stolen credit cards. Hence, online situations require more concrete verification of the people involved. One approach is to ask companies and individuals to verify their physical identity and obtain a digital certificate. This certificate is installed on the computer and automatically transmitted during the transaction. The electronic side of this process is relatively secure and easily handled with today's technology. The problems lay on the human side. Who will be the certificate authority? Would you trust the certificate from some start-up company you have never heard of? Or would you be more trusting if the U.S. post office issued the certificate? Of course, the use of certificates means that companies could track every purchase an individual makes on the Internet. In 1999, Intel provided an additional level of identification by installing a unique identifying number on every Pentium III processor. Hence, theoretically it would be possible to track actions by any machine on the Internet. After a public outcry concerning privacy, Intel chose to leave the numbers in the processor, but designed special software required to access the numbers.

well. Some of these combinations cross international boundaries (e.g., Daimler and Chrysler). Some of these trends were fueled by the high stock market valuations, which provided capital to the successful firms and punished the weaker ones.

One of the important keys to these mergers was the improved capability of information and communication technology. Without the IT structure, it would be exceedingly difficult to manage these combined firms. Most of the combinations also resulted in a loss of middle-management jobs. The remaining workers relied on technology to improve their productivity. The newly centralized firms also relied on communication technology to provide customer service across the country.

## Decentralization and Small Business

Today, technology makes it possible to split firms into smaller managerial units that make decisions at lower levels (decentralization). In addition to faster communication, technology makes available low-cost hardware and software to each division. It is now possible to operate a company as a collection of small teams and maintain complete management statistics without the need for hundreds of bookkeepers and accountants. In the past, with limited information technology, small divisions were expensive to maintain because of the cost of collecting and processing the basic accounting and operating data.

Within a firm, operations can be decentralized into teams of workers. In this situation, departments operate relatively independently, "selling" services to other departments by competing with other teams. They often perform work for outside firms as well—essentially operating as an independent business unit within the corporation.

There has also been an increase in the number of employees working for small businesses. This change was most dramatic from the mid-1980s to the early 1990s, when the largest U.S. firms shed almost 10 percent of their workforce (Fortune 500 from 1989 to 1993). This pattern changed from 1992 through 1998. As the entire economy grew, Bureau of Labor Statistics (BLS) and U.S. census figures show that the largest tier of companies increased their employment by 64 percent, whereas the other firms gained 58 percent.

Decentralization and smaller businesses can eliminate layers of middle managers in an organization. One goal of decentralization is to push the decisions and the work down to the level of the customer, to provide better customer service and faster decisions. Information systems enable executives to gather and manipulate information themselves or with automated systems. As a result, there is less need for middle managers to prepare and analyze data.

## Temporary Workers

So what happens to the people who are no longer needed as middle-level managers? At various times in the past, some companies provided a form of lifetime employment for their workers. As long as workers continued to do their job and remained loyal to the company, their jobs would be secure. Even in more difficult times, when employees were laid off, they were often encouraged (through extensions of unemployment benefits) to wait until the economy improved and they could be rehired. Companies in other nations, especially Japan, had stronger commitments to workers and kept them on the payroll even in difficult times.

Today, in almost every industry and in many nations (including Japan), companies increasingly rely on a temporary workforce. Individuals are hired for specific skills and tasks. When these basic tasks are completed, the employees move on to take other jobs. Increasingly, even executives are hired because of their specific expertise. Consultants and other professionals are hired on a contract basis to solve specific problems or complete special assignments.

In many ways, it is more difficult to manage a company that relies on temporary workers. Special efforts must be made to control quality, keep employees working together, and ensure that contract provisions are met. Technology can play an important role in these situations. It can improve communications, maintain easy (but controlled) access to data and contracts, and help to institute corporate standards. The Internet is beginning to play this management role—finding contract workers, negotiating the work, and distributing the finished products.

To individual workers, a firm's reliance on temporary workers means that to achieve a position with more responsibility and command higher rates of pay, workers will need to possess more analytic skills than other potential employees. Even as a manager, you will need your own competitive (professional) advantage. Along with additional education, your use and knowledge of technology can give you an advantage. For example, personal productivity tools such as word processors and spreadsheets enable workers to complete jobs faster and with better quality. At the next level, programming tools such as Power Builder and Visual Basic and database management systems (see Chapter 5) enable you to create custom systems with the help of previously written modules. Knowing how to use information technology to communicate (Chapter 6) and solve problems (Chapters 8 and 9) will help you get jobs and help you perform them more efficiently and with better quality.

## Internationalization

Several events of the early 1990s demonstrated the importance of international trade: closer ties forged with the European Union, creation of the North American Free Trade Agreement (NAFTA), and the continued relaxation of trade restrictions through the General Agreement on Tariffs and Trade (GATT) and the World Trade Organization (WTO). Although barriers to trade remain, there is no doubt that the international flow of trade and services plays an increasingly important role in many companies. Even small firms are buying supplies from overseas and selling products in foreign markets. Trade also brings more competition, which encourages firms to be more careful in making decisions.

As Figure 1.6 shows, the role of exports and imports has expanded rapidly in the United States since 1970. In European nations, international trade is even more important. Today, internationalization is a daily fact of life for workers and managers in almost every company. Even small businesses have links to firms in other nations. Many have set up their own production facilities in other nations. Much of this global expansion is supported by technology, from communication to transportation, from management to quality control.

Communication facilities are one of the most prominent uses of information technology to support the move to international operations. Communication technology is especially important for service industries such as consulting, programming, design, marketing, and banking. Several years ago, services were often considered to be nontradable goods because they tended to have high transportation costs, making them difficult to export. Today, improved communication facilities through the Internet have made certain types of services easy to export. For example, financial institutions now operate globally. Although not on the same level as banks, software development is also beginning to achieve an international presence. Some U.S. firms are turning to programmers in Ireland, India, and Taiwan. Through the use of programmers in India, for example, a U.S.-based firm can develop specifications during the day and transmit them to India. Because of the time difference, the Indian programmers work during the U.S. night hours and the U.S. workers receive updates and fixes the next morning.

**FIGURE 1.6**
By almost any statistic, in almost every nation, the level of international trade has increased dramatically during the last 20 years. International trade brings more choices, more competition, more data, more complexity, and more management challenges.

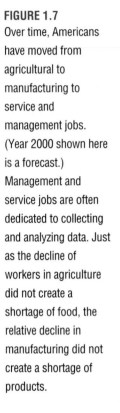

**FIGURE 1.7**
Over time, Americans have moved from agricultural to manufacturing to service and management jobs. (Year 2000 shown here is a forecast.) Management and service jobs are often dedicated to collecting and analyzing data. Just as the decline of workers in agriculture did not create a shortage of food, the relative decline in manufacturing did not create a shortage of products.

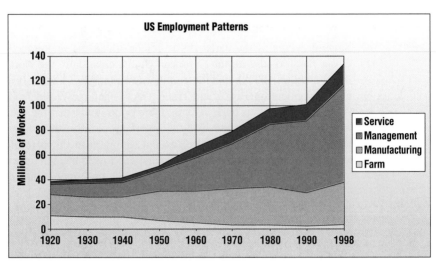

Internationalization also plays a role in selling products. Groups of countries have different standards, regulations, and consumer preferences. Products and sales techniques that work well in one nation may not transfer to another culture. Information technology can track these differences, enabling more flexible manufacturing systems that can customize products for each market.

The increased competition created by internationalization and decentralization requires corporations to be more flexible. Flexibility is needed to adapt products to different markets, choose suppliers, adopt new production processes, find innovative financing, change marketing campaigns, and modify accounting systems. Firms that attain this flexibility can respond faster to market changes, catch opportunities unavailable to slower firms, and become more profitable.

## Service-Oriented Business

Another trend facing industrialized nations is the move toward a service-oriented economy. As shown in Figure 1.7, in 1920 the U.S. census showed 29 percent of the employed were in farming. By 1990, that figure had shrunk to 3 percent. In the early 1900s, people were afraid that this trend would cause food shortages throughout the United States and the world. Improvements in technology in the form of mechanization, transportation, growing techniques, chemicals, and crop genetics proved them wrong.

A similar trend in manufacturing has produced similar consternation. Although the number of workers employed in manufacturing has varied over time, it is clear that the largest increase in jobs has been in the management, clerical, and service sectors. In 1998, 25 percent of the jobs were in manufacturing, with 72.5 percent in service and management jobs. The largest increase in new jobs has been in the management, clerical, and service sectors.

These trends represent changes in the U.S. economy and in demographics such as age characteristics of the population. The importance of the management, clerical, and service sectors has to be considered when we examine how MIS can benefit a firm and its workers. The goal is to gain a competitive advantage through better customer service. Even manufacturing companies are beginning to focus their efforts around the concept of providing services to the customer.

**RE-ENGINEERING: ALTERING THE RULES**

Many companies are managed by rules and procedures. It would be virtually impossible to do otherwise—the cost of an intense evaluation of every single decision would be overwhelming. Hence, upper-level managers establish procedures and rules and an organizational structure that automatically solve typical problems. More complex problems are supposed to be identified by managers and forwarded up the chain-of-command for answers.

This type of management creates a fixed approach to operations and to solving problems. However, the business environment rarely remains constant. Over time, new technologies are introduced, new competitors arrive, products change, old markets shrink, and new markets arise. At some point, firms that have been guided by relatively static methodologies find their methods no longer match the marketplace. Hence, they decide to **re-engineer** the company: beginning from scratch, they identify goals along with the most efficient means of attaining those goals, and create new processes that change the company to meet the new goals. The term *re-engineering* and its current usage were made popular in 1990 by management consultants James Champy and Michael Hammer. Many of the underlying concepts have been in use for years.

Sometimes re-engineering is undertaken by internal management as a means to improve the company. For example, in the early 1990s, Compaq Computer altered its strategy and re-engineered its operations and management to cut millions of dollars in costs and save the company. Sometimes re-engineering is forced on the company when it is taken over by another corporation. In a few rare cases, managers continuously evaluate the firm to make several small changes instead of relying on a major overhaul.

Re-engineering can be a highly complex process, requiring thousands of hours of time to analyze the company and its processes. In addition to the complexity, re-engineering often faces resistance because it results in a change in the organization's structure, which affects the authority and power of various managers.

Like any management technique, re-engineering is not guaranteed to work. A report by CSC Index, a major re-engineering consulting company, which surveyed 497 large companies in the United States and 124 in Europe, noted that 69 percent of the American

---

**Reality Bytes**     **1–5**    **Making Money on the Internet**

For years, much of the content on the Internet has been offered free to users. Yet, it costs money to create and maintain web sites, and someone has to bear this cost. The two basic choices are (1) charge users for the content, or (2) sell advertising space. Increasingly, web sites are turning to advertising revenue. In 1998, marketers spent slightly over $2 billion on Internet advertising. Experts were predicting substantial increases in advertising. Only a few elite companies such as *The Wall Street Journal* have been able to make any money through subscriptions. With the expansion

of the Internet, even more exciting possibilities exist. For example, many vendors have discussed embedding Internet access into everyday appliances. One expert, Mr. Cutler of Net.Genesis, suggests the possibility of companies providing free Internet-enabled toasters, where the toaster would burn a new ad into your toast each morning. He suggests: "You see that ad impression while you are buttering your toast. In exchange for your time, you get a free toaster. How badly would Procter & Gamble love to be able to target you at that key moment?"

and 75 percent of the European companies have already undertaken re-engineering projects. Several of these projects have not been successful. CSC Index notes that three factors are necessary for success: (1) overcome resistance by managers who are afraid of losing jobs or power; (2) earn strong support by upper management; and (3) aim high and go for major changes instead of small rearrangements.

Re-engineering has a close relationship with management information systems. In many cases, the new processes will rely on new computer systems to transfer and manipulate information. The important tie between re-engineering and information technology is that it is not sufficient to install new computers; the company must also re-engineer its underlying processes. A common situation occurred throughout the 1980s and 1990s when companies purchased millions of dollars of personal computers but failed to reorganize business operations to capitalize on computerization. As a result, the companies showed little or no gain in productivity from the use of the computers. For automation to be useful, managers need to understand how the computers will alter the tasks and management of the firm.

## MANAGEMENT AND DECISION LEVELS

To understand management, re-engineering, and information systems, it helps to divide the organization into three levels: strategy, tactics, and operations. Each level has unique characteristics, which use different types of support from information technology. These levels were explained by Robert Anthony in 1965. In 1971, Gorry and Scott Morton added a detailed explanation of how information systems at that time could support the various levels of management. Figure 1.8 is an updated picture of the typical pyramid shape of most organizations involving operations and tactical and strategic decisions. As is typical with most management models, the various levels are not strictly delineated. Some problems will encompass all levels of the firm. Similarly, making a change at one level may have unexpected repercussions on the other levels. Classifying a problem by its most relevant level makes it easier to concentrate on a solution. Once the primary problems are solved, the other effects are easier to handle. This text begins by discussing operations and works up to strategy. The cases in each chapter will help you identify problems at each level.

**FIGURE 1.8**
There are three primary levels of decisions in business. Business operations consist of tasks to keep the business operating on a day-to-day basis. Tactical decisions involve changes to the firm without altering the overall structure. Strategic decisions can alter the entire firm or even the industry. Information system tools exist to help with each type of decision.

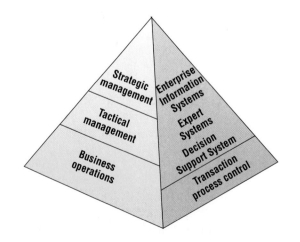

## Operations

The *operations level* consists of day-to-day operations and decisions. In your first job, you will typically concentrate on the problems that arise at this level. For example, in a manufacturing firm, machine settings, worker schedules, and maintenance requirements would represent management tasks and decisions at the operational level. Information technology at this level is used to collect data and perform well-defined computations. Most of the tasks and decisions are well **structured,** in the sense that they can be defined by a set of rules or procedures. For example, a clerk at Wal-Mart follows the procedures in the guidebook to deal with typical operations. Common problems are anticipated, with actions spelled out in the guidebook.

Summarized in Figure 1.9, managers in other disciplines, such as accounting, marketing, or finance, also face operational decisions. Personal productivity tools, such as spreadsheets, word processors, and database management systems help managers collect and evaluate data they receive on a daily basis. The use of these tools is reviewed in Chapter 2.

An important task at the operations level is to collect data on transactions and operations, hence **transaction processing systems** are a crucial component of the organization's information system. The data collected form the foundation for all other information system capabilities. As discussed in Chapter 4, an important characteristic of transaction processing systems is the ability to provide data for multiple users at the same time. A special class of transaction processing software designed for factory operations is called *process control* software.

Database management systems are increasingly used to control data and build systems to share data. Their role is explained in Chapter 5. Chapter 6 shows how communication networks are used to provide access to data throughout the organization.

Increasingly managers work in teams—either with workers in the same department or across departments and sometimes companies. Increasingly sophisticated software tools are being developed to help integrate data in these collaborative arrangements. These integration tools and *enterprise resource planning systems* are described in Chapters 7 and 8.

Operational decisions are often the easiest to understand. They deal with structured problems over relatively short periods of time.

| Sector | Operations | Tactics | Strategy |
|---|---|---|---|
| Production | • Machine settings<br>• Worker schedules<br>• Maintenance schedules | • Rearrange work area<br>• Schedule new products<br>• Change inventory method | • New factory<br>• New products<br>• New industry |
| Accounting | • Categorize assets<br>• Assign expenses<br>• Produce reports | • Inventory valuation<br>• Depreciation method<br>• Finance short/long term | • New GL system<br>• Debt vs. equity<br>• International taxes |
| Marketing | • Reward salespeople<br>• Survey customers<br>• Monitor promotions | • Determine pricing<br>• Promotional campaigns<br>• Select marketing media | • Monitor competitors<br>• New products<br>• New markets |

**FIGURE 1.9**
Each functional area of management faces the three categories of decisions and problems. Only a few examples are presented here.

## Tactics

As you move up in your career to project leader or department manager, you will encounter a different level of decision making, where the types of problems will depend on your specialization, but some common features will stand out. At the *tactical level,* decisions typically involve time frames of less than a year. As shown in Figure 1.10, these decisions usually result in making relatively major changes but stay within the existing structure of the organization.

A manufacturing tactical-level decision might involve rearranging the work area, altering production schedules, changing inventory methods, or expanding quality control measures. These changes require time to implement and represent changes to the basic methods of the firm. What distinguishes them is that they can be made without altering the overall characteristics of the organization. For example, in most cases, expanding quality control measures does not require the firm to expand into new industries, build new facilities, or alter the structure of the industry. Much of the information for making tactical decisions comes from the transaction records that have been stored in the computer. Computer tools to help analyze this type of data are called **decision support systems (DSSs),** and they are described in detail in Chapters 8 and 9.

Other types of problems occur in business that involve more complex models. For instance, **diagnostic situations** consist of spotting problems, searching for the cause, and implementing corrections. Examples of these situations include responding to problem reports from operations to identify the cause of the problem and potential solutions. For instance, a marketing manager might be asked to determine why the latest marketing approach did not perform as well as expected. Tactical-level decisions tend to involve specialized problems and can often be solved with the help of an expert. Chapter 10 presents **expert systems** to make this knowledge more accessible to an organization.

## Strategy

The next step on the pyramid moves up the corporate ladder to executive-level decisions. Although you may never be a CEO, you might be in a position to advise upper-level management about strategic opportunities—especially in small businesses. **Strategic decisions**

| DECISION LEVEL | DESCRIPTION | EXAMPLE | TYPE OF INFORMATION |
|---|---|---|---|
| Strategic | • Competitive advantage, become a market leader <br> • Long-term outlook | • New product that will change the industry | • External events, rivals, sales, costs quality, trends |
| Tactical | • Improving operations without restructuring the company | • New tools to cut costs or improve efficiency | • Expenses, schedules, sales, models, forecasts |
| Operations | • Day-to-day actions to keep the company functioning | • Scheduling employees, ordering supplies | • Transactions, accounting, human resource management, inventory |

**FIGURE 1.10**

Each decision level affects the firm in different ways. Each level uses and produces different types of information.

involve changing the overall structure of the firm to give it an advantage over the competition. They are long-term decisions and are unstructured. In other words, they are usually difficult and risky decisions. Examples of strategic decisions in the manufacturing arena include building new factories, expanding to new products or industries, or even going out of business. Strategic decisions represent an attempt to gain a competitive advantage over your rivals. Because of the complexity and unstructured nature of executives' decisions, it is difficult to determine how information systems can help at the strategic level. However, Chapter 11 explores information system techniques that firms have used to gain a competitive advantage.

## AN INTRODUCTION TO STRATEGY

Firms are constantly searching for ways to gain an advantage over their rivals. Finding these opportunities is hard: it requires extensive knowledge of the industry, and it requires creativity. Managers also have to be willing to take risks to implement strategic options. Strategic uses of IT often involve the use of new technology and development of new software. Being the first company to implement a new idea can be risky. However, it can also bring substantial rewards.

Strategic uses of IT are discussed in detail in Chapter 11 because you need to understand the technology before trying to solve difficult problems. On the other hand, to stimulate the imagination needed for creativity, it helps to begin thinking about the basic ideas right from the start. Many cases used throughout the book illustrate how firms have used technology to gain substantial advantages. These examples should help you solve other problems. If you can recognize a pattern or similarity between your problem and actions taken by other firms, the association may help you create a solution.

Michael Porter noted that often the first step in searching for competitive advantage is to focus on *external agents,* or entities that are outside the direct control of your company. Porter's Five Forces model in Figure 1.11 illustrates that typical external

**FIGURE 1.11**

In analyzing strategies, Michael Porter focuses on the five forces: threat of new entrants, threat of substitute products or services, bargaining power of suppliers, bargaining power of buyers, and rivalry among existing competitors. Competitive advantage can be obtained by using these forces or altering the relationships between these external agents.

SOURCE: Adapted from Michael Porter, *Competitive Strategy: Techniques for Analyzing Industries and Competitors,* (New York: Free Press, 1980).

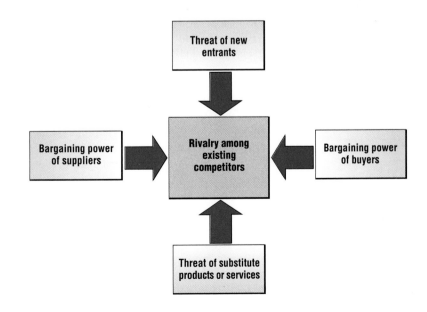

## Reality Bytes    1–6    Baxter Healthcare/American Hospital Supply

Hospitals use a large amount of routine supplies such as bandages and antiseptics. Originally, they purchased them from various suppliers, held them in inventory, and distributed them throughout the hospital as they were needed. This relationship is shown in Figure 1.10. American Hospital Supply (AHS) was one of these suppliers. To gain an advantage over their competitors, AHS created a new system and made an offer to the hospital managers. AHS placed computer terminals in hospital locations where the supplies were used (emergency, operating rooms, nursing stations, etc.). As shown in Figure 1.11, these terminals were connected to the AHS computer.

As hospital personnel removed supplies, they recorded them on the terminals. The computer kept track of the amount of supplies in each location. A list would be printed at the warehouse, and drivers delivered the necessary supplies to each location in the hospital. Monthly usage statistics were sent to the hospital.

The hospital gained because the facility did not need to maintain extra inventory, which saved money and space. Fewer hospital employees were needed because the supplies were delivered directly to the needed locations. Additionally, the hospital received detailed usage records.

To offer this service, AHS incurred higher costs—largely the cost of creating and maintaining the information system. What did AHS gain in return? As long as it was the only company offering this service, AHS gained a competitive advantage by providing a new service. Hospitals were more likely to choose AHS over the rivals. But what would happen if a competitor created a similar system? Would the hospitals stay with AHS or switch to the rivals?

Although the answer depended on the prices, hospitals had a strong incentive to stay with AHS. They would encounter various *switching costs* if they chose another supplier. For example, daily operations would be disrupted while the system was changed. Employees would have to be retrained to use the new system. Managers who used the monthly usage reports would have to adapt to the new system. A rival would have to offer strong price advantages to overcome these costs.

Of course, over time Baxter had an incentive to cut its costs to maintain higher profits. In the process their delivery service might suffer. Some hospitals apparently experienced problems and returned to in-house stock rooms to eliminate shortages of basic supplies.

agents are customers, suppliers, rivals, and governments. Competitive advantages can be found by producing better quality items or services at a lower cost than your rivals. Also, many firms have strengthened their positions by building closer ties with their suppliers and customers. An excellent example of this situation is provided by Baxter Healthcare, as illustrated in Figures 1.12 and 1.13. Information technology can be used to exchange information with suppliers or customers. Over time, the customers and suppliers will come to rely on this information and the capabilities you provide. Even if a competitor eventually offers similar ties, your new partners (customers and suppliers) will be reluctant to deal with a different firm because it would be difficult to change their systems and processes.

It can be difficult to identify strategic opportunities, and it requires practice to learn to analyze a complex problem. Figure 1.14 can be used to organize your thoughts as you approach strategic problems. Additional techniques and ideas are discussed in Chapter 11.

Information technology can also play a role in helping managers seek competitive solutions that might not directly employ the new technology. This support for strategic decisions typically consists of gathering, analyzing, and presenting data on rivals, customers, and suppliers.

**FIGURE 1.12**
American Hospital Supply began as an intermediary that bought various medical supplies and distributed them in bulk to hospitals. The hospital distributed supplies throughout the hospital and was responsible for maintaining its own inventory.

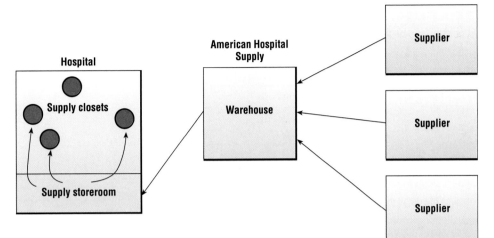

**Typical Supply Relationship**

**FIGURE 1.13**
American Hospital Supply changed the industry by providing a just-in-time inventory delivery service. Supplies then were delivered directly to where they are used within the hospital. AHS could offer this system only by maintaining a computer link between supply usage and the local warehouse. The computer data also provided summary reports to management. By purchasing AHS, Baxter Healthcare gained immediate access to that sales data.

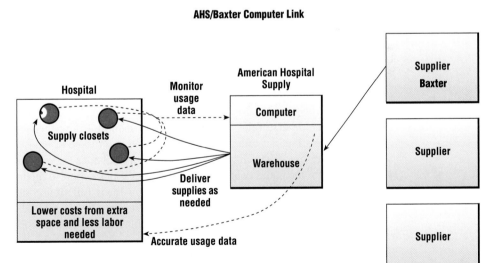

**AHS/Baxter Computer Link**

**FIGURE 1.14**
A useful method to analyze strategic problems is to begin by listing all of the strengths and weaknesses of the organization. Then analyze each category in detail. You will often have to perform additional research to answer the detailed questions.

| STRENGTH | |
| --- | --- |
| Source of strength | |
| Value of strength | |
| How can it be developed? | |
| What could undermine it? | |
| Development costs | |
| Additional benefits (opportunities) | |

| WEAKNESS | |
| --- | --- |
| Effect on company | |
| Possible solutions | |
| Cost of solution | |
| Result and cost of leaving as-is | |

**MANAGEMENT INFORMATION SYSTEM ROLES**

Information systems do not magically appear in an organization. Considerable effort, time, and resources must be devoted to building and maintaining information systems. One of the most important considerations in designing information systems is to solve the right problem. Identifying business problems and potential solutions is the main purpose of *systems analysis,* described in Chapter 3. These techniques can also help you analyze business cases and problems in other business functions. Chapter 12 introduces the main techniques used to build information systems. It focuses on the advantages and disadvantages of techniques to build information systems, such as *systems development life cycle, prototyping,* and *end-user development.*

The diverse roles of the MIS department are described in Chapter 13, along with problems that are often encountered. A common issue in many firms today is centralization versus decentralization: should major decisions be made by a core group of managers for the entire company, or should decisions be left to the managers within each subdivision of the firm? For many years business functions, including MIS roles, were centralized. As businesses have pursued decentralization in the last few years, managers have searched for new information technologies that can support both centralized and decentralized operations.

Chapter 14 outlines some of the social impacts of information technology. Users and managers need to remember that business information systems can also adversely affect workers and consumers. Firms, managers, and developers have responsibilities to ensure that information systems continue to benefit everyone.

## SUMMARY

Information technology is altering jobs, businesses, and society. Managers who understand and use this technology will be able to improve companies and advance their personal careers. Information systems consist of hardware, software, people, procedures, and collections of data. These components work together to provide information and help managers run the firm, solve problems, and make decisions. Studying information systems will also teach you to analyze business operations and solve problems.

The role of a manager is changing, but at a basic level all managers spend time organizing resources, planning, motivating workers, and communicating with other employees and managers. Several business trends will affect individual jobs, business operations, and society. Important trends include specialization, management by methodology and franchising, decentralization, the increased importance of small businesses, the use of temporary workers and consultants, the growing international scope of business, and the rise in service-oriented businesses. Information technology is used to support these trends and provide new management alternatives.

As is true of many problems, management and information technology can be studied by breaking them down into smaller pieces. The three basic levels to management are operations, tactics, and strategies. The operations level is concerned with day-to-day operations of the firm. Tactics involve changes and decisions that improve operations but do not require a major restructuring of the firm. Strategies are designed to give a firm a competitive advantage.

Strategy typically involves examining external forces: rivals (competitors within the industry), customers, sup-

pliers, potential new competitors, and potential substitute products or services. Information technology can be used to strengthen links strategically between customers and suppliers. It can also be used to create new products and services and to improve the quality of the operations.

Information technology can be the foundation of a business, but it can also be expensive. It is important that the information system be designed and organized to match the needs of the firm. Designing and creating effective information systems is a complex task, and several techniques have been developed to analyze organizations and build information systems. Common techniques include the systems development life cycle, prototyping, and end-user development. Business managers need to understand the strengths and limitations of the various methodologies to ensure that companies get an information system that meets their needs.

### A MANAGER'S VIEW

To be a successful manager, you must understand the roles of a manager in a modern company. There are several views of managers: as organizers and planners, as decision-makers, or as facilitators and team leaders. As a worker and a manager, you need to understand several trends in business and how they affect the ways managers do their jobs. You also need to know how information technology can be used to make you a better manager. Technology is helpful in personal tasks, collecting data, sharing information, analyzing problems, making decisions, and giving your company a competitive advantage.

## KEY WORDS

| | | |
|---|---|---|
| data, 7 | information, 7 | re-engineering, 19 |
| databases, 6 | information technology (IT), 6 | software, 6 |
| decision process, 10 | knowledge, 7 | strategic decisions, 22 |
| decision support systems (DSSs), 22 | management information system, (MIS), 6 | structured decisions, 21 |
| diagnostic situations, 22 | | systems analysis and design, 8 |
| expert systems, 22 | people, 6 | transaction processing system, 21 |
| hardware, 6 | procedures, 6 | wisdom, 7 |

## WEB SITE REFERENCES

### General Searches

| | |
|---|---|
| AltaVista | www.altavista.com |
| Excite | www.excite.com |
| Hotbot | www.hotbot.com |
| Infoseek | Infoseek.go.com |
| Lycos | www.lycos.com |

| | |
|---|---|
| Meta Crawler | www.go2net.com |
| Savvy Search | www.savvysearch.com |
| Search | search.cnet.com |
| Yahoo | www.yahoo.com |
| Web Crawler | www.webcrawler.com |

### People and Businesses

| | |
|---|---|
| Anywho | www.anywho.com |
| BigYellow | s15.bigyellow.com |
| Knowx | www.knowx.com |
| Switchboard | www.switchboard.com |
| Whitepages | www.whitepages.com |
| Zip2 | www.zip2.com |

## REVIEW QUESTIONS

1. What is the main purpose of MIS?
2. Why do students who are not MIS majors need to study MIS?
3. Describe how six basic trends in today's business environment are related to MIS.
4. Describe the five components of a management information system.
5. What is meant by the phrase *management by methodology?* How will it affect you in the next five years?
6. Describe the three basic levels of management decisions.
7. How can an understanding of the levels of management decisions help you solve business problems?

8. What is the purpose of re-engineering? What are the costs and benefits of re-engineering?
9. Using the information given in your text and the knowledge you have gained in your previous business classes, explain why the concepts in this text are important to all students of management.
10. Outside the business environment, what are some uses of computers?
11. How are information systems used at the various levels of business management?
12. What is the main purpose of system analysis?

## EXERCISES

1. Interview a local manager (or a student who has recently graduated) to discover which business trends most affect them. Are there any other patterns that affect their industry?
2. Using the resources of your library (government data, annual reports, business publications, etc.), find statistics to document at least two business trends. Draw graphs to reveal the patterns.
3. Choose one large company. Using annual reports, news articles, trade journals, and government data (e.g., 10K reports), research this company. Identify any changes that have been made in response to business trends in the last few years.
4. Choose a specific industry. Read news articles and trade journals to identify the major companies in that industry. Extend your research to include the primary international firms in the industry. Compare the growth rates of the two types of firms during the last five years.

5. Identify three common decisions within a specific industry. Identify one decision at each level (operations, tactical, and strategic).
6. Interview a recent graduate in your major (or a relative or friend). Find out what they do on a daily basis. Ask them what their managers do. Do managers have operations tasks to perform as well as management duties? For instance, does a manager in an accounting firm work on tax returns?
7. As an entrepreneur, you decide to open a fast food restaurant. You can purchase a franchise from one of the established corporations (as discussed in the McDonald's case) or create your own restaurant. Compare the choices by identifying the decisions you will face with each approach. What data will you need to collect?
8. Think of a part-time job you have or have had. How does your manager break down his or her time

among categories of communication, traditional management, networking, and human resource management? What issues have you felt your manager has dealt with effectively? On what issues could your manager spend time to improve?

### 💾 C01Ex09.txt

9. The data disk contains a text file for this problem. You have been hired as a consultant to a fast food store. The store manager has listed the cash received and the number of orders for each half hour of the day during one week of operations. Read the file into a spreadsheet.

   *a.* Format the columns, then compute daily and weekly totals.

   *b.* Create two line charts: one for cash, one for orders. Show transactions by the half hour. (There should be seven lines on each chart.) Highlight the line for Saturday.

   *c.* Create a separate schedule that shows the cumulative cash and orders through the day.

   *d.* Draw a graph for the cumulative cash flow. Indicate on the graph when the manager should take the cash to the bank (any time the total exceeds $2,000).

   *e.* The manager wants an estimate of the number of workers needed at any time of the day during the week. Create a table that displays the total number of counter workers and kitchen staff needed at each half hour (two columns per day). For every 25 orders during a half hour, we need two kitchen workers. For every 15 orders during the half hour, we need one counter worker.

### Rolling Thunder Database

10. Install the Rolling Thunder Bicycles database. Look through the various forms. List each of the main forms and briefly describe the purpose of each form.

11. Using the Rolling Thunder help files or the description available on the Internet site, describe the goals of the firm and outline the basic operations.

12. Using Internet sources, identify the competitors to Rolling Thunder Bicycles.

13. Using Internet, financial, and government sources, estimate the size of the market (total sales and number of bicycles) for quality bicycles.

14. Locate at least five sources for additional information about bicycles and bicycle components on the Internet. List and briefly describe the sites.

## ADDITIONAL READING

Anthony, Robert N. *Planning and Control Systems: A Framework for Analysis.* Cambridge: Harvard University Press, 1965. [Early MIS]

Booker, Ellis. "Baxter Gets PC Smart, Ousts Dumb Terminals," *Computerworld,* April 3, 1989, p. 33. [Baxter Healthcare]

Gorry, G. A., and M. Scott Morton. "A Framework for Management Information Systems," *Sloan Management Review,* Fall 1971, pp. 55–70. [Early MIS]

"Health-Care Guys Can Make Good on Retail IT," *PC Week,* August 21, 1995, p. 11. [Baxter Healthcare]

Leavitt, Harold J., and Thomas L. Whisler, "Management in the 1980's, *Harvard Business Review,* November 1958, pp. 41–48 [Prediction of decline in middle management]

Luthans, Fred. *Organizational Behavior: A Modern Behavioral Approach to Management.* New York: McGraw-Hill, 1973. [Management]

McWilliams, Gary. "Lower-Priced PCs Drove Strong Sales in December," *The Wall Street Journal,* January 8, 1999. [Sales data for PCs]

Mintzberg, Henry. *The Nature of Managerial Work.* New York: Harper & Row, 1973. [Management]

Nash, Jim. "Just What the Doctor Ordered," *Computerworld,* June 1, 1992, p. 79. [Baxter Healthcare]

Porter, Michael. *Competitive Strategy: Techniques for Analyzing Industries and Competitors.* New York: Free Press, 1980. [Strategy]

Rohde, David, and Neal Weinberg. "Can e-rate make the grade?" CNN, February 16, 1999. [Money intended for Internet access for schools wasted]

Sloan, Alfred. *Adventures of a White-collar Man.* New York: Doubleday, 1941. [Management]

# CASES  *The Fast Food Industry*

Restaurant franchising is a system in which a producer or marketer of a service, the franchisor, sells others, the franchisees, the right to duplicate a concept and use the trade name. The franchisor provides sales and other support within a specified territory for an agreed period of time. For example, a franchise may include the name, decor, menu, management system, accounting system, and usually the information system. Supplies are ordered from preapproved sources. Managers often receive training at corporately sponsored institutes.

Due to rapid growth during the 1970s and 1980s, franchise chains account for roughly 25 percent of restaurant outlets and 43 percent of industry sales. The introduction of restaurant alternatives is expected to slow new unit growth and sales through the 1990s. Restaurants that want to continue high-growth and above-average sales have already focused on the international markets. New domestic initiatives include operating units in nontraditional markets and dual-branding, where several restaurant chains or services operate in the same location.

The simplest franchise type involves a contract between a supplier and a business owner. The business owner agrees to sell only one version of a particular product. For example, McDonald's sells only Coca-Cola soft drinks. Conversely, product–trade name franchising, which accounts for 52 percent of all franchise sales and 33 percent of all the franchise units in the United States, involves selling products to distributors who resell them.

The fastest growing type of franchise is the prototype or package franchise in which a whole mode of business operations including the product or service, inventory system, sales and marketing methods, and record-keeping procedures are sold to the franchisee. Package franchising has grown ten times faster than product–trade name franchising, 11.1 percent versus 1.1 percent on average per year.

Through franchising, a business can grow quickly and achieve a higher market penetration than a single owner business. Franchises are often entrepreneurs who lack the knowledge to start a business. Franchising allows those individuals to adopt a business concept without starting from scratch. Franchises also face less risk than encountered when starting a business because the concept behind the franchise has already proven to be profitable on a limited scale. Thus, the five-year survival rate for franchises is much higher than that of start-up businesses (85.7 percent vs. 23 percent).

The franchiser's revenues are in the form of a start-up fee, ranging from $10,000 to $600,000 depending on the size and market share of the franchise. This includes a license for the use of the trade name, managerial training and support, and royalties that amount to 3 to 8 percent of gross sales.

Additional initial outlays include rent, inventory legal fees, equipment, insurance, and licenses. These can amount to ten times the start-up fee. In the case of McDonald's they can reach $500,000. The average initial cost of $330,000 per franchise limits the ability to enter this. Franchisers may also require that purchasers have experience in the particular franchise or in the segment represented.

| | |
|---|---|
| McDonald's | $45,000 |
| Subway | $10,000 |
| Domino's Pizza | $1,000 |

Start–up Franchise Fees

### Financial Analysis of Franchise Industry

Franchise restaurants are an $800-billion-dollar industry employing more than 8 million people. One out of every three dollars spent in the United States on food services goes to franchise restaurants. In 1996, the industry showed a 1.7 percent increase in revenues, continuing a decade-long trend in which the industry benefitted from a strong economy. Industry growth measured in terms of the increase of total domestic units, however, has been slowing over the past two years, from 7.9 percent in 1994 to 5.9 percent in 1995.

Profit levels for most fast food franchises averaged 14.6 percent in 1995. Pizza and chicken chains showed a faster growth rate than burger chains due to the more health-conscious consumer. Even though sales of burgers are outpacing pizza and chicken, burger sales nevertheless grew a healthy 7.2 percent in 1995.

### Stock/Investment Outlook

The growth rate for the fast food industry is about 15 percent per year. Investment projections for the largest franchises are optimistic. Analysts project that sales for Wendy's and McDonald's will increase by 17 percent and 14 percent respectively for the next five years.

Investors can expect a continuation of the recent trend toward mergers and acquisitions. The early 1990s saw a large number of initial public offerings from small franchise chains. Many of the more successful mom-and-pop franchises are acquired by corporate giants.

Long term, the investment prospects are favorable. The national trend toward two-income households has been a boon to the restaurant industry as a whole. Today's working parents eat out far more than their parents did. In 1996, 51.9 percent of all spending on food took place in restaurants; this is compared to 48.1 percent on groceries. Conversely, in 1972, only 38.2 percent of spending occurred in restaurants while 61.8 percent went to groceries. With their targeted marketing and expanded menus, the larger restaurant franchises have positioned themselves to take advantage of the social trend toward dining out.

### Potential for Growth of Franchise Industry

Growth in the entire franchise industry is expected to continue with expansion from 41 to 50 percent of all retail sales. Sales are expected to reach $2.5 trillion by the year 2010. Even though the domestic market for the fast food restaurant industry has matured and competition is tight for consumer dollars, companies are continually searching for new areas for growth. These include:

**Niche marketing in the United States**

Marketing toward children

Health-conscious and nutritionally balanced meals

Home meal replacement (traditional family meals with the ease of fast food)

**Mergers and Considerations**

Wendy's purchase of Tim Horton's, Hardees, and Roy Rogers

Boston Market's purchase of Einstein Bros. Bagels

**Dual-branding, where several restaurants operate at the same location.**

Taco Bell and KFC locations under one roof

Dunkin' Donuts and Baskin-Robbins

Arby's and p.t. Noodles

**Nontraditional operations**

McDonald's operations in Wal-Mart stores and gas stations

Little Caesar's Pizza outlets in Kmart stores

**International development**

Companies such as McDonald's, KFC, and Burger King continue aggressive development of markets in Asia and South America.

**Value offerings**

Consumers want value, so prices will be kept low. Many restaurants will focus on combo value offerings or value menus.

Wendy's 99¢ value menu

McDonald's combo menu, which offers standard combinations of popular items at a slightly reduced price

Franchise growth can be somewhat attributed to the changing demographics in the United States. The elderly, seeking convenience, will be making up a bigger portion of the U.S. than ever before. The 21 percent of the population over 55 has access to 50 percent of domestic income. By the year 2000, aging baby boomers' expenditures will increase by 90 percent.

### Competitive Structure of the Franchise Industry

The fast food industry is highly competitive and fragmented. The largest ten chains make up approximately 15 percent of all units and account for only 23 percent of sales. McDonald's remains the industry leader with more than 15.9 billion dollars in sales and more than 11,000 units in the United States. Burger King, Hardee's, Pizza Hut, KFC, Wendy's, and Taco Bell follow.

Mergers have changed the competitive structure of the industry. In 1995, Wendy's merged with Tim Horton's, Canada's largest national chain of coffee and baked goods. In addition, Wendy's purchased 40 Roy Rogers restaurants in New York from Hardee's in 1995 and 35 Hardee's in the Detroit area in 1996. Wendy's also plans to purchase 37 Rax restaurants in Ohio and West Virginia. These stores will be converted into either Tim Horton's or Wendy's. Wendy's ended 1996 with approximately 5,000 Wendy's units and 1,300 Tim Horton's units.

Boston Market was one of the fastest growing restaurant chains with sales of approximately $384 million in 1994. This represents an almost 150-percent increase over 1993. It also more than doubled its unit growth between 1993 and 1994, jumping from 217 units to 534 units. Boston Market focuses on home-style entrees, vegetables, and salads. However, their rapid growth resulted in a loss of control and the firm closed many stores by the end of 1998.

A chief competitor to the franchise food industry is grocery stores. They have targeted busy students and working parents by offering more prepared foods, deli counters, and eat-in dining areas.

### Technological Investment and Analysis in the Fast Food Industry

Technology has impacted the growth of the franchise industry. Improvements have included electronic systems, which help track inventories and sales. These systems yield more efficient operations and ease in the transmission of information between owner and franchisor. Electronic Data Interchange (EDI) is also being used by some franchises such as car rentals and hotels to communicate regarding reservations and customers.

Prospective franchisers can also use the Internet to find key locations for their business by perusing demographics and market research reports rapidly and at a low cost. Constructing Web pages to advertise to prospective owners is another use of technology. Lastly, because starting a franchise network requires a lot of communication comprised of training and support, leaps in telecommunications technology have helped make the global exchange of information easier than ever. This development has allowed easier monitoring of the uniformity of the franchisee.

The role of research and development in the fast food industry is generally limited to the test marketing of new products and improvement in food taste, calories, and consistency. Fast food companies constantly test the market acceptance of new menu items. Usually several restaurant locations serve as a test market to check the popularity of a new menu item. This type of market research helps keep the company ahead of the competition by adjusting to consumers' changing food tastes. Research also includes food science experimentation to improve the cost, taste, texture, shelf life, and fat content of menu items.

### Recommendations for the Future of the Fast Food Industry

The fast food industry faces many challenges over the next five years. While there is plenty of room for growth in the international market, sales will continue to lag in the United States. Companies will have to fight to increase or even keep their market share. In an effort to increase domestic market share, companies must focus on nontraditional markets and niche marketing. They must also focus on dual-branding. Careful attention will have to be given to delivery speed and customer service. As competition continues to tighten, there will be an increase in the number of mergers between companies, such as the Wendy's and Tim Horton's merger.

## CASE  *McDonald's*

McDonald's has worked hard to be more than a restaurant chain. It has become a marketing icon and is part of the routines of millions of people. Its success is so far-reaching that it has developed its own culture and identity. McDonald's has become a symbol of the success and desirability of American popular culture.

### TECHNOLOGY INVESTMENT AND ANALYSIS

#### Networks

Networks are particularly important to McDonald's because they provide a mechanism to manage the franchises

spread over large geographic areas. Networks reinforce the centralization of power by enabling headquarters to communicate with the franchises. This ensures standardization and quality control through the analysis of inventories and franchises. Networks achieve these functions at a comparatively low cost and without the time constraints of more mainframe-based communications.

### Smart Card Technology

Both McDonald's and Burger King are testing smart card technology in selected markets. The cash value of each card is stored on a computer chip or a magnetic strip on the back of each card. Value can be added to the card through machines that accept cash or through ATM-like machines that add value by transferring funds out of a customer's bank account. Customers can use the cards, instead of cash, to make their food purchases. Corporate goals for smart card implementation include cost savings in relation to money handling, reduced shrinkage, and increased loyalty through incentives and premiums. Smart cards eliminate the need for merchants to communicate with banks for authorization of purchases.

McDonald's is testing this technology at 870 restaurants across Germany. A payment system lets customers pay for goods using stored-value smart cards. Customers at McDonald's Deutschland, Inc. restaurants will be able to pay for goods by swiping smart cards through small, countertop terminals. They also will be able to add value to their smart cards by downloading money electronically from their bank accounts at touch-screen terminals in the restaurants. The terminals will lead users through the process of downloading new money to the cards.

McDonald's Deutschland continues to use smart card terminals in 55 stores earlier this year. During the first ten weeks of the trial, 30,000 transactions were conducted, using Hewlett-Packard Co.'s (HP's) VeriFone unit, which provides the terminals.

Though smart cards are catching on in Germany, there has not been an easy way to add value to the cards. According to Rolf Kreiner, senior vice president of marketing at McDonald's Deutschland, by letting customers not only buy goods but also add value to their cards, McDonald's is hoping to lead a trend toward the wide-scale acceptance of smart cards in Germany. The German smart-card payment infrastructure, known as GeldKarte-System, has about 40 million cards in circulation. McDonald's has committed to use VeriFone's SC552 smart card reader, which supports GeldKarte-System cards.

The system that will let users add value to their cards will be separate from the smart card readers and will be called VeriFone's Transaction Automation Loading and Information System (TALIS). The system will let users add value to their cards separate from the smart card readers. While customers wait for TALIS terminals to connect to their banks, the screens flash advertising and marketing messages.

VeriFone's TALIS touch-screen terminals are equipped for two cards, permitting consumers to "transfer" monetary value from a debit or credit card to a smart card after first tapping in a personal identification number. Once the smart card has been filled with stored value, it can then be inserted into a smart card reader at the point of sale to make payment on goods or services.

Technologically, smart cards were designed to function in place of credit cards in the fast food environment. Historically, credit card transactions were too slow in the fast food service environment. Their associated costs were too high in the face of small margins. Smart cards are an important step in resolving these issues. They enable restaurants to leverage the sales enhancing the impact of the ease of credit card use. Authorization and settlement technology are rapidly improving and the costs of network connectivity are decreasing.

### Internet Sites

McDonald's first announced a Web presence in 1994 with McDonald's interactive, an area in NBC Online on America Online. In 1995, the company developed and implemented a web site called McFamily (www.mcdonalds.com). It is aimed at families, perceived by McDonald's as its most important target market. The site features "seasonal ideas for fun family activities such as block parties, travel games, and household safety information." The Auditorium sponsors monthly guest speakers, including celebrities and parenting experts, and a Hey Kids area houses a gallery with McArt submitted by children with downloadable games and contests. The goal of all of these web pages is to enhance the brand image that McDonald's presents to families. McFamily includes a section on helping others. This section features information on Ronald McDonald House and other related children's charities. This section also features information on McDonald's efforts to preserve the environment.

The McDonald's web site cannot be used to sell food. However, it can capture revenue through the sales of merchandise related to McDonald's sponsorships. The McStuff for You section offers gear from McDonald's racing teams and the Olympic Games. The web site is used to collect customer information and profiles through online surveys.

### Data

Decision-makers at McDonald's Corporation realize that consumer preference is paramount. The chain is imple-

menting a restaurant-level planning system, dubbed Made For You, which lets each restaurant eliminate its inventory of foods prepared in advance. Instead, workers make sandwiches based on actual demand without sacrificing any of the efficiency.

About 800 McDonald's restaurants use the system, which consists of PC-based cash registers running in-house software. Orders are routed to monitors at different food preparation tables to balance the workload among employees.

In McDonald's restaurants without the new system, workers must anticipate the demand for each type of sandwich in advance and place them in bins. When a customer wants a sandwich that is not premade or one with a different topping, the person at the register shouts out the order and workers move out of the assembly line for the special request. This slows the process and extends the customer's wait.

McDonald's introduced the new system in March 1998 at a meeting for its franchisees. The company is encouraging its 12,400 U.S. restaurants to incorporate the system, but the actual decision is left to each franchise. The technology eases the workload and could add up to a percentage point to the company's profit margin because it enables the restaurant to sell more food faster, according to Douglas Christopher, a financial analyst with Crowell Weedon & Co.

Wal-Mart and McDonald's have joined together to share retail space. These two companies have been partners since 1993, with more than 700 restaurants in Wal-Mart stores around the country. Now, McDonald's has taken this one step further. It actually uses Wal-Mart's clerks and registers to sell McDonald's food.

In several test locations, when Wal-Mart shoppers pull their carts up to the checkout, there is a mat on the counter displaying McDonald's products, much like what you would see at one of the restaurants. Each product, from hamburgers to Happy Meals, has a code number that the clerk scans into the Wal-Mart system while ringing up the customers' purchases. The orders are automatically relayed from the register to the kitchen using software jointly developed by McDonald's and Wal-Mart. The food is brought to the customers as they leave the store. Since the food appears on Wal-Mart's registers and receipts, customers can pay for it with a single credit card purchase. At the end of the day, the companies go through the receipts and tally up McDonald's portion of the proceeds.

This process only works in Wal-Marts with a McDonald's kitchen somewhere in the store, whether it be in a restaurant or a stand-alone counter. Currently, there are almost 800 McDonald's outlets in Wal-Marts around the country. McDonald's hopes to continue implementing these systems as extensively as possible.

"It's an inevitable process," says Ross Telford, vice-president of retail practice at NCR, the Dayton, Ohio–based company that has based its business on supplying point-of-sale (POS) systems and helping vendors and retailers such as Wal-Mart, JC Penney, and Qantas Airways capture, process, and analyze customer data. According to Telford, individuals are starting to use one another's environments and skills to reach as many potential customers as possible.

The Wal-Mart/McDonald's partnership is part of a much larger, industrywide trend toward the cost-effective use of information at the cash register to increase profits. Known as *real-time cross-marketing,* the concept enables the company to use information technology to get more than one sale out of every transaction. As the buyer produces his or her checkbook or wallet, the retailer offers another product that fits with the customer's original selection, or one that matches a profile of the customer's previous purchases stored in the database. Matching a customer's current or past purchases with new ones and completing the sale requires both skill and tact. First, the information must be found; the product must then be presented in a way as to make the customer feel as if the company is not intruding. "Acquisition of detailed data is always a challenge. Even more challenging is how to use the data without being intrusive," says Steve Keller, director of general merchandising and industry marketing at NGR.

To manage its inventory better, McDonald's has bought supply-chain software from Manugistics Corporation. This acquisition will enable McDonald's to better manage inventory across the United States by sharing demand and supply information among its restaurants, suppliers, and distributors.

## QUESTIONS

1. What is McDonald's strategic/future direction?
2. What are McDonald's critical success factors?
3. What are McDonald's core competencies?
4. Upon which technologies has McDonald's relied?
5. What has caused a change in the use of technology within McDonald's?
6. How has this change been implemented throughout the franchise?
7. How successful has the technological change been?
8. How has McDonald's use of technology impacted the financial performance of its stock?

## ADDITIONAL READING

Davey, Tom. "Personalized Service at Lower Cost—Hotels and Restaurants Turn to Transaction Processing and Real Time Communications to Get a Strategic Edge," *Information Week,* September 14, 1998, p. 173.

Essick, Kristi. "Put a Big Mac on my Smart Card, Please," *Computerworld,* August 24, 1998, p. 45.

Frank, Diane. "The New ROI in Point of Sale," *Datamation,* November 1997, pp. 73–77.

Gallagher, Sean. "Getting More Miles from IT," *InformationWeek,* September 9, 1996, pp. 124–127.

"Germans to Buy Big Macs with VeriFone's Smart Cards," *Newsbytes News Network,* August 17, 1998.

"McDonald's McCyberSpace," *Electronic Market Report,* September 5, 1995, p. 4.

"McDonald's Supply Chain," *InformationWeek,* April 13, 1998, p. 30.

Nash, Kim S. "McDonald's IT Plays Catch-Up With Rivals," *Computerworld,* December 14, 1998, p. 1.

Schien, Esther. "Telecom Tango: Telecom Deregulation in Central and South America Will Encourage U.S. Business Emigration," *PC Week,* February 16, 1998, pp. 73–74.

"Smart Cards and Big Macs," *InfoWorld,* August 24, 1998, p. 51.

## CASE *Rainforest Café*

Steven Schussler was an owner of a chain of nightclubs. He also loved exotic birds. For the benefit of his pet birds, he turned his house into a rainforest habitat. The project turned out so well that he decided to apply the rainforest idea he had developed into a rainforest theme restaurant. Since the prototype was already in place, he could use his home to convince potential investors to commit to the project. They did. The result is the multi-outlet, multimillion-dollar enterprise known as Rainforest Café.

### Technological Investment and Analysis

Rainforest Café "uses eight Profit Series POS workstations with five preparation printers" in each restaurant. Rainforest executives chose the Profit Series manufactured by HSI for a number of reasons. First, the HSI Profit Series did not require proprietary hardware, thus allowing systemwide integration in existing and new restaurants alike. Rainforest executives wanted to work with a mature company like HSI, which could grow with them and meet the company's future needs. The Profit Series system was user friendly. This made training easy, lowered costs, and increased flexibility.

The point-of-sale system utilized by Rainforest Café simplifies the inventory tracking. The system indicates what sells the most, what needs to be ordered, when it needs to be ordered, and how much needs to be ordered, thus lowering inventory costs. This saves time and eliminates ordering mistakes that could result in running out of needed goods.

Rainforest Café also uses a computer system to calculate waiting times for tables to within seven minutes. With this knowledge, restaurant patrons can utilize their time more efficiently, allowing them to shop or do whatever they desire while waiting for their tables. The timing system also accounts for part of the increased table turnover.

## QUESTIONS

1. What trends are driving the strategic direction for the Rainforest Café?
2. Upon which systems has the Rainforest Café been built and why?
3. How has Rainforest Café used its web page to present its business directives?
4. What challenges and opportunities is the industry facing?
5. How important are Rainforest Café's databases to its continued success?

## ADDITIONAL READING

Schwartz, Mathew. "Which Way to the Web?" *Software Magazine,* September 1998, pp. 70–76.

## CASE *Dave & Buster's*

Dave Corriveau met James Corley in Little Rock, Arkansas. Corriveau considers himself the "fun-and-games guy." He was still quite young when he opened up his own business in Little Rock. It was a game parlor and a saloon. In 1976, he opened a larger version named Slick Willy's World of Amusements. It has been rumored that Bill Clinton was among those that frequented the place. The 10,000-square-foot business generated sales in excess of $1.2 million while Corriveau was still in his early twenties.

During the same time, Corley was a general manager for T.G.I. Friday's in the same town. He aspired to open up his own restaurant. He liked the location in which Slick Willy's was operating, a renovated train station. Corley approached Corriveau to request financial support in opening his restaurant. Corriveau agreed, and Corley opened right next door with a walkway connecting the businesses. Corley was also in his early twenties.

The walkway between these two businesses is probably the best thing that ever happened to the two entrepreneurs. The walkway enabled customers to migrate easily between the restaurant and the game parlor and saloon. Customers who initially came to one of the establishments would end up walking to the other establishment. They came to eat something and then stayed to play a couple of games. Sometimes they came to play a couple of games and then stayed to eat. It was good business and the two owners soon realized the potential that existed for a complex that would combine both businesses under the same roof.

The Slick Willy Restaurant was sold to raise money. Corriveau and Corley then moved to Dallas. They were in Dallas a little over two years before they were able to open up their first place. In 1982, inside a 40,000 square foot building located next to an expressway, Dave & Buster's (D&B) was born.

### Technology Investment and Analysis

D&B provides a PowerCard for customers to use. The card provides convenience to the customer by taking away the burden of carrying around a bucket of coins and allows D&B to make gradual increases in the amount they can charge for a game. Previously, prices could be raised only in whole increments (one token at a time). The card has done away with that by allowing incremental increases of 0.1 through 0.9 at a time. The customer simply swipes the card through a scanning mechanism located in front of each machine, and the credit amount is automatically deducted from the card.

The system has the capability of tracking what games have been played with each card and how much has been spent. Customers can verify the amount they have on their card by using analyzer/rechargers that are located throughout the arcade area. These analyzer/rechargers also allow customers to put more money on a card without having to stand in a line. The tokens are still used for some of the ticket redemption games that involve skill activities with the tokens.

A discount on the games is offered to those who have spent over a certain amount of credits on the same card. Members can sign up for the card by filling out an application with some particular information, and they are then given a card with their name on it. The "gold" card gives the customer a 10-percent discount on the amount required to play the games.

The card offers bonuses to customer through a lottery-type system that matches the numbers on their card with a randomly drawn number by the computer. Credits are awarded accordingly to the card. The PowerCard system does have certain limitations. The card can only be used at the issuing store, the credits are nontransferable, and no cash back is allowed on any remaining credit balance of the card. Furthermore, customers can only get their bonuses if they see an attendant at one of the desks and not at the analyzer/rechargers.

### Recommendation for the Future

Other PowerCard bonuses should be considered. Whereas additional game-buying power is certainly a fun incentive, it might also be useful to give incentives that customers can take home. These incentives could be like boardwalk and game prizes—stuffed toys, toy jewelry, and so on.

## QUESTIONS

1. What technology tools are Dave & Buster's using to keep its focus on expansion?
2. What are the technological forces that are driving this direction?
3. Why do you think Dave & Buster's would choose not to have an Internet site?
4. What challenges and opportunities is the theme-restaurant industry facing?
5. How important is data to the corporation's continued success?
6. How will the capture and maintenance of customer data impact the corporation's future?

## ADDITIONAL READING

"Late Earnings Roundup: Dave & Buster's Reports Income," *Newsbytes,* September 9, 1996, p. NEW09090021.

## DISCUSSION ISSUE

### *Why Don't Computers Understand English?*

Ever since the invention of computers, people have dreamed of communicating with them the same way we communicate with other humans. Businesspeople often complain about how hard it is to learn to use computers. Imagine how easy it would be if you could just type in a couple sentences in English (or some other natural language) and get the results you want. Advances have been made to develop natural language interfaces. However, there are some problems. As the following interaction between a human and a computer demonstrates, some problems may result.

Bowman:   Who are our best clients?

HAL:   I do not understand the word *clients.*

Bowman:   I mean customers.

HAL:   I cannot compute the mean of customers. To calculate averages, you must specify a numeric attribute. For example, *average income of customers.*

Bowman:   No, no. I do not want the average.

HAL:   Please restate the question as a positive statement. You want . . .

Bowman:   Who are our best customers?

HAL:   Searching . . . There are no customers named *Best.*

Bowman:   No, I want the top customers.

HAL:   Searching . . . The following customers match your request:

| Name | City | Phone | Account Balance ($) |
|---|---|---|---|
| Mike Top | Ames | 222-2222 | 1452.35 |
| Sidra Top | Gainesville | 444-4444 | 3352.92 |
| Susan Top | Fargo | 333-3333 | 1093.52 |

Bowman:   Wait a minute.

HAL:   Entering sleep mode for one minute. Further input ignored until 13:42.

Bowman:   No!

HAL:   13:42. Please enter your request.

Bowman:   Why are all of the customers named Top?

HAL:   Searching . . . Unable to answer question. There is an incorrect premise. There are currently 7,354 customers. Only three of them are named *Top.*

Bowman:   I get it. Okay. Which customers have the most sales?

HAL:   Searching . . . There are no customers with sales.

Bowman:   What?

HAL:   Rephrasing result: There is no salesperson named *customers,* so *customers* has no sales.

Bowman:   No. Which customers have bought the most?

HAL:   Searching . . . There are no products called *most.*

Bowman:   Arghh! Which customers have spent the largest amount of money?

HAL:   Searching . . . Unable to access customers' computers. Please supply the proper passwords.

Bowman:   What?

HAL:   Retrying access . . . Incorrect passwords. Notification has been received from four customers that security violation has been logged. Network security command has shut off our access to the EDI network. Details have been forwarded to the computer security supervisor.

Bowman:   No! Cancel the request.

HAL:   Query canceled.

Bowman: Why did you try to access the customers' computers?

HAL: The request required calculation of total corporate spending by each of the customers. That data is stored on the customers' computers.

Bowman: Okay, try this: Which customers have bought the most products from us?

HAL: Searching . . . This company sells no products called *most*.

Bowman: Nuts. Which customers have spent the largest amount of money on all of our products?

HAL: Searching . . . The following customer matches your request:

| Name | City | Phone | Purchase | Date |
|------|------|-------|----------|------|
| Robert Jones | Atlanta | 777-6666 | 8734.99 | 12/12/98 |

Bowman: It's about time. Thank you. I quit.

HAL: The time is 14:37. Closing the session. Logging off.

## QUESTIONS

1. Did Bowman finally get what he wanted? What did he want? There are at least three possibilities: (1) the most expensive item ever purchased by a customer; (2) the most amount of money spent at any one time by a customer; (3) the highest total purchases by a customer over some specified time period.
2. Can you write a question that Bowman could ask that will give him the information he wanted—with no room for misinterpretation?
3. Assuming that it would be possible, what would be the drawbacks of making computers "more like humans"?

One of the first lessons you have to learn in dealing with computers is the importance of being precise. The second lesson is that computer software is created by humans—analysts who make many decisions about the expected user interaction. Software designers generally attempt to build systems that match the jobs and needs of the users. However, the software is usually less flexible than humans, so people will typically have to adjust their own processes to adapt to the computer.

# *Finding Information*

Think about your education for a minute—consider all of the classes students take. Many of the classes focus on specific skills (reading, writing, arithmetic, and so on). Yet, a common thread in all of these classes is learning to find information. You learned how to use a dictionary, an encyclopedia, newspapers, the library, a phone book, maps, and so on. Now, imagine a world where all of this data is stored in digital form on computers. We are not quite there, but the Web is rapidly beginning to provide the capability of searching for virtually any information.

Computers offer several advantages for searches. They are fast, they can search full text so they rarely miss material, and the search is automatic so it is inexpensive and up to date. On the other hand, computer searches generally lack human intelligence, so the computer does not truly understand what you are searching. Consequently, the computer may not find what you really want, or the search may return thousands of responses, which makes it hard to answer your questions.

The key to becoming efficient with computer searches is to understand how the computer organizes the search. This appendix presents the basics of computer searches and gives you hints on how to find what you want. The first section lists some of the common web search engines. The second describes the most common search methods using Boolean techniques. The third section provides some hints on how to narrow your search and find exactly what you want. The fourth section gives you ideas on where to start when you have a general topic but do not know exactly what you want to find.

## WEB SEARCH ENGINES

Several companies provide free search engines for use on the Web. Some popular sites are listed in Figure 1.1A. The full-text engines function by automatically scanning pages posted on the Web and building indexes of key-words. Your search looks up the keywords in the index and retrieves the Internet address of the matching pages. Sometimes a page will no longer exist even though it is still in the index.

| FULL-TEXT WEB SEARCHES | |
| --- | --- |
| AltaVista | www.altavista.digital.com |
| Excite | www.excite.com |
| Hobot | www.hotbot.com |
| Infoseek | www.infoseek.com |
| Lycos | www.lycos.com |
| Search | www.search.com |
| **CATEGORY WEB SEARCHES** | |
| Yahoo | www.yahoo.com |
| **PEOPLE AND BUSINESSES** | |
| ATT | www.tollfree.att.net |
| Bigyellow | s15.bigyellow.com |
| Switchboard | www.switchboard.com |

**FIGURE 1.1A**

WEB SEARCH ENGINES

These companies use advertising revenue to cover their costs, so you can search for free.

Note that each search engine has different methods for entering Boolean conditions. Some require commands to be in uppercase (e.g., AND, OR). Some use symbols (e.g., &, +). You will have to read the specific documentation for each system.

Some of the search engines (e.g., Lycos) provide a numeric rating that attempts to indicate how well the page matches your search condition. Most likely pages are listed first.

## BOOLEAN SEARCHES

The most basic possible search is to enter a single word and tell the computer to retrieve all the information related to that one word. And every once in a while, you will have a topic where you know exactly which word to use. On the other hand, a search for the word *autarky* on Hotbot returned "only" 868 matches. Even the word *onomatopoeia* resulted in 1,791 matching pages. Both of these words describe well-defined and relatively obscure topics—yet they both returned more data than you are willing to read.

Almost every search you perform will need to use more than one word. The power of a Boolean search lies in how you combine the words. Consider a search with two words (white, knight). There are three basic options: (1) Treat the words as a phrase where the document must contain exactly that phrase: "white knight." (2) Return documents that contain both words in any order: white and knight. (3) Return documents that contain either word: white or knight. The first method is the most restrictive and treats the phrase as a single word. Most Web systems use the quotation marks to indicate a phrase. The second method is the most common. The computer searches for documents that contain all of the words you enter. If you do not specify the connector (and, or), most web systems assume you want all of the words (and). The third approach can be dangerous—it widens the search. You would never use the example given here because both words are far too common, and one or the other would be found in millions of documents. Some systems support modifications of these commands. For example, you might be able to search for documents where the two words appear within words of each other.

The real power of a Boolean search is that you can form complex searches using the algebra that you learned in school. Any word (or phrase) can be connected by AND, OR, or NOT. You can also group terms together by enclosing them in parentheses. Figure 1.2A uses a truth table to show the basic logic.

Consider the example shown in Figure 1.3A. Say you are going to be transferred to an office in Medellín, Colombia, for two years. You decide to search the Web to learn more about Medellín. What happens if you ask the search engine to find all references to Colombia? You will be flooded with several thousand articles containing that word. Even the city Medellín returns thousands of matches. Your next step is to narrow the search by providing a more specific topic. Say you add the word *terrorism*. Then you will get a more reasonable number of responses (430).

There is another problem, however. If you are looking for the word *terrorism*, you should also include other words that refer to the same topic, such as terrorist, bombing, and kidnap. In other words, you want to search for all articles that refer to Medellín AND (terrorist OR terrorism OR bombing OR kidnap). One useful trick is to know that most search engines match parts of words. Instead of entering *terrorism* and *terrorist*, you can just enter the word *terror*, which will match both of those words. You should always use root words in your search

| **A** | **B** | **A** AND **B** | **A** OR **B** | NOT **A** |
|---|---|---|---|---|
| T | T | T | T | F |
| T | F | F | T | F |
| F | T | F | T | T |
| F | F | F | F | T |

**FIGURE 1.2A**
TRUTH TABLE
An AND statement is true only if both components are true. An OR statement is true if at least one of the components is true.

| Colombia | 278,851 |
|---|---|
| Medellin | 8,587 |
| Medellin AND terrorism | 430 |
| (terror OR bomb OR kidnap) | 598,795 |
| (terrorism OR bombing OR kidnap) | 320,063 |
| Medellin AND (terror OR bomb OR kidnap) | 830 |
| Medellin AND (terror OR bomb OR kidnap) AND American AND (dead OR death) | 482 |

**FIGURE 1.3A**
SAMPLE BOOLEAN SEARCH
The number on the right is the count of the number of documents that matched the search clause. Note the use of parentheses to group terms.

phrases (such as *bomb* instead of *bombing*). The fourth and fifth rows in Figure 1.3A show the difference—the root words return almost twice as many matches. Your full search is given by the last condition in Figure 1.3A. Your query can include AND and OR connectors, but you should always use parentheses to indicate how the phrases should be combined.

## YOU KNOW WHAT YOU ARE SEARCHING FOR

This topic should be easy. As long as you know what you are looking for, just tell the computer, and it will find it. Life, however, is rarely that easy. First, you need to be able to describe what you want in a few key words. Second, the real problem is that the authors of the web pages and articles may not have used the same words that you choose. You need to think about which words and phrases are most likely to be used.

The first step is to write down a list of words that describe your topic. Then run some initial searches to see how many pages are returned. If the number is too large, add more search terms (connected by AND) to restrict the search. If no matches are found, delete search terms, or add new terms connected by an OR. If the initial articles do not match what you want, throw out your search words and start over.

Once you have a core group of articles, read a few of them at random and look for new search ideas. If the page contains a keyword list, consider adding some of them to your search list. When you find the results you want, save your search list. It is a good idea to keep a search journal. You might have spent several hours searching for information. Do not discard your work. Use your word processor to keep a journal. Whenever you do a search, enter the date, the search topic, the search engine, and the final search condition into the journal. If you need to find similar information again, you can save time by referring to your journal.

Consider an example. You read somewhere that ITT was involved in a corporate merger. Hilton Hotels wanted to buy out ITT to gain control of their Sheraton Hotels. ITT directors did not like the idea and sought out a third company, which purchased them, becoming what is known as a "white knight." You want to find the name of that company. To make it more interesting, say that you are not certain about many of the details. You only remember that ITT was a participant in some corporate merger that resulted in a white knight takeover.

Figure 1.4A shows your search strategy and the resulting matches. Clearly, searching for ITT is too broad. If this were the only information you had, you would be better off going directly to the ITT web site and seeing if they had information on a merger. But, as a second attempt, you add the words: corporate merger. You might narrow the search by requiring them to be a phrase (instead of separate words), but that might be too narrow. Once you add the "white knight" phrase, the list is narrowed considerably. It is now easy to scan the articles until you find the answer (Starwood Lodging).

## YOU HAVE A VAGUE IDEA ABOUT WHAT YOU WANT

How can you find something when you do not know what you want? Yet, in practice, you will often find that you want information about a topic, but you do not yet know enough to ask specific questions. Without detailed questions, a computer search would return way too much data. So, you first need to find resources that provide a general introduction to the topic and show how it is organized.

If you are really uncertain about where to begin, you should first look through the categories provided by the

| ITT | 81,801 |
| ITT corporate merger | 908 |
| ITT corporate merger "white knight" | 26 |

**FIGURE 1.4A**

WEB SEARCH FOR ITT MERGER

Knowing that the merger involved a "white knight" significantly narrows the search. It is easy to scan the 26 matches to learn the details.

search engines. In particular, Yahoo uses people to categorize sites that they find. These categories are arranged hierarchically, so you can start with general topics and work down to more detail. The process is similar to looking through a table of contents for a book. The advantage of this approach is that human intelligence has already organized and sorted the basic data, making it easier for you to find information based on concepts. The drawback is that it is nowhere near as complete as the automated searches. Consequently, it makes a good starting point.

In other situations, or after your initial search, you will have a vague idea of what you want to find. You can still run searches on key words—just be prepared to receive thousands of matches. One useful technique is to select some of these matches randomly and use them to help refine your search. If the document matches what you want, look for key words and phrases that you can add to your search condition. If the document does not contain information you want, look for key words that you can tell the search engine to avoid. By continually refining your search, you should eventually get closer to the information you want.

Consider the example used in the last section, but this time assume you do not know as much information. For instance, you might start out with an interest in "white knight" takeovers. Figure 1.5A shows the progression of the search. You begin with "white knight" and get thousands of matches. Adding the term *corporate* reduces the list considerably, and you decide to scan some of the results. You notice that many of these pages refer to topics that do not interest you—they refer to companies in Canada and India, or they refer to historical concepts (real knights). Your third pass asks the search engine to ignore pages with those references, and the list is cut in half. After a little thought, you realize that the word *corporate* by itself is insufficient—for example, you are getting matches with companies that have "white knight" in their name. Adding the word *merger* reduces the list to about 100 matches. Skimming these entries, you notice several articles on Germany; so you add "Germany" and "foreign" to the re-

| | |
|---|---|
| "white knight" | 8399 |
| "white knight" corporate | 913 |
| "white knight" corporate NOT (history, Canada, India) | 465 |
| "white knight" corporate merger NOT (history, Canada, India) | 103 |
| "white knight" corporate merger NOT (history, Canada, India, Germany, foreign) | 79 |

**FIGURE 1.5A**
WEB SEARCH FOR A TOPIC
After reading some of the items from the second search, you decide to rule out some topics. Adding the word *merger* restricts the list even further. Removing some additional topics (Germany and foreign) reduces the list to a manageable number.

stricted list. The query now returns only 79 matches. Although that might seem like a large number of items to read, remember that you started with a vague topic. You will have to read many of these items to make a decision about what you want to learn. Once you make up your mind, you can modify your search to narrow the topic.

Interactive searching is the key to finding information. You add terms to restrict the list. You skim random articles to find new terms. Look for terms to restrict the list (add with AND), to expand the list (add with OR), or to be excluded (add with NOT). You could also use a thesaurus to find synonyms that writers might have chosen. When you find an article that interests you, use its list of keywords to find related articles.

## INTERNET CHANGES THAT CAUSE COMPLICATIONS

While the search engines are powerful, they were designed to handle a specific type of data: static pages of text. Increasingly, companies are creating web sites based on database systems. At these sites, the data is stored in a database, and specific pages are built on the fly in response to a customer query. For example, if you go to a site that sells computer products, the items are all listed in the company's database; they are therefore generally not accessible to the search engines. Hence, if you ask a search engine to find every store that sells a specific type of printer, the search engine will probably miss most of the stores. Instead, you would have to search for printer sales and hope that the company has at least a few pages that will be found by the search engines.

### EXERCISES

1. Using Internet resources and search engines, find the name of the person who was the lead prosecutor for President Clinton's impeachment trial.
2. Using three different search engines, enter the answer from exercise 1 and list the number of matching documents returned by each engine.
3. Find three Internet sites that provide financial and background information about companies.
4. Run the search in Figure 1.3A in two different search engines. How do they differ in syntax for entering the Boolean conditions?
5. You have been asked to start a recycling program for the toner and ink jet cartridges used in your company offices in three cities: Boston, San Francisco, and Dallas. Using the Internet, find a company that can provide these services in each of the three cities. (It would be better if the same company can be used in all three cities.)

# PART 1

# *Personal Productivity and Business Operations*

**How do information systems help managers perform basic tasks?** Computers are particularly useful in helping managers with personal tasks and routine transactions. These systems have been in use for several years, and many businesses could not survive without them.

All managers perform tasks like writing, scheduling, calculating, and graphing. One of the most powerful uses of information systems lies in helping managers with these personal applications. Hundreds of tools exist to help managers with their daily tasks.

Another key role of managers is to analyze the business to solve problems and identify new opportunities. Several systems analysis techniques have been developed to help us understand complex systems. The methods and diagrams can be used by managers to understand how their actions affect the entire company.

The heart of any company is its daily operations. Whether the company manufactures products or provides services, basic operations must be performed continuously. These operations give rise to transactions with suppliers, customers, employees, other firms, and governmental agencies. Transactions must be recorded, aggregated, and analyzed. Information systems are crucial to maintaining, searching, and analyzing transactions.

A firm could have many separate transaction-processing systems. Data might be collected from thousands of sources and stored in hundreds of locations in the firm. A database management system can help managers find data. It makes it easier to share data with other workers. A database management system provides several tools to create reports and build input forms with minimal programming.

CHAPTER 2

# *Personal Productivity*

Small businesses are beginning to rely on microcomputers because of their low costs and off-the-shelf software applications.

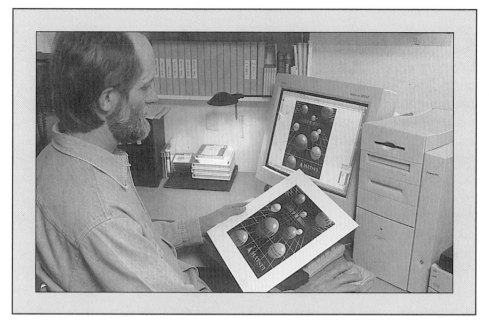

## SMALL BUSINESS

Despite its founding in Jeff Bezos' garage, Amazon.com doesn't fit the Web startup stereotype of twenty-somethings in ponytails. Bezos was a systems development executive at Bankers Trust in New York in the late 1980s—the bank's youngest VP ever. Yet, when the explosive growth of the World Wide Web caught his eye, he saw an even bigger opportunity: online commerce. Two years later, Bezos, CEO of the Internet bookstore Amazon.com, is one of a crew of young entrepreneurs using cyberspace technology to take market share from traditional businesses with strong consumer and industrial franchises.

This type of analytical thinking is not foreign to Bezos, a former Wall Street investment firm worker. "I always wanted to start a business, but my wake-up call was when I found out the Internet was growing at a 2,300 percent rate," he says. "That's a market that nothing compares to. Then I sat down and made a list of 20 possible products to sell on the Web, and books were the biggest commodity."

The thing about books, says Amazon.com Inc. owner Bezos, is that there are so many of them. At any given time, there are 1.5 million English-language books in print plus another 3 million worldwide. No other consumer commodity item comes close (music is a distant second, with about 200,000 titles available). Add to that the fact that even the largest real-world bookstores house only about 170,000 books and you discover what appears to be an opportunity for an ideal electronic-commerce business.

**OVERVIEW** The past decade has given the typical manager an incredible array of tools—both hardware and software—to improve day-to-day work. At first glance, it might seem that the value of the computer depends heavily on each manager's specific job. Marketing managers, financial analysts, CPAs, and retail store managers all appear to have different uses for computers because their jobs are different. They might even need different types of computers. However, many jobs have similar features, so hardware and software tools have been created to

**FIGURE 2.1**

Every manager must perform certain basic personal tasks, including searching for data, communicating, scheduling, writing, and various computations. Several software packages have been designed to help with these basic tasks.

help with specific personal tasks. Most managerial jobs involve four basic functions: research, analysis, communication, and organizing resources. Managers perform several common tasks, including data searches, computations, writing reports and memos, drawing graphs, communication, and scheduling workers and appointments. Common application software packages were created to help managers with these tasks.

**INTRODUCTION**

Why do you care how computers work? After all, it is easy to use a photocopy machine without understanding how it works. Automobiles cost more than most computers, yet you can buy an automobile without knowing the difference between a manifold and a muffler. You can also make telephone calls without understanding fiber-optic cables and digital transmissions.

On the other hand, when you buy an automobile you need to decide if you want options such as power windows, a turbo charger, or a sunroof. Similarly, many options are available for telephone services. If you do not understand the options, you might not end up with the car, telephone service, photocopier, or computer that you need. Or, you could end up paying extra money for services that you will not use. To choose among the various options, you need to know a little about how computers work.

Computers are typically discussed in terms of two important classifications: hardware and software. *Hardware* consists of physical items; *software* is the logical component, such as a set of instructions. Of course, many functions can be provided in either software or hardware and a computer user often cannot tell which has been used, and most often does not care. The one main difference is that it is easier to make changes to software than to hardware—especially because software patches can be transmitted across the Internet.

**TYPES OF DATA**

Computers are used to process five basic types of data: numbers, text, images, sound, and video. Because of limited speed and storage capacity, early computers could only handle simple text and numbers. Only recently have computers become fast enough and inex-

## Trends

The first computers were simple pieces of hardware. Like all computers, they had to be programmed to produce results. Programming these machines was a time-consuming task, because all of the pieces were connected by individual wires. Programming the computer consisted of rearranging the wires to change the way the pieces were connected. As computer hardware improved, it became possible to program the processor without having to change the internal wiring. These new programs were just a list of numbers and short words that were input to the machine. These lists of commands were called *software,* because they were easier to change.

Programmers soon learned that some tasks needed to be performed for most programs. For example, almost every program needs to send data to a printer or retrieve information stored on a disk drive. It would be a waste of time if every programmer or user had to write a special program to talk to the printer. By writing these common routines only once, the other programmers could concentrate on their specific problems. As a result, every computer has a basic collection of software programs called an *operating system.* The operating system handles jobs that are common to all users and program-

mers. It is responsible for controlling the hardware devices, such as terminals, disk drives, and printers.

As machines became faster and added new capabilities, operating systems evolved. These new capabilities have changed the way that we use the computer. The early computers could only recognize individual characters and numbers, so keyboards were used to type information for the computer. Printers that could handle only characters and numbers were the only way to get output from the computer. Eventually, television screens were used for output, but most of this output remained as characters. With the introduction of microcomputers, low-cost graphics hardware allowed the television screens to display pictures that were created by the computer. Today, many operating systems are completely graphical, which enables users to work with pictures and icons.

As the use and capabilities of computers expand, the ways we use computers change. Early programs were written by users. Later programs were written so users followed steps and answered questions in a fixed order. Eventually, users were given some control over the programs through the use of menus. More recent software focuses on an event-driven approach, where the user controls the sequence and the software responds to these events.

pensive enough to handle more complex sound and video data on a regular basis. As computers continue to improve, these new capabilities will alter many aspects of our jobs and society.

As always, the business challenge is using technology to add value. For example, putting music and video footage in an accounting presentation might be entertaining, but in many cases it would not add value to the presentation itself. On the other hand, holding meetings with digital video links could save money by eliminating travel for a face-to-face meeting. You need to understand the concepts and characteristics of these emerging technologies so that you understand their merits and costs and learn to identify worthwhile uses.

### Object Orientation

One of the most important concepts to understand with existing computers is that all information is represented as **binary data.** Binary data may be written as a collection of ones and zeros, and the name is shortened to *bits.* A set of 8 bits is called a *byte.* Data that are not in binary form are converted during data entry with various **input** devices. **Output** devices then change this data back to a form that humans can understand. Even complex objects can be represented by binary data. Figure 2.2 illustrates the five basic data types.

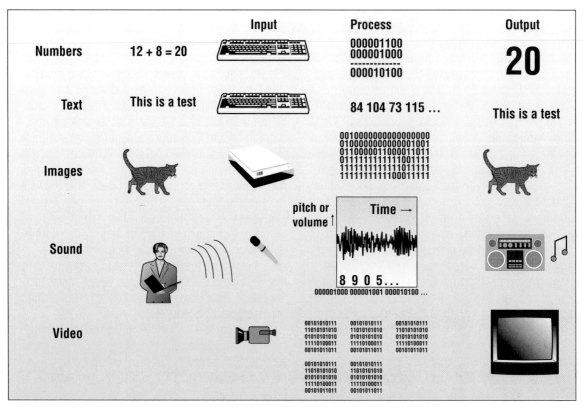

**FIGURE 2.2**
FIVE BASIC TYPES OF DATA
Because processors only deal with binary data, each format must be converted or digitized. Computer peripheral devices are used to convert the binary data back to the original format.

Recent software development has strongly embraced the concept of *object orientation*. The designers create objects for each software package. Each object has its own *properties* and *methods* or *functions*. Users can change properties and call the predefined functions. Although objects can become complex, most software begins with the five basic data types as fundamental objects. Software designers are beginning to standardize the properties and functions of these five data types. Once you learn these basic features, it is easier to use software.

Each of the basic data types has its own characteristics. Numbers have a precision and usually a scaling factor. Text has a typeface and display size, as well as appearance attributes such as bold, underline, and italic. Pictures can be described by their resolution and the number of colors. Digitized sound is based on a specified sampling and playback rate, and fits into frequency and amplitude ranges. Video combines the attributes of pictures with a frames-per-second definition. Any computer program dealing with these objects must understand their basic attributes. As a manager, once you understand the attributes it will be easier to use most new software packages.

Along with the attributes, several predefined functions can operate on each data type. Basic functions dealing with numbers include totals, calculations, and comparisons. Standard methods to manipulate text include searching, formatting, and spell-checking. Methods dealing with pictures involve artistic alterations such as color or lighting changes, rescaling, and rotation. Existing functions for sound and video are often limited to recording, playback, and compression/decompression.

**FIGURE 2.3**
NUMERIC PRECISION
If you tell a
spreadsheet to display
two-decimal digits, it
performs the additions
in the full precision of
the data—and displays
the data in the right
column. If you really
want two-digit
precision, you should
use the Round ($\times$, 2)
function to round-off
the data before
adding—giving the
results in the middle
column.

| PRECISION | ROUND OFF BEFORE ADD | ROUND OFF AFTER ADD |
|---|---|---|
| 5.563 | 5.56 | 5.56 $^{-}$ |
| 0.354 | 0.35 | 0.35 |
| + 6.864 | + 6.86 | + 6.86 |
| 12.781 | 12.77 | 12.78 |

Most application packages create their own objects as combinations of the basic data types. For example, graphs consist of numbers, text, and pictures. As a result, all of the attributes and functions that apply to the basic types also apply to derived graph objects. Hence, graphing packages can perform calculations on numbers, select fonts for displaying text, and enable you to set colors and rotation for the graph. Other applications, such as slide shows, provide additional functions, like controls for how one slide is replaced by another (e.g., fades, dissolves, and wipes).

The point is, once you understand the properties and functions of the basic data types, you can learn how to use any new application by concentrating on the new objects, their attributes and functions. This approach is especially true since many applications are designed and built using object-oriented methods.

Of course, the process of learning how to use new software would be much easier if software designers always chose the same set of commands to perform the same functions. Although the world does not quite work that way, you can come close by purchasing software *suites,* which are a combination of software packages sold by a single company. Commands to perform basic functions, such as setting text attributes, are the same for all the suite's applications. The suites also make it easier to exchange data between applications.

## Numbers and Text

Numbers and text are still the most common type of computer data used in business—for example, each cell in a spreadsheet can display a number or text (labels). Most business reports consist of tables of numbers with supporting text.

Computers handle numbers differently than do humans. Our base 10 (decimal) numbers are first converted to base two (binary). However, some decimal numbers do not convert to an exact binary value, so you will occasionally run into round-off problems. Most of the time the computer uses enough precision to avoid problems, but if you are dealing with very large or very small numbers, the errors can accumulate.

As shown in Figure 2.3, you must be careful with round off—particularly within spreadsheets. Consider the first column of numbers with three decimal digits. What happens when the format command tells a spreadsheet to display those numbers in the third column with only two decimal places? The computer will perform the addition first, and round off the displayed result, which means the total will appear to be incorrect. If you really want only two digits of precision, you should use the Round function to convert each number before it is added, as shown in the second column. Precision of calculations is important in business. For example, the 1999 European Union standards require that all monetary conversions be computed to six digits to the right of the decimal point.

Alphabetic characters are represented internally by numbers. The simplest method is to number the characters alphabetically, so *A* is 65, *B* is 66, and so on. These numbers are then stored in binary form. Two basic complications exist. First, large IBM machines use a different numbering sequence (EBCDIC) than do most other computers (ASCII). Fortunately, most existing methods of transferring data to and from IBM machines automatically convert between these numbering schemes. The second problem is that different countries use different characters. Today's hardware and software can be configured with special character sets for each country, but it can cause problems in conversion of files for people in different nations. These problems are gradually being solved by a new standard method of encoding characters known as Unicode. **Unicode** is an international standard that defines character sets for every modern (living) language, and many extinct languages (e.g., Latin). Unicode solves most difficulties with phonetic languages such as Japanese or Chinese by using a two-byte code for every character, so it can handle up to 65,000 characters. Most recent hardware and software can handle Unicode, but if you need to use foreign-language characters you should test the software carefully.

Figure 2.4 illustrates one of the more important properties of text: its typeface. You can choose from several thousand typefaces to achieve a desired style. Be careful with your choices. Some choices are obvious; for example, do not use a script typeface to write a business report. Also, serif fonts are typically used for printed material, and sans-serif fonts are used for very small or very large presentations. Other choices are more subtle and may require the assistance of a professional designer. You will also have to choose font sizes. The basic rules of thumb are that most printed text is displayed at 10 to 12 points. It is also useful to know that letters in a 72-point font are approximately one inch tall.

## Pictures

Pictures, graphics, and icons are used to display graphs and charts. Pictures are sometimes used as backgrounds or as icons in presentations that are used to help the audience remember certain points. In fact, almost all of the computer work that you do today is based on a graphical perspective. Video screens and printers are designed to display

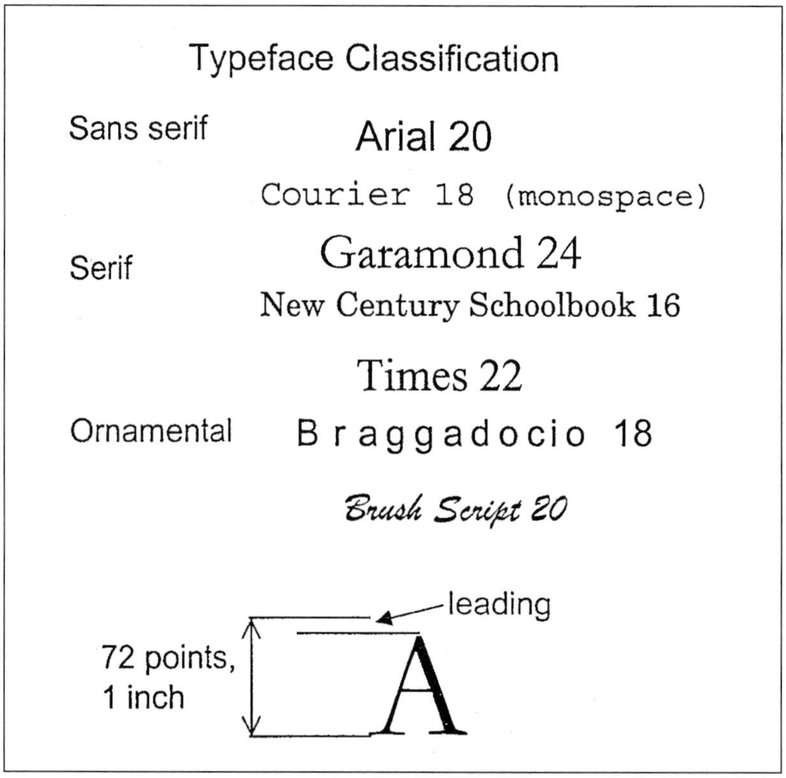

**FIGURE 2.4**
Typefaces fall into two main categories: serif and sans serif. Serifs are little curls and dots on the edges of letters. They make text easier to read; however, sans-serif typefaces are useful for overheads and signs because the added white space makes them easier to see from a distance. Ornamental typefaces can be used for headlines. Size of fonts is measured in points. Characters in a 72-point font are about 1 inch tall, and most books and newspapers use a font between 10 and 12 points.

everything, including text, in a graphical format. The graphical foundation provides considerably more control over the presentation. For example, you can change the appearance of characters or combine figures and graphs in your reports.

Two basic ways to store images are bitmap or vector format. The easiest to visualize is bitmap (or raster or pixel) format. A **bitmap image** is converted into small dots or *pixels (picture elements)*. If the picture is in color, each dot is assigned a (binary) number to represent its color. This method is often used to display photographic pictures where subtle changes in color (such as blends) are important. Bitmap pictures are evaluated in terms of the number of colors and resolution of the picture. Resolution is often measured in *dots per inch (dpi)*. You will encounter certain problems with bitmap images. Consider what happens if you create a bitmap picture in a square that has 50 pixels per side. How do you make the image larger? Use larger dots? Then the lines are very rough. How can you stretch the picture into a box that is 100 by 200 pixels? Although these operations are possible, they do not usually produce good results.

Historically, each graphics software package created its own file format for saving image files. Hence, it is easy to find more than 50 different formats on one computer. These differences cause problems when you attempt to exchange files. Your colleagues might not have the same graphics software and might not be able to convert your images correctly. With the Web, it is crucial that everyone be able to read the same graphics files. Hence, two major formats are used for sharing image files: GIF and JPEG. GIF files tend to be smaller, but they support only 256 colors. Hence, GIF files are often used for icons, while JPEG files are used for more realistic photographs. A third standard (PNG) began gaining acceptance in 1998. PNG files combine the advantages of both GIF and JPEG formats. However, remember that all three of these formats are bitmap formats.

When you need to change the size of pictures and keep fine lines and smooth edges, it is better to store pictures in vector format. **Vector images** consist of mathematical descriptions instead of dots. In most cases, they take up less storage space than bitmaps do. For example, a line is described by a statement such as: *line from (0,0) to (10,10) in yellow*. Do not worry, you do not have to be a mathematician to use vector images. Most of the current drawing packages store their work in vector format. Web browsers are beginning to support a new Internet vector image format that provides faster image transfers and scalable images.

In recognition of the usefulness of digital images, Kodak created a standardized system to convert photographs to digital (bitmap) form and store them on optical disks. The system is known as **Photo-CD.** Several commercial firms convert photographs to a Photo-CD format. Depending on how you want to use the pictures, you can choose among the resolutions listed in Figure 2.5. All of the resolutions use 24-bit color. Higher resolution means that fewer pictures can be stored on one compact disk (CD).

**FIGURE 2.5**
PHOTO-CD
RESOLUTIONS
Bitmap images are evaluated by their resolution and number of colors. Photographic quality requires 24-bit color (16.7 million colors). The Kodak Photo-CD standards define six levels of resolution, each requiring more bits of storage.

| Image Pac | Name | Resolution (v × h) | Dots per Inch at 3 × 5 |
|---|---|---|---|
| Base/16 | Thumbnail | $128 \times 192$ | 40 |
| Base/4 | Thumbnail | $256 \times 384$ | 80 |
| Base | TV | $512 \times 768$ | 160 |
| Base*4 | HDTV | $1024 \times 1536$ | 300 |
| Base*16 | Digital Print | $2048 \times 3072$ | 600 |
| Base*64 | Pro | $4096 \times 6144$ | 1200 |

Two basic methods are used to convert pictures into a computer format. One is to use a scanner that examines a photograph and identifies the various pixel colors. The second method is to use a digital camera. The basic difference between the two methods is convenience. However, scanners currently provide better resolution (more pixels) than digital cameras do. Most scanners are capable of at least 600 dpi, whereas most digital cameras operate at about 100 dpi. If you want to display the resulting pictures on a web site, 100-dpi resolution is probably acceptable. If you want to print the digital photographs, you will need 300 to 600 dpi (and sometimes higher) to get satisfactory images.

## Sound

Digitized sound is a relatively new feature for personal computers. Some companies are using sound capabilities much like telephone answering machines. You can use your computer to send **voice mail** messages to coworkers. There are tools that will even read e-mail and fax messages over the phone so managers can stay in touch while they are away from the computer. Software also enables users to attach voice notes to spreadsheets or documents. Colleagues can play back your comments while they read the report. Music and sound effects can be incorporated into presentations to make them more interesting. Increasingly, voice input is being used both to control the computer and for dictation.

Increased storage capacity and declining costs make it easier for sound to be stored in digital format. The conversion of sound to digital form is best illustrated with CDs.

Sound consists of two basic components: volume (amplitude) and pitch (frequency). These two values are changed over time to produce words and music. To digitize sound, volume and pitch are measured several thousand times per second. The resulting binary numbers are stored in sequence. The challenge is to sample the source often enough so no important information is lost. The music (or speech) is reproduced by synthesizers that convert the numbers into the appropriate sounds and play them through amplifiers and speakers.

If you intend to use music in your presentations, you need to understand the two basic ways to store music data. One basic format is to digitize the raw sound waves by measuring the amplitude and frequency. These files can rapidly become huge, but the method can capture any sound. For music (not voice), there is a second means of storing files. Many musicians today create music using electronic keyboards. Much like typewriter keyboards, these music keyboards transmit numbers indicating which key has been pressed, how hard, and for how long. This process is supported by several standards known as *musical instrument data interchange (MIDI).* By transmitting these numbers and messages to a synthesizer, the music can be re-created.

The difference between the two methods is like the difference between a tape recorder and sheet music. Digitized wave files are like tape recorders in that they record everything exactly as it was created. MIDI files are like sheet music—they tell a synthesizer which notes to play, and the synthesizer creates the music on demand. In addition to taking up less disk space, MIDI files are easy to modify and can be printed as sheet music. In using music files, you will have to make a choice between the two formats. The MIDI format takes substantially less space, but you need a synthesizer to reproduce it. Sampled music requires less sophisticated hardware. Also, with MIDI files, because of differences among synthesizers, you might get different sounds if you play the presentation on a different machine.

## Video

The use of computerized video signals is still in its infancy. Several recent technological changes will lower the cost of digitized video, which will ultimately increase its use in business. One use with incredible possibilities is the ability to transmit motion pictures over standard telephone lines. For instance, physicians can send images to specialists for consultation. Engineers can use video transmissions to diagnose problems over the telephone. Managers can carry on face-to-face conversations. Computer imaging tools also make it easier for workers to create animated presentations for demonstrations or for analyzing designs and layouts.

Although it is possible to convert motion picture and television signals to binary form, the conversion results in a tremendous amount of data. The process is similar to that for single pictures, except standard movies display 24 frames (images) per second, while U.S. televisions display 30 frames per second. Perhaps you have heard of *high-definition television (HDTV)*. The U.S. government, in cooperation with industry leaders, has defined standards for HDTV broadcasts in the United States; other countries use different standards. Television broadcasts are being converted to digital form for transmission. In the United States, Hughes Corporation established the first commercial digital TV broadcasts in 1994 with direct broadcast satellites to small satellite receivers with special decoders to convert the signals back to standard TV format. Much like audio CDs, HDTV provides improved quality with bigger yet sharper pictures, less interference, and more channels. Another major advantage to digital signals is that they can be compressed, allowing broadcasters to send more channels within the same space. With digital technology, cable TV companies can broadcast 500 channels over existing connections. Major television networks began the conversion to HDTV in 1998. Traditional analog broadcasts are scheduled to cease after 20 years.

Digital video signals also enable you to alter the image. In fact, it is now common to create entire digital scenes that never existed in nature. These techniques are commonly used in marketing. They are also used by engineers to develop and market-test new products.

## Multimedia

The combination of the five basic data types—text, numbers, sound, video, and images (animation)—is known as **multimedia.** In its broadest definition, multimedia encompasses virtually any combination of data types. Today, it typically refers to the use of sound, text, and video clips in digitized form that are controlled by the computer user. Multimedia applications tend to use huge amounts of data.

Available multimedia applications include encyclopedias and similar presentations, including discussions of animals, cities, and historical figures. To date, there have not been many commercial management applications of multimedia, although some educational courses have made good use of multimedia tools. For example, anatomy classes and medical courses have access to multimedia explorations of the human body. Some software tools even enable students to perform "surgery" on a multimedia "patient" and observe the results. Some people have used multimedia tools to build presentations. They are useful for initial designs in marketing because an initial video presentation can be created in a few days, instead of months. Multimedia tools are also being used in business training.

Currently, multimedia presentations are difficult to create. The techniques required are similar to those used in creating movies. In fact, if you want to learn how to create a professional multimedia presentation, it would be wise to take a course in filmmaking. It is easier to edit presentations on a computer than on film, but the concepts of scripts, storyboards, camera angles, lighting, movement, and aesthetics still apply.

You need several hardware tools to create multimedia presentations. You will need an optical disk drive, a sound board that records and plays back digitized sound, a high-resolution color display system, and a computer with a fast processor and plenty of memory. Additionally, to create your own video images, you will need a camera and a video capture board to digitize the images.

Several software tools are specifically designed to create multimedia presentations (e.g., Adobe Premier for video editing and Adobe After Effects for animation). Look for tools that can handle large projects, manage all of the data types you need, and are easy to use. In particular, look for tools that enable you to make extensive changes, so that you can move scenes around, copy portions of one scene to use as a foundation for another one, and so on. You can buy images, sound clips, and even video clips to make your job easier, but remember that film studios spend millions of dollars to create films.

One major business use for multimedia tools is for training. A human resources department is often responsible for creating and administering training for all the employees. Computer-based training provides the ability to offer training to individuals on their schedule. It also provides a consistent approach that can be tested and verified for accuracy.

Computer-based training makes it easier to track employee progress to determine which staff need refresher courses and to help in promotion decisions. Because of the flexibility in scheduling, it gives the employees the ability to plan their own education and choose their own direction in the company. All of these benefits can be achieved at lower cost with computer-based training than with traditional training methods.

If computer-based training lessons are used by enough people, it can be a cost-effective teaching technique. However, it can also be expensive and time-consuming to create the individual lessons. Because of the costs, computer-based lessons may not be updated as often as conventional handouts and textbooks. Additionally, because the tools are not yet standardized, companies run the risk of creating lessons using hardware and software that may rapidly become obsolete, requiring the project to be discarded or rebuilt from scratch. Despite these drawbacks, computer-based training can be a useful technique to train employees. As the variety and quality of software tools and libraries improve, it will become easier and cheaper to build lessons.

## Size Complications

To understand the importance of the five types of data, it helps to examine the size of each type. For many years, computers predominantly handled numbers and limited text. Over time, usage has gradually changed to include images, sound, and video. The more complex data types require much greater storage space, processing power, and transmission capacity.

Consider a typical, single-spaced printed page. An average page might contain 5,000 characters. A 300-page book would hold about 1.5 million characters. Now, consider a picture. At 300 dots per inch, a full 8.5 by 11–inch page would require a little over a million bytes if it were scanned in black and white. A photograph in Kodak Base*16 resolution with 16 million colors (24 bits per pixel) would require 18 **megabytes** (million characters) of storage space. Fortunately, most pictures have a lot of repetitive (or empty) space, so they can be compressed. Even so, high resolution pictures often fill more than one megabyte of space. Kodak's compression technology reduces Base*16 images to 4.5 megabytes.

Sound and video require considerably more storage space. Remember that thousands of numbers are being generated every second. A typical CD holds 650 megabytes of data, which can store 72 minutes of stereo music. The current standard for digitizing telephone conversations generates 64 kilobits per second, almost half a megabyte per minute. Video generates approximately 3 megabytes of data every second. However, some compression systems reduce the amount of data needed to transmit video. They start with the first frame and store just the parts that change for each succeeding frame. To address this issue, Intel has a software-based technology called Indeo that compresses and decompresses video pictures in real time. It reduces a one-minute video to about 9 megabytes on average. Several other companies are producing customized processors that will convert and compress

**FIGURE 2.6**
SIZE COMPLICATIONS
Video is the most
troublesome. Even with
compression, full-
screen video fills up
2 GB in 10 minutes.

| OBJECT | RAW | COMPRESSED |
|---|---|---|
| Text and numbers | 5K/page | 0.6 KB/page |
| Image (300 dpi, 24-bit color, 4 × 6 in.) | 2 MB | 0.5 MB |
| Sound (44.1 KHz stereo) | 150 KB/sec | 100 KB/sec |
| Video (NTSC 30 fps, stereo sound) | 25 MB/sec | 3 MB/sec |

video signals faster. These techniques also provide automatic picture scaling, to let the user choose the size of the final picture—from a small window up to the full screen. Figure 2.6 summarizes the basic size characteristics for the standard data types.

Finally, many companies are experimenting with multimedia applications. The combination of these data types requires a computer having a large amount of storage capacity and fast processing speed. Multimedia applications are typically stored and distributed on CD-ROMs.

**HARDWARE COMPONENTS**

Certain hardware components are needed regardless of the job. The four main components are devices that handle: input, processing, output, and secondary storage. Of course, for each component, there are hundreds of options, which means you can tailor a computer to your specific job. The features and costs of each component are continually changing, so it is difficult to derive simple rules that you apply when choosing a computer for your job. However, the basic roles of the four components are likely to remain relatively constant for the next few years. One trend that you have to remember is that the hardware industry changes rapidly, especially for small systems. Most computers that you buy today will have a short economic life—perhaps only three years. At the end of that time, each component will have changed so much that you will typically want to replace the entire computer.

The relationship among the four components is summarized in Figure 2.7. Note that the process subsystem consists of **random access memory (RAM)** and at least one processor. In many ways, the **processor** is the most important component of the computer. It carries out instructions written by various programmers. It uses RAM to temporarily store instructions and data. Data and instructions that need to be stored for a longer time are transferred to *secondary storage*. The capabilities, performance and cost of the computer are affected by each of these components.

You need to know three important characteristics to evaluate each component: speed, capacity, and cost. As illustrated in Figure 2.7, each component operates at a different speed. For example, how fast can you type? If you type 60 words per minute, then the computer receives five characters in one second, or one character every two-tenths of a second. However, the processor runs much faster. Some processors can perform more than 300 **million instructions per second (MIPS).** Between each of your keystrokes, the computer processor could execute 60 million instructions! The same concept applies to most output devices because their speed is often measured in characters per second. Speed of most secondary storage devices is measured in **milliseconds** or thousandths of a second. That's still pretty slow when compared to billionths of a second (**nanoseconds**) that measure processor speed.

Why are there secondary storage devices? Why not just store everything in high-speed RAM? The main reason is cost. Although prices vary, memory chips cost somewhere around $1 per megabyte. Typical storage devices cost $0.05 per megabyte or less. Also, there are two basic kinds of memory chips: static and dynamic. Dynamic chips cost less but lose their contents when the power is turned off, so they are not useful for long-term storage.

## Processors

Processors come in a wide variety of formats. Some computers use one processor that consists of a single silicon chip (*microprocessor*). Others use several different chips to make up one processor. Still other computers use multiple processors. The critical point to remember is that each type of processor is unique. Each manufacturer creates its processor in a certain way and designs it to follow a specific set of instructions. For in-

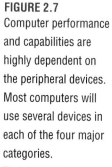

**FIGURE 2.7**
Computer performance and capabilities are highly dependent on the peripheral devices. Most computers will use several devices in each of the four major categories. Technological progress in one area often results in changes to all four types of components.

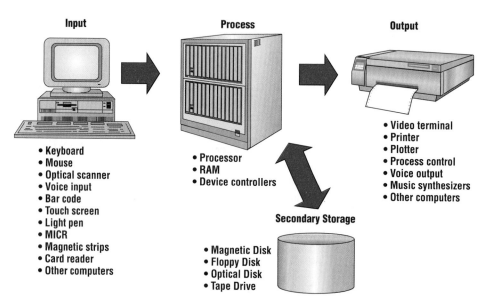

**Input**

- Keyboard
- Mouse
- Optical scanner
- Voice input
- Bar code
- Touch screen
- Light pen
- MICR
- Magnetic strips
- Card reader
- Other computers

**Process**

- Processor
- RAM
- Device controllers

**Output**

- Video terminal
- Printer
- Plotter
- Process control
- Voice output
- Music synthesizers
- Other computers

**Secondary Storage**

- Magnetic Disk
- Floppy Disk
- Optical Disk
- Tape Drive

---

### Reality Bytes     2–1    Building Processors and Memory Chips

Building processors and memory chips involves growing silicon crystals and slicing them into wafers. The internal circuits are then etched onto these wafers using chemical deposition techniques. The catch is that cramming more storage on a chip requires finer and finer circuit lines. Common RAM chips in 1994 held 4 megabits of data, with leading-edge chips at 16 megabits. Because of capital costs, manufacturers will only produce new chips if they can gain four times the amount of storage.

Researchers in the mid-1990s were beginning work on a 1-gigabit chip (64 times the storage of a 16-megabit chip, or 3 generations improved). For this chip to work, it needs lines that are 0.15 microns wide (1/200,000 of an inch).

Using conventional laser lithography to etch patterns onto the chip becomes difficult as the lines get smaller. Conventional methods rely on a mask to

cover parts of the chip that are then exposed to laser light, which removes a photoresistive material on the uncovered sections. The main difficulty with small sizes is that the light waves are too wide. Modern chip technology relies on ultraviolet rays because they are narrower, but they are still 0.193 microns wide. Manufacturers are experimenting with smaller wave x-rays or electron beams.

A second problem is that the etching size is coming closer to the size of a single molecule, which brings in quantum physics effects, where atoms randomly "tunnel" through barriers.

Some companies, like Cray Computer, have switched from silicon to gallium arsenide (GaAs), because it has smaller molecules that allow finer etchings. The GaAs chips also operate faster. However, GaAs crystals currently are more difficult to work with.

stance, a processor made by Intel works differently than one made by Motorola. As a result, instructions written for one processor cannot be used directly by the other processor. Note that some companies (especially in the personal computer world) produce "clones" of the leading chip manufacturer. For example, Advanced Micro Devices and Cyrix/IBM make chips that are compatible with Intel processors and can run the same programs.

### Comparing Processors

Whenever you buy a computer, you want to have some idea of how fast it can operate. Because all of the components interact, it is hard to measure speed. It is even harder to make comparisons among different types of processors—especially when they operate differently. Nonetheless, it is difficult to justify spending the money for a new computer if you have no idea of what can be gained. Hence, there are several measures of speed. Some measures focus on individual components, others attempt to evaluate the entire system.

Because the processor is an important factor in the speed of a computer, a commonly used measure is the number (millions) of instructions they can complete in one second (MIPS). A slightly more accurate measure is the number (millions) of **floating point operations per second** (MFLOPS), which evaluates the processor's performance in terms of mathematical computations. Other measures, called *benchmarks,* have been created to compare different computers under a variety of situations. Although benchmarks give a better indication of performance than do MIPS or MFLOPS for certain tasks, they are more complex to administer and they tend to change over time. They are useful if you can find one to match your application and you want to compare several machines at the same point in time.

Some people use the internal clock speed as a measure of processor performance. For example, the Intel Pentium II processor was available at different clock speeds, such as 200 MHz, 300 MHz, and 400 MHz. Although the clock speed does directly affect the performance of the processor, you must be careful to use it only to compare processors from the same family. For instance, a Pentium II at 233 MHz is faster than a Pentium processor running at 233 MHz. Clock-speed comparisons between manufacturers are essentially meaningless.

Price is another important feature of processors. Consider the approximate measure of price and performance shown in Figure 2.8. Because the recent numbers are hard to see, they are printed in the accompanying caption. The graph shows the average cost of buying one million floating point operations per second (cost/MFLOPS). The costs are approximate because they include peripheral equipment. Despite these approximations, it

---

**Reality Bytes          2–2   My Computer Is Faster than Yours**

Manufacturers continually look for ways to produce faster computers. On the high end, manufacturers such as IBM have been building massively parallel computers for high-performance tasks. For example, in 1998, IBM sold a version of their RS/6000 computer called Blue Pacific to Lawrence Livermore laboratory for use in testing nuclear weapons. The machine can perform 3.9 trillion calculations per second and contains 2.6 trillion bytes of memory.

The system contains 1,464 nodes, each with four processors, for a total of 5,856 processors working together. The computer is a descendant of the Deep Blue machine that IBM used to defeat world chess champion Gary Kasparov in 1997. IBM sold the Blue Pacific computer for $94 million. IBM is reportedly working on a newer version capable of 10 teraFLOPS (trillion floating point operations per second).

**FIGURE 2.8**

Computer performance has improved considerably in the last 10 years. One measure of performance is millions of floating point operations per second (megaFLOPS). The continual performance improvements in microcomputers and RISC-based workstations has resulted in dramatic declines in cost per MFLOPS. In 1998, the numbers were as follows: supercomputer $8, midrange $67, and microcomputer $17.

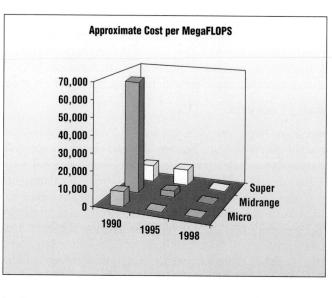

is clear that the price drop over 10 years has been enormous. Much of this decline was driven by the expanding performance of microcomputers. Today, the important conclusion is that for most applications, processing time is free.

The important features of the table and graph are the speed and prices of the microcomputers. Notice how the personal computer speeds compare to those of the larger computers. Although these machines are designed and used for different purposes, because the differences are so large, we would expect this pattern to affect the way businesses use computers. These changes will be examined in later chapters.

In the mid-1980s, the Intel 80286 machines performed at a fraction of 1 MFLOPS. Today, the Intel Pentium II machines can process over 100 MFLOP. Intel has developed its own rating system to help personal computer buyers understand the potential value of new processors. Some examples are shown in Figure 2.9. The numbers do not signify any absolute level of performance but are designed to allow comparison to earlier Intel chips. For example, a Pentium II/400 is about 4.5 times faster than a Pentium/120. There are many differences among the chips, and without the iCOMP measure, it would be hard to tell which chip might be faster.

The catch is that these numbers represent only the speed of the *processor,* but system performance also depends on the speed of peripheral devices, amount of system memory, and type of internal connectors (buses, as described next). Nonetheless, the graph does illustrate the improvements made for each generation, with the 386 popular during 1989–1993, the 486 during 1993–1995, the Pentium from 1994–1997, and the Pentium II from 1997 on.

### Random Access Memory

As processor speed has improved, RAM has become a crucial factor in system performance. Because disk drives are mechanical, they are the greatest bottleneck in a computer system. Hence, modern operating systems try to hold as much data as possible in RAM. Although RAM speeds have remained relatively constant in the last few years, RAM price has dropped substantially. In relative terms, RAM is virtually free. For a couple hundred dollars, you can easily buy enough RAM to hold several applications and their data in RAM at one time.

### Connections

Even if two computers have the same basic components, it is still possible for one machine to be substantially faster than the other. The reason is that the components need

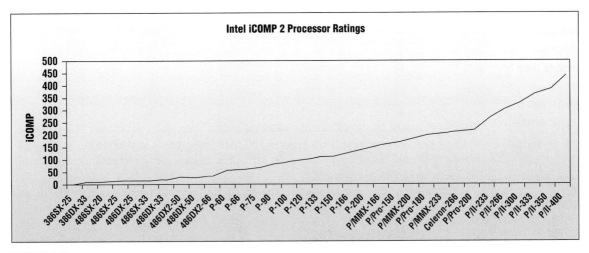

**FIGURE 2.9**

To assist buyers, Intel provides a measure of its own processors. The rating is an index that measures relative performance. A processor with a rating of 200 would generally be about twice as fast as a processor with a rating of 100. Of course, your other devices also influence the overall system speed, so just buying a faster processor does not guarantee that your machine will run faster.

to exchange data with each other. This communication requires an electrical connection. Most computers have special slots that form the connection between add-on boards and the processor *bus*. Various manufacturers make boards that fit into these slots. The processor can exchange data with these other devices, but it is constrained by the design of the bus. For example, even if a processor can handle 64 bits of data at a time, the bus might not have the connections to allow it to transfer that much data at a time. Each computer manufacturer has to choose how to design the bus. Standards enable users to exchange cards and devices from one computer with another. The problem is that a bus designed for today's computers will eventually become obsolete as the processor improves. At some point, the standards need to be changed. In the personal computer market, standards for the bus have been gradually evolving. The original, IBM-designed bus, known as the *Industry Standard Architecture (ISA)* still exists in some computers today—despite the fact that it was designed to transfer only 8-bits at a time. With the introduction of the Pentium processor, the industry has generally adopted an Intel-sponsored design known as *Personal Computer Interconnect (PCI)* bus. PCI was also designed to make it easier for users to set up their computers. In conjunction with the operating system, the computer determines which cards the computer contains and configures them automatically—a process known as *plug-and-play*. In the past, users had to read obtuse documentation and set switches on every card, hoping that a new card did not conflict with an existing one. New varieties of the bus are being tested today, but there is no clear successor to PCI.

One interesting connector was introduced on personal computers in 1998. Known as an IEEE 1394 or *firewire,* it was originally developed to connect game machines. It can transfer data at extremely high speeds and easily connects several devices. It is gaining rapid acceptance for consumer devices such as digital video cameras.

### Parallel Processors

In the past, when processors were more expensive, designers used only one processor in a machine. Today, many computers contain multiple processors. Although it can be a desirable

**FIGURE 2.10**
Some computations must be performed in sequence, so there is little to be gained with multiple parallel processors. In this example, the second computation (yyy) must wait for the first one to finish.

$$
\begin{array}{rr}
23 & xx \\
+54 & +92 \\
\hline
xx & yyy
\end{array}
$$

feature, you must be careful when evaluating parallel-processing machines. If a computer has four processors and each can process 100 MFLOPS, then it is tempting to say that the computer in total can process jobs at 400 MFLOPS. Indeed, many computer companies advertise their computers this way.

Can a computer with four processors really do your job four times faster? The answer is that it depends on your job. Consider an example. A computer with two processors has to add two sets of numbers together. Each processor works on one pair of numbers and finishes in half the time of a single processor. Now, the same two computers have to work the problem in Figure 2.10.

Notice that the second calculation depends on the outcome of the first one. The second one cannot be computed until the first one is finished. Even if we assign one processor to each calculation, the parallel-processing machine will take just as long as the single processor.

A parallel-processing computer is faster than a single processor only when the job can be split into several independent pieces or there are several jobs and each processor can be assigned to different jobs—several examples are presented (see Parallel Processing Examples). There is one more problem: The computer has to spend some time assigning jobs and collecting the results. For a small number of processors, this may not be a major problem. However, some companies are selling computers that contain as many as 32,000 separate processors. Seymour Cray of Cray Computer Corporation, in 1994 indicated that by 1999 he wanted to produce a machine with 32 million processors, capable of performing 1 quadrillion (billion, million) operations per second. Two important questions should leap into your mind at this point: (1) For what types of jobs would these massively parallel computers be useful? (2) How much will the computer cost? As a partial answer for the first question, at the end of 1994, another computer manufacturer, NEC announced that the firm could build a machine that performed 1 trillion operations per second. However, analysts estimated that it would cost $100 million and would probably never be built because no one would buy one at that price. Although there are many interesting uses for supercomputers, companies are increasingly faced with the question of determining how much value such expensive machines could contribute. An additional answer to the question comes by noting that Cray Computer filed for bankruptcy in 1995. In 1996, Cray Research (the leading supercomputer manufacturing company) was sold to Silicon Graphics, Inc. In the continuing effort to build faster machines, IBM has stepped in with its Big Blue massively parallel system. In 1997, the computer beat the reigning chess champion. In 1998, IBM announced that processor improvements raised its performance to 100 gigaFLOPS; and that by 2000 they expect to produce a machine reaching 1 teraFLOPS in speed. Pricing was not announced.

Some of the commercial uses for massively parallel machines are listed here (see Parallel Processing Examples). The common feature is that the tasks can be split into thousands of smaller pieces, and there is a huge amount of data to examine. Two other users of supercomputers are: (1) governments for code breaking, and (2) special-effects studios, such as Industrial Light & Magic.

## Parallel Processing Examples

According to a study by International Data Corp, the total revenue for manufacturers of massively parallel computers was approximately $261 million in 1991. Partly because of high cost, partly due to lack of commercial objectives, massively parallel machines were largely limited to facilities performing scientific research. They are used to simulate molecules in chemistry and to study weather patterns. However, commercial use of the machines is increasing.

Chevron Oil Field Research uses a Maspar Corp. MP-1 for oil exploration. Chevron uses the parallel processors to search huge quantities of 3-D seismic data. A typical survey consists of 2,000 tapes holding 200 MB of data each.

NASA used a Maspar Corp. MP-1 to improve the initial images from the Hubble Space Telescope. The lens on the $1.5-billion telescope was not ground correctly and the initial images were blurry. With 8,192 processors, the MP-1 delivers 650 megaFLOPs (million floating-point operations per second). Software analyzes each portion of the image and estimates the amount of spherical distortion from the lens to correct the image. The process takes about three hours per picture and would not be practical without the massively parallel system.

The OnLine Computer Library Center provides computer support for 11,000 member libraries. It maintains a card-catalog database of more than 24 million books. Roger Thompson is in the process of converting the database search system to run on a parallel computer to shorten the search times.

Dow Jones News/Retrieval is a division of the company that publishes *The Wall Street Journal.* They created a search system called DowQuest that uses a Thinking Machine Corp. computer with 32,000 processors. The system is a database that stores full-text articles from more than 184 publications (e.g., *The Wall Street Journal, Barron's,* and *Fortune*). The system asks users for a search topic, then each processor searches a portion of the database. The results are immediately presented to the user. The user can then prioritize the list, or select one or two articles. The system then uses the rankings and the words in the chosen articles to perform another search of the database. With this iterative search, the system is better at finding related articles that might use synonyms. The parallel processors make the search significantly faster, giving the user more opportunities to revise the conditions.

By using thousands of low-cost processors instead of one or two expensive, high-speed processors, massively parallel systems can be cheaper to use. A benchmark comparison of the Oracle Corp. database provides one example. The best large-computer performance in 1992 was 419 transactions per second, costing about $50,000 per transaction. The same process on a 64-node NCube parallel machine yielded 1,073 transactions per second at a cost of $2,482 per transaction—a substantial improvement in price and performance.

## Input

Because of the variety of data types, many input devices are available. The purpose of an input device is to convert data into electronic binary form. Keyboards are the most common method of entering new text and data. Note that you can purchase different types of keyboards to suit individual users. For example, some keyboards enable you to change the layout of the keys. Keyboards have their own "feel"; some individuals prefer sensitive keys using a light touch, others like stiffer keys to support their hands. Some manufacturers have gone further and have experimented with keyboard designs that accommodate nontraditional placement of the hands. Figure 2.11 provides one example.

**Ergonomics** is the study of how machines can be made to fit humans better. One of the main conclusions of this research in the computer area is that individuals need to be

**FIGURE 2.11**

There have been increasing complaints about injuries caused by repetitive typing tasks. Several manufacturers have experimented with new keyboard designs that are claimed to relieve physical stress.

able to adjust input (and output) devices to their own preference. Forcing people to adapt to rigid devices can lead to complaints and even physical injuries. Since the mid-1980s, many workers have encountered a disabling condition known as *repetitive stress injury,* which some people claim results from extended use of tools that do not physically match the worker.

Although there is limited scientific study of these injuries and causes, some people have found relief after ergonomic changes to their work environment. Complaints typically involve back pain, eye strain, headaches, arm and shoulder pain, and finger or wrist pain due to carpal tunnel syndrome. Common ergonomic suggestions include adjustable chairs, foot rests, arm rests, adjustable keyboards, high-resolution low-flicker monitors, and improved lighting.

Of course, all of these adjustments cost money—especially if they are added as an afterthought. The key to the problem is to evaluate individual requirements and adjust the environment *before* installing computers.

### Pointing Devices

With the increased use of graphics and pictures, it is common for computers to use pointing devices for input. A mouse is the most popular device in use today, although light pens, touch screens, and digitizer tablets are heavily used in some applications. Touch screens are commonly used for displays that involve customers or other atypical computer users. Many tourist bureaus, hotels, and shopping areas use computer displays with touch screens to give directions to visitors. Besides the fingerprints, the biggest problem with touch screens is that the tip of your finger is often too large to be a useful pointer. For more detailed use, an engineer who is designing a wiring diagram for an automobile would use a digitizer tablet with a special pen to draw fine lines and select individual points that are close together.

### Scanners

When you are dealing with pictures, it is often helpful to have a scanner convert a paper-based image into digital (bitmap) form. For certain types of images (line-drawings and text), there is vector tracing software to convert the bitmap image into vector form.

The quality of a scanner is measured by the number of pixels per inch that it can distinguish as well as the number of colors. Most scanners can read at least 600 dots per inch. More dots mean better resolution: finer lines and sharper pictures.

Scanners also can be used to input text and data into a computer. The scanner first converts the page into a picture of dots. Then **optical character recognition (OCR)** software examines the picture and looks for text. The software checks each line and deciphers one character at a time. Although OCR software is improving, it is not 100-percent accurate. Some systems automatically look up each word in a dictionary to spot conversion errors and improve accuracy. Even then, users report about a 95-percent accuracy rate—which is highly dependent on the quality of the original document.

### Pen-based Systems

A new category of computers is being created. Some handheld, notebook-size computers use a pen as the primary input device. The pen is used to point to objects on the screen, make changes to documents, and even write notes. In some cases, the machines can convert handwriting to computer text—much like OCR converts typed papers. Of course, deciphering individual handwriting is much more difficult than reading typed characters, and the accuracy of data can be limited. Despite the hype about potential applications for traveling managers (and salespeople), the first versions of pen-based computers did not sell well. As processors, storage, and display technology and telecommunications improve, we will probably see more acceptance of pen-based handheld computers.

### Sound

Sound is initially captured with a microphone that converts sound pressure waves into electrical signals. A *sampler* then converts these signals into numeric data that can be stored on the computer. Musical **synthesizer** technology is used to convert the numbers back to electrical signals that can be heard with speakers. Sound boards can be purchased for personal computers that contain both the sampler and synthesizer technology. Digital sound conversion occurs on almost every long distance telephone call you make. Your voice is converted to 1s and 0s to be sent across fiber-optic telephone lines.

### Speech Recognition

As long as computers have existed, individuals have dreamed of being able to talk to them and have their words translated into text. Today, computers can digitize and record speech, and they can convert spoken words into computer text. Some problems still exist,

---

**Reality Bytes    2–3    Sears Uses Speech Recognition to Cut Costs and Improve Service**

In 1999, speech recognition systems began gaining acceptance in mainstream applications. For example, Sears faced increasing problems in their customer service operations. They had 3,000 telephone operators in 800 stores, covering phones seven days a week 12 hours a day. It was difficult and expensive to find and train employees. Additionally, customer service was somewhat lax as noted by Jan Drummond: "We had customers listening to as many as 20 rings before they got an operator. We were missing calls and customers were going to Circuit City and other competitors." Sears installed the new speech recognition system that interprets customer requests and routes them to the correct department. It recognizes even heavily accented speech, and accepts synonyms for products, like "fridge" for refrigerator. By reducing the need for operators, the system paid for itself in three months.

## Speech Recognition Examples

Public familiarity with voice recognition devices increased in 1993 when Sprint Corp. began selling a voice-activated calling card that recognizes user commands to dial up to 10 numbers. In a similar vein, several car phones offer voice-dialing as a safety feature for drivers. AT&T eliminated 2,000 telephone operator positions with the use of voice recognition.

The U.S. Bureau of Labor Statistics replaced paper reports by using a voice recognition system to collect monthly data from 390,000 businesses.

Auralogy S.A., a French software company, developed a system to teach foreign languages. If the program does not recognize a student's phrase, it uses a pronunciation lesson to assist the student.

ADGA Quebec Ltd. is an engineering firm that uses voice recognition to train airport ground personnel how to use and respond to radio orders.

and the systems need to be trained to a specific user. Common problems include the use of homonyms, variations in speech patterns or dialects, and the effects of punctuation on meaning.

In 1998, several companies introduced speech recognition systems for under $200 that perform very well at converting speech into computer text. Initially, speech recognition systems were adopted by occupations that require note taking along with two hands to do the job. Quality control inspectors and surgeons use them regularly. As performance continues to improve, we will see an expanded use of speech recognition systems among all users.

### Video Capture

As technology improves, companies are increasingly adding video clips to presentations. Probably the most common use of video lies in computer-based training (CBT). Users interact with scenarios described in video clips to solve problems or learn new techniques. Digital video transmissions are also being used for communication.

Because computer monitors and television sets are loosely based on the same technology, it would seem easy to merge the two. However, computer monitors deal with different types of video signals. Computers need special video boards to convert and display TV signals on the computer monitor. These cards accept standard coaxial video output from a VCR, camcorder, and television receiver. Not only can the signal be displayed on a monitor but also converted to digital form and saved or replayed. Hence, you can change the images, add text and graphics, or design special effects such as a metamorphosis that turns a person into a car *(morphing)*.

The fact that computer monitors use signals differently from televisions causes an additional challenge in an international environment. The United States, Europe, and Japan have different television signals. Videotapes recorded in the United States cannot be played on European VCRs. That means that a video capture board built for the U.S. market might not work in other countries. A few boards, however, support several different signals. So, if you are dealing with offices in different countries, be careful when purchasing video hardware and software to ensure that it supports all of the standards you need.

## Output

Most people are interested in two types of output: video and paper copy. Video output is created by a video card and displayed on a monitor. The quality is measured by the **resolution,**

**FIGURE 2.12**

COMMON VIDEO RESOLUTIONS

Note that higher-resolution video cards require larger monitors. Current video cards also contain features to increase the speed of 3-D imaging. Monitor size is viewable space measured in inches along the diagonal.

| Video | # Colors | Resolution | V-RAM | Monitor |
|---|---|---|---|---|
| VGA | 256 | $640 \times 480$ | 150KB | 10 in. |
| SVGA | 65K | $800 \times 600$ | 1 MB | 12 in. |
| XGA | 16.7M | $1024 \times 768$ | 2 MB | 14 in. |
| Super XGA | 16.7M | $1280 \times 1024$ | 4 MB | 16 in. |
| No name | 16.7M-4B | $1600 \times 1280$ | 6–8 MB | 20 in. |

which is the number of pixels and colors it can display. Resolution is established by the video card, but higher resolutions require larger, more sophisticated (and more expensive) monitors. Common personal computers today can support 1,024 horizontal and 768 vertical dots at 16 million colors, which requires a video card with 2 megabytes of memory. Some video cards support as many as 2 billion colors. This level of color is called **true color**, because it exceeds the range of colors that can be distinguished by the human eye. True color requires 32 bits (4 bytes) per pixel to attain this level of color. Computer projection systems used for meetings and presentations use high-intensity light to project an image onto a screen. In addition to resolution, they are evaluated by the intensity of the light, measured in lumens.

High-resolution screens with multiple colors can display beautiful pictures and excellent quality text. As indicated in Figure 2.12, they do have some drawbacks, however. They are relatively expensive, especially because large-screen monitors (19 inches or more) are often needed to display text in a legible size. Because high-resolution true-color screens require over 15 times more data than the older video boards, the higher-resolution boards can also be slower. Manufacturers have compensated by building special hardware and software to accelerate them. Accelerators for 3-D imaging are particularly useful for intensive graphics.

The other common output device is the printer. Printers come in many different forms. Three popular formats are laser, ink jet, and dot matrix. In all three cases, the output is created by printing dots on the page. Resolution is measured by dots per inch. Common resolutions include 300 and 600 dpi, and 1,200 dpi lasers are available. In contrast, standard typesetters, such as those that are used to print books, operate at resolutions of at least 2,400 dots per inch. Again, higher-resolution devices are more expensive. Also, the increased amount of data being displayed takes longer to print (for the first copy).

Laser printers operate much like photocopiers. A multifaceted mirror reflects a laser light onto a drum. This drum rotates and picks up the toner (dry ink). As the paper feeds through, it is given an electric charge that attracts the toner. The toner is then heated and fused to the paper. It is not crucial that you understand the process; the important point is that there are few moving parts in laser printers. As a result, they are relatively trouble free and significantly quieter than older types of printers. Because they use toner instead of ribbons, they are often cheaper to operate.

Dot matrix and ink-jet printers have a print head that moves across the page and prints each character or graphics dot. A dot matrix printer has wires that physically press a ribbon to the paper to print dots and form each character. An ink-jet print head does not touch the paper but relies on electrostatic charges to attract the ink from a nozzle to the paper. Both printers operate more slowly than laser printers, but prices tend to be lower. More importantly, it is easier to create color output with ink-jet printers because they use liquid ink instead of dry toner. Color laser printers exist, but be sure to check the cost of printing a page. Approximate comparisons of the three major types of printers are displayed in Figure 2.13.

FIGURE 2.13
PRINTER
EVALUATIONS

Printers are evaluated
in terms of initial cost,
cost per page,
resolution, and speed.
There are many types
of printers, led by laser,
ink jets, and dot matrix
printers. Prices vary
depending largely on
speed and resolution.
Technological changes
are leading to new
varieties of printers
than can produce full
color at a cost of
around 5 to 10 cents
per page.

| PRINTER | INITIAL COST (DOLLARS) | COST PER PAGE (CENTS) | QUALITY (DOTS/INCH) | SPEED (PAGES/MIN.) |
|---|---|---|---|---|
| Laser: B&W | 600–200,000 | 0.6–3 | 300–1200 | 4–8–17–100+ |
| Laser: Color | 2,500+ | 5–75 | 300–1200 | 0.5–8 |
| Ink jet: B&W | 100–2,000 | 5–50 | 300–600 | 0.25–7 |
| Ink jet: Color | 200–2,000 | 25–150 | 300–720 | 0.1–4 |
| Dot matrix | 100–500 | 1.5–3 | 100–300 | 0.5–2 |

## Secondary Storage

Except for prices (declining) and capacity (increasing), typical secondary storage devices have changed little during the last few years. Secondary storage is needed to hold data and programs for longer periods. Secondary storage is evaluated by three attributes: capacity, speed, and price. The values for different types of storage are summarized in Figure 2.14.

The device most commonly used today is the magnetic hard drive. *Magnetic hard drives* consist of rigid platters that store data with magnetic particles. Data is accessed by spinning the platters and moving drive heads across the platters to access various tracks. Hard drives come in a variety of sizes, ranging from 2 to 15 gigabytes (billions of bytes). One thousand gigabytes are called a *terabyte* (trillion bytes). Typical drive prices range from $0.04 to $0.15 per megabyte (and up). **Access speed** is the time needed for the drive to move to a particular location and begin transferring data. Typical access speed is around 10 milliseconds.

With the increasing importance of data, companies are searching for ways to prevent loss of data by providing continuous backups. One straightforward method is to install an extra disk drive and keep duplicate copies of all files on this *mirror drive*. If something goes wrong with one of the drives, users simply switch to the other drive. A second method of protecting data is known as a **redundant array of independent drives (RAID).** Instead of containing one large drive, this system consists of several smaller drives. Large files are split into pieces stored on several different physical drives. At the same time, the pieces can be duplicated and stored in more than one location. In addition to the duplication, RAID systems provide faster access to the data, because each of the drives can be searching through its part of the file at the same time.

On personal computers, another common storage device is the floppy disk drive. These use thin, removable disks to store data. They operate similarly to magnetic hard

---

**Reality Bytes    2–4   How Small Can It Be?**

As manufacturers strive to make all of our devices more intelligent, there is an increased need for miniaturization. For example, digital cameras typically use flash cards (nonvolatile RAM) to store pictures, but they have limited capacity. So in 1998, IBM introduced a miniature hard drive. The microdrive is about one inch in diameter, weighs 0.7 ounces, and holds about 340 megabytes of data.

**FIGURE 2.14**

Disk drives are evaluated in terms of capacity, speed, initial cost, and cost per megabyte—especially for removable media. Many drives are available in each category so a range is displayed for each feature. Note there has been a strong downward trend in hard drive costs in the last few years.

| DRIVE | CAPACITY (MEGABYTES) | SPEED (MILLISECONDS) | INITIAL COST (DOLLARS) | COST/MBYTE (DOLLARS) |
|---|---|---|---|---|
| Magnetic hard | 2,000–18,000 | 9–15 | 200–2,000 | 0.02–0.15+ |
| Removable hard | 100–1,500 | 12–20 | 200–400 | 0.05–0.20 |
| Floppy | 1–120 | 80–200 | 50–100 | 0.02–0.35 |
| Solid State/RAM | 2–1,000 | 0.00006–0.006 | 50+ | 25.00–100.00 |
| Tape | 250–2,000 | sequential | 300–5,000+ | 0.04–0.15 |
| CD-ROM | 650 | 100 | 50–150 | 0.001 |
| CD-Recordable | 650 | Slow write | 350–500 | 0.002 |
| DVD | 8,000 | 150 | 300 | 0.004 |

drives but are much slower. Typical capacity is around 1.5 megabytes per disk, which costs less than 5 cents per megabyte when bought in quantity. However, the access speed is around 100 milliseconds, or 10 times slower than hard drives.

Magnetic tapes are also used to store data. Their biggest drawback is that they can only store and retrieve data sequentially. That means you have to search the tape from the beginning to find any data. A single tape can hold a gigabyte of data at a cost of 4 to 10 cents per megabyte. Because of these two features, tapes are most commonly used to hold backup data.

With the increased use of images, sound, and video, there is a need for substantially greater storage capacity for data files. Optical disks have provided substantial capacity at relatively low costs. The optical (or magneto-optical) disk drive uses a laser light to read data stored on the disk. There are three basic forms of optical drives: CD-ROM, CD-R (recordable), and erasable. **CD-ROM** stands for *compact disk-read only memory,* the format used to store music CDs. The ROM portion of the name means that you only can read data from the disk. A special machine is required to store data on a CD-ROM. One side of a CD can hold 650 megabytes of data and costs less than a dollar to produce in

## Upgrade Decisions

Not counting printing and input devices, we can think of the computer as four major subsystems (processor, memory, secondary storage, and video). These four systems strongly affect the computer's performance. With current system designs, it is possible to upgrade a computer by replacing one or more of these components. How much you gain in speed depends on the improved speed of the new component and on how you use the computer.

For example, Mark VanName and Bill Catchings *(Computer Shopper)* note that for a typical user task that might take 100 seconds, about 60 seconds will be used by the processor and memory, 20 in the disk drive, and 20 in the graphics subsystem. Assume you buy a new video card that can display information

twice as fast as the old one. The time spent in the video subsytem would be cut from 20 to 10 seconds, but that's only a 10-percent increase in system speed. On the other hand, if you doubled your processor/memory speed, you would cut 30 seconds from the overall time.

Keep in mind that not all machines and people use the subsystems in the same proportions. If you work on highly graphic-intensive applications, you might gain even more by buying a faster video subsystem.

Finally, note that after about three years, virtually all of the subsystems will be outdated. In such a case, upgrading one or two components might not be sufficient. To seriously improve system performance, you will want to upgrade the entire computer.

quantity. The biggest drawback is that a *fast* access speed is 200 milliseconds (one-fifth of a second). Hence, it could take a full second to find five different pieces of data. CD-ROMs are most useful for storing large quantities of data that will not change. CDs are available that contain text, pictures, sound, and video for an entire encyclopedia.

Manufacturers have tried to improve the access speeds on CDs, but they are limited by the existing standards. In the 1980s, to ensure compatibility, the major manufacturers agreed on how data would be stored on CDs. As part of this process, they decided to maintain compatibility with audio CDs, so that computer-based CD readers could also play musical selections. Although this decision helped create multimedia applications, it currently limits the speed of CDs. To meet the standards, the CD must spin at a predetermined speed. This spin rate is a major factor in determining access times, because data can only be found and retrieved when it is spun under the read head. A common method to speed up CDs is to build in two spin rates: the standard speed to read the data and a faster rate (two, three, or four times faster) to search the CD indexes.

CD-R drives enable users to record data onto a CD-ROM disk. These drives can only write data once—the data cannot be erased. They use a special disk that can be read by standard CD-ROM drives. The process can take an hour or more to record data. Hence, a CD-R drive is useful for making one or two copies of data. To create multiple copies of a CD for distribution, it is better to pay a company to create a standard CD-ROM.

It is possible to purchase a CD-erasable drive, which enables you to create and change data on the disk. However, the **DVD (digital video disk or digital versatile disk)** is a significantly better technology. DVD was created to distribute digitized video. Compared to CD, the strengths of DVD are: (1) increased capacity; (2) significantly faster access speeds; (3) standards for audio, video, and computer data; and (4) the ability to record data. The standards are evolving, but a double-sided DVD should hold at least 6GB of data.

The biggest drawback to all forms of disk drives is that they are sensitive mechanical components. They can be damaged if dropped, they wear out with use, and there are physical limits to how fast they can store and retrieve data.

Due to speed constraints and the declining costs of memory chips, some applications are beginning to use memory chips as secondary storage. Although the cost can be as high as $30 per megabyte, data can be stored and retrieved a thousand times faster. One increasingly common version is the PCMCIA (Personal Computer Memory Card International Association) card that is used with laptop and notebook computers. PCMCIA cards are about the size of a thick credit card, ranging from 3-mm to 16-mm thick. The cards can hold 20 megabytes of data in a type of memory chip that does not lose its contents when the power is turned off.

## OPERATING SYSTEMS

Computers follow instructions called software that are written by programmers. Every computer needs one special type of software known as the operating system. The **operating system** is software that is responsible for communication among the hardware components. The operating system is also a primary factor in determining how the user deals with the machine.

In the past, you had no choice about the operating system; when you bought the computer, the manufacturer included its proprietary system. Today, with almost any computer, you can choose between at least two operating systems (proprietary and UNIX). With personal computers you can choose between UNIX and a version of Microsoft Windows (e.g., Windows 98 or Windows 2000). Approximately 95 percent of the buyers use Windows. Today, differences among operating systems generally revolve around three areas that affect you directly: multitasking, user interface, and security.

Anyone who spends substantial time online or reads financial publications has heard of Amazon.com. Amazon took the Internet by storm, scaring even Barnes & Noble, one of the largest booksellers. Not as many people have heard of the Internet Bookshop Ltd. (www.bookshop.co.uk)—despite the fact that in 1997 it carried the second largest number of books on the Internet. Interestingly, despite the global nature of the Internet, perhaps the greatest challenge faced by the company is the fact that it is located in Cambridge, England. More than 40 percent of the company's sales come from U.S. customers. But, Amazon is better known, does not have to charge international shipping, and its products are priced in dollars instead of pounds sterling. The Internet Bookshop emphasizes global sales, since 80 percent of its sales are outside of the United Kingdom. However, the process is complicated because the site must be offered in multiple languages and customer support representatives need to be bilingual. Shipping costs are still a substantial problem. Currency issues are minor, because credit card companies convert currencies at favorable exchange rates. Darryl Mattocks, the founder, sums it up when he observes that "Ideally, the Internet provides the communication highway across the continents, but then you face all the problems that a regular business does."

Historically, each computer manufacturer created its own operating system tailored for that specific hardware. Knowing how to use one set of operating system commands might not help if a user bought machines from different vendors. Likewise, changing vendors typically required purchasing new application software. AT&T researchers began to solve this problem when they created a hardware-independent operating system. It is known as *UNIX* and is designed to work with computers from many different manufacturers. However, UNIX is not a complete standard, and application software must generally be rewritten before it can function on different computers. Standards have been an important contributor to the declining cost of personal computers, which has led to their widespread use throughout the world.

Another approach to the compatibility (portability) problem is being taken by Microsoft Corporation, which created an independent operating system originally called *Windows NT*. Now known as *Windows 2000,* it was designed to operate on a variety of hardware platforms. It was also designed to be relatively easy to adapt to processors that might be invented later. A key difference with the Windows 2000 operating system is that application software written for one version will run without changes on other computers, regardless of the processor used. For example, a small company could begin by using personal computers. As the company grows, the amount of data increases. The company could switch to a RISC-based computer running Windows 2000, simply by copying the application software and data to the new machines. This *scalability* can be a useful feature for any company because it minimizes the problems and trauma arising from changing computer systems.

**APPLICATION SOFTWARE**　The main reason for buying a computer is its application software. It is good software that makes your job easier. Regardless of your job, you will always perform certain tasks. As a manager and decision maker, you first have to gather data (research). Then you analyze the data and determine alternatives (involving calculations). Next you will make decisions and implement them (requiring writing, communication, and organizing resources). Each of these tasks can be supported by computer resources. The trick is to use the appropriate tools for each task. The objective is to use the tools to make you more productive in your job.

The catch is that productivity is a slippery problem in business—especially with respect to computer tools. One measure of productivity involves efficiency: Can you perform tasks faster? A second, more complicated measure of productivity involves effectiveness: Can you make better decisions? Early uses of computers focused on improving efficiency by automating manual tasks. The tools were often justified on the basis of decreased labor costs. Today, managerial uses often focus on effectiveness, which is harder to measure.

An important concept to remember with application software is that it was created by teams of designers and programmers. In the "old" days, when software was custom-written for specific companies and users, users could tell the designers how the software should behave. Today, we are moving rapidly to off-the-shelf software that is created to support the needs of millions of different users. In creating the software, designers had to make thousands of decisions about what the software should do and how it should appear. Sometimes their final choices might seem strange, and software does not always work the way you might prefer. Some issues can be resolved by customizing the software to your particular situation. Other times, just remember that you acquired the software for a tiny fraction of the price you would have paid for custom software.

## Research: Databases

Almost any job involves workers searching for information. This search could involve any of the five basic types of data. Computers have made it substantially easier to find, compare, and retrieve data. Two important strengths of a *database management system (DBMS)* are the ease of sharing data and the ability to search for data by any criteria. In terms of productivity, a DBMS can make you both more efficient and improve your decisions. It improves efficiency by providing easier and faster data retrieval. By providing more complete access to data, a DBMS helps ensure that your decision incorporates all relevant data.

One complication with research is that you must first determine where the information is located. It could be located on your personal computer, the group's networked server, the company's central computers, a computer run by the government, or one purchased from another company. Unless all of these databases are connected, you must first determine which database to search. Chapter 5 focuses on the use of database management systems. Most DBMSs can handle numbers and simple text well. Only recently have they begun to tackle large text files, pictures, sound, and video. Internet search engines help you do research, but they only support data stored in one format.

## Analysis: Calculations

Almost everyone performs computations in a job. Although simple calculators are useful, they have some drawbacks. For example, it is difficult to go back and change a number entered previously. Also, calculators cannot save much data, and it is hard to print out the results. Finally, because of their small screens, they can display only a few numbers at a time. Spreadsheets were initially designed to overcome these limitations. These features are designed to make you more efficient at making calculations.

Most people find spreadsheets useful because their disciplines began with models on paper that used columns and rows of numbers. For instance, most accounting systems and financial models were designed for ledgers in this way. Whenever software mimics the way you already work, it is easier to learn.

Spreadsheets have many additional features. Graphs can be created with a couple of mouse clicks. Most packages enable users to modify the graphs by adding text, arrows, and pictures. Spreadsheets also perform various statistical and mathematical analyses. You can perform basic matrix operations such as multiplication and inversion. Statistics capabilities include multiple regression to examine the relationship among different variables. Linear programming can be used to search for optimum solutions to problems. These additional features are designed to help you make better decisions by providing more powerful decision-evaluation tools.

## Communication: Writing

The primary gain from word processing is increased efficiency. Word processors improve communication by making it easier to revise text, find writing errors, and produce legible reports. Word processors today also include a spell-checker, a thesaurus, and a grammar-checker. Although they are not the same as having a human editor correct your writing, they are all useful tools for writers. Grammar-checkers use standard measures to estimate the reading difficulty level of your writing. For instance, if you write an employee policy manual, you want to make sure that an average employee can understand it. Most word processors also have outline tools that help you organize your thoughts and rearrange a document, improving the communication.

The proliferation of word processors creates additional advantages. At some point, a company finds that almost all of its reports, data, and graphs are being created and stored on the computer. If this transition is handled carefully, managers can use the computer to search for any prior reports or data. It also becomes easier to send reports and notes to

---

### Reality Bytes    2–6    International Notations

Most applications today have the ability to use characters that are not found in the U.S. alphabet. For instance, in France or Mexico, you might need to use an acute mark (é). However, different software packages handle the characters differently, so you might have trouble converting a document from one word processor to another or to a different computer. For example, if a French subsidiary is using *WordPerfect* and the Canadian headquarters is using *Microsoft Word,* they can both print reports using the special characters. However, the document might change when the Canadian users attempt to retrieve a French document electronically.

Additionally, if you work for an international organization, remember that people in different countries write dates differently. For example, 5/10/93 means May 10, 1993, in the United States but would be interpreted as October 5, 1993, in Europe. Most word processors enable you to choose how automatic dates should be displayed.

Numbers are also handled differently in European nations. The use of commas (,) and points (.) is reversed from the U.S. version where commas separate thousands and the decimal point delineates the fractional component. (126,843.57 in the United States should be denoted as 126.843,57 in Europe.)

Two other problems often arise with spreadsheets: currencies and denoting billions. When you transfer documents to other languages or fonts, be sure to check any currency symbols. A few systems will automatically change the symbol to the local units (e.g., change $ to £), but unless the numbers are converted by exchange rates, these changes would be incorrect. A second complication arises when a graphing package or spreadsheet automatically converts numbers to billions. In the United States and France, the number 1 billion has 9 zeros. In the United Kingdom (and nations like India), 1 billion has 12 zeros. An automatic conversion of 2,700,000,000 to 2.7 billion would result in a misinterpretation if the graph is sent to Great Britain.

other managers. It sounds as though companies would use less paper and rely on electronic transmissions. Most organizations have not made it to this stage yet, and some people believe we never will. In fact, the use of personal computers has dramatically increased the usage of paper by U.S. companies.

Software companies have continued to add features to their products. The biggest trend in word processors is the addition of desktop publishing features. **Desktop publishing (DTP)** provides more control over the final print. For example, you can choose a typeface to convey a certain image. You can include graphics images, tables, special characters, equations, and borders. You can automatically build an index and a table of contents. One problem that some companies have experienced with desktop publishing is that it appears to decrease the efficiency of employees. It takes employees longer to create reports because they spend more time experimenting with layouts and presentation. The trade-off is that the reports now contain more information or communicate it better so that the effectiveness has improved and managers can make better decisions. Be careful when you communicate with documents that will be transferred to other nations. Even if the language is the same, some systems will replace characters with the local alphabet—which can be a major problem with currency signs.

One interesting impact of low-cost computers is that it is increasingly difficult to evaluate organizations by the quality of their publications. Even small groups can afford to produce high-quality reports and brochures. In the past, people tended to dismiss poorly typed and handwritten papers because they obviously came from small organizations. Now, one person can produce a report that looks like it came from a major organization.

## Communication: Presentation and Graphics

In many cases, the difference between a good report and an outstanding report is the presence and quality of the artwork. Graphs and pictures are used to communicate information and feelings. Charts and graphs are easy to create, store, and modify using graphics software. Even if you are not an artist, you can buy **clip art** that was created by someone else and use it in your reports or charts. By using existing art libraries, reports and presentations can be created in a few hours. In the past, reports and presentations took days or weeks to finish by a staff of artists. By improving the appearance, a well-designed graphic can also improve communication and decision making.

To create or modify your artwork, you need a graphics package and an input device such as a mouse that enable you to draw on the computer screen. Most commercial artists use scanners so they can draw the original on paper and convert it to computer form. The digitized form enables you to make very precise changes, since you can *zoom* into a specific area. Zooming is helpful if you need to force lines to meet exactly or you want to make changes to small items, such as eyelashes on a person.

Color often presents problems to computer artists. Colors on display screens are usually different from those generated by the printer. If you are serious about exact color matching, the Pantone® color standard is supported by some printers (especially those used by commercial printshops), graphics software, and even some monitors. By choosing colors according to these definitions, you are assured of getting the precise color on the final copy. Some software packages also support color separation. In modern four-color presses, color is created based on four different masks (cyan [blue], magenta [red], yellow, and key [black]—abbreviated CMYK). Other colors are created by blending portions of these colors, as controlled by the masks. Software that supports color separation can use a special machine to print the separate masks, which go directly to a commercial printing press.

**Reality Bytes    2–7    MP3 Alters the Music World**

For many years, a few large recording/distribution companies controlled the music industry. The company signed musicians, arranged production of the music, promoted the artists, and earned money from distributing the CDs. However, the consumer saw little of most of these activities. Instead, most consumers bought CDs form the local music store chain. The introduction of Internet-based music stores like CDnow does not change this model. Conceivably, the Internet stores may increase competition, which could slightly lower prices and increase selection. On the other hand, a relatively new audio technology offers the ability to alter the status quo radically in the music industry. That technology goes by the name *MP3.* It stands for an audio compression technology that can reduce the typical stereo song to about 4.5 MB. That means a typical CD could be stored in about 80 MB versus the 650 MB the CD requires. The MP3 format does result in a slight, but generally unnoticeable, production quality. The significance of the storage size is that MP3 makes it possible to download songs over the Internet. And this capability scares the music industry. For starters, Diamond Multimedia introduced an audio player called Rio in 1998. The music industry fought to keep this device off the market. Their primary argument was that they were concerned about music piracy. However, the MP3 format is readily available to everyone and inexpensive to use. Hence, any band can now create music to sell and distribute over the Internet—circumventing the existing music industry. Today, you can easily find MP3 audio files on the Internet for free or minimally priced download. In fact, in 1998, MP3 became the second most common search term on the Internet search engines (behind sex). Common MP3 sites include: www.mp3.com, www.audiofind.com, and www.hot100.com/music.

Although you do not have to be an artist to incorporate artwork into your reports and documents, you do need an element of artistic sensibility. The goal is to use art to enhance your presentation, not clutter it. Knowing what looks good and using restraint are signs of artistic talent. Remember that faster does not always mean better. Use some of the time savings to put more thought into your presentations.

## Communication: Voice and Mail

All jobs require communication—with co-workers, managers, and customers or clients. Word processors help with reports and memos, but much of our communication is less formal. Everyone is familiar with answering machines for telephones. Businesses have taken this concept a step further by using voice mail systems. Voice mail systems record messages much like an answering machine, but they store the messages in digital form on computers. They usually give the caller control over where the message is sent. Most people in the United States have dealt with systems that direct you to press buttons on the telephone to make choices. Some voice mail systems enable you to send the same message to several people. Some systems also enable you to skip messages or fast forward to the end.

Networked computers can be used to send messages directly to other users. These **electronic mail (e-mail)** systems are typically used to send written notices to various people. They can be used to send pictures, facsimiles (faxes), or even voice messages if the computers have sound boards and speakers. The basic problem with any communication system is that sooner or later it becomes cluttered with junk mail. One of the advantages of text e-mail is that the recipient can have the computer scan the messages to search for items that are important or interesting. With the appropriate *mail filters,* junk mail can be discarded automatically. Messages also can be retrieved and stored for future reference or forwarded to other people.

## Organizing Resources: Calendars and Schedules

An important task of managers is to organize company resources so that they are used most effectively. An important function is scheduling workers. Schedules involving line workers entail making sure that there are enough employees to get the job done, but no extra employees. Schedules involving managers typically involve meetings and require trade-offs between competing demands for a manager's time. Several software tools are available to improve both types of scheduling and make more efficient use of the human resources.

Most managers spend a considerable amount of time in meetings. In fact, it becomes difficult to keep track of appointments, set up new meetings, and reschedule meetings. The process is even more difficult when some participants are traveling or are based in another city or country.

Several software packages store appointments and schedules on electronic calendars. Electronic calendar and scheduling software enables data to be shared with other people. For instance, each person in a department would use the electronic calendar to keep track of his or her personal, departmental, and corporate appointments. To schedule a meeting with departmental members, the manager selects an approximate time, specifies the priority of the meeting, and fills in the participants, location, and subject information. The calendar software then searches each personal calendar for the best time for the meeting. It overrides lower-priority meetings and places the complete notice on each person's calendar in a matter of seconds. Employees have to check their calendars periodically to see whether meetings have been added or changed.

## The Paperless Office?

You might think that with increased use of electronic data, there would be less need for paper. So far, the opposite has happened. According to *The Economist,* in the 1990s in Britain the use of paper increased by 65 percent over 10 years. From 1993 to 1998, despite the growth in use of personal computers and the Internet, paper usage increased by 13 percent. Worldwide, paper use doubled form 1982 to 1998. Some people might argue that electronic capabilities helped hold down the increased use of paper, but there is little evidence to support this claim.

Why would the use of paper increase? First, corporate information systems and the Internet have made it easier to create and distribute information. Second, the current electronic displays are generally not as readable or as portable as paper copies. Consequently, people retrieve the data they want and print it out.

Today, electronic displays are approaching the point where they might eventually be able to replace paper copies. Screen resolution has been a big factor in readability. Conventional monitors operate at about 100-dpi resolution. Newer technologies will produce 200-dpi resolutions, which will produce good quality text at traditional book sizes. Portability is also improving, although battery life is still an important issue.

There are still unresolved issues about future compatibility. Properly cared for, paper documents will last for decades. While electronic data can service for years on CDs or DVDs, the hardware and software to read them may disappear in a short time.

## SUMMARY

One of the original purposes of computers was to make it easier to perform basic tasks. Over time, as computers have become more powerful, they have come to support increasingly complex tasks. Today, in addition to increasing efficiency, computers can help you make better decisions. One major change is in the type of data routinely processed. The five major types of data are numbers, text, images, sound, and video. To handle more sophisticated data and more difficult tasks, computer hardware and software have grown increasingly complex.

To choose a computer that best meets your needs, you must evaluate the four basic hardware components: input, processor, output, and secondary storage devices. Each component is measured by slightly different characteristics. Input devices are selected based on the specific task (such as a keyboard for typing, mouse for pointing, or a microphone for voice input). Processors are often selected based on speed and price. Output device quality is appraised by resolution and color capabilities as well as initial and ongoing costs. Secondary storage is evaluated based on speed, capacity, and price.

Although computer hardware and software are becoming more complex, operating systems are being improved to make them easier to use. Through graphical user interfaces and standardized menus, operating systems make it easier to use common applications. When choosing an operating system, you should also evaluate its ability to run several applications at once (multitasking).

### A MANAGER'S VIEW

Many tools available for personal computers will help you in your daily tasks. Every manager needs to write reports and memos. Most also deal with numbers on a regular basis. Calendars, schedules, and personal notes are used by most executives. Contact managers and phone lists are particularly important for sales managers.

You need to know how to use all of these tools. You also need to keep up with changes in the industry. Many times in your career, you will need to purchase computer hardware and software. You can make better decisions if you understand the technology and trends.

Application software is the primary source of improved productivity. Packages exist to assist in research, analysis, communication, and organizing resources. Database management systems are used for research and data sharing. Spreadsheets and other analytical tools assist in calculations. Word processors, desktop publishing, drawing packages, voice mail, and e-mail are used for communication. Electronic calendars and scheduling software are used to help organize human resources. There are hundreds of other software applications for specific tasks, but most people begin with these basic tools.

## KEY WORDS

access speed, 66
binary data, 47
bitmap image, 51
CD-ROM, 67
clip art, 72
desktop publishing (DTP), 72
digital video/versatile disk (DVD), 68
electronic mail (e-mail), 73
ergonomics, 61
floating point operations per second (FLOPS), 57

input, 47
megabyte, 54
million instructions per second (MIPS), 55
milliseconds, 55
multimedia, 53
nanoseconds, 55
operating system, 68
optical character recognition (OCR), 63
output, 47

Photo-CD, 51
processor, 55
random access memory (RAM), 55
redundant array of independent drives (RAID), 66
resolution, 65
synthesizer, 63
true color, 65
Unicode, 50
vector image, 51
voice mail, 52

## WEB SITE REFERENCES

**Free News Sources**

Associated Press
CNN
Ecola
ESPN

wire.ap.org
www.cnn.com
www.ecola.com
espn.go.com

| | |
|---|---|
| Fox News | www.foxnews.com |
| Internet News | www.internetnews.com |
| MSNBC | www.msnbc.com |
| News.com | www.news.com |
| Newshare | www.newshare.com |
| USA Today | www.usatoday.com |
| United Press International | www.upi.com |
| Wired | www.wired.com |
| ZDNet | www.zdnet.com |

**Almost Any Magazine or Newspaper (many charge for access)**

| | |
|---|---|
| *Business 2.0* | www.business2.com |
| *Fortune* | cgi.pathfinder.com/fortune |
| *The Economist* | www.economist.com |
| *Wall Street Journal* | wsj.com |
| *Washington Post* | www.washingtonpost.com |

## REVIEW QUESTIONS

1. Describe the differences between hardware and software.
2. List and describe the five basic types of data. How much space would it take to store a typical example of each type of data?
3. Explain why speed and cost are important characteristics of computers.
4. What current processor gives the best performance for the price? Explain your answer.
5. The computer for Letterman Co. has three 100-MIPS processors. Is it safe to assume that this computer operates at a constant rate of 300 MIPS (100 MIPS * 3)? Explain your answer.
6. List and describe four common input devices. Using the knowledge you have gained thus far, what do you think is the most common type of input device? What input devices do you think will become more popular in the future?
7. List and describe two common output devices. Give an example of their use in business.
8. What is a secondary storage device? Give two examples of secondary storage devices.
9. Assume you are an employee for XYZ company. The director of MIS for XYZ company wants you to evaluate two different secondary storage devices to determine which best fits the needs of XYZ. What criteria will you use in your evaluation of the two storage devices?
10. What is multitasking? Give some advantages of multitasking. What are some potential problems of multitasking?
11. How does a graphical user interface (GUI) help end users operate their systems more effectively?
12. Identify at least three possible uses for a massively parallel-processing supercomputer. Explain how the tasks can be split into the necessary pieces.
13. You find that your company's staff now spends more time producing reports than they did before using personal computers. Should you get rid of the computers?
14. On a quick tour through a company, you notice that only 10 percent of the personal computers were being used. The rest sat on desks, either turned off or running a weird screen saver. Based on these numbers, you are thinking about selling half the machines and asking workers to share. Is this a good idea?
15. How do computers improve productivity in communication? What is the difference between increased efficiency and effectiveness (better decisions)?

## EXERCISES

1. Why don't companies build processors that follow the same instructions?
2. Estimate the current costs of operating these printers (cost per page): laser, dot matrix, ink jet, and color laser.
3. Give three reasons why the use of personal computers could increase the usage of paper.
4. A software package enables you to define rows of data, but it uses an integer to count the rows. This value is stored in 2 bytes. If half the values can be negative, what is the largest positive value that can be held in the 2 bytes? If the counter is increased to 4 bytes, what is the largest positive value?

5. You have just been hired in a new job, and you will need a personal computer in your work. The company will pay up to $3,500 for hardware and software. Your new boss is willing to let you choose whatever components you want. Using current business and computer magazines, select the basic hardware and software elements you will need. At a minimum, your software should include an operating system, word processor, graphics package, and a spreadsheet program. You might not need to purchase a printer. Describe the basic components you chose. Be sure to justify any unusual choices.

6. Using reviews in computer magazines, identify at least two software packages in the following categories: word processor, spreadsheet, graphics, calendar, communications, and database management. Identify five major features of each package. Find the current lowest price (and source) of each product.

7. You have just been asked to explain word *processors, spreadsheets,* and *graphics packages* to a computer novice. In particular, he wants a *reference sheet* that will help him.

**CO2Ex08.txt**

8. You are trying to decide on raises for your departmental employees. The accompanying table lists the performance evaluations they received along with an estimate of the percentage raises that you wish to give. To review your spreadsheet skills, enter the formulas necessary to complete the table, including the totals and averages. Also, create a graph that displays the percentage raise and the performance evaluation for each employee. (One extra credit point is given for identifying all of the employees.)

9. Estimate the storage space (number of bytes) required for each of the following items:
   a. A telephone book with 10,000 entries consisting of names, addresses, and phone numbers. Use your phonebook to estimate the average length of an entry.
   b. A fax transmission of a 30-page report at high resolution (200 by 200 bits per inch). What is the raw size? What is the size if you can use a compression algorithm that reduces each page to one-twentieth the original size?
   c. You have a 4 by 6 inch color photograph scanned in high resolution at 2,400 dots per inch and 16 million colors (24 bits for color). How far (percentage) would you have to compress this image to fit into 4 MB of available RAM?
   d. Kodak has a system that transfers photographs to a CD-ROM. Using the Base*16 resolution and the compression ratio described in the text, how many pictures can be stored on a CD-ROM that holds 650 MB? How many Base (TV) resolution pictures could be stored?
   e. If you wanted to store your favorite half-hour television show in digital form, how many bytes of storage would it take? Extra credit: How much space would it take if you remove the commercials? (Hint: Time the commercials.)

10. To review your word processing skills, write a short report to the CEO similar to the one shown here. It should include a properly formatted table. If possible, use a laser printer and a proportional typeface. Use a larger font for the title, and include the underline and bold attributes.

| Renovation Schedule | | | |
|---|---|---|---|
| | | **EST. RENOVATION DATE** | |
| **FACTORY** | **MANAGER (PHONE)** | **START** | **END** |
| Spindle Prod. #7 | Sanchez (4327) | 4/9/01 | 6/7/01 |
| Planing #1 | Mirabel (1135) | 12/13/01 | 3/20/02 |
| Chair Assembly #12 | Gruntag (7893) | 6/3/01 | 9/17/02 |
| Upholstery #16 | Bachnel (8876) | 10/5/01 | 12/11/01 |
| Spring Prod. #3 | Coorda (3352) | 8/9/01 | 9/8/01 |

To:        J. Kevorkian
From:
Date:

After talking with the engineers and plant managers, the renovation committee has arrived at the enclosed schedule. With this schedule, we believe that we can complete the needed renovations *without disrupting production.* As you can see, it will take us almost a year to finish the remodeling. It is possible to speed up the process, but we would have to sacrifice production—which would cause us to be late on the **Werner contract** and we would be forced to pay a penalty fee.

11. A spreadsheet is an important tool that can be used to manage your personal finances. A simple plan that you can implement is a personal balance sheet. The top of the balance sheet includes your income. In it you can list all of the money that you have coming in each month. The bottom of the balance sheet is your expenses. Using it, you can list all the expenditures that you were required to make each month. Your instructor has a disk with a sample outline that you can fill in with your personal data. Of course, you can enter additional lines in each category.

### C02Ex11a.xls, C02Ex11b.xls

a. An important part of financial analysis is the ability to compare your financial statement to those of others. Several sample worksheets are included on the sample disk. Examine several worksheets. They are each listed by student name. How do these worksheets compare to your income and expenses?

b. Graph the most significant items in your worksheet. These would include those items that seem to have the most variance or the widest range of dispersion. What difficulties occur when you graph these items against the totals in each category?

### Rolling Thunder Database

12. Using the Export Data form, copy the data to a spreadsheet and create graphs for the following situations. (Choose the type of graph you feel is best suited to present the data.)
    a. Sales by model type
    b. Sales by month
    c. Sales by model type for each month
    d. Sales by state
    e. Sales by employee by month

13. Using the existing forms, enter data for a new bicycle order.

14. Design a small web site (include some forms and graphics) that could be used to advertise the products manufactured by Rolling Thunder Bicycles.

15. Find at least two other bicycles (e.g., on the Internet or from a dealer). Create a spreadsheet comparing the features and costs with a similar bicycle built by Rolling Thunder Bicycles.

16. Find at least five web sites on which Rolling Thunder Bicycles might advertise their bicycles. Briefly describe the type of people who might see those ads, and why they would be interested in Rolling Thunder Bicycles.

## ADDITIONAL READING

Adams, S., R. Rosemier, and P. Sleeman. "Readable Letter Size and Visibility for Overhead Projection Transparencies, *AV Communication Review,* 1965, pp. 412–417. [An early discussion of creating good presentations]

D'Amicao, Mary Lisbeth, "Electrolux Shows Net Fridge, *Computerworld,* February 16, 1999. [Appliances connected to the Internet]

Hamilton, David P. "Memory-Chip Man Must Tame Electrons," *The Wall Street Journal,* June 21, 1994, p. B10. [Building memory chips]

Lieberman, David. "Software Goes on a Search-and-Locate Mission," *Electronic Engineering Times,* January 25, 1999, p. 44. [Improved imaging/vision technology (www.imaging.com)]

"Science: The Numbers Game," *Time,* February 20, 1988, pp. 54–58. [Short history of computers]

Simonds, D. and L. Reynolds. *Computer Presentation of Data in Science: A Do It Yourself Guide,* Boston: Kluwer Academic, 1989. [Ideas for presentations]

Stix, Gary. "Toward 'Point One,'" *Scientific American,* February 1995, pp. 90–95. [Designing memory chips]

# CASES *Entrepreneurial Businesses*

The entrepreneurship industry is a thriving and vibrant industry. After years of being thought of as oddballs, entrepreneurs are not only getting respect, they are admired and sought after. An *entrepreneur* is someone who starts a business for himself or herself, and also has a new way of doing things or a new product.

Entrepreneurs used to be thought of as people who couldn't make it in corporate America, or with strange personalities; the word had a less-than-positive connotation. This attitude has changed markedly in the past 15 years. Nothing has brought about change in attitudes faster than when the countries in Asia seemed to be passing the United States in productivity and ideas, with effective processes such as just-in-time becoming the norm in large companies. Suddenly, corporate America moved too slowly and entrepreneurship style of thinking was needed; the entrepreneur then became the desired state of mind for companies that wanted to succeed. How big is entrepreneurship these days? Venture capitalists (companies that look for ideas in which to invest) have poured millions of dollars into nothing much more than an idea and a prototype of the product. Only the volatility of the stock market threatens to dry up the liberal financing currently available for the entrepreneurship industry.

Entrepreneurship is so popular these days that a new type of entrepreneur is popping up: the well-to-do entrepreneur. For example, Alex Mandl, the second in command at AT&T, quit his job in late 1997 to work at a start-up wireless communications company. He spent his first week hiring a secretary and trying to install a new phone system. Why did he do it? A team of venture capitalists had an idea, and they hired Mandl to do everything else. He also received a $20-million bonus plus a stake in the company to sign. But mostly, when we say *entrepreneur* we mean a person who is risking his or her livelihood to start his or her own business from scratch.

## Stock/Investment Outlook

Investment in entrepreneurs is a risky proposition, to say the least. The great majority of new businesses fail within the first five years. Moreover, these businesses are usually small and not publicly traded. Therefore, investing in them means contributing to the business directly in return for equity. In order for that to happen, entrepreneur-driven businesses can require at least tens of thousands of dollars.

With such a bleak outlook, who would invest and why? Venture capitalists, that's who (along with friends and family of the person(s) starting the business). Venture capitalists specialize in looking for good investment opportunities. Again, why invest in a start-up? If the concept seems reasonable, usually the person trying to get the funding is putting everything on the line, having already asked for money from everyone he or she knows. Therefore, investors know that if the business fails, it is probably not for a lack of trying. Venture capitalists, moreover, can provide general business guidance and advice so that the new business can avoid the common problems. The payoff: if the business makes it, the return can be quite handsome. In return for the investment, venture capitalists own a piece of the company.

A successful entrepreneurship can be quite profitable. In 1997, *Forbes* survey of the Forbes 400 richest Americans contained 72 percent of first-generation entrepreneurs (think Bill Gates, Michael Dell). Of course, there are no guarantees of success.

In short, investing in entrepreneur-headed businesses is something generally left to the rich and the experts. Personal investing in a small, entrepreneur company should be done with the expectation that you will lose all the money. Therefore, most people should limit this to family and friends starting businesses.

## Potential/Prospective for Growth

The growth in the entrepreneurship industry is surprising. The lure of big profits and the ability to be your boss entices a lot of people. The potential for growth has been very good lately. Years of a healthy economy have loosened the purse strings of many venture capitalists, and it is easier than ever to get money for your new business (but you still need a good plan and perseverance). Luckily for entrepreneurs, the market volatility of the second half of 1998 has only made venture capitalists cautious, not running scared.

Assuming the business gets off the ground, the potential for growth depends on a number of factors, including the need for the new product or service, the state of the economy, how the product or service is priced, marketed, and delivered, and the customer service.

With today's technology, however, it is easier than ever to compete with big companies offering similar services or products. There are even associations to help entrepreneurs get business advice, find mentors, and make business contacts. Therefore, combining the change in attitude toward entrepreneurs, the good economy, and the venture capitalists, the chance for growth is better now than it has been in years. This also means that there may be more competition now than ever for investors' dollars, and there is always the fact that most businesses fail to make it.

## Competitive Structure

The competitive structure of those in the entrepreneurship industry changes. Since they are not all selling the same product or service, or even going after the same type of client, the competitive structure of the entrepreneur's business depends mostly on the product or service they resemble most, or the product or service they are trying to replace. If this is a completely new product or service, which few are, there are no competitors. In that case, however, customers need to be convinced that this is a new product or service they need or want, and store buyers have to be convinced to give up some store shelf space for the new product.

In short, getting a new offering off the ground is an extremely difficult endeavor, especially for entrepreneurs lacking the power (and money) of multinationals, who also come out with new products. In that sense, there is competition. Entrepreneurship is so well thought of in this day and age, that many major manufacturing companies, from drug to toy makers, have allowed and even encouraged entrepreneur-like behavior in order to come up with new products and markets. Once these big companies do have a new product, they have a lot more clout in stores than a small company in asking for shelf space. Therefore, the competitive environment is usually stacked against a competitor. If the new offer from the entrepreneur is a good idea and executed well, the product or service will easily sell itself once the company starts growing. It will usually take some time before the big companies come in to compete with a successful entrepreneur. There are many reasons for this, from believing that entering that market may not be worth it, to the internal delays faced by large companies.

## Role of Research and Development

Research and development is the reason entrepreneurs start a business for themselves. Entrepreneurs have the vision of a product or service that is unique enough to warrant their full attention and financial support. The idea for a necessary product, for example, may come from simply saying "wouldn't it be great if something existed that . . . ?" In that case, a little research needs to be done. Not only product research, but also market research: would people be willing to pay for this concept? How much? How often would they buy it? As previously mentioned, some big companies make entrepreneur-like behavior a process. These companies realize that "thinking outside the box" means more than just putting out today's fire in the most efficient way.

For example, Merck and Company, the huge pharmaceutical company, has tried to standardize the invention process. The scientists who develop drugs in Merck's laboratories are encouraged to take a chunk of time and devote it to scouting for ideas outside the company and create and follow up on drug projects of their liking. They can then make a case to a Merck board to finance the research or buy it from the outside. How are they rewarded? Usually through handsome payoffs in stock options, according to the *New York Times*. Therefore, research and development is part of an entrepreneurship business.

## Technological Investment and Analysis

Although the amount of technological investment in an entrepreneur company depends on the main product of that business, there is no doubt technology and technological advancements have made being an entrepreneur easier and lowered the barriers to entry. Ironically, it is especially in the field of technology where entrepreneurs have done best in the recent memory. Companies such as Dell, Microsoft, and Netscape were all started as entrepreneurial businesses. In fact, Silicon Valley, the hotbed of computing-related innovations in the United States, is filled with venture capitalists looking for the next Netscape. While a person selling a service or a simple product might not need to keep abreast of the latest technology to survive originally, that business will need it down the road if the business grows.

It is easy to see that new technology is more than desirable for an entrepreneur, it can be critical to the success of a new entrepreneurial company. In fact, technology can deliver the competitive advantage that is driving the new business. Consider, for example, the Internet's leading compact disc and video store, CDNow. CDNow, which sells millions of dollars a year of CDs, went public in 1998, yet was started less than five years ago by two twin brothers in their twenties. To this day, CDNow remains a virtual store, with no warehouse or inventory. It simply passes the order to the distributor, who ships it out. The people that work at CDNow work on customer service and web page design, but do not have the overhead and lease costs of a normal record store. The advent of new technology like the Internet has created successful new businesses.

At the very least, technology can help a small entrepreneurial company compete with the big company on many levels. Using technology such as web sites on the Internet, combined with software packages to do everything from the payroll, to professional-looking presentations and proposals; a single person with a computer can appear as professional and competitive as a much larger company. A technology setup of this kind, while not cheap, is certainly within reach of most small businesses. This has lowered barriers to entry in many industries.

To summarize, technology has not only lowered costs and barriers to entry, and increased efficiency for entrepreneurs, technology has been the key to many new entrepreneurial businesses.

### Recommendation for the Future

Entrepreneurs need to be prepared for the worst, but work hard for the best. A good idea or product is not enough to make a successful business. Entrepreneurs need mentors, they need to think of their possible competitors (if it was so easy for me to start this business, what stops others from starting them if mine becomes successful?), and they should look at technology to give them an edge (or at the very least, make their lives easier). Technology also helps because the never-ending barrage of technological advances are constantly providing new entrepreneurial opportunities.

Entrepreneurs need to do their research and development to make sure that their concept is not only a viable one, but one that consumers need or demand. One place to start looking is to use new technology to capitalize on current consumer (among other) trends. For example, the Internet has grown partly due to the fact that it makes data gathering so much faster in a time when people seem to have less and less spare time. Now that the country has realized how important entrepreneurs are to keep the country productive and innovative, it's time to take charge and lead the way.

## CASE *Amazon.com*

### Technological Investment and Analysis

Amazon.com uses its talented workforce to create its web pages and to think of new ideas. By having the technology created in-house, Amazon.com can control the programs more easily and keep its secrets from competitors. The disadvantage is that by keeping the technology creation in-house Amazon.com is limiting itself to its small workforce to create its new product.

Amazon.com uses the Secure Netscape Commerce Server for handling online sales. Customers can enter their credit card number online using any that supports the Secure Sockets Layer specification. If the customer does not have this technology they can fax in their order. Online electric commerce has increased at a rapid pace due to its beneficial effects on the efficiency and competitiveness of service-oriented and sales companies. Amazon's inventory system is run on separate computers and is not directly connected to the web site.

As more business and households purchase computers, the larger the audience there will be for Amazon.com. Some people maintain that putting a credit card number on the Internet is no more dangerous than giving a credit card to a waiter in a restaurant. On the other hand, Kevin Mitnick, a computer hacker, stole 20,000 credit card numbers from just one site before being arrested. This is one reason that Amazon.com has to stay on the leading edge of technology.

### Technological Innovations

#### Internet sites

To be successful as an Internet company, "the lesson is be first, be dominant, and be the recognized leader," according to Bill Burnham, the e-commerce analyst for CS First Boston. Among cyber-merchants that offer recommendation services, Amazon.com has an edge over competitors because its service, though complex, can be accurate.

Buying items on the web is a part of the direct channel. It is growing at a rate comparable to that of the Internet itself. Interestingly, web sales have enhanced or added to sales at more traditional outlets. It has not replaced them. For example, Amazon.com has not stopped people from visiting bookstores.

Web-based buying is particularly suited to products where instant access to updated pricing and configurations is advantageous. Sites can be expanded beyond this to provide a range of information, including special discounts, information on product availability, setup help, troubleshooting tips, driver updates, warranty information, and chat areas.

In competition with the Internet site of Amazon.com, Barnesandnoble.com is expanding its offerings in the business-to-business environment. Barnesandnoble.com continues to upgrade its intranet bookselling service. The Barnesandnoble.com service includes subscriptions to more than 42,000 newspapers and magazines, in addition to the books already offered. The publications are sold through a partnership with electronic-commerce subscription vendor RoweCom in Cambridge, Massachusetts. RoweCom will also add direct account debiting and detailed financial reporting to corporate users. This will enable Barnesandnoble.com to better track company expenditures on books and publications.

According to Michael Donahue, Director of Business Solutions, Barnesandnoble.com signed up 25 corporate customers in the service's first two months. Customers use specially developed tools to make links from their intranets to the Barnesandnoble.com business site. This enables them to put up specific titles for their employees to see.

Another alternative to simply buying books on a web site is the opportunity normally linked to bookstores, that is the ability to browse and sample the books. Silicon Valley–based BookBrowse has launched a new web site that publishes excerpts from popular USA bestsellers, as well as many top fiction and nonfiction titles. In addition to excerpts, book summaries, author biographies, and reviews help with the book-buying process.

| STOCK | ANNUALIZED RETURN (%) |
|---|---|
| 1. Amazon.com | 496 |
| 2. Yahoo | 214 |
| 3. MindSpring | 152 |
| 4. EarthLink | 143 |
| 5. @Home | 135 |
| 6. America Online | 109 |
| 7. CMG | 108 |
| 8. Onscale | 93 |
| 9. Broad Vision | 57 |
| 10. Mecklermedia | 52 |

Top ten performing companies based on stock price.

### Overall design aspects of Amazon.com

Amazon.com's web site is divided into four main areas. Each of these areas can be accessed via the tabs at the top of the default screen. The simplified and low-bandwidth graphics allow customers to easily select the type of media they are interested in purchasing, books, music, videos, or gift merchandise. This same simple design is used in each of the four main areas, so the user will not have to relearn navigation commands once they have become accustomed to their preferred media choice (i.e., they have bought books at Amazon.com before but are now interested in purchasing a CD).

One of the more powerful features used by Amazon.com is affinity lists. When you look at a book, CD, or movie, the site automatically lists similar books that were purchased by people who bought the item you are looking at. These lists help consumers find similar items, and they encourage customers to purchase more items.

### Books

The site for books is the default page customers will view when they visit Amazon.com's web site (http://www.amazon.com). Amazon.com has placed immediately reachable search fields to enable customers to go right to the products they are searching. Additionally, navigation buttons have been placed conveniently at the top of each page to other book pages on their site, such as Book Search, Browse Subjects, Bestsellers, Recommendation Center, Award Winners, Kids, Featured in the Media, and Computers and Internet. These navigation buttons are a good help to those visitors that are simply "browsing the aisles" and not certain about the exact book they are interested in purchasing. Amazon.com also spotlights certain books on the default page in an effort to draw the customers' attention to the most recent books, or books Amazon.com wants the customer to know about. This product placement is similar to POP displays, or end-of-aisle displays in a traditional retail store.

Book Search allows the customer to conduct a more detailed search of Amazon.com's database of products than the search field located at the top of every main area default page. Searches can be as refined by author, title, format (hard or softcover), or subject.

Browse Subjects categorizes book titles into 24 main topics, ranging from children's books to horror stories, from arts and music to mystery and thrillers. By choosing the subject of book in which the customers are interested, they will be taken to pages filled with subcategories, recommendations, and new book announcements (all within that subject field).

Bestsellers lists contain the country's most popular books. They are categorized by soft/hard cover, fiction/nonfiction, and printed/not-yet-printed. These lists are compiled from the sales data Amazon.com receives. An interesting feature that Amazon.com has placed here is the "Amazon.com Hot 100" which updates the bestsellers' results every hour.

The Recommendation Center provides customers with interactive sections to help them pick out their purchase. These interactive sections ask questions about what type/style/author of books the customer likes and, based on their answers, helps bring up suggestions for purchase.

Award Winners collects books that have won various prizes, medals, and commendations and presents them to the customer.

The Kids section provides customers with the ability to further narrow the type of book best suited to a certain range of children's ages. This can be a great help to parents or relatives who are interested in purchasing a book as a present for a child but do not want to buy something too easy or too complex for the child's reading level.

Featured in the Media consolidates each month's selected reading lists from leading media sources, such as the *Oprah Winfrey Show, The New York Times, Time, Entertainment Weekly,* and *The Atlantic Monthly.* Customers familiar with these media sources can reach their anticipated lists here, within easy reach for ordering.

The Computers and Internet section presents computer and Internet-related books for quick reference. The pages also have links to other computer-related web sites that are related to the books Amazon.com has to offer.

### Music

Amazon.com also sells music on its web site. The music section of the site uses the same theme as the book area, simplicity. Just as the book area allows users to search for the book they want to purchase, customers can search for the CD they want to buy. Navigation buttons are located in the same location as in the book area, allowing customers to access these sections: Browse Styles, Chart Toppers, In the Media, and Recommendations.

Browse Styles offers genre-specific music in 14 main categories, complete with reviews, editors' picks, articles, interviews, best-sellers, and lists of recommended essential titles.

Chart Toppers includes the most popular and current music, all offered at a 30 percent discount. The area will also feature the Billboard Top 30 and CMJ college radio chart and national music charts from the United Kingdom, Germany, Japan, and Brazil.

In The Media features CDs from 20 leading media outlets, including *Rolling Stone, Spin, NPR, Entertainment Weekly, The Tonight Show,* and the *Late Show with David Letterman.*

Recommendation Center offers a computerized recommendation service that is based on the user's preferences and favorite artists.

## Data

The growing reliance on computers, shared databases, and centralized information-collection systems has increased the need for conformity in the way data is collected, structured, and stored. While this uniformity can contribute to the more efficient operation of databases, it can also represent an inconvenience. Departments maintaining data that will be merged with data from other departments generally must adhere to companywide standards, whether they like it or not. That can be especially daunting in the case of a merger or acquisition. In these cases, information managers suddenly find themselves marching to a different drummer or, worse, multiple drummers. When it comes to extranets, on which companies share data with other companies, the issue can escalate from an inconvenience to a major stumbling block.

To address these issues, a number of Internet companies, including Junglee, owned by Amazon.com, and Jango, owned by Excite Inc., have developed technology to enable companies to collaborate over the Internet. Excite uses Jango's technology to develop a virtual online store that is an aggregation of multiple stores. Agent software resides on the main portal server and goes to a variety of web sources to identify requested information. Based on rules guided by the source, the agents parse the resulting data to provide the key pieces of information needed by the user. This removes the necessity for all relevant information to reside on a single server.

The advantage of this technology is that it removes the necessity for an actual relationship to exist between the information provider and the informational-retrieval system. Any change made by the information provider could cause the system to break down, depending on the accuracy of the technology that parses the web pages.

A third approach, pioneered by Isadra Inc. in Palo Alto, California, is a two-part system that involves a cooperative relationship between the data source and the portal or information hub. One piece resides on the same server as the data source; the other at the hub or portal. Working together, the two provide the conformity needed to find and parse information without requiring the source data to be the same.

Amazon.com announced the acquisition of Junglee and Planet All to diversify its electronic commerce offerings. Junglee produces technology for aggregating job listings, retail product information, and other online data. It also manufactures Internet price-comparison software as well as comparison shopping services on various Internet sites. Amazon also acquired PlanetAll, which offers a web-based calendar, address book, and reminder service that enables users to maintain contact with friends and associates. Amazon offered a total of $280 million in stock for both companies, of which about $185 million went to Junglee's management and investors and $93 million went to Planet All. These acquisitions enabled Amazon.com to expand its services by helping customers locate other Internet stores. Profit will come from Internet store commissions.

Junglee earned widespread praise when it introduced its JobCanopy service late last year. The system treats online information as a vast, distributed "virtual database" and applies a series of data wrappers that can gather information from a variety of sources, such as employers' recruiting sites. The technology formats the data in a uniform manner, enabling online publishers to reuse the aggregated information quickly and easily. A number of online newspapers, including the *Washington Post,* the *Boston Globe* and the *Wall Street Journal Interactive Edition,* now use JobCanopy to supplement their employment listings.

Junglee exploited its potential by adapting its technology to allow comparison shopping for books, clothing, home electronics, and other product categories. Consumers can enter a book author and title and Junglee will return price, availability, and shipping information from a number of participating retailers. Yahoo, Snap, Go2net, and several other web publishers currently use the Junglee system to supplement their e-commerce offerings.

Junglee is exploring XML as a means to aggregate this type of data format it on the fly using tools such as Internet Explorer's client-side data-binding technology. Junglee's XMLizer, currently available as a demo on the company's site, delivers XML-formatted product information to an Internet Explorer 4.0 browser. Users can reformat the data to get the view they would find most convenient. As web publishers and merchants adapt XML to structure their data, and as both Netscape and Microsoft deliver XML-compliant browsers, this approach will increase the power of Junglee and other comparison-shopping tools.

Once industries agree on specific tagsets for structuring their header data, Junglee will be able to automate the data-gathering process further. Currently, Junglee must build custom-designed data "wrappers" to analyze HTML-formatted data. This is a time-consuming, manual process that Junglee adapts for each participating retailer. Comparison-based services such as Junglee promise to be successful where "online malls" failed. In addition to aggregating price, availability, and other product information, the virtual database can provide views of the information not readily available in any other form. Differences in search interfaces can make it difficult to do straight-ahead comparisons. Junglee's technology irons out these incompatibilities, giving the consumer a single, coherent way to understand information. XML searching will enable Junglee to give customers more options regarding the best way to view products and speed up the process by doing more work on the client side.

Junglee technology could present problems for Amazon.com, however. Book selling is generally a commodity market. The Junglee technology can push prices down even further by giving consumers an easy way to find the lowest price for a given title. Jeff Bezos recently told the *New York Times* that Amazon would deemphasize price-based comparisons, claiming that "we don't think that customers find price comparisons very useful."

What this means is that if comparison-shopping services are successful, corporate publishers that publish catalogs will want their products to show up on the list that Junglee produces.

Amazon.com has also acquired Bookpages Ltd., a U.K.-based online book retailer; Telebook, an online bookstore concern in Germany; and the Net-based Internet Movie Database directory site. The online retailers Bookpages and Telebook have become fundamental components of its expansion into the European marketplace. The Internet Movie Database supports Amazon.com's entry into online video sales.

The acquisition of Bookpages in the United Kingdom and Telebook in Germany provided distribution centers to enable Amazon to slash their shipping costs for their European customers. Currently it costs $30 per shipment plus $5.95 per book for a delivery time of one to four days between Amazon's U.S. operation and a customer on another continent. Bookpages ships books to any European destination for about $3.35 per book, with a maximum charge of $16.70 and a four-day delivery time. Bookpages' catalog offers all 1.2 million U.K. books currently in print.

Telebook operates not only in Germany, with 400,000 German titles, but also in Spain, where its subsidiary Libro Web offers a million titles in Spanish, German, English, and Dutch. Another Telebook subsidiary operates in South Africa. Amazon.com paid $55 million in cash and stock for the three companies, although the individual amounts were not broken out.

The movie database content will become the backbone for what Amazon.com CEO Jeff Bezos called a "best-of-breed video store." His goal is to add to the company's established franchise in books and music CDs. The movie database site will offer in greater detail the same kind of background and review material for movies as Amazon.com's site provides for books.

According to Colonel Needham, managing director of the Internet Movie Database, "The general direction of the database will remain unchanged. We will still be the most comprehensive movie information source on the Internet. However, we will be able to add new features as a result of having the resources of Amazon."

The Internet Movie Database is one of the 500 most visited sites on the Web, according to Media Metrix, and offers data on 140,000 movies. It began in 1990 as a Usenet newsgroup maintained entirely by volunteers. It was transferred to the Web in 1995 and became a business in 1996.

Amazon.com paid $55 million in cash and stock for the three companies, though the individual amounts were not broken out. Amazon.com's stock closed at $91.75 after the purchases, a jump of $9 over the price it commanded before the purchases and a smaller-than-expected first-quarter loss of 40 cents per share were reported.

### Future Acquisitions

Amazon.com's emphasis during the next year could be to continue to increase its market share of online audio CD sales while maintaining its market share in book sales. The next target for Amazon.com could also be online software sales. Software, like books, CDs, and videos, is an information-rich commodity. It is easy to order online and products can be shipped straight from the distributor to the customer.

Amazon.com's three recent purchases indicate that it prefers to acquire best-of-breed companies with strong brand names rather than develop them internally. The leading brand names in Internet software sales are Software.net and Egghead.com. With current market valuations pushing half a billion dollars, these companies could be too expensive to acquire. Another possibility is the privately held start-up Chumbo (http://www.chumbo.com). Like Amazon.com, Chumbo has many retail partnerships with other companies. It hosts a co-branded online software store and shares a percentage of the store's revenue, just as Amazon.com does with its Associates program.

The recent hiring of Jimmy Wright, Wal-Mart's logistics chief, as vice-president and chief logistics officer provides access to logistics and supply-chain control techniques. This addition suggests that Bezos takes seriously the challenges of establishing a powerful, rapid supply-and-distribution network.

## QUESTIONS

1. What forces are driving the strategic direction for Amazon.com?
2. Upon what technologies has Amazon.com relied?
3. How has Amazon.com financed its development efforts?
4. What alternatives exist for the service Amazon.com is providing?
5. What does the corporation's web page present about their business?
6. How will technology continue to impact the book-selling industry?
7. How important is data to the corporation's continued success?

## ADDITIONAL READING

"Amazon.Com: The Wild World of E-Commerce," *Business Week,* December 14, 1998, p. 106.

"Amazon.com to Offer Links to Other Net Stores," *Newsbytes,* December 7, 1998.

"Amazon.Com Turns to Sun," *InternetWeek,* August 3, 1998, p. 15.

Catchings, Bill, and Mark L. Van, "Abandoning Childish E-Commerce Myths," *PC Week,* December 21, 1998, p. 40.

Champy, Jim. "Why Web Won't Kill Middlemen," *Computerworld,* January 25, 1999, p. 54.

Hanrahan, Timothy. "Lessons Learned," *The Wall Street Journal,* December 7, 1998, p. R16.

Karlgaard, Rich."It's the Software, Stupid," *Forbes,* August 10, 1998, p. 37.

Koenig, Steve, and Aaron Ricadela, "Online Sales Hit Record Level," *Computer Retail Week,* December 7, 1998, p. 1.

Lombardi, Rosie. "Viable E-Business Model Is Still a Closed Book," *Computing Canada,* December 7, 1998, p. 34.

Nee, Eric. "Surf's Up," *Forbes,* July 27, 1998, pp. 106–114.

Rabinovitz, Jonathan. "E-Commerce Grows Up," *San Jose Mercury News,* October 25, 1998, pp. D1–D2.

## CASE *Peapod*

Thomas and Andrew Parkinson founded Peapod in the Technical Center at Northwestern University in Evanston, Illinois, in 1989. It was created on the premise that people are too busy to spend hours each week in the grocery store. Peapod has since become the number-one online grocery shopping and delivery service in the world, with most of its recognition coming in the past two years.

The founders, with backgrounds in sales and brand and product management, saw a growing market consisting primarily of women in upper-middle class, dual-income families (with median income exceeding $60,000 per year), between the ages of 30 and 54. Many have children and are too busy living their lives to spend time each week on a little-favored task, grocery shopping.

The Parkinsons determined that this market would be willing to pay a premium for the time savings and convenience of having someone else do their grocery shopping for them, leaving them time for jobs, families, and other obligations. From this concept, the Peapod tagline evolved: "Smart Shopping for Busy People." This business idea has continued to thrive. The response from a 1995 survey by Andersen Consulting has shown that approximately 30 percent of consumers would pay a service fee for electronic ordering and grocery delivery services.

### Technological Investment and Analysis

The Peapod consumer software is based on a three-tier architecture, which has positioned Peapod at the forefront of Internet computing. The first tier, the client layer, is located on the member's computer. The client layer utilizes instructions from the application server in order to create the user's interface, run the application, and return the input to the Peapod server. The two remaining tiers, the application and the database, are centrally maintained and manage all of the logic and data associated with the Peapod application.

Peapod believes that this "thin client" architecture has many advantages. The overall application performance is strong relative to other consumer network applications with comparable levels of interactivity. A major factor in the performance of a network application is the utilization of the narrow bandwidth connection between the consumer's computer and the server. Peapod makes efficient use of this bandwidth by performing certain processing on the member's computer and by exchanging only application-relevant information between a member's computer and the Peapod server (Prospectus).

It is also believed that this architectural structure offers a high degree of scalability. Efficient interaction between the Peapod server and the member's computer and the processing of certain application activities on the clients' side reduces the processing requirements of the Peapod server. The separation of the application and the database enables Peapod to isolate and optimize the different processing requirements of those layers. As the membership base expands and the number of simultaneous users increases, Peapod can integrate additional application servers without impacting the rest of the application architecture.

Another advantage is the functionality and flexibility of the application. Because the application logic and data is maintained centrally, Peapod can change much of the content and appearance of the software without having to modify or upgrade the software on the member's computer. For example, in 1996, Internet e-mail features were added to the application without any interruptions in client service or modifications to the customers' software. The centralized application logic also enables Peapod to present interactive marketing events and customize application appearances to individual members.

The new version of Peapod software, Version 5.0, will be based on Microsoft's ActiveX technology and will be designed to offer an even greater level of integration with the Web. Peapod will be able to incorporate web site content, such as HTML documents or Shockwave animated images, into its consumer interface. With this new version, Peapod will be able to adapt its consumer software to support new technologies.

Peapod software is easily accessible via the Internet or from a Peapod diskette. Once the software is downloaded to the member's computer, members can then access the Peapod servers via direct dial-up or the Internet. The Peapod client software currently supports both Windows and Macintosh user platforms.

Peapod has designed and integrated several business support systems with its shopping application in order to facilitate the administration of services. The fulfillment management application, installed at each of Peapod's fulfillment centers, enables Peapod field operations managers to access and print member orders according to store layout, manage delivery time availability, and update store-specific product offerings. The Peapod accounting system provides the billing, processing, and collection functions, which include the electronic link of the processing of member credit card payments and funds transfer.

The next release of the fulfillment management applications will incorporate handheld scanning technology to enhance and streamline the order picking and packing functions and electronically integrate the actual member order with the Peapod accounting systems.

Peapod's services are vulnerable to weaknesses in the communications medium (the Internet), which may compromise the security of confidential electronic information exchanged with members. Disruptions of service or security breaches could cause losses to Peapod, reduce member satisfaction, and deter new members from joining as a result of lack of confidence in online commerce. Peapod has taken some steps to address these and other privacy concerns. It has restricted access to its database, limited the type of information it has made available to third parties, required each employee to sign a nondisclosure and confidentiality agreement, and implemented data security systems at the main data center.

## Technological Innovations

### Telecommunications

Peapod remodeled its web site in 1998 so that a variety of Internet-accessible devices, besides the standard PC/Web browser combination, will be able to shop in Peapod's virtual supermarket. The new site complements its SuRF proprietary shopping system. SuRF combines the multimedia capabilities of the World Wide Web with Peapod's WinSurfer application controls. This enables Peapod to offer shopping functionality and performance that are superior to those available from standard Internet technologies. This is particularly true considering the Internet's narrow bandwidths and conventional modem speeds.

### Data

Peapod developed a way to track how individuals respond to particular promotions, not just if they respond. The software is called Universal Event Processor (UEP). It not only knows that you buy diapers, but it also knows that you immediately used a two-for-one electronic coupon for raisin bagels even though you had never purchased bagels before, or that you ignore ads for cheese unless you're buying wine. "It's routine to search databases for people who conform to a specific profile. We wanted to create a system that automatically tracked the actual transactions that resulted," says Thomas Parkinson, Peapod's chief technology officer.

"We found, for example, that we could sell five times as much Keri hand lotion by running a banner ad whenever a customer clicked on bananas," Parkinson says. This may seem illogical but it is invaluable marketing information.

Peapod says it's too early to tell whether this has made individual consumers more loyal to Peapod. Nonetheless, it helps Peapod sell more goods, and the UEP has led data-hungry consumer goods manufacturers to Peapod's door.

Kraft Foods, Bristol-Myers Squibb Co., and Kellogg Co. use Peapod to test consumer tastes and behavior. They have seen on average a 10 percent to 15 percent increase in sales when they run a targeted banner advertisement. This is twice as much as with targeted electronic coupons, Tim Dorgan said. He is an executive vice-president at Peapod, who oversees market research for consumer goods companies.

## Recommendation for the Future

Peapod must build brand identity and awareness. This is to be accomplished by aggressively marketing its services, through promotion and advertising, to increase brand name recognition. Peapod will stress the functionality, quality, convenience, and value of its services in order to build on its brand identity.

Peapod must provide a superior member experience. Peapod is committed to providing its members with user-friendly, highly functional, and cost-effective shopping tools, convenient delivery and pick-up service, and exceptional product quality, each of which ensure member satisfaction and loyalty. Peapod will continue to gather consumer preference information so it can introduce more personalized services to its members which will attract new members, retain existing members, increase member usage, and increase Peapod's share of members' household purchases.

Peapod must expand into new geographic markets and further penetrate existing markets. Peapod believes that it can achieve competitive advantages in various markets by being the first to build a substantial online membership base. Peapod is currently in talks with grocery retailers in a dozen new markets that could come online in 1997. To take advantage of economies in fulfillment and advertising, Peapod plans to penetrate these markets quickly by opening multiple fulfillment centers in each new market.

The company considers numerous factors when determining which new markets in which to expand. Factors include size, population density, prevalence of personal computer users, demographic composition, market conditions, availability of a high-quality grocer, and other general economic factors.

Peapod must build interactive marketing services and leverage its database. Peapod has pioneered, in partnership with consumer goods companies, innovative interactive marketing services consisting of advertising, promotion, and market research services. The company has a relationship with The M/A/R/C Group, a national marketing research organization, to develop and market custom and syndicated research applications that will bring the research benefits of Peapod to the marketplace.

Peapod plans to continue to use its database and online shopping channel to develop new services for its interactive marketing clients. As Peapod's membership increases, it is believed that consumer goods companies will find the interactive marketing services a more valuable and cost-effective research tool.

Peapod must work with retail partners in evolving the retail model. Peapod has been working closely with the retail partners to expand their roles in the fulfillment of member orders. This partnership has also been leveraged to improve product distribution and order fulfillment to reduce costs, improve quality and enhance scalability. Technological support for these goals include the recent development of a handheld scanner which will be used to expedite the order picking and packing functions. Peapod has recently initiated efforts to license its technology to retailers on an international basis and in select U.S. markets.

Peapod has also been developing new options for the customer in order to lower their costs. In Houston, Peapod and its retail partner, Randalls, have implemented a drive-through pick-up option. This option reduces the member's delivery fees and creates additional scheduling flexibility by allowing members to pick up their own orders at their convenience. Peapod plans to incorporate this option in existing and future markets.

Peapod must leverage its membership and technology into other online services. Peapod recently entered into agreements with Geerlings & Wade, Inc., a national direct marketer of premium wines, to offer an online wine store and Firefly Greetings, L.L.C., a provider of personal greeting cards and specialty products, to offer an online gift and specialty products center. Future plans include the partnership of Peapod with nongrocery retailers to offer additional online services that would appeal to the company's membership base. Peapod also plans to make its services accessible on a national basis via the Internet. These companies have agreed to pay Peapod development, management, and transactional fees so that these new services can be introduced in the next Peapod software version.

The next major step is to move online shopping from the computer to the television. Dispatch Interactive Television is testing this system and hopes to introduce it sometime in 1997. Dispatch Interactive believes that this service should expand quickly once it is available in all households, not just the ones with home computers.

## QUESTIONS

1. What forces are driving the strategic direction of Peapod?
2. To accomplish this service, upon what technologies must Peapod rely?
3. What has caused a change in the use of technology in the grocery industry?
4. An analysis of Peapod's financial information will produce what conclusions?
5. What does the Peapod's web page emphasize?
6. What role does data play in the future of the corporation?

## ADDITIONAL READING

Bicknell, David. "Virtual Mall Is Master of the Aisles," *Computer Weekly,* October 1, 1998, p. 30.

"Entrepreneurs: A Special Section," *New York Times,* September 23, 1998, pp. D1–D15.

"Food Delivery Services Look for Market to Peak by 2000," *Electronic Advertising & Marketplace Report,* September 23, 1997, p. 3.

Grover, Mary Beth. "Go Ahead: Buy the Dream," *Forbes,* June 15, 1998, pp. 146–150.

Hof, Robert D. "Customizable Web Sites," *Business Week,* October 5, 1998, pp. 176–177.

Johnson, Andrew. "Peapod Launches Secure Firewall for Web Servers," *PC User,* February 21, 1996, p. 12.

Muchmore, Michael W. "Virtual Supermarkets," *PC Magazine,* November 18, 1997, p. 41.

"Peapod Expanding," *Computerworld,* August 17, 1998, p. 33.

"Peapod's Customer-Tracking System," *Computerworld,* August 10, 1998.

Useem, Jerry. "The New Entrepreneurial Elite," *Inc. Magazine,* December 1997, pp. 50–55.

## DISCUSSION ISSUE

*Are Graphs Misleading?*

Graphics images convey ideas. As such, they are not always precise. Hence, there are many ways in which graphics can be misleading. In order to avoid sending the wrong impression, you need to examine each image carefully. Look at both the detail and the overall perception that is conveyed by the graph. Consider an example where the CEO (Mr. Cruddock) has called a meeting to discuss sales for the different divisions. Kwilla-June Holmes (the head of marketing) has stated that the dog food division should be sold because its sales and profits are lower than those of the other divisions. The head of the dog food division (Vic) is also at the meeting.

Holmes: And this graph shows the sales for the last three years for each of our product divisions. Notice that the dog food division is lower than the others.

Cruddock: Uh, I can't quite read that graph. Are those bars made up of little dogs?

Holmes: *(smiling)* Yes they are. The new graphics package let me put different objects in for the bars.

Cruddock: Hmmm. Well, is the top supposed to be at the dog's head or the tail? The tail is quite a bit higher . . .

Holmes: Ah. I guess I don't know.

Vic: Our actual sales numbers are slightly below the other divisions, but only by 2 to 5 percent. Because she used those tall thin candles for the bars in the wax division, it makes it look higher compared to the wider bar for the dog food division.

Holmes: Sure, sure. I'm not criticizing your department. It just has less sales. Let's look at the next graph. Here I created four graphs—one for each division. Each graph has sales for the last five years. One bar for each year. Oh, notice that all the bars in the dog food graph use the dog symbol and are the same width, so it should be easier to compare.

Cruddock: Now, in this graph, it looks to me like the dog food division is doing better than the others. See how the sales for all five years are near the top. But in the cat food division they have two good years, but the other three are quite a bit lower. Maybe we should solve the cat food problems first.

Holmes: But. Oh, I see the problem. Look at the numbers on the left. See, all of the numbers for cat food are higher than those for dog food. These graphs are just designed to show what happened in each division over five years. Let's just look at one graph at a time. See how the dog food division hasn't changed much. Its sales have stayed flat.

Vic: Wait a second, that's not right. Here, I've got the actual sales numbers. We've increased sales by an average of 6 percent each of the last five years. Are you sure you have the correct numbers in your graphs?

Holmes: Oh yes. I took them out of your report to Mr. Cruddock. See, check the numbers on the Y-axis.

Vic: Well, something's wrong with your graph.

Holmes: Maybe the next graph will make it clear. These four pie charts show the breakdown of expenses for the last two years for the wax products division and the dog food division. See this slice that I exploded out from the pie, it's personnel expense. Notice that it takes a much bigger share of the pie in the dog food division, and it's even larger in the next year. This increase in labor cost is expensive because the division is not really growing.

Vic: Now wait a minute. I thought we settled that. We have been growing, that's why we hired more people. And . . .

Cruddock: Hang on. Ms. Holmes, the slices for personnel in the dog food division appear to be smaller than the slices in the wax products division. Why do you say that the dog product's costs are higher?

Holmes: Oh that. I scaled the pie charts to match the overall sales of the division. Notice that the entire pie for the wax products division is larger than for the dog food. What I'm saying is you need to compare the percentage of the cost in each case, not the actual size of the pie. I wanted to be sure to include all of the information. It's a little confusing at first . . .

Vic: It's not confusing. It's just wrong. I don't know what you're trying to do, but I'm not putting up with these inane graphs. Just look at the actual numbers. Sure, we're not as large as the other divisions, but we're a whole lot more stable. We've had five straight years of growth.

Cruddock: Ms. Holmes, thank you for the presentation, but I'm inclined to agree with Vic. There might be some problems in the dog food division, but I don't really understand your graphs. Next time, be a little more careful when you create them.

## QUESTIONS

1. Do you think the graphs created by Ms. Holmes accurately portray the status of the dog food department?
2. Do you think graphs with pictures are more interesting than simple bar graphs?
3. Do you think changing the size of the pie charts is a good way to show how the total expenses are higher for the wax products division?
4. Can you find graphs in newspapers and magazines that use pictures instead of bars to display the data? Are they more interesting? Are they misleading?
5. Do you think Ms. Holmes deliberately made the graphs so they are misleading?
6. Can you find a graphics package that enables you to draw graphs such as those created by Ms. Holmes?

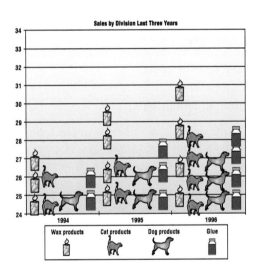

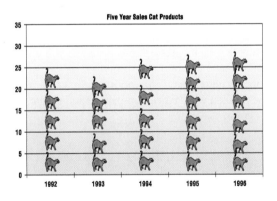

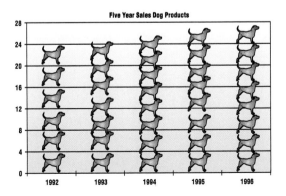

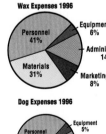

# *Displaying Data*

Computers make it easy to do certain things, such as writing reports and drawing charts. But conveying information and persuading people requires more than just writing a report and slapping in a chart. The purpose of a chart is to communicate ideas. Different types of charts exist to highlight different relationships. Your job is to choose the chart that most clearly describes the important concepts. You must also pay attention to the overall layout and style of the chart. For example, color, typeface, and white space all affect the viewer's perception of the graph.

## COLUMN OR BAR CHART

One of the most important steps in presenting information is to choose the correct type of chart. Several common types exist that highlight typical business re-lationships. Choosing the wrong type may mislead the reader and will make it difficult for others to under-stand your comments.

The four most chart types are column, line, pie, and scatter. The column or bar chart is used to com-pare values by categories. For example, Figure 2.1A shows the sales for the Rolling Thunder Bicycle com-pany by the type of bicycle. The chart could have been drawn with horizontal bars, but charts that involve money typically place amounts on the vertical axis.

Every chart must have certain features. For exam-ple, it must have a title, and the axes must be labeled. If there are multiple categories of data, a legend will be used to identify each category. For instance, you could add another set of columns to Figure 2.1A to show sales for the next year. This additional set of bars would be marked with a different pattern and perhaps a different color.

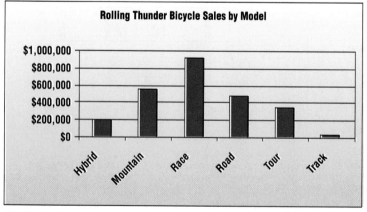

**FIGURE 2.1A**
COLUMN CHART
Column and bar charts are used to compare categories of data. In this case, sales by each type of bicycle.

## PIE CHART

Pie charts are used to show how some total value is broken down into its constituent parts. For example, Figure 2.2A displays the same data that was shown in Figure 2.1A—the sales by type of bicycle. Although the two charts show the same type of data, they convey different information. The column chart focuses on the actual sales level for each model. The pie chart highlights the relationships across the model types. The emphasis is on the percentage contributed by each model as opposed to the total dollar level. Also note that pie charts can display only one set of data at a time.

## LINE CHART

Whenever you want to show how data changes over time you need to use a line chart. The horizontal axis displays time and the vertical axis displays the business data. As shown in Figure 2.3A, the different categories are shown with different markers or different line styles. Color can be used to differentiate the categories; however, you have to be careful to choose colors that people can see clearly. Each output device may display colors differently, so you will have to test your graph colors to be sure they come through correctly. Also, keep in mind that some people have difficulty distinguishing colors.

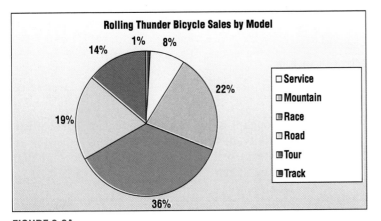

**FIGURE 2.2A**
PIE CHART
This pie chart shows how the different bicycle models contributed to the
overall sales.

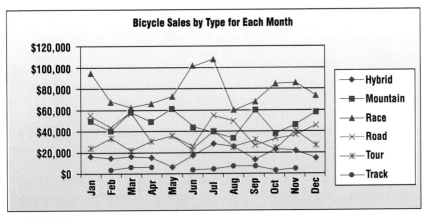

**FIGURE 2.3A**
LINE CHART
Time is displayed on the horizontal axis of a line chart. Categories are shown by different
matters or different line styles.

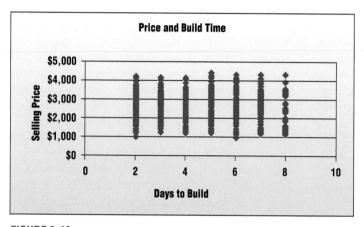

**FIGURE 2.4A**
SCATTER CHART
Scatter charts are useful for displaying relationships between noncategorical data. Randomly scattered results like those shown here indicate no correlation between the two variables.

## SCATTER CHART

Scatter charts are particularly useful for examining the relationships between noncategorical variables. A noncategorical variable is one that can take on virtually any value. The example in Figure 2.4A compares the selling price of the bicycle to the number of days it took to build each one. As a manager, you might be interested to learn whether the company charges more money for bicycles that are harder to build. In this example, the results show virtually no correlation between price and time.

You can compare three variables using a surface chart in three dimensions. The control variables are generally placed on the *x* and *y* axes, while the dependent variable of interest rises from the page.

## STYLE AND ORNAMENTATION

As Edward Tufte points out his book *The Visual Display of Quantitative Information,* graphing software offers many temptations that should be avoided. Whenever you build the chart you should always first ask yourself: What is its purpose? You should then make sure that every option you choose highlights that purpose. Avoid cluttering your graph with excess lines, images, or garish color schemes.

Although it is true that design requires some artistic creativity, in virtually every situation, conveying accurate information is far more important than splashy effects. The goal of any design is to strive for elegance.

## EXERCISES

1. Create the graph in Figure 2.1A, and add another series for a second year of data.
2. Search the Internet and business publications and find an example of a chart that you believe conveys information easily and effectively. Find another example of a chart that does a poor job. Briefly explain what you like and dislike about each chart.
3. Use the export data form in Rolling Thunder bicycles to generate sales by state. Create a column chart and a pie chart for this data. Briefly explain why one chart is better than the other one.
4. Using Bureau of Labor Statistics data, plot the unemployment rate and the hourly wage rate over three years.
5. Using the data in exercise 4, draw a new chart to examine the relationship between the unemployment rate and the hourly wage. Explain what happens when you use the axes values that are automatically chosen by the graphing package.

CHAPTER 3

# *Solving Problems*

Ben & Jerry's is well
known for its interesting
ice cream flavor names.
The web site describes
the current flavors along
with the company's
involvement
in social issues.

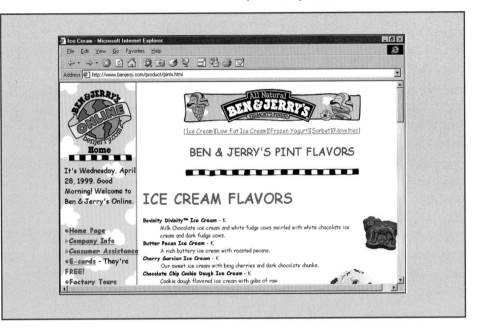

## BEN & JERRY'S

Ben & Jerry's Homemade, Inc., is a publicly held corporation that was founded in 1978 by charismatic visionaries Ben Cohen and Jerry Greenfield. The corporation had its modest beginning when Cohen and Greenfield took a $5.00 correspondence class on making ice cream. Together, they opened up an ice cream shop in a renovated gas station in Burlington, Vermont. Since then, Ben & Jerry's has grown into a multimillion-dollar powerhouse that is known worldwide for its plethora of frozen yogurt treats and ice cream novelties in traditional and unique flavors.

Although most of Ben & Jerry's success can be attributed to their array of innovative flavors made with the freshest Vermont milk and cream, some individuals argue that the company's idealistic business philosophy has contributed equally to its success. Ben & Jerry's Homemade, Inc., operates in a socially conscious manner where the co-founders' values influence the corporate mission statement and strategy. Among publicly held companies, Ben & Jerry's Homemade, Inc., donates the highest percentage of its annual pretax earnings to community organizations and social causes.

**OVERVIEW**   Throughout your career, you will face many business problems. Some will be easy to solve; others will be more complex. The problems that are the hardest to solve are those that have impacts in several areas. It becomes especially difficult to find the cause of the problems. You need to develop a method that will help you understand and solve problems.

Fortunately, several methods already exist to analyze problems and evaluate alternatives. MIS workers commonly use two types of techniques to examine business problems and build information systems. One technique focuses on identifying the business objects, determining how they are related, and analyzing the data that managers need. A second technique focuses on business processes and activities. This methodology is based on systems theory and is valuable for understanding complex

**FIGURE 3.1**

As a manager, you need to analyze the business to solve problems and make the firm more efficient and effective in pursuit of its goals. Understanding the business is crucial to using MIS to its full potential. The systems approach is used to analyze business decisions, solve problems, and design new computer systems to support the business.

transactions. It is commonly used to highlight flows of data or products as they travel through the system.

You will learn how to analyze a complex business system by dividing it into pieces. A *system* can be described as a collection of processes that have inputs and produce outputs. It also can be described in terms of the properties and functions of various business objects. This chapter presents diagramming techniques that will help you analyze the systems you study. You will learn to identify common systems problems.

Solving problems often entails learning to ask the right questions. Questions can help organize your thoughts and encourage you to consider new directions when looking for answers. The chapter provides hints on how to approach cases and application problems. The first step is to search for the primary problems and their cause. Once the main problems have been identified, the next step is to choose the proper tools and implement a solution. Also, it is important that you learn how to test your work to avoid costly errors.

**INTRODUCTION**

A common theme arises when talking with businesspeople who hire recent college graduates. Many people believe that although college students are bright, they have trouble dealing with unstructured problems. In most courses, you learn a specific tool in each section and complete assignments at the end of the chapter using that tool. At most, you might have a comprehensive final or a final paper that requires you to analyze the problem and select from the tools in the course to solve that problem.

In the business world all you see are symptoms. Before you can make a decision or develop a solution, you first have to use all of your knowledge to determine the causes and nature of the problem. How do you determine the cause of the problem? How do you know whether the solution involves accounting, production management, marketing, or some combination of many disciplines? Where do you start?

Solving unstructured problems is a technique required in any discipline. Physicians use symptoms to identify causes every day. An automobile mechanic needs to determine whether your car's problems are due to electrical, fuel, or transmission errors. In business, you often need to determine whether a problem should be approached through marketing, finance, human resources, accounting, or information systems. Models and the systems approach help you classify problems and identify their causes and organize decisions.

Hundreds of years ago, almost all businesses were small shops with few employees. The managers were also the owners. Management and problem solving were focused on day-to-day operations. As firms became larger and more complex, new management structures were created to enable a small group of managers to control the organization. Larger businesses and more complicated management structures led to more complex problems and a need for more and better information.

In the early days of computers, they were primarily used for simple mathematical computations. The programs were technical, but involved well-defined problems. The initial uses in business were to automate repetitive manual tasks such as bookkeeping and tracking customer data and orders. As computer prices dropped, the machines were used for more complex business tasks. Today, a main function of computers is to provide information to manage the firm.

Several problems quickly arose in creating these new information systems. New software projects were usually over budget and late. Worse yet, the new systems were hard to use and not very helpful. Part of the problem was that individual programs written by different people could not work together. New systems often did not solve business problems because the designers did not fully understand how the business operated.

In response to these problems, MIS researchers used general systems theory to create a new way to design software. The goal of the systems approach is to first determine how the business system works, and then use computer hardware and software to make it work better. The process of re-engineering extends this idea to the entire organization and seeks to redesign the company.

A more recent problem is the need to create new systems faster and with fewer errors. Companies are searching for ways to create a base set of systems definitions that can be used over again, instead of starting every system from scratch. Although the goal has been around for years, it has proven to be elusive. Systems designers are hoping that object-oriented design techniques might be an answer to this problem.

## OBJECT-ORIENTED DESIGN

One way to begin your analysis of a business is to focus on the business objects: what they are and what they do. Objects could be anything from people to raw materials to data files or schedules. The key to **object-oriented design** is to focus on defining what an object is and what it can do. A *class* is a generic description of a set of objects. This distinction is not crucial in this book, but you might want to know there is a difference. For example, the Bicycle class describes any bicycle that could be built by the company. A specific bicycle (e.g., serial number 15) is an object.

### Properties and Functions

Objects are defined by a set of properties (or attributes). The properties define the object. They also represent data that will be collected for each object. Consider the small example of a banking system. One primary object will be Accounts. A generic Account object would have basic properties such as: Account Number, Account Name, Client, Manager, Date Opened, Beginning Balance, Current Balance, and Interest Rate.

Each object also has functions which describe actions that can be performed by the objects and define how to alter the object. In the bank example, there would be functions to Open Account, Close Account, Accept Deposits, Pay Withdrawals, and Pay Interest. Note that each type of account could have a different method for computing interest payments. One account might compound them daily, another weekly, and so on. With the object-oriented approach the properties and functions are combined into the definition of the object. The goal is to describe a system so that if you change a function, you only have to change one object. All of the other objects and processes remain the same.

## Object Hierarchies

Objects are related to each other. Typically there is a base class of objects and other objects are *derived* from the base definitions by adding properties and altering functions. This process results in an **object hierarchy,** illustrated in Figure 3.2, that shows how the classes are derived from each other. The bank example has several types of accounts with each of these categories containing further subdivisions.

Figure 3.2 also shows detail in the classes by including some of the properties and member functions. The accounts have elements in common that they **inherit** from the base class (account), such as the balance attributes. Each level adds additional detail. Each account class also contains member functions to perform operations, such as paying interest. Because the interest computations can be different for each of the accounts, the method is stored with the original definition of each account.

**FIGURE 3.2**

Objects: Encapsulation, hierarchy, inheritance, polymorphism. Object-oriented design focuses on individual objects and the data within the organization. Processes are secondary and they are usually embedded in the object. By encapsulating these definitions, the objects can be used to develop related systems with less effort. It is also easier to modify a system by making small changes to an object's behavior.

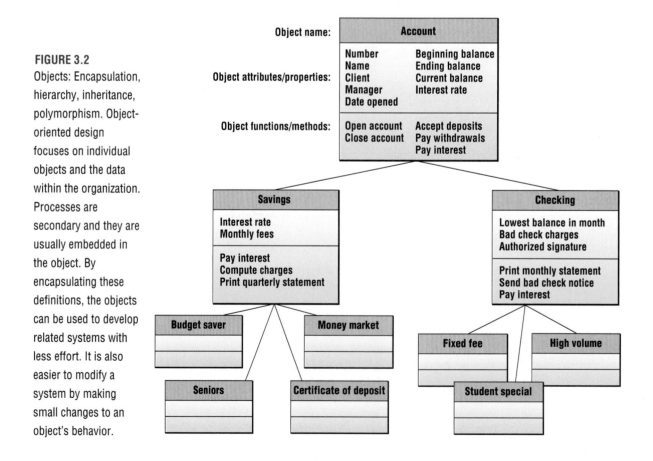

## Events

Another aspect of modeling objects is that they are often used in an event-driven approach. When some business event occurs, an object function is called or a property is modified. As a manager, you need to think about possible events and how they influence the objects you control. In the banking example, a customer's deposit triggers a credit to her account. This change might then force an update in a daily report object. This chain of events defines the business operations. As a manager, you are likely to be asked to identify the major objects and the events that affect your area of expertise in the company.

To see the usefulness of the object approach, consider what happens if the bank decides to collect additional data for the checking accounts. The only change needed is to add the new data items (and the associated functions) to the checking account class. All checking accounts will then inherit those properties and functions. None of the other operations are affected. Changes to the information system will only affect the specific accounts; the rest of the system will remain the same.

**ANALYZING SYSTEMS**

To solve business problems, you first have to understand how the business operates. The basic idea is that systems consist of smaller, interdependent **subsystems.** Each subsystem can be broken into smaller sections with more details. By examining each piece and its interactions, it is easier to determine the cause of problems and to derive a solution.

Several techniques have been created to help analyze systems. A useful new method is based on the unified modeling language (UML). UML was designed to assist in creating object-oriented information systems. It asks you to identify the primary objects in the system in terms of their properties and the methods or functions that they can perform.

---

**Reality Bytes     3–1   Software Bugs**

Software is difficult to create. Design and development require creativity, attention to detail, perseverance, and time. Yet, demand for new software is high—consumers and businesses continually want new products and features. Competition and the need for money drive firms to release software to market as fast as possible—often skimping on testing. Combined with increasing complexity, software often ends up with several bugs and incompatibilities. One organization (BugNet) tracks reports of bugs and vendor responses. For 1998, they were disappointed that even in the best case, vendors fixed fewer than 85 percent of the major reported bugs. Software bugs arise from many causes. One of the most difficult situations is interaction with other software. It is nearly impossible for a developer to test every combination of hardware and software. Another major problem is

that the tools (operating system and programming languages) contain bugs. A substantial portion of a programmer's time is spent finding work-arounds for problems created by other software. Users are understandably upset over bugs. You would not accept an automobile if you had to tear it down and rebuild it once a year. Yet, it is relatively common to have to reload software and even reformat computers annually. On the other hand, 90 years ago when automobiles were first being developed, you might have been willing to accept a shaky car—on the grounds that it was better than the alternative. The same situation exists today with computers. Until someone finds a way to develop more stable computer software, people will continue to accept some level of problems—as long as the bugs can be circumvented, and there are no other alternatives.

Most of today's information systems rely heavily on database management systems to collect and share the underlying data. An important strength of this approach is that you rarely need to worry about how data gets from one point in the company to another. Managers simply retrieve the data from the database as needed. The UML design techniques are useful in this environment because they focus on collecting and manipulating the data stored in each object.

The Rolling Thunder Bicycle company will be used to illustrate the analysis process. After carefully reading the analysis, you should have a good understanding of how the company operates. Pay particular attention to the data collection: Where is data collected and exactly what data needs to be stored?

## Divide and Conquer

Most problems are too complex and too large to deal with all at once. Even if you could remember all the details, it would be hard to see how everything was supposed to fit together. A crucial step in analyzing a system is to carefully break it into smaller pieces or a collection of subsystems. Each subsystem is separate from the others, but they are connected through the data they collect.

Figure 3.3 presents the initial business model for Rolling Thunder Bicycles. In UML terms, it is known as a *Use Case diagram.* It shows the primary business processes in the organization: (1) Order Entry, (2) Assembly and Shipping, (3) Purchasing and Receiving, (4) Accounting, and (5) Product Management. Note that additional processes such as Personnel Management could also exist. However, only these five will be used in this information system.

Commonly, the top-level business diagram is divided into the processes that are already defined within the company. For example, many businesses are split by functional area: accounting, finance, marketing, human resource management, and so on. A few companies are split by products, such as baby products, personal hygiene, detergents, and so on. Each subsystem can then be *exploded* into a more detailed figure. The goal is to identify the processes or business activities that take place within the subsystem. In a large, complex company, this division could continue for several levels. There are no concrete rules for how far to subdivide each process. However, it is helpful to break them down far enough so that a final process can be described on one page or screen.

A system for a large organization could require hundreds of pages to show all the detail. Although it is unlikely that you will have to draw or maintain such a large diagram,

**FIGURE 3.3**
ROLLING THUNDER
TOP-LEVEL BUSINESS
SYSTEM (USE CASE)
DIAGRAM
These are the five processes involved in the information system. Note that the retail store, customer, and manufacturer objects are drawn outside the main system.

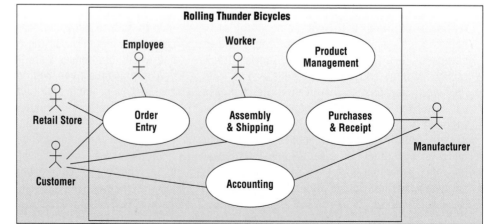

you should know there are computer tools to help keep track of these drawings. An automated tool called **computer-aided software engineering (CASE)** helps a systems analyst draw diagrams on the computer screen. That way the analyst can have the computer keep track of the pages and the various levels. By pointing and clicking with a mouse, the analyst or user can see how the subsystems are related and retrieve any desired information about the system. The CASE tool analysts share their work. They also keep track of the detailed definitions and comments.

## Showing Object Interactions with Collaboration Diagrams

The individual business processes can be described in more detail by using sequence diagrams or interaction diagrams. The choice of diagram technique depends on your focus. If you need to describe a process in step-by-step detail where timing and conditions are important, then you can use a sequence diagram—or write out the steps in text. On the other hand, with most business problems it is more important to focus on the collection of data. Hence, the Rolling Thunder Bicycle case will be developed using collaboration diagrams.

A collaboration diagram can focus on interactions by displaying the individual object classes used within a process. Remember that a class defines an object in terms of properties and the functions that it can perform. For example, the Bicycle class would contain properties for the serial number and the date it was ordered. A typical function would be the ability to add a new bicycle order.

### Order Entry at Rolling Thunder Bicycles

The order-entry process is shown in Figure 3.4. Notice that the Bicycle, BikeTubes, and BikeParts objects are central to the process because the order is where the bicycle is first defined. The other classes (BikeSizes and Components) are secondary and are used to help determine the proper size of the bicycle and set its price.

Keep in mind that each of the external actors (represented by stick figures) also represents an object related to the process. The company will need to collect data on most of these external objects. We will define simple functions for them as well, such as adding a new customer. However, because they are outside the system, we will not attempt to define their behavior, such as specifying how often a customer should buy a new bicycle.

Notice that association lines connect the classes. For example, the Bicycle class is joined to the BikeParts class. In this case, the BikeParts object shows exactly which components are chosen for a specific bicycle.

**FIGURE 3.4**
ROLLING THUNDER
ORDER-ENTRY
PROCESS
As shown on the connecting lines, various actions can trigger the use of functions that are defined by the classes.

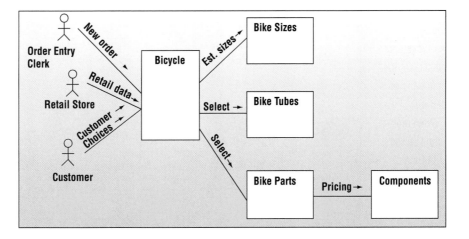

Specifying the related functions at various points shows interactions. For example, the order-entry clerk triggers a new order function, which tells the system to create the base data for a new order. Similarly, selecting a part for the bicycle (e.g., a front tire) sends a message to the Component class to recalculate the price of the bicycle.

### Manufacturing at Rolling Thunder Bicycles

Figure 3.5 shows the primary classes involved in the manufacturing process. Notice that the activities are more detailed in this diagram. As each employee completes a task, the date and time are recorded by the appropriate function. As parts are installed, the Component class adjusts the inventory quantity on hand (QOH). Note that a single employee could perform the roles of assembler, painter, and installer. However, the jobs are displayed separately to highlight the details of the manufacturing process.

The details of the manufacturing steps could be shown in a different (sequence) diagram. If there were problems within manufacturing, it would be helpful to specify the exact order of the assembly steps, and note the dependence of each phase. For example, managers might want to know the average time it takes to assemble a frame as well as if the installers are waiting on the painters. At the moment, this specific data is not collected by the system, so the current diagram is sufficient.

### Purchasing at Rolling Thunder Bicycles

Figure 3.6 shows the general purchasing process used by the company. The actual purchase relies primarily on two classes: PurchaseOrder to record the base data about the purchase, and PurchaseItems to record the quantity and price of the items ordered. The process becomes more interesting when shipments are received. When the dock worker enters the shipment into the system, the inventory quantity on hand is updated, and a notation is recorded in the ManufacturerTransaction object. The accounting system will eventually examine this table and pay the bills at the appropriate time.

**FIGURE 3.5**
ROLLING THUNDER
MANUFACTURING
PROCESS

The assembler uses data from the BikeTubes and TubeMaterial classes to design and build the frame. When the frame is painted, the painter records the date in the system. As tubes and parts are installed, the inventory quantity on hand (QOH) is adjusted. When the installer signifies the completion of the bicycle, it is shipped and the customer is billed.

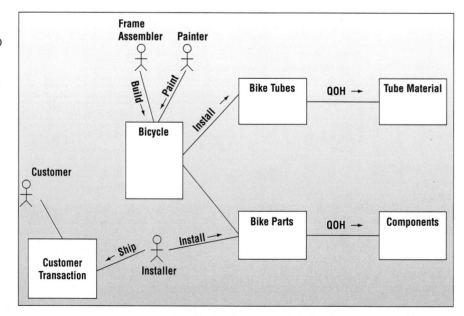

### Rolling Thunder Bicycle Summary

At some point, the system designers will provide more details about the classes used in these various processes. Likewise, the various functions will have to be defined precisely so they can be programmed into the system. Each of the processes described will eventually have a data-entry screen to enable workers to enter the needed data rapidly. Each function or event trigger will be implemented in a programming section.

The classes will be defined in more detail. In particular, each class will have several properties. These properties represent the data that will be stored within that class. In Chapter 5, these classes are created as tables within a database. Figure 3.7 shows the details for some of the classes used in the Rolling Thunder Bicycles database. This figure is a **class diagram,** which displays the classes, their properties, and the associations or relationships among the classes. The classes are drawn as rectangles with the class name at the top, followed by the list of properties. You can also include the functions embedded in each class, but they are not shown here. Finally, the classes are related to each other based on the properties. The connecting lines show these associations. Typically,

**FIGURE 3.6**
ROLLING THUNDER
PURCHASING
PROCESS

Ordering is straightforward. Just note that as items are received at the loading dock, the inventory quantity is updated, and the payable function triggers an entry in the ManufacturerTransaction class to ensure the manufacturer is paid.

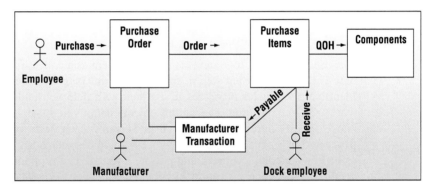

**FIGURE 3.7**
SOME CLASSES FOR
ROLLING THUNDER
BICYCLES

These classes will eventually become tables in the database application. The properties will become columns in the table. For example, each Bicycle has a SerialNumber, CustomerID, ModelType, and so on.

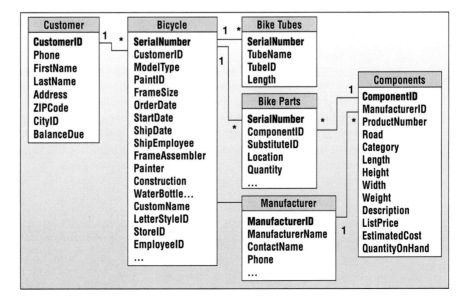

the associations are marked with notes to indicate the type of relationship. For example, one (1) customer can order many (*) bicycles. However, only one customer can order a given bicycle.

Notice that the class diagram is a model of the firm. The classes represent real objects in the company. These classes hold the data generated by the firm. Chapter 5 explains how to use these tables to obtain answers to common business questions.

**PROCESS ANALYSIS**

If you are examining a transaction-processing system or dealing with a system that is largely noncomputerized, you should consider creating a process diagram. The purpose of a process diagram is to describe how the individual processes interact with each other. It concentrates on the business activities instead of the objects.

A data flow diagram is a process-oriented technique used for investigating information systems. The method can be used to look at the "big picture" and see how a system works in total. It also can be used to examine the details that occur within each process. Examining organizations at both levels provides a relatively complete picture of the problems and potential solutions. The use of systems analysis is illustrated by evaluating a small system for a zoo.

## Input, Process, Output

One useful approach to systems is to look at them as a collection of processes or activities. The most important step in solving problems is to find the cause of the problems. Identifying the major processes in a system will help you understand how the system works. Examining input and output objects helps you spot problems and trace them back to their source. As illustrated in Figure 3.8, systems receive **input,** which is **processed** to produce **output.** The process could be mechanical, such as manufacturing using raw materials, workers, and power. Alternatively, it might be a process involving symbolic processing instead of physical activity. For example, accounting systems receive sales data and process it into cash-flow statements. In many cases, there are two types of input and output: physical and data. Physical flows are often accompanied by data. For instance, raw materials are shipped with an invoice that describes the products and the shipping information. Systems theory can be used to examine both types of flow. However, this is an MIS text, so most of the problems presented here deal with flows of data.

Systems are described by collections of these processes. Each system operates in an environment that is somewhat arbitrarily defined by the boundaries of the system. For most problems, anything directly controlled by the firm is considered part of the relevant system. Everything else exists in the environment outside of the firm. The environment typically includes at least the physical space, laws, customs, industry, society, and country in which the firm operates. The firm can influence the physical environment, laws, and customs, but it does not have direct control over them.

**FIGURE 3.8**
Each system can be decomposed into three major components: input, process, and output.

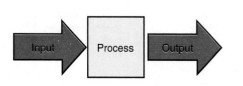

Consider the example of a zoo: input and output are less concrete because a zoo primarily produces services instead of products. Figure 3.9 shows the basic inputs of food, money, and health data for potential new animals. Output objects include education, educational materials, and baby animals for other zoos. For most purposes, the system boundary is relatively clear. Visitors, suppliers, and other zoos are outside the direct control of the zoo, so they are in the environment. If the zoo was operated by a governmental agency, it would be harder to identify the boundary. Government systems tend to reach into many different areas, and it can be hard to identify their exact limits, especially since they can be extended or contracted by political decisions.

If a system is entirely self-contained and does not respond to changes in the environment, it is called a **closed system.** An **open system** learns by altering itself as the environment changes. Systems are almost never completely closed because closed systems cannot survive for long. However, some systems (or companies) are more responsive to changes in the environment than others.

Most large firms face a certain amount of inertia. It is easier for these firms to keep operating the way they always have than to continually introduce changes. But if a firm becomes too static, it can no longer respond to changes in the environment. Much like the U.S. railroad companies in the 1960s, closed firms will lose ground to firms that are more open and responsive to the environment. Remember that a key component of strategy is to search the environment for potential advantages.

## Divide and Conquer

Most problems are too complex and too large to deal with all at once. Even if you could remember all the details, it would be hard to see how everything was supposed to fit together. A crucial step in analyzing a system is to carefully break it into smaller pieces or a collection of subsystems. Each subsystem is separate from the others, but they are connected and interdependent.

Figure 3.10 shows the five primary subsystems within the zoo. Of course, there could be many possible subsystems for the zoo. The actual division depends on how the organization operates. Each subsystem is defined by identifying the input and output flows. How do you know how to divide a system into smaller parts? Fortunately, most

**FIGURE 3.9**
SYSTEM BOUNDARY
AT THE ZOO
As we build systems, we must identify the components that make up the primary system. There will be many other entities that interact with the system. However, these entities are beyond our control, so they are outside of the system.

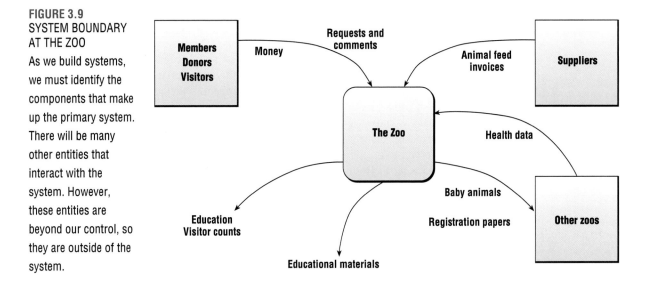

**FIGURE 3.10**
PRIMARY
SUBSYSTEMS
OF THE ZOO
The first step in
analyzing a system is
to identify the major
subsystems. In most
organizations, this step
is relatively easy
because the
organization will
consist of several
departments or
functions.

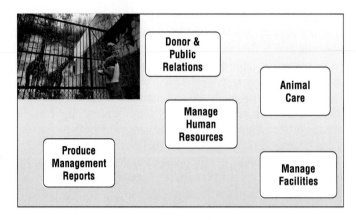

complex systems have already been subdivided into different departments and tasks. Many companies are organized by business functions: accounting, finance, human resources, marketing, MIS, and production. Others are split into divisions according to the type of product.

Once you have determined the major components of the system, each subsystem can be divided into even smaller pieces. An accounting department, for example, might be split into management reporting, tax management, quarterly reporting, and internal auditing groups. Each of these areas might be split into even more levels of detail. At each step, the subsystems are defined by what they do (process), what inputs are used, and what outputs are produced.

There are some drawbacks to the divide-and-conquer approach. It is crucial that you understand how the components work together. If a project is split into small parts and given to independent teams, the teams might lose sight of the overall goals. Important components might not be completed, or the individual pieces might not meet the overall objectives of the system.

## Goals and Objectives

Subsystems have goals or purposes. A goal of a manufacturing firm might be to sell more products than any rival (increasing sales). Or it might be to make as much money as possible for its owners (increasing revenues). Another goal might be find an entirely new area in which to sell products (new market segments). The system should define its goals. If the system does not have a goal, it has no purpose, and there is no way to evaluate it. In fact, by definition, it would not be a system. When you observe a system, you will need to evaluate performance, which means you have to identify the goals.

Typical spreadsheets give us the ability to ask "what-if?" questions. For example, you might want to know what happens if you increase sales commissions by 10 percent. Goals help focus the answer by providing the ability to ask questions about *Why?* and *So what?* The answer to the *What-if?* question involving commissions might be that revenue increases by 5 percent. But what does that result mean? If we also know that a goal of the company is to increase profits, we could look more carefully and find that increasing commissions by 10 percent leads to a 3-percent increase in profits. That result is important because it brings the system closer to one of its goals. Hence, it would make sense to increase the commissions.

It is clear that to solve business problems, you must first identify the organization's goals. The catch is that there are often conflicting ways to measure the goals. For in-

While parents shop at the D&W supermarket in Holland, Michigan, they can rest assured that their children are safe. The store offers a separate playroom for the children. To ensure their safety, a special bracelet is placed on their wrists. The bracelet contains a radio frequency ID (RFID) tag so that if the child leaves the room, an alarm sounds. The store also provides a similar bracelet for parents, so they do not accidentally leave the store without their children, or intentionally leave the store to get free baby-sitting services. The service is just one example of the use of RFID technology. Companies are also using it for a variety of purposes: to track equipment such as computers, to give people access to secure areas, to time runners in marathons, and to identify animals such as pets and cattle. In 1997, Mobil Cor-

poration introduced an RFID tag to enable customers to purchase gas just by driving up to the pump. Texas Instruments, a manufacturer of the tags, notes that they cost around $2 each, and expect the price to drop to about 50 cents. Several people have suggested placing the tags in jewelry or other objects that people carry, which would provide an easy means to track individuals. For example, stores could track customers as they shop, and businesses could track employees. In January 1999, Professor Kevin Warwick, director of cybernetics at the University of Reading, became the first person to be implanted with an RFID tag. For the nine days in which the chip was implanted in his arm, the intelligent office building automatically recognized him, gave him access to restricted areas, and turned on lights for him.

stance, improved customer satisfaction or product quality might be useful goals. But how do we measure them? Managers who measure customer satisfaction by the number of complaints they receive will make different decisions than those who actively survey customers. In other words, the measurement of our performance with respect to the goals will depend on the data we collect.

## Diagramming Systems

We often represent systems graphically to gain insights and spot problems. We also use diagrams to communicate. Communication is of critical importance in MIS and all areas of business. Users describe their problems to systems analysts, who design improvements and describe them to programmers. Ideas and comments can be misinterpreted at any step. We can minimize problems by using a standard diagramming technique. The data flow diagram approach presented in this section is commonly used because it focuses on the logical components of the system and there are few rules to remember, so almost anyone can understand the diagrams.

Although you could invent your own diagramming technique, a method called a **data flow diagram (DFD)** has been developed to represent information systems. It is designed to show how a system is divided into smaller portions and to highlight the flow of data between those parts. Because there are only three graphical elements (five if you count the dashed control flows separately), it is an easy technique to learn. The DFD illustrates the systems topics in this chapter.

The basic elements of a DFD are external entities (objects), processes, data stores (files), and data flows that connect the other items. Each element is drawn differently, as shown in Figure 3.11. For example, data flows are shown as arrows. **Feedback** and control data are usually drawn as dashed lines to show that they have a special purpose.

**FIGURE 3.11**

Only four or five objects are used to create a data flow diagram. External entities are objects that are independent and outside the system. Processes are functions and actions applied to data. A data store or file is a place to hold data. Data flows are shown as solid lines with arrows to indicate the data movement. Control flows are marked with dashed lines.

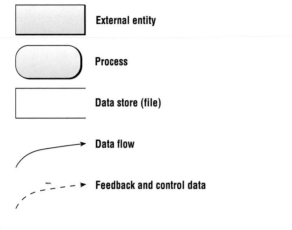

**External entity**

**Process**

**Data store (file)**

**Data flow**

**Feedback and control data**

Figure 3.12 presents the main level of subsystems for the zoo. Notice that it contains external entities, processes, and data flows. This level generally does not show data files or control flows. They can be incorporated in more detailed presentations.

### External Entity

When you identify the boundary of a system, you will find some components in the environment that communicate with your system. They are called **external entities.** Although each situation is different, common examples include customers, suppliers, and management. External entities are objects so they are labeled with nouns.

In the zoo example, the primary entities are management, certification agencies, other zoos, and members of the public (visitors, donors, and members). All relevant external entities need to be displayed on the first-level diagram.

### Process

In a DFD, a process is an activity that involves data. Technically, DFDs are used to show systems that involve data, not products or other materials. However, in business today, virtually all physical processes have data-processing counterparts. When customers buy something, they get a receipt. In a manufacturing process, the amount of raw materials being put to a machine, measures of the volume of output, and quality control values are recorded. The DFD process is used to represent what happens to the data, not what occurs with the raw material.

Because processes represent actions, they are typically labeled with verbs, such as *Sell products,* or *Create tax reports for management.* There are two important rules involving processes. First, a process cannot invent data. That means every process must have at least one flow of data entering it. Second, a process cannot be a black hole; every process must transfer data somewhere else. If you look at your DFD and find one of these two problems, it usually means that you missed a connection between the processes. On the other hand, processes that do not export data might be data stores or external entities.

### Data Store

A data store or file is simply a place to hold data for a length of time. It might be a filing cabinet, reference book, or computer file. In a computerized system, data is likely to be stored in a database management system (DBMS). Chapter 5 provides more detail on the capabilities and uses of a DBMS. For now, it is important to note that data is a valuable

FIGURE 3.12

The zoo: Level 0. The primary processes and data flows of the zoo.

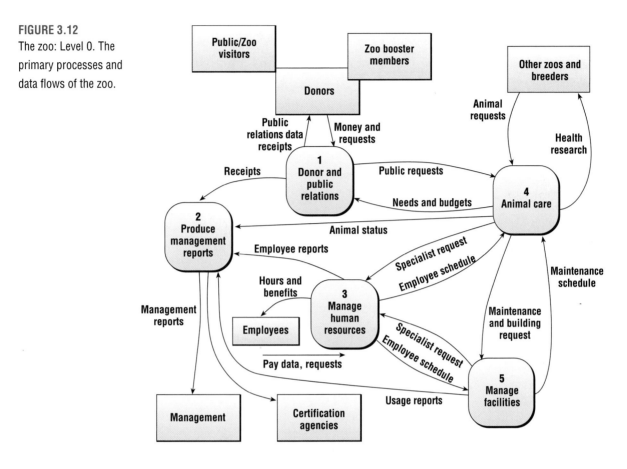

resource to any company. In drawing a DFD, try to list exactly what needs to be stored, how long it should be held, and who should be able to read or change the data.

### Data Flow

The data flows represent the inputs and outputs of each process or subsystem. The data flows are easy to draw. They are simply arrows that connect processes, entities, and data stores. Be sure to label every data flow. The diagram might seem obvious *now;* however, if someone else reads it or you put it away for several months, it can be hard to figure out what each flow represents.

### Division of the System

A DFD provides an excellent way to represent a system divided into smaller components. First, each task is shown as a separate process. The data flows between the processes represent the inputs and outputs of each subsystem. Second, the DFD for a complex system would be too large to fit on one page. Hence, the DFD is displayed on different pages or levels. The top level or *context diagram* acts as a title page and displays the boundaries of the system and the external entities that interact with the system. The next level (*level zero*) shows the primary subsystems. Figure 3.12 is an example of a level zero diagram. Each of these processes is then exploded into another level that shows more detail. Figure 3.13 is the exploded detail for the first process (donor and public relations). These explosions can continue to any depth until you have displayed all the detailed operations needed to explain the system.

**FIGURE 3.13**

Each process can be expanded into more detail. This diagram shows the interactions with various members of the public. Note that data flows from the higher level must appear on this level.

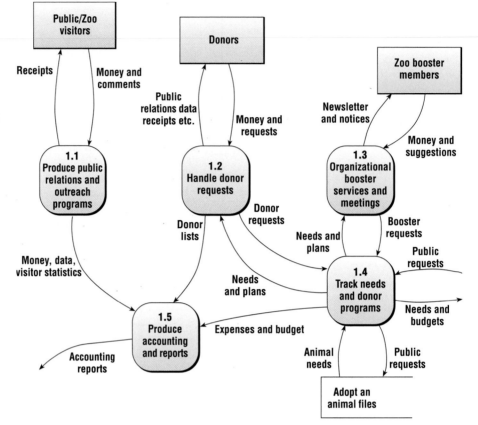

## Data Dictionary

In any project, you need to remember additional pieces of information about each object. You might want to keep a sample report for a *management tax report* data flow, along with any deadlines that must be met. For data stores, you need to record information such as who controls it, who needs access to the data, how often it should be backed up, and what elements it contains.

A **data dictionary** or **repository** contains all of the information that explains the terms you used to describe your system. A good CASE tool will maintain the dictionary automatically and help you enter longer descriptions for each item. Without these tools, you will have to keep a notebook that contains the full descriptions. For convenience, the entries should be sorted alphabetically. A word processor can be used to hold and print the dictionary. Figure 3.14 shows sample entries for the zoo system.

## Summary: How Do You Create a DFD?

The first step in creating a DFD is to identify the environment and boundaries of the system by asking the following questions. What problems do you need to solve? What areas do you want to avoid? What are the goals? What are the main external entities? The second step consists of identifying the primary processes that define the system. Keep the list short (fewer than 10). Then answer, What are the main activities in the system? What are the inputs and outputs of each process? How are these processes in-

**FIGURE 3.14**
SAMPLE DATA
DICTIONARY ENTRIES
(PARTIAL)

A few sample entries
from the zoo's data
dictionary. A data
dictionary records
details on all of the
organization's objects.
It is typically organized
by type of object. It is
easiest to maintain if it
is stored in a computer
database.

| PROCESS | DESCRIPTION . . . |
|---|---|
| Animal care | Feed, clean, and vet care |
| Donor and public relations | Handle public requests and provide educational information |
| Employee relations | Schedule employees, process benefits, handle government reports |
| Facility management | Handle maintenance, new construction, planning |
| Produce management reports | Collect data and produce summary reports for management |
| **ENTITIES** | |
| Certification agencies | Government and private agencies that create rules and regulate zoos |
| Donors | People and companies who donate money to the zoo |
| Employees | Primary (paid) workers, full-time and part-time |
| Other zoos and breeders | Zoos we trade with and share data with |
| Public/zoo visitors | Daily visits, we rarely keep data on individuals |
| Zoo booster members | Members who donate money and time for minor benefits |
| **DATA** | |
| Accounting reports | Standard (GAAS) accounting reports for management |
| Certification reports | Reports for certification agencies; produced annually |
| Facility reports | Summaries of work done and plans, mostly weekly |
| Needs and budgets | Budgets and special requests from animal care |
| Public requests | Suggestions and comments from the public |

terconnected by the data flows? The third step is to look at each process in more detail and draw an expanded subsystem on a new page. What activities take place within a given process? What detail is needed in the reports and data inputs? The fourth step is to build the control flows. What processes are used to monitor progress toward the goals? What additional data is collected to monitor the environment and the system's performance?

The key to analyzing systems is to start small. You can begin with one detailed subsystem and build your way up, or you can describe the general system processes and work down by adding increasing levels of detail.

**ASKING QUESTIONS**   The key to solving business problems is to ask the right questions. In any realistic situation, you, as a manager, will never have enough information. Most of the time, several people will be involved, each with his or her own perspectives, opinions, and biases. Although most people will not deliberately withhold information, they may not know what information is important.

You will often have to talk to the people involved at least twice. The first interview will determine the scope of the problem and identify the components of the system. When you understand the basic problem, you usually have to return and ask more specific questions to learn the details and to clarify conflicting points. You also need to try out possible

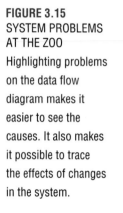

**FIGURE 3.15**
SYSTEM PROBLEMS
AT THE ZOO
Highlighting problems
on the data flow
diagram makes it
easier to see the
causes. It also makes
it possible to trace
the effects of changes
in the system.

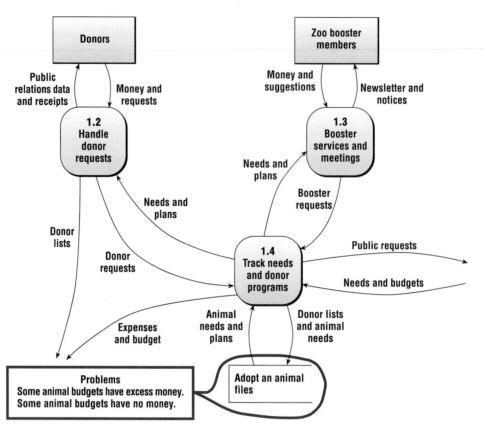

solutions to determine their strengths and drawbacks. Sometimes you can have a good solution, but the people directly involved will be able to suggest improvements.

Questions serve another useful purpose. They can be used to suggest new alternatives to decision makers. This is why it is important to ask questions even when you
already know the answer. Communications among people can be challenging. Each
person has a mental picture of how the system works. There is no guarantee that
everyone works from the same viewpoint. Questions force people to think about their
view of the problem. Sometimes solving a problem is as simple as asking the right
questions to define it correctly. The main point to remember is that when you approach a business problem, do not start by looking for answers; first look for the important questions.

How do you know which questions to ask? The first step is to find a goal and stick to
it, which generally leads to the first question: What is the primary objective? Then, if you
run into conflicts or decisions: How does this action help achieve the objective? Use
questions to stay focused on the goal. Another approach is to think of various alternative
solutions or models. Then use questions to choose among them. Questions typically include: How do the solutions differ? Are the underlying assumptions reasonable? What
happens if something goes wrong? For illustration, consider the problem encountered at
the zoo. As marketing manager, you find there is a problem in the budgets stemming
from donations. Although there are some quick-and-dirty solutions, you really need to dig
deeper to find the source of the problem. Figure 3.15 shows the subsystems that are affected by the problem.

---

**Reality Bytes　　3–3　Problems at the Zoo**

As a marketing manager at the zoo, you notice there is a problem. Some of the animal budgets contain more money than they need. Other animal budgets have no money at all. Your first response to this "problem" is to simply pull money from the large accounts and put it into the accounts with no money. Then your assistant reminds you that the accounts "promise" donors the money will be spent on the animals they specify, and it would be unethical to transfer money in the accounts. So, you need to ask: Is this the entire problem, or is it just a symptom? Why did this event occur? Does it happen often? You decide to use the DFD to trace where the money and animal requests come from. First you check to see whether total donations have changed. You examine the process that handles donor requests and verify that account balances are correct and that no major mistakes were made. You

eventually work back to the donor groups and the booster members. On questioning several prominent members, you find that some animals are more popular than others. Everyone wants to sponsor the lions and giraffes. No one wants to give money to sponsor the binturong.

On looking further, you find that the marketing department tracks only the total donations. It does not look at the breakdowns by animal. As a result, marketing promotions continue to push the "cuddly" animals, even though those animals do not need more money. You considered a proposal to change the promotions so the zoo can shift money among accounts at will. However, your legal staff advises that it might be illegal as well as unethical. You finally decide that you need to build a better feedback loop and improve the information system so that marketing knows which animals to "sell."

---

**SOLVING BUSINESS PROBLEMS AND CASES**

One of the goals of this text is to help you move a step closer to the business world and its unstructured problems. It takes time to develop your own approach to identify the important issues and search for alternative solutions with unstructured problems. Figure 3.16 illustrates one basic approach to solving problems. A useful way to learn how to solve business problems is to begin by working with smaller cases. These cases represent more compact, slightly better-defined business problems. Each chapter contains exercises and cases that reflect situations you might encounter in business. Many of these problems are loosely defined. You might be given a set of numbers and asked to create a report. In some cases, you will have to decide what problems need to be solved. Then you need to select appropriate tools to produce the report. Remember that in business, presentation is important because you will be judged both by the context and the appearance of your work.

### Solve the Right Problem

One of the first complications you encounter with unstructured problems is that there could be several problems. Especially with cases, it is not always clear which problem is the most important. You must be careful to identify causes instead of just symptoms. That is where systems theory is useful. It encourages you to look at all the components of the system. Keep in mind that almost no business runs perfectly. Some minor problems are not worth the cost to fix them. You will have to evaluate each problem and determine which ones are the most important. Remember that it is crucial to focus on the goals of the system. If there are multiple goals, you will have to assign priorities and determine how your plans relate to the goals.

**FIGURE 3.16**
You should develop a systematic plan for solving problems. The steps outlined here provide a starting point. Each step leads to increasingly detailed analysis.

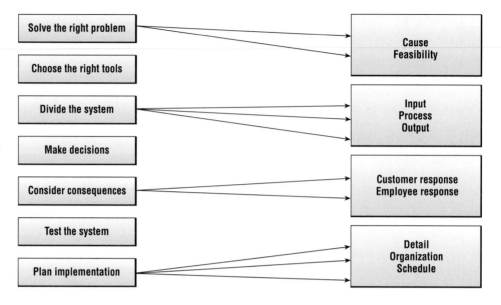

## Choose the Right Tools

When the only tool you have is a hammer, everything looks like a nail. That's an old saying that has often been applied to MIS. Many students quickly see the value of spreadsheets, so they try to solve all their problems using a spreadsheet. Sometimes the exercise is easier to do with a database management system, or even a word processor. When you encounter a new business problem, stop for a minute and decide which tool is best for the job. For example, Chapter 5 examines the differences between spreadsheet problems and situations where a DBMS is a better choice. Chapter 7 shows how to combine the results of several tools.

## Divide the System: One Step at a Time

At first glance, many problems appear to be too difficult. Or you might have trouble finding a solution to a case. The trick is to split the problem into smaller pieces. For cases, use systems theory and data flow diagrams to identify the components of the system. For exercises and problems, work one step at a time. Collect the data, perform computations, create graphs and then create the final report. If the problem is structured appropriately, try to keep the individual components separate. If you need to make a change in one section, it should not interfere with the rest of the project.

## Making a Decision

Once you have evaluated the alternatives, you must make a decision. For most problems, you can only afford to pursue one option. Your choice should be clearly defined and the relative advantages and disadvantages spelled out in detail. You also need to include a solid action plan that describes each step of your proposal. If possible, you should estimate the potential costs. At least identify the items that must be purchased, even if you do not know the costs. Also, if it is relevant, you should identify the people who will be in charge of implementing your plan.

## Reality Bytes          3–4    Union Pacific Merger Problems

In the 1980s and early 1990s, Union Pacific was one of the few railroad companies recovering from the doldrums of the 1960s and 1970s. Investments in infrastructure improvements and information technology made Union Pacific one of the leading long-haul carriers for products across the United States. Managers and the company received awards for their innovation and use of technology to improve the company. In 1997, Union Pacific purchased Southern Pacific Rail. Problems first arose in Texas and the Gulf region, where Union Pacific was having problems providing cars for transporting oil and grain. As Union Pacific struggled with the merger and handling the new schedule requirements, average train speed dropped form 16.5 to 14.1 mph. Retailers and shippers complained about the delays and sought alternative shipping methods, resulting in a loss of over $300 million in rev-

enue to Union Pacific. By July 1998, Union Pacific had not solved all of its problems. Shippers were concerned about the backlog of holiday imports stacking up in Los Angeles docks. One customer, David Krakauer of Worldwide Dreams, LLC, noted that a shipment of purses and accessories from Hong Kong took eight days to travel from California to New York instead of the normal five days. In an attempt to solve its problems, Union Pacific eventually decided to decentralize some of its operations. Paul Broussard, a transportation consultant notes that "Union Pacific pushed centralization beyond the point of reasonableness. Now it has learned the hard way that it has to do something to restore its control in the field." After doubling in size through acquisition, John Bromley a Union Pacific spokesman noted that "The railroad is too large to operate from one location."

### Consider the Consequences

Any time a system is changed, it is important to examine the participants to see who might be adversely affected and to identify how external agents might respond to the changes. For example, if you design a new system that alters the work flow within the company, some jobs and middle-level management tasks may be altered or eliminated. Although companies routinely alter jobs and occasionally reduce their workforce, a good plan will include a means to retrain workers for new jobs within the company whenever possible. Effects on external agents are more difficult to identify and harder to resolve. For example, a manufacturer might consider skipping over the retail channel and selling products directly to the final consumer. With this approach, the manufacturer could offer a lower price to consumers. However, the existing retail outlets would be upset at the additional level of competition. Many times the retailers add support through product demonstrations, comparisons with competitive products, training, and repair services. In these cases, a new system that irritates the retailers or skips them completely could be disastrous.

### Implementation

In business, creative ideas are always useful, but without a detailed implementation plan the idea alone will not be used. Consider an idea for a new product. The idea itself is not worth much until you find a way to manufacture, market, and distribute the product. Similarly, in MIS it is easy to say that a company can achieve significant gains by installing a new computer system. However, the idea is more valuable and the project more likely to succeed if you include a detailed implementation plan. MIS implementation plans include hardware and software requirements, along with training, changes required in various departments, and timetables for installation. Chapter 12 explains the process in more detail.

## Evaluating Technology Projects: Initial Questions

- Does the project fit with the business goals and management style?
- Does the project improve the competitive position of the firm?
- How long will any competitive advantage last?
- What value or reward is created by the system?
- What level of technology is needed to create the system (experimental, leading edge, established, or old-hat)?
- What is the probability of technical success (actually building the system)?

- What is the probability of commercial success (making money once the project is technically successful)?
- What are the costs involved in creating the system:
  - Monetary?
  - Time?
  - Additional capital, marketing, and management?

### Hints for Solving Business Problems and Cases

Cases are often used to illustrate business problems and to show the role played by information. As you progress in your business education, you will encounter more cases. The purpose of this section is to provide an approach to solving cases. Cases tend to be less structured than typical textbook exercises. With cases you not only have to solve the problem, you have to identify the cause of the problem, then decide what tools to use to address it. The accompanying box lists some questions to pursue when you begin your study of a new business situation.

Treat cases as if they are real business situations. First, familiarize yourself with the situation and the symptoms (read the case). Next, create a system view of the organization (read the case again and take notes). Divide the system into components connected by data flows. Sketch the process. You do not always have to draw a complete data flow diagram; any picture will make it easier for you to see the relationships between the components. Look for basic system problems such as defective subsystems, inputs not matching outputs, and weak interaction with the environment.

Remember that you are looking for causes of the problem. A symptom where reports contain errors could have many possible causes. Perhaps the system is not collecting accurate data. Maybe two departments are interfering with each other and altering the data. Possibly a clerk or a computer program is making the wrong computations. To find the cause in this case, you need to follow the data from the source to the final report and determine where the errors first arise. Most cases are complicated by the fact that there are many symptoms and sometimes more than one cause. A DFD can help you sort out the various relationships.

There are two difficult aspects to any business problem: identifying the true problem and trying to come up with a solution. With practice, you can learn to understand systems and determine causes. Solutions, however, often require creativity. There is no easy way to learn creativity. The best way is to examine what other companies have done to solve their problems. Often, problems that you encounter will be similar to those at other firms. Each chapter in this book carries cases of how actual companies have approached various problems. You can find more case situations in common busi-

## Elements of Good Business Analysis

1. Identification of the root causes of problems.
2. A solid grasp of the strategic components of the problem.
3. Identification of the critical success factors.
4. An evaluation of the financial implications.
5. Thorough discussion of implementation.
6. Realistic analysis of the expected results.
7. The effect on future growth and continued development.
8. The effect on the human resources.
9. An understanding of the target markets.

## Reality Bytes     3–5     Organization of Case Analysis

When you write up your case analysis, the following format will be useful. Check with your instructor to see if he or she wants changes or additional features.

### Problem description

- Statement of the facts and problems
- Identify the most important problems and causes

### Plan

- Describe the new system
- Implementation plan
- Contingency plan for problems that might arise

### Advantages

- Show how your plan will solve the problems
- List any additional opportunitites that you might be able to pursue. In particular, look for new directions that might give your firm an advantage over the rivals.

ness publications such as *Computerworld, Fortune, Business Week,* and *The Wall Street Journal.*

Finally, remember there can be many different answers to any case. You might find that it is easy to suggest that a company should "buy a new computer system." Although that statement is undoubtedly true, it is not very helpful. You really need to add more detail. The best answers describe the nature and cause of the problem, provide a detailed plan, and explain how the plan solves the problem and provides additional advantages.

A typical case will be written as a report to the managers of the company involved. The accompanying box lists some of the elements that are required for a good analysis of business problems. Organization of case analysis presents a useful way to organize your presentation, beginning with a summary of the problems and a discussion of the causes. The solution should then be spelled out in detail. An implementation section should explain exactly how to arrive at the solution. This section includes a step-by-step plan of action that lists when to take each action, and specifies who is in charge. The report should also estimate the costs of the solution and describe the anticipated benefits. Some reports may need to include a contingency plan. If you make a risky suggestion that could backfire, it would be wise to give the company another option.

## SUMMARY

Solving business problems and cases can be a difficult task. It is wise to start by searching for causes of problems. You can begin your search by dividing the problem into smaller pieces using either an object-oriented design or a data flow process design.

It is easier to solve problems once you have learned to analyze and diagram business systems. You can begin by examining each module to be sure that it is performing the task it was designed to do. Other sources of problems include the connections between the modules, missing or inappropriate feedback and control mechanisms, and the failure to interact with the environment. You begin to solve problems by asking questions. As you begin your study of business problems, it is important to begin collecting a list of questions that you can ask whenever you start a new case.

When presenting a solution, focus on a complete description of the plan. Make sure you choose the correct tools for each job. Explain how your approach will solve

> ### A MANAGER'S VIEW
>
> All managers need to solve problems. You will eventually gain experience and develop your own style. Object design and systems theory provide useful starting points because they encourage you to break a system into smaller pieces that are easier to understand. The methods also help you focus on the causes of problems instead of the symptoms.
>
> Knowledge of the object and systems approaches will make it easier for you to communicate with analysts for MIS when you are creating a new information system.

the problems and provide new opportunities for the organization. If you are creating a new system, be sure to test it thoroughly. Leave enough time in the development schedule both to test each component individually and to test the complete system.

## KEY WORDS

class diagram, 103
closed system, 105
computer-aided software engineering (CASE), 101
data dictionary, 110
data flow diagram (DFD), 107
external entities, 108
feedback, 107

file transfer protocol (FTP), 129
hypertext markup language (HTML), 127
inherit, 98
input, 104
Internet service provider (ISP), 129
intranet, 126
object hierarchy, 98

object-oriented design, 97
open system, 105
output, 104
portable document format (PDF), 128
process, 104
repository, 110
subsystems, 99

## WEB SITE REFERENCES

**General Shopping Sites**

| | |
|---|---|
| Bizrate | www.bizrate.com |
| City Search | www.citysearch.com |
| Microsoft/MSN | shopping.msn.com/msnlink |
| Net Market | www.netmarket.com |
| Netscape | excite.netscape.com/shopping |
| Shop the Web | shoptheweb.amazon.com |
| Sidewalk | national.sidewalk.msn.com |
| Web Market | www.webmarket.com |
| Yahoo | shopping.yahoo.com |

**Any Traditional Store**

| | |
|---|---|
| Macy's | www.macys.com |
| Sears | www.sears.com |
| Wal-Mart | www.wal-mart.com |

## Auctions

| | |
|---|---|
| eBay | www.ebay.com |
| Lycos | auctionconnect.lycos.com |
| Price Line | priceline.com |
| Yahoo | auctions.yahoo.com |

## REVIEW QUESTIONS

1. Describe all steps involved in the systems method.
2. What are the five elements of a data flow diagram (DFD), and how is it useful in MIS?
3. What two important roles do processes have in a data flow diagram?
4. Explain how object-oriented design is different from the data flow approach.
5. How do object hierarchies make it easier to modify systems?
6. How does encapsulation make it easier to build and modify systems?
7. What is meant by the phrase "divide and conquer"? Why is it important in analyzing and designing systems?
8. Why is it so important to ask questions when you are trying to solve a systems problem?
9. List and describe some helpful hints that can be used when you are solving business problems and cases.
10. Define the major forms of testing used in systems design.

## EXERCISES

1. Write down five questions that you might ask whenever you approach a new case.
2. Interview a manager (or a friend who has a job). Identify the major processes involved in the job. Draw a diagram to show how the processes are related and to show the relevant inputs and outputs of each process.
3. Draw an object hierarchy to illustrate your job.
4. Choose one subsystem in the zoo example and add another level to the data flow diagram. If possible, interview a manager or worker at an actual zoo.
5. Draw a data flow diagram to illustrate the course registration process at your school. Compare your diagram with those drawn by two other students.
6. Create a list of objects that would be involved in the course registration process at your school. Briefly describe some of the attributes and functions used by each object.
7. Read current business periodicals and find examples of three companies that have experienced system problems. Classify the problem in system terms (subsystem, mismatched inputs, etc.). Draw a small diagram to illustrate the problem.
8. Find an article that describes the operations or problems of a company. Write five questions that you would want to ask the CEO (or other officers) of that company if you were hired as a consultant to improve the company's operations.
9. In the bank account example, the bank wants to add a special type of checking account for people who are more than 50 years old. The interest rate will be tied to their age: a one-eighth point increase for every five years over 50 (50 = +1/8, 55 = +2/8, 60 = +3/8 . . .). Change the object hierarchy and add the appropriate properties and functions.

 **Rolling Thunder Database**

10. Identify the processes and activities of the Rolling Thunder Bicycle Company.
11. Diagram the overall system, showing the major subsystems, the flow of products, and the data flows.
12. Identify the primary objects involved. Specify a name, primary attributes, and possible functions for each object.
13. Identify possible constraints or bottlenecks in the system.
14. Identify the primary external objects that interact with Rolling Thunder Bicycles.

## ADDITIONAL READING

Weinberg, Gerald. *Rethinking Systems Analysis and Design,* Boston: Little, Brown, 1982. [Insightful book on the difficulties of systems analysis and design]

Whitten, Jeffrey L., and Lonnie D. Bentley. *Systems Analysis and Design Methods,* New York, NY: Irwin/McGraw-Hill, 1998. [Basic introduction to analysis and design]

# CASES *Specialty Retail*

Retail sales have been strong during the past few years, especially in light of the mature and saturated retail market in the United States. While sales have not been phenomenal, they have risen by about 4 percent annually throughout most of the 1990s. Much of this growth can be attributed to the good economy of the last six years, marked by low interest rates, low inflation, and low unemployment (resulting in an increase in disposable income). Standard and Poor's predicts the economy to keep growing but at a slower pace. These factors, plus a strong consumer confidence index, all mean continued growth for the specialty retail industry; but at a moderate pace overall.

Actually, given the economic indicators, a good question is: Why are sales not growing even faster? The biggest culprit—new shopping and spending trends from consumers. For example, recent studies indicate mall shopping is on the decline, with the average mall visit dropping in duration by more than a third. This may be partly because consumers are more pressed for time. As consumers have less time to shop, they are more likely to purchase only what they need and leave.

The Internet has also helped with precision shopping. In fact, Internet shopping has many advantages, which are not lost on the consumer. However, since home computers with Internet access are not universal in the United States, Internet shopping so far has made only a small dent in overall retail spending. As more consumers become equipped with Internet access and security becomes more standardized, however, Internet shopping will take a bigger bite of the retail shopping pie.

An important spending trend is the increased spending toward leisure and entertainment, reducing spending for retail shopping. This has not been lost on the sellers of entertainment and leisure services, as evidenced by the skyrocketing prices of big concert tours, plays, and unusual vacation packages. For example, concert tours in the past few years from such acts as the Eagles, Rod Stewart, Fleetwood Mac, and U2 have charged from $60 to more than $100 for their top tickets.

One last trend affecting large specialty retailers looking to merge with each other comes from the federal government. The Federal Trade Commission has blocked two retail mergers in the past couple of years, one of which was the proposed merger of specialty retailer Office Depot with Staples. This type of restriction has helped keep specialty retailers from monopolizing the niche market they serve.

## Stock/Investment Outlook

The investment outlook is best for those companies that seem to be the future of specialty retail. The term "specialty retail" seems to imply a small store or chain. However, if we consider businesses such as Toys "Я" Us and Bed Bath and Beyond specialty stores, the picture changes.

The future looks brightest for those companies poised to take advantage of the recent trends in specialty retailing: superstores and "category killers." By attempting to stock every item in a certain line of merchandise, superstores/category killers gain the ability to charge really low prices. Office Depot is an example of a category killer in the office supply area. Other examples of category killers include Toys "Я" Us and Circuit City.

Those large specialty retailers poised to become the leaders in their category have the best investment outlook. As far as small specialty retailers go, those with the best outlook are retailers who seem to be serving a new trend or increasing need. IKEA furniture stores, for example, have found a hungry U.S. market for reasonably priced, stylish furniture.

## Potential/Prospective for Growth

One advantage specialty retailers will always have is that their fortunes do not necessarily move in step with that of the economy. By definition, a specialty retailer sells products only in specific categories serving niche markets. Therefore, a specialty retailer can make money as long as their niche market is profitable, regardless of the state of the economy as a whole. Likewise, a good economy is not enough to guarantee success for a specialty retailer.

## Competitive Structure

Specialty retail stores are normally thought of as small stores competing for a small piece of the pie, the majority of which is owned by a few large players. While this is certainly partially true, this can change depending on your definition of a specialty retailer. Certainly businesses such as Toys "Я" Us, Staples, The Limited, and Radio Shack sell primarily one type of merchandise, yet they are large businesses. Therefore, specialty retailers can appear on both ends of the spectrum in size.

Consider the small specialty retailers. These can be either a national chain or mom-and-pop (or regional) stores. If it is a national chain, this is usually because there is a nationwide market for the niche products they sell. This usually means that one or a few large specialty retailers have the lion's share of the market. An example of this might be the smaller FAO Schwartz stores competing against Toys "Я" Us. Smaller retailers generally compete (especially against category killers) by focusing on something slightly different from the large category killer they are up against. For instance, they may have only high-end (or more expensive) merchandise. FAO Schwartz, for example, focuses on more expensive (and more profitable) merchandise, while Sharper Image's toys are geared toward adults.

The large retailers have found that they can only remain on top by never resting on their laurels and carefully following overall retail trends such as everyday value pricing (e.g., Home Depot). Some retailers seem happy to give up the leadership in order to retain their profitability. Borders Books and Music and Barnes and Noble's are two examples of bookstore chains that are not trying to capture the other's customers by undercutting each other in prices. Therefore, the competitive structure depends on the niche market you are examining. In general, there are a few large players taking up a large share of the market, with the rest of the retailers fighting for the remainder, which often comprises more than half of the market.

### Role of Research and Development

Research and development has an important role in specialty retailing, although not in the traditional sense of R&D. Like all retailers, specialty retailers must do research regarding market conditions and keeping tabs on the competitors. Unlike general retailers, specialty retailers have to pay extremely close attention to trends within their niche. For example, a retailer that sold only typewriters and carbon paper would be hard-pressed if they did not plan adequately to change once personal computers started becoming popular in the 1980s. General retailers can afford to be slightly behind the trends and still survive, since they do not make their entire living from one smaller section of the population.

Development is similar. Specialty retailers need to develop new concepts and new ideas for growth to keep from being passed by or stagnating. Development of faster and cheaper ways of doing business can also help. Dell Computers (a direct computer retailer and manufacturer), for example, has reaped great profits from developing a fast assembly and delivery method in the time-sensitive market of home computers. The role of development in specialty retailing consists of refining the concept and shopping experience of customers to keep pace with changing demands.

### Technological Investment and Analysis

Specialty retailers are poised to take advantage of technological improvements in different ways. For innovations in issues that all retailers face, such as inventory management, specialty retailers (especially the smaller ones) let the bigger, general retailers pay for research, and then the specialty retailers follow suit. Specialty retailers, especially the smaller ones, can be quick adopters of technological advancements and improvements, sometimes using new technology in innovative and unintended ways in order to gain a competitive advantage over their rivals.

For example, one small high-end men's apparel store in Washington, D.C., uses digital cameras to store pictures of outfits that clients purchase. That way, if a client needs to buy a new shirt to match a previously purchased set of pants, a simple call may be all that is needed. The salesperson will pull up pictures of outfits purchased in the computer and make recommendations. General retail innovations such as EDI or Internet shopping have been quickly accepted by specialty retailers.

The Internet especially seems to be a powerful tool for specialty retailers. A specialty retailer on the Internet does not need a store or a catalog to present itself professionally to customers. The Internet also allows customers from all over the world to shop at a store, even if the business has only a few locations. According to Standard and Poor's, a commitment to information systems is emphasized in specialty retail, particularly the bigger chains. Information technology helps stores reduce and control costs and can provide key information about the business. For example, the use of point-of-sale data can tell retailers quickly what is selling and what isn't, allowing for better response time to trends.

### Recommendation for the Future

Specialty retailers need to keep abreast of the latest market trends in the general economy, in retailing, and most importantly, in their niche. They must also exploit improvements in technology to keep up with their nimble competitors; even the large specialty retailers have smaller competitors who could turn operations around quickly. A more targeted and dedicated marketing approach seems to be the next trend in retail marketing, for example, and this is not lost in the least on specialty retailers. Standard and Poor's sees improvements in store design, customer service, merchandise quality, and technology as coming trends.

Some of these trends are already occurring, with sales clerks making suggestions for more merchandise based on previous purchases and demographics. With the Internet and the lack of time to shop, specialty retailers will have to work hard to keep customers. Location will again become important. Stores should be prepared for customers or offer to deliver the merchandise through the mail for free if it is not available. Only enhanced service such as this will keep a high margin and highly profitable customer coming.

## CASE *Ben & Jerry's*

### Technological Investment and Analysis

Ben & Jerry's currently utilizes technology in the following areas: customer database management, manufacturing, web site development, and multimedia. By examining each area individually, we can determine how the company should continue to invest in technology in the future.

Customer database management is a tool for satisfying customer needs and demands. The company currently uses its database for two primary reasons: 1) to discover what customers think of new product ideas and 2) to involve customers in social concerns.

Most of the database records are collected from the Franchised Scoop Shops that send in the names of people who want to be placed on the Ben & Jerry's mailing list. When placed on the mailing list, customers are sent catalogues and newsworthy updates on company happenings. By using the customer databases, the company builds valuable relationships between people and products.

In its manufacturing, Ben & Jerry's uses a very advanced system to emphasize efficiency and productivity for the user. The system ultimately creates a better link between production and storage areas. The business planning and control groups use Ethernet and networking products.

The use of system architecture allows employees to exchange and analyze data. Through this system, the company allows its engineers and designers to share product development information so that the progress can be evaluated constantly. Systems architecture also offers pattern recognition and process learning. Thus, if employees spot inefficient trends during the manufacturing process, proper adjustments can be made that are more effective for the company.

Although the manufacturing process is constantly updated to improve efficiency, Ben & Jerry's also invests much time and effort into further web site development. The web site is an area of continuous technological growth and investment. The company's current web site features an interactive page with an animated tour guide helping visitors around the site in order to answer their questions. The range of interactive information that can be gathered on the site is useful in building long-term relationships with Ben & Jerry's customers.

Finally, the company focuses its resources equally on the expanded use of multimedia applications in its day-to-day operations. Specifically, Ben & Jerry's utilizes videoconferencing to maintain close teamwork and communications between employees who are more geographically scattered as the company expands into the worldwide market.

### Recommendation for the Future

Since Ben & Jerry's manufactures products in the mature stage of the product life cycle, the company should now focus on strengthened market share and building brand loyalty. Ben & Jerry's super premium ice cream product already has an established customer base. The company will gain new customers only if consumers choose to switch super premium brands. In this stage of the product life cycle, emphasis must be placed on customers by building brand loyalty and creating customer satisfaction through the use of technology.

The company can build brand loyalty through the effective use of web site development and database marketing. The Ben & Jerry's web site currently uses several innovating frames to encourage customer interaction with the product and the company. By increasing the number of interactive elements on their web site, keeping the site current with product information, and, most importantly, marketing their site among prospective clients, Ben & Jerry's will be able to maintain high customer loyalty among their target markets.

The real key to Ben & Jerry's future success lies in the company's ability to use and maintain customer databases effectively. Currently, Ben & Jerry's uses its customer databases to gather customer feedback and to introduce customers to social concerns and volunteer organizations. Although these are major current concerns of the company, Ben & Jerry's can use customer feedback in the future in other areas as well. For example, customers may recommend additional channels of distribution for the company, international opportunities, and new growth areas.

As technology grows, Ben & Jerry's should stay aware of increasingly new methods of adding to its customer database. In addition to Scoop Shops, sites such as grocery stores and restaurants where customers purchase the products, the company now has the opportunity to use the Internet to maintain contact with old and new customers alike. By expanding the method of creating additional customer databases, the company can find out more information about consumer habits and therefore gain more accurate marketing knowledge.

If Ben & Jerry's decides to focus on the customer first, super premium ice cream will not enter the declining stage of the product life cycle. The company must understand the importance of customer feedback and the use of technology to utilize it appropriately.

### QUESTIONS

1. What is the strategic direction for Ben & Jerry's ice cream?
2. What are the critical success factors and core competencies factors for Ben & Jerry's ice cream?
3. Upon what technologies has Ben & Jerry's relied?
4. What has caused a change in the use of technology at Ben & Jerry's?
5. Are there replacement products for Ben & Jerry's ice cream?
6. What does the corporation's web page present about its business directives?
7. How important is data to the corporation's continued success?

## ADDITIONAL READING

"Discovery Channel Multimedia Partners with Ben & Jerry's Team to Cross-Promote CD-ROMs," *Multimedia Business Report,* January 17, 1997, p. 4.

Holland, Kelly. "Yummie!" *Business Week,* November 3, 1997, p. 50.

"Raspberry Rebels," *The Economist,* September 6, 1997, pp. 61–62.

## CASE *The Limited, Inc.*

On August 10, 1963, Leslie Wexner borrowed $5,000 from his aunt to finance the opening of a small women's clothing store in Columbus, Ohio. On his first day, Wexner sold $473 worth of merchandise. In the span of 34 years, Wexner's aunt's investment of $5,000 has become a multibillion dollar company. One man's vision, perseverance, and business savvy have made The Limited a leading specialty retailer in the United States.

Growing from one store in the 1970s to a multistore, multibrand corporation has been the result of several strategic and operating efficiencies. Many new stores were opened in the 1970s. The Limited built a distribution facility in Ohio, next to the company headquarters. This allowed The Limited to have inventory shipped directly to the distribution center for prepackaging, price tagging, and store-order fulfillment. Additionally, the company acquired better control over inventory, storage, and shipping costs. The corporation has since opened additional distribution centers to accommodate the thousands of retail stores existing today.

Another strategic initiative that contributes to overall brand perception and success is storefront saturation. Whenever possible, The Limited will lease several contiguous spaces in new malls and act quickly to reposition their different stores in clusters in mall relocation and remodeling. This strategy causes the customer virtually to be surrounded with stores that are owned by The Limited. Otherwise, distractions like a cookie shop or a bookstore, for example, might flank a brand new Limited store. This retail space strategy leads to internal efficiencies also. Contiguous stores can share break rooms, inventory rooms, management, and other resources. Interior passages between stores (for instance, connecting a Structure and an Express) gives the customer the illusion of a much larger store, and keeps customers inside Limited stores and out of the rest of the mall.

### Technological Investment and Analysis

The Limited employs thousands of people, has almost 20 self-managing subsidiaries, and has managed to accumulate several billions of dollars in assets. Technology has helped The Limited manage inventory, manage product lines, control day-to-day activities at the retail stores, and provide information to management enabling them to grow the business.

How can a retailer know each customer? Winners in the consumer information market will be expert managers of that data. Building upon the successes of data warehousing in other business fields, retailers will have to find data about customers, analyze it, and proactively use that knowledge to increase profitability and retain market share.

Also changing is retailers' use of the Internet to market goods, distribute corporate information, and attract customers. Specialty retailers like booksellers, wineries, T-shirt shops, and travel services have capitalized on doing business on the Internet. Technology will continue to play a vital role in determining the future of any retailing enterprise. The Limited is no exception. But being large and a market leader has led The Limited to take a somewhat conservative approach to technology.

Data, hardware, and software are the building blocks of information technology. The integration of these objects enables a company to work, predict results, and make money. Most sales and customer data is collected at the point of purchase. Hardware enables stores to scan inventory items into an IBM terminal–based cash register programmed with custom sales tracking routines and inventory modules. The sale is computed, payment is made, and the customer leaves. Nightly, store management closes the day's transactions, and enters cash and payment balancing information to reconcile the day's activity. Leased-line connections from the store to central data repositories in Columbus, Ohio, make the transfer of sales data. Inventory levels are adjusted, shipping orders are formulated, and data is stored for management review. A warehousing strategy is used to store data. In turn, the data is mined to provide reports on store sales, product line productivity, and patterns of consumer behavior.

The same principles are in operation in data warehousing. Intelligent handling systems track incoming goods, fill orders for stores, and monitor inventory levels. This hardware must be available to all levels of employees. Systems are also in place to automatically alert management of late shipments and deteriorating inventory levels. To make sure that the information stays current, custom software solutions track the flow of goods. Intranet-based database applications ensures smooth delivery to all warehouse personnel.

PC-based utilities are employed to manage employees, share information between store and corporate management, and facilitate client/server automation. These systems answer questions regarding future shipments and price and product availability. Home office users share information through local and wide area networks. The Limited's corporate campus is several blocks long and wide. Traditional memos and nonelectronic communication would be inefficient and costly.

The Internet could play a very important part in the future of The Limited's information technology focus. The Limited started a web site in 1997. It is used primarily to distribute marketing and financial information. Newly developed commerce solutions could be plugged into the existing distribution channels with little infrastructure change.

Knowing customers and their tastes is crucial to the development of brands that customers will buy. Web-enabled questionnaires and marketing forms could gather this critical information. PCs are being bought and used in the home and office internationally every year. Persons at home, work, or at an interactive kiosk in a store could volunteer information that could be used to feed decision support systems. Management would then have the ability to peer through the technology and see beyond quantitative data. Customers' feelings toward products could be analyzed.

A virtual store on the Internet requires a fraction of the overhead required for a physical store. Once established, transaction processes would record the sale, produce entries in the data warehouse, and, by default, collect marketing data. This same interactive information could be modified into back-end management applications to monitor and predict sales results. This would leverage the IT expenditure to gain sales insight.

Over the last three years, developments in collaborative GroupWare and software have made sharing information across the enterprise less costly, more effective, and a valuable part of the information chain.

Support systems must be integrated to manage and share information. A typical software suite like Lotus Notes could be used by all members of the information chain. Since an intranet-based information solution would be integrated into the supply chain, the same technology could be used to examine the front (marketing) and back (financial and operational) ends of the data. Employees would be able to share data, comment on contributions and new data, import and export raw data into other software application suites, such as Microsoft Office, and generate variations of reporting for more departmental and personal uses.

Data models could be built to answer questions regarding the profitability of the Internet commerce project or any other business decision. External sources could supply the static inputs and industry paradigms. Internal data could be applied to the model logic, and the outflows would answer management hypotheses. Modeling enables companies to examine data through the use of constructed scenarios without actually executing the components of the model. As a testing ground for ideas, a model enables companies to query a set of data in countless ways not otherwise possible.

Technology will enable The Limited to answer questions regarding the profitability and effectiveness of the Internet. First, a descriptive model must be constructed to evaluate the effect of Internet commerce on supply and distribution chains, pricing, market segmentation, and information management. Assuming an enterprise information system has been installed, inputs from all aspects of this marketing channel could be considered. The model would evaluate the inputs and produce a set of descriptive outputs for management review. These sets of data would complement a decision support system designed to evaluate the effectiveness of the project.

### Recommendation for the Future

The specialty retailing industry entered the technology arena late. As a result, these retailers continue to make investments in technology to catch up. The Limited has the financial and management resources to test and deploy an Internet commerce system and should do so immediately. Their main competition, The Gap, Inc., has already made such a bold move. In November 1997, The Gap launched an online store that markets and sells all merchandise found in their stores. Sensing that their primary market is the same user demographic surfing the Internet, The Gap was the first large specialty retailer to establish itself on the Internet.

The Limited must continue to refine its presence on the Internet. The younger, contemporary market is easily impressed with trends and marketing savvy. As a matter of viability, The Limited must act now to capture and maintain a sizable and influential market share.

### QUESTIONS

1. What is the strategic direction of the corporation, and who drives this direction?
2. Upon what technologies has the corporation relied?
3. How is customer data collected?
4. How successful has the technological change been?
5. What does the corporation's web page present about the business?
6. What role does data play in the future of the corporation?

### ADDITIONAL READING

Izmirlian, Robert J. "Retailing: Specialty; Industry Survey," *Standard and Poor's,* January 22, 1998.

"Limited Leans on NCR," *Computerworld,* December 15, 1997, p. 37.

"Limited Taps NCR," *Computerworld,* November 24, 1997, p. 37.

Newton, Nell. "Industry Snapshot: Retail & Wholesale," http://www.hoovers.com.

Shein, Esther. "Intranet Logistics Goes High Fashion," *PC Week,* September 8, 1997, pp. 29–30.

## DISCUSSION ISSUE

### *Resistance to Change*

Changing the way an organization operates can have many repercussions. Sometimes it is difficult to decide which effects are important and which ones are major. Similarly, many people dislike change simply because it creates short-term problems and forces alterations in their lives. Any new plan faces these problems and more. Sometimes even more than planning, overcoming these objections requires persuasion. Listen to a typical conversation at a company that distributes musical merchandise.

Jake:  We've got this great idea! We can put the team together and sell direct to the consumers. We'll computerize the entire inventory system and install an order-entry system that can be accessed with telephones or personal computers.

Elwood:  Sure, Jake, that way customers can buy directly from us, skipping the retail outlets.

Jake:  Yeah, Elwood. It'll be great. We'll be able to charge lower prices and still make more money. In addition, we'll know exactly what's hot and what's not selling. No more messing around with sales estimates. We'll have the exact numbers.

Aretha:  I don't know, you'd better think about your actions. Think!

Murph:  Aretha's right. We're not set up to handle the direct distribution. Besides, from my sales experience, most customers like to have their purchases immediately.

Jake:  We've got that worked out, Lou. We'll use overnight delivery to get them the stuff the next morning. In the worst case, they have to wait maybe 20 hours.

Elwood:  Plus, for new music, we're planning ahead for some new tricks.

Jake:  That's right. With our computer system, the customers can listen to a few cuts over the phone before they decide. That's more than they can do in any retail store. Even better, with the new recordable disks, we could transfer the data directly over the phone to their disks. We collect the money up front, the customers get to sample the music, and they get copies immediately.

Aretha:  I'm not convinced, Jake. What about the costs? We need a huge new computer system. Plus, someone has to pay for these phone calls. What's to stop people from tying up a phone line for hours listening to different cuts?

Jake:  Those are minor details. Once we get the computer system in, we can program anything we want. We can limit the length of each call. With the new phone services, we can even place limits on the number of calls we accept from each phone number to stop repeat callers who don't buy anything.

Murph:  But what's going to happen to the distribution department? We've got sales people, managers, and a big shipping department.

Elwood:  Well, if Aretha's really worried about costs, we can save a ton of money by cutting most of those departments.

Murph:  But some of those people have been with us for 15 years. I'm not being sentimental, but those folks have a lot of knowledge and experience that we shouldn't just toss out.

Jake:  Hey, hey. We're not just going to throw people away. In fact, after two years, we'll probably be bigger than we are now. We'll need all of those people. They'll just be doing different things.

Aretha:  Sure, Jake. *If* your plan works. *If* the retailers don't get too upset. *If* the customers actually want to buy products this way. *If* we can get the workers retrained. *If* our competitors don't cut prices and knock us out of business. Then maybe we'll be better off. It sounds too risky to me.

Murph:  She's got a point, Jake. If this plan fails, we're dead. Besides millions in costs, we'll lose sales. Even worse, we'll never get back into the retail stores. They'll be so upset at us that they'll never carry our products again. We have to be careful.

Aretha:  Isn't there some way we can do this without betting the entire company?

Jake:  Come on, folks. We have to be bold! Think about the future. We have a chance to be the first and the best. Opportunities like this don't come along every day. We need a positive outlook.

### QUESTIONS

1. Are Aretha and Murph being overly cautious, or are their comments correct?
2. Is there a way to tell whether people's comments are serious or people are merely worried about jobs and resisting change? (Hint: Does it matter?)
3. If you were running this company, would you take the risk and go with Jake and Elwood's plan?
4. What additional information might you want to collect?
5. What other problems might be encountered? Are there additional benefits?

# *Creating Web Pages*

One of the strengths of the Web is that it is easy to use. The user interface is straightforward. You see a page of text and graphics. Clicking a link brings up a new page. Search engines help you find additional pages. Anyone can learn to use the Web in a few minutes. The Web is a good method for presenting and sharing information with colleagues and other workers. Increasingly, most of the information you create as a manager will be shared through web sites. Many companies set up servers that are accessible only to employees. These systems are called **intranets** to indicate that they contain information available only to insiders.

It is relatively easy to create web pages. The basic steps are outlined in Figure 3.1A. The first two steps are perhaps the most difficult: determining content and defining a style. In a business situation, choosing content might be easy—creating it is what takes the time. For example, the accounting team might decide to create a web site to post weekly financial data as common financial reports. The hardest part is collect-ing and formatting the data. The next step is to choose a style, which consists of the page layout and color scheme. Once you have the content and the layout, you can use a word processor to create the text and tables, and add graphics to each page. Each page is stored as a separate file. You can easily link pages together so users can jump to related information. Once you have tested your work, you can transfer the pages to a web server.

## STYLES

Presentation is an important aspect to any job. When you make a presentation to the CEO, you want to look your best. When you build a web site, you want to create a style that reflects the purpose of the site. Probably the two most important design issues are consistency and subtlety. Choose a color scheme, layout, and fonts that convey a specific image. Then apply that style to every page. You might want to hire a graphics artist to help you design the initial style.

The best way to make sure that every page uses your style is to define a style sheet. A style sheet enables you to set every aspect of the page design, including margins, typefaces, colors, and backgrounds. The style sheet is saved as a separate (.css) file. Every page that contains a <LINK> tag with that file will use that style. When you want to change the style of your web site, you simply change the style sheet, and every page will automatically use the new settings.

Some tools such as Microsoft's Visual Interdev will help you define a style sheet. The alternative is to find a style sheet file and modify it to create your own style. The key to creating and using styles is that every element on your page must be named. You can create styles for any of the standard tags described in the next section, or you can create separate styles that you can apply to any text or section.

- Determine the content
- Define a style
- Create each page
  - Text
  - Graphics
- Link the pages
- Test your work
- Transfer pages to a web site

**FIGURE 3.1A**
STEPS TO CREATING A WEB SITE
The first two steps often require the most work. Many tools exist to help with the later steps.

## CREATING PAGES WITH HTML

Pages on the Web are created using a simplified page layout language: **hypertext markup language (HTML).** Several tools exist to help you create HTML documents, so you do not have to memorize the syntax. In many cases, the simplest solution is to use your word processor—the leading ones have tools to help you create web pages.

The main feature of HTML is that every element on your page is denoted with a tag. That is, each element is surrounded by a marker. For example, basic text is marked with the paragraph tags: <P>Sample paragraph.</P>. Other styles include headings, block quotes, and citations. With a word processor or other visual development tool, you simply type the text, then highlight it and select the appropriate style. When you save the document, the tool adds the necessary tags. Figure 3.2A shows a very basic HTML page. You can create text or edit the page with a simple editor (e.g., Notepad), but then you have to memorize the tags. It is generally easier to use a visual-editing tool. Many sources on the Internet provide information about the various HTML tags if you want to learn how to build a page by hand.

## GRAPHICS

For many years, graphics were a pain to share. Each software package defined a unique file format, so it was hard to share images unless your colleagues had the same hardware and software. The Web deals with this issue by defining three common types of graphic file formats: Grahpics Interchange Format (GIF), Joint Photographic Experts Group (JPEG), and Portable Network Graphic (PNG). To share images, your software must convert them into one of these three formats. The last one (PNG) is relatively recent and is supported only by the newer browsers and a limited number of graphics packages. However, the PNG format is the most versatile because it was designed specifically for the Web. GIF files support a limited number of colors and are typically used for icons. JPEG files are useful for images such as photographs that consist of multiple colors and subtle changes. The newest browsers also support a vector-image format that is much faster and produces better images for simple graphics and charts.

You can create your own image files—if you have the appropriate hardware and software. Scanners are used to convert photographs. Line art and icons can either be scanned or redrawn with a graphics package.

Size is the most important issue with web graphics. If your site will only be used in-house on a high-speed network, you can use large, fancy images. If people will access your pages across the Internet using phone lines, you need to keep image files to fewer than 50,000 bytes.

Images are placed on the HTML page with an <IMG> tag. For example: <IMG SRC="myfile.gif" WIDTH=350 HEIGHT=200>. Again, the visual tools will help you place an image on a page, so you do not have to memorize the syntax of the tag.

To be complete, we need to mention animated GIF files. You have undoubtedly seen them on the Web. Animated GIF files display different images in one spot, enabling you to create simple motion effects. Some sites have so many animated files that they resemble pinball machines. Avoid this effect—most people find it annoying. In fact, it is generally better to avoid animated GIF files unless you absolutely need to call attention to some spot on the page.

```
<HTML>
<HEAD>
<TITLE>Sample HTML Page</TITLE>
</HEAD>
<H1>Section One</H1>
<P>This is a sample paragraph on a sample page.</P>
</BODY>
</HMTL>
```

**FIGURE 3.2A**
BASIC HTML PAGE
Each element is surrounded by tags. A word processor will insert the tags automatically—you simply mark the text and save the file as an HTML page.

## LINKS

Links are one of the most useful features of the Web. Users can find related information by clicking on a link. Links are also used to download files. A link consists of two parts: the text displayed in the browser and the name of the new page/file. Visual page editors make it easy to create links. Just highlight the text in the browser, click a link icon, and enter the name of the new page or file. In HTML, links are marked with an anchor <A> tag. For example: <A HREF="annual.htm">Annual Results</A>.

When you jump to a new page, you can also pick a specific location within that page. Simply add a marker <A NAME="sales"> within the new page, then specify the marker in the link reference: <A HREF="annual.htm#sales>Annual Sales</A>. Again, visual tools make it easy to enter these items. The HTML is shown here to help you understand how the system works.

One problem with links is that if you delete or move a file, users may click on a link and receive an error message. If you rename or delete a file, you need to find and update all of the references to that file in your other pages. Current visual-editing tools help with this task by searching for broken links. Some tools will graphically portray your web site by showing the links from each page. Even with these tools, it is time-consuming to change the files on your web site.

## ADDITIONAL FILE TYPES

If you are building a web site for internal use, you can use some additional features to provide more information to your colleagues. For example, if the company has standardized on Microsoft software products, you can include spreadsheets or slide shows on your web

site. When someone clicks on the file reference on your page, the file will be transferred to his or her machine and displayed in the browser. The file is easy to add with a standard link tag. For instance: <A HREF="ftp://myfile.xls"> Quarterly spreadsheet</A>.

Adobe has created the **portable document format (pdf)** type that is useful when you need precise control over the layout of your documents. Many governmental agencies (e.g., the IRS) use pdf to distribute electronic copies of common forms. Most browsers can display and print the documents exactly as they were created. You generally need Adobe Acrobat software to create the forms, and the browsers need Acrobat Reader to display them. The reader software is free, but you have to purchase the software to create the files. Once they are created, you link them into your web site the same way you would any other file.

## PUBLISHING DOCUMENTS TO THE WEB

As indicated by Figure 3.3A, when you have created all of your pages and tested the links, you need to copy the files to a web server. Many types of computers can function as web servers, and they all have slightly different methods for accepting your pages and for assigning security permissions. If you are building a site for internal use, your MIS department will run a server and explain how to transfer the files. If you are publishing pages for external use, the server

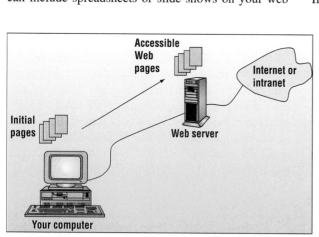

**FIGURE 3.3A**
PUBLISHING WEB PAGES
Files are created on your computer. They must then be transferred to a web server. You can use FTP or Microsoft Front Page extensions if they are available.

can be run by your company, or you can lease space on a server run by an **Internet service provider (ISP).** The ISP will have its own rules and procedures for publishing web pages.

Today, probably the easiest mechanism is if your server is set up to support the Microsoft Front Page publishing system. Several development tools can automatically communicate with the server using this system. Once you have the pages designed on your computer, you simply click an icon and enter the name of the server. Your PC then contacts the server and transfers the files automatically.

If the Front Page system is not available, you will generally use the Internet **file transfer protocol (FTP)** to transfer the files to the server. You need to know the Internet name of the server, an account name, and the corresponding password. The FTP software enables you to select the files and transfer them to the server. You might have to set security permissions so that the web server can retrieve the pages (but not alter them). The details depend on the server.

If you have a powerful enough computer system on your desk (for example Windows 2000 or UNIX),

you can run your own web server. You simply set aside a directory for public access. Then to publish data, you copy the files into that public directory. This approach is generally used only for sharing files with co-workers. It requires someone (probably you) to manage the web server and to maintain adequate security precautions. Security problems are minimized by allowing only internal workers to access the machine.

## EXERCISES

1. Create three web pages that are linked. Include at least one image.
2. Create a style sheet for your web pages.
3. Create a web site that will hold all of your assignments for this course. Create a main page with links to all of the future assignments.
4. Find an ISP and determine the costs of creating a web site for a small business. List the additional features (and costs) that are available.
5. Create a basic promotional web site for the Rolling Thunder Bicycle company.

CHAPTER 4

# Operations and Transactions

TRANSACTION DATA
As a large retailer, Home Depot recognizes the importance of collecting quality data and automating the transaction-processing system.

## HOME DEPOT

Bryan Kahlow stepped back for a second to survey his work. He and his father-in-law had constructed a new deck. After receiving estimates in the $3,000 to $4,000 range, Bryan decided to investigate the possibility of completing the job himself. Of course, not being much of a handyman he knew that he needed a lot of help.

On a Saturday, the two men attended a short class at the neighborhood Home Depot store. There they learned all of the steps necessary to complete a deck. They were even given the name and phone number of their instructor, to call in case they ran into trouble along the way. After two days of diligent work, they constructed a new deck. This was made possible by the friendly and courteous staff at Bryan Kahlow's Home Depot.

A high level of customer service is what has helped Home Depot revolutionize the home improvement industry. Skilled contractors formerly dominated the industry. Now the industry includes many do-it-yourselfers eager to save time and money and achieve a sense of accomplishment.

**OVERVIEW**  Every business must perform certain basic tasks. Figure 4.1 illustrates how businesses keep track of sales and bill customers, monitor and pay employees, record expenses, and order supplies. The data collected from these transactions is also used to make all the other decisions in the firm. If there are major mistakes in these day-to-day operations, the company will not survive. Because of the tremendous amounts of data involved, the data must be carefully collected and organized.

Most companies already have computerized transaction-processing systems. As a manager, you most likely will not be asked to create a new system. However, there are many times when you will have to evaluate the existing system to locate problems. You will also be asked to suggest improvements, both to decrease costs and to provide better information. It is particularly important to reevaluate transaction systems when a company is changing—whether growing rapidly or undergoing structural changes through re-engineering.

**FIGURE 4.1**

Transaction processing involves collecting data from the business operations and from external "partners." Through analysis and consolidation, this data is converted to information that enables managers to make better decisions.

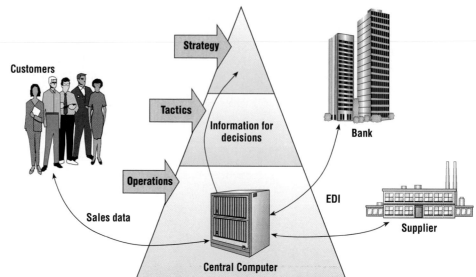

The key to collecting data is to capture it as close to the source as possible, with techniques such as point-of-sale data collection, process control, and electronic data interchange. Collecting data is a straightforward job that computers have performed for years. However, using computers does not guarantee the data will always be correct. As a manager, you have to understand the importance of maintaining the integrity of the data. Factors that complicate the task of collecting and maintaining accurate data include multiple users, huge quantities of data, summarization, and time requirements.

Because of the importance of transaction data, accounting systems were one of the earliest tasks that were computerized. In many companies, financial data collection is still the largest focus of MIS. To understand the potential opportunities and problems and how MIS helps organizations, it is important to understand some elements of accounting. Human resource management is a second area that uses transaction processing heavily. Both situations illustrate the importance of collecting, storing, and protecting key information for any company.

**INTRODUCTION**

All decisions require information, but this information does not simply materialize. It must be collected, stored, and maintained. These activities take place at the operations level of the firm and are called **transaction processing.** Whenever two people make an exchange, it is called a *transaction.* Transactions are important events for a company. Examples include making a purchase at a store, withdrawing money from a checking account, making a payment to a creditor, or paying an employee. Data from these events needs to be saved for future use because these events involve other people. Imagine what would happen if you bought an item from someone but that person later stated that you did not pay the full amount due. Your records of the transaction would help you prove that you did indeed buy the item. The first step for computers in any firm is to capture and store this basic data. The computers also must provide a way to retrieve data and produce reports so the data is useful to decision makers. Of course, the hard part is knowing which data will be needed in the future.

## Trends

Because of legal ramifications, businesses have always collected data about transactions. Paper documents have been stored for years. Even today, copies of important transactions are kept on paper. However, paper records cause problems: It takes time to make copies, they require large amounts of storage space, and they deteriorate over time. More importantly, it is difficult to use the data contained in paper records. Imagine the work involved if all sales records are on paper and you want to compute annual sales totals for each salesperson.

Accounting systems were created to generate information from the transaction data. With a paper system, transactions are recorded in a daily journal and posted to a general ledger. The accounting profession has designed reports (e.g., balance sheets and income statements) that are routinely created from this data.

Businesses quickly recognized the value of using computers to process transactions. The *back-office tasks* of computing sales totals and posting information to the accounting ledger were viewed as important uses for the computer. They were also easy to computerize. Through the 1960s, most business computers were primarily producing basic accounting reports. Raw data was punched into the computer by hand, and the computer produced totals and updated the general ledger. In effect, the computer was used as a giant calculator to automate the production of printed reports that were structured as they were before the advent of computers. The primary reason for using the computer was speed and accuracy. It was justified because it was cheaper and less error-prone than hiring thousands of people to produce the reports.

As computer capabilities increased in the 1970s, the role of the computer also increased. In transaction-processing systems, the most important change was to use the computer to collect the raw data. In retail sales, the cash register was replaced with a computer terminal and a bar-code scanner. Whenever a customer purchased an item, the transaction data was immediately sent to the main computer. This automation eliminated the need to hire a person to enter the data at the end of the day. Together with fewer errors, these *online transaction systems* provided better service to the customer. Because sales were recorded immediately, the sales clerk could quickly determine whether an item was in stock. The systems also provided virtually instantaneous sales data to the managers. If some item was selling rapidly, the system could tell the employees to restock that item on the shelves.

The 1980s resulted in even more integration. Most of the changes occurred in the way data was processed into information. The largest transaction-processing change was the dramatic drop in hardware prices. This change enabled more businesses to use computers to process transactions with computers. Today, almost all businesses use computers to keep track of their transactions and produce reports and information from that data.

Several **change-drivers** have started as data-collection tools and expanded to alter the firms and industries that used them. Classic examples include bar-code scanners in retail stores, handheld mini-terminals or notebook computers by delivery firms and salespeople, and reservation systems by the travel and entertainment industries.

Toward the end of the 1990s, the year 2000 problem drove many companies to replace their old customer transaction software with complete packages that (1) could handle four-digit dates, (2) provide all common accounting and personnel tasks, and (3) provide an integrated view of the data within the organization.

From the standpoint of how executives manage a company, transaction data has even more uses. Most transactions occur between the company and people outside the company (e.g., customers, suppliers, and competitors). Hence, transactions provide a way to measure the progress of the company. Companies are often measured by the amount of sales (customer transactions), costs (payments to suppliers and employees), and market share (compared to competitors). All of this information is used to show managers the status of the company and identify where problems exist. It is used to make decisions regarding day-to-day operations as well as to set future directions for the firm.

Firms also have many internal transactions. All companies keep records on employee evaluations and promotions. Larger companies produce products in various divisions and need to track orders and shipments among the divisions. Sometimes companies use a *chargeback system* to allocate managerial costs among departments. This internal data is needed for legal purposes and it is used to make decisions within each department.

Looking at internal processes, accounting and human resources are two subsystems in every company that make heavy use of transaction-processing systems. They also demonstrate the importance of integrating transaction data throughout the company.

## THE VALUE AND COST OF INFORMATION

Virtually any data could be collected by a company; however, it would be absurd to measure and save every piece of data. For example, it is technically possible to monitor exactly where every employee is located at every minute. But why would you want this data? It costs money to collect and store data. In addition, the more data you have, the more difficult it is to find the specific pieces that you need. The goal is to collect data that will be useful. How do you know today what data will be useful tomorrow or next year? One method that is often used to answer this question is to look at the types of decisions that organizations make.

Transaction processing highlights the difference between data and information. Numbers that are collected and stored are raw data. When managers make decisions, they retrieve data and process it to provide pertinent information. If you collected all the sales transactions for a retail store, the data simply would be stored as a collection of numbers. Perhaps a manager wishes to evaluate a particular store. The manager might examine the sales levels for the last five years. The computer would accumulate all the sales **data** to produce the totals for each year. The resulting **information** might show a downward trend that would lead to a decision to emphasize a different approach or even to close the store. The *value of information* is its ability to improve decisions.

In the event of a store closing, you might ask how we chose to look at five years of data. Why not more? The answer is that we always face a trade-off. Collecting more data might lead to more accurate forecasts, but it is expensive to collect, store, and analyze extensive amounts of data. Also, beyond some point, additional data merely serves to confirm the results; it does not really provide more value. Perhaps with five years' data, we can forecast sales within 10 percent. Adding more data might improve the forecast to 7 percent. In many cases, the difference will not affect our decisions, so it would not be worth the cost. Of course, all of these details are difficult to evaluate ahead of time.

One method of making decisions has been formalized with the use of statistics. When you perform tests of hypotheses, you are making a decision. As displayed in Figure 4.2, a simple hypothesis test begins by assuming the mean is at some level (e.g., zero). All tests are subject to error. A Type I error arises when you reject a null hypothesis that is actually true. You select the probability that this event will occur, which leads to the choice of a critical test value. You then gather the data and estimate basic parameters. If your test value falls above the critical level, you would reject the null hypothesis.

A second type of error can arise: you might accept (fail to reject) the null hypothesis when it is actually false. In the example, the true mean might be equal to five, but your data leads you to believe the mean is zero. The probability of this Type II error is measured as the area under the curve to the left of the critical value in the distribution for the mean equal to five.

**FIGURE 4.2**

More information decreases errors. Any statistical test risks two types of errors. Changing the critical value simply trades off between the two errors. With more information, the distribution narrows and the probability of making either type of error decreases. But it costs money to acquire additional information.

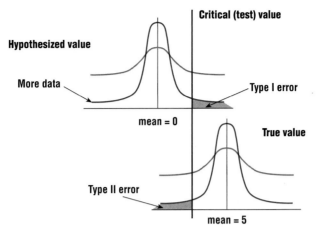

One fundamental theory in statistics states for a given amount of information, if you attempt to decrease the probability of one type of error, the probability of committing the other type of error will increase. This problem can be observed by moving the critical value line to the left or right. As the area under one of the solid curves decreases, the area under the other one will increase. However, if you collect more information by increasing the number of observations, the underlying curve will change to the (tighter) dotted line shown in the graphs. In this case, the probability of both errors decreases to the shaded areas. Statistically, you can make better decisions by increasing the amount of information. Of course, from a business standpoint, the next questions you encounter are: How much does it cost to acquire the additional information and what are the potential gains?

For example, you can produce a product in several color combinations. You need to determine the colors and run production in July for year-end (Christmas) sales. How many items should be produced in each color set? You survey customers and examine past sales to answer this question. The accuracy depends on the number of customers you survey and the amount of data you have. But it costs money to collect, save, and analyze the data. How much the information is worth depends on the value of the additional accuracy in making the decision. The situation is even more complicated when you do not know exactly what decisions will be made in the future.

**DATA CAPTURE**    The basic components of a transaction-processing system are illustrated in Figure 4.3. The focus is twofold: accomplishing the transaction and capturing data. Data capture consists of gathering or acquiring data from the firm's operations and storing data in the computer system. Entering data into the computer can be time-consuming and difficult. For instance, banks have invested heavily in automating the collection and recording of transaction data. Yet, because many transactions are based on paper, clerks still spend considerable time entering data. First, tellers enter the data into their terminals. Then a bank staffer reads the dollar value written on checks and deposit slips. The bank staff works through the night, typing the amount into a machine that codes the number on the bottom of the check so it can be read by other computers. Automated teller machines (ATMs) and debit cards save some of these steps, because the customer enters the initial numbers directly into the computer. Although the numbers must still be verified by an employee, the American Bank Association estimated that it costs banks $1 to process every check, but only $0.50 to

**FIGURE 4.3**
Data that is captured at the operations level is used throughout the firm to make decisions. If there are problems in the data or in providing access to the data, all of the decisions will suffer.

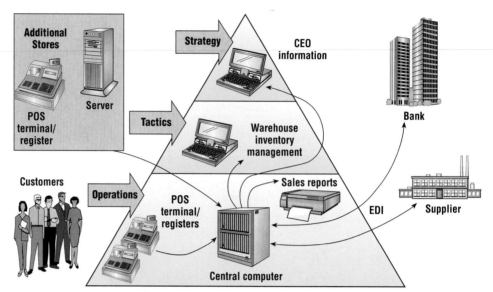

process ATM transactions. In 1995, several banks, led by Citicorp, dropped all customer fees for electronic transactions but levied fees on teller-assisted transactions. Banks now charge fees on the use of ATMs at other banks, to encourage customers to deal with only one bank, and to collect money from noncustomers.

As the volume of transactions increased, businesses looked for faster and more accurate ways to get data into the computer. Three basic methods are used to collect data, depending on its source. The data-collection method consumers are most familiar with is **point of sale (POS),** where the sales register is actually a computer terminal that sends all data to a central computer. On assembly lines, robots and manufacturing equipment can collect data, such as quality control measures, and return it to a computer. Typically the computer also can send control instructions to these machines. This exchange of data between manufacturing machines and computers is known as **process control.** The third way to collect data automatically involves the exchange of information with organizations outside the firm, especially suppliers and customers. Instead of dealing with paper records such as purchase orders, it is possible to send orders electronically through a process called **electronic data interchange (EDI).**

EDI represents a computer connection between various companies. Sometimes the connection is a private link between two companies; in other cases it can involve a network that connects computers between several firms.

## Point of Sale

Several devices have been created to capture data at the point of the sale. Some companies rely on keyboards to enter data, but high-volume areas have switched to bar-code scanners. All consumers are familiar with bar-code scanners that read the universal product codes (UPCs). The scanner reads the code and sends it to the computer, which looks up the corresponding name and price. The computer prints the receipt, stores the sale information, and automatically decreases the inventory count.

Another type of scanner is used by the U.S. Postal System, which uses **optical character recognition (OCR)** to read handwritten zip codes, allowing mail to be processed

SALES DATA
Collecting transaction data at the point of sale ensures accurate data, speeds transactions, and provides up-to-the-minute data to managers.

and sorted faster. Even so, the post office hires thousands of workers to type in data that the scanners cannot read. Banks use a process called **magnetic ink character recognition (MICR)** to process checks and deposit slips. MICR readers are more accurate than straight OCR because they pick up a stronger signal from magnetic particles in the ink. A few companies are using speech recognition technology to enable workers to enter data by speaking to the computer. Speech recognition enables the users to enter data while leaving their hands free to do something else.

Several advantages arise from using automated data entry. Directly capturing data means fewer errors occur because the machines make fewer mistakes. Sometimes it is not easy to collect data at the source.

POS systems also have built-in error detection methods to make certain the numbers are read correctly. By collecting the data immediately, it is easier to find and correct mistakes. If a clerk using a POS system enters an incorrect product number (or the scanner reads it incorrectly), the error can be caught immediately.

With POS data collection, the computer performs all necessary computations immediately. Hence, the job is easier for clerks and fewer errors will occur. For example, a retail store might give discounts to certain customers. With a POS system, the employees do not have to keep track of the customers or discounts, because the computer can look up the discounts and apply them automatically. Similarly, prices are maintained and changed by the computer. To hold a sale, you simply change the price in the computer (one place) and put up a new sign. Of course, when there are thousands of items and prices, there are still plenty of opportunities for errors.

POS systems also can provide better service to customers. Because the sales data is captured immediately, the managers and clerks always know the inventory levels. If a customer calls to learn whether a product is in stock, the clerk can instantly determine the answer. With most systems, it is possible to tell the computer to hold that item until the customer picks it up. Some companies even connect their store computers together. If you find that one store has run out of a particular item, the clerk can quickly check the other stores in the area and tell one to hold the item for you.

A few companies even enable customers to bypass the clerks entirely. Taco Bell is experimenting with a touch-screen order system. Customers place their own orders by touching items on the screen. When the order is entered, the customer pays a clerk. Similarly, grocery stores are implementing self-serve checkouts—to cut employee costs. Mail-order companies use a similar type of system, but have phone order clerks to answer questions and enter the data.

Transactions entered via the Internet are the ultimate in data collection. Customers enter the data themselves, thereby reducing the vendor's cost and collecting the data immediately. If the system is easy to use, it can also reduce errors because customers have a strong incentive to enter the data correctly and verify the choices.

## Process Control

Manufacturing firms often deal with a different type of data. Most factories use machines that can be connected to each other and to computers. The computers can exchange data with the production machines. If you want to alter your product, you would need to change the manufacturing settings on several different machines. If the production line has 10 machines, each with five control items that need to be set, it could take several hours to reset the entire production line. Even a minor change in the product means that someone has to set each of the machines correctly. By connecting the machines to a computer, the computer can store the appropriate settings. When you make a change in the product, the computer sends the correct settings to all the machines. Computers are often used to monitor the progress of the production line. The data is used to identify problem spots and to help the firm meet production goals. Figure 4.4 illustrates the basic concept of individual machines controlled from one location. Although the concept seems simple, factories have found it difficult to carry out this idea on a large scale.

Technology also can be used to collect data from manufacturing machines. With this communication, the computer can constantly monitor production levels. Managers can keep track of hourly and daily production, and even track individual products. If a customer wants to check on the progress of a special order, the manager can determine how much of the product has been produced and when it is likely to be completed.

Process control computers can also be used to monitor quality in the manufacturing process. Sensors can automatically measure almost any characteristic. They can check for items such as thickness, weight, strength, color, and size. These measurements can then be passed to a computer. If the computer notices a trend or a major problem, it can notify the operators. In some operations, the computer can send messages to the machine causing the problem and reset its controls to correct the problem automatically.

**FIGURE 4.4**

Process control is the control of production machines from centralized computers. The computers monitor data from the machines and make continuous adjustments. The central control enables designers to specify all production settings from one location.

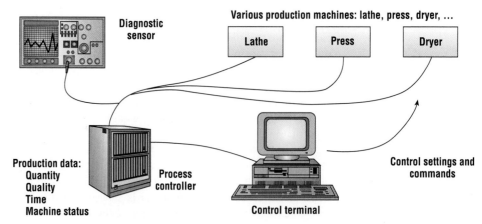

Diagnostic sensor

Various production machines: lathe, press, dryer, …

Lathe          Press          Dryer

Production data:
Quantity
Quality
Time
Machine status

Process controller

Control terminal

Control settings and commands

Two basic difficulties exist with process control. First, the large number of machines makes it difficult to establish standards, making it harder to connect the various machines together. Second, production machines can produce an enormous amount of data. Some machines can generate billions of bytes of data per hour. This large amount of data requires efficient communication lines, high-speed computers, and a large storage capacity. Despite these complications, process control can provide enormous advantages. It enables companies to change production processes and alter products faster and more often. It provides better information and control over quality. It enables manufacturers to create products that match the needs of individual customers: mass customization.

## Electronic Data Interchange (EDI)

EDI is a form of automated data entry that supports operations by transferring documents between firms electronically. The essence of EDI is the ability to transfer data among computers from different companies. There are two basic methods to accomplish the transfer: (1) send the data directly from one computer to the other or (2) send the data to a third party that consolidates the data and sends it to the proper location. Early EDI implementations were based on direct connections as individual firms experimented with the technology. In both methods, there are two important considerations: establishing the physical links and transferring data in a format compatible to all users.

For EDI to work, each company must translate its data into a form that can be used by the other companies. If one company like Sears or GM takes the lead and requires suppliers to send data via EDI, then they are free to define the base transaction objects. Suppliers must translate their objects into the appropriate EDI structure. Yet, a supplier might need links to several customers. If each customer used different EDI definitions, the supplier must have a conversion system for each link. Someday it might be possible to create standards for EDI connections, forcing everyone to conform to one type of data definition. Although there is some progress in this area, firms with existing EDI systems will be reluctant to spend the money to convert their data.

Data conversion might sound like an easy task, but it is complicated when the transaction systems were created over long periods of time and were poorly documented. In many cases, the programmer might have to search major portions of the corporate systems to find the appropriate data definitions. Once the appropriate data is found, it can be hard to modify. Existing programs might expect the data to maintain specific formats. Making changes to the data can require rewriting other programs.

### Proprietary EDI

As displayed in Figure 4.5, most of the early EDI systems were created independently: One large company required suppliers to provide data and accept orders electronically. The goal was to cut the costs of transactions and speed up the ordering process. EDI arrangements also enabled manufacturers to improve quality control and to implement just-in-time inventory systems. Suppliers were "encouraged" to adopt the EDI systems by threatening a loss of sales if the vendors did not comply.

With proprietary systems, the lead firm establishes the standards in terms of the hardware and the types and format of data to be exchanged. From the standpoint of the lead firm, these controls ensure that they are able to connect to each supplier with one standard technique.

To a supplier, proprietary systems created by one company can lead to problems. Imagine what happens when the supplier sells to several firms, and each firm requires the use of a different EDI system. In addition to the hassles of providing data in the proper format for

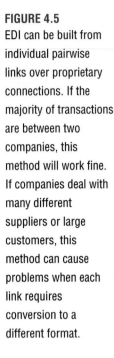

**FIGURE 4.5**
EDI can be built from individual pairwise links over proprietary connections. If the majority of transactions are between two companies, this method will work fine. If companies deal with many different suppliers or large customers, this method can cause problems when each link requires conversion to a different format.

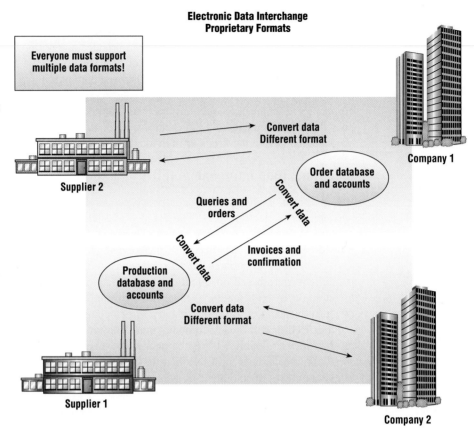

each customer, the supplier's employees would have to learn how to use several different systems. Purchasers face similar problems unless all of their suppliers follow a standard.

## Commercial EDI Providers and Standards

Multiple proprietary systems lead to confusion and higher costs. Consequently, companies have formed groups to define common methods to exchange data among companies. As shown in Figure 4.6, third-party providers (such as banks) have begun operating as clearinghouses for EDI transactions. In both cases, the objective is to establish common hardware and software requirements so that any company following the standards can share data with other companies.

Communication standards enable firms to share the data and automate basic transactions. However, to provide useful information, companies need to integrate this data into their management information systems. Sending purchase orders over phone lines is faster than using traditional mail, but firms can gain more advantages if the resulting data can be tied directly to their internal accounting systems.

There are two primary standards for EDI messages. The UN sponsors the Edifact standard; the United States defined the ANSI (American National Standards Institute) X12 definition. Figure 4.7 shows the overall structure of an EDI message. A significant difference between the standards is in the numbering system used to represent the types of messages, segments, and data elements. Figure 4.8 presents a partial list of the segment types available in the X12 standard. The standards also specify the exact format of the data required in each segment type.

**FIGURE 4.6**
When many companies need to exchange data with several other firms, it is best if they can agree to a common EDI transaction format. In some cases, a central or regional company can coordinate transfers among all parties. This method is especially beneficial to small companies.

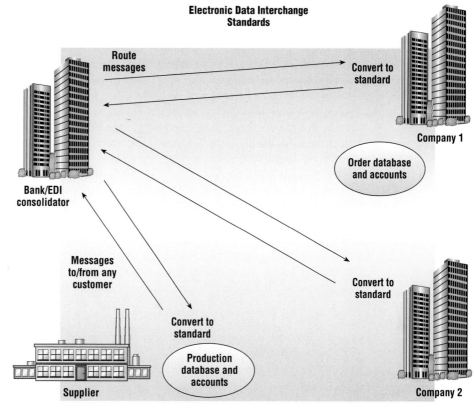

**Electronic Data Interchange Standards**

Route messages

Convert to standard

Company 1

Order database and accounts

Bank/EDI consolidator

Messages to/from any customer

Convert to standard

Convert to standard

Company 2

Production database and accounts

Supplier

**FIGURE 4.7**
EDI STANDARDS
UN Edifact and U.S. ANSI X12 standards are similar in format; each message consists of segments and detailed data lists. Each message, segment, and data element are defined by numbers from a predefined list of possible transactions. There are substantial differences in the numbering system used for the segments and data elements.

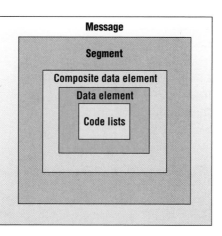

**Message**

**Segment**

**Composite data element**

**Data element**

**Code lists**

## Additional Features and Problems

Taken to its full capabilities, EDI enables firms to handle all communications among other firms electronically. It enables managers to create and review orders without relying on paper printouts. Having data available electronically means that several people can work with the same form at the same time. In most companies, purchase orders and invoices are examined and altered by several people. If the form is processed on the computer, each person has access to the data at the same time. It is also much easier to store and search the electronic data. Eventually, even prices and negotiations could be handled electronically, making it much easier to sort and compare bids from various suppliers.

Some unresolved issues with EDI's security and ethics need further consideration. What happens when a company denies that it placed an order? How do we protect the communication links so people cannot intercept orders? Reading, changing, or deleting your competitor's orders could destroy its business. Although these actions are illegal, they can be difficult to prevent or uncover. Privacy issues also arise in conjunction with EDI. If consumer transactions are captured electronically and stored, an enormous amount of personal information will be available. What will prevent a company from acquiring or selling a list of all the items you purchase along with your salary and your home address? These questions are addressed in more detail in Chapter 14.

**FIGURE 4.8**

SAMPLE SEGMENT CODES FOR ANSI X12

A partial list of the codes used within X12 EDI messages. Only the number is transmitted. Each segment specifies the format of the additional data.

| | |
|---|---|
| 104 | Air Shipment Information |
| 110 | Air Freight Details and Invoice |
| 125 | Multilevel Railcar Load Details |
| 126 | Vehicle Application Advice |
| 127 | Vehicle Baying Order |
| 128 | Dealer Information |
| 129 | Vehicle Carrier Rate Update |
| 130 | Student Educational Record (Transcript) |
| 131 | Student Educational Record (Transcript) Acknowledgment |
| 135 | Student Loan Application |
| 139 | Student Loan Guarantee Result |
| 140 | Product Registration |
| 141 | Product Service Claim Response |
| 142 | Product Service Claim |
| 143 | Product Service Notification |
| 144 | Student Loan Transfer and Status Verification |
| 146 | Request for Student Educational Record (Transcript) |
| 147 | Response to Request for Student Educational Record (Transcript) |
| 148 | Report of Injury or Illness |
| 151 | Electronic Filing of Tax Return Data Acknowledgment |
| 152 | Statistical Government Information |
| 154 | Uniform Commercial Code Filing |
| 161 | Train Sheet |
| 170 | Revenue Receipts Statement |
| 180 | Return Merchandise Authorization and Notification |
| 186 | Laboratory Reporting |
| 190 | Student Enrollment Verification |

### Using the Internet for EDI

The entire purpose of EDI is to share data with business partners. Sharing data requires a communication link and standards that define how the data will be interpreted. The ANSI and Edifact definitions describe how the data should be organized. However, communication links are equally important. Increasingly, companies are using the Internet as a primary link to other firms. The main strength of the Internet is that it is widely available throughout the world. Standardization enables any firm to participate at a low cost.

Web sites are used to advertise and display information about products and their availability. Search engines enable companies to find components and potential suppliers quickly. EDI transactions such as orders and request-for-prices can be handled over the Internet as e-mail messages. The Internet can also host secure communication channels between two partners. These links can be used for high-volume exchanges of data.

The one catch with the Internet is that currently there are no service guarantees. While messages are rarely lost, they might be delayed. Periodically, various segments of the Internet become overloaded and it can be difficult to transfer data. If these interruptions are infrequent, you could resort to manual methods such as fax machines and telephone calls. Plans for improving the Internet include the ability to specify (and purchase) dedicated bandwidth, so that companies can ensure a certain level of service. So far, the strengths of the Internet far outweigh the potential drawbacks. Even up to 1999, the biggest commercial use of the Internet was for business-to-business sales.

## DATA QUALITY

As you can see, a transaction-processing system can become quite complex. Problems are going to occur in any system—especially because all business organizations change over time. That means the computer system has to change to match the business. It is virtually impossible to change the system at exactly the same time as the business, so problems will occur. Other problems arise simply because the systems are so complex. Many processes involve humans who make mistakes. If you understand what types of problems might arise, they will be easier to solve.

The key to data quality is to focus on quality throughout the process. At input, data should be collected as close to the source as possible. For processing, data should be available to all users in a form they can use without having to reenter the data. In terms of output, reports should be linked to the databases so they always use the most recent data. Figure 4.9 lists the primary measures of data quality that you

| DATA QUALITY ATTRIBUTE | DESCRIPTION AND PROBLEMS |
|---|---|
| Integrity | Errors in data entry. Missing data. Failure to make updates. |
| Multitasking Concurrency | Data altered by two people at the same time, creating incorrect results. |
| Volume | Cost, difficulty of searching, transmission costs, errors harder to find, system overload. |
| Summaries | Too much detail is overkill when you only need summaries. With only summaries, you cannot recover the details. |
| Time | Many reports and decisions are subject to deadlines. Different departments getting data at different times can cause sequencing errors and additional delays. |

**FIGURE 4.9**
Maintaining data quality is crucial to managing a firm. Several problems make it difficult to build good transaction-processing systems.

need to consider. In examining an information system, if you detect any of these problems, they are clues that you should search for ways to improve the transaction-processing system.

## Data Integrity

One of the most important concepts in information processing is the issue of data integrity. **Data integrity** means keeping data accurate and correct as it is gathered and stored in the computer system. There is little value in an information system that contains out-of-date or inaccurate data. A common complaint among shoppers today is that stores using bar-code scanners might have a different price in the computer than the amount displayed on the shelf. It is easy to change prices in the computer; it is more difficult to change the signs in the store. Shoppers will feel cheated if the computer tries to charge them a higher price than the amount listed on the shelf. Some states, such as Michigan, have passed laws requiring that the scanned price cannot be higher than the amount listed on the package or display. Similar errors cause problems when the computer shows more items in stock than actually exist.

The first step to ensure data integrity lies in its capture. Each item must be correctly entered and the complete information recorded. It is sometimes possible to check the data as it is entered. Item code numbers usually include a check number that is based on the other digits. In the item code 548737, the first five digits add up to 27, so the number 7 is included as the last digit. If the person or machine makes a mistake entering one of the digits, they will probably not add up to 7, so the computer can immediately determine that there is an error. Sophisticated methods exist to catch mistakes involving more than one digit.

Even with machine entry of data, validity problems can arise. What happens when a shipment arrives, but the receiving department forgets to record it? The same problem occurs when a clerk holds an item for a customer and does not record it in the computer. Data integrity can be destroyed by indiscriminately allowing people to change the numbers in the computer. It is one of the main reasons for creating secure computers and controlling access to each piece of information.

## Multitasking, Concurrency, and Integrity

A useful feature offered by more sophisticated operating systems is the ability to perform more than one task at a time. In many situations it is useful to have several jobs running at the same time. What happens if you are searching a huge database and your boss calls and asks you for a sales figure? With a multitasking computer operating system, you could switch to a new program, look up the number, and allow the database to continue searching in the background.

If you use a multitasking operating system, it is important that your application software understand that other applications might be running at the same time. Each application needs to protect its data files from **concurrency** problems. Concurrency arises when applications attempt to modify the same piece of data at the same time. If two people are allowed to make changes to the same piece of data, the computer system must control the order in which it processes the two requests. Mixing the two tasks will result in the wrong data being stored in the computer. These problems can be avoided by only using software that was specifically written for multiuser (or multitasking) computers.

---

**Reality Bytes    4–1    Low Technology Equals Low Sales in the Furniture Industry**

The furniture industry is at an interesting stage of development. For years the retail side has consisted of small local stores, with a few larger regional businesses. The manufacturing side has been fragmented with hundreds of small manufacturers, generally relying on individual workers. Consequently, customers are not very happy with the industry. For example, Douglas McAuley ordered $70,000 worth of furniture and waited five months to receive only one piece. On a smaller scale, Cathy Marshik had to wait 12 weeks to receive the furniture she ordered from Pottery Barn. In comparison, she notes that when she bought her Jeep Cherokee, she was able to drive it home the same day.

Given the increased incomes in the 1990s and the increase in home ownership, you expect to see large increases in furniture sales over that time. However, as a percent of consumer spending, furniture sales dropped from 1.2 percent in 1980 to 1 percent in 1998. At the same time, the nation's largest furniture retailer (Heilig-Meyers Co.) lost $55.1 million in 1997 and Levitz Furniture, Inc., filed for bankruptcy.

A large part of the problem stems from the manufacturing side. Only three furniture manufacturers have revenues of over $1 billion, and together their market share is only 20 percent. Most of the work is still done by hand. The large number of options—particularly variations in upholstery, also complicates production.

---

**FIGURE 4.10**

CONCURRENCY AND DATA INTEGRITY

Multiuser and multitasking systems can cause problems with concurrent changes to data. Two processes cannot be allowed to change the same data at the same time. Most systems will lock out transaction B until transaction A is completed. If a system becomes very busy, you can sometimes encounter delays while you wait for other users to finish their changes.

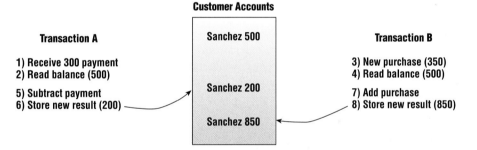

Consider the case of a mail-order firm shown in Figure 4.10. On the left side, customer Sanchez sent a payment on his account. At the same time the clerk begins to process the payment, Sanchez calls a second clerk and places a new order. The figure shows what happens if both transactions continue and interfere with each other. What should the final balance be? Does the computer have the correct number?

To solve this problem, the application program must know that several people might try to access the same piece of data at the same time. The software locks out all users except one. When the first process is finished, the other users can try to gain access again. To keep data accurate, applications used by many people at the same time must be written to handle these concurrency problems. Early personal computers were designed for only one user, so much of the software did not prevent concurrency problems. Software designed for computer networks generally handles this issue. When you use this software, you will occasionally receive a message that says a piece of data you desire is currently being used by another person. If you get this message, simply wait for a few minutes and try again. When the first person is finished, you should be able to proceed.

## Data Volume

A common problem experienced by a growing business is the increase in the amount of data or data volume. Consider the huge databases handled by Information Resources that processes data from supermarket checkouts, or United Parcel Service that tracks every package every day.

As the business grows, there will be an increase in the number of transactions. As the price of a computer drops, more applications are placed on the computer. Additional transactions become computerized. Several problems can be created from this increase: (1) processing overload or system slowdowns; (2) greater difficulty in making sure the data is accurate; (3) insufficient storage within the computer system; and (4) data not captured fast enough.

Visa International processes more than 6 billion electronic transactions a year. By 2000, the company expects to handle 15 billion annual transactions. There are 18,000 banks offering Visa cards, used by 10 million customers. So much data is generated on a daily basis that Visa cannot keep transaction data online beyond six months. All older records are moved to backup storage, making them inaccessible for additional research or decisions.

Sloppy practices and huge datasets can lead to inaccurate data. As the system slows down or the computer runs out of storage space, people avoid using it, so data is no longer up to date. With the increase in volume and the computerization of new types of data, it is more difficult for programmers and managers to check the data. If parts of the computer system are too slow, data may not be captured fast enough. As a result, some data might be lost. A tremendous amount of information is stored in raw data. The raw data could be analyzed to offer new services or improve the quality of existing services. However, the huge volumes require too much storage space and too much processing time.

Careful planning is required to avoid these problems. At best, new computers and storage usually take a month or two to purchase. It could take a year or more to evaluate and purchase a large, expensive central computer. The MIS department would like to forecast the demands that will be placed on the computers at least a year in advance.

## Data Summaries

Another situation is commonly encountered in transaction-processing systems. In almost any company today, managers complain of having too much data. Consider the situation of a marketing manager who needs to determine the best way to increase sales for next year. Think of the amount of data that is readily available. The firm's transaction-processing system can provide detailed records on sales of every item every day, by each salesperson, broken down by city, for at least the last five years. Scanner data from marketing research firms lists itemized sales by grocery store for every product. There is also internal data from consumer surveys, production, and responses to promotions. Demographic data is available from the government.

To deal with this much data, managers are forced to rely on summaries. The marketing manager may only see a list of sales totals by each salesperson. That total might or might not include merchandise that was returned. Imagine what happens if returns are *not* included in the totals, but the manager believes that they were included. An unethical salesperson could sell extra merchandise to a friend (boosting the totals), and then return the merchandise the same day (because the returns are not subtracted from the list).

The problem multiplies as the information travels through different levels in the organization. Higher-level managers in the firm deal with data that has gone through several types of summarizing at each lower level. By the time they finally receive the information, the reports might not contain the information that is needed. The details might have been deleted or the summaries might carry the wrong set of information.

## Time

Time is another aspect of information quality in transaction-processing systems. The information system must furnish the information at the time it is needed for decision making. An information system that is overloaded or not producing properly summarized data will not be able to provide information at the right time. Consider the data needed to file tax forms. The government has a time limit for filing tax forms. Managers would be understandably upset if their computer system could not produce the annual accounting reports in time to calculate taxes. Similarly, it is difficult to place orders for new merchandise when the only available data is a three-month-old sales report.

Problems with timeliness generally arise because data is not captured early enough. The sales report might be delayed because too many people are needed to enter the data and make some of the computations. A POS system could provide a detailed sales list almost instantly. Other delays arise when the system cannot distribute data to everyone at the same time, so reports end up sitting on someone's desk.

**THE ROLE OF ACCOUNTING**  Accounting systems are important because they extend throughout the company and because they focus on money. They are used to collect data and evaluate performance. Accounting systems also enable managers to combine the many divisions into an integrated picture of the entire company. Accounting systems also provide controls over the data to ensure accuracy and to prevent fraud. The primary purpose of accounting is to collect the financial data of the firm, ensure that it is accurate, and create standard reports. It is hard to capture all of the elements of an accounting system in one illustration, but Figure 4.11 summarizes the essential components of an accounting system. The accounting transaction system can be examined in terms of inputs, outputs, and processes.

### Input and Output: Financial Data and Reports

Raw financial data is collected by the accounting department and stored in an **accounting journal.** Modern accounting requires the use of a double-entry system to ensure accurate data. In a double-entry system, at least two entries must occur for every transaction. Generally, one entry records the effect of the money (e.g., cash, accounts payable, accounts receivable), and the other refers to a specific category (e.g., sales, office expenses, commissions). Each entry includes the date, amount of money, account number, the name of the person or firm involved, perhaps a comment, and the name of the person making the entry. The journal's purpose is to record all the transactions.

Journal entries represent raw data. To be useful, this data must be transformed into information. The first step is to categorize the data by *accounts* or categories, which is the purpose of the **general ledger.** The ledger is a collection of accounts that break the data into specific categories. Common categories include *accounts receivable, accounts payable, inventory,* and *cash.* Although there are some standards, each company can define its own **chart of accounts,** which allows owners and managers to examine data on whatever categories are important to their firm.

**FIGURE 4.11**
Transaction processing is a major function of the accounting system. The accounting system collects data throughout the company and produces consolidated (centralized) reports that are used for planning and management.

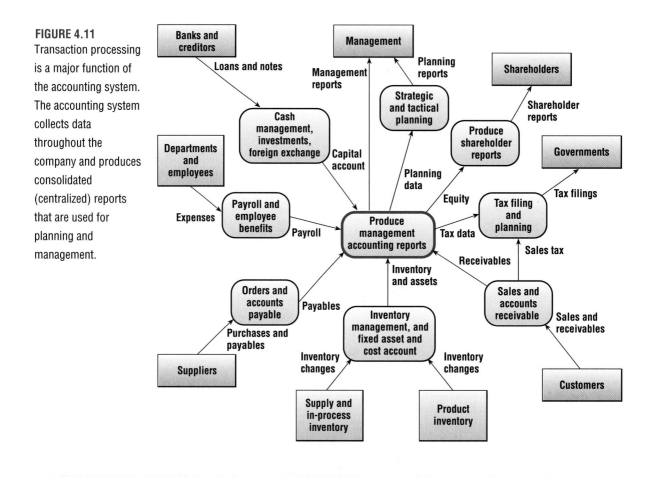

For managers to make comparisons between divisions and other firms, accounting systems produce standardized reports. Most companies produce *balance sheets, cash flow statements,* and *income statements* every quarter. These reports are produced following standard accounting rules to enable owners, managers, and investors to compare the financial positions of various companies over time.

## Purchases, Sales, Loans, and Investments

One of the primary purposes of accounting is to record the financial transactions with external organizations. In addition to collecting the raw data, the accounting system contains controls that minimize fraud by limiting access to the data. The system also creates summary and detail reports to monitor key information.

Managers often build **exception reports** into the accounting system that are triggered when some event occurs. If sales in some region suddenly drop, if there is a major increase in the cash balance, or if inventories fall below a defined level, a message will be sent to the appropriate manager. The manager typically responds by searching the recent summary reports for a possible cause.

## Inventory

Most organizations need to control inventory carefully. Retail stores find it hard to sell items that are not in stock. Manufacturing firms need to receive and process parts as cheaply as possible. Inventory control consists of knowing exactly what items are available and where they are located. The system also needs to determine when to place new orders. It must then track the orders to make sure each item is delivered to the appropriate location at the right time. With EDI, the inventory control system can monitor current sales and automatically place orders with the supplier.

Manufacturing firms use these systems to implement just-in-time inventory control. The computer system monitors the current production requirements, keeps track of deliveries, and electronically sends orders to the suppliers. The suppliers then deliver the parts just as they are needed on the production line.

Automated inventory control systems also help identify and prevent theft. By recording all movement of items from receipt to sales to shipping, management knows exactly how many items exist. Consider a retail store like a bicycle shop. The computerized inventory notes that there should be three *Cateye computers* in stock. Yet, when a customer asks to buy one, you notice there are only two left. If there is no mistake in your inventory report, you conclude that someone stole one of the items. Although the system did not prevent the speedometer from disappearing, it does show which items are susceptible to theft. It also helps control theft by employees, who will be less likely to steal if they know that the items are carefully monitored.

---

**Reality Bytes    4–4   Chrysler Races to Produce Accounting Reports**

SEC regulations state that companies must file their quarterly 10-Q report within 45 days of the start of the quarter. Many large companies routinely take three to four weeks to close the books and file reports. In the first quarter of 1998, Chrysler Corp. figures it set a record by closing its books and filing the report in nine days. Why does it matter? In the past, it used to take 30 days and cost $500,000 each quarter. Additionally, the fast processing enables managers and investors to receive information earlier to help them make better decisions.

## Reality Bytes 4–5 Small Business Accounting

Small businesses have to be especially careful when they attempt to computerize their information systems. The accounting records are the logical first step. Many owner/managers of small businesses use their checkbooks as the primary accounting system. To these managers, it seems logical to organize their entry into computers the same way. Some "personal financial" software packages make it easy to enter all of the checks into the computer and print out monthly reports. These methods are based on single-entry accounting systems.

Consider a small construction company that builds single-unit residential housing. The owner records his payments (checks) in the personal financial package Quicken. At the end of the month, he uses the bank statement to enter the deposits and cleared checks to balance his checkbook. He uses a code number to keep track of which house the expense is applied to but finds that he sometimes enters the wrong number. Some payments to subcontractors apply to work done on more than one project. As a result, he has difficulty tracking the true cost of each house, making it difficult to make decisions about the construction techniques.

## The Accounting Cycle

An important aspect of accounting systems is that they produce information in specific cycles. Firms are required to produce reports that reflect the financial condition of the firm at the end of every quarter. Accounting systems are based on these requirements. For the most part, managers operate from quarterly reports, with intermediate monthly reports for some items. Because of the volume of data in the detail, most companies only keep current statistics and summary reports on file. Older data is shuffled off the system to make room for the current numbers. As a result, managers may not have easy access to detailed data from prior years.

## Process: Controls, Checks and Balances

### Double-Entry Systems

An important objective of accounting systems is to maintain the integrity of the financial data. The goal is to prevent mistakes and discourage fraud. Double-entry accounting provides a method to locate mistakes in data entry. If an amount is entered incorrectly, the account totals will not balance.

Because many transactions involve outside organizations, mistakes can be caught by sharing data. Every month firms receive a statement from the bank. The totals can be compared to changes in the firm's cash account. Similarly, companies typically send receipts when they receive payments from each other. Auditors periodically send verification requests to suppliers and customers to make sure the data was recorded correctly. EDI strengthens this approach, because transaction data is transmitted in computer form among the companies.

### Separation of Duties

Another type of control is the separation of duties. A manager in the purchasing department might be responsible for choosing a supplier of parts. Only the accounting department can authorize the transfer of money to the supplier. The objective is to minimize fraud by requiring a potential thief to deal with multiple employees.

---

**Reality Bytes    4–6   Features to Look for in Accounting Software**

**SMALL BUSINESS BASICS**

**General Ledger**

Sample chart of accounts that can be modified.
Optional automatic posting to the ledger so you don't forget.
Automatic data entry for often-used vendor account numbers.
Define fiscal years instead of forcing calendar year.
How many months can be "open" at once?
Can entries be posted for prior months or prior years?
Audit trail.
Track expenses by departments and allocate portions of bills.

**Accounts Receivable**

Granting discounts for early payments.
Charging interest for late payments.
Multiple ship-to addresses.
Sales tax (by state and locality).
Automatic payment reminder notices.
Automatic entries for monthly maintenance fees.

The ability to add notes to invoices.
Carry invoice details month-to-month, not just total balance.

**Accounts Payable**

Check reconciliation support.
Automatic recurring entries.
Monitoring and automatic notices of payment discounts.
Ability to select bills to be paid from the screen.
Ability to make payment by item, not just total bill, in case of dispute.

**General Features**

Support for printers.
Require special preprinted forms?
Custom reports.
Custom queries.
Security controls, access to various modules by password.
Technical support costs?

---

Many banks take this concept a step further. They require employees (especially tellers) to take their vacations every year. Several instances of fraud have been revealed when the employee was no longer at the job to keep the fraudulent mechanism running.

### Audit Trails

An **audit trail** is important to accounting systems. It enables investigators to track backward through the data to the source. A cash-flow statement might indicate that the company has spent twice as much money this month as last. To find out why, trace backward and find all of the raw entries that make up the number. Together with dates and amounts, the raw journal entries can contain the identity of the person responsible for the entry. By keeping this identification data, it is possible to list every article that affects an item on a report.

**HUMAN RESOURCES AND TRANSACTION PROCESSING**

Every company has employees. Companies collect hundreds of pieces of data for each employee—some for management purposes, others because they are required by law. For years, the human resources (HR) department focused on filling out and storing forms. The enormous amount of paperwork alone begs for computerization just to cut down on storage space needed. Computerized databases also enable managers to find specific data on employees. Early HR software emphasized these two benefits. Modern HR software is expanding beyond simple forms to improving data collection and providing better analyses. To illustrate the problems presented by large-scale transaction processing systems, consider the three areas of input, output, and processing.

## Reality Bytes    4–7    Tektronix Uses Euro Introduction to Improve Operations

By the end of 1998, most firms had their hands full with year 2000 corrections. Yet, they also faced additional changes. Several years before, the European Union agreed to move to a standard currency called the euro. By January 1999, all companies doing business in Europe had to be able to accept payments denominated in euros. Bills and coins are scheduled to be introduced in 2002, replacing national currencies. Paul Brennan, director of Tektronix's European operations, notes that planning for the changes caused them to identify several opportunities. For example, the common currency enabled them to consolidate billing operations known to one European center. But he notes that the introduction of a single currency had a larger impact elsewhere. "The biggest impact of the euro I've seen is that it's forcing companies to rethink their pricing," Brennan said. "In our measurement instruments business, where we had different mark-ups in different markets—we had to rethink our pricing." For example, with different currencies in each nation, Tektronix was able to charge different prices in each country. Changing to a single currency would emphasize these price differences, making them hard to explain to customers. Tektronix decided to adopt a new pricing strategy that more accurately reflected costs in each nation. Hence, basic prices will be the same, but firms will be given discounts for paying earlier. Most of the larger companies in Europe began the preparations in 1994/1995. However, Brennan notes that some firms were not as prepared for the change: "On the other hand, [small and midsize enterprises] don't know anything about the euro or its implications. You'd think they were Americans."

## Input: Data Collection

Figure 4.12 illustrates the basic components of a human resources management (HRM) transaction-processing system. Note that the system is even more complex because the data comes from all areas of the company. To understand how the HRM systems became so complicated, begin with the obvious data that needs to be collected: numbers related to the payroll. For hourly workers, the system needs to collect and monitor hours worked. For many sales tasks, the system must compute sales by employee to determine commissions. Professional service firms often ask employees to track their time in terms of billable hours for work that is charged back to clients. In all three situations, as the number of employees increases, it becomes increasingly difficult to collect all of these statistics and verify their accuracy. It also becomes harder to find specific pieces of data.

Think about paychecks you have received. In addition to the payment amount, there could be 10 to 20 other numbers on the pay stub. Companies monitor and report several types of payroll taxes, including federal, state, local, Social Security, and health. Also, firms monitor employee benefits, such as health care and retirement. Most firms also handle employee deductions for employee purchases, savings plans, stock purchases, parking, meal plans, and other options. In some situations, companies must garnish wages and forward them to a third party.

Human resources departments also track days taken for vacations, personal time, and illness. In larger companies, HRM provides training courses and offers testing of critical skills. Employee attendance and performance data is stored and incorporated into evaluations.

With the increasing use of merit pay, the system must also track employee evaluations. Some performance measures are tied to productivity or output within the employee's department, so HR must relate employee work schedules to production and quality measures.

**FIGURE 4.12**

Most employees know that human resources management (HRM) deals with payroll and benefits. But HRM also collects data and produces reports for myriad government reports, oversees employee evaluations, and tracks job applications. The department also handles training and education opportunities.

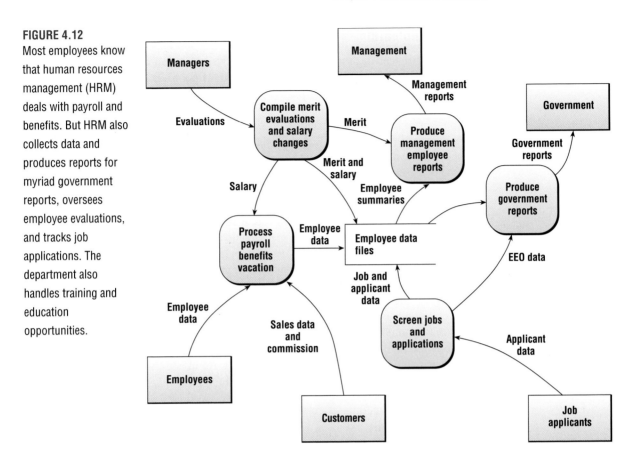

Most companies use a centralized HRM department to advertise job openings and to screen the initial applicants, verify credentials, and keep basic employment and hiring data.

## Output: Reports

The human resources department also produces several reports related to payroll. Along with printing checks, HRM must provide expense reports and forecasts to the accounting system. Periodic reports are created for job vacancies and analyses of employee performance and morale.

HRM departments also spend a great deal of time creating reports for various government agencies. All companies must file various economic reports dealing with employment. Tax-withholding data must be filed regularly with federal, state, and local agencies. HRM departments create equal employment opportunity reports detailing characteristics of their workforce, job applicants, and hiring decisions. Then there are various reports required by the Occupational Safety and Health Administration (OSHA) regarding injuries and exposure to various hazards. If employees need to be certified, companies file aggregate reports with the various regulatory agencies. All of these reports have deadlines.

In addition to the standard reports, the human resources department is responsible for maintaining compliance with all relevant employment laws. Hence, HRM staff must continually monitor the employment data and evaluate it for exceptions and problems.

## Process: Automation

The human resources department is a busy place. Keep in mind that the data and reports apply to every branch of the company. Even standard items such as paychecks become complicated when the company is split into several divisions scattered across the country. Also, remember that accuracy is crucial. Employees can become upset if their paychecks are wrong. Errors with government reports can lead to fines and lawsuits. Equally importantly, companies with good HRM departments are able to offer additional benefits to employees. With a good information system, they can offer cafeteria-style benefits where each employee selects a personal combination of benefits.

Small businesses have long complained about the burdens imposed by government reports and data collection. To alleviate some of the hassles and expense, several companies specialize in automating the data collection and report writing. Consider payroll: Because of the constantly changing laws, many companies rely on an outside agency to collect data and print the paychecks. One of the largest providers is Automated Data Processing (ADP). Even if a company chooses to maintain its own payroll records, it typically purchases the software from a third party instead of trying to keep up with the annual changes using internal programmers.

Several companies sell software that automates HRM data handling and produces government-required reports. From economics to equal employment to OSHA reports, the basic HRM reports are being computerized. You still need to collect the data in the proper format and convert it to the purchased software. In addition to saving time in producing reports, the packages often contain the essential government rules and can analyze the data to spot potential problems.

Some newer technologies are being used to simplify data gathering. In particular, companies are searching for ways to make it easier for workers to deal with the HRM department. A system created by PRC, Inc., uses touchtone phones and a voice-response system to enable workers to make changes directly to their base information, like changing their address or tax withholding. Another approach is to install PC-based kiosks and use the Internet, so that employees can look up information, sign up for training classes, or modify their personal data whenever they wish. Other companies are using similar software and the corporate network to allow workers to perform basic HR tasks from their desks or from home.

PeopleSoft, Inc., exemplifies the overall trend in computer support for HRM, by moving HR management off centralized databases and onto personal computer–based applications. The new technologies cut human resource management costs, make it easier for managers to get information, and enable companies to offer new benefits.

---

**Reality Bytes    4–8   IRS Embarrassment**

In February 1998, the IRS sent routine CP-49 notices to 3,000 people stating that their income tax refund had been withheld to offset money they owed on their taxes. For example, Kenneth L. Steen was expecting a $513 refund. The letter informed him that he owed $300,000,007.57. The IRS stated that a "human programming error" caused the problem, and that corrections were sent. The IRS spokesman noted, "Obviously, it's embarrassing to have that kind of thing go out."

## SUMMARY

Every organization must perform certain basic operations: pay employees, pay bills, monitor revenue, and file government reports. Operations are relatively structured, short term, and easy to computerize. They form the foundation of the company. MIS supports operations by collecting data and helping to control the underlying processes.

Transaction-processing systems are responsible for capturing, storing, and providing access to the basic data of the organization. The goal is to capture the transaction data as soon as possible. Common collection methods include point-of-sale devices, process control, and electronic data interchange. Because data collection is a well-defined task, it has been computerized in most organizations for many years. Because data is the foundation for all other decisions, transaction-processing systems must maintain data integrity and minimize the threats to the data.

Financial data has always been important to any business organization. Accounting systems have been created over many years to help collect data, maintain its accuracy, and provide standardized reports to management. Financial checks and balances—such as double-entry accounting, separation of duties, and audit trails—are used

to maintain data integrity. Processing of accounting information leads to monthly, quarterly, and annual information cycles in most businesses.

Human resources systems illustrate the problems entailed in transaction processing: maintaining accurate databases and producing timely reports, and supporting employee and management needs at a low cost. They also show that good transaction-processing systems can provide additional benefits by offering new services.

### A MANAGER'S VIEW

Transaction processing is a crucial task in any company. Managers are responsible for ensuring the quality of the transaction data.

Managers quickly recognized the value of using computers to collect and maintain transaction data. Two primary transaction systems in most companies are for accounting and human resources management.

As a manager, you need to watch continually for problems or potential improvements that might arise in the transaction-processing systems. Because of the volume of data, mistakes are quickly multiplied. Likewise, even small improvements in efficiency or cost can provide substantial benefits.

## KEY WORDS

accounting journal, 147
audit trail, 151
change-drivers, 133
chart of accounts, 148
concurrency, 144
data, 134
data integrity, 144

electronic data interchange (EDI), 136
exception reports, 149
general ledger, 148
information, 134
magnetic ink character recognition (MICR), 137

optical character recognition (OCR), 136
point of sale (POS), 136
process control, 136
transaction processing, 132

## WEB SITE REFERENCES

Microsoft Expedia
Sabre Travelocity

**General Travel Reservations**

expedia.msn.com
www.travelocity.com

**Discounts**

Bestfares
Priceline
The Trip
TravelHUB

bestfares.com
www.priceline.com
www.thetrip.com
www.travelhub.com

**Individual Airlines**

| | |
|---|---|
| American | www.aa.com |
| Delta | www.delta-air.com |
| Northwest | www.nwa.com |
| Southwest | www.iflyswa.com |
| United | www.ual.com |

## REVIEW QUESTIONS

1. Describe three methods of data capture.
2. What is meant by the term *data quality*? Give three examples of problems with data quality.
3. Why is data volume an important issue in transaction-processing systems? Will newer, faster machines automatically solve the problem?
4. What is meant by *concurrency,* and why is it a problem in a multiuser environment?
5. Why are so many transaction-processing systems based on accounting methods?
6. How does the accounting cycle affect decisions and operations in a typical firm?
7. What is the difference between data and information?
8. Briefly describe three ways to collect data at the point of sale.
9. How is data collection at the factory level different from data collection about consumers?
10. Why are standards so important for EDI?
11. Why is it so important to capture data close to its source?
12. How much data is represented by one terabyte? How many textbooks (the size of this one) could be stored in one terabyte of storage space? (Hint: Forget about pictures—how many words are on an average page?)
13. Why do managers and executives rely on summaries? What problems can arise with summarized data?

## EXERCISES

1. Consider a medical example related to testing. One hundred sick people are in your office. Based on their symptoms and medical statistics, you know that 90 of them have disease A and 10 of them have a rare disease B. You do not know which people have each illness, but both groups will die without treatment. Fortunately, there is a 100-percent cure for both diseases. However, if you give the wrong treatment to a person, he or she will die. You have a test available to indicate whether a person has disease A or B. The test is accurate 80 percent of the time. How many people will you test? Why? What is the important characteristic of this problem? How is it related to the testing of information systems?
2. Find information on at least two accounting packages that could be used for a business with 100 to 150 employees. Identify the strengths and weaknesses of each package. Are the packages tailored to specific industries?
3. Visit at least three retail stores in your area and determine how they handle transaction processing for sales. How many checkout counters are available at each store? By counting the number of customers in a 10- to 15-minute time interval, estimate the total number of sales transactions occurring for a given day.
4. Visit a local store or factory and identify a primary set of transaction data. Describe at least three reports that a manager would want to see based on this data.
5. Go to the library and research a particular industry. Identify the major transactions that would be experienced by a typical firm in this industry. How often do the transactions occur (daily, weekly, monthly)?
6. Because of the importance of transactions, there is a large number of cases involving fraud and other legal problems with sales and other transactions. Pick an industry and find articles in business and trade journals that identify problems of this nature. How will computerization of the transactions affect fraudulent transactions? Why would the computerization make it easier or harder to detect these problems?
7. Using articles from business, trade and computer magazines, identify three companies (in different industries) that are using imaging systems for transaction data. How large are the companies? How much storage space is used by the data?
8. Data collection can be difficult for certain industries. For example, government agencies, transportation companies, hospitals, and agricultural entities all have unique problems in collecting data. Choose one

of these industries, research a firm in that industry, and explain the problems the managers encounter and how technology is being used to overcome the difficulties and collect data.

 **Rolling Thunder Database**

9. Identify the major transaction-processing components in the system.
10. Identify transaction-processing operations that need to be added to the system.
11. What features are used in the database and the forms to ensure quality of transaction data?
12. What additional data quality features should be added?

13. Explain how additional data quality features can be provided with training, procedures, and manual controls.
14. For each major transaction type, identify the sequence of steps that are performed and determine which ones are time critical.
15. For each major transaction type, estimate the frequency of the transaction and the volume of data involved.
16. Identify any transaction forms that could be improved to make them easier for clerks and other users.
17. Using the existing forms, perform the following tasks for Rolling Thunder:
    a. Take a bicycle order.
    b. Assemble a bicycle.
    c. Create a new purchase order.
    d. Record the receipt of purchases.

## ADDITIONAL READING

Bleakley, Fred. "Electronic Payments Now Supplant Checks at More Large Firms," *The Wall Street Journal,* April 13, 1994, pp. A1, A9. [Costs of handling checks]

Kirkpatrick, David. "Why the Internet Is Boosting IBM's Mainframe Sales," *Fortune,* January 11, 1999, p. 148. [Transaction processing requires computing capacity]

Winslow, Ron. "Four Hospital Suppliers Will Launch Common Electronic Ordering System," *The Wall Street Journal,* April 12, 1994, p. B8. [EDI for hospitals, including costs]

# CASES  *Retail Sales*

The retail sales industry encompasses all sales to end-product users—the consumers of the world. This industry is large and getting even larger as new and innovative means of reaching buyers continue to be developed. Presently, much media focuses on the Internet as a new medium for retail sales. The big question is whether people will buy over the Internet. Retail sales currently take place in department stores, warehouse stores, specialty stores, via mail-order, and in many other venues.

## Financial Analysis of Retail Industry

Retail sales have been robust for the past few years. Low inflation, rising income, falling unemployment rates, and an increase in consumer spending have led the drive in the retail sales industry bull market. In 1996, according to Reuters News Service, retail sales rose 5.3 percent, compared with 4.9 percent, 7.5 percent, and 5.6 percent for prior years. Using the returns of the Standard & Poor's 500 as a measure of performance, the general retail industry has recently shown return rates to be 21 percent higher on average over the S&P. Historically, normal valuation is only at 0.5 percent over the S&P 500.

Retail sales are generally cyclical in nature. Holiday sales are a significant measure of consumer sentiment. The National Retail Federation reports 1996 December holiday market sales posted a 0.6-percent increase, which was above industry expectations of a 0.4-percent increase. The 0.6 rise was a 2.5-percent increase relative to December 1995 sales.

## Stock/Investment Outlook

Retailers were expected to have problems in 1997, despite high levels of consumer confidence, because of the high levels of consumer debt and personal bankruptcy. According to NatWest Securities group, and by historical benchmarks, the growth in retail sales would begin pulling back. It was likely that consumer demand for luxury items was at a peak. With a slowdown in the economy, consumers may not be willing to purchase many unnecessary items. To economists, the numbers tell an old story: too many stores, too few consumer dollars.

## Potential/Prospective for Growth

The retail industry encompasses an extremely competitive and broad marketplace. The advancement in new retail avenues is ongoing. The up-and-coming Internet online retail industry grew by an estimated 50 percent in 1995, a rate much faster than the growth of retail in general. Over $2.2 trillion was spent in retail in 1995, with over $50 million of that amount in online retail shopping.

The National Retail Federation believes that by the year 2005, 25 percent of basic merchandise could be bought on the Internet. While the use of online shopping will continue to increase, most retailers and consumers agree that online shopping will never be a complete replacement for the physical experience of browsing.

In addition to Internet access, there is competition among stores to develop the shopping environment for the future. An example of research at work is a present collaboration between JC Penney and Nordstrom. It proposes interactive home shopping through a consumer's television screen. This service would allow consumers to view merchandise on screen and make purchases through their television remote controls. Interactive home shopping networks are already in place; few allow the purchase of consumer goods through remote control.

Retailers who don't place information technology and research and development as top priorities will get squeezed out in the scramble to catch up. Retail industries must keep up with the changing demands, character, and demographics of their customers.

## Competitive Structure

The retail sales industry is highly competitive in all areas. There are single store, franchise, and large retail outlets. Sandra Shaber of the WEFA group calls it either a "price business" or a "We've got a gimmick business." Barriers to entry are not always high. There are always many trials of new concepts in progress. Retailers must react quickly to consumer preferences in the industry.

## Role of Research and Development

Much research and testing of Internet web sites is presently underway. It is not clear which concepts will work and how consumers will respond. Utilizing data warehousing technologies to obtain, gather, and analyze customer data/purchasing habits is being developed to the fullest by Kmart Corporation. For example, in developing their idea of "Retail 2000," Kmart is researching cart scanning. With this process a whole cart is scanned at once to determine prices for checkout. Kiosks will allow customers to order products directly from a manufacturer. Marketing research and development is always underway in this industry.

## Technological Investment and Analysis

Retailers have invested in many of the newest technologies. Technological improvements have allowed many retailers to thrive in this competitive industry. Tracking customer information via smart cards and computer programs designed for efficient stocking and warehousing, have helped retailers cut costs and increase marketing capabilities. Web sites with online shopping capabilities allow for an extension of the store hours to 24 hours. Information technology allows retailers to transact business deals around the clock and from any location on the globe.

### Recommendations for the Future of the Retail Industry

Retailers must continue to take advantage of and innovate with the most up-to-date information technologies. They must seek ways to cut costs in a very competitive industry where much of the competition is based on overhead, inventory, and shipping costs.

### CASE  *Home Depot*

### Technological Investment and Analysis

Future growth for Home Depot will be contingent upon its ability to expand into new markets. The principles that built the company are the traits that will assure its future success. Increased customer loyalty, expanding services within the store, and improving the product line will allow the company to operate more efficiently.

One of the ways Home Depot seeks to improve operating efficiency is through the implementation of a computer-assisted ordering system. This system reduces the time spent by associates ordering inventory and increases inventory availability. This leads to higher sales (the required items are in stock and on the shelves when the customers want them) and higher inventory turnover (inventory items that are not required are not sitting in a warehouse).

In order to provide better means of communication between individual stores and the home office in Atlanta, the company decided to move ahead quickly in the areas of communications and networking. In moving to a more open system, they installed HP9000 UNIX processors from Hewlett-Packard in the stores and connected them to headquarters using a TCP/IP (Transmission Control Protocol/Internet Protocol) connection. This is now the standard in open communications interconnections.

The transition from in-store processors to a central TCP/IP hub was not terribly difficult, but Beach Clark, manager of network architecture at Home Depot, ran into problems in finding an off-the-shelf package that would meet Home Depot's needs. To be effective, the package had to be capable of handling data transport to (and from) the stores since the file transfer application for the Data General proprietary environment was not suitable for the TCP/IP network. Additionally, the package had to run in real time instead of processing in batch mode.

Corporate Microsystems (CMI) received the contract for its Mlink Advanced Communications Manager Software, which runs on a UNIX platform and delivers TCP/IP support. Mlink software offered capable data collection and downloading, connections for all the stores to the headquarters data, and coordination of e-mail between stores. By continuously polling stores for updates in areas such as price or inventory, the system was continuously updated instead of waiting until batch download was performed in the evening. Best of all, the system could run unattended and unobserved thereby minimizing operator interaction. The system has improved all levels of communication and information processing between the stores and headquarters, and improved inventory management.

Home Depot hopes to increase its customer base and improve customer service in its present markets. Implementing technological improvements in inventory management and improving its computer network will help keep inventory on hand and will reduce costs. Additionally, customer spending habits, rush orders, and general company information can be communicated between individual stores and the home office instantly.

### QUESTIONS

1. What forces are driving the strategic direction of the corporation/organization?
2. Upon what technologies has the corporation relied?
3. How did the corporation fund, purchase, and implement the technological program of advancement?
4. Are there replacement products for what Home Depot sells?
5. What can you learn from an examination of the corporation's web page about their business direction of the organization?
6. What challenges and opportunities is the industry facing?
7. What role does data play in the future of the corporation?

### ADDITIONAL READING

Dalton, Gregory. "Application Server Strategy Hits Bumps on Way to Lower Costs—Home Depot on Middle Road," *Computer Reseller News,* August 3, 1998, p. 42.

Hohman, Robin Schreir. "Marimba Solves Home Depot Dilemma," *Network World,* February 1, 1999, p. 29.

"Home and Garden Tips Focused for You," *Newsbytes,* January 4, 1999.

Karpinski, Richard. "Home Depot Picks Its Spots," *InternetWeek,* September 28, 1998, p. 13.

Litt, Mona R. "Solid Foundation for the Home Depot Network," *Network Computing,* January 15, 1997, pp. 88–91.

Sliwa, Carol. "Easing the 'Middle-Tier' Traffic Jam: Securities Firm Leads with Agent Technology," *Computerworld,* December 21, 1998, p. 14.

Stedman, Craig. "ERP with Fewer Consultants: Reebok, Home Depot Plan Bulk of Work In-House to Best Meet Business Needs," *Computerworld,* February 1, 1999, p. 40.

———. "Retailers Adopt Different Strategies for Installing SAP R/3," *Computerworld,* January 25, 1999, p. 9.

Stein, Tom, and Jeff Sweat, "Focus Shifts from Technology to Managing Relationships—Supply Chains Emerge as Both a Tool, Philosophy," *Computer Reseller News,* November 16, 1998, p. 102.

Turek, Norbert. "Decision Into Action—Closed-Loop Systems Are Making Retailers More Responsive to Inventory Adjustments," *InformationWeek,* October 26, 1998, p. 85.

Wilder, Clinton. "Consensus Builder—Ron Griffin Applies Technology to the Bottom Line, and Bottom-Line Thinking to the Retail Industry," *InformationWeek,* December 21, 1998, p. 38.

## CASE *Toys "Я" Us*

In 1957, Charles Lazarus saw the baby boom generation in the making. He observed that this was going to lead to a huge demand for baby products, in his mind, mainly furniture. The idea of selling just furniture did not last long. The furniture sold well, but Charles Lazarus got a lot of customers asking the same question, "Don't you stock any toys for my baby?" This led to the first "toy supermarket," which was also opened in 1957. In the mid-1970s, Toys "Я" Us became a public company, and since that time has targeted other markets. These stores include Kids "Я" Us, which concentrates mainly on kids' clothes, Babies "Я" Us, which markets products for younger-aged toddlers, and Books "Я" Us, which sells books.

### Technological Investment and Analysis

The company's primary technology includes Unisys mainframes, IBM processors, and thousands of personal computers. Operating systems include DOS, Windows, and Windows 2000 all running under one protocol with IBM AS/400 midrange systems. Toys "Я" Us uses a wide area network based on satellites, some local area networks, and third-party networks.

It is important for the company to keep in constant contact with all locations. At the same time, Toys "Я" Us tries to maintain a decentralized focus, giving individual stores the autonomy needed to respond to local markets around the world.

Joseph Giamelli, Vice-President of Information Systems, international division, has decided to upgrade to Windows 2000 running on IBM AS/400 servers. This transition is intended to bring clients and distributed servers together under one standard open platform for Toys "Я" Us stores around the world. With over 400,000 AS/400s in place, it is the largest installation of data warehouses. As far as training goes, Giamelli states that, "By going in with the AS/400, I just had to train people on the application, so I eliminated the technical knowledge required and focused on the business model."

Also involved in the upgraded system is a global data warehouse that will acknowledge 12 different languages and currencies. The length of time to remap data to the data warehouses in 12 languages and currencies was just six months. This upgrade will allow all software from around the world to run on the same platform and still allow all activities to be analyzed by the head office. Toys "Я" Us analysts will be able to run better reports on a global basis by item, vendor, and category.

### Technological Innovations

### Telecommunications

Toys "Я" Us hopes to expand its customer base with its web site, which offers services that are not available in stores, such as the ability to search for gifts by age and price range. The web site was put online in 1998. Purchases can be gift-wrapped and shipped with a personalized note.

Toys "Я" Us is facing competition from Web startups Etoys and Toys.com. By focusing on wrapping and other services, the company is looking to attract upscale consumers.

The Toys "Я" Us web site is linked to the company's back-end inventory and fulfillment systems by commerce server software from InterWorld Corp. The Kmart system, which is also connected to back-end systems, uses Dell servers running IBM's Net.Commerce web server software.

### Recommendation for the Future

Integrating the company's databases and yet putting decision-making power in the local store managers' hands gives Toys "Я" Us a competitive edge. While operating locally, stores have the benefit of knowledge about the entire Toys "Я" Us system. The company must expand into more countries, creating and expanding market share.

### QUESTIONS

1. What has been the catalyst for change at Toys "Я" Us?
2. What technologies have the corporation relied upon?
3. How has this technological change been implemented?
4. What is the financial ability of Toys "Я" Us to embark on a major technological program of advancement?
5. What does the corporation's web page present about their business?
6. Is the toy industry oligopolistic or competitive?
7. How important is data to the corporation's continued success?

## ADDITIONAL READING

Dalton, Gregory, and Clinton Wilder, "Kmart, Toys 'Я' Us Turn to Internet for Sales Boost—Retailers Seek Larger Customer Base," *InformationWeek,* July 20, 1998, p. 30.

Garvey, Martin J. "AS/400 Gamble," *InformationWeek,* March 24, 1997, pp. 105–107.

LaMonica, Martin. "At Toys 'Я' Us, Help Desk Application Is No Plaything," *InfoWorld,* October 5, 1998, p. 60.

Leong, Kathy Chin. "Toys 'Я' Us Restructures for E-Comm," *InternetWeek,* June 8, 1998, pp. 47–49.

Musich, Paula. "Toy Story: Toys 'Я' Us Plays New Kind of Software Distribution Game," *PC Week,* October 21, 1996, pp. 1–3.

Orenstein, David. "Retailers Struggle to Keep Techs," *Computerworld,* November 2, 1998, p. 39.

"Transforming Toys 'Я' Us," *Computer Retail Week,* September 21, 1998, p. 3.

## CASE  *Walgreens*

Walgreens is the largest and most visited drugstore chain in the United States. It provides most types of prescription and nonprescription drugs. Walgreens also has a large variety of items used on a day-to-day basis such as milk, film, soda, batteries, school supplies, bread, chips, bandages, toothpaste, deodorant, and chocolates. Walgreens's success can be attributed to convenience but also to its successful logistics, distribution, and inventory systems.

### Technological Investment and Analysis

Electronic data interchange (EDI) technology is used for the distribution/inventory system at Walgreens. The distribution/inventory system of Walgreens is the most automated in the industry, making heavy use of bar coding and radio frequency technology to track and transmit distribution/inventory information. Logistics, inventory, and distribution have always been important parts of the retail business. In the mid 1980s, many retailers discovered that one of the success factors for their businesses were logistics, inventory, and distribution.

One of the newer techniques used in retailing today is continuous replenishment. This technique focuses on eliminating duplicate inventory in the channel of distribution by increasing predictability and trust between buyer, seller, and any third-party support agencies. Continuous replenishment often hinges on moving from push strategies to pull strategies. Continuous replenishment applies the use of new information technology and new methods of materials handling designed to speed information and

cut cycle times up and down the pipeline. This technique has been adopted not only by Walgreens but also by many of its competitors such as Wal-Mart and Target.

The thinking process for continuous replenishment starts at the planning and forecasting stage, which is done in conjunction with key vendors. The process requires the ongoing sharing of point-of-sale information. It concentrates on optimizing logistics planning to get shipping and receiving in sync with selling floor trends. The system targets reduction of time and inventory throughout the whole supply chain to realize cost savings and productivity gains for both the retailer and the supplier.

Managing distribution to get the right merchandise to the right stores at the right time in the right amount, makes a big difference. Cost and productivity benefits are realized by distributing lean up-front quantities to the stores, replenishing exactly and frequently based on SKU level sales.

A concept currently being used by Walgreens for the distribution of their products is that of cross-docking. In the cross-docking system, the product is not consigned to storage but rather continuously flows across the dock until it is resorted and moves to a store. In this system, the distribution center becomes a sorting rather than a holding area. In some cross-docking systems, the merchandise is held at the dock less than half the day before it is moved to the store. The tighter the window on cross-docking, the greater the inventory savings and the more careful the coordination between buyer, seller, and third party needs to be.

The process saves everyone money. Workers in the warehouses only touch the product once, to audit and move it from truck to truck. Communications technologies such as EDI are a critical link in this type of system.

Good asset management requires knowledge of what the company owns and where these assets are located. The inventory and tracking of data prevent property loss and theft. Asset management is made easier by technologies such as bar codes, radio frequency tagging, laser coding, and newly developed desired state software management. These technologies assign identification tags on company assets that are to be tracked, using relevant data in a central information system.

To speed the store checkout lane at Walgreens, barcode technology is used. By moving bar coding into the warehouse, operations in the areas of receiving, stocking, and retrieval are now more efficient. Incorporation of bar codes with efficiency-driven programs like cross-docking and advanced use of EDI helps raise productivity levels. "It's a technology whose time has come," said Charlie Hunter, distribution center manager at Harvest Foods, Little Rock, Arkansas. For example, when the merchandise is taken out of the warehouse, the mainframe database is updated on a real-time basis.

Another tool used in the retailing industry for inventory control is laser technology. This tool is similar to bar

---

| ADVANTAGES OF BAR CODES FOR INVENTORY MANAGEMENT |
| :--- |
| 1. Improves inventory accuracy from receiving to shipping. |
| 2. Provides immediate availability of inventory information. |
| 3. Reduces the percentage of data entry errors. |
| 4. Creates a permanent audit trail. |
| 5. Reduces inventory levels previously inflated to compensate for errors. |
| 6. Increases inventory turns. |
| 7. Reduce shipment errors. |
| 8. Improves relationships with customers and suppliers. |
| 9. Reduces internal costs due to the elimination of errors, reduction of inventory levels, and accurate shipments. |
| 10. Takes costs out of all stages of the industrial/ commercial channel. |

coding. The laser produces a permanent code without the use of inks or solvents. They can be placed anywhere in the product. It is a low maintenance, inkless operation, with minimum downtime, maximum flexibility, and accurate, consistently reliable coding at high speeds.

The chief advantage of these types of systems is that there is a constant interactive flow of up-to-date inventory information. Any mistake is flagged immediately. If there is a discrepancy, it is known immediately rather than when a quarterly inventory review is done. Previously, everything was reactive. Now, armed with up-to-the-minute information, product coding allows Walgreens to make timely and accurate decisions, and become a more responsive partner to the customer. Using bar codes to identify inventory cuts distribution costs for Walgreens.

The company has also been successful at increasing the sales per employee and at reducing long-term debt, dropping to zero by 1995.

### Technological Innovations

#### Networks

AT&T provides connections for companies like Walgreens to enable them to communicate instantaneously with their stores and pharmacists. In 1998, AT&T experienced a major T-1 shortage. The shortage presented major problems since AT&T's standard frame relay backup options were rendered useless by the fact that the switches, rather than the physical routes, were out of service.

AT&T officials worked to discover the root cause of the failure. AT&T Chairman and CEO C. Michael Armstrong said in a briefing with reporters that the company would not charge customers for frame relay service until the network was restored and the root cause was identified and fixed.

Some users thought AT&T had an obligation to go even further. In January, AT&T announced service-level agreements (SLAs), which included 99.99-percent availability for the frame relay network. At the time, AT&T Data Services Vice-President Steve Hindman promised a four-hour mean-time-to-repair guarantee. If this failed, customers would receive free ports and permanent virtual circuits (PVCs) for a month.

An AT&T spokesperson said the SLAs had slipped past the scheduled March general availability date. He confirmed some larger customers had been given the guarantees anyway.

During this downtime, nearly all users reported that they did not have enough backup lines to keep their networks running. Many resorted to unusual measures. One giant pharmaceutical company called in a fleet of six jets to keep its networks of papers, services, and products working. Some of the pharmaceutical company's 80 sites had ISDN backup; others only had 9.6Kbps modems. Only half of the company's orders were able to get through via dial-up, so the company brought in the planes to fly paper orders to distribution centers. The company did not get its frame relay fully restored until Wednesday morning of the week of outage.

Walgreens does have financial protection because it contracted for a Service Level Agreement from AT&T. Ray Sheedy, Walgreens's director of corporate telecommunications, said 278 of the company's stores connected via AT&T were down for 24 hours. Walgreens' mail-order locations in Tempe, Arizona, and Orlando, Florida, which are ordinarily on the AT&T network, had backup frame relay capacity with MCI. Sheedy said Walgreens cannot afford dual networks in stores and indicated that ISDN is too expensive to run to individual stores and is not available everywhere.

Most analysts stressed the importance of discovering the root cause to prevent similar problems from occurring. Steve Sazegari, president of Tele.Mac, a Foster City, California, consulting firm, noted that data traffic typically spikes on Monday, the day this outage occurred, since this is the day order-entry systems accept weekend mail orders and transactions.

"These switches were never put under this kind of test in a public network before," Sazegari said. "Unlike a fiber cut, which could be avoided through rerouting, eliminating an impact on the rest of the network, this switching interruption had an impact upon the whole networking structure."

### Internet Site

The Extensible Markup Language (XML) is a World Wide Web Consortium standard for tagging Web content to exchange data. The standard lets users make fields that name data. Search engines use those fields to make more accurate return lists.

This technology enables companies to attach data within a document. So internal users can find and share information easier by tagging each important data piece with a name. Pete Van Valin, team leader for Web systems at Walgreens, hopes to have XML up and running within 12 months on the company's web site. Currently, employees must place meta tags in their HTML documents. The goal is to automate the process with XML. Van Valin is still evaluating tools.

Tagging is essential to get a hold of all the information generated from the intranet's 10,000 users. His team has developed a list of standards and best practices for intranet documents but has not completed formal training on tagging. "Tagging is all about precision. When that precision happens, it's ideal," Microsoft's Tuchen says.

### Search Tools

Walgreens uses several search tools to help employees find information faster. Autonomy uses for Bayesian logic to track word patterns in documents. This is based upon the relationship between multiple variables and includes the extent to which one variable impacts the other. Rather than searching for individual words, Autonomy's engine examines patterns of words within documents, marking their occurrence together. For example, if a user wants to search for information on Microsoft's Wolfpack, he or she is not interested in information about wolves in the wild. Because of the user's marked pattern, Autonomy's Agentware system will know that this request is dealing with software and Microsoft.

Semio uses visualization to help users understand their search options. It offers a search tool that indexes text, makes clusters of content, and then generates visual maps of those clusters for search results. For example, if a user searches on "NT," SemioMap will display the returns that directly pertain to that result, and then map out related concepts such as Windows, Microsoft, and operating systems. This gives users a sense of the hierarchy of their searches.

To be successful at companies like Walgreens, searching mechanisms will have to incorporate the following:

1. They will have to become more user-friendly and simplify search, extending beyond Boolean search mechanisms.
2. They will have to gather and process external information as well as they gather internal data.
3. Embedded agents will have to analyze search paths and offer other ways to find information.

They will have to study data-gathering behavior, store that information, and be able to build suggested query lists based on that information.

4. They will have to incorporate standards such as XML.

### QUESTIONS

1. What forces are driving the strategic direction of the corporation/organization?
2. What technologies have the corporation relied upon?
3. What has caused a change in the use of technology in the corporation/organization?
4. How successful has the technological change been?
5. What challenges and opportunities is the industry facing?
6. What are some of the other services Intercom Plus's data can enable Walgreens to perform?

### ADDITIONAL READING

Hoffman, Thomas. "Walgreens Heals Prescription Net," *Computerworld,* April 20, 1998, p. 43.

Tadjer, Rivka. "Wanted: Technical Talent," *CommunicationsWeek,* June 2, 1997, p. 105.

"Walgreens Signs Deal to Simplify EDI with Vendors," *PC Week,* January 5, 1998, p. 69.

### DISCUSSION ISSUE

## *Are Standards Helpful?*

It can be difficult to combine information. One problem is the differing types of data—spreadsheets, word processor documents, databases, and graphics. A bigger problem is that there are many different brands of software in each category. There are more than a hundred different word processors available and they all store the documents in a different format. Similarly, each commercial graphics package uses its own method to store the data. The problem becomes even worse when there are different brands of hardware involved. Then the data has to be transferred physically from one computer to another. Although there are data converters, the data is often modified slightly.

One answer to these problems is to choose standard software for everyone in the company to use. By using only one brand of each type of software, it is easier to share data with other people in the company. It is also easier to combine information from the different types of software. However, there are some problems with standardization. The director of MIS (George) has just called a meeting with the head of the accounting department (Sam) and the director of marketing (Jenny).

**George:** Hi, Sam and Jenny. Thanks for coming. When I talked to you earlier, I mentioned that the MIS staff has been receiving a lot of calls from your departments. It's great that your employees are using the new computers. But we're starting to see some problems with the software. Sam, how many different graphics packages are you using?

**Sam:** Let's see. I guess about half are using Microsoft PowerPoint. The rest are using some version of Corel Draw, and a couple people are using Adobe Illustrator. But they're working on special projects.

**George:** Jenny, what about the marketing department? I hear you have around eight graphics packages.

**Jenny:** That's not quite true. The administrative assistants are using PowerPoint for basic presentations and Excel for graphs. We produce some early advertising drafts with our two publishing packages. But one of those is on a PC and the other runs on a Mac. The marketing staff members use whichever graphics package they first learned, so I guess there could be five or six. What's the problem?

**George:** Well, we've been getting a lot of calls from your folks as they try to share information. One of the marketing people wanted to create a report with last year's sales figures and a graph. It took us a while to find the data, and then we had to spend three days converting the graphics. And the accounting department has been screaming for a year about not being able to get access to all of the data they want. It seems everyone in the company is stashing away data in their own databases and computers. So, we've decided to choose standard software for the entire company. We just made a bulk purchase of all the software we need for the company. We'll start distributing it next week.

**Jenny:** Wait a minute. That's crazy. Who picked this software? Don't we get to vote? What's wrong with a little freedom?

**Sam:** I can see where it'll save money. And we really do need a corporate graphics library. I've seen 20 different versions of the corporate logo, and I know people keep creating new versions for their own software.

**George:** That's right. And we'll be able to provide better training and help for everyone because there will be less software we have to handle.

**Jenny:** Oh come on. How much money can you really save? Besides, I don't think my department can get by with only one graphics package. We do too many different things. We have to have a separate system for our advertising staff, and all of our copy writers use their own systems at home, and . . .

**George:** We know there are going to be some problems at first. We've chosen the most flexible packages we can find. We can do everything you need using just one software package.

**Jenny:** I doubt it. Besides, then it'll be impossible to use. Plus, my staff are already familiar with the software they use now.

**George:** We know it will take some time. We have training sessions scheduled for the next month. I have sign-up sheets here. We want you to get everyone in your offices signed up and in a class within the next month.

Despite the problems, the company changes to four standard software packages. A year later, there is another meeting.

**Jenny:** George, I told you it wouldn't work.

**George:** Well, if your staff would just cooperate a little longer, we can still work out the small problems. Besides, we did gain the advantages I promised. The MIS department is spending less on software, training, and support than we have in the last three years.

**Jenny:** Right. That's because the software and support are all coming out of my budget now. My staff know better than to call you for help. They just call the software company support lines. The phone calls are costing a fortune, but at least we get answers.

**Sam:** At least everyone can share their work now. We spend a lot less time converting figures and documents, and there are fewer touch-ups. I think the standard software policy is working well.

**Jenny:** Oh sure. Just because they picked the software you like. But you're stuck now. I just read where the database company you people chose is filing for bankruptcy. And George, remember that graphics package you picked? It's two years out of date. It doesn't handle Object Linking and Embedding in Windows 95 and won't run on Windows NT. So now what do we do? Pick *more* standard software?

**George:** Calm down. There have been a few minor problems, but Sam's right. The system is working fairly well.

Jenny: Sure, that's easy for you to say. Have you talked to the other departments lately?

Sam: Look. Can't we compromise a little? I don't really care about word processors and graphics packages. I just need access to spreadsheets and databases. Let's standardize on those and you folks in marketing can use whatever graphics packages you want.

Jenny: Oh come on. I don't see what the problem is anyway. The new versions of the software we have can share data with all of the other software. I have a package that will convert documents between 30 different word processors and 20 graphics packages. It's not perfect, but it's easy and it's fast. I still don't see why we can't just buy what we want. If you want to read my data, you can convert it to whatever format you need.

George: But then we're back where we started. I think we'll just stick with this software for a while longer. It's going to be too hard to change now. Maybe next year we can look for a new graphics package.

Jenny: Sure, and maybe you should look for a new job.

## QUESTIONS

1. Do you think everyone in a company should use the same word processor? What are the advantages? What are the drawbacks?
2. Does everyone at your university use the same software? How is student software chosen? Is there a committee? How often does it meet? When was the last time your school changed software? How often do software vendors upgrade their software?
3. Do you think George is right in enforcing the corporate standard? Can you think of a compromise for Sam that will make everyone happier?
4. How difficult is it to convert documents among different word processors? What software packages are available to help?
5. Do you think this problem is common in business? Is there anything businesses can do to minimize the problem?

# Accounting Review

The primary purpose of accounting is to track the financial transactions in an organization and provide reports that summarize the financial position of the organization. Standardization is a key aspect to modern accounting. To be able to compare financial statements from various firms, investors (owners) and managers need to know that each organization measures variables the same way. Consequently, the accounting profession has created a large set of rules for classifying transactions and for producing reports. Only the most elementary forms are reviewed here.

## GENERAL LEDGER

Every financial transaction is defined in two categories: money and a classification account. For example, if the firm purchases something, the accounting system records how it was bought (cash, credit, etc.) and the type of item (supplies, inventory, and so on). It is the classifications that provide the detailed information about the firm. All account classifications are defined in the general ledger.

Accounts are organized by the basic accounting equation: Assets = Liabilities + Owner's Equity. *Assets* are claims that the firm has on others. *Liabilities* are claims that the firm owes to others. *Owner's Equity* is the difference, which is owed to the owners or investors. These are the three primary classification accounts in the general ledger. The other accounts are simply increasing levels of detail within these three accounts. For example, assets are divided into current assets versus property, plant, and equipment. Similarly, liabilities are split into current liabilities and long-term debt. In general, current means items due within one year—although there are specific accounting rules for determining the classification of various items.

Although the primary categories are standardized, each firm will have a different set of accounts at the more detailed levels. In general, firms within an industry tend to have similar sets of accounts. For example, accounts in a retail firm focus on sales, purchases, and inventory. Whereas accounts in a manufacturing firm focus on production, capital costs (plant and equipment), and long-term contracts. In modern accounting systems, the general ledger is stored as a database. Each account classification is numbered, where detailed accounts have longer numbers. The numbers are used internally and do not appear on the financial statements.

## BALANCE SHEET

The balance sheet is the standard method for presenting the current financial status of the firm. It is a report that summarizes the three basic account totals and shows the total values of the various accounts at a particular point in time. Figure 4.1A shows a typical balance sheet.

The balance sheet shows the totals for the primary account categories (assets, liabilities, and owner's equity), along with the totals for the first level of details. Balance sheets and other financial information are readily available for American firms through the SEC EDGAR files at http://www.sec.gov.

## EARNINGS OR INCOME STATEMENT

Most firms are in business to make money. The amount earned is displayed on the earnings statement (sometimes called an income statement). Earnings are computed over a period of time (usually a year, a quarter, or a month). Generally, most earnings come from sales. The statement deducts the cost of goods

| ASSETS | |
|---|---|
| **Current Assets** | |
| Cash and cash equivalents | $    47,794 |
| Receivables | 399,319 |
| Inventories | 1,714,229 |
| Prepaid expenses | 71,855 |
| Deferred income tax benefits | 28,583 |
| Total Current Assets | 2,261,780 |
| **Property, Plant and Equipment** | |
| Land | 779,873 |
| Buildings | 2,325,388 |
| Fixtures and equipment | 2,877,019 |
| Leasehold improvements | 831,364 |
| Subtotal | 6,813,644 |
| Less accumulated depreciation and amortization | 2,552,723 |
| Net property, plant and equipment | 4,260,921 |
| Goodwill, net of accumulated amortization | 1,611,812 |
| Other Assets | 401,502 |
| **Total Assets** | **$8,536,015** |

| LIABILITIES AND SHAREHOLDERS' EQUITY | |
|---|---|
| **Current Liabilities** | |
| Accounts payable | $1,186,845 |
| Accrued payroll and benefits | 301,656 |
| Current portion of self-insurance reserves | 108,263 |
| Income taxes payable | 11,293 |
| Other current liabilities | 412,342 |
| Current maturities of long-term debt | 100,935 |
| Total Current Liabilities | 2,121,334 |
| Self-insurance reserves, less current portion | 390,661 |
| Deferred income taxes | 349,041 |
| Other liabilities | 163,927 |
| Long-term debt and capital leases less current maturities | 3,201,970 |
| Shareholders' equity common stock of $1.00 par value | 299,778 |
| Additional paid-in capital | 269,205 |
| Retained earnings | 2,320,322 |
| Less cost of treasury stock; 26,171,962 shares | (580,223) |
| Total Shareholders' Equity | 2,309,082 |
| **Total Liabilities and Shareholders' Equity** | **$8,536,015** |

**FIGURE 4.1A**

BALANCE SHEET FOR AMERICAN STORES

It shows the primary account totals (assets, liabilities, and owner's equity); along with the first level of account detail.

| Sales | $19,138,880 |
|---|---|
| Cost of merchandise sold | 14,039,263 |
| Gross profit | 5,099,617 |
| Operation and administrative expenses | 4,317,576 |
| Restructuring and impairment | 13,400 |
| Operating profit | 768,641 |
| **Other income (expense):** | |
| Interest income | 5,647 |
| Interest expense | (216,710) |
| Shareholder related expense | (33,913) |
| Total other income (expense) | (244,976) |
| **Earnings before income taxes** | 523,665 |
| Federal and state income taxes | (243,045) |
| **Net earnings** | $    280,620 |
| Basic earnings per share | $        1.02 |

**FIGURE 4.2A**

EARNINGS STATEMENT

Sales and cost of goods sold are generally the largest components. Investors often focus on the earnings per share.

sold, which usually consists of the purchase price of the items, shipping, and storage costs. Administrative expenses are listed separately. Additional revenue and costs arise from interest income and expense. Income taxes (federal and state) are always shown as a separate computation. Net earnings are useful, but for comparison, most investors are interested in earnings per share, which is computed by dividing net earnings by the number of outstanding shares. Figure 4.2A shows a typical earnings statement.

## CASH FLOW

The cash flow in an organization can be an early indicator of potential problems or future success. A troubled firm might be able to hold off problems by selling assets, not paying liabilities, or reducing the number of employees. However, the cash-flow statement shows the major sources and uses of cash. It will reveal all of these potential problems. The report is an excellent source of information about the immediate financial problems or successes in the organization.

Figure 4.3A shows a cash-flow statement. Notice the major categories: earnings, changes in assets, changes in liabilities, investments, and changes

| | |
|---|---:|
| **Net earnings** | $280,620 |
| Depreciation and amortization | 468,869 |
| Net (gain) loss on asset sales | (722) |
| Self-insurance reserves | (26,201) |
| Other | (100,078) |
| **(Increase) decrease in current assets:** | |
| Receivables | (80,441) |
| Inventories | 11,313 |
| Prepaid expenses | (15,829) |
| **Increase (decrease) in current liabilities:** | |
| Accounts payable | 335,560 |
| Other current liabilities | 16,137 |
| Accrued payroll and benefits | (24,150) |
| Income taxes payable | (9,997) |
| Total adjustments | 574,411 |
| Net cash provided by operating activities | 855,031 |
| **Cash flows from investing activities:** | |
| Expended for property, plant and equipment | (996,288) |
| Proceeds from sale of assets | 39,447 |
| Net cash used in investing activities | (956,841) |
| **Cash flows from financing activities** | |
| Proceeds from long-term borrowing | 500,000 |
| Payment of long-term borrowing | (160,000) |
| Net addition to (reduction of) debt and leases | 279,101 |
| Proceeds from exercise of stock options | 44,164 |
| Repurchase of common stock from major shareholder | (550,000) |
| Issuance of common stock for over-allotments | 95,914 |
| Cash dividends | (97,042) |
| Net cash provided by financing activities | 112,137 |
| Net increase (decrease) in cash | 10,327 |
| **Cash and cash equivalents:** | |
| Beginning of year | 37,467 |
| End of year | $ 47,794 |

**FIGURE 4.3A**
CASH FLOW STATEMENT
By focusing on the sources and uses of cash, the report is a good indicator of current problems and successes.

in financing. Increases in cash flow due to increases in net earnings are clearly a good sign. Increases due to changes in short-term assets usually arise from improved collection of accounts receivable. Changes due to liabilities, investments, or financing could signify problems within the firm. In particular, watch for one-time changes due to reorganizations or changes in tactics.

## EQUITY STATEMENT

Investors and owners are ultimately concerned about their equity. Over the last time period, how much did the firm add to their holdings? This information is displayed in the equity statement. Generally, the most important contribution is the retained earnings—which consists of the corporate profits (net earnings) that were not used for other purposes. Additionally, a firm may pay dividends, and it might repurchase stock. Treasury stock consists of stock held by the company—often as a result of a repurchase, but it is also used in director and employee compensation plans.

Figure 4.4A shows an equity statement. It is slightly more complex than those shown in introductory accounting textbooks because regulations require that firms disclose the effect of stock compensation plans. Hence, a modern equity statement shows the effect of the various stock option plans.

## ACCRUAL VERSUS CASH ACCOUNTING

Accounting would be a fairly simple field if every business operated on a cash basis—where all revenues and costs were settled immediately at the time of a transaction. In reality, expenses and revenues rarely occur at the same time. To gain a fair picture of the firm's operations, the accounting system needs to match the expenses and revenues over a defined period of time. In a simple example, a firm might purchase supplies and pay employees to work on a project in December. Yet the firm does not receive payment for the project until it is completed—in January. If we recorded the transactions on a cash basis as they were paid, it would appear that the firm lost money in the first year, and then earned a huge profit in the second year. It makes more sense to match the

| | COMMON STOCK | ADDITIONAL PAID-IN CAPITAL | RETAINED EARNINGS | TREASURY STOCK | TOTAL |
|---|---|---|---|---|---|
| **Balances at year-end 1996** | $299,778 | $212,672 | $2,136,744 | ($113,767) | $2,535,427 |
| Net earnings--1997 (52 weeks) | | | 280,620 | | 280,620 |
| Stock options and ESOP | | 5,983 | | 24,704 | 30,687 |
| Directors' stock compensation plan | | 3,931 | | 86 | 4,017 |
| Dividends ($.35 per share) | | | (97,042) | | (97,042) |
| Stock purchase incentive plans | | 10,425 | | | 10,425 |
| Purchase of shares incl. ESPP buyback | | | | (967) | (967) |
| Stock repurchase from major shareholder- | | | | (550,000) | (550,000) |
| Stock issuance for over-allotments- | | 36,194 | | 59,721 | 95,915 |
| Balances at year-end 1997 | $299,778 | $269,205 | $2,320,322 | ($580,223) | $2,309,082 |

**FIGURE 4.4A**
EQUITY STATEMENT
Amounts are in thousands. Note the effect of a major purchase of stock from one shareholder (in the notes, the company stated that they bought the stock from the founder).

costs and revenue. In this case, the sales revenue would be counted in December when the contract was made and the work performed—even though the actual cash is not received until next year. As a result of the accrual basis, some costs and revenues are spread over multiple time periods. Accountants make adjusting entries at the end of every period to allocate these costs and revenues properly.

## EXERCISES

1. Create an income statement, cash flow statement, and balance sheet using a spreadsheet.
2. Using the sales and cost data from Rolling Thunder along with bicycle industry averages, create a basic income statement and balance sheet for Rolling Thunder.
3. Using the SEC Edgar files on the Internet, find a balance sheet for a company that interests you. Copy it to a spreadsheet. Create an estimated balance sheet for the next year. Assume a 5 percent increase in sales, a 4 percent increase in costs, a 6 percent increase in receivables, the same tax rates, no increase in debt or stock, and a 1 percent increase in purchases of plant and equipment.
4. Find a balance sheet for a large manufacturing company (e.g., John Deere). Find a balance sheet for a similarly sized retail firm (e.g., CVS). Discuss the similarities and differences in the balance sheets.
5. Find an accounting textbook, or search the Internet, to describe three major accrual changes that are made in accounting.

CHAPTER 5

# *Database Management*

As a leader in the development of the airline reservation systems, American Airlines was one of the first to take advantage of the Internet for booking flights. Access to the AA database provides consumers with more information and control over their travel.

## AMERICAN AIRLINES

In early 1977, hearings were held in Washington regarding airline deregulation. The hearings proceeded without event for much of the day. Phil Bakes, the legal counsel for Senator Ted Kennedy, remembers sitting in the hushed hearing room as a panel of airline witnesses finished testifying. As he glanced up from his seat, he noticed an unfamiliar, tough-looking man coming right at him. "You academic pinhead!" the man shouted. "You don't know anything. You can't deregulate this industry, you're going to wreck it. You don't know a thing!"

And so it was that this distinguished legal mind and other spectators got their first public introduction to Robert Crandall, Vice-President and future President and CEO of American Airlines.

While Crandall lost this initial fight over airline deregulation, from that day on the rest of the airline industry knew he was a force to be reckoned with. Almost twenty years later, Crandall once again thrust himself into the spotlight, but this time with visions to change the airline industry forever.

In the spring of 1996, Crandall announced that American Airlines and British Airways were pursing an alliance. In a sense, it could be classified as an operational merger in that they would cooperate on pricing, sales, and marketing, and share revenues; yet they would retain separate entities. The rest of the industry immediately protests in fury, claiming this would cause monopoly-like conditions and shut almost everyone out of the U.S. European gateways. Yet, Crandall, with his slicked-back hair and tireless spirit, decided he would take on government, his competitors, industry nay-sayers, and all others, to push through the merger.

**OVERVIEW**  Collecting and sharing data is a crucial aspect of any job. Data collection is a fundamental step in transaction processing. Data management also integrates the divisions of a company, supports teamwork, and helps to control the organization. A primary role of information systems is to collect data and make it available to managers throughout the

**FIGURE 5.1**

Without a DBMS, data can be scattered throughout the company, making it more difficult to share information. Inconsistent data, duplication, and errors are common. A DBMS maintains data through a common interface. Data definition, access, consistency, and security are maintained by the DBMS.

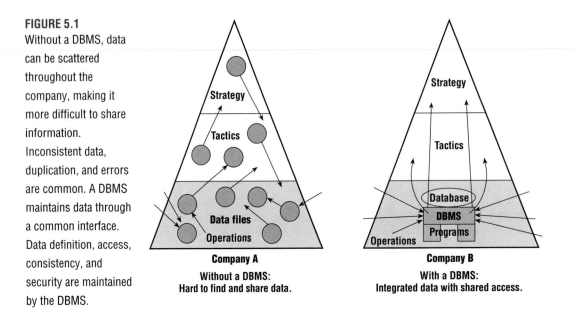

company. As shown in Figure 5.1, when data is not integrated but controlled and protected by separate divisions, it becomes impossible to run a firm efficiently.

Companywide databases are used to set standards and make it easier for managers to access and compare the data held by various departments. With standards and well-defined databases, managers can use query languages like SQL or query-by-example to ask questions and retrieve data in any manner. As long as the data exists in the database, managers can ask any type of question and examine the data in any way they need.

For you to obtain the full advantages of databases, they need to be designed carefully—often with the help of a database professional. Once the data tables are established, it is straightforward to create data-entry screens and reports. Current database systems help users build complex reports and applications simply by placing details on the screen with a mouse.

Databases are typically supported and managed through software known as a *database management system (DBMS)*. Database management systems provide controls over the data to ensure its accuracy and control who can use or alter the data. DBMSs are designed to deal with multiple users at the same time. They have internal provisions for backup and recovery of data.

Because database management systems are so powerful, they contain many options and controls, which can be intimidating when you first encounter a DBMS. The key is to focus on the components that you need first and worry about the other details later. As a manager, the most important feature you need to learn is how to retrieve data from an existing database.

**INTRODUCTION**    Database management systems are one of the most important tools in MIS. They have changed the way that computer applications are developed, and they are changing the way that companies are managed. The database approach begins with the premise that the most important aspect of the computer system is the data that it stores. The purpose of a database management system is to provide shared access to the data, answer questions, and create reports from the data.

## Trends

In the 1960s and 1970s, companies typically built their own transaction-processing systems by writing programs in COBOL. These programs consisted of millions of lines of code. Each program created and used its own set of files. As companies expanded, more programs were created—each with its own format for files. Whenever a manager wanted a new **report** or additional information, a programmer had to modify the old code or create a completely new program.

A database management system (DBMS) presents a different approach to data, reports, and programming. The most important task is to define and store the data so authorized users can find everything they need. Report writers and input screens make it easy to enter data and create reports without relying on programmers. Data is stored in a special format so that it can be shared with multiple users.

The early forms of DBMS (hierarchical and network) limited the way in which data could be stored.

The most severe limitation is that you needed to know exactly how you were going to use the data *before* you started collecting it. Database designers had to know exactly what questions people might ask regarding the data.

In the early 1970s, E. F. Codd created a flexible approach to storing data, known as the *relational model* that avoided these problems. Today, relational databases are the dominant method used to store and access data. Relational databases have a *query system* that enables managers get answers to questions without relying on programmers.

Early databases were designed to handle business types of data, such as customer names and account data. Some modern database systems can store entire books, pictures, graphs, or even sound clips as types of data. A few companies are working on **object-oriented DBMSs** that enable users to create their own data types and continue to manipulate and search the data.

A crucial factor with databases is that they can become massive. Several companies have indicated that their databases contain several terabytes (trillions of bytes) of data, as illustrated by American Express. Even small companies deal with databases with megabytes (millions of bytes) of data. The size of the database greatly affects its performance and the ability of users to find the data they need. Large databases need to be designed and maintained carefully to ensure that they run properly.

Another important characteristic of databases is that they are designed to help users to examine the data from a variety of perspectives. Instead of simply printing one type of report, they enable users to ask questions and create their own reports. Figure 5.2 illustrates how a DBMS is used in an organization. It collects data for transaction processing, creates reports, and processes ad hoc queries for managers. Figure 5.2 also indicates that databases usually require programmers to define the initial database and maintain programs to perform basic operations. The overall design is controlled by the database administrator.

Not all database systems are successful. Just as businesses fail, so do projects. There are many cases of information system projects that have failed. The failed reservation system of Continental Airlines provided an interesting comparison to American Airlines. Although database projects are often easier to complete than projects using traditional programming techniques, it is still important to evaluate the business first and decide whether or not the project is reasonable.

### Relational Databases

The goal of a relational DBMS is to make it easy to store and retrieve the data you need. All data is stored in **tables,** which consist of **columns** with **rows** of data. Each table has a

**FIGURE 5.2**

MIS EMPLOYEES
AND DATABASES

The database administrator is responsible for defining and maintaining the overall structure and data. Programmers and analysts create applications and programs that collect data and produce reports. Business operations generate data that fills the database. Managers use the application programs and ask ad hoc questions of the data.

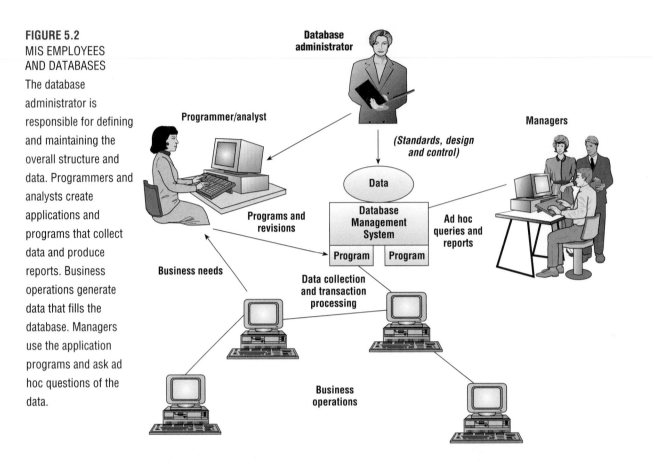

## Database Terminology

When E. F. Codd created the relational database model, he deliberately introduced new terms to describe the way that databases should store information. His terms are *attribute, tuple,* and *relation.*

Although Codd's terms are precisely defined mathematically, they can be confusing. As a result, many people use the slightly easier words: *column, row,* and *table.*

Before relational databases, several different terms were used to refer to the various parts of a database. The problem is that many of the terms had several definitions. Common terms include *field, record,* and *file.* You should avoid these terms.

name and represents objects or relationships in the data. For instance, most businesses will have tables for customers, employees, orders, and inventory.

Besides storing data, a modern DBMS has several useful tools. Input screens are built to help users enter data. Reports can be created by laying out data, text, and graphics on the screen—often with no programming. You can get answers to questions with a query language or even by pointing to tables and data on the screen. You can establish security conditions by granting or denying access to portions of the data. Most systems include an application generator that can tie input screens, queries, and reports together with a menu system. A complex application can be created by typing a few titles on the screen, without writing a single line of traditional program code.

**FIGURE 5.3**
CREATING TABLE DEFINITIONS
Tables are defined so that they can be linked by common columns. For a given row in the Orders table, you can find the corresponding customer data by locating the row with the matching phone number. In practice, this matching is handled by the DBMS query system.

**Customer Table**

| Phone | Name | Address | City |
|---|---|---|---|
| 312-555-1234 | Jones | 123 Main | Chicago |
| 502-555-8876 | Smith | 456 Oak | Glasgow |
| 602-555-9987 | Juarez | 887 Ribera | Phoenix |
| 612-555-4325 | Olsen | 465 Thor | Minneapolis |

**Orders Table**

| Customer | Date | Salesperson | TotalSale |
|---|---|---|---|
| 502-555-8876 | 3-3-99 | 2223 | 157.92 |
| 602-555-9987 | 4-4-99 | 8152 | 295.53 |
| 612-555-4325 | 4-9-99 | 8152 | 132.94 |
| 502-555-8876 | 5-7-99 | 3345 | 183.67 |

## Tables, Rows, Columns, Data Types

If you understand how spreadsheets work, it is easy to comprehend relational databases. A single spreadsheet consists of rows and columns of data. Each column has a unique name, and a row contains data about one individual object. A database consists of many of these tables that are linked by the data they contain.

In a database, each table contains data for a specific entity or object. For example, most companies will have a table to hold customer data. There are certain attributes or characteristics of the customers that we want to store. In Figure 5.3, each customer has a phone number, name, address, and city. In practice, there will be more columns.

Figure 5.3 also illustrates one of the most important features of a database system: Relational databases are specifically designed to allow many tables to be created and then combined in interesting ways. If you only had one table, you could use a spreadsheet or virtually any filing system, assuming it could handle the number of rows you needed. However, most business problems involve data stored in different tables. In the example, customers can place many different orders. Each order is stored in a separate line in the Orders table.

Notice that the tables are joined or linked by the customer phone number. The phone number is the **primary key** column in the customer table. Each row in a table must be different from the rest; otherwise, it is a waste of space. Consequently, each table must have a primary key. A primary key is a set of one or more columns that uniquely identifies each row. If someone gives you a key value (e.g., phone number), you can immediately locate the appropriate row and find the rest of the data for that entity (name, address, city).

Each primary key value must be unique, so in this example no two customers can have the same phone number. In the Orders table, the key consists of the customer phone number plus the Date column. Keys that use more than one column are called **concatenated keys.** For this key to be unique, customers can place only one order per day. In the real world, we could avoid this problem by creating a column for Order_Number as the key.

Unlike a spreadsheet, each database column can contain only one type of data at a time. For example, in the Date column you can store only dates. You would not be allowed to put names or totals in this column. Most relational databases were designed to hold business types of data. The basic choices are text, dates (and times), numeric, and objects (graphics, video, and sound). Some systems enable you to be more specific about how to store numeric data. For instance, you might want to store data with only two decimal places for monetary values. Whenever possible, dates should be stored in a date format instead of text. That way you can perform arithmetic on the values. For example, a formula like (today + 30) could be used to find a due date that is 30 days from today.

## Problems with a File Approach

**ADVANTAGES OF THE DATABASE APPROACH**

To store data on a computer with a file-based programming approach (e.g., COBOL), the programmer has to create a file. To use this file later, the programmer has to know exactly how it was created. Consider the portion of the simple data file shown in Figure 5.4. It is difficult to determine the meaning of the data stored in this file. For instance, the middle set of numbers may represent a customer ID number. However, where does it stop? Is the first address supposed to be 351 Main Street, or is it 1 Main Street? There is no way to answer this question by looking at this data file. To use this data, a programmer has to locate the file definition or program that originally created the file. Hiding somewhere in that program is a description of how this file is supposed to be read.

It gets worse. Imagine what happens when there are thousands of data files and hundreds of programs, and constant changes, as in a reservation systems. If the programmers are careful, even this situation can be dealt with. However, consider what happens when the data needs to be shared among several programs or multiple users. In Figure 5.5, there are only two programs and four files. Notice that the customer file is used by both programs. One dark and stormy night the program that prints customer bills encounters an error and crashes. It displays an error message on the operator's terminal. The operator promptly calls the programmer who is on duty that night. The programmer crawls out of bed, goes to work, and looks for the problem. To solve the problem, our sleepy programmer has to modify the customer file. That leaves three choices. First, if she just changes the file and this program, the invoice program will fail at some point in the future (in the middle of the night). Second, she could change all the programs that use the customer

**FIGURE 5.4**
SAMPLE DATA FILE
Simple files. In a non-DBMS approach, data is often stored in files that are hard to read. To correctly retrieve the data, you need to find the file definition that is probably stored in an application program. If one program is changed, all other programs that use the file will need to be altered.

> Jones John 223452351 Main Street Smith Abdul 987635323 Elm Street Markan Martha 151257362 Oak Street Stein Joshua 736346542 East Way
> . . .

**FIGURE 5.5**
PROGRAMMING DIFFICULTIES
Significant problems arise in a programming environment when multiple programs try to share the same data files. The problem is multiplied when there are thousands of programs and data files.

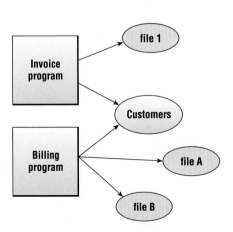

file, but it means spending several hours searching through every program to see whether it uses the customer file. Third, she can copy the customer file and modify it for the billing program. That way the billing program will be able to finish tonight and the other programs will not be affected. Of course it means creating duplicate data, but someone else can solve that problem later.

## The Database Management Approach

### Focus on Data

The database management approach is fundamentally different from the older programming methods. As noted in Figure 5.6, the most important aspect is the data, not the programs. The problems that were created with the old methods are avoided by focusing our attention on the data. Whenever someone needs a computer application, the first step is to identify the data that will be needed. Then a database management system is used to store the data. It takes care of storing the raw data, as well as information about that data. Everything you want to know is stored within the DBMS, not in an application program. This situation is illustrated in Figure 5.7. The goal of the DBMS approach is to collect accurate data and make it available to users. The system should also minimize unnecessary duplication of data.

### Data Independence

Defining the data separately from the programs is called **data independence.** The main advantage is that it is possible to change the data without having to change the programs. For instance, you might want to add a second phone number to the customer data. With a DBMS, you can make this change, and it will not affect any of the existing programs. Similarly, the reports can be modified without having to change the data. That means when the programmer is called in at 3 A.M., she only has to change one program. All the other programs will be unaffected. Besides making the programmer's life easier, the database is more likely to be accurate and there will be less duplication of data.

Data independence means that the data and programs are separate, which makes it possible to alter the database tables as needed, without destroying the programs. As the business grows, you might decide to collect additional data, such as keeping track of sales

**FIGURE 5.6**
DBMS AND PROGRAM/FILE COMPARISON
The database management approach has many advantages. The ability to separate the data from programming is an especially powerful advantage. It means that programs can be altered without changing the data. Similarly, new data attributes can be added without affecting existing programs. The DBMS also provides powerful development tools like report writers and input screens that make it easy to rapidly generate applications.

| DBMS Advantages | Program/File Advantages |
|---|---|
| Focus on data<br>*Data is crucial, programs change* | Existing MIS knowledge |
| Data independence<br>*Ability to change programs and data* | Support for legacy data |
| Data integrity<br>*Accuracy, time, concurrency, security* | High-speed code for some applications; can run on existing/older hardware |
| Speed of development<br>*Report writers, input forms, data manipulation* | |
| Flexibility and queries<br>*User control without programs* | |

**FIGURE 5.7**
DBMS APPROACH
The database management system controls all access to the data. Programs and queries are controlled by the DBMS. Security, consistency, and integrity rules are always maintained by the DBMS.

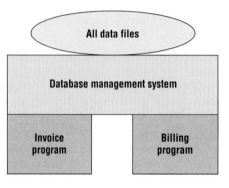

by salesperson or by sales route. As the company expands and changes, the underlying tables can be expanded and new tables can be added—without interfering with the existing tables or current programs. Just be careful to avoid deleting tables or removing entire columns. Of course, as the business changes, managers will undoubtedly want to modify the reports to add the new information.

### Data Integrity

As discussed in Chapter 4, data integrity is an important consideration in designing and maintaining databases. Data integrity means that the database holds accurate, up-to-date data. If there are business limits on certain values, the database should force the data entry to abide by those rules. For example, prices will always be positive numbers. Another integrity concept is the importance of identifying missing (null) data. Computations should be able to skip missing data. From a manager's viewpoint, an important integrity design element is naming columns carefully. The columns should have names and descriptions so that the users understand what is stored in the database. If a column is simply labeled *Revenue,* users might wonder if that means revenue from all products, all divisions, the current year, or perhaps just monthly totals. All of this information is stored with the database in the data dictionary.

An important component of database integrity is that the data needs to be consistent. For example, consider a table that describes products for sale. Perhaps the products are grouped into categories (cleaning supplies, paper goods, clothing, etc.). Each item belongs to only one category. What happens if the categories are not entered consistently? The *Cleaning Supplies* category might be entered as just *Cleaning,* or maybe as *Clean Supplies,* or even *Cl Sup.* These variations in the data make it difficult to search the table based on that category because the user would have to know all of the variations. A good DBMS supports rules that can be used to minimize these problems. However, when dealing with databases, it is good practice to be careful when you enter data to ensure that your entries are consistent.

Consider the problems faced by the Central Intelligence Agency (CIA). Agents collect and store data on thousands of variables for hundreds of countries. Plus, they search large blocks of textual material, which causes many problems. Different words can be used to describe the same concepts; the same word can have different meanings; and words can be misspelled. These inconsistencies make it difficult to search the database. Therefore, the CIA database tools have to be powerful and capable of finding matches based on inconsistent and incomplete data. Chapter 10 illustrates other tools available that the CIA uses to overcome these problems.

### Speed of Development

It is possible to create an entire database application without having to write a single line of traditional programming code. As a result, an application can be built in a fraction of the time it would take to create it by writing COBOL programs. Studies indicate that most systems can be created 10 times faster using a DBMS—if the data already exists in the database. As the commercial database products (such as Oracle, Ingres, Informix, and DB2) continue to add features, they can be used to solve even more complex problems.

Keep in mind that it is possible to use traditional programming tools (such as COBOL) in conjunction with the DBMS. If complex reports or complicated calculations are involved, it is sometimes easier to use a traditional programming language. These programs retrieve the base data from the DBMS and print their own reports or store computed values in the database for later use.

Recall that one of the most important steps of developing a solution is to break the problem into smaller pieces. One major piece of any problem is the data. A DBMS makes this portion of the problem easier to solve. By putting the DBMS in charge of maintaining the data, keeping track of security, automatically supporting multiple users, and printing reports, the developer can concentrate on solving the specific business problems. By starting from scratch with COBOL, each of these features would have to be rewritten for every application that was designed, which would be expensive.

### Control Over Output

Another strong advantage of database management systems is their ability to provide many different views of the output. In fact, a primary objective of the relational database approach is to store the data so that users can retrieve it any way they need. The other feature of databases is that they are designed to make it easy to combine related data. An older programming/file approach generally limits the user to using data in only one way.

With a DBMS, output can be created from report writers, which make it easy to format the data; some systems even draw graphs. The other common method of retrieving data is to use a query language such as **query by example (QBE)** or **SQL.** Queries enable managers to search for answers to questions without using a programmer to write special programs.

**QUERIES**     Most of the time, managers will be dealing with databases that have been created by someone else. You will need to learn how to retrieve data to answer questions. It might be nice to be able to ask questions in a natural language (such as English), but it turns out to be hard to make computers understand these questions, and you might not always be certain that the answer is what you asked for. A DBMS provides at least one method of asking questions and retrieving data. Two common methods are QBE and SQL. SQL is an international standard method for retrieving data from database management systems. It is supported by most of the major commercial relational database management systems. By the way, according to the most recent definition, the name SQL is just three letters and not an acronym. *QBE* stands for query by example and is a visual method of examining data stored in a relational database. You ask questions and examine the data by pointing to tables on the screen and filling in templates. Queries can only answer questions for which you have collected the appropriate data.

Regardless of the method used to look up information in a database, there are four basic questions you will answer, as listed in Figure 5.8. It does not matter in which order you think of the questions. With some methods (such as QBE), it is easier to choose the tables first. With other methods (such as SQL), it is sometimes easier to choose the output first. In many cases, you will switch back and forth among the four questions until you have all of the components you need. As you learn more about databases, keep these four questions handy and write down your answers before you attempt to create the query on the DBMS.

## Single-Table Queries

Consider a simple customer table, that contains columns for CustomerID, Name, Phone, Address, City, State, and AccountBalance. Each customer is assigned a unique number that will be used as a primary key. The AccountBalance is the amount of money the customer currently owes to our company. The table with some sample data is shown in Figure 5.9.

**FIGURE 5.8**
FOUR QUESTIONS TO CREATE A QUERY
To create a database query, you will always have to answer these four questions. In many cases, there will be only one table (or view), so the second and last questions are easy.

- What output do you want to see?
- What tables are involved?
- What do you already know (or what constraints are given)?
- How are the tables joined together?

**FIGURE 5.9**
A SAMPLE TABLE FOR CUSTOMER DATA
CustomerID (abbreviated to CustID) is the primary key and is used to uniquely identify each customer.

| CustID | Name | Phone | Address | City | State | AccountBalance |
|--------|------|-------|---------|------|-------|----------------|
| 12345 | Jones | 312-555-1234 | 123 Main | Chicago | IL | 197.54 |
| 23587 | Smitz | 206-656-7763 | 876 Oak | Seattle | WA | 353.76 |
| 87535 | James | 305-777-2235 | 753 Elm | Miami | FL | 255.90 |

## Query by Example

Query-by-example systems that were designed for graphical user interfaces (GUIs) are especially easy to use. Microsoft's Access illustrates a common approach. The basic mechanism is to make selections on the screen—typically by pointing to them with a mouse. You then fill out a template like the one shown in Figure 5.10.

With a QBE approach, you will first be asked to choose the table that contains the data you want to see. You will be given a list of tables in the database and you select the one you need. Once you have selected the table, you choose the columns that you want to display in the result. You use the QBE screen to specify totals, sort the results, and place restraints (criteria) on the data.

Most of the time, you will want to see only some of the rows of data. For instance, you want a list of customers who owe you the most money. You decide to restrict the listing to customers who have account balances greater than $200. With QBE, you enter the appropriate restriction in the column as shown in Figure 5.11. You can specify other conditions for the other columns. Placing them on the same row means they will be interpreted as AND conditions. If conditions are placed on separate rows, results will be computed for rows that match at least one of the criteria (OR condition). Figure 5.11 shows the QBE screen, which tells the DBMS to display the ID, City, and AccountBalance for customers who live in Denver and have account balances of more than $200.

If you are searching a text column, you might want to look for a single word or part of a word in a sentence. There is a pattern-matching command called LIKE that enables you to search for parts of text. For example, to assign customer accounts alphabetically to your salespeople, you might need a list of customers whose names start with the letter *S*. In the name column, you would enter the constraint: LIKE "S*". The asterisk (*) will match any characters that follow the letter *S*. You also can use a question mark (?) wildcard character to match exactly one character. Note that some database systems use the SQL standard percent sign (%) and underscore (_) instead of * and ?.

Another useful condition is the BETWEEN statement. If you have a table of orders and want to get a list of orders placed in June and July, you can enter the condition for sales_date: BETWEEN #6/1/99# and #7/31/99#.

There is one additional feature of relational databases that you will find useful. In many cases, data will be missing from your database. Perhaps you do not have the phone numbers of all of your customers. Or, maybe the marketing department has not yet set a price for a new product. Missing data is represented by the NULL value in relational databases. So if you want a list of all the customers where you do not know their phone numbers, you can enter the condition for the phone column: IS NULL.

**FIGURE 5.10**

**QUERY BY EXAMPLE FOR THE CUSTOMER TABLE**

Checking the Show box ensures that the column will be displayed when the query is run. Conditions are entered in the Criteria row. Conditions entered on the same row are connected by an "And" clause. Conditions on separate rows are combined with an "Or" clause.

| Field: | CustomerID | Name | Phone | Address | City | State | AccountBalance |
|---|---|---|---|---|---|---|---|
| Total: | | | | | | | |
| Sort: | | | | | | | |
| Show: | [X] | [X] | [X] | [X] | [X] | [X] | [X] |
| Criteria: | | | | | | | > 200 |
| Or: | | | | | | | |

**FIGURE 5.11**

QUERY BY EXAMPLE QUERY

List the customers from Denver with an AccountBalance of more than $200. Results of the query can be sorted in Ascending or Descending order. Multiple levels of sorts are created by selecting additional columns. You will use multiple column sorts when the first column contains several identical values. For example, sort by City, Name.

| Field: | CustomerID | Name | Phone | Address | City | State | AccountBalance |
|---|---|---|---|---|---|---|---|
| Total: | | | | | | | |
| Sort: | Ascending | | | | | | |
| Show: | [X] | ☐ | ☐ | ☐ | [X] | ☐ | [X] |
| Criteria: | | | | | Denver | | > 200 |
| Or: | | | | | | | |

## SQL

Another method of retrieving data from a DBMS is with the query language SQL. Although some people find SQL more difficult to learn, it has two advantages. First, it is a standard language that is supported by many different database systems, so the commands will work the same in many situations. Second, it is easier to read than QBE, so it is easier for your colleagues to understand your queries.

SQL is a moderately complex language. There are only a few major commands in SQL, but each command can have several components. We will use only a few simple SQL statements. You can take a database class to learn more SQL details. We will start by looking at data in a single table, to introduce the SELECT statement. Then you will learn how to combine data from several tables.

The standard command for retrieving data in SQL is SELECT. To be clear, we will write SQL command words in uppercase, but you can type them into the computer as lowercase. The simple form of the command is shown in Figure 5.12. The four parts are written on separate lines here to make the command easier to read.

The first step is to decide which columns you want to see. These columns can be listed in whatever order you want. The column names should be separated by commas. If you want to see all the columns, you can use the keyword ALL or an asterisk (*). Next, you need to know the name of the table. The SQL command to retrieve all of the customer data is SELECT * FROM Customers. The result can be sorted by adding the ORDER BY clause. For example, SELECT * FROM customers ORDER BY City.

To get a list of customers who live in Atlanta with account balances greater than $200, you need to add a WHERE clause. The command becomes SELECT * FROM Customers WHERE (AccountBalance > 200) and (City = "Atlanta"). Notice the similarity to the QBE command. Of course, with SQL, you need to remember (and type in) the names of the tables and columns. NULL values and BETWEEN commands are also available in SQL.

## Computations

Many business questions involve totals or other calculations. All database systems have some mechanism to perform simple calculations. However, these facilities are not as complex as those available in spreadsheets. On the other hand, the database versions are generally easier to use and can operate on millions of rows of data. Typical functions are listed in Figure 5.13.

**FIGURE 5.12**
The SQL SELECT command is used to retrieve and display data. It is the foundation of many of the other SQL commands.

| | |
|---|---|
| **SELECT** | columns |
| **FROM** | tables |
| **WHERE** | conditions |
| **JOIN** | matching columns |
| **ORDER BY** | column {ASC│DESC} |

**FIGURE 5.13**
DATABASE CALCULATIONS
QBE and SQL can both perform calculations on the data. In addition to these aggregation functions, new columns can be created with standard algebraic operators (+ − * /).

| | |
|---|---|
| SUM | total value of items |
| AVG | average of values |
| MIN | minimum value |
| MAX | maximum value |
| COUNT | number of rows |
| STDEV | standard deviation |
| VAR | variance of items |

**FIGURE 5.14**
Query by example overall AccountBalance average for the Customer table. This query counts the number of rows (CustomerID) and computes the overall average of the account balance.

| Field: | CustomerID | Name | Phone | Address | City | State | AccountBalance |
|---|---|---|---|---|---|---|---|
| Total: | Count | | | | | | Avg |
| Sort: | | | | | | | |
| Show: | X | ☐ | ☐ | ☐ | ☐ | ☐ | X |
| Criteria: | | | | | | | |
| Or: | | | | | | | |

## Query by Example

Although most database management systems provide a means to compute totals and averages, there is no standard method for entering the commands. Typically, the commands are displayed on a menu. Access uses an extended grid, which is shown in Figure 5.14. You point to the row you want to calculate and type in the desired function. The example shows how to get the number of customers and the average account balance.

**FIGURE 5.15**
QBE AccountBalance average for Atlanta customers for the Customer table. This query computes the average account balance for those customers living in Atlanta.

| Field: | CustomerID | Name | Phone | Address | City | State | AccountBalance |
|---|---|---|---|---|---|---|---|
| Total: | count | | | | where | | Avg |
| Sort: | | | | | | | |
| Show: | X | ☐ | ☐ | ☐ | X | ☐ | X |
| Criteria: | | | | | Atlanta | | |
| Or: | | | | | | | |

**FIGURE 5.16**
SUBTOTAL CALCULATIONS
One powerful capability of query systems is the ability to compute summary statistics for subsets (groups) of data. This query computes the average account balance for customers and lists the results for each city in the database.

| Field: | CustomerID | Name | Phone | Address | City | State | AccountBalance |
|---|---|---|---|---|---|---|---|
| Total: | | | | | Group By | | Avg |
| Sort: | | | | | | | |
| Show: | ☐ | ☐ | ☐ | ☐ | X | ☐ | X |
| Criteria: | | | | | | | |
| Or: | | | | | | | |

Calculations are generally combined with the selection criteria. For instance, you might want the average account balance for all customers who live in Atlanta. The QBE screen for this question is displayed in Figure 5.15. The only change you have to make is to type *Atlanta* into the city column. Combining selection clauses with calculations enables you to answer many different questions.

Another useful feature is the ability to divide the rows into groups and get subtotals or other calculations for each group. If you know there are 10 cities in the database, you could run the average account balance query 10 different times to get the values for each city. An easier method is to use the GROUP BY option and run the query once. This time, instead of specifying the city, you indicate that cities are to be treated as groups. Then the DBMS will find the average account balance for each city. You do not even have to know which cities are in the database. The group by method used by Access is shown in Figure 5.16.

## SQL

SQL can also perform simple calculations. If you have columns for Price and QuantitySold, the value of items sold can be found by computing SELECT Price * QuantitySold. The standard functions listed in Figure 5.13 are available. To compute the total of the accounts, you would enter SELECT AVG(AccountBalance) FROM Customers.

The group by clause is also available. The command becomes SELECT AVG(AccountBalance) FROM Customers GROUP BY City. Although it might be more difficult to remember the command and the column names, using SQL has two advantages over QBE. First, SQL is a defined standard. The commands you learn for one DBMS will generally work the same on another DBMS. Second, SQL statements are sometimes easier to read. Some QBE commands are not easy to understand, especially if selection criteria are connected by AND or OR commands displayed on separate lines. Many QBE systems

**FIGURE 5.17**

MULTIPLE TABLES
The true power of a database lies in the ability to combine data from multiple tables. Actual databases can have hundreds or thousands of related tables. Notice that each table is related to another table through matching columns. You should be able to draw lines between column labels that will connect each of the tables.

**Customer**

| C# | Name | Phone | City | Acct |
|---|---|---|---|---|
| 12345 | Jones | 312-555-1234 | Chicago | 197.54 |
| 29587 | Smitz | 206-676-7763 | Seattle | 353.76 |
| 87535 | James | 305-777-2235 | Miami | 255.93 |
| 44453 | Kolke | 303-888-8876 | Denver | 863.39 |
| 28764 | Adamz | 602-999-2539 | Phoenix | 526.76 |

**Orders**

| O# | C# | S# | ODate | Amount |
|---|---|---|---|---|
| 117 | 12345 | 887 | 03-03-99 | 57.92 |
| 125 | 87535 | 663 | 04-04-99 | 123.54 |
| 157 | 12345 | 554 | 04-09-99 | 297.89 |
| 169 | 29587 | 255 | 05-06-99 | 89.93 |
| 178 | 44453 | 663 | 05-01-99 | 154.39 |
| 188 | 29587 | 554 | 05-08-99 | 325.46 |
| 201 | 12345 | 887 | 05-23-99 | 193.58 |
| 211 | 44453 | 255 | 06-09-99 | 201.39 |
| 213 | 44453 | 255 | 06-09-99 | 154.15 |
| 215 | 87535 | 887 | 06-09-99 | 563.27 |
| 280 | 28764 | 663 | 06-27-99 | 255.32 |

**Salespeople**

| S# | Name | YearHired | Phone | Commission |
|---|---|---|---|---|
| 255 | West | 1975 | 213-333-2345 | 5% |
| 452 | Zeke | 1994 | 213-343-5553 | 3% |
| 554 | Jabbar | 1991 | 213-534-8876 | 4% |
| 663 | Bird | 1993 | 213-225-3335 | 4% |
| 887 | Johnson | 1992 | 213-887-6635 | 4% |

**ItemsSold**

| O# | Item# | Quantity |
|---|---|---|
| 117 | 1154 | 2 |
| 117 | 7653 | 4 |
| 117 | 3342 | 1 |
| 125 | 8763 | 3 |
| 125 | 1154 | 4 |
| 157 | 7653 | 2 |
| 169 | 3342 | 1 |
| 169 | 9987 | 5 |
| 178 | 2254 | 1 |

**Items**

| Item# | Description | Price |
|---|---|---|
| 1154 | Corn Broom | 1.00 |
| 2254 | Blue Jeans | 12.00 |
| 3342 | Paper towels 3 rolls | 1.00 |
| 7653 | Laundry Detergent | 2.00 |
| 8763 | Men's Boots | 15.00 |
| 9987 | Candy Popcorn | 0.50 |

automatically build the corresponding SQL statement for you. It is a good idea to check this statement to make sure you placed the conditions correctly on the form.

## Joining Multiple Tables

The true strength of a database management system lies in its ability to combine data from several tables. Part of the Customer table is shown in Figure 5.17, with additional tables that show a list of orders placed by those customers and the salespeople involved.

Notice that the tables were designed so they can be connected. For example, the Orders table can be connected to the Customers table by matching the customer number (C#). The Orders table can be matched to the Salespeople table through the salesperson number (S#). Once you have joined the tables together, the database system retrieves and displays the data as if it were stored in one table.

The chief advantage to using multiple tables is that you can connect tables that have a one-to-many relationship. For example, each salesperson may be associated with many different orders. Instead of repeating the salesperson information on every order, we only needed to include the salesperson's ID (S#) number. Joining the tables together tells the DBMS to automatically look up the corresponding data from the Salespeople table.

### Query by Example

Most people find that database systems that use graphical QBE commands to join tables together are much easier to use than straight SQL commands. With a DBMS like Access you join the tables together by pointing to the column name in one table and dragging it to the matching column in the other table. As shown in Figure 5.19, the DBMS displays the connection between the two columns. Whenever you want to retrieve data from more than one table, you must first join them together.

## SQL

In SQL, connections between tables are typically made with the INNER JOIN clause in the FROM statement. For example, to join the customers and orders tables by equal customer numbers and get the combined data, use the command SELECT * FROM Customers INNER JOIN Orders ON Customers.C# = Orders.C#

Notice that both tables must be listed in the FROM statement. Always remember that if you list more than one table, the tables must be joined. The dot before the column (C#) separates the table name from the column name (table.column). You can use this form any time you type in a column name, but it is only required when there might be confusion about which table the column is in. In the example, both tables have a column called C#. To keep them straight, we have to specify which table we want to use.

## Examples

We now have the basics to begin asking questions of the data. Start with an easy one. Which customers (C#) have placed orders since June 1, 1999? The query and result are shown in Figure 5.18. Notice that customer number 44453 has placed two orders. Some systems will show you the order number twice; others will automatically delete the duplicates.

It can be difficult to remember each customer's number, so it is better to use the customer name and have the DBMS automatically look up the customer number. This second query is shown in Figure 5.19. Note that the Customer table is joined to the Orders table by the matching values of C#.

Now, try a more complicated query: List the salespeople (sorted alphabetically) with the names of the customers who placed orders with that salesperson. This question sounds difficult, but the command is easy when you join all three tables together. The query and the result are shown in Figure 5.20. Notice there is no entry for the salesperson (Zeke) who has no orders at this point.

**Question:** **Which customers (C#) have placed orders since June 1, 1999?**

**QBE:**

| Field: | C# | ODate | | | | | |
|---|---|---|---|---|---|---|---|
| Total: | | | | | | | |
| Sort: | | | | | | | |
| Show: | [X] | [X] | ☐ | ☐ | ☐ | ☐ | ☐ |
| Criteria: | | > = 6/1/99 | | | | | |
| Or: | | | | | | | |

**SQL:**  SELECT   C#, ODate     **Result:**  44453   6/9/99
       FROM   Orders                   44453   6/9/99
       WHERE   ODate > = 6/1/99      87535   6/9/99
                                   28764   6/27/99

**FIGURE 5.18**
QBE AND SQL
QBE and SQL are based on the same fundamental concepts. You build each query by asking the same four basic questions.

**Question:** What are the names of the customers who placed orders since June 1, 1999?

**FIGURE 5.19**
Multitable queries showing shared columns. Queries that use more than one table are slightly more complex. Because columns can have any name, you must tell the database system how the tables are connected.

**QBE:**

| Customers | Orders |
|-----------|--------|
| C# | O# |
| Name | C# |
| Phone | S# |
| City | ODate |
| AccountBalance | Amount |

| Field: | **Name** | **ODate** | | | | | |
|--------|----------|-----------|--|--|--|--|--|
| Total: | | | | | | | |
| Sort: | | | | | | | |
| Show: | ☒ | ☐ | ☐ | ☐ | ☐ | ☐ | ☐ |
| Criteria: | | > = 6/1/99 | | | | | |
| Or: | | | | | | | |

**SQL:**  SELECT  Name
         FROM    Customers INNER JOIN Orders ON Customers.C# = Orders.C#
         WHERE   ODate > = 6/1/99

**Result:**  Kolke
             James
             Adamz

**Question:** List the salespeople (sorted alphabetically) along with the names of the customers who placed orders with that salesperson.

**FIGURE 5.20**
Multitable queries with several joins. More complicated queries follow the same basic rules. Note that some database management systems can automatically switch displays between QBE and SQL. This feature is useful so that you can check the joins and the criteria to be sure they are being interpreted correctly.

**QBE:**

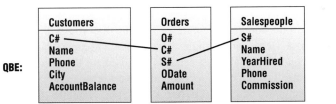

| Customers | Orders | Salespeople |
|-----------|--------|-------------|
| C# | O# | S# |
| Name | C# | Name |
| Phone | S# | YearHired |
| City | ODate | Phone |
| AccountBalance | Amount | Commission |

| Field: | **SalesPeople.Name** | **Customers.Name** | | |
|--------|----------------------|--------------------|--|--|
| Total: | | | | |
| Sort: | | | | |
| Show: | ☒ | ☐ | ☐ | ☐ |
| Criteria: | | | | |
| Or: | | | | |

**SQL:**  SELECT    SalesPeople.Name, Customers.Name
         FROM      SalesPeople INNER JOIN
                   (Orders INNER JOIN Customers ON Customers.C# = Orders.C#)
                   ON SalesPeople.S# = Orders.S#
         ORDER BY  SalesPeople.Name

**Result:**

| | |
|---------|-------|
| Bird | Adamz |
| Bird | Kolke |
| Bird | James |
| Jabbar | Smitz |
| Jabbar | Jones |
| Johnson | James |
| Johnson | Jones |
| West | Kolke |
| West | Smitz |

**FIGURE 5.21**

Computations and subsets. Totals and other computations can be entered on the QBE form. Be careful about the WHERE criteria. In this example, we want the condition to be applied to each data line, so we specify the WHERE label. Some systems might try to apply the condition to the overall total, which would use the SQL HAVING label.

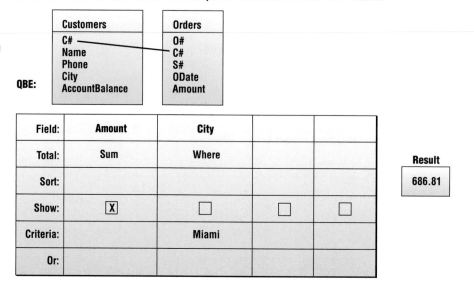

**Question:** What is the total amount of orders placed from customers who live in Miami?

| Field: | Amount | City | | |
|--------|--------|-------|--|--|
| Total: | Sum | Where | | |
| Sort: | | | | |
| Show: | [X] | ☐ | ☐ | ☐ |
| Criteria: | | Miami | | |
| Or: | | | | |

**Result**

686.81

**SQL:**  SELECT   Sum(Amount)
FROM   Customers INNER JOIN Orders ON Customers.C# = Orders.C#
WHERE   City = "Miami"

One more example and you should be ready to work on problems by yourself. Say your firm is thinking about opening a new office in Miami, and your manager wants to know the total amount of orders placed from customers who live in Miami. This command uses the SUM function and is shown in Figure 5.21.

## Views

There is one important feature of queries that you will find useful. Any query can be saved as a **view.** For example, if you have a complex query that you have to run every week, you (or a database specialist) could create the query and save it as a view with its own name. The important point is that the view can now be treated like any other table. In the example, you might define a view that combines the tables for customers, orders, and salespeople, and call it SalesOrders. Then, to get the total sales from customers in Miami, you run the query on the SalesOrders view and you no longer have to worry about joining tables because the query has already performed the step.

The advantage of views is that you can look at the data in different ways without having to duplicate the data. As a manager, you can create complex views so your employees can look up information using much simpler commands. Think of a view as a mirror. If you stand in front of a three-way mirror in a clothing store, you get different views of yourself although there is still only one person.

**DESIGNING A DATABASE**

In any large project, the most important first step is to determine whether the project is going to be economically and technically feasible. At this point, it is also crucial that the top levels of management fully support the project. If there is hesitation on the part of the executives, the rest of the organization will be less likely to cooperate. Also, when the project runs into delays and additional expenses, it will be difficult to obtain the additional support needed to finish the project. The developers of the Sabre reservation system obtained this support by explaining the potential advantages of the system.

An important step in dealing with databases is the initial definition when you decide exactly what columns to put in each table. If it is done correctly, the tables fit together and you can retrieve any combination of data you need. It is also easy to make additions and changes to the tables. On the other hand, if the tables are not defined correctly, you will end up with a mess. You will not be able to collect and store some of the data you need. You will have trouble getting answers to some types of questions. It can be time-consuming to redefine tables and reports to fix the problems. Because defining tables is so important, everyone who uses a database should have some idea of what is involved. However, to become an expert you really need to take a database management course.

## Data Definition

The first step in defining tables is to identify the information that you will need to make your decisions. You can begin by collecting or designing the input forms and reports that will be used. Then the data items displayed on these forms and reports will be organized into tables.

There are some rules that each table must obey. First, every table must have a primary key, which is one or more columns that uniquely identify each row. Often we create an ID number (such as an order number) to use as a short primary key. Improperly chosen database keys can result in costly errors.

The second rule is there can be only one value stored in each cell. For example, if there is a column for the phone number, it cannot hold a home phone number and a business phone number at the same time. In this case, the solution is to create two columns: Home-Phone and WorkPhone. But what if there are more phone numbers, such as a fax number or an answering service number? How many phone number columns should we create? If most people have only one phone number, it would be a waste of space to create columns for five phone numbers. This problem is an example of repeating columns. If you do not know how many columns to use, you should create a new table to hold those columns. In this example, you could have a phone table, like the one shown in Figure 5.22. Notice that the columns for the primary key are underlined and must include the original customer number (C#). There is no wasted space if a customer does not have a certain type of phone number. For example, there is no entry for a business phone for customer number 44.

---

### Internationalization: Zip Codes

Databases often contain addresses (of customers, suppliers, employees, etc.) that typically use zip codes. In the United States, zip codes typically consist of five digits, so it is tempting to set up a Zip-code column that restricts input to five integers. However, bulk mail is often cheaper if it utilizes nine-digit zip codes (zip + 4).

Even more importantly, if your addresses might someday include international data, you have to be more careful in column restrictions. For instance, Canadian and British postal codes include alphabetic characters in the middle of the code. Some areas (such as Hong Kong) do not use any postal codes.

Similarly, when you set up databases that include phone numbers, be sure to allocate enough space for area codes. If international phone numbers will be listed, you need to add three extra digits on the front for the international country code.

**FIGURE 5.22**

TABLE DEFINITION
For the database
approach to work
correctly, all of the
tables must be
carefully defined. A
technique known as
normalization is used
to properly define the
tables. In this example,
customers might have
many different types of
phone numbers. We
say that phone number
is a repeating attribute.
Repeating attributes
must be converted into
rows in a new table.
Hence we split the
initial table into two
tables: Customers and
Phones.

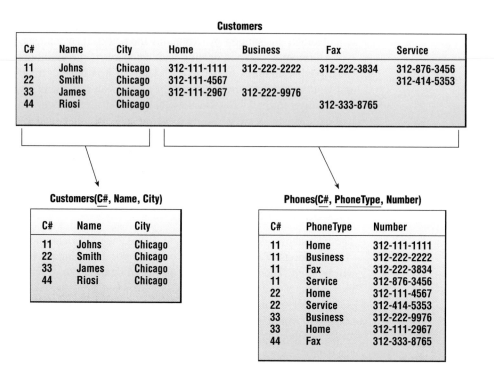

**Customers**

| C# | Name | City | Home | Business | Fax | Service |
|----|------|------|------|----------|-----|---------|
| 11 | Johns | Chicago | 312-111-1111 | 312-222-2222 | 312-222-3834 | 312-876-3456 |
| 22 | Smith | Chicago | 312-111-4567 | | | 312-414-5353 |
| 33 | James | Chicago | 312-111-2967 | 312-222-9976 | | |
| 44 | Riosi | Chicago | | | 312-333-8765 | |

**Customers(C#, Name, City)**

| C# | Name | City |
|----|------|------|
| 11 | Johns | Chicago |
| 22 | Smith | Chicago |
| 33 | James | Chicago |
| 44 | Riosi | Chicago |

**Phones(C#, PhoneType, Number)**

| C# | PhoneType | Number |
|----|-----------|--------|
| 11 | Home | 312-111-1111 |
| 11 | Business | 312-222-2222 |
| 11 | Fax | 312-222-3834 |
| 11 | Service | 312-876-3456 |
| 22 | Home | 312-111-4567 |
| 22 | Service | 312-414-5353 |
| 33 | Business | 312-222-9976 |
| 33 | Home | 312-111-2967 |
| 44 | Fax | 312-333-8765 |

The process of defining tables correctly is called data **normalization.** You can learn more about normalization in a database course. The first steps of normalization are described in the appendix. If you want a hint, an important rule is that "every nonkey column must depend on the whole key and nothing but the key." Roughly, it means that each table should refer to only one object or concept. You should be able to give each table a name that reflects what is stored in the table. If you have trouble coming up with a simple name, the table might not be defined correctly, and you might have to split it into multiple, simpler tables. An introduction to the process of normalization is presented in the appendix to this chapter.

## Data Input Screens

Rarely is data entered directly into the database's tables. Instead, input forms are used to enter some data automatically and to present a screen that is easier for users to understand. It is common to use colors and boxes to make the screen easier to read. Input screens can be used to perform calculations (such as taxes). Longer descriptions and help screens can be included to make it easier for the user to remember what goes in each column. A sample form is shown in Figure 5.23.

Many times, input screens look like existing paper forms. Consider a typical order form, which first collects customer information such as name and address. It also contains lines for items ordered, descriptions, and prices. These are usually followed by subtotals and totals. If these forms exist on paper, it is easy to create them as a DBMS input screen. If you are creating a completely new form, it helps to draw it on paper first to get a feel for what you want it to look like.

Most input forms begin as a screen that is empty except for a menu line or some other help message. Three types of information can be placed on an input screen: (1) sim-

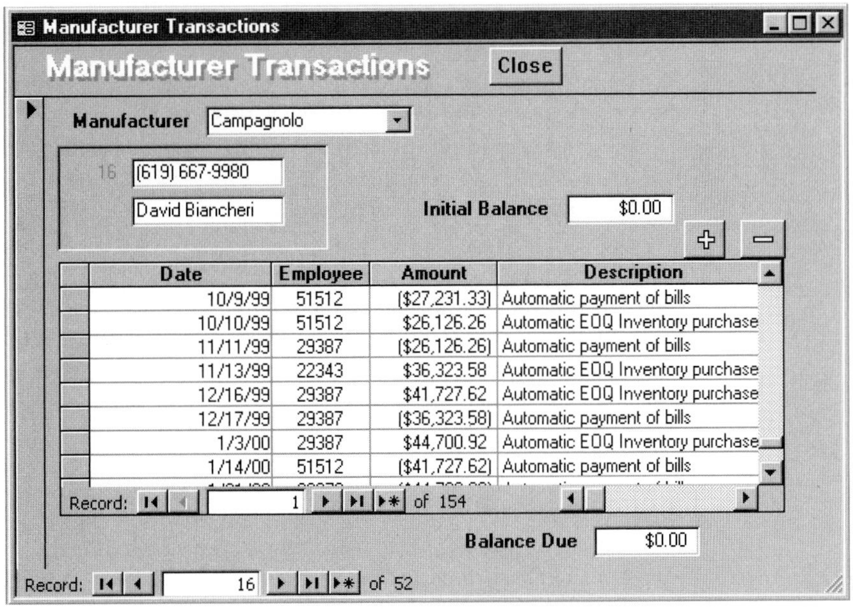

**FIGURE 5.23**

DBMS INPUT FORMS
Input forms are used to
collect data from the
user and perform basic
computations.
Subforms or scrolling
regions are used when
there is a one-to-many
relationship.

ple text, (2) input blanks, or (3) data retrieved from the database. A Windows-based DBMS can also include pictures, graphs, sound, and video.

Paper forms have labels to tell the user what is supposed to be entered into each blank. For instance, many paper forms ask for a name: NAME _____. The label (NAME) tells you what you are supposed to enter on the blank line. A DBMS input form works much the same way. The first step is to type in the various labels. Move the cursor to a spot on the screen and type in a label or sentence that will tell the user what needs to be entered.

Most database systems automatically enter some types of data, such as the current date. If necessary, users can change the date, but it saves time by enabling them to press ENTER to accept the displayed value. The same situation holds for sequential items like order numbers, where the DBMS can automatically generate each unique order number.

After you have typed in the basic labels, the next step is to add the data-entry boxes. Just as you would type a blank line on a paper form, you need to tell the DBMS exactly what data will be entered by the user. For instance, move the screen cursor to a position next to the Date label, then tell the DBMS to enter data at that point. You will specify the name of the column where the data will be stored. You can also specify default values. A **default value** is a value that is automatically displayed by the computer. For the case of the date, the DBMS will let you enter a name like Date() that will display the current date.

When a DBMS prints out data, it can be formatted in different ways. You can control the way the data is displayed by using a format command. A date might be displayed as 10/24/1999 by entering the format MM/DD/YYYY. There are several common date formats; most firms tend to use one standard format. Note that many European firms use a format that is different from the common ones used in the United States.

The next section of the order form contains basic customer information. This data is stored in the Customer table, not the Orders table. When you select the Orders table, you might have to indicate that the Orders and Customer tables are connected to each other by the phone number. Now, place the text labels on the screen (customer name, address, etc.). Then, place a data entry box after each label.

Next, you can add the Sales table; it is connected to the Orders table by the order number. Type in the column names for Item#, Description, Price, and Quantity. The DBMS input form will define this part of the table as a **scrolling region** or subform. To users, this subform will behave somewhat like a spreadsheet. They can see several rows at a time, and keys (or the mouse) will move the screen cursor up and down as users enter data into any row.

The only items entered in the sales table are the Item# and the Quantity ordered. The Description and Price can be found by creating a *look-up* in the items table. If the clerk using this screen types in the item number, the description and price will appear. With a good DBMS, it is possible to define a *pop-up form* or *combo box* in case the clerk does not know the number. This way, by pressing a certain key, a table listing each Item# and Description will be displayed in a window on the screen. The clerk can then scroll through the list to find the item.

## Reports

Most of the time, the data listed in one table is not complete enough to help managers make decisions. For example, a listing of a Sales table might provide only phone numbers, item numbers, and the quantity ordered. A more useful report would print sales grouped by customer. It would also compute total sales for each customer. Because this report relies on data from several tables, it is best to base the report on a view.

The view for the sales report example needs four tables. An OrderReport view is created that joins the Customer table to Orders by C#, Orders to ItemSold by O#, and ItemsSold to Items by Item#. The DBMS will have a "create report" option to create the sales report. The report will be based on the OrderReport view. The report writer consists of a blank screen. You can put simple text statements anywhere on the page. You also can place data values on the page, and you can compute totals and make other calculations.

Most reports can be broken into categories. For example, there might be report titles that appear only at the front of the report (such as cover pages). Other information, such as the report title, date, and column labels, will be repeated at the top of each page. All of these items are called **page headers.** Similarly, there can be **page footers** at the bottom of each page. Reports may also contain group **breaks.** For instance, the sales report needs subtotals for each customer, so you need to break the report into subsections for each customer. Generally, you can specify several levels of breaks. For instance, you might break each customer order into totals by date. Each break can have a *break header,* a **detail section,** and a *break footer.* In the example shown in Figure 5.23, the customer name is printed on the break header. There is a detail line that lists the item information. The subtotals are displayed on the break footers. The report design or layout is illustrated in Figure 5.24. The report with sample data is printed in Figure 5.25.

To create this report, you first tell the DBMS that the report will contain one break based on customer phone number. You also define the variable *subtot,* which is price multiplied by quantity. Now you move the cursor to the top of the screen and type in the titles for the top of the page. Then place each column and variable on the report. You can format each item to make it look better. For example, you might want to format dates as MM/DD/YYYY so that all four digits of the year are displayed. Similarly, you can add dollar signs to the subtotals and totals.

When you have finished creating the report, you can print it. When you print this report, it should be sorted by customer name. The DBMS will also enable you to print the report so that it contains data just for one month. Notice that only five or six lines are needed to create a complex report. Without the DBMS report writer, it would take a programmer several hours to create this report, and it would be much harder to make changes to it in the future.

## Putting It Together with Menus

If you are creating a database for yourself with just a couple of input screens and reports, you can probably quit at this point. On the other hand, for more complex databases or for projects other people will use, it would be wise to make the system easier to use. *Application generators* are tools that enable you to combine the various features into a single application. The resulting application can be used by selecting choices from a menu, much like users do with commercial software. The important design feature is that you can create the entire application without writing any programming commands.

Consider a simple example. As a manager, you need a sales report printed every day that shows the best-selling items. Every week you want a list of total sales for each employee to bring to your sales meetings. You also send letters to your best customers every month offering them additional discounts. You want to put your secretary in charge of printing these reports, but you do not have time to explain all the details about how to use the database program. Instead, you create a simple menu that lists each report. The secretary chooses the desired report from the list. Some reports might ask questions, such as which week to use. The secretary enters the answers and the report is printed.

The first step in creating an application is to think about the people who will use it. How do they do their jobs? How do the database inputs and reports fit into their job? The goal is to devise a menu system that reflects the way they work. Two examples of a first menu are shown in Figure 5.26. Which menu is easier for a clerk to understand? The one that best relates to the job. Once you understand the basic tasks, write down a set of related menus. Some menu options will call up other menus. Some will print reports; others will activate the input screens you created.

Once you know how you want the menu structure to appear, you fill in the menu templates in the application generator. To create a menu, you type in a title and fill in the choices. Then you assign an action to each choice. Usually you just pick from a list of actions and type in specific data such as the name of the report and how you want it sorted. When you are finished, the application generator creates the application.

**FIGURE 5.25**
SAMPLE REPORT
Reports are often
printed by groups or
breaks with subtotals
for each group. With
a report writer, the
layout, typefaces, and
computations are easy
to change.

## Orders by Customers

| Name | ODate | Description | Price | Quantity | Extended |
|------|-------|-------------|-------|----------|----------|
| **Adamz** | | | | | |
| | 5/6/99 | Corn Broom | $1.00 | 2 | $2.00 |
| | 6/27/99 | Blue Jeans | $12.00 | 1 | $12.00 |
| | 6/27/99 | Paper Towels, 3 rolls | $1.00 | 3 | $3.00 |
| | | | | | **$17.00** |
| **James** | | | | | |
| | 4/4/99 | Corn Broom | $1.00 | 4 | $4.00 |
| | 4/4/99 | Men's Boots | $15.00 | 3 | $45.00 |
| | 6/9/99 | Blue Jeans | $12.00 | 1 | $12.00 |
| | 6/9/99 | Laundry Detergent | $2.00 | 1 | $2.00 |
| | | | | | **$63.00** |
| **Jones** | | | | | |
| | 3/3/99 | Corn Broom | $1.00 | 2 | $2.00 |
| | 3/3/99 | Laundry Detergent | $2.00 | 4 | $8.00 |
| | 3/3/99 | Paper Towels, 3 rolls | $1.00 | 1 | $1.00 |
| | 4/9/99 | Laundry Detergent | $2.00 | 2 | $4.00 |
| | 5/23/99 | Corn Broom | $1.00 | 1 | $1.00 |
| | | | | | **$16.00** |
| **Kolke** | | | | | |
| | 5/1/99 | Blue Jeans | $12.00 | 1 | $12.00 |
| | 6/9/99 | Blue Jeans | $12.00 | 1 | $12.00 |
| | 6/9/99 | Candy Popcorn | $0.50 | 5 | $2.50 |
| | 6/9/99 | Paper Towels, 3 rolls | $1.00 | 2 | $2.00 |
| | | | | | **$28.50** |
| **Smitz** | | | | | |
| | 5/6/99 | Candy Popcorn | $0.50 | 5 | $2.50 |
| | 5/6/99 | Paper Towels, 3 rolls | $1.00 | 1 | $1.00 |
| | 5/8/99 | Men's Boots | $15.00 | 1 | $15.00 |
| | 5/8/99 | Paper Towels, 3 rolls | $1.00 | 4 | $4.00 |
| | | | | | **$22.50** |
| | | **Grand Total:** | | | **$147.00** |

**FIGURE 5.26**
DESIGNING MENUS
FOR USERS
Which menu is easier
for a secretary to
understand? When
designing applications,
you should organize
the application to
match the processes
users perform.

| MAIN MENU |
|-----------|
| 1. Setup Choices |
| 2. Data Input |
| 3. Print Reports |
| 4. DOS Utilities |
| 5. Backups |

| CUSTOMER INFORMATION |
|----------------------|
| Daily Sales Report |
| Friday Sales Meeting |
| Monthly Customer Letters |
| |
| Quit |

**DATABASE**
**ADMINISTRATION**

Managing a database can be a complex job. Often there are hundreds of choices that need to be made *when* the database is designed. Someone needs to be in charge of defining the data, making sure that all useful facts are captured, and managing security for this valuable asset. Databases have to be evaluated and fine-tuned on a regular basis. Someone has to keep track of these maintenance changes and decide when major updates should be installed. A **database administrator (DBA)** is usually appointed to manage the databases for the firm. The DBA needs to know the technical details of the DBMS and the computer system. The DBA also needs to understand the business operations of the firm.

The database administrator is responsible for all operations involving the database. These duties include coordinating users and designers, establishing standards, and defining the data characteristics. When new programs are created, the DBA makes sure they are tested and documented. The DBA also schedules backups and recovery, and establishes security controls.

In a few large companies, an additional person known as the *data administrator (DA)* is charged with overseeing all of the data definitions and data standards for the company. In this case, typically several DBAs are used to monitor and control various databases. The DA is responsible for making sure data can be shared throughout the company.

### Standards and Documentation

In any company of moderate size, many different databases will be used by hundreds of workers. These databases were created at different points in time by teams of employees. If there are no standards, each piece will be unique, making it difficult to combine information from multiple databases or tables. The marketing department may refer to *customers,* whereas management calls them *clients*. The DBMS needs to know that both terms refer to the same set of data. Also, someone has to determine the key values for each table. Consider the Customer table. One department might assign identification numbers to each customer. Another department might use customers' phone numbers, and a third department might use the customer names. To prevent confusion and to be able to combine information, it is best for all users to use only one of these methods to identify the customers.

---

**Reality Bytes        5–2    International Trade on the Internet**

For decades, one of the factors in Japan's success as an international economic powerhouse was the "sogo shosha" or trading companies. Itochu is one of them. The company has 7,000 employees in 220 offices worldwide. These employees have knowledge of local cultures, languages, and business practices. That expertise is crucial in building the contacts to establish and expand the business. One question faced by many of these companies is how to take advantage of the Internet without losing their clout. That is, one of the strengths of the Internet is its ability to cut out the middlemen to reduce costs. Itochu faced the problem by creating a separate company, Itochu Internet Corp (IIC), to automate

their contacts. For example, they built a web site to handle orders for the company's Tex-Mart division. The division buys and sells textiles. The web site database enables buyers to specify the desired fabric composition, manufacturing details, and even the specific mill. The initial projections for the division are modest. The anticipated 1997 revenue is less than $1 million which is a minor fraction of Itochu's $18 billion revenue in textiles. However, the web site is expected to cut delivery times to days instead of weeks. More importantly, the online system will provide better information and data analysis. Particularly important is its ability to produce graphs and highlight historical trends in textiles.

There are other standards involved in the database process. It is easier to use a database if all input screens have similar characteristics. For instance, the base screen might use a blue background with white characters. Data that is entered by the user will be displayed in yellow. Similarly, certain function keys may be predefined. ESC might be used to cancel or escape from choices. F1 might be used for help and F3 to display a list of choices. If each application uses keys differently, the user will have a hard time remembering which keys do what with which database.

Likewise, it is helpful to standardize certain aspects of reports. It might be necessary to choose specific typefaces and fonts. Titles could be in an 18 point Helvetica font, whereas the body of reports could be printed in 11 point Palatino. To provide emphasis, subtotals and totals could be printed in boldface, with single and double underlining, respectively.

One of the crucial steps in creating a database is the definition of the data. Many important decisions have to be made at this point. Besides the issues of what to call each item, the DBMS has to be told how to store every item. For instance, are phone numbers stored as 7 digits, or should they be stored as 10 digits, or perhaps stored with the 3-digit international calling code? Postal zip codes pose similar problems. The United States uses either a five digit or nine digit zip code, but is considering adding two more digits. Other countries include alphabetic characters in their codes. Someone has to determine how to store this information in the manner that is best for the company.

There are many other aspects of database design that need standards to make life easier for the users. However, whenever there are standards, there should be a mechanism to change these standards. Technology always changes, so standards that were established five years ago are probably not relevant today. The DBA constantly reviews and updates the standards, and makes sure that employees follow them.

Even though databases are easy to use, they would be confusing if the designers did not document their work. Picture a situation where you want to find information about customers but the designers named the table *Patrons*. You might never find the information without documentation.

Documentation can assume many forms. Most DBMSs allow the designers to add comments to each table and column. This internal documentation can often be searched by the users. Many times it can be printed in different formats so that it can be distributed to users in manuals. Because it is maintained in the database along with the data, it is easy to find. It is also easy for the designers to add these comments as they create or change the database, so the documentation is more likely to be current. It is up to the DBA to ensure that all designers document their work.

## Testing, Backup, and Recovery

One advantage of the DBMS approach is that it provides tools such as report writers and application generators that end users can employ to create their own systems. Although it is easier for users to create these programs than to start from scratch, the programs still need to be tested. Corporate databases are extremely valuable, but only if the information they contain is accurate. It is the responsibility of the DBA to keep the information accurate, which means that all software that changes data must be tested.

Most companies would not survive long if a disaster destroyed their databases. For this reason, all databases need to be backed up on a regular basis. How often this backup occurs depends on the importance and value of the data. It is possible to back up data continuously. With two identical computer systems, a change made to one can be automatically written to the other. If a fire destroys one system, the other one can be used to continue with no loss of information. Obviously, it is expensive to maintain duplicate facilities. Many organizations choose to back up their data less frequently.

The main point of backup and recovery is that someone has to be placed in charge. Especially in small businesses, there is a tendency to assume that someone else is responsible for making backups. Also, remember that at least one current copy of the database must be stored in a different location. A major disaster could easily wipe out everything stored in the same building. There are some private companies that for a fee will hold your backup data in a secure, fireproof building where you can access your data any time of the day.

## Access Controls

Another important task in database administration is the establishment of security safeguards. The DBA has to determine which data needs to be protected. Once basic security conditions are established, the DBA is responsible for monitoring database activity. The DBA tracks security violation attempts and monitors who is using the database. Because there are always changes in employees, removing access for departed employees and entering new access levels and passwords can be a full-time job.

**DATABASE AND SPREADSHEETS**

A common problem faced by computer users is understanding the difference between spreadsheets and databases. As spreadsheets get easier to use and continue to offer new features, it gets more tempting to use the spreadsheet for every job. Although spreadsheets and databases both store data in rows and columns, they are designed to solve different problems. You need to understand the comparative advantages of each tool to use them wisely. As explained in Chapter 7, you might want to combine both tools to solve problems.

## Data Storage versus Calculations

The main purpose of a database is to store different tables containing large amounts of data. The DBMS provides tools to combine the data from these tables. It is possible to perform calculations on the data; however, most calculations apply to sets of data, not just to one item. For example, databases are commonly used to calculate totals. On the other hand, spreadsheets were primarily designed to perform calculations. They are not good at storing large amounts of data, and it is difficult to combine information that is stored in different spreadsheets.

## Illustration

To illustrate the difference between the tools, consider the three tables in Figure 5.27: Customers, Products, and Sales. The Customer table contains typical data such as phone, name, and address. Likewise, the Products table lists product numbers, descriptions, and prices. The Sales table identifies products that were bought by each customer. It holds the customer phone number, a product number, date, and the quantity purchased.

You want to produce a report that lists the customers who spent the most money last month. Producing this list means that you have to look at the Sales table first. Get the product number for each item sold this month. Look up the price in the Products

**FIGURE 5.27**
SAMPLE
COMPARISON
OF SPREADSHEET
AND DBMS

You are given three lists (tables) of data. You are asked to find the best customers (highest sales total). This problem is difficult to solve if you only have a spreadsheet. A DBMS can provide an answer with a single query. Problems that involve combining data from multiple tables are best solved with a database management system.

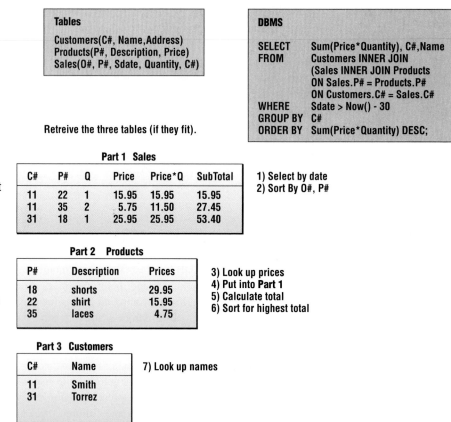

**Tables**

Customers(C#, Name,Address)
Products(P#, Description, Price)
Sales(O#, P#, Sdate, Quantity, C#)

Retreive the three tables (if they fit).

**Part 1  Sales**

| C# | P# | Q | Price | Price*Q | SubTotal |
|----|----|---|-------|---------|----------|
| 11 | 22 | 1 | 15.95 | 15.95 | 15.95 |
| 11 | 35 | 2 | 5.75 | 11.50 | 27.45 |
| 31 | 18 | 1 | 25.95 | 25.95 | 53.40 |

**Part 2   Products**

| P# | Description | Prices |
|----|-------------|--------|
| 18 | shorts | 29.95 |
| 22 | shirt | 15.95 |
| 35 | laces | 4.75 |

**Part 3   Customers**

| C# | Name |
|----|------|
| 11 | Smith |
| 31 | Torrez |

**DBMS**

```
SELECT      Sum(Price*Quantity), C#,Name
FROM        Customers INNER JOIN
            (Sales INNER JOIN Products
            ON Sales.P# = Products.P#
            ON Customers.C# = Sales.C#
WHERE       Sdate > Now() - 30
GROUP BY    C#
ORDER BY    Sum(Price*Quantity) DESC;
```

1) Select by date
2) Sort By O#, P#

3) Look up prices
4) Put into **Part 1**
5) Calculate total
6) Sort for highest total

7) Look up names

table and multiply that price by the quantity sold. This value is then added to the total for the customer. When all the sales have been searched, sort the list by the customer totals. Finally, use the Customer table to look up the names that go with these customer numbers.

For small amounts of data, this problem can be solved using either a database or a spreadsheet; however, the spreadsheet approach is much more difficult. It involves several complicated instructions to combine the information from the three tables. With a good database, this list can be created with one or two statements. Additionally, consider what happens if there is a large amount of data. Perhaps there are thousands of customers, hundreds of products, and thousands of sales per day. It is probably not possible to store each table in a single spreadsheet. Now you have to search even more spreadsheets to combine the information. What happens if you start with a small store, but it expands? With the spreadsheet approach, you have to rewrite the entire system. With the database, you simply add more data. The commands and reports do not change.

On the other hand, if you need to perform complex analyses on the sales data, you might be better off using a spreadsheet. Perhaps you want to examine a statistical moving average and some regression statistics. Then you want to display these projections in a graph. Although it is possible to produce this type of report with a database, the statistics computations might not be available. However, the calculations are relatively easy with a spreadsheet. Because the spreadsheet also can produce the graphs, the entire report can be produced without having to leave the spreadsheet.

## Security and Data Integrity

Another important difference between databases and spreadsheets is that databases have stronger controls for data security and integrity. With most database management systems, users are asked to identify themselves (with usernames and passwords) before they can use the database. The designer can then give each user (or group) access to specific data items. For instance, consider a typical purchasing department. A security problem that has arisen in some companies is that a clerk in the purchasing department might create a fictitious supplier. The clerk then places orders with this company, fakes the receipt of products, and collects the "payment." A DBMS could be used to prevent this problem. Clerks would have the ability to create new purchase orders and correct mistakes in existing orders. However, they would not be given the ability to create new "suppliers." The DBMS would not allow purchases from companies not listed in the supplier table, so this scheme would fail.

Although spreadsheets can be encrypted, you generally are forced to give a user complete access to the spreadsheet. With some simple commands, a user can—accidentally or purposefully—delete entire rows and columns in the spreadsheet. Similarly, it is hard to set integrity constraints in a spreadsheet. What happens if a user accidentally enters a negative number for a sale price? Both of these situations are easy to control with a good DBMS. The designer sets the appropriate conditions, and the DBMS handles the rest.

**COMPLEX DATA TYPES AND OBJECT-ORIENTED DATABASES**

Modern database management systems can deal with data types that are more complex than simple text, dates, and numbers. Today, there are many applications where you might want to store large quantities of text, such as a book or last year's tax report. Similarly, many reports include graphs and pictures.

## Text

One problem that is being faced by many companies today is that the majority of reports are now created on computers. However, they are created on individual personal computers and stored independently in each department. There is a tremendous amount of information and analysis contained in each report. It would be useful if managers could search the old reports by computer and combine information from them to create new reports. Similarly, there is an enormous amount of information published each year that might be useful to have accessible via the computer. Another method to handle searches of large amounts of text is to use an intranet where the information is stored on internally accessible web pages, which are linked and can be indexed by a search engine.

Some databases can now hold entire documents as a single piece of data. Typical search commands enable users to find documents based on keywords or phrases. By storing the text in the database, several people can have access to the data at the same time. By keeping the data in the same place, it is easier to see what reports are available, and making backups is easier because they are maintained by the DBMS.

---

**Reality Bytes    5–3    Natural Language Processing Provides Help to Decipher Vagueness in Words**

Today's corporation faces an avalanche of textual information. Letters, field reports, wire-service stories, memoranda, e-mail messages, faxes, and legal documents flood corporate offices each day from any number of sources. Word processing has helped to save and organize internally generated information on disks. However, finding the information that is needed even when it is stored in a compatible source can present serious problems.

Today major computer companies such as IBM and Digital Equipment Corporation are investing vast resources in trying to discover a process that will enable them to find specific pieces of data among the vast collections of unorganized text.

Database systems enable the computer to process data that fits naturally into lists of structured records. The format enables each item to be stored with an index. Based on location, the database system can quickly find and relate data to other items.

Unfortunately, straight lines of text do not provide such a neat indexing scheme. Sentences and paragraphs convey ideas that make sense to the trained mind but are extremely difficult for the computer to grasp. As a result, textual analysis has been called the next frontier of information processing.

Much of the research in textual analysis has been funded by the U.S. military and intelligence communities. Verity, Inc.'s, workstation-based Topic enables scientists to scan National Science Foundation files on research projects and grants. General Electric uses a GESCAN machine to examine notes on phone calls to a customer hotline and identify patterns in reported problems.

Information Dimensions, Inc., in Columbus, Ohio, has established leadership in large-scale text retrieval. Its Basis software can identify text in which word combinations occur. Verity adds the advantage of weighting keywords by relative importance. Text management systems bring the benefit of collecting large amounts of information without deciding ahead of time how to organize or search it. With the reduction in the cost of storage and the high cost of organizing the data, this presents a more cost-effective way to store data. Money is only spent to access data when the information is needed rather than indexing all the data whether it is needed or not.

## Pictures and Graphs

In many cases it is useful to store pictures and graphs in a DBMS. For instance, some companies store employee photographs in a database. Whenever a security guard brings up an employee record, the person's picture is displayed on the screen for additional verification. Pictures of products can be incorporated into reports to produce custom catalogs or more appealing letters. Engineers store diagrams directly in the database. Whenever they need to make a change to a component, the DBMS can bring up the correct diagram and save the changes so other engineers can see the new version immediately. Along the same lines, databases are beginning to store video clips.

## Objects

There has been a movement to define databases in terms of objects. Objects can be defined by the users to match real-world entities. In some respects, there is little difference between objects and relational tables. However, remember that with objects, not only is the class defined, but so are the commands that work on those objects. For example, an engineer might define a *blueprint* object to hold diagrams. The engineer might define commands to search, add, and subtract blueprint objects. The search command would enable engineers to compare portions of diagrams based on their graphics content. An automobile engineer might ask the computer to find all blueprints that use a particular suspension system—based on how the blueprint is drawn. Similarly, perhaps an ADD

**FIGURE 5.28**

SAMPLE OBJECT DATABASE

Each table represents a separate object, and each object can contain different types of data. The patient data might contain a photograph, and the x-rays can be stored in the online database so they are accessible to several physicians in different locations. The physician comments might be voice recordings.

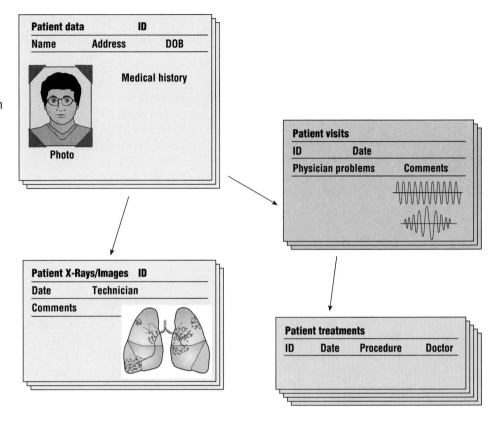

command would take smaller diagrams from different engineers and piece them together to create a complete blueprint. Similarly, as Figure 5.28 shows, a doctor might use an object-oriented database to store information related to patients. Of course, creating these commands is still difficult. In any case, a true object-oriented DBMS allows the user to create databases that closely reflect the way they work, which makes them easier to understand and to use.

The term *object-oriented* means designers create their own objects, along with commands (methods or actions) that affect the objects. Many existing object-oriented databases do not allow relational queries. Instead, they rely on predefined relationships.

**COMMERCIAL DATABASES**

Many types of information are impossible or expensive for individual firms to collect. Governments collect an enormous amount of data from individuals and from companies. There are private research companies that offer detailed data on almost any subject, such as customers, competitors, and international markets. Much of this data is available in commercial databases. You might want to trace the stock prices of six companies during the last five years. You can use your computer to call a computer owned by a commercial data service. Then you search for exactly the data you need and copy (download) it to your computer. Your spreadsheet and graphics software can be used to analyze the data. Several companies specialize in providing business data for computer users. Most of the data is now accessible over the Internet. The private companies generally charge fees for access to the data.

An enormous amount of information is available in commercial databases. Most of the data collected by different government agencies is available on tape, optical disk, and through private companies that maintain commercial databases. For example, demographic

---

**Reality Bytes    5–4    I Know What You Did Last Summer**

GeoCities is one of several Internet companies that provide individuals with free web space. To obtain the web space, you must first fill out a questionnaire providing some personal information. The personal information included education, income, marital status, occupation, and other personal interests. The site is popular, ranking in the top 10 percent of visited sites. GeoCities promised people that they would not release the personal information without permission. In 1998, the FTC accused GeoCities of lying to its users and deliberately releasing the data to advertisers. Jodie Bernstein, director of the FTC's Consumer Protection Bureau notes that "GeoCities misled its customers, both children and adults, by not telling the truth about how it was using their personal information." The FTC was particularly worried about the "GeoKidz Club," where advertisers used contests to collect data from children. GeoCities settled with the FTC by agreeing to alter its privacy statement in order to explain what information it collects and how distributes it. The company also agreed to obtain parental permission before collecting data from children age 12 and under.

---

data on customers from the census bureau is available in many forms. Stock prices can be purchased from many different companies. Individual corporate data such as profit statements and other reports can be obtained electronically. The results of all legal cases in the United States are stored in computer databases as well. Westlaw and LEXIS-NEXIS provide online searches of cases and results. With a modem, a subscriber can copy these cases to a computer and they can be included in reports to clients. The variety and amount of information available continues to increase at a rapid rate. A considerable amount of data is also available on CD-ROMs.

## Advantages

Lawyers and accountants can use these sources instead of traditional libraries of books and periodicals. Besides saving trees, there are several advantages to using computerized databases instead of traditional books. It is possible to squeeze several hundred books on one optical disk. These disks can be carried with portable computers to a client's office. In seconds, the computer can search the text for any phrase. Not only is the computer faster, but it is complete—you do not have to worry about accidentally missing some information. The commercial database companies can provide up-to-date information. Many of the databases are updated daily or weekly. It is impossible to change information in books that rapidly. Lastly, with dial-up services, you only pay for exactly the data that you use.

## External versus Internal Data

There are a couple of things to keep in mind when using databases that are created by someone external to your company. First, you have to pay for *usage* of the database. That means you have to be efficient and not waste time while you are connected to the database. Some ideas for efficient search strategies are outlined in the next section.

Another consideration with external data is that you are dependent on someone else for the accuracy of the data. Although some items can be verified through other sources, much of the data cannot be tested. Fortunately, most commercial database firms are extremely careful about providing accurate data. Additionally, remember that the data available from commercial databases is available to anyone willing to pay the price, including your competitors. You typically need to supplement the commercial data with additional research.

Commercial databases are useful for data that changes quite often. For example, it would be extremely expensive for you personally to keep track of current stock market prices. You can buy data for individual stocks from a variety of sources. Similarly, various governmental agencies collect economic and demographic data that you can purchase. In both cases, it would be difficult to collect similar data on your own, and if you could, it would be extremely expensive.

Privacy presents an additional problem with large, centralized databases. Government agencies are particularly troublesome because their databases contain detailed personal data.

## DATABASE SEARCH STRATEGIES

Many modern databases, especially the commercial ones, are huge. If you are not careful, you might ask a question that takes several hours and thousands of dollars to answer. It would be silly to go to a large university library and ask for a list of all books in the subject area of business. This list would contain several thousand entries. Similarly, any time you search a large database, you need to have some idea of the size of the response.

Many databases are text based. They hold written information that you can search by words or phrases. To find the information you want, you need to write down a list of keywords that describe your topic. With some systems, such as Verity's Topic, you provide weights for each word to indicate its importance. The system then ranks each document it finds based on those weights.

The hardest part of searching textual databases is coming up with a list of possible keywords. You need to think about the words that are related to your topic. You might want to use a thesaurus if you have trouble thinking of related words.

Most of the large database systems provide you with a count of the number of items that match your keywords. You can use this number to tell you when to narrow or widen your search. If the computer says there are several thousand items that match your selection, you should narrow the search to a more specific topic. So you will add additional words (using AND). On the other hand, if the computer finds no items that match your conditions, you will have to try different keywords. Split phrases up into separate words, get rid of some AND conditions, and add synonyms using an OR phrase.

It takes practice to learn what combinations of keywords work best. Some companies hire specially trained librarians to help with these searches. It is a good idea to learn how to search for information in these large databases. Because of their significant advantages, eventually all important data will be stored and searched by computers.

Several companies are taking another approach to dealing with the problem of costly online searches. In many cases, it is possible to buy CD-ROMs that contain the popular databases. Because you can search a CD-ROM as often as you want for a one-time cost, you begin your search there. After you have narrowed down the topic and obtained the base data, you run a quick check with the online services to collect recent additions or changes.

## SUMMARY

Everyone needs to search for information. Computers make this job easier, but someone must set up and maintain the databases to ensure their integrity. There are many ways to search databases, and relational database management systems are a popular method. They are increasingly used as the foundation of the information system. They make it easy to share data among users while maintaining access controls. Equally importantly, the databases are easy to alter as the organization changes. Sophisticated databases can handle all the data types in use today, not just simple numbers and text.

It is relatively easy for users to obtain data using SQL or query-by-example tools. Because SQL is a recognized standard query language, it is worth remembering the basic elements of the SELECT command. The syntax is easy (SELECT columns, FROM tables, WHERE conditions, ORDER BY columns). Just remember that whenever you use more than one table, they must be joined by related columns.

An important step in databases is to design them correctly. The trick is to split the data into tables that refer to exactly one concept. Most organizations have a database administrator to help users create the initial database tables, define standards, establish access rights, and perform backups and testing. Once the tables have been defined, users can create input screens, reports, and views by using graphical tools to draw the desired items on the screen.

**A MANAGER'S VIEW**

Every manager needs to do research. Sometimes you will have to summarize and evaluate transaction data. Sometimes you will use external databases to evaluate the industry and your competitors.

Database management systems provide important capabilities to managers. One of the most useful is a query language, such as QBE or SQL, that enables you to answer questions without the need for hiring an MIS expert. A DBMS also speeds the development of new systems and provides basic features such as report writers and input forms.

It is important to choose the right tool for each job. Databases excel at handling huge amounts of data and sharing it with other users. On the other hand, spreadsheets are designed to perform calculations and create graphs. One indication that a problem should be solved using a DBMS instead of a spreadsheet is when several tables of data are involved.

Every day, more information is stored in commercial databases. In many ways, they are becoming the libraries of the future. Almost any type of reference data you can imagine can be searched electronically. Just remember that you have to pay to access this data, so you have to design your search strategies carefully to save money.

## KEY WORDS

| | | |
|---|---|---|
| breaks, 192 | normalization, 190 | report, 173 |
| column, 173 | object-oriented DBMS, 173 | row, 173 |
| concatenated keys, 175 | page footers, 192 | scrolling region, 192 |
| data independence, 177 | page headers, 192 | SQL, 179 |
| database administrator (DBA), 195 | primary key, 175 | table, 173 |
| default value, 191 | query by example (QBE), 179 | view, 188 |
| detail section, 192 | | |

## WEB SITE REFERENCES

**Shopping Services**

| | |
|---|---|
| America's Automall | www.aautomall.com |
| Autobytel | www.autobytel.com |
| Cars@cost | www.carscost.com |
| Dealer Net | www.dealernet.com |
| Edmunds | www.edmunds.com |
| Kelley Blue Book | www.kbb.com |
| Microsoft Carpoint | carpoint.msn.com |

**Manufacturers**

| | |
|---|---|
| DaimlerChrysler | www.daimlerchrysler.com |
| Ford | www.ford.com |
| General Motors | www.gm.com |
| Honda | www.honda.com |
| Nissan | www.nissan-usa.com |
| Suzuki | www.suzuki.com |
| Toyota | www.toyota.com |
| Volkswagen | www.vw.com |

## REVIEW QUESTIONS

1. How does data independence make it easier to design and maintain computer applications?
2. What is the purpose of normalization, and why is it important?
3. What is the purpose of a primary key? What is a concatenated key? Why do we use concatenated keys?
4. What tasks are performed by a database administrator?
5. Would you prefer to use QBE or SQL to access a database? Why?
6. What is a view in a database?
7. What four questions do you need to answer in order to create a database query?
8. How do you join tables with QBE? With SQL?
9. How do you enter restrictions or constraints with QBE? With SQL?
10. How do you perform computations with QBE? With SQL?
11. What is the purpose of an application generator in a DBMS?
12. Do you think users can create their own reports with a DBMS report writer? What limitations does it have?
13. Why are standards important in a database environment?
14. What types of problems are better suited to using a DBMS instead of a spreadsheet?
15. What are the advantages of using an external commercial database, compared to developing and maintaining the database yourself? What are the drawbacks to both methods? What types of data are best purchased from external databases?

## EXERCISES

**C05Ex15.mdb**

It is best to answer the first 15 exercise questions using a DBMS, but if one is not available, you can use the tables in the text and write your queries by hand. If you have a DBMS that handles both QBE and SQL, you should do the exercise with both methods.

1. List the customers who live in Seattle and have an account balance less than $500.
2. List the customers who live on Main Street or whose last name begins with the letter *J,* in descending order of account balance.
3. What is the total amount of money owed us by customers who live in Miami?
4. How many orders have been placed by customers from Denver? How many of those were placed in March 1999?
5. What is the largest order ever placed?
6. Which set of salespeople has placed the most orders: those who were hired before 1993 or those hired in 1993 or later? Hint: Use two separate queries.
7. List the names of the salespeople who sold orders worth more than $200 in descending order of the amount.
8. Calculate the total commissions owed to salesperson Johnson. Hint: You need to compute the total of commission times order.amount.
9. Get the name and phone number of customers who bought laundry detergent in June 1999.
10. Create a list of items that have been sold, along with the total quantity sold of each item, sorted by that quantity. Hint: Use *GROUP BY*.

11. Which (if any) salesperson sold jeans to Adams in Phoenix?
12. Create an input screen that enables a clerk to update information and add new customers to the database.
13. Using the tables in the chapter, create an order-entry input screen that can be used by a clerk who knows nothing about databases. Note: Depending on the DBMS, it might be difficult to compute the order.amount total.
14. Create an inventory report that lists all of the products, group them by category, and within each category, sort them by ID number.
15. Create the customer order report that is described in the chapter. Hint: First create a view that joins the appropriate tables together.
16. For any business, choose five entities (objects) that might be used as database tables. Identify primary keys for each table.
17. Using the CD-ROM resources at your library or perhaps access to an online database service, identify which company was the first one to issue corporate bonds with a maturity of 100 years. Include the source of your answer. Hint: It was after 1990.
18. Using the CD-ROM resources at your library or perhaps access to an online database service, how were the U.S. airlines doing in 1992? Which airline(s) had positive earnings? What major problems did the airlines face?
19. With the cooperation of a local small business, create a database for that company. Note that you should verify the initial layout of the tables with your instructor or someone who has studied database design.

 **Rolling Thunder Database**

Create queries to answer the following questions. (*Difficulty level: 1 = easiest*)

20. How many bicycles have been built of each type? *(2)*
21. What is the most popular type of tubing used in the bicycles that were ordered? *(3)*
22. What is the most expensive bicycle that was sold? *(2)*
23. Who spent the most money on bicycles? *(3)*
24. Which customers still owe us money? *(2)*
25. Which employee (name) installed the most bike parts? *(3)*
26. What is the total salary cost? *(2)*

27. What is the average price we paid for Shimano XT derailleurs (rear)? *(4)*
28. List all of the managers (check their title) and the employees (names) who work for them. *(5)*
29. List the purchase orders where TotalList does *not* equal the computed total of the individual items. *(4)*
30. List the component items that had *no* sales in March. *(5)*
31. Compute the list price of the component items for bicycle with serial number = 841. *(2)*
32. Compute the sales by model type by month. *(5 Hint: Crosstab)*
33. Compute sales by month. *(2)*
34. Compute the total sales taxes we owe to each state (for 1999). *(2)*
35. List all of the employees hired before 1993. *(1)*
36. List all of the bicycles ordered in March 1999 that used the LetterStyle "Flash." *(1)*
37. What is the value of our current inventory of Shimano components? *(2)*
38. List all of our employees (ID) who were involved in a transaction with a manufacturer worth more than 100,000. *(1)*
39. List all of the retail bicycle stores in your state. *(2)*

## ADDITIONAL READING

Jacobs, April. "Database Minds the Stores: Pizza Hut Uses App to Track Franchise Quality," *Computerworld,* August 24, 1998, p. 31. [Moving store evaluations to database improves decisions]

Mayer, Merry. "New DNA Database Extends the Long Arm of Law Enforcement," *Government Computer News,* October 19, 1998, p. 47. [Government database to identify criminals]

"Microsoft Gets Reality Check on Warehouses," *PC Week,* October 27, 1997, p. 90. [Data warehouse sizes expand to 100-500 GB, and almost one-fifth larger than 1 terabyte]

Post, Gerald. *Database Management Systems: Designing and Building Applications,* Irwin/McGraw-Hill, 1999. [How to design databases and use them to build business applications]

Tiboni, Frank. "FEMA Automates Property Inspection Scheduling," *Government Computer News,* November 9, 1998, p. 14. [Emergency agency uses telephone registration and database to help disaster victims in less time]

# CASES *Airlines*

The airline industry is an important component of to-day's global economy. Over 1.25 billion passengers per year rely on the world's airlines for business and vacation travel. Approximately a quarter of the world's manufactured exports by value are transported by air. Since the first jet airliner flew in 1949, use of commercial aviation has expanded more than 65-fold.

The industry is mature but is still changing and growing. The passenger segment of the airline industry is the largest and in 1995 accounted for over $69 billion in revenues or 73.7 percent of the industry's total revenues. Other major segments include freight and express (9 percent), charter (3.5 percent), and mail (1.3 percent). Economically, the airline industry is an imperfect oligopoly, in which a few carriers dominate in long-haul passenger traffic, while several dozen small carriers compete for short-haul flights. The Department of Transportation classifies air carriers by the size of their revenue base. In the United States, 34 carriers have a fleet of 25 or more aircraft.

Airline industry demand is cyclical. Travel generally follows economic activity. Economic models for forecasting airline traffic are commonly based on projections for gross domestic product (GDP), disposable personal income, and consumer confidence levels. While air traffic volume reflects economic factors, the cost and convenience of alternative modes of transportation also impacts air traffic. Demand for discretionary travel, such as vacations, tends to be more price sensitive. In recent years, corporate travel budgets have also become price sensitive. Higher fares stifle air traffic demand, whereas low fares spur greater demand.

The federal government stopped regulating airlines in 1978. Since deregulation, the industry has grown significantly more concentrated. Since 1985, mergers have played a significant role in this concentration. Between 1986 and 1987, Texas Air merged with Eastern and People's Express, Northwest Airlines with Republic Airlines, and Delta with Western. Industry consolidation has resulted from slowing traffic growth and the exhaustion of conventional cost-cutting measures. Mergers offer savings opportunities through the consolidation of administrative, distribution, and maintenance operations. Bankruptcies in the 1990s, most notably Pan American and Eastern, have also led to the consolidation of the industry.

All major airlines with the exception of Southwest operate through hub-and-spoke networks. In this hub system, passengers are gathered from surrounding "spoke" cities to a central hub airport where they must transfer to the second leg of their flight. This enables densities to be built for the longer portion of the flight, better matching equipment to demand. Competitive challenges are rare

---

| **MAJOR AIRLINES** |
| --- |
| Annual revenues exceed $1 billion |
| American, United, Delta, Northwest, Southwest, and U.S. Airlines |
| Each has fleets of 300 or more aircraft |
| **NATIONAL AIRLINES** |
| Annual revenues are between $100 million and $1 billion |
| More regional in focus with smaller seating capacities |
| **REGIONAL AIRLINES** |
| Annual revenues are less than $100 million |
| Computer lines and startup carriers |

---

once an airline is established in a hub. This has led to the stabilization of airfares and profit margins.

Despite deregulation, the Federal Aviation Administration (FAA) still imposes safety standards on carriers. It certifies aircraft and airlines and establishes age and medical requirements for pilots. A series of tragic airplane crashes in 1996 pushed air safety to the forefront. The crash of a Valu-Jet airplane in the Florida Everglades in May was followed in July by the mysterious explosion and crash of TWA's flight 800 over the Atlantic Ocean. The ValuJet crash prodded regulators to tighten their scrutiny of startup airlines and the practices of maintenance contractors. Certification of a new airline now takes twice as long as before. The number of aircraft that a new airline can operate is also limited based on the carrier's financial and managerial resources.

The Department of Transportation (DOT) levies civil penalties against airlines that engage in fraudulent marketing practices and violate code-sharing rules. It also decides airline ownership and control issues. Internationally, the DOT plays an important role by negotiating bilateral aviation treaties with foreign nations.

## Financial Analysis

Over the past three years, the growth rate in the airline industry has averaged 6.7 percent each year. In 1997, the growth rate averaged 7.1 percent per year, with an average load factor of just over 70.6 percent. Compared to other transportation industries, this rate is high, due to the fact that regional and international airlines continue to increase their service to underserved destinations.

The airline industry includes high barriers to entry. It requires a huge capital investment, especially for purchasing aircraft but also for labor, gate fees, advertising, fuel, and so on. Nonetheless, the airline industry is easier to enter now than it was before 1978 when deregulation was passed. Flight equipment accounts for more than 62 percent of total airline assets.

A newer trend for start-ups, as well as major carriers, is to lease planes instead of buying them. If aircraft are purchased, tax implications occur such as charges for depreciation and financing costs such as interest or preferred dividend payments. Among major airlines, depreciation averages 4.7 percent. For Southwest Airlines, depreciation increased 4.9 percent compared to an increase in the percentage of owned aircraft.

An important measure is yield, or the revenue generated per passenger mile (RPM). Comparing the absolute yield level for different carriers is only useful if the carriers have a similar mix of flights. Another consideration is revenues from nonfare sources. Since these can account for as much as 10 percent of an airline's total revenues, this contribution can make the difference between an operating profit and loss.

Industry revenues are strongly linked to corporate earnings and disposable income. The second and third quarters, along with holidays, have commonly been the times when demand was highest and operating conditions most favorable. From 1990 to mid-1994, the industry suffered $12 billion in losses. In the third quarter of 1995, the airline industry reported record profits of nearly $2.4 billion. Total operating revenues increased by 3.6 percent while total operating expenses increased by 3.3 percent. At the same time, passenger revenues increased by 6.2 percent along with freight and express revenues, which increased by 16.4 percent. The rate of return on investment rose by 6.8 percent. As a result of these factors, the operating profit margin increased by 3.1 percent along with a net profit margin that increased by 2.9 percent.

The outlook is even more promising for the worldwide airline industry. The profits for 1995 reached a net figure of $5.2 billion dollars, based on international service revenues of $129.6 billion dollars. Net profit of 4 percent of revenue set an all-time record for the industry. International revenues for 1996 reached $140 billion dollars, resulting in a $6.0 billion net profit or 4.3 percent of revenue. With the airline industry's new profitability, and provided that the airlines continue to focus their efforts on the balance sheets, this industry will become a very attractive investment in the next century.

The airline industry is expected to continue to grow in pace with the U.S. economy. As the outlook

for corporate profits and personal income growth improves, continued profits also appear likely. Forecasters warn, however, that this industry is highly cyclical, and thus is prone to overcapacity resulting in high levels of competition.

Airline stocks are the most cyclical on Wall Street. Investors tend to bid up shares of airlines when they look weakest and substantial losses are incurred. Once profits are returned, investors move on, dumping stocks with depressed price/earnings ratios. Investors tend to favor growth airlines with wide profit margins rather than those with a strong service performance and a young fleet. The biggest rally gains in equity airlines go to the *worst* airlines because investors anticipate a bigger gain from a depressed base in that carrier's bottom line.

### Potential/Prospective for Growth

The airline industry remains one of the fastest growing sectors of the world economy. Passenger and freight traffic is expected to increase at an average annual rate of 5 percent to 6 percent between 1997 and 2010. This is significantly greater than the expected growth of global GDP. By 2005, the number of people traveling by air could exceed 2.5 billion a year. Growth in air travel will be led by the Asia market. Demand for this region is anticipated to grow by an average of 8.6 percent annually between now and 2010.

Experts attribute the rapid rate of growth to the increasing disposable incomes of consumers and the decreasing fares being charged. Airfares today are 70 percent less after adjustment for inflation than they were in 1970. As world economic growth continues to accelerate, so should growth in the airline industry. A significant change in the structure of the industry is *open skies*. This term refers to the process of internationally deregulating air transportation services, an area of many regulations and restrictions.

For instance, the United States and Canada signed a new bilateral air services agreement in February 1995. The deal allows for unlimited nonstop air services between two-thirds of the 100 largest U.S. cities and any major Canadian cities that previously did not have air services. This new agreement should greatly expand air traffic between the two countries, with projections for growth to 20 million passengers annually. The United States has also been negotiating *open skies* agreements with several European nations, with discussions focused on initiating new transatlantic routes, increasing flight frequency on existing routes, and lifting pricing restrictions. Some airlines are also adding transarctic routes over newly opened Russian airspace offering substantial time savings from the United States to Europe.

Another area for substantial growth is the regional airline market. Largely overlooked during deregulation,

| CITY | CODE | DEPARTURES/DAY |
|------|------|----------------|
| Dallas/Fort Worth | (DFW) | 370 |
| Los Angeles | (LAX) | 342 |
| Cincinnati | (CVG) | 255 |
| Leading regional airports in 1995. | | |

this market has become a bottom-line profit booster for the national airlines, feeding passengers into their hubs. During the 1970s, the regional airline industry was made up of local commuter airlines serving local cities and connecting outlying communities to metropolitan areas.

After deregulation, national and major airlines ended service to smaller communities, concentrating on higher yield routes. The smaller commuter airlines began to acquire larger turboprop aircraft and replace the major airlines on these low-yield routes. In the 1980s, commuter airlines grew through industry consolidation and code sharing with larger airlines. In the 1990s, they grew into large regional carriers serving numerous cities and operating turbojet aircraft. This has enabled them to service new routes previously not possible without the longer-range regional jet aircraft.

Technological advancements have enabled code sharing, which is a major key to growth in the regional airlines. This enables them to take advantage of a single ticket source by using the ticket codes of the larger national airlines. This facilitates the coordination of schedules through a smooth transfer of passengers from one airline (regional) to another code-sharing partner (national). Code sharing has contributed to the consolidation of smaller commuter carriers into larger regional carriers. The number of regional carriers has decreased 51 percent to 124 carriers in 1995. The average trip length has doubled from 121 miles in 1978 to 223 miles in 1995. The number of passengers has grown from 11.3 million in 1978 to 57.2 million in 1995.

In 1995, the two largest regional airlines were Simmons Airlines, Inc., an American Eagle carrier, and ComAir, Inc., a Delta Airlines carrier. Simmons flies a fleet of 92 turboprops out of Dallas/Fort Worth and Chicago O'Hare, serving more than 50 cities with 586 flights per day and carrying 4.98 million passengers. ComAir flies out of Cincinnati and Orlando, serving 79 cities with 680 flights per day.

### Competitive Structure

Ten major airlines (airlines with annual revenues over $1 billion) currently account for more than 75 percent of all operating revenue and 90 percent of passenger revenue. The other 10 percent are made up of more than 100 airlines. The market share of other airlines has been increasing at the expense of the major ones.

The competitiveness in the airline industry was enhanced by the deregulation in 1978. Deregulation allowed airlines to fly wherever they wished. It also allowed new small airlines to compete with the existing major airlines. Some small airlines, such as Southwest, have done well with point-to-point, short-haul, and high-frequency operations.

Airlines do not sell a tangible product but simply supply transportation. Aside from offering certain frills, the service airlines provide is basically undifferentiated. Some of these frills include more legroom, better food, newer movies, telephone service, and most recently, hookups for fax and online communication. Frequent flier programs and rewards are also used to set apart airlines from their competitors.

Airlines use frequent flyer programs to build brand loyalty and distinguish themselves from the competition. Frequent flyer programs have been developed in an attempt to gain customer loyalty and promote repeat business. Frequent flyers represent only 8 percent of the total number of passengers, but the miles they fly equal 45 percent of all miles flown. Satisfying these passengers can be key to an airline's success.

Passenger pricing is directly available to consumers and corporations, particularly due to consumer access to fares on the Internet. In sum, the airline industry is highly competitive. Airlines compete with each other on both service and price. For business travelers, the frequency of flights is the time of day is critical. Schedule reliability also influences airline selection. Smaller airlines unable to obtain gate space during peak travel times are unable to attract business travelers.

Besides competing with each other, airlines compete with a variety of other transportation modes, including automobiles, railroads, and buses.

### Role of Research and Development

Safety is an area the airline industry is always seeking to improve. The weakest link in air safety has been the human factor. Airlines continually seek advances in technology and training to help diminish this problem. In developing new, more reliable systems for aircraft and more advanced simulators for pilot training, the airlines can help the pilots identify and avoid problems before they become irreversible.

Airport capacity is another crucial issue facing the industry. It's usually cheaper to expand existing airports rather than to build new ones; thus it is crucial to squeeze more capacity out of existing airports. The FAA is responsible for making decisions regarding flight paths and determines when an airport is overcrowded. With the development of the Global Positioning System (GPS), a new system called free flight may reduce congestion and save time, energy, and the need for new airports.

## Technological Investment and Analysis

Technology presents tremendous potential to cut costs and simplify the process of air travel. The airline industry has improved its operating efficiency by applying new information and communication technologies. Staffing levels can be cut because computers, modems, and ATM-like machines allow for fast and efficient communication and ticket distribution.

In 1995, airlines established home pages on the World Wide Web. These sites display information about schedules and fleets, contain financial and promotional material, give listings of in-flight movie offerings, and let travelers check the status of their frequent flyer accounts. Since 1996, because of ticketless travel, ticket purchases can be made on the Web. Once the reservation is paid for, passengers can board the airline by showing a valid driver's license. This eliminates the security surrounding ticketing stock as well as the accounting procedures required to track the used tickets.

In 1997, 2 percent of air travel was made through Internet bookings. As travelers use the Internet to obtain frequently sought information, airlines are cutting customer service operators. The Internet makes airfares publicly available and comparable on the World Wide Web. This enables consumers to compare and shop prices.

Airlines are using technology to reduce operating costs. Early in 1995, for example, the airline industry realized the partial elimination of the traditional paper ticket. The "electronic ticket" was its replacement. It brings significant savings to airlines in ticket distribution costs. By the end of 1998, almost 40 percent of travel was booked on electronic tickets.

The Airline Smart Card is another new product. It will provide frequent travelers with the ability to quickly identify themselves, board a flight, obtain a ticket, and pay for other products and services. It will also save airlines in ticket distribution costs, allow more passengers the use of self-service facilities, and provide better means of identification.

It is predicted that most airline Smart Cards will eventually be co-branded cards. This means that they will be issued by banks or credit card companies and will also contain airline industry applications. The cards will have the capability to allow up to 10 airline applications. Space will also be allowed for immigration data for some governments.

All majors, with the exception of Southwest Airlines, are part of an intricate computer system that allows travel agents to book flights for customers. The nation's 30,000 travel agents sell 85 percent of the tickets. Major airlines are able to offer a high concentration and variety of flights along with the availability that makes it easier for agents to schedule. In addition, major airlines are able to offer more incentives to travel agents who sell the airlines seats. Earlier in 1995, most major airlines imposed a $50 cap on all seats over $500 sold by agents.

Many airlines form alliances through code sharing. Code sharing allows airlines with a market presence in one region to extend their services to those in another. This allows cost cutting through shared counters, gate space, noncompetitive computer software, and bulk purchases.

## Recommendation for the Future

For airlines to survive in this highly competitive industry, they need to strive to become as cost efficient as possible. Only with low costs can airlines compete with low fares. The use of technology can be used to cut costs and provide convenience as shown with the use of electronic tickets and smart cards.

In order to gain a competitive advantage in the industry, airlines should seek to gain access to emerging markets in Asia, such as China. As these Asian countries become more involved in the global marketplace, their rate of economic growth will rise, which will lead to a greater demand for air travel. For an airline that is able to capture this market, the returns will be considerable.

A method that could be utilized to capture this market is the Smart Card. If an airline introduces the card from the start, other airline's procedures would seem tedious in comparison. Consumers would not want to switch from using the Smart Card due to the costs and inconvenience. Thus, the new market would be captured, at least, for a limited time.

## CASE   *American Airlines*

### Technological Investment and Analysis

The first move American Airlines Decision Technologies (ADDT) Group made was to closely align itself with the SABRE Technologies group, to apply the expertise of the people already on that staff. As this newly defined group began to take shape, they realized their first hurdle would be to create the appropriate core modules in relational databases, and make sure the standalone systems could interact with the core. They settled on four core modules, which they felt would cover a larger percentage of the areas addressed by the decision support tools.

1. **Aircraft Records.**   As John Simmons, a director of the group explained, "It keeps track of hours, cycles, components, the airframe, the engines, and tells you exactly where you stand, whether a part is attached to an aircraft, or in a shop or a warehouse."
2. **Materials.**   This module encompasses inventory, purchasing, warehousing, warranty tracking, and related activities.
3. **Training Module.**   This system tracks mechanic and inspector licenses, as well as

recurrent training requirements. The module provides a clear history of all personnel records.

4. **Production Control.** This module develops the package for a specific aircraft's base visit and then transfers the package electronically to mechanics anywhere in the world.

These modules were put into place in 1992 for American's own fleet. Sabre technologies built an interface that tied the module into mainframe applications as inventory control, flight scheduling, and financial analysis. Johnson explained the power of the tools when they are programmed to work as one:

> A mechanic can look up a part number at a terminal on the floor of the hangar and order the part; the front end interfaces with the mainframe to order the part, get it delivered to him, document the cost, assign the cost to the specific airplane he's working on, and change the decrement inventory. The inventory system then automatically reorders, to maintain current inventory levels.

Equally impressive are the labor reports, which allow a mechanic to log onto and off of a work card and indicate which piece of work is in process. This provides a real-time status of hours, materials, and labor for any ongoing project. The history database enables a mechanic to examine 20 to 30 airplanes and predict with a very large degree of certainty the exact parts that are going to be needed. This means that airlines do not have to stock everything needed for an airplane, which has a major impact on the levels of inventory that need to be maintained.

These technological strides keep American Airlines ahead of all the competitors. British Airways (BA) could not help but notice that the technologies that American was developing were those that directly addressed the main problems BA was facing. Areas like efficiency, usage, and maintenance were presenting serious problems for BA, while American was transforming itself into a technologically driven engine. If BA wanted to buy the technologies, not only would they have to make a major outlay of cash, but they would actually be supporting one of their competitors. This was due to the fact that BA would need to pay American personnel as consultants to get the systems running.

American has begun to develop technologies that would further implement the AA/BA concept of seamless travel through the alliance. Perhaps the program that promises the most obvious and appreciated results is American's newly developed AAccess electronic ticketing. Most of the major airlines went to the option of electronic ticketing in 1997. This means that the consumer does not need a hard copy or paper ticket but just has to check in at the gate with a picture ID to claim their boarding pass. American believes the AAccess program will take this concept to a new level, allowing a traveler to go from their home computer to an airplane seat without any intervening stops inside the terminal.

The AAccess system combines online reservation and electronic ticketing with gate readers that allow e-ticketed passengers not checking bags to board their aircraft at 21 U.S. airports merely by inserting any credit card to identify themselves. This distinguishes the system as the only one that does not require the traveler to stop at a ticket or gate counter. American has begun testing airport kiosks that will be called AAccess self-service devices. At selected test airports, passengers will be able to change their seats, check their AAdvantage mileage, or make their own upgrades. These innovations make American more attractive as a potential partner with British Airways.

### Technological Innovations

### Telecommunications

American Airlines has leveraged Web technologies to reduce call center volume, sell vacant seats, and expand its affinity marketing programs. At the same time, the company is deploying intranet tools to knit together its distributed enterprise, which at any given time can have personnel spread across 115 different cities worldwide.

"What we've done is put the primary burden for developing the Internet strategy on the department heads," says Scott Nason, American's Vice-President of information technology. "If you are running the operations department, it is your and your manager's job to figure out how to run your department better."

By pushing business managers to take responsibility, American has come up with solutions to difficult problems. An ever-increasing appetite for call center ticketing support has been satisfied through Internet electronic commerce. Dead inventory is being reduced through discount sales at its NetSavers site.

"The number of people buying online is still small, but there will be ongoing cost implications and broader marketing implications for the distribution of product from here on," said John Samuel, American's managing director of interactive marketing.

### Data

American Airline's Revenue Accounting Data Access Resource (RADAR) started as a departmental data mart for use by 40 accountants in March 1997. It is now accessed by more than 100 users in diverse departments such as marketing and security. The data mart took about nine months to build.

RADAR consists of a Sybase IQ 11.5 running on a Sun Enterprise 5000 12-way server, which pulls data from a mainframe ticketing system that each year issues more than 125 million pieces of travel-related documents. The front end is IQ/Objects from IQ Software, which translates GUI-driven commands into valid SQL for custom, ad hoc queries.

RADAR development required several months of raking through data, looking for corrupted index. The finished data mart has 20 tables and completes the average query in seven minutes, with about 40 percent of queries being done in less than four minutes. The return on investment has exceeded expectation. During its first week RADAR saved $60,000 by spotting improper ticketing procedures. American Airlines says that the $400,000 project has paid for itself many times in straight cost savings.

### Recommendation for the Future

In the fourth quarter of 1995, American placed sixth among all companies in World Wide Web advertising. The important thing is not just that American is reaching people on the Web but that they are providing a service that the consumer wants. One example of this is easySABRE, American's consumer-oriented version of the reservation system that had previously been available only to travel agents. Consumers can now access this service online. In 1995 alone, American sold 1.6 million tickets through this medium. In addition, millions have signed up for NetSAAvers on the American Airlines web site. Through this service, consumers are alerted to specials once a week via e-mail, helping to fill seats that would have otherwise remained empty. Also, by selling tickets directly to the consumer, American keeps the percentage that would otherwise go to a travel agent.

### QUESTIONS

1. What is the strategic, future direction of the corporation/organization and what forces are driving this direction?
2. Upon what technologies has American Airlines relied?
3. What caused a change in the use of technology at American Airlines?
4. How successful has the technological change been?
5. What does the corporation's web page present about its business directives?
6. How important is data to the corporation's continued success?
7. How will the capture and maintenance of customer data impact American Airlines' future?

### ADDITIONAL READING

Adhikari, Richard. "E-Commerce Impact—Companies Are Finding New Ways for Web Technology to Expand Their Businesses," *InformationWeek,* July 27, 1998, p. 77.

"American Taps Speech," *InformationWeek,* December 14, 1998, p. 34.

Frook, John Evan. "Future Trend: Getting Personal with Customers," *InternetWeek,* June 22, 1998, p. 11.

Furger, Roberta. "The Skies Just Got Friendlier," *PC World,* October 1996, p. 256.

Lasky, Michael S. "United versus American: Airline Software," *PC World,* November 1996, p. 104.

Manes, Stephen. "A Fatal Outcome from Misplaced Trust in 'Data'," *The New York Times,* September 17, 1996, pp. B11, C9.

Messmer, Ellen. "Revamped Web Site to Take Flight at American Airlines," *Network World,* June 15, 1998, p. 39.

Neil, Stephanie. "Airline Rides the Technology Tailwinds," *PC Week,* April 27, 1998, pp. 94–96.

Sullivan, Kristina, B. "Net to Help with In-Flight Emergencies," *PC Week,* April 21, 1997, p. 94.

"Surf to Fly," *Computerworld,* March 3, 1997, p. 59.

Tebbe, Mark. "American Airlines' Web Strategy," *PC Week,* September 30, 1996, p. N13.

## CASE   *Southwest Airlines*

Look! Up in the sky! It's a bird. It's a plane. It's . . . Shamu? Sound crazy? If you have ever flown on Southwest Airlines, nothing seems more natural than munching peanuts inside a black-and-white painted killer whale. There's more: Imagine sitting in an aisle seat. Just as you lay your head back, a bunny-suited flight attendant pops out of the overhead bin and yells, "Surprise!" Or at the end of a trip, your flight attendant requests: "Please pass all the plastic cups to the center aisle so we can wash them and use them for the next group of passengers." These are examples of the unconventionality that characterizes Southwest Airlines. The unconventional approach carries over to the operations as well—making Southwest one of the most profitable airlines.

### Technological Story

While most airlines rely on independent travel agents to write up a great majority of their tickets, Southwest has steadfastly refused to connect with the computer reservation system that the agents use. Agents who wish to book a Southwest flight have to pick up the phone like anyone else or go to the Southwest home page. Many try to persuade customers to pick another carrier or to make the call themselves. The result is that nearly half of all Southwest tickets are sold directly to passengers, with an annual savings to the airline of about $30 million. The percentage of Southwest tickets sold by agents is in the "mid-40s," which is far below the industry average.

Southwest Airlines, which only participates in the Sabre CRS, offers electronic booking options to agencies with more features than the web site. Southwest's Direct Access software product, which enables non-Sabre agents to dial into the airline's computer system, gives an agent more information and allows cancellations.

In 1996, Southwest Airlines became one of the first airlines on the Internet, offering "26 different types of information" from its own site, the Southwest Airlines Home Gate. The ultimate goal for the carrier was to add a booking capability so passengers could make ticketless reservations from their home personal computers. Southwest's strong customer orientation led them to invest in this customer-focused technology.

Once it added the option of bookings at the web site, the company expected it to build gradually. The company advertised for the service, both online and in other media. So far it has proven to be very successful. As with other Web booking systems, Southwest's site accepts only bookings from a browser that can encrypt data.

### Technological Investment and Analysis

In 1994, in a move that significantly improved the productivity of business travelers, Southwest Airlines and McCaw Cellular's Claircom Communications unveiled the world's first broadly available air-to-ground commercial fax and data service through the AirOne Communications Network. Prior to this, the wealth of data services accessible by computer on the ground were not available to the air traveler. Through the same AirOne system that delivers clear and reliable telephone calls from a plane, passengers can attach to electronic networks to get the latest news, weather, sports, and travel information or even play video games.

The AirOne system, installed throughout the Southwest fleet, provides high-quality, digital air-to-ground service using AT&T's Long Distance Service. Passengers on all Southwest's planes can access electronic mail networks and information networks such as Compuserve, Prodigy, and Dow Jones. The AirOne System offers the most comprehensive fax and data services in the market. It can be used to send and retrieve faxes, data, and electronic mail through conventional laptop computers, portable fax machines, and personal data assistants such as the Palm Pilot.

In the above example, Southwest Airlines demonstrated that they recognized ahead of time the significant demand for this type of service because of the increased productivity and accessibility it provided to the business traveler. By providing this type of service, the airline has attracted the businessperson who does not pay out of his or her own pocket, and as a result, does not choose an airline based exclusively on low fares. This person was not exactly the company's target market before. Southwest was the first airline in the world to make this type of communication technology broadly available to its customers. This service is consistent with Southwest's history of providing POS (Positively Outrageous Service.)

Previously, the airline had a vision that there would be a demand for ticketless travel. Their strong customer orientation, once again, led them to invest in something that would benefit the company as well. Electronic tickets provide a significant reduction of cost compared to printing, mailing, and processing paper tickets. Even more savings are generated from avoiding commissions. Before the introduction of electronic booking, approximately 40 percent of the airline's tickets were sold by agents. This is well below the industry average of 80 percent. Now that number is even smaller.

Southwest used Object Design, Inc.'s ObjectStore, an object database management system software to help build a ticketless reservation system into its Home Gate corporate web site. The company was looking for a system that would make the online booking process easy to use, responsive, and quick to build. Object technology was quickly chosen and ObjectStore was selected after an exhaustive search, mainly due to the product's virtual memory mapping technology and the company's reputation. Southwest Airlines' 10 GB database stores passenger, fare, confirmation, and schedule data.

Home Gate is easy to use. Customers simply click on the departing location, their destination, travel date, and approximate departure time. Home Gate looks up the fare and schedule information and returns relevant information. The customer can then make a reservation, type in his or her credit card number, and purchase the ticket. The system provides a confirmation number. The passenger simply shows a driver's license at the gate to obtain a boarding pass. The purchasing process is secured through encryption technology. The ObjectStore database is designed specifically for building Internet and Intranet applications. In the expanding Web environment, the product supports rapid development of applications, including those that call for extended data types such as image, free text, video, audio, HTML, and Java software objects.

Southwest's newest investment is shifting from Sabre Group's SAAS-hosted TPF reservation system to an in-house system developed in partnership with Hewlett-Packard. The system being developed is a hybrid of mainframe and client/server technology that combines a central inventory database with local schedules and fares databases using a proprietary operating system.

## Technological Innovations: Network

Southwest migrated from a legacy multiprotocol network to a routed TCP/IP network in 1998. While the frame relay WAN is currently in its infancy phase and handles primarily operational traffic, it is eventually slated to handle passenger reservations and updates. The WAN currently transports traffic from operational applications such as e-mail, accounting and procurement and links the check-in terminals at 51 airports, nine reservations hubs, Southwest's headquarters, and 20 additional locations.

## QUESTIONS

1. What is the strategic direction of Southwest Airlines?
2. What is causing a change in the use of technology at Southwest Airlines?
3. What does the corporation say about its financial ability to embark on a major technological program of advancement?
4. What does the corporation's web page present about its business directives?
5. How will technology impact the industry?
6. What role does data play in the future of Southwest Airlines?

## ADDITIONAL READING

Cravotta, Nicholas. "Network Health Remedies Frame Relay Bottlenecks," *Network,* April 1, 1998.

Dash, Julekha. "Soft Skills Soar at Southwest," *Software Magazine,* April 1998, p. 14.

Dryden, Patrick. "Airline's Network on Standby," *Computerworld,* November 24, 1997, pp. 53–55.

Garvey, Martin J. "RS/6000 Moves Up—S70 Line, Solutions Focus Make IBM More Attractive for New Users' ERP Apps," *InformationWeek,* December 21, 1998, p. 22.

Hoffman, Thomas. "Airline Turbocharges Schedule Efficiency," *Computerworld,* March 25, 1996, pp. 1–3.

Karpain, Gregory. "Ticketless Travel Takes Off, Thanks to ODBMS Technology," *Databased Web Advisor,* August 1997, pp. 38–41.

Melymuka, Kathleen. "Sky King," *Computerworld,* September 28, 1998, p. 68.

"Middleware Deal," *Computerworld,* December 7, 1998, p. 51.

Shein, Esther. "Web Spinning New Help Desk Assistance," *PC Week,* September 1, 1997, pp. 85–87.

## DISCUSSION ISSUE

### *Who Should Control Corporate Data?*

An interesting problem arises with the emphasis on the data provided by the database approach. Who should control the corporate data? Remember that standards are needed in order to keep the data consistent and make it useful to everyone. On the other hand, the data often comes from individual users and departments. If the production department has its own collection of information, perhaps the staff should have more control over that information. Listen to Ilsa, the production manager, as she discusses her new database with Rick, the database administrator.

Ilsa:  Rick, I have to talk to you.

Rick:  Uh-huh. I saved the first report for you.

Ilsa:  We have the new robots installed. They'll be connected to the computers by the end of next week. We need to store the measurement information to use it for quality control. Also, we need access to the inventory and production schedule databases so we can configure the robots for each production run. Only we're having some problems with the database team. They said management won't let us use the customer data. We need you to talk to them.

Rick:  Yeah. Well, I try not to stick my neck out. These rules were created by a committee three years ago. We all agreed to them. You knew the rules going into this project.

Ilsa:  I can understand how you feel. Before all this started, I thought I had everything I needed. But we've changed. We didn't know about the robots three years ago. We can't live in the past. I tried to go straight to marketing, but the staff said you're the only one who can help us. They seem upset that they don't own the data anymore.

Rick:  Listen. Nobody owns anything here. And we all have problems. You know what it was like before. If it weren't for these standards, you wouldn't even be able to ask for the customer data. It was so poorly managed that even marketing couldn't use it. It took us almost a year to clean it up and test all the data. We can't just give you open access to it now. I'm not going through that mess again.

Ilsa:  There must be something you can do. Look, if we can't get access through you, we'll just have to go around you. We can build our own cus-

Rick:  tomer and orders database. It'll just take longer and cost us more money.

Rick:  Sure, but how are you going to keep it up to date? And how are you going to fit it in with the existing data? You'll end up duplicating everything we've already done. Pretty soon we'll be right back to the mess we had three years ago. I can't allow you to do that.

Ilsa:  We don't have any choice. Our work is too important to the company. OK, we can't do it without your help. So why can't you help us? There must be some way to set up our databases to match with yours. We'll promise not to hurt your data. We'll do whatever tests you need.

Rick:  It's not that easy. Maybe we can work it out, but we can't possibly finish it by next week. See, I have to play by the rules too. If I start changing the customer database, then marketing will be in here screaming. If I touch inventory, management will be on the phone. Plus, accounting has a bunch of changes they want me to make. I don't think your modifications will match theirs. They've been complaining about security and insufficient audit trails. I have to coordinate these changes. We'll at least need a committee and several meetings.

Ilsa:  All I'm asking for is a chance. Remember, Rick, this problem's bigger than both of us. Sometimes we can't play by the rules; they need to be changed.

## QUESTIONS

1. Do you think Rick is being too restrictive? Should he just give Ilsa what she wants?
2. What do you suppose will eventually happen if Ilsa "goes around" Rick and builds her own database? What if everyone else in the company does the same thing?
3. Is there a compromise by which both Rick and Ilsa can get what they want?
4. How could a good database management system help?

# Data Normalization

## INTRODUCTION

Database management systems are powerful tools, with the ability to present data in many ways. They are used by managers to answer many different types of questions. However, this flexibility is not automatic. Databases need to be carefully designed; otherwise, managers will not be able to get the information they need. Poor design also leads to unnecessary duplication of data. Duplication wastes space and requires workers to enter the same data several times. *Normalization* is an important technique to design databases.

To understand the process of normalization, consider a small example. We want to build a database for a small video rental store. We begin by thinking about who will be using the database and identifying what data they will need. Consider the situation of the checkout clerks. They first identify the customer, then record each movie to be rented. The computer should then calculate the amount of money due along with any taxes. Figure 5.1A shows a sample input screen that might be used.

The important point to note is that the data will have to be stored in more than one table. Each entity or object on the form will be represented by a separate table. For this example, there are four objects on the form: Customers, Videos, Rental, and VideosRented.

Before explaining how to derive the four tables from the form, there are some basic concepts you need to understand. First, remember that every table must have a primary key. A primary key is one or more columns that uniquely identify each row. For example, we anticipated problems with identifying customers, so each customer is assigned a unique ID number. Similarly, each video is given a unique ID number. Note that we might have more than one copy of each title, so we have also assigned a copy number to each video. There is one drawback to assigning numbers to customers: We cannot expect customers to remember their number, so

we will need a method to look it up. One possibility is to give everyone an ID card imprinted with the number—perhaps printed with a bar code that can be scanned. However, we still need a method to deal with customers who forget their cards.

The second aspect to understand when designing databases is the relationships between various entities. First, observe that there are two sections to the form: (1) the main Rental which identifies the transaction, the customer and the date, and (2) a *repeating section* that lists the videos being rented. Each customer can rent several different videos at one time. We say there is a *one-to-many* relationship between the Rental and the VideosRented sections. As you will see, identifying one-to-many relationships is crucial to proper database design.

In some respects, designing databases is straightforward: There are only three basic rules. However, database design is often interrelated with systems analysis. In most cases, we are attempting to understand the business at the same time the database is being designed. One common problem that arises is that it is not always easy to see which relationships are one-to-many and which are one-to-one or many-to-many.

## NOTATION

It would be cumbersome to draw pictures of every table that we use, so we usually write table definitions in a standard notation. The base customer table is shown in Figure 5.2A, both in notational form and with sample data.

Figure 5.3A illustrates another feature of the notation. We denote one-to-many or repeating relationships by placing parentheses around them. Figure 5.3A represents all the data shown in the input screen from Figure 5.1A. The description is created by starting at the top of the form and writing down each element that you encounter. If a section contains repeating data, place

## Green's Video Store

| | | | |
|---|---|---|---|
| **Green's Video Store** | + | − | **Close** |

**Customer** | Washington ▼ | **TransID:** | 1

502-777-7575 | **RentDate:** | 4/18/99 11:03:56 AM

Elroy | Washington

95 Easy Street

Smith's Grove | KY | 42171

| Video ID | Copy # | Title | Rent |
|---|---|---|---|

| | VideoID: | Copy# | Title: | Rent: |
|---|---|---|---|---|
| ▶ | 1 ▼ | 2 | 2001: A Space Odyssey | $1.50 |
| | 6 | 3 | Clockwork Orange | $1.50 |
| * | | | | |

Record: ⏮ ◀ | 1 | ▶ ⏭ ▶* | of 2

| | |
|---|---|
| **SubTotal** | $3.00 |
| **Tax** | $0.18 |
| **Total** | $3.18 |

Record: ⏮ ◀ | 1 | ▶ ⏭ ▶* | of 16

**FIGURE 5.1A**

The order form is used in almost any firm. We need to determine the best way to store the data that is collected by this form.

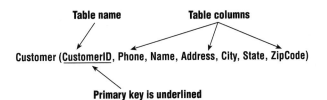

Table name | Table columns

Customer (<u>CustomerID</u>, Phone, Name, Address, City, State, ZipCode)

Primary key is underlined

| CustomerID | Phone | LastName | FirstName | Address | City | State | ZipCode |
|---|---|---|---|---|---|---|---|
| 1 | 502-666-7777 | Johnson | Martha | 125 Main Street | Alvaton | KY | 42122 |
| 2 | 502-888-6464 | Smith | Jack | 873 Elm Street | Bowling Green | KY | 42101 |
| 3 | 502-777-7575 | Washington | Elroy | 95 Easy Street | Smith's Grove | KY | 42171 |
| 4 | 502-333-9494 | Adams | Samuel | 746 Brown Drive | Alvaton | KY | 42122 |
| 5 | 502-474-4746 | Rabitz | Victor | 645 White Avenue | Bowling Green | KY | 42102 |
| 6 | 615-373-4746 | Steinmetz | Susan | 15 Speedway Drive | Portland | TN | 37148 |
| 7 | 615-8884474 | Lasater | Les | 67 S. Ray Drive | Portland | TN | 37148 |
| 8 | 615-452-1162 | Jones | Charlie | 867 Lakeside Drive | Castalian Springs | TN | 37031 |
| 9 | 502-222-4351 | Chavez | Juan | 673 Industry Blvd. | Caneyville | KY | 42721 |
| 10 | 502-444-2512 | Rojo | Maria | 88 Main Street | Cave City | KY | 42127 |

**FIGURE 5.2A**

NOTATION FOR TABLES

Table definitions can often be written in one or two lines. Each table has a name and a list of columns. The column (or columns) that makes up the primary key is underlined.

RentalForm(<u>TransID</u>, RentDate, <u>CustomerID</u>, Phone, Name, Address, City, State, ZipCode, (<u>VideoID</u>, Copy#, Title, Rent))

**Repeating section**

**Causes duplication**

| TransID | RentDate | CustomerID | LastName | Phone | Address | VideoID | Copy# | Title | Rent |
|---------|----------|------------|----------|-------|---------|---------|-------|-------|------|
| 1 | 4/18/99 | 3 | Washington | 502-777-7575 | 95 Easy Street | 1 | 2 | 2001: A Space Odyssey | $1.50 |
| 1 | 4/18/99 | 3 | Washington | 502-777-7575 | 95 Easy Street | 6 | 3 | Clockwork Orange | $1.50 |
| 2 | 4/30/99 | 7 | Lasater | 615-888-4474 | 67 S. Ray Drive | 8 | 1 | Hopscotch | $1.50 |
| 2 | 4/30/99 | 7 | Lasater | 615-888-4474 | 67 S. Ray Drive | 2 | 1 | Apocalypse Now | $2.00 |
| 2 | 4/30/99 | 7 | Lasater | 615-888-4474 | 67 S. Ray Drive | 6 | 1 | Clockwork Orange | $1.50 |
| 3 | 4/18/99 | 8 | Jones | 615-452-1162 | 867 Lakeside Drive | 9 | 1 | Luggage Of The Gods | $2.50 |
| 3 | 4/18/99 | 8 | Jones | 615-452-1162 | 867 Lakeside Drive | 15 | 1 | Fabulous Baker Boys | $2.00 |
| 3 | 4/18/99 | 8 | Jones | 615-452-1162 | 867 Lakeside Drive | 4 | 1 | Boy And His Dog | $2.50 |
| 4 | 4/18/99 | 3 | Washington | 502-777-7575 | 95 Easy Street | 3 | 1 | Blues Brothers | $2.00 |
| 4 | 4/18/99 | 3 | Washington | 502-777-7575 | 95 Easy Street | 8 | 1 | Hopscotch | $1.50 |
| 4 | 4/18/99 | 3 | Washington | 502-777-7575 | 95 Easy Street | 13 | 1 | Surf Nazis Must Die | $2.50 |
| 4 | 4/18/99 | 3 | Washington | 502-777-7575 | 95 Easy Street | 17 | 1 | Witches of Eastwick | $2.00 |

**FIGURE 5.3A**
CONVERTING TO NOTATION
Repeating sections are indicated by the inner parentheses. If we try to store the data this way, notice the problem created by the repeating section: Each time a customer checks out a video we have to reenter the phone and address.

parentheses around it. Preliminary keys are identified at this step by underlining them. However, we might have to add or change them at later steps. Notice that CustomerID is marked with a dashed line to indicate that in the RentalForm, it is not the primary key, but it might be used as a key in another table. Because TransID is unique for every transaction, there is no need to make CustomerID a key. We can already see some problems with trying to store data in this format. Notice that the same customer name, phone, and address would have to be entered several times.

Remember that some repeating sections are difficult to spot and might consist of only one column. For example, how many phone numbers can a customer have? Should the Phone column be repeating? In the case of the video store, probably not, because we most likely want to keep only one number per customer. In other businesses, we might want to keep several phone numbers for each client. Data normalization is directly related to the business processes. The tables you design depend on the way the business is organized.

into tables. The first step is to split out all repeating sections. Think about the problems that might arise if we try to keep the repeating VideosRented section with the customer data. If we design the database this way, we would have to know how many videos could be rented by each customer, because we would have to set aside space before hand. If we do not choose enough space, we will have to throw out transaction data. If we set aside too much, there will be wasted space. Figure 5.4A illustrates the problem.

The answer to this problem is to pull out the repeating section and form a new table. Then, each movie rented by a customer will fill a new row. Rows do not have to be preallocated, so there is no wasted space. Figure 5.5A uses the notation to show how the table will split. Notice that whenever we split a table this way, we have to bring along the key from the prior section. Hence, the new table will include the TransID key as well as the VideoID key.

When a table contains no repeating sections, we say that it is in *first normal form.*

## FIRST NORMAL FORM

Now that we have a way of writing down our assumptions, it is relatively straightforward to separate the data

## SECOND NORMAL FORM

Even if a table is in first normal form, there can be additional problems. Consider the RentalLine table

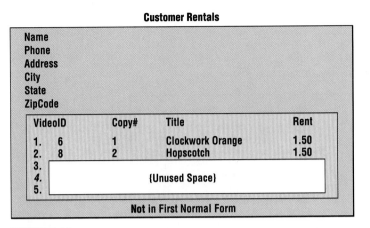

**Customer Rentals**

Name
Phone
Address
City
State
ZipCode

| VideoID | Copy# | Title | Rent |
|---------|-------|-------|------|
| 1.  6 | 1 | Clockwork Orange | 1.50 |
| 2.  8 | 2 | Hopscotch | 1.50 |
| 3. | | | |
| 4. | | {Unused Space} | |
| 5. | | | |

**Not in First Normal Form**

**FIGURE 5.4A**

A table that contains repeating sections is not in first normal form. If we try to store data in this form, we are faced with the question of deciding how many videos might be rented at one time. We will waste a lot of space with missing data.

RentalForm(TransID, RentDate, CustomerID, Phone, Name, Address, City, State, ZipCode, (VideoID, Copy#, Title, Rent))

RentalForm2(TransID, RentDate, CustomerID, Phone, Name, Address, City, State, ZipCode)

RentalLine(TransID, VideoID Copy#, Title, Rent)

**RentalForm2**

| TransID | RentDate | CustomerID | Phone | LastName | FirstName | Address | City# | State | ZipCode |
|---------|----------|------------|-------|----------|-----------|---------|-------|-------|---------|
| 1 | 4/18/99 | 3 | 502-777-7575 | Washington | Elroy | 95 Easy Street | Smith's Grove | KY | 42171 |
| 2 | 4/30/99 | 7 | 615-888-4474 | Lasater | Les | 67 S. Ray Drive | Portland | TN | 37148 |
| 3 | 4/18/99 | 8 | 615-452-1162 | Jones | Charlie | 867 Lakeside Drive | Castalian Springs | TN | 37031 |
| 4 | 4/18/99 | 3 | 502-777-7575 | Washington | Elroy | 95 Easy Street | Smith's Grove | KY | 42171 |

**Note: replication**

**RentalLine**

| TransID | VideoID | Copy# | Title | Rent |
|---------|---------|-------|-------|------|
| 1 | 1 | 2 | 2001: A Space Odyssey | $1.50 |
| 1 | 6 | 3 | Clockwork Orange | $1.50 |
| 2 | 8 | 1 | Hopscotch | $1.50 |
| 2 | 2 | 1 | Apocalypse Now | $2.00 |
| 2 | 6 | 1 | Clockwork Orange | $1.50 |
| 3 | 9 | 1 | Luggage Of The Gods | $2.50 |
| 3 | 15 | 1 | Fabulous Baker Boys | $2.00 |
| 3 | 4 | 1 | Boy And His Dog | $2.50 |
| 4 | 3 | 1 | Blues Brothers | $2.00 |
| 4 | 8 | 1 | Hopscotch | $1.50 |
| 4 | 13 | 1 | Surf Nazis Must Die | $2.50 |
| 4 | 17 | 1 | Witches of Eastwick | $2.00 |

**Note: replication**

**FIGURE 5.5A**

Splitting a table to solve problems. Problems with repeating sections are resolved by moving the repeating section into a new table. Be sure to include the old key in the new table so that you can connect the tables back together.

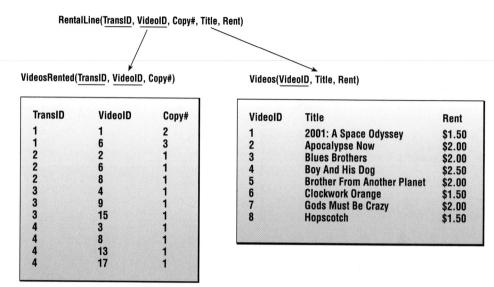

**FIGURE 5.6A**

SECOND NORMAL FORM

Even though the repeating sections are gone, we have another problem. Every time we enter the VideoID, we have to reenter the title. That would waste a lot of space. There is a more serious problem: If no one has rented a video yet, we have no way to find its title since it is not yet stored in the database. Again, the solution is to split the table. In second normal form, all nonkey columns depend on the whole key (not just part of it).

in Figure 5.5A. Notice there are two components to the key: TransID and VideoID. The nonkey items consist of the Copy#, Title, and the Rental rate for the movie. If we leave the table in this form, consider the situation of renting a movie. Every time a movie is rented (new TransID), it will be necessary to enter the VideoID, Copy#, *and* the title and rental rate. It means that we will be storing the video title every time a video is rented. Popular movies might be rented thousands of times. Do we really want to store the title each time?

The reason we have this problem is that when the TransID changes, the movie title stays the same. The movie title depends only on the VideoID. It is tempting to say that the same problem arises with respect to the rental rate. Indeed, in some video stores, the rental rate might depend only on the VideoID. However, what if the store offers discounts on certain dates, or to specific customers? If the rental rate can vary with each transaction, the rate would have to be stored with the TransID. The final choice depends on the business rules and assumptions. For now, we will assume that rental rates are like the title and depend only on the VideoID.

When the nonkey items depend on only part of the key, we need to split them into their own table. Figure 5.6A shows the new tables.

When each nonkey column in a table depends on the entire key, we say that the table is in *second normal form.*

## THIRD NORMAL FORM

Examine the RentalForm2 table in Figure 5.5A. Notice that because the primary key consists of only one column (TransID), the table must already be in second normal form. However, a different problem arises here. Again, consider what happens when we begin to collect data. Each time a customer comes to the store and rents videos there will be a new transaction. In each case, we would have to record the customer name, address, phone, city, state, and zip code. Each entry in the transaction table for a customer would duplicate this data. In addition to the wasted space, imagine the problems that arise when a customer changes a phone number. You might have to update it in hundreds of rows.

RentalForm2(<u>TransID</u>, RentDate, <u>CustomerID</u>, Phone, Name, Address, City, State, ZipCode)

Rentals(<u>TransID</u>, RentDate, <u>CustomerID</u>)

Customers(<u>CustomerID</u>, Phone, Name, Address, City, State, ZipCode)

**Rentals**

| TransID | RentDate | CustomerID |
|---------|----------|------------|
| 1 | 4/18/99 | 3 |
| 2 | 4/30/99 | 7 |
| 3 | 4/18/99 | 8 |
| 4 | 4/18/99 | 3 |

**Customers**

| CustomerID | Phone | LastName | FirstName | Address | City | State | ZipCode |
|------------|-------|----------|-----------|---------|------|-------|---------|
| 1 | 502-666-7777 | Johnson | Martha | 125 Main Street | Alvaton | KY | 42122 |
| 2 | 502-888-6464 | Smith | Jack | 873 Elm Street | Bowling Green | KY | 42101 |
| 3 | 502-777-7575 | Washington | Elroy | 95 Easy Street | Smith's Grove | KY | 42171 |
| 4 | 502-333-9494 | Adams | Samuel | 746 Brown Drive | Alvaton | KY | 42122 |
| 5 | 502-474-4746 | Rabitz | Victor | 645 White Avenue | Bowling Green | KY | 42102 |
| 6 | 615-373-4746 | Steinmetz | Susan | 15 Speedway Drive | Portland | TN | 37148 |
| 7 | 615-888-4474 | Lasater | Les | 67 S. Ray Drive | Portland | TN | 37148 |
| 8 | 615-452-1162 | Jones | Charlie | 867 Lakeside Drive | Castalian Springs | TN | 37031 |
| 9 | 502-222-4351 | Chavez | Juan | 673 Industry Blvd. | Caneyville | KY | 42721 |
| 10 | 502-444-2512 | Rojo | Maria | 88 Main Street | Cave City | KY | 42127 |

**FIGURE 5.7A**

THIRD NORMAL FORM

There is another problem with this definition. The customer name does not depend on the key (TransID) at all. Instead, it depends on the CustomerID. Because the name and address do not change for each different TransID, we need to put the customer data in a separate table. The Rentals table now contains only the CustomerID which is used to link to the Customers table and collect the rest of the data.

The problem in this case is that the customer data does not depend on the primary key (TransID) at all. Instead, it depends only on the CustomerID column. Again, the solution is to place this data into its own table. Figure 5.7A shows the split.

Splitting the table solves the problem. Customer data is now stored only one time for each customer. It is referenced back to the Rentals table through the CustomerID.

The four tables we created are listed in Figure 5.8A. Each table is now in *third normal form*. It is easy to remember the conditions required for third normal form. First: There are no repeating groups in the tables. Second and third: Each nonkey column depends on the whole key and nothing but the key.

Note in Figure 5.8A that we could technically split the Customers table one more time. Because zipcodes are uniquely assigned by the post office, the city and state could be determined directly from the zip code (they do not depend on the CustomerID). In fact, most mail order companies today keep a separate zip code table for that very reason. For our small video firm, it might be more of a nuisance to split the table. Although we can purchase a complete zip code directory in computer form, it is a very large database table. For small cases, it is often easier to leave the

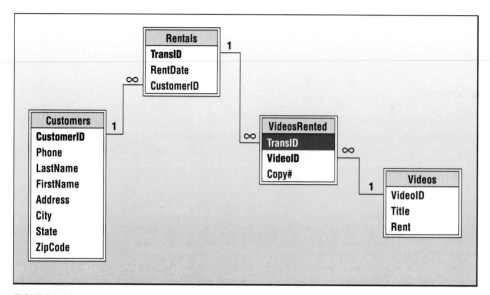

**FIGURE 5.8A**
THIRD NORMAL FORM TABLES
There are no repeating sections and each nonkey column depends on the whole key and nothing but
the key. This figure also shows the relationships between the tables that will be enforced by the
DBMS. When referential integrity is properly defined, the DBMS will ensure that rentals can be made
only to customers who are defined in the Customers table.

three items in the customer table and use the database
to assign default values so clerks can simply press
ENTER and accept the common values.

### CHECKING YOUR WORK

To double-check the tables, first look for items that
might be one-to-many relationships. They should be
signified by keys (underlined). For instance, in the
VideosRented table, each transaction can show rentals
for many videos. If you find you have to add a new
key, you will have normalize the table again.

When you are satisfied the keys adequately represent the one-to-many rules of the business, go through
each column and ask: Does it depend on the whole
key and nothing but the key? If not, split the table into
smaller pieces.

Finally, be sure that the tables can be rejoined to
create the original form or report. Notice in Figure
5.8A that you can draw lines that reconnect all of the
tables. If you find a table standing alone, it generally
means that you forgot to bring along a key value when
you split the table. Be especially careful when you are

pulling out repeating sections to carry along the key
from the main table.

Another way to test your tables is to look at the
table names. Each table should represent one entity or
object. If you have trouble deciding what to name a
table, it might be because the table is trying to describe more than one entity—like the RentalForm2
table in Figure 5.5A. You will also see similar problems as you try to enter data into the tables. If you
find yourself entering the same data more than once,
you probably made a mistake.

### EXERCISES

1. A friend of yours has just opened a photofinishing
   operation. She wants you to create a database system to help her run the business. The basic processing is straightforward: A customer drops or mails
   in one or more rolls of film. A clerk records the
   basic data on the customer and the film. The rolls
   are assigned a number, sorted, and run through
   the processor. Processing varies slightly depending
   on the type of film, film speed, and processing

| EIS Project #:<br>Date initiated:<br>Date ECC involved:<br>Date ECC finished: | Client:<br>Principal contact:<br>Phone:<br>Contact address:<br>City, state, zip: | Phone:<br>Billing address:<br>City, state, zip: |
|---|---|---|
| Site location: latitude      longitude<br>Site address:      City:      State:      Zip:<br>Site description: | | |
| Proposed development description: | Proposed activities (standard list):<br>Drain wetlands<br>Fill<br>Build roads<br>Store waste | |

| Comments and Responses | | | | | | |
|---|---|---|---|---|---|---|
| Date received | Category | Source | File | Response date | Person | Title |
| | | | | | | |
| | | | | | | |
| | | | | | | |

options. Your friend wants to keep track of which clerk performed the processing and match the names with any complaints that might arise. She also wants to offer a frequent-buyer program to reward the most active customers. It is also important to track the chemical usage for the processing—both to keep track of orders and expenses, and to make sure the processors always have fresh chemicals. The clerks are also responsible for cleaning the processing equipment. Create a set of normalized tables for this company. Identify attributes where possible. (Hint: Obtain a film mailer that lists various options.)

2. You have been hired by an environmental consulting company (ECC) that specializes in creating environmental impact statements (EISs) for large projects. It needs a database to track the progress of each EIS. The company is particularly concerned about tracking public comments, questions from state and federal officials, and the responses to all of these comments. All comments are scanned and stored as digital files. Create a list of normalized tables needed to build this database.

3. Using your experience with video stores, extend the example presented in this chapter to include more data. For example, the store wants to let parents limit the videos their children can rent based on the movie's rating.

4. The Rolling Thunder company wants to offer cafeteria-style benefits to its employees. Each year, employees would get to select items such as health insurance, dental benefits, child care, and so on. Employees would have a fixed amount of money to spend on the various items. Diagram a form that could be used to enter the data, then define the tables that would be added to the system.

5. Create a small database to track the grades you receive in your classes. You should record each assignment, the due date, and the grade received. Design the system so that it can handle all of your courses.

# PART 2

# *Business Integration*

**How do information systems help managers integrate business tasks?**
A hundred years ago, there were very few large businesses. As firms
became larger, owners needed a way to manage and control the huge
number of employees. Managers needed assistance with hundreds of
daily operational decisions. The primary approach was to build a hierarchical structure where each division was divided into ever-smaller departments. With guidelines and standard procedures, each
department was independent and was responsible for its
own operations.

Technology provides managers with virtually instantaneous communication. This communication enables
managers to integrate the business operations. Managers can reorganize the business to solve problems
from a broader perspective. Technology also enables
managers to integrate information in different formats from multiple
locations around the company.

# Networks and Telecommunications

Fisher Scientific products are used by scientists throughout the world. Information technology and the Internet enable scientists to obtain up-to-date information on products, prices, and orders.

## FISHER SCIENTIFIC

In 1902, Chester G. Fisher, 22, of the Western University of Pennsylvania opened his own business. He saw a need for someone to supply scientific laboratories so he purchased a local storeroom to begin a scientific supply business. Laboratory work was based on simple experiments involving solid, liquid, and gaseous measurement. Fisher's earliest products included microscopes, burettes, pipettes, litmus, balances, and calorimeters.

In 1978, Fisher installed computer terminals at his major customers' sites, enabling them to place orders directly and receive immediate order verification. Customers were able to look up information on past purchases and other financial information. A year later, Fisher expanded this system to increase the speed and accessibility of the customers' terminals.

In 1994, Fisher Scientific became the first catalog distributor in the industry to have the majority of its product offering available to its customers on CD-ROM and for purchase on its web site. Fisher's spending on computer technology has increased its efficiency and enabled it to win large preferred supplier agreements such as the Department of Defense for handling smaller instrumentation and operational products.

**OVERVIEW**   "The network *is* the computer." Scott McNealy, CEO of Sun Microsystems, built his company on this philosophy. In any business, buying computers and collecting data is not enough. To produce information, we must be able to share. As illustrated by Figure 6.1, networks are used to share data, software, and hardware and to communicate throughout the company. The ultimate goal is to eliminate distance as a factor in managing a business.

The importance of teamwork is easy to understand. Why would anyone disagree? Why would a company (or a nation) not have a state-of-the-art network? Like many questions in MIS, there are two basic problems: cost and changes in technology. Most networks rely on cables to transmit data. Installing cables in a building is time-consuming, expensive, and disruptive. Additionally, there are several possible ways to link computers together. As we gain knowledge and technology improves, companies eventually have to

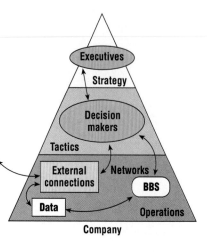

**FIGURE 6.1**

Managing an organization requires communication. Increasingly, communication uses computer networks to collect data, transmit messages, store collective knowledge, search for answers, coordinate work, and connect to external agents.

replace components in their networks. Managers need to plan and predict how the company will grow and how technology might change. Between the costs and uncertainties, there is plenty of room for disagreement and several decisions to be made.

Consider the brief history of networks in most companies. Years ago, companies installed lines for telephones. Then they installed lines for dumb terminals connected to central computers. Then they installed lines for video. Then they installed **local area networks (LANs)** to connect personal computers. Every time the company grows, it has to expand these networks.

Consider the dream of a full-service, integrated network that would combine voice, fax, computer data, images, and video on one integrated system. We would like instant access to the system from anywhere in the world. We could send or receive any type of data anywhere, then copy it, edit it, search it, and route it to additional people. Oh yes, we would have access to the network 24 hours a day with no failures, no transmission errors, and no loss of data, and it would cost very little.

We actually come close to having all of these capabilities today, except that the cost of using such networks is not as low as in our dream. In the early 1960s, it was technically possible to build a network of videophones. But it was too expensive—not enough people were willing to pay the price. Over time, technology improved and costs declined so that telecommunication companies are now building networks to carry video data; thus, as a manager, you need to be aware of the changing capabilities of networks, but you must also evaluate the benefits and compare them to the costs.

**INTRODUCTION**

Communication is important to companies. There are two major categories of communication: internal and external. Internally, communication is used to keep the business running as one cohesive organization. Messages and data constantly travel among workers and managers. Workers collect data and share it with colleagues and summarize it for managers. Managers use the data to make decisions and change the organization. Changes are implemented as new policies and procedures, resulting in messages that are distributed throughout the company. External communications are important for many reasons, including collecting data about customers and suppliers and providing information to shareholders and governmental agencies.

To understand the importance of telecommunications, note that AGS Information Services (a consulting firm) estimates that 48 percent to 68 percent of corporate technology budgets are spent on telecommunications. Some firms, like travel agents and broker-

## Trends

The telephone system was originally designed to transmit sound by converting sound waves into electrical signals. Certain limitations were built into the system to keep costs down. An important feature of the phone system is its ability to handle multiple phone calls on one line. In the very early days of telephony, phone calls were connected by giant switchboards that required separate physical connections for each call. Over time, these switchboards were replaced with electronic switches. Today, the switches are the heart of the phone system network. Most of the switches in the United States are actually dedicated computers. To carry voice calls, the switches first convert the electrical signal into packets of digital data. These packets are then sent to the appropriate destination.

Another major change is the use of cellular telephones. In the 1980s, cellular telephone networks were installed in U.S. cities. They enable people to carry portable telephones, which transmit and receive signals with radio waves instead of wires. Computers are used to identify phones and maintain connections.

A more recent trend that will affect personal communications is the rapid growth of cable television. Over 60 percent of U.S. households can receive cable television. In 1996, the government removed almost all barriers in the telecommunications industry. Consequently, the major cable television providers are considering using their systems to transmit phone calls, and the phone companies are attempting to transmit television programs over the phone lines. The competition could be interesting. Cable television uses wiring that can carry more data (or channels). However, the cable systems do not have the routing capability of the phone companies.

Originally, computers were expensive. As a result, most companies owned only one computer. Because input and output were located at one point, there was little reason to transmit data. Eventually, video terminals and personal computers were placed on managers' desks, and these computers needed to share information.

The late 1980s saw a significant increase in the number of companies connecting computers with local area networks (LANs). Many computers are also connected across longer distances. These connections often use the services of the telephone companies. The digital phone switches make it easier to transmit computer data.

Some companies are experimenting with radio networks that connect portable personal computers without wires. At the other end of the scale, several countries are investing money in high-speed computer networks. These communication lines will make it easier for researchers and businesses to exchange information.

The defining trend of the 1990s is the use of the Internet. From 1994, commercial use of the Internet grew exponentially. Substantial improvements were made in browsers, web site capabilities, and transmission speed. Technologically, the Internet is simply a large global network created by the acceptance of standards. In practice, the Internet capabilities have the power to change society. We have only begun the process, and tomorrow's managers need to understand the capabilities of networks.

age firms, rely heavily on telecommunications and spend even more for them. Telecommunications expenses represent 2 percent to 7 percent of these businesses' total operating budget—which amounts to more than $10 million a year for a $500 million firm.

Sharing data and resources can cause problems. For example, there are security issues concerning who should be able to use and change the data. Additionally, there are political problems regarding ownership and control over the data. These concerns are multiplied in an international environment, because national governments may impose constraints on how companies can use the data they collect.

The objective of a network is to connect computers transparently, so that the users do not know the network exists. The network provides access to data on central computers, departmental computers, and sometimes on other workers' personal computers. Networks can create shared access to fax machines, modems, printers, scanners, and other special-ized hardware. To the user, it does not matter where these devices are located. The net-work makes them work the same as if they were on any desktop. Department stores were early users of networked systems that enabled tracking sales by each store.

## Sharing Data

Sharing data, which is one of the most obvious uses of networks, also makes profound changes in the way an organization works. For hundreds of years, companies have been organized as hierarchies, divided into smaller organizations that are easier to manage. Dupont and General Motors quickly learned that as the size of an organization increases, it becomes increasingly difficult to manage, so their executives invented the structure of the modern corporation. Much like a military organization, dividing the company into subsections with well-defined tasks enables top executives to focus on direction while lower-level managers implement solutions. In this type of organization, data flows up and down the hierarchies, whereas limited data flows across the various departments. Enter-prising managers often build informal connections with managers in other departments to improve their personal access to data.

Implementing networks in a corporation changes the way employees and managers communicate. A well-designed  information system can radically increase the flow of data throughout a company. Managers can see customer and marketing data immediately as it is collected. Employees in one department can easily share data with other depart-ments. Globally located firms can use networks to operate on problems around the clock, sharing data and bringing in teams as each day begins around the world. Changing the way people communicate has the ability to alter the entire structure of the company. In particular, the increased flow of data across organizational lines reduces the importance and power of the hierarchical structure. It also means that managers have to trust employ-ees. By giving employees access to the data they need, jobs can be accomplished faster and with higher quality. A network also facilitates the use of teams. In particular, it en-ables informal teams to spring up throughout the company to solve problems as they arise. Instead of waiting for a higher-level manager to appoint a team, employees can use the network to ask questions, notify others involved, and find in-house experts.

### Transactions

One of the most important reasons for connecting computers is the ability to share data. Consider a retail store with five checkout registers. Each register is actually a computer. If these computers are not connected, it is difficult to compute the daily sales for the store. At the end of the day, someone would have to manually collect the data from each computer and enter it into another computer. Also, imagine what would happen if a cus-tomer asked a clerk to determine whether a product was sold out. The clerk would have to check with each of the other clerks or perhaps call the storeroom. Collecting data from point-of-sale devices was a primary motivation for installing computers in the retail envi-ronment. A simple network is shown in Figure 6.2.

Connecting the firm's computers enables a central database to maintain the current inventory and sales data. Current sales totals will be available instantly from any termi-nal. When a customer asks whether an item is in stock, the clerk simply looks up one number. If several stores are connected with the network, the clerk's computer can in-stantly check inventory at the other store as well. Similarly, the manager can get daily sales figures from each location without leaving the office. Increasingly, consumers are gaining direct access to merchants and banks. Consequently, automated bill payments are becoming increasingly popular.

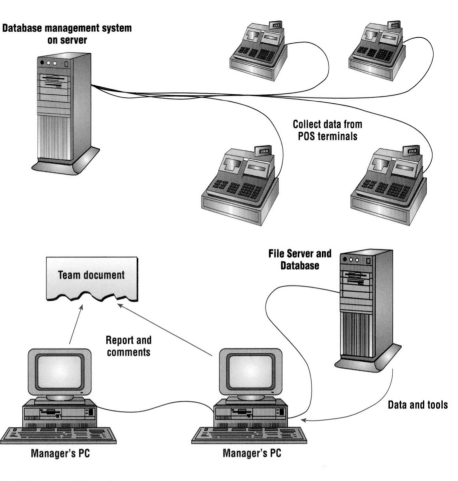

**FIGURE 6.2**
NETWORK FOR
TRANSACTION
PROCESSING
Networks are often
used to collect data in a
central database. From
there, the data can be
queried and analyzed
by managers.

**FIGURE 6.3**
NETWORK FOR
DECISIONS AND
COLLABORATION
The file server holds
basic data and software
tools. Managers
retrieve data and create
reports. The reports
can be shared with
other managers. With
collaborative software,
revisions are
automatically tracked
and combined to form
the final document.

## Decisions and Searches

Many types of data need to be shared in a company. Look at the problem from a manager's viewpoint. Each level of management has its own decisions to make and each requires information from the rest of the company. Consider a situation in which a manager is told to close down 3 out of 200 stores. Selecting those stores can be a tough decision. It requires knowing sales volume for every store and projected future sales as well as operating costs. The manager will bring the basic information to a personal computer to create graphs and evaluate models. It is possible to collect all of the data from each store by hand and enter it into the computer. However, it would be much more efficient if the manager could simply transfer the data directly from the central database to the personal computer. Not only is this method faster, it prevents errors. The database should have the most recent information. Additionally, all managers will use the same data. A portion of a network for making decisions and sharing work with team members is illustrated in Figure 6.3. Without networks and centralized data sharing, many companies experience problems when managers have different versions of the data. American Express implemented a LAN in its human resources department to help the staff consolidate information and process data more efficiently.

## Messages

Computer networks can be used to send messages to other people, much like telephone or mail systems. This technique is called *electronic mail* or **e-mail** for short. By connecting computers, one person can send a message to any other user connected to the mail system.

**FIGURE 6.4**
**NETWORKS FOR**
**COMMUNICATION**

E-mail messages and scheduling are two common forms of communication in business. With e-mail, one machine holds the mail for the group. Mail is held until the recipient logs on and can receive the message. For scheduling, each user maintains a personal calendar. To schedule a meeting with a group of people, the computer examines the calendars for the desired participants to locate an open time slot.

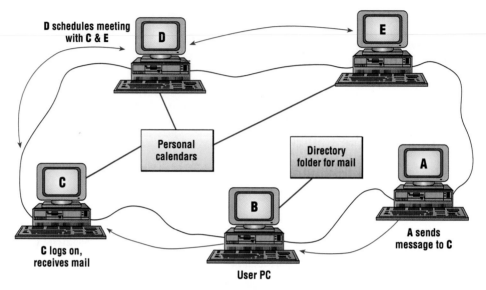

Current mail systems enable you to send files, pictures, or even sound to other computer users. As shown in Figure 6.4, e-mail systems often rely on one machine to hold messages, which are then distributed to other computers when the users sign on.

Many companies have their own internal e-mail systems. Common interoffice communications (such as meeting notices) are sent over the computer. E-mail is much faster than traditional mail. Many times it is more convenient than using telephones because there are never any busy lines with e-mail. E-mail users can send or receive messages at any time. Electronic messages can be sent to many people at the same time by creating a mailing list. Messages can be stored, retrieved, and searched for later usage. In most systems, the computer can automatically notify you when the recipient reads your message. You never have to worry about whether your message was received.

Voice mail systems, which resemble answering machines, have some of these same advantages. However, e-mail takes less space to store. More importantly, e-mail can be scanned electronically to search for key topics. Similarly, there are e-mail filters that automatically read your mail and focus on the topics you have chosen. They cut down on the amount of junk e-mail messages.

There are also public networks that enable organizations to communicate electronically. The most popular is the Internet, which is a worldwide data communications network that links together millions of computers. With this system, managers can easily communicate with researchers at universities and with other managers around the world. Sometimes, people are too easy to reach by e-mail; executives and researchers are increasingly swamped by e-mail messages.

There are some drawbacks to e-mail. For one, some people are still reluctant to use computers, so they do not check the computer often enough to keep up with their mail. Another problem is that in 1991, the U.S. courts ruled that public transmission systems such as e-mail are not subject to the same legal protections for privacy as paper mail and phone calls. Unless the laws are rewritten, therefore, it is legal for employers (and almost anyone else) to read everyone's e-mail messages. Of course, the fact that it is legal does not make it ethical. The best solution to open communication systems is to encrypt the messages. Most word processors and spreadsheets make it easy to encrypt the files when they are saved. An interesting twist on this situation is that some courts have ruled that

---

**Reality Bytes        6–1    Be Careful What You Say on the Internet**

The Internet has become an important source of financial information for investors, particularly small investors who do not want to pay the fees charged by full-service brokerage firms. Current and historical data is easily available from government agencies and individual companies. But today's investors are never satisfied with current data. People are always searching for rumors, tips, and insight that will help them guess which companies might succeed. Hence, hundreds of sites and chat rooms have evolved to share and spread rumors. Hundreds of people have created newsletters and e-mail lists to promote stocks. In October 1998, the Securities and Exchange Commission (SEC) filed charges against 44 of these promoters.

For example, the SEC alleged that George Schleiben, publisher of his own online newsletter (http://www.pennystock.com), failed to disclose that he received about $100,000 in compensation from the companies he promoted. Mr. Schleiben notes that he did disclose he was being paid, but he never specified how much. Some of the charges against other people were more serious, including claims that some individuals spread false information about companies in an effort to drive up their stock prices. Even the SEC admits that it is impossible to police all of the messages on the Internet. The bottom line is that you must be careful about trusting messages, tips, and information from the Internet.

---

public officials *cannot* encrypt their messages; in fact, in some situations, it is illegal for public officials to communicate via e-mail at all.

### Bulletin Boards, Newsgroups, and Chat Rooms

An electronic *bullentin board system (BBS)* is similar to a physical bulletin board, except that people access it from computers. The BBS allows users to post comments, pictures, and files for other people to view or copy. Bulletin boards are usually organized by topics, and you can search them for specific phrases or comments. They are a useful way to disseminate information that is of interest to many different people. Today, bulletin boards can be accessed as web sites from the Internet. In other words, a bulletin board is a type of web site, with the main feature that it is designed to have many people post information.

A **newsgroup** is an Internet feature similar to a bulletin board in that it carries comments from many people. It is designed to be copied from server to server so that the comments are available to a wide audience. Internet newsgroups are useful when you are searching for people with experiences similar to your own. However, they are a bad place to put company information.

A *chat room* is a specialized web site that enables participants to type comments and see other responses in real time. It is similar to a bulletin board but more transitory—messages are usually not saved. So you can see only messages from people who are currently connected to the room. Chat rooms have not had much use in business.

Overall, the purpose of these three systems is to enable people to send and retrieve electronic messages from others. The difference lies in the level of central control and monitoring. More highly monitored newsgroups are generally more accurate and more valuable in business. For example, the HRM department could run a newsgroup to provide information about benefits. Employee questions and answers could be posted in the newsgroup or through a BBS because answers to one person might be valuable to other employees.

### Calendars and Scheduling

Managers spend a great deal of time in meetings. Yet, sometimes the greatest challenge with meetings is finding a time when everyone can get together. Several software packages use computer networks to solve this problem. Managers enter planned meeting times and scheduled events into their personal electronic calendar file, where each event is assigned a priority number. For example, a time allotted for a haircut would be given a low priority; a meeting with a supervisor would receive a higher rating. If the CEO wants to set up a meeting, the CEO tells the computer which people are to be included, sets a priority level, and gives an approximate time. The computer then uses the network to check everyone else's schedule. When it finds an open time (overriding lower priority events if needed), it enters the meeting into each person's calendar. The entire process takes a few seconds.

### Teamwork and Joint Authorship

In any job, it is rare for one person to work alone. Most businesses are arranged as teams. Within the team, individual people are given specific assignments, and each team member contributes to the final product. For instance, the marketing department might have to prepare a sales forecast for the next six months. Each person could work on a specific sales region or product category. These individual pieces would then be merged into a single document. If the computers are networked, the manager's computer can pull the individual pieces from each of the individual computers. Also, each team member can be given access to the others' work to ensure that the reports use the same data and assumptions.

**Groupware** is software that enables several people to work on the same document. Each individual computer has access to the master document. When one person makes a change to the document, the change is highlighted for everyone to read and approve. With existing international networks, each person might be located in a different country. Lotus Notes is a groupware product that makes it easy for employees to combine data and communicate interactively with each other. Microsoft distributes a product called Net-Meeting, which combines several groupware tools and enables managers to participate in meetings across a network. It is described in more detail in the appendix to Chapter 7.

### Backup

Another important reason for sharing data over computer networks is that most people are not very good at maintaining backup copies of their work—especially on personal computers. If each computer is attached to a network, there are two ways to set up an automatic backup system for individual personal computers. The older method relies on individual workers saving their files to a central file server. The network manager then makes daily (or hourly) backups of the data on the central server.

A newer method is significantly safer because it is virtually automatic and does not require users to remember to transfer their files. It does require users to leave their machines running. At a predetermined time, a central computer with a large backup capacity connects to the individual machines and copies the files that have changed. This data is then stored somewhere safe (such as a tape or optical disk). If a computer or a person accidentally deletes a file, the backup computer can restore the file and send it back to the personal computer. With the communication network, the backup process is almost completely automatic.

## Sharing Hardware

Hardware items are also often shared through communication networks. For example, networks are used to provide users access to special output devices, such as high-speed printers, plotters, or color printers. Networks can be used to give people access to special computers, such as when an engineer needs to use a high-speed supercomputer.

### Printers

A common use of networks is to give users access to high-speed, high-quality printers. Even if each computer has a small personal printer attached, some jobs need to be handled

**FIGURE 6.5**
NETWORKS FOR SHARING HARDWARE
The workstations use the server to perform backups. Files are picked up by the server and transferred to tape. The LAN administrator can reload a tape and restore files as needed. Networks are often used to share printers and storage devices. Networks can be used to share access to supercomputers—even if they are in a different city or different country.

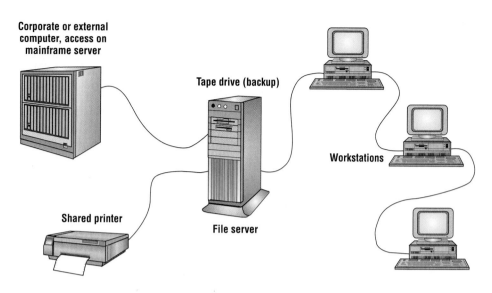

Corporate or external computer, access on mainframe server

Tape drive (backup)

Workstations

File server

Shared printer

by a high-speed laser printer. Some printers even provide collating and stapling of documents. For instance, at $5,000 each it would be expensive to buy color laser printers for everyone who might need one, yet it might be reasonable to buy one for a department to share. With a network, users can choose from among two or three different printers by selecting them on the screen. Figure 6.5 shows some of the hardware devices that are often shared.

Another advantage is that if one printer breaks down, users can send their jobs to another printer on the network. Think about what happens if there is no network and your printer breaks down. You have to copy the file to a floppy disk and interrupt someone else's work to borrow their computer to send the file to another printer. What happens if you are using a special software package that no else has on his or her computer? You will probably have to physically move a printer from another computer desk to yours, connect the hardware, print your document, and return the printer. When you are on a network, you simply select a different printer from a list displayed on your computer and go pick up the output.

### Storage Devices

The arguments used for network printer sharing can be applied to sharing storage devices. For instance, the firm's finance department may require access to large financial databases. Financial data and stock prices for most U.S. companies can be purchased on CD-ROM disks. It would be expensive to buy copies of the data disks for every person in the finance department. It makes more sense to connect the finance computers and the CD-ROM drive together on a network, then whenever someone wants to look up information in the database, the computer uses the network to transfer the information from the optical disk.

### Special Processors

Special computers that are relatively expensive can be attached to a network to save costs and make it easier for users to access these machines. Parallel-processing computers and other supercomputers can perform calculations thousands of times faster than ordinary computers, but they are expensive. Consider a small engineering company. For the most part, the engineers use their workstations to develop their designs. They occasionally need to run simulations or produce detailed graphic images. Both of these tasks could take many hours to perform on individual client computers. The company can cable each engineer's workstation to a network that can access a supercomputer. When an engineer needs to perform high-speed calculations, the job is sent directly to the supercomputer. The results are returned via the network to the workstation so they can be added to the final report. More likely, a university could own the supercomputer, and the firm would lease time to run each job. If the network is deigned properly, it makes no difference where the machine is located.

## Sharing Software

At one time, networks were used to share software, which cut down on the disk space required by individual machines. When disk drives cost $1 per megabyte, it was cheaper to store one copy of a 200 megabyte program on a central server, rather then eat up space on 20 client machines. Today, disk space is essentially free so the storage cost issue is less important. On the other hand, it takes time to install individual copies of software. Sharing one copy on the network server makes it easier to install and upgrade software.

Consider the same example if all of the computers were connected to each other with a network. One of the computers could be chosen to store all of the software. This machine would be a **file server.** Each application package would only be stored on the file server, which would conserve space on the other 24 machines. To use the software, your computer takes the application package from the file server and loads it into the RAM on your computer. Only one new copy has to be installed to update the software for all users.

The issue of buying 25 copies of an application package is a little trickier. It depends on the software company and how often the software is used. Each software company has its own license requirements. In some cases, if all 25 people want to use the software at the same time, you will still have to buy 25 copies. In other cases, if only 10 people will be using the software at the same time, you would have to buy a license for only 10 users, then any group of 10 people can use the software. The software automatically counts the number of current users. When it reaches 10, no one else is allowed to use that package. The amount of money that can be saved depends on how many people will be using each package at the same time. These network license agreements are especially useful for experimenting with software that only a few people will use at one time.

Of course, the server-based approach does not work in all cases. Portable computers require their own software so they can be used when they are not connected to the network. Another drawback to the server-based approach is that it places greater demands on the network. Sometimes the network is too slow or too unreliable to share software.

## Voice and Video Communication

A major cost of telecommunications in business is for telephone calls. Despite the total expenditures, there is little doubt about the value of communication and phones. Phone calls are almost always cheaper than in-person visits. With the rapidly declining costs of phone calls, cost is less of an issue. Even cellular phone costs are dropping rapidly; some experts predict that within a few years, almost all calls will be made over the cellular networks instead of traditional phone lines.

Since the mid-1980s, companies have experimented with video communication or teleconferencing. The ultimate objective is to decrease travel costs by connecting people with video links. Several large companies built teleconferencing rooms that provide video links to similar centers. With several video links, participants at each center can see and hear the others, as well as view documents at each location. The centers have been useful for companies that routinely conduct business in fixed locations, such as a U.S. company with a manufacturing plant in Southeast Asia.

With improvements in technology and faster transmission of data at lower costs, it is becoming feasible to run full-service networks to each desk. These links enable workers to communicate with others using voice, pictures, computer data, or video across the same line. Although these links are technically feasible today, they are somewhat expensive.

As Internet speeds improve and costs continue to decline, you will have more opportunities to use these technologies. Currently, one of the greatest difficulties with using these technologies over the Internet is that you may randomly experience delays from some link. But newer versions of the Internet protocols are being released that support guaranteed levels of service. Soon you will be able to conduct video meetings by reserving a certain level of speed at a set time.

## COMPONENTS OF A NETWORK

At some point in your career, you might be responsible for purchasing a local area network. Similarly, you might experience problems when some component of an existing network fails. In both cases, you need to be familiar with the major components of a LAN. Illustrated by Figure 6.6, computer networks contain four basic components: computers, transmission media, connection devices, and software. In practice, there are many varieties of the components. Also, several companies manufacture each of these products, hence, sometimes products do not work well together. As a result, it can be confusing and difficult to create a computer network. It can also be difficult to track down the source of problems.

## Computers

Virtually any type of computer device can be connected to a network. Sometimes only simple terminals and printers will be used for input and output. At other times, personal computers are linked. Sometimes there will be several large central computers connected together. In some cases, all of the computers will be similar. In other cases, one computer will be faster and larger than the others.

The earliest computer networks consisted of one computer with several terminals and printers attached to it. These networks were fairly simple, because all of the work was performed by the one computer. Substantially more problems are involved in connecting several computers together. For starters, each computer needs to know that the others exist and that they have a specified location (address) on the network. The computers

**FIGURE 6.6**

LAN COMPONENTS
A local area network consists of four major components: computers, transmission media, connection devices, and software. Each computer and shared peripheral must be connected to the transmission media. Network operating system software controls access to files and controls the flow of data on the network. The personal computer operating system must be modified to recognize the LAN services and process communication between the personal computer and the LAN.

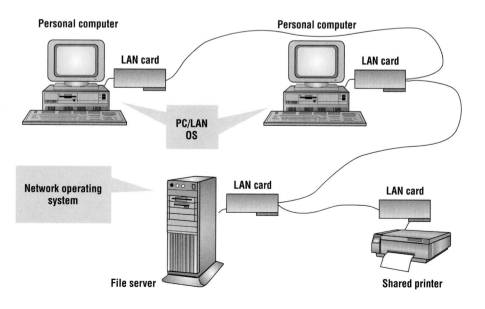

need to know how to send and receive information from each other. To work together, they need connection devices (LAN cards) and special software.

Computers attached to networks tend to perform one of two functions: servers or clients. *Servers* are computers that store data to be used by other computers attached to the network. *Clients* are computers used by individual people. Sometimes a computer is used as both a client and a file server. Networks where many of the machines operate as both clients and servers are called **peer-to-peer networks.**

### Servers

Consider a human resources management (HRM) department that wants to create a network of computers. This department wants to use one computer to store the data files for the employees, as well as data about training classes, new jobs, benefits, and work schedules. Managers want employees to use the computers to look for information about their jobs. On the other hand, there is some information (such as salaries) that only managers should be able to see. Before the network, each type of information was stored on a separate computer. An employee would have to check four different computers in order to find all of the basic information. However, the salary information was stored on only the manager's computer, so no one else could use it. Figure 6.7 shows the situations before and after the installation of a network.

The department wants to buy one larger computer and use it as a file server. It will have a much bigger and faster hard disk to store all of the data files. The other computers will be used to look up any information on the file server. In this manner, employees can find all of the information they need by using one computer. Yet, there is a slight problem: The manager still wants to prevent the employees from seeing the salary data.

Actually, there are two complications for the file server. First, any computer that stores files for the others must be able to talk to them all at the same time. Second, the file server needs to have security provisions so that some information can be accessed only by authorized users. In other words, the file server has to be able to function as a multiuser computer. Remember that personal computers were originally designed to work with only one person at a time. For personal computers to function as file servers, they need a multiuser operating system. This operating system has to understand the network, provide file and printer access to the attached computers, and provide security for each of the files.

**FIGURE 6.7**
SAMPLE NETWORK FOR HRM
Before installing the network, human resources management workers had to move to different machines to perform each task or data had to be duplicated across each machine. After the network was installed, each workstation had equal access to any database. Access can be improved by adding more client computers or by connecting the network to workers' desktop machines.

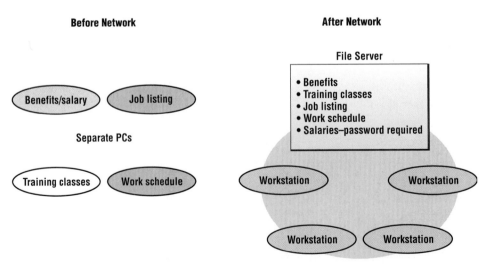

### Client Computers

The networked computers could be any type of machine. Because these computers are typically used by individual people at their own desks, they are often call *client computers*. These computers need to access the network and be able to send information to at least one other computer. A **network interface card (NIC)** (or LAN card) is installed in each computer. These cards are connected together by some transmission medium (e.g., cable). Additionally, the personal computers might need special driver software to connect the operating system to the network.

In 1999, Microsoft began encouraging organizations to switch to their Windows 2000 operating system (which was originally called Windows NT). While there were several reasons for the switch, the most important is that Windows 2000 was designed to function better in a networked environment. In particular, it supports both client and server functions and has a reliable security system. The system makes it easy to create a personal web site on your computer, and to control who can see and use the files on your computer.

With this peer-to-peer system, you can make a file available to others. To do this, you simply put it into a directory where read or write permissions have been given to the appropriate workers. They can then find the file using a Web browser. If they know the name of the file, they can open it directly using the **universal naming convention (UNC).** For example, if the file *May2000.xls* is stored on the server *Accounting* in the *Distribution* directory, an authorized user can open it with the name: \\Accounting\ Distribution\May2000.xls.

When you tell the application software to read a file from a server, several things happen. First, your workstation sends a message to the file server. The server decides whether you have the proper authority to use that file. If so, it sends the file over the network to your computer. All of these messages are hidden from you, and you can treat the file server just as if it were a high-capacity hard disk drive.

## Media

All communication requires a transmission medium. There are many different ways of connecting computers. As illustrated in Figure 6.8, common methods include electric

**FIGURE 6.8**
Signals can be sent via several types of media. They can be carried by electricity, light waves, or radio waves. All of these methods have advantages and disadvantages. Fiber-optic cabling offers the fastest transmission rates with the least interference, but because it is relatively new, the initial cost tends to be higher.

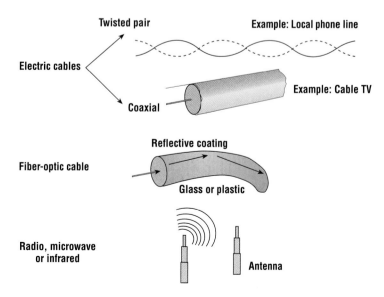

wires, light waves, and radio waves. From a computer management perspective, there are some distinct advantages and disadvantages of using each of these methods. In many ways, the choice of communication medium is the most important aspect of selecting and installing a network. All of the other components can be changed fairly easily. Cables are often buried underground or run through the walls and ceilings of buildings. Once a media choice is made, it can be expensive to change your mind and install new cabling.

### Electric Cables

The two basic types of electric cables are twisted pair and coaxial. *Twisted pair* is the oldest form of electrical wiring. Since electricity must travel in a closed loop, electrical connections require at least two wires. Twisted-pair wires are simply pairs of plain copper wires. There are many examples of twisted-pair wires in households, such as telephone cables. Twisted pair is the cheapest type of cabling available. Another advantage is that some businesses have extra, unused telephone wires in buildings. In a few cases, these extra wires can be used to connect computers, which reduces the cost of installing new wires.

Twisted-pair wires have certain disadvantages. This type of cable cannot carry much information at one time. Plus, data transmitted on twisted-pair wires is subject to interference from other electrical devices. Interference can distort or damage a telecommunications signal. For instance, it is best to avoid running twisted-pair wires next to electric power lines and electric motors, because these devices produce electromagnetic radiation that can interfere with the signal. On the other hand, it is possible to put several twisted pairs into the same diameter as one coaxial cable. The overall transmission speed can be increased by sending portions of the message along each wire.

Coaxial cables were designed to carry more information than twisted pairs, with lower chances of interference. *Coaxial cable* (often shortened to *coax*) consists of a central wire, surrounded by a nonconductive plastic, which is surrounded by a second wire. The second wire is actually a metallic foil or mesh that is wrapped around the entire cable. This shielding minimizes interference from outside sources. Cable television signals are transmitted on coaxial cables. Coax is capable of carrying more information for longer distances than twisted pair.

Despite the strengths of coax cable, twisted pair dominates most LAN installations today. The main reason is because of the engineering developments that enable multiple pairs to carry data at higher speeds. It is cheaper to bundle multiple twisted pairs than multiple coax lines.

### Fiber Optics

A relatively recent invention (early 1970s) in communication uses light instead of electricity. Because light generally travels in a straight line, it could be difficult to use for communication. Fiber-optic cable allows light to travel in straight lines but still be bent around corners. A fiber-optic cable consists of a glass or plastic core that is surrounded by a reflective material. A laser light (typically infrared) is sent down the cable. When the cable turns, the light is reflected around the corner and continues down the cable. Fiber-optic cable provides the advantages of high capacity with almost no interference. The limitation in using fiber is the higher cost of the cable and the cost of the connectors and interface cards that convert computer electrical signals into light. For example, NICs for coaxial or twisted-pair cables can be purchased for

A thin fiber-optic cable can carry as much data as 900 single copper wires, with minimal interference and superior tensile strength.

around $80, whereas NICs for fiber-optic lines that run directly to personal computers cost around $700 (in 1999).

### Radio, Micro, and Infrared Waves

Radio, microwave, and infrared transmissions do not require cables. These communication methods are called **broadcasts.** The signal can be picked up by any receiver or antenna that lies in its path. However, microwave and infrared transmissions require clear line-of-sight transmission. The major advantage of broadcast methods is portability. For example, computers can be installed in delivery vehicles to receive information from corporate headquarters. On a smaller scale, individuals can carry around small computers (e.g., handheld computers). These computers can communicate with each other and with a central database via a broadcast network. For example, physicians in hospitals could carry small computers that would automatically receive information for each patient when the physician enters the room. Any instructions could be sent directly from the physician's computer to the nursing station. Commodity traders have also found portable computers and radio networks to be useful.

There are two potential drawbacks to broadcast media. First, it is more important to provide security for the transmissions. Second, broadcast transmissions carry a limited amount of data. The two problems are related. Because it is a broadcast method, the signals sent by one computer can be received by any other computer within range. There is no way to prevent other computers from physically receiving the signal.

The problem of limited capacity arises because only a small number of radio frequencies can be used to carry data. Most of the radio and television frequencies are already being used for other purposes. Figure 6.9 shows some of the major frequency allocations in the United States. The Federal Communications Commission (FCC) allocated the personal communication service (PCS) bands in late 1993 for use by personal communication devices such as laptop computers and personal digital assistants

**FIGURE 6.9**

ELECTROMAGNETIC
FREQUENCY
SPECTRUM

Communication
techniques are
essentially the same on
all media, because all
waves physically have
similar properties.
However, the different
frequencies affect the
communication
performance. Shorter
wave lengths (higher
frequencies) can carry
more data. Some
waves can travel longer
distances. Others are
more susceptible to
interference. In any
case, there are a finite
number of frequencies
available for
communication. Hence,
the frequency spectrum
is allocated by
governmental agencies.

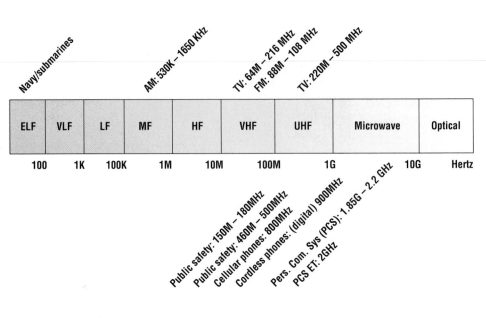

(PDAs). To provide these frequencies, the FCC had to take them away from existing users. Imagine what would happen if computers suddenly started sending information over the same radio frequency as that used by your favorite radio station. You would not be able to hear the voices on the radio, and the computers would miss most of their data because of the interference.

All governments allocate the frequency spectrum for various uses, such as radio, television, cellular phones, and garage door openers. The PCS frequencies were auctioned off to the highest bidders in 1994, raising more the $65 billion. The frequency problem is even more complicated when the signals might cross political boundaries. As a result, most broadcast telecommunications issues are established with international co-operation. Some of the overcrowding problems are being mitigated through the use of digital transmissions that cram more calls and more data into the same amount of frequency space.

Despite these problems, an increasing amount of business communication is being carried over radio networks. For example, from 1982 to 1993, the use of cellular (radio) phones expanded from almost zero to 13 million subscribers in the United States and 30 million worldwide in 70 countries. These numbers do not seem large compared to the worldwide estimate of 550 million telephone users, but the number of cellular phone users will undoubtedly increase. For starters, Motorola (a leader in radio communication) estimates that 40 million U.S. employees work away from the office for extended periods, as does 40 percent of the global workforce. Additionally, in many cases, it is much easier to connect people over radio networks instead of installing cables. As noted in *The Economist* (October 23, 1993), the $1,000 average cost of providing a radio network to a home or business is falling rapidly. In comparison, in places such as Italy or China, it costs $2,000 or more to install a basic copper wire (twisted pair) to a home.

Motorola is leading the way in selling satellite phone services (Iridium), but several other companies are close behind. While these phones will work anywhere in the world, they are still expensive. The $3,000 phone cost will probably decline, but the $2 to $3 a minute charge will keep them in a niche market for several years.

Small hand-held computers like these from 3Com provide important portability to businesspeople. Some also support mobile access to the Internet.

### Transmission Capacity

To understand the difference in the amount of information that can be carried by the various media, consider a simple example. It's a hot day outside and you spray water on yourself with a garden hose (about 1 inch in diameter). On the other hand, if you want to put out a house fire, you will need more water, so you use a fire hose (3 inches in diameter). If you need enough water to supply a factory, you will want to use an even larger pipe (10 inches in diameter). The amount of water supplied by each method is loosely equivalent to the raw amount of data that can be carried by twisted-pair, coaxial, and fiber-optic cables. However, the amount of data is not related to the diameter of the cables; in fact, optical cables are thinner than the electrical cables and carry substantially more data.

Capacity of transmission media is measured by the number of bits of data that can be sent in 1 second. In raw form, twisted-pair wires can carry about 1 million bits per second (denoted 1 Mbps). Coaxial cables typically carry 10 Mbps, while fiber-optic cables can carry more than 100 Mbps. These numbers can be improved by using multiple cables, signal compression, and other advanced transmission methods. For example, a standard transmission protocol that uses multiple twisted-pair wires known as *10Base-T* can carry up to 10 Mbps. A newer method called *Fast Ethernet* is capable of transmitting data up to 100 Mbps. Fiber-based LANs using Gigabit Ethernet can carry data at rates up to 1,000 Mbps (or 1 Gbps).

In the long run, fiber-optic cables offer the greatest potential bandwidth. Long-distance carriers rely heavily on fiber-optic lines. In 1994, there were about 1.3 million long-distance calls in progress at any point in time. Researchers are working hard to design new fiber-optic cables and switches that can carry more signals. State-of-the-art research has enabled the switches to send more than 300 billion bits per second down a single fiber in the lab.

To see the effect of bandwidth, consider an example involving two computers. You have three items that you wish to send: a small text file, a picture, and 10 seconds of a video. The text file consists of 10,000 bytes (or 80,000 bits). The picture is a bit image of about 500,000 bytes, or 4 megabits. The video generates about 1.5 megabytes per second for a total of 15 megabytes (or 120 megabits). How long does it take to send the raw data using each of the three cables? The times are displayed in Figure 6.10, assuming that the transmission can use the entire bandwidth. In practice, networks are considerably less efficient (sometimes as low as 20 percent to 50 percent of capacity). Notice that it does not really matter how the text file is transmitted. On the other hand, only the fiber-optic cable carries the video data in less than 10 seconds, so it is the only method that can show the raw, uncompressed video in real time. Other methods will force the digitized video to be shown in slow motion. One of the main reasons we do not have good video telephones yet is that twisted-pair wires cannot carry enough data to transmit real-time *raw* video data. So how are the phone companies going to deliver television signals? By compressing each picture into less data.

Transmission times become more important when more than two computers are involved, and when you want to send more than one item. For example, think about what will happen if you install a slow (1 Mbps) network for 60 users in a department. What happens when they all arrive at work in the morning and turn on their computers at the same time? Say the computers all go to the file server and ask for a copy of a word processor program (about 2 million bits). In the best case, it takes 2 minutes (2 seconds times 60 people) for everyone to get started. In reality, it is more likely to require at least 10 minutes. Now imagine what happens if there are 600 users on the network!

You want to use the fastest communication line that you can afford. The next important question is: how much difference is there in price? Cable costs are measured per foot. For the most part, there is little difference in prices between multiple twisted-pair wires and coaxial cable. The actual prices depend on the specific cable—especially the type of outer coating. In general, coaxial cable costs about the same as industry-standard cat 5 twisted pair (around $0.35/foot). Fiber-optic cable is more expensive (about $1.75/foot). However, in most cases the cost per foot does not matter. In most LAN situations, there will be only a couple thousand dollars difference between a "cheap" alternative and a faster one. Typically, it costs more for the labor to install the cable.

**FIGURE 6.10**
TRANSMISSION
SPEED AND TIME
Raw transmission speeds over single wire (pair) with no compression and no overhead. Compression techniques have raised each of these levels, so 10 Base-T provides 10 Mbps over twisted-pair. Similarly compression enables transmission of 100 Mbps over coaxial lines. Fiber-optic transmissions are still being improved. Experimental rates of raw data transmissions have been reported in excess of 10 gigabits per second.

| | | | TWISTED PAIR 1 MBPS | COAXIAL 10 MBPS | FIBER OPTIC 100 MBPS |
|---|---|---|---|---|---|
| ITEM | BYTES | BITS | SECONDS | | |
| Text | 10,000 | 80,000 | 0.08 | 0.008 | 0.0008 |
| Image | 500,000 | 4,000,000 | 4 | 0.4 | 0.04 |
| Video-10 sec. | 15,000,000 | 120,000,000 | 120 | 12 | 1.2 |

Transmission rates for radio-based methods depend on the amount of frequency available. A typical speed for transmission over microwave transmissions from small satellite dishes is 57,600 bits per second. Cellular phone speeds are comparable to standard phone transmissions (around 33,300 bits per second).

### Combinations of Media

To gain the advantages of each type of media and to deal with networks created a section at a time, most large networks use several types of media at the same time. For example, fiber-optic cables are typically used as a *backbone* to connect networks over longer distances between buildings or between floors in large buildings. Use of the nonelectrical cables between buildings also helps isolate the network from lightning strikes.

Many companies initially built smaller LANs in various departments throughout the company. As shown in Figure 6.11, a fiber-optic backbone can be used to connect these individual networks into one large network to make information available to everyone in the company. Typically, each smaller LAN is connected to a *router* and the routers are connected together with fiber-optic cable. The individual LANs could use twisted-pair, coaxial, or even radio connections. The router is used to convert the appropriate signals into a standard signal that can be handled by the other routers. Messages can then be sent from one workstation on a LAN to any other workstation in the company regardless of the LAN or media being used. In many ways, routers are just small computers that accept different types of signals and send (route) them to the appropriate subnetwork. This design has four major advantages. First, most of the traffic is maintained locally within each department. Second, given the appropriate security access, managers can get access to the same data and resources regardless of the computer they use. Third, if one part of the network (or a computer) fails, the other segments are unaffected and continue to operate. Fourth, one segment can be changed and updated at a time. It is not necessary to change the entire company's hardware or software at once. Each department can have exactly the resources they need.

**FIGURE 6.11**
CONNECTING NETWORKS
Several challenges arise if you build an enterprise network. An enterprise network often connects many smaller networks established in different departments, buildings or even nations. The hardware and software components must follow standards so they can communicate. An MIS team has to manage the overall structure to maximize efficiency, avoid duplication, and solve problems.

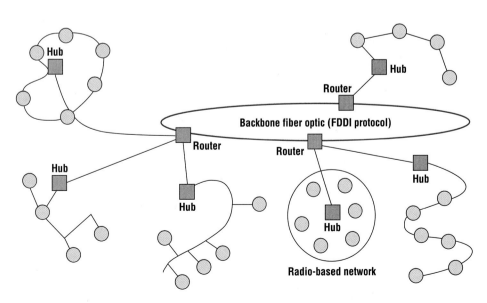

## Connection Devices

Keep in mind that transmission speed in networks depends on the speed of all the components. As a result, it takes substantially longer to transfer files and messages than would be indicated by the published transmission speeds. In particular, as the number of computers increases, the network has to work harder at coordinating the computers. This coordination can generate an enormous amount of messages being transmitted.

In order to connect the cables (or receive radio waves), the computer needs a special communication card. This NIC or LAN card translates computer signals into messages that can be sent on the network. Each network has certain *protocols* or rules that must be followed when sending messages.

Other connection devices are often required to connect different networks. In a business, each department might have its own network based on coaxial cable. Each department would have its own file server and printer. In order to share information with other departments, the departmental networks would have to be connected to each other. This connection could use fiber-optic cable and would require a special device (router or *gateway*) that converts the electrical coaxial signals into light. Routers are used to connect different types of networks together regardless of the type of cable. They can also convert protocols to connect different types of networks.

A *hub* is a small network device used to split a cable. The hub splits a single cable that is run from the router into separate cables, which are then run to individual computers.

Routers are crucial to improving efficiency in large networks. In may respects, a router works like a post office. It examines the destination address of each packet of information and selects the best way to send that packet. Routers improve performance by choosing the path of the message and segmenting large networks into smaller pieces. For example, router segments might be assigned to each department of a large company, where each department has its own server. Most of the messages stay within the specific department, so they do not take up bandwidth across the entire company. Only messages that truly need to be sent to other areas will be transmitted outside the departmental segment. *Switches* perform a similar task but isolate communications down to one line. So your communication would have full use of a line for a period of time. Modern routers combine the function of both switching and routing to take advantage of both techniques.

## Software

Because most personal computer were designed as stand alone machines, the older (DOS) operating systems cannot provide data to several users at the same time, and they cannot send information to or receive it from other computers.

Any computer used as a file server needs to employ a multiuser operating system. For example, Novell is a company that specializes in selling hardware and software for networks. Novell sells a multiuser network operating system (NOS) called NetWare that runs on the file server. It is also possible to use minicomputers as file servers. All of the minicomputer manufacturers provide software to use their machines as file servers for personal computers. Operating systems such as Windows, 2000, UNIX, and OS/2 can handle multiple users and function as file servers.

Most personal computers also need special LAN software. Generally, this software is purchased from the same company that provides the operating system for the file server. It runs in the background on the workstation so that it can send and receive information on the network. Its job is to identify messages sent to each computer and put the incoming messages into the proper format for the workstation computer. It also converts the data so that it can be sent in the proper format for the file server to understand. If there is a printer on the network, the workstation software intercepts the workstation printer output and passes it to the network printer.

**ENTERPRISE NETWORKS**

Many large companies have hundreds of local area networks. Connecting personal computers is only the first step in building a telecommunications system. The next step is to facilitate communication across the company and interconnect the LANs. A network that connects various subnetworks across a firm is called an *enterprise network.*

Several types of data need to be collected and shared throughout a company. Basic transaction-processing data such as accounting and HRM data need to be collected and aggregated for the firm. Management decisions and questions need to be communicated with all employees. Planning documents and forecasts are often prepared by interdisciplinary teams.

Although it is easy to agree that all computers in a company should be able to share data, several problems arise in practice. Various departments often use different hardware, software, and network protocols. It becomes more difficult to identify the cause of problems in a network as it becomes larger. Likewise, adding more components tends to slow down all transmissions. Network management issues multiply. Small tasks such as assigning usernames and maintaining passwords become major chores when there are thousands of users and hundreds of file servers. Security becomes increasingly complex, especially when corporate data is carried across public networks. Upgrading network components can become a nightmare, resulting in either complete replacement across the firm or incompatibilities between some divisions. Even simple network functions like e-mail can quickly bog down a system when there are 50,000 users.

Enterprise networking requires a combination of standards and special hardware and software to translate data from one system to another. It also requires investing in more network personnel to install, upgrade, and manage all of the components.

As enterprise networks spread across large distances, they tend to involve wide area networks. A *wide area network (WAN)* differs from a LAN because of the geographical distance that it covers. More specifically, a WAN involves links that are controlled by public carriers (e.g., telecommunication companies). Few individual firms can afford to build their own long-distance networks. Although some companies do have their own satellite connections, it is almost impossible for a company to install its own cables for any distance.

To establish WAN lines, you simply call a telecommunication company or other commercial contractor. Each has several offerings in a wide range of prices, all of which

---

**Reality Bytes    6–3    Hewlett-Packard Medical Division Sales Over the Internet**

Using the Internet to sell products online could easily cut sales cost by 15 percent. The Internet can also open the market to customers you did not reach before. On the other hand, companies like Hewlett-Packard's (HP's) medical division have spent years and millions of dollars creating a traditional marketing and sales staff. The 500 sales professionals and dozens of distributors generate more than $1 billion of sales a year. Some hospitals are suggesting that they want simple, one-clicking ordering over the Internet to avoid salespeople and distributors completely. The dilemma for Hewlett-Packard is that they cannot risk alienating salespeople and distributors, which might reduce their sales.

Yet HP must placate their customers to avoid losing them to other companies. Hence, HP is rolling out a web site that will let major companies place orders online. HP is pricing the items in line with existing sales channel prices and contemplating paying salespeople commissions from the online purchases. James Cyrier, HP's head of marketing, notes that "We have a big direct-sales force calling on hospitals, and it would be very demotivational for them if customers placed an order through this new e-channel, and they didn't get paid. At the same time, selling online could be more cost-effective. So maybe we will end up passing the savings on to the consumer."

change over time. Typically, you lease a line with a fixed amount of bandwidth or transmission capacity. For instance, a T1 line can transmit up to 1.544 Mbps. A T3 line can carry about 45 Mbps. Higher speed digital (OC) lines are also available from some carriers. On the lower end, if your carrier offers Integrated Services Digital Network (ISDN), you can lease digital lines that start at transmissions of 128 Kbps. Most of these choices involve communication from one fixed point to another, such as a connection from headquarters to a factory or warehouse. You can use the line to carry any type of data that you wish. However, all of your hardware and software must meet the standards supported by the public carrier.

## The Need for Standards

**STANDARDS**    **Standards** are important with networks. There are many different types of computers and various network types. Each computer and network company has its own idea of which methods are best. Without standards there is no way to connect computers or networks produced by different vendors. Standards are also supposed to protect the buyers from obsolescence. If you install network equipment that meets existing standards, you should be able to buy products in the future that will work with it.

Unfortunately, there are many standard-setting organizations. Each major country has its own standards organization (such as ANSI [The American National Standards Institute]). There are several international organizations, such as ISO and the ITU (International Telecommunications Organization, renamed form CCITT) charged with defining computer and communications standards. Additionally, manufacturers of computers and

---

**Reality Bytes    6–4    Internet Advertising: The Beginning of a New Industry**

By the end of 1998, 50 percent of U.S. households had personal computers. Probably half of them were connected to the Internet. As people spend more time online, there is increasing incentive for businesses to use the Internet for advertising. The Internet is an interesting target for advertising because it offers a mix of features. For example, individuals use the Internet to search for specific topics, so businesses can target viewers with a great deal of precision. At the same time, popular sites receive millions of viewers a day—much like television. Additionally, the Internet offers some capabilities to track individual users—particularly repeat customers. Also, Internet advertising offers a future not available in any other method: the ability to track responsiveness to the ad via click-through percentages, that is, the number of people who immediately responded to an advertisement. By the end of 1998, more than $2 billion were spent on Internet advertising. Another interesting feature of advertising on the Internet is that the publishers (web sites) are so willing to modify their sites to accommodate advertiser wishes. In the traditional magazine and television world, no one would ever volunteer to change content in response to a marketer. Yet, an interesting Internet example can be found at Scott Adam's web site. (Scott Adams is the creator of the *Dilbert* comic strip.) DoubleClick (an Internet marketing company) persuaded Scott Adams to add a financial portfolio section on his web site for his cartoon characters. This section is full of ads for Datek Securities, Inc., an online stock trading company. When asked why he was willing to change his site to accept advertising, Scott Adams summarized the attitude of many Internet entrepreneurs: "Many people have asked why the Dilbert Zone has sold out and accepted advertising. The reasons are complicated, involving many philosophical and ethical issues. For the slower students, I can summarize it this way: They give us money. We like money."

telecommunications equipment try to define their own standards. If one company's products are chosen as a standard, they gain a slight advantage in design and production.

It is not likely that typical managers will be involved in the issues of setting and choosing communication standards. Yet, as a consumer, you need to be aware that there are many standards and sometimes variations on the standards. (In this industry, the word *standards* does not mean there is only one way to do something.) When you are buying telecommunications equipment, the goal is to purchase equipment that meets popular standards. It is not always easy to decide which standards will become popular and which ones will be abandoned.

## A Changing Environment

Why are there so many standards? It would be far simpler if everyone could agree to use one standard and build products that are compatible. The problem with this concept is that technology is continually changing. Thirty years ago, phone companies never considered using digital transmission over fiber-optic cables, which is the dominant form of long-distance transmission used today.

As each technology is introduced, new standards are created. Yet, we cannot discard existing standards because it takes time for firms to convert to the new technology. Additionally, as manufacturers gain experience with a technology, they add features and find better ways to use the products. These alterations usually result in changes to the standards. An additional complication is that many companies are modifying their products at the same time. It is hard to determine in advance which changes are worthwhile and should be made standards.

The net result is that standards can be useful, but managers have to be careful not to rely too much on a standard. First, remember that even if two products support a standard, they still might not work together well. Second, if you choose a standard for your department or company, remember that technology changes. Corporate standards should be reevaluated every year or so to make sure they are still the best solution.

**OBJECT ORIENTATION**  At the foundation of any telecommunications system, there is a means to transfer raw bits of data. In fact, the ISO communication model is built around this fact. A primary purpose of standards is to ensure that machines can be physically connected to provide this transfer of binary data. Yet, workers are increasingly interested in transferring entire objects. Hence, each computer needs to be able to not just transfer the object but also be able to read and display the attributes and to use its base functions.

Today, it is generally possible to transfer objects between computers, but there is no guarantee that each computer will be able to evaluate or use the object. In many cases the objects are simply stored as binary files, awaiting transfer to a computer or user with the appropriate software and hardware to use the object.

The **World Wide Web (WWW)** represents a step toward an object-oriented approach to telecommunications and data transfer. With the Web, every computer and its files are treated as objects. To run the Web, each computer needs client software that is capable of understanding a base "markup language," as well as a "universal" address system. The addressing system provides a means of identifying objects (what they are and where they are located). The markup language contains commands that are used to define functions and attributes of the various objects. Currently, objects are limited to predefined text, graphics, sound, and video formats.

Lotus Notes is another method that enables users to share and integrate objects over a network. Lotus Notes is loaded on the network, with copies running on each user's workstation. It primarily works as an enhanced mail system that makes it easy for users to mail data from a variety of objects, including spreadsheets, word processors, and voice annotation. The resulting "message" can be modified by the recipient; notes can be added, spreadsheets changed, or graphs inserted. The resulting message object can be modified by other users in the workgroup who have the proper authorizations. Lotus Notes maintains all of the objects in a database, which enables users to search for phrases, comments, or other objects. Lotus Notes is discussed in more detail in Chapter 7.

## NEW TELECOMMUNICA-TION SERVICES

Recent and ongoing changes in the telecommunication systems will eventually produce major changes in the way we deal with telephones, computers, and televisions. The older phone system was designed to carry voice or sound. These systems are limited in their ability to transfer computer data. With voice-based systems, the computer's electrical signals have to be converted to sound with a **modem.** The phone system converts the sound to new electrical signals that are then transmitted over the phone lines. A key issue with modems is the speed at which they can transmit basic data. Because of the way the telephone system was designed, there is a limit to how fast data can be transmitted over ordinary phone lines. Existing modems are close to this limit. Current high-speed modems can transmit raw data at 33,300 bps. However, data-compression techniques (squeezing files into fewer bits) can increase the effective transmission speed. Some modems are available today that use compression to transmit in excess of 200 Kbps. Of course, to get these high speeds both the sender and receiver have to have similar modems, and they need a high-quality phone connection.

In the last few years, phone companies have converted their systems to a digital (computerized) system known as Integrated Services Digital Network (ISDN). With this system, all transmissions are sent as digital (binary) signals. As a result, computer transmissions are faster and less subject to errors and interference. The binary computer signals are converted directly to signals for the phone system. Low-speed computer communication over ISDN lines is around 128,000 bps. Devices similar to modems are used to convert the computer signals into appropriate digital telephone signals. Again, compression methods can increase the effective speed of these devices. Additionally, it is possible to rent high-speed ISDN connections that can transfer millions of bits per second and are

## Reality Bytes    6–5    The Last Mile

In the 1980s, the federal government broke up AT&T. The breakup left AT&T in charge of long distance telephone service while seven "Baby Bell" companies provided local service. Several of the local companies have merged, but they still mostly have a monopoly on providing phone service to individual homes. In the mid-1990s, Congress passed laws to encourage competition at the local level. However, would-be competitors have repeatedly complained about the lack of cooperation from the local monopolies in providing service for the "last mile" of service from the phone company office to individual houses. Over a two-year period, AT&T spent $4 billion to move into the local markets but gained only $65 million in revenue. In 1998, AT&T took action to circumvent this problem by purchasing TCI, the nation's largest cable television company. The plan is to offer combined telephone, television, and Internet service over the high-capacity coaxial lines. The merger would give AT&T end-to-end access to more than 20 million homes. Currently, long-distance providers must pay the local Bell companies an access charge of 4.6 cents per minute for every long distance phone call placed.

limited more by how much you are willing to pay than by the technology. One advantage of ISDN services is that they utilize existing phone lines—customers simply purchase new connection devices. ISDN links are fast enough to connect LANs across common phone lines, so that a user in Chicago would have the same access as a user in Los Angeles. As shown in Figure 6.12, one feature of many digital systems is that they break information into small pieces, call *packets*. These packets contain a destination address along with the message and are carried to the appropriate location and reassembled. Even voice conversations can be broken into pieces. This method grants the telecommunication company greater control over the usage of its lines and better utilization of available transmission capacity.

Computer networks are beginning to employ a packet-switching system in which packets can be sent over different routes at different times. The system is known as **Asynchronous Transfer Mode (ATM).** With high-speed routers it can offer transmission speeds in excess of 150 Mbps. With the appropriate devices, it can also carry sound, fax, and video on the same lines intermixed with computer data. Development of ATM networks is fairly new, and considerable work on perfecting them remains to be done. However, ATM networks offer significant gains in transmission speed and capacity for all transmission forms.

The rapid growth of the Internet led to the development of a new telecommunication service: **digital subscriber line (DSL).** DSL comes in several varieties, such as Asymmetric DSL (ADSL), which has a relatively high-speed download rate (from 1 Mbps to 6 Mbps), but a slower upload speed (up to 640 Kbps). Implementation of DSL requires that customers live within a couple miles of a phone company switching point. New switching equipment is also required. To encourage competition, the FTC is requiring the local phone companies to allow outside firms to lease space in the switch buildings. The technology enables customers to obtain reasonably fast communication lines at substantial cost savings. For example, a leased T1 line at 1.544 Mbps could cost as much as $1,000 per month, a 1 Mpbs DSL line might cost $100 per month. However, the distance limitations and need for new equipment are limiting factors in the adoption of the technology.

The importance of the new switching equipment arises from the fact that the entire phone system was based on providing simple voice services. To cut costs and provide service to more customers, the phone company restricted bandwidth for each household to about 2,000 Hz of frequency range. The equipment automatically cut off low and high frequencies. Only a small set of mid-range frequencies was used. In comparison, the new SDL equipment uses a digital signal and carries substantially more data on the existing lines.

**FIGURE 6.12**

Packet-switched networks operate by partitioning all messages into small packets. Each packet contains a destination and source address, along with sequencing instructions. The packets can be separated and sent over different routes. At their destination, the original message is automatically restored by the network. Packets provide efficient use of transmission networks because they can mix packets and route transmissions over empty routes.

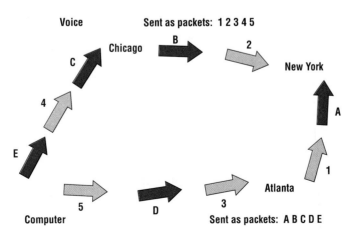

**THE INTERNET**    The **Internet** is a loose collection of computer networks throughout the world. It began as a means to exchange data among major U.S. universities (NSFnet of the National Science Foundation), and connections to various military organizations and U.S. defense suppliers (Arpanet of the Advanced Research Projects Agency). No one knows how many computers or networks are currently connected by the Internet. The numbers have been increasing exponentially since the early 1990s, so any number is likely to be wrong within a few days. To give you some idea of the Internet's astounding growth, in January 1993, there were 1.313 million host computers. In January 1994, there were 2.217 million hosts located in more than 70 countries. By January 1999, 4.757 million hosts were registered. Current statistics are available at http://www.domainstats.com. Another 80 nations have e-mail access to the Internet. Remember that these are servers. Millions of more client computers are connected. In 1994, over 20 million people had access to at least e-mail services. As of mid-1994, commercial use (as opposed to university and government use) accounted for 50 percent of the Internet usage. International usage expanded so that since mid-1994, more than 50 percent of the networks on the Internet are located outside the United States. In 1998, Charles Lee from GTE estimated that by the year 2010, about 1 billion computers will be connected to the Internet. Increasingly, firms are talking about embedding Internet capabilities into common appliances.

Best estimates are that in 1998, consumers bought about $8 billion worth of goods over the Internet, which is a relatively small amount when compared to traditional sales. On the other hand, trade between businesses amounted to $43 billion. Job sites are also becoming popular.

What exactly is the Internet? At heart, the Internet is just a communication system for computers. It is defined by a set of standards that allow computers to exchange messages. The most amazing aspect of the Internet is that there really is no single person or group in charge. Anyone who wishes to connect a computer to the Internet simply agrees to pay for a communication link—via an Internet service provider (ISP), and to install communications hardware and software that supports the current Internet standard protocols. The person or company is given a base address that allows other computers to identify users on the new computer. Standards are defined by a loose committee, and addresses are controlled by another small committee. The committees are convened purely for the purpose

---

**Reality Bytes    6–6    Intel versus Hamidi**

In 1995, semiconductor giant Intel fired an employee named Hamidi. Mr. Hamidi now heads an organization called Former and Current Employees of Intel that is critical of management policies at Intel. In 1998, Intel filed a lawsuit against Mr. Hamidi, claiming he sent at least six mass e-mail messages to employees at Intel, and that he ignored requests to stop. Mr. Hamidi states that he began sending e-mail messages after Intel blocked employees from accessing his organization's web site (www.faceintel.com). Intel claims that the unwanted messages (spam) waste Intel's resources and employee time. Mr. Hamidi and the ACLU argue that his freedom of speech entitles

him to send e-mail messages. Coeta Chambers, an Intel attorney, responded that "the First Amendment might give one a right to use a public forum or to walk up and down a sidewalk. But it doesn't make us let him come on to our property and use our equipment to deliver his messages." In the past, other court cases have supported Internet service providers who blocked users from sending mass e-mail messages. For example, Cyber Promotions, Inc., was banned by several Internet providers and paid Earth-Link Network $2 million. But the Intel case is believed to be the first one involving a company blocking third-party access to its e-mail system.

of speeding the process; all decision making is up to the organizations connected to the network. Participation in the Internet is voluntary, and there are few rules, just standard practices and agreements. From a business or consumer viewpoint, there are two primary aspects to the Internet: establishing a connection and using the Internet.

## How the Internet Works

The Internet is a communication system; it is a method of connecting computers together. So the first step in determining how the Internet works is to understand how your computer connects to others. As shown in Figure 6.13, the Internet has a hierarchy of service providers. Individuals pay a local **Internet service provider (ISP)** for access to the Internet. In turn, local ISPs pay an upstream *network service provider (NSP)* for access to their systems and features. Each connection must be made over a communication link. Local links are typically made over telephone wires, but cable companies also provide service over their coaxial lines. A few companies provide satellite download data but still rely on the phone lines for uploading data. Most ISPs also utilize phone company lines to connect to their NSP, but they lease dedicated, full-time lines that provide faster service. The largest NSPs also provide backbone service. That is, they route communications over their own fiber-optic lines that are installed across the United States. Increasingly, NSPs are also phone companies. Some started as phone companies and expanded into the Internet, others started with the Internet and gradually offered voice services.

You should understand the foundations of the Internet because someone has to pay for each connection. Current pricing policies are to charge for the initial communication link and for the point-of-contact Internet service. For example, an individual pays the phone company for the local phone line and pays the ISP for basic services. The ISP pays the phone company for the next link and pays the NSP for access services. Figure 6.14 lists some of the largest providers in each category. You can check with them for current prices and services.

The charging mechanism is similar for companies that wish to establish web sites. The catch is that the costs are higher because the company needs faster communication services. The phone company charges more money for a faster link (e.g., $1,000–$3,000 per month for a T1 line). The ISP also charges more money for the increased traffic because it needs faster equipment and faster connections to the NSP.

**FIGURE 6.13**
INTERNET
CONNECTIONS
Each computer must
be connected to others.
The Internet has a
connection hierarchy.
Companies and
individuals typically use
phone company lines
to connect to an ISP.
The ISP connects to an
NSP, which routes data
over the high-speed
backbone network to
the destination NSP,
down to the other ISP,
and to the final
computer. Each step
may involve several
computers.

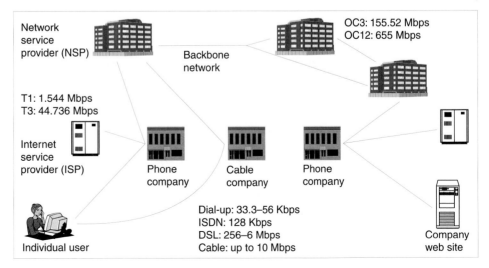

**FIGURE 6.14**
LEADING INTERNET
PROVIDERS
There are thousands of
ISPs and cable
companies. This list
provides only some of
the large companies in
each category.

| BACKBONE PROVIDERS | | |
|---|---|---|
| AT&T | Sprint | |
| GTE | Worldcom/MCI | |
| Qwest | | |
| **NETWORK SERVICE PROVIDERS** | | |
| AT&T | Qwest | |
| Cable & Wireless | Sprint | |
| IBM | UUNet | |
| **PHONE COMPANIES** | | |
| Competitive local exchange carriers (CLECs) | | |
| Regional Bell operating companies (RBOCs) | | |
| **CABLE COMPANIES** | | |
| Intermedia | | |
| Regional | | |
| TCI | | |
| **SATELLITE** | | |
| Direct Satellite | | |
| **INTERNET SERVICE PROVIDERS** | | |
| America Online | Digex | MindSpring |
| Ameritech | EarthLink | NETCOM |
| AT&T WorldNet | Erols Internet | Pacific Bell |
| Bell Atlantic | FASTNET | Prodigy |
| Bell South | GridNet | Southwestern Bell |
| CompuServe | IBM GlobalNet | Sprint Internet |
| Concentric Network | Microsoft Network | UUNET |

The Internet service connection business is completely based on economies of scale. The high-speed fiber networks (OC3 and OC12) can handle a vast number of transmissions, but they carry a high fixed cost. The backbone providers make money by selling smaller increments of bandwidth to the ISPs, which incorporate a sufficient profit. Why do we need local ISPs? Many of the NSPs are backbone providers and increasingly they also offer ISP services. So far, the local ISPs survive by providing local service and features such as web site development.

## Internet Features

As a giant communication system, the Internet offers some advantages. But all features are available only because they are offered by the owners of the computers that are attached to the Internet. Some organizations offer free services; others charge for them. There are three basic types of services: (1) mail, (2) access to data and to computer time, and (3) electronic commerce.

Before you can use any of these services, you must be able to locate a particular computer. Technically, every computer is given a unique number, assigned by the ISP. Originally, the numbers were 32-bit numbers, typically written as four bytes separated by dots. For example, 161.6.28.18 was assigned to a specific machine. However, 32-bit numbers will identify a maximum of 4 billion machines, fewer in practice because some values cannot be assigned. Hence, an Internet committee designed a new numbering system consisting of 128 bits, which allows for more than 1,000 numbers to be assigned to every person likely to live on the planet. The new system is known as IP v6 and will be phased in gradually. Every computer or device has a unique number. If you know its number, you can send e-mail or retrieve data—whatever the owner allows.

Of course, numbers are difficult for most people to remember. So, the Internet utilizes a system where a *domain name server (DNS)* converts names to numbers. Anyone can apply for a name and pay a nominal fee (e.g., $70 for two years) to use that name. Of course, names must be unique, so there is sometimes a fight over popular names. Names are followed by a suffix such as .com, .edu, or .gov. Several organizations have suggested adding more suffixes, arguing that it would provide for more possible names. One interesting feature of the names is that each country is given a specific suffix. Some of the countries sell names using their unique suffix. For example, the small nation of Tuvalu allows companies to use its suffix (.tv) for a fee.

Whatever you do on the Internet, your IP number follows you because it is used to route the data back to your machine. Hence, any computer that you deal with can learn the number of your machine. It is one of the reasons people worry about privacy on the Internet. Some techniques can be used to hide this number, but they are cumbersome and not very successful.

## Internet Mail

One of the most popular features on the Internet is electronic mail. Virtually every machine on the Internet is capable of sending and receiving mail for registered users. As long as all participants have the appropriate software, they can send files, pictures, even sound as their message. One company even sells an Internet "phone" system that enables two people to talk to each other using the Internet links. Another sells a service that enables you to transfer real-time video images—as long as both sides have a video camera and capture card.

The Internet offers two other services similar to e-mail: discussion groups (listserv) and newsgroups (news). Discussion groups send electronic journals to anyone who "subscribes" to the list. Typically, there is no fee for subscribing. Editors control the "publication" of a group. Comments are sent first to the editor, who decides whether to include them. Newsgroups are similar, but more open. Anyone can submit a comment at any time to a newsgroup, which represents a giant, global bulletin board. There are thousands of established topics, ranging from science to alternative lifestyles to anything you can imagine. The comments are usually uncensored and might or might not be accurate. Some people have found newsgroups useful for addressing complex computer problems. With millions of people on the Internet, there is a good chance that someone else has already encountered your problem and might have a solution. Newsgroups and web sites provide useful tools to managers, especially to small business managers who have limited resources.

Although messages on the Internet tend to be uncensored, be careful. If you somehow manage to insult a few thousand people, you could find yourself immersed in hundreds of thousands of mail messages that overwhelm your computer account. Also, avoid using the Internet for personal use while working for a company. In the United States, companies have the legal right to monitor your messages. In extreme situations, the computer manager can revoke accounts from people who abuse the system. Even more importantly, some hiring managers have been known to search the Internet for messages that you posted—to check you out before making a job offer.

In terms of commercial usage, there is an Internet proposal to encapsulate EDI messages from the International (Edifact) and U.S. (ANSI X12) standards inside regular mail messages on the Internet. When this standard is approved, firms will be able to transmit their EDI messages along existing Internet links. This system should make it much simpler for firms to communicate. The Internet provides a standard, worldwide data link. By connecting to one point, a firm can reach any other company on the Net. By using one of the two standards (specified in the mail header), the firms can easily exchange data.

## Access to Data on the Internet

Anyone with a computer connected to the Internet has the ability to give other users access to data stored on that computer. Read that sentence again. The owner has control over the data. Unless someone specifically grants you access to data, it is basically illegal to try and get the data, or even to use the person's computer.

### WWW: World Wide Web

The World Wide Web is a first attempt to set up an international database of information. As discussed in the appendix to Chapter 1, today's challenge lies in finding the information you want. Sites are built as pages that contain links to other pages. Making a choice in one page will usually connect you to another computer on the Internet and bring up its WWW pages. From there you can look at library catalogs, pictures, or whatever information is provided by that Web server. The initial versions of the Web were developed at CERN, the European particle-physics laboratory, where the staff wanted to make it easier for researchers to share their work.

The easiest access to the Web is with a *browser* such as Internet Explorer or Netscape. Browsers present a page of information that contains links to other pages on the Web. The

---

### Reality Bytes    6–7   The Internet in Vietnam

The Internet is truly an international network. All it takes to use the Internet is a computer, a phone line, and a connection device (modem or router). Computers and connection devices have become relatively inexpensive and are easily available worldwide. In some countries the problem lies in obtaining phone service. Many developing nations experience problems with availability and reliability of the telephone and electrical power services. In many nations, including Vietnam, the phone services are run by the government, which means prices are set by governmental agencies. In the richest city in Vietnam (Ho Chi Minh City), the average per capita income is about US $1,000 per year. In 1998, the government reduced Internet charges from US $1.70 per hour to about US $0.80 per hour. About 15,000 subscribers were paying the higher rate. Authorities said they wanted to increase the usage to about 50,000 people. Like other developing nations, the government is trying to balance three issues: (1) the benefits citizens gain from the Internet, (2) the need to obtain revenue to purchase new equipment, and (3) the social effects caused by introducing an open communication system.

page can contain text, graphics, video, and sound clips. By selecting highlighted words, you can move to other systems, trace topics, and transfer data. Pictures are displayed automatically, and most operations can be completed by selecting items with a mouse.

## Locating Data on the Internet

Because the Internet is so large and is growing rapidly, it can be difficult to find useful data. Additionally, organizations are constantly changing the type of information they provide. The data available is constantly changing, making it impossible to provide an up-to-date listing. So how do you find anything on the Internet?

Several tools can help you find data on the Internet. You might purchase a book that lists some of the major databases. It can be a useful starting point, because some databases have been provided for several years. However, an easier method is to use one of the electronic search tools provided by Internet organizations.

The World Wide Web is a graphic-based Internet search tool. Many web sites contain links to other sites so you can find related data. Some companies provide search engines that help you search for specific topics. Common search sites include Yahoo, AltaVista, Lycos, and Excite. Lycos (the Wolf spider) was created in 1994 by Michael Mauldin at Carnegie Mellon University. It searches web sites, catalogs each page it finds, and records

## Establishing an Internet Site

Although it is still challenging to make sales over the Internet, many companies are using the Internet to market their products and to build closer links to their customers. Some web sites get as many as 100,000 hits (visits) a day. Although only about 7 percent of American households are connected to a network, the profile user is a valuable customer. The average U.S. user is a 31-year-old male making $65,000 a year. Seventy percent of users have a college degree. These demographics are not surprising, because network connections require about $2,000 in computer equipment and a network connection. America Online (AOL), one of the leading private networks, charges about $22 a month.

Building a site on the Internet requires that you have a fairly powerful computer. It also entails buying a router that can connect to the network at high speeds and paying communication costs. Forrester Research estimates that building a web site costs $60,000 to $120,000 the first year. However, you can often lease space on someone else's machine for around $5,000.

The difficult part of building a web site is attracting visitors. Internet users are notoriously fickle. Many are searching for entertaining sites. Others look for customer support or in-depth product infor-

mation. Mahesh Murthy, who designed marketplaceMCI, notes that "If you bore users the first time, they'll never come back and you've lost them. Then you've wasted your resources." He points out that "entertaining" web sites have to change constantly and offer new connections, games, and features.

Actually building a web page is becoming easier as companies introduce new software. Web pages are based on a standardized format know as Hypertext Mark-up Language (HTML). Several word processors now support this format, and other tools make it easy to add video and graphics. HTML is a set of commands that tell the browser how to display the text. Complete documentation is available on the Web. Interactive sites are built using a special programming language called *Java*. Generally you need to hire trained programmers (Webmasters) to build complex interactive web sites.

It can be hard to measure the value of building a web site. Because it is difficult (and against custom) to charge for access to individual sites, you can receive thousands of visitors a day and see no direct profit. Reaching new customers, encouraging repeat buying, and providing better customer service are all possible goals of an Internet site. But they are all difficult to quantify in terms of profits.

the links for future searching. AltaVista was created by Digital Equipment Corporation to search thousands of sites based on complex criteria you enter. One key difference with Yahoo is that it organizes information by topics, and the structure and many sites are reviewed by humans. Hence, a search on Yahoo will not return the millions of matches produced by an automated system such as AltaVista. However, if you have only a vague idea of what you are searching for, Yahoo is a good staring point because you can use the topics to help refine your ideas.

A few specialized web sites operate as pointers to other sites. Traditional magazine and newspaper organizations maintain links to relevant data. For example, *The Wall Street Journal* provides many links to business sites.

## Security Concerns on the Internet

Although security is an issue with all computer networks, the Internet presents a special challenge. In particular, the Internet is not owned by anyone and is really just a loose connection of computers. Virtually anyone can connect a computer to the Internet—even serving as a host computer or a router.

Because of the design and size of the network, messages are rarely sent directly from one computer to another. In almost all cases, messages are passed through several other computers or routers on the way to their destination. As indicated in Figure 6.15 it is possible for someone to join the Internet and spy on all conversations that pass through that section of the network. Users on the starting computer who log in to the destination computer via Telnet will have to enter their username and password on the destination computer. Yet that information will pass, unprotected, through the interloper's computer. With a simple monitoring program, the eavesdropper could collect hundreds or thousands of accounts and passwords a day. The other difficulty is that security is the responsibility of each machine operator.

Today, this aspect of Internet security is relatively easy to handle: simply encrypt your transmissions. Web transactions can be automatically encrypted with a secure server. E-mail can be encrypted with add-in software such as Proctor Good Privacy (PGP). As explained in Chapter 14, these encryption systems provide a high level of security. In essence, encrypted Web transmissions are far more secure than any other means of communication.

There is another important security issue regarding data on the Internet. How do you know what data is authentic? A tremendous amount of "fluff"—information that is of du-

**FIGURE 6.15**
INTERNET SECURITY CONCERNS
Data passes through many unknown servers. Any machine connected could read the data, destroy it, or fabricate a different message. Encryption techniques are available but not yet employed by the mainstream of Internet users. Rapidly changing automatic password generators are available for secure logins across insecure networks.

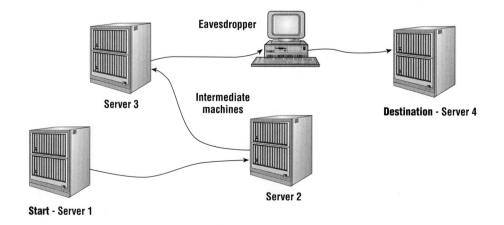

bious value—exists on the Internet. Additionally, many of the comments are purely personal opinions, which might or might not be accurate. As a user of the Internet, it is your responsibility to verify all "facts" and comments that are important to you. In some cases, you can use the source of the data to determine its validity, but it is still relatively easy for hackers to alter the apparent source of their messages. Encryption Techniques can prevent this *spoofing* by authenticating individuals on the Internet, but to date not many people use them.

Figure 6.16 summarizes the security and trust issues. For now, be careful about believing information on the Internet. Try to deal with reputable companies that have a presence in the "real" world. Remember that you will have trouble resolving disputes with vendors in different countries. Several scams have been created through the Internet. Stock manipulation schemes in particular have been popular. In October 1998, the U.S. SEC charged 44 people with using the Internet to manipulate the stock market, largely by providing false or misleading information.

## Browsers, Cookies, Certificates, ActiveX, and Java

Accessing the web requires the use of browser. A browser is a piece of software designed to display information in a standard format. The browser has the ability to display text, graphics, and video. It has several capabilities for formatting text such as setting typefaces, tables, and page layout. It also has internal programming language that gives web site developers more sophisticated control over your computer.

As the use of the Internet has expanded, web site developers have developed increasingly sophisticated techniques for communicating with your computer. Some of these techniques raise important issues for you as a user and for the company as a web site developer. To understand some of these issues so that you can make informed decisions you need to know a little bit about how the web works.

Initially, the web was designed to display simple pages of text and graphics. Each page contains links to other pages. However, to the web server, each page is independent. More importantly, web servers were never designed to keep track of individual sessions. In other words, you might go to web site and look at three pages. To the web server, each page that you request is independent. That is, the server sees three separate but related requests. As long as we are interested only in simple text and graphics, this technique works relatively well.

Problems begin to arise when the web is used for electronic commerce. For example, if you go to an online store, you may want to select several items, place them into a virtual shopping cart, and then pay for them. These activities require that the web server keep track of who you are, which items you selected, and how much they cost. That is, your activities are logically related into a session.

To create sessions, the Web server needs to know who you are each time you select a page. The most common way of identifying users for a session is for the web server to

**FIGURE 6.16**
INTERNET SECURITY AND TRUST
Security can be strong—as long as site operators are careful. Trust requires knowing the customers and vendors. Certificates can be obtained to verify identities. Or, third-party firms, like the credit card companies, will assume the risks in exchange for money.

| Security | Trust |
|---|---|
| • Each transmission is encrypted. <br> • Security on individual servers is the responsibility of vendor. | • Is the vendor legitimate? <br> • Is the customer legitimate? <br> • Tranditional sales rely on credit card companies to cover these risks. <br> • Future: certificates to verify your identity. |

send a small piece of information to your browser. Your browser then stores this data and returns it to the server each time you select the page at that server. This piece of data is called a *cookie.* A cookie generally contains an ID number, the site to which it should be sent, and an expiration date. Some computer users worry about the use of cookies, because they are concerned that web site developers might use cookies to track user activities. However, because a cookie is designed to be returned only to one site, it is not very useful for this purpose. If you are concerned about this minor possibility, browsers enable you to reject cookies set by web sites. However, if you reject all cookies, you will not be able to participate in most electronic commerce activities.

The issue of identification is becoming increasingly important on the Web. How do you know that the vendor at the other end of your connection is legitimate? How does the vendor know that you are a real person? In some cases vendors may require additional information about you, such as your age. How can a vendor verify these individual details? Technologically, there is an answer to these situations. Whether you are a customer or a vendor, you can install a digital certificate on your computer. This certificate must be obtained from an authorizing company, such as Verisign. When you purchase a digital certificate, you must verify your identity with a traditional mechanism such as a driver's license. Once the digital certificate is installed on your system, it verifies who you are. Digital certificates are effective means for identifying people on the Web; however, there is great potential for a loss of privacy.

As people turned to the Web for more sophisticated applications, developers created techniques to provide more detailed control over the browsers and your computer. Two powerful technologies are ActiveX controls from Microsoft and Java applications that originated with Sun Microsystems. The primary issue with these technologies is that when you go to a web site that uses them, you give more control to the web site developer. In particular, if your browser downloads an ActiveX control, the program has access to your entire computer. So you need to be very careful when accepting ActiveX controls. In particular, you should never accept the control unless it comes with a digital certificate, which states who created it. Java applications are less dangerous because they have access to only a limited set of features on your computer.

## Internet 2

Originally, the U.S. government funded much of the Internet design and development. By 1995, the U.S. government had discontinued almost all funding, and the Internet was largely financed and controlled by private organizations. From 1994, the commercial use of the Internet increased exponentially. In 1996, 34 university participants decided that they needed faster connections (the number of participants expanded to 100 in 1999). With the support of the government and industry, they began creating Internet 2 (http://www.internet2.edu). When the original Internet was developed, most traffic was simple text, and the bulk of the communications were via e-mail. There was little need for high-speed connections, and delays in delivering e-mail did not matter since most people did not read their mail immediately.

The two most important proposed features of Internet 2 are high-speed connections and quality-of-service provisions. The overall objective is to provide a transmission network that can support full-speed video and other high-bandwidth applications. To understand the change, consider that most existing "high-speed" Internet connections are in the range of 1 Mbps to 50 Mbps. The Internet 2 calls for gigabit connection points.

A related, but more fundamental, change is the ability to specify a desire level-of-service quality. Currently, if traffic increases on the Internet, all communications slow down.

This situation is annoying but not troublesome for simple tasks like sending e-mail. On the other hand, full video transfer requires a constant minimum level of transmission capacity. So participants need a mechanism to tell all components that a specific set of messages should take priority to receive a certain level of service. Some people have suggested that the system should enable participants to pay a fee to gain their desired levels of service, for each type of message. For example, basic e-mail messages would be free if there is no rush in delivering them. But to reserve a time slot for videoconferencing, participants would pay an additional fee. Then all of the Internet 2 components would give the video packets a higher priority. So far, there has been no agreement on whether additional fees should be charged, or on how the quality-of-service issues can be resolved.

Although the system is being designed for academic and government users, the industry participants (e.g., Cisco) ultimately intend to transfer any useful technologies to the commercial Internet. Businesses could find many uses for high-speed connections and service-quality guarantees. For starters, better video transfer may finally open the way for desktop videoconferencing to replace travel to meetings.

**ELECTRONIC COMMERCE**

As the percentage of U.S. households equipped with personal computers passed 50 percent, companies have become increasingly interest in using the Internet to sell products directly to consumers. The possibilities are enticing. The Internet gives companies the opportunity to save money by skipping the middle level of distributors and retailers. It also provides the ability to track customer preferences more closely and give them accurate and up-to-date information on products and options.

From a marketing perspective, the buying process has been defined in three basic steps: (1) prepurchase information gathering, (2) the purchase itself, and (3) postpurchase support. These steps are listed with examples in Figure 6.17. The Internet can be used to support each of these areas. The level of support in each area depends on the industry, type of product, and capabilities of the customers. Note that the process differs depending on whether the customer is a retail consumer or another company. For example, sales to other companies are generally repetitive and typically require additional documentation and billing procedures.

Creating a web site requires access to a server that has a full-time connection to the Internet. Initially, basic servers simply presented static pages, with text and limited graphics that rarely changed. Gradually, more sophisticated services have been introduced that add a higher degree of interactivity. One of the most important features is the ability of the

| PREPURCHASE | PURCHASE (REQUIRES INTERACTIVE) | POSTPURCHASE |
|---|---|---|
| • Static data sites<br>　Promotion<br>　Product specifications<br>　Pictures<br>　Schematics<br>　Pricing<br>　FAQs<br>• Interactive sites<br>　Configuration<br>　Compatibility<br>　Complex pricing | • Transmission security<br>• User identification<br>• Product selection<br>• Payment validation<br>• Order confirmation | • Service<br>　Revenue generation<br>　Problem tracking<br>　Sales leads<br>• Resolve problems<br>• Answer questions<br>• Product evaluation<br>　Modifications<br>　Tracking customers |

**FIGURE 6.17**
ELECTRONIC COMMERCE
Web sites are commonly used to support the three main phases of marketing.

web site to connect to the corporate databases. In this situation, the Web simply becomes a front-end or client computer to the back-end database server. The strength of the Web is that it provides a standardized user interface that is accessible anywhere in the world.

## Prepurchase Information

Prepurchase information is one of the easiest things to provide with a web site. Whether supporting end consumers or other businesses, the information tends to be relatively static and can be stored on virtually any Web server. Common features include product specifications, pictures, schematics, and prices. For static sites, lists of frequently asked questions (FAQs) can provide additional information to prospective customers. More interactive sites provide configuration and compatibility data. Surveys and monitoring of web site access provide data on customer preferences and activities.

Relatively static sites are easy to create and can be hosted on virtually any server. Today, many ISPs provide free basic web site space. Because these sites are easy to create and to host, they are one of the most common elements of e-commerce.

One of the greatest strengths of using a web site for prepurchase information is that it is relatively inexpensive. Additionally, the information is available worldwide 24 hours a day. It is also relatively easy to change the data, particularly since the data needs to be updated in only one location. For example, it is much cheaper to update a photo on a web site than to reprint and ship an entire catalog.

The most challenging aspect to providing prepurchase information is getting customers to come to your site. Web search engines make it relatively easy for customers to find the site, so motivated customers may search you out. However, companies are increasingly trying to attract customers. Hence, web site advertising is becoming more common—both on the Web and in more traditional media. Think about the number of advertisements you see that include a web address. Today, it is difficult to find even a newspaper ad that does not have a web address. Companies also advertise on other web sites. For example, the big search engines are some of the most popular sites on the Internet, used daily by millions of people. These portal sites sell ad space to other companies, who hope that viewers will click-through to learn more about their products.

## Purchase Mechanisms

Purchasing products over the Internet requires a substantially more interactive web site. The purchase mechanism also varies depending on whether the customer is an end consumer or another company. Online purchase mechanisms need five basic elements: (1) transmission security, (2) user identification, (3) payment validation, (4) product selection, and (5) order confirmation. When the customer is another company, the steps are the same but can be more complicated. In this situation, the company generally wants the ordering to be more automatic (e.g, EDI) and requires automated notification of the order status and shipping times. Companies also want more sophisticated billing features, such as itemized monthly bills, the ability to dispute individual times, and credit terms.

Transmission security is important on the Internet because unencrypted transmissions could be intercepted by thousands of people. Encryption is used to ensure that no one can intercept and read or change the order and financial data. Providing secure transmissions requires the use of a secure server. Browsers are already configured to accept the security conditions of the server. Server security is established by purchasing an authentication certificate from a security provider such as Verisign. The certificate ensures that your company exists and encrypts transmissions with the browser.

User identification depends on the type of customer. Commercial customers can purchase authentication certificates, which provide a relatively strong means of identifying people and organizations on the Internet. Retail customers are generally identified by their credit card data. The credit card number, expiration date, and billing address must be provided and verified to minimize the possibility of fraud. For both personal and commercial customers, particularly for repeat customers, you can also establish usernames and passwords to identify the customers.

Currently, payment validation is straightforward but can be expensive. Commercial customers are generally billed on a monthly cycle. So once you identify the customer, the system simply adds the purchase data to the billing system. Payments can then be made directly to your firm, or to your bank through an EDI mechanism. The EDI systems are relatively fast and highly reliable. Individual consumer payments are generally made using credit cards, which must be processed through a bank or credit card agency. Banks typically collect fees based on the value of the transaction (e.g., 1 to 5 percent). Some companies are working on more direct payment methods that transfer money directly. Chapter 14 discusses some of the possibilities and issues related to these mechanisms.

Any transaction requires that your web site identify the specific items and quantities being purchased. For retail consumers, the best method is to enable them to choose from a list. Virtual shopping carts are common: when customers see an item they wish to purchase, they click an icon and the ID number is added to the shopping cart. The most interactive sites enable customers to see if the item is in stock before they select it. Simpler systems are more static and require the customer to enter the product ID number directly. This method can lead to unacceptable errors but might be faster for commercial customers who repeatedly purchase the same items. In both cases, the system needs to look up the current price of each item and compute the necessary taxes and shipping costs.

The actual purchase mechanisms are relatively complex, particularly since you must be careful to provide security and minimize errors. Consequently, it is often wiser to purchase software that runs your web site somewhat automatically. Several companies sell servers specifically designed to generate interactive e-commerce sites: notably Microsoft and Netscape. For relatively uncomplicated sites, you can also lease space on a commercial mall site, which provides the underlying facilities. All you have to do is enter your database with product descriptions, images, and prices.

Order confirmation is related to the selection of the products. At a minimum, you should provide a list of the items purchased, the inventory status, the price, and the total value of the order. It is also helpful to provide an order number generated by the system. Then, if questions arise, it is easy to locate the specific order. For many retail consumers, the order number is an important feedback mechanism that verifies the purchase was accepted. Order confirmation is generally more complex for commercial customers. They often need detailed information on each purchase and its current status. In these situations, many sellers provide the purchaser with direct access (read only) to the order database, so purchase managers can check status and billing amounts at any time.

## Postpurchase Support

Postpurchase support consists of providing service, resolving problems, answering questions, and evaluating products. Some products require more service than others. In cases where the service generates continuous streams of revenue, a web site can be useful at tracking customers, providing additional information, and generating leads for new sales. The resolution of complaints is an important part of service for any product. Some problems are relatively easy to solve and can be handled with a support database and perhaps an online expert system that walks the consumer through possible solutions. In more complex cases, the system can track complaints, identify causes, and rapidly inform engineers of potential problems. Similarly, the information obtained through the service site can be used to spot consumer trends and provide ideas for product improvements.

In general, a postpurchase web site is relatively easy to create. Much of the content can be static—as long as there is an extensive, easy-to-use search system. Obtaining comments from consumers utilizes a straightforward, form-based site. About the only danger is that your competitors will have equal access to the information you provide. Most of the time, it will not be an issue, but you should be careful to protect comments and information returned by customers.

## Digital Content

All three of these areas become more important in the case of digital content. And more content is being converted to digital format every day. Computer software is still probably the leading item in digital content. But you can also purchase music and download it directly to your computer or a specialized player (e.g., MP3 format). Newspaper and similar information are available online. It is possible to purchase entire books online and download them either to your computer or a specialized player. With increased bandwidth and read/write DVD machines, videos will also become available online. In all of these cases, the entire transaction, including delivery of the content, takes place online. Of course, the biggest issue with digital content revolves around copyright protection and piracy. What will stop people from copying the content and either giving it away or selling it at a reduced price? Although worldwide laws prohibit these actions, the software, music, and video industries have seen that the laws are only useful against large-scale operations. Several technologies have been proposed for physically limiting the copying of digital content. However, technologically, any copy system can be defeated. Hence, in 1998, the United States passed a new law making it a criminal offense to circumvent copy-protection systems. It will take time for all the aspects of this law to be interpreted by the courts.

In any case, digital content is a natural fit for e-commerce. By keeping the entire process online, there are fewer costs. There are no traditional shipping costs—only the Internet connection cost, which is a fixed cost. The manufacturer receives all of the revenue because no distributors or retailers are involved. New content can be purchased instantly (depending only on the download time). The identical content is available worldwide. Patches or additions are available online. Additionally, the manufacturer has stronger ties to the final consumer, making it easier to sell upgrades or related products.

One interesting feature of digital content distributed on the Internet is that it breaks the power of the distributors. Historically, in book, music, and video publishing industries, a few large firms have controlled the distribution of content. Although anyone might write a book, a song, or create a video, it is difficult to distribute it without the backing of one of the large publishers. With digital content, it is easier to create the final product and relatively inexpensive to distribute it. Of course, there is still a place for publishers—in terms of conducting market research, improving the content, and promoting the products. Just because someone writes the next great American novel and puts it on the Internet does not mean anyone will find it or bother to pay for it. Nonetheless, some authors are already putting their work on the Internet—sometimes for free, sometimes with a free introduction and payment required for successive content. It is likely that new marketing models will be developed over time.

## GLOBAL TELE-COMMUNICATIONS

Business firms in the 1990s are becoming more dependent on international markets. This internationalization increases the demands on the telecommunications system. The international transmission of data is becoming part of the daily business routine. A manufacturing company may have factories in several different countries, with the headquarters located in yet another country. Supplies have to be sent to factories. Finished and intermediate products have to be tracked. Customer demands have to be followed in each country. Quality control and warranty repair information have to be followed from the supplier through the factory and out to the customers. Financial investments have to be tracked on stock markets in many countries. Different accounting and payroll rules have to be provided for each country. Basic accounting and financial data have to be available to management at any time of day, in any part of the organization.

Creating networks across international boundaries creates many problems. Some of the complications are technical, some are political or legal, and others are cultural.

## Technical Problems

The biggest technical complication is that each country may have its own telecommunications standards. For example, in the western European nations, the telephone systems are managed by governmental agencies call Postal Telephone (PTT) companies. Because PTTs are publicly run, national governments have a habit of insisting that communication equipment be purchased from manufacturers within their own nation. Despite the standards, there are still technical incompatibilities among the various nations.

In developing nations, the communications equipment may be antiquated. The older equipment will not be able to handle large amounts of data transfers, and there may be an unacceptable number of errors. Also, the government-controlled power supplies may not be reliable enough to run computers and network equipment.

One possible way to avoid the public telecommunications hassles is to use microwave transmissions through satellites. This approach can be more reliable but can be expensive unless you have huge amounts of data to transfer. For developing nations located in the southern hemisphere, there may not be adequate satellite coverage. Many of the satellite channels available to developing nations are used and controlled by the individual governments. It is generally not economically feasible to put up a new satellite, and most governments would object if you attempted to bypass their control.

To transmit more than simple text and numbers, there are more potential problems to consider. The United States, Europe, and the Pacific Rim all have different video standards. Televisions made for the U.S. market, therefore, will not function in Europe. If a company creates a multimedia marketing presentation in the United States, it will probably be difficult to show it to clients in France. These incompatibilities are about to get worse with the introduction of high-definition television (HDTV) or digital television. Each of the national groups is working with a different technique.

## Legal and Political Complications

Some important problems can be created when a firm wants to transmit information across national boundaries. These transfers are call **transborder data flows (TBDFs).** The problem arises because the information has value to the sender. Because it has value, some governments have suggested that they would like to impose a tariff or tax on that value. Besides the cost of the tariff, the issue raises the possibility that the national governments may want to monitor the amount and type of data being transferred. Most businesses are reluctant to allow anyone that must access to their information. Some countries go further; for example, France made it illegal to encrypt data.

Another important issue revolves around typical marketing data about customers. It is common for marketing departments to maintain huge databases. These databases contain customer names, addresses, phone numbers, estimated income levels, purchases, and other marketing data. Problems have arisen because the western European nations have much stricter laws concerning privacy than does the United States. In most European nations, it is illegal to sell or trade customer data to other companies. It must also be stored in protected files that cannot be seen by unauthorized employees or outsiders. In most cases, it is the responsibility of the company to prove it is meeting the requirements of the law. In many cases, this requirement means that customer data must be maintained on computers within the original nation. Also, this data cannot then be transmitted to computers in other countries. As a result, the multinational company may be forced to maintain computer facilities in each of the nations in which it does business. It also needs to impose security conditions that prevent the raw data from being transmitted from these computers.

There is one more important political issue involving international computer centers. Many nations, especially the developing nations, change governments quite often, as well as abruptly. There are many nations where terrorist activities are prevalent. Oftentimes, large multinational companies present tempting targets. Because computer centers tend to be expensive, special security precautions need to be established in these countries. Probably the most important step is to keep the computer center away from public access. Several U.S. security specialists publish risk factors and suggested precautions for each country. They also provide security analysis and protection—for a fee.

A host of other political complications affect any multinational operation. For example, each nation has different employment laws, accounting rules, investment constraints, and local partnership requirements. Most of these can be surmounted, but they usually require the services of a local attorney.

## Cultural Issues

All of the typical cultural issues can play a role in running multinational computer networks. The work habits of employees can vary in different nations. It may be difficult to obtain qualified service personnel at some times of day or night. These issues can be critical for computer networks that need to remain in operation 24 hours a day. In many nations, it is still considered inappropriate to have female managers when there are male subordinates. Collecting information may be exceedingly difficult or even culturally forbidden. In some countries, you will lose a customer if you try to obtain marketing data such as age and income.

In some nations, the connections between suppliers and customers are established by culture. For instance, in Japan, distribution of products is handled by only a few large firms. These companies have established relationships with the suppliers and retail outlets. In any country, it can be difficult for an outside firm to create a relationship between suppliers and customers. Trying to build computer networks with the various companies could cause severe repercussions. The established firms may think you are trying to steal their knowledge or information.

## Comment

Creating international data networks can lead to many problems. There is no easy solution to many of these problems. However, international networks do exist and they will

---

### Cultural Differences in the World

If you invite people to a party at seven o'clock, your guests will consider it polite to turn up on the dot in Germany, 5 minutes early in the American Midwest, an hour early in Japan, 15 minutes afterward in the UK, up to an hour afterward in Italy, and some time in the evening in Greece. I deliberately avoided the more emotive word "late," because there is nothing wrong in it. It is the accepted convention.

SOURCE: John Mole, When in Rome . . . *A Business Guide to Cultures & Customs in 12 European Nations*, AMACOM: New York, 1991, p. 155.

increase in the next few years. In many cases, firms have to operate in the international evironment in order to succeed. There is no choice. The company must build international telecommunications networks.

As the European Union increases the amount of interdependence between western and eastern European nations, there will be even more reasons for companies to operate in many nations. The same holds true for the conversion of the Eastern European nations to market economies. The companies that take the lead in international computer networks will face many problems, but if they succeed, they will create the foundation necessary to be the leaders in their industry.

## SUMMARY

One of the most important concepts in MIS is the necessity of sharing data. Computer systems designed to be used by many people simultaneously are more complex than single-user systems. Because of this complexity, more problems arise. Hardware and software have to be designed to be shared. Someone has to be in charge of controlling access to the machines and data. Standards have to be established to ensure compatibility among pieces of equipment.

Local area networks are an easy means to share data between users. They provide access to transaction data collected by central computers. They are used to send messages between users through e-mail and bulletin boards and to schedule meetings on electronic calendars. They make it easier for teams to share data, results, and reports for projects. LANs also make it easier to create backups of personal computer data.

As the use of personal computers increases, LANs are frequently used to connect them together and to give individual users access to data stored on central computers. Many organizations have chosen to organize their networks as a collection of client computers that access data from a few servers. Most communication is between the client personal computers and the server. Computers can also be connected as peer-to-peer machines to transfer data directly to each other, without the use of an intermediary.

Changes in the telephone industry are having profound effects on the connection of computers across long distances. As the availability of ISDN and DSL increases, it will become easier (and possibly cheaper) to connect computers across phone lines at much higher speeds. Even the television cable companies are considering new facilities for connecting computers.

Increasingly, the Internet is used as a foundation for building networks, giving workers access to internal data and to data on web sites around the world. Consequently, the Internet browser is becoming the standard means of finding and displaying data. Today, you share data by creating Web-formatted files and storing them on your Web server.

The telecommunications facilities and prices on which we rely in industrialized nations are not always available in other nations. Additionally, there are incompatibilities between equipment produced for various nations. Political restrictions are another source of complications when transferring data across international boundaries.

---

### A MANAGER'S VIEW

All workers need to communicate, both through formal channels with reports and informal conversations with other workers throughout the company. Telecommunication systems compensate for the barrier of distance.

Computer networks facilitate several types of communication: written, voice, image, and even video. Basically, networks are simple connections among machines. As a manager, you need to know how to use networks to share data. You also need to watch for network problems and incompatibilities.

---

## KEY WORDS

Asynchronous Transfer Mode (ATM), 251
broadcasts, 241
digital subscriber line (DSL), 251
e-mail, 231
file server, 236
groupware, 234

Internet, 252
Internet service provider (ISP), 253
local area network (LAN), 228
modem, 250
network interface card (NIC), 239
newsgroup, 233

peer-to-peer network, 238
standards, 248
transborder data flows (TBDFs), 265
universal naming convention (UNC), 239
World Wide Web (WWW), 249

## WEB SITE REFERENCES

### Financial News and Quotes

| | |
|---|---|
| Big Charts | www.bigcharts.com |
| Bloomberg | www.bloomberg.com |
| Dun & Bradstreet | www.dnb.com |
| Dow Jones | www.dowjones.com |
| Quote.com | www.quote.com |
| Reuters | www.reuters.com |
| SEC Edgar | www.sec.gov/edgarhp.htm |
| Security APL | www.secapl.com |
| StockPoint | www.stockpoint.com |
| Thomson | rtq.thomsoninvest.net |
| Wall Street Journal | wsj.com |

### Discount Online Trading

| | |
|---|---|
| E*Trade | www.etrade.com |
| DLJdirect | www.dljdirect.com |
| Ameritrade | www.ameritrade.com |
| Datek | www.datek.com |
| Suretrade | www.suretrade.com |
| Charles Schwab | www.schwab.com |
| Discover Brokerage Direct | www.discoverbrokerage.com |

## REVIEW QUESTIONS

1. Identify three main items that can be shared with networks.
2. What business reasons do users have for sharing data?
3. List the main components of a network.
4. Explain the concept of an enterprise network.
5. Why are standards so important in networks?
6. What new telephone services are available and how do they affect businesses?
7. What problems arise with global telecommunications?
8. Discuss the advantages and drawbacks of e-mail compared to traditional mail. Compared to telephones.
9. What is a bulletin board system? Give an example of how it can be used in business.
10. How are electronic calendars used to schedule meetings? How does their use affect workers?
11. Explain what advantages are gained by sharing printers with a LAN.
12. What do you gain by storing software on a file server?
13. List the types of transmission media available. How do they compare in transmission rates and cost?
14. What software is needed on personal computers to connect them to a LAN?

## EXERCISES

1. **First, get permission from your LAN administrator,** then conduct a performance test of your LAN. Have five students start an application program at the same time: Measure the time it takes for the package to be loaded for all five users. Now, try the same experiment with 10, 20, 30, and as many users as you can find. Graph the results.
2. Using magazine reviews and advertisements, how many major network operating system choices can you find for a 10-user LAN?
3. Using catalogs and advertisements, estimate the hardware and software costs of installing a LAN for 10 users and one file server. Provide a detailed list of the items you need to purchase. What is the cost of some application packages (word processor, spreadsheet, database, etc.). Will you need to license all of the software for 10 users?

4. Use your LAN to send a message to at least five students in your class. If you have access to a BBS or USENET, post a message on the system and reply to anyone who responds to the message.

5. As a group assignment, set up a small database on a LAN. For example, create an input screen to record product orders and create reports that display customer and inventory data. Using the LAN, have three people enter data at the same time. Make sure the database handles multiple users correctly; see whether the values are correct. Also, note whether there are any performance changes when one, two, and three people enter data simultaneously. Can two people enter orders for the same customer at the same time? What about entering the same product for different customers at the same time? Can a fourth user retrieve accurate reports at the same time orders are being taken? Are the reports automatically updated after the orders are entered? Have one user view the base table data while the orders are created. Does the user screen update automatically when the data is entered?

6. As a group assignment, write a short paper (one or two pages) on the uses of LANs. Using current periodicals, each group member should find an article on local area networks and summarize that article in one paragraph. Each person types in his or her summary with a word processor. Using a LAN, send the individual pieces to one member, who assembles them into a final document for printing.

7. Assuming that you have money, choose an automobile that you would want to buy. Use the Internet to fine the list price and estimated dealer invoice of the automobile. Is it possible to purchase the automobile over the Internet? Can you apply for a loan using the Internet? Be sure to specify the address of any data you find.

### Rolling Thunder Database

8. Design a network for the Rolling Thunder Bicycle Company. Identify who will need access to the network, how many workstations you need (and where to place them), the data, input forms, and reports users will need. Using the existing data, estimate the storage requirements and transmission needs. Specify how changes and growth will affect the type of network needed.

9. Match purchase orders with receipts. Verify total expenditures match. Determine whether any employees were in charge of both purchases and receipts.

10. Choose a bicycle and list all of the people who were involved with its production and shipping. Assume we received a problem/complaint on a bicycle. How would a network facilitate handling this type of query?

11. Describe how the Internet could be used to increase sales or cut costs at Rolling Thunder Bicycles.

12. What network problems would you encounter in a manufacturing environment?

## ADDITIONAL READING

Borzo, Jeanette. "At Last, European Telecom Gets Competitive," *Computerworld,* February 16, 1999. [Competition in telecommunications spreads to Europe]

Diederich, Tom. "Survey Cites Bandwidth, Convergence as Top Issues," *Computerworld,* February 12, 1999. [Issues involved in improving the Internet]

Evans, J. "Losing $21.5 Million: As Easy as ABCNews.com," *The Industry Standard,* November 2, 1998, p. 26. [Major web sites losing money]

"Hitting the Mail on the Head," *The Economist,* April 30, 1994, p. 69–70. [Postal statistics]

Kahn, Robert E. "The Role of Government in the Evolution of the Internet," *Communications of the ACM,* August 1994, p. 15–19. [Early days of the Internet]

Schwartz, Nelson P. "The Tech Boom Will Keep on Rocking," *Fortune,* February 15, 1999. [Recent telecommunications changes, and forecasts]

"The Swelling Tide of Information," *World Press Review,* January 1999, p. 11. [Telephone usage in China]

Wiggins, R. "How the Internet Works," *Internet World,* 8(10), 1996. [Basic explanation of terms and connection points]

# CASES *Wholesale Trade*

The wholesale industry is a broad and fragmented industry with multiple channels of distribution and more than $250 billion in annual sales. Wholesalers market to a number of distribution channels including retail outlets, small distributorships, national, regional, and local distributors, direct mail suppliers, large warehouses, and manufacturers' direct sales force. The industry is focused primarily in the food, health, and industrial maintenance and repair sectors.

## Industry and Market Analysis

The wholesale industry's customers have increasingly focused on reducing overall costs by dealing with fewer suppliers and maintaining relationships with those that can offer a broad product selection, automated order processing, and advanced services such as inventory management and nationwide support. To remain competitive, it has become increasingly important for distributors to provide customers with wider product selection, lower costs, and value-added service.

The principal means by which wholesalers compete with manufacturers and other distributors is by providing local stocks, efficient service, account managers, competitive prices, several catalogs, extensive technical and application data, procurement process consulting services, and other efforts to assist customers in lowering their total costs.

The wholesalers' advantage lies in their ability to supply products faster and allow smaller inventories to be held by the customer. Basically, wholesalers allow customers to have access to one-stop shopping, thereby reducing the number of suppliers and transactions required to obtain the supplies needed.

## Financial Analysis

Since 1990, producer prices have been falling, limiting the wholesale industry's ability to increase prices. In the absence of price inflation, industry consolidation will likely continue as it has over the past decade. Bottom-line gains are coming from increased productivity, not from increased prices.

## Stock/Investment Outlook

The investment outlook for the wholesale sector is neutral. The lack of inflation has a negative impact on profits given the companies' traditionally low profit margins. Only productivity gains and premiums paid for outright purchases are likely to influence the stock prices of wholesale companies.

## Potential/Prospective for Growth

Growth in the wholesale industry is not expected to be strong. The industry is threatened by advances in communications and freight systems. Growth in individual companies will mostly be through acquisitions. Some overseas growth is possible since American companies are often at the forefront of utilizing new technologies to increase productivity.

## Competitive Structure

The competitive structure of the industry has been changing. The wholesale industry now competes with more companies than ever before as manufactures are able to reach more customers directly. Internally, competition has not allowed prices to rise and has focused on productivity gains and industry consolidation. One of the most consolidated areas is drug wholesalers, where three companies now account for over 50 percent of the industry's sales.

## Role of Research and Development

The ability of wholesalers to succeed depends on their ability to increase productivity. Research and development to increase productivity depends on creative and thoughtful use of the many off-the-shelf products available. These technologies include bar-code scanners, wireless communications, data warehousing, and Internet communications.

## Technology Investment and Analysis

Wholesalers are using technology to provide many types of value-added services to the distribution of hard goods. Some of the services include sophisticated, continuous replenishment programs for customers, warehouse and inventory management, customized labeling, barcoding, and special packaging. All of these services are communications intensive, requiring powerful computer systems and data warehousing and management.

## Recommendation for the Future

The wholesale industry is under threat from the globalization of the world economy. Advances in communications, transportation, and data warehousing technology are decreasing the time and space that separate retailers and consumers from manufacturers. The speed with which these technological advances have been adopted varies from industry to industry. A definite trend toward the elimination of the middle person is in place. It is only by offering unique, value-added services in addition to the physical movement of goods that the wholesale industry will have opportunities for future success.

## CASE *Fisher Scientific International*

### Technological Story

The years 1995 and 1996 saw the beginning of several information technology developments. The strategic objective was to maximize return on assets by increasing sales volume through all global trade channels. The Fisher Technology Group, dedicated to the development and support of advanced technology for businesses over computer networks, introduced developments to expand Internet services and develop other electronic solutions to increase business productivity.

### Technological Investment and Analysis

SupplyLink manages the entire product procurement process and centralizes all supplier information, making internal referencing of vendors' products more efficient. Integrated SupplyNet is a customer-specific electronic catalog that enables customers to maintain existing contracts with suppliers, including net prices.

Another leading-edge technology development of Fisher's Technology Group is ProcureNet, an online mall of more than 50 scientific suppliers run by Fisher. Even Fisher's competitors are lining up to participate. ProcureNet (www.procurenet.com) is the first public, business-to-business electronic mall that allows actual transactions to occur. ProcureNet enables vendors to create electronic storefronts to maximize exposure for their company and actually sell over the Internet. This site was developed by the Fisher Technology Group. Its main software product Cornerstone, on which ProcureNet is based, is available for sale to companies that need this technology function. Cornerstone operates much like its own catalog division. It includes online product descriptions and ordering and availability information.

The quality of this Internet commerce product has been so well-received that IBM and Oracle plan to resell Fisher's software as part of their own Internet commerce products. This new business area will help Fisher offset downtrends in the laboratory markets and give Fisher a new area for future growth.

Given the high margins and after-sale consulting revenue that is involved with software licensing for Internet commerce products, this area could prove to be Fisher's most profitable area yet. The incentive for the Fisher Technology Group is that for every dollar of licensing products shipped, there are probably 10 dollars of consulting and service revenue to follow. Given the alignment with IBM, Fisher has a high-profile distribution mechanism to launch its future marketing efforts. Fisher Technology Group's recent acquisition of UniKix will add to their expertise and capabilities in the electronic commerce area.

### Technological Innovations: Telecommunications

Fisher Scientific launched a new Internet commerce site based on IBM's Net.Commerce server. It performs real-time contract pricing and payment processing, and manages EDI transactions, according to Mark Munson, general manager of Fisher Scientific's ProcureNet.

The Trilogy and IBM servers calculate pricing and other variables in real time in order to accommodate the nuances of business relationships. Variables include volume discounts, delivery logistics, multiple-supplier outsourcing, automated replenishment, sales forecasting, and reporting.

### Recommendation for the Future

The Fisher Technology Group has laid the groundwork for a promising start in the Internet commerce business. This should be developed further to help Fisher diversify its revenues across different industries and further focus on its competencies. Fisher has the jump on other business-to-business sites on the Web and should seize the opportunity to be the first to market a top-quality product. This focus will help Fisher stay close to its customers by making the procurement process the most convenient and efficient in the industry.

### QUESTIONS

1. What are the core competencies for Fisher Scientific?
2. Upon what technologies has Fisher Scientific relied?
3. What has made Fischer so successful in developing changes in the use of advanced technology for the sales of its products?
4. What conclusions can be reached by analyzing Fisher's financial trends?
5. What does the corporation's web page present about their business direction?
6. How is technology impacting the special parts industry?

### ADDITIONAL READING

Frook, John Evan. "E-Commerce Receives Real-Time Pricing Boost," *InternetWeek,* August 3, 1998, p. 8.

## CASE   *W. W. Grainger Company*

When drifting along the Edens Expressway just north of Chicago, a large sign spelling the name W. W. Grainger is visible. In fact, this name is visible no matter what state you live in. W. W. Grainger provides the products that keep the electricity flowing to all areas of America's buildings—hand and power tools, the lights which illuminate offices and classrooms, and cleaning, safety, and sanitary supplies.

### Technological Investment and Analysis

In 1981, Grainger redefined their method of retrieving and replenishing inventory when they installed their Automated Storage and Retrieval System (AS/RS) at the Niles, Illinois–based RDC. This massive 10-aisle system was designed to supply over 60 percent of the replenishment stock to forward picking locations at a rate of 210 pallet loads an hour.

This AS/RS has greatly increased efficiencies in getting product to the customer as well as to the branches. Although the AS/RS helped in expediting inventory, this was only one component in improving customer service and efficiency. The other component was expediting information.

Information transmission has been enhanced through the use of satellite communications. Grainger utilizes a satellite communications network, which substantially reduces its reliance on phone lines by linking stores and other facilities together via a network control center. This was enhanced in 1995–96 when Grainger completed the installation of IBM minicomputers at each brand, office, and distribution center. The Grainger network enables all potions of the business to be linked by satellite network to provide the convenience of instant product availability information and real-time inventory management for more than $1 billion of inventory.

The network has decreased Grainger's response time through the almost instantaneous transmission of information. This expedites the completion of sales transactions and the initiation of stock replenishment, which, in turn, increased levels of customer satisfaction. It has also enabled Grainger to distribute software across the network with greater effiency.

Grainger offers their general catalog on CD-ROM, free to Grainger customers. In 1996, the company introduced a web site. With the introduction of their web site, Grainger became one of the first business-to-business web sites to accept orders over the Internet. Grainger's state-of-the-art technology helps Grainger customers to instantaneously look up products. When doing so, they utilize a guided interactive search engine, by description, brand name, specification, manufacturer's model number, and Grainger stock number to check the company-specific pricing.

Grainger has integrated the CD-ROM catalog version with Datastream products. Datastream is a leading manufacturer of computer software programs such as MRP2 and Maintain It (purchasing and preventative maintenance software programs). Now users of these Datastream products can click on an icon and immediately be transferred to the Grainger CD-ROM catalog (ECAT [electronic Catalog]).

Utilizing Grainger's web site (http://www.grainger.com), customers can now order online 24 hours a day, seven days a week, to find more than 200,000 products quickly and easily. This provides the customer with fast and cost-effective paperless services. In addition, customers can utilize the web site for inquiries and feedback. Grainger's Internet site has dramatically increased the number of companies using Grainger's distribution system.

Barbara M. Chilson, Grainger's Vice-President and General Manager, Electronic Commerce, stated "Grainger's Internet commerce convenience was created in response to feedback received from our customers." Grainger's Online Catalog (Web Cat) also allows multiple users per account to order online. This provides a significant advantage to larger companies, which often give more than one employee purchasing responsibility.

Items such as the CD-ROM catalog and Web Cat give customers greater access to products in the general catalog. The CD-ROM version enables customers to access more than 500,000 product cross-references. The Internet provides over 1 million cross-references. Other electronic services include Electronic Data Interchange (EDI), Electronic Funds Transfer (EFT), and computerized maintenance management programs with built-in interface to the Grainger CD-ROM catalog.

According to James T. Ryan, Grainger's Vice-President of Information Services, "The company is continually upgrading its information systems to better serve its customers." In 1995, Grainger started moving major applications from the mainframe into a more distributed client-server network. Every branch now uses minicomputers and "intelligent" workstations. As a result, Grainger is now positioned to respond much faster to customer needs with more computing power resident at the branch level.

Technology has enabled increased products, services, and locations. Grainger's direct sales focus is shifting from servicing resellers, other distributors, and small customers to integrated supply chains, national accounts, and medium to large customers. Grainger has been careful not to make the critical mistake of ignoring its smaller customers, who up until the mid-1980s had been the largest source of Grainger's profit. To ensure that smaller customers were not neglected, Grainger piloted a telesales project in 1996. It was designed to further penetrate the accounts for whom direct mail alone was not sufficient.

Realizing that Integrated Supply was more than a fad, Grainger formalized a new division—Grainger Integrated Supply Operation (GISO). With GISO, a customer uses Grainger to supply some or all of its maintenance, repair, and operating supplies. According to Donald E. Bielinski,

Senior Vice-President of Marketing and Sales, "Most GISO customers are large corporations because GISO customers typically order about $1 million of product per location per year from Grainger. Currently, annual orders of less than $1 million are not cost effective for Grainger to fulfill within the GISO program."

As technology improves, Bielinski estimates it will become cost effective for the company to accept smaller orders. Bielinski estimates the national market for integrated supply to be around $2 to $3 billion. GISO is paying off. Grainger recently signed American Airlines at its Dallas-Fort Worth airport operation and Fel-Pro, out of Skokie, Illinois, as GISO customers. GISO currently has about 40 customers. Looking to the future, Bielinski adds that "Grainger will continue to work on the three major areas that any distributor must constantly strengthen. This includes continuing to improve the physical movement of products, the flow of information, and the efficiency of transactions." In keeping with Bielinski's iteration of the critical factors for future growth, it seems that technology has found a home with Grainger. The use of technology will allow Grainger to meet its customers' as well as its own internal goals.

One of the largest benefits to developing electronic mediums such as the Grainger web site and CD-ROM catalog is to improve customer service and cut costs of producing catalogs. The web site affords customers access to Grainger round the clock from all corners of the globe. In addition, the web site and CD-ROM can help reduce the costs of catalog distribution. In 1995, more than 2 million copies of the general catalog were distributed to businesses nationwide. Given the freight charge to ship a catalog approximately five inches thick, the savings from shipping only a CD-ROM are substantial.

Not only do freight costs decrease when more users go online or utilize the CD-ROM catalog version, but costs are also saved on producing the catalog (paper version versus CD-ROM). Since 1995, Grainger has also produced the general catalog once a year instead of twice (spring and fall). This has also helped to reduce the cost of producing catalogs and enabled them to direct the money back to the company.

### Technological Innovations: Telecommunications

W. W. Grainger is teaming with SAP to let customers use the R/3 application to buy products from Grainger via the Web. Grainger views the web as a growth vehicle for business-to-business sales. The web site accounts for less than 1 percent of Grainger's total sales but is growing as much as 100 percent a quarter.

Grainger will use electronic-catalog technology from Requisite Technology, Inc., to provide the online content for all its Web initiatives. Requisite will also provide catalog technology to support Grainger's web site

and intranet, which sales representatives use to get information to fulfill orders and answer customers' questions.

One initiative includes a project with systems integrator Perot Systems to aggregate MRO products from Grainger and other distributors into a single Web portal for sales to small businesses. Grainger will form a subsidiary to manage the initiative, which should start early next year.

### Recommendation for the Future

Grainger must continue to focus on technology to improve efficiencies, increase customer service levels, effectively manage inventory, and facilitate access to existing markets. In short, they must implement technology that will improve distribution processes as well as give them the upper hand against current and future competition. Technology is being used to align customer needs with the company vision. Technology has taken Grainger from 347 branches to the virtual store, which can be accessed anytime from anyplace.

Grainger believes the key to integrating technology and the customers' needs lies in the ability to align investments in technology with the company's business objectives. In doing so, Grainger's success will be determined by how well it anticipates the needs of their customers and how well they respond to those needs. A key factor for Grainger's future is the decision to follow other companies and customers across national boundaries into the international marketplace.

### QUESTIONS

1. What is W. W. Grainger's strategic direction, and who or what forces are driving it?
2. What are the critical success factors and core competencies for Grainger?
3. What technologies have driven the process?
4. How has this technological change been implemented?
5. How successful has the technological change been?
6. What does Grainger's web page present about their business direction?

### ADDITIONAL READING

"E-Commerce Gains Ground with Purchasing Staff," *PC Week,* January 5, 1998, p. 69.

Frook, John Evan. "Blue-Collar Business on the Web," *InternetWeek,* September 14, 1998, p. 43.

Machlis, Sharon. "Supplier Seeks Sales via Web Searches," *Computerworld,* September 14, 1998, p. 20.

Tadjer, Rivka. "Purchasing Nirvana?" *InternetWeek,* September 22, 1997, pp. 55–58.

Wilder, Clinton. "Online Supplies Purchases Via R/3— W. W. Grainger Teams with SAP on Electronic-Commerce Initiative," *InformationWeek,* September 14, 1998, p. 32.

## DISCUSSION ISSUE

### *International Data Flows*

Operating in an international environment adds several complications to MIS. Technical difficulties include problems created by differing standards and complications that arise because of transferring data over long distances. However, cultural differences and different legal environments can cause even more problems. Techniques such as marketing systems and inventory methods that work well in the United States will usually have to be changed to support the variations in other nations. Listen to the head of marketing (Toni) discuss strategy with one of her department managers (Millie) and Dobbs, the MIS manager assigned to the project.

Millie: The way I see it, we should set one marketing plan and use it across all the markets. Besides cutting costs, I don't think there's much difference between the markets anyway.

Dobbs: Oh come on, Millie. We'll have to translate all of the promos and the packaging anyway. I don't see where it'll cut costs.

Millie: Well, Dobbs, for starters, it'll cut down on the number of meetings we need. More importantly, a single focus cuts down on the production diversity. For example, if we choose to focus on quality in all markets, we can limit the number of options and colors and concentrate on the base set. Plus, it'll simplify the data we need. By collecting the same data from each market, it will be easier to collect data and to perform the marketing analyses.

Toni: Speaking of marketing data, could we get back on track? We need to identify the data you want to collect. For starters, we'll need to set up focus groups in each major city. Then track initial sales by store, along with our competition. To select initial markets, we'll also need to get geographic-based consumer data such as incomes, spending, and population by region.

Dobbs: Whoa. Slow down. Sure, that's the way we've worked in the United States, but I think we're going to have trouble in Europe.

Millie: How so? I don't see where it'll be much different. Overall income distributions and basic economic indicators are about the same.

Dobbs: I'm not worried about the marketing differences right now—just the data collection. For example, France has limits on what data we're allowed to transfer out. Legally, we should set up a separate database facility in France, and we might need another one in Germany.

Millie: So where's the problem, Dobbs? We'll have offices in each country anyway. Because we use PCs in every office, we'll just set up the local data in each office. You can build a communication network, right? Then we just transfer everything back here and do what we want.

Dobbs: Sure, from a technology standpoint, we can do that. But what I'm trying to say is that we're not supposed to do it that way. France says we're not supposed to export this data.

Toni: Well, I don't see how we can work that way. At some point, the managers in the United States are going to need to look at that data. What are we supposed to do? Fly to Paris every time we have a marketing decision?

Millie: Those rules sound crazy. Does anyone actually obey them? Maybe we should just set it up the way we want. What can they do to us anyway?

Toni: Dobbs, isn't there some way we can transfer the data without the government knowing about it? I mean, we're going to be sending tons of data back and forth. I can't believe they can monitor all of it.

Dobbs: I don't know much about their laws yet. I just know the French government doesn't want us to transfer the data. I suppose we could think about using a coding scheme so no one can tell what we're sending. We do have to be careful though. France also has pretty strict rules about private companies not being allowed to encrypt data. Still, you're right about the amount of data. I imagine my staff could cook up something that'll work. But I'm not sure we should work this way, Toni.

Millie: Look, Dobbs, what's the worst that can happen? If they complain, we'll just apologize and tell them that we'll do it their way. It's not like were stealing anything. We still pay lots of money to collect the data and organize it. How can anyone care about where we store it? Toni, it'll make it a lot easier to handle the marketing end. We can't afford to run each nation separately. The combined data will let us make decisions faster and cut our costs. Plus, it'll give you more control over the day-to-day decisions.

Toni: Well, that's true. No matter who I send to head these departments, I'll still need to check the data and verify their decisions. If I had to travel to each agency, I'd spend all my time in airports. I don't see where we have much choice. Dobbs, check into it a little more, then come back with some options for us. We want to be careful, but we've got a right to use that data.

Dobbs:   All right, it's a little risky, but I think we can do it. Just don't tell everyone about how we're going to be transferring the data. We'll set it up to look like the data is staying in France. We can use the backup data. We'll keep the transmission time as short as possible. Once we get the data in the United States, if anyone asks, we'll just say we got if from somewhere else.

## QUESTIONS

1. Do you agree with the group decision?
2. Is there any other way for the marketing department to operate the way they want, but still leave the data in France? What are the trade-offs?
3. If you work for the marketing department or the MIS department and you are asked to help set up this new system, what would (or could) you do?
4. What is the probability the company will be *caught?*
5. Do you think nations should be allowed to set up laws that restrict the transfer of data? What are the advantages and disadvantages to the country?

# *Technical Definitions*

## INTRODUCTION

In many ways, computer networks and telecommunications are highly technical fields. They are also rapidly changing fields, with new products being introduced daily. As a result, the industry has created its own terminology. Of course, the terminology changes as fast as the industry, so no description can ever be up-to-date. Nonetheless, managers might find it useful to be familiar with some of the basic technology.

There are also a few standard products available for computer networks. Although the capabilities and purposes are similar, some technical differences among the choices can affect purchase decisions.

## DIRECT CONNECTIONS

One of the earliest methods of connecting terminals to computers was with direct physical connections. For example, each terminal would be wired directly to the computer—typically with twisted-pair cable. Eventually, to provide some flexibility, these terminals were wired directly to a *front-end processor,* shown in Figure 6.1A. This processor was a simple communications device that accepted all of the terminal wires and then assigned each user to an open communications *port* on the computer. This device decreased the number of physical access ports required on the computer. Although the front-end processor had to physically connect to every terminal, by reassigning terminals to different computer ports, the computer needed only enough ports to handle the expected number of simultaneous users. Because not all users were expected to be on the computer at the same time, the cost of the computer was reduced.

One of the biggest drawbacks to direct connections is that separate lines had to be run from each terminal to the front-end processor. In addition to the high installation costs, many of these lines sat unused for extended periods of time.

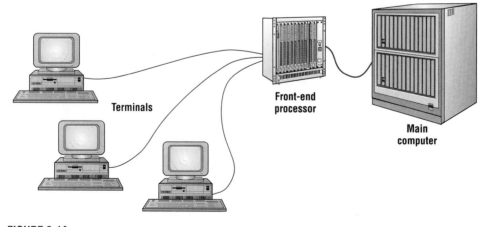

**FIGURE 6.1A**
DIRECT-CONNECT (STAR) NETWORKS
Early networks connected terminals through individual lines to a front-end processor that controlled
and organized the signals for the main computer.

## SWITCHED NETWORKS

There are various switched networks. At heart, they are all based on providing individual connections between any two computers (or telephones). With these systems, each device must be connected directly to a switch. The switch maintains addresses (phone numbers) for each device. The early switches actually made physical connections between devices. For example, if your terminal requested a connection to a specific computer, a physical link between the two was established and dedicated to your use. A small example of a switched network is displayed in Figure 6.2A.

Modern switches provide logical connections that do not rely on a single physical line. In particular, many of the systems are *packet switches.* Packet switches chop every transmission into small pieces. Each piece contains a source and destination address as well as a sequence number. When the switch receives a packet, the switch determines the best route and sends the packet on to the next switch. The final switch reassembles each packet in the proper order and delivers the total message to the destination machine. The packets for a single session might follow hundreds of different paths before reaching the same destination. The process happens so fast that none of the users can tell that the packets were ever separated. Modern phone systems are based on packet-switched networks.

A relatively new transmission protocol known as Asynchronous Transmission Method (ATM) is a virtual circuit–switching network that runs at very high speeds. Using high transmission speeds and preventing collisions, it offers high-speed transfers for many simultaneous users. When requested, it opens a connection between two machines. This connection can follow any path across several switches, but the same path is used for the entire session.

## SHARED-MEDIA NETWORKS

Shared-media networks evolved from early radio networks—such as the ALOHANET created by the University of Hawaii to connect users on different islands to the university computer. Although this system was based on radio waves and avoided the high cost of installing cables, today the most popular shared-media network is *Ethernet,* which is based on coaxial or twisted-pair cables.

In many ways, a shared-media network is like a room full of people trying to talk to each other. The limitation of sharing the media (the air in the room) is that only one person or computer can talk at a time. As a result, there need to be *protocols* that establish rules of behavior to avoid common problems. The protocols need to cover four situations: (1) providing a means to address each recipient and sender, (2) determining who is allowed to talk (initiate a conversation), (3) determining how long a single sender can talk at one time, (4) providing what to do if there is a *collision* when two machines (or people) try to talk at the same time. Figure 6.3A illustrates how the various computers are

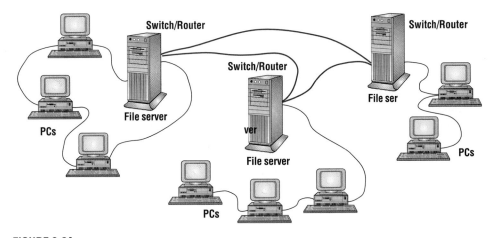

**FIGURE 6.2A**

In a switched network, each terminal makes a connection to the nearest switch which routes the message through other switches to the desired terminal. Sophisticated switches can reroute a message if there is a problem with one connection.

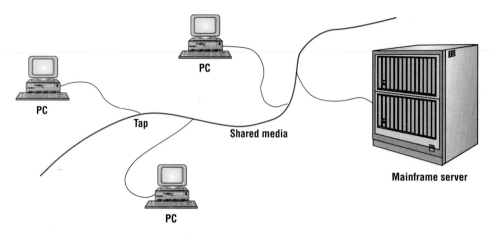

**FIGURE 6.3A**

With a bus (Ethernet) network each device is connected to a common transmission medium. Only one device can transmit at a time. Standards define when a device can transmit, how to specify a device, and how to tell whether the line is busy.

connected to a single cable in a shared-media or *bus* network. Radio networks are often built the same way, except the transmissions occur with radio frequencies through the air instead of through cables.

Ethernet is one of the earliest protocols to resolve these problems. It has been standardized by several national and international standard-setting bodies so that a network can be built from equipment provided by different vendors. The Ethernet protocol is also known as CSMA/CD, which stands for *Carrier-Sense, Multiple-Access/Collision Detection.* In this system, any LAN card is allowed to transmit on the network, but first it must examine the media to see whether another card is currently transmitting (carrier-sense). If so, the second card must wait until the line is clear. Users are prevented from tying up the line for extended periods by restricting the length of time each card can transmit at any one time. This time interval is a *tunable parameter* that can be set by the LAN administrator to provide better service under different conditions. Once the line is clear, the card can begin transmission. Because of multiple access, sometimes two computers will attempt to initiate a conversation at the same time and a collision occurs. When any card detects a collision, it immediately stops transmitting and waits a random length of time before trying again. Addressing on Ethernet is handled by each interface card. Every interface card must have a unique identification number. The numbers are assigned at the time the card is manufactured.

One of the biggest drawbacks to CSMA/CD is that as the number of users increases, there will be more collisions. With many collisions, the computers end up spending more time detecting collisions and waiting than they do transmitting. It is also the reason why a high-speed medium is important to this method. The faster that every transmission can be sent, the sooner the line is clear and ready for the next user.

A second method of dealing with shared media, known as a *Token-Ring* network, is shown in Figure 6.4A. The protocols here are slightly different. In this case, there is a special data packet known as a *token.* There is only one token available, and it is passed around a *ring* to each machine. A machine is allowed to send a message only if it holds the token. The message contains a source and destination address, and each machine examines the address to see which packets it should keep.

The drawback to Token-Ring networks is that the computers have to continually pass the token, and they have to wait until they receive the token before transmitting. This overhead results in slower transmissions than Ethernet networks when there are only a limited number of users. However, as the number of users increases, there are no collisions with the Token Ring, so performance does not deteriorate as rapidly as under Ethernet.

In practice, the differences among network types is not as great as the theory might indicate. Of course, most networks are designed in segments to avoid putting thousands of users on the same shared media. By building a LAN in segments, most traffic remains within a smaller network and only a few messages are shared on the network backbone.

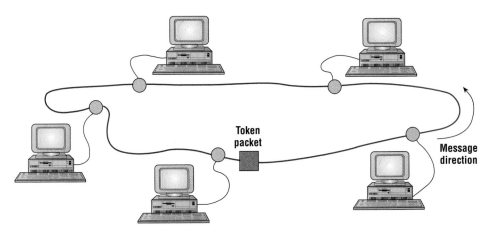

**FIGURE 6.4A**

A token-ring network operates with a unique protocol. A machine is allowed to transmit data only if it holds the token packet. Messages are passed between machines until they reach their destination. Based on defined intervals, the token is passed around the ring to each machine. If a machine has nothing to send, it passes the token on. This sequential method is relatively efficient for large networks.

| BRAND/VENDOR | TYPE | MEDIA |
|---|---|---|
| ATM | Switched/Token | Fiber optic (others later) |
| Digital | Ethernet | Coaxial/Twisted pair |
| FDDI | Token Ring/Dual | Fiber optic |
| IBM | Token Ring | Twisted pair |
| Novell | Ethernet | Coaxial/Twisted pair |

**FIGURE 6.5A**

A brief comparison of networks that are commonly available. Offerings change constantly, so contact the vendors for specific data.

## CHOOSING NETWORK DESIGNS

For the most part, it is rare that you will make a direct decision between the various networks types. Because there are only a limited number of network vendors, the most common practice is to identify the business needs of the users and then see how existing vendors can meet those needs. The focus of the decision is on features and prices, not on the type of network offered. For comparison purposes, a few of the popular networks are listed in Figure 6.5A

## ISO REFERENCE MODEL

Although there are differences in network communication system, they all have a common form that can be studied using the ISO Reference Model. In this model, there are seven basic layers to network communications: Physical, Data link, Network, Transport, Session, Presentation, and Application. Any communication between two computers must deal with these seven layers in some fashion. The basic structure is illustrated in Figure 6.6A. Each layer serves a specific purpose. Also, each layer tends to add data to the layer above.

The primary advantage of the OSI model is that it breaks the communication problem into smaller pieces. As long as each piece follows the appropriate standards, you can choose components from different vendors. As new components are introduced, you should be able to upgrade the appropriate section without replacing the entire network.

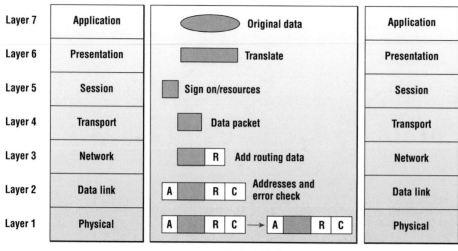

| Layer 7 | Application | | Application |
| Layer 6 | Presentation | | Presentation |
| Layer 5 | Session | | Session |
| Layer 4 | Transport | | Transport |
| Layer 3 | Network | | Network |
| Layer 2 | Data link | | Data link |
| Layer 1 | Physical | | Physical |

Physical Media

**FIGURE 6.6A**

The ISO Reference Model illustrates how data from an application on one machine is translated through seven layers, transmitted to another machine and converted to the new application. Networks involve more than just transmitting data.

## Physical Layer

The purpose of the Physical layer is to make the connection between two machines. It is directly related to hardware. There are standards to specify constraints on voltage, type of wire, frequency of signals, and sizes of physical connectors. Raw data bits are transferred at this stage.

## Data Link Layer

The Data link layer is concerned with transmitting error-free data to the correct destination. This level is primarily directed to hardware specifications. Standards refer to error-checking methods and means of identifying addresses. Most networking protocol standards (Ethernet, Token Ring, FDDI [fiber distributed date interface]) define standards through the Data link layer.

## Network Layer

The Network layer is concerned with routing messages to the appropriate location. In particular, it selects the appropriate path for a message in networks where there is a choice. Its main advantage is that it separates the higher layers from the physical transmission of data. The Network layer handles connections across differ-

ent machines and multiple networks. The Internet Protocol (IP) is an example of a Network layer standard.

## Transport Layer

The Transport layer is responsible for providing transparent services to the session layer. It hides the details of establishing connections and transmitting data. It breaks the message into packets and reassembles them on the receiving side. The Transport layer ensures that message packets are delivered correctly, in the proper order, and with no duplication or lost data. Sample protocols at this layer are TCP and Novell IPX.

## Session Layer

The Session layer is the user interface to the network. It handles user identification at logon time and enables the user to select remote hardware and software. It is handled in software, by the operating system and network specific packages. For instance, you might be asked to specify which file server you want to use.

## Presentation Layer

The Presentation layer handles encryption and compression. Data is translated into formats that can be used by the two machines.

## Application Layer

The Application layer translates the underlying data into a meaningful context. It ensures that applications can talk to each other and retain the meaning of the data. For example, a sales database on one computer might provide sales data to your computer. Even though it might be reformatted and translated into a spreadsheet application, it still represents sales data.

Above the Transport layer, many existing networks use proprietary techniques to establish connections. For example, logon commands and procedures depend on the manufacturer of the network and the computer equipment. At the presentation and application layers, there are few standards. Perhaps the closest we come today is with the use of dynamic data sharing in Windows, which is described in Chapter 7. Software that is written to Windows definitions can share data with similar software. Hence, applications can share data directly, even over networks.

## EXERCISES

1. If the equipment is available, build a network cable and test it.
2. If the equipment is available, run a network monitor and identify usage patterns over the course of a day or a week.
3. If the equipment is available, use a network sniffer to identify the number of bad packets on various segments of a network. Identify possible causes.
4. Write a plan for upgrading a network of 1,200 users. They are currently using six routers on twisted pair segments at 10 Mbps and an FDDI backbone at 100 Mbps. The workers are in two buildings and the organization needs the ability to set up video meetings and transfer large binary files.
5. Identify the current plans of the Internet2 group, and list the technologies and hardware available at each level of the ISO model.

CHAPTER 7

# *Integration of Information*

Ford used cross-functional teams, supported by a powerful information system, to design the 5.0-liter V-8 Explorer in about one-third of the time required in the past.

## FORD MOTOR COMPANY

In 1996, Alex Trotman, President, CEO, and Chairman of the Board of Ford Motor Company hosted a Ford family meeting. Trotman has hosted the Ford family every year since his appointment as CEO in 1993. Approximately twenty Fords gathered to tour the facilities, drive new models on the test track, lunch with the board of directors, and drill Trotman on everything from sales in Latin America, productive capacity, and environmental issues to—important to the Fords—dividends.

The Ford family received roughly $88 million in dividends in 1995. Trotman knows the value of keeping on the good side of the Ford family. Although the company is publicly held, the family exerts significant influence on it. They are also protective of their investment. One outside director said, "With all this cash, if it weren't for the family, I'd take over this company." After former chairman and CEO Donald Petersen rubbed the family the wrong way, he retired prematurely. Trotman, however, hopes to retain the Ford family support. He needs it now more than ever as he attempts to "win the world over" all over again.

**OVERVIEW**    Some companies work together with a great deal of synergy. In others, departments operate independently and managers battle each other constantly. As illustrated by Figure 7.1, teamwork, cooperation, and sharing are crucial to ensure profitability for most companies. Manufacturing can improve quality and cut costs by examining every step of the production process constantly. Marketing is more effective when there are close ties between sales, production, and distribution. Finance needs to know details of current sales, marketing plans, and cost projections throughout the company.

**FIGURE 7.1**

To simplify management, firms are often split into departments. Yet, they must be able to work as a single, integrated company. Information systems can help managers improve the integration and control of their firm.

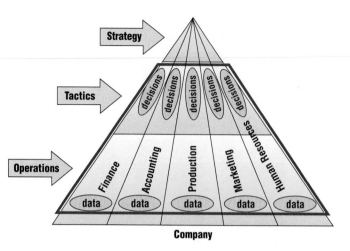

Cooperation and teamwork seem like obvious concepts, why would companies have problems with them? One problem has always been the difficulty of sharing information throughout a firm. As a manager, how do you find the data you need without being deluged by tons of data? It is especially difficult when most data takes the form of printed corporate reports. How are teams supposed to work together when they rely on phone calls, meetings, and office mail to communicate?

A primary task of management is to keep the company focused on a common goal with everyone working together. Information systems play a major role in this task. Creating communication networks is one step in the process of integrating the corporate components by the same data to all users via phone and data communication. Another helpful technique is the ability to capture data from different sources and view the data from different perspectives using enterprise resource planning systems.

Various software packages have been designed to handle the different types of information: word processors for text, spreadsheets for computations, databases for storing numbers, and graphics packages for pictures and graphs. Most business reports and analyses need elements from each of these packages. The goal is to collect this data from different locations and combine it into one report. An important concept involved in combining this data is the difference between static and dynamic integration. With **static integration,** you simply copy results from one system into another. If the original data changes, it does not affect the copy. Conversely, **dynamic links** can be created so that if the original data changes, the "copy" is automatically updated as well.

**INTRODUCTION**     Coordinating the many aspects of business requires a wide variety of information from many sources. Perhaps you need to make a decision about how to market a new product. You would retrieve a variety of customer data from the sales database. You would use reports from the production team and a collection of graphs created from the initial marketing surveys. You could use a spreadsheet to analyze this information along with various marketing strategies. Along the way, you would probably use accounting data to create graphs to display costs and projected profits for the various cases. Finally, you would use a word processor to create a formal report for your supervisors that describes the choices and your analysis. The report would contain your writing along with the graphs, spreadsheet tables, and some of the data.

Integrated data could be something as simple as a graph and table from the human resources department that you have included in your financial reports. That way you can see the overall patterns in the data and still have the raw numbers handy. Similarly, there are

## Trends

Consider a sample business decision involving different types of data. You are working as a manager at a large department store. Three reports are produced daily by the central computer: the daily sales report (Figure 7.2), returned merchandise log (Figure 7.3), and a commission report (Figure 7.4). At the end of each week, you create a report that evaluates the profitability of each department in the store (e.g., housewares, women's clothing, and shoes). You also maintain a line graph that shows this net sales number for each week. At the end of the month, you write several pages of comments about the trends and the monthly activities. The report includes copies of the data and your graphs. It is sent to upper management. A small example is shown in Figure 7.5.

To see how the use of computers is changing, consider how this report might have been produced by managers at different points in time. Figure 7.6 highlights the differences in processing information in three time periods. In the 1970s, the central computer kept track of all sales. Each night, the computer printed three basic reports. At the end of the week, a manager computed the net sales by hand and drew the graph on graph paper. A secretary would then type the report on a typewriter and staple the graph at the end of the document.

In the 1980s, personal computers with spreadsheets and word processors were introduced to the business world. At this point, the manager entered the numbers from the reports into a spreadsheet. These numbers were usually entered by hand. The spreadsheet could perform the necessary calculations and create the graphs with only a few commands. A word processor was used to type the report. The spreadsheet printouts and the graphs were stapled into the final report.

Today, the process can be even simpler. First, a database management system holds the sales data. Spreadsheet commands can be used to retrieve exactly the data that is needed. The spreadsheet performs the desired calculations and produces the graphs. The report is still typed on a word processor; however, the spreadsheets and graphs are automatically copied into the word processor document. This process is facilitated by software suites that consist of software packages designed to exchange data.

Think about what happens if some of the original data is changed. For instance, just before you send the report to management, someone calls and says that the sales figures for half the items in the housewares department are wrong. In the 1970s example, the manager had to recompute all of the totals, redraw the graphs, and rewrite the report. The 1980s manager had to change the numbers in the spreadsheet, rewrite sections of the report, and print the new graphs. With a truly integrated system, you would simply tell the word processor to reprint the report. The word processor would automatically tell the spreadsheet to get the new data, update the graphs, and transfer the results to the final copy.

The most recent trend in integrating information comes through the use of windows-oriented software and graphical user interfaces. One of the primary objectives of these operating systems is to enable you to run several different types of software at the same time (multitasking) and to share data between each package. When software vendors create software for these operating systems, they follow some standard rules. These rules allow each piece of software to "talk" to the other software you own and exchange data. As a result, you can combine information from any word processor, graphics package, or database system that follows the rules.

many times where you will want to include pictures in a word-processing document. In terms of databases, there are many situations in which you want to store images. An automobile insurance company could store photographs of the cars they insure. If a client's car were damaged, those pictures could also be saved.

A difficulty that arises when you are trying to integrate information is the diversity in hardware and software. For example, each software package uses its own format to store data files. As a result, there are more than 50 different formats for word-processing documents. The problem multiplies rapidly when you consider that most of these formats change with each software revision. To integrate these different types of information, you

**FIGURE 7.2**
Businesses create many different reports. Begin with this small excerpt of the daily sales report. It itemizes sales for each department.

| DAILY SALES REPORT | | | FEBRUARY 16, 2001 | |
|---|---|---|---|---|
| DEPARTMENT | ITEM # | Q-SOLD | PRICE | VALUE |
| House | 1153 | 52 | 2.95 | 153.40 |
| | 5543 | 13 | 0.59 | 7.67 |
| W. Clothing | 5563 | 1 | 87.32 | 87.32 |
| | 7765 | 4 | 54.89 | 219.56 |
| | 9986 | 2 | 15.69 | 31.38 |
| Shoes | 1553 | 2 | 65.79 | 131.58 |
| | 6673 | 1 | 29.39 | 29.39 |
| **Total Sales** | | | | **660.30** |

**FIGURE 7.3**
To evaluate customer service and quality, the store tracks returned merchandise and produces a daily report by item number.

| RETURNED MERCHANDISE LOG | | FEBRUARY 16, 2001 | |
|---|---|---|---|
| ITEM # | Q | PRICE | VALUE |
| 1153 | 3 | 2.95 | 8.85 |
| 3353 | 6 | 27.59 | 165.54 |
| 4453 | 2 | 15.95 | 31.90 |
| 8878 | 1 | 24.95 | 24.95 |
| **Total** | **12** | | **231.24** |

**FIGURE 7.4**
Managers compute daily sales by employee and determine the commission based on each employee's commission rate.

| COMMISSIONS | | | FEBRUARY 16, 2001 | | |
|---|---|---|---|---|---|
| EMP # | NAME | DEPT | SALES | RATE | AMOUNT |
| 1143 | Jones | House | 543.95 | 5% | 27.20 |
| 2895 | Brown | M. Clothing | 775.35 | 4% | 31.01 |
| 4462 | Smith | W. Clothing | 1,544.52 | 5% | 77.23 |
| 7893 | Torrez | Shoes | 876.93 | 6% | 52.62 |
| 9963 | Cousco | M. Clothing | 589.47 | 5% | 29.47 |

**FIGURE 7.5**
The weekly sales analysis report requires selecting and aggregating data from each of the other reports. The text, data, and graph are combined into a final document.

**Weekly Sales Analysis**    2/11/01 – 2/17/01
Manager comments are written in the first 10 pages, along with comments on special events.

**Department Analysis**

| Dept | Sales | Returns | Commissions | Net |
|---|---|---|---|---|
| House | 4,113.58 | 25.35 | 205.68 | 3,882.55 |
| Women's clothing | 54,221.92 | 998.52 | 3,024.64 | 50,198.76 |
| Men's clothing | 28,664.48 | 356.24 | 1,421.58 | 26,886.66 |
| Shoes | 10,225.31 | 853.47 | 592.36 | 8,779.48 |
| **Total** | **97,225.29** | **2,233.58** | **5,244.26** | **89,747.45** |

Sales and Net Sales

**FIGURE 7.6**

Methods used to create integrated reports have changed over three decades. With simple transaction systems, managers computed the totals, drew graphs, and had secretaries type the report. With personal computers, middle managers reentered data into spreadsheets and used a word processor to print the final report. With an integrated system, top managers use a personal computer to query the database, draw the graphs, and produce the final report.

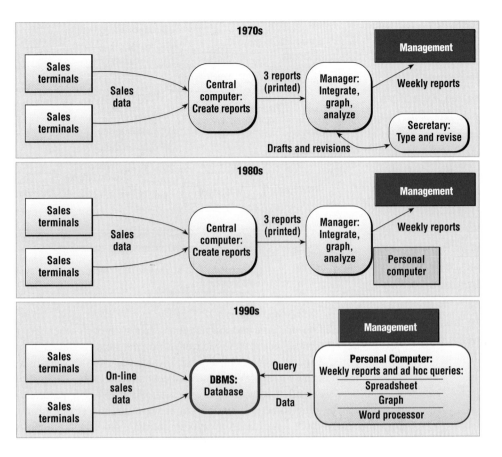

need software that can read many different file types, or the software needs to use a common format.

One trend in software is the adoption of enterprise systems that are designed to hold data in a central database. These systems provide consistent data across the company. A trend in personal productivity software is toward packages that work together by sharing data through links. When the underlying data changes, the software automatically picks up the new data and updates the document. The concept is similar to a spreadsheet formula that refers to other cells. The key difference is that you can refer to data in different programs, such as transferring data from a spreadsheet into a word processor. With a network, the data can be located in different departments throughout the business.

**INTEGRATION IN BUSINESS**

For a business to be successful, it needs to integrate information from all aspects of the organization. Figure 7.7 shows that modern management techniques of just-in-time production and mass customization require a high degree of internal integration, as well as strong links to suppliers and customers.

Most companies are split into functional departments, with varying degrees of independence. However, there are always pressures and decisions that affect the entire organization. For instance, changes in products or manufacturing schedules clearly affect the marketing department. Because these changes will probably alter the cash flows of the company, the accounting and finance departments also need to be aware of the changes.

In the 1960s and 1970s, computer systems were built for individual departments and areas within the company. In many companies, these systems became islands. They were

**FIGURE 7.7**

Total data integration begins with the vendors, tracks data through all operations of the firm, and incorporates information from customers. Each area in the firm has easy access to data from any other location. This integrated data is used to make better decisions by enabling managers to focus on the "big picture" instead of local solutions.

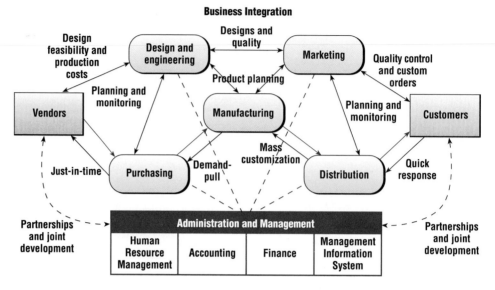

focused on one task and did not share data with each other. For instance, the accounting department collected the basic transaction data and produced the necessary accounting reports. Anyone in the company who wanted to use this data relied on paper printouts of the standard reports. When spreadsheets arrived in the 1980s, the basic accounting numbers were often rekeyed into spreadsheets in other departments. Besides wasting employee time to retype numbers that were already stored on a computer, this practice caused more errors from mistyping the data. Additionally, consider what happens when the accounting department changes the numbers: some users of the data might not get the updated versions, and people would attempt to make decisions on outdated data.

Computer use in most companies began with transaction-processing systems. Because transaction systems are structured and there is considerable experience at this level, it is a logical place to begin. However, it is also tempting to treat each transaction separately: (1) Payroll services can be purchased from a specialized data-processing company, so the data will be handled separately from the other corporate data. (2) A sales order-processing system might be constructed independently of the inventory control system. (3) Process control systems to handle manufacturing tend to be isolated because the data (e.g., robotic control signals) are different from that used in the rest of the company. (4) Similarly, the corporate accounting system is often developed as a standalone product. Journal entries are created by copying data in reports produced by other systems. Although each of these transaction systems offers management advantages to their respective departments, it is difficult for managers to use data from other departments. Also, independent systems make it difficult for executives to share data and evaluate interrelationships between the departments.

The amount of data integration needed in a company often depends on the management structure of the firm. Some firms are highly decentralized, so that each business unit makes its own decisions and functions independently of the others. Typically in these situations, only accounting data (profit/loss) are integrated and reported to upper management.

On the other hand, some organizations are much more integrated. In your economics courses you were shown the difference between vertically and horizontally integrated firms. Consider a vertically integrated firm such as an oil company that functions at different levels of production (including oil exploration, drilling, transportation, storage, and

---

**Reality Bytes          7–1    National Bicycle Industrial Co., Ltd. (Japan)**

Japan's National Bicycle Industrial Company uses a highly integrated computer-driven manufacturing system to build custom bicycles. The computer handles just-in-time inventory, computer-aided design, and robot processing. When customers purchase Panasonic bicycles, their measurements are entered into the computerized ordering system. They also enter their choice of gearing, handlebar size, pedals, brakes, and color preferences. In all, there are 11,232,860 possible combinations. The specifications are sent by network to the factory, where bar-coded parts are delivered to the robot (and a few human) builders. The inventory levels are monitored by the computer, which automatically places orders with the suppliers. With this system, an entire bicycle is built in 8 to 10 days, with about 60 semicustom bicycles produced every day.

---

retail sales). Although an oil exploration team may not need access to daily fuel sales in New York state, they do need to forecast future demand for oil. Likewise, the retail sales division does not need to know the daily costs associated with drilling for oil, yet they might need to track deliveries and communicate with the corporate office.

Consider a horizontally integrated firm such as Wal-Mart with retail stores in many different cities. They achieve lower costs by combining the buying power of all the stores. By coordinating sales, warehouses, and distribution, Wal-Mart can negotiate better prices with manufacturers. Additionally, Wal-Mart reduces operating costs by standardizing management practices (and information systems) across all the stores. By integrating information from all stores, it is easier for Wal-Mart to forecast customer demands. Also, by networking the store information systems, managers who experience higher sales of certain products can request shipments from stores that are not selling the item as rapidly.

Manufacturing firms can gain additional benefits from integrating data. Benefits like just-in-time inventory, total quality management, and mass customization can only exist with the tight integration of data. The National Bicycle Industrial Company of Japan illustrates how integrated data is used to provide customized products to mass markets.

**ENTERPRISE RESOURCE PLANNING**

**Enterprise resource planning (ERP)** is the current state of the art in integrated information in business systems. The systems incorporate data from financial accounting, logistics, and human resource management. The field is dominated by large, expensive software packages from companies such as SAP, Peoplesoft, Oracle, Lawson, and J. D. Edwards. The systems use databases, processes, and rules to provide up-to-the-minute data on the major financial issues in a firm. One of the key points of ERP systems is that they run on top of a DBMS; hence, all of the data is centralized and accessible via DBMS queries and reports.

ERP systems handle all of the financial accounting systems. They also emphasize purchasing, human resource management, and investment management. The systems are tailored for specific businesses and can focus on areas such as manufacturing, research and development, and retail sales.

One of the primary strengths of the ERP systems is that they were designed to handle data for large companies operating in an international environment. In the late 1990s, many companies chose to install commercial ERP systems instead of trying to modify their existing systems to handle the year 2000 problem.

Many organizations have experienced high costs and long implementation times when converting to ERP software. The challenges are great: you must replace the entire financial accounting system, reorganize the business operations, train everyone, and then learn to evaluate the data. ERP vendors responded to these problems by creating preconfigured versions of the tools—complete with implementation tools and templates to help quickly customize the systems. The systems are targeted at midsize firms ($100 million to $1 billion in revenue). Faster implementation means lower implementation and consulting costs, less disruption to the company, and quicker access to the benefits of the ERP software. Of course, "rapid" does not mean you can install a complete ERP system next week. The following table provides sample installation times.

| COMPANY | VENDOR | TIME |
| --- | --- | --- |
| Cognex | PeopleSoft | 6 months |
| Robinson Nugent | PeopleSoft | 8 months |
| Imperial Holly | PeopleSoft | 8 months |
| Dopaco | SAP | 8 months |
| Borden | PeopleSoft | 9 months |
| Rehrig | QAD | 10 months |
| CIDCO | PeopleSoft | 11 months |
| Yuwasa-Exide | Baan | 11 months |

## International Environment

Several features are important to firms operating in an international environment. First, all menus and reports should be available in several languages, so clerks and managers can use the language they prefer. Second, the system should handle currency conversion automatically, so managers can view reports in any currency. Similarly, conversions should be capable of being fixed at a point in time—so that when items are transferred they can be valued at the exchange rate in effect at that time, even if the rate changes later.

A more complex feature for the international environment is the ability to produce reports following the rules of individual nations. For example, a company with subsidiaries in many nations would need to produce reports that follow the rules (e.g., depreciation) for each specific nation, and then produce consolidated reports following the rules of the home nation.

A third complicating factor arises from taxes. In addition to the rates, the rules and procedures vary by nation. The rules are particularly important for payroll and benefit applications. A good enterprise application automatically incorporates the rules for each nation and state.

## Financial Accounting

The accounting system is a core feature of an ERP. Eventually, all transactions must be recorded in the general ledger accounts. The accounts fulfill the standards required by each nation. They are used to create the standard accounting reports. The systems provide flexibility by enabling managers to create their own subaccounts and subledgers, which are used to create reports on additional topics. An important feature of the accounting system is that standard accounting reports can be generated at any time for any section of the company. The ERP system automatically uses the most up-to-date data.

In addition to standard financial accounting, the systems manage assets and provide common treasury functions such as cash management. The systems also provide basic audit trails and other accounting controls. To make them easier to use, most ERP systems provide enterprise (or executive) information system (EIS) capabilities. Managers can examine data at virtually any level of detail. From summary values, they can drill down to more detail.

## Logistics

Logistics consists of the operations required to purchase materials, deliver them to the warehouses and factories, and sell and distribute products. It incorporates traditional MRP analysis, quality control, accounts payable, and accounts receivable.

In today's manufacturing companies, logistics is an important component of just-in-time inventory and demand-driven production. Using an integrated system, the marketing department gets up-to-the-minute data on customer demands. Marketers can cooperate with designers and engineers to develop new products. The specifications can be transferred to the production machines and raw material orders can be generated for vendors. Purchasing and payments can be tracked and generated over EDI networks—including the Internet. As orders are generated and inventory levels change, the accounting data is automatically updated—providing instant analysis of profitability.

For service-oriented companies, logistics involves service management tasks. The ERP systems can track customers, identify repeat customers, monitor service contracts, help salespeople with call management, and handle automatic billing and accounts receivable issues.

## Human Resource Management

Payroll is a complicated function, particularly in a multinational environment involving different rules and currencies. Even in a single state, the issues of benefits, state and federal rules, and legal issues arising from child support make handling payroll a complex task.

Today's HRM departments handle such additional tasks as recruitment, training, travel, and organizational planning. Each step must be documented and requires a variety of federal and state reports. In addition to these basic tasks, most of the major ERP systems enable HRM departments to offer Web access to basic data. For example, employees can use the Web to check on their taxes, change their withholding status, and sign up for benefit plans and training sessions.

## Integration

Integration is probably the most important feature of the ERP systems. All the data is stored in a central database; hence, data is entered only one time (but into a double-entry accounting system). All reports are generated from the base data. Custom queries and reports can be generated through the DBMS.

Consider a simple example. A manufacturing plant takes an item from inventory. The system instantly adjusts the inventory quantity-on-hand. It also updates the financial value of the inventory holdings on the general ledger and any subledgers that utilize that figure. New orders can be triggered automatically with the orders and payments sent through common EDI mechanisms. All of the changes are made automatically. When managers request reports, the new data is automatically incorporated and displayed using current currency conversions.

The key point to remember is that all of the transactions and accounts are integrated. Managers can request reports utilizing any combination of data at any time—and each report will use the most up-to-date information.

Most of the major ERP systems also utilize distributed hardware and software. Hence, the database can be split into many pieces stored in different locations. As

**FIGURE 7.8**
ERP INTEGRATION
Although data can be distributed, it is still integrated across the organization. Changes in one item (inventory) cause changes in all related databases. Reports are generated from current data.

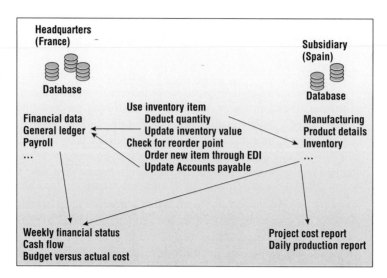

changes occur in one location, they are automatically distributed across the network to the other locations. The company can add a subsidiary with its own processing support. Yet, all of the new data is readily accessible to managers throughout the company.

Figure 7.8 provides a simple example of data integration. When a factory uses an inventory item, the system reduces the current inventory count. It also changes the inventory valuation in the general ledger. The item usage might trigger a purchase through the EDI system, which must also be recorded, along with the accounts payable change. Since the databases are shared across the organization, all changes are automatically included when new reports are generated.

Remember that all of the modules are integrated. So manufacturing schedules developed in the production module automatically provide data to the payroll system and personnel systems. Then the financial data (e.g., wages) is linked back to the general ledger, which provides updated data for all financial reports.

## WORKGROUP INTEGRATION

Cooperation and teamwork have always been important in managing a company. Today, as firms remove layers of middle management and as they focus on teamwork, integration and sharing become crucial. Making decisions requires input from different people. Problems that arise are solved by creating a team of workers—often from different disciplines.

Picture yourself as a manager in a modern corporation. In addition to your day-to-day tasks, you will be asked to serve on various teams to solve problems. You could be working with three or four different groups simultaneously. How do you organize your work? How do you remember the status of each project? How do you keep in touch with the team members? How do you keep track of documents, comments, and revisions for each team? How do you know which team members are falling behind and need more help? Now assume that the team members are scattered across different locations. You cannot afford to schedule meetings every week. How do you keep the project moving and make sure that all important ideas are incorporated in the final decision?

Software tools known as **groupware** have been created to help answer these questions and make it easier for teams to work together. Groupware tools are designed to make it easy for several people to work on a document at the same time, regardless of where each one is located. There are three key components to groupware: (1) communication, (2) compound documents, and (3) databases. Groupware uses these three components to integrate and share different types of data across an organization.

## Reality Bytes     7–3   Four Main Groupware Categories

*Basic groupware* (Lotus Notes)—Basic groupware combines a sophisticated messaging system with a giant database containing work records and memos. It changes the way information flows in an organization. Traditional e-mail requires you to know to whom you are forwarding your idea. With Lotus Notes, the memo is forwarded instead to the appropriate bulletin board. Anyone interested in that subject can then check the bulletin board within their time frame.

*Workflow software* (ActionWorkflow, PRocessIT from NCR)—Work flow software is designed to remake and streamline business processes, eliminating much of the form-filled, paper-clogged bureaucracy. It focuses on the steps that make up

processes and redesigns those steps. Work is routed automatically from employee to employee.

*Meeting software* (GroupSystems from Ventana Corporation)—Meeting software enables meeting participants to interact simultaneously through the computer. Studies have shown that people read faster than they speak. Thus, the software dramatically speeds the process toward consensus by not waiting for individuals to speak individually. This also ensures that everyone gets a chance to take part.

*Scheduling software* (Network Scheduler 3 from Powercore)—Scheduling Software coordinates a workgroup's electronic datebooks and identifies when they can meet.

## Communication

To share data effectively, everyone involved on a team project should be connected to the others via a network. The network could be a small LAN connecting members of a department, or it could be an enterprise network that connects everyone in the company across the nation or world. Depending on the problem, the network might include radio links to traveling salespeople, or it could contain ties across the Internet to divisions in other countries.

An important aspect of the network is that it must be able to handle large transfers of data efficiently. Most groupware products operate by sending constant updates across the network. These updates can include text, images, sound, and even video clips. Remember that the more complex data types can be huge, and they require high-speed network links.

One simple use of groupware products is basic e-mail and scheduling. However, groupware products extend e-mail in several ways. Users can mail documents created with other software packages. The mail system enables recipients to sort and organize each piece of mail so that it is easy to find later. Each piece of mail can be related to other documents, so project data can be stored in one location. Users can comment on mail messages, store the comments with the original, and forward them to other workers. Some systems have a mailbox for each user that can automatically handle text, fax, and voice messages. All of these messages are sent to one address, making it easier for senders and for the recipient.

## Compound Documents

**Compound documents** are a key focus of groupware tools. Almost everything the user does is stored in a document. These documents can contain text, images, graphs, sound, and even video clips. Each document can be revised and shared with other members of the team. Just remember that everyone who wants to view a complex document must have access to the hardware and software needed to re-create the various elements. For team projects, each team member might be responsible for various elements of a document. For instance, one worker could find the basic data and enter it in a database. Another worker could use a spreadsheet to analyze the numbers. A third team member might create the various graphs and artwork, whereas a fourth documents the analysis and writes the conclusions.

Computers are used increasingly to support team work and workgroups. Data, comments, and analysis are created and shared through networks of computers.

The contributions of each worker are stored in a central document. As one worker updates and revises the document, the changes are automatically noted for the other team members. Colors are often used to highlight changes recommended by each worker.

## Databases

Databases are a crucial element to the groupware approach. Their key contribution is to enable workers to share access to the same documents at the same time. Each member of the team can work on the same document. As the document is updated by one person, the changes are immediately available to everyone else on the team. The database system automatically records who was responsible for each change. It provides security features by controlling who is allowed to make changes and who is allowed to see the document.

The database approach enables users to search the various documents and link them together. From a base document, users can find related documents easily and share them with colleagues. Users can search for documents based on titles, topics, or subjects. Users can also do full-text searches or search the documents alphabetically.

The database approach also makes it possible to build new applications with minimal programming. By maintaining complex objects, groupware tools enable designers to create systems that collect and share data across the organization. Groupware tools have been especially useful in automating the workflow in service-based organizations. Think about the steps and people involved in creating a legal document, an accounting report, or a management-consulting analysis. It is difficult to automate this process with conventional MIS tools. However, groupware tools work well because they focus on the final document. Contributions from individuals are immediately available to the rest of the team, and comments can be added or changed at any time by any member of the team.

## Applications

Groupware tools have been successful in several areas. Applications can be classified into four primary types: (1) automation of teamwork, (2) discrete business solutions, (3) enterprisewide systems, and (4) extending the enterprise.

### Automation of Teamwork

Communication is essential to teamwork. Teams are often formed to solve specific problems to work on special projects. For example, to solve a problem with cost overruns in a warehouse, you would create a team that consisted of, at the minimum, an accountant, the warehouse manager, warehouse employees, a purchasing manager, and a production manager. The team would collect data, evaluate alternatives, and recommend solutions.

E-mail enables teams to share ideas, review work, and share comments with other members of the team. Providing 24-hour access to communication ensures that people can work whenever it is convenient for them. It also supports workers in different time zones. Providing support for complex documents, recording comments, and tracking votes, enables groupware to function as a substitute for face-to-face meetings. The expanded use of video will further decrease the need for meetings.

Groupware tools enable managers to allocate tasks to the team members and then monitor the progress of each worker. By tracking changes and comments of each member, the system shows managers the contributions of each person.

Groupware products are oriented toward knowledge management. Knowledge consists of more than simple data elements. It is the product of data, rules, observations, insights, and comments by various members of the team. By storing all of these comments, the system makes them available to future teams. Then if a similar problem arises, workers can review the solutions and comments of earlier teams. Think about what typically happens when a problem arises. Managers appoint one or two experts who solved similar problems in the past. But what happens when these experts leave? Although we might keep their earlier reports, we would know only the answers to the problem. On the other hand, if all problems had been analyzed and discussed with groupware tools, think of the stored knowledge that would remain available to future managers. All of the comments, suggestions, criticisms, assumptions, and notes would be stored and arranged by topic.

### Discrete Business Solutions

Applications can also be designed for individual projects or discrete solutions. Individual departments can create their own applications, providing greater communication and support within each department. By focusing on complex documents, the tools improve productivity in service jobs—an area that has always been difficult to automate. For instance, a groupware application would be useful in a legal department. The application would track individual cases and enable managers to oversee schedules and comment on specific cases.

Given the initial network and software, workers in each department could build their own applications with support from specialized MIS personnel. Although groupware tools require the purchase of additional software for each user, they generally run on existing hardware and common networks. By using existing software applications and hardware, the costs of using workgroup software are relatively low.

A key feature of workgroup tools is that users control the entire development process. Once the groupware has been set up, users create the documents, choose topics, and create links among documents. Each team or department controls the outcome. Better yet, documents and linkages change over time to meet changing needs of the organization—without requiring programming or manual changes by MIS personnel.

### Enterprise Solutions

By standardizing on hardware, software, and communication protocols, groupware tools serve to connect the entire organization. The system can connect workers from different locations. It provides equal access to mobile workers regardless of their current location.

**Reality Bytes     7–4     Chasing Stock Market Advice on Chromatics**

Chromatics Color Sciences International (CCSI) Inc. is a small company trying to market a device to diagnose jaundice in newborns. For the most part, it is just another small company trying to succeed. However, in 1997, an anonymous stock pundit using the screen name "Skipard" began saying wonderful things about the company and encouraging people to invest. He urged readers by suggesting that the way to get rich in the market was to "find the idea, be right, bet it big . . . and pray like hell." Several people responded and purchased high-risk shares in the small company—many buying stock using margin loans. Even Skipard took his own advice—buying 400,000 shares. In April 1998, the stock price hit $17. By July the price had fallen to $5.50.

In the meantime, a writer going by the name "Mr. Pink," who admittedly was selling the stock short, had posted several messages critical of the company and of Skipard. After considerable online name-calling by both people ("pond scum," "slimeball"), Mr. Pink revealed the identify of Skipard and posted the following message on a Yahoo finance message board: "Anyone upset about losing millions on CCSI should call Skip Davidson at [his home phone number]. Or send him a package with a gift to [his full home address]." Mr. Davidson and his wife fled their home for five days because of obscene phone calls and death threats. In response to many problems, Chromatics asked the SEC to investigate trading irregularities by short sellers.

It enables employees to work from home. By being accessible to all workers, it is easy to create ad hoc problem-solving teams consisting of workers from different departments.

By capturing all important communications and analyses, groupware tools can serve as a form of corporate memory. To learn how a particular decision was made three years ago, someone need only pull up the associated documents. In addition to the raw data and the ultimate decision, the system contains comments, criticisms, and viewpoints from workers throughout the company. Along the same lines, managers can review all comments to get a better understanding of the corporate culture. They can also monitor statements for potential legal problems, such as discriminatory or inflammatory comments.

### Extending the Enterprise

Because of their ease of use and ability to handle complex documents, groupware tools can be used to build links to other companies, suppliers, and customers. Improving ties to suppliers and customers can cut costs, speed product development, improve quality, and provide better customer service. Beyond these simple changes, closer relationships can also alter the way the business operates. Groupware systems can change business processes such as purchasing and production. As discussed in Chapter 11, information systems can provide a competitive advantage by changing the basis of competition. Closer ties to customers can keep out competitors, and closer ties to suppliers can lock out potential competitors by minimizing their access to materials.

Of course, building ties through groupware products requires that all companies involved have similar technology. Hardware and networks need to be compatible. Each company must use the same groupware tools, especially because there are few standards. The various companies might also have to use the same basic software tools (word processors, spreadsheets, and graphics packages). At a minimum, they will need to be able to store documents in some common format.

## Workgroup Example

To understand how groupware works, consider the example of an engineering consulting firm. As illustrated in Figure 7.9, the firm has its headquarters in San Francisco, but a team is working with a client headquartered in Stamford, Connecticut. The engineering

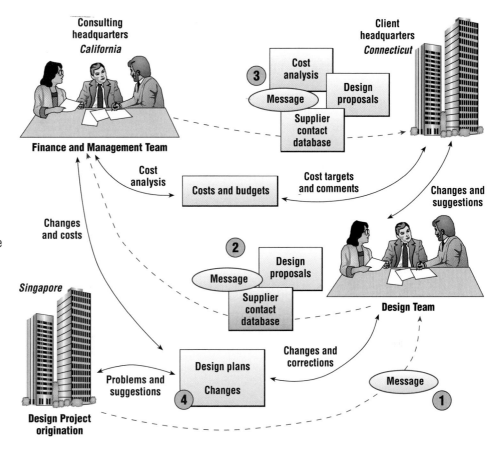

**FIGURE 7.9**
WORKGROUP
EXAMPLE

A design firm uses teams to design a project for the client. The teams working in different areas can share their changes and comments with groupware tools. (1) Message and problem are sent to the design team. (2) The design team forwards two proposals to the finance team. (3) The finance team analyzes the costs and budget effects. (4) The client makes a choice and design team makes changes and notifies the project leader.

firm is designing a plant for the client's site in Singapore. Much of the work is being performed by three engineering teams: the design team working at the client's headquarters in Connecticut, the finance team in California, and an on-site project team in Singapore.

Consider what might be a typical day. At noon, the project team encounters a problem with the design when they cannot obtain some special components specified in the original design. The project team tracks down two alternatives, and at 6:00 P.M. the project leader sends an e-mail message to the design team noting the problems and asking for guidance. Three hours later, at 8:00 A.M. in Connecticut, the design team consults with the client and draws up two sets of modifications to the plans. At 1:00 P.M., they add initial designs and comments to the message and send a message to the finance team in California.

The finance team takes the proposed changes and begins an analysis of the costs. Using the supplier contact database supplied by the project team, the finance team revises the budget estimates and schedule and attaches a copy of two spreadsheets to the new design. The client goes over the changes and new costs with the design team and chooses one of the options.

At 4:00 P.M. the next day, the design team revises the main design, orders the components, and notifies the project leader. Three hours later, the project team arrives at work and begins implementing the changes. An acknowledgment message is sent to the design team with the daily progress reports.

All of the messages, designs, spreadsheet analyses, and databases are transferred through the corporate network of the design firm. The related documents are tied together. For instance, the design team can retrieve the cost spreadsheets or the supplier contact database by clicking on icons in the report. There are separate LAN servers for each of the three locations. The files are replicated on each server; as changes are made in one location, they are automatically forwarded to the other servers. At any time, a person in each location can call up the related documents and check the progress or comments of the other teams.

## Problems with Sharing Documents

Although groupware tools make it relatively easy to share documents and coordinate workers, there are some problems that managers need to avoid. Even companies that are highly advanced in their use of technology have reported problems. Figure 7.10 summarizes the basic issues.

Compatibility of data and software tools is the most important issue. In most cases, all users need the same software tools. Many times, they will need the same versions of that software. There are tools that convert data files to different formats; however, if you want to keep the exact page layout or take advantage of special features on one product, you will need to use the same software.

Similarly, everyone using a document will need the same fonts. Because fonts are generally software-based, it is not a serious problem because they can be distributed to other users. However, in any organization some users will insist on collecting and using obscure fonts that might not be available to everyone else. One solution to this problem is offered by Adobe in the form of a software product called *Acrobat*. It is a document viewer that always displays documents the same way, even when a recipient does not have the same hardware, software, and fonts as the document's creator. All information about the document (such as fonts and graphics) is stored within the document. Acrobat also contains a full-text search engine that enables users to search all of their documents.

The problem of compatibility worsens for more complex data such as sound and video. To reproduce these objects on different machines requires each machine to have the appropriate (matching) hardware and software. In some cases, if a user does not have the appropriate hardware, the document will not open.

With dynamically linked documents, users need access and network paths to all of the relevant documents. This problem is especially important when documents are moved to other machines. With some systems, if a piece of software is unavailable, portions of the document will be blank. There is a related problem with sound and video. Even if the network connections are available, they might be too slow to support the amount of data. This problem is most common with mobile links and ties to outside companies and across international links.

Another problem exists because of concurrency—allowing several people to modify the same document at the same time. There are several solutions to this problem. The most com-

**FIGURE 7.10**
PROBLEMS WITH SHARING DOCUMENTS
There are several technical hurdles to overcome to make it easy to share documents. One solution is to require everyone to use the exact same hardware and software. But the continual introduction of new hardware and software updates makes it difficult to achieve this harmony.

---

Everyone needs current/same version of the software.
- Data conversion tools exist.
- To get the exact layout you need the same versions.

Everyone needs the same fonts, displays, sound cards, and video drivers.
- Different hardware adjusts and converts but does not always produce the same results.
- If a driver (e.g., sound) is missing on one machine, the document might crash.

Everyone needs access and network paths to the linked documents.

Transmission time can be a problem with video and sound.

Concurrency: Multiple changes at the same time.
- Who made what changes? Good software keeps track by user and time.
- One user might be locked out of a document while others make changes.
- Replication minimizes lockouts but causes conflicts when two people change the same data on different servers. Which version should survive?

mon method used by groupware tools is to replicate the data across the organization. Each file server contains a copy of the documents. When a document is updated on one machine, the changes are sent to the other machines. The problem is that users might make changes to the same document on different machines. Then someone has to decide which version should be saved. The process is relatively automatic, but occasionally the computer cannot determine which change should be kept and you will be asked to decide which version to retain.

## INTEGRATING WITH LEGACY SYSTEMS: A DATA WAREHOUSE

In many ways, the design and implementation of an information system is easier if you are starting a new company or rebuilding one completely. With older (legacy) systems, existing data and software might be incomplete and inconsistent. Valuable information and processes are embedded in these systems; we cannot just throw them away and start over. Yet, it can be more difficult to retrieve data from these systems and integrate it into new management systems.

As business operations and management change, information systems need to be updated. Management emphasis on teamwork is a significant change in the last few years. The improved integration features of current software fit nicely with the changes in management toward teamwork and integration across the enterprise. The problem is that few companies have the opportunity or the money to completely redesign their information system to take advantage of these new features. As a result, they need to utilize the data stored in their **legacy systems.** This data must be made accessible to decision makers so it can be analyzed. To meet this need, some companies are creating a data warehouse. A **data warehouse** is a single consolidation point for enterprise data from diverse production systems. The data is typically stored in one large file server or a central computer.

Many older transaction-processing systems store data in their own files, without using a database management system. Although transaction systems produce standard reports, managers often need to use the base data to perform additional analyses or in-depth searches. Before the widespread use of networks, managers often entered data from each report into their own spreadsheets. Installing a network offers the ability to share data across the company. However, the data must be stored in a format that is accessible to the managers. Figure 7.11 illustrates how a data warehouse copies the transaction data into a central, shared location.

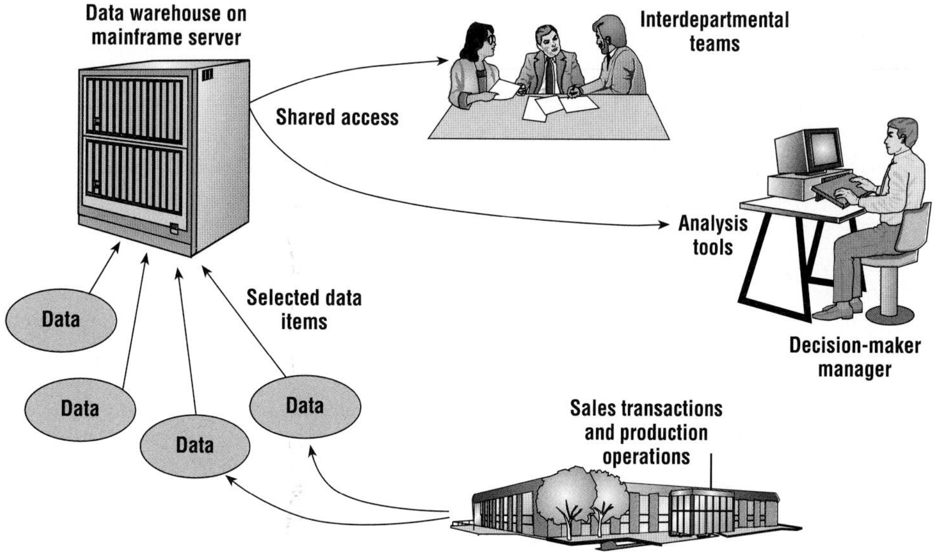

**FIGURE 7.11**
DATA WAREHOUSE
A data warehouse is commonly used as a method to provide data to decision makers without interfering with the transaction-processing operations. Selected data items are regularly pulled from the transaction data files and stored in a central location. DSS tools query the data warehouse for analysis and reporting.

## Building a Data Warehouse

The goal of a data warehouse is to hold all of the data needed by managers to make decisions. Hence, the first step is to determine the data needs and models that managers use. The next step is to identify the data sources that are available in the company. This step can be difficult when the data is stored in hundreds of different files, scattered across many different machines. It requires analyzing company data sources in depth and documenting the business processes.

Once the data needs and data sources have been identified, the data must be transformed and integrated so that it can be searched and analyzed efficiently by the decision makers. In many cases, the data warehouse is created as a static copy of the original data. Instead of building a link to the original data files, it is easier to copy the data into new files. Special programs are run periodically to update the data warehouse from the original data.

The next step is to document the data warehouse. *Metadata* is used to describe the source data, identify the transformation and integration steps, and define the way the data warehouse is organized. This step is crucial to help decision makers understand what data elements are available. It also enables managers to find new data.

Once the data warehouse has been defined, programs are written to transfer the data from the legacy systems into the data warehouse. In some cases, managerial applications are created and distributed. Applications can be written for decisions that occur on a regular basis. For instance, finance decisions involving cash flow must be made every month or every week, and rely on standard data. On the other hand, applications for ad hoc decisions will have to be created as they are needed. U.S. West and Chase Manhattan Bank illustrate how a data warehouse can overcome problems with large, unconnected databases.

---

**Reality Bytes    7–5    Data Consistency—Building a Data Warehouse**

U.S. West is one of the "baby bells" formed from the initial breakup of AT&T. It provides telephone services to people in 14 states. In 1991, U.S. West decided to consolidate the multiple terabytes of data held in the separate corporate databases. Part of the decision was driven by desperation. Because the data was not connected, orders for new service and resolution of complaints often required manual searches. Worse, phone lines and switches were not being freed up quickly enough when a customer moved or dropped services. Consequently, in fast-growing regions, U.S. West was having trouble allocating new lines. Even though the capacity was available, service personnel had no easy way to find the open switches and lines. Every database had different formats, so street addresses from one file could not be matched to addresses in the customer database. U.S. West put together a team of four full-time project managers and part-time support from 18 managers. With the help of Apertus Technologies, Inc. in Minneapolis, the team created rules, data structures, and relationships among the data items. Apertus developed an object-oriented program to analyze the data and automate part of the process. To reduce the complexity and obtain results faster, U.S. West narrowed the problem to six databases in the fastest growing cities. Nonetheless, after four years, managers estimate they are only halfway through the project.

Chase Manhattan Bank in New York faced similar problems in reconciling myriad customer accounts. The bank's new database would pull data from 70 databases operated by 18 different business units. The goal was to consolidate all customer data so managers could retrieve and analyze data by households. The initial process required the efforts of 22 people over four years just to clean names and addresses of 20 million records. Chase used software from Innovative Systems that contains a list of 2.4 million names and more than 60,000 rules to identify duplicate names and addresses.

## Limitations of a Data Warehouse

A data warehouse represents a subset of the total data in the company. In most cases, it is a static copy, not a dynamic link. Consequently, managers might not always have the most current data. Similarly, data not transferred to the data warehouse will still be difficult to find and use. Data warehouses are not always stored in relational database management systems. Instead, they are collections of files and the data items are extracted and transmitted to managers' personal computers. This type of system is relatively easy to use: managers do not have to learn data access commands (SQL or QBE). However, it is less flexible than using a database management system. Decision makers will be unable to get additional data or to compare the data in some previously unexpected way. The success of a data warehouse depends on how well the manager's needs have been anticipated.

## OPEN SYSTEMS: INTEGRATION WITH DIFFERENT SYSTEMS

Integrating data is difficult enough if everyone uses the same hardware and software. Integration is considerably more complex when it involves hardware from different manufacturers. Figure 7.12 illustrates some of the problems with integrating data across different systems. The problems are even more severe when the systems are owned by different people, such as suppliers or customers.

The entire technology industry is aware of these problems. Consequently, a variety of standards are designed to make it possible for different hardware and software to share data.

## Hardware

In the early days of computing, there were almost no standards. Hundreds of different companies built their own hardware that was completely independent of all the other computers. In the 1960s and 1970s, this process changed due to the dominance of IBM. As long as a company stayed with basic IBM hardware, data could be transferred among departments and different companies. Other companies built hardware that was compatible with these IBM machines. However, there were still many different computer companies that used incompatible hardware and software. Even IBM itself created new machines that were not directly compatible with other primary IBM computers.

**FIGURE 7.12**
Data integration with diverse technology. It is possible to share data even though users have different hardware and software applications. At a minimum, each person must be able to connect to the network, and the software must be able to store data in a common format. Typically, the data will be transferred in ASCII format, which results in the loss of formatting and layout information.

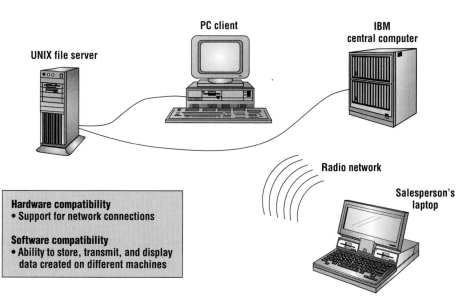

Hardware compatibility
• Support for network connections

Software compatibility
• Ability to store, transmit, and display data created on different machines

AT&T was one company that encountered problems in dealing with hardware and software from different vendors. Consequently, AT&T developed an operating system known as *UNIX*. The goal was to make this system run on hardware from different vendors. That way, it would always be possible to share data between various machines. Today, you can buy a version of UNIX for almost any type of computer. The catch is that there are several variants of UNIX, and they are not completely compatible with each other.

An ultimate goal of creating an *open system* is to separate software and data from the hardware. If a company needs a new computer, it would be ideal to simply buy a new machine, copy all of the software and data to it, and have everything work correctly. From the beginning, however, UNIX only solved part of this problem—just the data and commands were transferable among systems. Software generally needed modifications to run on new hardware.

With the advent of personal computers, the situation worsened. For a while, there were many different computer companies, all with incompatible hardware and software. By the mid-1980s, most companies (excluding manufacturers in Japan) focused on two types of computers: IBM-compatible and Apple Macintosh. Most companies focused on IBM-compatible machines. Just as in the 1960s and 1970s, this dominance of one machine made it easier for people to share data and software, but only because the machines were built exactly alike.

To expand their capabilities, computer companies are continually experimenting with new designs and new methods of building computers. One important example is the introduction of reduced instruction set computer (RISC) processors that perform more limited computations, at much higher speeds than traditional processors. The problem is that to gain speed, these processors are not completely compatible with existing designs; hence, they cannot run the huge amount of software available for typical personal computers.

## Software

To take advantage of breakthroughs in hardware design, we need a way to use common software and data on different types of hardware. Several companies are working to solve this problem. Microsoft was one of the first to provide a commercial solution with its Windows NT operating system (now called Windows 2000). This operating system was designed from the bottom up to run exactly the same on different types of hardware. The hardware manufacturer makes a few changes to a hardware-interface layer that makes it compatible with a new processor. Application software runs the same on any hardware, so data can be shared with any user. However, software vendors generally have to sell separate versions of software for each hardware platform.

The problem is even more complex when dealing with divisions in different nations. Several businesspeople have remarked that people outside the United States are slower to adopt new technology. For instance, if a software package is upgraded, it is most likely to be adopted by the U.S. departments of a company, whereas the overseas workers will continue to use the old version. Data integration becomes difficult when departments are using different versions of the operating system and the application software.

## Open Standards

The common-hardware and Windows 2000 approaches have one major problem. They are based on *proprietary* definitions. In the case of hardware, the entire computer was defined by IBM. In the case of Windows 2000, the interface is defined by Microsoft. Other computer vendors are reluctant to use these definitions because they must pay royalties to the owners of these definitions.

To combat this situation, several organizations have attempted to define *standards* and *protocols* that will enable hardware and software to work together. By making the standards definitions public, all companies can use them without royalty payments and lawsuits. Over the years, several important standards have been created that have made it easier to share data.

The drawback to the open-standards approach is that it takes considerable time to develop the necessary standards. Additionally, each vendor has an incentive to push its own definitions. It can take years for competitors to agree on a standard. By that time, the definition might be obsolete. The competition between vendors often leads to the creation of two or more competing standards-setting organizations.

Despite these problems, standards are essential to creating integrated systems. They are especially important when you are linking machines that are owned by different organizations, such as ties between suppliers and customers. Today, the Internet is an important set of standards for sharing documents—particularly when you want to share documents with users in other organizations. Internet standards cover many aspects of sharing data, including hardcore network definitions (TCP/IP), text and graphics display (HTML), and data exchange (XML).

To a manager, the entire issue of computer standards can be confusing. The most basic issue is that it would be wonderful if everyone could immediately agree on a single standard for every definition. That way we could buy hardware and software from anyone

## Reality Bytes     7–6   Trane

As a subsidiary of American Standard, Trane manufactures residential and commercial heating and cooling systems. Their manufacturing plant in Clarksville, Tennessee, typically produces mid-range commercial units up to 130-ton capacity. These units are typically used for heating and cooling at small stores, such as fast food restaurants.

Like many other manufacturing companies, Trane has moved to just-in-time deliveries with many of its suppliers. The assembly line is automated and demand-driven. Turning to the computer terminal at the start of the line, an operator can call up a specific order. The computer system generates instructions throughout the line and parts are tagged for that assembly. Four-and-a-half hours later, the designated heating/cooling unit rolls off the line and into a truck for delivery.

In an effort to improve efficiency, the plant operates with only two levels of managers. The central computers of the 1980s were outsourced and replaced with an IBM AS/400 mid-range computer. By 1997, the AS/400 was replaced with a series of LAN file servers. Managers rely on the PC-based information systems to communicate and share

data with workers in the plant and throughout the company.

Don Combs, manager of the MIS department, observes that this level of operation can be achieved only through the use of corporate standards for all information systems. As new technologies are added, new standards have to be implemented. For example, the plant vice-president decided that all operations would go to a paperless environment. Meetings are held in rooms with PC-based projection equipment and PCs connected to the LAN. No one is allowed to bring paper to the meetings. New standards were created for the selection of scanners, graphics file formats, and supporting software to convert and store paper documents that came from outside sources.

Combs is searching for groupware and e-mail tools that will further reduce the use of paper and improve the flow of information throughout the company. He is particularly concerned about the need to attach binary documents (e.g., images and spreadsheet files) to mail messages that can be sent throughout the company. In early 1996, few software packages provided the standards needed to enable seamless exchange of binary documents over the mail system.

and know that it would work together on any of our computers. This utopia will probably never exist because of changes in technology and the constant competition among manufacturers to gain an advantage. In reality, we are forced to guess which technology will succeed and which standard will eventually dominate the others. Choosing incorrectly can result in ownership of *orphaned* products that are no longer supported. You also end up changing hardware, software, and data more often, which results in expensive and disruptive conversions.

Unfortunately, there is no simple rule that will tell you how to choose a direction or standard. Some companies avoid the issue by avoiding new technology and waiting until it is clear which technology will win. Some managers simplify their choices by always buying from the market leader. Both strategies can cause problems: In particular it means that you will always be a follower instead of a leader. While there are advantages to being a follower, it makes it difficult to use technology to gain an advantage over your competition.

**GROUP DECISIONS**      A different type of groupware tool is designed specifically to help groups (or teams) make decisions. Many business decisions involve a group of people. Often, one person might be responsible for the final decision, but meetings are used to enable everyone to have a say, analyze the potential effects on each area, and persuade others to accept a decision. Decisions that involve groups of people have additional complications. Someone has to organize and control the meeting. During the meeting, people compete to make comments and get their opinions heard. Someone has to take notes of the meetings and votes have to be counted.

Information systems can help with group decisions. Groupware tools can be used to share data and documents. Message systems can be used to share comments and early drafts of work. Bulletin boards can be used to let everyone express opinions and evaluations. In the late 1980s, an additional tool known as a **group decision support system (GDSS)** was defined. A GDSS is designed to help managers reach a consensus during meetings.

## Features of a GDSS

Most versions of a GDSS use a special meeting room like the one shown in Figure 7.13, where each participant is seated at a networked computer. A facilitator operates the network and keeps the discussion moving in the right direction. Before the meeting, the primary decision maker meets with the facilitator to establish the objective of the meeting. They set up sample questions and design the overall strategy.

Typical meetings begin with a brainstorming session, where participants are asked to think of ideas, problems, and potential solutions. They type each of these into categories on their computers. The basic ideas and suggestions are stored in a database and shared with the group through the networked computers.

In terms of discussion and comments, the facilitator can choose individual items and project them on a screen for the entire group to analyze. Participants can write comments or criticisms of any idea at any time. This system is particularly helpful if many participants come up with ideas and comments at the same time. The computer enables everyone to enter comments at the same time, which is faster than waiting for each person to finish speaking.

Another feature of using the computer for the entry of ideas and comments is that they can be anonymous. Although each comment is numbered, they are not traced back to

**FIGURE 7.13**
Group decision support systems can be used to coordinate meetings, record notes, take votes, and encourage participation. As shown in this system by Ventana Corporation, each participant enters data in a PC, with summary results displayed on the central screen.

the original author, so people are free to criticize their supervisor's ideas. Anonymity reduces embarrassment and encourages people to submit riskier ideas.

At various points, the facilitator can call for participants to vote on some of the ideas and concepts. Depending on the software package, there can be several ways to vote. In addition to traditional one-vote methods, there are several schemes where you place weights on your choices. The votes are done on the computer and results appear instantly. Because it is so easy to vote, the GDSS encourages the group to take several votes. This approach makes it easier to drop undesirable alternatives early in the discussion.

One useful feature of conducting the meeting over a computer network is that all of the comments, criticisms, and votes are recorded. They can all be printed at the end of the session. Managers can review all of the comments and add them to their reports.

In theory, a meeting could be conducted entirely on a computer network, saving costs and travel time if the participants are located in different cities. Also, if it is designed properly, a GDSS can give each participant access to the corporate data while he or she is in the meeting. If a question arises about various facts, the computer can find the answer without waiting for a second meeting.

## Limitations of a GDSS

Perhaps the greatest drawback to a GDSS is that it requires participants to type in their ideas, comments, and criticisms. Most people are used to meetings based on oral discussions. Even if they have adequate typing skills, a GDSS can inhibit some managers.

Along the same lines, in a traditional meeting, only one person speaks at a time, and everyone concentrates on the same issues at the same time. With a GDSS, your focus is continually drawn to the many different comments and discussions taking place at the same time. People who type rapidly and flit from topic to topic will find that they can dominate the discussions.

In terms of costs, maintaining a separate meeting room with its own network and several computers can be expensive. Unless the facility is used on a regular basis, the computers will be idle a great deal of the time. When you factor in the costs for network software, the GDSS software, and other utilities, the costs multiply. One way to minimize this problem is to lease the facilities that have been established by a couple of universities and some companies (e.g., IBM).

The use of a GDSS also requires a trained facilitator—someone who can lead discussions, help users, and control the GDSS software on the network. Hiring an in-house specialist can be very expensive if there are only a few meetings a year. Again, using facilities from an outside agency can reduce this cost, but it means that someone outside your company is watching and controlling your meeting. Although most facilitators are scrupulously honest, there might be some topics that you do not want to discuss with nonemployees.

One way to overcome these limitations is to alter the approach to meetings. Instead of requiring everyone to get together at the same time in one room, meetings could be held via network discussion groups. Each participant could read messages, add comments, and vote on issues electronically at any time from any location. Again, the Internet offers possibilities to provide these facilities, but it could be a few years before organizations and managers can accept the changes required.

## SOFTWARE TO SUPPORT INTEGRATION

At the high end, ERP systems are designed to provide most of the functions necessary to integrate data across the organization. These tools work well for transaction processing and traditional production-oriented companies. For service organizations and decision-oriented tasks, groupware tools are more useful. Many of these tools ultimately utilize existing personal productivity software such as a word processor, spreadsheet, and graphics package. The network and groupware tools transfer data among workers, but workers still need the traditional tools to create and modify the data. Software companies have been adding features to these packages to make them more useful for workgroups. Three of the most important features are (1) linked documents, (2) protected documents that display corrections by multiple people, and (3) annotation capabilities to record notes for other users.

---

### Reality Bytes    7–7    Integrating Data to Monitor Customers

To help reduce criminal activity, particularly drug-related crimes, the U.S. government requires companies to report all cash transactions involving more than $10,000. Yet, law-enforcement officials and legislators decided that even more detailed monitoring might be needed. In December 1998, the FDIC published a rule instructing all banks to monitor their customers for evidence of illegal activities. The rule suggested that banks should verify customer identities and sources of income. Within two days of its publication, the rule had drawn nearly 3,000 complaints from the public, most sent by e-mail. Typical responses were harshly opposed to the rule: "The majority of U.S. citizens are NOT criminals dealing with large amounts of cash, are NOT tax evaders, and DO NOT DESERVE the prying of banks into our affairs."

However, this "know your customer" rule has strong support from law enforcement. For example, John Varrone from the U.S. Customs Services states, "I think it's critically important that the banking industry self-police, in addition to what law enforcement does, to maintain the integrity of the system."

Regulators suggest that the rule is simply a formalization of good banking practices, where managers are increasingly observing customers to help increase sales. They also suggest that individual banks will have the flexibility to interpret the rules to match their own situations. But customers have their own concerns. One customer, Jeanne Miller, wrote: "If they have to charge me $27 to stop payment on one check, imagine what they will charge me to spy on me and my banking activities."

## Documents

Windowing operating systems have a *clipboard* used to import or export data between different software packages. As an example, say that you are writing a report using a word processor in one window. You have displayed a graph using a graphics package in a second window and would like to put it in the report. Using a mouse, you click the pointer on the graph window to make it active. You then choose the cut option to move the image or copy icon to copy the graph. This copy is temporarily stored on a clipboard. Now, you switch to the report and paste the copy of the graph from the clipboard. The graph will be included when the report is printed. However, remember that unless you make a dynamic link, if you change the graph using the graphics package, you will have to go back and recopy the graph into the report.

Historically, the earliest type of integration in the personal computer world occurred within spreadsheets. In many firms, users spend too much time reentering data into spreadsheets that came from other computers. Today, it is easy to automatically retrieve data from a database and insert it into a spreadsheet.

Spreadsheets are capable of creating dynamic links to other software packages, especially to databases. With these tools, the original data is stored in a database management system. The spreadsheet is used as a report writer to produce computations and graphs. Whenever the original data is changed, the spreadsheet and its graphs are automatically updated.

As illustrated in Figure 7.14, a company may keep a central database that records all of the sales data. The database tracks customers, salespeople, inventory, and actual sales. This data is used to produce standard monthly sales and accounting reports. On the other hand, the marketing department has a spreadsheet to predict sales for the next three months. It uses the sales data for the last three months along with some economic variables. Likewise, the purchasing department combines the inventory and sales data in a spreadsheet that helps purchasers decide when to reorder each product. At the start of each day, the marketing and purchasing departments print out their spreadsheets. Because the spreadsheets are dynamically linked to the central database, they automatically have the current data. Therefore, end users simply start their spreadsheets and print the reports that are needed.

Microsoft Excel provides three methods of obtaining dynamic data links from a database: (1) copy a query and edit, paste special, paste link; (2) Microsoft Query activated with data, get external data, new query; and (3) pivot tables which utilize the query system but provide additional features.

**FIGURE 7.14**
SPREADSHEET LINK TO DBMS
One of the biggest problems users encountered with early spreadsheets was the need to type data from existing reports into the spreadsheet. With dynamic linking (and networks), (1) the spreadsheet can issue a query to the DBMS, (2) receive the data, and (3) perform the computations automatically. (4) The spreadsheet can query the DBMS at regular intervals to (5) collect changes in the data.

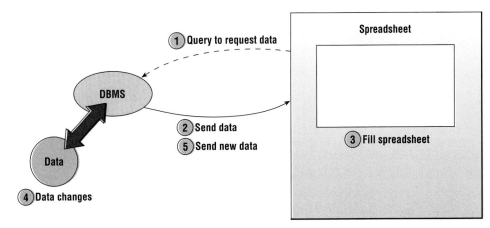

## Microsoft Pivot Tables

Microsoft **pivot tables** are the most advanced means of retrieving data and examining it in a spreadsheet. A pivot table is essentially a means of examining data from a variety of viewpoints. To use this program, you first set up a query to retrieve the detailed data you want to examine. The pivot table then provides several functions to help you define groups and examine subtotals.

On starting the pivot table wizard, your first step is to find your data. Typically, it will come from a database stored somewhere on the network. Then create a query to extract exactly the data you want. The query wizard uses QBE and SQL methods similar to those described in Chapter 5. In selecting data, look for natural groupings. In the Rolling Thunder example, you might want to examine sales by model type, by state, and by month. So from the Bicycle table, select the ModelType, SaleState, SaleDate, and SalePrice. You can use the Month( ) function to convert the SaleDate to a month number. You can also restrict the data to examine a single year.

Once the data is selected, set the basic structure of the pivot table by indicating which items are rows (ModelType and SaleState), columns (Month), and central data (SalePrice), which is automatically summed. Figure 7.15 shows the resulting pivot table. Notice that an additional group was created to display results by quarter instead of month. The groups were created by highlighting three months at a time and creating a new group. The strength of the pivot table is that the detail (e.g., monthly) data still exists and can be displayed quickly by selecting the "show detail" option.

## Protected Changes

Most service organizations operate in a teamwork environment because it takes many people to complete a project. Each team generates several documents that are read and modified by each person. Even spreadsheets and charts go through several revisions. In a system that relies on paper, each person marks changes and insertions on a separate copy. A coordinator is then responsible for integrating the changes and producing the final document.

Three basic issues arise when many people simultaneously work on a document. First, everyone needs to have a current version of the document. Second, we need to know who made each change in case there are questions or additional discussion issues. Third, we need to keep a record of the changes so everyone knows the current status of

| Sum of Sale Price | | Quarter | Month | | | |
|---|---|---|---|---|---|---|
| ModelType | SaleState | Quarter1 | Quarter2 | Quarter3 | Quarter4 | Grand Total |
| Hybrid | | 49,11.21 | 38,365.38 | 58,022.29 | 53,507.33 | 199,006.21 |
| Mountain | | 138,419.65 | 150,297.45 | 133,240.00 | 141,669.80 | 563,626.90 |
| Race | | 215,602.55 | 231,187.01 | 243,694.51 | 238,500.00 | 928,984.04 |
| Road | | 145,108.33 | 112,108.20 | 111,749.85 | 120,901.80 | 489,868.18 |
| Tour | | 79,222.71 | 89,869.80 | 81,602.01 | 95,506.07 | 346,200.59 |
| Track | | 7,703.77 | 7,450.00 | 15,125.00 | 4,750.00 | 35,028.77 |
| Grand Total | | 635,168.22 | 629,277.84 | 643,433.66 | 654,835.00 | 2,562,714.72 |

**FIGURE 7.15**

PIVOT TABLE FOR ROLLING THUNDER SALES

The detail is currently hidden. By clicking one of the title buttons (ModelType, SaleState, Quarter), you can select the option to display details and the table will expand to show the individual items. Traditional spreadsheet functions can be used to format or graph this data.

the document and what was changed. Electronic documents provide advantages over paper in all three of these areas.

With a network, it is easy to share a document so that many people can retrieve it at the same time. By keeping one central copy, everyone will be working with the latest version. However, the single-copy approach raises a problem when you need to know who is making changes. Current software resolves this problem by enabling you to protect the document. Once the protection option is set, all changes are marked. As shown in Figure 7.16, insertions are marked with an underscore and deletions with a strikeout line. Changes made by each person are marked in a different color.

Periodically, the coordinator or team leader can unprotect the document and run the tracking tool (tools, track changes, accept or reject changes). This tool searches for the marked changes and makes it easy to incorporate or reject each suggested change.

## Annotated Documents

The third issue in teamwork is more complex and difficult to automate. Particularly for large projects, it is helpful to track the changes that were made at various stages. Detailed changes are rarely necessary. Instead, it is more important to summarize the changes and indicate why they were made. Summary and explanation cannot be automated. What you need to do is keep notes to describe the various changes. You can store these notes as a separate document, as additional pages within the document, or you can incorporate them directly into the document in the form of comments.

As shown in Figure 7.17, comments can be added as either text or voice recordings. Technically, with the appropriate hardware (video camera and capture board) and editing software, it is even possible to place a video note into a document. However, video is more useful for presentations than for simple notes.

**FIGURE 7.16**
TRACKING CHANGES
Once a document is protected, insertions are marked with an underscore and deletions with a strikeout. Each person's changes are marked in a different color. When desired, a search tool makes it easy to incorporate or reject each change.

> The results from the fourth quarter indicate that the sales promotion was ~~very~~ successful. Based on these results, we should ~~consider~~ implement~~ing~~ a similar strategy next quarter.

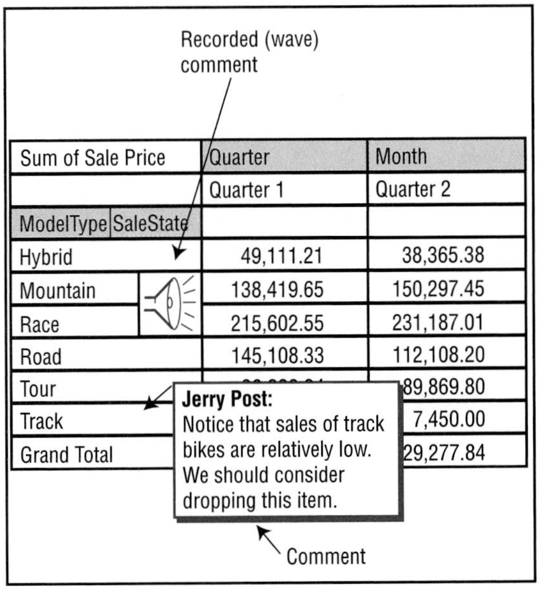


**FIGURE 7.17**
ANNOTATIONS AND COMMENTS
Individual items and changes can be marked with text comments. With the appropriate hardware, voice comments can be added to any document as well.

## SUMMARY

Working together and sharing data are crucial in today's companies. MIS can help teams work better with tools designed to integrate data across an organization. Managers need to know how to use a variety of tools, from data sharing over networks, to dynamic linking, to groupware products.

Enterprise resource planning systems are commercial systems designed to collect and share data across the company. Most of them concentrate on transaction-processing data with a special focus on accounting systems. However, the consistent data provides a solid foundation for additional analysis.

Workgroup software like Lotus Notes combines many features to facilitate work on group projects. It supports communication, document sharing, integration of data types, and tracking individual changes.

Group decisions can also be supported with GDSS software that is used to facilitate meetings. Its primary feature is that all managers can contribute at the same time. It also tracks comments for each idea and supports several types of votes and rankings.

Integration often requires combining data from many different locations. Networks enable you to dynamically link the work done by different people. However, if everyone in a company uses different software, it becomes difficult to combine the information because each software package stores data in a unique format. As a re-

sult, companies generally create standards for how the data will be stored and accessed. Although these standards are often necessary, several problems can arise when some users have special needs or the standards need to be changed.

At the personal computer level, software supports dynamic links that automatically update final documents as the underlying data changes. Microsoft pivot tables provide a flexible method of retrieving and examining data queries. Locking documents and tracking changes is useful to monitor the changes suggested by team members. Annotation facilities provide a mechanism to keep a log of changes and record the reason for the change.

---

### A MANAGER'S VIEW

Teamwork is an increasingly important aspect of management. Integration of business units so they work together is another important issue. Effectively managed, the techniques can cut costs, improve quality, and improve response time.

Several tools will help you integrate data and share information. Enterprise systems collect and integrate transaction data across the organization. Workgroup software helps team members share documents. Group DSS software assists in meetings and discussions. Software suites enable users to integrate data and track changes.

---

## KEY WORDS

compound document, 293
data warehouse, 299
dynamic links, 284
enterprise resource planning
  (ERP), 289

group decision support system
  (GDSS), 304
groupware, 292

legacy system, 299
pivot table, 308
static integration, 284

## WEB SITE REFERENCES

| | |
|---|---|
| **Bureau of Labor Statistics** | **Common Statistics** |
| Bureau of Labor Statistics | www.bls.gov |
| Census Bureau | www.census.gov |
| FedStats | www.fedstats.gov |

**General Reference Sites**

| | |
|---|---|
| Congress | lcweb.loc.gov/global/legislative/congress.html |
| Congressional Quarterly | www.cq.com |
| Copyright Office | lcweb.loc.gov/copyright |
| Executive Branch | lcweb.loc.gov/global/executive/fed.html |

| | |
|---|---|
| IRS | www.irs.gov |
| Judicial | www.uscourts.gov |
| Laws | law.house.gov |
| Legislative votes | pathfinder.com/cgi-bin/congress-votes |
| Library of Congress | www.thomas.loc.gov |
| Patent Office | www.uspto.gov |

## REVIEW QUESTIONS

1. What is meant by the concept of integrating information in business? Give an example of problems that can arise if business information is not integrated.
2. How do enterprise resource planning systems integrate data across the company?
3. What are the primary features and capabilities of an enterprise resource planning system?
4. What tools exist to support workgroup coordination and teamwork?
5. How does a data warehouse support integration? Why are they needed in many organizations?
6. What problems are you likely to encounter when attempting to integrate data across the entire company? How might you solve these problems?
7. What is the goal of open systems? How does it affect sharing data and integrating the business operations? Will we ever see completely interchangeable hardware and software?
8. Describe three features of group decision support systems.
9. What software tools exist to support a team working on a common document?

## EXERCISES

1. Describe a report for which you would use a spreadsheet as the base for integrating other information.
2. Sometimes dynamic integration can cause problems. Identify three situations in which you would be better off using static instead of dynamic integration of data.
3. Create a spreadsheet and draw a graph. Now, copy them into a word processing system's document and dynamically link (embed) them. Make changes to the original spreadsheet to make sure the graph and the word processor's document are updated. Does your software require extra steps to make sure the changes are recorded in each location?

**CO7Ex04.mdb**

4. Using a DBMS and a spreadsheet, create the sample report displayed in the spreadsheet discussion section. The sales and returns are stored in the DBMS and the DBMS should be used to compute the totals by region.
5. As a group project, assume that each person in the group is a manager of a different department. Each person creates a spreadsheet to list the salespeople in his or her department (4–10), their hours worked, total sales, and commissions. Compute the totals for each column. Once the individual spreadsheets have been created and stored on separate computers, the group will create a composite spreadsheet that brings in the data from each individual spreadsheet. Compute the corporate total and draw pie charts for each column. If possible, use dynamic linking across the network to capture the data from the individual spreadsheets.

**DeptStor.mdb**

6. Using a DBMS, spreadsheet, and word processor, create the four reports shown in the introduction: daily sales report, returned merchandise log, commissions report, and weekly sales analysis. If possible, use tools that support dynamic integration.
7. Using current business publications, find an example of a company that is experiencing problems with integrating data. Alternatively, find an example of a company that has an excellent system for integrating information. Identify data that is shared dynamically and data that is shared through static copies. (Hint: Companies are more likely to report successes than problems.)
8. Using a graphics-oriented DBMS, create a small catalog report that includes pictures and text descriptions.
9. Find descriptions of the top-selling software packages (spreadsheet, database management system, word processor, graphics). Be sure to include version

(edition) numbers. What types of integration do they support? Will they share data with software written by other companies? Can each package dynamically link to any of the other packages? Will it link as both a client (accepting data) and server (sending data)?

10. Find a business situation that could benefit from the use of a groupware product. Describe the problems that exist and how they can be overcome with the groupware tools.

 **Rolling Thunder Database**

11. Extract sales and cost data by model type and create a spreadsheet to analyze it. (Hint: Use the Extract Data form.) Write a short report discussing profitability and any trends. Include graphs to illustrate your comments. Your spreadsheet should look at monthly sales by model and monthly material costs by model. Be sure to compute profit margins and examine percentages.

12. Assume that Rolling Thunder is experiencing problems with quality control. Suddenly there are several complaints about the components. Write a report describing all of the data and reports we would need to help us resolve these problems.

13. Top management needs an analysis of purchases and deliveries from vendors. Begin by using queries to extract the appropriate data to create a basic spreadsheet. Write a report analyzing the data; include graphs to illustrate your points.

14. Describe how an ERP solution could improve operations at Rolling Thunder. What operations would you implement first?

15. Using Microsoft Excel, build a query to get information about sales in November and December. Create a graph to compare the two months. Then using Microsoft Word, write a short report about your conclusions and link the graph dynamically.

| Vendor | Purchases— Order Total $ | Percent of Vendor Total | Received $ | Receipts % of Purchase | Avg. # Days to Deliver |
|--------|--------------------------|-------------------------|------------|------------------------|------------------------|
|        |                          |                         |            |                        |                        |
|        |                          |                         |            |                        |                        |
|        |                          |                         |            |                        |                        |

## ADDITIONAL READING

Moad, Jeff. "Packages Rate Interest," *PC Week,* February 15, 1999. [Royal Bank of Canada adopts SAP]

Stedman, Craig. "Customer Data Faces Rough Road to Factory—How Do You Use Info and Keep it Private?" *Computerworld,* September 28, 1998, p. 1. [Challenges of integrating data from customers into a production system]

Weston, Randy. "ERP Users Find Competitive Advantages," *Computerworld,* January 19, 1998, p. 9. [Summary of ERP benefits]

# CASES  *Automobile Industry*

The automobile manufacturing industry is an increasingly competitive industry with respect to a number of factors. Automobile companies compete on quality, price, development, appearance, size, special options, safety, and financing terms.

Three types of automobile manufacturers dominate the industry:

1. Original equipment manufacturers (OEMs)— Supply such inputs as windshields, seats, and brake systems directly to another stage in the assembly process.
2. Aftermarket/replacement parts—Manufacture parts such as brake pads and batteries, supplied to assemblers and to the replacement market.
3. Capital goods—Provide manufacturing and assembly line equipment to the assemblers.

## Financial Analysis

In the past few years, the automobile industry has benefited from certain factors. The first is the improved economic conditions in the United States. The second, a result mostly of favorable exchange rates, is a cost advantage in comparison to vehicles manufactured in Japan (or those vehicles containing significant amounts of parts manufactured in Japan).

Automakers and suppliers are also affected by the season. Operating results vary primarily because of the variability in types and numbers of vehicles sold in different seasons. In addition, results are affected by new product launches, sales incentives, and costs of materials and production changes.

Manufacturers have also benefited from the increased demand for trucks and sport utility vehicles (SUVs). The high-end models of these vehicles have substantially higher profit margins than basic cars. Sometimes as much as $10,000 profit for an SUV versus $500 for a car.

## Stock/Investment Outlook

U.S. automobile manufacturers continue to struggle to come out on top in terms of quality and market share. In 1994 and 1995, operating revenues increased while net income decreased, lowering returns on investment.

Stock prices vary greatly in the auto industry. Stocks linked directly to the automotive industry fell out of favor in the late 1990s. The industry and stock prices tend to be highly dependent on the overall economy. The relatively lower prices in the late 1990s were an important factor in the worldwide industry consolidations.

## Potential/Prospective for Growth

In the recent past, quality has become the main focus point in the domestic auto industry, and vast improvements have been made. Nonetheless, the perception persists that U.S. automobiles do not have the same high standard as certain foreign manufacturers.

Several trends in automotive manufacturing are setting the stage for future growth. As the industry responds to demands for safer vehicles and environmentally safe vehicles, emerging innovations are flourishing. A Dataquest report suggests three main sectors for growth:

1. Advanced driver information and communication systems. Examples include keyless entry, navigation systems, and near obstacle recognition. Such products will enhance the driver's awareness of his or her own personal safety as well as the safety of road conditions through power steering, electronic brakes, and collision avoidance.
2. Powertrain electronics. Examples include active suspension.
3. Body control electronics. This includes, for instance, black boxes for autos and security systems.

The next generation of smart cars will enable its passengers to automatically keep pace with the vehicle in front and signal emergency services to an exact location of an accident without driver action.

Moving past the year 2000, production capacity will likely continue to exceed demand. Europe has become the primary battleground for car manufacturers, with unified Germany now the biggest single market. Eastern Europe and South America offer limited growth as well as high risk during the late 1990s but will become significant markets in the years 2000 to 2010. China, India, and the Asian countries represent the greatest opportunities and challenges to Japanese, U.S., and European manufacturers.

## Competitive Structure

Automobile manufacturing remains a highly competitive industry ranging from the big three automakers to a variety of suppliers. In addition, a number of foreign automotive companies are investing in North America. U.S. automakers are also taking advantage of new management tools and techniques.

One such trend is the just-in-time (JIT) manufacturing system, which essentially shifts inventory costs from the automakers down to the suppliers. Automakers are also using the system to reduce the number of suppliers. American automakers traditionally utilized thousands of different suppliers in short-term contract relationships, basing them on cost. Today, by implementing JIT, manufacturers reduce the number of suppliers by establishing long-term relationships with fewer suppliers.

Most European car manufacturers have significant positions only within Europe. U.S. companies tend to have major shares domestically and in Europe, while only two major Japanese companies can claim to be truly global. Although the industry is concentrating, no single company is close to dominating the market and, in fact, seven companies have between 10 percent and 15 percent. A variety of alliances and joint ventures have been utilized as a means of growth.

Consolidation will dramatically alter the profile of the entire industry over the next 10 to 15 years. Ford is trying to move further up market with the acquisition of the Aston Martin, Jaguar, and Volvo brands. Facing tough Japanese competition in the U.S. market, Ford is set to challenge General Motors (GM) for second place in Europe with the purchase of 51 percent of Mazda.

Consolidation in supplier relationships will also dramatically alter the profile of that industry over the next 10 to 15 years. Ford had 2,300 direct suppliers in 1995 and expects to reduce this figure to 1,150 by the year 2000. Chrysler intends to reduce its direct suppliers from 2,000 to 1,500 over the same period. BMW recently announced its intention to reduce from its current figure of 1,400 line suppliers to just 200.

## Role of Research and Development

Research and development in the domestic automobile manufacturing industry never ceases. Automakers and suppliers continuously strive to improve their products to remain ahead of competition in the United States and in other countries.

Ford has a lofty goal: the global standardization of environmental systems and processes at all Ford facilities worldwide. Ford is standardizing its operational procedures while still striving for consistency and continuous improvement in its facilities. This program is called Ford 2000.

Automobile pollution is a worldwide problem. Automobiles currently have 80 percent of the global personal transport market and 55 percent of goods transportation. Their effect on the environment is large. Noise and solid waste also contribute to environmental deterioration. According to the study done by Harvard University, more than 500 kg of every car produced ends up in landfill sites, accounting for 4 percent of total rubbish weight.

Recycling is another way to deal with the pollution problems that cars pose. About 75 percent of current cars are steel and therefore are easily recyclable. The remain-

ing 25 percent consist of plastic, glass, and rubber. Legislation will force reductions of the latter to 15 percent by 2002 and to 5 percent in the longer term. Alternatives to plastics include resin-bonded flax, which can be used as agricultural fertilizer when the car is eventually recycled. Green networks are being built to collect batteries, catalytic converters, and bumpers and recycle them directly in the production of new vehicles.

Reducing fuel consumption is a major research area. Engines are being developed with reduced friction, more efficient combustion, and better ignition. Diesel cars are an alternative; work also continues on small electric cars. Engines capable of using renewable fuels such as Soya oil have been in existence since the 1970s. These renewable fuels will not become cost effective, however, unless there is a large change in oil prices or in the presence of government incentives.

Weight reduction is another area of research. In the future, car bodies may be composed of lighter, high-strength steels, alloys, polymers, and composites.

## Technological Investment and Analysis

Motoman, Inc., Fanuc Robotics, and other robot manufacturing companies have been making sales to automobile manufacturers. Robots are capable of completing jobs humans have difficulty with or find tedious and boring and often make fewer errors. They are usually operated from familiar Windows-based PCs.

In order to speed up the design cycle, the big three U.S. automakers bring their electronics suppliers into the design cycle at much earlier junctures than in the past. According to Alex Popovic, automotive marketing manager at National Semiconductor Corp., "The sooner we [suppliers] get involved, the more cost-effective and better-performing system the customer gets." Early supplier involvement has another advantage in the automotive market. In advance, the system people can design diagnostic techniques that will help reduce the automaker's future warranty costs. Alex Popovic states, "We try to eliminate problems in silicon and increase the accuracy of the diagnosis of problems."

Most of the 1.1 million employees working for Chrysler, Ford, and General Motors are expected to eventually use Web applications. The big three automakers are proving that intranets and extranets can open communications in the supply chain, improve international communications, and save money on support. The automakers are also looking to networking as a way to lower costs and improve profit margins. The big three are already among the leaders in providing Web access to their employees.

Members of the Automotive Industry Action Group trade association are working to help GM, Ford, and Chrysler overcome Year 2000 problems and problems at parts makers that threaten to disrupt the supply chain. A Year 2000 problem at even a small company could cripple a giant automaker because most companies tightly manage their business partners and use JIT inventory. These efforts are important because most of the automobile industry is running on old legacy computer systems and applications.

### Recommendation for the Future

Although the automotive industry has had its ups and downs in the recent past, automakers and suppliers must continuously improve their processes in order to survive in today's market. This means taking advantage of the latest technology to cut costs.

Quality control must also be a major goal of U.S. automobile manufacturers. This increasingly means giving customer service long after the completion of the sale.

## CASE  *Ford Motor Company*

In late 1995, Elena Anne Ford, the great great granddaughter of Henry Ford, became the first member of the fifth generation to go to work for Ford. The event is a small reminder that the Ford family is a constant presence. The special Class B stock the Fords own gives them 40 percent of the shareholder votes.

The Fords also have a strong board of directors presence—with seats being held by Edsel B. Ford II, William Clay Ford, and William Clay Ford, Jr. Edsel and his cousin Bill, Jr., have also been mentioned as possible candidates to become CEO. However, Bill, Jr., resigned from the company in 1995 to succeed his father as chairman of the finance committee of the board, a position reserved for an outside director. In the 1920s, Henry Ford spoke of the opportunities available to young people if they work hard. It does not hurt, he should have added, if they answer to the name of Ford. Ford is still considered a family enterprise even though it is publicly held.

### Technological Investment and Analysis

The global computer network, Global Studio, will allow team members throughout the world to work online with one another and effect changes in the design and manufacture of vehicles instantaneously. Coupled with other technology being implemented, the global network system will also help avoid lengthy and expensive product simulations, enable designers to view products being developed in other parts of the world, replace sketches and clay models as design tools and stages, and facilitate global communication. The Global Studio will allow teams to share data on a variety of subjects, including ergonomic studies, air-flow analyses, crash simulations, digital mockups, and general and group engineering review.

Ford has encountered difficulty in implementing the process. Information technology (IT) has more than 5,000 people who labor to support 7,000 engineering workstations and 85,000 PCs. Migration to the new system has been difficult, and convincing the system users of the advantages of Global Studio has been a laborious task. IT director Bill Powers has even encountered resistance from IT personnel.

To facilitate the retraining process and ensure further integration of the worldwide systems, Powers has permanently moved the head engineers from each of Ford's systems to the Systems Integration Center in Dearborn, Michigan, where they will work to establish the best infrastructure for the company. The integration issue is likely to become more difficult as employees are forced to work as a team and understand elements that previously did not fall into their jobs. Smaller teams may be able to integrate faster, but as "larger units grapple with issues of time, costs, redundancy, and training, Powers is likely to discover many issues forming that could slow down the re-engineering effort."

The implementation of the Global Studio is also severely limited by technological parameters such as bandwidth, which limits the amount of information that can be sent at once. Local communication laws define what can and cannot be done and the infrastructure and the capabilities of each country vary significantly.

In 1996, Ford launched a project called C3P, or CAD/CAM/CAE and Product Information Management. The system is intended to assist Ford in cutting prototype costs by 50 percent, improve efficiencies by 20 to 30 percent, and eliminate one-half of the company's costly late development design changes. Before C3P, "it used to take two to three months to build, assemble, and test a prototype of a car's chassis. "Using the C3P technologies, Ford can do all that in less than two weeks," says Richard Riff, a C3P project officer. The system should help Ford reduce its product development lead time even further.

While developing the Global Studio, Ford has also had to contend with issues of security. Ford uses the Total Control Security Server, a system that manages sign-on requests originating from a SecureID card, a separate device from Security Dynamics. The SecureID card is a changing "lock and key" device that generates one-time passwords for user authentication. The credit card–sized device, which is synchronized with the security server, generates a new six-digit number every 60 seconds on a LCD display creating a cryptographic key. When an employee types in the number displayed and his or her unique PIN to request remote access, the security server runs an algorithm using the time and the cryptographic key, then matches up the number to the card it comes from. If all the pieces fit together, the server accepts the sign-on.

## Technological Innovations

### Network

Ford's intranet connects about 120,000 of Ford's computers around the world to web sites containing proprietary company information such as market research, rankings of suppliers' parts, and analyses of competitors' components. The chief benefit of this network is that it has enabled Ford to bring new models into full production in 24 months compared with 36 months before.

The intranet is expected to save the company billions of dollars during the next few years. Ford plans to use its intranet to achieve manufacturing on demand. This would be a process that involves coordination of delivery and assembly of thousands of components. The company plans to manufacture most of its vehicles on a demand basis by 1999. This will require linking its 15,000 dealers around the world to the intranet.

### Telecommunications

Ford has a pilot test in which consumers in Houston and Boston can use the Internet to buy used Fords, Mercurys, and Lincolns (www.fordpreowned.com).

Ford Motor Co. finds it far more difficult to sell those cars than new models. Many used cars come off multiyear leases and have up to 36,000 miles on the odometer.

### Data

In 1998, Ford Motor Co. awarded an outsourcing contract to Ryder Integrated Logistics, Inc., to design and manage an integrated JIT supply-chain and transportation system for Ford's 20 North American manufacturing plants.

Ford is starting a project that will integrate its plants' individual supply-chain systems. It will connect them to suppliers for real-time information about component and part inventories, as well as real-time tracking of deliveries. The system will help Ford "squeeze out" the cost of transporting parts and components to its plants.

The consolidated system would let Ford managers monitor when plants in the same area need deliveries of similar auto parts. Currently, each plant's shipments are delivered individually by separate trucks. Managers will be able to coordinate parts transportation to multiple plants in the same region using just one truck.

### QUESTIONS

1. What is the strategic direction of Ford Motor Company?
2. What was the catalyst for change at Ford?
3. Upon what technologies has Ford relied?
4. How successful has Ford's technological change been?
5. What role does data play in the future of Ford Motor Company?
6. How will the capture and maintenance of customer data impact Ford's future?

### ADDITIONAL READING

Bicknell, David. "Car Firms Test-Drive an Extranet," *Computer Weekly,* October 2, 1997, p. 32.

Brull, Steven V. "Networks That Do New Tricks," *Business Week,* April 6, 1998. p. 100.

Dalton, Gregory. "Ford Turns to Extranet—Automaker Sees Netscape Applications Helping It Expand Visteon Parts Business," *Information Week,* August 10, 1998, p. 30.

"Ford Selects Intelisys' E-Commerce System," *Electronic Buyer's News,* October 26, 1998, p. 80.

Madden, John. "Ford Explores Outsourcing: May Contract Bulk of U.S. IT Operations," *PC Week,* April 27, 1998, p. 8.

Sliwa, Carol. "Intranet Apps Applauded," *Computerworld,* March 23, 1998, p. 47.

Suris, Oscar. "Behind the Wheel: At Ford Motor, International Product Development Will No Longer Need Travel Agents, Just Computers," *The Wall Street Journal,* November 18, 1996, p. R14.

Warren, Liz. "Top Gear," *Computer Weekly,* March 7, 1996, pp. 34–36.

"Wiring in High Gear," *Communications News,* September 1997, p. 20.

### CASE   *General Motors Company*

*I ask you to think back to the 1980s for the moment. . . . GM was even called a dinosaur. We have since restructured our company, lowered our costs, improved our quality, wholeheartedly embraced lean manufacturing and common processes, and produced an entire new line of exciting cars and trucks.*

—John F. Smith, Jr., President and CEO of General Motors, in a speech delivered to The Executives Club of Chicago on April 17, 1997.

Obviously, information systems and computer services play a very important role in such processes. The push toward a consistent information system (IS) infrastructure has been a great challenge for GM since 1984 when GM bought EDS, a highly successful data-processing firm for $2.5 billion. After 12 controversial years, GM spun off EDS and started to look for a chief information officer (CIO) to build an internal information strategy and management capability.

Effective June 28, 1996, GM named Ralf J. Szygenda, former CIO of Bell Atlantic, vice-president and CIO. Szygenda had to face two major challenges. One was to impose order on highly autonomous information systems groups within GM's operational units. The other was to ensure that outsourcing vendor EDS provides the best service at the best price as it seeks to build its non-GM business after being spun off from GM. Szygenda's main work was to develop and implement an information technology strategy that would help CEO Smith fully achieve his four top priority goals: getting common, systems running lean, competing on a global basis, and growing the business.

## Technological Investment and Analysis

In the early 1980s, when GM owned 40 percent of the U.S. auto market with revenues exceeding $100 billion, the company did not have a unified information system that would satisfy its needs. Even though GM had used a scheme called electronic data interchange (EDI) to order parts automatically from suppliers since the concept was proposed in the early 1970s, different divisions and sections within divisions used different computers and software.

Thus, GM was forced to handle many tasks manually whereas a unified computer system would prevent the need for much of that work. For instance, if two sets of engineers were not using the same computers to communicate with each other, they would often have to reenter the data and change their formats.

Roger Smith (GM's CEO from 1981 to 1991) envisioned a setup where everyone at GM would be connected to one network. Design, engineering, administration, payroll, health insurance, and financing departments, the factories and the telephones would all be integrated into one system. Smith thought that data processing was at the heart of General Motors and should be handled only by an internal group.

Since GM did not have strong IS capabilities, Smith decided to solve the problem by going outside of the company and hired Salomon Brothers to assist him with the acquisition of a computer services company. Out of several potential candidates, Smith chose Electronic Data Systems for several reasons. First, it was a highly successful (if small, by GM standards) data-processing firm, and second, it had a corporate culture which minimized the red tape and bureaucracy that Smith hated so much. EDS merged with General Motors in 1984 and immediately assumed control of GM system and inventory. Overnight, thousands of GM workers became EDS workers.

The integration of EDS into General Motors turned out to be a painful and long-term process. Aside from the clash of cultures and resentment of EDS's intrusion into GM turf, there were professional complaints about GM's new subsidiary. When GM acquired EDS, the computer company had no automotive experience and little background in distributed systems. Also, EDS lacked experience in management control systems, robotics, computer-aided design, and manufacturing, which were all a large part of GM's computer systems. GM personnel complained that EDS mishandled parts supplying, often buying far too many or too few of an item, resulting either in overstock or factory delays.

However, EDS scored successes in consolidating purchases, improving payroll databases, and standardizing PC systems at GM. Ever since the merger, EDS tried to move to commercial packages. Automakers have been notorious for developing homegrown software, and GM led its competitors in this regard.

EDS coordinated the project for GM North American Operations called Consistent Office Environment (COE). COE was a three-year plan focused on replacing a hodgepodge of desktop models, network operating systems, and application development tools with a shorter and hence more manageable list of vendors and technology platforms. COE represented the fastest and largest IS infrastructure upgrade in GM's history, which laid the foundation for the implementation of a common business communication strategy across General Motors. The goal was to change the way GM handled information on the desktop, in the workgroup, and across the enterprise. In 1993, GM had 27 e-mail systems, 10 word-processing programs, five spreadsheet applications, and seven business graphics packages.

All the contracts for COE were, by design, signed within 90 days of one another in mid-1993. The contracts were structured on a per-user/per-month basis, allowing GM to ramp up the new system without incurring capital spikes.

Obviously, COE was a landmark for the few lucky vendors tapped by GM/EDS to supply hardware and software components. For example, Lotus Development Corp., which supplied its Notes groupware platform, is said to have made its largest single Notes sale to date to EDS for the project. Similarly, Compaq Computer Corp., which got the nod to supply the desktop and laptop system, was believed to be looking at one of its largest non-government sales ever.

In June 1996, GM filled its top information systems job with Ralph Szygenda, former chief information officer at Bell Atlantic Corp. Before joining Bell Atlantic, Szygenda had been CIO at Texas Instruments. In his new job, Szygenda chairs GM's Corporate Information Council, which includes the IS heads from GM's business sectors. Szygenda reports to GM Vice Chairman Harry Pearce. Szygenda's job was to develop and manage GM's global information technology strategy as well as its relationship with outsourcers, most notably EDS.

Szygenda faced two major challenges. One was to impose order on the highly autonomous information systems groups within GM's operational units. The other challenge was to ensure that outsourcing vendor EDS provided the best service at the best price as it built its non-GM businesses. Szygenda had to rely on EDS for much of his IS needs, at a time when the newly liberated systems integrator was focused elsewhere.

Usually, getting a lower price from an outsourcer is good news for a CIO. But it could be more complicated for GM's CIO because lower earnings for EDS could drive down the value of EDS stock held by GM pension funds. That, in turn, could require GM to make special payments to those funds in compensation. The CIO is not responsible for the pension fund, but GM's contracts are important to the vitality of EDS. Therefore, GM has to phase in the shift of its business to EDS's competitors.

"Despite this semi-captive relationship, EDS is responding well to our cost-reduction effort. We need to align all of our investments in information systems with our business priorities [while] running information systems and services like a business," Szygenda said in late December 1996.

Szygenda was pleasantly surprised to find 2,200 IS employees "hidden" within GM and not shipped off to EDS. Among the handful of corporate IS staff, he picked Raymond Kahn to head year 2000 compliance efforts for the company's 2 billion lines of code, a project estimated to cost hundreds of millions of dollars. But most of the new IS executives were to come from outside to assist Szygenda in accomplishing his mission.

Although GM management had been imposing tighter controls on IS for several years, Szygenda wanted to cut hundreds of millions of dollars more from GM's current information technology budget of more than $4 billion. To achieve this goal, he decided to hire 300 new CIOs who would help him in this effort by finding common software, processes, and expertise that can be reused across the company.

Integration and common global product development is critical to GM's prosperity. Because of EDS, GM's IT infrastructure was in relatively good shape, but applications were developed piecemeal by GM's units, leading to about 7,000 separate systems. Szygenda wanted to see at least half of GM's $4 billion IS budget go to developing applications. He wanted to finish GM's struggle to standardize and to collaborate globally.

GM took a step toward common systems in December 1996 when it announced it would standardize on EDS's Unigraphics CAD/CAM solid modeling software. Shortly after that, GM began automatic translations of solid model data with its suppliers, which use a variety of CAD/CAM systems, to cut costs and product development time. Another major step toward unified IS would be a complex business software system.

General Motors is thinking about purchasing R/3 from the German company SAP. R/3 ties together and automates the basic processes of accounting: taking orders, checking credit, verifying payments, and balancing the books. SAP's R/3 is becoming the new standard equipment of global big business.

An intranet is helping GM to develop products more efficiently. GM engineers need to share knowledge. If they do not, dozens of people end up writing the same bug fix or working with out-of-date versions of objects, simply because they do not know what their co-workers have done. Without a process for tracking changes and revisions, all large projects can get out of control.

GM's Powertrain Control Center uses its intranet to coordinate the work of more than 300 engineers all over the world. Prior to the intranet Web servers, GM engineers filed paper documents and distributed them via the internal mail system. In 1994, they installed a UNIX-based shared file server, but it lacked data organization, control, and file naming standards. Now, using the Continuus/Web intranet solutions, instead of completing dozens of disjointed efforts, everyone works with consistent standards, procedures, documentation, and code.

Colleagues, whether in Michigan or Münich, can access this document with their Netscape Communications Corp. Netscape browsers. An e-mail notification system automatically sends users a message every time a document that concerns them changes.

They use a second intranet to deploy executable files—the code that runs the black boxes. Customers, including manufacturing companies, the GM service organization, auto dealers, and assembly plants, use the software to program the Powertrain and transmission controllers.

The intranet does not solve all of the problems, however. GM engineers still wrestle with incompatibility issues, such as reconciling the different UNIX and Windows file formats and tools. Nor does the intranet help them balance the need for security with the need for usability. So, the Continuus intranet solution has not yet helped GM to reach its ultimate objective: moving its "entire" software development process to a single database and communicating all that information through a Web server. But it accomplished an important interim goal: consistency.

Another area of GM's business that needed standardization and efficiency improvements was communication with the dealership network. GM has never had one common communications system in place for its dealerships. The old Dealer Communication System, which dated back to 1975, forced the dealers to take piecemeal technical downloads that took hours, and then cut and paste the messages into a cohesive format. To improve communications and information exchange between GM headquarters and its dealer network the company asked EDS to introduce a new dealership automation program. The system was named GM Access.

EDS chose Novell rival Microsoft Corporation's Windows NT Server as the lynchpin of the program to link all the dealerships nationwide. This decision to deploy two network operating systems rather than standardize on one reflects industrywide trends.

The main objective of the GM Access Program was to distribute data about the availability of new cars quickly to GM's car dealerships via a satellite network. The satellite network was supposed to replace the outdated X.25 network, which took hours to download information.

General Motors started to install Notes at its 8,500 U.S. dealerships as the platform for GM Access in the first half of 1996. Dealers will use Notes to check inventories, locate specific vehicles matching customer requirements, and find information on pricing, incentives and service. Notes is estimated to help reduce by 30 percent the time it takes to get sales and service information to GM dealers.

The GM Access program allows dealers to access inventory data that is no more than 24 hours old, read service manuals and technical bulletins, and get recall notices and parts availability information. Access will also let dealers use an online search engine to find individual models or configurations. This information will be downloaded within 14 seconds to the dealerships to increase efficiency and get consumers the most up-to-date information. GM Access will also allow GM and its dealerships to standardize the entire system. Previously, Pontiac, Buick, and GMC all submitted their paperwork differently, which was an administrative nightmare.

In addition, to cut the time it takes to get information to its dealerships, General Motors decided to use an emerging technology called IP Multicasting. IP Multicasting, which broadcasts data from one main site to multiple receiving stations, was more efficient than creating an individual link from the central site to every remote location. "We went from transmitting a 1M-byte file to a very limited number of dealers in roughly 30 minutes to sending that same file to 500 dealers in three minutes," said Wayne Stein, a project manager at Electronic Data Systems.

IP Multicasting lets GM provide dealerships with timely software updates, sales incentive data, service bulletins, and car availability information. In the past, this was done by numerous point-to-point transfers or by mailing diskettes to dealerships. All 8,500 GM dealerships nationwide were scheduled to be online by September 1997.

GM is using the Internet extensively in its advertising effort focused on increasing brand equity. GM was a true pioneer in the automotive industry when it started to broadcast its messages through the Back Web channel. GM first used "push" technology in the end of 1996 to send an animated advisory to subscribers of Back Web's GM Channel, announcing the launch of the 1997 Buick Regal. A click on that notice sent users to the Regal's own web site, which included video clips and chat areas. "We see a whole slew of different experiments to see how this aids the branding efforts for GM," said Larry Lozon, senior vice-president and director of GM's new-media strategy arm.

While the Internet advertising succeeds in attracting new customers, GM is also using the Net to make it easier for its customers to get financing. GM's financial division, General Motors Acceptance Corporation, became the first automotive financial services company to offer an online credit application on the Internet in 1996.

In addition to promotion and customer services activities, the Internet is expected to be used extensively in areas such as market research and employee training. In the near future, by clicking on a picture of a red Corvette, a market analyst at General Motors might be able to call down a profile of red Corvette buyers. If he wants to break that up by region, he might circle and click on a map. All in the same motion, he might view a GM sales-training film to see whether the sales pitch is appropriate, given the most recent market trends.

### Technological Innovations

#### Network

GM has begun a two-year global rollout of an ambitious IT architecture that will provide up to 175,000 GM users with Web access. Called GM OnLine, the rollout includes new applications as well as Compaq Computer PCs.

"GM OnLine is a new integrated intranet infrastructure that gives our users access to the Internet," said GM CIO Ralph Szygenda. "It will be our platform for knowledge-sharing and collaboration, and will be the nucleus of a number of new applications in the future." Besides the Compaq Windows NT-based desktops, GM OnLine includes Lotus Domino, Microsoft Office, and Tivoli Systems' TME 10 enterprise management system.

#### Telecommunications

GM has launched its response to web sites such as Auto-by-Tel and Microsoft CarPoint, which let consumers shop for cars online. GM enables customers to configure and price GM cars and trucks on its corporate web site (www.gm.com) and divisional sites such as www.buick.com and www.pontiac.com.

Dealers will still be utilized. Web users will be directed to the nearest GM dealer stocking the model in the desired color and with the desired options. The customer will receive online the manufacturer's suggested retail price and financing terms from General Motors Acceptance Corp., GM's credit unit.

Nevertheless, price negotiation, ordering, and payment will still be handled at the dealerships by traditional means. GM does have long-term plans to link from the Web into dealer inventory systems to enable online ordering, says Craig Norwood, interactive retail systems manager at GM in Warren, Michigan.

The configuration application will run on the Web-enabled version of Signature Plus interactive selling software from CWC, Inc., in Mankato, Minnesota. GM dealers in North America already use a customized client-server application from CWC called Prospec to configure, locate, and order cars from GM. The GM web site application is the first customer deployment of the Web version of Signature Plus.

### Data

GM is evaluating several data-mining products for projects the company plans for this year and next, involving several GM divisions, including its GMAC loan division and its credit card division.

GM has experimented with data mining on a few scientific projects, but it is only recently that the automaker has tried to use data mining in production work to solve problems. Some of these problems are database marketing and using customer data and warranty information. For example, if GM can use warranty data to identify very specific problems, GM can fix those processes or parts and save on future warranty expenses.

### QUESTIONS

1. Where does General Motors see itself heading?
2. Who or what forces are driving this direction?
3. Upon what technologies has General Motors relied?
4. What has caused a change in GM's use of technology?
5. How has the technological change been implemented?
6. How successful has the technological change been?
7. What does General Motor's web page present about its business directives?
8. How will the quality of the customer data impact the corporation's future?

### ADDITIONAL READING

Adhikari, Richard. "Groupware to the Next Level—Collaboration with Customers and Suppliers Means Fewer Mistakes and Fast Turnarounds," *Information Week,* May 4, 1998, pp. 106–110.

Bicknell, David. "Car Firms Test-Drive an Extranet," *Computer Weekly,* October 2, 1997, p. 32.

Caldwell, Bruce, and Marianne Kolbasuk McGee. "Magnitude of Change," *Information Week,* August 11, 1997, pp. 42–48.

Caldwell, Bruce, Stuart J. Johnson, and Clinton Wilder. "NT Server Rollout: Two-Way Electronic Communications Will Link GM Dealerships and Divisions," *Information Week,* May 20, 1996, pp. 15–17.

"Disciplined Approach," *Information Week,* August 11, 1997, p. 56.

"Intra-National Intrigue," *Computerworld,* October 26, 1998, p. 72.

King, Julia. "The Challenge of a Lifetime," *Computerworld,* November 17, 1997, p. 12.

McGee, Marianne Kolbasuk. "GM Prepares Rollout of Integrated Intranet Platform—Plan Calls for Huge Desktop Procurement," *Information Week,* April 20, 1998, p. 26.

Schwartz, Jeffrey. "GM Taps Notes 4 for E-Mail and Groupware," *CommunicationsWeek,* January 8, 1996, p. 1.

Wallace, Bob. "GM Readies Fast Fiber Net," *Computerworld,* December 7, 1998, p. 4.

### DISCUSSION ISSUE

## Telecommuting

The last few years have given rise to a substantial increase in the capabilities of personal computers as well as improved telecommunications facilities. Many people have also observed that the type of work performed today is radically different from the manual labor required several years ago. A large portion (perhaps as much as 50 percent) of the U.S. workforce provides information services. Because this information is easy to transmit, it is theoretically possible for millions of workers to perform their current jobs from their own homes. They would not have to go to an office in order to work. However, there are many issues that need to be resolved before telecommuting becomes commonplace. Here, Paul, a financial analyst, is asking his boss (Duncan) for permission to work at home. The CEO (Leto) also has to be convinced.

Paul:      Duncan, I've been reading about some companies that are allowing the employees to work at home. They work on PCs and trade information with the firm's computers by connecting over the phone lines.

Duncan:   Yes, I've heard of that. In fact, I ran into a friend at a convention who has some employees working at home.

Paul:      Well, I'd like to try it. You know I live out by the desert and have to drive about 50 miles to get to work. By working at home, I'd save gas and I'd be able to spend more time on my work. I already have a fast PC and a modem. Most of my job is spent analyzing numbers, and I can get those by dialing in from home. There's really no reason for me to come here every day.

Duncan: I know you spend a lot of time at the computer, but I'm not sure. I'd really prefer to have you here, so I can keep an eye on your work. You've been doing a good job, but sometimes I need to check your calculations.

Paul: I've already thought of that. I'll get a separate phone line in my house for the computer. That way you can call me whenever you want. With this new software on the LAN, we can even work on the same project at the same time. All of the information on my screen will show up on yours, too. So, we can talk on the phone, and I can show you step-by-step how I did the calculations.

Duncan: Hmmm. That might work. But what about distractions? Don't you have two children?

Paul: Sure; on the other hand, there'll be fewer distractions from the other workers. Plus, I can start earlier and work later at night. Look, how about if we try it for a month as an experiment? If it doesn't work out, I'll come back in. If it doesn't work, you'll have a good excuse when someone else asks. If it works, you can offer the option to other employees. Just think of the office space you'll save.

Duncan: That's an interesting thought, but I'll have to clear it with the CEO. I'll set up a meeting...

*At the meeting with the CEO...*

Duncan: Those are the basic advantages. I'm willing to try it as an experiment...

Leto: Well, I'm not. I think it's foolish. Paul, you chose to live that far away and you knew how long the drive was. We'd have no way to keep track of your work if you stay at home. For instance, with all that *extra* time, you'll be tempted to moonlight for some other company. We need your full attention on this job.

Paul: I like this job. I promise I'll spend all my time working on this job. And you or Duncan can still follow everything I do. He just has to call me. Plus, the firm's computer holds all of my work, so you can always see what I'm working on and how fast it's getting done.

Leto: There are still too many problems. What about security? You work with some top-level information. How can we allow you to transfer all of this data to your home computer? What if some neighbor decides to look through your PC files?

Duncan: But Paul takes work home now. I don't see the difference.

Leto: I still don't like the idea. Maybe we can trust Paul, but what about the next person? What happens when everyone wants to work at home? If I let Paul do it, but no one else, I'll end up with discrimination complaints.

Paul: Eventually, I think everyone will end up working at home. There are a lot of qualified workers out there willing to work part time who can't commute to the office. We'd just be starting the new style earlier than some other companies.

Leto: Maybe so, but I think the risk is way too high. If we let our employees stay home, they might work and they might not. If they don't, we're dead. It would take too long to pinpoint the problem. Duncan, you and the other managers would just hide the delays from me. By the time all of the managers told me the problem, it would be too late. Maybe next year. . . .

## QUESTIONS

1. Do you think that Leto is too strict? What advantages does telecommuting provide to the company? What advantages to the workers?
2. As a new employee, do you want to work for a company where most of the people work out of their homes? Would you accept a lower salary to work for such a company?
3. What type of jobs would be easier to perform with telecommuting? What jobs would not work well?
4. What changes will managers have to make in order for telecommuting to succeed?
5. Do you think more companies will support telecommuting in the next 5 years or 10 years? What pressures will persuade companies to use telecommuting? What social practices will lean against it?
6. What problems would be experienced by telecommuting workers? The employers?
7. If 25 percent to 50 percent of the workers eventually telecommute, how will society be changed?

# *Interactive Online Meetings*

For years, businesses have been run with meetings. Ask any manager how much time he or she spends in meetings. Telephones, voice mail, and facsimile machines can handle some of the simpler communication demands. However, traditional meetings still play an important role in management. Today, managers have better options for meetings. The personal computer can be used to share documents, text messages, voice, and even video. Microsoft NetMeeting illustrates the capabilities of this software.

## HARDWARE REQUIREMENTS

Virtually any computer can be used to run NetMeeting, however, the more advanced features require additional hardware. For example, you will need a good sound card and microphone to communicate with voice. Similarly, you will need a small video camera and a video capture card to send and receive images. It is also beneficial to have a relatively large, high-resolution video screen. You will want to display several items on the screen at one time. Perhaps the most important component is the speed of your network connection. Text and voice can be handled relatively well with dial-up connections. If you need interactive drawing in video, you will want a higher speed connection, for example, LAN, cable modem, T1, or a DSL communication speeds.

## SOFTWARE REQUIREMENTS

A nice thing about Microsoft NetMeeting is that currently the basic software is free. To use NetMeeting, all of the people who wish to participate in the meeting should download and install the current version of the software. If users wish to share documents, the participants should also have the same document software, for example, Microsoft Word or Excel.

## STARTING THE MEETING

One of the meeting participants is the host, who starts the software, selects the call option, and hosts the meeting. At that point, all of the other participants start a new call and enter the name of the person hosting the meting. This name can be a machine name, IP address, or e-mail address. For security purposes, as each person calls, the host decides to accept or reject the call. As a caller is accepted, each can see a list of the other participants, as shown in Figure 7.1A.

## COMMUNICATION TOOLS

One of the most basic communication tools is the chat screen. As shown in Figure 7.2A, when each person types in a comment, the message is displayed on a screen for everyone to see. The biggest drawback to the chat screen is that everyone has to type the message. The greatest advantage is that the chat room keeps a record of everyone's comments. Of course, if the participants use a speech recognition system, their spoken comments can be sent to the chat room automatically.

The whiteboard is a more sophisticated mechanism to share information. It is a simple graphic screen that is shown on each machine. As each person types, or even draws, those notations are transmitted to all of the participants. As shown in Figure 7.3A, participants can use the whiteboard to sketch ideas.

If you are interested in voice communication and do not need to keep a record, NetMeeting enables you to use the computer sound card much like a telephone. Spokesman comments are digitized and transmitted to the other computers. Of course, only one person can speak at a time.

In a similar manner, when systems are equipped with a video camera and card, images can be transmitted to the other participants in the meeting. By opening

**FIGURE 7.1A**

MICROSOFT NETMEETING

One person acts as a host. When others call, the host decides to accept or reject the call. Once the meeting is established, the communication tools are activated through the menu.

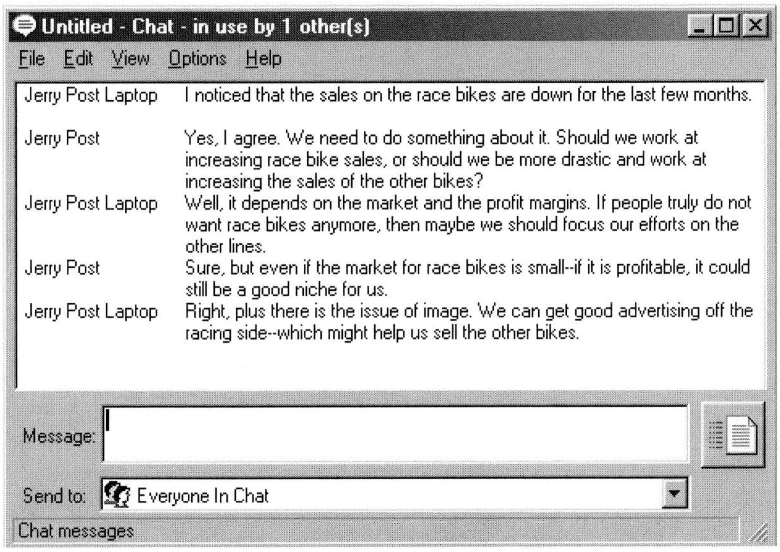

**FIGURE 7.2A**

CHAT SCREEN

Comments are displayed on each participant's screen. They can be saved for later use but are difficult to reorganize.

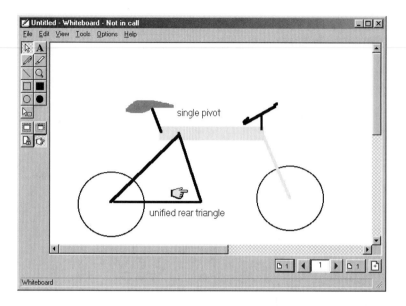

**FIGURE 7.3A**
WHITEBOARD

The whiteboard is used to share graphical information with all of the participants.
Each person can make changes or annotations on the screen. The hand pointer
can be used to point out features without altering them.

multiple windows, you can see several participants at one time. The quality of the picture depends primarily on the connection speed.

A simple file transfer mechanism exists for transferring existing work to the other participants's computers. For example, an initial document can quickly be distributed to each person. Or a summary of the meeting could be saved in a file and sent.

NetMeeting also includes a more sophisticated method for sharing documents. In fact, the collaboration tool is one of the strongest features in NetMeeting. The process begins when one person opens an application and selects the Share Application tool. When this option is selected, the image of the application, for example, a word processor, shows up on each participant's screen. The real fun begins when the Start Collaborating tool is selected. At this point, each participant can make changes to the document. Actually, only one person can make changes at a time, but all the changes are displayed on everyone's screen. Users can take turns making changes. In this fashion, several people can write a document to-

gether. If you are making changes to an existing document, you should set the software to track changes for the document. Then, each person's changes will be highlighted in a different color, so everyone can see the modifications. Once everyone is satisfied, the owner of the document can tell software to incorporate changes. Figure 7.4A shows the basic results using Microsoft Word.

Each of these tools is a useful feature in its own right. Together, they form a powerful communication tool. For example, while you are working on a document, you could be discussing the changes using the sound system or watching video of someone's actions. With sufficient communication speed, the system is better than a traditional meeting in many ways. Through the computer, several people can work at the same time. In a typical meeting, only one person can speak at a time. Additionally, the computer system provides a record of the comments along with the finished product. Finally, the system removes distance as a factor. Meeting participants can be located virtually anywhere in the world.

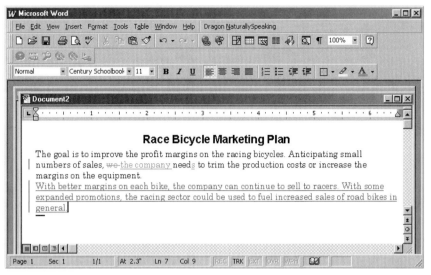

**FIGURE 7.4A**
SHARED APPLICATIONS

Through collaboration, participants can work on a document—and highlight each change.
The final document can be distributed to each participant.

## EXERCISES

1. Pick a topic and set up a net meeting with three other people. Use the whiteboard to draw a figure. Save the chat screen and the whiteboard. If you have the hardware, test the voice (and video) capabilities.
2. Test NetMeeting over a dialup connection with at least one other person. Compare the speed to a LAN connection. What capabilities work? Which ones would you avoid on the dialup connection?
3. Use NetMeeting to write a short report with two other people sharing a Microsoft Word document. For example, have each person write a paragraph on the features of SAP.
4. Will managers use tools like NetMeeting? Or will they stick with traditional meetings? What features of traditional meetings does NetMeeting not provide?
5. Survey friends, relatives, and managers. Explain the features of NetMeeting, and ask if they would use it instead of convening traditional meetings.

# PART 3

# *Decisions and Models*

**How do information systems help managers make better decisions?**
Business decisions can be complex. Complexity can arise from several areas, including: the use of huge amounts of data, difficult mathematical formulations, uncertain relationships, detailed linkages to multiple business units, and physical or procedural constraints. Middle-level managers in all functional areas face complex problems. Various models have been created to help you analyze these problems and evaluate alternative answers. Information technology provides several tools to help managers collect data, evaluate models, evaluate output, and make decisions.

Ongoing research into artificial intelligence has led to additional tools to solve specific problems. Expert systems, robotics, and neural networks are sophisticated tools to tackle complex problems.

Strategic analyses represent some of the most difficult decisions a manager can face. Strategy represents fundamental changes in the operations of the business. Information systems are used to search for useful changes. Information systems have also been useful in creating a competitive advantage.

CHAPTER 8

# *Models and Decision Support*

**OVERVIEW**

**INTRODUCTION**

**DECISIONS**

**BIASES IN DECISIONS**
Acquisition/Input
Processing
Output
Feedback
Models and Information Systems

**INTRODUCTION TO MODELS**
Physical
Process
Business Modeling

**WHY BUILD MODELS?**
Understanding the Process
Optimization
Prediction
Simulation or "What-If" Scenarios

**DECISION SUPPORT SYSTEMS: DATABASE, MODEL, OUTPUT**

**BUILDING MODELS**
Assumptions
Identifying Input and Output Variables
Processes and Equations
Software

**LIMITATIONS OF MODELS**
Model Complexity
Cost of Building Models
Problems with Modeling

**A BUSINESS MODEL: ENTERPRISE INFORMATION SYSTEMS**
Description of an EIS
How Does an EIS Work?
Advantages of an EIS
Limitations of an EIS

**SUMMARY**

**KEY WORDS**

**WEB SITE REFERENCES**

**REVIEW QUESTIONS**

**EXERCISES**

**ADDITIONAL READING**

**CASES: COMPUTER HARDWARE INDUSTRY**

**DISCUSSION ISSUE: EMPLOYEE PRIVACY**

**APPENDIX: FORECASTING**
Structural Modeling
Time-Series Forecasts
Exponential Smoothing
Seasonal and Cyclical Components
Exercises

Michael Dell has been a leading force in the personal computer industry for several years. His company led the way in personalized computers for every customer. The company is also an innovator in the use of the web for direct sales.

## DELL COMPUTER CORPORATION

Many people get a first job during high school, but few are as successful as Michael Dell was. Dell made $18,000 selling newspapers in one year. He identified the newspaper most purchased by newlyweds and new families in the area and targeted that particular segment.

He tracked this market segment via the city marriage license bureau, lists of new home purchases, and other sources. Later that year, he bought a BMW with $18,000 cash. The ingenuity and persistence Michael Dell demonstrated at an early age indicated a strong entrepreneurial spirit. The formation of Dell Computer occurred only two years later.

With competitors attempting to copy Dell's sales model, Dell focused on another direct route, the Internet. Compaq, Packard Bell, and other companies that sell through retailers allow "surfers" to browse through a product line catalog on the Internet. But while consumers look through Compaq's product line, others are purchasing PCs through Dell's homepage. Dell has revenues in excess of $1 million a day in Internet sales.

**OVERVIEW** How can information systems help you make better decisions? Providing the necessary data is one step. We have already seen how personal and operations-level decisions can be improved with better access to data. Yet, some tactical business decisions are more complex. Sometimes just having the data is not enough. For example, choosing advertising alternatives, identifying investment opportunities, and determining merit pay raises are difficult decisions. Each of these decisions affects many areas of the company and involves several variables.

To deal with complexity, we build models. Models help managers visualize physical objects and business processes. As illustrated in Figure 8.1, information systems help you build models, evaluate them, and organize and display the output.

**FIGURE 8.1**
Tactical decisions often require complicated analysis. Problems utilize forecasts, optimization and in-depth analysis. Information systems provide support through datamodeling and presentation tools. Managers use information system tools to build, evaluate, and maintain various models.

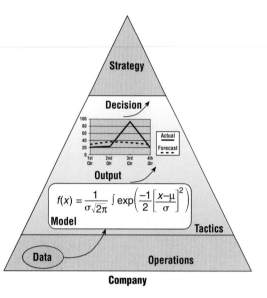

**FIGURE 8.2**
SAMPLE MODEL
Models come from several disciplines, including this one from economics. This model illustrates how a firm uses industry price and internal cost curves to determine the optimal quantity to produce.

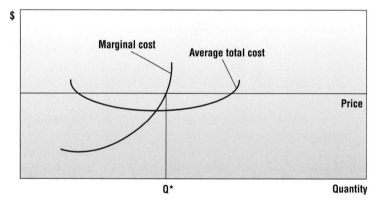

**INTRODUCTION**

What subjects are you required to study? Many of them are outside your major field; some may not seem relevant to the job you hope to have. Why do you think these subjects are required? One reason is to show you how various disciplines solve problems and make decisions. Every academic discipline has created models that describe an approach to problems and identify common solutions. Psychologists create models of how humans behave and interact. Sociologists concentrate on models of groups and societies. Economists have models that attempt to explain how people, firms, and governments interact using money and prices. Financial models help you evaluate various investments. Marketing models of consumer behavior help you decide how to promote and sell products and services. General management models examine the organization of firms and interactions between workers. The point of each subject is to learn these models and recognize the problems they solve. Regardless of the job you eventually perform, you will be amazed at the number of models that will prove useful.

A **model** is a simplified, abstract representation of some real-world system. Some models can be written as mathematical equations or graphs; others are subjective descriptions. Figure 8.2 shows a simple economic model that can be used in business to determine the best level of production for a firm. In actual practice, the process will be much more complex.

## Trends

Through the 1970s, computers were largely used to assist with transaction processing. Support for making decisions was generally limited to the basic reports produced from the data. Computers were too expensive and programming too difficult to be used by every manager. As personal computers became commonplace through the 1980s, managers began transferring data from the corporate central computers to their personal computers.

Personal computers gave managers the ability to quickly examine the data from many different perspectives. They made it easy to compute totals and other statistics. Control over data on their personal machines also gave managers the ability to get reports and analyses faster. Spreadsheets gave managers the ability to create graphs quickly and easily. Managers now have the tools to evaluate data instantly and in detail. Combining basic statistics with graphs, it is easier to identify patterns and see trends. Spreadsheets also enable analysts to build models that can be used to examine the effects of changes using various assumptions and interrelationships between factors.

Another important trend that occurred during the 1980s and 1990s was the increased competitiveness experienced in most industries. Every decision became more important. Winning in business now requires that answers be more precise and decisions be made as rapidly as possible. More options need to be evaluated, and potential solutions have to be measured against corporate goals.

Our knowledge of business has also increased during the last decade. Academics and businesses have created more complex models or ways of approaching problems. Computers are used to analyze the corporate data using these models.

**FIGURE 8.3**

BUSINESS DECISIONS

Tactical decisions often involve attempts to improve efficiency. Models play an important role in these decisions. Several MIS tools are used to support tactical decisions. Most are classified as decision support systems (DSSs).

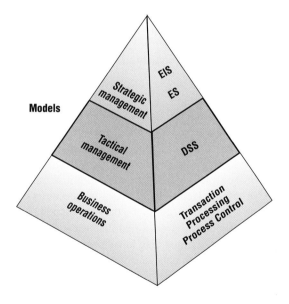

Information systems typically provide three levels of support for tactical decisions. First, they provide the data for the models. Second, technology provides support for building, evaluating, and analyzing models. Third, information systems provide the means to display the results in a variety of formats—especially graphs.

**DECISIONS**     The many levels of decisions and problems in business require many different types of models. Figure 8.3 should refresh your memory of the business decision levels. Operations problems tend to be well-defined and relatively easy to solve. They are largely supported by transaction-processing systems that collect the data. Managers at the tactical level who make less-structured decisions use this database.

What separates operations problems from tactical level decisions? Of course, there is no hard and fast line. Yet, there are some indicators that will help you classify problems into the appropriate level. First, look at the time frame. If the decision only affects the business for a day or two, it is probably at the operations level. Decisions with a time frame of around a year or less are likely to be tactical in nature. The real key is the complexity of the model involved in making the decision. More complex, less structured models lead us to classify the decision as tactical. Detailed examples of tactical decisions in various business areas are presented in Chapter 9.

Why do you care about the level of the decision? The basic reason for the classification is to make it easier for you to solve problems. If you can identify a problem as transaction oriented, you know that the solution will focus on the collection and integrity of the data. If a problem falls in the tactical decision level, the solution probably entails improving the decision support system (DSS). A major component of a DSS is the model.

**BIASES IN DECISIONS**

Making decisions can be difficult. If we ask managers to glance at a few pieces of data and make a decision, they will make mistakes. We know that people have **decision biases** and difficulties assessing data. If you understand these biases, it becomes clear that we need an organized means to evaluate data and make decisions. Additionally, as a manager, you should be aware of some of these problems, both in your own evaluations and when you make presentations to other managers.

Barabba and Zaltman analyzed decision making at General Motors and noticed that several common problems arose. In particular, they were concerned about decisions being made regarding the development of new automobiles. Figure 8.4 summarizes the biases in four primary categories: acquisition (input), processing, output, and feedback.

### Acquisition/Input

The first type of bias arises from the way we perceive data. People tend to place too much emphasis on events they just observed or on major events that receive news coverage. For example, many people are afraid of flying, whereas statistically, heart disease is a much more likely problem. People often misinterpret data statistically. They tend to discard data that does not fit their prior beliefs, thinking that it is merely an "outlier." Similarly, managers often have trouble identifying correlations between events. Even if two events happened at the same time, it does not mean they are related. If you put a new sales manager in a region and sales increase, does that mean that the sales manager was responsible? Perhaps. But the increase might also have been attributable to a change in consumer incomes. We need to evaluate the data carefully to make the correct determination.

### Processing

In processing or evaluating data, people make several common mistakes. They have difficulty being consistent from one decision to another. In evaluating new car options, managers might first prefer a streamlined, aerodynamic look. Several months later, they might decide that the aerodynamic look is too harsh and ask designers to add rounded corners and other aspects to soften the look. Similarly, we do not always incorporate new information. If some decision has traditionally been made one way, it is hard for managers to change their methods—even though the environment has changed. Complexity causes similar problems. When faced with complex decisions under uncertainty, people tend to simplify the problem by ignoring some aspect. Hundreds of variables might affect our forecast of sales for next year. Yet, many times

**FIGURE 8.4**

BIASES IN DECISION MAKING

Without models, people tend to rely on simplistic "rules of thumb" and fall prey to a variety of common mistakes. These errors can be minimized with training and experience in a discipline. They can also be minimized by having computer systems perform much of the initial analysis.

| ACQUISITION/INPUT | | |
|---|---|---|
| **BIAS** | **DESCRIPTION** | **EXAMPLE** |
| Data availability | Ease with which specific instances can be recalled affects judgments of frequency. | People overestimate the risk of dying due to homicides compared to heart disease. |
| Illusory correlation | Belief that two variables are related when they are not. | Ask any conspiracy buff about the death of JFK. |
| Data presentation | Order effects. | First (or last) items in a list are given more importance. |
| **PROCESSING** | | |
| Inconsistency | Difficulty in being consistent for similar decisions. | Judgments involving selection, such as personnel. |
| Conservatism | Failure to use new information completely. | Resistance to change. |
| Stress | Stress causes people to make hasty decisions. | Panic judgments and quick fixes. |
| Social pressure | Social pressures cause people to alter their decisions and decision-making processes. | Majority opinion can unduly influence everyone else: mob rule. |
| **OUTPUT** | | |
| Scale effects | The scale on which responses are recorded can affect responses. | Ask a group of people to rate how they feel on a scale from 1 to 10. Ask a similar group to use a scale from 1 to 1,000. |
| Wishful thinking | Preference for an outcome affects the assessment. | People sometimes place a higher probability on events that they want to happen. |
| **FEEDBACK** | | |
| Learning from irrelevant outcomes | People gain unrealistic expectations when they see incomplete or inaccurate data. | In personnel selection you see how good your selection is for candidates you accepted. You do not receive data on candidates you rejected. |
| Success/failure attributions | Tendency to attribute success to one's skill and failure to chance. | Only taking credit for the successes in your job. |

we simplify the problem by assuming that few things will change, and we simply project a 10 percent increase. In a related manner, people often look for simple rules, as long as they can be "justified." Finally, all of our decisions are affected by stress and social pressure. Faced with the pressure of a deadline or competition, people will rush and make decisions differently than if they took the time to study the problem.

## Output

Decisions are sometimes biased by the format of the output. Scales on graphs affect our interpretation. For instance, presenting results on a small handheld screen can give a different impression and lead managers to choose a different option than they would if they saw the graph on paper. Worse yet, people often choose outcomes based on wishful thinking. Some managers examine a list of possible outcomes and gravitate to the one with the best outcome. They sometimes think that if everyone simply tries hard enough, they can reach the best outcome. Sometimes this attitude is helpful to push the company higher. Other times it causes serious problems when managers ignore more likely outcomes.

## Feedback

Managers should alter their decision-making technique based on how well they perform on each decision. Unfortunately, we sometimes incorporate the feedback incorrectly. For example, when hiring new workers, you might congratulate yourself on choosing good workers. Yet, you rarely receive data on the candidates you rejected, so you do not really know if you made the best decision. Similarly, many people only take credit for successes. Either deliberately or unintentionally, they downplay their failures.

## Models and Information Systems

There is nothing inherently good or bad about these biases, they simply exist in most people. The first step to overcoming them is to recognize their existence. The second step is to carefully collect accurate data. Finally, the biases point out the need for models. When correctly used, models can provide consistency and improve decisions by minimizing individual biases. Of course, poorly designed models might simply incorporate and institutionalize these same biases.

Information systems can help minimize problems with data acquisition. By providing access to the data and sorting it in different ways, managers get a complete picture of the situation. By making it easy to perform statistical tests, managers do not have to rely on their intuition.

If we could computerize the entire decision-making process, processing and feedback biases would be minimized. However, most situations are difficult to automate. Chapter 10 examines a few of the complex situations that we can automate. In other cases, we rely on managers to use an appropriate model. As computers become more powerful and less expensive, managers can evaluate more complex models. Simulation tools also enable managers to examine the potential outcome of their solutions *before* they are implemented. By looking at more options and evaluating the outcomes, managers identify better decisions.

The strength of information systems lies in their ability to present results in a variety of formats. By viewing results from several different perspectives and in different formats, a manager gets a clearer picture of the problems and potential solutions.

**INTRODUCTION TO MODELS**

As defined earlier, a *model* is a simplified, abstract representation of some real-world system. It is simplified because we cannot handle all of the details of the real system. In fact, simplification is a major reason to build models. However, it must contain enough features of the original system that it behaves the same way. Models represent systems, so they are built from a collection of related subsystems.

## Physical

Models are used for many different purposes, and there are several different types of models. Most people are familiar with physical models. Movie studios build physical models so they can destroy them without injuring people or expensive property. Archi-

## Reality Bytes    8–1    It Is Better to Crash and Burn in Simulations

Engineers have always known that it is better to practice and experiment before trying a new strategy in the real world. Pilots and astronauts train in realistic simulators to learn to handle dangerous situations without risking lives or expensive equipment. Business managers are just beginning to gain some of the tools needed to test their ideas before committing to a real-world trial. At the high end, Advanced Competitive Strategies (ACS) (www.competing.com) offers computer software called ValueWar to help managers participate in complex war games. As managers adopt strategies and challenge each other, the computer projects the effect on costs and revenues. Similar products are available from Innovation Associates (www.arthurdlittle.com/ia) and Booz, Allen & Hamilton (www.bah.com), who have applied their experience with military war games to the business environment.

tects construct models to help clients and builders visualize a building and its surroundings. Automobile designers build models (prototypes) so they can test consumer responses. Engineers build models to test specifications and examine aerodynamic properties. In the case of a physical model, generally the goal is to create a model that can be constructed cheaply that behaves like the original system.

Physical models have limitations. They can be expensive to build, especially as you try to add more detail. A small-scale model of a building that concentrates on size and wall placement can be easy to create. But if you want to add details such as interior trim, window treatments, and furniture, you need to hire talented artists to work with the small scale. Even more importantly, physical models are relatively difficult to change. For instance, automobile designers once built full-size clay models of new designs. The clay enabled them to make minor style changes, but large changes (such as length) essentially required starting over.

The declining costs and improved capabilities of technology have given designers new tools with which to build models. In particular, computer-aided design (CAD) tools make it easy to create visual models of physical items. As shown in Figure 8.5, these systems enable designers to create realistic, three-dimensional images of virtually any physical item. They are used to design buildings, landscapes, automobiles, airplanes, machinery, and all of the related components. Designers and clients can view the objects from any angle, under different lighting conditions. With high-resolution displays, the designs look like photographs of a real product.

CAD systems overcome two of the major problems with physical models. It is easier to add details, and it is much easier to make changes to the designs. In many cases, the designer can try out various changes and immediately see the effect. This interactivity can significantly speed the design process.

CAD systems provide two additional advantages. First, they make it easy to share the designs. With networks, designers from several countries can work on the same design at the same time. Automobile manufacturers have used these techniques to cut years from their development cycles. Second, most CAD designs are more than simple drawings. The objects are stored internally as mathematical relationships. At a simple level, consider a three-dimensional drawing. The design is actually stored as a set of coordinates in three-dimensional space. The designer can use this mathematical representation to perform various tests of the model. For example, CAD systems can estimate the heating and cooling systems needed for each architectural design. They can be used to

**FIGURE 8.5**
COMPUTER-AIDED
DESIGN
Designers traditionally
build models before
attempting to create a
physical product. CAD
systems make it easier
to create diagrams and
share them with
multiple designers.
Portions of drawings
can be stored and used
in future products.
Sample products can
be evaluated and tested
using a variety of
computer simulations.

estimate the weight of an automobile. They can also be used to test the aerodynamic effects of a design.

## Process

It is relatively easy to see the uses for models of physical items, but they are only one type of model. Other models are symbolic or descriptive. Recall the data flow diagram techniques presented in Chapter 3, which are used to display business processes. These diagrams are models of the underlying system. Models of processes have been used for many years, especially in manufacturing. Figure 8.6 illustrates a small process for handling custom orders. Engineers use process models to evaluate the flow of materials and products through the production process. They examine diagrams and mathematical models to identify problems and improve efficiency and quality.

Process models often use drawings and pictures to represent the various objects. However, at heart they typically use mathematical equations to represent the process and the various relationships. For example, an operations engineer would model a machine as a mathematical formula that converts raw materials and labor into products. Using equations for each step of the production process, the engineer could search for ways to reorganize production to make it more efficient or to improve quality.

## Business Modeling

We build models of a business or business process to help managers make decisions. Most businesses are far too complex for any single person to understand all of the details. Consequently, a variety of models may be created to present a simplified view of the business. In particular, one of the original purposes of accounting was to create a standardized model of the financial aspects of business. Another common model of business is the practice of dividing the company into functional areas. For example, a manager with experience in the finance department of one company can usually apply knowledge and problem-solving skills to finance departments in other companies and even other industries.

In the early to mid-1900s, two popular modeling techniques were derived from engineering concepts. Many companies used time-study models and work process flows to

**FIGURE 8.6**

Simple model of evaluation of custom orders. Data flow diagrams are useful models of business processes. They focus on relationships among entities and the various processes. Each process can be modeled to any desired level of detail.

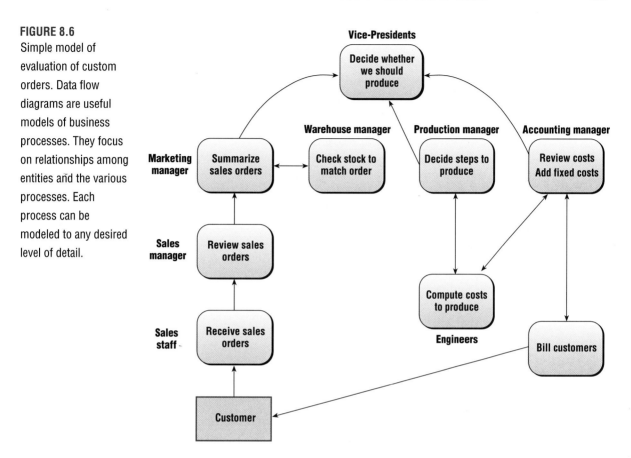

evaluate their firms and change their processes. The objective of these methods was to measure the business processes by the amount of time spent on each task and by tracing the number of steps each item followed. By identifying the redundant steps or the components that took the most time, managers would know which items needed to be changed.

In the 1990s, one modeling technique that gained increasing attention became known as **re-engineering.** The objective of this technique is to analyze and model the critical business processes and make major changes to the operation of the business. The underlying assumption is that small changes over time can eventually cause a business to be misaligned with the ideal target. Hence, the purpose of re-engineering is to make fundamental changes to the firm, improving efficiency and quality while better meeting the needs of the customers. The key feature in re-engineering is building a model of the business processes and creating an improved model from scratch. For example, the small model in Figure 8.6 could be used to track the number of orders and amount of time products spend in each department. Backlogs and redundant reviews could be identified and eliminated, making the process more efficient.

**WHY BUILD MODELS?**

Of the thousands of models in business, some are simple rules-of-thumb that managers use to make quick decisions. Others are highly abstract, often expressed as detailed mathematical equations. Some models are incredibly detailed and require thousands of data variables, like economic forecasting models. Other models are descriptions of situations or behavior, such as motivational recommendations based on personality types. Why do we have so many different models?

The basic goals are summarized in Figure 8.7. The main reason we need models is because reality is too complex and hard to understand. Models help us simplify the world. They help us search for similarities in different situations. Models also enable managers to predict how changes might affect the business.

Consider a small example. You have an older car that has about 80,000 miles on it. You received a small raise in your job and are thinking about purchasing a newer car. Your initial impressions are swayed by the hundreds of automobile commercials you see and you would really like to buy a new car. You checked prices and dealer invoice costs using the Internet and are excited about buying a new car. On the other hand, you know that new cars lose 10 to 15 percent of their value as soon as you drive them off the lot. A friend suggested that you should keep your old car for another year, but you are worried that it might lose too much value by next year.

You have just created a model. Part of the model is based on historical sales data, which tells you how fast new cars depreciate in value. Another part of the model uses economic data to estimate the potential value of your used car if you keep it and add miles for another year. To make an informed decision, you could create a simple forecast of automobile prices to estimate what might happen to new car prices next year. You could then create a spreadsheet to analyze the cost of buying a new car. By using standard discount functions, you could compare the total cost of your choices.

As the decision maker, it is up to you to determine which models to use and to make sure they actually apply to the situation. Once you have selected the appropriate model, you apply whatever data you have, evaluate the results, and make the decision.

## Understanding the Process

One of the primary reasons for building models is to help understand how the world behaves. Without a model or idea, how can you determine how things work? Citicorp uses a model to determine how well the banking firm is serving customers. By comparing the model results both to actual practice and to their corporate standards, Citicorp managers get a measure of the quality of their service. Models that explain how things work can be used to solve other problems. Models are also used to determine cause-and-effect relationships.

**FIGURE 8.7**
MODEL BUILDING
The four primary reasons for building and using models. Descriptive, graphical, and mathematical models can be used for each of these purposes. However, mathematical models tend to be emphasized for optimization and simulation.

*Understand the Process*
Models force us to define objects and specify relationships. Modeling is a first step in improving the business processes.

*Optimization*
Models are used to search for the best solutions: Minimizing costs, improving efficiency, increasing profits, and so on.

*Prediction*
Model parameters can be estimated from prior data. Sample data is used to forecast future changes based on the model.

*Simulation*
Models are used to examine what might happen if we make changes to the process or to examine relationships in more detail.

Some models are accurate and work well in a wide variety of situations. Other models seem haphazard and generate incorrect results. One reason for the difference is that some processes are harder to understand. For example, most of the physics models that you know are concrete and work well in daily situations. On the other hand, weather forecasters have many models, but it seems that they are wrong a lot of the time. One of the reasons is because weather depends on the entire biosphere, which is exceedingly complex. Similarly, some economic models are highly accurate. We know that if the government increases taxes on gasoline, the price will rise. Some economic models will even tell you how fast and how far the price will rise—within a few tenths of a cent. Yet economic forecasts for an entire economy are often wrong because the system being modeled is much more complex.

Along with the difficulty in understanding complex processes, some processes can never be modeled accurately. Sometimes there is too much variability in the underlying process. As a simple example, consider a roulette wheel with 38 possible numbers. Even if we build a model to explain how a roulette wheel works, it will not help us predict which number will show up next (unless the wheel is broken or rigged). The roulette wheel was designed to be a system with a large random component. We can model how it will behave on average over time, but that does not help us determine the next outcome. Many systems in the real world have large, random components, particularly if they involve subjective choices by people. We might be able to predict on average how a group of 50,000 consumers will respond to a marketing approach, but randomness makes it difficult to predict how one specific consumer will react.

## Optimization

In business, an important reason for building models is to help us make the *best* choice possible. Without a model, we can experiment, and we might get lucky enough to make a

---

### Reality Bytes 8–2 Federal Express Optimizes Problems

Some of the more complicated decisions faced at Federal Express (FedEx) involve routing packages and assigning planes and pilots to routes. A myriad of regulations must be followed, and even minor changes could result in saving millions of dollars. So, in June 1998, Federal Express replaced its laborious manual decision procedures with a new computer system. The goal was to find more efficient routes and increase productivity. Within a few weeks, however, pilots were screaming. They were often routed across time zones in two hemispheres and given back-to-back transatlantic and transpacific flights. Oftentimes they had to travel for hours in shuttles and taxis to change aircraft. Even worse, many of the pilots lost their hometown layovers. By August, FedEx acknowledged the problems and backed off from the system.

For years, the pilots were one of the most valuable assets to FedEx. Many grew their careers along with FedEx and had tremendous loyalty to the company. In exchange, work rules were relatively loose and pilots were given a fair amount of flexibility and freedom. By August 1998, the pilots were so upset they finally agreed to join a union.

Tom Ivaskiv, CEO of Ad Opt Technologies, which developed the Optimizer, notes that the system has worked well at other airlines. However, other airlines had many more specific rules regarding flights and pilots. At FedEx, there were few official rules, which gave the Optimizer more freedom to find better solutions, but which caused problems for the pilots—particularly the pilots who had less seniority. Some of the pilots agree with Mr. Ivaskiv. For example, pilot Ron MacGarvey notes that "the Optimizer does essentially whatever they tell it to do. It's very efficient at what it does, but they have taken some very loosely worded work rules we had and ratcheted them down to where they're untenable."

**FIGURE 8.8**

OPTIMIZATION MODEL
Optimization models
are formed by
identifying the control
variables and the
output or goals. With a
mathematical model, it
is possible to locate a
maximum or minimum
point for the goal. Many
problems are complex
and highly nonlinear
problems do not always
have a solution.

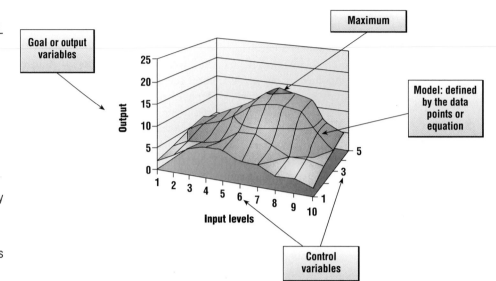

decision that gives us good results. But if we really want to find the optimum choice, we must first build a model that accurately describes the underlying process. Then we can find a solution for the model that gives the best result. Figure 8.8 illustrates the basic concepts with a simple model using two-input variables.

There are many examples of optimization models in business operations. For instance, how many tellers should a bank have on duty at one time? What is the blend of fuels that will produce the lowest-cost gasoline? What price should a company charge for a new product? The teller problem can be analyzed with a queuing theory model. Fuel blending is typically analyzed with a mathematical programming approach. The pricing problem uses models from marketing research and economic models of prices, costs, and profits.

**Optimization** is a complex subject that typically evaluates mathematical models to find a "best" solution. The average business manager will not be expected to create his or her own mathematical optimization models. On the other hand, you will be expected to know that models exist to solve certain types of problems, and you should know how to apply these basic models. Computer software can be used to solve the model and evaluate the alternatives.

## Prediction

An important use of models is for **prediction.** If a model is reasonably accurate, it can be used to predict future outcomes. For instance, in the used automobile example it would be possible to estimate how the price of used cars changes over time.

Prediction first requires that you have a model that describes the situation. Then data is collected and statistical techniques are used to estimate the **parameters** of the model for the specific problem. Next you fill in any parameters that you already know, and the model provides a prediction. Sometimes the prediction will be a specific number, other times it will be a range of possible values. Occasionally predictions are descriptive, such as "prices will increase slightly."

Statistical methods and **descriptive models** can be used to describe situations. Descriptive statistics such as means and variances are useful to help managers identify and classify problems. Prediction techniques such as regression and time series forecasting are used to examine the data, identify trends, and predict possible future changes. To use statistics effectively requires a model of the underlying system. For instance, to use regression methods you first identify the dependent variable and a set of possible indepen-

**FIGURE 8.9**

PREDICTION MODEL
Several statistical
techniques exist for
analyzing data and
making forecasts. Two
common methods are
regression and moving
averages. Both
methods require
substantial amounts of
data. Choosing
between the two
requires some
expertise in statistical
analysis, but many
times we display both
methods to show a
range of possible
outcomes.

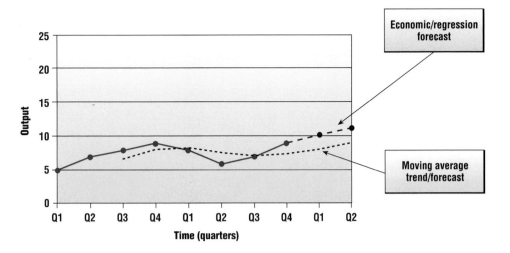

dent variables. These choices come from the underlying model. Figure 8.9 illustrates how a spreadsheet or graphics package can be used to display the results of a forecast. With an integrated system, the results from a statistical model could be fed to the graphics package, automatically updating the graph for changes in assumptions.

## Simulation or "What-If" Scenarios

**Simulation** is a modeling technique with many uses. Once a model is created, managers use simulation to examine how the item being studied will respond to changes. With simulation, various options can be tested on the model to examine what might happen. For example, engineers always build models of airplanes and engines before they try to build the real thing. The models are much cheaper. In fact, most engineers today start with mathematical computer models because they are cheaper to create than physical models and can contain more detail. Additionally, they can perform experiments on models that would not be safe to perform in real life. For example, an engineer could stress a model of an airplane until it broke up. It would be dangerous and expensive to try such an experiment on a real plane. Similarly, a business model could examine what would happen if prices were increased by 20 percent, without worrying about losing real money.

### Business Trends

Models are closely related to one of the business trends discussed in Chapter 1: management by methodology. To manage a large business and ensure consistency, many companies have created methods (or processes) for each task. For instance, a package-delivery company will have specific instructions for delivery people, clerks, and other line workers. Management reports are created a certain way each week or month and routed to a specified list of managers.

These rules make it easier to train new employees, provide more consistent service, and enable man-

agers to control the company. But how do managers create the rules? Trial and error (or experience) is one possibility. However, for more complex problems, managers begin with a model of the business. Depending on the situation, the model might be used for optimization, prediction, or simulation. By using a model, managers can examine and test alternative methodologies without harming the actual business. As the resulting methodologies are implemented, reactions can be used to alter the underlying model, improving it for future use.

**FIGURE 8.10**

Simulation models explore many alternatives. This example shows how output might change in response to a control variable for three scenarios. The first step in simulation is to identify the input (control) and output variables. Then a (mathematical) model is built that measures the response of the output variables to changes in the inputs. The model is examined for several different levels of each input variable.

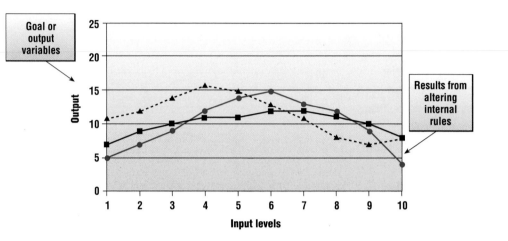

Most simulation models are mathematical instead of descriptive models, because they are easy to evaluate. Mathematical models contain parameters, or variables that can be controlled by the managers. For instance, you might use a spreadsheet to create an accounting model of an income statement and balance sheet. When you create the spreadsheet, production quantity and price of your products are controllable parameters that affect the income and profits of the firm. You could use the model to investigate decisions, like the effect on profits if you increase production. Costs will increase, but so will revenue from sales. The net result depends on the specific details of the firm and the model. Figure 8.10 presents sample output from a simulation. Spreadsheets are often used to analyze small models and graph the results. More sophisticated simulation packages can support more complex analysis and will automatically create graphs and pictures to show interrelationships.

The more complex the model, the more alternatives that can be simulated. In the last example, a more detailed model might enable you to investigate alternatives such as increased overtime, hiring another shift, building additional plants, or subcontracting the work to another firm.

**DECISION SUPPORT SYSTEMS: DATABASE, MODEL, OUTPUT**

By now you should have an inkling of how MIS can help you make decisions. **Decision support systems (DSSs)** were created to help managers make **tactical decisions.** As illustrated in Figure 8.11, a DSS provides support in three main categories: data collection, analysis of models, and presentation.

Notice that data collection is typically performed by the transaction-processing system. Thus, if the transaction system is not working properly, the DSS will not work either. Also note that a fundamental difference between a transaction system and a DSS is the support for creating and evaluating models.

You cannot make good decisions without data, so databases are a fundamental component of a DSS. The issues of data quality and availability raised in Chapters 4 and 5 apply equally well to DSS. However, decision support systems require more than just collecting and storing the data. It is important that the data be easily accessible to the decision maker. To make rapid, competitive decisions, the decision maker needs to retrieve data and transfer it to the model. Similarly, the predictions, simulations, and even the model itself need to be shared with colleagues.

It is sometimes difficult to get access to the transaction data within the company's legacy systems. For starters, the transaction-processing systems were designed to collect and store huge amounts of data very quickly. The systems often cannot handle the additional load

**FIGURE 8.11**

DECISION SUPPORT SYSTEMS

A DSS provides support for tactical-level decisions. It has features to query data, analyze and store models, and present results. Some systems are designed to solve specific problems. Other systems use standard components (e.g., database management system, spreadsheet, and graphics packages) with applications that are tailored to each problem.

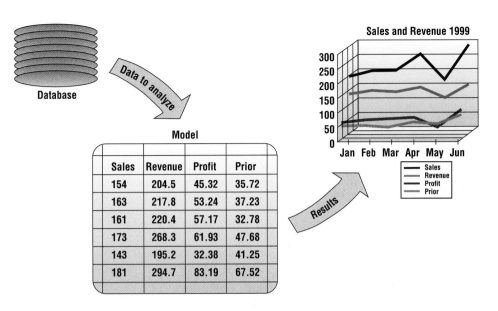

| Model | | | |
|---|---|---|---|
| Sales | Revenue | Profit | Prior |
| 154 | 204.5 | 45.32 | 35.72 |
| 163 | 217.8 | 53.24 | 37.23 |
| 161 | 220.4 | 57.17 | 32.78 |
| 173 | 268.3 | 61.93 | 47.68 |
| 143 | 195.2 | 32.38 | 41.25 |
| 181 | 294.7 | 83.19 | 67.52 |

of providing searches and aggregations needed for making decisions. Additionally, data collected from different parts of the organization may be stored in incompatible formats. Consequently, to support decision making, many companies have created data warehouses. A **data warehouse** consists of data that is collected from the transaction-processing systems. The data is reformatted and consolidated so that it is consistent. The database is designed so that it provides the fast searches and aggregations needed by decision support systems.

Software packages exist to create and analyze many types of models. Specific models and modeling software are discussed in more detail in the following sections and in Chapter 9. Spreadsheets continue to add more analysis tools. More powerful standalone packages are available to perform statistical and mathematical analyses.

At first glance, it might seem strange to include output as a characteristic of a DSS. Yet, if the system cannot produce output in a format that is easy to understand, then it will not be useful. Graphs are an important feature of DSS output. Most people find it easier to spot trends and relationships on a graph than from a table of numbers.

When you are generating output to be used to make decisions, you should remember one feature of the corporate world: Few decisions are made by one person. A large part of the decision-making process involves persuading other people that you are right. Reports that are concise, accurate, and visually appealing can be persuasive.

Decision support systems can range from simple spreadsheets to complex, integrated systems designed to share decisions across the organization. Sometimes individual managers build their own systems. Some systems can be purchased from outside vendors. Other systems can be built and coordinated by the MIS department.

## BUILDING MODELS

Once managers have access to the data, they can build models to analyze the data and solve problems. Building models is an extension of the systems approach presented in Chapter 3. A model is built as a collection of subsystems that match the real-world system. Each subsystem consists of inputs, processes, and outputs. In mathematical models, these relationships are expressed with equations. As explained in Chapter 3, the first step is to decompose the problem into smaller pieces. The next step is to identify input and output variables. The third step is to define the processes and determine how they behave mathematically. The resulting model equations are usually programmed into the computer.

## Assumptions

A key feature of all models is the **assumptions** made by the builder. Models are designed to be simplifications of reality, which means that some details have been left out. Models are generally built for specific situations; they may not apply in every case. Modelers use explicit assumptions to highlight the situations where the model can be used effectively. Whenever you evaluate models, a key place to begin is to look at the assumptions. Be careful; sometimes not all assumptions are spelled out.

Students sometimes complain about studying unrealistic models. These complaints often arise because of the assumptions in the model. Keep in mind that it is far easier to understand a model if you start with a smaller, simpler version. As you modify assumptions, the models become more realistic, but they also become more complex.

## Identifying Input and Output Variables

In a model, each subsystem receives data through input variables, processes the data, and alters the output variables. Output variables are chosen with respect to your goals. Profit will be a typical output variable for a firm. There are also output variables for the various departments. For instance, quantity produced and quality ratings are common output variables for a manufacturing department. As long as the company has well-defined goals, it is relatively easy to identify the relevant output variables.

Input variables can be almost anything. In production systems, they might be quantities of raw materials, labor hours, or money invested in capital equipment. Marketing departments looking at sales relationships would examine input variables such as prices, promotions, consumer demographics, and quality ratings. Notice that output variables (e.g., quality) for one system will be input variables to other systems.

As shown in Figure 8.12, a major task in many models is to identify the important input variables. Statistical techniques (such as factor analysis and multiple regression) are often used to identify and determine weights for input variables. Statistical packages (like SAS and SPSS), and some spreadsheets have made it much easier to use statistical tools. However, statistics can only be used effectively if you understand the model. You cannot test every possible variable and hope that the statistics reveal useful relationships. You need a model to determine which variables *cause* changes in others.

**FIGURE 8.12**
MODEL BUILDING
To build models, you first identify each subsystem by specifying the processes, inputs, and outputs. Assumptions are made to simplify the problem. For mathematical models, you identify the variables that can be controlled and define the equations that specify the relationships. Use statistical techniques to estimate model parameters and make forecasts. Simulations can then be used to test assumptions and evaluate alternatives.

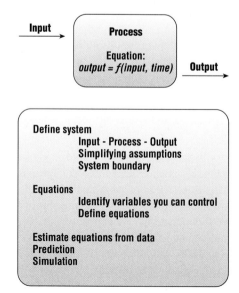

## Processes and Equations

Functions or processes take the input data and transform it into outputs. For instance, consider metal-working machines that can take blocks of aluminum, roll it out, cut it, and produce aluminum cans. Inputs would be the aluminum blocks, electricity, the number of machines, and human labor. Output is measured by the number of cans. Based on the characteristics of the machine, a production function determines how many cans will be produced from the inputs. The equation in Figure 8.13 is one possible example of the relationship.

Notice that if any of the inputs is zero, there will be no output, and output can be increased by increasing any of the inputs. The actual values of the coefficients will depend on how we measure the variables and on the machines being used. The specific values could be statistically estimated from test runs of the machine at different combinations of the inputs.

An important question arises with this example: How do we know which type of equation to use? It is not enough to know the variables, you also have to know how they fit together. Perhaps a linear equation (e.g., $Q = 9.4\,A + 1.5\,E + 4.3\,L$) would provide a better explanation of the process. A major question in modeling involves choosing the appropriate equations to explain the underlying relationships. Advanced statistical techniques offer some help in choosing functions. But the best method is to understand the process thoroughly. In this case, the engineers who designed the machine should know which mathematical model best describes the machine.

In other situations, the best method to determine the proper relationships is to refer to an expert. Recall that this chapter began by noting that one of the goals of a business education was to teach you the various models used in each discipline. Other people have already created thousands of models for you to use. You just have to understand them and know when to apply each model. To help you out, some common models and applications will be examined in Chapter 9.

## Software

Once you understand models and the modeling process, it is easier to see how MIS can help build and evaluate models. Clearly the first step is to provide easy access to the data. Data is used to identify input variables, estimate model equations, and drive simulations. However, decision support systems go a step further and help the decision maker create and evaluate various models. There are two basic categories of DSS software: generic and preprogrammed.

### Generic Modeling Tools

The advantage to generic modeling tools is that they can be applied to any situation or business. The drawback is that you have to build the models yourself. For example, SAS is a collection of software packages that can be used to build a complete DSS. The tools include a DBMS, advanced statistical analysis, graphing support, and optimization techniques. It contains the base tools you need to create and evaluate complex models. But by themselves, the SAS programs know nothing about finance, marketing, accounting, or other business models. You apply your knowledge and equations to create the model. Other statistical software packages help you model and statistically evaluate the processes within an organization.

Spreadsheets can also be used as generic modeling tools. Current versions provide some statistics capabilities (regression), can solve small optimization problems, and can be used for simulations that involve a small number of variables. They are particularly

**FIGURE 8.13**
PRODUCTION
EQUATION

Simple production relationship that shows how output ($Q$) changes in response to three input variables: capital assets ($A$), energy ($E$), and labor ($L$).

$$Q = (6.5)\,A^{0.7}\,E^{0.1}\,L^{0.2}$$

## Reality Bytes　　8–3　The Wala Group

In the last decade, people have increasingly sought healthier diets. As nutritionists have recommended foods lower in fat, consumers have increased their purchases of chicken and turkey. This increased demand has affected the entire meat-production industry. Managers in the industry face new decisions at every step from growth to processing to marketing and distribution. The process is complicated because of the high level of integration. Decisions at one level strongly affect the outcomes of the other steps. For example, growers can produce larger birds, but it takes more time, and the birds may not produce the final components (e.g., amount of breast meat or leg meat) that are demanded by consumers. As a manager, how can you evaluate the choices and examine all of the interactions? Remember that even a small savings in cost—a few pennies per pound—can amount to millions of dollars a year.

The answer lies in gaining a better understanding of the bird physiology. The Wala Group in Minneapolis is a leader in this research. From the foundations of biology and nutrition, their researchers built a mathematical model of growth. By analyzing the nutritional input value of the feed, the model can predict the exact growth of the bird, including the various components. For example, based on what the bird is fed, the system will predict the final composition of bird meat, such as breast weight, wings, and amount of fat. Using a complex mathematical optimization process, the model can identify the best way to feed the birds.

But their system goes even further. The Wala Group's CAMERA system "optimizes the meat production process with respect to the net income of the operation. This optimization enables business managers to improve their bottom-line results by fine-tuning the many trade-offs between cost reduction, revenue and income generation, and meat throughput that exist in the meat supply chain." With research backed by two patents, the CAMERA system enables managers to examine every aspect of the production process. By modeling and optimizing the entire process on the computer, the system enables managers to evaluate alternatives, avoiding the time and risk of experimenting in the real-world production system. The system works because the Wala Group's researchers have already performed the experiments and built a mathematical model of the entire process.

useful for finance and accounting problems because they have several predefined functions that are commonly used in those areas.

There are several other generic modeling tools. You can purchase simulation tools such as GPSS, SIMSCRIPT, and MODSIM III. As shown in Figure 8.14, some tools enable you to build a complete graphical representation of the process and run the simulation by drawing objects on the screen and defining the interrelationships. For instance, a traffic engineer could test a traffic light system by drawing streets, cars, and the lights on the screen. After defining how each object behaves, the computer will run the simulation and display the actions on the screen. Available tools such as IMAGINE-IT are specifically designed to help managers model the business organization. These tools are useful for re-engineering because managers can test and evaluate the effects of changes without disturbing the actual operations.

To maximize production, minimize costs, and improve quality you need to know more about how the control variables influence the outputs. To gain this understanding, you can perform experiments, varying each control level and measuring the output variables. One problem with experiments, however, is that they cost money and time. For instance, to conduct an experiment with a machine, a manager has to take it off the production line and pay someone to try the many input combinations, measure the output variables, and analyze the results.

With any process, it is generally impossible to evaluate every combination of input levels because there are too many possible settings, and it would be too expensive to test them

**FIGURE 8.14**

OBJECT-ORIENTED SIMULATION

A simple example of custom manufacturing. Each object (parts list, purchase order, etc.) and each process are defined in detail by the modeler. The simulation system generates orders, makes shipments, and orders inventory according to programmed rules. The simulator collects a wide variety of statistics that can be displayed graphically (as in Figure 8.10) or in tabular reports.

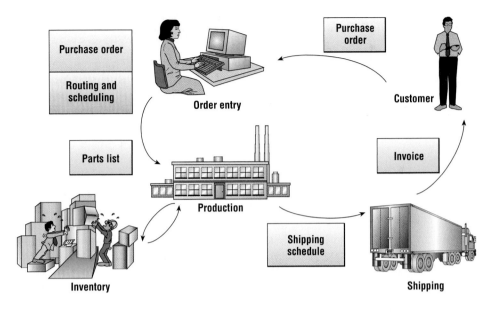

all. Consequently, statisticians have devised several methods to evaluate processes using a smaller set of data. Each technique has certain advantages, examines slightly different combinations of input data, and uses a different statistical technique to analyze the data.

Information systems can be used to help analyze processes, design the appropriate experiment, and analyze the results. One tool specifically designed for this purpose is a personal computer package called DOE-Wisdom from Madcat Software. DOE-Wisdom helps the worker choose a design method. It then selects the appropriate control levels to be tested and asks the decision maker to perform the experiments and enter the resulting data. The software automatically performs several analyses of the data and presents the results in tables and a variety of graphs. Using the data from the experiment, the software then builds a model of the process. In addition to the graphical presentation, the software helps the designer evaluate predictions using the model.

With a graphics-based simulation package, the objects are displayed on the screen and the simulator moves the objects so the decision maker can see the resulting interactions. For example, this process could be used to display the flow of information or products through various steps in the company. As illustrated in Figure 8.14, the object can be modified at each step, or new objects can be created. By adding timing attributes, the simulator can portray the actual movement. The analyst can alter various parameters and see how they affect the overall system, looking for bottlenecks and solutions to problems.

In the example, the primary function of the customer object is to generate purchase orders. The timing and frequency of orders is a control parameter. The orders are processed by the order-entry department, which schedules the jobs and sets timetables for the production department. The order-entry department evaluates a small optimization function to set priorities for various jobs depending on the customer, type of product, and marketing objectives. In this situation, production is treated as a black box, which is not concerned about how production actually converts inputs into final products. In a real company, configuring optimal production lines and schedules is an important area of simulation and optimization. The inventory department uses models to determine quantities and delivery times so that the production line always has the items it needs. In the last step, the shipping department consolidates shipments by geographic area and distributes the products to the customer.

## Building Quality Models in Spreadsheets

Many models are built using spreadsheets. In many respects, spreadsheets are similar to more traditional computer programs. Yet, designers rarely include comments that explain their intentions. Hence, when spreadsheets are passed to other users, there is enormous potential for mistakes and problems. You need to consider these problems when you create a spreadsheet and you should check other users' spreadsheets for them.

One common problem is the use or misuse of absolute and relative addresses (using the dollar sign to keep a cell reference from changing). Say that cell B1 holds the current hourly wage rate. Other cells can use that value to compute the cost of workers: =B1*C7. To be safe, the formula should be written as: =$B$1*C7. Without the absolute address, copying the formula to a new location will cause the B1 pointer to change, yielding incorrect results. These changes can be hard for later users to spot.

Be on the lookout for hidden columns, hidden rows, or hidden worksheets. Current spreadsheet software enables users to hide portions of the spreadsheet. There might be errors in these hidden segments—look for missing rows or columns. First save a backup copy, then "unhide" all of the rows and columns.

Beware of formulas in which the cell references have been changed to "hard" numbers or literals. Walter Schmidt, a CPA, recalls the time he gave a spreadsheet to a client that computed the interest expense deduction for the client's taxes. At some point, the client discovered that the interest deduction was too low. On investigation, Schmidt learned that one of the client's employees had changed a cell reference to a constant value. When the spreadsheet was changed, the formula did not pick up the changes, leading to the wrong number.

Most current spreadsheets can present a "map view" of the spreadsheet, in which special characters indicate the purpose of each cell: value, formula, or label. These characters can help you spot formulas in which the entire cell has been accidentally replaced by a constant. You will still have to check individual formulas by hand. Other tools enable you to see how each cell depends on (or is used by) other cells. These tools are useful to spot cells that are no longer needed and to highlight circular references.

You can also protect spreadsheets by locking cells containing formulas. That way users will not accidentally overwrite your model.

Another useful trick is to make sure that any operations performed on columns have a "nice" starting and ending point. Place a line in the cell above the first row and after the last row. If the data range from B10 to B20, place a line in B9 and B21. Then any column operations should include the lines: SUM(B9:B21). The lines will not affect the computation. More importantly, if someone tries to insert a row before the first entry (B10), the new value will be included in the final total. If the original cell range only extended from B10 to B20, inserting a row before B10 would not update the total.

Cells and ranges should be given names. Then, instead of referring to a cell by its address, formulas will use the full name, making it easier to understand the purpose of the formula. Names are especially useful when you are linking spreadsheets.

Current spreadsheets make it easy to add notes to any cell. Use the notes to document the purpose of the cell and to answer questions that co-workers might have when they look at your spreadsheet. Be sure to reference the source of all equations and models.

---

Each of these physical objects has attributes such as capacity, time required to complete a job, and cost. They have internal functions, typically created from optimization and scheduling models. The functions respond to the data objects and produce the desired outputs that are sent to the next step.

In a graphical simulation, the computer randomly generates customer orders. As the orders pass through each stage, the computer executes the processing that takes place, adding a random time element to simulate human variances. At each step, the computer monitors the number of transactions taking place, the amount of time spent waiting because of delays, and the cost of the operations. These values are displayed on graphs. The person analyzing the model can alter underlying parameters to see what happens. For instance, if the order-entry scheduling system is changed, you would want to know how it will delay production and how it will affect delivery times, as well as total costs. Likewise, you could examine the effects of decreasing the inventory levels.

Like any simulation, the greatest difficulty lies in creating the underlying models. Each component (order entry, production, inventory, and shipping) must be defined mathematically. After specifying the inputs and outputs, the internal rules and procedures need to be written as mathematical statements. Most of the time, as you make the model more realistic, the number of variables and complexity of the model increases. But once the base model is constructed, it can be used to analyze a wide variety of problems.

### Preprogrammed and Specific Models

Because some situations occur in many different businesses, several companies have designed models and created software to help you solve specific problems. Some models are *add-ins* that run with other software (such as spreadsheet macros). Other versions are *standalone* and handle the complete problem from collecting data to evaluating models to producing output. In finance there are thousands of software packages that will capture stock market data, evaluate different finance models, and track your portfolio with graphs and summary statistics.

One feature to look for with preprogrammed models is how much control you have over the underlying model. If your problem has a slightly different twist, you might want to modify the model by altering the input variables or even the equations. As with any software, try to arrange a trial period to evaluate the software and make sure it can be applied correctly to your specific problem.

How do you find software packages to help model your specific problem? Probably the easiest place to begin is with magazines or journals that are aimed at your particular specialty. For instance, accounting magazines regularly evaluate and carry advertisements for accounting software. Magazines have reviews for almost any topic in which you might be interested. Another source of advice is user groups and web sites that carry discussions on the topics you need. Also, some commercial firms (such as Datapro) publish notices and evaluations of a wide variety of software.

## Model Complexity

LIMITATIONS OF MODELS Several problems can arise with models and simulation. These issues are summarized in Figure 8.15. First, there might be so many alternatives that it could take years to examine all of them. The catch is that more complex models tend to be more realistic, but they also take longer to evaluate. Of course, a faster computer can speed up the evaluation of the alternatives.

## Cost of Building Models

It can be expensive to build detailed models. Sometimes, it might be cheaper to make a decision (even if it is wrong) than to spend the money to build and evaluate the model. Unless you have a lot of spare time on your hands, it is probably not worthwhile to build a mathematical model to determine the optimal time for students to buy used textbooks, for example. The cost of building models is sometimes hidden. Creating a complex new model from scratch can take considerable time. In many cases, it is not possible to create a new model in time to make a decision. The trick is to build the base models ahead of

**FIGURE 8.15**
MODELING
LIMITATIONS
While models are very useful, they do have limitations. Managers must always remember that forecasts, simulations, and recommendations are only as good as the underlying model. These cautions do not mean we should discard models, only that we must be careful.

| Model complexity |
| Cost of building model |
| Errors in models |
| • Data |
| • Equations |
| • Presentation and interpretation |

time so they are available whenever a decision must be made. But then, how do you know whether you are spending too much on the models when you do not know whether they will be useful?

## Problems with Modeling

The other major problem is that models are not the same as reality. G. H. Hardy (a superb theoretical mathematician) once stated (*A Mathematician's Apology*) that he felt sorry for applied mathematicians because no matter how good they were, no matter how complex the models they built, the model could always be criticized because it did not accurately reflect the real world. Remember that predictions and simulations from models do not have to be 100 percent correct. Some variables could be incorrect, relationships can be missed, or results might be misinterpreted. However, these are not sufficient reasons to discard the entire process of modeling and simulation. Even a partial understanding is better than none. In many cases, simulations enable us to investigate situations that would be impossible with any other technique. But, it is important to understand the models being used so that you know which variables are important and which ones can be ignored. Several real-world problems have been traced to errors in using and applying models.

Three fundamental errors often arise in mathematical models: (1) flaws in the data, (2) flaws in the equations, and (3) flaws in display or interpretation of the results. Data errors can arise because of missing data, errors in collecting the data, or using the wrong data to build the model. Some models, especially those that rely on statistics, are highly sensitive to the database that was used to build the model. If someone tries to apply the model to a different problem area, it could give incorrect results. Similarly, if a model is tested with one set of data, but the actual system is exposed to completely different conditions, the model cannot be expected to provide completely accurate results.

Models based on mathematical equations can be extremely complex. For example, some economic models contain thousands of equations. It is difficult to ensure that all of the equations are correct and that they actually represent the way the original system works. Errors in even one equation could lead the decision maker to make major mistakes. Even for small models, you may hear horror stories from people who have lost money because of errors in their spreadsheet equations.

Presentation errors can also be difficult to spot. Chapter 2 raised the issue of the interpretation of graphics. Research has shown that people are sensitive to graphics features such as scale, dispersion, and color. Errors in interpretation can be the most difficult to spot, especially because different people can reach different conclusions when looking at the same output. One solution would be to have several different people examine the results. By combining their interpretations and discussing the results, you stand a better chance of avoiding misinterpretations.

## Reality Bytes    8–4    **Modeling and Simulation Problems**

The Hartford Civic Center Coliseum roof collapsed on January 18, 1978, from snow and ice. Apparently the wrong model was chosen when the beam construction was being simulated. After the collapse, the simulation was rerun with the correct model and it predicted the crash.

In development of the Handley-Page Victor aircraft, a wind-tunnel model, aerodynamic equations from a resonance test, and a low-speed flight test all indicated that there were no tailplane flutter problems. Unfortunately, all three models contained errors, and the tailplane broke off during the first flight test, killing the crew.

On April 1, 1991, a Titan 4 rocket booster blew up on the test pad. Extensive 3-D computer simulations missed a combination of subtle factors that contributed to the engine failure.

**FIGURE 8.16**

The Pilot Balanced ScoreCard by Pilot Software is a highly evolved form of an Executive Information System (EIS). The screen shown is a top level view of the four major perspectives of a business: customer, financial, internal, learning and growth. From this screen, a manager can drill down to better understand all major aspects of a business.

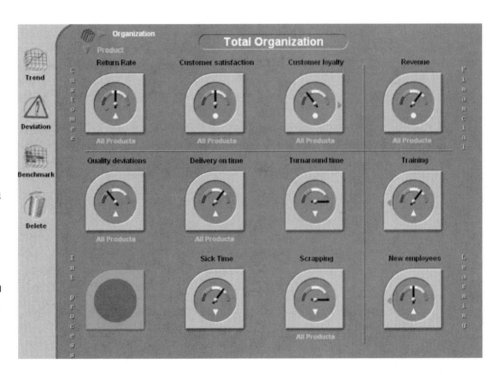

**A BUSINESS MODEL: ENTERPRISE INFORMATION SYSTEMS**

Many companies have moved beyond simply collecting data and are striving to produce systems that provide useful data to the executives and are also easy to use. An **enterprise (or executive) information system (EIS)** is designed to use the existing transaction data and display it in a form that is easy for top-level executives to access. To achieve this objective, the EIS is based on a model of the entire company. In most cases the output from the model is presented graphically, and the executives retrieve information by pointing to objects on the screen. A small portion of a sample EIS is shown in Figure 8.16.

## Description of an EIS

The first screen of an EIS can be a graphical representation of the company. A CEO can then point to a portion of the company on the screen and get reports for that division. If there is a problem or a decision to be made, the executive can **drill down** to get more detailed data by pointing to another object. For example, if the main screen shows that current sales in the west region are low, the executive can focus on the west region and bring up the last few quarters of sales data. The EIS will graph the data to highlight trends. The manager can then dig deeper and bring up sales by departments or check the sales performance of each employee, highlighting unusually high or low sales figures. By pointing to customers, the CEO can get current profiles on the main customers and examine their recent purchases. With a good EIS, the executives can retrieve this information instantaneously by pointing to objects on the screen.

## How Does an EIS Work?

For starters, for an EIS to work, it must be connected to the transaction-processing system or data warehouse, since it is the source of the data. Many of these systems are created with special software (e.g., Pilot) that simply grabs data from the corporate databases. In one sense, the EIS is a complex model of the firm. Figure 8.17 illustrates how executives can "visit" different divisions on the computer and retrieve the data immediately. For the EIS to be useful, the computer model must be a faithful representation of the actual company.

As a model, the EIS display has inputs of raw materials and people. Outputs are typically measured by traditional accounting standards of profits, costs, and growth rates. The

**FIGURE 8.17**
ENTERPRISE
INFORMATION
SYSTEM

As industries become more competitive, managers search for ways to evaluate and improve the overall operations. Enterprise systems collect data from across the firm and make it available to managers and top executives. Managers can start with an overview of the firm and drill down to various levels and departments to get more detailed data.

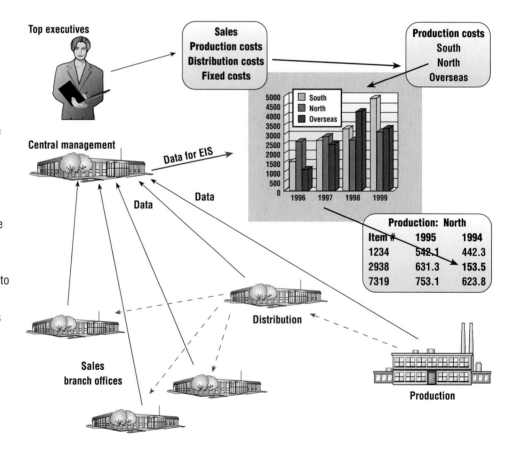

EIS maintains budgets and forecasts and can compare them to actual values. The functions and processes are determined from the individual departments. For instance, there could be a production model that describes the manufacturing output. An EIS at McDonnell Douglas has a graphics screen that displays portions of airplanes as they are being built. As a wing is completed, it is drawn onto the computer model.

## Advantages of an EIS

The primary goal of an EIS is to provide easy access to corporate data for the executives. Instead of waiting for a report, the top executives can retrieve the data as soon as it is available. Also, because all the data is accessible from the same system, it is easier to examine data from different departments to produce a better view of the big picture. Another useful feature is that the executive's use of the data is nonintrusive.

Imagine that you are CEO of a company, and you do not have an EIS. The monthly reports have just indicated that one of the warehouses is not running smoothly. You want to find out what the problems are. You suspect the warehouse manager is part of the problem, but you need to be sure. What do you do? The most direct approach is to go visit the warehouse. But what happens when you show up at the warehouse? It is likely that the manager and the workers will change the way they work. Your attempts to collect data have altered the way the system runs, so you will not get the information you wanted.

Other options include sending other people or asking for additional information via the chain-of-command. Although useful, these methods will be slower and the information you receive will be colored by the perceptions of the people collecting the data. For example, many people will try to focus on what they think you want to hear.

The EIS minimizes these problems by providing instant access to the corporate data. The executives can produce reports and examine departments without interfering with the operations of the company. Graphs can be created automatically. The executives can set up different scenarios or simulations. Most of these activities are accomplished simply by pointing to objects on the screen.

## Limitations of an EIS

The concept of an EIS sounds good: Give the top executives immediate access to all of the corporate data. In practice, an EIS is rarely that comprehensive and is usually difficult to implement. One of the biggest limitations is that in many companies, the corporate data is

---

**Reality Bytes     8-5   Dow Chemical Reorganizes Data and Company**

By implementing a data warehouse, Dow Chemical was able to reorganize business divisions and shut down or sell underperforming assets. In terms of basic transactions, the warehouse resulted in a 43 percent gain in reporting productivity, and 70 percent faster report generation. The system also provided new ways of looking at data. Instead of simple profit-and-loss statements, the tool provides value-based measurement—providing detailed data on total shareholder return from products and services. Mike Costa, a client manager at the Midland, Michigan, firm notes: "Our objective was to generate an income statement that takes into account recovering investment capital." This process means that managers need to drill down and see how each product and service is generating costs and revenues. The process is known as a value-based information system (VBIS). The company is now planning to expand the process into forecasting and planning. Costa observes: "We are going to try to use the same approach we used for VBIS, using data mining tools to help [the] forecasting process."

handled by older COBOL-based programs. It is difficult to translate this data into a database that can be searched by the executives. Many systems simply copy portions of the data into a small database. This method typically provides only a small subset of the data.

There is also a trade-off between ease of use and the flexibility of the EIS. An EIS is easiest to use if the designers know ahead of time exactly what questions might be asked. Executives can then click on each item they wish to see. However, if the managers stray from the predefined report, they have to create complex queries.

In addition, although the graphical interface and drill-down capabilities are elegant and easy to use, and EIS is expensive to create and maintain. Integrating the data and formatting it for ease of use requires programmers and analysts behind the scenes to anticipate management needs and keep the system up-to-date.

Overall, most top executives find it easier to ask lower level managers for basic reports and information. A few executives believe that day-to-day details and computer usage should be left to lower level managers. Standard reports are already produced by the transaction-processing system. Other questions can be investigated by midlevel executives. Many top executives believe this system leaves them free to concentrate on long-run strategy.

## SUMMARY

Managers make many different decisions. Every business discipline builds models to help people analyze problems and make decisions. Some models are straightforward; others are complex. Some are described by statements subject to interpretation; others are defined by mathematical formula. Businesses use models to improve their processes, evaluate choices, and forecast the future.

Management information systems can help managers collect data to drive the models. Software tools help managers design and evaluate models. Word processor and graphics software are used to create the final reports. Decision support systems combine elements of these three tools to make it easier for managers to evaluate options, make decisions, and persuade others to accept the decision.

It is unlikely that you will have to design your own theoretical models from scratch. On the other hand, you will be responsible for understanding the basic business models. You also will have to decide which model is needed to analyze and solve various problems. Once you have determined the appropriate model, a variety of software is available to help apply the model. Generic tools such as spreadsheets, statistics, and optimization packages

> ### A MANAGER'S VIEW
> Tactical-level decisions can be complex. Managers need to make forecasts, improve operations, and search for ways to reorganize the business. Making snap decisions based on "gut instinct" rarely leads to effective solutions. Rigorous analysis can involve mathematical and statistical evaluation of operations data. Models are tools that are used to make better decisions. Although they have limitations, models can provide insight into the business. Managers use decision support systems to collect data, evaluate models, present the results, and make better decisions.

rely on managers to supply the model. Some specific problems can be analyzed with prepackaged systems.

In many ways, enterprise information systems are models of the entire business. They are designed to make it easy for higher level managers to monitor the performance of the firm, identify problems, and retrieve data from the corporate databases. EISs are graphically oriented to make them easier to use and to enable them to create graphs and images of the corporate performance.

## KEY WORDS

assumptions, 344
data warehouse, 343
decision biases, 332
decision support system (DSS), 342
descriptive model, 340

drill down, 352
enterprise (or executive) information system (EIS), 351
model, 330
optimization, 340

parameters, 340
prediction, 340
re-engineering, 337
simulation, 344
tactical decisions, 342

## WEB SITE REFERENCES

### Computer Manufacturers

| | |
|---|---|
| Apple | www.apple.com |
| Compaq | www.compaq.com |
| Dell | www.dell.com |
| Gateway 2000 | www.gateway.com |
| IBM | www.ibm.com |
| Silicon Graphics | www.sgi.com |
| Sun | www.sun.com |

### Software Companies

| | |
|---|---|
| Adobe | www.adobe.com |
| Computer Associates | www.cai.com |
| Corel | www.corel.com |
| Microsoft | www.microsoft.com |
| Novell | www.novell.com |
| Oracle | www.oracle.com |
| SAP | www.sap.com |
| Tucows (shareware) | www.tucows.com |

## REVIEW QUESTIONS

1. What are the primary reasons for creating business models?
2. What are three uses of models?
3. Describe three problems you might encounter when using models.
4. How are tactical-level decisions different from operations-level decisions?
5. List the three major components of a DSS.
6. List the major steps involved in building or using a model to solve a problem.
7. What is the major difference between generic and application-specific modeling tools?
8. What is the primary purpose of an enterprise information system?
9. List three advantages of an EIS.
10. What is the role played by assumptions in building models?
11. What is meant by the term *drill down* in an EIS?
12. How does re-engineering use models to improve a company?

## EXERCISES

1. Find examples of five models. List the discipline (such as economics or marketing), give an example of how modeling is used, and classify the use (optimization, prediction, simulation).
2. Find three software packages that would be useful for building decision support systems. Evaluate each in terms of the three DSS components. Are the packages generic or specific to some discipline?
3. Choose a local retail firm and identify three models that could be used by the manager to run the company. Which of these models is the most important to this firm? List the assumptions, input and output variables, and processes involved for this model.
4. You have just been hired by Eli Lilly to design a new EIS. As a first step, you need to determine the primary structure of the company. Using resources available at the library, create an outline of how the EIS will function. In particular, build a hierarchical chart that describes the primary screens and how they are related.
5. Interview a manager in your community to see what kinds of models he or she uses to make decisions. (Hint: Do *not* ask the manager to describe the models they use.) Are the models mathematical, descriptive, or heuristic (rules of thumb)? Could some of the decisions be improved by using better models? How difficult would it be to create and use these models? Who selected and created the models currently being used?
6. A marketing manager has asked you to help design a DSS for the marketing department. Every month

marketers need to evaluate the effectiveness of their advertising campaigns and decide how to allocate their budget for the next month. They advertise only in the local area and have four basic choices: radio, television, local newspapers, and direct mail. Each month, they conduct random phone interviews to find out who sees their advertisements. They can also purchase local scanner data to determine sales of related products. Each month, the media salespeople give them the Arbitron ratings that show the number of people (and demographics) who they believe saw each advertisement. They also receive a schedule of costs for the upcoming month. As a first step in creating the DSS, identify any relevant assumptions and input and output variables, along with any models that might be useful.

7. A government official recently noted that the government is having difficulty processing applications for assistance programs (welfare). Although most applications are legitimate, several facts they contain have to be checked. For instance, welfare workers have to check motor vehicle and real estate records to see whether the applicants own cars or property. The agency checks birth, death, and marriage records to verify the existence of dependents. They sometimes examine public health data and check criminal records. It takes time to check all of the records, plus the agency needs to keep track of the results of the searches. Additionally, a few applicants have applied multiple times—sometimes in different localities.

The office needs to randomly check some applications to search for fraud. Every week, summary reports have to be sent to the state offices. A key feature of these reports is that they are used to convince politicians to increase funding for certain programs. Describe how a DSS could help this agency. (Hint: Identify the decisions that need to be made.)

### Rolling Thunder Database

8. Identify five models that could be used to improve the management of the Rolling Thunder Bicycle company. What data would be needed to evaluate the models?
9. Identify shipments where receipts do not match the original order. Provide a count and value (and percentages) by supplier/manufacturer.
10. Using basic accounting, list costs and revenues by month. Provide any graphs and tables to illustrate trends or patterns.
11. Analyze sales and discounts by employee and by model type. Are some employees providing higher discounts than others? Are we discounting some models too much or not enough?
12. List a tactical-level decision in each of the main divisions of the company. How often is the decision made? Who makes it? What information is used? What types of analyses need to be performed?

## ADDITIONAL READING

Barabba, Vincent, and Gerald Zaltman. *Hearing the Voice of the Market.* Harvard Business Press: Cambridge, MA, 1991. [Overcoming design biases at GM]

Bowerman, B. L., and R. T. O'Connell. *Forecasting and Time Series.* Duxbury Press: Belmont, CA, 1979.

Dangermond, Jack, and Adena Schutzberg. "Engineering, Geographic Information Systems, and Databases: A New Frontier," *Journal of Computing in Civil Engineering,* July 1998, pp. 121–122. [Uses of GIS]

Madden, John. "HP Reaps Harvest of Information," *PC Week,* February 8, 1999. [HP builds 1 terabyte data warehouse and decision tools to analyze financial data]

Neil, Stephanie. "Blue Cross Dissects Data to Improve Care," *PC Week,* February 8, 1999. [BCBS uses data warehouse and online application processing DSS to improve service]

Plain, Stephen W. "Trading Up," *PC Week,* February 16, 1999. [DSS tools for personal investing]

Wilkinson, Stephanie. "PC Apps Help to Take a Byte Out of Crime," *PC Week,* February 23, 1998. [GIS and imaging tools help police predict and solve crimes]

# CASES *Computer Hardware Industry*

The computer hardware industry is a maturing industry in rapid and constant transition. For example, in 1997, Intel had sales of about $25 billion. Yet, more than 90 percent of Intel's revenue came from products that did not even exist the previous year. This represents product life cycles at their shortest.

Growth in computer hardware spending has been largely driven by business purchases. The computer hardware industry can be divided into three segments: 1) systems and servers (including mainframes and supercomputers), 2) personal computers (PCs) and 3) workstations. Of the $600 billion spent on information technology in 1996, 40 percent was spent on hardware.

### Financial Analysis

The significant growth of the computer hardware industry has dramatically increased revenues to companies in the industry. Profit margins are much slimmer in the United States due to fierce competition and the price wars waged for the sake of market share. Nonetheless, computer hardware companies are expanding internationally where profit margins are certainly higher.

Due to the very fast market cycle, inventory turnover is very high. Any company with lower inventory turnover than its competitors will quickly have balance sheet problems.

### Stock/Investment Outlook

The outlook for the computer hardware industry is positive. The continued build-out of LANs and WANs (also called client-server computing) in business settings creates a need for PCs. The increasing consumer interest in Web access is also very positive for the industry. In 1996, the number of Web users increased by 115 percent. Almost 50 percent of U.S. households have a PC, but far fewer do worldwide. Thus, the PC market is nowhere near saturation.

Stock in computer hardware companies will be volatile. Since the technologies involved are changing fast, hopes and fears will also be rising and falling in step. Expectations of future earnings and success will be difficult to gauge. Will Microsoft and Intel dominate the markets further? Will there be successful challenges to their hegemony? Will technological breakthroughs in other areas such as communications or physics change the industry? Computer hardware will never be as staid as breakfast cereals.

### Competitive Structure

The top 10 PC suppliers control 65 percent of the market; and competition is fierce. In fact, the PC market in some ways resembles a commodity market; top vendors target market share over margins. Also, new entrants to the industry have slowed and the product offerings of existing vendors have widened.

"Wintel" is an acronym for the Microsoft Windows–Intel hegemony that dominates the PC market. Worldwide, 83 percent of PCs use the Windows operating system and 85 percent of all PCs use an Intel microprocessor. This is a concern of many, including some at the U.S. Department of Justice. One feature of this market domination, unlike other monopoly situations, is constant innovation.

Intel and Microsoft spend 13 percent of their combined sales on R&D. This is far ahead of other computer hardware vendors, who only spend 3 to 5 percent of sales. Yet, with this constant innovation and improvement comes ever shorter product life cycles. In fact, the need or perceived need to upgrade PC systems has benefited the entire industry.

### Potential/Prospects for Growth

The tremendous increases in PC power and flexibility and the ability to amplify PC strengths by networking, in local area networks (LANs) and wide area networks (WANs) has made the PC segment the largest. This segment is the biggest in both units and dollars. Between 1991 and 1995, PC shipments increased at 20 percent annually. Shipment growth of 15 percent annually should continue.

Large systems and services account for about 35 percent of the spending on computer hardware. Certainly mainframe sales have dropped, but sales of servers have increased. Servers are needed to enable the creation of LANs and WANs.

Workstations constitute only 5 percent of spending on computer hardware. Workstations combine powerful processors, networking, and graphical user interfaces. They are put together in packages aimed at certain intensive professions like engineering, 3-D animation, and scientific applications. The increasing power of PCs has infringed on the market segment where UNIX vendors dominate.

### Technology Investment Analysis

The investment in technology is particularly pronounced in the manufacturing aspect of computer hardware. Due to the fierce competition in the industry, cost control is very important. The price differentials between direct PC sellers and retail PC sellers have narrowed greatly because of the control of costs. The increased competition means there is less room for error by those in the industry.

The technical and scientific feats of further innovation in processor speeds and storage capabilities demands ever more complicated manufacturing constraints. Constant advantage must be gleaned from the latest technologies in manufacturing and research.

### Recommendation for the Future

In the future, the computer hardware industry will have to broaden, in order to satisfy market needs. Presently, PCs fit this description: one type fits all. There is really only one type of PC with a few interchangeable parts of varying degrees of newness. Does one have a 450 MHz microprocessor or a 700 MHz microprocessor? In many ways, it does not really matter.

Upgrading can be a costly nuisance. Who will design and create simpler, task-specific machines? Which companies will ensure that old software can talk to new software by making translators? The industry would do well to follow the auto industry. In the auto industry, it is no longer one car for all people but a different car for every individual.

## CASE  *Dell Computer Corporation*

### Technological Investment and Analysis

In 1997, Dell extended its use of technology by incorporating a service that electronically links Dell with larger corporate customers. Purchases of Dell products can be made directly through corporate accounting systems of a suitably outfitted corporation or institution.

Dell Computer also focuses on the server market. Servers account for 6 percent of the company's system revenue. The company currently ranks fourth in server sales behind IBM. Beginning in 1997, Dell Computer made stronger efforts to move up in rank by cutting server prices by 16 percent on its mid-range and high-end Pentium Pro processor–based PowerEdge network servers. The price cuts place Dell PowerEdge servers as much as 30 to 35 percent lower than comparable systems offered by Dell's major competitors.

In 1997, Dell Computer announced that it would enter the workstation market with delivery of Windows NT–based workstations in 1998. The company targeted the financial services, software development, and mechanical CAD/CAE/graphics markets. Workstations integrate hardware and software into a solution for specialized tasks such as financial analysis, computer-aided design, or software development.

Dell Computer also entered the international arena. In 1997, the company moved into 10 markets in Asia enabling customers to purchase a computer online in Aus-

tralia, the United States, Hong Kong, New Zealand, Thailand, Korea, Malaysia, Singapore, Taiwan, and Japan. Dell Computer has various web pages for different countries, each developed in local languages and local currencies. To cut costs, computers are manufactured in foreign plants rather than in the United States.

Around 1995, Dell attempted to expand its customer base by marketing PCs through discount retail electronic stores. This approach was a disaster for Dell. The biggest problem was that the computers sent to the stores quickly went out of date. Sales were low, and the stores wanted to return the old computers to Dell. After a short time, Dell backed out of the market and today focuses on selling customized systems, where each person can select the desired options, and the machine is custom-assembled.

### Technological Innovations

#### Network

Dell has not chosen the same strategy that Compaq has for networks. Compaq markets components of networking that are tied to the server; these include the things that go in the box, the network adapters, and so on. You could make a case that things attached to the server could be sold easily. But Compaq must convince the reseller to sell the Compaq server and the Compaq router or the Compaq switch, rather than the Cisco or 3Com or Bay Networks product: That is not easy. Larger network users have already bought into architectures, and customers will need a compelling argument to switch vendors. Dell is therefore committed to pursuing only the server market.

CEO Michael Dell believes his company's strategy is appropriate and will be sufficient to make it the number-one server supplier. He says that Dell's own efforts have been helped by the move toward a standardization of products with the introduction of Microsoft's Windows NT. The company will continue to push for industry standards and does not see itself as a technology innovator.

#### Telecommunications

Dell's telecommunication plans are broad. They include customized web sites for business customers. These let a company's employees buy computers directly over the Internet based on automated policies. Dell is also focusing on automated service and support based on the latest configuration information of a company. The vendor is currently designing a workflow capability that will automate the purchase-approval process within businesses.

### QUESTIONS

1. Who or what forces are driving the strategic direction of Dell Computer?
2. What has been the catalyst for change at Dell Computer?

3. What caused a change in the use of technology at Dell Computer?

4. How successful has the use of technology been at Dell Computer?

5. Does Dell have the financial ability to embark on a major technological program of advancement?

6. What does the corporation's web page present about their business directives?

7. How important is customer data to Dell's continued success?

## ADDITIONAL READING

"The Billionaires' Club," *PC Magazine,* December 1, 1998, p. 9.

"Breakfast with Michael Dell," *VAR Business,* September 28, 1998, p. 111.

Darrow, Barbara. "Michael Dell—Dell Says He Still Enjoys Taking PCs Apart and Reassembling Them, Maintaining What Colleagues Say Is a Fascination with the Technology," *Computer Reseller News,* November 16, 1998, p. 126.

Davey, Tom. "Dell Turns To Servers—Chairman and CEO Michael Dell Discusses the Vendor's Plans for High-End Servers and Online," *Information Week,* April 27, 1998, p. 156.

"Dell Inks Big E-Commerce Deal," *InternetWeek,* February 15, 1999, p. 9.

"Dell Strengthens Server Leadership with Price Cuts of Up to 16 Percent," *The Wall Street Journal,* May 15, 1997.

"The Direct Route," *InfoWorld,* June 2, 1997 pp. 1, 19.

"The Entrepreneurial Bone," *PC Magazine,* February 23, 1999, p. 30.

Gallant, John. "A Dollop of Michael Dell—On Servers and More," *Network World,* May 4, 1998, p. 20.

Girishanker, Saroja. "The *InternetWeek* Interview—Michael Dell, Chairman and CEO, Dell Computer," *InternetWeek,* April 13, 1998, p. 8.

McWilliams, Gary. "Michael Dell's Newest Role: Private Investor," *The New York Times,* December 16, 1998, p. B1.

Pendery, David, Dan Briody, and Ephraim Schwartz. "What Dell Does Best," *InfoWorld,* April 6, 1998, p. 1.

Trommer, Diane. "Michael S. Dell—Direct-sales Mega-maven Continues to Recast Biz Models," *Electronic Buyers' News,* December 21, 1998, p. 48.

## CASE *Gateway 2000, Inc.*

Ted Waitt founded TIPC (Texas Instruments PCs) Network in August of 1985 after dropping out of college. He brought in his friend Mike Hammond to work the technical side of the business. Contrary to popular belief, the pair started their business in an empty office on the Waitt cattle farm and not in a barn.

The company sold upgrades and accessories to owners of Texas Instruments (TI) PCs. Waitt's grandmother guaranteed the $10,000 loan which founded TIPC. Norm Waitt, Ted's older brother, joined the company in early 1986 to take care of the company's finances. In 1987, Texas Instruments reportedly offered its customers a chance to upgrade their old machines to IBM-compatible PCs for $3,500.

Waitt and Hammond saw this as a great opportunity, since they knew they could do the same for a lot less. The first Gateway computer had two floppy drives, a deluxe color monitor, and more memory than most PCs at the time. The $2,000 asking price was comparable to other models, but the Gateway PC offered far greater performance.

Gateway's marketing capitalized on a distinctive cow motif—which established an early brand identity in a market where PCs were typically seen as commodities.

### Technological Story

The MMX processor was introduced in January 1997. Through diligent research, Gateway was able to capitalize on the new technology. Gateway was able to offer PCs with the new processor to consumers prior to many of its competitors. Consumer demand decreased in the fourth quarter of FY1996 in anticipation of the MMX introduction.

Gateway capitalized on the introduction of the MMX processor by immediately offering the new processor as soon as consumers demanded it. Gateway experienced greater-than-expected demand in the first quarter of FY1997 for PCs with this new technology. This greater-than-expected demand is also a sign to the rest of the industry that demand was strong for the new processor.

### Technological Investment and Analysis

Gateway has an advantage over the competition with outstanding technical support. Gateway continues to provide extensive training for its support staff with each new technological introduction to ensure that the service level remains high. The support staff must be aware of new products' capabilities and nuances in order to provide the most complete technological support available.

In 1998, Gateway created a new sales channel through retail stores. However, the stores carry only demonstration computers. Salespeople explain features and options and provide the customer with a hands-on experience. To purchase the computer, the clerks then enter the specifications into the Gateway computer system. The customer's system is custom assembled at a factory and shipped to the customer.

## Recommendation for the Future

Gateway must continue monitoring the ever-changing technology environment in order to remain a step ahead of the competition by offering consumers the latest new technology. Gateway must also continue to invest in the extensive training of their support staff in order to maintain their competitive advantage in customer support. A lapse of foresight could result in a serious setback to the company.

Gateway 2000, Inc., has displayed the ability to aggressively develop new PCs with the latest technology and pass along the savings resulting from improved technology directly to the consumer. This management style will enable Gateway 2000 to continue the growth the company has experienced thus far.

## QUESTIONS

1. What forces are driving the strategic direction for Gateway 2000, Inc.?
2. Upon what technologies has Gateway relied?
3. How has Gateway changed its use of technology over time?
4. What does Gateway's web page present about its business directives?
5. What role does data play in the future of Gateway 2000?
6. How will the capture and maintenance of customer data, particularly from customer calls for support, impact the corporation's future?
7. How do the retail stores Gateway introduced in 1999 compare to Dell's failed retail attempt?

## ADDITIONAL READING

Abel, Amee. "The Solo 2500SE Leads the Way for High-Value Notebooks," *Computer Shopper,* September 1998, p. 234.

Berlind, David. "Get Ready for Software with Cow Spots: Gateway Looks Beyond Hardware," *Computer Shopper,* September 1998, p. 108.

"Gateway G6-333," *Computer Shopper,* September 1998, p. 181.

"New Gateway 2000 Customer Support Subsidiary Locating in Hampton: New Call Center Will Add 300 Jobs," *EDGE: Work-Group Computing Report,* December 30, 1996, p. 9.

Wolf, Marty. "Shopping Daze: Buying a Computer Led to an Epiphany," *Computer Reseller News,* January 25, 1999, p. 46.

## DISCUSSION ISSUE

## *Employee Privacy*

An important issue for many employees today is the extent to which companies monitor their employees' use of telephone and computer communications systems. As an example, let's listen to a hypothetical discussion between Edgar and one of his employees.

Edgar: Miles, I understand you have been using electronic mail a lot lately.

Miles: Sure. I've been working on the Robestat project, and I've been asking some of my old colleagues and a couple of professors for advice. I'm building a fairly complex model and I needed some help with the math and the statistics. The e-mail system is fast and my friends aren't charging us for the advice. Besides, I thought the e-mail system was cheaper than regular mail. Is there a problem with the cost?

Edgar: Not exactly. The work you've been doing on the project is fine. That's not the problem. The problem is that you've also been using the system for personal use on company time.

Miles: I don't think I know what you're talking about.

Edgar: Do you know someone named Madeline at the University of San Francisco?

Miles: Well, sort of, but . . .

Edgar: The computer records show that in the last month, you sent her an average of five messages a day, and received about two a day from her.

Miles: Uh, sure. But she's just one of the colleagues I mentioned. We've, uh, been discussing parts of the project. She does some research for me at the library. I haven't given her any details about the project or any confidential data.

Edgar: That's not the real problem. But Miles, you're not quite telling me the whole story are you?

Miles: I, uh, don't know what you mean.

(*Edgar turns to a terminal and types a command.*)

Edgar: Well, let's see. How about this message you sent yesterday:

Dearest Madeline: I really miss you. I had a great time at the party last weekend. I can't wait to see you again. I have a boat reserved for the weekend. Just the two of us. Come with me, and we can watch the sun rise over Alcatraz. What do you say? Miles;>)

There's a lot more of this drivel here. I can't find anything about the project, unless you count this silly reference to some chase through the library.

Miles: But . . . where did you get those? You can't read those. They're personal property.

Edgar: Not that it matters, but we routinely monitor everyone's use of the computer. The point is that you've been using company resources for your personal use. Besides, some of these messages sound a bit immoral to me. This company doesn't need workers like you. Clean up your desk. We'll mail your final check to your home address. Here's security. They'll escort you out.

Miles: But, but, wait a minute. You can't do that. You can't read my mail messages—that's illegal. You can't tell me what I can or can't do on my time. You can't do this, I'll sue the company. I'll sue you. I'll . . .

Edgar: Go ahead. We'll win, just like all the other companies have won. It's our computer, we can do what we want. Security, I'm through with him.

*(Miles is ushered out.)*

Miles: Wait, wait! What if I pay the cost of the messages? It can't cost more than a couple cents each!

Most people know that it is illegal to intercept people's mail or to tap phone lines. Even the police need a warrant from a judge to violate privacy in this manner. However, many people are not aware that these legal protections do not extend to broadcast communication systems. Also, employees are often unaware that companies can routinely monitor their computer usage and read electronic mail messages. Similarly, companies are allowed to monitor phone calls on the systems they own.

## QUESTIONS

1. Even if it is legal, do you think companies should read employee e-mail? Explain your answer.
2. What does the company gain by reading employee e-mail? What does it lose?
3. Do you think Miles was wrong to use the e-mail system the way he did? Would you fire him?
4. Do you think cost of the message system is an important issue?
5. Assume that you want to change the laws and restrict the ability of companies to monitor their employees' use of the information systems. How would you write a law to protect employee privacy, yet still protect the interests of the companies?

# *Forecasting*

Think of what you could accomplish if you could see the future. Of course, no one can truly predict future events. However, in many situations a forecast can provide a good idea of the possibilities. Of course, forecasting patterns for the near future is much easier than predicting what might happen several years out.

Forecasting is used in many areas of business. Marketing forecasts future sales, the effect of various sales strategies, and changes in buyer preferences. Finance forecasts future cash flows, interest rate changes, and market conditions. The HRM department builds forecasts of various job markets, the amount of absenteeism, and labor turnover. Strategic managers forecast technological changes, actions by rivals, and various market conditions. Sometimes these forecasts are built on intuition and rules of thumb. But, it is better to use statistical techniques whenever possible.

The science of forecasting is dominated by two major approaches: time-series forecasting that identifies trends over time, and structural modeling that identifies relationships among the underlying variables. Many forecasts require the use of both techniques.

As shown in Figure 8.1A, by focusing on the underlying model, structural modeling seeks to identify the cause of changes. For example, if consumer income increases, the demand for our product shifts out, which results in more sales. If we know the shapes of the supply and demand curves, it is straightforward to predict how sales will increase.

Figure 8.2A shows a time-series approach to the same issue of sales forecasting. In some ways it is simpler. We know nothing about the underlying model and have simply collected sales data for the past few months. The data is plotted over time. By fitting a trend line to the data, it is clear that sales are increasing. Assuming that this trend continues, it is easy to forecast sales for the next period.

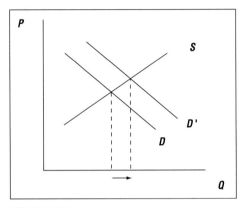

**FIGURE 8.1A**
STRUCTURAL MODEL FORECAST
The underlying model helps explain the causal relationships, making it easier to forecast the effect of changes. Here, an increase in income shifts the demand curve, which causes increased sales ($Q$) even at higher prices.

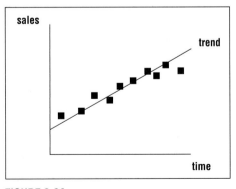

**FIGURE 8.2A**
TIME-SERIES FORECAST
Sales change over time. The trend line provides a forecast of future values. But it assumes that underlying factors behave as they did in earlier times.

It is often tempting to say that structural models are "better" than time-series forecasts. After all, the model provides an understanding of the causal relationships. So we know that the increase in sales is occurring because of increasing consumer income. While this knowledge is valuable, the structural model does not tell us how fast income will increase in the next period. Hence, we end up using time-series techniques to estimate the trends in consumer income. Consequently, we need both techniques. As much as possible, find a structural model to explain the problem. Then use time-series methods to estimate the underlying trends. Plug these forecasts into the structural model to determine the outcome of the desired variables.

## STRUCTURAL MODELING

Modeling an underlying structure provides the most information and knowledge about a problem. Consider a simple physics problem: If you throw a ball at a certain angle, with a certain force, how far will it travel? You could try several experiments, timing each event and measuring the outcome. You could then use this data to make a forecast of future attempts. However, if you know the underlying model of gravity (e.g., Newton's equations), then it is easy to determine the outcome of any attempt.

Many economic models have been developed to determine relationships that apply to business decisions. For instance, cost models are used to determine supply relationships, and consumer preferences generate demand curves. Demand for a product can be expressed as a function of several variables: price, income, and prices of related products. These relationships can be estimated with common statistical techniques (e.g., multiple regression).

Figure 8.3A presents the basic steps in using a structural model to forecast sales demand. First you need a model—in this case, a basic economic model. Then you need to collect data for each of the variables in the model. It is best if the underlying variables change over time, and you will need observations from several points in time. It is best to have at least 40 observations, but you get better results with more data. Next you use regression analysis to estimate the values of the model parameters. Finally, you plug in estimates of the independent variables to obtain a forecast of the future sales.

## TIME-SERIES FORECASTS

When you do not have a structural model, or when you need to forecast the value of an underlying variable, you can use time-series techniques to examine how variables change over time. The basic process is to collect data over time, identify any patterns that exist, and then extrapolate this pattern for the future. The approach assumes that the underlying pattern will remain the same. For example, if income has been gradually increasing over time, it assumes that this increase will continue.

| Model | $Q_D = b0 + b1\ Price + b2\ Income + b3\ Substitute$ | | | | |
|---|---|---|---|---|---|
| | Time | Quantity | Price | Income | Substitute |
| | 1 | 24926 | 134 | 20000 | 155 |
| Data | 2 | 26112 | 150 | 21000 | 155 |
| | 3 | 27313 | 142 | 22000 | 135 |
| | 4 | 26143 | 141 | 21000 | 150 |
| Estimate | $Q_D = 1114 - 0.1\ Price + 1.2\ Income - 1.0\ Substitute$ | | | | |
| Forecast | $33318 = 1114 - 0.1\ (155) + 1.2(20000) - 1.0\ (160)$ | | | | |

**FIGURE 8.3A**

FORECASTING PROCESS USING A STRUCTURAL MODEL

Collect data and use regression to estimate the underlying parameters. Then plug in estimates of the future values of the independent variables to forecast the value of the dependent variable (quantity).

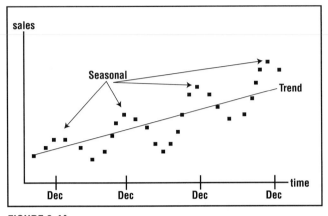

**FIGURE 8.4A**

TIME-SERIES COMPONENTS

A trend is a gradual change over time. Seasonal patterns show up as peaks and troughs at annual intervals. Other cycles are similar but cover longer time periods and are usually less regular. Random change is shown because the cycle and trend are not perfect.

Figure 8.4A shows that a time-series consists of a number of observations made over a period of time. Four types of patterns often arise in time-series data: (1) trends, (2) cycles, (3) seasonal variations, and (4) random changes. A trend is a gradual increase or decrease over time. A cycle consists of up and down movements relative to the trend. Seasonal variations arise in many disciplines. For instance, agricultural production increases in the summer and fall seasons, and many industries experience an increase in sales in November and December due to holiday sales. Random components are variations that we cannot explain through other means. In some cases, the random component dominates the others, and forecasting is virtually impossible. For example, many people believe this situation exists for stock market prices.

## EXPONENTIAL SMOOTHING

Random variations make it difficult to see the underlying trend, seasonal, and cyclical components. One solution is to remove these variations with exponential smoothing. Exponential smoothing computes a new data point based on the previously computed value and the newly observed data value. The weight given to each component is called the *smoothing factor*. The higher the smoothing factor, the more weight that is given to the new data point. Typical values range from 0.2 to 0.30, although it is possible to use factors up to 1.0 (which would consider only the new value and ignore the old ones). Lower values (down to 0.01) put more weight on previous computations and result in a smoother estimate.

Current spreadsheets (e.g., Microsoft Excel) have procedures that will quickly estimate the moving average for a range of data. You simply mark the range of data, highlight the output range, and supply the smoothing factor. As shown in Figure 8.5A, it is then easy to graph the original and the smoothed data.

How do you choose the smoothing factor? The best method is to apply several smoothing factors (start with 0.10, 0.20, and 0.30), and then examine the accuracy of the result. The accuracy is typically measured as the sum-of-squared errors. For each smoothed column of data, compute (actual − smoothed)*(actual − smoothed) to get the squared-error on each row. Add these values to get the total. Now compare these totals for each of the smoothing factors. The smoothing factor with the smallest error is the one to use.

In practice, most data will have a trend component. In these cases, you need to use double exponential smoothing. Perform the first smoothing as usual and find the best smoothing factor. Then perform a second smoothing on the new (smoothed) column of data using the same smoothing factor. Figure 8.6A

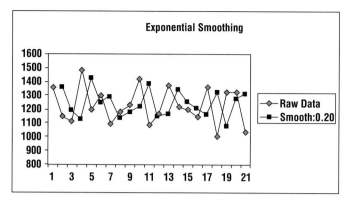

**FIGURE 8.5A**

EXPONENTIAL SMOOTHING

The smoothed data is computed by Excel by applying a smoothing factor to each new data point.

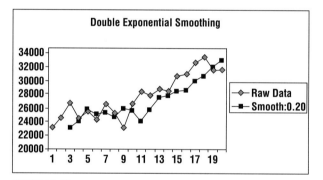

**FIGURE 8.6A**

DOUBLE EXPONENTIAL SMOOTHING

When there is a trend, you need to smooth the data a second time.

shows that the result follows the basic trend line but still incorporates the cyclical variations in the data.

The smoothed data can be used to forecast the dependent variable for future periods. It is wise to stick with forecasts only one or two periods ahead. Longer range forecasts are less likely to be accurate. The basic formula is given in Figure 8.7A. You need the smoothing factor ($\alpha$) and the number of time periods ahead to forecast ($\tau$). Then you take the smoothed values at the last data point (single and double) and plug them into the formula. The result is a forecast that incorporates a linear trend along with the basic cyclical variations in the data.

If you want a forecast that utilizes only the trend (and none of the cyclical variations), you can use a simple regression technique. Use standard regression techniques with the observed data as the dependent ($Y$) variable and time ($t$) as the independent variable. Then use the computed parameters to estimate the predicted value at any future point in time. Again remember that linear trends may not continue for extended time periods, so keep your predictions down to a few periods. Figure 8.8A illustrates the process, using Excel to obtain the regression coefficients. The result is the prediction along the trend line, which ignores cyclical variations.

Once you compute the trend factor, you can subtract it from the original series to identify the cyclical, seasonal, and random components. Use the spreadsheet to plug in values for each time period and compute the trend line. Then subtract these values from the original series. If you plot the new series, you will

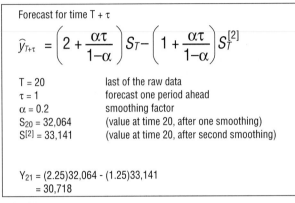

Forecast for time T + τ

$$\widehat{y}_{T+\tau} = \left(2 + \frac{\alpha\tau}{1-\alpha}\right)S_T - \left(1 + \frac{\alpha\tau}{1-\alpha}\right)S_T^{[2]}$$

| | |
|---|---|
| T = 20 | last of the raw data |
| τ = 1 | forecast one period ahead |
| α = 0.2 | smoothing factor |
| $S_{20}$ = 32,064 | (value at time 20, after one smoothing) |
| $S^{[2]}$ = 33,141 | (value at time 20, after second smoothing) |

$Y_{21}$ = (2.25)32,064 - (1.25)33,141
  = 30,718

**FIGURE 8.7A**

FORECASTING WITH DOUBLE EXPONENTIAL SMOOTHING

Plug your values into this formula to estimate future values
of the data.

| Time | Quantity | Trend | Difference |
|---|---|---|---|
| 1 | 24917 | 24484 | 432 |
| 2 | 26152 | 24983 | 1169 |
| 3 | 27297 | 25482 | 1816 |
| 4 | 26157 | 25980 | 177 |
| 5 | 26710 | 26479 | 231 |
| 6 | 26103 | 26977 | −874 |
| 7 | 27981 | 27476 | 505 |
| 8 | 26327 | 27975 | −1647 |
| 9 | 24913 | 28473 | −3560 |
| 10 | 28524 | 28972 | −448 |
| 11 | 29774 | 29470 | 303 |
| 12 | 29136 | 29969 | −833 |
| 13 | 29332 | 30468 | −1136 |
| 14 | 30306 | 30966 | −660 |
| 15 | 32133 | 31465 | 669 |
| 16 | 33329 | 31963 | 1366 |
| 17 | 34522 | 32462 | 2060 |
| 18 | 34769 | 32961 | 1808 |
| 19 | 33355 | 33459 | −104 |
| 20 | 32684 | 33958 | −1274 |
| 21 | | 34456 | |
| 22 | | 34955 | |
| 23 | | 35454 | |
| 24 | | 35952 | |

$$Y_t = b_0 + b_1(t)$$

Use regression to estimate $b_0$ and $b_1$.

| | Coefficients | Std Error | t Stat | P-value |
|---|---|---|---|---|
| Intercept | 23985.81 | 652.48 | 36.76 | 2.2E–18 |
| Time | 498.60 | 54.47 | 9.15 | 3.4E–08 |

Plug t into equation to estimate new value (on trend):

$Y_{21}$ = 23,986 + 498.6* (21)
  = 34,456

Result is the prediction on the trend, with no random factors
and no cycles.

**FIGURE 8.8A**

FORECASTING WITH LINEAR TRENDS

Use regression to estimate the two parameters. Then plug in the desired time value to obtain the
predicted trend value for any new time period.

see the data without the trend. It should be easier to see seasonal and cyclical patterns on this new chart.

## SEASONAL AND CYCLICAL COMPONENTS

Two powerful methods exist to decompose time-series data into its trend, seasonal, and cyclical components. They are Box-Jenkins and Fourier analysis. You can purchase tools that will perform the complex calculations for these methods. Unfortunately, it would take many pages to describe either one of these techniques, so they are beyond the scope of this appendix. Just remember that it is possible to perform much more detailed analyses (and forecasts) of time-series data. If you need them, hire an expert, or take a separate class in time-series forecasting.

## EXERCISES

1. Obtain a three-year set of monthly data from the Bureau of Labor Statistics web site (http://stats.bls.gov) that is not seasonally adjusted (e.g., Producer Price Index). Transfer the data to a spreadsheet. Plot the data and include a trend line.
2. Plot the sales data from the table. Draw one graph with a trend line and a second chart with three-period exponential smoothing.
3. Using the regression functions in the spreadsheet, estimate the trend line and produce a forecast for four periods ahead.
4. Use double exponential smoothing (damping of 0.3) and plot the new data.
5. Use the formula in Figure 8.7A to forecast sales for the next four periods using double exponential smoothing.

| | JAN. | FEB. | MAR. | APR. | MAY | JUN. | JUL. | AUG. | SEP. | OCT. | NOV. | DEC. |
|------|------|------|------|------|-----|------|------|------|------|------|------|------|
| 1998 | 414 | 382 | 396 | 530 | 551 | 396 | 365 | 415 | 424 | 485 | 684 | 802 |
| 1999 | 457 | 432 | 465 | 598 | 632 | 424 | 392 | 476 | 489 | 555 | 768 | 883 |
| 2000 | 505 | 477 | 534 | 636 | 696 | 466 | 442 | 506 | 531 | 610 | 825 | 973 |

SALES DATA FOR THE REMAINING EXERCISES

# CHAPTER 9

# Decisions in Business Areas

The instant recongnition of a FedEx delivery shows the dominance that FedEx has in the minds of consumers. The company achieved its position through good management, dedicated workers, marketing, and innovative use of information systems.

## FEDERAL EXPRESS

Federal Express promises to deliver packages overnight absolutely and positively. Its extensive fleet of trucks and planes, Memphis distribution hub, and Cosmos II computer system enable it to accomplish these objectives. Cosmos II keeps track of 14 million online package deliveries every day. When a customer service representative keys in a package's registration number, the system can track the package from its dropoff at any Federal Express office to its ultimate destination. The advantages that this system provides have been indispensable in Federal Express's rise to be the leading provider of overnight package delivery around the world.

A key component of the system is the menu-driven Supertracker bar-code scanner. Worldwide, 60,000 Supertrackers scan packages every time a package changes hands. Data is stored in the Supertracker and relayed back to the minicomputers in the dispatch station when the Supertracker is replaced in its cradle in the van. At the end of the business day, the Supertracker is returned to a mechanical cradle in the dispatch station where its information is downloaded to the central computer. This transfer enables the master database to be automatically updated each night.

The Supertracker system provides more information than just the location of packages. Early access to the number of packages headed toward each destination enables management to allocate delivery personnel and trucks to each day's routes. Monitoring the number of pickups in a region also assists management in its efforts to evaluate advertising and other programs in an area. Quantitative measures of pickups and deliveries can also be used to evaluate offices and personnel against standards from other offices and areas.

**FIGURE 9.1**

Management is often analyzed and taught as a collection of disciplines. Each functional area has its own tactical decisions and its own models. There are similarities between all of these models. Information systems support tactical decision making with access to data, evaluation of models, and presentation of results.

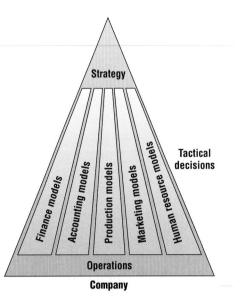

**OVERVIEW**

It is easiest to understand the importance of models by briefly examining models from various business disciplines. You will study most of these models in greater detail in other disciplines. However, in order to see how MIS supports different tasks, we need to look more closely at those tasks. As illustrated in Figure 9.1, each discipline uses models to evaluate tactical decisions.

As you read these examples, notice that although the models are different, the support from MIS is similar in each case. Look for the DSS components: database, modeling tools, and presentation support. Once you learn the basic MIS tools and learn how to deal with models in general, you can apply these techniques to any modeling problem.

**INTRODUCTION**

Every discipline has its own set of models that characterize how it approaches problems. Models are revised and new ones are created. The study of management includes models from many areas, such as accounting, finance, marketing, human resources management, production management, economics, and statistics. Depending on your career inclinations, you will be exposed to models from other disciplines, including psychology, art, education, philosophy, and history.

To demonstrate how MIS can help you create and evaluate models, this chapter will illustrate models from some of the important business functions. Even if you are not an expert in each subject, you should be able to understand the main concepts of the models. The problems illustrated in this chapter are small enough so that they can be solved with generic software available to you (i.e., spreadsheet, database, and word processor). In the business world, the databases are much larger, the models more complex, and the reports can run to hundreds of pages.

Each business discipline has its own way of modeling business problems. This approach is characterized by the different objects that are used and the techniques they employ. For instance, accounting defines several standard objects, such as transactions, reports, journals, and accounts. In production management, the focus is on operations and products, with the goal of optimizing production (cutting costs, increasing efficiency, or improving quality). In each of the following examples, you should identify the primary use of the model as discussed in

## Trends

Every business must perform certain functions. Every company needs to account for its sales, market its products or services, reward and motivate its employees, and make investment decisions. In a small company, these functions are often performed by one or two individuals. In the development of corporations, large firms found it beneficial to create specialized departments to perform these functions. Today, with the help of information technology, many firms are working to integrate these functions across the company.

One trend stands out in the United States and in European nations: Business has become more competitive. In almost every industry, profit margins have been shrinking. For example, Sears' managers estimate that between 1980 and 1995 average gross margins in U.S. retailing fell by 10 percentage points (*The Economist,* March 4, 1995). In turn, the retailers have pushed manufacturers for lower prices. The emphasis on prices is strongly emphasized in retailing by the strength of discount outlets. *Discount Merchandiser* (June 1993) reported that discount stores (and wholesale clubs) in 1992 sold 22.7 percent of general merchandise such as clothing, housewares, and small appliances in the United States.

Companies are also facing more competition from international rivals. The reduction of barriers in Europe led to consolidation of retailing across West-

ern Europe. Between 1990 and 1993, European firms opened 610 stores in nations other than their home country. Four of the top five food retailers in Spain are now owned by French companies (*The Economist,* March 4, 1995).

The essence of competition is that it forces companies to become more efficient. Managers have to make better decisions. Management mistakes always cause problems. With competition, they are more likely to cause the company to fail.

Researchers have been studying businesses for many years. Our knowledge of how to manage a business and solve typical problems has increased considerably during the last 30 years. Until recently, many of these solutions have been difficult to apply. Part of the problem is the lack of trained managers, and part has been due to the difficulty of evaluating and using the various models.

In the past, only large firms were able to hire specialists to build models and solve problems for that company. They were also able to afford the expensive computer time needed to collect the data and solve the models. With increased capabilities and low prices of personal computers, these same models are now available to all business managers. With the standardized computer platform, specialists have created packages that enable managers to use complex models without needing to be experts in the area.

Chapter 8. Look for similarities between the applications. They will lead to a better understanding of how information systems can help managers use models to make better decisions.

## Transaction Processing and Tactical Management

ACCOUNTING A large portion of the resources in accounting departments is devoted to transaction processing. Systems are designed to capture data and produce standardized reports. Tracking the financial data provides a model of the business—especially the financial aspects. Order processing, inventory, accounts receivable, and accounts payable model the acquisition and sale of products from the firm. Fixed asset reports and depreciation track the purchase, operating costs, and remaining value of major assets of the firm. Payroll, withholding amounts, and tax records monitor employee activities and payments.

Accounting departments also support tactical management throughout the company. Standard reports such as cash-flow analysis, income statements, and balance sheets provide an indication of the current financial status of the firm. By comparing current and prior reports, managers can spot trends and make changes to correct problems. Operating budgets and capital spending plans are created to help managers compare alternatives and plan future expenditures. Similarly, the accounting departments are in charge of tax-management tactics to minimize tax bills and avoid penalties.

Models and analyses are important aspects of any manager's job. Spreadsheets are powerful tools for building models and analyzing data.

MIS support for transaction processing is explained in Chapter 4. The fundamental component is the use of databases to store the data, control shared access to authorized users, and produce reports for managers. In addition to providing access to the data, MIS supports tactical management with decision support systems that evaluate the various models and produce graphs and reports. Most organizations have customized accounting software packages to collect data, produce reports, and perform comparisons. Increasingly, the data can be transferred to personal computers on which models can be created and evaluated using spreadsheets and other financial modeling tools.

If there are failures in the MIS support for accounting transaction systems, some common symptoms will be observed. Reports will be delayed and inaccurate. Managers will complain about not being able to get the data they need. Meetings may degenerate into discussions of the true values of the basic financial numbers. Some managers will be forced to use their own time to adjust reports and create graphs to make comparisons. In extreme cases, departmental managers will begin keeping their own accounting records.

## Control Systems

Because of their responsibility for the accuracy of the financial data, accounting systems also provide important control systems to minimize theft and fraud. Financial statements produced on a regular basis track the major expenses and revenues of the firm. Capital budgeting is used to monitor and allocate purchases of expensive items. Similarly, accounting systems are often responsible for analyzing costs and benefits from projects and to monitor project expenditures on a regular basis. Reports on the changes in financial position display the major sources and uses of funds in the firm. Unexpected or overly large changes in these reports could be indications of problems. Similarly, departments

## Business Trends

As a current or future manager, you might be asking "Why do I need to learn so many different models? I can always find an employee to take care of the details; my job is to make decisions . . ." Although this philosophy might have worked in the past, it is likely to cause serious problems in current and future jobs because of the changing business environment.

As competitive pressures increase, businesses are downsizing and decentralizing. Most growth is occurring in small business and franchise operations. In each situation, there is less need for "middle managers," and more demand for managers who collect their own data, perform analyses, and

make decisions. Individuals who can efficiently perform these tasks without relying on subordinates will earn promotions and bonuses.

With increased specialization, you will probably focus on models within your discipline. However, models from other areas can sometimes lead to ideas and solutions to other problems. For instance, an investment model from finance might be used by a marketing manager as a foundation for selecting a mix of promotional strategies. Additionally, few jobs are rigidly defined in one discipline. Almost all managers need to understand the basic accounting, marketing, economic, and human relations management models.

and projects are expected to submit and follow budgets. Variances from the budgeted amounts are closely monitored in an effort to control expenses.

MIS support for accounting controls comes from maintenance of historical data to use for comparisons and from assisting in evaluating the basic accounting models. Spreadsheets are often used to draw graphs for highlighting trends and evaluating variances between budgeted and actual expenses.

Errors in accounting control systems can be serious. If the controls are inadequate, there is increased potential for fraud or theft. For example, a county government in Tennessee lost thousands of dollars from 1990 to 1992. An employee created a fictitious company that allegedly sold several products to the government. The money was paid to the company and pocketed by the employee and no products were delivered. Better control systems and information management could have identified the discrepancy between expenses and deliveries.

Control systems can also be too strict—to the point where it is more expensive to provide the accounting paperwork than to suffer the loss. For example, most departments are allocated petty cash to spend on small items each year because it is too expensive to record small expenditures. The costs of generating purchase orders and tracking payments through a paper-based accounting system often exceed $50 per order.

### Strategic Support

Virtually every firm has its own accounting system. Although certain standards have to be met, each system is created and customized to fit the specific situation of the firm and its management and owners. These systems are defined and maintained by the accounting departments. However, because the firm changes over time, so will the accounting system. It is up to the accounting department to modify its systems as the company changes or as the *generally accepted accounting practices* are modified.

Accounting systems are used to evaluate potential mergers and acquisitions. By creating a standard financial model of the firm it is possible to compare firms, even if they are in different industries.

**FIGURE 9.2**
DANA CORP.
AUTO PARTS

Traditional cost
accounting totals
expenses in a limited
number of predefined
categories. It is difficult
to determine how
much it really costs
to make a product—
especially if there are
multiple products.

SOURCE: "A New Tool for
Managing Costs," by
Terence Pare, *Fortune,*
June 14, 1993,
pp. 124–129.

| Salaries | $371,917 |
|---|---|
| Fringes | 118,069 |
| Supplies | 76,745 |
| Fixed Costs | 23,614 |
| Total | $590,345 |

The accounting department is also responsible for evaluating strategic alternatives in terms of accounting and tax policies. Occasionally a firm will alter its financial structure to take advantage of changing tax laws or because of changes in the market.

MIS support for strategic changes is more complicated. Decision models can be used by managers to evaluate the various choices. Any company undergoing restructuring would want to examine changes in cash flows, costs, and profitability. With a computerized model of the financial system, these changes could be simulated to identify potential problems and benefits.

## Example

The foundations of traditional cost accounting systems were designed in the 1920s. The traditional methods identify costs according to basic categories, such as salaries, fringe benefits, supplies, and fixed costs. This method works well for a manufacturing firm in which most of the costs are due to labor, and the company produces a few products using the same processes. Through the 1960s, most large U.S. manufacturers fit this mold, and the standard accounting methods worked well. Today's manufacturers produce a much wider array of products and spend more on supplies, capital, and fixed costs than on labor. As explained by Terence Pare in *Fortune,* consider a company that makes two types of pens: one black, the other purple. Ten times as many black pens are produced as purple ones. It takes eight hours to reprogram the machines to switch pens, which is the major overhead cost. In traditional accounting, the overhead costs are allocated to each pen based on the levels of production, so 91 percent of the switching costs will be allocated to the black pens and 9 percent to the purple ones. This method understates the costs of producing the low-volume purple pens.

An accounting method that is better at identifying costs for complex manufacturing processes was designed by professor Robert Kaplan, called **activity-based costing (ABC).** The fundamental difference is that ABC allocates costs by examining a detailed breakdown of the production activities. In the example of the pens, each activity carries a cost. Production of purple pens would entail activities such as processing orders, buying supplies, and reprogramming the production machines. The production system is decomposed into its various subsystems, as explained in Chapter 3. Only now, using ABC, each activity or subsystem carries a cost. The cost of producing an item is obtained by adding the costs from each subsystem that it uses.

Figure 9.2 illustrates a traditional approach to accounting for costs. It identifies costs for each major category. The ABC method is shown in Figure 9.3. Notice the increased amount of detail. In particular, the cost attributed to each process is itemized. As illustrated in Figure 9.4, these values are found by breaking the production process into smaller subsystems and then estimating the costs attributable to each step.

**FIGURE 9.3**
ACTIVITY-BASED
COSTING

Activity-based costing
pushes accounting to
more detailed levels.
Instead of simply
recording the total
costs (bottom row), we
estimate the costs at
each processing step.
This detail provides a
better picture of where
and how costs are
incurred.

| | SALARIES | FRINGES | SUPPLIES | FIXED COSTS | TOTAL |
|---|---|---|---|---|---|
| Process sales order | $91,253 | $28,969 | $18,830 | $5,794 | $144,846 |
| Source parts | 85,882 | 27,264 | 17,722 | 5,453 | 136,320 |
| Expedite supplier orders | 45,450 | 14,429 | 9,379 | 2,886 | 72,143 |
| Expedite internal processing | 31,465 | 9,989 | 6,493 | 1,998 | 49,945 |
| Resolve supplier quality | 29,987 | 9,520 | 6,188 | 1,904 | 47,599 |
| Reissue purchase orders | 28,498 | 9,047 | 5,881 | 1,809 | 45,235 |
| Expedite customer orders | 17,481 | 5,549 | 3,607 | 1,110 | 27,747 |
| Schedule intracompany sales | 11,194 | 3,554 | 2,310 | 711 | 17,768 |
| Request engineering change | 10,524 | 3,341 | 2,172 | 668 | 16,704 |
| Resolve problems | 10,488 | 3,330 | 2,164 | 666 | 16,648 |
| Schedule parts | 9,696 | 3,078 | 2,001 | 616 | 15,390 |
| Totals | $371,917 | $118,069 | $76,745 | $23,614 | $590,345 |

**FIGURE 9.4**
ACTIVITY-BASED
COSTING

The data flow diagram
is a useful tool to
display processes and
the flow of data (or
products) through a
system. Activity-based
costing assigns costs
to each process by
categories such as
salaries, fixed costs,
and so on.

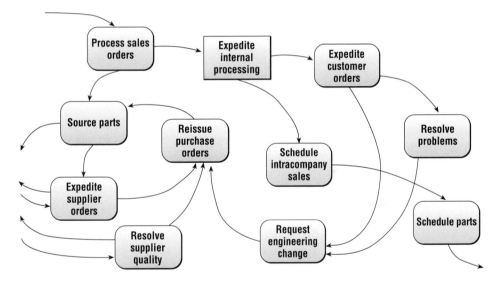

**FINANCE**   The many models in finance are classified into two general categories: investment and corporate financial management. Most of the financial decisions in a firm occur at the tactical level. However, tracking external financial markets is typically a transaction-processing problem.

## Investments

Managing portfolios of financial instruments is probably the best-known finance activity. Thousands of potential investments exist for individual and corporate funds. Each investment must be evaluated on the basis of current price, price trends, estimated risk, and maturity date. Evaluation of these components often requires a substantial amount of additional data. To estimate the future price of a particular stock, analysts examine the current and prior financial statements of the firm as well as international economic conditions.

Sports fans love to wear hats and jerseys from their favorite teams. And manufacturers are happy to provide them. The catch is that businesses cannot just slap a logo on a hat and sell it. The logos of teams are trademarks, and each sale generates royalty payments to the team. In the NFL, one firm (NFL Properties) tracks the $300 million annual sales and monitors the licenses to ensure firms receive the proper payments. NFL Properties tracks 31 teams, plus the NFL logo itself, on about 3,000 products, sold by 300 licensees.

Until 1997, this data was tracked manually, entered into a basic general ledger system, and then transferred to a spreadsheet for analysis. Sanjiv Satyarthi, the IT director, noted, "We used to send out paper forms, one per month per product to licensees, which was terribly slow and caused errors because they were handwritten." The IT department had to write custom reports to retrieve the data—adding weeks to the analysis process.

NFL Properties implemented a new sales database, with online application processing (OLAP) tools to transfer data to spreadsheets. In May 1998, it also added a Web-based extranet to collect reports from the 60 largest licensees. In addition to collecting the data, the tools enable the firm to analyze sales. For example, Ralph Carras, vice-president of finance notes, "If you know a particular jersey is doing well, then you can isolate the reasons behind it and create more products like it in the future."

They also look at industry changes, trends in the market, and general economic data. Can you picture how much data is involved? Just consider prices of financial instruments. Even if you restrict yourself to 1,000 stocks and record hourly prices each day, you will collect 2 million prices a year. When you include the international markets, the amount of data increases substantially.

Through the 1980s, many Wall Street banks and investment firms hired financial analysts who became known as *rocket scientists* or *derivatives geeks.* Their job was to create models of the various markets. These models analyze the changing prices and look for certain features that indicate the best stocks to buy and sell. Some of the models operate virtually automatically. As the models monitor the prices, they evaluate thousands of rules and automatically generate buy and sell orders. These computer systems have changed the way large financial institutions deal with investments. They enable analysts to monitor more investments, identify changes, and make decisions faster. Some systems use the Black-Scholes equations to estimate pricing for derivatives (financial instruments that are based on some underlying market, such as options). As an illustration of the difficulty of models, note that several firms lost millions of dollars in the derivatives market in 1994 and 1995. Some of the clients claimed they lost money because they did not have access to or understand the models created by the brokerage firms.

An excellent summary of the techniques and tools available to investment professionals is contained in a series of articles (Survey: Frontiers of Finance) in the October 9, 1994, issue of *The Economist.* For example, Olsen and Associates, a Zurich company, has a financial model that predicts exchange rates for 53 pairs of currencies. Using the model has produced annual returns of more than 10 percent on top of the interest rate costs. The system uses second-by-second data on foreign exchange rates collected since 1986. It is updated every month with more than 50 megabytes of data from Reuters and an equal amount from Knight Ridder and Telerate. Trading recommendations are made by the system at least hourly.

Smaller versions of these systems are available to individual investors and small businesses. Primary stock market price data is available through online services such as

**FIGURE 9.5**

FINANCIAL MARKETS Information is the entire essence of a financial market. Its purpose is to bring buyers and sellers together. With thousands of investments and millions of buyers and sellers, brokers are surrounded by data. The problem lies in properly analyzing and evaluating this data.

Dow Jones News/Retrieval or from data broadcasts that can be received with a special modem. Investment analysts sell commercial versions of their modeling software that provide automatic monitoring, trend graphs, and investment advice.

At heart, finance relies heavily on information. As indicated in Figure 9.5, stock markets have to keep track of the base trading data and provide information to investors. Increasingly, they are being called on to handle computerized trading, where the investors trade electronically. Creating these systems can be difficult For example, in March 1993, the London Stock Exchange scrapped its Taurus project to computerize their operations. After six years and around £400 million ($600 million), the exchange decided the new system would not work (*The Economist,* June 12, 1993, p. 90).

## Corporate Finance

Corporate financial officers have to make many decisions beyond managing investment portfolios. They are often responsible for capital budgeting, cash management, credit control, economic forecasting, and financial performance analysis. Each of these tasks uses a specific set of models. Economic models are used to forecast future conditions. Financial performance models are correlated to the economic results. Cash-flow models are based on careful monitoring of budgets and historical revenue and spending patterns. Customer credit is granted or denied based on evaluations of the current customer balance, payment history, and estimates of their ability to pay.

One obvious level of MIS support is the computerized databases that monitor the firm's financial transactions. MIS also provides access to data from external sources, such as various government agencies, stock markets, financial institutions, and credit agencies. The reports generated from these databases play an important role in financial decisions. For example, the financial officer relies on exception reports to make sure the firm has enough cash on hand to meet its payment obligations. If a department suddenly goes over budget, or if revenues fall short of predicted levels, the finance department needs to make adjustments to the investments to increase the cash holdings.

---

**Reality Bytes    9–2    A Market of One?**

Marketers and advertisers have noticed several trends in the last couple of years. For example, one big advertiser states "Now, when you put up a single [TV] ad, it gets one-third the size of the audience it used to get." Coupled with increased prices for TV commercials, "the cost-effectiveness of mass media has been lost."

Some people have suggested that the Internet offers the ability to identify individuals, so that marketers might be able to create a market by finding all of the individuals who might be interested in the product. However, not everyone is as optimistic. For example, Jeff Levy, CEO of RelevantKnowledge, a Web-measurement company, observes, "This is not the ultimate medium. The Web has been pitched as

'you can know everything about everybody'" and place "a customized ad for every single person. . . . That will never happen."

The new medium is causing both excitement and uncertainty. Web site publishers are anxious to receive more advertising dollars—expecting business to begin spending more than the average $700,000 now allocated to Web ads. On the other hand, web sites are nervous about alienating customers with large, complex, slow-to-download adds preferred by marketers. Yet, money is a strong motivating factor, as indicated in the comments from one Web publisher to group of advertisers: "Just tell us what you want us to do, and we'll do it."

---

Financial management also uses forecasting and simulation to evaluate alternatives. When financial planners lay out investments for the future year, they need to forecast the cash flow at various points in time, which entails estimating monthly revenue and expenses. New investments and projects have to be scheduled properly to make sure returns and maturity dates provide adequate cash flow.

Several computerized financial modeling tools are available, such as the Interactive Financial Planning System (IFPS). Similar to spreadsheets but geared toward financial models and scheduling, IFPS enables financial analysts to monitor transactions, evaluate models, and examine the results of various simulations.

It can be difficult to identify problems in financial information systems. One common symptom is when a firm consistently has problems meeting its cash-flow needs. However, this symptom could also be caused by the rapid growth of a company or by considerable variation in demand for the company's products. Similarly, inaccurate economic and financial forecasts could be symptoms of problems in the information systems. Or they could be random errors caused by unpredictable events. Likewise, it is unreasonable to blame the information system if it fails to pick winning investments every time, because it is difficult to guarantee success. Nonetheless, if several of these problems show up in a firm, it would be wise to dig deeper to determine whether the financial staff is receiving the information and modeling support they need.

## Example

A common problem in finance is the necessity to derive projected financial statements for future years. In particular, financial analysts are often interested in balance sheet and income statement projections to examine future earnings potential. Consider the simple balance sheet and income statement presented in Figures 9.6 and 9.7. Although real-world statements contain more detail, these examples will illustrate the model.

The balance sheet and the income statement are interrelated. Additions to retained earnings on the income statement will be added to the total retained earnings in the balance sheet. Interest paid on the bonds and accounts payable from the balance sheet will appear on the income statement. Similarly, if the amount of common stock changes,

**FIGURE 9.6**
BALANCE SHEET
FOR 1999
Projected financial statements. A common modeling problem in finance involves taking current financial data and making forecasts for the next period.

| Cash | $ 33,562 | Accounts Payable | $ 32,872 |
|---|---|---|---|
| Receivables | 87,341 | Notes Payable | 54,327 |
| Inventories | 15,983 | Accruals | 11,764 |
| Total Current Assets | 136,886 | Total Current Liabilities | 98,963 |
| | | Bonds | 14,982 |
| | | Common Stock | 57,864 |
| Net Fixed Assets | 45,673 | Retained Earnings | 10,750 |
| Total Assets | $182,559 | Liabilities + Equity | $182,559 |

**FIGURE 9.7**
INCOME STATEMENT
FOR 1999
Projected financial statements. Beginning with the current balance sheet and income statement, the objective is to determine the financial impact of an increase in sales. First, sales and costs will change. These changes might require additional funds, so we need to determine how much money will be needed for next year and the best way to obtain that money.

| Sales | $97,655 | Tax Rate 1999 | 40% |
|---|---|---|---|
| Operating Costs | 76,530 | Dividends 1999 | 60% |
| Earnings before Interest and Tax | 21,125 | Shares Outstanding 1999 | 9,763 |
| Interest | 4,053 | | |
| Earnings before Tax | 17,072 | | |
| Taxes | 6,829 | | |
| Net Income | 10,243 | | |
| Dividends | 6,146 | | |
| Additions to Retained Earnings | 4,097 | | |
| Earnings per Share | $ 0.42 | | |

changes in dividends will appear on the income statement. These interrelationships do not matter much for data in the current year, because those numbers are not likely to change. However, they will play a role on the projected statements for the following year.

The first step in creating the projected statements is to forecast some of the underlying numbers, such as sales and operating costs. Various statistical and marketing techniques can be used to derive these figures. They are commonly expressed as percentage changes from the prior year. We also need to forecast the effects of these changes on the balance sheet. The simplest method is to assume that the underlying financial ratios will remain constant. For instance, if sales increase by 10 percent, the basic balance sheet accounts (cash, accounts receivable, etc.) should also increase by 10 percent. The model can be made more realistic by using a more sophisticated method.

With a spreadsheet, it is relatively easy to add these forecasts to the income statement and balance sheet. First make the changes to the sales and costs. By using a separate cell to hold the percent increase, it will be easier to experiment with different values. The second step is to compute the forecasts on the balance sheet entries for cash, accounts receivable, inventories, accounts payable, and accruals. Now, because increased sales result in more income, you need to increase the balance sheet entry for retained earnings by the amount gained from the income statement. Use a formula to combine the old value with the gain for the next year. Of course, it is not likely that the balance sheet will continue to be balanced. In order for the firm to increase sales, it will have to obtain more capital.

There are several ways to increase capital, such as issuing more stock or selling bonds. In a real-world setting, you would examine both methods to see which provides the greatest contribution to profits. Figure 9.8 illustrates the steps needed for the sales of bonds.

**FIGURE 9.8**
FINANCIAL
PROJECTIONS

For most companies, a spreadsheet can be used to estimate changes to the balance sheet and income statement. First, compute the increase in sales and costs. Then estimate the effects on cash, accounts receivable, accounts payable, and accruals. Compute the change in retained earnings, and use the balance sheet to estimate the need for additional funds. If funds are raised through bond sales, the interest expense increases, altering the income statement. This circular relationship should converge to a stable solution.

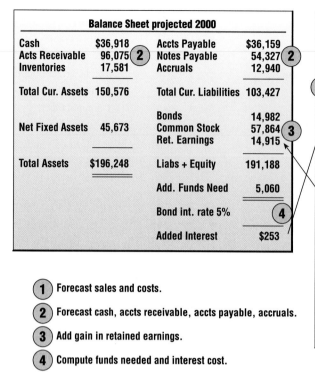

**( 1 )** Forecast sales and costs.

**( 2 )** Forecast cash, accts receivable, accts payable, accruals.

**( 3 )** Add gain in retained earnings.

**( 4 )** Compute funds needed and interest cost.

**( 5 )** Add new interest to income statement.

Notice that no matter which method you choose, there is a feedback relationship between the income statement and the balance sheet. If a spreadsheet is used for the computations, it will indicate that there is a **circular reference.** In other words, the amount of bonds needed will depend on the retained earnings, but the retained earnings depend on the interest cost of the bonds. In this situation, the feedback is normal and the circular reference does not mean there is an error. However, it will take the spreadsheet a few tries to come up with the correct answer. You will have to tell the spreadsheet to recalculate several times. The values should eventually **converge** to a final solution. They converge in this example because the transmission factor is set by the interest rate, which is less than 100 percent. In some situations, the multiplier may be greater than one, in which case the numbers would **diverge** and would never reach a solution. Feedback systems that diverge are **unstable** and will not survive.

**MARKETING**  Marketing departments are responsible for market research, sales forecasting, management of the sales staff, advertising, and promotion. In some firms they also process orders and manage the design of new products and features. Processing orders is essentially a transaction-processing task. The others involve tactical or strategic questions that are more complex, so we will focus on those tasks.

## Research and Forecasting

An enormous amount of data is available for market research. Figure 9.9 presents some of the common data available for marketing purposes. Internally, the marketing department maintains records of sales and basic customer attributes. With some firms, there can

**FIGURE 9.9**
COMMON MARKETING
DATA SOURCES
There are three primary
sources of marketing
data: internal
collections, specialty
research companies,
and government
agencies. Detailed data
is available on the
industry, customers,
regions, and
competitiors.

| INTERNAL | PURCHASE | GOVERNMENT |
|---|---|---|
| Sales | Scanner data | Census |
| Warranty cards | Competitive market analysis | Income |
| Customer service lines | Mailing & phone lists | Demographics |
| Coupons | Subscriber lists | Regional data |
| Surveys | Rating services (e.g., Arbitron) | Legal registration |
| Focus groups | Shipping, especially foreign | Drivers license |
| | | Marriage |
| | | Housing/construction |

be a longer distance between the firm and the final customer. For instance, manufacturers typically sell products to wholesalers, who place the products in individual stores, where they reach the final customer. In these cases it is more difficult to identify customer needs and forecast sales. There will be delays in receiving sales data because the retailers and wholesalers typically place bulk orders. Additionally, it is more difficult to identify customer preferences because their purchases are filtered through other companies.

Marketing departments also have access to data that is collected by other firms. In a manufacturing environment, marketers might get raw sales data from the wholesalers and retailers. On the retail side, with the pervasiveness of checkout scanners, it is now possible to buy daily and hourly sales records from thousands of stores in various cities. This data contains sales of your products as well as rivals' products.

Several marketing models are used to evaluate consumer preferences, forecast sales, and analyze promotion opportunities. For instance, attribute models enable marketing researchers to analyze the importance of product attributes. Consider an automobile. It has measurable attributes such as gas mileage, color, number of seats or doors, price, and cargo space. It also has subjective attributes encompassing style, performance, handling, and ride. Which of these attributes are most important to consumers? What trade-offs are customers willing to make? For example, how much gas mileage are they willing to give up for better performance?

Models have also been designed to help marketers choose among the various promotion alternatives. A key concept in marketing today is the use of *target marketing,* in which the goal is to find the consumers who are specifically interested in your products. Advertising and promotions should highlight the relevant features for the people who will see them. To perform target marketing, you need to know which product features appeal to each group. You also need audience characteristics for each advertising method. For instance, who reads newspapers regularly, and how do they differ from people who watch television sitcoms?

Along with data collection, MIS can help evaluate the models. Computers are used to identify categories and to perform statistical analyses. Marketing survey data is combined with statistics about advertising media. Data from warranty registration cards, discount coupons, and checkout scanners is analyzed to spot changes in preferences, evaluate the effectiveness of promotional campaigns, and provide leads for future promotions. Additionally, in some businesses information systems can be used to track thousands of products and their current status in each market.

Errors or failures in marketing information systems can have serious consequences. Errors in processing orders will result in products not delivered correctly and will create

Marketing decisions often entail determining customer preferences. Interviews and data collection are an important first step. Analyzing conflicting data is a challenge that often requires sophisticated decision support tools.

irate ex-customers. Errors in models such as incorrect forecasts or erroneous target information will result in a decline in sales. However, because there are many possible causes of declining sales, more detailed questions are needed to spot the cause. It is difficult to spot errors in the marketing models or in the data being used and it is important that these components be thoroughly tested.

## Customer Service

A major focus of marketing is to improve service to the customer. Information systems and decision support systems are useful for identifying consumer demands and keeping track of customer attributes.

## Example

Consider the fictional company Inchiki, which sells customized watches. Inchiki buys watch components from a group of suppliers. The watch faces and bands are customized for specific companies. For example, companies buy watches with their own logos to give as sales incentives and rewards. Tourist locations buy watches to sell as souvenirs. Sporting teams and special-events organizers also buy them for the similar reasons.

The marketing department initially determines that monthly sales reports do a good job tracking company sales, but they need more marketing information. In particular, marketing needs a way to measure the effectiveness of marketing promotions. They decide to create a marketing information system to track Inchiki's sales, sales by competitors, and the results of a weekly customer survey. The survey is from the final customers who buy the watches. The survey teams ask customers about quality, style, and value. The results are summarized by a number between 1 and 100, where 100 is the best score. All three promotions will be tested. First, marketers will run with no promotions for six weeks, then each promotion will be tested separately for six weeks each.

**FIGURE 9.10**
ANALYSIS OF
MARKETING
PROMOTIONS
Three different
promotions were tested
and we examined the
effect on sales,
competitor sales, and
customer satisfaction.
Even with this limited
data set, it is difficult to
determine the effect of
each promotion from
the raw data.

| | WEEK | OUR SALES ($) | COMPETITION SALES ($) | CUSTOMER SURVEY RATING |
|---|---|---|---|---|
| No promotion | 1 | 36725 | 86524 | 45 |
| | 2 | 37564 | 87349 | 46 |
| | 3 | 35835 | 86783 | 42 |
| | 4 | 38256 | 88653 | 48 |
| | 5 | 38698 | 89875 | 47 |
| | 6 | 37865 | 85762 | 43 |
| Promotion 1 | 1 | 38854 | 87654 | 47 |
| | 2 | 38933 | 88534 | 47 |
| | 3 | 39452 | 92576 | 46 |
| | 4 | 38762 | 93765 | 46 |
| | 5 | 38896 | 91543 | 47 |
| | 6 | 37602 | 89243 | 46 |
| Promotion 2 | 1 | 38210 | 89456 | 48 |
| | 2 | 39786 | 90765 | 52 |
| | 3 | 42986 | 88976 | 54 |
| | 4 | 43140 | 89653 | 55 |
| | 5 | 43976 | 89763 | 56 |
| | 6 | 43786 | 89076 | 54 |
| Promotion 3 | 1 | 47532 | 88753 | 42 |
| | 2 | 43876 | 90753 | 41 |
| | 3 | 42087 | 92764 | 38 |
| | 4 | 40123 | 93765 | 36 |
| | 5 | 38742 | 94109 | 37 |
| | 6 | 35673 | 93875 | 36 |

**FIGURE 9.11**
PROMOTION RESULTS
Marketing analysis.
Regression analysis of
the data in Figure 9.10
provides an indication
of the differences
between the
promotions. In
particular, the negative
signs on coefficients
for promotions 1 and 3
could indicate
problems.

With no promotions:

$$sales = 20{,}865 + 342 * consumer + 339 * week$$

*consumer survey average = 45*

Promotion 1:

$$sales = 42{,}370 - 62 * consumer - 211 * week$$

*consumer survey average = 47*

Promotion 2:

$$sales = 13{,}448 + 501 * consumer + 545 * week$$

*consumer survey average = 53*

Promotion 3:

$$sales = 44{,}808 + 98 * consumer - 2067 * week$$

*consumer survey average = 38*

After the six-month experiment is completed, the new system has collected enough data to begin modeling how product promotions affect sales at Inchiki. The results of the survey are displayed in Figure 9.10. Based on this data, a marketing research consultant estimated the effects of the three types of promotions. These four equations represent a model of how sales respond to the different promotions. The estimated equations are shown in Figure 9.11.

**FIGURE 9.12**
PROMOTION
ANALYSIS

From the chart, it is clear that promotion methods 1 and 3 will generate lower sales if they are run for more than five weeks. Promotion 2 looks like the best way to increase sales. One question that needs to be answered is the cost of running promotions for only four weeks.

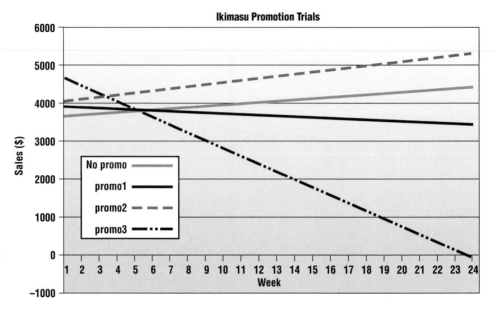

Although the results from the equations are strong, they can be difficult to interpret and understand. The equations are entered into a spreadsheet to see what happens with each promotion. Figure 9.12 shows the graph generated from the model. For any promotion running more than four weeks, it is clear that promotion 2 is the best bet. In fact, the other methods are worse than running no promotion at all! If marketers run the promotions less than four weeks, method 3 appears to produce the highest level of sales. However, at the end of the promotion, it looks like it would be a good idea to start up promotion 2 to recover from the declining trend. Keep in mind that the model only reflects sales; it does not include the cost of the promotion. To make a good decision, Inchiki will have to subtract the costs of the promotions and create a new graph.

## Employee Records

**HUMAN RESOURCES MANAGEMENT**

For many years, payroll records were the only items computerized in human resources management (HRM) departments. It is easy to measure the advantages of using the computer to compute taxes and other withholdings and to print the checks. Most of the older payroll systems were highly centralized and were not designed to provide data to managers throughout the company. Today, software from such companies like Austin-Hayne is moving HRM data away from the inaccessible mainframe files and making it available to managers using everyday web browsers and personal computers.

In the process, the role of HRM has expanded in today's legal environment. There are more laws and rules that govern hiring and release of workers. Personnel reports have to be filed with various governmental agencies. Additionally, many firms are moving away from straight hourly salaries and focusing on merit pay. HRM departments are often responsible for providing new training, monitoring employee progress, and maintaining an inventory of employee skills.

A computerized listing of employee skills will be especially helpful in full implementation of the 1993 Family Leave Act. This U.S. law permits employees to take extended (unpaid) leaves for a variety of reasons. The law requires companies to offer the employee an equivalent job upon returning to the company. With thousands of employees, a computerized listing of jobs and skills will help HRM staff find employees to take

This HRM compensation system by Austin-Hayne provides access through web browsers. Managers use the tools to analyze performance and compensation.

over the job vacated by the employee on leave. It can also be used to search for equivalent new positions when the employee returns.

HRM departments are also beginning to take advantage of the Internet when it comes to hiring. In particular, employees are asked to submit their resumes electronically. Skill-matching software then compares individual skills to the job requirement lists and performs the initial sort of the applicants.

## Performance Evaluations

A substantial change in the past few years has been the shift from fixed pay rates and standardized raises to a merit pay system that rewards workers based on their performance. This method uses regular performance appraisals to evaluate each employee. These appraisals can be computerized. When each department is given a budget for raises, the manager evaluates each person on the basis of performance, position within the salary range, years of service, and other factors. Computer software can help the manager evaluate various raises. It enables the manager to try out various possibilities, check for consistency, and stay within budget. The software also can automatically monitor compliance with nondiscrimination laws.

## Example

An important HRM task in any organization is the need to allocate raises. Using a merit pay system, each employee is evaluated on the basis of factors related to his or her job. Typically, each manager is given a fixed amount of money to allocate among the employees. The goal is to distribute the money relative to the performance appraisals, provide sufficient incentives to retain employees, and meet equal employment opportunity guidelines. Many of these goals are conflicting, especially with a finite amount of money available. To set the actual raises, managers need to examine the raw data. On the other hand, a graph makes it easier to compare the various goals.

A few specialized software packages can help you determine merit raises. However, as shown in Figure 9.13, it is possible to create a small system using a spreadsheet. A

| | | | | **MERIT PAY** | | | | **RAISE POOL** | | **$10000** | | |
|---|---|---|---|---|---|---|---|---|---|---|---|---|
| | **PERFORMANCE** | | | **PCT** | **SALARY RANGE ($000)** | | | **CURRENT** | **MERIT** | **MARKET** | **TOTAL** | |
| **NAME** | **R1** | **R2** | **R3** | **PERF.** | **HIGH** | **LOW** | **AVG.** | **SALARY** | **$100** | **ADJUST.** | **RAISE** | **RAISE %** |
| Caulkins | 9 | 7 | 6 | 73% | 37.5 | 28.4 | 36.4 | 35.8 | 733 | | 733 | 2.0% |
| Jihong | 3 | 6 | 7 | 53% | 18.9 | 15.4 | 16.3 | 17.9 | 533 | | 533 | 3.0% |
| Louganis | 8 | 7 | 7 | 73% | 30.2 | 26.7 | 28.9 | 29.5 | 733 | | 733 | 2.5% |
| Naber | 9 | 8 | 8 | 83% | 23.2 | 19.5 | 21.4 | 19.8 | 833 | | 833 | 4.2% |
| Spitz | 3 | 4 | 3 | 33% | 22.4 | 17.3 | 18.4 | 17.5 | 333 | | 333 | 1.9% |
| Weissmuler | 5 | 4 | 6 | 50% | 60.4 | 32.5 | 45.2 | 53.2 | 500 | | 500 | 0.9% |
| Department | 6 | 6 | 6 | | 32.1 | 22.2 | 21.9 | 21.7 | 3665 | | 3665 | 2.4% |
| Corporate | 5 | 6 | 5 | | 124 | 9.2 | 18.9 | 18.9 | | | | |

**FIGURE 9.13**

MERIT PAY ANALYSIS

With a merit system, salary increases should be related to performance evaluations (denoted in r1, r2, r3). Managers are typically given a fixed pool of money to distribute among the employees. Employee raises should be based on merit evaluations, current salary, and the salary range for the job. Market adjustments are often paid to attract workers in high-demand fields. A spreadsheet can be used to model the effects of various policies. In this example, the manager has allocated $100 for each merit percentage point. The rest of the money will be given as market adjustments. The effects of the adjustments can be seen in the graph displayed in Figure 9.14.

**FIGURE 9.14**

PERFORMANCE EVALUATION

Using a separate y-axis for the two types of data and overlaying line plots on the bar chart makes this graph easier to read. If this graph is dynamically linked to the salary table, the manager can make salary changes and instantly compare the raises to the performance ratings.

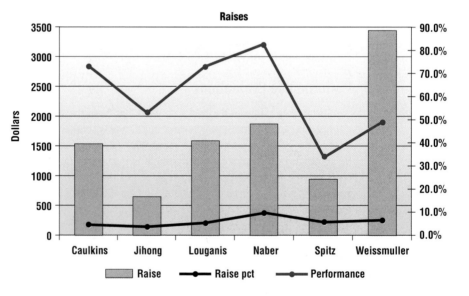

spreadsheet that can display a graph alongside the data tables is particularly useful. Assume that the company wishes to give a certain portion of the raise based on the average performance ratings. The amount of money per point (currently $100) can be changed. Each person can be given an additional market adjustment raise. The total departmental raises cannot exceed the allocated total ($10,000).

The goal is to fill in the market adjustment column so that the raises match the performance appraisals. As illustrated by the graph in Figure 9.14, the manager can evaluate

---

**Reality Bytes**    **9–3**    **Knowing the Right Codes Pays Off for Laguna Medical Systems**

John W. Mohler makes millions of dollars a year—enough to own a townhouse on the Pacific, several exotic cards, and a yacht. He makes the money from Medicare, but he is not a medical doctor. His company, Laguna Medical Systems, makes its money on contingency-fee deals with hospitals. He promises to examine their billing systems and, by recoding their data, obtain higher benefits from insurance programs. His software and people analyze the data looking for more accurate codes to describe treatments. His company then takes 25 to 40 percent of the new money.

Medical insurance payments are based on diagnostic related group (DRG) codes that specify the exact nature of the treatment. In 1997, the federal government filed several complaints against some hospitals—notably Columbia Healthcare—for misfiling claims based on the DRGs. Consequently, in 1998, Healthcare managers were leery of Laguna's "revenue maximization" strategies. So Mr. Mohler

changed his marketing and focused on compliance. He notes "This turned out to be the best year we ever had. You go with what's hot, and if compliance is hot, then that is where you direct your efforts."

Mr. Mohler notes that for years hospital errors typically enabled his consultants to find as much as 4 percent additional revenue for a hospital. In 1997, the Inspector General of the Department of Health and Human Services sent hospitals a memo stating that firms working on a contingency basis have "little incentive" to find errors that would result in less money. He also noted that the process was "ripe for upcoding, unbundling and other manipulation increases," which might be fraudulent. On the other hand, Mr. Mohler's perspective is that "I don't think there are any hospitals that are intentionally committing fraud. What is really disagreeable to me is that you have a system that is so complex, there is no one who understands it, including the government."

---

both absolute dollar raise or the percent increase. The total departmental raises should be equal to $10,000. By displaying the graph next to the last columns in the spreadsheet, it is possible to watch the changes as you enter the data. This immediate feedback makes it easier to set the raises you prefer.

**GEOGRAPHIC INFORMATION SYSTEMS**

Many aspects of business can benefit by modeling problems as geographical relationships. For instance, to choose the site of retail outlets, you need to know the location and travel patterns of your potential customers. Manufacturing can be made more efficient if you know the locations of raw materials, suppliers, and workers. Similarly, locations of distribution warehouses need to be chosen based on retail outlets, manufacturing facilities, and transportation routes. Thousands of other geographical considerations exist in business, such as monitoring pollution discharges, routing and tracking delivery vehicles, classifying areas for risk of crimes and fire, following weather patterns, or tracing migration paths of fish for commercial fishing. **Geographic information systems (GISs)** have been designed to identify and display relationships between business data and locations. Arc Info and MapInfo are two of many commercial GIS packages available.

A GIS begins with the capability of drawing a map of the area in which you are interested. It might be a world or national map that displays political boundaries. It might be a regional map that emphasizes the various transportation routes or utility lines. It might be a local map that displays roads or even buildings. An oil exploration company might use a map that displays three-dimensional features of a small area. A shipping company could use ocean maps that display three-dimensional images of the ocean passageways. The level of detail depends on the problem you wish to solve.

## Maps and Location Data

There are two basic ways to create and store the underlying maps: as pictures or as digitized map data. Digital map data provides the most flexibility. Besides being easier to change, digital maps enable you to zoom in and see more detail. Each item is stored by its location as measured by latitude and longitude and sometimes its elevation. Most U.S. digital maps are based on data that the Bureau of the Census created for the 1990 national census, known as TIGER. The Bureau of the Census has every road and house number entered into a giant database. Because of privacy reasons, they will not sell house locations, but you can get the range of street numbers for each city block. The U.S. Department of Defense has digital data available for many areas, including international locations and often includes elevation data. The U.S. Geological Survey topographical maps are also being converted to digital systems. However, keep in mind that the systems being mapped are constantly changing, so even digital maps often contain missing, incomplete, or inaccurate data, as the United States learned when it accidentally blew up the Chinese embassy in Belgrade because the CIA maps were out of date.

Once you have the base maps, the objective is to overlay additional data on the maps. For example, you can obtain census data that displays average consumer characteristics such as income, house price, and number of autos within each geographic area. The GIS could be used to plot different colors for each income level. Next you can overlay the locations of your retail stores. If you are selling a high-price item like Cadillac you want to locate the stores in areas of higher income.

Although you can buy base geographical data, how do you know the location of your retail stores? Or, how do you plot the locations of delivery vehicles, or police cars, or trains? The easiest answer today is to use the **Global Positioning System (GPS),** which is a set of satellites maintained by the U.S. government. A portable receiver tuned to the satellites will identify your location in latitude, longitude, and elevation (if it can reach

---

### Reality Bytes    9–4    Welch Allyn

Your physician probably uses Welch Allyn's blood pressure and heart monitor tools. The 2,000-employee company is known for its precision instruments. Their marketing and sales staff were supported by the financial department—led by Kevin Cahill. When someone had a question about sales, the financial staff searched the databases and sent the raw data to the managers by e-mail. The managers then analyzed the data. Cahill notes that the system was not very effective: "We were using a hodgepodge of systems and Lotus spreadsheets. It took tons and tons of paper to support managers throughout the company." So he replaced the system with a 30-MB shared database and an executive information system (ESSBase). "It was our belief that if people did not have access to meaningful

data, there were opportunities that we were missing," Cahill says. "People had incorrect information, nonexistent information. Today people have become more productive."

In addition to providing better information, the system has made the financial department more efficient—be reducing the closing time for the $300 millon company from 10 days to five. Like many other companies, Welch Allyn had difficulties in standardizing and cleaning up the data for the new system. "When you put in a system like this, you find that the raw data in many cases is not as accurate as you thought," Cahill says. "We have been cleansing the data from the transaction systems and in some cases completely re-engineering the way the data is organized."

four satellites) within 50 feet. Several handheld units are available for a few hundred dollars. If you work for the Department of Defense, you can get receivers that will identify your location within a few millimeters, but you need appropriate security clearances to obtain these receivers. In 1996, the U.S. government announced that it would enable consumer use of full-resolution measurements in "five to 10 years." Civilian models that combine signals from U.S. and Russian satellites provide that resolution now, but cost about $8,000.

As a model, the GIS makes it easier to spot relationships among items. Visual presentations are generally easy to understand and are persuasive. A GIS can be an effective means to convince management that neighborhoods have changed and that you need to move your retail outlets. A GIS can also be used for simulations to examine alternatives. For example, a GIS oriented to roadmaps can compute the time it would take to travel by different routes, helping you establish a distribution pattern for delivery trucks.

## Example

Consider the problem faced by a manager in a small retail chain that has stores located in 10 Florida cities. It sells a combination of hard goods (such as cleaning supplies, snack items, and drapery rods) and soft goods (mostly clothing). For the most part, profit margins for soft goods are higher than for hard goods. However, total sales of hard goods seem to be better than those of soft goods—except in certain stores. The manager has been unable to find a reason for the difference, but a friend who has lived in Florida longer suggested that there might be some geographical relationship. The basic numbers are presented in Figure 9.15.

Because there are only 10 cities, it might be possible to identify patterns in the data without using a GIS. However, an actual firm might have several hundred or a few thousand stores to evaluate. In this case, it is much more difficult to identify relationships by examining the raw data. It is better to use a GIS to plot the data. Different colors can be

| CITY | 1980 POP | 1990 POP | 1980 PER-CAPITA INCOME | 1990 PER-CAPITA INCOME | 1980 HARD-GOOD SALES (000) | 1980 SOFT-GOOD SALES (000) | 1990 HARD-GOOD SALES (000) | 1990 SOFT-GOOD SALES (000) |
|---|---|---|---|---|---|---|---|---|
| Tampa | 271,523 | 280,015 | 6441 | 15,081 | 767.4 | 851.0 | 953.4 | 1009.1 |
| Tallahassee | 81,548 | 124,773 | 6310 | 14,578 | 595.4 | 489.7 | 843.8 | 611.7 |
| Perry | 8,254 | 7,151 | 5727 | 11,055 | 300.1 | 267.2 | 452.9 | 291.0 |
| Orlando | 128,291 | 164,693 | 6735 | 16,958 | 425.7 | 509.2 | 691.5 | 803.5 |
| Ocala | 37,170 | 42,045 | 6175 | 12,027 | 359.0 | 321.7 | 486.2 | 407.3 |
| Miami | 346,865 | 258,548 | 6084 | 16,874 | 721.7 | 833.4 | 967.1 | 1280.6 |
| Jacksonville | 540,920 | 635,230 | 6767 | 15,316 | 990.2 | 849.1 | 1321.7 | 1109.3 |
| Gainesville | 81,371 | 84,770 | 6150 | 13,672 | 365.2 | 281.7 | 550.5 | 459.4 |
| Fort Myers | 36,638 | 45,206 | 6483 | 16,890 | 535.2 | 652.9 | 928.2 | 1010.3 |
| Clewiston | 5,219 | 6,085 | 7645 | 13,598 | 452.0 | 562.5 | 367.6 | 525.4 |

**FIGURE 9.15**
GEOGRAPHIC SALES DATA
We suspect that sales of hard and soft goods are related to population and income. We also want to know whether there are regional patterns to the sales.

**FIGURE 9.16**
GEOGRAPHIC-BASED
DATA
It is difficult to display
this much data without
overwhelming
managers. Notice that
the sales (radar)
graphs use size and
shape to highlight total
sales, and the changing
sales mix. Income is
color-coded in a
smaller graph. Notice
in the sales graphs that
the northern counties
experienced a greater
increase in sales in
hard goods compared
to the southern
counties.

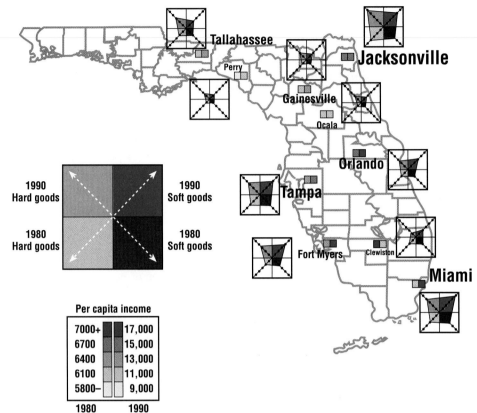

used to highlight large increases in sales. By overlaying this data with the population and income data, it is easier to spot patterns. In Figure 9.16 notice that there is a correlation between population and total sales. Also, notice that sales in the northern cities are concentrated more in hard goods than in the southern cities.

## SUMMARY

Managers use many different models to solve problems. Each discipline might have hundreds of different models. You will use many different models in your career. Keep in mind that there are similarities among many of the business models, and distinct patterns in how MIS provides support for those models. Foremost in MIS support is the ability to retrieve the data needed to evaluate the models. The graphics capabilities of personal computers contributes enormously to the ability of managers to evaluate choices, interpret the results, and make decisions.

Every day, new software packages are created to help managers design and evaluate business models. Some of these tools are designed to solve specific tasks, such as a marketing management package to evaluate customer surveys, or a financial investment system to monitor and identify trends in the prices of financial instruments. Other generic tools, such as spreadsheets, can be used to build whatever model you create.

## A MANAGER'S VIEW

Middle-level managers continuously face tactical-level decisions: How can operations be reorganized to improve the business? Each discipline has its own set of problems and creates its own models. Information systems help managers make tactical decisions by providing data, evaluating models, and presenting output in a variety of formats. As you study models in your chosen discipline, remember the tools that MIS provides. Learn to use them. They will help you make better decisions, and they will help you understand the models. Many times, building a simple spreadsheet and experimenting with changes in the data will help you understand a model and how it is used to solve business problems.

## KEY WORDS

activity-based costing (ABC), 374
circular reference, 380
converge, 380

diverge, 380
geographic information system
  (GIS), 387

Global Positioning System
  (GPS), 388
unstable feedback, 380

## WEB SITE REFERENCES

**Computer Industry News**

| | |
|---|---|
| ACM Digital Library | www.acm.org/dl |
| Computer Economics | www.computereconomics.com |
| Computerworld | www.computerworld.com |
| Domain Stats | www.domainstats.com |
| Federal Computer Weekly | www.fcw.com |
| Gartner Group | www.gartner.com |
| IDG | www.idg.com |
| IEEE | www.ieee.org |
| Infoworld | www.infoworld.com |
| Internet.com | www.internet.com |
| Internet2 | www.internet2.org |
| InterNIC | www.internic.net |
| Network Solutions | www.networksolutions.com |
| PC Week | www.zdnet.com/pcweek |
| World Wide Web Consortium | www.w3.org |
| ZDNet | www.zdnet.com |

## REVIEW QUESTIONS

1. Describe the use of models in the disciplines of accounting, finance, marketing, human resources management, and production.
2. What similarities exist between sample models presented for the various departments?
3. What is a circular reference in a spreadsheet? Does it always mean there is an error in the spreadsheet?
4. What does it mean to say that a feedback loop *diverges*?
5. How are computers used to help manufacturing firms design products and control the manufacturing process?
6. Describe three decisions in finance that could benefit from the use of a DSS.
7. How can a DSS help the HRM department support laws that affect employees?
8. How is a geographic information system different from a package that just draws maps?
9. Describe four examples of businesses that would benefit from the use of a GIS.

## EXERCISES

1. Use the accounting example of activity-based costing. Build a spreadsheet that computes the ABC schedule in the text. Now, create a second version of the table to use for next year's forecast. Salaries are projected to increase by 5 percent in every area, except in *process sales orders,* where they will increase by 6 percent. New fringe benefits will add another 1 percent to everyone's benefits. Supplies are expected to change as follows: process sales orders, source parts, and schedule parts will increase by 5 percent. Reissue purchase orders, expedite customer orders, resolve supplier quality, expedite supplier orders will

rise by 7 percent. The others will decrease by 4 percent. Fixed costs will be the same in all areas, except request engineering change and resolve problems, which will decrease by 20 percent. Given these changes, compute the new totals. Create a set of graphs that will show how these changes will affect the company.

2. Build the balance sheets and income statements shown in the finance example. Convert the example so that the increase in capital is financed through the sale of stock (assume the price stays the same). In this example, is it better to issue stocks or to sell bonds?

3. From the marketing example, compute a new set of numbers and draw a similar graph given the costs of the promotions: Promo 1: $1,000 up front, Promo 2: $300 per week, Promo 3: $1,000 up front. (Advanced option: Use statistics to estimate the equations in the text.) Trivia question: What does *inchiki* mean?

4. Use a spreadsheet to create the example from the HRM section. Fill in the market adjustment column so that raises match the performance appraisals. Remember, total raises cannot exceed $10,000.

5. For one discipline (accounting, finance, marketing, human resources, economics, production management), find three models. List the assumptions, input and output variables, and the model or equations. Describe a business example where each model would be used.

6. For each of the models in the previous exercise, build a spreadsheet that evaluates the model and presents the output in a manner that makes it easier to make the decision. For most models, you should be able to draw a graph.

7. Interview a local manager to find a specific problem that can benefit from the use of a model. Obtain sample data (from the manager, or industry averages, or make it up if it's proprietary). Create a DSS to evaluate the data. How does the decision compare to the manager's (or your) initial guess?

8. Find four sources of data that you might use in a DSS for financial investments. Is the data available in computer form? Is it up to date? Optional: How much does it cost?

9. Create an example of a spreadsheet that contains a circular reference. Show two examples, one that converges to a stable solution, and one that diverges.

10. Describe three examples of how a geographic information system can be used to improve decisions. No more than one of them should be in a government agency.

 **C09GIS.xls**

11. Using the sample GIS data and the picture, can you identify any other potential relationships? What

other information would you like to see? Can you measure how the different factors affect sales? (Hint: Use statistical techniques.)

 **DeptStor.mdb**

You are a midlevel manager for a small department store. You have collected a large amount of data on sales for 2001. Your transaction system kept track of every sale (order) by customer. Most customers paid by credit card or check, so you have complete customer data. Walk-in customers who paid cash are given a separate customer number, so you still have the sales data.

You are trying to determine staffing levels for each department. You know that the store becomes much busier during the end-of-the-year holiday season. For summer months, you have thought about combining staff from the departments. From conversations with experienced workers, you have determined that there is a maximum number of customers that can be handled by one person in a department. These numbers are expressed as monthly averages in the table.

You are thinking about combining workers from some of the departments to save on staffing—especially over the spring and summer months. However, working multiple departments makes the sales staff less efficient. There are two considerations in combining staff members. First, if any of the departments are reduced to a staff of zero, sales in that department will drop by 10 percent for that month. Second, total staffing should be kept at the level defined by the monthly averages. If average staffing (total across all departments) falls below the total suggested, then sales in all departments will fall by 2 percent for each tenth of a percentage point below the suggested average.

| DEPARTMENT | CUSTOMERS/MONTH |
|---|---|
| Clothing—Children | 180 |
| Clothing—Men | 150 |
| Clothing—Women | 180 |
| Electronics | 200 |
| Furniture | 150 |
| Household | 250 |
| Linen | 300 |
| Shoes | 300 |
| Sports | 400 |
| Tools | 340 |

12. Using the database and a spreadsheet, determine how many workers we need in each department for each month. Present a plan for combining departments if it can save the company money. Assume that sales members cost an average of $1,000 a month. Two queries have already been created by the MIS department and are stored in the database: SalesbyMonth and SalesCountByMonth. The first totals the dollar value; the second counts the number of transactions.

13. Write a report to upper management designating the appropriate sales staff levels for each department by month. Include data and graphs to support your position. (Hint: Use a spreadsheet that lets you enter various staffing levels in each department in each month, then calculate any sales declines.)

### CO9Ex15.html

14. Obtain the data on the latest advertising campaign from the web site (or direct from the HTML file if a web site is not set up for you). For each product category, compute net profit: Net = Revenue − Cost − Advertising expenses − Employee cost (assume employees are hired at the suggested average level).

### Rolling Thunder Database

15. **Production model.** Evaluate the daily production levels and capacities. Identify any bottlenecks in production. Is there excess capacity in any of the steps?

16. **Production model.** Evaluate our inventory strategy. Determine whether it is feasible to operate with a just-in-time inventory for some of the components or tubing. (Hint: How often do we use each part? How large are part orders/deliveries? How much do we spend on each order? How much money do we tie up in holding inventory? Do we ever run out of parts?)

17. **Production model.** Management wishes to cut costs. Based on 1999 orders, evaluate the effect on production of altering the number of assembly stations. Consider values of 4, 5, 6, and 7. Perform a similar analysis for paint stations. We particularly want to examine how these changes would affect the average number of days to build a bicycle.

18. **Marketing model.** Managers are thinking about expanding production facilities and would like to know the value of such an expansion. If we increase the capacity of assembly, painting, and shipping, we will probably need more order takers. How busy are the current order lines, and how many new order-entry clerks should we hire if we want to expand produc-

tion by 10 percent (also consider 20 percent and 40 percent increases). (Hint: Estimate how long each order call will last by the length of time it takes to fill out the order form. Also consider the number of calls that arrive at the same time—busy periods. Consider looking at other firms/industries.)

19. **Marketing model.** Evaluate existing sales by location. Try to obtain external data on demographic characteristics for our customers. Present a marketing plan describing our customers and the types of bicycles they purchase. Provide suggestions on how we might expand our sales by locating similar customers.

20. **Forecast model.** Management wants to know how many bicycles can be sold in the next year. Using internal data, economic data, and industry trends, provide a forecast for the number of bicycles that could be sold (with no production constraints). If possible, provide a breakdown by type of model or frame material.

21. **Finance model.** Extract the appropriate financial data and build a spreadsheet to compute the standard financial ratios. Compare the ratios to other medium-size manufacturers. Based on this analysis, what changes should be made to improve the financial performance of the firm?

22. **Finance model.** The firm wants to expand production next year and wants to create another assembly station. The initial cost of the equipment is $50,000. The purchase will entail additional repair and maintenance costs of $100 per month for the next five years (the estimated life of the equipment). Should we buy it?

23. **HRM model.** Build a spreadsheet to compare the production/output of each employee. Compare the production to the salary. Could we reduce the size of the workforce?

24. **HRM model.** Assume that management allocates a 5 percent increase in salaries across the company (excluding managers and the CEO, whose raises are determined by the board). Create a merit evaluation for each of the employees (make up the data if it does not exist). Then determine the new salaries for each worker, based on his or her merit evaluations, level of experience and current salary. You cannot exceed the overall 5 percent increase for the company. Use any necessary graphs and analysis to explain your choices.

25. **Accounting model.** Build a report that creates the standard income and balance sheets. Create/assume data as necessary, such as outstanding stock.

26. **Accounting model.** Analyze the cash flow. Determine whether there are problems with the existing procedures.

27. **Accounting/Finance model.** Forecast cash flow needs for the next year. Suggest investments and schedule maturities, receipts, and payments to minimize costs for the coming year.

28. **Accounting/Finance model.** Create an application to track financial investments and cash flow needs.

29. **Teamwork.** Most of these models/questions can be combined and solved as an integrated model by a team.

## ADDITIONAL READING

"Frontiers of Finance," *The Economist,* October 9, 1993 (Survey pp. 1–22). [A survey of financial techniques, models, and some existing applications]

Pare, Terence. "A New Tool for Managing Costs," *Fortune,* June 14, 1993, pp. 124–129. [A discussion of activity-based accounting]

"Wall Street: Refugees from Physics Find Joy as 'Derivatives Geeks'," *Scientific American,* April 1994, pp. 126, 128. [Physicists on Wall Street]

Worcester, Barbara A. "EIS Used as Data-Management Tool," *Hotel & Motel Management,* November 3, 1997, pp. 78–79. [EIS in the hotel industry]

# CASES *Package Delivery*

The secret to being a successful package delivery company is timeliness, efficiency, and affordability. In the last 20 years, guaranteed two-day and overnight delivery has made drastic changes in businesses' perception of "timely." Pony express delivered messages for several years, until the telegraph rendered it obsolete. Many think that fax machines and e-mail may do the same thing to the overnight market. So far this has not been the case. The industry has continued to change nonetheless, hastened by the march of technology.

As manufacturers and sellers have focused on driving costs down in a more competitive marketplace, inventory management has become an increasingly important issue. The package delivery industry has responded with products and services to make inventory management more efficient and effective. The industry offers many different price structures, timing options, and tracking information options for a variety of different needs.

## Financial Analysis

While moderate to high market growth continues in the industry, prices have declined because of fierce competition. Technological advances and efficiencies have enabled the industry to continuously cut costs. United Parcel Service (UPS) and Federal Express (FedEx), the two most technologically advanced companies, have reported profit increases greater than yearly sales increases.

## Stock/Investment Outlook

The stock projection for the package delivery industry is positive for the next few years. Most of the large delivery companies are rated a buy or outperform for the next three to four years. Those companies that are competing on price, such as Airborne Express, may face a bleaker future than those that have prepared to offer technologically differentiated services, such as UPS or FedEx. Other carriers, such as Emery and DHL, have identified niches with heavier packages or international delivery.

## Potential/Prospects for Growth

The package delivery market continues to grow 3 to 5 percent each year, and competition is fierce among the established players. Alternative messaging devices, including the Internet, fax machines, and e-mail, may decrease document delivery growth in the future. Alternatively, Internet usage may increase package delivery growth as more individuals purchase from the Internet and as business conditions continue to get more efficient and less dependent on location.

Alliances between manufacturing and delivery companies are becoming increasingly prevalent and important. Also, the growth of the Internet as a commercial outlet and means of distribution may increase the importance of package delivery. Recently, UPS joined the online computer services Compuserve and Prodigy. The software for FedEx is preinstalled on Apple and IBM personal computers.

With the decrease in air transportation costs, an increasing amount of lower-value and heavier manufacturing products are being shipped by airfreight. Increasingly, carriers market their service not as airfreight, but as "time-definite" transportation. Pricing is based upon the speed with which the shipment is delivered and the distance it travels. This contrasts with trucking, where rates are set by weight and distance. This strategy has served to narrow the price difference between these two modes of delivery.

The other major area for growth is international, especially in Southeast Asia. Those companies with the resources to build new facilities and new networks in this region gain a substantial advantage over competitors without these resources.

## Competitive Structure

The U.S. market is made up of seven large companies, dozens of smaller entities, and the U.S. post office. The biggest shake-up in the package delivery industry occurred when UPS, the sleeping giant, awoke. For years, UPS was the industry cash cow. It owned the package delivery market and was a very staid company trying to do one thing well—mass-produced delivery. After the upstart FedEx began the new overnight market, UPS slowly began to transform itself to expand into that and other markets. One of the ways UPS transformed itself was to increase the marketing department from seven to 600 people, in order to attract and keep corporate customers.

Given the high cost of entry, the oligopoly in the marketplace will continue. Billions are needed to develop facilities in trucking, delivery, computer, and air networks. These costs keep new companies from entering or becoming a dominant force in the marketplace. As time goes on, more buyouts, mergers, and alliances may further restrict the number of players.

Mergers will continue to play an important role in the consolidation of the industry. FedEx acquired Flying Tigers in 1988. Airborne formed an alliance with Roadway to complement its strengths. Airborne brought planes to the table; Roadway had a well-established truck network.

| CARRIER | FORECAST | | | GROWTH RATE | |
|---|---|---|---|---|---|
| | **1995** | **1996** | **2000** | **1993–95** | **1995–2000** |
| FedEx | 142,768 | 151,741 | 191,531 | 8.3% | 6.1% |
| UPS | 70,343 | 98,498 | 158,807 | 27.1% | 17.7% |
| Other | 997,853 | 1,027,060 | 1,284,986 | 11.6% | 5.2% |
| TOTAL | 1,210,964 | 1,277,300 | 1,635,326 | 11.9% | 6.2% |
| FedEx/UPS share | 17.6% | 19.8% | 21.4% | | |
| Freight Capacity in Metric Tons—Annual | | | | | |

PACIFIC RIM–U.S. CARGO CAPACITY DEPLOYMENT

Source: MergeGlobal, Inc., *Aviation Week & Space Technology,* August 26, 1996.

The post office has also increased its role and tenacity in the marketplace. The post office enjoys several advantages that other companies do not have. It has an entire restricted market, daily mail delivery, and a well-established infrastructure, including trucks and airplanes.

### Role of Research/Development

The role of research and development in the package delivery industry is to develop new technologies that will cut the cost of shipping or provide better services to customers. Recent initiatives include new software installed at customer sites that allows the customers to track packages themselves. Other software links package label printing with customer databases to track shipped packages better. Most of the focus lies in improving efficiency through distribution and planning.

### Technological Investment and Analysis

FedEx and UPS are leading the industry in technological spending. They are attempting to integrate all facets of the delivery process. They want their customers to use their software for creating shipping labels, tracking packages, and billing. Eventually these delivery companies want to become the shipping departments for corporations. Once FedEx and UPS have introduced their software into customers' routines, it is more difficult and troublesome for customers to switch to other delivery services. This is similar to the way some travel companies have set up sites as in-house corporate travel departments.

Assets that provide the means to move goods physically are undifferentiated and generically available to all players. Technology has emerged as the method to distinguish a company's products, improve its service quality, and lower costs. As such, it has become increasingly important to manufacturers and sellers to be able to access real-time information about the status of parts, materials, and finished goods in a world of just-in-time inventory management.

Technology is increasingly being used to manage complex physical networks, enhance asset utilization, and reinforce the reliability and predictability of package delivery. Technology is the leading component of the effort to add extra value for service and mitigate the downward spiral on prices. In spite of this focus on technology, the package delivery business, even more than that for standard letters, is a labor- and capital-intensive business.

### Recommendation for the Future

The future appears bright for those companies with the resources to continue their expansion into Asia and onto the Internet. These are growth areas and should be exploited with the latest technology.

As more companies cut costs and reduce the number of employees through outsourcing, they may outsource their shipping department to the larger package delivery companies as well. This is a service area of the business that could be expanded by the larger companies. Smaller package delivery companies will have to find specific niches, such as transport for heavy items, valuable items, or dangerous items, in order to survive (e.g. Emory, DHL, and Airborne).

## CASE *Federal Express*

The Pony Express was a pony relay mail system between St. Joseph, Missouri, and Sacramento, California. It operated between April 1860 and October 1861. The system comprised 100 stations, 80 riders, and between 400 and 500 horses.

Two technological breakthroughs led to the end of the Pony Express: the connection of the East and West by the intercontinental railroad in 1861, and the completion of the intercontinental telegraph in 1861. These advancements enabled Americans to send messages across the country in minutes and send packages and freight in weeks as opposed to several months. The march of technology continues.

### Technological Investment and Analysis

An extranet is a network that uses Internet protocols to connect to customers and suppliers in a secure environment for secure communications and data exchange. It is different than the Internet in that selected information from an organization's intranet is made available to its external users. In other words, the extranet is the integration of the intranet and the Internet. The Federal Express site lets customers key in their account and airbill numbers, then tap into the overnight courier's own operational system to track the progress of their shipments.

High-volume corporate customers can handle their shipments automatically by integrating their order and warehousing data systems with FedEx's intake, billing, and package tracking software. FedEx is a leader in the use of the Internet for providing information to customers and improving efficiency.

In late 1996, FedEx terminated its development of a version of its FedEx Ship software for Lotus Notes. The company decided to focus its attention on the development of its web site. FedEx Ship for Notes would have required that users have a Notes or a basic Windows client.

FedEx utilizes the Internet to provide information to its customers, enable customers to make orders, and give customers the ability to track their packages. At this time the Internet has not replaced the customer call center, which provides the same services to FedEx customers. However, for its customers who currently use a PC to dial into FedEx, the Internet will eliminate the need for customers to have FedEx ordering and tracking software installed on their PC. The software allowed FedEx customers to make an order and track their package by linking to the FedEx mainframe over the telephone lines via a modem or EDI. Federal Express's web site allows customers to track their shipments, locate the nearest drop-off sites, request a pickup, and ask for an invoice adjustment.

Approximately 5 million customers per month visit the site, which opened in November 1994. Handling 900,000 tracking requests online each month is cheaper than fielding them in the FedEx call center. Setup costs for the web site were minimal, as FedEx modified applications were already in development for its proprietary InterNetShip network. The web site, which is protected by a firewall, runs on Netscape Commerce Server software hosted by dual Sun SPARC Web servers. Secure Socket Layer (SSL) security protects information sent over the Web.

The exponential growth of the use of FedEx's web site is creating the need for FedEx's IS department to serve its external customers. "'(Customers) expect everything to work perfectly all the time and they get very frustrated," said Susan Goeldner, manager of Internet technologies at Federal Express. "Unlike internal users, who are hostage of IS, external customers demand immediate attention. And if they don't get it, they go elsewhere."

Relations between IS and marketing at FedEx have not always gone smoothly, according to Goeldner. But the need to create a viable presence online has driven them together. Federal Express is trying to focus the IS department on the strategic need for Internet commerce. Given the growth of PCs in the business world, electronic commerce over the Internet is a viable way to capture customers and reduce costs.

An experimental courier route planning system project is underway. FedEx is using geo-coding and geo-positioning technology to plot a courier's pickups and deliveries on a map route by longitude and latitude. One use of the map is to show the courier the exact route she followed and to suggest possibilities for more efficient sequencing. Soon to follow are shortest time path estimates. These will help station managers to plan the work of couriers under supervision. Preliminary estimates show that a five to 10 percent productivity improvement is possible, and almost all of it goes to the bottom line.

Another application involves plotting an entire station's deliveries by route number on the station's service area map. This will reveal operating problems in the route structure. Since customer volumes are always changing, and new customers appear and old ones disappear, route balancing is a constant challenge. Couriers' routes are currently plotted by hand, but when the geo-coding experiment is completed, it is likely that a computer program can be devised to do the task more effectively.

### Technological Innovations

#### Network

Federal Express uses a set of package tracking and shipping application programming interfaces (APIs) that will link corporate networks, intranets, and World Wide Web sites directly to internal FedEx applications that hold shipping status information. Such tight links with customers' systems can make electronic commerce easier and faster, said Michael W. Janes, FedEx's vice president of marketing for logistics and electronic commerce. To provide a higher level of customer support, the Memphis-based delivery giant is investing millions of dollars to install distributed application and management software.

#### Telecommunications

Federal Express's FedEx.com site began in the spring of 1995 but did not add the ability to track packages until April 1996. The site has had to add servers and bandwidth as traffic increased, particularly during the UPS strike in August 1997. During this time, the number of hits doubled on the site from 140,000 per day to 280,000 per day.

The company uses ten 200 MHz Sun Microsystems Ultra 2 Web servers running Netscape Enterprise Server 3.5.1: five running Solaris 2.6 and five running 2.5.1.

Although FedEx does not break out details on how many packages are shipped or tracked through FedEx.com alone, the company says that 2 million of the current daily average of 3 million packages are shipped or tracked via the web site or through FedEx's Windows software over a proprietary data network.

Federal Express is beta-testing the FedEx intraNet-Ship. This is a workgroup-enabled extranet application that will link to customer intranets and automate package-tracking and authorization processes. Full implementation was scheduled for January 1998. FedEx intraNetShip will run on customer servers and will interface with FedEx.com, the package carrier's web site. The application is designed to centralize policy management at user sites and standardize authorization procedures. It represents an expansion of FedEx's Internet strategy, from Web-based package tracking and other services to a model based on server applications at customer sites.

Federal Express is also beta-testing software (caliber system) that lets corporate customers take a virtual peek inside packages in transit to reveal their contents and value. The application establishes a central administrator who can parcel out inventory, packing, and shipping instructions to appropriate departments and not only track the path of the package but also the contents and value of the box, according to Rohan Champion, vice-president of strategic alliances at Federal Express.

### Recommendation for the Future

FedEx should continue its web site development and focus on customer service. The extranet will eventually lead to cost savings as well as better integration of data for its internal and external customers.

With the purchase of Caliber System, Federal Express will be able to utilize its technology in order to capture more revenues and profits. The airfreight business has very low margins and Federal Express has proven to be a leader in its industry. However, the inventory management and logistics businesses have wider margins, which will enable Federal Express to better utilize its fixed assets. The outsourcing of corporate warehousing, ordering, and shipping functions will provide a growing market for Federal Express to capture more revenues and better profit margins.

### QUESTIONS

1. What has been the catalyst for change at Federal Express?
2. Upon which technologies has Federal Express relied?
3. How successful has technological change been at Federal Express?
4. What does the corporation say about its financial ability to embark on a major technological program of advancement?
5. What does Federal Express's web page present about its business directives?
6. What challenges and opportunities is the package delivery industry facing?
7. How important is the collection and evaluation of data to the future of Federal Express?

### ADDITIONAL READING

Basch, Reva. "What on Earth is an Extranet?" *Link-Up,* February 17, 1997, p. 248.

Davis, Beth. "FedEx Signs BMC for App Management, *InformationWeek,* September 7, 1998, p. 40.

Deck, Stewart. "FedEx Pilots Expect Relief," *Computerworld,* February 1, 1999, p. 16.

———. "Mark FDX Opts for Oracle8 DB," *Computerworld,* January 25, 1999, p. 14.

———. "System Implementation May Contribute to Pilots' Strike at FedEx," *Computerworld,* October 26, 1998, p. 24.

"FedEx Builds Technology Campus," *Electronic Buyers' News,* October 26, 1998, p. 80.

"FedEx Enhances Internet Shipping," *Electronic Buyers' News,* January 11, 1999, p. 52.

Machlis, Sharon. "And Don't Do It Too Often: To Redesign or Not to Redesign?" *Computerworld,* October 26, 1998, p. 43.

Moad, Jeff. "FedEx Tracks Customers on the Move: Uses an Intranet Decision-Support Application to Chart Letter and Package Drop Points," *PC Week,* November 30, 1998, p. 110.

"Online All the Time," *InformationWeek,* December 21, 1998, p. 26.

Pereira, Pedro. "FedEx Opens Doors to World," *Computer Reseller News,* October 21, 1996, p. 55.

Vijayan, Jaikumar. "Capacity Planning More Vital than Ever," *Computerworld,* February 15, 1999, p. 64.

Walsh, Mark. "The Air Bill Joins the 8-Track," *Internet World,* August 1997, p. 43.

Wasserman, Todd. "Strike Threat Worried Few—Contingency Plans in Place to Handle a FedEx Pilot Walkout," *Computer Retail Week,* November 23, 1998, p. 2.

### CASE *United Parcel Service, Inc.*

The chief information officer for UPS, Ken Lacy, has a daunting task at hand. Simply put, he has to take an enormous, geographically sprawled company and update its central nervous system. He has to do this in a hurry, too, because the competition is ferocious. Federal Express, UPS's most feared competitor, has the potential to corner the parcel delivery market much like Kleenex or Xerox did in their markets. "Go FedEx this for me, would you?" or, "I just got a FedEx from my uncle in Baltimore," are phrases that Lacy or, more importantly, Lacy's boss Chairman and CEO Kent Nelson, never wants to hear.

Lacy has the company's support and backing as well as the company's cash to spend. In a time of deregulation, more competition, and cost cutting, investments in technology must show results.

### Technological Investment and Analysis

New facilities in Georgia and New Jersey house what UPS claims is the largest database in the world, the DB2 database. The DB2 database has more than 7,000 gigabytes of records, the tracking information regarding all UPS packages shipped in an 18-month period. This kind of computing power translates into information regarding senders, receivers, billing, bar codes, time sent, estimated destinations, and other information for more than 4 billion packages.

The new Atlanta site is primarily backup for the New Jersey operations in case of disaster or expansion needs. Input into these new centralized computing facilities is through DIADs, or delivery information acquisition devices, specially developed for UPS by Motorola. These devices are handheld by the delivery person and feature 1.5 MB of RAM, digital signature capability, and an optical coupler. The optical coupler is used to transfer information and signatures into the DVA or DIAD Vehicle Adapter, where data is then transferred via cellular phone or modem. UPSnet makes the transfer of data to the data facilities in New Jersey and Atlanta. UPSnet does this via a network of 500,000 miles of dedicated cables, more than 200 switching nodes and a UPS satellite.

Outsourcing of certain functions needing expert advice and creating partnerships that support the needs of information systems are also underway. For example, to send all the information from the delivery trucks through the DVA using UPS TotalTrack, UPS has alliances with more than 90 local and regional cellular carriers including AT&T Wireless Communications, AirTouch Cellular, Southwestern Bell Mobile Systems, Pacific Telesis, GTE Mobilnet, and others. Northern Telecom switches provision UPSnet's dedicated cables directly linked to the central computing facilities. Several types of products from several companies result in a 100 percent uptime for the network.

Users of UPS MaxiTrac dial through lines provided by AT&T and Sprint. For data warehousing, UPS has chosen EMC Corp. and a system developed by Hewlett-Packard Co. and Oracle Corp. UPS's existing mainframes were not meeting the speed and availability needs required to service the vast amounts of data, but with the help of EMC, data warehousing will now be state of the art. These cooperative agreements have helped lessen UPS's technology-related responsibilities and have focused UPS's energies on more core issues.

The final implementation of UPS's technological initiative is the development and upgrading of software application products. One of the results of this initiative is UPS Online. This service is a Windows-based system that lets customers manage finances related to the package, track the status of their package, and print out shipping summaries. This system will integrate UPS into the customers' daily operations while providing more valuable information, allowing the customer to react to situations in real-time.

Another new product is the UPS web site. On the site, a browser can find information about the company, what is new in the company, employment information, news releases, and a host of other information related to UPS. The customer can also find on the site a service that will, using bar codes, locate where the package is in the delivery process. In this way, even the casual, noncompany-related customer could have access to most of the information that users of UPS Online would have. If all goes as planned, the Internet and the UPS web site will also serve as a center where transactions will occur without the security hazards still present on the Web. The Internet potential is great and UPS wants to be one of the first companies capitalizing on its potential.

Another new product is the improved help desk that will service both internal users as well as external users in an attempt to "empower our [employees and customers] to become as independent as possible in using technology." The help desk function was not a formal organization five years ago, but as the volume and the sophistication of UPS and its software grew, and as the need for support for these new technologies grew, an operation was launched to service the need.

With the internal and external operations combined, the help desk receives approximately 70,000 calls a month, a dramatic increase compared to approximately 14,000 calls a month in 1991. The external operation is run by 130 front-line experts and the internal group is run by 65 first-line consultants in the Mahwah, New Jersey, campus.

The intimidating task of supporting all the software at UPS is, in turn, supported by Windows-based Expert Advisor from the Software Artistry company. Previously, the help desk function was supported by IBM's mainframe-based Infoman, but its limitations became too apparent as the move to PC-based operations from mainframe operations came about.

Expert Advisor allows UPS to store more data online to assist helpers solve problems in a standardized manner quickly and efficiently. The help desk technicians no longer have to flip through binders full of information to solve an issue. Rather, they just have to type it into Expert Advisor. With its dynamic ability to constantly update and incorporate new diagnostic tools and solutions into the system, Expert Advisor has developed the help desk function into a real value-adding arm at UPS.

UPS has therefore taken steps to initiate and seek new technologies as well as react to industry forces. These technologies all have an element of risk involved as significant funds have been allocated for the acquisition of new equipment, new software, and new employees. However, it is clear that UPS is trying to innovate to keep its market share and profitability.

### Technological Innovations

### Telecommunications

In 1998, UPS launched an Internet-based delivery service that the company says could make life a lot easier for firms wanting to send sensitive documents on tight deadlines. The service is called UPS Document Exchange. It is a suite of delivery and information management services that provides a choice of two Internet delivery services: UPS OnLine Courier and UPS OnLine Dossier.

UPS OnLine Courier uses either the UPS web site or a separate software package and allows customers to send documents to anyone, regardless of the e-mail software package, operating system, or hardware being used on either side of the delivery process. UPS OnLine Courier is built on an open environment.

"It has a PDF (portable document format) and Adobe PDF built into it, so if the recipient doesn't have the same software as you do, it won't hinder their ability to read it. That's a benefit of the Courier," said Joan Schnorbus, a UPS spokesperson.

UPS OnLine Dossier takes UPS OnLine Courier a step further by using a double-encryption process and offering insurance. The document will self-destruct if tampered with. UPS OnLine Dossier authenticates identities using digital certificates, which are required by both sender and receiver.

UPS is developing another service for corporate customers. This service integrates UPS package-tracking capabilities directly with the customers' web sites. The move allows consumers to obtain tracking information for their orders from the site where they ordered rather than by jumping to UPS.

### QUESTIONS

1. What has been the catalyst for change at the United Parcel Service?
2. What are the critical success factors and core competencies for UPS?
3. Upon what technologies has UPS relied?
4. What caused a change in the way UPS used technology to meet the business needs of its customers?
5. How does the corporation's web page support its business directives?
6. How important is the analysis of data to the corporation's continued success?
7. How will the capture and maintenance of customer data impact the corporation's future?

### ADDITIONAL READING

Beizer, Doug. "When You Need It Now," *PC Magazine,* September 1, 1998, p. 40.

"Cyberscope: Tracking Santa's Helpers," *Newsbytes,* December 1998.

Enright, Greg. "UPS Ships Online Delivery System," *Computing Canada,* July 6, 1998, p. 29.

Gable, Gene. "Two Brilliant Ideas, or Two Megaflops?" *Publish,* May 1998, p. 26.

Holt, Stannie. "ERP Vendors to Boost Shipping: Companies Strive for 'Seamless, Paperless' Supply Chain," *InfoWorld,* April 13, 1998, p. 19.

Kramer, Matt. "Web-Bound Attachments Remove Some Burden from E-Mail Servers," *PC Week,* November 23, 1998, p. 36.

Marlatt, Andrew. "Internet Emerges as Alternative to Overnight Mail, Faxes," *Internet World,* November 2, 1998, p. 54.

"Quality Stuff," *Computerworld,* July 27, 1998.

"UPS Buys Part of TanData," *InformationWeek,* October 19, 1998, p. 20.

"UPS Creates Wireless Industry Group," *Electronic Buyers' News,* September 28, 1998, p. 58.

"UPS Delivers a Lawsuit to Postal Service," *Network World,* October 12, 1998, p. 6.

"UPS E-Commerce; www.ec.ups.com," *Electronic Buyers' News,* June 8, 1998, p. 62.

Williams, Paul. "The Virtual Receptionist," *Newmedia,* May 5, 1998, p. 22.

Winter, Richard, and Kathy Auerbach. "VLDB: the Big Time," *Database Programming & Design,* August 1998, pp. S2–S9.

### DISCUSSION ISSUE

*Simulation*

Geordi is head of marketing for a new product introduction, which is code-named: red-clay. Tasha is the head of finance and accounting. Deanna is the person who developed the red-clay product and is responsible for the overall project. They are in the middle of a small argument over whether they should begin production of the product.

Geordi: According to the computer simulations, by running these ads at the target 18–24 year old group, we can expect an initial response rate of 19.2 percent. But we're also interested in repeat purchases. By extrapolating the statistics from our experiences with the *big-sky* product, we anticipate repeat buying of two items a month by 5 percent of the target group. If the product gains momentum, long-run market share should stabilize around 35 percent. At this point, there is insufficient data to determine whether the product will be fully accepted.

Tasha: In other words, we're supposed to risk the entire project based on these numbers generated from the computer. I don't like it.

Deanna: Actually, we believe the values are low. In my discussions with the participants after the study, I sensed that they were much more enthusiastic than the numbers indicate.

Geordi: In fact, Tasha, we deliberately chose conservative values to use in the simulations. If Deanna is right, this product could be hot. We might even show a major profit in the first six months.

Tasha: But, that's all speculation. This model has no relationship to reality. I could just as easily find 10 people who hate the product. I was talking to my niece the other day, and she says it's revolting.

Deanna: Now Tasha, you know we can't make decisions based on the responses of one person. We scientifically selected the participants . . .

Tasha: That was just an example. I'm much more concerned about these computer projections. I don't understand how the computer produced these results. Instead of wasting time with simulations, I think we should talk to real people.

Geordi: If you want, I can print out the computer model equations for you. But they're from state-of-the-art market research, and they might be hard to follow. Plus, last time I checked, there were 50 pages of equations.

Tasha: Are you saying that consumers have to compute 50 pages worth of equations to decide whether they want to buy this product!?

Geordi: No, no. The equations are just used by the computer to describe how customers behave.

Tasha: But how do we know the equations are right? Are you saying the computer can tell you whether I will buy the product?

Deanna: No, of course not. But we don't need to predict responses of individuals. We focus on how the entire target group will respond.

Tasha: We don't seem to be getting anywhere. I still don't see how we know whether the computer is right. If it's wrong, we lose a lot of money. I don't see how the computer can analyze every possibility. For instance, what happens if the product appeals to the 15- to 18-year-old group? Won't that create a negative status effect on our target group?

Geordi: We talked about that possibility early on, but we don't think it's important enough to include in the model. There are hundreds of minor possibilities, but we don't have time to include all of them.

Tasha: In other words, your model only includes things *you* thought were important. That's even worse. Why didn't you just make up the sales projections, instead of hiding them behind some phony model?

Deanna: I sense that we have reached an impasse. Perhaps we should take a break and come back later. Geordi, perhaps you could prepare a small demonstration of the model. And Tasha, remember that we still have to make a decision. We can't always predict the exact future; sometimes even a little information is better than none.

## DISCUSSION QUESTIONS

1. Is Tasha right—are simulations just a way for Geordi to invent whatever numbers he wants?
2. How accurate can we make the results from models and simulations? How easy would it be to force a model to produce the results we want?
3. What would you gain by manipulating simulations and models to produce the results you want? What are the costs (short run and long run)?
4. Is it possible to verify the accuracy of simulations and models? Are some models easier to evaluate than others?
5. What knowledge or background do you need to evaluate models? Do you think managers can accurately evaluate models from other disciplines (such as accountants evaluating marketing models)?
6. Should we distrust all models and simulations? What uses do they have?

# Financial Definitions

Several standardized methods have been created to analyze business financial data. These numbers are easily computed from the standard reported accounting data. The various financial ratios are particularly useful to highlight potential problems. The ratios can be compared against industry averages that are published by various companies.

The basic definitions are presented here with brief comments on their usage. You can find more detailed analysis and interpretation in any introductory finance textbook.

## BASIC ACCOUNTING REPORTS

The balance sheet summarizes the firm's assets, liabilities, and owner's equity (net worth) at a particular point in time. The income statement details the receipts and profits during a specified time period. The statement of owner's equity or retained earnings statement covers the same time period as the income statement and displays the changes in ownership data.

## Interpretation

### Profitability Ratios

There are many ways to evaluate profitability in a firm. Some people look at gross profit (income); others rely on net income. Profit margin is a common measure, but it varies considerably by industry. Return on assets and return on equity more closely reflect the earnings received by investors. The DuPont method shows these two values are closely related. The DuPont method also highlights a key feature of ROA. Firms can increase ROA by increasing their profit margin (possibly selling products at a higher price) or by increasing their turnover (dropping the price and selling more items at lower profit). A quick examination of these two values will tell you a key strategy of the firm.

### Liquidity Ratios

Liquidity ratios evaluate whether a firm can meet its short-term obligations. Higher values mean it is easier to cover current expenses, but values that are too high imply too much money is sitting idle. The quick ratio is the most conservative, where values greater than 1.0 imply a firm can pay off current debts almost immediately.

### Activity Ratios

The activity ratios indicate how well the firm is handling day-to-day operations. In particular, a low *asset turnover* would imply the firm has excess capacity. A low *inventory turnover* implies they are not handling inventory very well or that sales are dropping. A low *average collection period* indicates that the firm is slow to collect from its customers. As usual, *high* and *low* are relative terms and must be compared to industry averages.

### Debt Ratios

The basic *debt ratio* indicates the share of financing that came from borrowing instead of equity (stocks). This value is highly variable. Some managers prefer to borrow heavily; others rely on equity. Relatively high values imply that it will be difficult for the firm to borrow additional money—an important piece of data if you are looking to invest heavily in new technology. The *times interest earned* ratio measures the firm's ability to pay interest costs from operating income. If the ratio is low, the firm is struggling to cover its debt payments.

BALANCE SHEET

| ASSETS | | CLAIMS | |
|--------|--|--------|--|
| Cash | | Accounts Payable | |
| Securities | | Notes Payable | |
| Receivables | | Accruals | |
| Inventories | | Bonds Payable | |
| *(total)* | Current Assets | Provisions for Taxes | |
| | | *(total)* | Total Liabilities |
| | | | |
| Gross Plant & Equip. | | | |
| *less* Depreciation | | Common Stocks | |
| | Net Plant & Equip. | Retained Earnings | |
| | | *(total)* | Total Net Worth |
| | | | |
| *(add)* | Total Assets | *(add)* | Total Claims |

INCOME STATEMENT

| | | |
|--|--|--|
| Net Sales | | *(gross sales – returns and discounts)* |
| *less* Cost of goods sold | | *(inventory, purchases, transportation, etc.)* |
| | Gross Profit | |
| Selling costs | | |
| General & administrative | | |
| Building leases | | |
| *(total)* | Operating expenses | |
| *(subtract to get)* | Gross operating income | |
| *(less)* | Depreciation | |
| *(equals)* | Net operating income | |
| *(add)* | Other income | *(royalties, etc.)* |
| *(equals)* | Gross income | |
| Interest on notes payable | | |
| Interest on mortgage | | |
| Interest on bonds | | |
| *(total)* | Other expenses | |
| *(subtract to get)* | Net income before taxes | |
| *(subtract)* | Federal income taxes | |
| | Net income | |

STATEMENT OF RETAINED EARNINGS

| | |
|--|--|
| *(Starting)* | Retained earnings |
| *(add)* | Net income |
| *(equals)* | Total |
| *(subtract)* | Dividends |
| *(equals)* | Ending retained earnings |

FINANCIAL RATIO
CALCULATIONS

| **PROFITABILITY** |
|---|
| Profit margin = $\dfrac{\text{Net income before taxes}}{\text{Net sales}}$ |
| Earnings per share (EPS) = $\dfrac{\text{Net income after taxes + dividends}}{\text{Number of shares outstanding}}$ |
| Return on equity (ROE) = $\dfrac{\text{Net income after taxes}}{\text{Equity (book value)}}$ |
| Price earnings ratio (P/E) = $\dfrac{\text{Average market price per share}}{\text{EPS}}$ |
| **LIQUIDITY** |
| Current ratio = $\dfrac{\text{Current assets}}{\text{Current liabilities}}$ |
| Quick (or Acid) test = $\dfrac{\text{Current assets – Inventories}}{\text{Current liabilities}}$ |
| **ACTIVITY RATIOS** |
| Asset turnover = $\dfrac{\text{Net sales}}{\text{Total assets}}$ |
| Inventory turnover = $\dfrac{\text{Cost of goods sold}}{\text{Inventory}}$ |
| Average collection period = $\dfrac{\text{Accounts receivable}}{\text{Sales per day}}$ |
| **LEVERAGE RATIOS** |
| Debt ratio = $\dfrac{\text{Total debt}}{\text{Total assets}}$ |
| Times interest earned = $\dfrac{\text{Income before taxes + Interest charges}}{\text{Interest charges}}$ |

DUPONT ANALYSIS

$$\overbrace{\text{Profit margin} \times \text{Total asset turnover}}$$
$$\text{ROA} = \frac{\text{Net income}}{\text{Sales}} \times \frac{\text{Sales}}{\text{Total assets}}$$

$$\overbrace{\text{ROA} \times \text{Leverage}}$$
$$\text{ROE} = \frac{\text{Net income}}{\text{Total assets}} \times \frac{\text{Total assets}}{\text{Common equity}}$$

## EXERCISES

1. Find a balance sheet and income statement (try http://www.sec.gov/edgar), copy the data into a spreadsheet, and compute the basic financial ratios.

2. Choose two similar-sized firms in different industries (check the Fortune 500 list), and compare the DuPont ratios to see if they pursue different strategies.

3. Find profit and debt ratios for three different industries (try *Wall Street Journal* or Hoover). Briefly explain why the values are different in each industry.

4. Find a small firm and a large firm in the same industry and briefly describe the differences in their basic financial ratios.

5. Find financial data on one firm and compute its basic financial ratios for the last five years (using quarterly or annual data). Describe any patterns or trends.

# CHAPTER 10

# *Complex Decisions and Artificial Intelligence*

Mrs. Fields is recognizable around the nation. Managing the stores entails making many difficult decisions. Mrs. Fields relies on expert systems to help managers make better decisions.

## MRS. FIELDS, INC.

In 1977, Debbie Fields opened a small cookie store in Palo Alto, California, defying conventional wisdom that "No one will pay 75 cents for a cookie." The store specialized in chocolate chip cookies made from a recipe generous in chocolate chips. It became an overnight success. Mrs. Fields cookies struck a responsive chord in the taste buds of the Palo Alto residents. Today, these cookies are available nationwide at more than 635 licensed franchises.

Randy Fields, the "mister" in Mrs. Fields cookies, was a Stanford graduate with a great deal of programming experience. From the beginning, he insisted on the implementation of computers throughout the stores. Even so, problems began to develop in his efforts to keep track of the rapidly expanding chain of stores.

As the company continued to grow, more than 20 people were serving on the headquarters staff. The sales-tracking system required managers to key in sales information on Touch-Tone telephones. It worked fine with 25 locations. However, by 1985 it was falling apart under the burden of 136 stores. In addition, Mrs. Fields cookies had just bought a 70-store chain in the East that would have to be immediately integrated into the reporting system. Thus, Randy Fields made the timely decision to hire Paul Quinn, an expert in systems development, to head the MIS area.

The vision for Mrs. Fields cookies was to grow so quickly that no one would be able to catch up. With such an aggressive mission, the owners needed more than just an information management system to stay on top. Quinn had an idea. Because Mrs. Fields had started from an idea that defied conventional wisdom, why not remain innovative in the design of the new computer system? To answer this question, Randy Fields and Paul Quinn embarked on a program to develop an integrated store system that would use expert systems technology.

**OVERVIEW**    What functions do computers perform best? The short answer is: basic computations and processing large sets of data. Modern computer systems are also good at creating graphs and reports. All of these traits are useful for building transaction-processing and decision support systems. But in these situations, the computer is relatively passive. Designers and managers perform all of the analysis and "thinking." The computer provides data, performs calculations, and produces output at the direction of the managers. Can computers do more?

Most people do not have perfect recall and cannot perform billions of mathematical calculations per second. However, people can solve problems and make decisions, and they can deal with symbolic and subjective data. To make decisions in an uncertain world, we make judgments and guesses.

There are certain tasks that people do very easily: recognize a family member across a street, know the difference between a tree and a flower, communicate in a spoken (natural) language, learn new tasks. So far, it has been difficult to create computer systems that can perform these types of tasks.

Most experts believe we are a long ways away from creating machines that can *think*. However, computers can help with certain complex problems. In particular, diagnostic problems are common in business. A machine might need repairs and you have to find the cause, or sales are slipping in one region and you want to find the best method to increase them. You could turn to a consultant or expert to help solve diagnostic problems.

Consider a related question: What functions do machines perform better than humans? To use machines wisely, we must analyze their capabilities and compare them to the relative advantages of humans. Of course, scientific progress continually improves technology and expands the capabilities of machines. Several techniques, like the neural network illustrated in Figure 10.1, have arisen from research into artificial intelligence. Each new technique raises similar questions. How can the technology be used to solve problems and make better decisions? Is the technology cost effective? Sometimes new technology is exciting and it is easy to forget that it must be carefully analyzed to determine its true value.

**FIGURE 10.1**
COMPUTER ANALYSIS OF DATA AND MODELS
Research into "intelligence" has led to some decisions that can be analyzed and "solved" by computers. Expert systems and neural networks are two tools that are being used to help make decisions. These tools are used to make faster, more consistent decisions.

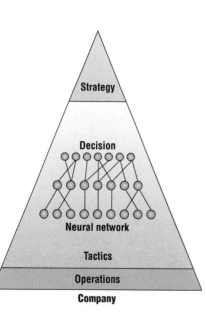

**INTRODUCTION**　Few business problems are straightforward. In these cases, we simply create a set of rules or procedures to follow. A computer can often be programmed to follow these basic procedures. As long as the business behaves in a predictable manner, the rules apply and the computer can handle the details. However, many business problems are less structured and cannot be solved so easily. Additionally, problems often involve data that is not well defined. For example, it is straightforward to create a computer system to handle inventory because the computer can easily keep track of item numbers and quantity sold. Consider

## Trends

As businesses began to use computers, the easy problems were solved first, such as the highly structured transaction processing systems discussed in Chapter 4. But from the earliest days of computers, people have dreamed of machines that could solve more complex problems. One recurring question is whether or not machines can ever solve problems the same way as humans. Some of the earliest professional comments on artificial intelligence (AI) came from discussions by British mathematician Alan Turing and his co-workers in the 1940s. Books by Hubert Dreyfus provide a quick, critical review of the history of AI research.

At first (1957–1962), researchers tried to define intelligence and attempted to write programs that could solve general problems. In particular, a great deal of effort and money was expended on software that would automatically translate documents—especially from Russian to English. However, after spending about $20 million, the researchers gave up in 1966. Two additional groups of AI researchers were busy: Newell, Shaw, and Simon at Carnegie and Papert and Minsky at MIT. Newell, Shaw, and Simon created a "General Problem Solver" that could prove some basic theorems in mathematics, when it was given the basic assumptions and prior theorems.

When it became impossible to extend the early research into more general problems, AI research changed directions. From 1962 to 1967, research focused on "Semantic Information Processing" (which was the title of a book by Marvin Minsky). Researchers also began to suggest that to create intelligent machines, they first needed to understand how the human brain worked. So they began to build models of human thought. An interesting program called STUDENT was written by Brobow, a graduate student working under Minsky. STUDENT could solve basic algebra "story problems" by examining key words (*is* for *equals, into* for *divide*, etc.).

Research again changed from 1967–1972 as workers focused on narrower subjects. Another MIT researcher (Weinograd) created a program called SHRDLU. SHRDLU displayed a set of geometric figures (boxes, pyramids, circles) and would answer questions or manipulate them in response to written commands. Within its limited area, it could understand fairly complex written statements.

From 1972 to 1977, research again narrowed its scope and focused on specific problems or "knowledge domains." The foundations of expert systems came from this early work. Feigenbaum at Stanford created Dendral, a system that contained rules and complex knowledge of chemical reactions.

The years from 1977 to 2000 have seen an expansion of research in AI, including robotics, pattern matching, language comprehension, and voice recognition. We have also seen the commercialization of many of the AI innovations, especially expert systems and speech recognition.

In the early years, researchers were optimistic about the possibilities presented by "thinking machines." In 1953, Turing suggested that by the end of the century, we would have "intelligent" machines. As technical advisor for the 1967 film *2001*, Marvin Minsky assured Kubrick that Turing was pessimistic, and we would see "intelligent" machines well before the end of the century. In 1957, Herbert Simon also suggested that his General Problem Solver would eventually show signs of intelligence. Although these predictions were overly optimistic, the ideas and results of this research have led to computer systems capable of solving more complex problems.

the more difficult problem faced by a manager who has to decide where to locate a new plant. Some attributes are measurable, such as distance from suppliers, cost of land, and taxes. Other features are difficult to quantify: quality of the labor force, attitudes of government officials, and long-run political stability of the area.

Many problems involve nonnumeric data and complex interrelationships among the various factors. Without computers, businesses often call in experts or hire consultants to help solve these problems. Special software programs called **expert systems (ESs)** provide many of these features.

From the beginning, researchers and computer designers have known that humans perform some tasks much better than computers can. These differences led researchers to investigate how people solve problems and investigate how humans think. The research into techniques that might make computers "think" more like humans is known as **artificial intelligence (AI).** There is some question as to whether it will ever be possible to build machines that can think the same way humans do. Nonetheless, the research has led to some useful tools that perform more complex analysis and can solve difficult problems. These tools attempt to mimic the processes used by humans in a simpler form that can be processed by a computer system.

For example, humans are very good at recognizing patterns, so techniques have been created to help machines identify patterns. Engineers are continuing to work on robots that can see, pick up diverse objects, and walk. Research continues into speech recognition and machine vision. In addition to application in manufacturing, these capabilities would make it easier for humans to communicate with machines.

## SPECIALIZED PROBLEMS: COMPLEX, REPETITIVE DECISIONS

Imagine your life as a top-notch manager. Co-workers perceive you as an expert and value your advice and problem-solving skills. You are constantly answering questions and there are always more problems than you can handle. You are using decision support systems and integrated information technology to perform your job better and more efficiently, but it is not enough. Can technology help you with more complex decisions and problem solving?

From another perspective, when you encounter new problems with different, complex models, it would be helpful to have an expert assist you with applying and understanding the models. Yet experts or consultants are expensive and not always available. Can you somehow capture the knowledge and methods of experts and use technology to make this knowledge available to workers throughout the company?

Expert systems have proven useful for many problems. The goal of an expert system is to enable novices to achieve results similar to those of an expert. The users need to understand the basic problem, learn the terminology, and be able to answer questions. For example, a typical patient would not be able to use a medical expert system because the questions and terms would not make any sense.

Think of an expert system as a consultant in a box. The consultant can only solve certain specific problems. For example, perhaps a retail store manager needs to estimate buying patterns for the next few months. The manager might call a marketing consultant to survey buyers and statistically search for patterns. The consultant will ask questions to determine the basic objectives and identify problems. Similarly, a production manager might be having problems with a certain machine. The manager might call a support line or a repair technician. The advice in this situation will be quite different from the marketing example, because the topics (or domains) of the two problems are different. It would be difficult to create one computer program that could help you with both types of problems. On the other hand, there are similarities in the approach to the two problems. Com-

Exsys is one of the leading suppliers of expert system development tools. One of their latest releases builds expert systems that run as a web site on the Internet. Companies could use this system to provide advanced advice to customers 24 hours a day.

puterized expert systems are designed to solve narrow, specialized problems. Each problem can be relatively complex, but it must be reasonably well defined. Many business problems fall into this category, and expert systems can be built for each problem.

## Diagnostic Problems

Several problems in the world can be classified as diagnostic situations. These problems arise when the decision maker is presented with a set of symptoms and is asked to find the cause of the problem, as well as solutions. Consider a firm that uses a complex machine. If the machine breaks down, production stops until it is fixed. Additionally, maintenance tasks have to be performed every day to keep the machine running. The company hires an engineer to perform these tasks. The engineer also knows which adjustments to make if various symptoms appear. This system has been working well, and the company wishes to expand to other locations with a franchise system. The problem is that there is only one engineer, and it would be too expensive to have a highly trained engineer at each location.

One possible solution would be to set up a phone link between the franchises and the engineer. One person at each franchise would be trained in the basics of the machine. If problems arise, the person could call the engineer. The engineer would ask specific questions, such as "What do the gauges show?" The answers will lead the engineer to ask other questions. Eventually, the engineer makes recommendations based on the answers.

Of course, if there are many franchises, the engineer will be too busy to solve all of the problems. Also, if the businesses are located in different countries, the time differences may not allow everyone enough access to the engineer. A better solution is to create a computerized expert system. All the expert's questions, recommendations, and rules can be entered into a computer system that is distributed to each franchise. If there is a problem, the on-site person turns to the expert system. The system asks the same questions that the engineer would and arrives at the same recommendations.

## Expert Systems Applications

### DIAGNOSTIC PROBLEMS

Many situations present a set of symptoms. Experts analyze these symptoms and search for a common cause. Interpretations are sometimes vague, use incomplete data, and can be hard to express in "rational" terms.

### SPEED

Some decisions are only moderately complex but are made hundreds or thousands of times. The ability to make these decisions rapidly (and correctly) improves customer satisfaction and can lead to an advantage over the competition.

### CONSISTENCY

From operational to legal consequence there are many advantages to making decisions consistently. Presented with the same basic inputs, the firm needs to reach the same conclusion, regardless of irrelevant factors.

### TRAINING

Automated support for repetitive decisions can be useful for training new employees. As the workers use the system, they will learn the business rules that make up their job.

Expert systems also have the ability to explain their recommendations. While running the ES, the user can ask it to explain why it asked a particular question or why it arrived at some conclusion. The ES traces through the answers it was given and explains its reasoning. This ability helps the user gain confidence in the decisions, allows mistakes to be corrected, and helps the users remember the answer for future reference.

The business world offers many examples of diagnostic situations, such as identifying causes of defects, finding the source of delays, and keeping complex equipment running. The common characteristic is that you are faced with a set of symptoms, and you need to find the cause.

### Speedy Decisions

Other situations can benefit from the use of expert systems. Even if a problem is not exceedingly complex, you could use an expert system to provide faster responses or to provide more consistent recommendations. Several advantages can be gained from making decisions faster than your competitors do. If you can identify a trend in stock prices before anyone else, you can make a higher profit. If you can answer customer questions faster, they will be more likely to shop with you in the future. If you can provide a loan to a customer sooner than anyone else, you will do more business.

Transaction-processing systems keep much of the basic data that you need to make decisions. Decision support systems help you analyze that raw data. Both of these tools enable you to make decisions faster than trying to make the decision without any computers. However, it still takes time for a human to analyze all of the information.

Consider the case of a bank loan. In order to get a loan, you go to the bank and fill out a loan application form. You tell the loan officer why you want the loan and provide basic data on income and expenses. Depending on the amount of money involved, the banker will probably check your credit history, get appraisals on any collateral, and perhaps get approval by a review officer or loan committee. All of these actions take time.

Now, consider the steps involved with a computerized process. First, you need to tell the bank that you want a loan. Instead of driving to the bank, you could use the telephone.

## Reality Bytes    10–1    Software Shopping Bots

As a precursor to agent technology, several web sites have created software robots or "bots" that are programmed to check specific sites looking for data. In particular, several bots have been created to compare prices of common products, such as music and books. Popular sites that run bots include www.webmarket.com and Junglee purchased by Amazon (shoptheweb.amazon.com). Some retailers are reluctant to deal with the bots. For example, Jason Olim, founder of CDNow, Inc., notes "We're simply not interested in working with the bots. It's too expensive to try and serve a customer who's only going to shop with us one out of every three times because of a 50-cent savings." So he blocks the bots from his site, which is easy because most bots obey a tag within a web page that tells them to ignore it. Other companies play different games, such as lowering the base price to attract shoppers, but raising hidden prices such as shipping and handling. Retailers are justifiably concerned about the bots when they are owned by a competitor. The major example is the purchase of Junglee by Amazon.com.

With a pushbutton phone, you enter information directly into the bank's computer. The computer would give you a choice of loan types (car, boat, personal, etc.) and you push a button to select one. You enter the amount of money you want to borrow. The next step is to check your credit history. Your income, expenses, and credit record are available to the bank from national credit reporting agencies. The bank might also have its own database. The bank's computer could be connected to credit agency computers to collect additional data on your credit history.

To make the final decision, the bank needs a set of rules. These rules take into account the size of the loan, the value of the collateral, as well as your income, expenses, credit history, and existing loans. When the bank has determined the proper rules, the computer performs the analyses. If the bankers trust the rules, the computer could make the final decision. For example, there would be no need for a loan officer to be involved in simple decisions, such as making small car loans to customers with large savings accounts. With an expert system, a bank can cut the loan-approval period down to a few minutes on the phone.

Many other decisions need to be made rapidly. The first step in all of these cases is to make sure that the transaction-processing system provides the necessary raw data. The second step is to create a set of rules for making the decision. The difficulty lies in finding these rules. For some problems, there are well-defined rules that can be trusted. For other problems, the rules may not exist. In this case, the company will probably still need a human to make the final decision.

### Consistency

The example of the bank loan demonstrates another advantage of expert systems. Business decisions are subject to a wide variety of nondiscrimination laws. An expert system can be used to provide consistent decisions. The rules followed by the ES can be set up to avoid illegal discrimination. Businesses also have credit ratings, which are often determined by Credit Clearing House (CCH). CCH uses an expert system to make the "easy" decisions, which speeds up the process by allowing humans to focus on the more complicated cases. It also leads to consistent application of the rules.

Consider the loan example. If each loan officer makes individual decisions, it is hard to determine whether they are consistent with corporate policy. Each individual decision would have to be checked to make sure it was nondiscriminatory. On the other hand, a committee could spend several weeks creating a set of lending rules that can be verified to be sure they are legal and ethical. As long as the bank employees follow the recommendations of the ES, the outcome should not be discriminatory. Because there should be few cases where the loan officer overrules the ES, managers will have more time to examine each of these circumstances.

Many business decisions need to be performed consistently to avoid bias and to treat people equally. Loans, pricing, raises, and promotions are some examples. However, there can be problems with using a computer system to enforce standards. The main difficulty lies in creating a set of rules that accurately describe the decisions and standards. For example, it might be useful to have a set of rules regarding raises and promotions, but think about what happens if an employee's job does not fit the basic rules. Organizations continually change, which means the rules have to be monitored and changed regularly.

## Training

Training employees is closely associated with problems of consistency. All organizations must train employees. If the tasks are complex and the decisions highly unstructured, it can take years for employees to learn the rules and gain the experience needed to deal with problems. Two features of expert systems help employees learn. First, employees learn what questions need to be asked. In particular, after using the system for a while, certain groups of questions will occur together. Second, most expert systems have provisions for explaining their answers (and the motivation for each question). At any point, an employee can ask the expert system why it asked a certain question or why it reached a conclusion.

**DECISION SUPPORT SYSTEMS AND EXPERT SYSTEMS**

Consider a small example. You wish to fly from Miami to Phoenix for Thanksgiving. You go to a travel agent who uses a computer reservation system to display the basic flight information. If there are seats available on the flights that you prefer, the computer records your name and prints a ticket. But, what happens if there are no open seats on the flights that you prefer? The computer system simply displays a message. You and the travel agent then have to find alternatives. The computer system is passive. It only provides basic information about schedules, availability, and prices.

Perhaps the computer designers have built a more sophisticated system that has decision support features. Now, when you have trouble finding a flight, the travel agent asks the computer to display a list of all open seats, sorted by price. It shows a graph of available seats arranged by price and departure times. A well-organized presentation of the data can make it easier for you to choose a flight.

Can the computer do even more? Look at the problem from another perspective. Why do we have travel agents? In the early days of flight reservation systems, the travel agent was necessary because passengers did not have access to computer terminals. Also, the agents needed special training to use the software. Today, it is easy to use the Internet to make your own reservations. Does that mean we do not need travel agents anymore? That's a question many people are asking. However, consider a situation when you want to book a vacation to a tropical island. Which resort should you choose? Does one offer better features? Is the food or service better at one? Which resort best fits the activities you prefer? You need the additional data and knowledge of someone who has been to the resorts. You need reliable information from someone that you trust.

Figure 10.2 indicates how the additional knowledge of the travel agent can make a difference in your decision. If this knowledge were incorporated into the computer sys-

**FIGURE 10.2**
Expert systems are designed to help novices achieve the same results as experts. An expert uses symbolic and numeric knowledge along with rules to analyze a situation and make a decision. Knowledge engineers create a computerized knowledge base that is used to assist novices.

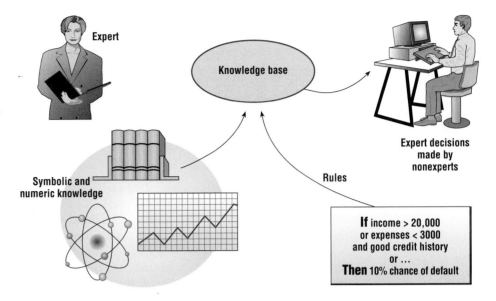

**FIGURE 10.3**
DSS VERSUS ES
An expert system has a different goal and a different approach than a decision support system. A DSS is used by a trained decision maker to collect data, analyze models, and produce output. An ES is built to provide advice to nonexperts and guide them to make a better decision.

|  | DSS | ES |
|---|---|---|
| GOAL | Help user make decision | Provide expert advice |
| METHOD | Data-model-presentation | Asks questions, applies rules, explains |
| TYPE OF PROBLEMS | General, limited by user models | Narrow domain |

tem, it would become an expert system. Such a system would enable a novice traveler to make decisions as well as the experienced travel agent.

In practice, there is no solid line between decision support and expert systems, but Figure 10.3 highlights the primary differences. One of the most important differences is that the expert system evaluates rules and suggests a result or action. In the case of expert systems, users must always be careful to understand how the expert system is evaluating the choices. If the system is using short-term rules, but the users prefer to focus on the long term, use of the expert system can lead to problems.

**BUILDING EXPERT SYSTEMS**

At first glance, you would suspect that expert systems are hard to create. However, except for one step, which is hard, tools exist to make the job easier. Expert system shells help nonprogrammers create a complete expert system. The area that causes the most problems when you are creating expert systems is finding a cooperative expert who fully understands and can explain the problem. Some problems are so complex that it is difficult to explain the reasoning process. Sometimes the expert may rely on vague descriptions and minor nuances that cannot be written down. Even though expert systems can deal with these types of problems, it might take too long to determine the entire process. Also, if you transfer the expert's knowledge to a computer, the expert might worry about losing his or her job.

Most expert systems are built as a knowledge base that is processed or analyzed by an inference engine. A **knowledge base** consists of basic data and a set of rules. In most situations, an *inference engine* applies new observations to the knowledge base and analyzes the rules to reach a conclusion.

The basic steps to create an expert system are (1) analyze the situation and identify needed data and possible outcomes; (2) determine relationships between data and rules that are followed in making the decision; (3) enter the data and rules into an expert system shell; (4) design questions and responses. A **knowledge engineer** is often hired to organize the data, help devise the rules, and enter the criteria into the expert system shell, or supervise programmers as they create an expert system.

## Knowledge Base

A knowledge base is more than a simple database. It consists of data but also contains rules, logic, and links among data elements. In most cases, it contains less structured and more descriptive data. For example, an ES for medicine might have a list of symptoms that contains items like "high temperature," and "intense muscle pain." This knowledge base is the reason why the problem must be narrow in scope. Even narrow, well-defined problems can require large amounts of information and thousands of rules or relationships. The real challenge in building expert systems is to devise the knowledge base with its associated rules.

There are three types of expert systems in use today. They are defined by how the knowledge base is organized: by rules, frames, or cases.

### Rules

The heart of a rule-based ES is a set of logical rules. These **rules** are often complicated. Consider some of the rules that might be needed for an ES to evaluate bank loans, as shown in Figure 10.4. This example has been simplified to keep it short. There will usually be hundreds of rules or conditions to cover a wide variety of situations. Rules are often presented as If . . . Then . . . Else . . . statements. They can include Boolean conjunctions such as AND, OR, NOT. Figure 10.5 presents a portion of a **decision tree** that visually displays the rules.

The difficulty with any ES lies in determining these rules. Some of them will be easy. Others will be complex. Most of them will come from the expert. Unfortunately, most people do not usually express their thoughts in the form of these rules. Although we might follow rules of this sort, they can be difficult to express. It is even more difficult to remember all the rules at one time. For instance, say you have lived in the same place for five years and a new person moves into the neighborhood. She asks you to describe the best ways to get to school, the mall, and the grocery store. Then she asks you for the best

---

First, compute the monthly income before taxes.

Next, compute the monthly payment of the loan.

If the payment is greater than 5% of income:

    Compute total of other loans payments.

    Compute payments as percent of monthly income.

    If this percent is less than 25%:

        If the new loan is less than 10%, make loan.

        Else:

          If total monthly expenses are less than 40% of income, make the loan.

        Else:

          If less than 50% and has been a customer for more than 5 years or if less than 60% and has been a customer for 10 years and has lived at the same address for 5 years, make the loan.

**FIGURE 10.4**
SAMPLE RULES
FOR BANK LOAN

shortcuts if one of the roads is closed. This problem is relatively simple, but can you sit down right now and provide a complete list of all the rules?

### Frame- and Case-Based Reasoning

Another type of expert system uses a more complex type of information known as a frame. A rule-based expert system connects relatively small chunks of data based on numbers and keywords. A frame-based system deals with entire frames or screens of data at one time. Marvin Minsky, one of the pioneers in AI research, emphasized the importance of frames. A *frame* consists of a related set of information that humans group together. Sometimes groupings can be arbitrary. In the lending example, one frame might consist of all of the basic customer data (loan amount, purpose, credit history, monthly payment, etc.). It could also include a picture of the item to be purchased.

Frames can be linked through hypertext, where selecting a keyword on one frame leads to a related frame. In the loan example displayed in Figure 10.6, a loan officer might

**FIGURE 10.5**
Decision tree for sample bank loan expert system. Parts of a knowledge base are often expressed as a decision tree. Each answer to a question leads to additional questions and eventually to a decision. Notice that questions sometimes require numeric answers but can also rely on subjective comments.

**FIGURE 10.6**
FRAME-BASED ES FOR BANK LOAN EXAMPLE
Instead of asking hundreds of detailed questions, some decisions are better suited to the use of frames. Each frame contains a group of related items. On analyzing the data, the ES uses internal rules to present the next frame.

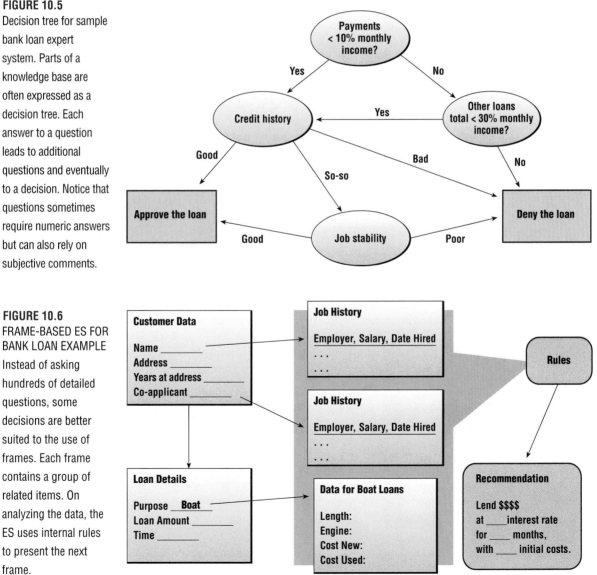

select the keyword *boat* to bring up a frame listing additional conditions to be examined for boat loans. Frames can also be linked through logic rules. After the loan officer enters the base data on the initial loan screen, the inference engine evaluates the data and displays new screens to collect additional data or to make a recommendation. In this situation, a frame-based system operates much like a rule-based system, but with larger chunks of data. Frames are objects that can contain attributes and other objects. Frames can be defined that perform specific functions or operations.

In some ways, **case-based reasoning** is an extension of the frame concept. The difference lies in the type of data contained in each frame and in how the users interact with the system. Entire cases or situations are described in a type of database. As workers encounter problems and develop solutions, they write a short description of the situation. These cases are then available to solve future problems. When a manager encounters a problem, he or she asks the expert system to search the cases for similar situations. If the system finds a related case, the manager can retrieve the solution that was used. Many times, the initial workers will also leave notes and descriptions of related problems. Rather than match by exact words, the system attempts to match situations by concepts. It uses a distance measure to determine which cases are closest to the problem being investigated.

Case-based reasoning is particularly applicable to the higher-level components of business. For many years, strategic planners have tried to capture and record specific instances of an activity. If different problems in business could be identified, codified, and searched, it would be easier to train new managers to participate in strategic solutions for the business. The difficulty, of course, is categorizing the variables. Previously, someone had to categorize all of the individual cases by using a keyword system. The user would then search for a case by using the predefined set of keywords.

In case-based reasoning, the case approach is conceptual rather than based on individual words. As a result, the traditional Boolean rules do not work well. Through categorization, case-based reasoning connects situations and allows searching to be accomplished on larger components by searching for concepts and ideas instead of keywords.

## Knowledge Engineers

With the importance of descriptive data and complex rules, it can be difficult to determine how an expert system should function. In many cases, it is difficult for human experts to express how they make decisions. Once these obstacles are overcome, the data and rules need to be described in a form that the computer can understand and evaluate.

With the increasing use of expert systems, ES specialists have advanced during the last few years. Knowledge engineers are trained to deal with experts to derive the rules needed to create an expert system. The engineers also convert the data and rules into the format needed by the expert system. The format varies depending on the type of expert system being created. Some systems require a series of if-then rules; others operate from decision trees or tables, and some require the engineer to build and link frames.

When several experts are involved in a problem or when it will take considerable time to develop the system, it will be better to hire a knowledge engineer to design and build the expert system. When workers thoroughly understand the issues and with some additional training, they can be the knowledge engineers and build their own system.

## Creating an ES

There are two basic ways to create an expert system: (1) hire a programmer to write custom software or (2) use commercial ES shell software to evaluate rules. For some problems, you can also buy a prepackaged solution, but the system was originally created by one of these two basic methods.

Older expert systems were typically written using a special language such as LISP or Prolog. These languages work well with text data but require specially trained programmers, making it very expensive to create an ES this way. These two languages are still in use today, but programmers are also using object-oriented languages like C++ to build expert systems.

More commonly today, an ES is built from an **expert system shell.** This program provides a way to collect data, enter rules, talk to users, present results, and evaluate the rules. To create an ES, you must know what data you need and all of the rules. Once you express this knowledge base in the format used by the shell's inference engine, the shell takes care of the other problems. Many ES shells are available on a wide variety of computers.

To understand how to create an ES, consider the bank loan example. A typical dialogue with the user (the loan clerk) appears in Figure 10.7. Notice that the ES begins by asking some basic information-gathering questions. The responses of the user are underlined. Once the basic data is collected, the ES performs some computations and follows the built-in rules. Notice that the ES follows the rule that asks for the other loan payments. However, the loan clerk does not know about this rule, so he or she asks for clarification. This ability to ask questions is a powerful feature of expert systems.

Once you have collected all of the rules involved in the problem, you enter them into the ES shell. The shell lets you type in the questions you want to ask the user. You define

**FIGURE 10.7**
BANK LOAN SAMPLE SCREEN

An expert system carries on a dialogue with the user. The ES asks questions and uses the answers to ask additional questions. The user can ask the ES to explain a decision or a question. Hence the ES can be used for training purposes.

```
              Welcome to the Loan Evaluation System.
What is the purpose of the loan?   car
How much money will be loaned?   10,000
For how many years?   5

The current interest rate is 10%.
The payment will be $212.47 per month.

What is the annual income?   24,000

What is the total monthly payments of other loans?
Why?

Because the payment is more than 10% of the monthly income.
What is the total monthly payments of other loans? 50.00

The loan should be approved, because there is only a 2% chance of default.
```

the calculations and tell the shell how to look up any other information you need (e.g., the interest rates for auto loans). You then enter the conditions that tell the shell what questions to ask next. If there are many rules with complex interactions, it is more difficult to enter the rules into the shell. However, as illustrated in Figure 10.8, it is generally easier to use a shell than to have programmers create the system from scratch in LISP or Prolog.

One advantage of ES shells is that you generally have to enter only the basic rules and data. As the user enters the data, the shell performs the calculations and follows the rules. The shell also automatically answers the user questions. You do not have to be a computer programmer to create an ES with a shell. With training, many users can create their own expert systems using a shell. However, there are many dangers inherent in ES development, so it helps to have someone evaluate and test the resulting system.

## Reasoning

Expert systems usually perform two types of reasoning: forward chaining and backward chaining. **Forward chaining** is where the shell traces your rules from the data entry to a recommendation. In the bank example, forward chaining is used to display the questions and perform the calculations. For example, when the ES realizes that the payment amount is greater than 10 percent of the customer's monthly income, the corresponding rule is utilized. The ES works down the list of rules and evaluates each condition. If the condition is true, the ES does whatever the rule says, and we say that the rule has been fired or

**FIGURE 10.8**
EXPERT SYSTEM
DEVELOPMENT
Once the knowledge is provided by an expert, there are two basic methods used to build an ES. One method is with an expert system shell, or software that already knows how to store and evaluate rules and handle the user interface. The other approach is to hire programmers and write the entire ES from scratch. Special-purpose languages like LISP and Prolog make the job a little easier, but custom programming is still expensive and time consuming.

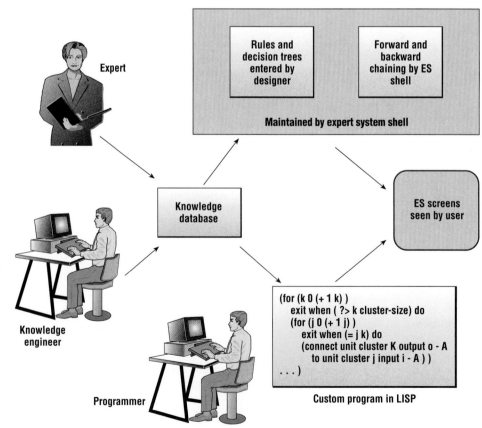

```
(for (k 0 (+ 1 k) )
   exit when ( ?> k cluster-size) do
   (for (j 0 (+ 1 j) )
      exit when (= j k) do
      (connect unit cluster K output o - A
       to unit cluster j input i - A ) )
   . . . )
```
**Custom program in LISP**

*triggered.* Eventually, if all the rules have been entered correctly, the system follows the rules and reaches a conclusion. Generally, the system will present some information indicating how sure it is of the decision. In the example, it uses historical data to indicate only a 2 percent chance of default on the loan.

With **backward chaining,** the user enters a "conclusion" and asks the expert system to see if the rules support that conclusion. Consider the lending example using the decision tree displayed in Figure 10.5. The bank is investigating the possibility of discrimination and has pulled representative applications from several categories of borrowers. For each of the applicants, the manager wants to determine whether that person should have been granted a loan. A backward chaining expert system begins with the hypothesized conclusion (e.g., that the applicant should have been granted the loan). It examines rules by looking at the conclusion and decides whether the premise supports the conclusion. For example, it might note that there is a poor credit history, hence the loan could not have been granted on the strength of past credit. So the ES next evaluates job stability. If job stability was "good," it traces back and reexamines the credit history. If it finds that credit history was "bad," it concludes that the applicant should not receive the loan. The backward chaining continues until the conclusion is found to be supported or rejected, or there is insufficient data to make a decision.

As you attempt to create an expert system, you should take a broad look at the rules before you begin. Some tasks and decisions simply cannot be described in enough detail to justify the use of an expert system.

## Limitations of Expert Systems

Expert systems are useful tools that can be applied to several specialized problems. However, several important drawbacks arise in their design and use. First, they can only be created for specific, narrowly defined problems. Some complex problems contain too many rules with too many interactions. It quickly becomes impossible to express all of the interrelationships. For example, it is currently impossible to create a medical diagnostic system that covers all possible diseases. However, smaller systems are in use that help determine drug dosages and other treatments such as radiation levels for cancer patients.

Another problem that users and designers have encountered is that it can be difficult to modify the knowledge base in an expert system. As the environment or problem changes, the expert system needs to be updated. The changes are relatively easy to make if they affect only a few rules. However, many expert systems use hundreds of interrelated rules. It is not always clear which rules need to be altered, and changes to one rule can affect many of

### Common Limitations of Expert Systems

- *Fragile Systems:* If the underlying process changes or the environment generates changes, the rules need to be revised. Changes in one rule might force us to rebuild the entire system.
- *Mistakes:* Who is responsible when an expert system makes a mistake? The expert? Several experts? The novice operating the ES? The company that uses it? The company who created it? The knowledge engineers who built it?
- *Vague Rules:* Many times the domain expert cannot completely describe the rules.
- *Conflicting Experts:* If there are conflicting experts or rules, who will decide? Which one is right?
- *Unforeseen Events:* What happens if the ES faces an unexpected problem or a new event? Experts solve these problems through creativity and learning. Expert systems cannot.

the others. In essence, as the situation changes, the company is forced to completely re-design the expert system. In fast-changing industries, it would cost too much to continually redesign an expert system. In the lending example, a policy change based on monthly in-come would be relatively easy to implement. On the other hand, some changes in policy would force a complete redesign of the expert system. For instance, a bank might decide to grant loans to almost everyone but charge riskier people higher interest rates.

Probably the greatest difficulty in creating an expert system is determining the logic rules or frames that will lead to the proper conclusions. It requires finding an expert who under-stands the process and can express the rules in a form that can be used by the expert system.

## Management Issues of Expert Systems

Creating and building an expert system involves many of the same issues encountered in building any other information system. For instance, the problem must be well defined, the designers must communicate with the users, and management and financial controls must be in place to evaluate and control the project.

However, expert systems raise additional management issues. Two issues are partic-ularly important: (1) if an expert transfers knowledge to an expert system, is there still a need for the expert, and (2) what happens when the expert system encounters an excep-tion that it was not designed to solve?

The answer to the first question depends on the individual situation. In cases where the problem is relatively stable over time, it is possible to transfer expert knowledge to software—enabling the firm to reduce the number of experts needed. If this action results in layoffs, the experts will need additional incentives to cooperate with the development of the system. In other cases, the firm will continue to need the services of the experts, to make changes to the ES and to solve new problems. Before starting an ES project, managers need to determine which situation applies and negotiate appropriately with the experts.

The second problem can be more difficult to identify. Consider what happens when workers rely on an expert system to make decisions, and management then cuts costs by hiring less-skilled workers. The new workers do not understand the system or the procedures—they simply follow decisions made by the rules in the ES. If an exception arises, the ES may not know how to respond or it may respond inappropriately. A cus-tomer then would be left to deal with an underskilled worker who does not understand the process and cannot resolve the problem.

**Reality Bytes    10–3    Italian Government Uses Expert System to Handle Emergencies**

Governments around the world are increasingly concerned about the environmental impact of acci-dents such as chemical spills. Italy had adopted the Sistema di Gestione Rischio Chimico (SIGRIC) ex-pert system to help them analyze potential problems and deal with emergencies. The system utilizes a geographic information system (GIS) with mapping details at the provincial and local levels. By analyz-ing a three-dimensional digital terrain model (DTM) and diagnostic wind field model (DWM), the system can analyze the impact of a wide variety of events (e.g., chemical spills and explosions) and predict the direction and level of potential damages. In an emergency, the expert system (RTXPS) will ask rel-evant questions and direct the personnel to take the appropriate actions to solve the problems. A set of simulation tools can be used to analyze new installa-tions and potential problems.

**ADDITIONAL SPECIALIZED PROBLEMS**

Further research in artificial intelligence examined how humans are different from computers. This research led to tools that can be used for certain types of problems. Some of the ideas come from the early days of computers, but it has taken until now for machines to be developed that are fast enough to handle the sophisticated tasks. Ideas in AI have come from many disciplines, from biology to psychology to computer science and engineering.

Humans are noticeably better than computers in six broad areas: pattern recognition, performing multiple tasks at one time, movement, speech recognition, vision, and language comprehension. Some of these concepts are related, but they all represent features that would make machines much more useful. Even with current technological improvements, most observers agree that it will be several years before these features are available.

## Pattern Recognition and Neural Networks

One of the early issues in AI research was the question of how human brains worked. Some people suggested that to make intelligent computers, the computers would have to work the same way as the human brain does. An important conclusion from this research is that humans are good at pattern recognition.

Humans use pattern recognition thousands of times a day. It enables people to recognize co-workers, to spot trends in data, to relate today's problems to last year's changes. Many problems in business could benefit from machines that could reliably recognize patterns. For example, what characteristics do "good" borrowers have in common? How will changes in the economy affect next year's sales? How are sales affected by management styles of the sales managers?

Pattern recognition is used by people to solve problems. It is one of the reasons teachers use cases to teach students to solve business problems. If you notice that a problem is similar to a case you have seen before, you can use your prior knowledge to solve the problem. Imagine how useful it would be if an expert system could recognize patterns automatically.

One current technique that is used to spot patterns is the use of neural networks. Initial study indicated that the brain is a collection of cells called *neurons* that have many connections to each other. Each of these cells is relatively simple, but there are approximately 100 million of them. In some respects, a neuron resembles a simple computer. It can be at rest (off), or it can fire a message (on). A neuron responds to other cells (input) to send messages to other neurons (output). A collection of these cells is called a **neural network.** Human neural cells are actually more complicated, but researchers have focused on this simplified form.

---

## Business Uses of Research in Artificial Intelligence

**Expert Systems:** Building systems that help novices achieve the results of experts.

**Pattern Recognition:** Identifying patterns in sound, vision, and data. Driven by neural network research.

**Voice and Speech Recognition:** Recognizing users by voice, and converting spoken words into written text.

**Language Comprehension:** Understanding the meaning in written (or spoken) text.

**Massively Parallel Computers:** Performing thousands of tasks simultaneously to solve complex problems.

**Robotics and Motion:** Building machines that have a high range of movement, physical sensitivity, and the ability to navigate.

**Statistics, Uncertainty, and Fuzzy Logic:** Finding ways to solve statistical problems easier. Dealing with associations and comparative data.

A common current example is a bank that uses a neural network to spot credit card fraud. In some cases, Mellon Bank's neural network identified fraudulent patterns even before the human investigators spotted them. It is faster and more accurate than an earlier expert system. The original expert system looked at a limited number of variables and indicated 1,000 suspects a day, which was far more than actually existed and too many for the investigators to keep up with. The new neural network system examines more variables, lists fewer false suspects, and adjusts its methods on its own.

A finance manager might use a form of pattern recognition to search for patterns in the financial markets to forecast future movements. Of course, with thousands of other people searching for patterns, the patterns would not last very long. Similarly, a banker might use pattern recognition to classify loan prospects.

Neural networks can be built with software. Also, computer chips are available today that function as neural networks. Neural networks can be measured in two ways: by (1) the number of neurons and (2) the number of interconnections between the individual cells. It is fairly easy to increase the number of cells, but the number of possible interconnections increases very rapidly. For instance, if there are four cells, there are six possible connections. With 10 cells, there are 45 connections. With 1,000 cells, there are half a million connections. In general, if there are $N$ cells, there are $N(N-1)/2$ possible connections. For many purposes, not every connection is needed; but with millions of cells, a neural network would incorporate a large number of connections. Most existing networks use only a few thousand cells.

Figure 10.9 presents a version of how a neural network converts an array of input sensors into a hidden layer and then stores patterns on an output layer. One useful feature of the neural network approach is that it is fairly good at identifying patterns even if some of the inputs are missing.

**FIGURE 10.9**
NEURAL NET FOR PATTERN MATCHING
Input cells convert data to binary form. The required hidden layer recodes the inputs into a new internal representation. The connections represent outputs from the lower layers. When total input levels exceed some value, the receiving cell fires. Any cell can be connected to many other cells. Input weights are determined by training. The output cells are triggered when total input levels from the connections exceed some threshold. Note that a pattern can be recognized even if some input cells are wrong.

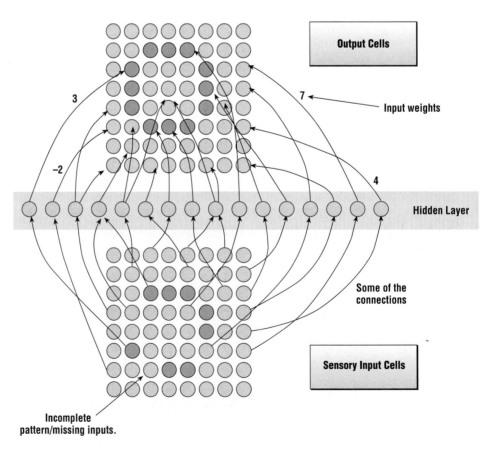

What can neural networks do that cannot be done with traditional computers? The basic answer is "nothing." However, they provide a new way of thinking about problems. More importantly, with hardware specifically designed to process neural networks, some difficult problems can be solved faster than with traditional computers. The primary objective of neural networks is the ability to store and recognize patterns. A well-designed network is capable of identifying patterns (such as faces or sounds) even if some of the data is missing or altered. The army has designed a neural network system to process visual data that can drive a vehicle at speeds up to 55 miles per hour.

Another advantage that researchers hope to achieve with neural networks is the ability to simplify training of the computer. The discussion of expert systems noted that changes in the business often mean that knowledge engineers have to redesign the entire expert system. A neural network has a limited ability to "learn" by examining past data. Feeding it proper examples establishes the interconnection weights that enable the network to identify patterns. In theory, neural networks have the ability to learn on their own. In practice, the learning stage is the most difficult component of building a neural network. Most times the designer has to understand the problem and provide hints to the network, along with good sample data. In many ways, training a neural network uses basic properties of statistics related to data sampling and regression.

## Machine Vision

Machine vision has many uses in manufacturing environments. Machines are used in optical character recognition, welding and assembly, and quality control. Mechanical sensors have several advantages over humans. They do not suffer from fatigue, they can examine a broader spectrum of light (including ultraviolet and infrared), and they can quickly focus at many different levels (including microscopic).

On the other hand, traditional computer systems are literal in their vision. It is hard for computers to compare objects of different sizes or to match mirror images. It is hard for machines to determine whether differences between objects are minor and should be ignored or if they are major distinguishing features.

The Department of Defense has funded Carnegie Mellon University to develop software that is used to automatically drive vehicles. One system (Ranger) is used in an army ambulance that can drive itself over rough terrain for up to 16 km. ALVINN is a separate road-following system that has driven vehicles at speeds over 110 kph for as far as 140 km.

Say you are shown a picture of your instructor, and someone adds or subtracts features to it, such as bigger eyebrows, longer hair, or glasses. In most cases, you would still recognize the face. Computers would have difficulty with that problem because they see pictures as a collection of dots (or lines). How does the computer know which changes are important and which are minor?

If computers were better at pattern recognition, there would be thousands of uses for vision recognition systems in manufacturing and business. Neural networks have shown some success in solving these problems, but they are still somewhat slow and inaccurate. Again, problems that have a narrower scope are easier to solve. For example, the U.S. post office uses optical scanners to recognize handwritten zip codes on mail. Yet they rely on humans to read (and key in) addresses and cities.

## Voice and Speech Recognition

We hardly need to discuss the benefits of having a machine that can understand human speech. Most people can speak faster than they can type, so voice input to create and edit documents saves a considerable amount of time and money. Voice input is useful for hands-free operations. A quality control worker might need both hands to inspect a product. Speech recognition enables the worker to take notes that can be edited and printed later. Surgeons gain the same advantages. Additionally, voice input would eliminate the need for a keyboard, and possibly a monitor, making computers much more portable.

Two main types of speech recognition systems are available today. Both types are available on personal computers. The first type must be trained before it can be used. The user speaks a list of words and the computer stores the base patterns. With training, today's systems can recognize continuous speech with 90 to 95 percent accuracy.

A second form of speech recognition does not require training. Some systems can recognize a few words without additional training. For example, some phone systems recognize spoken numbers and a few key words.

Speech recognition is rapidly gaining acceptance as an input device. Modern systems examine pairs of words and sentence structure to reduce problems with homonyms. Punctuation is still a problem, but for data entry, the speaker simply inserts the correct punctuation by name. While speech recognition may never be *perfect,* it will be *acceptable.* The point is that because communication between humans is not perfect, we cannot expect communication between machines and humans to be perfect either.

## Language Comprehension

Related to voice recognition is the issue of language comprehension, or the ability of the computer to actually understand what we are saying. Technically the two topics are separate, since it might be possible to have a machine understand what we type onto a keyboard. Language comprehension exists when the machine actually understands what we mean. One test of comprehension would be the ability of the computer to carry on a conversation. In fact, Alan Turing, a British pioneer in the computer field suggested the **Turing test** for computer intelligence. In this test, a human judge communicates with a machine and another person in a separate room. If the judge cannot determine which user is the machine and which is a person, the machine should be considered to be intelligent. Some people have tested this concept (using specific topics). Other people have noted that perhaps you do not have to be intelligent to carry on a conversation.

Language comprehension would be useful because it would make it easier for humans to use computers. Instead of needing to learn a language such as SQL to access data, imagine being able to get answers to questions asked in English (or some other

**FIGURE 10.10**
VOICE RECOGNITION
AND PUNCTUATION
There are inherent
problems with voice
recognition.
Punctuation and
implicit meaning are
two difficult areas.
Even communication
between people has
frequent
misinterpretations.

See what happens when you give a computer the first set of instructions, but it does not hear the commas correctly and thinks you said the second line:

```
(1) Copy the red, file the blue, delete the yellow mark.
(2) Copy the red file, the blue delete, the yellow mark.
```

Consider the following sentence, which can be interpreted by humans but would not make much sense to a computer that tries to interpret it literally.

```
I saw the Grand Canyon flying to New York.
```

natural language). Of course, any natural language has its limitations. The greatest danger with language comprehension is that the machine will interpret your question incorrectly and give you the "right" answer to the "wrong" question. Figure 10.10 provides a simple illustration of the complexities of language comprehension. The first example involves the use of punctuation. A misinterpretation of the command can result in deleting the wrong file. Similarly, interpretation of a natural language involves understanding some basic concepts, such as the fact that the Grand Canyon cannot fly.

## Robotics and Motion

Modern manufacturing relies heavily on robots, and the capabilities of robots continually increase. Most existing robots are specialized machines that perform a limited number of tasks, such as welding or painting. In many firms, there is little need for a general-purpose robot that can "do everything." However, one area that remains troublesome is the ability of machines to move. Making a machine that can navigate through an unknown or crowded area is especially difficult. Some work is being done in this area. Liability is a major problem when robots attempt to move among people.

Although science fiction writers have already devised thousands of uses for "intelligent" robots, there is still a long ways to go. Part of the problem is that the concept of robots is closely tied to the issues of vision, pattern recognition, and intelligence. In order to navigate a crowded room, a robot needs to be able to see objects. It must also recognize each object and have a basic understanding of its characteristics. For instance, a robot needs to recognize and know the difference between a table and a wall to understand that it can go around a table but not a wall.

## Statistics, Uncertainty, and Fuzzy Logic

Many situations can benefit from the use of applied statistics. Statistics enable us to examine large sets of data and spot patterns and relationships. It also enables us to define the concept of uncertainty. In life, we can rarely predict any outcome with complete certainty. There is always a chance that some random event will arise, affecting our system and producing a different outcome. By assigning probabilities to various events, we can evaluate the effect of these random events.

The catch is that statistics is a relatively complex field, and it is often hard to apply in practice. Evaluating millions of data points, determining interactions, and estimating probabilities is not an easy task, even with top-of-the-line computer tools. These tasks often require the services of an expert in statistical analysis. Yet, people face uncertainty every day and manage to make decisions. Sometimes we might not make the "best" decision, but we have found ways to cope with the main issues. One common method of coping is our

**FIGURE 10.11**
SUBJECTIVE DEFINITIONS

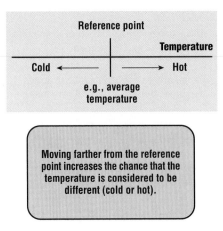

Many human tasks are characterized by subjectivity. When we say that the weather is "cold" we rarely specify an exact temperature. Instead, we are making a comparison to a reference point. Distances farther from the reference point provide a stronger impression of the change. Machine systems can be based on these principles using statistics or "fuzzy-logic" definitions. These interpretations often make it easier for people to deal with machines.

ability to use subjective and incomplete descriptions. When a person declares that "it is cold outside," listeners in the same area understand the statement. Yet, "cold" is a subjective term. Forty degrees can be cold to a resident of Arizona, but it would be considered "pleasant" to a resident of Wisconsin in mid-January.

It is possible to model these concepts with statistical definitions that involve means and standard deviations. However, it can be difficult to derive the underlying statistical functions and implement them for each situation. To overcome these limitations, Lofti Zadeh created a system that attempts to mimic the way humans perceive uncertainty. His definition of fuzzy sets and fuzzy logic use definitions of subjective terms such as *cold, hot, sometimes, fast,* and *slow.* The logic system defines a way to combine these terms to reach descriptive "conclusions." Figure 10.11 illustrates that the key is that each definition refers to a range.

In 1994, Charles Elkan showed that fuzzy logic is conceptually similar to more traditional methodologies. However, manufacturers (especially Japanese companies) have found it easier to design products using fuzzy logic. The fuzzy definitions also correspond with the way humans perceive the machine. Fuzzy logic is used in washing machine settings, elevator controls, and bullet train controllers (where operators can set controls like *hotter* or *faster).*

## DSS, ES, AND AI

The differences among decision support systems, expert systems, and artificial intelligence can be confusing at first. Take a simple problem and see how a computer system based on each method might operate. A common financial problem is to determine how much money to lend to customers. Any firm that grants terms to customers—not just financial institutions—must make this decision. Figure 10.12 discusses the differences among a DSS, ES, and AI approach to the inventory problem.

In a relatively simple system, the computer would retrieve data about the customer and the prior loans to that customer. Historically, loan officers used basic data and personal factors to make the lending decision. In some instances, these rules of thumb led to problems—with bad decisions and sometimes discrimination. The DSS could also be used to monitor existing loans and payments. As part of a transaction-processing system, it can notify managers when customers continually make late payments and help identify problem loans.

To improve consistency and reduce the decision time, many firms have moved to expert systems to help evaluate loans. Statistical analysis of prior loans is used to establish a

**FIGURE 10.12**
COMPARISON
OF TECHNIQUES
FOR A LOAN
A DSS can display
background data for a
loan for a loan officer
and can also monitor
customer payments.
An ES could help
managers decide if they
should make the loan
by evaluating more
complex rules. An AI
such as a neural
network can analyze
past loans and
determine the rules that
should be used to grant
or deny future loans.

| Decision Support System | Expert System | Artificial Intelligence |
|---|---|---|
| **Loan Officer** | **ES Rules** | **Determine Rules** |
| **Data**   Income   Existing loans   Credit report | **What is the monthly income?** **3,000** | **Data/Training Cases** |
| **Model**   Lend in all but worst cases   Monitor for late and missing payments. | **What are the total monthly payments on other loans?**   **450**    **How long have they had the current job?** **5 years**    . . . | loan 1 data: paid   loan 2 data: 5 late   loan 3 data: lost   loan 4 data: 1 late |
| **Output**   Name Loan  #Late Amount   Brown 25,000  5  1,250   Jones 62,000  1   135   Smith 83,000  3  2,435   ... | **Should grant the loan since there is only a 5% chance of default.** | **Neural Network Weights**    **Evaluate new data, make recommendation.** |

set of rules that are coded into the ES. In some cases, the ES can then be operated with Touch-Tone phones or over the Internet. In straightforward cases, the ES can make the final decision and approve the loan. In more difficult situations, the preliminary results and data can be forwarded to a human loan officer to factor in personal judgment and factors not considered by the ES.

Of course, the value of the ES depends heavily on the accuracy of the underlying rules (and the supplied data). These rules might change over time or as economic conditions change. A neural network can be used to examine the prior loans automatically to identify the factors that predict successful and unsuccessful loans. Once these factors are identified, they can be coded into the ES to automate the decision process. In this situation, the AI/neural network takes the place of (or supplements) the decisions of the human expert.

**MACHINE INTELLIGENCE**

What would it take to convince you that a machine is intelligent? The Turing test has been proposed as one method. Many other tests have been proposed in the past. At one time, people suggested that a machine that could win at chess would be intelligent. Today's chess-playing computers have beaten even the top human players. Another test proposed was the ability to solve mathematical problems—in particular, the ability to write mathematical proofs. An early AI program created in the 1950s could do that. Today, for a few hundred dollars, you can buy programs that manipulate mathematical symbols to solve equations.

Some people have suggested that intelligence involves creativity. Creativity is probably as hard to measure as intelligence. Even so, there are examples of computer creativity. A few years ago, a programmer developed a system that created music. The interesting feature of the program was that it allowed people to call on the phone and vote on the

---

**Reality Bytes**    **10–4    Canadian Farmers Use GPS and Expert System to Cut Costs**

Jim Robins is a farmer and founder of Precision Farming Solutions, a company that develops hardware and software systems for fertilizer applications. With a global positioning system (GPS) in the tractor, farmers always know exactly where they are in the field—down to a few meters. By sampling various sections of the farm, the system can identify the specific fertilizer needed for each section of the farm. "We use moisture probabilities and moisture levels on hills and midslopes, and low levels to target fertilizer rates based on potential yield in those areas," says Robins. The expert system then determines the amount of fertilizer needed at each area on the farm. As the farmer drives across the farm, the computer-controlled system monitors the tractor's location via the GPS unit and applies the proper amount of fertilizer. Robins notes, "In the first year, we basically broke even with a per acre net increase of between $6 and $12 and costs at about $10 per acre." The cost savings occur from using less fertilizer. Of course, the environment and consumers also benefit from the lower amounts of chemicals used.

---

music. The computer used this feedback to change its next composition. Not only was the computer creative, it was learning and adapting, albeit in a limited context.

Although there are limited business applications to much of this current research, there are two main reasons for staying abreast of the capabilities. First, anything that makes the computer easier to use will make it more useful, and these techniques continue to improve. Second, you need to understand the current limitations to avoid costly mistakes.

**OBJECT ORIENTATION**

A recent application of AI techniques has arisen in the context of the Internet. A key issue of the Internet is searching for data. Although the Internet dramatically improves communication, there are problems with maintaining the "interpretation" of the information from various systems.

Originally, most data on the Web was stored as standard pages of text using HTML. Search engines would simply scan these pages and build searchable indexes. Increasingly, the Internet is being used to store and transmit objects composed of data, pictures, spreadsheets, sounds, and video. From a pure transmission standpoint, any object can be decomposed into raw data bits and sent between computers. Where we run into problems is searching for the objects. Consider a simple example where you want to find a new printer, so you search the Internet for prices. Today, many vendors store the product descriptions and prices in a database, then build the HTML page on demand when you go to the site. Since the page is not static, the search engines do not index it.

One solution to this problem is to create software agents. **Agents** are object-oriented programs designed for networks that are written to perform specific tasks in response to user requests. The concept of object orientation is important because it means that agents know how to exchange object attributes, and they have the ability to activate object functions in other agents. The tasks could be simple, such as finding all files on a network that refer to a specific topic. One key feature of agents is that they are designed to communicate with each other. As long as your agent knows the abilities or functions of another agent, they can exchange messages and commands. General Magic is a pioneering company that created a standard programming language for agents. With this language, agents can transfer themselves and run on other computers. Agents also have a degree of "intelligence." They can be given relatively general commands, which the agents reinterpret and apply to each situation they encounter.

**FIGURE 10.13**

SOFTWARE AGENTS

A personal software agent might be used to book a vacation. It would take your initial preferences and communicate with other agents to find sites that matched your preferences. It might also be able to negotiate prices with competing resorts.

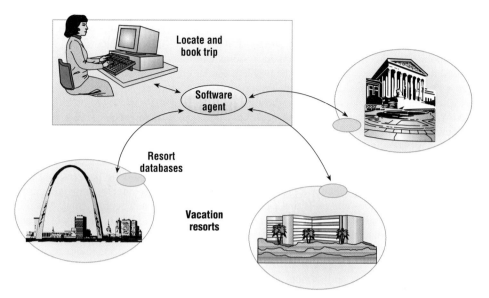

Consider an example illustrated by Figure 10.13. You have been working hard and decide to take a vacation. You want to go to a beach but do not have much money to spend. You are looking for a place where you can swim, scuba dive, and meet people at night. But you also want the place to have some secluded beaches where you can get away from the crowds and relax. You could call a travel agent and buy a package deal, but every agent you called just laughs and says that next time you should call three months ahead of time instead of only three days ahead. You suspect that a beach resort probably has last-minute cancellations and you could get in, but how do you find out? There are thousands of possibilities. If all of the resort computers had automatic reservation agents, the task would be fairly easy. You would start an agent on your computer and tell it the features you want. Your agent sends messages to all of the automated resort agents looking for open spots at places that matched your features. When your agent finds something close, it brings back details and pictures to display on your screen. When you decide on a resort, the agent automatically makes the reservations.

Notice three important features of software agents. First, the agents need to know how to communicate. It is not as simple as transmitting raw data. They must understand the data and respond to questions. Second, imagine the amount of network traffic involved. In the vacation search example, your agent might have to contact thousands of other computers. Now picture what happens when a thousand other people do the same thing! Third, all of the agents are independent. You, as well as other computer owners, are free to create or modify your own agent. As long as there are standard methods for agents to exchange attributes and activate functions, they can be modified and improved. For instance, you might program your agent to weight the vacation spots according to some system, or you might teach it to begin its search in specific locations.

Programmers have begun to incorporate expert system and other AI capabilities into these agents. By adding a set of rules, the agent becomes more than just a simple search mechanism. The more complex the rules, the more "intelligent" it becomes, which means you have to do less work. In fact, software agents have the potential to dramatically increase the research in AI. Currently, because of limited standards and the difficulty of creating them, there are few examples of useful agents. As increasing numbers of people use agents and begin demanding more intelligence, it will become profitable for researchers to work harder at building reliable, intelligent software.

## SUMMARY

Complex decisions, such as diagnostic problems, require more sophisticated computer tools. Expert systems can be used to solve complex problems if the problem can be narrowed down to a specific problem. Expert systems ask questions of the users and trace through rules to make recommendations. The systems can also trace backward through the rules to explain how they arrived at various questions or conclusions. Expert systems can be built using shells that contain the logic needed to process the rules.

Research into making machines more intelligent has led to several techniques and tools that can be useful in solving some problems. Pattern recognition is being studied with neural networks. Pattern recognition problems are involved in handwriting and voice recognition, vision systems, and in statistical applications. Researchers are also working on robotics and motion—especially combined with vision systems that will enable robots to navigate their way through new areas.

These techniques are still young and have many limitations. One of their most important uses will be the ability to improve the interaction between computers and hu-

### A MANAGER'S VIEW

Research in artificial intelligence has led to tools that are useful to managers. In particular, expert systems are used to make repetitive decisions rapidly and more consistently using novice employees. Although they are powerful, expert systems can only be used to solve problems in a narrow domain. Even then, they can be hard to modify as the business changes. Neural networks represent a new approach to using computers. They are much better than most other systems at recognizing patterns and have been applied in scanners, handwriting recognition, vision systems, and speech recognition. Advances in robotics, motion, and vision systems offer additional capabilities for specific problems.

mans. The better that computers can be adapted to humans, the easier it will be to use them. Voice recognition and language comprehension systems are important steps in that direction. Although current technology is still somewhat limited, considerable progress has been made over the last few years.

## KEY WORDS

agent, 430

artificial intelligence (AI), 410

backward chaining, 421

case-based reasoning, 418

decision tree, 416

expert system (ES), 410

expert system shell, 419

forward chaining, 420

knowledge base, 415

knowledge engineer, 416

natural language, 427

neural network, 423

rules, 416

Turing test, 426

## WEB SITE REFERENCES

**Movie Studios**

| | |
|---|---|
| 20th Century Fox | www.foxmovies.com |
| MGM Motion Pictures | www.mgm.com/movies |
| New Line Cinema | www.newline.com |
| Paramount Motion Pictures | www.paramount.com/motionpicture/homemp.html |
| Sony Pictures Entertainment | www.spe.sony.com/movies |
| Universal Pictures | www.universalstudios.com |
| Walt Disney Studios | disney.go.com/StudioOperations |
| Warner Brothers Movies | www.movies.warnerbros.com |

## REVIEW QUESTIONS

1. What types of problems are particularly well suited to expert systems?
2. What are the major differences between a decision support system and an expert system?
3. Do you think consumers would be happier if major decisions in banks were made by expert systems? Or would customers prefer to use a bank that advertised all decisions were made by humans?

4. What steps are involved in creating an expert system?
5. What research is being done in artificial intelligence?
6. Describe three situations that could benefit from the use of pattern recognition.
7. What tasks can benefit from existing voice recognition technology?
8. What are the three basic types of expert systems?
9. How is backward chaining used in expert systems?
10. How is case-based reasoning different from rule-based expert systems?
11. What is the Turing test? Do you think it is a reasonable test?
12. Why is it so hard to create a machine that can understand natural language?

## EXERCISES

1. Interview local managers or search the recent literature to find three diagnostic problems that could benefit from the use of expert systems. Where would you find an expert to assist with each of the situations?
2. What would it take to convince you that a computer system was intelligent? How close are existing computer systems to this standard? Do you think we might see intelligent machines within the next 5 or 10 years? Within your lifetime?
3. Interview an expert in some area and create an initial set of rules that you could use for an expert system. If you cannot find a cooperative expert, try researching one of the following topics in your library: fruit tree propagation and pruning (what trees are needed for cross-pollination, what varieties grow best in each region, what fertilizers are needed, when they should be pruned), requirements or qualifications for public assistance or some other governmental program (check government documents), legal requirements to determine whether a contract is in effect (check books on business law).
4. Search the computer literature to find the current state-of-the-art in voice and speech recognition. How many words can the best system recognize? What about continuous speech? Does it require training?
5. For the following problems identify those that would be best suited for an expert system and those that would use a decision support system. Explain why.
   - Investing in the stock market.
   - Annual evaluation of suppliers and negotiation support.
   - Choosing a marketing campaign.
   - Customer telephone support lines for questions and problems (not orders).
   - Monitoring and identifying causes of inventory shrinkage.

6. Describe how artificial intelligence techniques could be used to enhance software agents. What additional capabilities could they be given? Give an example of the application of a "more intelligent" agent.
7. Assume that you have a software agent to handle your personal mail and other tasks on the Internet. Write a set of rules for your agent to follow.
8. Describe a situation, other than the vacation search example, where you would want to use software agents to perform some task. Describe the features of all agents, including attributes and functions that they can perform.
9. Who will pay for the creation of software agents? What about the use of the agents? Should (or could) users be charged every time their agent calls another one? What about network usage? What would happen if your agent used your telephone to connect to thousands of other agents?

 **Rolling Thunder Database**

10. Identify an area in which an expert system could help. Be specific and explain the advantages of using an ES for that area. Where would you find an expert to assist with creating the knowledge domain?
11. Describe how new technologies might be used to improve decisions at the Rolling Thunder Bicycle company. What experimental and future technologies should we watch closely? If you could create an "intelligent" computer system for the company, what would it do and how would it be used to increase profits?
12. Do some research to identify complex decisions that are involved in designing and building bicycles.
13. What pattern-matching types of decisions arise at Rolling Thunder that could benefit from the use of neural networks?
14. What aspects of customer service might be automated with expert systems? What are the potential advantages and disadvantages?

## ADDITIONAL READING

Bylinsky, Gene. "Computers That Learn by Doing," *Fortune,* September 6, 1993, pp. 96–102. [Examples of AI in business]

Dreyfus, Hubert L. *What Computers Still Can't Do.* Cambridge, MA: MIT Press, 1992. [Update of the 1972 and 1979 books on the difficulties of AI and the current limits of technology, including critical review of history of AI research]

Edmonds, Ernest, L. Candy, R. Jones, and B. Soufi, "Support for Collaborative Design: Agents and Emergence," *Communications of the ACM,* July 1994, pp. 41–47. [Software agents]

"Expert Systems in Diagnosis," *Business Line (India),* January 27, 1999. [Researchers developed an expert system to aid in diagnosis of cervical spondylosis]

Genesereth, Michael, and S. Ketchpel, "Software Agents," *Communications of the ACM,* July 1994, pp. 48–53. [Software agents]

"A Processor Looks to Combat Fraud Using Tools from a Debit Warehouse," *Debit Card News,* January 18, 1999, p. 1. [Deluxe Corp. uses neural network to detect debit card fraud]

"Roadway to Increase Traffic with Mexico," *Plain Dealer,* November 14, 1998, p. 2C. [Roadway Express uses expert system to speed shipments through customs]

"Walker Digital Gets Patent for Online Opinion Market," *The Wall Street Journal,* January 20, 1999, p. B9B. [Jay Walker, head of Priceline.com patents system to match experts with those needing expert service]

# CASES *Franchises*

Franchising is a system in which a producer or marketer of a product or service, the franchisor, sells others, the franchisees, the right to duplicate a concept and use a trade name while providing sales support in a certain territory for an agreed-upon length of time. The location can involve the right to exclusivity. The amount of support varies from providing the product to resell, to extensive sales training, to control over business operations.

The first and simplest of three types of franchises involves a contract between a supplier and a business owner. The latter agrees to sell only one version of a particular product, for example, McDonald's sells only Coca-Cola soft drinks.

A second type of franchise, product trade name franchising, involves selling products to distributors who resell them. Product trade name franchising accounts for 52 percent of all franchise sales and 33 percent of all the franchise units in the United States.

Third, the fastest growing type of franchise is the prototype or "package" franchise, in which a whole mode of business operations including the product or service, inventory system, sales and marketing methods, and record-keeping procedures are sold to the franchisee. Package franchising has grown 10 times faster than product trade name franchising (11.1 percent versus 1.1 percent on average per year).

## Financial Analysis

The franchisor's revenues are in the form of a start-up fee, ranging from $10,000 to $600,000 depending on the size and market share of the franchise, the trade name, managerial training and support, and royalties that amount to 3 to 8 percent of gross sales.

For example, the start-up fees for a McDonald's, Subway, and Domino's are $45,000, $10,000, and $1,300 respectively. Additional initial outlays include rent, inventory, legal fees, equipment, insurance, and licenses. These can amount to 10 times the start-up fee and, in the case of McDonald's, can reach $500,000. The average initial cost is $330,000. There may be additional conditions before beginning; franchisers can require that purchasers have experience in the particular franchise or in the business segment it represents.

Besides covering the costs needed to acquire a franchise, the buyer needs to commit to making the system work. Franchisees who fail typically bypass immersing themselves in the business and instead attempt to be merely managers. The training program for McDonald's, for example, can take months and require a degree from Hamburger University for completion.

Financially, the outlook for investing in a start-up franchise is modest profit and growth until market share increases. Due to substantial competition in low barrier-to-entry industries such as restaurants, cleaning services, and food delivery, franchise operators must keep their prices competitive. Therefore, in order to be profitable and generate a considerable return on assets, a large volume of sales must be generated. Market penetration is the goal.

Franchisors do not expect franchisees to produce substantial returns immediately. Because franchisees face low profit margins due to stiff competition, they often experience salary decreases. On average, an owner's salary falls from $66,000 to $35,000 when leaving corporate America. Their workweek also increases.

Nevertheless, despite these statistics, franchising has continued to be a popular field, creating 170,000 new jobs in 1995. This can be attributed to the feeling of autonomy franchisees attain, which accounts for their high level of job satisfaction. Additional components include recent corporate layoffs, which have left many qualified middle managers ready to undertake new challenges.

## Stock/Investment Outlook

Investing in franchise stocks allows one the ability to choose which industry in which to invest and the desired levels of business maturity, ranging from new businesses to established, "graying" enterprises. Obviously, risk and, therefore, potential returns are higher on new ventures. Some of the risk is diversified because the investment represents a stake in a multitude of independent stores located in different areas of the country such that unfavorable economic conditions in a specific area will not be detrimental to franchisers in different territories.

Franchise stockholders need also to be aware that sometimes when a franchise is successful and the franchisor raises sufficient capital, he or she may begin repurchasing some of the slow growth. This is a long-term strategy for growing the franchise.

## Potential/Prospective for Growth

Currently, 8 million people are employed by franchises. Forty-one percent of retail sales are attributed to franchises. By franchising, a business can grow quickly and achieve a higher market penetration than a sole proprietorship.

For the franchisee, who is often an entrepreneur lacking the knowledge of how to start a business, franchising provides an opportunity to adopt a business concept without having to start from scratch. The franchisee also faces less risk in starting a business because the concept behind the franchise has already proven to be profitable on a limited scale. Hence, the five-year survival rate for franchises is much higher than that of start-up businesses (85.7 percent versus 23 percent).

### Competitive Structure

Franchises can achieve higher efficiency than individual small businesses and "mom and pop" stores. Franchisors do not have to be concerned with internal competition because the franchise contract stipulates how many units can coexist within a particular area. Additionally, franchise owners who leave to open a related business are often precluded from opening one within a specified vicinity of their former operations.

A liability of this form of business occurs when franchisees find more efficient ways to manage their businesses in their particular markets or feel a slightly altered product mix would be more profitable. They are often unable to implement these ideas due to the restrictions imposed by the franchiser who has a commitment to standardization within his franchise.

The amount of control that a franchisor can exert is stipulated in the contract; most franchisees are required to submit monthly, quarterly, and annual financial reports to the franchisor, while certain owners may be required to purchase supplies from a select list of vendors.

### Role of Research and Development

Franchising has experienced considerable growth in the past two decades with currently 670,000 franchise units (5,000 franchises) operating in the United States. A new franchise opens every 6.5 minutes per business day.

According to the International Franchise Association, franchise sales are growing at 10 percent per year. Sales are expected to reach $1 trillion by 2000.

The highest growth has been in the nonfood retail sectors, such as lodging and services. One reason for this growth has been the ability of franchisors to adapt their businesses most effectively to service emerging market trends.

### Technological Investment and Analysis

Technology has also impacted the growth of the franchise industry. Improvements in the technology available to small business owners have been dramatic. They have included comprehensive systems for tracking inventories and for tracking sales. Better and more varied communications tools have made the transmission of information between owner and franchisor much easier and more effective.

The wealth of information and services available to small business owners has also rapidly broadened. The Internet is a prime reason. The Internet also provides a means for small business to reach target customers regardless of location.

### Recommendation for the Future

As many U.S. franchises, most notably in the food industry, have matured and reached market saturation, franchisors have expanded internationally. Besides international expansion continuing into the future, some other key trends are predicted for the franchise industry. Steady growth is expected to continue: retail sales from franchising will go from 41 percent to 50 percent, and sales are expected to reach $2.5 trillion by the year 2010. Franchises that are expected to thrive in the next 20 years are providers of home services such as cleaning, food delivery, and senior care services.

In conclusion, although franchising is a risky business venture for the franchisor as well as the franchisee, it has continued to expand. This can be attributed to the ability of franchisors to raise capital and replicate a business idea that has proven to be effective. Franchising has also benefited from international expansion, allowing it to continue its growth despite market saturation in certain industries. Lastly, technological advances have increased efficiency in the transfer of information, contributing to franchise growth while changing demographics and the current political situation have had offsetting effects on the industry.

### CASE *Mrs. Fields Cookies*

The year is 1977. Randy Fields, Debbi's new husband, is at work giving financial advice to a client. Debbi has just returned home from a history class that she's taking at a local community college. She has been wondering what impact her life will make. She decides to make another batch of her chocolate chip cookies. Since she's been doing this so long, she knows she's good at baking cookies, and enjoys doing so. The light bulb in her head suddenly shines bright, "Why not open a small cookie shop where she can bake and sell her cookies?" Since Randy's clients like them so much, she's sure that many others will, too. The first hurdle was to convince Randy that her idea would work.

### Technological Investment and Analysis

Trying to create a new management system that would continue to allow Debbi the control that she wanted, but would be more cost efficient, was necessary. Randy's philosophy was that the best management structure would be built as flat as possible, meaning not too many people would be involved, and not a great deal of paperwork would be necessary.

The early years of Randy's management information systems department were full of basic implementations that were very useful. The use of phone mail allowed Debbi to leave personal messages to each of the store managers at all of the stores. The form mail program was an "e-mail" system created by the MIS department to allow personal messages to be typed up by store managers and sent to Debbi at corporate headquarters. Debbi promised a response to each message within 48 hours. Now she was able to communicate with each of her stores without actually visiting them. Visiting was time intensive; Debbi logged about 350,000 commercial air miles in 1986.

Improvements to the existing system included a corporate database that operated on IBM computers. IBM-compatible PCs, which soon interfaced with the cash registers, linked each store to corporate headquarters. The MIS group developed its own applications to perform various functions at the store level, such as production planning, staff scheduling, financial reporting, hiring practices, lease management, training, and baking schedules. This group of programs was labeled Retail Operations Intelligence (ROI), and was so successful within the company that the company decided to sell the software to the general public. The implementation of the ROI system gave Debbi the opportunity for the hands-on management that she wanted, allowing her to maintain control over individual store operations from one central office.

The ROI system simplified the role of the store managers to the point of being told what, where, how, and when to do something. With the business focusing primarily on selling cookies, the new technology was able to tell a store manager how many cookies needed to be baked and sold at a certain time during the day. This helped to eliminate a great deal of waste, consequentially cutting cost. It also provided store managers with more time to focus on customer needs by alleviating administrative details.

The main strategy of the MIS department at Mrs. Fields Cookies was to assist in solving any business problems the company faced. The problem with this strategy was that at the rate the business was expanding, problem solving would not be helpful in the prevention of new problems that would arise. Paul Quinn, the director of MIS, reported directly to Randy Fields. He was not concerned about problem prevention but wanted to be aware of the issues dealing with cost efficiency and the benefits of any implementation of information systems coming from his department. Problem solving can be good for present situations. But analyzing the big picture and the possibilities for the future are just as important, especially when it involves a business of the size and reputation of Mrs. Fields Cookies.

Quinn's definition of MIS strategy had to do with anything that would promote sales and control food and labor costs. Quinn wanted to know not only how a new technique would cut costs and save the business money, but also how it would develop new sales for the business and put the company in a better position to take advantage of opportunities.

At the corporate level, Quinn implemented a Return on Investment System for the business as it moved out of the 1980s into the 1990s. No longer was the company growing at such a fast rate and seemingly trying to flood the market. Many viewed the ROI system to be an expert system (ES).

Randy Fields made the following statement about his belief in the use of ES at Mrs. Fields Cookies:

> We couldn't run our business without information technology—not a single facet. Who we hire is determined by an expert system. What we make at each store is determined by an expert system. How we schedule our labor in each store is determined by an expert system. How we communicate internally is routed by an expert system. . . . What's left? At the store level, everything that the manager does that's related to control and administration has been "offloaded" to a machine. So the manager's job is to think about people.

With the implementation of the ROI applications, control by one person was eliminated at the store level. Also, implementation of these applications took some of the burden off of the shoulders of Debbi as she had tried to maintain control over everything for so long.

The ROI system includes 12 applications, each with the purpose of decreasing the time and cost spent on each function by the company. Four of the more important applications include Interview, Training and Testing, Automated Troubleshooting, and Form Mail. These four applications help decrease the time managers spend completing these tasks and not being able to offer customers the best service.

The Interview application requires that the first part of a job applicant's interview process take place on a computer. The basic questions asked give the company an understanding of the type of person who was applying. The computer program probes the intention of the applicant and the reason for applying to work at Mrs. Fields. It pinpoints inconsistencies provided by an applicant, such as a 17-year-old who lists an educational background up to graduate school. The program produces a list of concerns about the candidate. Upon completion of the computer interview, it ranks the applicant in areas of education, honesty, and salesmanship, among others. After the computer interview, the applicant is given the opportunity to "audition" as a performer in front of customers. The manager then decides if the applicant will be hired.

Each employee, from manager to baker, engages in continuous training and evaluation by using the Training and Testing systems application. Again, the system asks several questions based on experience and performance to test and evaluate individual skills learned, and to train to develop new ones. Once an employee completes a training module, their records in human resources are updated automatically at corporate headquarters.

Automated Troubleshooting is a maintenance module used mainly by the store manager to deal with problems concerning faulty or broken store equipment. If the answers entered in the system do not lead to a solution for the problem, a function is added that requests an outside call for assistance. Each store has a file with the product service group at corporate headquarters, listing information about each piece of equipment at the store. This information is used to contact the product vendor to request any type of repair that is needed.

The Form Mail application is used mainly by store managers to maintain communication with corporate headquarters. Debbi is also able to send memos to each of the stores with the use of this application. It was a basic e-mail system developed in the early 1980s.

## QUESTIONS

1. What is the strategic direction of Mrs. Fields Cookies?
2. Who or what forces are driving this direction?
3. What has been the catalyst for change for Mrs. Fields Cookies?
4. Upon what technologies has Mrs. Fields Cookies relied?
5. What caused a change in the use of technology in the corporation?
6. How has this change been implemented?
7. Who has driven this change throughout the organization?
8. How successful has the technological change been?

## ADDITIONAL READING

Prendergast, Alan. "Learning to Let Go," *Working Woman,* January 1992, pp. 42–44.

Sandberg, Jared. "At Thousands of Web Sites, Time Stands Still (neglected Web sites)," *The Wall Street Journal,* March 11, 1997, p. B1.

## CASE *Blockbuster Video*

On a typical night in America, if there is nothing to watch on regular television, people can simply switch among dozens of channels to watch a movie on cable or choose a pay-per-view movie. This does not mean leaving the house. Alternatively, improvements in video technology such as laser discs or digital videodiscs (DVDs) are beginning to provide other options. Running to the local video store has become less necessary than it used to be.

In today's society, going to the local video store to rent a movie with friends and family has been a source of entertainment. Video rental is still a relatively new technology. One of the pioneers in this key home entertainment industry is Blockbuster Entertainment Group.

### Technological Investment and Analysis

A partnership between the Blockbuster Entertainment Group and Sony Electronics, Park Ridge, New Jersey, to promote and demonstrate the new digital videodisc technology may portend how supermarkets can tie in to the product launch.

Select Blockbuster stores in major markets installed in-store demonstration kiosks with Sony DVD players in April 1997. Meanwhile, purchasers of the Sony hardware units received coupons for free DVD rentals at Blockbuster. According to Benjamin S. Feingold, president of Columbia TriStar Home Video, Culver City, California, similar demonstration programs could be made available soon to supermarkets.

"Over time I'm sure we will develop various types of promotional programs for various accounts in conjunction with Sony Electronics," he said. "But in the beginning, there may be inventory issues about how much hardware and software is available. Over time we would expect that there would be promotional opportunities available for almost every class of trade that wants to be in the business."

The Blockbuster-Sony partnership is noteworthy because Viacom's ownership of Paramount Pictures is in direct competition with Sony's Columbia and TriStar units. "Blockbuster is committed to being a leader in developing the entertainment software experiences that exceed the expectations of our members," according to Tom Byrne, Blockbuster's vice chairman.

According to John Briesch, president of Sony's Consumer A/V Group, "We believe people already expect the latest in home video entertainment from Blockbuster, so it makes sense for them to be one of the first retailers in the country to demonstrate the incredible video and audio experiences only available from DVD." "Once people have an opportunity to experience our new DVD video player, we believe they will immediately understand the excitement that DVD offers," he said.

### Technological Innovations

### Telecommunications

Modern audiences demand a technological touch in movies, advertising, and television. All of these enhancements are expensive to develop and to transmit. A company such as KWCC, the special-effects house behind the films *Clear and Present Danger* and *Judge Dredd,* uses dedicated Silicon Graphics (SGI) workstations that run into the hundreds of thousands of dollars. These houses charge $2,000 to $12,000 per second of screen time for performing their digital special effects. To make waves with digital photos, Web graphics, or printed documents, eye-catching effects must be included. Everyday tasks look dull by comparison if some splash is not included, whether it's adding color to e-mail, animations to the home page, or a personal touch to photos and videos.

### Internet

An agreement has been signed by General Electric's NBC and Intertainer, Inc., to enable individuals to request, on-demand, rebroadcasts of NBC programming like *Late Night with Conan O'Brien* and *Dateline*. NBC said it will partner with Intertainer, Inc., to provide content from the programming it owns to Intertainer's on-demand broadband video entertainment and shopping service.

In the process, NBC and GE Capital's Equity Capital Group will pay $3 million in cash for 6 percent of privately held Intertainer. NBC and GE Capital will also have the option to purchase up to 19 percent of the Santa Monica, California-based company for about $75 million in the next 18 months. Details regarding the shows NBC will bring to the upcoming Intertainer service were not immediately finalized and were going to be subsequently revealed. Intertainer's service will be delivered through a high-speed cable or phone line and will provide movies, music, television programming, shopping, and informational programming to a user's personal computer or television set.

The Intertainer service is based upon the concept of any on-demand video service. Customers will be given the ability to watch what they want, when they want. Intertainer's service is personalized through intelligent agent technology from Firefly Networks. The agent "reads" users' preferences and provides prompts and suggestions leading them to personalized movie, music, television, or interactive shopping program options. Intertainer is available to consumers through their personal computers or televisions, initially through distribution provided by two of its original partners, Comcast and U.S. West.

Today, six mass media giants dominate the entertainment and information field. These companies are News Corp, Viacom, Seagram, Walt Disney, Time Warner, and Sony.

April 1997 was a low point for Viacom, Inc., and Sumner Redstone, its chairman. The stock price was down and the Blockbuster video retail chain was struggling. Since this time, Redstone has engineered a turnaround that has raised Viacom, Inc., to new heights.

According to Redstone, Blockbuster is fixed because he cut deals with the Hollywood studios that enable more hit movies to be in his stores. Still, Viacom remains a work in progress. Its UPN Network is losing money. Redstone says he would like to sell Blockbuster and Spelling Entertainment, and will likely make more acquisitions, too. "But we will not re-leverage," he concludes quickly.

Amid increasing concern at Viacom about reducing the company's $8 billion debt, rumors persist that Blockbuster Video will be sold. The success of *Titanic* helped to increase revenues by 12 percent at Viacom for the latest quarter of 1998. However, profits from continuing operations were down 83 percent, due to the continuing losses at Blockbuster.

Redstone sold half of USANetworks to Seagram for $1.7 billion. The money went toward reducing Viacom's debt. Yet Viacom's stock did not move from the low 30s.

The logic for selling Blockbuster revolves around the commitment of Viacom's Paramount film subsidiary to embrace Divx, a new home video format for digital videodiscs. The format requires users to buy an encoded disc for about $5. After that, it is a pay-per-view deal. The disc player is hooked up to a phone line. The movie cannot be watched without dialing in. After a 48-hour viewing period, a charge is incurred for subsequent screenings. If the system catches on, the reduced likelihood that people will buy tapes will cut into rentals. Advanced an estimated $20 million by the format's developers, Paramount is already licensing films for production in the Divx format.

### Competitor

The Hollywood Video rental chain paid $100 million to acquire the Internet-based video concern Reel.com, Inc. Wall Street responded favorably to Hollywood Video, increasing its stock price by 13.28 percent in one day of trading.

Hollywood Video is the second largest video store chain in the United States, with more than 1,000 superstores in 43 states. Each store carries about 10,000 titles and 16,000 videocassettes. Reel.com offers 85,000 VHS titles for sale, more than 1,200 DVD titles for sale, and 35,000 video titles for rent. The cyberstore is also the leading video-only store on the Internet.

The acquisition enables Hollywood Video to leverage its base of 25 million members, industry knowledge, and studio relationships to a new and rapidly growing distribution channel. Because of the uniqueness of an individual customer's taste in movies, the Internet, together with the PC's information processing capabilities, are positioned to create a substantial increase in movie consumption through matching, collaborative filtering, and customized recommendations.

### Recommendation for the Future

In its quest to become the neighborhood entertainment source, Blockbuster will use its extensive consumer database to select the product mix. "The goal is neighborhood retailing and the customization of each product for each store," says marketing manager Baskin. "The key is to cater to the local market and service the local customer." Baskin says the chain has the "strategic advantage" of knowing the entertainment buying habits of half of the households in the United States. Managers at individual locations will have the most input on which products to stock. "Having unmatched demographic information is a great guide, but it's not a silver bullet," says Baskin. Blockbuster tried to diversify by expanding into music stores. It even attempted to add book sales—tailoring the titles to specific locations. In 1999, after consistently losing money, Blockbuster sold all of the music stores.

Blockbuster's greatest strength in the last two years has been its unique association with Viacom, which enabled Blockbuster to change its purchase arrangement. The deal provides Blockbuster with thousands of copies of new releases at minimal cost—enabling the stores to guarantee hot titles will be in the store.

Blockbuster needs to continue to invest in technology. The demand for home entertainment will remain consistent. At this point in time, home entertainment includes television programming, movies, compact discs, and books. However, what is important today does not necessarily determine what will be important in the next two, five, or seven years.

## QUESTIONS

1. What is the strategic direction of the Blockbuster Entertainment Division of Viacom?
2. What are the critical success factors and core competencies for the Blockbuster organization?
3. Upon what technologies has Blockbuster relied?
4. What has caused a change in the direction of the use of technology at Blockbuster?
5. How successful has the technological change been?
6. What does the corporation's web page present about its business directives?
7. How does technology impact the challenges and opportunities that the home video industry is facing?
8. How will the capture and maintenance of customer data impact Blockbuster's future?

## ADDITIONAL READING

Hamblen, Matt. "Web Site Gives Pay-Per-View a Fighting Chance," *Computerworld,* June 30, 1997, p. 6.

Harrington, Mark. "Blockbuster Exits PC Business, Closes Stores," *Computer Retail Week,* October 13, 1997, pp. 1–2.

"Hollywood Video Reels Out $100Mil in Acquisition," *Newsbytes,* July 31, 1998, p. NEW07310025.

Marcus, Ann M. "Four on a Match," *PC Entertainment,* March 1996, p. 14.

"NBC: Let Us Intertain You," *Newsbytes,* August 3, 1998, p. NEW08030032.

Pepper, Jon, and Cesar Alvarez, "Hollywood Comes Home," *Computer Life,* July 1998, p. 58.

Serwer, Andrew. "Viacom Wants an Oscar for Fixing Blockbuster," *Fortune,* April 27, 1998, p. 485.

"Wave Aims to Be Blockbuster Video of E-Commerce," *Newsbytes,* June 25, 1997, p. NEW06250072.

## DISCUSSION ISSUE

### Who Owns Knowledge?

There is an important ethical question involving expert systems. Remember that developing an ES requires the assistance of a cooperative expert. Why should an expert cooperate? Listen as Alvy (the CEO) tries to get Annie (the expert) to participate in a new ES project.

Alvy: Hi, Annie. We've got a new project I think you're really going to like. You get to show off a little. We're going to build an expert system to handle quality control. I asked my VPs, and they all said you're the best. Whenever they have a question, they come to you. Your knowledge is going to be the foundation for the new expert system.

Annie: Well, it's nice to know that everyone likes my work. But, I'm a little worried. I heard about the new project, and I've done some reading on expert systems. It seems to me that when you've built your new system, you won't need me around anymore. Are you saying I need to look for a new job?

Alvy: No, no. We really love your work. That's why you've been chosen for this project. It's really quite an honor. We'll take you off your normal duties for a while so you can devote time to the developers, but we want you here.

Annie: But what will I be doing when the system is complete? It took me 15 years of hard work to learn everything. I still have 10 years to retirement. I'm not sure it's possible, but if your fancy new machine takes everything I know, then what's left for me? What are you planning? Drain all my knowledge and throw me away like an empty beer can?

Alvy: Whoa, slow down. I don't really know how this stuff works, but the programmers are just going to ask you a bunch of questions. We're planning on taking at least six months. After that, it'll be another year before the system is completely tested and ready to go. We've got plenty of time to worry about what happens after that.

Annie: That's not good enough. I've invested a lot of time and energy. I've always worked hard for this company. If I'm going to lose my job in a year, I want to know now. I'd be better off if I start looking now.

Alvy: You're blowing this situation out of proportion. I never said anything about you losing your job. When the project's over, it may change a little. We'll have to see how everything works out. When we get out of this recession and get that new plant built, I'll be looking for a manager. It's long term, but if you keep up the good work, you'll be on the short list for that job.

Annie: Hey, I don't need your empty promises. You've been talking about that plant for 10 years. The way I see it, you need me for this expert system. If I walk out of here today, you don't get your system, and I get a new job somewhere else doing what I love.

Alvy: Come on, you've been a loyal employee for years. You've struggled with us through the hard times. It won't be much longer, and I'll be able to reward you the way I always intended. Besides, we trained you. You got all that knowledge from our company. We paid you through all those years. Now we want to use that information. You never complain when the VPs ask you questions.

Annie: Well . . . I don't know . . .

Alvy: Look, I didn't realize it would bother you so much. We don't need to nail this down today. Why not take the afternoon off and think about it? Call Susie in MIS if you want more information on what the programmers need. Let's get together again next week. In the meantime, I'll talk to the VPs and the directors and see whether we can scrape together a raise or a bonus or something.

## QUESTIONS

1. Do you think Annie should go along with Alvy's plan? Will she be able to keep her job? Will the job be the same?

2. Do you think the company should be able to force Annie to participate? How can they make her participate?

3. Do you think this situation is realistic? Do you think you might someday be in Annie's shoes? What can you do to avoid that situation?

# APPENDIX

# *Optimization*

Many problems in business require optimization, such as finding the least cost or the most profit. These problems typically have three components: an objective, a set of variables that you can control, and a set of constraints or limits. Mathematicians have created several powerful techniques to solve these types of problems. If the problem is not too large, it can be handled in a spreadsheet with Excel's Solver.

Today, the most challenging aspect of an optimization problem is setting up the problem. Once you have defined the problem correctly, it can be solved almost instantly with today's computers.

## SAMPLE PROBLEM

It is easiest to see the process by setting up a sample problem. Consider a problem with three facto-

ries. Each factory has different costs of production, so label them *cheap, intermediate,* and *expensive.* Part of the cost is reflected in the quality of their output. The cheap factory tends to produce lower quality products. Each plant can produce a limited amount of output per time frame (e.g., one day). To keep it simple, output will be measured in kilotons. Figure 10.1A shows the basic parameters for the three factories.

Now, say that two orders arrive that both need to be filled over the same time period. The details of the orders are shown in Figure 10.2A. To meet the quantity and quality specifications, you will have to mix output from the three factories. The ultimate question is: What is the cheapest way of allocating production from each factory to fill the two orders?

| FACTORY | MAX OUTPUT | COST OF OUTPUT | QUALITY |
|---|---|---|---|
| Cheap | 100 | 75 | 2.0 |
| Intermediate | 100 | 100 | 2.5 |
| Expensive | 100 | 120 | 3.0 |

**FIGURE 10.1A**
FACTORY PARAMETERS
Production at the expensive factory costs more, but quality is higher.

| ORDER | TOTAL QUANTITY | MIN. QUALITY |
|---|---|---|
| Order 1 | 100 | 2.5 |
| Order 2 | 150 | 1.5 |

**FIGURE 10.2A**
ORDER SPECIFICATION
You will have to mix output from the three factories to provide the desired quantity and quality.

## PROBLEM DEFINITION

This problem is an optimization problem because the goal is to choose output variables that produce the least cost solution. The problem contains several constraints in the form of limits on production and specifications for the order. The basic description of the problem is shown in Figure 10.3A. The most important step in setting up the problem is to realize there are six control variables contained in the amount of production from each plant that is given to each order.

## SPREADSHEET LAYOUT

Some optimization systems enable you to enter the problem definition as it is written in Figure 10.3A. However, if you want to use Excel's Solver for the problem, it is easier to first lay out the problem in the spreadsheet. This step makes it easier to change values later and examine the effects of changes.

As shown in Figure 10.4A, you want to define a column for each of the control variables. Leave a blank cell (row) that will hold the actual value (solution) for

---

**Variables:** things you can control
Output from each factory (c, i, e) given to each order (1,2):
Qc1, Qi1, Qe1, Qc2, Qi2, Qe2

**Goal:** objective function
Minimize total cost:
Cost= 75 Qc1 + 75 Qc2 +100 Qi1 + 100 Qi2 +120 Qe1 + 120 Qe2

**Constraints:** restrictions or limits
Plant Limit C:   Qc1 + Qc2 <= 100
Plant Limit I:    Qi1 + Qi2 <= 100
Plant Limit E:   Qe1 + Qe2 <= 100
Quality Order 1: Qc1 + Qi1 + Qe1 = 100
Quality Order 2: Qc2 + Qi2 + Qe2 = 100
Quality Order 1: 2.0 Qc1 + 2.5 Qi1 + 3.0 Qe1 > 250 (2.5* 100)
Quality Order 2: 2.0 Qc2 + 2.5 Qi2 + 3.0 Qe2 > 225 (1.5* 150)

---

**FIGURE 10.3A**
PROBLEM DEFINITION

Note the six variables that we need to solve. The goal is to minimize total cost. The answer must meet the constraints on the plants and on the orders.

---

= C3*C2 + D3*D2 + E3*E2 + F3*F2 + G3*G2 + H3*H2

= C4*C2 + D4*D2

| | Variables | Qc1 | Qc2 | Qi1 | Qi2 | Qe1 | Qe2 | | | Limit |
|---|---|---|---|---|---|---|---|---|---|---|
| | | | | | | | | Constraint | | |
| Objective | 0 | 75 | 75 | 100 | 100 | 120 | 120 | | | |
| Plant C limit | | 1 | 1 | | | | | 0 | <= | 100 |
| Plant I limit | | | | 1 | 1 | | | 0 | <= | 100 |
| Plant E limit | | | | | | 1 | 1 | 0 | <= | 100 |
| Order 1 | | 1 | | 1 | | 1 | | 0 | = | 100 |
| Order 2 | | | 1 | | 1 | | 1 | 0 | = | 150 |
| Quality Order 1 | | 2 | | 2.5 | | 3 | | 0 | > | 250 |
| Quality Order 2 | | | 2 | | 2.5 | | 3 | 0 | > | 225 |

**FIGURE 10.4A**
SPREADSHEET LAYOUT

Put each control variable (*Qc*1, *Qc* 2, . . . *Qe*2) in a column. Put the objective function parameters in a row. Define each constraint in a row, where the total is compared to a limit value.

each variable. Then put the parameters for the objective function on a new row. Finally, create rows for each of the constraints. Each constraint has parameter values that will be multiplied by the variable and summed for each row. This total is compared to the limit value.

Start with the objective function. You must define a cell that contains the total cost value (which will be minimized). Multiply each cost parameter by the amount that will be produced and compute the total. For example, $75 * Qc1 + 75 * Qc2 + 100Qi1$ and so on. Each parameter (75) and variable ($Qc1$) is defined by the appropriate cell (e.g., $C3 * C2 + D3 * D2$). Currently the total is zero because there is no solution yet and all of the quantities are zero.

Define the constraints similarly. For instance, for factory C, add the amount produced for order one ($1 * Qc1$) to that produced for order two ($1 * Qc2$). This total must be less than or equal to the capacity of factory C (100). On the plant C row, you put a 1 in the columns for $Qc1$ and $Qc2$. Then you enter the value 100 in the limit column. In the constraint column, you enter a formula to add: $1 * Qc1 + 1 * Qc2 + 0 * Qi1$, and so on. The other constraints are defined just as easily.

## EXCEL SOLVER

The next step is to start the Excel Solver and tell it where to find the three components (control variables, objective function, and constraints). Figure 10.5A shows the basic form for the Solver. Use the total value for the objective function as the target cell. The "changing cells" are the control variable cells that you set aside earlier.

You must add each constraint separately. When you click the Add button, enter the cell for the computed value (the constraint column), choose the appropriate inequality or equality sign, then set the cell for the limit value. Technically, you could enter the inequality similar to the way it is shown in Figure 10.3A; however, it is better to use the method shown in Figure 10.5A. That way it is easy to change the constraint parameters and the limit values. Entering new values in the spreadsheet is much easier than editing the inequality in the Solver.

## SOLUTION

Once you have the three components entered, you simply click the Solve button. The Solver will tell you if it finds an acceptable solution. If not, you probably have infeasible constraints, and you should double-check all of the constraints. If necessary, start with a simpler problem with few constraints; then add constraints until you find the problem. In some cases, there might not be a feasible solution. For example, what would happen if the two orders required a total of 450 kilotons? This problem could not be solved because the total output of the three plants is only 300.

The solution to the sample problem is shown in Figure 10.6A. The Solver fills in the control values for the solution. The spreadsheet then computes the total cost and the value for each constraint. Notice that because all the constraints are satisfied, the solution is feasible. Also note that the expensive plant is used to produce only 50 kilotons. Remember that the total plant capacity was 300, and the total of the two orders was only 250. Hence, the solution makes sense because the slack is at the most expensive factory.

What happens if costs change, or if the customers change their quality specifications? You simply change the parameters in the spreadsheet, restart the Solver, and click the Solve button.

## LIMITATIONS

One issue you might encounter is a limit on the number of variables or constraints. The actual limits within the Excel Solver change with new versions, but it is unlikely that it will be able to handle problems with more than a couple hundred variables and constraints.

If you look carefully at the sample problem in Figure 10.3A, you will notice that the objective function and the constraints are all linear. For example, there are no quadratic or other nonlinear terms. These types of problems are relatively easy to solve. On the other hand, if you have nonlinear constraints, the problem is considerably more difficult to solve. Although the Excel Solver can handle some degree of nonlinearity, it will probably not work on complex problems.

In these situations, you will have to find dedicated optimization software to handle your problem. Fortunately, several commercial software packages can handle very large, complex optimization problems.

| | Variables | Qc1 | Qc2 | Qi1 | Qi2 | Qe1 | Qe2 | | | Limit |
|---|---|---|---|---|---|---|---|---|---|---|
| | | | | | | | | Constraint | | |
| Objective | 0 | 75 | 75 | 100 | 100 | 120 | 120 | | | |
| Plant C limit | | 1 | 1 | | | | | 0 | <= | 100 |
| Plant I limit | | | | 1 | 1 | | | 0 | <= | 100 |
| Plant E limit | | | | | | 1 | 1 | 0 | <= | 100 |
| Order 1 | | 1 | | 1 | | 1 | | 0 | = | 100 |
| Order 2 | | | 1 | | 1 | | 1 | 0 | = | 150 |
| Quality Order 1 | | 2 | | 2.5 | | 3 | | 0 | > | 250 |
| Quality Order 2 | | | 2 | | 2.5 | | 3 | 0 | > | 225 |

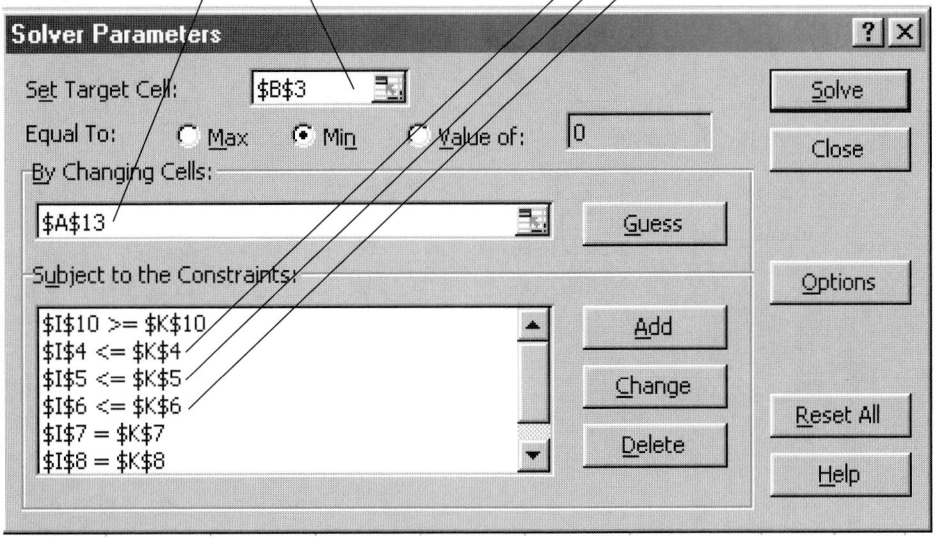

**Solver Parameters**

Set Target Cell: `$B$3`

Equal To: ○ Max  ● Min  ○ Value of: `0`

By Changing Cells: `$A$13`

Subject to the Constraints:

```
$I$10 >= $K$10
$I$4 <= $K$4
$I$5 <= $K$5
$I$6 <= $K$6
$I$7 = $K$7
$I$8 = $K$8
```

Buttons: Solve, Close, Guess, Options, Add, Change, Delete, Reset All, Help

**FIGURE 10.5A**

EXCEL SOLVER

You need to tell the Solver where to find the three elements: objective function total, control variables, and the constraints.

| | Variables | Qc1 | Qc2 | Qi1 | Qi2 | Qe1 | Qe2 | | | Limit |
|---|---|---|---|---|---|---|---|---|---|---|
| | | 28.555 | 71.445 | 41.327 | 58.673 | 30.118 | 19.882 | Constraint | | |
| Objective | 23500 | 75 | 75 | 100 | 100 | 120 | 120 | | | |
| Plant C limit | | 1 | 1 | | | | | 100 | <= | 100 |
| Plant I limit | | | | 1 | 1 | | | 100 | <= | 100 |
| Plant E limit | | | | | | 1 | 1 | 50 | <= | 100 |
| Order 1 | | 1 | | 1 | | 1 | | 100 | = | 100 |
| Order 2 | | | 1 | | 1 | | 1 | 150 | = | 150 |
| Quality Order 1 | | 2 | | 2.5 | | 3 | | 250.7813 | > | 250 |
| Quality Order 2 | | | 2 | | 2.5 | | 3 | 349.2188 | > | 225 |

**FIGURE 10.6A**

SOLUTION

The Solver fills in the values for the control variables (28.555 to 19.882). The spreadsheet then computes the total cost and the value of each of the constraints. Notice that each constraint is satisfied, indicating a feasible solution.

## SUMMARY

The power of optimization is that it can identify a precise solution. You do not have to rely on rules of thumb or guesswork. In many cases, even a seemingly small change can result in saving thousands or millions of dollars. For instance, AT&T improved their switching network by embedding an optimization routine that determines the best method to route phone calls.

## EXERCISES

1. Build the spreadsheet to solve the problem in the text. Test it to see that you get the correct answer. Now, change the quantity in order 1 to 125 and the quality in order 2 to 1.75. What are the new production values?
2. Identify three business problems (that are not used in this book) that would benefit from mathematical programming tools.

3. A company wishes to develop new software that is estimated to require 30,000 elements (e.g., lines of code). It can hire full-time staff who can create 15 elements per day, part-time workers who produce 10 elements a day, or contract with an outside company to produce 25 elements a day. Full-time workers cost $200 per day, part-timers $160 per day, and contract workers $400 per day. Because of a hiring freeze, the project cannot use more than 1,000 days of full-time employees (e.g., 3 employees for a year). However, because of management involvement, at least 500 days of full-time work is required. The directors are tired of paying for contractors so they will not authorize spending more than $180,000 on contractors. How many days of full-time, part-time, and contract work is needed to minimize costs?

# Strategic Analysis

American Airlines uses its Sabre web page (http://www.sabre.com) to provide information about the company and to list flight schedules and make flight and hotel reservations for customers on the web.

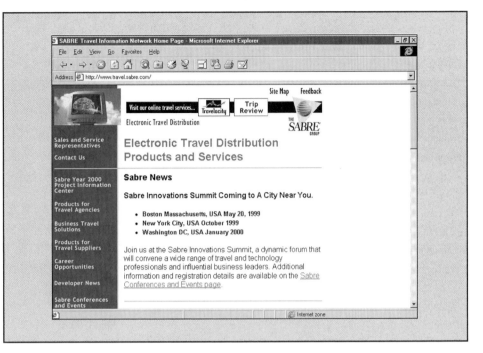

## AMERICAN AIRLINES SABRE

In their efforts to be competitive for the business and pleasure traveler, airlines have placed increasing demands on their reservation systems. The requirement for instantaneous response is a given. However, travelers are intensifying their demand for preassignment to their seats, preissued boarding passes, and more varieties of in-flight menus and movies.

Today travelers even want "one-stop" reservations for all their needs. Hotels and rental car agencies have linked themselves to the reservation systems to enable travelers to complete all of their travel arrangements at one location and through one computer system. Frequent-flyer and hotel programs are similarly linked together. Joint arrangements encourage travelers to stay at participating hotels after flying on a particular airline. When they do so, bonus points are given in award programs that involve linked fly/stay weekends.

To meet these increasingly sophisticated reservation demands, American Airlines developed the Sabre system. This strategic business tool is an advanced database system that provides instantaneous reservation service to travel agents across the country. Specific pricing categories can be introduced, complicated connections planned, and seats reserved all in one action. By enlisting a large number of travel and ticket agencies, American Airlines can use its information system to ensure that its seats and flights are filled first.

Ticket agents are more likely to book flights that are listed first. At one time, Sabre always listed American's flights first, increasing the likelihood that the reservations would be made on American instead of competing airlines.

The strength of the Sabre system is its ability to link a number of smaller databases instantaneously. Currently, American is involved in an extensive development program that will further improve this ability. American is experimenting with image processing, expert systems, cooperative processing, local area networks, and a corporatewide office automation network. These new techniques will further improve Sabre's ability to book the entire itinerary for a trip through one reservation system.

**FIGURE 11.1**
STRATEGIES
Managers are
increasingly being
asked to find ways
to give their firm an
advantage over
the competition.
Information systems
can help identify areas
that can provide a
competitive edge.
Information systems
can also directly
provide services and
advantages that are not
offered by your rivals.

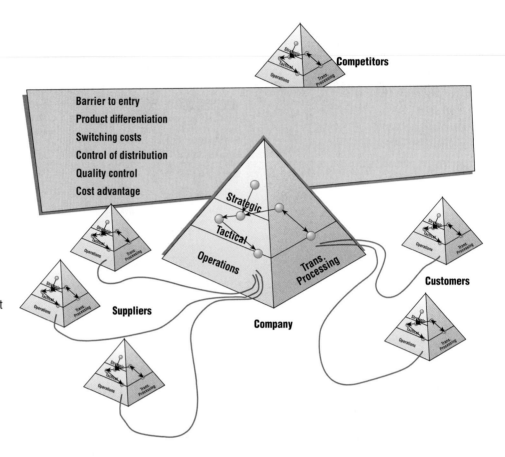

- Barrier to entry
- Product differentiation
- Switching costs
- Control of distribution
- Quality control
- Cost advantage

**OVERVIEW**   As the world economy has become more competitive, firms have become more ambitious in seeking a means to gain a strategic advantage. As illustrated by Figure 11.1, they are searching for methods that make them unique. Finding these opportunities can be difficult. Information technology is a tool that has proved useful at providing a competitive edge through innovative products, better service, lower costs, and improved quality.

Setting strategic directions is often performed at the top management levels of the firm. Because only a few students will become corporate leaders, it might seem that this chapter is not as important to you. Besides the fact that you might be one of the few who run a major firm someday, there are two basic reasons why you need to understand the strategic uses of information technology. First, strategy requires creativity. Having more people in a firm searching for competitive advantages means more ideas. Even if it is not part of your job description, good ideas are likely to be rewarded. Second, recall that many jobs are in small businesses. In a small business, you do not have the luxury of hiring specialists to focus on strategic questions. All managers are expected to contribute to the growth of the firm.

**INTRODUCTION**   In some ways, information systems designed for competitive advantage are not much different than transaction processing and decision support systems. In many cases, advantages over your rivals can result from changes in the basic transaction-processing systems and business methods. The real difference with strategy lies in its goal: to change the way the business operates and gain an advantage over the other firms in the industry.

Creating strategic systems requires that you understand the entire firm and its relationship with external agents in the environment, such as suppliers, consumers, workers,

## Trends

Ideas and concepts for managing businesses are constantly changing. Many current practices are often traced to Alfred Sloan, who drove the consolidation and expansion of General Motors from 1920 to 1956. Management techniques evolve over time and ideas come from many sources. Through the 1950s, many companies focused on making production more efficient. In the 1950s and 1960s, U.S. firms expanded into wider markets, both nationally and internationally. In the 1970s, managers were preoccupied with the economic changes brought on by oil price rises and consequent shocks of high inflation and high interest rates. The 1970s and 1980s also saw the emergence of increased international competition—for example, between 1960 and 1985, U.S. imports as a percent of GDP increased from 5.6 percent to 11.5 percent.

Despite these general trends, most companies find it difficult to change. As a result, as the business environment changes, a company might lose its focus, or new competitors may appear. Periodically, executives need to examine the overall position of the firm to see whether there might be a better strategy or a new way to gain an advantage over rival firms. Michael Porter, in his book *Competitive Strategy: Techniques for Analyzing Industries and Competitors,* took the lead in showing executives how to reexamine their business and search for competitive advantages.

Through the 1960s and 1970s, the use of MIS was largely governed by its capabilities and the immediate needs of the organizations. The most common MIS objective was to save money and time by automating transaction-processing tasks. The projects were evaluated on the basis of how much money they could save. Eventually, managers came to realize that computer systems have other advantages. A new technology might enable the firm to provide better service to customers. The company that is the first implementer of a technology might find it easier to attract customers, giving it a competitive advantage over the other firms. For example, the first banks that installed ATMs to provide 24-hour access gained an advantage over its competitors. Warren McFarlan was one of the first writers to analyze how information technology could be used to gain a competitive advantage.

Several classic cases are commonly used as examples to illustrate the strategic uses of information systems. The earliest examples come from the airline industry. In the 1960s and 1970s, United Airlines and American Airlines spent millions of dollars to develop online reservation systems Apollo (1971) and Sabre. The Apollo system was spun off in 1987 and renamed Covia. In 1988, Covia, British Airways, SwissAir, and KLM formed Galileo. These systems did more than simply sell tickets—they kept track of customers and flights. When the airline industry was deregulated new competitors appeared (such as People's Express). Despite having higher operating costs, the larger airlines were able to survive many of these challenges by using their information systems. With their reservation systems, they were able to charge different prices for different passengers (business and tourist class). Another competitive feature of their systems was that they listed their own flights first. Congress eventually decided this practice was unethical because they were charging other airlines to list flights on the system. The reservation systems are also used to track frequent flyers, which encourages customers to use one airline.

and rivals. Many systems have been devised to help you analyze and create corporate strategies. A common thread in gaining a competitive advantage is to improve the ties and communication with suppliers and consumers. Electronic communication can provide automatic data collection, minimize errors, and create faster responses.

Information systems can provide a competitive advantage through increasing the barriers to entry and controlling distribution channels. Services from information systems can be used to differentiate your product from the others in the market or even to create entirely new products. Computer systems might give you an edge by being the lowest cost producer or through improved quality management.

Designing strategic systems can be a dangerous task with many opportunities to fail. One complication is that development costs are high. Some strategic systems use new technology, which carries higher costs and a greater risk of incompatibilities and other problems. It is also important to remember that attempts to monopolize a market are illegal, and strategic systems can sometimes come close to breaking the antitrust laws.

The most difficult aspect of strategic systems is coming up with ideas that might give you an advantage. One way to get ideas is to see what firms in other industries have done. You never know when some of the techniques and tricks used by other companies might be useful to you.

**THE COMPETITIVE ENVIRONMENT**     One of the important trends facing most businesses today is the increased level of competition. Improved telecommunications and faster delivery services mean that local firms

---

### Business Trends

Business statistics indicate a clear trend toward the increased importance of service-oriented firms. Service firms are well suited to certain strategic uses of information systems. In particular, product differentiation, product quality, and new products are typically useful strategies. In many service industries, information is the primary product, so technology is especially valuable.

The financial industry provides several strategic examples, such as the Merrill Lynch Cash Management Account, ATMs, or new financial instruments created by brokers. Similarly, Federal Express uses tracking information to differentiate its service from its rivals' offerings. Likewise, the airlines used their reservation systems to give them a competitive advantage in transportation services.

---

Competition is increasing in many industries, but it is particularly intense in the restaurant and fast food industry. Competition encourages firms to hold down costs, provide more variety, and provide new and better service to customers.

face competition from regional, national, and international firms. Local firms have to compete against national mail-order companies, which offer wide selections, next-day delivery, and low prices. The Internet, home shopping channels, and toll-free phone numbers make it easier for consumers to compare prices, putting pressure on all firms.

Large national retailers and franchises put pressure on local stores. They also compete against themselves for market territories. Their size gives them leverage in dealing with manufacturers. By purchasing in large quantities, they can negotiate lower prices. Their high volume also makes it easier for them to buy from foreign producers.

Several international trends are creating increased competition. The international search for lower manufacturing costs puts pressure on firms to cut their costs. For instance, the Japanese have moved production to other Asian nations to build television sets. Decreasing trade barriers throughout the world also creates larger markets. As Eastern European economies rebuild, as the European Union takes shape, and as Mexican incomes increase, consumers will be able to buy more products. Although the prospect of these increased sales is enticing to U.S. manufacturers, there are some complications. If a competitor becomes established first, it will be a stronger and tougher competitor in the United States. New firms will arise or expand in these international markets, giving them a stronger base to increase sales in the United States, providing for increased competition.

**EXTERNAL AGENTS**    Competitive advantage can be gained by establishing or changing relationships between the firm and its **external agents.** External agents consist of suppliers, customers, rivals, potential new entrants, substitute products, and sometimes the government. Figure 11.2 portrays these relationships in Porter's **five forces model.** From a systems perspective, each of these entities is outside the control of the firm. Yet, they strongly affect the company. Through improved ties to these agents, they become part of your system, which can be used to improve the competitive position of the firm. Figure 11.3 illustrates the various relationships that exist with modern companies.

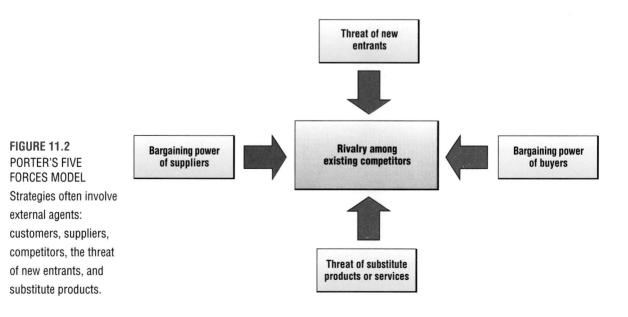

**FIGURE 11.2**
PORTER'S FIVE
FORCES MODEL
Strategies often involve
external agents:
customers, suppliers,
competitors, the threat
of new entrants, and
substitute products.

**FIGURE 11.3**

PRODUCTION CHAIN
Modern companies
have ties to hundreds
or thousands of
entities. Sometimes
a company will own
several pieces of the
production chain
(vertical integration).
Sometimes the
company might expand
horizontally by building
related businesses.
Each linkage requires
communication and
offers the possibility
for strategic gain.

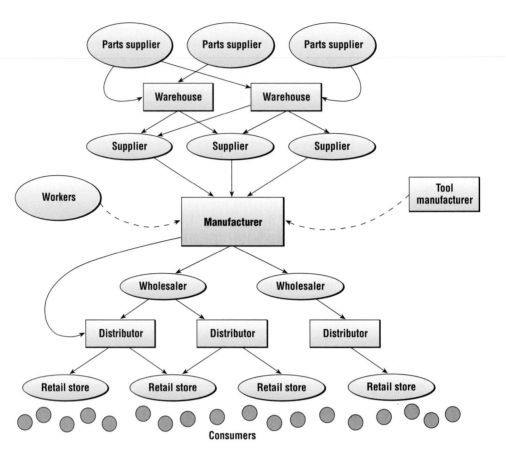

## Customers

To a retail outlet, customers are likely to be individual people. A large manufacturer may have several levels of customers, ranging from wholesale firms that buy in bulk, then sell to distributors, which deliver products to retailers, where the final customer purchases the product. Having more intermediate levels between the manufacturer and the customer can make it much harder to manage the firm.

An important goal in any company is to satisfy the customers. If there are many layers of buyers between the company and the ultimate consumer, it can be difficult to determine what the customer wants. Similarly, the layers create delays that make it difficult for the retailer to order and obtain the products. For example, with older, slower manufacturing processes, merchants have to place most orders for the Christmas season around July—five or six months before the sales would occur. What happens if the economy changes or some event causes people to suddenly demand a different product? The retailer, manufacturer, and customers all suffer as a result of these long lead times.

The intermediate layers also cause confusion about what the customers want because it is hard to identify the customer. To the manufacturer, is the customer the wholesale firm that buys the products, the retailer, or the final consumer? It is often wise to focus on the final consumer, but the manufacturer has to consider the needs of the retailer as well. For example, in the bicycle industry, one company found a new way to package its bicycles so that they could be assembled (by the retailer) in half the normal time. This particular situation helped both the retailer and the final consumer, but imagine what happens when the manufacturer receives conflicting demands from the various "customers."

A common strategic goal is to "get closer to the customers." Information systems can be used to strengthen the ties among the customers, manufacturers, and various intermediaries. For example, you could build electronic ordering systems, with terminals in the retail stores to capture current sales levels. The systems could also be used to send new product information to the customers, or collect feedback on various attributes, or provide immediate answers to question from retailers and customers.

## Suppliers

Suppliers can provide individual parts, entire products, or even services (such as a bank that lends money). Three major issues involving suppliers are price, quality, and delivery schedules. Just as with customers, problems can arise when there are many layers of suppliers. For instance, increased layers can result in longer delays between ordering and delivery because the supplier has to contact its supplier, who contacts its supplier.

Quality management is also more difficult when there are several layers of suppliers. A fundamental element of **total quality management (TQM)** states that quality must be built into every process and item. Picture the problems that arise if quality is measured only in terms of the output at the manufacturer. When a defective product is found, there is no information about the cause. How can the problem be corrected? Managers need to know where each component came from and evaluate the quality as soon as possible. For instance, if there is a defective product, you could check each component to determine its original manufacturer. The manufacturer could be notified of problems, and you could search other items for similar defects. The manufacturer could use this data to identify problems with individual production lines.

Information systems can be used to build electronic ties to suppliers. Common uses of these systems include placing orders, tracking shipments, monitoring quality control, notifying partners of changes in plans, and making payments. Electronic links provide faster responses, better record keeping, and fewer errors. They also offer the potential strategic benefits described in the next section.

## Rivals, New Entrants, and Substitutes

The goal of a strategic approach is to derive a competitive advantage over the **rivals,** or other firms in the industry. There could be many competitors or just a few larger rivals. The competition could take place in a small town, across a nation, or worldwide. One of the first steps in any strategic analysis is to identify the primary competitors and to assess their strengths and weaknesses.

One issue to remember about competition is that it never stops. Coming up with one strategic idea is not good enough. For example, American Airlines and United Airlines spent millions of dollars to build reservation systems as strategic systems. Today, all major airlines have access to these systems, and each airline must continually work to improve its system to provide new enticements to customers. Similarly, automobile companies designed computerized diagnostic systems to improve services offered by repair shops. Today, all of the manufacturers have essentially the same systems. In some cases, they might offer improvements over your ideas, which will put the originator at a disadvantage. However, the firm that first implements a new strategy can gain recognition and market share. It is important to remember that companies must continually improve and seek new opportunities.

A related issue is the concept of potential competitors or entrants in the business. In some cases, you might identify the major rivals, implement a strategy, and then immediately lose everything as new firms enter your business. Entrants might build their firms from scratch, such as the way Burger King built new stores in the same areas as McDonald's restaurants. Alternatively, other firms may increase the sales of products that are similar to your products. Substitute products are related economically by the degree to which consumers are willing to use one product instead of the other. A classic example comes from the late 1970s, when the U.S. economy faced high inflation rates and banks were subject to limits on the interest rates they could pay on deposits. Merrill Lynch, the stock brokerage firm, introduced a service enabling customers to store their money in a wide variety of financial instruments that paid significantly higher interest rates than did checking accounts, and still write checks on the account. Many larger customers took their money away from banks and put it in these asset accounts. These new accounts were perceived as close substitutes for traditional bank services, and people transferred huge sums of money out of the banking system.

The key point is that you need to take a broad look at your firm and the industry. Know who your competitors are and how they operate. Are there other products or services offered by other industries that might attract your customers? If you make a change in the way you do business, find out how it will affect your rivals. Determine how changes will alter the industry. Will they provide an opening for firms in other industries?

## Government Regulations

In any economy, government intervention has a strong influence on the firm. There are myriad government agencies, regulations, taxes, and reports. The situation multiplies for multinational firms that are subject to the regulations of many nations. These agencies and regulations can have strong effects on the profitability of a firm. Generally, an individual firm has no control over government regulations, but sometimes suggestions can lead to modifications. For instance, it is now possible to submit some documents to government agencies in computer form. In fact, some reports (such as 10K or 10Q financial reports) are *required* to be filed electronically. Electronic forms can decrease your storage costs and make it easier to find documents that have been stored for long periods of time.

## IS TECHNIQUES TO GAIN COMPETITIVE ADVANTAGE

Competitive advantage may be achieved with many techniques in business. Information technology is one area that may provide several opportunities. In general, there is no reason to believe that MIS techniques are better than other methods. However, some firms have experienced considerable success from using these techniques, so they are well worth considering. Additionally, the rapid changes in technology often lead to competitive advantages if your firm is the first to find a creative use for the new technology. The other side of the coin is that untested new technologies may not work as planned. Hence, the pioneer is taking a risk: If the project fails, the development costs may put the firm at a competitive disadvantage.

The fundamental mechanisms for gaining competitive advantage are barriers to entry, switching costs, lower production costs, product differentiation, control over distribution channels, innovation, and quality control. These techniques are illustrated in Figure 11.4. The question we wish to examine is how information systems can take advantage of these techniques.

## Barriers to Entry

A fundamental concept of economics is that in order to make extra profits, you need some mechanism to prevent other firms from entering the industry. Otherwise, as soon as your firm develops a strategy that pays higher returns, other firms will flock to the industry and drive the prices and profits down. Figure 11.5 summarizes the common **barriers to entry.** One common way that information systems create barriers to entry is from their cost. Con-

**FIGURE 11.4**
METHODS TO GAIN
COMPETITIVE
ADVANTAGE
Examining the
production chain
highlights several useful
techniques. Barriers to
entry keep out potential
competitors and
substitutes. Ties to
suppliers can cut costs,
improve quality, and
lock out competitors.
Control over distribution
provides stronger
markets and keeps out
competitors. Building
ties to customers builds
loyalty, improves
products, and increases
margins. Creating
switching costs keeps
customers loyal.

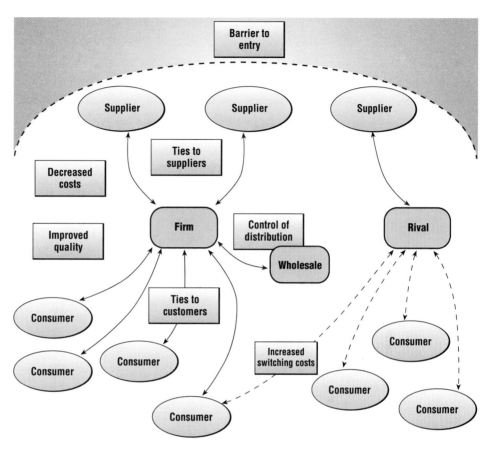

**FIGURE 11.5**
SOURCES OF
BARRIERS TO ENTRY
There are several
methods to build
barriers to entry. Be
careful. Many attempts
to erect barriers are
considered illegal under
antitrust legislation.

- Economies of scale (size)
- Economies of scope (breadth)
- Product differentiation
- Capital requirements
- Cost disadvantages (independent of size)
- Distribution channel access
- Government policy

sider what happens when you create a new information system that provides additional services, like banks did with ATMs. Customers soon expect all firms to offer those services. If a new company wishes to enter the industry, it will have to spend additional money to buy the computers and create the systems to offer those services. The information system raises the cost of entering the industry. A classic example of this situation was the introduction of People's Express Airlines in 1981. The CEO of People's Express stated that he knew the airline needed a reservation system to compete effectively with other airlines, but after raising $100 million to start the airline, the top management found it impossible to raise the additional $100 million needed to create the reservation system.

## Reality Bytes     11–1    People's Express Airline (Classic Case)

In 1981, Donald Burr's People's Express Airlines was the darling of the airline industry and American management. In four years the fledgling airline grew to a $2 billion company. People's Express was cited in *In Search of Excellence* as an ideal American business because of its flat organizational structure and compensation plan that based reward on stock growth. All employees, whether "customer representatives" or pilots, were viewed as equally valuable to the company. Growth seemed to be unlimited and the airline could not process applications or reservations fast enough. Yet, on January 18, 1985, People's Express Airlines declared bankruptcy. Soon thereafter, the parts of the empire that Burr constructed were auctioned off and the routes redistributed.

The basic philosophy driving People's Express was to make air travel available to everyone. At its peak, People's low fares brought thousands of students, the elderly, and the middle class through Newark, New Jersey. The waits were horrendous and the service was chaotic. Yet the $29 fare made the hassle worth it, particularly when the other airlines were charging five times as much. People's fares allowed the carrier to book and fly full planes.

As long as the flights were full, the profits were easy to calculate: Determine the price of the fuel and the equipment and employee cost per flight of the plane; determine a per flight fare that would provide a profit when the expenses were subtracted; and repeat this formula across the flight pattern. Keep the fares so low that the flight would always be booked. By developing the demand in this new market segment, Burr felt that he had found a formula for success that could not be broken.

This approach looked promising until American Airlines used its Sabre reservation system to implement "yield pricing." Through advance ticketing and other restrictions, American was able to discount seats that would otherwise have gone unsold because of People's low fares. The flying public now had a choice. They could continue to fly on People's Express Airlines and deal with the chaos and the crowds, or they could make reservations and fly on American Airlines with comfort. Besides, they could fly directly and not go through Newark. The snack and soft drink were free. The remainder of the seats were sold at full price to businesspeople who could not plan far enough ahead to make advance reservations.

People's vision was a good one. It centered on cost-cutting and motivating the workforce. Certainly over-expansion and the lack of a marketing focus contributed to the failure of People's Express. However, a third major factor was the failure to integrate technology into solving its business problems. Before its first plane left the ground, People's decided not to duplicate American and United Airline's sophisticated reservation systems. Instead, the carrier opted for "a big, dumb computer" that stored passengers' names but could not do sophisticated pricing.

Another reason People's shied away from technological development was that the airline lacked the internal expertise to build or even buy a reservation system. In 1983, the carrier contracted with NCR Corporation to build a system to handle yield management. After 18 months, the project failed. According to Burr, the failure was due to poor communication on both sides and a lack of management attention.

Computer systems might also be used to create more direct barriers to entry. For instance, as a manufacturer you could build a computer system that is tied to retail stores. The stores would use the system to place orders, and to inquire about products, warranties, and delivery schedules. You might be able to forbid the stores from using the system to connect to any other manufacturers. If the stores gain advantages from the new system, they will end up placing more orders from you, and you will keep out potential competitors. However, you will have to be careful not to violate antitrust regulations.

## Distribution Channels

Controlling **distribution channels** is a method of gaining competitive advantage that is similar to creating barriers to entry. The Japanese economy has long been a classic example of controlling distribution channels, although the role of information systems is minimal. In Japan, sales relationships are developed over long periods of time, and companies have many interrelationships and ties. In particular, distribution of products from manufacturers to retailers is controlled by a few large companies that are loosely organized into support groups. If you want to sell products in Japan, you must build a relationship with one of these companies. American executives have often complained about the problems they experience in dealing with these distributors, which creates a barrier to selling U.S. products in Japan. Although there is disagreement on the cause of the problems, the ability to control distribution channels can be an effective strategy to maintain market share and deter rivals. The distributors gain power through their close personal ties to the customers. For example, in Japan, most new automobiles are sold by salespeople who call on customers at their homes.

Information systems can be used to control distribution channels. As a manufacturer, you could build a computer link to the retail stores. In addition to providing faster ordering and more information, you encourage the store to order directly from your company and avoid competitors. For example, Levi Strauss, the jeans manufacturer, has installed such a system in some retail chains. Assume that you work for a competitor and you call on the retail store to convince the buyers to carry your products. Probably the first question you will be asked is whether the store can order your jeans through the Levi Strauss computer link. If the answer is "no," the store manager is going to be less willing to buy your products.

Now, imagine the confusion that can result for the poor retail manager who wishes to sell similar products from three companies. What happens if each company has its own private computer link? Does the manager need to have three different computer terminals and learn three different systems?

Partly because of the loss of access to distribution channels and partly because of the confusion resulting from having multiple systems, attempts are being made to standardize some electronic relationships. An important component of electronic data interchange (EDI) is to define standards so that managers only have to work with one system and everyone has reasonable access to that system. If EDI does become standardized, there will be fewer opportunities to control distribution channels with information systems. However, businesses might still be able to gain a competitive edge by providing better, more sophisticated electronic services through the links. For example, expert systems might be used to provide faster responses to retailer and consumer questions.

One of the interesting aspects of the Internet is its ability to alter traditional distribution channels. In particular, the Internet could eventually become the major distribution system for digital data, such as books, music, software, and videos. Some traditional organizations fear this change as a loss of control. For example, in the U.S. music industry, a handful of firms have controlled the production and distribution of most music. In 1998, the firms attempted to stop the expansion of digital music (e.g., MP3 format), but the courts did not support this interference. Consequently, it is now relatively easy for anyone to create music in a commercial format and distribute it cheaply over the Internet. The same industry-altering effects can occur within the book industry—if a standard digital reader ever becomes acceptable.

## Switching Costs

An interesting strategic capability of information systems is their ability to create **switching costs** for your consumers. Consider the case of a brokerage firm that creates a system that enables you to manage your accounts with your personal computer. You buy and sell financial instruments and write checks against your account. The computer automatically tracks your portfolio, notifies you of major changes, and automatically sweeps uninvested cash into interest-bearing assets. At the end of the year, it prints a complete summary of your transactions for tax purposes.

Now, what happens if another broker offers you the same capabilities? Will you switch to a new firm? You might, but it depends on what other incentives the company offers. If everything else is the same, most people would be reluctant to change since they incur costs to switch. For example, you would have to learn how to use the new system. Additionally, you would have to reenter your investment data and program new reports and graphs. If you are one of the first firms to create a new system, the deterrence of switching costs can be a powerful tool to maintain your market share. Figure 11.6 summarizes the tools to create competitive advantages as practiced by companies in the classic cases.

## Lower Production Costs

In some cases, an effective strategy is to become the lowest-cost producer. If you can consistently sell your product for lower prices than your competitors do, you will have an important advantage. However, consumers need to believe that your products are as good as the competition's.

Computer systems have long been used to decrease costs. Transaction-processing and accounting systems decrease administrative costs. Robots and process control systems can be used to control manufacturing costs. Inventory systems are used to track parts and reduce inventory ordering and holding costs. Marketing systems might be used to create better target marketing, with the advantages of improved response and lower marketing costs. Financial systems that control investments and cash flow also can result in decreased costs.

**FIGURE 11.6**
**GAINING A**
**COMPETITIVE**
**ADVANTAGE**
Several classic cases illustrate some important methods of acquiring a competitive advantage. Understanding these cases will help you identify potential strategies in other situations. They will also help you communicate with IS professionals.

*Barriers to Entry*
The additional costs of creating a sophisticated information system make it harder for firms to enter the industry. Classic case: People's Express.

*Distribution Channels*
Control over distribution prevents others from entering the industry. Case: Movie distribution to theater chains.

*Switching Costs*
Consumers are reluctant to switch to a competitor if they have to learn a new system or transfer data. Classic case: Baxter Healthcare.

*Lower Production Costs*
Using technology to become the least-cost producer gives an advantage over the competition. Classic case: Wal-Mart.

*Product Differentiation*
Technology can add new features to a product or create entirely new products that entice consumers. Classic cases: Federal Express and Merrill Lynch.

*Quality Management*
Monitoring production lines and analyzing data are important aspects of quality control. Improving quality leads to more repeat sales. Classic case: Digital Equipment Corp.

*The Value Chain*
Evaluating the entire production process identifies how value is added at each step. Combining steps or acquiring additional stages of the value chain can lead to greater profits. Case: Boeing Information Systems.

## Product Differentiation and New Products

Another strategic use of information systems is the ability to create new or different products. If you can add features to your product so that consumers believe it is different from the competition, you will be able to make more money. A classic case of using technology to create a new product is portrayed by Merrill Lynch.

A classic case of using information systems to modify a product for competitive advantage came from Federal Express—an overnight package delivery company. Federal Express was the first major delivery company to track individual packages. The service places bar codes on every package and scans them every time the package is moved. By storing this data in a central database, Federal Express employees can tell customers exactly where any package is located. Besides decreasing the number of lost packages, this system provides a new service for customers. Nervous customers can use the information to determine when a package will be delivered. The information system tracks the current location of each package. When the system was created it provided a unique service to customers. To consumers, Federal Express is offering not just package delivery but also information on the location of the package. This **product differentiation** will help attract customers and might allow the company to charge higher prices.

In some cases, information systems can be used to create entirely new products or services. For example, many banks offer "sweep accounts" to customers who place large sums of money in their bank accounts. There are variations, but the purpose of a sweep account is to automatically place money into higher-interest-bearing assets. For instance, you might need cash available during the day to cover any withdrawals. But if you do not make major withdrawals at night, the bank could lend your money to someone for overnight use. The bank needs a sophisticated information system to keep track of which

---

**Reality Bytes    11–2   Merrill Lynch Cash Management Account (Classic Case)**

Until the 1970s, banks and other financial institutions were treated differently by the government than stock brokers such as Merrill Lynch. Financial institutions could not sell stocks, and there were limits on interest rates that could be paid to depositors. Brokerage companies focused on investments in stocks. In this environment, Merrill Lynch created its Cash Management Account (CMA). For a minimum sum of $25,000, investors could open a new account with Merrill Lynch. The account was similar to a bank account. The money could be placed in risk-free government bonds or it could be used to purchase stocks and bonds. The money could be obtained with minimal problems, including writing checks against the account. In short, the CMA became a bank account for medium and large investors. The primary advantage to the CMA over traditional bank accounts was that there were no government restrictions on the interest rates. As commercial interest rates rose in the late 1970s and early 1980s, huge sums of money left the banking industry and were deposited in the CMA.

Merrill Lynch used its information system to offer additional features, such as automatic transfers between accounts, overnight repurchases and sales of government bonds, and automatic investments and sales of stocks. All the investment options were controlled by individual investors. Banks could not offer these services because of governmental restrictions, and other brokerage firms did not have the information systems. This use of information technology gave an advantage to Merrill Lynch.

While Merrill Lynch was not known for other innovations, it is one of the largest financial institutions in the United States, with a balance sheet comparable to Citicorp's. In 1995, the brokerage firm had 44,000 employees and operated in 31 countries. The 1994 profit amounted to 18.6 percent return on equity.

customers are participating, monitor what limits they have imposed, and automatically transfer the money to the borrower's accounts. (As a side note, you might wonder who wants to borrow money for just one night. There are many possibilities, but two major players are governments and large banks. Some interesting international possibilities also arise by lending across time zones.) Customers receive more interest, borrowers have access to more funds, and banks make money on the transaction fees and interest differentials. These accounts can only be provided by investing in new information systems.

## Quality Management

Firms can gain a competitive advantage by offering higher-quality products. Through the 1980s, surveys indicated that owners reported fewer problems with automobiles manufactured by Japanese firms compared to those produced by U.S. manufacturers. This difference in quality gave the Japanese firms a competitive advantage. Similarly, Motorola is one of the leading proponents of total quality management. The company is constantly encouraging its suppliers to work at improving quality through the entire manufacturing process.

Information systems have a role in improving quality management. For starters, they can be used to collect data about quality measures. If quality measures come directly from production machines, there can be an overwhelming amount of data. In other cases, quality measures might be collected electronically from your suppliers. Collecting data seems like an obvious idea, but the huge amount of data complicates the process. In many cases, manufacturers have trouble identifying the original source when a component fails. Often, just knowing which suppliers cause the most problems is a useful step in quality management. This data can also help the supplier. Failure data can be used by the supplier to pinpoint the source of problems. Since 1992, nations in the European Union (EU) have been requiring firms to improve quality by complying with the statements in the ISO 9000 (International Organization of Standards) directive. ISO 9000 requires companies to measure quality at all stages of production. Any firm that wishes to sell products or parts to firms in the EU must build an information system to monitor quality and provide information to customers.

---

### Reality Bytes    11–3    Digital's Use of Expert Systems (Classic Case)

In the 1970s, Digital Equipment Corporation was experiencing problems with installation of its computers. Many times, various components were purchased and delivered that would not work together. Similarly, installers found that the delivered equipment was often missing necessary cables. The basic problem was that Digital offered many computers, each with different options. Additionally, new versions of hardware typically required different cables and were often incompatible with earlier models. As the number of combinations multiplied, it became impossible for salespeople to keep track of which components worked together and which options were needed for each package. Although the installers and customer service representatives would eventually solve the problems encountered by each customer, the time, money, and negative images were detrimental to Digital.

To combat these problems, Digital created an expert system called Xcon, that evaluates every order. As new models and peripherals are created, the engineers add the requirements to the expert system. The expert systems works as an engineer to evaluate each sale and make sure the necessary components are included. Use of this system improved the quality of the final product along with reducing costs, giving Digital an advantage over its rivals. The system has an average success rate of 90 percent, versus about 70 percent for human operators. Because of this success, Digital continues to expand its use of expert systems throughout the company, with hundreds of expert systems in use today.

No machine is perfect. There is always an element of error in the output. The difficult part is to determine which errors imply that the machine needs to be readjusted. Decision support systems can be used to improve quality. **Statistical quality control (SQC)** is an important tool. Several statistical calculations and graphs are used to determine whether fluctuations are purely random or represent major changes that need to be corrected.

Expert systems can also be employed to control errors and locate the source of the problems. Consider a production line that has 50 major machines. Additionally, several hundred parts are purchased from external suppliers. The final product has thousands of parts and hundreds of assembly operations. Total quality management requires that quality be monitored at each step of the process. A typical problem facing a machine operator is that a machine might stray off the baseline and need to be corrected. The operator faces several questions, such as: Which adjustment should be made? Should we overcorrect to compensate for the prior errors? Was the problem caused by this machine, or did earlier operations contribute? If corrections are made now, how will they affect other machines down the line? An experienced operator might be able to answer some of these questions. On the other hand, an expert system might be helpful at solving the more complex problems. Digital used expert systems to improve quality and cut the cost of installing minicomputers. Digital's weak performance in the 1990s also illustrates the difficulty in maintaining a competitive advantage—as the market changes.

## The Value Chain

One method of searching for areas that might provide you with strategic benefits is to examine the entire **value chain** of the industry. As shown in Figure 11.7, the key feature of a value chain is to examine each step of production and determine how value is added at each step. If some steps show larger increases in value than others, they will be key points to target for strategic action. The second objective of value chain analysis is to encourage decision makers to examine the bigger picture in the industry. In many cases, a firm can benefit by expanding its operations beyond its traditional activities. For instance, an automobile manufacturer (Ford) might buy a car rental agency (Hertz). Now the manufacturer can control a large consumer of its products and control the sale of the used vehicles.

**FIGURE 11.7**
VALUE CHAIN
The value chain illustrates the essential operations in a business. Every firm has operations for purchasing, production, shipping, marketing, and customer service. These processes are supported by the organization of the firm, human resources management, technology development, and procurement services. Providing services desired by customers contributes to the profit margin of the firm.

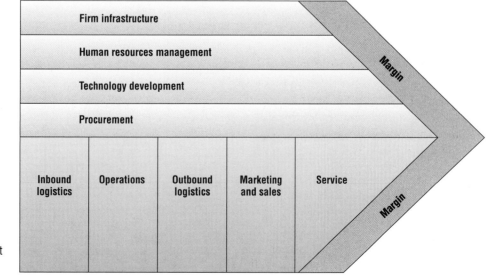

Industry and academic leaders are constantly searching for ways to improve organizations and gain a competitive advantage. Illustrated by Figure 11.8, one method to organize the search is to examine the primary processes of the firm: research, engineering and design, manufacturing, logistics and supply, marketing, sales and order management, service, and general management. Each of these processes has its own inputs, outputs, and objectives. Analyzing them in detail enables managers to spot problems and to search for innovative opportunities.

The following sections present general ideas for each of these processes that have generated interest and some success. Most of them use technology to improve the process or to help the processes work together better. Keep in mind that in any firm, there can be many ways of improving processes. Relying on information technology is not always the best answer.

Just coming up with a new corporate strategy is difficult, but it is not enough. As indicated by Figure 11.9, an effective strategic plan must also describe the changes in the process, identify the new data needs, and describe how the information system will be changed to support the new strategy. Figure 11.10 summarizes the capabilities of IT to support innovation.

## Research

Research in firms varies enormously depending on the industry and the overall corporate strategy. At a minimum, most firms at least have a product development team that is constantly searching for new products or improvements in existing products. Some companies, like 3M, DuPont, AT&T, or Intel, spend considerable sums of money on basic research to create entirely new products. To these firms, strategic advantage comes from being the leader in the industry with a constant cycle of new products.

IT support for research takes the form of computer analysis and modeling, statistical analysis of data, project management and budgeting, and workgroup technologies that make it easy for researchers to collaborate and share information with each other and with managers throughout the company.

**FIGURE 11.8
PROCESS
INNOVATION**

Production consists of the processes of supply logistics, manufacturing, and sales management. These processes are directly supported by design, engineering, and marketing. Research and customer service support all of the processes; top management organizes and controls the firm. Technology can provide innovations in all of these processes.

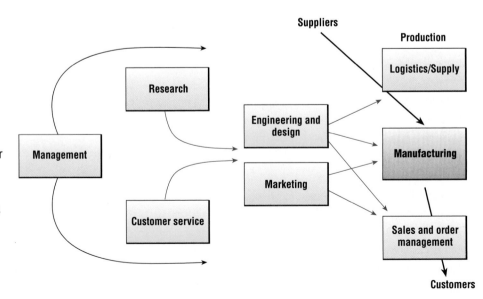

## Engineering and Design

Engineering and design processes are responsible for converting theoretical research into new products. Engineers establish manufacturing procedures, design new equipment, and coordinate suppliers with production. In particular, the design process must optimize the production line to minimize costs and retain high quality.

**FIGURE 11.9**
DEVELOPING
STRATEGIES

Market measures and firm performance measures are used to highlight problems and opportunities. Corporate strategies are developed from process improvements and innovations. Potential strategies are evaluated and prioritized. Processes are re-engineered and new systems are designed and implemented.

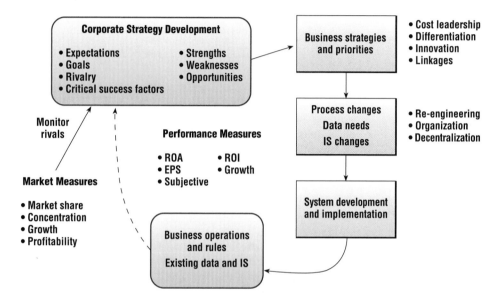

**FIGURE 11.10**
THE SEARCH
FOR INNOVATION

Information technology provides many opportunities for improving the fundamental business processes. IT is used to improve communication, decrease costs, reduce design times, monitor customers and rivals, and improve customer service.

| AREA | INFORMATION TECHNOLOGY SUPPORT |
|---|---|
| Research | Analysis and modeling, project management, workgroup support, databases, decision support. |
| Engineering and Design | CAD/CAM, testing, networks, workgroup support. |
| Manufacturing | Mass customization, links from customers and suppliers, robotics, quality monitoring, expert systems for maintenance, production databases, business integration tools. |
| Logistics and Supply | Just-in-time linkages, forecasts, models, links for design, transaction processing. |
| Marketing | Frequent buyer databases, target market and media analysis, survey design and analysis, multimedia promotion design, links between customers and design teams. |
| Sales and Orders | Portable computers for salesperson contact, expert systems for order customization and configuration, workgroup tools for customer support. |
| Service | Phone support systems, location monitoring and scheduling of service people, expert system diagnostics, databases. |
| Management | Enterprise information systems, links to service providers (accountants, consultants, etc.), e-mail, bulletin boards, decision support systems, personal productivity tools, workgroup support. |

Support for engineering and design takes the form of CAD/CAM systems that make it easy to create, modify, store, and share new designs. If these systems are coupled to integrated design databases, engineers can more easily reuse prior results. Tying into production databases enables the engineers to model and test various aspects of their designs. Engineers can also be supported with expert systems that help them analyze production aspects of their designs. As General Motors engineers design new cars, software helps them improve the layout to simplify production and to use existing components. Engineers are also being supported by workgroup technologies that make it easy to share designs and receive input from teams of workers throughout the company.

## Manufacturing

There are four key features to production: costs, speed or timing, quality, and flexibility. Competing through lower costs and higher quality are time-honored means of gaining a competitive advantage. They might not be sufficient today. Increasingly, firms are turning to **mass customization** in an attempt to gain market share. Twenty or 30 years ago, the large firms in an industry were content to build huge plants, gain economies of scale, and aim at the mass market. This approach tended to leave niches open for competing firms. The problem with this strategy is that it allows rival firms to gain a toehold, which they might use to build market share and eventually compete directly against your primary market. Today's firms are trying to shift production fast enough so that they can cover virtually all of the niche markets.

Mass customization requires an IT system that links the sales system directly to the production line and through to supply. It also involves heavy use of robotics that are configurable directly from one computer. Other uses of IT include expert systems for maintenance and diagnostics. Japanese firms have long been proponents of preventive maintenance. If you wait until a machine breaks, it is too late. Expert systems can be used to schedule routine maintenance and spot problems before they cause problems. IT systems are also heavily used to monitor quality and suggest improvements.

## Logistics and Supply

The implementation of just-in-time (JIT) inventory systems is largely credited to Japanese manufacturers. Today they are used by manufacturers worldwide. Manufacturers attempt to cut costs by holding minimal inventories. Instead, inventories are maintained by the suppliers, who deliver the products to the assembly line just as they are needed. The system can only work if the suppliers and factories are linked electronically—often there is only a one- or two-hour delay between ordering and delivery.

Suppliers are often involved in the design phase. Their knowledge is useful in identifying supply availability, costs, and substitutability of components. Sometimes, it is difficult to locate suppliers for equipment. Computer networks such as IndustryNet help firms connect with potential suppliers, and identify equipment, parts, and prices.

## Marketing

A well-known application of IT to improve marketing is the use of frequent-buyer databases that identify major customers. More traditional point-of-sale transaction systems can be leveraged by identifying preferences and rapidly spotting patterns or trends. At the tactical level, expert systems are used to help analyze data and perform statistical trend analysis. Geographic information systems are being used by leading firms to identify patterns and possibilities for new sales. Information systems can also be used to link firms

| Reality Bytes | 11–4 | Tracking Your Competitors |
| --- | --- | --- |

As a manager of a large company, would you like to know when your competitor's managers visit another company? You can find out with online government data. When pilots fly one of the 10,000 corporate planes, they file flight plans indicating their destination and time of arrival. In 1997, to help companies track their planes—particularly in bad weather—the FAA put the data on the Internet.

One company (www.TheTrip.com) provides real-time tracking and historical data for (1) any flight based on an airplane, or (2) all takeoffs and landings at a specific airport. The site charges fees for some of this data. Similar data and tools are also available from Dimensions International (www.dimen-intl.com). Information on individual airplanes and corporate ownership can be found at www.landings.com. Access to the data can run $100 per month. And, in a reverse privacy issue, the subscriber list is given to the FAA.

more closely to external marketing firms for research data, communication, and development of promotional materials.

Multimedia tools are being used by leading firms to develop initial ideas for advertising and promotional campaigns. Companies such as General Motors are also using video tools and computer dissemination of video to link customers and marketing departments closer to the design team.

## Sales and Order Management

Sales and order management are often handled simply as an operations or transaction-processing area. However, in the last 10 years, several firms have used technology to gain a competitive advantage by improving the way they handle sales and orders. Frito-Lay's use of handheld computers is a classic example. The systems enable managers to more closely track their own sales, sales of competitors, and other external factors because sales people can enter data immediately. For certain industries, the concept can be extended further to installing workstations at the customer sites that tap into your central databases. Federal Express and Baxter Healthcare both used this technology to gain a leadership position.

Leading firms are also using expert system to assist customers in choosing the products and options that best match their needs. These systems assist order-takers and improve sales by matching customer needs. Expert systems are similarly used to improve configuration and shipping.

Workgroup technologies, e-mail, and expert systems all combine to give more power to the frontline workers dealing directly with customers. Resolving problems and meeting customer needs faster can improve customer satisfaction and cut costs.

## Service

Service industries and service-based processes (like accounting, MIS, and law) have their own problems and opportunities. Technology is used to support services with on-site, portable computers. These systems enable workers to have complete access to information almost anywhere in the world. Leading companies are building specialized databases to support their service workers, such as the "answer line" databases that support General Electric and Whirlpool customer service representatives.

Systems are built that monitor locations of service personnel, enabling firms to identify the closest workers to problems and to fine-tune schedules throughout the day. Complex products are increasingly being sold with internal diagnostic systems that automatically notify service departments. Similarly, companies are cutting costs and reducing repair time by building expert systems to diagnose problems.

## Management

One of the more dramatic IT support mechanisms for management is an enterprise information system. By giving top managers better access to data, it allows them to identify and correct problems faster. More sophisticated models can be built to examine alternatives—especially to analyze the potential reactions of rivals in a competitive situation.

Larger firms are building electronic links to their strategic partners, for instance, by providing electronic access to corporate data to accounting and legal firms. These links enable the external partners to keep a closer eye on the firm, speeding the identification of problems and assisting them in spotting broad patterns and opportunities.

Executives are also increasingly turning to electronic conferencing tools and workgroup software, even e-mail. With these systems, executives can cover more areas and deal with more people than through the phone or through face-to-face contact. Some studies have shown that in traditional conversations managers spend as much as 50 percent of the time on personal chit-chat. Electronic systems (although they might be less personal) tend to be more efficient. On the other hand, some companies have been restricting employee access to electronic networks (especially the Internet) because they waste too much time on personal communications.

Another approach taken by management is the move toward standardization: the effort to make all jobs similar, routine, and interchangeable. By reducing jobs to their most basic level, they become easier to control and easier to support or replace with information technology. Franchises make good use of this concept. At the same time, management jobs in some companies are being reformulated as teams of knowledge workers. In the past, managers worked on fixed tasks within the corporate hierarchy. Today, you are more likely to be hired for your specific skills and knowledge. As the needs of the company change, you will work with different teams at solving problems and creating new products and services. Personal computers and client-server technologies are often used to support

---

**Reality Bytes     11–5   Performance Measurement**

Most managers quickly learn the importance of strategy. With experience, they learn to formulate new ideas and focus on the search for competitive advantage. The ultimate challenge then lies in implementing and executing the strategy. An effective measure system is an important aspect of implementation that is often missing. The measurement system provides the link between the plan and the objectives. However, it is difficult for managers to absorb huge amounts of data from across the organization. Hence, a useful approach is to define critical measures for four areas: customer connectivity, internal process efficiency and effectiveness, individual and group innovation and learning, and financial data. Aspects of these four groups can be measured and presented on an information system in the form of gauges. By monitoring these areas, managers obtain an overview of how well the company is performing and how well it is moving to the new strategies.

these management teams. Instead of relying on one central computing facility, each team has its own set of resources, which are shared over networks throughout the company.

**COSTS AND DANGERS OF STRATEGIES**

Strategic uses of information systems can be seductive. There are many interesting cases in which companies have created innovative information systems. Inventing strategic alternatives requires a considerable amount of creativity. It is easy to get caught up in the excitement of designing new approaches and to forget about the risks. Evaluation of any project requires weighing the risks against the potential gains. Although it is often difficult to measure the potential gains and risks, it is important to consider all consequences. By their nature, strategic changes can alter the entire course of the firm. Figure 11.11 summarizes the skills, organizational effects, and risks involved with several strategies.

Robert Morison and Kirtland Mead ("A Hard Look at Strategic Systems") pointed out that it is easy to misinterpret the various classic cases regarding strategic use of technology. For example, in many cases, the true strategy does not lie in the computer system; instead, the gains came from changing the way the business operates. For instance, the gains experienced by American Hospital Supply (Baxter Healthcare) came about because they improved the way their customers (hospitals) handled supplies and inventory. The computer system facilitated this change but was not necessarily responsible for it. In other words, rather than search for a *killer* strategic computer system, it is wiser to identify ways to improve the overall business.

| STRATEGY | SKILLS AND RESOURCES REQUIRED | ORGANIZATIONAL REQUIREMENTS | RISKS |
|---|---|---|---|
| Differentiation | • Strong marketing<br>• Product engineering<br>• Basic research skills<br>• Distribution channel acceptance and cooperation | • Internal coordination, R&D, production, and marketing<br>• Incentives for innovation<br>• Resources to attract creative and skilled labor | • Competitors imitate<br>• Customers do not accept differences<br>• Cost is too high |
| Cost Leadership | • Continued capital investment<br>• Process engineering<br>• Continuous quality improvement<br>• Tight supervision of labor and costs<br>• Products designed for low-cost production<br>• Low-cost distribution | • Tight cost control<br>• Frequent, detailed control reports<br>• Highly structured organization<br>• Incentives based on quantitative measures | • Competitors imitate<br>• Technology changes<br>• Lose production or distribution advantage |
| Customer-Supplier Links | • Influence with partners<br>• Communication channels<br>• Standards or agreements | • Flexibility to respond to customers<br>• Service-culture<br>• Ability to adapt to emergencies | • Security threats<br>• Changing standards<br>• Competitors copy with more links |

**FIGURE 11.11**

Implementing strategy can be difficult, costly, and time consuming. Firms generally choose one primary strategy and then build the resources and shape the organization to best support that strategy.

## High Capital Costs

One of the important considerations in strategic analysis is the cost. Strategic changes often involve implementing new technology before any of your competitors. Yet new technology tends to carry high costs. Manufacturers of technology may not have reached economies of scale, and they might have monopoly power over prices through patent rights. Additionally, the IS teams will have less experience with the technology, so it will take longer to implement and may result in missteps and require additional testing. For instance, Morison and Mead report, "It took six years and $350 million before American Airlines' Sabre travel agency reservation system started paying off." As Figure 11.12 notes, these costs might take away money from other projects.

It can be difficult to estimate the cost of major projects, especially when they involve new technologies. There are many examples of MIS projects going over budget and beyond deadlines. Additionally, strategic projects often require major capital outlays up front, but increased revenues do not appear until much later.

A big question with new technology is trying to decide when it should be implemented. There is an inherent conflict. If you offer an innovative service from the technology before your competitors, you can gain a competitive advantage. However, if you wait, the costs will be lower. In making this decision, you will also have to guess what action your competitors will take.

## When the Competition Follows

Another difficulty with strategic systems is that much of the advantage comes from creating a service that is not offered by your rivals. Once you introduce the service, your rivals will watch the customer response closely. If the customers begin to switch to your firm, your rivals will undoubtedly create a system to offer the same services. At that point, you lose most of the competitive advantage. Even worse, you might end up with an escalating "war" of technology. Although the competition is good for the customer, the increased expenditures can cause problems for the company if the ideas do not work as well as you expected.

The gains to technology occur from when you first implement the strategy to the point that your rivals follow. For example, almost all of the major overnight delivery services now provide the ability to track shipments. If the system is easy to create, you may

**FIGURE 11.12**
DANGERS OF
STRATEGY
When developing and choosing strategies, you must always remember that innovations can be risky and often carry high capital costs. Although it may be exciting to spend millions of dollars on technology, it can destroy the firm if you do not have enough resources to support research and operations.

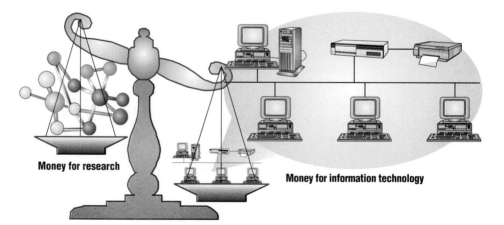

**Money for research**

**Money for information technology**

not gain much. However, it is likely that customers who switched to your firm will stay, so you can gain a larger share of the market.

On the other hand, if your strategic ideas do not pay off, your rivals will gain, because you will likely lose most of the money invested in the project. Some firms use this tactic to great advantage. They allow smaller firms to take the risk and experiment with new technologies. If the project succeeds, the large firm steps in with more money and more clout and creates their own, improved version. About the only risk they take is that the smaller firm might become successful enough to grab a serious share of the market.

## Changing Industry

An intriguing problem that can arise is that even if your strategic project succeeds, the company might lose because your project has changed the industry. Consider an insurance company that sells software to companies to allow them to track insurance deductions and payments to workers. The insurance company decides that it can add a program to compute payroll, so the companies could drop their existing payroll software. These features appear to give the company an edge over its rivals in the insurance industry. The problem is that there are many more companies that create payroll software, and it is very simple for these companies to add insurance capabilities to their existing software. The actions of the insurance company encourage the payroll software firms to move into the insurance market. Illustrated in Figure 11.13, the insurance company suddenly has hundreds of new competitors and could lose customers.

**FIGURE 11.13**
CHANGING INDUSTRY AND GOVERNMENT INTERVENTION
A complication with strategy is it might alter the industry. A firm in Industry 1 might use IT to attract customers from a different industry. Because of this expansion, the firm gains new competitors (from Industry 2). While competition is often beneficial, you must thoroughly analyze the effect of the new competition before embarking on changing the industry. In a related manner, sometimes changes in government regulations alter relationships between industries, as in the telephone and cable-TV markets.

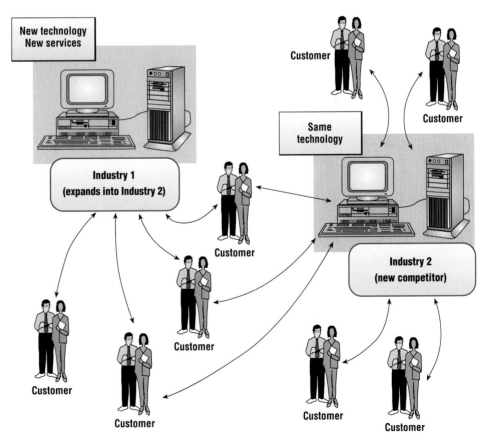

## Sharing Data

One common technique in strategic systems is to share your data with customers and suppliers. Two questions arise from this situation. First, do you really want suppliers and customers to have access to the data? Second, can you control their access to protect other data? Security and control issues are examined in detail in Chapter 14. The main point to think about here is what might happen as your customers gain access to your data. Consider the situation of a supplier to General Motors. To save costs and improve communications, GM wants you to connect your computer to the GM factory computers. GM intends to use the links to place orders, monitor quality data, and track shipments. Are you willing to give GM access to your computer? Can you control the information that the large corporation is allowed to see? Maybe when checking on their order, GM will also be able to determine how much you are producing for other companies. Or maybe GM will gain access to your supplier lists and raw material prices. Even if the GM managers are ethical and do not reveal this data to anyone else, you still might worry. What happens when you have to negotiate prices with GM the next time? If the corporation has access to your data, you might be concerned that it could influence the negotiations. Figure 11.14 illustrates the need for security systems that will enable you to control the access to your data.

## Government Intervention

You have to be careful when considering strategic maneuvers. Many potential strategies violate **antitrust laws.** For example, many barriers to entry are illegal, as is price discrimination. In fact, attempts to monopolize a market are forbidden by the Sherman Antitrust Act. Price fixing and other forms of collusion are also outlawed. Information system agreements between competitors could be scrutinized by the Justice Department or the Federal Trade Commission.

If government agents choose strict interpretations of the laws, it could complicate many information system issues. For instance, firms might be discouraged from forming consortiums that define standards. Agreements to share disaster backup facilities might be outlawed. Computer links to customers might be seen as limiting competition. So far,

**FIGURE 11.14**
SECURITY
COMPLICATIONS
Improving communication and sharing data are common themes in using technology for competitive advantage. This need to share data with "outsiders" makes it more difficult to protect your internal data. Security systems can provide some protections, but the more outsiders who are involved, the more difficult it is to provide adequate security.

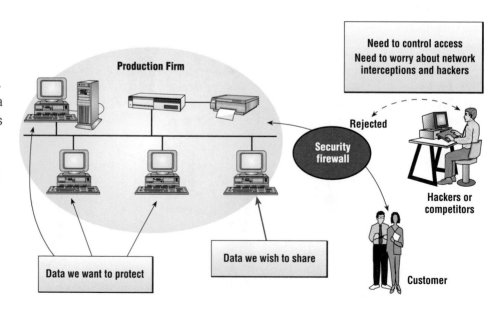

the U.S. agencies have allowed all of these activities to proceed without interference. However, there is always the chance that other nations or different political administrations will view the issues differently.

In the 1980s, the government was relatively lenient about antitrust issues, including those regarding information systems. However, one interesting case arose with the airline reservation systems. For many years, American Airlines and United Airlines had the leading reservation systems. Other airlines could list flights on the systems, but they had to pay money for each ticket sold through the system. A conflict eventually arose, because the airlines that created the system programmed it to list their flights first. Flights from other airlines were often listed on separate screens, so travel agents and customers were encouraged to choose flights from the airline that built the system. Although this mechanism did not directly violate antitrust laws, Congress decided to pass a new law, making the practice illegal. Lawmakers decided that as long as the other airlines had to pay for access to the system, everyone should have an equal chance at being listed first. The point is that even though the initial action was not illegal, Congress has the ability to pass new laws and remove the advantages, so you cannot assume that the benefits will last.

**OPERATIONS, TACTICS, STRATEGY**

Strategic plans involving information technology are not created from thin air. The systems are based on improved or expanded use of operations- and tactical-level systems. Consider the airline reservations systems, which began life as transaction-processing

---

### Reality Bytes    11–6    The New Economy?

In the late 1990s, particularly with the enormous growth and excitement generated by the Internet, many people were arguing that a new economy was being shaped. Some of their arguments were used to "explain" the sky-high prices being paid for Internet IPO stocks. Other people used the analysis to claim that business strategy needed to change. While there might have been some truth to the statements, it was dangerous to base your entire company on them—as some managers and entrepreneurs who followed the hype learned. The problem is that there are no easy answers to business success. The basic myths/statements were:

1. Grow or die.
2. You must be virtual.
3. Go global.
4. Capital is easy.
5. Everybody is an entrepreneur.
6. Technology makes life easier.
7. You must be on the Web in a big way.

The *Inc.* article presents many examples of managers who attempted to follow these ideas and en-

countered problems. For example, Jonathan Katz is CEO of Cinnabar, a $17-million company that creates scenery and special effects for movies, commercials, and theme parks. The company was enthusiastic about technology. Managers and employees quickly realized the value of cell phones and e-mail. Whenever a problem cropped up, employees used the electronic communication to contact clients and production studios to straighten it out. The problem is that at the start of 1997, Cinnabar's commercial and film business started to drop. After a great deal of thought, Katz realized that "my people had become complacent and too reliant on the convenience of electronic communication like faxes, e-mail, and telephones. The real heart of our business, which came out of direct contact with our clients, was not happening." He told the employees to put away the cell phones and e-mail, and pay personal visits with directors, producers, and art directors. In the last quarter of 1998, Cinnabar's commercial business increased by 50 percent.

systems, reducing costs and making it easier for people to get the flights they want. Similarly, banking systems like ATMs and debit cards were targeted at improving transactions. Yet, these systems all had a strategic component: Being the first organization to implement these systems led to better customer service and increased market share.

Tactical-level systems can also provide strategic advantages. Making better decisions faster creates improved products, more loyal customers, and lower costs. Building decision support systems, enterprise information systems, expert systems, and AI techniques helps to reduce the bureaucracy of middle management. Two important strategic consequences arise: (1) more control and authority are pushed down to customer service agents, enabling them to solve problems faster and meet the needs of the customer; and (2) top executives gain more information and control over the business—making it easier to identify problems, enact new strategies, and respond faster to changes in the business environment.

Overall, there are two important lessons to be learned regarding strategic uses of technology: (1) computer systems can provide value beyond simple cost cutting; and (2) strategic gains are often fleeting, requiring continual upgrades and investment in new technology. Because new technology is expensive, and innovations do not always succeed, it can be risky being on the leading edge. Each firm needs to decide *when* it should adopt new technology. Being first carries not only high costs and more risk but the opportunity for greater rewards, as well as a certain image. Being a technology follower has the advantage of reducing costs. Each industry contains both types of firms.

## SUMMARY

Information systems can provide benefits beyond traditional cost saving. Competitive advantages can be gained by creating barriers to entry and gaining control over distribution channels. Using information systems to build ties to suppliers and customers can provide lower costs and better quality products. Computer systems also provide incentives for customers to remain with your company if they incur costs of learning new systems and transferring data when switching to a competitor. Information systems can also be used to differentiate your products from the others in the marketplace. Similarly, innovative services offered with the help of technology can entice customers and expand your market.

You can search for competitive advantages by examining Porter's external forces of rivals, customers, suppliers, substitute products, and new entrants. You can also search for strategies in research, engineering, and design. In manufacturing, you can look for ways to decrease costs and improve logistics. In marketing, potential gains can be found in better understanding of customer wants, as well as sales and order management. Services can be supported through better information flows and workgroup products. Management can be helped with better data and better decision tools.

### A MANAGER'S VIEW

With increased competition, every manager is being asked to identify ways to improve the company and find an advantage over the rivals. Gaining a competitive edge is not easy. Examining the entire value chain is a useful place to start. Information systems can provide data and evaluate models to help you identify strategic applications. Information systems can also provide direct advantages by creating a barrier to entry, gaining control over distribution, cutting costs, improving quality, and improving ties between suppliers and customers.

Strategic systems face many risks. They tend to be expensive and difficult to create. Any gains created may disappear when competitors pick up the technology and imitate your offerings. Additionally, making strategic changes to your firm might alter the industry, which might adversely affect your firm. And if these problems are not enough to discourage you, remember that attempts to monopolize a market are illegal, so you have to make sure that your plans do not violate governmental regulations.

## KEY WORDS

antitrust laws, 472

barriers to entry, 456

distribution channels, 458

external agents, 453

five forces model, 453

mass customization, 466

product differentiation, 461

rivals, 455

statistical quality control (SQC), 463

switching costs, 459

total quality management (TQM), 455

value chain, 463

## WEB SITE REFERENCES

**Bookstores**

| | |
|---|---|
| 2MillionBooks | www.2millionbooks.com |
| A1 Books | www.a1books.com |
| Amazon.com | www.amazon.com |
| Barnes & Noble | www.barnesandnoble.com |
| Barnes & Noble College | www.bkstore.com |
| Borders | www.borders.com |
| Internet Bookshop | www.bookshop.co.uk |
| Varsity College Bookstore | www.varsitybooks.com |

## REVIEW QUESTIONS

1. Briefly describe four techniques that can be used to gain competitive advantage.
2. How is strategic analysis related to the environment aspect of the systems approach?
3. What are external agents?
4. What are the costs and dangers of strategic implementations?
5. For a large manufacturing firm, who are the customers? How many different types of customers can there be?
6. Why are barriers to entry important to gain a competitive advantage?
7. How does control over distribution channels give a firm a competitive advantage?
8. How can information systems be used to gain control over distribution channels?
9. How might EDI limit firms from gaining control over the distribution channels?
10. What are switching costs, and how can they give a company a competitive advantage?
11. How can information systems be used to enhance product differentiation and create new products?
12. What role is played by information systems in improving quality management?
13. What is the value chain and how is it used to search for competitive advantage?

## EXERCISES

1. Consider a small service firm such as a physician, dentist, accountant, or lawyer. Is it possible for such an office to use computers to gain a competitive advantage? To start, identify the customers, suppliers, and rivals. Do you think the "natural" switching costs are high or low; that is, how often do customers switch to competitors? Which of the major techniques do you think would be the most successful (barriers to entry, switching costs, quality control, lower prices, ties to customers or suppliers, etc.)?

2. How long can firms maintain an advantage using an information system? Research one of the classic cases and find out how long it took for the competitors to implement a similar information system (for example, Merrill Lynch and its Cash-Management Account, American Airlines and the Sabre System, Levi-Strauss and its Levi-Link ordering system, or Federal Express and its tracking system). Find out when the system was implemented, identify the competitors, and find out when they implemented similar

systems. Did the original company continue to update its strategy? Collect data on sales and profits for the firms to see whether there were major changes.

3. Choose a country other than the United States, Canada, Japan, or a Western European nation. (In particular, select a developing nation perhaps in South America, Africa, Eastern Europe, or Southeast Asia.) Research the communication and information system facilities available to firms in that country. Do you think firms in the United States have a competitive advantage over those firms? If so, what could the firms (or nations) do to overcome that advantage? How will the countries compare five years from now?

4. Read through the industry cases for each chapter in the book. Identify the firms that have chosen to be technology leaders and those that are followers. What other differences can you find between the firms (profits, sales, employees)?

5. Pick an industry. Find two firms in the industry— one a technology leader, the other a follower. Get the financial information on those firms for the last five years. Find analyst summaries of their operations. Compare the two firms. Are there differences in finances, operating methods, or customers?

## Rolling Thunder Database

6. Identify the competition in the industry. Who are existing rivals? Who are potential rivals? Be sure to define the industry carefully. Consider using SIC codes.

7. Perform a value chain analysis of the company. Could they improve profits by expanding vertically or horizontally? Are there additional products we should consider offering?

8. What data do we collect? Can it be used to achieve greater value? Would other firms be interested in our data? Are there possibilities for alliances with other companies?

9. We have the opportunity to purchase a chain of retail bicycle stores. Evaluate the strategic aspects of this proposed acquisition. What will be the effect on the information systems? Can the existing information system be used to improve the operations of the retail stores? What additions and improvements would be needed?

10. Is there any way to increase ties to the customers using technology to gain a competitive advantage?

## ADDITIONAL READING

Andrews, K. R. *The Concept of Corporate Strategy,* 3e. Burr Ridge, IL: Richard D. Irwin, 1987. [Basic text on designing corporate strategy]

Melymuka, Kathleen. "State Street Bank's Change in Direction Required a New IT Approach," *Computerworld,* February 15, 1999. [Changing strategy with information technology]

Porter, Michael. *Competitive Advantage: Creating and Sustaining Superior Performance.* New York: Free Press, 1985. [Early discussion of strategy and competitive advantage]

Wah, Louisa. "Welcome to the Edge," *Management Review,* November 1998, pp. 24–29. (Managing in the face of change and chaos)

# CASES *Travel Industry*

The travel and tourism industry is growing fast. This is due both to social factors that make demand for travel increase and also to technological advances that make travel possible and less expensive. The swelling of the middle class in developing countries, years of prosperity in the United States, and lower prices have increased the demand for travel significantly.

While it is difficult to determine the economic impact of tourism, the World Travel and Tourism Council, an industry lobby group, placed it at $3.6 trillion in 1996. This was about 10 percent of the world's gross product. Especially hot growth segments include package tours and cruises. Average tourist spending is expected to grow by 8 percent annually for the next five years, according to *The Economist*. This has led to demands from groups such as the World Travel and Tourism Council and local and national governments to spend money on improving infrastructures, which will support tourism. Some countries, such as Canada, have responded by increasing their spending on tourism dramatically.

With this fast growth, the hotel business has matured. Hotels, once mostly independent businesses, are quickly joining chains. They are, in effect, being branded. Information technology, such as the Internet and electronic ticketing, is also changing tourism by changing the way tourism is being sold. Nothing has made the globalization of travel and tourism grow faster than cheap airline tickets, however. Technology has made the biggest impact in that area. It was less than 30 years ago that Pan Am flew the first 747 from New York to London.

Even with all these factors and trends, however, there are great risks. Hotels and airplanes are still big investments that can prove to be expensive failures. Also, the tourism part of travel (as opposed to business travel, a small but very profitable segment of the travel and hospitality industry) is basically a luxury. This means that a recession, especially if it affects a large area such as the one that began in Asia in 1998, can be devastating to the travel industry.

Surprisingly, the recession in the industrialized countries in the early 1990s only slowed down the growth of tourism but did not stop it. Tourism is also highly sensitive to external shocks. Caribbean islands are a paradise one day, but a hurricane can turn away tourists very quickly. Another example is the attacks suffered by European tourists in Miami in 1992. This hindered European visitors to South Florida for a few years.

One way to combat external dangers and to address the issue of depleting or destroying natural attractions is to create the tour environment from scratch. Theme parks are such places. These destinations are custom-built to entertain and delight visitors. As technology advances and popular destinations become more and more crowded, these artificial worlds may grow in their market share.

## Stock/Investment Outlook

The outlook for companies in the travel and tourism industry is good. Certain companies positioned to take advantage of current trends in the travel and tourism industry will be star performers.

As far as airlines are concerned, those that look to be the best investment are those forming code-sharing alliances, which allow them to book travel on their partner's routes. This allows airlines to cover more territories by banding together. Thus, American Airlines' partnership with British Airways and other airlines seems to bode well for them; just like United Airlines' partnership with a handful of international airlines seems like a smart move.

Mergers and acquisitions in the hotel industry are frequent. Branding helps hotels smooth out demand. The recent spate of hotel mergers (especially outside the U.S., where hotels are less likely to be part of a chain) is mostly a result of overbuilding of hotels during the 1980s and technological improvements making economies of scale more significant.

Cruise ship companies are also good investments, in light of their increasing popularity. Carnival Cruise Lines and Royal Caribbean, the two largest cruise companies, are both expanding and building larger ships to accommodate and take advantage of this boom in cruising.

## Potential/Prospects for Growth

With the next few years looking rosy in the travel and tourism industry, the potential for growth ranges from moderate to high, depending on the market segment. The growth in the cruise ship segment looks to be very good, assuming companies can keep in mind why many people choose cruises: they are relatively inexpensive (usually everything except liquor and gambling is included), and they provide a relaxing atmosphere with entertainment. Cruise ship operations are also more predictable than hotel operations, with generally high occupancy rates, a captive audience, and more predictable costs. This bodes well for both the major cruise lines and smaller cruise lines that offer good alternatives.

The growth in the airline industry looks moderate. While airline travel is increasing and is expected to continue increasing, the market is saturated and mature in some areas (such as flying within the United States). Newly formed alliances, deregulation abroad, and more foreign governments freeing up their airspace mean changes, challenges, and opportunities. Those airlines forming alliances with international airlines look to be the ones with the most to gain. The American–British Airways alliance is an example. Also, with airlines courting lucrative business travelers more, they should remain flying.

Hotels are also expected to grow as a whole. Those hotels that are not part of major chains will need to identify special niches to do well in an era of branding, buy-outs, mergers, and consolidation. There are, however, many aspects an independent hotel or small hotel chain can offer that would lure travelers, as long as they market this difference properly.

## Competitive Structure

For different reasons, most of the tourism and travel industry used to be fragmented. The airline industry was fragmented due to government regulations, the difficulty of growing in a less advanced technological age, and less powerful planes. The hotel industry was fragmented due to difficulties operating geographically dispersed properties in an efficient and consistent way. The cruise industry was first injured by the long-haul passenger jet, which all but replaced the cruises to Europe a few decades ago. However, once shorter-term and more affordable cruises were offered to the Caribbean from South Florida, the industry revived.

Currently, as the entire industry grows and matures, the competitive structure is moving toward an imperfect oligopoly. There will be a few major players in each segment of the travel and tourism industry, while there will be large number of small players fighting for the rest of the pie. The major players will offer competitive prices for their services, while the smaller players will offer a slightly different angle. This process can be slower in segments where government intervention is a significant factor, such as international flights.

## Role of Research and Development

Research and development is an important component of this industry. R&D affects some segments more than others. Research and development has led to the realization by airlines, for example, that business travelers are less price sensitive than leisure travels. Hence, airlines have devised elaborate pricing strategies for available seats. R&D has led to technological advances like the jet airplane, hotel and airline reservation systems, jumbo cruise ships, and multiple kinds of rides in theme parks.

Research and development of a concept has allowed Las Vegas to develop from a place where only gamblers went, to a vacation mecca for the whole family. Developers in Las Vegas realized that the popularity of theme parks such as Disney World was not something that appealed only to children. By making each hotel almost its own theme park for adults, and placing all the hotels near each other, Las Vegas has been able to attract thousands of visitors to its city.

Airlines have used research to develop things such as frequent flyer programs to create loyalty, low weekend getaway fares to sell tickets on poorly sold routes, Saturday night requirements to differentiate passengers, and more fuel efficient, longer lasting, bigger, and safer planes.

By branding themselves, hotels can give a customer a familiar setting and a perception of quality, no matter where in the world the traveler is. Even the same hotel chain sometimes has different offerings, or sub-brands. Each one is targeted and positioned to appeal to a different type of traveler; for example, a person that is looking only for the bare necessities and is very price sensitive, to the extended-stay business traveler that may be on a multimonth assignment outside his or her hometown. Another hotel innovation is the time-share business, which has slowly gained ground in acceptance.

## Technological Investment and Analysis

Without technological advancement, the travel and tourism industry would still be mostly for the rich. The driving force behind industry growth has been the refinement of the jet airplane. Before the jet airplane, most vacations were either close to home or they required one of two things most people did not have or were not willing to part with: a lot of money or a lot of time. The jet airplane allowed prices to come down for flying, making faraway destinations more affordable for middle-class consumers. The newest revolution in technology with regard to tourism is the Internet.

Information technology is changing the way tourism is being sold. Travel agents find cheap tickets and package tours on their computer screens through one of the two major airline and tour reservation systems: Sabre or Galileo. Sabre is currently trying to expand beyond their core users of travel agents and have set up their own web site for retail customers: http://www.travelocity.com. Galileo, meanwhile, has taken a different approach, concentrating on serving their main set of users: the travel agents that book most of the travel in this country. Now, with the Internet, customers can make their own searches and purchases directly through the computer, not only through Travelocity, but with a myriad of online travel agents as well. Sophisticated computer reservation systems help hotels track their customers' spending and preferences over time, giving the company a better idea of the lifetime value of the customer to that hotel chain.

The airlines use a yield management formula to differentiate ticket prices for the same flight, thereby yielding what they hope will be the greatest amount of revenue per each flight. Without computers, calculating this in an efficient manner on a nationwide level would be impossible.

Theme parks are another development that would be impossible without the application of technology. These wonderlands of artificial reality are created solely for entertainment and leisure. Customers come back more than once, because the attractions change. Technology is used to find more and different ways to entertain and delight crowds. Technological developments will be one of the main avenues for developing new sources of revenues and profits.

### Recommendation for the Future

Companies in the travel and tourism industry must look at current trends while keeping one eye on the future to remain competitive. When the industry was highly fragmented, complete information was harder to come by for travelers, sheltering many businesses from competition. Those days are gone. The technology is available now to take advantage of location, services, convenience, and value. An unaffiliated business with no apparent advantage is best served affiliating themselves with a chain. For example, a nondescript hotel in North Miami Beach, in an area where hotel rooms are plentiful and many new ones are being built, will have difficulty thriving in the future. Even if the hotel does not become part of a chain, the least it might do would be to develop a web page, list itself in as many search engines and Web directories as possible, and advertise in nontraditional (as well as traditional) channels where there is less competition.

### CASE *The Sabre Group*

There is an underground complex of reinforced concrete surrounded by cement walls four-foot thick. It is fireproof, earthquake-proof, flood-proof, and blackout-proof. The roof is made up of three-and-a-half feet of reinforced concrete covered by five feet of hard-packed dirt. The facility can withstand tornadoes and can operate for up to three days without outside electricity or water.

Such a place exists in Tulsa, Oklahoma, and it is home to the Sabre Secure Computer Center. Sabre is one of the largest real-time computer systems in the world, and its importance in the airline industry warrants such secured facilities.

### Technological Investment and Analysis

Sabre installed IBM's System/390 Parallel Enterprise Server. Its many features make this high performer ex-

tremely cost efficient. According to Terrell B. Jones, the CIO of the Sabre Group, the group was attracted to the new server for a number of important reasons. First, the new server is environmentally friendly: it is air cooled instead of water cooled, and it uses considerably less power than previous units.

According to Dennis Erkine, Managing Director, Distribution Planning for Holiday Inn, in his experience, "Replacing a water-cooled 9021-900 with a new eight-way S/390 G3Enterprise Server can reduce energy bills by 97 percent, while increasing capacity by 10 to 15 percent. At the same time, the R84 takes 94 percent less floor space than the 9021-900 and can cost 70 percent less to maintain." As such, the server's price-performance ratio is in the range that the people at Sabre were searching for.

Additionally, the transition to the new system was extremely easy. In less than twenty-four hours the new system was in place and functioning correctly, and no one even noticed that the transition had been made. According to Jones, "Since it was an unannounced product, we never told anyone it was there! And, it performed so well that no one ever knew it was there—which is exactly the result we wanted."

According to IBM, some of the features that make the 390 Parallel Enterprise Server better than other servers are the following:

1. The cost of computing with S/390 CMOS processors is lower than the cost of using other processors.
2. Operating costs are reduced through the use of CMOS air-cooled processors, consumption of energy is lowered.
3. Maintenance costs are reduced.

In addition, because more than 4,000 S/390 CMOS processors are installed worldwide, repairs and maintenance to the system will be easier than if the system were a unique, in-house system developed specifically for Sabre.

Because Sabre has become available on the Internet, IBM's new system is even more exceptional in that it has characteristics catering to the new emphasis on Internet accessibility. It uses powerful servers for network computing and is especially designed for client-server environments. It has new features such as the cryptographic coprocessor and the full-duplex open system adapter (OSA), which deliver secure connections to ATM, Ethernet, Token Ring, and FDDI local area networks.

These features, when used with facilities such as the Internet Connection Secure Server for OS/390 and native gateways for CICSTM, DB2, IMSTM, and the MQSeries products, enable the S/390 platform to serve new and existing applications over the Internet. Clearly, the new IBM server is the ideal application for the Sabre system.

## Technological Innovations

### Telecommunications

Sabre Group owns Travelocity, the successful Web-based travel agency. It runs with a three-tier architecture. In the first tier are the site's Web servers. It uses Silicon Graphics' Origin 200 servers running Netscape Enterprise Server, which handle the static HTML pages.

The second tier consists of transaction-processing servers, which handle the dynamically generated HTML pages showing reservations and other information. These SGI Origin 2000 servers run proprietary software to access the third tier, the company's immense Sabre Reservations System, a 7-terabyte database that runs on eight IBM S1360 mainframes and is affectionately referred to as Mother Sabre. The Sabre Reservations System, which runs a proprietary transaction protocol, provides at most a three-second response time anywhere in the world.

Although bandwidth has not been a bottleneck, Travelocity added a new Internet connection in 1998, a T3 (45 Mbps) from UUNet Technologies. The site already was running a 2-Mbps link from Sprint and a 10-Mbps connection from MCI.

### Data

Sabre Technology was one of the first companies to adopt Informix's object-relational database for its data warehouse. Its object-relational technology speeds execution times for complex queries and makes the system easier to program, according to Sabre officials.

Sabre chose the Informix system because its Data-Blade modules can execute in parallel and process many sources simultaneously. Its warehouse will eventually cull information from 80 sources ranging from passenger reservation to ticketing systems and will house up to 8 terabytes of data. Thirty developers are writing logic to clean the data and load it correctly.

The warehouse promises to be commercially significant for Sabre and its customers. By knowing who is flying where, when, and for how much money, Sabre can gather valuable data to sell to airlines and other businesses, such as travel agencies, hotels, and real estate firms.

With the new relational database, Sabre could find, for example, who is flying to a specific city in the next three weeks. This information could be very valuable to all kinds of associated industries, such as hotels and entertainment.

Sabre intends to consolidate on a single database for both transactional and warehouse purposes because the cost of maintaining two databases is prohibitive, he explained. The existing 4-terabyte TPF database has the capacity to handle more than 1 billion transactions daily.

## Recommendation for the Future

Several opportunities for future revenue growth have been identified. Increasing the use of Sabre in foreign countries, offering new products in emerging distribution channels, such as corporate direct distribution and the Internet, expanding participation of travel providers in Sabre, and providing technology solutions products and services more broadly are just a few of the ideas for increasing revenue.

In terms of enhancing technology and operating capabilities, Sabre has budgeted approximately $100 million during the next five years to enhance Sabre's core operating capabilities. According to the company, "The goals of this development effort are to accelerate new product development, increase flexibility, power, and functionality for subscribers and associates, improve data management capabilities, raise capacity levels, and lower operating costs."

In terms of Sabre's presence in the hotel and automobile rental market, current progress illustrates that the company is attempting to make the process of reserving a room or a car easier. According to a recent article in a Fort Worth, Texas, newspaper, "Sabre travel agencies worldwide with clients requesting a stay at Motel 6 can now reserve the room electronically at one of the motel chain's more than 200 properties.

The agreement between the Sabre Group and Motel 6 marks the first time the motel chain has used a global distribution system to make reservations. Motel 6, which owns, operates, and is affiliated with more than 700 hotels in North America, plans to add additional properties to Sabre in the coming year." According to the article, "Direct Request for Hotels" properties are listed in Sabre and give agencies the ability to access and request information on participating locations while using preexisting formats. When a customer requests a room reservation Sabre sends a fax message with all the booking information to the appropriate hotel. Sabre then electronically reads information from the hotel's file and updates the reservation automatically. Clearly, more innovations in the hotel and car rental industry are forthcoming.

### QUESTIONS

1. What forces are driving the strategic direction of Sabre?
2. What has been the catalyst for change at Sabre?
3. What are the critical success factors and core competencies of the Sabre group?
4. Upon which technologies is the Sabre system built?
5. What has caused a change in the use of technology at Sabre?
6. How successful has the technological change been?

## ADDITIONAL READING

"Abacus, Sabre file IPOs: Wired Reduces Shares but Boost Price," *Electronic Marketplace Report,* October 15, 1996, p. 5.

Anderson, Jennifer. Doug Beizer, and Trever Dawes, "Ticket to Ride," *PC Magazine,* April 21, 1998, p. 40.

Deck, Stewart. "Sabre in Privacy Hot Seat," *Computerworld,* July 13, 1998, p. 6.

Dillon, Nancy. ". . . while Climbing Storage Management Mountain," *Computerworld,* March 2, 1998, pp. 31–32.

Friedman, Matthew. Mainframes back in Mainstream," *InternetWeek,* September 15, 1997, p. 22.

Girard, Kim. "Storage Snafu Grounds Sabre for Three Hours," *Computerworld,* June 29, 1998, p. 16.

Hamblen, Matt. "Sabre Deems Outsourcing Deal a Success," *Computerworld,* December 1, 1997, p. 6.

Hoffman, Thomas. "Sabre Group Hastens Y2K Plans," *Computerworld,* March 2, 1998, pp. 31–32.

Joachim, David. "Travel Apps Branch Out to Internet," *InternetWeek,* April 20, 1998, p. 23.

Karpinski, Richard. "Commerce One Brings Aboard Travel Services," *InternetWeek,* February 15, 1999, p. 10.

Klein, Stephen. "Industry Surveys: Airlines," *Standard and Poor's,* May 14, 1998.

Madden, John. "Sabre Eyes Warehouse Space," *PC Week,* July 6, 1998, p. 10.

Ouellette, Tim. "Sabre Flies Big Iron in Heavy Traffic," *Computerworld,* March 10, 1997, pp. 43–44.

Palmeri, Christopher. "This Might Not Fly," *Forbes,* April 20, 1998, p. 200.

Roberts, Mark. "Dream Factories: A Survey of Travel and Tourism," *The Economist,* January 10, 1998.

## CASE *American Express*

American Express Company has long been the widely recognized leader in the worldwide travel and corporate financial services arena. Until five years ago, American Express relied mostly on its strong brand name to maintain its position in the industry. The reality was that the company had been losing market share in the credit card business to Visa and MasterCard over the past 10 years, and had overexpanded into many different corporate divisions that did not work well together.

With the appointment of Harvey Golub to CEO of American Express in 1992, a series of major restructuring projects began, with the objectives of strengthening the company's capital position and refocusing on its core businesses in order to improve efficiency and produce higher returns. Golub eliminated the brokerage, investment banking and life insurance units and focused on the company's three principal operating divisions.

### Technological Investment and Analysis

The primary goal for American Express is to build long-term relationships with its customers through products and services that offer superior service and value. This enhances the value of the American Express brand name. The company has been successful on several fronts in the development of new and innovative technology that can be translated into legitimate products and services to upgrade the support and benefits given to customers. To a great extent, American Express has transcended beyond simply using technology to improve its operation and services to the point where technology itself has become product for American Express to develop and market.

One driver is for the company to find ways to strengthen its relationships with merchants and to increase the number of merchants that accept its card. Technology furnishes American Express with a means of extending more assistance to merchants. This includes providing a low-cost way to set up Web store fronts for merchants, enabling merchants to access card member spending information, and providing real-time authorization for American Express card purchases. Through these tools, American Express is able to offer a higher level of service to their merchants then they might receive from other vendors. It also helps justify the company's discount rate, which is higher than the industry average.

The common thread is to leverage technology to establish a permanent link between the customer and American Express. Uniting customers with American Express systems and products prevents those customers from developing their own systems or using those of a competitor.

American Express, with Microsoft, has launched an online travel reservation system designed for corporate customers. Called American Express Interactive (AXI), the system is based primarily on Microsoft software, including the Internet Information Server, SQL Server, and Windows NT. The AXI software is aimed at companies that use American Express as their business travel agency. The software can be integrated with American Express's proprietary travel management software, which includes a low fare search tool and an automated expense reporting system.

AXI enables corporate employees to negotiate and book airfares, rental car rates, and hotel rates from their desktops. It is designed to load data from computerized reservation systems via the Internet or corporate intranets. The system can be customized for each company to reflect its individual travel policies and procedures.

With travel generally being the third-highest controllable expense for a firm, the ability to control costs and to enforce compliance with corporate travel policy provides a significant benefit to customers. Chrysler is one of a half dozen companies using AXI; they project a 50 percent savings in processing fees, cost of transactions, and an increase in the number of people complying with the company policies through the use of the system.

At American Express's Smart Card Center of Excellence, the company is leveraging its technology and customer databases to develop stored value cards. The company is forging alliances and partnerships with other companies to market the cards. Unlike other debit cards, the transactions on American Express smart cards go through the company's central processing centers. These enable the company to collect its discount rate in exchange for transferring the credit risk from the merchant to American Express.

The company has joined with American Express, Hilton Hotels, and IBM to test the use of smart card technology to support ticketless travel. Customer information, as well as hotel and travel preferences and loyalty programs, would reside on a microchip. The chip will allow the cardholder to use a machine at the airport to immediately register for a flight. Information contained in the card will verify the electronic reservation and confirm traveler identification, eliminating the need for a boarding pass. The card can also be used to register for a hotel room by machine and will subsequently serve as the room key. It will be capable of carrying stored value in multiple currencies and has the potential to be coded with the user's fingerprints and even be used as a passport.

By taking an early role in the development of smart cards, American Express has positioned itself to reap the revenue rewards once the smart card market becomes viable. According to David Boyles of American Express, "Our goal is to give value and convenience through globally operable, multifunctioning cards."

American Express is implementing an innovative marketing program called CustomExtras. This program is designed to treat each card member as a "market of one," in which personalized offers are made to selected customers. One-to-one marketing utilizes three technologies: customer databases, interactive media, and systems that support mass customization. Through the use of these technologies, American Express can learn specific details on customer spending patterns, form a deeper relationship with those customers, and provide them with customized products and services. Companies spend a great deal of time and money to acquire customers; one-to-one marketing protects that investment and more fully develops the amount of business that can be conducted with those customers.

With the increasing recognition that mass marketing is an inefficient approach (a 3 percent response rate is considered good in the industry), the goal of one-to-one marketing is to make more selective, cost-efficient solicitations that generate a much higher response rate. Within the industry, the market for products and services that support one-to-one marketing is forecasted as one of the largest growth areas for technology in business.

The overall strategy for American Express through these initiatives is to maintain that ideal customer relationship. "All this enables us to follow our customers as they move from phone or paper-based customer support or transactions to the use of the Internet to handle their travel activities, all the way to the use of smart cards," according to Andrew Bartels, Vice-President of Encrypted Payments at American Express.

American Express is funding the technology expenditures through a combination of new business development and improved margins through improved processes. The company has greatly reduced costs and has eliminated less profitable noncore divisions. Revenue has increased consistently over the past few years as a result of these and other efforts. The company is very strongly capitalized and has the resources necessary to support technology spending. Per their 1996 annual report, American Express maintains the goal of having a cost structure that creates freedom for company investment programs, product design, and pricing.

With the primary objective of increasing customer card business with the company, American Express can measure its success based on levels of consumer spending using its card products. It can also measure the success of its one-to-one marketing strategy based on card member response rates to solicitations sent out by the company.

One of American Express's strategies has been to improve the technological support for its financial advisors division. The goal is to increase both productivity and the level of customer service. American Express intends to provide advisors with laptops that will provide remote access to client and product data. It previously took from 50 to 60 days for a financial plan to be delivered to a prospective client; it is expected that better technological support will reduce that turnaround time to 24 hours with the help of the new systems. Prior to these improvements, 15 to 20 percent of customers did not act on the plan or take the plan's recommendations to other product providers. Once the technological improvements are complete, American Express can measure the number of customers accepting financial plans in the future to determine if any improvement in acceptance rates has been attained.

A key use of data involves the American Express CustomExtras one-to-one marketing program. This program begins with the company's collection of all card member purchase records and other information, which is stored in a marketing database. Proprietary software selects merchant offerings and other American Express promotions that fit a customer's profile. Those offerings and promotions are then printed on the monthly bill. Through the use and evaluation of this stored data, American Express can tailor its marketing to the individual customer.

American Express has reinvented itself as a corporation that actively partners with other companies to develop new revenue opportunities. No longer the imperial standalone company it once was, American Express now engages in partnerships, and cobranding efforts designed to build both their U.S. and overseas markets. These partnerships quite often involve technology companies.

The tremendous amount of data from the high-profile client base held by American Express gives the company the ability to develop more effective marketing strategies. This information is used both to market its own products and services and for increasing card member spending. By utilizing their database and a closed-loop network, American Express is able to store and use this information to identify customer spending patterns, assist in budget planning, and increase efficiency. One primary use of the data is for target marketing, in which specific merchant offers are targeted to those customers most likely to take advantage of them, based on their previous spending behavior. American Express also makes customer purchase data available to merchants through a Windows-based software product designed by the company.

Rather than simply rely on its own proprietary distribution systems, American Express utilizes many other types of distribution networks, including brokerage, direct marketing, and online systems to attract and service its customers. American Express also utilizes a vast worldwide electronic network. This enables the company to increase charge volume and enables it to hold down fraud and minimize bad debt. This network provides the infrastructure needed to access a multitude of markets, many of which have opportunities for expansion.

American Express has two goals for its information technology: reengineer the company and develop new products. According to American Express CIO Allan Loren, "We're changing distribution channels." The Internet helps to distribute new products and expand the transactional capabilities of the company. The overall intent for technology is to better service the customer and maintain a solid position in a highly competitive business environment.

The most recent data for American Express identifies its allocation of IT expenditures as follows:

- For reengineering and new product development (50 percent)
- Maintenance of existing technology (40 percent)
- For determining new directions for the company (10 percent)

American Express uses a closed-loop network to collect and use customer information for target marketing. Point-of-sale transactions feed a massive parallel database for use across the organization. For the CustomExtras program, the company has deployed a second database, running on a mainframe with relational database software. This database draws data from the first database and uses it to track purchases, rewards, and promotions. It manages the printing of billing statements with customized offers and messages. As a follow-up, the American Express marketing database tracks customers' activities regarding offers and promotions. Whenever a customer acts on an offer, American Express shares the results with the merchant.

Teamed with Hewlett-Packard, American Express has introduced a new electronic commerce program (ExpressVault) designed to enable merchants to conduct business over the Internet quickly and securely. It combines HP's computing and security technologies with American Express's payment processing system. ExpressVault enables merchants to add online commerce features to web sites; it also protects transaction, database, and web site information against unauthorized access and provides real-time processing for American Express card transactions.

### Technological Innovation

#### Network

At the core of the American Express Company financial services business, the IDS division employs 8,500 advisers who work out of remote field offices as well as home offices and sell a broad range of financial products and services to clients throughout North America.

Financial planning is an increasingly lucrative business for Amex. Its advisers work with individuals and families to develop long-range financial goals for retirement, education, illness, disability, or estate planning.

Until five years ago, financial planning was a paper-intensive business. Advisers met with prospective clients, typically at the client's home or business location. They gathered relevant data on client assets, liabilities, and goals, and then reported back to the local regional office. At the regional office a clerk entered information and uploaded it to the legacy mainframe-based application in Minneapolis. Weeks later, a rudimentary financial plan would be mailed to the adviser, who would go back to deliver it to the client and meet with him or her to tailor the plan to his or her precise needs. Depending on the client, this could go on for three or four iterations.

Today, AdvisorLink has changed everything. This remote application encompasses a wide range of applications specifically designed for field advisers. Under its umbrella, new functionality is added either via in-house development projects or software purchased from third parties. AdvisorLink brings together internal "best practice" processes and technology that the firm believes will give its advisers a significant competitive edge over other financial services firms.

The internal proprietary adviser service software, written in Smalltalk, resides on advisers' laptops and processes client plans locally. Although client data is still uploaded to legacy systems, the turnaround time for completing sophisticated financial plans has been cut from weeks to days.

The adviser directs the initial data gathering of goals, income, assets, and debt from the client. The client then uses the new software to develop customized plans that specifically tie the client's long- and short-term goals to existing and future assets. Rather than relying upon the boilerplate results that came from the previous legacy application, the new software gives the adviser the opportunity to tailor a plan more precisely. When the plan is complete, the adviser meets with the client, validates the results, and conducts "what if" scenarios to ensure that the client is happy with the results. At any time, the client can request adjustments and the adviser can make them on the spot. This has shortened dramatically the processing time for sophisticated financial plans.

### Telecommunications

On the consumer side, American Express promotes travel, dining, and entertainment. To do so, it has invested money in a company that is using the Internet to help consumers find places where they can do all of these things. American Express has entered an investment and joint marketing agreement with CitySearch, Inc., the developer of online city guides. CitySearch supplies maps and information for 16 cities, including New York, Portland (Oregon), San Francisco, Washington, D.C., Chicago, Sydney, and Toronto. In doing so, it covers news about sports, the arts, entertainment, community activities, shopping, recreation, and weather. CitySearch also helps small and medium-size businesses develop web sites and helps to host these sites. It gathers this information from its newspaper partners in each city.

### Security on the Internet

On May 31, 1997, Visa International, Mastercard, and American Express, with most of the major players in electronic commerce and internetworking, unveiled the Secure Electronic Transactions (SET) standard. SET was set up to revolutionize online transactions and make the Internet safe for electronic commerce. Unfortunately, the implementation of this technology has moved more slowly than expected. The difficulties have surrounded both business and technical reasons.

The point of SET is to increase consumer confidence in the security of online transactions. Both credit card holders and merchants are issued digital certificates, which are verified by a certificate authority to make a transaction. Neither the merchant nor the consumer can be anyone other than who they purport to be, greatly reducing the threat of impersonation fraud.

The difficulty comes in the requirement that merchants using SET install expensive new software and build their businesses around a complex transaction infrastructure. Current online merchants have not exactly been lining up to get on the SET bandwagon. In fact, one year later, the attempted standard still had not seen a single operational deployment. SET's biggest shortcoming is the client channel. Vendors like VeriFone and IBM have developed SET wallet plug-ins for the popular Web browsers. Yet, Internet users do not favor external plug-ins.

In the meantime, electronic commerce continues to grow on the Net, protected by Secure Sockets Layer encryption. While not as secure as SET, for many consumers, it is secure enough.

### Free Internet e-mail

American Express introduced a free Internet e-mail service, AmExMail, in April 1998. The service, available only to American Express customers, was developed with the help of Colorado Springs, Colorado-based electronic messaging firm, USA.Net. The new e-mail system uses USA.Net's mail engine architecture. This purchase makes American Express the first major business outside the Internet industry to offer free e-mail. Services such as AmExMail have become more common among companies seeking to build close ties to their customers. This is an important way for a credit card company, such as American Express, to keep its customers active and be able to share new information with them.

Other free e-mail services, such as Four11, Hotmail, and WhoWhere have been partnering with or purchased by larger companies, including Yahoo, Microsoft, and Qualcomm, respectively; these deals have linked free e-mail to already existing Internet products or services.

AmExMail will continue to be operated by USA.Net, a firm that will continue to offer free, ad-supported e-mail services. In April 1997, American Express announced the purchase of a minority interest in USA.net, which is privately held. American Express has been testing the service since November. The AmExMail service is free to any Internet user, but American Express cardholders will get toll-free customer service support and 10 Mbytes of mail storage space, compared to 5 Mbytes for noncardholders.

### American Express Travel

American Express Travel and Entertainment is a Web-based travel solution that integrates a company's travel policies and directives with the reservations system. Reservations that do not comply with policy directives are flagged, and "preferred supplier" services are emphasized. AXI's linkage to Microsoft's Expedia software means users can take advantage of added features such as airline seat maps for seat selection and access to international destination information. The travel system can operate in multiple environments, with multiple computer reservations systems and an Internet, intranet, or extranet connection.

American Express Travel online provides an easy-to-use reservation system, access to vacation and last-minute travel specials, and excellent customer service. As such, the service is good for travelers without a lot of special needs. As such, it does not offer the more specialized services of the ability to book flights using frequent-flier miles or to book more than five legs of a business trip.

The AmEx reservations system is driven by Internet Travel Network (ITN). All reservations are sent to American Express Travel Related Services. This provides several advantages, including options to purchase tickets. AmEx provides the ability to change an itinerary worldwide through AmEx offices or through its toll-free number. Ticketing is available 24 hours a day, but customer service is available on a more limited schedule.

To use the system, each user must register and establish a profile, which is identical to the ITN profile and stored for future use. For security reasons, the credit card number cannot be stored from one session to another.

The site's vacation packages, including many different suppliers and certified vacations, are guaranteed to be at the lowest prices available. The drawback of the vacation packages is that the prices quoted are for fixed tours; fares will increase drastically if many changes are made.

### American Express retirement services

The American Express retirement services has instituted natural language query software on its ExpressLink extranet to eliminate the necessity for retirement planners and benefits administrators to learn basic query software. The query tool, which required users to download some data to a desktop and to point and click on the data elements they wanted, scared some users away. In its place, the natural language software returns an answer for queries typed in plain English or suggests alternatives that can help users find what they need. Some users accustomed to the older querying tools found the new option slow and awkward; however, they feel it would be most beneficial for those users who had never used any query tools previously. The ExpressLink service costs $2,500 plus a $1,500 annual support fee.

Amex used English Wizard, a natural language tool from Linguistic Technology Corporation in Littleton, Massachusetts, to develop the ExpressLink extranet. The extranet went live in 1997 and is used by about 60 external users. Many individuals use ExpressLink to work on their 401(k) plans. In addition to the query tool, ExpressLink provides users with monthly reports online, the ability to check call center statistics, and access to send electronic mail to their account managers.

American Express is working with Mercantec to develop an economical way to establish Web-based storefronts. The companies will use Mercantec's SoftCart payment and virtual shopping software. American Express will handle the back-end processing and offer financial and marketing expertise. SoftCart offers companies a way to explore the possibilities of a Web store without making a major financial commitment. The partnership with Mercantec offers American Express a good entry point for offering Web. American Express will use SoftCart and a network of payment gateways to provide Web merchants with authorization for American Express and bank card purchases.

Unlike many companies that act as Web commerce enablers, American Express already has strong relationships with both merchants and consumers. In comparison, Visa and MasterCard work through affiliate banks. Many of these have faltered in the area of electronic commerce.

SoftCart features a relatively low-cost entry point for Web merchants, with a onetime license fee of $1,800. Monthly licensing is also available. Merchants can purchase a solution directly from American Express or work with integration partners, including ISPs that will implement the software on their networks. The product has limited availability.

### Data

American Express has enhanced an application for its corporate purchasing service. This will enable customers' purchasing data to be fed directly into their back-end SAP systems. The interface to American Express's AccountingLink application eliminates any manual intervention. This is particularly important because large clients process more than 1 million purchasing documents a year.

The goal is that customers of American Express's purchasing service will essentially outsource their accounts payable and purchasing operations to the vendor. This business will handle $4 billion in invoices and 15 million transactions in 1998 alone.

### Smart card

American Express and Visa International have formed a joint venture to focus on developing applications for smart cards to spur use of the technology in the United States. The companies hope that their smart-card applications will become the standards for the electronic-commerce industry, though their goal is to design open interfaces that will support competitors' systems.

Banksys SA in Belgium and ERG Ltd. in Australia are also partners in the venture, called Proton

World International. The company will continue to develop and license smart-card applications that were originally developed by Banksys, including the Proton electronic purse application used by 30 million people worldwide.

Credit card companies have been reluctant to push multifunction smart cards because they fear that they will cannibalize the credit card company's brand by replacing traditional credit cards. The commitment of New York City-based American Express and Foster City, California-based Visa indicates that these firms believe they have more to gain with smart cards than they have to lose.

"If you have a multifunction smart card, you can use it to gain entry to your office, take money out of the bank and ride mass transit," according to Jim Balderston, an analyst at Zona Research, Inc., in Redwood City, California.

In contrast, MasterCard International, Inc., supports the Mondex electronic purse system, which follows a different verification structure.

### Recommendation for the Future

For American Express, it is especially critical to meet the demands of its corporate customers to retain and grow in that lucrative market. Industry observers expect the number of commercial cards and charge volume to grow as much as 50 percent over the next few years. Some of that growth is anticipated to result from small businesses, which have limited technology to monitor and control expenses in-house. The ability of American Express, for instance, to develop an Internet system for purchasing cards ahead of its competitors is essential to capturing a large share of the small business market.

Technology is enabling American Express to attempt to see whether it can sell additional financial services to its card members. Of American Express's 20.5 million customers, only 250,000 of them have accounts with American Express Financial Advisors. The company should be able to use its customer database to develop marketing strategies to sign up additional cardholders for other financial services offered by American Express. An expert system would seem to be a possible option. An expert system could be designed to evaluate the data of those customers who are both card members and financial service customers. It would then extrapolate those patterns to identify other customers most likely to be interested in financial services.

Given the intense competition in the industry, technology must keep American Express in the position of meeting customer needs. Management recognizes this fact in its effort to leverage technology to improve customer service and efficiency.

### QUESTIONS

1. What has been the catalyst for change at American Express?
2. Upon which technologies does the corporation rely?
3. What has been the primary cause of change in the use of technology at American Express?
4. How successful has American Express been with this technological change?
5. How has American Express developed the financial ability to embark on a major technological program of advancement?
6. Are there long-term trends that seem to be problematic for American Express?
7. What does the corporation's web page present about American Express's business directives?
8. How will technology impact the industry?
9. What role does data play in the future of the corporation?

### ADDITIONAL READING

"American Express Links to Apps," *InternetWeek,* April 6, 1998, p. 7.

Block, Valerie. "Amex to Test Smart Cards with Hilton and IBM," *American Banker,* May 29, 1997, p. 1.

Cole-Gomolski, Barb. "Amex/Visa Deal to Push Smart-Card Technology," *Computerworld,* August 3, 1998, p. 6.

"EDS Inks Sale of ATMs," *PC Week,* February 1, 1999, p. 81.

Friedman, Matthew. "SET Standard Not Exactly Hitting the Fast Lane," *Computing Canada,* June 15, 1998, p. 26.

Girishankar, Saroja. "American Express Online Travel Service Flies High," *InternetWeek,* December 1, 1997.

Gupta, Udayan. "Sharing Data to Get an Edge," *Information Week,* September 9, 1996.

Kestelyn, J. "Emerging Standard Gives Smart Card Players Hope," *Intelligent Enterprise,* October 1998, p. 10.

LaPlante, Alice. "Commanding a Mobile Army," *Computerworld,* July 20, 1998, p. 55.

Mulqueen, John T. "Big Business Remains Bullish on E-Commerce," *InternetWeek,* July 13, 1998, p. 48.

"Online Travel Group," *Computerworld,* June 22, 1998, p. 41.

Pike, Bill. "American Express Coins Its Euro Strategy," *Enterprise Systems Journal,* December 1998, p. 26.

Stedman, Craig. "Amex to Users: Speak English," *Computerworld,* December 15, 1997, pp. 57–59.

Sweat, Jeff. "American Express Upgrades SAP Links," *InformationWeek,* April 6, 1998, p. 40.

"Visa and Amex Start Smart Standard War," *Computer Weekly,* August 6, 1998, p. 6.

## DISCUSSION ISSUE

### *Strategy or Power*

In looking at the various cases involving the use of the information systems to gain a competitive advantage, one pattern often emerges. Many of the examples (such as American Airlines and Baxter Healthcare) consist of suppliers using information systems to change the relationship with their customers. Although this change in the relationship can benefit both parties, the possibility always exists that one of the groups may eventually choose to abuse the power created by the change. In the following example, Oliver, Avery and Lamar work for an accounting firm. One of their clients is a small business run by Mitch and Abby.

Oliver: Look, we're starting to feel pressure in this business. We're having a lot of trouble keeping our smaller clients. Lately, even some of our larger clients have been complaining about the cost of our services. We need to find some way to expand our services and keep our current clients.

Avery: Well, Oliver, we've been looking at this problem for quite some time. There seem to be only a few options. Obviously, we don't want to cut our fees. We've cut our internal costs as far as we can. Based on economic projections, the number of accounting firms is increasing faster than the client base, so we can't expect things to get any better. But, Lamar here has an idea that has some merit . . .

Lamar: Thanks, Avery. I've been talking to our junior staff members and a couple of clients. It seems that a large portion of our time is spent just collecting data from some of our clients. Although most of the larger clients have computerized accounting systems, we still do taxes and audits from the printouts. For the smaller clients, we spend a lot of time just organizing their data. Sure, we charge them for our time, but as soon as a hungry competitor offers to do the paperwork for a lower price, the clients jump ship.

Oliver: Sure, that makes sense; because of our higher overhead, we can't price our services as low as some of these small firms. So what's the answer?

Lamar: Well, the main idea is to handle everything on the computer. Let's take our main computers and connect them to all of our clients. For the larger clients, we'll concentrate on getting direct access to their databases. Whenever we need data, we'll just pull it directly from the client computer, feed it into one of our auditing or tax packages, do some quick analyses, and create the final reports. It'll really speed up the process and cut down on errors. Plus, we'll be able to concentrate more on the analytical services, such as looking for better tax strategies.

Avery: That seems to fit with our goals of cutting costs and offering more services, but what about the small clients that don't use much in the way of computers?

Lamar: With the smaller clients, we'll offer a complete accounting system that runs from our computers. Basically, we'll provide their complete information system. With current telecommunications technology, it's easy to set up. It doesn't really matter where the computers are located. And we've already got most of the software we need.

Oliver: Okay, so we can run with lower costs. I still don't want to cut prices. How does this system help keep clients?

Lamar: Once the clients are on the system, they won't want to switch. Even if a competitor comes up with a similar idea, it would cost the clients too much time and effort to change to another system. Once we get them hooked, they're locked in.

Avery: Yes, that's the best part. Here's how I see the plan. We go to our customers and offer them a short-term discount to switch to the system. Tell them we want to use them as demo sites . . .

Oliver: I get it; we make the same offer to everyone, just to get them on the system.

Avery: That's right, plus we train their staff members. Get them used to the system. After a year or so, we start to raise our rates. In the meantime, we write a couple of reports showing how much the system is saving them. Collect a couple numbers that show how much we spent on training their people and setting up the system for them. Then, if they complain about their bills and start talking about switching to another firm, we give them a report showing how much it'll cost them to switch.

Lamar: Plus, we can tell them the costs are because of their increased business—part of which they earned because of getting better reports from us.

Oliver: And because we have all of their data, it should be easy to make these reports say anything we want. I like it . . .

*(Later, at one of the clients . . .)*

Mitch: Hi, Abby. Lamar from the accounting firm just made us an interesting offer. He said his firm is offering a new service. It will handle all of our accounting for a fixed fee. And they're offering a special deal if we agree to let them use us as a demo site . . .

Abby:  I don't know, Mitch. Maybe they found out we've been talking to other firms, and they're just trying to keep us interested.

Mitch:  Nah, I don't think that has anything to do with it. They've got a whole new system. Lamar was really excited. They're going to computerize everything.

Abby:  But we can't afford a big computer system. We've talked about it before . . .

Mitch:  That's the best part. We don't have to buy the computer. All of the records are kept on their computer. We just use a couple of smart cash registers that transfer the data over the phone lines.

Abby:  But what if we ever want to switch companies? How do we get our data?

Mitch:  Relax, I asked Lamar about that. He said it's like medical records. The accountants will give us whatever reports we want. If we ever switch companies, they'll give all of the data to the new firm.

Abby:  Well, maybe . . . And you said they're giving us a break on the prices? What do we have to do to get that? How can they afford it?

Mitch:  Lamar said that officially, we might have to let some potential customer wander through the store to check out the system. They won't see any of the data; they'll just make sure the system works. But don't worry, he hinted that it was just a formality. He's really looking out for us on this one—said he pulled a few strings to get us the offer. He hinted that they're making money because the new computer system is so efficient.

Abby:  Hey, I've got an idea. It sounds like they really want us to use this system. Maybe we can use that to negotiate with them a little . . .

Mitch:  Sure. Let's call Lamar and tell him it's still too expensive. We'll drop a hint that someone else made us a better offer for a similar service. Quick, what was the name of that company we talked to last week?

## QUESTIONS

1. Do you think the accounting firm's decision to use the information system to build stronger ties with clients is a good idea?
2. Do you agree with the accounting firm's approach to implementing the system and the plan to increase prices?
3. As a partner in the accounting firm, if you choose to go this route, how would you present and sell it to the clients?
4. Do you think Mitch and Abby examined all of the issues before making their decision? What else should they consider?
5. Do you think Mitch and Abby are taking the right approach in negotiating with Lamar? Is it ethical?
6. As a client, would you accept this offer, even if you know what the accounting firm is planning? What could you do to protect your interests?

# *Presentations*

As a manager, you will often have to give presentations. Two basic rules of presentations are (1) know your audience, and (2) be prepared. Most of your presentations can be made using computer projection systems. Modern presentation packages support color, graphics, animation, video, and sound. However, you must be careful to use the features to enhance your presentation—not to distract. Many audiences will find animation and sound to be too distracting. Presentation packages also help you be more prepared. For example, building the entire presentation ahead of time forces you to be prepared. More importantly, the systems also enable you to adapt to your audience. By building in hidden slides and activation buttons, you can jump to new topics or skip certain screens as the need arises.

## PRESENTATION FOUNDATIONS

The first question you must address in a presentation is to learn what size screen you will have. What resolution is supported by the projection device (640 × 480, 800 × 600, or 1024 × 768)? A related question is the size of text that can be read by the audience. If possible, go to the actual presentation room and try reading different font sizes from various locations.

The next step is to build a template that sets colors, typefaces, and backgrounds. Most presentation systems come with several predefined templates. One of the biggest decisions to make is whether you want a light background and dark text, or dark text on a light background. The choice depends on the mood you wish to set, the capabilities of your projection system, and the lighting in the presentation room.

Organization of your presentation is critical. Write an outline and test it with other people to be sure they understand what you are trying to communicate. Remember the presenter's rule: (1) tell the audience what you are going to say (introduction), (2) tell them, (3) tell them what you said (summary). The level of detail in the presentation and outline depends on the time factor and the difficulty of the material. As you develop the outline, try talking through the presentation to see how much time you will spend on each major section.

## BUILDING INDIVIDUAL SLIDES

Each slide will be tailored to the specific presentation. Common types of slides include titles, outlines or bulleted points, tables, charts, pictures, spreadsheets, animation, or video clips. You need to decide which slide best conveys each specific point. Note that images can enhance and highlight text. Icons and simple images can be used to help people remember your main points.

Be consistent when you build individual slides. Use the template to keep titles in the same locations. Use preset color schemes to highlight specific points. Keep your main points centered on the screen. Avoid cluttering the slides. When in doubt, put fewer words on each slide and use more slides.

## SLIDESHOW ANIMATION

Most presentation systems enable you to add animation effects to objects on the slides. For example, you can make each bulleted point fly in from the side. Before using any of these effects, be sure that you know your audience. Many people will quickly tire of the effect. Also, some people like to read ahead, and the effects may interfere. On the other hand, if you are building a standalone presentation and need to attract attention, a few animation effects may attract viewers. You can customize individual animations by setting delays and altering the item after the animation is complete (e.g., hiding, dimming, or changing colors). Finally, if you choose animated effects, pick one and stick with it. Do not use different effects on every slide.

If you want more control over animation, you will have to use an animation package like Adobe's After Effects. With a lot of creativity and effort, you can build a complete animated movie with these tools. However, keep in mind that the file size quickly becomes large. Even a 20 second clip can run to 100 megabytes or more.

## SLIDE TRANSITIONS

You can build more useful effects by controlling the transition between slides. Even in more formal presentations, these transitions are less distracting. In fact, the less obtrusive ones such as fades and wipes work as a signal to the audience that you are changing topics.

The transition effects are particularly useful if you build a slide show from a collection of images. Digitized photographs can appear on one slide and you can use transitions to fade in or dissolve to the next picture.

## AUDIO FILES

Audio files can be played in the background during a slide presentation, or they can be used as accents. Like animated effects, accent sounds (e.g., clicks) become annoying after a while, so use them sparingly. On the other hand, background audio tracks can add emotion and movement to a presentation—provided you do not have to talk over it.

In PowerPoint, background audio that plays across multiple slides is added in the Slide Transition menu. You might have to convert the file to a standard Windows wave (.wav) file. Other types of music can be played on individual slides, including MIDI files and audio tracks on a CD. With good audio software, you can convert files to the wave format or even create your own presentation CD that contains the tracks you need.

In addition to difficulties with file formats, you have to be careful with your use of sound clips. All commercial clips are protected by copyright laws, which limit how you can use the clips. Even if you purchased the CD, you might not have the right to use the sound clip in your presentation. Generally, if the presentation is to a small organizational group and not used to make money, you should be safe—as long as you paid for the initial copy. If you are using the presentation for marketing or to play to the public, however, you will have to pay fees for the use of the music. The same conditions hold for photographs and video clips.

The situation is even clearer on the Internet. You cannot use any sound, image, or other clip unless you have explicit permission to use it. Be sure that you have copyright permissions to use all of your material.

## EXERCISES

1. Build a slide show to sell your car (make up a car, or choose some other item if you do not own one).
2. Build a slide show of photographs with background music. For example, highlight your vacation photographs, a museum, or your friends.
3. Create the ugliest, most distracting slide show possible. Compete with your classmates to see which is worst.
4. Build a slide show to advertise the Rolling Thunder Bicycle company. Make it run automatically for one to two minutes, and then repeat.

# PART 4

# Designing and Managing Information Systems

**How do managers organize and control information systems?**
Because of their importance in a modern firm, information systems must be carefully planned, designed, and maintained. Business managers are increasingly involved in designing and organizing MIS resources. Managers need to understand the difficulties faced in systems development to understand the rules and processes. As technology changes, the organization of business operations and the MIS resources is changing. By identifying these changes, business managers can improve their operations and make better use of new information technologies.

Changes in technology and business cause fundamental changes in society. These changes affect everything from education to government to our daily lives as employees and citizens. Changing technology brings new responsibilities and problems. As managers and citizens we will face many new decisions. We must always remember our ethical responsibilities to other members of society.

# Systems Development

Air traffic control is a difficult job requiring intense concentration. Aging computer systems make the job more difficult, but the FAA has found it even more difficult to design and build a new air traffic control system.

## FEDERAL AVIATION ADMINISTRATION

Governmental control over aviation began in 1911, when Connecticut passed regulations governing the flights of planes. Although the federal government played an early role through the Department of Defense, control over civilian flights was not formalized until the creation of the Civil Aeronautics Board (CAB) in 1944 as a division of the Commerce Department. The Federal Aviation Administration (FAA) was created in 1958 and the CAB was merged into the new agency. In 1966, the FAA (and CAB) was made part of the Department of Transportation. The Airline Deregulation Act of 1978 effectively dismantled most functions of the CAB.

The FAA is charged with controlling civilian and military uses of U.S. airspace. The FAA is also responsible for modernizing the airways, installing radar, and training air traffic controllers. Probably their best-known function is control over commercial flights and routes to maintain safety and efficiency. With 50,000 flights a day among 300 major airports, the FAA has a huge task.

Despite the complications of size, weather, and delays, the airline industry has suffered relatively few disasters. The current accident rate is about one passenger fatality per 100 million passenger miles—far less than the accident rate caused by automobile traffic. Of the accidents that do arise, about half are typically attributed to human error, with one-third of those being caused by pilot error.

There are several other governmental agencies involved in aviation. The National Weather Service produces up-to-the-minute weather forecasts. The Federal Communication Commission allocates radio frequencies and rules. The National Ocean Survey creates the maps and charts used for navigation. The National Aeronautics and Space Administration supports aviation research. International flights are governed by the UN-sponsored International Civil Aviation Organization formed in 1944 and moved under the aegis of the United Nations in 1947.

The FAA has a computer system to help it control the thousands of daily flights. However, the system was created in the early 1960s. It has been patched and upgraded, but most of the hardware and software are based on decades-old technology. On several occasions, the FAA attempted to upgrade the facilities, but complications have forced the agency back to the old technology.

**OVERVIEW**

By now you should have some ideas of how MIS can help you in your job. Working as a manager, you will develop many ideas involving technology that you want to try. So how do you turn your ideas into an actual system? For complex systems, you will undoubtedly turn to experts for help: computer programmers and systems analysts. In order to communicate effectively with these people, you need to understand a little bit about how they do their jobs and the techniques that are available. Part of that understanding involves learning a little about the problems that are likely to arise when you develop computer systems. As illustrated in Figure 12.1, there are several different ways to create computer systems. Non-MIS managers are often involved in deciding which method to use, so you need to know the benefits, costs, and limitations of each method.

As a manager, you need to understand the problems and limitations facing MIS departments. You need to know why it can take MIS so long to create even small systems. Additionally, more and more often, managers and workers are expected to develop their own small systems (known as *end-user development*). The lessons learned from large MIS projects can help you create your own small system, particularly with implementation problems and solutions.

**INTRODUCTION**

There is a fundamental dilemma faced by anyone developing a computer application. Most problems are so large they have to be split into smaller pieces. The difficulty lies in combining the pieces back into a complete solution. Often each piece is assigned to a different team, and sometimes it takes months to complete each section. Without a solid plan and control, the entire system might collapse. Thousands of system development projects have failed or been canceled because of these complications.

Partly because of the problems that have been encountered in the past, and partially because of technological improvements, several techniques are available to develop computer systems. The most formal approach is known as the **systems development life**

**FIGURE 12.1**
It is not easy to create information systems to support business needs (strategy, tactics, and operations). Three basic techniques are systems development life cycle, prototyping, and end-user development. As a manager, you will participate in each of these methods. You will sometimes have to choose which method to use.

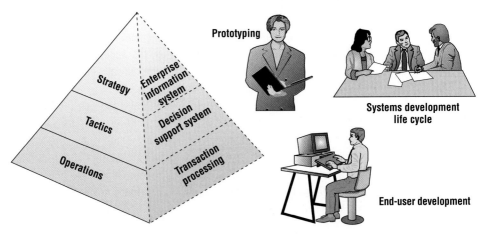

**cycle (SDLC).** As indicated in Figure 12.2, large organizations that develop several systems use this method to coordinate the teams, evaluate progress, and ensure quality development. Most organizations have created their own versions of SDLC. Any major company that uses SDLC also has a manual that is several inches thick (or comparable online documentation) that lays out the rules that MIS designers have to follow. Although these details vary from firm to firm, all of the methods have a common foundation. The goal is to build a system by analyzing the business processes and breaking the problem into smaller, more manageable pieces.

Improvements in technology improve the development process. The powerful features of commercial software make it easier to build new applications. Programmers and designers can work with larger, more powerful objects. For example, instead of programming each line in COBOL, a report can be created in a few minutes using a database management system or a spreadsheet. **Prototyping** is a design technique that takes advantage of these new tools. The main objective of prototyping is to create a working version of the system as quickly as possible—even if some components are not included in the early versions. The third method of creating systems, **end-user development** relies on users to create their own systems. This method typically uses advanced software (such as spreadsheets and database management systems) and requires users who have some computer skills.

It is important to be careful when you implement any new system. Case studies show that major problems have arisen during implementation of systems. In fact, some organizations have experienced so many problems that they will deliberately stick with older, less useful systems just to avoid the problems that occur during implementation. Although changes can cause problems, there are ways to deal with them during implementation.

**FIGURE 12.2**
EXAMPLES OF SYSTEM DEVELOPMENT METHODOLOGIES
Several companies specialize in developing systems, and they have built their own methodologies to coordinate teams, evaluate progress, and identify problems. All of these approaches are similar.

**Andersen Consulting,** a division of Arthur Andersen & Co., is the largest worldwide consulting firm in management information systems. It conducts major installations using a proprietary methodology called Method/1. Method/1 uses four phases in the development process: plan, design, implement, and maintain.

**McKinsey and Co.,** a strategic consulting firm, examines organizations with a copyrighted "Seven S" model. The seven S's are structure, systems, style, staff, skills, strategy, and shared values.

**Ed Yourdon,** a computer programmer credited with standardizing programming in replaceable components, applies a self-developed method of tools and techniques. His method uses graphical diagrams to model the hardware and software on which the system is based.

**Information Engineering Workbench (IEW), a** structured systems-development methodology, uses planning, analysis, design, and construction to increase the productivity of systems analysts. Developed by Knowledgeware, IEW uses object-oriented modeling concepts to involve the users in systems planning, analysis, and design. To increase the speed of the data-processing environment, the data-processing expenditure must be justified by its link to top management's directions and goals. By identifying how technology can best aid the strategic goals of the business, development is focused on systems that provide the most benefit for the company.

## Trends

In the earliest days, computers were used for simple mathematical computations. Most of the time, an individual recognized a problem to be solved, programmed the computer, and used the output. With only one or two people involved in the process, it was much easier to develop computer software. Everyone understood the problems and goals, so there were minimal communication problems. Because everyone knew how to program the computer, there was little reason to worry about creating an interface that was easy to use.

As computer use expanded to transaction processing, the situation changed, but only a little. Managers asked programmers to build systems that generated reports identical to the manually created reports already in use. Programmers concentrated on making efficient use of the computer. Data-entry clerks typed the data onto cards in a specific format. Final reports were sent to managers. The managers never actually used the computers. In fact, knowledge of computers was considered to be a menial, technical problem and something that good managers should avoid. In any case, there were few problems with communication because formulas, report layout, and data types could be copied from the existing manual system. Because managers only cared about the final reports, changes were written on the existing reports and programmers made the modifications. Since only a few trained people actually used the computer and because computer time was expensive, the user interface consisted of a few simple commands punched onto cards. The programs were short and simple, and programmers designed the systems in their heads or on a few scraps of paper.

Later, as computer use spread and computers were shared by large numbers of people, the separate professions of programmer and systems analyst evolved. Users would request help from the MIS department to solve a particular problem, and a team of analysts and programmers would be assigned. The analysts would interview the users at the start of the project and create system specifications for the programmers. A few days (or weeks or months) later, the MIS team would present what it believed was the completed project. Often users would express some disappointment in the results and adjustments would be made. Sometimes the system never did do exactly what the users wanted. As time elapsed, the business and the needs of the users would change. To control these changes, MIS departments began asking users to "sign off" on the project at various steps, agreeing not to change the specifications. This approach attempted to freeze the system while the analysts modeled it. Unfortunately, the actual business rarely stayed frozen.

Increasingly, firms are moving away from custom-written software. They are purchasing packages and hiring outside programmers to develop many components. In these situations, design issues generally consist of choosing and customizing the software to meet the individual needs of the organization.

There have been some spectacular failures in the development of computer systems. Projects always seem to be over budget and late. Worse, systems are sometimes developed and never used because they did not solve the right problems or they are impossible to use. Several design methods have been created to help prevent these problems. Each method has advantages and drawbacks. As a result, they tend to be suitable for different types of problems.

## Individual Programming

**EARLY METHODS**　At heart, development of information systems comes down to the work of individuals. Despite advances in technology, the emphasis on teamwork, and the use of methodologies, development of systems remains a craft. To understand the implications, consider that there can be a tenfold (or greater) difference in capability and productivity between programmers. Despite our best efforts, projects still fail. The success of any project depends on the skills and capabilities of the individual programmers and system analysts. Hiring, training, and keeping talented workers are crucial components in developing systems.

A few techniques were developed to assist individual programmers and analysts. For a short time, programmers were encouraged to visualize programs with *flow charts*. Although a few programmers still use flow charts, others first outline their plans using pseudocode. *Pseudocode* is used to describe the logic of a program or outline a system. It uses basic programming techniques but ignores issues of syntax.

These techniques are also used to communicate with users. Consider a system that requires complex logic or involved computations. Most programmers will not be experts in the interpretation of the equations, so they will rely on the users to verify the accuracy of the final system. As part of that process, the programmer or analyst will describe the program using pseudocode. The analyst will use the pseudocode to illustrate how the system will fit with the underlying business process. As a manager, there are situations in which you will want to check the pseudocode to verify that the program performs computations correctly. Figure 12.3 provides an example of pseudocode for developing a financial system that evaluates projects based on present-value costs. As an accountant or financial analyst involved with this project, you would be responsible for reading the pseudocode segments to make sure the logic and computations are correct.

## Top-Down and Bottom-Up Design

In the 1970s, there was considerable discussion of whether systems (and programs) should be designed following a top-down or a bottom-up approach. With a **top-down design,** the analyst begins by modeling the "big-picture" situation. Early methods called for analyzing the entire corporation. To save time, top-down analysis generally begins with the highest business level that will be affected by the system. As shown in Figure 12.4, the goal is to start at the top and list all of the business functions (marketing, accounting, etc.). All of these functions are broken into processes, each of which is supported by business activities. Eventually, a complete picture of the firm (or subsystem) is created that contains any desired level of detail.

**FIGURE 12.3**
PSEUDOCODE
EXAMPLE
Pseudocode is an initial step in designing a computer program. Programming commands are written in simple words without regard to syntax. Commands and comments are added to make the code easier for programmers and managers to understand.

---

*Project Evaluation (given a discount factor)*

Get list of cost items from the user

    (Description, value, time-incurred, probability-factor, category . . .)

Examine each item in the list:

Compute the present value of the cost:

    $PV = Cost / ( (1 + rate) \char`^ time)$

Multiply by the probability factor:

    $EV = Probability * PV$

If item is in a special category,

    Then add or subtract correction:

    category = Land         Add 10%

    category = Overhead    Subtract 5%

    category = Labor      Add 15%

End If

Accumulate the total value

End of list

Return the Total value

---

**FIGURE 12.4**
TOP-DOWN AND
BOTTOM-UP DESIGN
The top-down approach begins by examining the entire organization and seeks to improve the overall operations by making changes to the most critical areas. Bottom-up design identifies problems and solves them. By following standards and sharing data through a DBMS, the individual pieces should eventually fit together. Most organizations use a combination of the two methods: top-down to set long-term goals and maintain internal consistency and bottom-up to solve day-to-day problems and to get systems built on time.

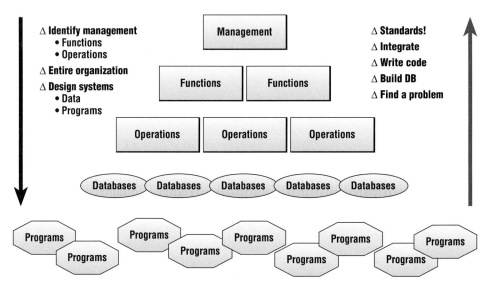

The main purpose of a top-down approach is to examine problems in the context of the entire system. It is particularly useful at comparing problems from different areas of the company. For instance, perhaps problems are found in marketing, accounting, and inventory management. Which problem should be solved first? Are the problems related? If a team works on one problem, can they use the same techniques to solve others? Because a top-down approach examines the entire system, it can answer these questions. The biggest drawback to the top-down approach is that it can take forever—literally. Because of the complexity and the continuous changes in most organizations, it is impossible to build a complete systems model of the organization.

A **bottom-up design** is somewhat like the advertisement: *Just do it.* Whenever a problem arises, the first objective is to solve it. If marketing, accounting, and inventory all need new systems, independent teams are assigned to develop them. The teams work closely with the individual departments but might not interact with each other. The advantage is that each problem gets solved relatively quickly and the users have control over how the system works. The drawback is that the company ends up with different systems that will probably not work together. For example, it will be difficult for the accountants to retrieve data from the marketing department.

Today, most people recognize that systems analysis and development requires a combination of features from both bottom-up and top-down designs. One common approach is to orient systems development to database management systems. The database administrator defines standards. The standards are designed from a top-down perspective to meet the needs of the entire organization. Teams of developers then solve the bottom-up problems of the individual departments. As long as they follow the database standards, the resulting systems should fit together.

Compare these problems to the **data flow diagram (DFD)** techniques introduced in Chapter 3. A DFD has only five elements (and two of those are arrows). It displays an overall view in the first two or three levels, and detailed descriptions are presented with additional levels. It can be built from the top down by starting at the context diagram and filling in each level for the entire company. It can also be built from the bottom up by working on detail views first and combining them into the final set of diagrams. Again, corporate standards are used to ensure that all designers use similar terms and that the pieces fit together.

## The Need for Control

**SYSTEMS DEVELOPMENT LIFE CYCLE**

SDLC was designed to overcome the problems that arose with large projects that involve many users and require thousands of hours of development by multiple analysts and programmers. Difficulties with runaway projects are shown in Figure 12.5. Figure 12.6 highlights some of the causes of the problems.

Before the use of the SDLC method, several related problems were common. It was hard to coordinate and control the various programmers and analysts, so there were duplicated efforts. Individual programmers created portions of a system that would not work together. Users did not always have much input into the process. When they did have

**FIGURE 12.5**
RUNAWAY PROJECTS
Managers fear runaway projects, but they still occur. Some projects end up two to five times over budget and behind schedule. Some projects are canceled because they never meet their objectives. Some fail because of design problems and conflicts among users, management, and developers. An important step in managing projects is to identify when the project becomes a runaway project.

△ **Technical measures**
 • 2 to 5 times over budget
 • 2 to 5 times behind schedule
 • Missing technical objectives

△ **Design problems**
 • Duplication of efforts
 • Incompatibilities
 • User/designer conflicts

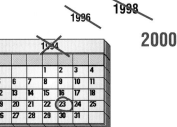

## Business Trends: Temporary Workers

One pattern that caused problems for MIS in the past was the high turnover in the MIS staff. Many times, projects were finished by completely different groups of MIS employees than the ones who began the project. This turnover created a strong need for control on projects to make sure the newcomers could understand the project, and to provide increased communication between the MIS department and the users.

As companies begin to rely on more temporary workers, the same problems arise. If MIS workers take family leaves, they are likely to be assigned a different job on return. Similarly, businesses are using more consultants to create the initial projects. Support and revisions are often performed by other employees. Although the outside contracts simplify the management involvement during the creation of the project, managers need to ensure that certain design standards are followed, and documentation is provided to allow the system to be modified later.

**FIGURE 12.6**
BUDGETS AND
SCHEDULES
In a 1994 study, only
16 percent of 8,000
projects met original
time and budget
estimates. For large
projects, the success
rate dropped to
9 percent. In 1999, it
was reported that 42
percent of U.S.
technology projects are
abandoned.
(*Computerworld,*
March 22, 1999.)

| TOP 5 REASONS FOR SUCCESS | TOP 5 REASONS FOR FAILURE |
|---|---|
| User involvement | Lack of user input |
| Executive management support | Incomplete requirements |
| Clear requirements | Changing requirements and specifications |
| Proper planning | Lack of executive support |
| Realistic expectations | Lack of technical skills |

SOURCE: Adapted from "Few IS Projects Come in on Time, on Budget," by Rosemary Cafasso, *Computerworld,* December 12, 1994, p. 20. Copyright 1994 by Computerworld, Inc., Framingham, MA 01701. Reprinted from *Computerworld.*

input, there were conflicts between users, and analysts did not know which approach to use. With long-term projects, programmers were promoted to other areas or left for different companies. New employees had to learn the system and determine what others had done before they could proceed. Similarly, new users would appear (through promotions and transfers), and existing users would change the specifications of the system. These problems often lead to runaway projects—projects that are significantly late and over budget. Even today, there are many instances of runaway projects.

These problems are related through the issue of control. It is impossible to prevent users from changing the specifications and to prevent employees from taking other jobs. Likewise, large projects involving many analysts and programmers will always have problems with coordination and compatibility. The goal of SDLC was to design a system that can handle all of these problems.

A key value in SDLC is project management. As shown in the appendix to Chapter 13, an important aspect of project management consists of identifying the dependencies among the various tasks. Project management tools exist to help evaluate these dependencies and show how the overall schedule is affected by delays in individual tasks.

### Introduction to SDLC

An important feature of the SDLC approach is that it is a comprehensive method. Some organizations (such as EDS) that specialize in systems development have hundreds of pages in manuals to detail all the steps and rules for using SDLC. Fortunately, it is possible to understand SDLC by looking at a smaller number of steps. As illustrated in Figure 12.7, the

**FIGURE 12.7**
SYSTEMS
DEVELOPMENT
LIFE CYCLE
Sometimes SDLC is
known as the waterfall
methodology because
each step produces
outputs that are used
in the next step. The
existing system is
studied for problems
and improvements. A
new design is analyzed
for feasibility. In-depth
analysis generates the
business requirements.
Systems design turns
them into a technical
design that is
implemented, creating
a new system. This
new system is analyzed
and the process
continues.

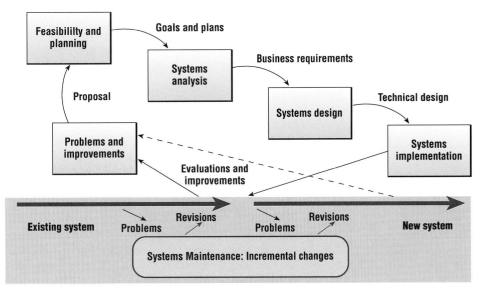

SDLC approach encompasses five basic stages: (1) feasibility and planning, (2) systems analysis, (3) systems design, (4) implementation, and (5) maintenance and review.

Actually, just about any systems development methodology uses these five steps. They differ largely in how much time is spent in each section, who does the work, and in the degree of formality involved. The SDLC is by far the most formal method, so it offers a good starting point in describing the various methodologies.

## Feasibility and Planning

The basic premise of *systems analysis* was presented in Chapter 3. The primary goal of the systems analysis stage is to identify problems and determine how they can be solved with a computer system. In formal SDLC methodologies, the first step in systems analysis is a **feasibility study.** A feasibility study is a quick examination of the problems, goals, and expected costs of the system. The objective is to determine whether the problem can reasonably be solved with a computer system. In some cases, maybe there is a better (or cheaper) alternative, or perhaps the problem is simply a short-term annoyance and will gradually disappear. In other cases, the problem may turn out to be more complex than was thought and involves users across the company. Also, some problems may not be solvable with today's technology. It might be better to wait for improved technology or lower prices. In any case, you need to determine the scope of the project to gain a better idea of the costs, benefits, and objectives.

The feasibility study is typically written so that it can be easily understood by nonprogrammers. It is used to "sell" the project to upper management and as a starting point for the next step. Additionally, it is used as a reference to keep the project on track, and to evaluate the progress of the MIS team. Projects are typically evaluated in three areas of feasibility: economics, operations, and technical. Is the project cost effective or is there a cheaper solution? Will the proposed system improve the operations of the firm, or will complicating factors prevent it from achieving its goals? Does the technology exist, and does the firm have the staff to make the technology work?

When the proposal is determined to be feasible, the MIS team leaders are appointed and a plan and schedule are created. The schedule contains a detailed listing of what parts of the project will be completed at each time. Of course, it is extremely difficult to estimate the true costs and completion dates. Nonetheless, the schedule is an important tool to evaluate the status of the project and the progress of the MIS teams. Figure 12.8 summarizes the role of planning and scheduling in providing control for projects.

## Systems Analysis

Once a project has been shown to be feasible and it is approved, work can begin on a full-fledged analysis. The first step is to determine how the existing system works and where the problems are located. The technique is to break the system into pieces. Smaller pieces are easier to understand and to explain to others. Also, each piece can be assigned to a different MIS team. As long as they work from the same initial description and follow all of the standards, the resulting pieces should fit back together. Of course, it still takes time and effort to integrate all of the pieces.

Diagrams are often created to illustrate the system. The diagrams are used to communicate among analysts and users, other analysts, and eventually the programmers. Data flow diagrams are a common method to display the relationships that were determined during systems analysis. The diagrams represent a way to divide the system into smaller pieces.

Graphics tools provide a useful way to communicate with the user and to document the user requirements. However, they do not speed up the development process. Producing, changing, and storing documentation can be a significant problem. Yet these tools are necessary because they make it easier for the user to control the final result. One increasingly common solution is to keep all of the documentation on the computer. This method reduces the costs, makes it easier for everyone to share the documentation, and ensures that all users have up-to-date information for the system.

At the end of the analysis phase, the MIS team will have a complete description of the business requirements. The problems and needs are documented with text, data flow diagrams, and other figures depending on the methodology followed.

**FIGURE 12.8**
DEVELOPMENT
CONTROLS

A complex system requires careful management. Without planning and control, any project will become a runaway. Control begins with a detailed plan and performance targets that enable managers to evaluate progress and identify problems. System control is provided by standardized practices and procedures to ensure that teams are producing compatible output. User input and control ensure that the final project will actually be useful.

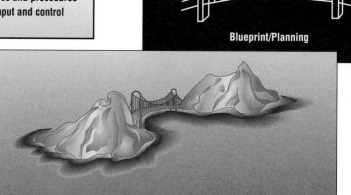

- **Detailed work plan**
- **Performance targets**
- **Practices and procedures**
- **User input and control**

**Blueprint/Planning**

## Systems Design

The third major step of the SDLC is to design the new system. During this step, the new system is typically designed on paper. The objective of *systems design* is to describe the new system as a collection of modules or subsystems. By subdividing the total project, each portion can be given to a single programmer to develop. As the pieces are completed, the overall design ensures that they will work together. Typically, the diagrams created during the analysis phase can be modified to indicate how the new system will work. The design will list all of the details, including data inputs, system outputs, processing steps, database designs, manual procedures, and feedback and control mechanisms. Backup and recovery plans along with security controls will be spelled out to ensure that the database is protected.

In traditional SDLC methods, managers and users will be shown various components of the system as they are completed. The managers will have to *sign off* on these sections to indicate that they meet the user needs. This signature is designed to ensure that users provide input to the system. If there are many diverse users, there can be major disagreements about how the system should function. Sign-offs require users to negotiate and formally agree to the design. It is relatively easy to make design changes at this stage. If everyone attempts to make changes at later stages, the cost increases dramatically.

In terms of physical design, some of the hardware and software will be purchased. Programmers will write and test the program code. In most large projects, the actual coding takes only 15 to 30 percent of the total development time. Initial data will be collected or transferred from existing systems. Manuals and procedures will be written to instruct users and system operators on how to use the system.

Once the designer has created base modules and sample inputs and outputs, the users are invited to a structured walkthrough. A **structured walkthrough** is a review process where the objective is to reveal problems, inaccuracies, ambiguities, and omissions in the systems design before the program code is finalized. The users are presented with a prototype or mockup of the proposed system. It is easier to spot problems and make suggestions by observing how the actual system might appear.

Design tools can be used to create prototypes of major system elements. For example, a designer can quickly piece together displays that illustrate how each screen might look and how the user will see the system. The number of walkthroughs used depends on the amount of time users and programmers can spend on reviewing the designs. The walkthroughs also provide management with feedback regarding the time schedule and anticipated costs of the project, because they are often scheduled in the original feasibility study.

The output of the design stage consists of a complete technical specification of the new system. It includes as many details as possible—sometimes leading to thousands of pages (or computer files) of description.

One of the difficulties in the design stage is sometimes called "creeping elegance." As the system is being built analysts, programmers, and users all want to include additional features. Although many of the features are good ideas, the continual evolution of the system causes additional delays. It also complicates testing, because changes in one section can affect the rest of the system.

## Systems Implementation

Systems implementation involves installation and changeover from the previous system to the new one, including training users and making adjustments to the system. The major

**FIGURE 12.9**
SYSTEMS
IMPLEMENTATION
When changing
operations with a new
system, you must be
careful to encourage
users to change. An
important step in
making a smooth
transition is to involve
the users at every step
of the design, and make
the system flexible
enough to adapt to
different users.
Education and training,
sufficient testing, and
formal plans all make
for easier
implementations.

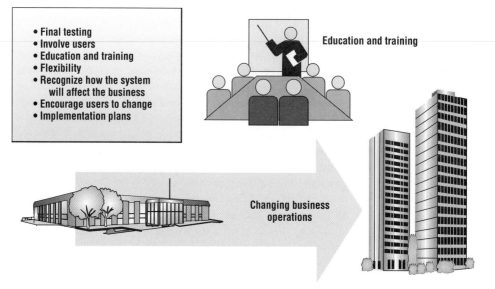

- Final testing
- Involve users
- Education and training
- Flexibility
- Recognize how the system
    will affect the business
- Encourage users to change
- Implementation plans

Education and training

Changing business operations

issues are summarized in Figure 12.9. Many nasty problems can arise at this stage. You have to be extremely careful in implementing new systems. First, users are probably nervous about the change already. If something goes wrong, they may never trust the new system. Second, if major errors occur, you could lose important business data.

A crucial stage in implementation is final testing. Testing and quality control must be performed at every stage of development, but a final systems test is needed before staff entrust the company's data to the new system. Occasionally, small problems will be noted, but their resolution will be left for later. In any large system, there are bound to be errors and changes. The key is to identify them and determine which ones must be fixed immediately. Smaller problems are often left to the software maintenance staff.

Change is an important part of MIS. Designing and implementing new systems often causes changes in the business operations. Yet, many people do not like changes. Changes require learning new methods, forging new relationships with people and managers, or perhaps even loss of jobs. Changes exist on many levels: in society, in business, and in information systems. Changes can occur because of shifts in the environment, or they can be introduced by internal **change agents.** Left to themselves, most organizations will resist even small changes. Change agents are objects or people who cause or facilitate changes. Sometimes it might be a new employee who brings fresh ideas; other times changes can be mandated by top-level management. Sometimes an outside event such as arrival of a new competitor or a natural disaster forces an organization to change. Whatever the cause, people tend to resist change. However, if organizations do not change, they cannot survive. The goal is to implement systems in a manner that recognizes resistance to change but encourages people to accept the new system. Effective implementation involves finding ways to reduce this resistance. Sometimes, implementation involves the cooperation of outsiders such as suppliers.

### Involve Users

An important process in reducing resistance to change is to involve the users in the design of the new system, which yields three main advantages. First, the users will get the system they need. Second, the users will understand the project better and it will be easier to use. Third, user contributions provide a sense of ownership, minimizing **user resistance** and promoting use of the final system.

At a minimum, user participation can begin by allowing users to design the reports and customize the input screens. Even moderately trained users can create report layouts and sample input screens using spreadsheets, word processors, or database management systems. Early involvement by users helps ensure that the users get worthwhile systems that are easier to use. Additionally, it gives them more time to adapt to the concept of change and see how it might benefit them.

Keep in mind that many computer systems are designed to improve the business operations and reduce costs. Often, these improvements arise by eliminating jobs. In these cases, it is hard to expect users to be enthusiastic about the new system. They are not likely to be cooperative if they are asked to help design the system that takes away their jobs. Even if employees are promised jobs in other areas, they are likely to be apprehensive about the changes. When jobs do need to be cut, experience from layoff specialists shows that it is best to determine job cuts up front and establish a clear policy before you begin implementing the new system.

### Education and Training

Anyone except aggressive risk takers will be nervous about a new system if they know nothing about it. A key component of any implementation strategy is user education and training. Even generic education courses that explain how computers work and how they can help are useful. Specific training classes on the actual system are even more useful. Many companies pay for training when it directly affects an employee's job. Companies also encourage workers to continue their general education by covering at least some of the costs.

Training classes give managers the chance to answer questions from the users and minimize the amount of misinformation floating through the grapevine. Additionally, the MIS development team gets feedback on the system and can make last-minute changes or record suggestions for future enhancements.

In some cases, a variety of training methods should be scheduled. Some experienced users may prefer a simple handout explaining the goals and the primary commands available. Some users will need extensive personal support and encouragement. Some companies are experimenting with video and multimedia training tools. For example, a personal computer tutoring system could be used to simulate the operation of the new system. Users can work at their own pace and are quizzed periodically to see whether they understand the basic operations. In addition to being accessible 24 hours a day, some people might feel more comfortable with computer training, especially if they can study at home or in their office. No one needs to know if they make mistakes, and they can ask "silly" questions without being embarrassed.

### Flexibility

It is important that systems be flexible so the users can adjust them. Simple things like being able to set screen colors, mouse sensitivity, and keyboard speed can be critical to keeping users happy. They are also useful for users with physical challenges. Some people have difficulty seeing certain colors and they are much more productive if they can choose their own colors.

The items that can be controlled by users will be different for each system. For instance, sometimes users may be allowed to change report titles or even calculations. In other cases, these variables may be governed by legal or security constraints. The key is to give the users as much control as possible while maintaining the integrity of the data. An added benefit from this flexibility is that if users are able to make their own changes, there will be less need for system changes later.

### Recognize How the System Will Affect the Business

Computer systems often change the way the business operates. These changes are not always anticipated. For example, when ATMs were installed in banks, the goal was to give customers easier access to their money. A second objective was to decrease the bank's operational costs by decreasing the workload on the human tellers. Early bank studies indicated that each ATM transaction cost the bank $0.50, whereas a human teller cost the bank $1 per transaction. Initially consumers were reluctant to change, but they eventually shifted transactions to the ATMs, primarily for simple deposits and withdrawals. However, human tellers are now dealing with more complicated transactions, making their jobs more difficult. As a bank manager, if you simply looked at the number of transactions processed by tellers before ATMs and after ATMs, you might conclude that the tellers were less productive. By failing to notice the change in complexity, you would make bad decisions.

In general, technology has traditionally created more jobs for society. However, they are almost always different jobs, usually in different industries. Hence, some workers can lose their jobs. Additionally, the newly created jobs may require more education, or might be in a different state, or even another country. Some workers will not want to change jobs. Others, especially in dual-income families, will have difficulty moving to new areas.

---

### Reality Bytes     12–2    Transaction Processing at Daiwa Bank

In 1995, Kiyoshi Maenaka returned to Daiwa Bank's computer department after spending seven years in a branch office. He found that almost nothing had changed in seven years. Later that year, Toshihide Iguchi, a bond trader working for Daiwa in New York, admitted that for 11 years he had been forging paper documents to hide his trading losses. Using documents that most U.S. banks had replaced with electronic systems years ago, Iguchi's scheme cost the bank more than $1 billion.

At the same time, Daiwa Bank was racking up more than $8 billion in bad loans. Bank operations in Japan have been extremely labor intensive but not necessarily customer-friendly. For example, an usher would show customers to their seats, but doors would close at 3 P.M., and ATM machines would be shut down at night. Even at some of the world's largest banks, loans would have to be signed by up to five people, and loan applications were routinely mailed between offices. It was not until 1998 that Sanwa, the world's ninth largest bank, bought a mainframe computer so it could start performing credit-risk analysis. Almost none of the Asian banks have systems in place to analyze customer needs to help with credit analysis and

marketing promotions. In contrast, Citibank, based in New York, with offices throughout the world, uses computer systems to monitor five types of risk, as well as the overall bank's involvement with any one customer, industry, or country. Citibank's director of regional operations in Singapore, Venky Krishnakumar, notes that "technology in operations is becoming the competitive weapon these days."

Other Japanese banks face similar problems. These problems are difficult to solve because of the Japanese culture and attitude toward employment and workers. For example, consultants from A. T. Kearney were called in by one bank to make its 30 processing centers more efficient. They found that most of the work was done by hand. For example, one employee was dedicated to taking deposit slips from an armored truck, sifting through them, and dividing them by transaction type. Other employees would sit at desks and shuffle transaction slips from various branches. When the consultants suggested improvements, the only thing the bank managers would accept was asking employees to stand up instead of sitting down. Daiwa Bank ultimately chose to outsource their operations to IBM, thereby avoiding many of the issues by starting from scratch.

**FIGURE 12.10**
CONVERSION
OPTIONS

When you implement a new system, there are several possible conversion methods. In most cases, direct cutover should be avoided because of the disruptions and potential for lost data. Parallel conversion entails running both systems simultaneously, which is safe but can become expensive and time consuming. With multiple stores or business units, pilot introductions of phased implementations are common. For pilot testing, designers can bring extra workers, managers, and systems designers to one location and work out the problems with the system. Once the system is running well, it can be implemented at other locations. With a phased implementation, a system can be introduced slowly throughout the company (e.g., by department). Projects can also be phased in by modules.

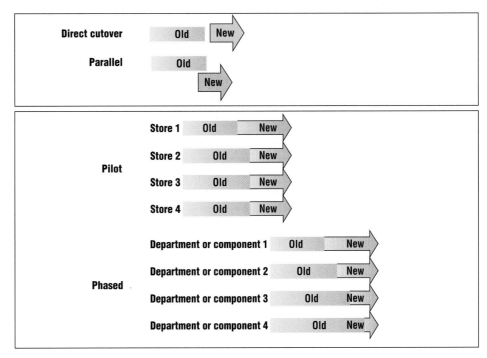

These changes have to be communicated to the users as soon as possible. The more opportunity employees have to adjust to the changes, the easier it will be for them. Several firms exist for the sole purpose of providing support for displaced workers. They help these workers search for new jobs and find educational or retraining opportunities.

### Encourage Users to Change

A common management technique is to make sure that the payment system incentives match the goals of the organization. Consider the situation of a bank teller. Perhaps a portion of the teller's pay is based on the number of transactions processed in a day. When ATMs are installed, if a manager concludes that teller productivity has declined, the tellers might be denied raises or promotions. A teller who foresees this problem would definitely resist the adoption of ATMs. One solution is to change the payment structure so the tellers are not penalized for the changing nature of their jobs.

Even if the business operations are not substantially altered, implementing a new system can cause reduced productivity while employees learn to operate the new system. Employees whose pay is based on performance will resist changes, because even a temporary decline in productivity will result in less money. A common solution is to provide additional training to help the users learn the system faster. During the training period, it might be appropriate to base employee pay on original productivity levels.

### Implementation Plans

Because implementation is so important, several techniques have been developed to help implement new systems. Direct cutover is an obvious technique, where the old system is simply dropped and the new one started. If at all possible, it is best to avoid this technique, because it is the most dangerous to data. If anything goes wrong with the new system, you run the risk of losing valuable information because the old system is not available. The various methods are displayed in Figure 12.10.

In many ways, the safest choice is to use parallel implementation. In this case, the new system is introduced alongside the old one. Both systems are operated at the same time until you determine that the new system is acceptable. The main drawback to this method is that it can be expensive because data has to be entered twice. Additionally, if users are nervous about the new system, they might avoid the change and stick with the old method. In this case, the new system may never get a fair trial.

Several intermediate possibilities are called phased implementation. For example, if you design a system for a chain of retail stores, you could pilot test the first implementation in one store. By working with one store at a time, there are likely to be fewer problems. But, if problems do arise, you will have more staff members around to overcome the obstacles. When the system is working well in one store, you can move to the next location. Similarly, even if there is only one store, you might be able to split the implementation into sections based on the area of business. You might install a set of computer cash registers first. When they work correctly, you can connect them to a central computer and produce daily reports. Next, you can move on to annual summaries and payroll. Eventually the entire system will be installed.

## Maintenance

Once the system is installed, the MIS job has just begun. Computer systems are constantly changing. Hardware upgrades occur continuously, and commercial software tools may change every year. Users change jobs. Errors may exist in the system. The business changes, and management and users demand new information and expansions. All of these actions mean the system needs to be modified. The job of overseeing and making these modifications is called **software maintenance.**

The pressures for change are so great that in most organizations today as much as 80 percent of the MIS staff is devoted to modifying existing programs. These changes can be time consuming and difficult. Most major systems were created by teams of programmers and analysts over a long period. In order to make a change to a program, the programmer has to understand how the current program works. Because the program was written by many different people with varying styles, it can be hard to understand. Finally, when a programmer makes a minor change in one location it can affect another area of the program, which can cause additional errors or necessitate more changes.

One difficulty with software maintenance is that every time part of an application is modified, there is a risk of adding defects (bugs). Also, over time the application becomes less structured and more complex, making it harder to understand. These are some of the main reasons why the year 2000 alterations were so expensive and time consuming. At some point, a company may decide to replace or improve the heavily modified system. There are several techniques for improving an existing system, ranging from rewriting individual sections to restructuring the entire application. The difference lies in scope—how much of the application needs to be modified. Older applications that were subject to modifications over several years tend to contain code that is no longer used, poorly documented changes, and inconsistent naming conventions. These applications are prime candidates for restructuring, during which the entire code is analyzed and reorganized to make it more efficient. More importantly, the code is organized, standardized, and documented to make it easier to make changes in the future.

## Evaluation

An important phase in any project is evaluating the resulting system. As part of this evaluation, it is also important to assess the effectiveness of the particular development process. There are several questions to ask. Were the initial cost estimates accurate? Was the project completed on time? Did users have sufficient input? Are maintenance costs higher than expected? The assessment items are summarized in Figure 12.11.

Evaluation is a difficult issue. How can you as a manager tell the difference between a good system and a poor one? In some way, the system should decrease costs, increase revenue, or provide a competitive advantage. Although these effects are important, they are often subtle and difficult to measure. The system should also be easy to use and flexible enough to adapt to changes in the business. If employees or customers continue to complain about a system, it should be reexamined.

A system also needs to be *reliable.* It should be available when needed and should produce accurate output. Error detection can be provided in the system to recognize and avoid common problems. Similarly, some systems can be built to tolerate errors, so that when errors arise, the system recognizes the problem and works around it. For example, some computers exist today that automatically switch to backup components when one section fails, thereby exhibiting **fault tolerance.**

An important concept for managers to remember when dealing with new systems is that the evaluation mechanism should be determined at the start of the project. Far too often, the question of evaluation is ignored until someone questions the value of the finished product. It is a good design practice to ask What would make this system a good system when it is finished? or, How can we tell a good system from a bad one in this application? Even though these questions may be difficult to answer, they need to be asked. The answers, however incomplete, will provide valuable guidance during the design stage.

Recall that every system needs a goal, a way of measuring progress toward that goal, and a feedback mechanism. Traditionally, control of systems has been the task of the computer programming staff. Their primary goal was to create error-free code, and they used various testing techniques to find and correct errors in the code. Today, creating error-free code is not a sufficient goal.

We have all heard the phrase, "The customer is always right." The meaning behind this phrase is that sometimes people have different opinions on whether a system is behaving correctly. When there is a conflict, the opinion that is most important is that of the customer. In the final analysis, customers are in control because they can always take their business elsewhere. With information systems, the users are the customers and the users should be the ones in control. Users determine whether a system is good. If the users are not convinced that the system performs useful tasks, it is not a good system.

**FIGURE 12.11**
EVALUATION
OF COMPLETED
PROJECTS
When projects are completed, the design team should evaluate the project and assess the development procedures. Cost and time estimates can be used to improve estimates for future projects. System performance issues can be addressed with future upgrades. It is important that the system achieve project goals and provide users with necessary tools and support.

| FEASIBILITY COMPARISON | |
|---|---|
| Cost and Budget | Compare actual costs to budget estimates. |
| Time Estimates | Was project completed on time? |
| Revenue Effects | Does system produce additional revenue? |
| Maintenance Costs | How much money and time are spent on changes? |
| Project Goals | Does system meet the initial goals of the project? |
| User Satisfaction | How do users (and management) evaluate the system? |
| SYSTEM PERFORMANCE | |
| System Reliability | Are the results accurate and on time? |
| System Availability | Is the system available on a continuous basis? |
| System Security | Does the system provide access to authorized users? |

## Strengths and Weaknesses of SDLC

The primary purpose of the SDLC method of designing systems is to provide guidance and control over the development process. As summarized in Figure 12.12, there are strengths and weaknesses to this methodology. SDLC management control is vital for large projects to ensure that the individual teams work together. There are also financial controls to keep track of the project expenses. The SDLC steps are often spelled out in great detail. The formality makes it easier to train employees and to evaluate the progress of the development. It also ensures that steps are not skipped—such as user approval, documentation, and testing. For large, complex projects, this degree of control is necessary to ensure the project can be completed. Another advantage of SDLC is that by adhering to standards while building the system, programmers will find the system easier to modify and maintain later. The internal consistency and documentation make it easier to modify. With 80 percent of MIS resources spent on maintenance, this advantage can be critical.

In some cases the formality of SDLC causes problems. Most importantly, it increases the cost of development and lengthens the development time. Remember that often less than 25 percent of the time is spent on actually writing programs. A great deal of the rest of the time is spent filling out forms and drawing diagrams.

The formality of the SDLC also causes problems with projects that are hard to define. SDLC works best if the entire system can be accurately specified in the beginning. That is, users and managers need to know *exactly* what the system should do long before the system is created. That is not a serious problem with transaction-processing systems. However, consider the development of a complex decision support system. Initially, the users may not know how the system can help. Only through working with the system on actual problems will they spot errors and identify enhancements.

Although some large projects could never have been completed without SDLC, its rigidity tends to make it difficult to develop many modern applications. Additionally, experience has shown that it has not really solved the problems of projects being over budget and late. As a result of this criticism, many people are searching for alternatives. One possibility is to keep the basic SDLC in place and use technology to make it more efficient. Other suggestions have been to replace the entire process with a more efficient development process, such as prototyping. Consider the assistance of technology first.

**FIGURE 12.12
STRENGTHS AND
WEAKNESSES
OF SDLC**
The SDLC
methodologies were
created to control
large, complex
development projects.
They work fairly well
for those types of
processes. SDLC does
not work as well for
small projects that
require rapid
development or heavy
user involvement with
many changes.

| STRENGTHS | WEAKNESSES |
|---|---|
| Control | Increased development time |
| Monitor large projects | Increased development costs |
| Detailed steps | Systems must be defined up front |
| Evaluate costs and completion targets | Rigidity |
| Documentation | Hard to estimate costs, project overruns |
| Well-defined user input | User input is sometimes limited |
| Ease of maintenance | |
| Development and design standards | |
| Tolerates changes in MIS staffing | |

**CASE TOOLS: CAN TECHNOLOGY HELP MIS?**

Software development with SDLC can be time consuming and expensive. In the past few years, several new software tools have been developed to help MIS in these tasks. They fall under the heading of **computer-aided software engineering (CASE).** There are two main categories of CASE tools: one for software development and another for maintaining existing systems. Similar to Kaiser Permanente, many companies have a substantial backlog of MIS projects that could take years to complete. They are searching for ways to help them design and build systems faster.

Sophisticated CASE tools, like Rose, Designer 2000, and IEF, combine both categories of features. For system development, CASE tools help analysts draw and maintain several types of diagrams, including data flow diagrams. Screen editors are used to design reports and data-entry screens. The software automatically creates a data dictionary that can be used to enforce design standards and share information among team members. CASE tools today can use all of this information to create the final source code. The computer does the actual programming based on the design specifications. Besides saving time, it eliminates one source of errors.

In terms of maintenance, some exciting software tools are available. The basic technique is called **reverse engineering.** In reverse engineering, the goal is to take older software (sometimes known as **legacy systems**) and rewrite it to modernize it and make it easier to modify and enhance. Reverse engineering tools consist of software that reads the program code from the original software. For example, if a programmer is asked to modify the payroll program, she could first use the CASE tool to examine the payroll software. This tool will put the payroll package into modern structured code, drop unused code, highlight the sections that are heavily used, and standardize all of the variable names. Some software can even create the underlying diagrams, input screens, and reports. Then the programmer can make changes to these design documents and rebuild the program automatically.

**Version control** tools also make it easier to design and modify systems and programs. Tools like *Source Safe* are a database that store different versions of the software. They also track who made changes to each component. If problems arise, it is relatively easy to go back to a prior version and start again.

One other tool that is available to the MIS department is a database management system (DBMS), usually coupled with a fourth-generation language. Using this tool instead of an older language such as COBOL can be as much as 10 times faster. It is easier to

## Kaiser Permanente HMO

Kaiser Permanente, the largest health maintenance organization (HMO) in the United States, is using computer-aided software engineering (CASE) technology to improve efficiency and cut administrative and health care costs. The systems development area views this as a better way to improve the quality of the systems in a shorter time frame than traditional programming.

Before the CASE program began at Kaiser, the programming backlog was more than 100 workyears.

As a result, the company implemented Texas Instruments' Information Engineering Facility (IEF) as its integrated CASE product. The changeover to CASE paralleled the purchase of intelligent workstations to replace terminals. Kaiser sees the CASE implementation as an essential component of its strategic plan to remain viable in the competitive health care market. CASE tools will enable Kaiser to respond more quickly to the demands of an increasingly demanding health care environment.

create sophisticated programs with fewer errors. The database systems also allow some portability so that if the company buys a new computer, the old data and software can be transferred to it with only minor changes. Finally, both end users and MIS workers can use the DBMS to answer many questions without needing to write a computer program.

One drawback to CASE tools is that they are relatively expensive, both for the software and the training for the MIS department. CASE tools increase MIS productivity, but only if the workers are fully trained in the development methodology.

**PROTOTYPING AND RAPID APPLICATION DEVELOPMENT (RAD)**

Prototyping has been proposed as a method to use for systems that are not overly complex and do not involve too many users or analysts. Just as automobile engineers design prototypes before attempting to build the final car, MIS programmers can build early versions of systems. These systems are then continually modified until the user is satisfied.

The first step in designing a system via prototyping is to talk with the user. The analyst then uses a fourth-generation language and a DBMS to create approximately what the user wants. This first step generally requires only a couple of weeks. The business user then works with the prototype and suggests changes. The analyst makes the changes and this cycle repeats until the user is satisfied or decides that the system is not worth pursuing. The emphasis is on getting a working version of the system to the user as fast as possible, even if it does not have all the details. Figure 12.13 illustrates the cycle involved in prototyping.

The major advantage of prototyping is that users receive a working system much sooner than they would with the SDLC method. Additionally, the users have more input so they are more likely to get what they wanted. Finally, remember that a large portion of MIS time is spent making changes. A system designed with the prototyping method is much easier to change because it was designed to be modified from the start.

In the early stages of design, a prototype is analogous to the scale models that automobile and aircraft designers use for wind-tunnel tests or to the cardboard scale models that architects use to show potential buyers what the finished building will look like. The initial mockup may not actually have any computer code. It might be a collection of input

**FIGURE 12.13**
PROTOTYPING
Prototyping typically involves one user and one developer. The developer interviews the user and designs an initial system using a DBMS. The user works with the prototype and suggests changes. This process repeats until the user or developer is satisfied or gives up.

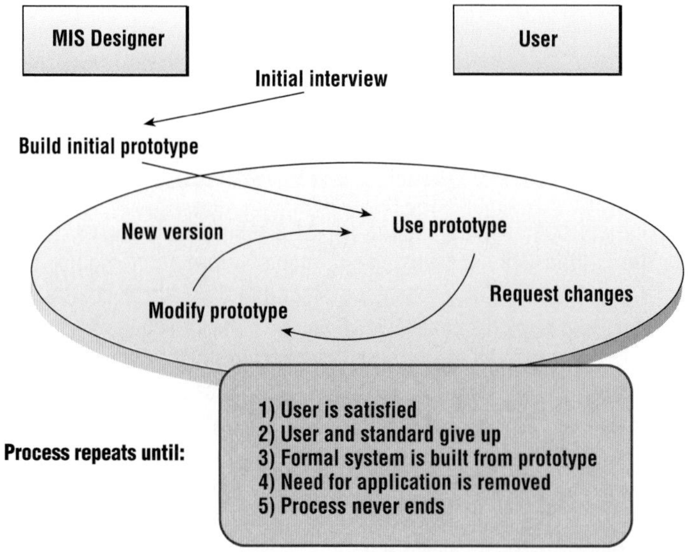

screens and reports that look like they were produced by the computer system. The primary value of these simulated results is to enable the user to actually see the planned results. Users often have difficulty telling designers what they want beforehand. They can react to sample output by saying what they like or dislike, or what needs to be added to the output to make it more useful to the end user.

With today's latest development tools, however, the prototype may be more than a mockup. It may be used to create a substantial portion of the final code. Using CASE tools and database management systems, error-free code can be generated almost instantly from the prototype descriptions. These tools also build documentation automatically, making it easier for the designer and the maintenance programmer.

Tools available for prototyping include presentation tools, which can show a series of computer screens and demonstrate the look and feel of the finished product. More powerful fourth-generation languages and database management systems can generate actual applications including input files, interactive screens, reports, and executable code without requiring programming. Other specialized tools such as expert system shells enable the designer to work with complex logical rules to create a finished product for certain types of applications.

The process of building a preliminary prototype, trying it out, refining it, and trying again is referred to as the *iterative process* of systems development. In the traditional SDLC approach, there was some iteration, but it is limited to a defined stage. The formal sign-off procedure was instituted specifically to restrict changes beyond some point in the development cycle. With the prototyping approach, iteration is planned and modern prototyping tools make it easy to modify the application. Further, because the prototyping tools allow a preliminary model to be created much faster, the user gets a working model much earlier in the design process. Therefore, the repeated changes are less likely to delay the completion.

Prototyping is especially helpful in situations where there will be heavy user interaction with the system, where the needed output is uncertain, and in some decision support

Developing systems is generally a team effort among MIS developers and business users. Groupware, CASE, and development tools are often used to facilitate communication and coordination.

applications where the logic is hard to determine in advance. Prototyping fosters a spirit of experimentation. It does not matter if there is some uncertainty regarding the path to the desired results or even uncertainty about the desired results. Prototyping enables you to try out a possible solution to see how it flies and to keep repeating this process until users are satisfied.

Prototyping does have some drawbacks and complications. First, problems arise if several users are involved. Imagine what happens if each user wants different changes and they cannot agree on how the system should behave. One of the reasons for user sign-offs in SDLC is to force users to agree before you create the system. For large projects, several different prototypes of reports and input screens could be used to help users evaluate the various choices.

There are some more subtle drawbacks to prototyping. Picture yourself as an MIS manager where the analysts all use prototyping exclusively. Most of the time the analysts are talking with the users and making simple changes. How do you know when the project is finished? How do you know whether the analyst is a hard worker or just making endless minor changes? How do you tell a user to stop making trivial changes? Under the SDLC method, you have predefined targets (milestones) and you know exactly what each person is supposed to accomplish. As a manager responsible for completing projects and allocating raises, which method would you prefer?

**Rapid application development (RAD)** bears some similarities to prototyping, but it attempts to maintain more control. The objective is to follow a more formal project approach but find the steps that can be reduced or performed at the same time. Using high-level languages, database systems, project management software, workgroup software, and CASE tools, highly trained programmers can build systems in a matter of weeks or months.

## DEVELOPING SYSTEMS REQUIRES TEAMWORK

Designing and developing systems is much easier if the entire system can be built by one person. In fact, that is one of the strengths of recent tools—they enable a single person to build more complex systems. However, many information systems—especially those that affect the entire organization—require teams of IS workers. As soon as multiple designers, analysts, and programmers are involved, we encounter management and communication problems. MIS researchers have measured the effects of these problems. One study by DeMarco and Lister showed that on large projects, 70 percent of a developer's time is spent working with others. Jones noted that team activities accounted for 85 percent of the development costs. There seem to be substantial areas for improvement in systems development by focusing on teamwork. One of the most difficult steps in creating any new system is determining the user requirements. What does the system need to do and how will it work? This step is crucial. If the designers make a mistake here, the system will either be useless or will need expensive modifications later. Prototyping and SDLC take different approaches to this problem. With SDLC, analysts talk with users and write reports that describe how the system will operate. Users examine the reports and make changes. This approach is time-consuming and difficult for users because they only see paper notes of the proposed system. Prototyping overcomes some of the problems by letting users work with actual screens and reports. But use of prototyping is hard to expand beyond one or two users.

Some companies overcome the problems of SDLC by prototyping each input screen and report with one or two primary users. Once the main concepts have been designed, the analysts formalize the system and get approval from other users. The designs are then given to programmers to create with the traditional SDLC development methods.

## Reality Bytes    12–3    Testing Programmers

By 2000, the demand for computer programmers was skyrocketing. Some estimates showed a shortage of about 300,000 people. Western Europe has a shortage of more than 500,000 IT workers. U.S. computer science and information system programs graduate approximately 30,000 new programmers each year—only one-tenth the number of people needed. Some of the additional people come from other disciplines. In many situations, it is easier to take someone who understands the application and train them to become programmers. Of course, these nontraditionally trained individuals can find it difficult to get other jobs. They must first convince potential employers that they have the needed skills. Likewise, from the standpoint of businesses, managers want some assurance that their employees are qualified.

The same situation exists for the increasing number of small contract-programming shops. Two types of answers have evolved because of these patterns. First, several of the major technology providers (e.g., Microsoft and Novell) offer certification programs. Workers who study a specific technology, pay about $100, and pass a test, can claim certification in a specific area. The second method is similar, some employers ask job applicants to take an exam on a specific technology. For example, the product Skiltest (www.skiltest.com) offers exams in several areas, like C++. The testing system, developed by Madcat software, presents the exams over the Internet. Job applicants review the particular technology on their own and then use their Internet browsers to take the timed exam. While there are no strict pass/fail guidelines, applicants with higher scores tend to be better programmers; hence, they are more likely to get the job.

Recall that an important reason for using SDLC is to obtain the views and agreement of many users. Using traditional interview methods and paper documentation, this process often takes several months. Each change has to be reexamined by other users, and disagreements have to be resolved.

A technique known as **joint application design (JAD)** was created to speed up the design stage. With JAD the main system is designed in an intense three- to five-day workshop. Users, managers, and systems analysts participate in a series of intense meetings to design the inputs (data and screens) and outputs (reports) needed by the new system.

By putting all of the decision makers in one room at the same time, conflicts are identified and resolved faster. Users and managers gain a better understanding of the problems and limitations of technology. The resulting system has greater value for users and managers because it more closely matches their needs. There is less need for changes later, when they become more expensive, so the system is cheaper to create.

The biggest drawback to JAD is that it requires getting everyone together at the same time for an extended period of time. Even for moderately complex systems, the meetings can run eight hours a day for three to five days. Most managers (and users) find it difficult to be away from their jobs for that length of time. Higher-level managers are also needed at these meetings to ensure the system provides the appropriate reports and information. Finally, the meetings can only succeed if they are led by a trained facilitator. The facilitator keeps the discussions moving in the right direction, minimizes conflicts, and encourages everyone to participate. At the end of the sessions, the systems development team should have a complete description of the proposed system. CASE tools are often useful in taking notes, building sample screens, and creating report layouts.

**FIGURE 12.14**
SDLC VERSUS
OBJECT ORIENTED
Initial design of an object-oriented approach takes more effort than with SDLC. However, once the objects are properly defined, it is much easier to create and implement a new system.

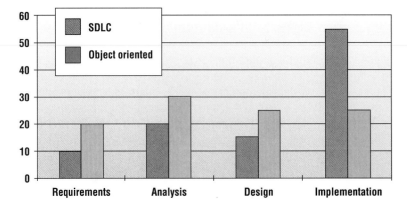

## OBJECT-ORIENTED AND EVENT-DRIVEN DEVELOPMENT

The concept of **object-oriented development** has received considerable attention during the past few years. In some ways, the base design techniques are not much different from traditional SDLC techniques. In other ways, object orientation requires a completely new way of thinking about systems development. The ultimate goal of the object-oriented approach is to build a set of *reusable* objects and procedures. The idea is that eventually, it should be possible to create new systems or modify old ones simply by plugging in a new module or modifying an existing object.

An *object* can be anything from an icon on a computer screen to an accounting statement. Objects have a set of characteristics or attributes, and methods or operations that can be performed on objects. Remember that properties and methods are *inherited*. New objects based on other objects acquire the same properties and methods. Designers need only define the additional properties and functions that make the new objects different. Once the base *classes* (collections of objects) are defined, new objects can be created with minimal effort.

One key difference between object orientation and other development methods is the way processes or functions are handled. With objects, all functions are *embedded* in the definition of the object—the object comes first. The object approach reverses the treatment of processes and data. With SDLC, illustrated by a data flow diagram, the emphasis is on processes, and data (attributes) is passed between processes.

One goal of an object-oriented approach is to create a set of information system building blocks. These objects and procedures could be purchased from commercial software companies (such as a spreadsheet from Microsoft or a database system from Oracle). MIS programmers or consultants can create additional objects tailored for your specific company or department. Once the basic blocks are in place, end users or MIS analysts can select the individual pieces to create a complete system. Hence, as Figure 12.14 indicates, less time is needed for implementation, as long as the analysis and design are performed carefully. On the other hand, the up-front costs of designing and building these objects can be quite high. Additionally, the tools and techniques tend to require substantial retraining of the existing MIS staff. Both of these types of costs have caused some companies to avoid object-oriented methods.

Although object-oriented techniques are still being developed, many companies are already headed in this direction. One effect of this type of development is that much of the traditional programming is moved to commercial companies that specialize in creat-

**FIGURE 12.15**
OBJECTS AND EVENTS
Most modern systems
are event driven in the
sense that the
programs are written
as small modules that
are triggered when
some event happens.
Instead of writing some
monolithic code that
controls every user
action, developers
create objects whose
functions are executed
in response to a
change in the business
environment or at the
direction of the user.

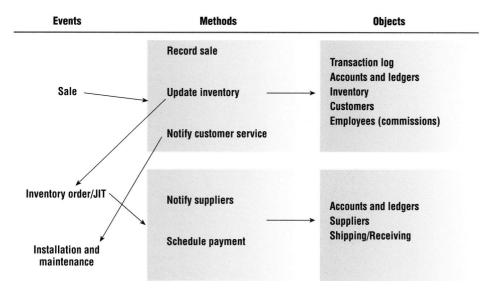

ing software components. Other companies hire analysts who focus on the business needs and put together the appropriate modules. These analysts need to understand business, be able to identify problems, and know how information systems can be used to solve them.

Another new feature of modern programming is the emergence of **event-driven systems.** In older programs, the programmer was responsible for building a complete, sequential program that defined and controlled every step taken by the user. Modern, window-based software does not follow a sequential process. Instead, actions by users generate events. The programs respond to these events and alter data or offer additional choices. Typical events include mouse clicks pointing to items on the screen, keystrokes, changes to values, or transmissions from other systems.

As a user, you will be asked to help identify important objects along with their attributes and functions. You will also want to determine specific events and rules. In any business application, the underlying business rules define interrelationships between the objects. As certain events occur, data elements will be changed or added. For example, as shown in Figure 12.15, when an item is sold, several actions take place: recording the sale, updating inventory levels, and perhaps notifying customer service. You cannot assume that the analyst or programmer automatically knows all of these rules. To get a system that works well, managers and users must communicate these relationships and events to the system designer.

**END-USER
DEVELOPMENT**

The term *end-user development* simply means that users do all of the development work themselves. In many ways, it resembles prototyping, except that users (instead of analysts from the MIS department) create and modify the prototypes. Clearly the main advantage is that users get what they want without waiting for an MIS team to finish its other work and without the difficulty of trying to describe the business problems to someone else.

Two basic reasons explain why end-user development is increasingly popular. First, most MIS organizations are facing a two- or three-year backlog of projects. That means that if you bring a new project to MIS, the designers will not even start on it for at least two years (unless you give up some other project). In fact, with the year-2000 changes, many MIS departments simply gave up on other modifications. The second reason is that software tools are getting more powerful and easier to use at the same time. Today it is possible for users to create systems with a spreadsheet in a few hours that 10 years ago would have taken MIS programmers a month to build with third-generation languages. As tools become more powerful and more integrated, it becomes possible to create even more complex systems. Reread the discussion of software integration in Chapter 7 and picture the reports you can create using off-the-shelf software. Five years ago, most users would not dream of being able to create these reports. Today, with windowing software you can build systems that share data with many users across the corporate networks—simply by pointing to items with a mouse. The advantages of end-user development are similar to those in prototyping. In particular, users get what they want, and they get working systems sooner.

The potential problems of end-user development are not always easy to see. Most of them arise from the fact that users generally lack the training and experience of MIS analysts and programmers. For instance, systems produced by end users tend to be written for only one person to use. They are oriented to working on stand-alone personal computers. The systems are often customized to fit the needs of the original users. Additionally, most users do not write documentation, so others will have difficulty using the products. Because of lack of training, users rarely perform as much testing as they should. The systems lack security controls and are hard to modify. Think about the problems you encounter when you are given a spreadsheet that was created by the person who held the job before you.

Other problems stem from the bottom-up approach inherent in end-user development. People in different areas of the company will wind up working on the same problem, when it could have been solved once by MIS. Data tends to be scattered throughout the company, making it hard to share and wasting space. Not following standards generates incompatibilities among systems, making it difficult to combine systems created by different departments or even by people within the same department.

End users are limited by the capabilities of commercial software. The initial systems may work fine, but as the company grows and changes, the commercial software might be unable to support the necessary changes. As a result, some users have created systems that produce incorrect answers, take too long to run, or lose data.

The last, and possibly most important, complication is that end-user development takes time away from the user's job. Some users spend months creating and modifying systems that might have been created by MIS programmers in a fraction of the time. One of the reasons for creating an MIS department is to gain efficiency from using specialists. If users are spending too much time creating and revising their own applications, the company needs to consider hiring more MIS personnel.

## WHEN TO CALL FOR HELP

The bottom line is that managers often have to decide which method is most suitable for developing a particular system. If the project is large and expensive, and affects important assets of the company, the choice of SDLC is fairly clear-cut. If a user simply needs computations for a one-time decision, it is faster and cheaper to have the user create the model using a spreadsheet. However, in many cases, there is not an obvious answer. A project might start out small, then suddenly grow. Similarly, a spreadsheet that was created by a user for one purpose might be passed around the company and used by others to make crucial decisions.

There is not much difference between projects created by end users and those that use prototyping. In a sense, virtually any project could be started by end users. As shown in Figure 12.16, the trick is to learn when to call for help by understanding the limitations

---

**Business Trends: Downsizing**

As businesses become smaller and shift increased responsibility down to lower levels of managers, these managers will become more responsible for determining their own information needs and for creating portions of information systems. As a manager, to get the information system that you need, it becomes increasingly important that you understand the process, advantages, and disadvantages of the systems development methods: SDLC, prototyping, and end-user development. At a minimum, you will be involved in the selection of the method, initial design, and implementation. As development tools grow more powerful, an increasing number of systems and modifications will be created by managers and other users.

---

**FIGURE 12.16**
WHEN TO CALL MIS FOR HELP
As companies struggle to cut costs, end-user managers are increasingly responsible for developing their own computer applications. As software tools improve, managers can develop complex systems. Yet, there are times when it is best to get help and approval from an MIS team—especially when the application involves critical operations.

Many people will use the system:
• PC versus central computer
• Need documentation
• Individual user differences
• Need to train users

Commercial software limitations

User time is expensive

Mission-critical application:
• Additional testing
• Many modifications
• Need security and control

Need to integrate:
• Use corporate data
• Tie to existing software
• Connect to network

Database integrity:
• Avoid duplicate data
• Verify changes to corporate data

of the methods. If the project is used by many people, affects critical portions of the business, or grows beyond the capabilities of prepackaged software, then MIS programmers can be called in to expand it, test it, create documentation, make it more flexible, or create an entirely new system.

Modern MIS departments have devised many ways to help users develop new systems other than the traditional analysts and programmers working on SDLC projects. Two methods that are discussed in more detail in Chapter 13 are moving MIS employees out to the departments and the creation of an information center. In both cases, the goal is to have MIS employees responsible for assisting users. This assistance can be offered in many forms, such as helping decide which hardware and software to purchase, answering questions about software, offering classes in using software and creating systems, testing user-developed systems for errors and incompatibilities, and building prototypes.

**COMBINING METHODOLOGIES**

In actual practice, most companies use a combination of the various methods to create systems. Figure 12.17 summarizes the features of the primary methods used to design and build information systems. Note that the methods are roughly listed in declining order of

**FIGURE 12.17**
CHOOSING DESIGN
METHODOLOGIES
With a wide variety of
potential applications,
we need several design
methodologies. Each
methodology has
advantages and
disadvantages and is
suited for different
applications. When
choosing a
methodology, you
should also consider
the training and
background of the
users and development
team. The chart shows
how each method
supports several basic
functions in the
development of
systems. The
appropriate software
tool can be found by
matching the project
characteristics to the
strengths of each
methodology.

|  | SDLC | RAD | OBJECTS | JAD | PROTOTYPING | END USER |
|---|---|---|---|---|---|---|
| Control | formal | MIS | standards | joint | user | user |
| Time frame | long | short | any | medium | short | short |
| Users | many | few | varies | few | one or two | one |
| MIS staff | many | few | split | few | one or two | none |
| Transaction or DSS | trans. | trans. or DSS | trans. or DSS | DSS | DSS | DSS |
| Interface | minimal | minimal | Windows | crucial | crucial | crucial |
| Documentation and training | vital | limited | in objects | limited | weak | none |
| Integrity and security | vital | vital | in objects | limited | weak | weak |
| Reusability | limited | some | vital | limited | weak | none |

control and formality. Keep in mind that these techniques can be combined so that projects gain the benefits of each method. For example, large projects that require control and oversight benefit from using SDLC and other MIS-controlled methods. Even in these projects, prototyping and JAD are often used for reports and input screens. An MIS analyst will meet with users and quickly build sample screens and reports using CASE tools and personal computer–based software. Users alter the designs and they are adjusted until the users are satisfied. Then the prototype designs are turned over to the SDLC team to be programmed into the main system.

Some projects might begin as end-user systems to solve problems within one department. As the application expands and more users become involved, a RAD or SDLC team might be called in to standardize processes, convert the data, and build a shared application for the entire company.

Similarly, a company might use SDLC techniques (especially standards and testing) to create an initial set of objects. Once these objects are created, a team can use prototyping and RAD techniques to build new systems. Likewise, companies will purchase prewritten components as much as possible. It is almost always cheaper to buy components that already exist. These components can range from application software such as database management systems to object libraries that can be customized for each company.

Any modern company with a large enough MIS staff is continuously experimenting with all of these design methods. Creating software is an expensive, time-consuming process. Firms are constantly searching for techniques and methodologies that will improve the process and lead to better systems.

## PURCHASING COMMERCIAL SOFTWARE

One important trend in the last few years is the growing importance of commercially available software. Hardware has been continually improving in performance. Many platforms are becoming standardized, like Microsoft Windows on personal computers and UNIX on mid-range workstations. These two trends encourage the development and acceptance of commercial software packages. For example, no company would try to write its own word-processing software because several low cost packages are readily available commercially. Increasingly, commercial packages handle many common tasks, especially transaction processing, financial reporting, and accounting tasks.

In the past, the trade-off between buying versus creating your own software was a shortage of acceptable alternatives and performance problems with "generic" applications. Both of these problems are minimized with faster machines and the widespread adoption of a few basic platforms. Today, several commercial applications exist to handle all of the basic tasks of managing a company. The software vendor is responsible for basic operations and for improving its product. By selling to many companies, the development costs are spread out and the software can be purchased for substantially less than it would cost for one company to produce the application. Individual companies modify the application to provide additional features that support their own business processes.

One important concept to remember is that even if you choose to purchase commercial software, you must still perform many of the basic feasibility and analysis steps, especially for complex, expensive software. Comparing and evaluating software can be just as time consuming as the traditional analysis stage in the SDLC methodology.

## SUMMARY

Systems development can be a difficult task. Many projects have failed because they cost much more than anticipated or they did not produce useful systems. Large projects are especially difficult to control because there can be conflicting goals, it is hard to ensure that subsystems work together, business needs change during the development process, and there is turnover among the MIS employees. The systems development life cycle evolved as a means to deal with the complexity of large systems and provide the necessary controls to keep projects on track.

Systems analysis techniques are used to break projects into manageable pieces. Various graphing tools, such as data flow diagrams, are used to display the relationships between the components. Systems design techniques use the results of the analysis to create the new system. The new system consists of interconnected modules. Each module has inputs, outputs, processing steps, database requirements, manual procedures, and controls. At various stages in the design process, managers and users are asked to sign off on the proposed system, indicating that they will accept it with no further changes.

In contrast to the rigid control embodied in the SDLC method, the prototyping approach is iterative and creates an early working model of the system. Users and managers can see the proposed input screens and reports and make changes to them. As the project develops, the prototype goes from a simple mockup to a working system. Prototyping is sometimes used in conjunction with SDLC during the design phase to lay out input screens and reports.

A third way to build systems is for end users to develop their own projects using fourth-generation tools such as database management systems, spreadsheets, and

other commercial software. As the capabilities of commercial software tools increase, users can develop more complex systems. The backlog facing MIS also encourages users to develop their own systems. The potential dangers of user development, such as lack of testing, incompatibilities, and unnecessary duplication, can be controlled by having MIS teams available to assist end users.

All three methods of developing systems involve five basic steps: feasibility and planning, systems analysis, design, implementation, and maintenance. Prototyping and end-user development typically focus on the design stage. However, managers need to remember that implementation problems can arise with any new system, regardless of how it was created. Similarly, there will always be a need to maintain and modify existing applications. It is easy to forget these steps when users develop their own software.

> ### A MANAGER'S VIEW
>
> As a manager in a large company, you will work closely with the MIS department to modify and build systems that support your operations. You need to be aware of the problems facing MIS staff to understand the reasons for their rules and methods. Managers are increasingly being asked to develop their own systems and to participate more heavily in the design of new reports and forms. The details of analysis, design, testing, and implementation will be useful regardless of the method used. As a manager, you also need to know the advantages and drawbacks of various development methods; you will often have to choose the method that is best suited to solving your problems.

## KEY WORDS

bottom-up design, 498

change agent, 504

computer-aided software engineering (CASE), 511

data flow diagram (DFD), 499

end-user development, 495

event-driven systems, 507

fault tolerance, 509

feasibility study, 501

joint application design (JAD), 515

legacy systems, 511

object-oriented development, 516

prototyping, 495

rapid application development (RAD), 514

reverse engineering, 511

software maintenance, 508

structured walkthrough, 503

systems development life cycle (SDLC), 494

top-down design, 497

user resistance, 504

version control, 511

## WEB SITE REFERENCES                                    MP3 Music

| | |
|---|---|
| 100hot.com | hot1.go2net.com/music |
| Audio Find | www.audiofind.com |
| Audio Forge | www.audioforge.net |
| MP3 Place | www.mp3place.net |
| mp3.com | www.mp3.com |
| Music Match | www.musicmatch.com |
| Songs.com | www.songs.com |

## REVIEW QUESTIONS

1. What is pseudocode, and why would a manager need to be able to read it?
2. What are the differences between top-down and bottom-up design? How do current methods use both techniques?
3. Why was the systems development life cycle method created and used?
4. What are three common methods to develop systems?
5. What are the major phases in the SDLC method?
6. Which stage of the SDLC method uses the most MIS resources today?
7. Why do legacy systems cause problems for MIS? How might reverse engineering help?
8. What activities are involved in systems analysis?
9. What activities are involved in the systems design stage?
10. What activities are involved in systems implementation?
11. How can resistance to change be managed?
12. Describe the major implementation techniques.
13. What are the drawbacks to the SDLC method?
14. How can CASE tools help the MIS department?
15. What types of projects are best suited to prototyping?
16. What are the advantages of prototyping over SDLC?
17. What projects are best suited to end-user development?
18. What is the purpose of the object-oriented approach to development?
19. Why is end-user development becoming more common?

## EXERCISES

1. If you have access to a CASE tool, use it to create the data flow diagrams illustrated in Chapter 3. Add another level of detail to the diagrams. Be sure to create the data dictionary. This assignment is best accomplished with teams. Assign one section of the diagrams to each team member.
2. Interview a local manager to determine the requirements for a new system. Explain which method would be the best approach to develop the system. Estimate how long it would take to complete the project and how much it would cost. Advanced option: Illustrate the new system with a data flow diagram. More advanced: Create the system.
3. Consider an information system for a firm that manufactures furniture. Every day, production managers get shipping invoices that detail the supplies that were delivered that day. Production orders come in from the marketing department, listing each product and the options that need to be included. Once a week, the production team gets a quality report from

sales outlets listing problems they have encountered with the products. Manufacturing is split into several component groups that are further split into teams. For instance, one component group makes sofas and recliners, another makes tables and chairs. Teams include frame groups, upholstery, woodworking, and finishing. Once a week, each team creates a report that lists the products that were completed, the materials used in each product, the statistical quality measures on each component, and the amount of time spent on each step. Using an object-oriented approach and based on what you know (or can find out) about furniture, create a list of objects that might be used in building an information system for this company. Show the relationships among the objects. Hint: One important object is *reports*.

4. Interview computer users to determine how they feel about their current system. Do they like it? What are the major advantages and drawbacks? How long have they used it? When was it changed last? Are there changes users want to see? Are they willing to accept changes? How are relations with the MIS workers? Who initiates changes, users or MIS? If users proposed a new project, how long would it take for MIS to get to it (how long is the backlog)? Team approach: Have each team member interview a different person (some users, some in MIS). Combine your results to get a picture of the entire company. Do users agree with each other? Does the MIS department agree with the users? Do they see the same problems? Hint: If you do not have access to another company, you can always find computer users in the university.

 **Rolling Thunder Database**

5. Rolling Thunder Bicycles needs a new web site. How should it be developed? What methodology could be used?
6. Write a plan to test the new web site being developed in the prior exercise.
7. Rolling Thunder Bicycles needs a new system to generate and track electronic orders (EDI) to its suppliers. What methodology should be used to develop the system?

## ADDITIONAL READING

"All 208 Million Tax Returns Get Electronic Scrutiny on Arrival," *Government Computer News,* March 6, 1995. [IRS]

DeMarco, T., and T. Lister. *Peopleware.* New York: Dorset House, 1987. [Hints and problems developing useful systems]

Jones, T. C. *Programming Productivity.* New York: McGraw-Hill, 1986. [Evaluating and measuring productivity, costs of teamwork]

King, Julia. "A Crash Course in Management," *Computerworld,* February 8, 1999. [Fifth in a series of articles following companies' preparations for the year 2000]

McConnell, Steve. *Rapid Development: Taming Wild Software Schedules.* Redmond, WA: Microsoft Press, 1996.

Naumann, Justus, and Milton Jenkins, "Prototyping: The New Paradigm for Systems Development," *MIS Quarterly,* Spring 1982. [Description, uses, and advantages of prototyping]

# CASES *Government Agencies*

Most U.S. citizens know the overall structure of the federal government: the president, Congress, and the Supreme Court. These groups are responsible for creating and interpreting the laws to govern the nation. What many people do not realize is that both the president and Congress are supported by a huge set of government agencies. These organizations form a bureaucracy that is ultimately responsible for carrying out the laws.

Governmental agencies have several unique problems. The most important one is that funding is subject to changes in the political climate. With each election, an agency runs the risk of having to change direction, cancel projects, or provide support for new tasks.

On the other hand, from an economic perspective, most government agencies are not subject to economic pressures. Consequently, they may not have the same incentives to economize and minimize costs that are faced by businesses.

The third critical feature of most government agencies is that they tend to serve large numbers of people, especially at the federal level. These large organizations collect huge amounts of data. Even today, much of governmental data is stored on paper.

Most governmental agencies have dealt with the size issue by maintaining large staffs, and combining decentralized management with centralized controls. Traditionally, government organizations have paid lower salaries than commercial businesses. Although the salaries are supplemented with benefits and job security, governmental agencies often face high turnover rates and changes in personnel. To compensate for these problems, the agencies rely heavily on procedures. There are rules for every conceivable circumstance. As new situations and decisions arise, new rules are created. Given these challenges, there is no surprise that most people perceive government agencies as large bureaucracies, filled with endless forms and strange rules.

There are many obvious uses for computers in government agencies. During a few minutes of observation, anyone can generate ideas that could improve agency performance, making life easier for the workers and citizens. However, the real challenges have always arisen in creating and implementing these ideas.

Although there are many success stories regarding computer implementation within government agencies, there are also some costly failures. The Federal Aviation Administration and the Internal Revenue Service cases present some of the difficulties that have arisen.

Be careful when you read these cases. Do not simply blame the problems on "typical government mismanagement." Many of these problems also exist within businesses. Always remember that we are searching for answers and methods that will overcome the obstacles and complications.

## Financial Analysis

The federal government employs 2.25 percent of the U.S. workforce. It spends annually over $1.5 trillion. In the first half of the 1990s, government revenues increased by 16.6 percent and expenditures by 10 percent. Unfortunately, on an average, expenditures were ranging 16 to 23 percent over revenues, pushing the deficit up to a little over 2 percent of the GDP; this is a 28 percent increase in the first half of the decade. The situation is not as bleak as it sounds. The European Community, in comparison, maintains on average a deficit of almost 5 percent of its GDP.

Other financial points of interest are:

- The U.S. economy has been growing at a general rate of 3 percent.
- Government expenditures will be 21 percent higher by 2002, growing at a rate that is slightly faster than the projected rate of inflation.
- The public is pushing the government to lower taxes.
- Medicare's trust fund is facing bankruptcy in just four years.
- By the year 2029, Social Security will exhaust its surplus and taxes will cover only 75 percent of promised benefits. To ensure solvency for the next 75 years, Congress will have to act now by either increasing the 12.4 percent payroll tax, or cutting benefits or both.

## Potential/Prospective for Growth

If the government wants to continue operating, it must be funded; so a certain amount of its growth is dependent on taxes. The amount of taxes that are raised is dependent on the economy. A report released by the Labor Department in early January 1997 shows that the economy was steadily growing. Unemployment rates were at a low of 5.3 percent. There was a 6 percent gain in average hourly earnings to $12.05. On average, weekly earnings increased 1.4 percent to $419.34. The average workweek for service, production, and manufacturing jobs rose 0.3 hours.

In contrast, the actual size of government is shrinking. The number of elected officials remains constant but the rest of the federal government is downsizing. Federal government employment peaked in 1990 and since has fallen by over 300,000 jobs. A review of employment figures shows that, in 1996, private-sector jobs grew by almost 2.5 percent but federal government jobs fell by 0.05 percent.

|  | **1995** | **1996** | **1997** | **1998** |
|---|---|---|---|---|
| Federal government | 2,821 | 2,756 | 2,699 | 2,685 |
| Feds, no postal workers | 1,978 | 1,901 | 1,841 | 1,819 |
| All private | 97,894 | 100,187 | 103,115 | 105,968 |
| Good producing | 24,275 | 24,492 | 24,935 | 25,260 |
| Service producing | 92,912 | 95,098 | 97,742 | 100,556 |
| Employment Figures (BLS), annual average in thousands. | | | | |

## Competitive Structure

Although an all-time low voter turnout might indicate a disgruntled attitude by the U.S. population, the U.S. federal government has no fear of being replaced. It has no competition as a government. However, in the area of investments, the government competes for dollars against the private sector. Among the major developed countries of world, the United States has one of the lowest rates of gross savings, so the competition for investment dollars is strong.

The other type of competition the government faces is within. The two major political parties are constantly competing for electoral votes and the ability to control government. The 1990s have seen reemergence of independent and third-party movements, but they have not had a significant impact.

## Role of Research and Development

The government is heavily involved in research. This section will focus only on research and development in the area of technology. One agency at the Congress's disposal is the Office of Technology Assessment. This agency was founded in 1972 and its primary task is to identify the effects of technology on society.

The Information Technology Management Reform Act of 1996 also promotes technological research. Through the Information Technology Acquisition Pilot Program, the Administrator of the Federal Procurement Policy (FPP) is authorized to "conduct pilot programs to test alternative approaches for the acquisition of information technology." Program parameters include:

- Each pilot program is limited to five years.
- Each agency conducting a pilot program must establish measurable criteria for evaluation.
- The FPP administrator must submit to Congress a detailed test plan before implementation.
- Each program's findings must be reported to the director of the Office of Management and Budgets (OMB) and to Congress.
- The OMD director will submit to Congress recommendations for legislation if the pilot program results show this type of action is needed.

- The FFP administrator can authorize a pilot program in which a private contractor "provides the federal government with an information technology alternative process."

## Technology Investment and Analysis

On July 16, 1996, the president's executive order on federal information technology (Executive Order 13011) was issued. It begins as follows:

> A Government that works better and costs less requires efficient and effective information systems. The Paperwork Reduction Act of 1995 and the Information Technology Management Reform Act of 1996 provide the opportunity to improve significantly the way the Federal Government acquires and manages information technology.

The White House is "reinventing government" according to their web page, and their solution involves information systems. Each agency is to have a chief information officer who will design, develop, and implement information systems. The CIO's goal is "to use information technology to improve the productivity of federal programs and to promote a coordinated, secure, and shared governmentwide infrastructure that is provided and supported by a diversity of private sector suppliers and a well-trained corps of information technology professionals" (Executive Order 13011). These systems are supposed to pay for themselves through the savings they create. They are intended to streamline and downsize government.

## Recommendation for the Future

The U.S. federal government must find ways to promote a higher savings rate in the country. Although foreign direct investment is high, an increase in the U.S. savings rate might lower the cost of capital. This would encourage economic growth, increasing tax revenues. In addition, the government must find ways to cut costs so the deficit can be reduced. Costly programs like Social Security and Medicare need to be reevaluated and restructured.

## CASE  *Federal Aviation Administration (FAA)*

The FAA is charged with overseeing all public (nonmilitary) flight operations in the United States related to safety and access to the air. They establish safety criteria, issue licenses for pilots, and create air worthiness certificates for planes. They also operate the air traffic control system throughout the United States. Funding for the agency is generated through user fees and taxes on aircraft fuel, tires, and airline tickets. By 1990, the Aviation Trust Fund held $41 billion, built up during the prior 20 years. The FAA is an executive agency and theoretically operates under the direct control of the U.S. president. However, tax rates and expenditures are established by Congress.

Air traffic control in the United States is an exceedingly complex problem. In 1994, the 300 major airports generated 50,000 flights a day. Air traffic control is responsible for scheduling the takeoffs, landings, and flight paths of all these flights. By 1990, 455 million passengers a year were flying on U.S. airlines.

Traffic control is organized into three levels: nationwide U.S. airspace, 20 regional air traffic centers, and individual airports. Air traffic control operators at each airport have immediate control over takeoffs and landings. Regional operators watch traffic within their defined airspace. Systemwide control is provided by the Central Flow facilities located in Washington, D.C. The Central Flow managers examine traffic across the entire United States and resolve conflicts and problems that arise among regions. The 40 traffic management specialists plan each day in advance, creating alternative routings for aircraft because of problems arising from snowstorms, accidents, and closed runways.

### Early Systems

The early traffic control system was built with hardware and software from Sperry-Rand/Univac, a computer company that was purchased in the mid-1980s by Burroughs. The combined company is now called Unisys. The airport-based traffic control computers were based on 256K bytes of main memory and performed 500,000 instructions per second. The original systems were installed in the early 1960s. The 20 regional centers had their own computers—IBM 9020 machines that were custom made for the FAA in the 1960s.

### Improvements

In 1981, the FAA was given approval for a comprehensive new system to upgrade the computer system. New airports, such as Dallas-Fort Worth, coupled with deregulation of the airline industry in 1978, led to huge increases in air traffic. The $12 billion plan called for replacement of 12 major systems over the course of 12 years. An additional 80 smaller projects were included in the plan.

By 1990, only 1 of the 12 systems had been replaced and the project was $15 billion over the original budget, and an average of four years late. The one project that was completed was known as Host, because it called for replacement of the mainframe computers at the 20 regional control centers. IBM installed its 3083 mainframes on schedule but was $16 million over budget. Even then, the 3083s were technologically obsolete at the time they were installed because the newer IBM 3090-class machines had been available for a year.

The FAA has been criticized several times for a lack of oversight and control in developing new systems. In 1980, the Senate Appropriations committee noted that "The FAA has no ongoing, well-defined, and systematic management approach to evaluating software and operational cost, capacity, and performance of the current system to meet projected short-range workloads."

The General Accounting Office (GAO), the watchdog of Congress, echoed that sentiment several times later.

### Advanced Automation System

One of the more visible components of the plan is the Advanced Automation System (AAS), which is designed to provide updated tracking displays to the controllers. It was supposed to be completed by 1990, but at that time was delayed until 1993. The system is designed to use IBM RS-6000 computers to display flight information, schedules, and current location along with weather fronts. The color systems will have higher resolution, be easier to read, and carry more information.

In 1994, an internal study of the AAS showed that the project was still two years behind schedule and probably would fall back another two years before completion. The project to that time has cost $2.3 billion and is estimated to eventually cost about $7 billion. David Hinson, FAA administrator, announced that he was replacing top managers on the project, dropping portions of uncompleted work, and demanding performance guarantees from the contractors. One system being canceled is the Area Control Computer Complex, which was designed to interconnect the host computers at the airport and regional levels.

### Problems

Air traffic controllers have been reporting problems with existing systems for years:

- In 1992, West Coast air traffic was delayed for several hours. An IBM 3083 at the regional station crashed. In the process, it removed the identification labels from the radar screens of controllers from Oregon to Los Angeles. The controllers switched to an older backup system but had to increase plane separation from the typical 3 miles up to 20 miles. Pilots and controllers used radio communication and manually filed flight plans to compensate. Ron Wilson, a spokesman for the San Francisco airport, notes that although there are frequent disruptions, "The FAA computer failures generally don't last long, just long enough to screw things up."

At Oakland, California, an average of three times a month the controllers' screens fail and controllers have a few seconds to memorize the position, speed, course, altitude, and destination of the 12 planes they are typically guiding. Then their screens go blank for at least 10 seconds. Sometimes when the screens come back online, they are missing critical data.

- Joel Willemssen, assistant director of the U.S. GAO's Information Management and Technology Division, reported that 70 percent of the 63 largest airports in the United States have experienced problems with blank or flickering computer screens. John Mazor, a spokesman for the Airline Pilots Association, notes the problems cause "delays, diversions, and—in the worst possible cases—accidents. It's not as dangerous as you might think, but it's not something you want to have happen to you."

- The Los Angeles basin region consists of 21 airports handling 6.5 million flights a year. The GAO notes that the FAA computers in the region have repeatedly suffered from the loss of critical data and slow responses because of the overload.

## Technological Investment and Analysis

According to a *Government Computer News* article in August 1995, "The Federal Aviation Administration will spend $65 million on Band-Aids . . . ." The truth of the matter is that the FAA has had big plans to rehaul its air traffic control system. Its largest project so far has been the Advanced Automation System (AAS). AAS is the FAA's air traffic modernization project that ideally would address all air traffic control difficulties from the enroute segment to digital tower control.

The first stage of AAS was scheduled to roll out in 1996, but the project is three years behind schedule and over budget. AAS is being designed to integrate all air traffic control data on a single workstation for the controllers. Currently air traffic controllers are using a mix of manual and automated plane and weather-tracking systems, making the process cumbersome.

Because the AAS is so far delayed, the FAA has not been able to roll out new technology fast enough to prevent breakdowns. Air traffic controllers are operating on IBM 9020E machines to process radar data from the aircraft. These machines, as well as most of the other air traffic systems, are more than 30 years old. Several of the FAA's machines are run on vacuum tubes and punch cards.

Many risks are involved in using these outdated systems. The controllers are well trained on these systems. Yet, as volume continues to increase, system failure becomes more and more of a concern. The FAA has faced serious outages in major markets with these machines. These outages often occur when the Display Channel Complex (DCC)—the center's mainframe computer that processes data into images displayed on a screen—shuts down. An outage can occur when any of the systems in the long line of processors malfunctions.

According to the FAA, however, outages simply cause the controllers to depend on backup systems and safety is never an issue. However, outages cause long flight delays as well as air traffic difficulties. The longer these systems are in use, the more frequent the outages will and have become, and the longer it will take to get them repaired. These serious problems facing the FAA must be addressed as soon as possible.

A second technology issue is airport and aircraft security. Due to bad planning and panic, implementation of airport security processes have proven to be costly and inefficient. Following the explosion of Pan Am Flight 103 in 1988, the industry was in a hurry to enhance airport security. The result was many different independent systems created haphazardly by the airports. These included features such as electronic screening of passengers and crew, secured doors with electronic ID card readers, video monitoring, and various computer systems to track employee security clearances. Because these functions were independently generated, most of the systems (hardware and software) were incompatible with one another.

Because of the sense of urgency following Pan Am 103, the FAA was unable to run pilot programs to test cost effectiveness. Maintaining these expensive systems, which many experts think are not even performing effectively, continues to be the responsibility of the FAA. These cost concerns are a major issue for the FAA given continuous financial difficulties and delays in advancing any of their technology. They will be forced to upgrade and maintain these systems while new ones are being developed.

The FAA does have a current plan to deal with risk management. According to a December 1995 *Federal Computer Week* article, the FAA is developing a sophisticated risk management plan using Akela's Security Analysis Support System (Sassy). This software uses customized parameters to fit a particular organization. It is used in other federal government agencies. Akela is currently compiling information based on area expertise and knowledge to create a product that will aid the FAA to assess risk areas in all types of security operations. The software can help to develop new strategies, evaluate possible options, and simulate potential threats. Possibly with the implementation of this software, the FAA can identify risks and formulate plans to address these risks in a timely and cost-effective manner.

A few key systems are instrumental in transmitting information from aircraft to controllers on the ground.

### Aircraft Monitoring System (ACMS)

The function of ACMS is to compile all the data from the various sensors on the aircraft and transmit them to the captain. ACMS reads present conditions and provides historical data to the captain. The captain can use the historical data to measure relative measurements and spot trends. The monitor is also extremely sensitive and can detect engine vibrations undetectable to humans. The information that is collected about the aircraft and the flight is interfaced with the systems in place at the ground stations. This ground system is called ACARS.

### Aircraft Communication Addressing and Reporting System (ACARS)

ACARS was introduced in 1976. It was intended to cut down the use of spoken radio messages to transmit information to the ground. It was thought that if the crew could save time by using data to transmit information to the ground, they could spend more time concentrating on flying the plane. ACARS directly interfaces with ACMS and also gives and receives messages directly to and from the pilot. The pilot punches his message, such as flight plans, in an alphanumeric keypad or touch screen, and this message is then relayed to the ground. The ground can also send messages such as weather conditions, estimated times of arrival, and assignment updates to the aircraft through ACARS. The tie between ACMS and ACARS is very important, yet there is still another system that connects the airlines—ARINC.

### Aeronautical Radio, Inc. (ARINC)

ARINC is a system commonly owned by all the domestic airlines that is used to keep in touch with one another. Because all airliners have the ACARS system, ARINC interfaces with this system and transmits messages from the individual ACARS Management Unit on each plane through VHF (radio waves) or satellite to ARINC headquarters. From there, the message is received by ARINC's Datalink Service Processor. The processor processes and controls the message on the ground. ARINC then searches for which antenna offers the best reception, and communication begins. This entire system operates much like a LAN.

For example, if United Airlines wanted to send a message to any plane on the ground or in the air, it can enter its message through its ACARS system. The message then goes through the United Airlines host system. It is then transmitted to the ARINC headquarters and ARINC can locate the plane, wherever it is, and send the message to the appropriate ground station. All informa-

tion must be formatted for ground-to-air transmittal since ARINC must transmit via radio or satellite. The marriage of these systems gives pilots and controllers quick access to almost any data.

The conversion to a completely new system must be done in a way that permits real-time operation. Shutdowns of the air traffic control system are not an option, so there must be a system in place to do the controlling while the switchover is made.

The importance of keeping these systems running cannot be underestimated. When a 9020E shuts down, controllers are able to see their air space sectors, but they are not able to transfer aircraft automatically to other controllers in control of other air sectors. These transfers then must be made manually. The controllers have to write the information down on a piece of paper and hand it to another controller.

### Technological Innovations

#### Network

The FAA replaced its system for acquisition management with a distributed architecture. The present system runs on 1980s-era minicomputers at 12 centers nationwide and processes more than 200,000 purchases per year. It was not updated for more than three years and was not year 2000 ready. Mounting problems in the old system led many FAA officials to revert to paper to track agency purchases.

The new system is called Acquire. It will use Oracle Corporations's Alert software and Discoverer/2000 querying tool. The FAA must also use Oracle federal purchasing software to get Acquire to run on a network that links headquarters to regional offices and field centers.

#### Telecommunications

The FAA is preparing a communications system overhaul aimed at readying the agency's infrastructure for the 21st century. The FAA Integrated Communications Systems for the 21st century (FICS-21) program will cost an estimated $2.75 billion.

FICS-21 will provide ground-to-ground transmission switching and network management control for voice, data, and video communications. The new initiative will replace at least 11 major programs, including FAA-owned and leased networks. FAA FICS-21 program manager Jeff Yarnell says it is a good time to rebuild the FAA's telecommunications infrastructure because many telecommunications contracts will expire around the year 2000.

### Recommendation for the Future

The goal of the FAA is to make operations a digital system. The air traffic control community is hoping to use and expand the capabilities of ACARS. There is a system currently in place called the Automated Terminal Information System (ATIS). All pilots must listen to the ATIS broadcast before taking off or landing. The broadcast is a tape that tells the pilot about wind direction and speed, visibility, runways in use, and other information that affects airport operations.

This broadcast was originally on an audio loop tape that the pilot would listen to prior to take off and landing. Just before landing, however, is a busy time in the cockpit, and listening to the ATIS can be very distracting to a pilot. By moving the information to a digital format, the pilot can download it into the ACARS system and then study it when there is more time to concentrate on it.

Expanding the role of ACARS is one of the many stepping stones to the future for the FAA. Currently, due to the new acquisition plan, the FAA has many contracts out for new technologies. The following are some of the high-priced contracts/projects the FAA currently has in gear.

### Global Positioning System (GPS)

GPS is a satellite-based navigation system that was developed by the Pentagon and previously available for use only in connection with military air travel. GPS allows pilots to navigate based on satellite signals instead of radar signals. It allows real-time flight planning for pilots. As more satellite technology becomes available, the integration of air traffic information as well as weather information and other data communication, will become a necessary technological step. Four dimensional GPS readings, longitude, latitude, altitude and time, allow an aircraft to come within 50 feet of any given target. Encryption technology is currently in place to protect security in the transmission of the satellite messages.

### Standard Terminal Automation Replacement System (STARS)

"STARS is the next big step in the FAA's comprehensive effort to upgrade air traffic control facilities across the nation; the new system will provide the platform for improvements to handle the ever-growing volume of air traffic safely and efficiently well into the 21st century," said FAA administrator David R. Hinson. STARS will standardize all air traffic control equipment at up to 172 FAA facilities as well as 199 Department of Defense facilities. STARS will supply new hardware and software to these facilities. The program will provide complete replacement for the aging systems currently in use. Display transmission will be the most important feature of the STARS program. The Automated Radar Terminal System (ARTS) that is currently in place is one that was developed in the 1970s and 1980s. The FAA believes that interim programs can extend ARTS life somewhat in the short term, but it is generally accepted that this system does not have the capabilities to take air traffic into the next century. ARTS software contains various versions and languages that are very labor intensive as well as expensive to support.

The STARS program is one that consists of a commercial standard system that the FAA believes will be much cheaper and easier to maintain. A key feature to the system is that one can extend the capacity of the system without having to reengineer the basic architecture. By essentially relying on commercially available software and hardware, the time to acquire the software will be cut down significantly while maintenance costs should also be much lower than those of ARTS.

### Computed Tomography Detection System (InVision CTX5000SP)

This new technology is designed to detect explosives in checked baggage. Existing technology is designed to spot objects that people may bring on the plane that are obviously threatening such as guns or knives. Currently, checked baggage is rarely scanned. CTX5000SP is an automated x-ray system that uses the CAT scan technology from the medical field. CTX5000SP first does a prescan of the object and points out areas of interest. It then takes slices from the identified area, as well as some random slices, and then creates a three-dimensional view of the slices. It can also display a full three-dimensional image. The console will fit the slices together and alert the operator and show the image and the location of the object in the bag by highlighting it in red. CTX5000SP was created in response to the crash of TWA Flight 800 in the summer of 1996.

The FAA awarded this contract to InVision Technologies for $52.2 million. InVision will supply from 54 to 100 explosive detection systems set to be installed later in 1997.

### Wide Area Augmentation System (WAAS)

WAAS is a system that is used in conjunction with GPS. Using a network of 36 ground stations to "distill" satellite GPS signals, WAAS will allow commercial aircraft to pinpoint a location within seven meters. With the use of WAAS/GPS, the FAA hopes it can close many of its ground control centers and allow pilots to fly more direct routes. These mechanisms are all a part of the vision of free flight.

### Free flight

Free flight is an ideal that the FAA is working to make a reality in the near future. Free flight would enable pilots to control their own navigation procedures like never before. The pilot would use the WAAS and GPS systems for navigational purposes and choose their own routes, speed, and altitude. Ground support will be held to a minimum and pilot flexibility will be hindered only when flights are in congested airport areas, when flights approach restricted air space, or if safety is at stake.

Two principles that drive the free flight plan are the protected and alert airspace zones. The sizes of these zones are determined based on aircraft speed, performance characteristics, communications, navigation and surveillance equipment. The protected zone is the zone closest to the aircraft. No aircraft should meet the protected zone of another aircraft. The alert zone is one that extends far from an aircraft's protected zone. The distance between planes will be monitored closely and if an instance occurs when a plane touches another plane's protected zone, the pilots and the air traffic controllers will determine if course corrections are needed. Under the free flight system, there will not be any interference until alert zones collide.

## QUESTIONS

1. What is the strategic direction of the Federal Aviation Administration?
2. What has been the catalyst for change at the Federal Aviation Administration?
3. With what technological changes has the FAA been forced to accommodate?
4. What has caused a focus on change in the use of technology at the FAA?
5. How has this technological change been implemented?
6. How successful has the technological change been?
7. Does the agency have the financial ability to embark on a major technological program of advancement?
8. How does the agency's representation of itself on its web page compare to what is actually being done by the FAA?

## ADDITIONAL READING

"Air Traffic Control—Good Progress on Interim Replacement for Outage-Plagued System, But Risks Can Be Further Reduced," *GAO Report,* October 17, 1996.

Deck, Stewart. "Air-traffic Union Puts Upgrades on Hold," *Computerworld,* February 1, 1999, p. 24.

"FAA's $500 Million Navigation Contract Takes Flight," *Federal Computer Week,* April 10, 1995.

"FAA Radar Glitches Found," *Computerworld,* November 2, 1998, p. 12.

"FAA Ready for Free Flight," *Advanced Transportation Technology News,* April 1996.

"FAA to Spend $65m on Stopgap Replacements for Old Computers," *Government Computer News,* August 7, 1995, p. 3.

Jackson, William. "FAA and GSA Renew Their Dogfight Over Air Traffic Control Modernization," *Government Computer News,* September 18, 1995, p. 73.

Leopold, George. "Study: GPS Can Fly as Commercial Air Navigator," *Electronic Engineering Times,* February 8, 1999, p. 18.

Murray, Bill. "FAA Document Management System Helps Users Stay on Track," *Government Computer News,* December 14, 1998, p. 36.

O'Hara, Colleen. "FAA Kicks Off ATC Upgrade," *Federal Computer Week,* December 7, 1998, p. 1.

———. "FAA Looks Abroad for Oceanic ATC Solution," *Federal Computer Week,* November 16, 1998, p. 6.

Ryan, Stephan M. FAA's Bailout Betrays Citizens, Benefits Lawyers, *Government Computer News,* September 18, 1995, p. 29.

Slabodkin, Gregory, Florence Olsen, and Frank Tiboni, "Poll: FAA Lacks Good Systems," *Government Computer News,* January 25, 1999, p. 6.

Tiboni, Frank. "FAA Begins Upgrade Project on Its Controller-Pilot Comm System," *Government Computer News,* February 8, 1999, p. 8.

———. "FAA Names AT&T Exec Daniel Mehan to Become its First Chief Information Officer," *Government Computer News,* January 25, 1999, p. 8.

———. "FAA Pulls Tracking App from Two Radar Centers," *Government Computer News,* November 23, 1998, p. 3.

———. "FAA Uses Patch to Prevent Air Traffic Lockups," *Government Computer News,* October 19, 1998, p. 46.

———. "Vendors Protest FAA Support Contract Award," *Government Computer News,* October 19, 1998, p. 49.

Walker, Richard W. "Readying for 2000: One Agency Story. Federal Aviation Administration on Target," *Government Computer News,* December 14, 1998, p. 47.

## CASE *The Internal Revenue Service (IRS)*

Between personal and business returns, the IRS processes more than 200 million tax returns a year. Some of the returns are simple one-page forms; others run to thousands of pages of supporting documents. Overall, the service handles more than 1 billion information documents a year. The IRS brings in more than $1 trillion in tax revenue a year. The IRS has 10 regional service centers that are responsible for processing and storing individual forms. In 1989, it cost the IRS $34 million just to store the paper documents.

Until 1990, all documents at the IRS were stored as paper records in a central warehouse. Documents were organized according to the year of filing. As a result, if a taxpayer had a problem or question that covered multiple years, the citizen had to schedule multiple meetings with IRS officials to correct problems for each of the years. In some cases, it could take weeks or months just to get the files. Occasionally, the IRS found it was faster to ask the taxpayer for a copy of the return. By the early 1990s, this problem was resolved by having each of the 10 service centers store digital images of the tax returns, making them available to agents on their terminals. Even so, the IRS knows that it needs more automation, especially the ability to scan the returns directly into a computerized information system.

Of course, automation sometimes creates additional problems, such as the situation faced by Dickie Ann Conn. The IRS determined that she owed $67,714 in back taxes. As a result, she was sent a bill for more than $1 billion in interest and penalties. On challenge, the IRS admitted that there was an error in the interest computation.

### IRS History of Automation Problems

The IRS seems like a logical candidate for improved automation. The benefits of faster processing, fewer mistakes, and easier access to data ought to save a considerable amount of money. The computer's ability to search the data, automatically match transactions, and analyze each return presents several additional opportunities that can either cut costs or raise additional revenue. Managers at the IRS are fully aware of the potential, and they have proposed several systems over the years. The problem has been in implementation and in getting Congress to support the plans.

In the late 1960s, the IRS knew that it needed to redesign its basic systems, and began planning for a system to be installed in the 1970s. Congress eventually killed the plan for two main reasons: it was too expensive and Congress was concerned about security and taxpayer privacy. The IRS then focused on keeping its existing computers running.

In 1982, the existing system was nearing capacity and the IRS established the Tax System Redesign program. It was a major redesign and consisted of three major components. According to the GAO, changes in management resulted in the system never getting past the design stage. A new assistant commissioner in 1982 embarked on the design of a new system that would carry the IRS through the 1990s. Initial costs were estimated at $3 to $5 billion over the entire project. The primary objective was to replace the old central tape-based system with an online database. Eventually, optical technology would be used to scan the original documents and store the data in the database. A new communication system would carry the data to any agent's workstation. By 1989, initial planning had already cost the IRS more than $70 million, with no concrete proposal or results.

The main computer systems were replaced at the IRS service centers in 1985. The change in the systems was almost disastrous for the IRS. The change delayed returns processing, leading to delays in refunds that cost the IRS millions of dollars in interest payments. IRS employees worked overtime but still could not keep up. Rumors were flying that some employees were dumping returns to cut down their backlog. Because of the delays and backlogs, the IRS managed to audit only about half the usual number of returns.

In 1986, the IRS initiated a plan to provide 18,000 laptop computers to make its field auditors more productive with its Automated Examination System (AES). Unfortunately, the service bought the Zenith laptops a full year before the software was ready. The system was written in Pascal and was delivered to agents in July 1986. The system was designed to help examine Form 1040 returns. Its biggest drawback was that it used 18 different diskettes, requiring agents to continually swap disks. From privatization efforts by the Reagan administration, the system was subcontracted to outside developers. As IRS funding was cut, programmers with experience in Pascal were cut. The system had to be rewritten in C.

A survey in 1988 revealed that 77 percent of the agents were dissatisfied with the software and it was used by only one-third of them. By 1989, the IRS revised the software and managed to reduce it to eight disks. Overall, by 1989, the AES project was more than six years behind schedule, and the GAO observed that it would be $800 million over the original budget. The IRS originally anticipated that the AES would produce $16.2 billion in additional revenue over nine years by making agents more productive. The GAO disputed those numbers, noting that "The IRS has been unable to verify that the use of laptops has actually resulted in the examination of additional returns or increased tax revenues."

In 1990, the White House cut funding for the program from $110 million down to $20 million.

### Tax System Modernization

By 1989, the IRS knew that it desperately needed to redesign its entire system for collecting taxes and processing information. In hearings before Congress, Senator David Pryor (D-Ark.) noted that the 1960s-era IRS computers were headed for a "train wreck" in the mid-1990s. The GAO estimated the original project would cost between $3 and $4 billion. The projected date for implementation slipped from 1995 to 1998.

The overall Tax System Modernization (TSM) design calls for a centralized on-line database, smaller departmental systems containing local information, that are tied together with a nationwide network. Tax return data would be entered with a combination of electronic filing and optical scanners.

By 1991, the estimated cost of the plan had expanded to $8 billion. Although it was anticipated that the system would cut $6 billion in costs, the plan was rapidly attacked by members of Congress. Three studies of the TSM plan by the GAO were released in early 1991:

- The GAO was concerned that optical technology was not sufficiently advanced to perform the tasks demanded by the IRS. The GAO urged greater emphasis on electronic filing.
- The GAO was concerned about management issues such as transition planning, progress measurement, and accountability.
- The GAO and Sen. John Glenn (D-Ohio) voiced concerns about security.

GAO official Howard Rhile notes that "This is a serious omission in view of the fact that the IRS intends to allow public access . . . to some of its systems and because concerns over the security of taxpayer information helped doom the first [IRS] modernization effort in the late 1970s."

Despite these misgivings, the IRS was committed to the TSM plan. Fred Goldberg, IRS commissioner, agreed with the GAO findings but observed that

> We have been running our business essentially the same way, using essentially the same computer and telecommunications systems design for 25 years. [Existing systems] will perform well and achieve incremental improvements for the next few years. . . . Our best judgment is that [OCR] technology will be there when we need it, by the end of the decade.

By 1992, the situation was worse. Shirley Peterson, the new commissioner of internal revenue, stated at a Congressional hearing that "Our systems are so antiquated that we cannot adequately serve the public. The potential for breakdown during the filing season greatly exceeds acceptable business risk. . . . Some components of these computers are so old and brittle that they literally crumble when removed for maintenance."

In December 1991, the IRS awarded a 12-year, $300-million contract to TRW to help manage the process and provide planning and system integration services.

The new system is ambitious, calling for 60 major projects, two dozen major purchases, 20 million lines of new software, and 308 people just to manage the purchasing. Despite their efforts, elements of the IRS modernization plan were stalled because of purchasing difficulties. In July 1991, the IRS awarded a billion-dollar Treasury Multiuser Acquisition Contract (TMAC) to AT&T. The goal was to standardize purchasing for the

IRS and the Treasury Department by routing all purchases through one vendor. The contract was challenged by other vendors and overturned. The contract was re-bid and AT&T won a second time. IBM (one of the original protesters) again objected to the process, noting that the IBM bid of $708 million was less than the $1.4 billion bid by AT&T.

In 1993, the IRS acknowledged that the TSM Design Master Plan needed to be rewritten. In particular, it had to focus on business aspects instead of technology. To better coordinate technical planning with IRS needs, the agency established a research and development center funded by $78.5 million of federal money but run by the private sector. The center is responsible for providing technical assistance and strategic planning for the TSM. The IRS also established a high-level "architect office" to evaluate technologies and their likely uses.

Through 1992, the IRS had spent $800 million on TSM. In 1993, new IRS estimates indicate that TSM will cost $7.8 billion above the $15.5 billion needed to keep existing systems running. The new system is expected to generate $12.6 billion in total benefits by 2008 through reduced costs, increased collections, and interest savings. Additionally, the improved processes should save taxpayers $5.4 billion and cut 1 billion hours from their time spent with the IRS.

The IRS asked Congress for a 1996 allocation of $1.03 billion, a substantial increase from the $622 million it spent on automation in 1995. However, Hazel Edwards from the General Accounting Office noted that "After eight years and an investment of almost $2 billion, IRS's progress toward its vision has been minimal."

IRS Commissioner Margaret Milner Richardson denies the GAO claims, noting "I think we have made significant progress, not minimal progress . . . but we do know we can and must do more."

The IRS situation represents a typical dilemma for Congress. The IRS claims that by spending more money, it will be possible to create a system that finally works. The GAO believes it is impossible to complete the entire project envisioned by the IRS. The GAO believes the IRS should focus on smaller projects that can be completed in one to two years.

### Electronic Filing

The IRS introduced electronic filing in 1986, when 25,000 forms were filed electronically. By 1990, 4.2 million people filed for tax refunds electronically. In 1992, the number increased to 10 million filers.

The primary target of electronic filing is the millions of individual taxpayers who will receive refunds. To control the process and ensure that documents are properly filed, electronic filing is only available through authorized tax preparers. The IRS is deliberately avoiding providing access to individual taxpayers. As a result, taxpayers who use the system pay an additional charge to the preparer. However, the electronic system provides for refunds within a couple of weeks.

Electronically filed returns cost the IRS one-tenth the processing cost of paper forms. They also eliminate the cost of paper storage. The IRS notes that it is able to store 800,000 returns on one side of a 12-inch optical disk.

For taxpayers with easy returns, the IRS is simplifying the process even further— providing for filing over the telephone. In a 1992 pilot, 117,000 Ohio taxpayers filed for refunds using Touch-Tone phone calls. The system was expanded nationwide in 1994. It can only be used by taxpayers who qualify to use the 1040EZ form. A replacement form (1040-TEL) must still be signed and filed with the IRS, along with the W-2 (withholding) statements.

### Automated Under-Reporter (AUR)

The Automated Under-Reporter (AUR) is another component of the TMS. The AUR is a system designed to monitor returns and identify people who are most likely to underpay their taxes. The system was first installed in 1992 at the Ogden, Utah, regional center. The system pulls data from the service center's Unisys 1180 mainframe. It is downloaded across a local area network to a Sequent Computer System S-81 minicomputer, and from there it is sent to one of 240 networked UNIX workstations on the employees' desks.

The system automatically matches distribution documents (such as 1099s and W-2s) with the filings of individual taxpayers. Mark Cox, assistant IRS commissioner for information systems development, notes that in trials with the AUR, "We've been able to cut down the rework of cases from 25 percent to less than 5 percent. We see this type of work enabling us to share in more of a connectivity mode."

The system uses an Oracle Corporation database running SQL to match data from various sources. It also performs basic tax computation and helps agents send notices to taxpayers. Managers note that although the new system has not improved the speed of the agents, it has cut down the error rates. As agents become familiar with the system, they expect productivity to improve.

In 1991, the Ogden center processed 26 million tax returns, collecting $100 billion in tax payments. It processed $9 billion in refunds. In 1992, it won the Presidential Award for Quality for improved tax processing by saving the government $11 million over five years.

### Currency and Banking Retrieval System

In 1988, Congress passed a new law in an attempt to cut down on crime (notably drug dealing) and to provide leads to people who significantly underreport their income. Every cash transaction over $10,000 is required by federal law to be reported to the IRS on a Form 8300. The IRS created the Currency and Banking Retrieval System to match these forms against the filer's tax return. The system automatically identifies people who had large cash purchases but claimed little income. However, because of a programming error, the system missed forms covering $15 million in cash transactions between 1989 and 1990.

The problem stemmed from the fact that the IRS used the same code number on the 8300 forms that it had been using on other cash transaction forms. The IRS later assigned separate codes for each form. But when programmers created the new matching programs, they did not know that there were now two codes for each transaction. The system was corrected in 1991 and by 1992 was used to process more than 1 million queries a year.

Jennie Stathis of the GAO notes that there are additional problems with the Form 8300. In particular, the filings are often incomplete or contain incorrect taxpayer identification numbers. The IRS is developing software that will allow businesses to verify the taxpayer ID numbers automatically before the customer completes the purchase.

### Document Processing System and Service Center Recognition/Image Processing System (SCRIPS)

In 1994, the IRS awarded a $1.3 billion contract to the IBM Federal Systems division to design a document processing system that by the late 1990s will convert virtually every tax return to digital form. A day after the contract was awarded, IBM sold the Federal Systems division to Loral Corporation for $1.52 billion.

The 15-year systems integration contract called for having the system online in 1996. The plan called for scanning incoming tax forms. Special software would digitally remove the form layout and instructions, leaving just the taxpayer data. OCR software would then convert the characters (including handwritten numbers) into computer data.

The system was scheduled for initial installation at the Austin, Texas, regional center in August 1995. Plans called for installing it at Ogden, Utah, Cincinnati, Ohio, Memphis, Tennessee, and Kansas City, Missouri by 1998.

Despite the popularity of electronic filing, the IRS still sees a need for the OCR system. The IRS anticipates receiving 252 million paper filings in the year 2001.

SCRIPS is a less ambitious project ($88 million) that was awarded in 1993 to Grumman Corporation's Data Systems unit. SCRIPS was designed to capture data from four simple IRS forms that are single-sided. SCRIPS was supposed to be an interim solution that would support the IRS until DPS could be fully deployed. However, delays have pushed back the delivery of the SCRIPS project.

Interestingly, Grumman Data Systems was the loser in the contest for the DPS contract. The IRS noted that Grumman failed a key technical test.

## Security Breaches

In 1983, Sen. John Glenn (D-Ohio) released an IRS report indicating that 386 employees took advantage of "ineffective security controls" and looked through tax records of friends, neighbors, relatives, and celebrities at the Atlanta regional IRS office. Additionally, five employees used the system to create fraudulent returns, triggering more than 200 false tax refunds. Additional investigations turned up more than 100 other IRS employees nationwide with unauthorized access to records. Glenn observed that the IRS investigation examined only one region and looked at only one of 56 methods that could be used to compromise security. He noted, "I'm concerned this is just the tip of a very large iceberg."

The IRS itself noted that the TSM program "greatly increases the risk of employee browsing, disclosure, and fraud," because of the online access to the centralized databases.

Margaret Richardson, commissioner of internal revenue, noted that the system used by the perpetrators was 20 years old and was used by 56,000 employees. It met all federal security standards, using passwords and limiting access based on job descriptions. The IRS found the problems in Atlanta by examining records of database access from 1990 to 1993. Because the system generates 100 million transactions a month, the data is stored on magnetic tape, making it difficult to search.

In 1989, the IRS arrested Alan N. Scott, of West Roxbury, Massachusets, for allegedly submitting 45 fraudulent returns via the new electronic filing system. The IRS claims the man received more than $325,000 in refunds.

The IRS requires tax return preparers to fill out an application before it issues an access code. Mr. Scott apparently used a fake taxpayer ID number and lied on the application form to gain the access number. The IRS claims he then submitted false returns using bogus names and taxpayer ID numbers to get refund checks ranging from $3,000 to $23,000.

IRS officials note that the electronic filings actually made it easier to identify the problem, because the computer could scan the data earlier than if it had been submitted by hand. Once the situation was identified, the IRS was able to immediately lock out further transactions from Mr. Scott's access number.

## IRS Budget

Like any Congressional agency, the IRS budget is set by Congress and approved by the president. In 1995, The Clinton administration asked Congress to increase the IRS budget by 10 percent—allocating the money to improving the information systems and procedures at the IRS to make them more effective. Congress responded by cutting the IRS budget by 2 percent. The Clinton budget called for $8.23 billion; the Congressional numbers cut the budget from $7.48 billion in 1995 to $7.35 billion in 1996. Congress did grant a slight increase in the budget for tax system modernization. Rep. Jim Lightfoot (R-Iowa) observed that "Without modernization, I think you're throwing good money after bad. The IRS is still working out of cardboard boxes. It's basically that bad."

## Recommendation for the Future

Do something. Anything. In 1998, congressional hearings into IRS dealings with the public revealed several problems within the IRS, and emphasized the negative perceptions the public has toward this important agency. The IRS eventually agreed to change some of its policies to improve its treatment of citizens. The 1998 IRS Restructuring and Reform Act was aimed at changing IRS attitudes and providing citizens a little more control in the tax-collection process.

Unfortunately, the IRS has been even less successful at implementing new technologies. By 1998, virtually all of the earlier development attempts were canceled. In late 1998, the IRS signed a 15-year development contract with Computer Science Corporation (CSC) worth $5 billion. CSC will be responsible for helping design new systems—so the ultimate goal has not yet been determined. Outside experts note that the contract does not necessarily solve all the IRS problems. The IRS must still deal with the contract management issues, and the IRS has not handled those very well in the past either.

In the interim, the IRS still needs to process millions of forms. In 1999, the emphasis shifted to electronic scanning of payment forms. Tax form data will continue to be hand-entered by clerks (having two clerks enter data from each form and checking for errors).

At congressional insistence, the IRS is also emphasizing electronic filing. In 1998, about 23 percent of individual returns were filed electronically. The congressional target is to have 80 percent filed electronically by 2007. However, neither Congress nor the IRS have provided incentives for individuals to file electronically. Currently, people have to pay a fee to file electronically. Generally, only people expecting a refund file electronically, because it does provide a slightly faster response.

## QUESTIONS

1. What problems have been experienced by the IRS in developing its information systems?
2. How are these problems related to the service's systems development methodologies?

3. The GAO thinks the IRS should place more emphasis on electronic filing. Is the GAO correct, or is the IRS approach better?

4. Are there any ways to speed up the development of systems for the IRS? What would be the costs and risks?

5. Are the IRS problems the result of technology or management difficulties?

6. What are the advantages and drawbacks to outsourcing the IRS information systems?

7. Why did the IRS choose private banks to develop the Electronic Payments System? Could this technique be used for other systems?

## ADDITIONAL READING

"All 208 Million Tax Returns Get Electronic Scrutiny on Arrival," *Government Computer News,* March 6, 1995.

"Automation Failed to Meet Requirements," *Government Computer News,* July 17, 1995, p. 6.

"Big Brother's Watching, But This Time It Could Be You," *Government Computer News,* December 12, 1994.

"CIO Says Goals Are Achievable," *Government Computer News,* January 25, 1999, p. 20.

Constance, Paul, James M. Smith, and Florence Olsen, "IRS RC Buy Is on Hold Yet Again," *Government Computer News,* July 3, 1995, p. 3.

Gleckman, Howard. "File Your Taxes—and Save a Tree," *Business Week,* February 1, 1999, p. 128.

"IRS Beefs Up Its Phone Filing System," *Government Computer News,* July 17, 1995, p. 8.

Masud, Sam. "New Bells Are Ringing at IRS," *Government Computer News,* October 16, 1995, pp. 44–45.

Mayer, Merry. "Interim Systems Will Tide IRS Over as It Modernizes," *Government Computer News,* January 25, 1999, p. 21.

McNamee, Mike. "A Kinder Gentler IRS?" *Business Week,* February 1, 1999, p. 128.

"Modernization," *Government Computer News,* January 25, 1999, p. 20.

Rothfeder, Jeffrey. "Invasion of Privacy," *PC World,* November 1995, pp. 152–161.

Thibodeau, Patrick. "Private Sector to Tackle IRS Mess," *Computerworld,* January 4, 1999, p. 4.

Smith, James M. "IRS Spends $1b for Next Five Years of Systems Support," *Government Computer News,* July 17, 1995, p. 82.

———. "Treasury's $109m PC Award Opposed; Sysorex Exec Claims Concept 'Where's AI hiding?'" *AI Expert,* April 1995.

## DISCUSSION ISSUE

### *Users Versus Developers*

One of the most difficult aspects of creating software is enhancing the communication between users and designers. Let's listen in on a typical discussion between an analyst (Khalil) and a manager (Charlie).

Charlie: But you said the entire project would be finished three months ago. Now you're telling me it will take another six months?

Khalil: Look, we were on schedule until a couple of my people quit. The real problem is that your staff kept changing their minds. When we started the marketing research system, you said we did not have to worry about tracking customer coupons. After everyone signed off on the requirements step, you suddenly decide to add these features. We had to go back and start over. That's why we're behind the original schedule.

Charlie: Wait a minute. We didn't care about the coupons until our competitor suddenly decided to expand operations in the Western region. I can't control what our rivals do. I don't remember "signing off" on anything. All I know is that once a month, you sent me a whole stack of papers to read that had nothing to do with my job. And after that first week of meetings, I never saw you for six months. If you had stopped in sooner, I could have told you about the coupons.

Khalil: This is a big project, and we have been busy. If you want the coupon tracking, we'll do it, but it's going to take another six months. You're lucky we can even squeeze it in. We've got other problems. Your employees can't agree on the form and content of some of these reports. We need you to pick one type. Also, to save time, we're going to skip this first report and just give you the combined data on this second report. We don't see any reason to duplicate the data. Last, we need to know the formula you use to make this calculation.

Charlie: No. We need all of the reports exactly the same as we use now. Don't change anything. I don't know the exact formula. I think Michele has it. Ask him. Uh oh, I have another meeting in two minutes. Don't change the reports, just add the coupon tracking. Oh, and we have a new employee (Jack) and he has some great new ideas. Be sure you talk to him.

*Six months later . . .*

Khalil:    Hi, I'm Khalil. What happened to Charlie?

Michele:    She was promoted to marketing VP. When are we going to get the marketing research system?

Khalil:    It's in alpha test now, but we're going to wait on the new 9350 series before implementing. We're having some I/O channel problems, plus I think the 9350 will support Token Ring directly.

Michele:    Huh? I don't know what you're doing, but we needed this system a year ago. We're desperate. Jack created this great spreadsheet program. It gives us some of the reports we want now, but your staff won't give us access to the data we need.

Khalil:    I can write a COBOL program to pull out some data for you, but we can't let your spreadsheets change any of the information. We can't trust the PCs, and there's no way to set up the security and integrity tests we need. You'd be better off waiting until we get the whole system running.

Michele:    Well, we can't trust you either. We're just going to keep working on the PCs. At least we have something. Anyway, I've got bigger problems right now. I just heard that we're expanding into New England by buying out another company. I have to fly out there and check out their marketing plans and hire a couple more staff members.

Khalil:    What? No one told me. We'll need a bigger computer, and we have to change . . . Wait. Do you know what computer that company is using?

## QUESTIONS

1. Whose fault is it that the marketing project is six months behind schedule?
2. Do you think the project will ever be finished?
3. Should the marketing department be given access to the corporate data? Should the staff be allowed to change the data?
4. Is there a solution to these problems—perhaps a different development method or different tools?
5. What can be done to improve the communication between the users and MIS department?

# *Visual Basic*

As a manager, for most business applications you will use existing software: spreadsheets, word processors, database management systems, and accounting systems. However, there will be times when you will want to customize some applications. Other times, you might hire someone to create small applications. In these situations, you might have to read some of the program code to make sure the computations are correct. In any case, it helps to have a basic understanding of computer programming.

Most modern computer languages perform a common set of elementary functions. When you learn a programming language, you focus on these primary features. Languages may differ in syntax (the name of a function, when to include parentheses, and so on). However, the logic is generally the same. Once you understand the logic of programming, it is relatively easy to read and understand a computer program. Learning to write your own code then requires practice. One of the easiest languages to use is Microsoft's Visual Basic (VB). It was designed to be readable and to minimize problems with syntax. It is a useful language to know because it is used in so many applications. All of the Microsoft software packages have a version available beneath the surface, which you can use to automate various tasks. It is also available as a standalone programming package.

## PROGRAMMING LOGIC

At heart, writing computer programs is an exercise in logic. At the high end, science and art become important issues, but the foundation of programming is logic and mathematics. When you write a program, simply think of the computer as a processor that executes each instruction that you give it. Unless you tell it otherwise, the processor examines each statement sequentially—performing the requested task and moving on to the next statement. Five primary types of statements are available: computations, conditions, loops, input, and output.

Computations usually involve numeric data. You can add (+), subtract (–), multiply (∗), and divide (/) numbers. Standard algebraic rules apply, so computations are performed from left to right, and you can use parentheses to change to order of computations. Additionally, you can also manipulate string (text) data. For instance, you can append one string to another: "John" & " " & "Smith" yields "John Smith".

## Computations, Variables, and Functions

Computations often involve variables. Think of a variable as a container that holds a value. For example, one statement might be $a = 32$, which assigns the value of 32 to the variable $a$. Then, a new statement could be $y = a/3 + 15$, which uses the value of $a$ to compute the value of the new variable ($y$). To minimize mistakes, variables should be declared before they are used. VB uses the Dim statement to declare a variable. For example, Dim $a$ as double. The main types of variables you will use are integer, double, string, and variant. An integer variable holds numeric data that does not contain fractions (1, 532, –2273, and so on.). A double variable holds numeric data that can contain fractions or digits to the right of the decimal point (3.14, –25.222, and so on). A string variable holds text ("John", "123 Maple Street", and so on). The variant data type is used when you do not know what type of data will be used, when you want to deal with special data (e.g., dates), or when you need to perform special tests, such as determining if the data is missing (null).

One important type of variable is called an *array*. An array is a variable that contains multiple values. For example, you might have an array that holds the sales for each month of the year. You could then obtain the values by number: SalesForMonth(1), SalesForMonth(2), up to SalesForMonth(12).

Every language has certain internal functions that perform common mathematical operations. For instance, VB uses the Sqr( ) function to compute the square root of a number. Additional functions manipulate string data, such as finding the number of characters in a string (Len), or converting a string to lowercase (LCase). Figure 12.1A lists the primary math and string functions that you might use. Additional functions, details, and examples are readily available from the VB Help system.

## Conditions

Conditions are used to tell the processor to make a decision. The most common conditional statement is the If-Then-Else statement. If the condition is true, one set of instructions is executed. If it is false, a second set is executed instead. Figure 12.2A provides an example of a conditional statement that computes an employee bonus based on a level of Sales. The actual condition can be relatively complex, containing Boolean expressions and multiple comparisons.

For situations when you have multiple values of one variable, it is easier to use a Select Case statement. As shown in Figure 12.3A, a business might give different discounts based on the type of customer. The same problem could be handled with multiple If-Then-Else statements, but the Select Case statement is much easier to read. Note the use of the Case Else statement to capture the values that are not predefined. Even if you think you know all possible values for Customer type, it is wise to include the Else statement in case someone adds a new type later and forgets to alter the Select Case statement.

## Loops

One of the strengths of a computer is that it can perform computations repeatedly. Loops are sections of code that can be performed more than once. Sometimes you know how many times you want to execute the loop. In this

| Math functions | |
| --- | --- |
| Abs | Absolute value |
| Atn | Arc Tangent |
| Cos | Cosine |
| Exp | Exponential |
| Fix | Returns integer portion |
| Int | Converts to integer |
| Log | Logarithm |
| Rnd | Random number |
| Sgn | Signum (−1, 0, 1) |
| Sin | Sine |
| Sqr | Square root |
| Tan | Tangent |
| **String functions** | |
| StrComp | Compare two strings |
| LCase, UCase | Convert to lowercase or uppercase |
| Len | Find length of a string |
| Format | Format a string |
| InStr, Left, LTrim Mid, Right, RTrim, Trim | Manipulate strings |

**FIGURE 12.1A**

INTERNAL FUNCTIONS

Math and string functions are commonly used in programs. Additional functions and details are available from the Help system.

```
If (Sales > 1000) Then
        Bonus = 100
Else
        Bonus = 0
End If
```

**FIGURE 12.2A**
CONDITIONS

One set of statements
is executed depending
on whether the
condition is true or
false.

```
Select Case Customer
        Case Customer = 'Corporate'
                Discount = 0.05
        Case Customer = 'Government'
                Discount = 0.10
        Case Else
                Discount = 0.01
End Select
```

**FIGURE 12.3A**
CONDITIONS WITH MULTIPLE
VALUES

The computer finds the matching
value for the Customer type, and
computes the appropriate
Discount.

```
total = 0
For month = 1 To 12
        total = total + SalesForMonth(month)
Next month
```

**FIGURE 12.4A**
LOOPS WITH FOR-NEXT

When you know how many times you
want to execute the loop, you can use a
For-Next statement.

```
month = 0
sales = 0
Do Until (sales > 100000)
        sales = sales + SalesForMonth(month)
        month = month + 1
Loop
```

**FIGURE 12.5A**

A loop you do not know how many times
to iterate. It repeats until some condition
becomes true.

case, you can use a For-Next statement. The example in Figure 12.4A computes the total sales for the year. It assumes that an array (SalesForMonth) holds the sales for each month. Note the use of the total variable: total = total + SalesForMonth(month). It is known as an accumulator because each time the statement is executed, the computer takes the current value (on the right-hand side) and adds the new monthly sales. The result is copied back to the total variable, providing a new total for the next time the statement is executed.

When you do not know how many times to iterate the loop, you can use a Do Until loop. Figure 12.5A provides an example that will tell you in which month the sales total reached 100,000. Notice the two accumulators: one for the sales total and one to count the months. Both of them have to be initialized (set to zero) before entering the loop. Failure to initialize accumulators is a common programming error. Also note that the increment statement (month = month + 1) inside the loop is crucial. If you forget this statement the loop will run forever—or until someone cancels your program.

## Input and Output

Before Windows, input and output required special statements, and programmers spent a great deal of time learning them and writing them. With Windows, it is still possible to write traditional input and output commands (InputBox, MsgBox, and Printer object commands). However, these commands are rarely used. You can read the VB Help system documentation to learn more about these commands.

With Windows, it is easier to let the underlying application handle the input and output. For example, you can retrieve and store values in spreadsheet cells, or as lines in a word processor document, or in boxes on a database or Visual Basic form. Then your code simply reads the data from the application, performs the necessary computations, and stores the data back

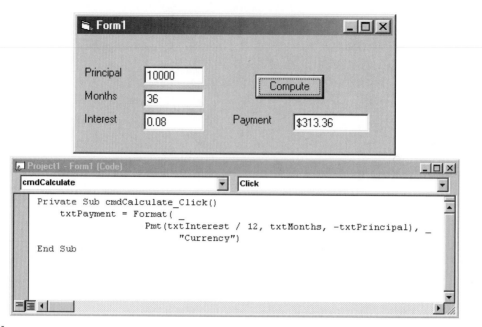

**FIGURE 12.6A**

A VB form uses text boxes for input and output. The boxes leave the user with control over the form and make it easier to write the program.

to the application. The user has complete control over the process and can use the application to format and print the results. This approach makes it easier to write programs and leaves the user in full control.

Retrieving and storing data within an application depends on the application. The easiest method arises with VB and database forms. Each form contains text boxes that are used to enter data and display results. The example in Figure 12.6A shows a simple form to compute the payment due on a loan. The user can enter the three items (principal, months, and interest rate) in any order. When they are ready, they click the Calculate button that executes your code. Your code stores the result in the Payment box. VB and Access forms make it easy to refer to textboxes: simply use the name that you gave the box (e.g., txtPayment) and treat it like a variable in your calculations. Spreadsheet cells and lines in a word processor are slightly more complex. The concept is the same, but the syntax is a little more complicated.

## VISUAL BASIC EXAMPLE IN EXCEL

Visual Basic runs as the macro programming language behind most Microsoft applications, including Excel. You can use it to write short programs that automate var-

| | |
|---|---|
| ALTA | 143 |
| SNOWBASIN | 154 |
| BRIGHTON | 113 |
| PARK CITY | 115 |
| DEER VALLEY | 120 |
| SOLITUDE | 137 |

**FIGURE 12.7A**
INITIAL DATA FROM
THE INTERNET
You want to use proper case for
the names to improve readability.

ious tasks. Consider the example in Figure 12.7A. You obtained a data file from the Internet that contains a list of cities. Unfortunately, the cities were entered in uppercase. To make them easier to read, you want the names to be in proper case, where the first letter is capitalized. Also, when there are spaces in the name, the next letter should be capitalized as well. You could just retype each name, but what if there are hundreds of them?

This type of repetitive task is what computer programs are designed to handle. With a few lines of code, you can fix the names. In fact, you can keep the program around in case you need it for similar problems in the future. As shown in Figure 12.8A, this program consists of two parts. The first part simply loops through the

```
Sub Macro 1()
' Keyboard Shortcut: Ctrl+Shift+U

  For Each c In Selection
     c.Value = PCase(c.Value)
  Next c

End Sub

Function PCase(txt)
' Convert a text value to proper case (first letter is capitalized)
  Dim i As Integer

  ' First make the entire string lower case
  txt = LCase(txt)
  ' Now capitalize the first letter
  Mid(txt, 1,1) = UCase(Mid(txt, 1, 1))
  ' Now search for a space
  i = 2
  Do While (i>0) And (i< Len(txt))
    i = InStr(i, txt,"")
    If (i > 0) And (i<Len(txt))Then
      Mid(txt, i + 1, 1) = UCase(Mid(txt, i +1, 1))
      i = i +1
    End if
  Loop

  PCase = txt
End Function
```

| | |
|---|---|
| Alta | 143 |
| Snowbasin | 154 |
| Brighton | 113 |
| Park City | 115 |
| Deer Valley | 120 |
| Solitude | 137 |

**FIGURE 12.9A**
RESULTS
Names are converted to initial capitals.

**FIGURE 12.8A**
CODE TO CONVERT TEXT TO PROPER CASE
The Macro1 routine gets each value from the spreadsheet and calls the PCase function to convert it.

cells you select and passes the value to the PCase function, which is the second part. The PCase function first converts the entire name to lowercase. Then it makes the first letter uppercase. Next, it searches the name for a blank space. If it finds one, it converts the next letter to uppercase. This search is repeated until there are no more spaces, or it reaches the end of the text.

The Macro1 routine is tied to an Excel keystroke combination: Ctrl+Shift+U. You convert the text by selecting the names in the spreadsheet and pressing the assigned keys. The names are converted to the proper case as shown in Figure 12.9A.

Even a few dozen names could take you a while to retype—and the retyping would probably introduce errors. These lines of code can be written in a few minutes, minimize errors, and be reused for other projects. Plus, it is a lot more interesting to write code than to retype names.

## EXERCISES

1. Copy the code from Figure 12.8A into Excel and test the macro.
2. Write a short macro program in Excel that adds all of the numbers between the values in cell A1 and cell A2 and puts the result in cell A5. For example, if A1 = 1 and A2 = 5, then add 1 + 2 + 3 + 4 + 5 to get 15. Hint: You can read or write to a cell with the command Range("A1").
3. Write an Excel macro that looks at each item selected to see if any cells are blank. If any are blank, display a message notifying the user how many blank cells there are. Hint: Use the IsEmpty function to test and the MsgBox command to display a message.
4. Briefly describe an application that could benefit from the use of a macro (i.e., it cannot easily be solved with a built in function).
5. Identify as many products as you can that use a version of Visual Basic as a programming language.

# Organizing Information System Resources

Fidelity Investments runs some of the largest mutual funds in the world. Managing investments for millions of people requires good information systems and careful organization.

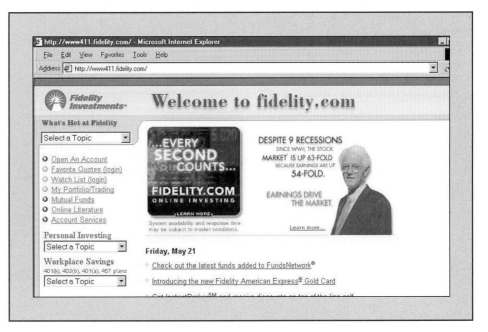

## FIDELITY INVESTMENTS

Edward Crosby Johnson III made the walk to 82 Devonshire with more on his mind than usual. It was the first day of winter in Boston, and he was evaluating his company's performance of the year. As the chairman of Fidelity Investments, the company was "his" because of his formal position of authority. It was also his because the Johnsons owned most of the privately held company, worth billions.

Most of all, Fidelity was Ned Johnson's because he had made the right decisions for Fidelity with remarkable regularity, building the firm into the world's largest mutual fund company, with over $400 billion in managed assets. It seemed fitting that Ned walked to work; it reflected his puritanical background and hatred of waste. Even though he had known wealth his whole life, a Brahmin sense of stewardship guided his behavior at all times, even when he managed other people's money.

**OVERVIEW**  The role of the MIS department is to help you achieve business goals. But before you start to think of them as your personal genie, keep in mind that the MIS staff works for the entire company. As illustrated by Figure 13.1, the challenge is to organize the MIS resources to support everyone with a minimum of conflicts.

In addition to systems development, many tasks need to be done to ensure that companies make efficient use of their MIS resources. But why should business managers care about how the MIS resources are organized? In smaller businesses, the answer is simple: There is no strong MIS department, so you have to do the job yourself. The answer is more complex in larger businesses that have well-established MIS departments. A basic answer lies in the fact that MIS departments face many challenges that impose constraints on their choices. Managers and users need to understand these constraints to learn why MIS departments cannot always fulfill their requests. Managers also need to determine the best method for building systems they need.

**FIGURE 13.1**
ORGANIZING
INFORMATION
SYSTEM RESOURCES
Making effective use of
information systems
requires organizing the
MIS resources:
Hardware, software,
data, and personnel. A
key decision involves
positioning the
resources in the
organization which
revolves around
decentralization versus
centralization. The goal
is to balance the need
for central control and
the value of
decentralized
decisions.

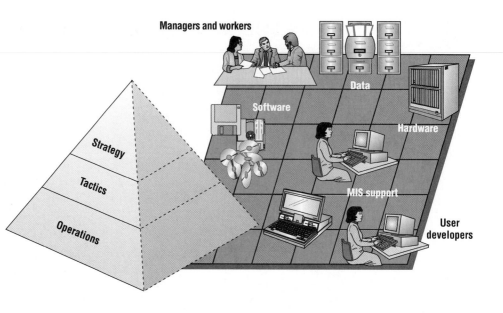

One of the key constraints facing MIS is that information within an organization needs to be accessible to everyone. There is a long history in U.S. companies of independent pockets of information being created that cannot be shared. In fact, there is a long-running conflict in many companies between individual demands and the corporate need to share data. The competing demands between this centralization and decentralization influence almost every aspect of how companies create and use information. Managers and users can play a key role in resolving the underlying conflicts.

## INTRODUCTION

The capabilities of application software are impressive. Because of these tools, business-people using personal computers are solving problems in a few hours that never would have been attempted five years ago. With these powerful tools available to the average businessperson, it is easy to wonder why a company needs an MIS department. That's a good question, and the answers keep changing through the years.

MIS departments provide many important services. For example, think about what happens when a new version of your word processor is released. Someone has to install the software, distribute the manuals, convert old document files to the new format, and show people how to use the new features. Now imagine the problems involved when there are 5,000 workers using this software.

According to statistics collected by *Computerworld,* large companies spend about 5 percent of their sales revenue on the MIS area. For a company with a billion dollars in sales, that amounts to $50 million a year spent on MIS. This money pays for personal computers, central computers, communications, software, and MIS personnel to manage it all. The primary tasks undertaken by the MIS department are software development, setting corporate computing standards, hardware administration, database administration, advocacy and planning, and end-user support.

Small businesses usually do not have a separate MIS department. That does not mean these duties are ignored. Even in small businesses, someone has to be responsible for these MIS functions. However, small businesses generally do not attempt to develop their own software. Even relying on commercial software requires that time be spent on determining data needs and evaluating software packages.

## Trends

There were few management issues with the earliest computers. They were big, required specially designed rooms, and highly trained programmers and operators. These computers were used for basic computations. As a result, the computers were placed in a central location. All data and software were stored with the computer. Because the early machines had limited communication capabilities, the MIS personnel were also located with the machines.

As the price of computers dropped and capabilities increased, they were used for more tasks. The machines, data, and software continued to be stored in central locations. Many companies put them in large rooms surrounded by glass, so managers could show visitors that the company was pursuing "modern" solutions. Eventually, companies realized that these "glass-houses" were a security risk. Most companies now hide their main computers behind locked doors and security guards.

In the 1970s, many companies purchased midrange computers. These computers were easier to operate and individual departments could afford to buy one for their own use. It represented the beginning of hardware decentralization. Many companies now had computers scattered throughout the firm. Software, data, and some MIS personnel followed the machines to the departments. In many cases, the hardware, software and data were incompatible with the central computers. As long as the machines and data were used only by a single department, the problems were minimal. However, many MIS departments spent a good portion of the 1970s trying to get these machines and user departments to share data.

In the 1980s, the move toward decentralization accelerated with the introduction of personal computers. The competition in microcomputer technology has created hardware that is as powerful as most large central computers at a fraction of the price. Most companies today have an average of slightly less than one computer per employee. The key concern is that as hardware becomes distributed throughout the organization, software, data and the need for support will follow. If computers and data are completely decentralized, it is difficult to share data among workers.

The local area networks of the late 1980s were a response to the need to share data and hardware. However, even with a LAN, there are many ways to organize the various information resources.

In the 1990s, as personal computers became increasingly powerful, even more data shifted to these machines. This increased control by individuals can alter the structure of the company, as the conflict between centralization and decentralization intensifies.

Probably the most important MIS decision facing business today is the issue of **centralization.** Because personal computers have a huge price/performance advantage over larger computers, there is a major incentive to decentralize the hardware. Yet, there are some serious complications with complete decentralization. Several strategies for organizing information resources provide the advantages of both centralization and decentralization. The management goal is to find the combination that works best for each situation. Before examining the alternatives, you need to understand the basic MIS roles.

**MANAGING THE INFORMATION SYSTEMS FUNCTION**

Many times in your career you will find yourself heavily involved with members of the MIS department. In the case of a small business, you might be in charge of the one or two MIS personnel. At some time, you might be the company liaison to an outsourcing vendor, MIS contractor, or consultant. In all of these situations, you will be responsible for planning, monitoring, and evaluating the MIS organization. You will have to make decisions and answer questions like: Is the MIS department doing a good job? Should the

## The Changing Role of MIS

The role of the MIS department has changed over time. In many respects, it is in the middle of a fundamental change. In the past, MIS departments focused on creating information systems and controlling data—particularly transaction data. Today, as explained by the Gartner Group (an IS consulting firm), the objectives of MIS are:

- Provide transparent access to corporate data.
- Optimize access to data stored on multiple platforms for many groups of users.

- Maximize the end-user's ability to be self-sufficient in meeting individual information needs.

These changes represent a shift in attitude. It moves toward the goal of increasing support for workers, not their replacement, so employees can do their jobs better on their own.

company be spending more money on MIS? Is it getting a good value for its current spending? Are there other methods that would be more efficient or save money?

As many companies have found, it is difficult to evaluate the MIS function. There are few objective measures. Changes in technology make the process more difficult. Innovations in hardware and software often make it easier to build and maintain information systems. However, there is a cost to buying new equipment. There is also a cost to continually retraining workers and modifying databases and reports. The goal of management is to find the appropriate balance between the need to update and the costs.

Management of information systems begins by understanding the roles of MIS. The MIS function is responsible for hardware and software acquisition and support. The MIS staff provide access to corporate data and build applications. They support end-user development with training and help desks. MIS workers set corporate data standards and maintain the integrity of the company databases. All of these functions have to be organized, performed, and evaluated on a regular basis.

The issue of new technology points out the importance of planning. The only way to control costs and evaluate MIS benefits is to establish a plan. Plans need to be detailed so actual results can be compared to the plan. Yet plans need to be flexible enough to adapt to unexpected events and new technology. You also need to formulate contingency plans for events that might occur.

One key issue in managing information technology is organizing the MIS function so that it matches the structure of the firm. Centralization versus decentralization has been a key issue in the organization of MIS resources. Networks and powerful personal computers have led to more options supporting decentralization of information. The increased options are useful, but they create more issues managers must examine. To understand the advantages and drawbacks of MIS options, we must first examine the roles of MIS.

**MIS ROLES** Good information systems do not simply materialize from thin air. Providing timely, accurate, and relevant information requires careful planning and support. Creating effective information involves maintaining hardware, providing software training and support, supporting end-user development, defining and controlling access to databases, establishing corporate standards, and researching the competitive advantages of new technologies. The basic roles of MIS are outlined in Figure 13.2.

**FIGURE 13.2**

MIS ROLES

The MIS department is responsible for hardware administration, software development, and training and support. MIS staff establish corporate computing standards, provide access to corporate data, and support end-user development. The MIS department also plays an advocacy role, presenting the IS benefits and strategies to the executive officers.

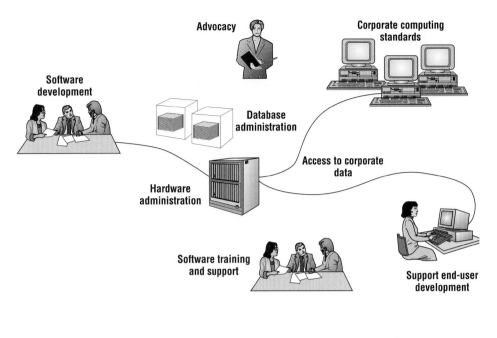

## Hardware Administration

Managers should not have to be computer experts to use their computers. Consider the work involved in buying a new computer. The computer industry has been changing rapidly, both with personal computers and with larger computers. Major changes occur in computer hardware continuously. For example, Intel (the designer of processors for most IBM-compatible personal computers) produced five major versions (plus additional variations) of microprocessors between 1982 and 1993. Each processor was more than twice as fast as the prior version and provided new features. Similar changes are constantly being made to the video capabilities, printers, networks, and storage devices.

Every time the hardware changes, there are new uses for computers. As computers gain speed and capabilities, they can be used to solve more difficult problems. As the price declines, computers can be used for even more tasks. An enormous amount of time is required for MIS watchers just to keep track of the changes in the industry. Someone has to keep abreast of these changes. It does not make sense for every manager to be an expert on the current state of computer hardware. Instead of duplicating this effort, it is best to make the MIS department responsible for maintaining current computer information.

When users want to purchase new computers, they can go to the MIS department for information and advice. Some businesses provide a company computer store to allow users to test new computers. The MIS department can then deliver and set up the computers with the appropriate software already installed. This specialization means that users do not have to spend large amounts of time keeping up with changes in the computer industry. It also allows companies to buy hardware and software in large quantities to get better discounts. By working with standard hardware and software, MIS staff can make sure that all the pieces will work together. The MIS department also takes care of repairing the existing computers. If a computer breaks down, someone has to identify the problem and install replacement parts or notify the vendor.

While computer reliability has increased considerably in the last ten years, installing, repairing, and modifying hardware is still an important job. Many companies rely on the original vendor or outside service firms to provide a rapid response to problems.

Hardware devices also need routine maintenance. Printers have to be cleaned and toner cartridges replaced. Disk drives need to be reorganized, reformatted, or re-aligned. Networks sometimes need to be reorganized because accounts are added or deleted almost daily. These small tasks can quickly multiply when there are thousands of users.

## Software Support

Software generally requires more support than hardware does. MIS staff can help users decide which software to purchase and then can install it. Users need to be trained to use various software features. Whenever workers change jobs or a company hires new work-ers, they need to be trained. Similarly, commercial software versions change almost every year, implying more training for users. Additionally, someone has to install the new copies on the machines, manuals have to be distributed, and data files sometimes have to be converted.

When users have difficulty getting the computer to do what they want, it saves time to have someone to call for help. Most commercial software companies provide tele-phone support for their products, although many of them charge extra for this support. In many cases, it is better for MIS to support users directly. Besides the possibility of lower costs, the MIS department has a better understanding of the business problems. Also, many users are now combining information from several packages. For example, you might put a spreadsheet and a graph into a word-processed document. If different compa-nies created the three programs and you have trouble, which one of the three software companies do you call? Your own MIS department will have experience with all three packages and should be able to identify the cause of the problems.

## Business Trends: Specialization

Just as in other areas of business, MIS jobs have become highly specialized. For instance, many advertisements for MIS jobs look like someone spilled a bowl of alphabet soup on the page. Companies often search for technical skills involving specific hardware and software.

Unfortunately, this approach to jobs causes problems for MIS personnel. In order to find other jobs or to advance in their current position, they have to acquire increasingly detailed knowledge of specific hardware and software packages. Yet, with rapid changes in the industry, this knowledge can become obsolete in a year or two. These changes mean employees have to continually expand their knowledge and identify software and hardware approaches that are likely to succeed.

On the other hand, businesses need to keep their current applications running. With thousands of hours invested in current systems, companies cannot afford to discard their current practices and adopt every new hardware and software system that shows some promise.

Network specialists can be involved in every aspect of the network, from installing and analyzing cables to configuring accounts and monitoring security over company networks. While communication is relatively straightforward, larger networks are much more difficult to install and maintain. Just tracking connection problems and identifying cables can be a full-time job.

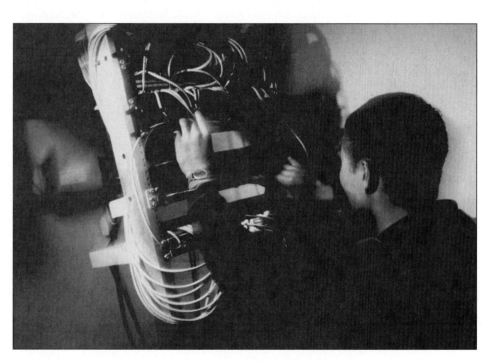

### Access to Corporate Data

In many organizations, massive data is stored on centralized computers. This basic data is often maintained by the MIS department. Users need this data for various reports. The marketing department may need the last 18 months of sales data in order to forecast the next 6 months. One important role of the MIS department is to help users access this information. Two basic items are needed to provide access to the data: hardware connections and software.

In terms of hardware, the MIS department is responsible for providing the physical connections between the machines. Besides the initial installation, considerable effort can be required to maintain these networks. Modern local area networks have many components scattered throughout the firm's buildings. Maintenance personnel need substantial expertise and patience to identify and correct problems that arise. Similarly, when someone wants to rearrange a large office, it might be necessary to change the network wiring. When computers are changed or someone wants access to other computers, the MIS personnel are responsible for changing the network.

In terms of software, the MIS department has to make sure that the information is provided in a format that can be used by the personal computers. MIS personnel have to be certain the users are authorized to access the data. The software has to maintain all necessary security provisions to make sure the data remains accurate. The personal computers also may need additional software to access the corporate network.

## Software Development

Chapter 12 explains the three common approaches to developing software: systems development life cycle, prototyping, and end-user development. Regardless of the method used, someone has to be in charge of each project. Also, because several projects are likely to be proposed at the same time, someone has to evaluate the feasibility of the projects and decide which ones should be undertaken first. Similarly, someone has to monitor the progress of all projects to keep them on track and avoid budget overruns.

The additional tasks of analysis and software design in the SDLC and prototyping methods have already been explained. The role of MIS personnel with end-user development is not as clear. Consider an extreme situation. If a company relies on prepackaged software and applications created by end users, would the company need an MIS staff? The basic answer is that someone still has to perform some of the MIS tasks, but he or she is likely to be an employee of an individual business unit instead of an MIS department.

## Support for End-User Development

Many application packages include programming capabilities. For example, a manager may create a spreadsheet to calculate sales commissions. Each week, new sales data is entered and the spreadsheet automatically produces summary reports. It would be better to have a clerk rather than a manager enter this new data. To make the clerk's job easier, the manager uses the macro capabilities in the spreadsheet to create a set of menus and help messages. Similarly, using a word processor's macro facilities, a legal department can create standard paragraphs for various contracts. With them, an assistant can type one word to display a prewritten warranty paragraph. In theory, even complex applications traditionally provided by the MIS department, such as accounting systems, could be programmed by end users with prepackaged software.

Several problems can arise from end-user programming. Techniques that are acceptable for small projects may lead to errors and delays with large systems. Programming major applications requires obtaining information from users and managers. Applications designed for corporate use require extensive checking of data and security provisions to ensure accuracy. The software often needs to run on different operating system and local networks.

The MIS department can provide assistance to minimize these problems. MIS personnel can assist end users in collecting ideas from other users. They can also help in testing the applications to verify the accuracy and make sure the software works with other applications. MIS can provide tools and help end users document their applications and move them to new operating systems or new hardware. Programmers can write special routines to overcome any limitations of commercial software that might arise. MIS staffs also maintain help desks or information centers to answer user questions and help users debug applications.

Training and education are increasingly important functions of the MIS department. With hardware and software changing on a daily basis, employees must constantly learn new tools and techniques.

## Corporate Computing Standards

Over time, MIS has learned that the firm gets into trouble if all of its people work independently. In the 1960s, applications such as payroll, accounting, and customer order processing were developed independently. During the 1970s, companies had to spend large amounts of money getting all of the pieces to work together. In the 1980s, personal computers arrived, and the problems got worse.

Reacting to the problems created by these incompatibilities, MIS professionals at different companies developed **standards.** If all vendors used standard formats for files, hardware connections, and commands, products from different vendors could be used together. Today, there are standards for everything: data, hardware, software, report layouts, and coffee pots.

It is unlikely that the computing world will ever see complete cooperation among vendors. Three factors prevent products from working together. First, standards are often ambiguous or incomplete. Human languages always have some ambiguity, and there is no way to determine whether the description actually covers every possible situation. A second problem is that standards incorporate what is known about a topic at the time the standard is developed. Computing technologies change rapidly. Often, vendors can produce better products by not following the standards. Then new standards have to be developed. A third problem occurs because vendors want to distinguish their products from the offerings of competitors. If there were standards that perfectly described a product, there would be only one way to compete: price. Many vendors find that it is more profitable to offer features beyond what is specified in the standards, enabling the developers to charge a higher price.

Even though it is not possible to create perfect industry standards, there are advantages to creating companywide standards. They enable firms to buy products at lower prices. Most large businesses have special purchase agreements with hardware and software vendors. Buying in bulk allows them to obtain better prices. Similarly, it is easier to fix hardware if all the machines are the same. Likewise, it is much more convenient to upgrade just one word-processing package for 200 computers, instead of 20 different brands. Similarly, training is less expensive and time consuming if everyone uses the same software and hardware. Finally, standards make it easier for employees to share information across the company.

The Internet and e-mail create additional demand for standards. To share a file on the Internet, you must store it in a standard format (e.g., HTML or PDF). People sometimes forget that a similar problem arises when attaching files to e-mail messages. Particularly when you send a file to someone in a different company, you need to remember that the recipient may not have the same version of software that you are using. If you attach a file in Word 2000 format, for example, the recipient needs to have Word 2000 to read it. Since some companies upgrade before others, it is generally safer to save attached files in either a standard format (HTML or RTF), or in a previous version.

Some organizations forget that standards cannot be permanent. Hardware and software change almost continuously; new products arrive that are substantially better than existing standard items. Similarly, as the business changes, the standards often have to be revised. Also, there are exceptions to just about any policy. If one department cannot do its job with the standard equipment, MIS must make an exception and then figure out how to support this new equipment and software.

## Data and Database Administration

Databases are crucial to the operation of any company. Keeping the databases up-to-date and accurate does not happen by chance. Larger organizations employ a **database administrator (DBA)** to be responsible for maintaining the corporate database. The DBA is responsible for maintaining the databases, monitoring performance of the database management system, and solving day-to-day problems that arise with the databases.

Companies also need someone to coordinate the definition of the data. Large organizations might hire a separate *data administrator (DA);* smaller companies will pass this role to the DBA. The DA is responsible for defining the structure of the databases. The DA has to make certain the data is stored in a form that can be used by all the applications and users. He or she is responsible for avoiding duplicate terms (e.g., customer instead of client). Additionally, the DA provides for **data integrity,** which means that the data must contain as few errors as possible.

The DA is also required to maintain security controls on the database. The DA has to determine who has access to each part of the data and specify what changes users are al-

---

### Reality Bytes    13–1    Changes in Information Technology Management

From 1994 to 1998, spending on information technology projects doubled as a percentage of corporate revenue. Much of this increase was due to the year 2000 work and the need to update systems to handle the introduction of the euro currency. Expenditures after 2000 are not expected to increase at the same rate, but Bob Silver, an executive vice-president at PaineWebber observes, "We do think technology is a competitive weapon, and we're going to continue to invest in it." He also states, "I'm very excited because I see major breakthroughs in being able to harness technology to solve some significant business issues. The Internet has given me lots of possibilities that I haven't had before from a speed-to-market standpoint." Yet much of this work will be done via outside contractors. Kurt Potter, an analyst with the Gartner Group, believes that by 2003, 50 percent of the IT work will be performed by external service providers—up from the 20 percent handled now. The Gartner Group also predicts that individual business units will control 65 percent of the IP budget by 2003—compared to the 60 percent under central control today.

lowed to make. Along the same lines, companies and employees are required by law to meet certain privacy requirements. For instance, banks are not allowed to release data about customers except in certain cases. European nations have much stricter privacy rules. If a firm operates a computer facility in many European countries, the company must carefully control access to all customer data. Some nations prohibit the transfer of customer data out of the country. The DA is responsible for understanding these laws and making sure the company complies with them.

Finally, because today's databases are so crucial to the company, the business needs a carefully defined disaster and recovery policy. Typically that means the databases have to be backed up every day. Sometimes, a company might keep continuous backup copies of critical data on separate disk drives at all times. MIS has to plan for things that might go wrong (fires, viruses, floods, hackers, etc.). If something does affect the data or the computer system, MIS is responsible for restoring operations. For instance, an alternate computing site might be needed while the original facilities are being repaired. All of this planning requires considerable time.

## Advocacy Role

The MIS department is headed by a single manager, who often is called the chief information officer (CIO). The CIO position might be a vice-president or one level below that. A major portion of this job involves searching for ways in which the information system can help the company. In particular, the CIO searches for and advocates strategic uses of MIS. The goal is to use the computer in some way that attracts customers to provide an advantage over the company's competitors.

Whenever a new technology is introduced, someone has to be responsible for deciding whether it will be worth the expense to make a change. If there is no one in this **advocacy role** who evaluates the existing systems and compares them to new products, an organization is probably not often going to get new equipment. Even when many users are dissatisfied with an existing system, they will have a better chance of acquiring new technology if they can voice their complaints through one highly placed person. Along these lines, the CIO is responsible for long-run planning in terms of information technology.

**MIS JOBS** A wide variety of jobs are available in MIS. Some of the jobs require a technical education, such as that for programmers. Specialized positions are available in data communications and database management. On the other hand, **systems analysts** require an extensive knowledge of business problems and solutions. Some entry-level operator jobs require only minimal training. On the other end of the scale, analysts may eventually become team leaders or managers. The entire MIS function is coordinated by chief information officers.

As you might expect, salaries depend on experience, individual qualifications, industry, location, and current economic conditions. Six basic MIS job tracks are shown in Figure 13.3: systems development, networks, database, user support, operations, and other specialists. Systems development includes several levels of analysts and programmers. Network management involves installing network hardware and software, diagnosing problems, and designing new networks.

Database management focuses on database design and administration. End-user support consists of training users, answering questions, and installing software. Operations consists of day-to-day tasks such as loading paper, mounting tapes, and starting long computer tasks. Many of these tasks are being automated. Entry-level operator jobs do not require a college degree, but there is little room for advancement without a degree. Specialist positions exist in larger companies and generally evolve from new technologies. For example, Web masters who would create and manage web sites were in high demand for two or three years. Then as

**FIGURE 13.3**
IS SALARIES

As in any field, salaries depend on experience. However, in IS they also depend heavily on technical skills. Programmer/analysts with current skills and experience in new technologies find it easier to get jobs and obtain higher salaries. Note that there is a wide variety of jobs in IS, each requiring different types of skills.

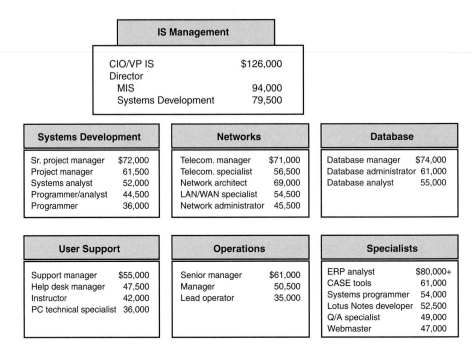

| IS Management | |
|---|---|
| CIO/VP IS | $126,000 |
| Director | |
| MIS | 94,000 |
| Systems Development | 79,500 |

| Systems Development | |
|---|---|
| Sr. project manager | $72,000 |
| Project manager | 61,500 |
| Systems analyst | 52,000 |
| Programmer/analyst | 44,500 |
| Programmer | 36,000 |

| Networks | |
|---|---|
| Telecom. manager | $71,000 |
| Telecom. specialist | 56,500 |
| Network architect | 69,000 |
| LAN/WAN specialist | 54,500 |
| Network administrator | 45,500 |

| Database | |
|---|---|
| Database manager | $74,000 |
| Database administrator | 61,000 |
| Database analyst | 55,000 |

| User Support | |
|---|---|
| Support manager | $55,000 |
| Help desk manager | 47,500 |
| Instructor | 42,000 |
| PC technical specialist | 36,000 |

| Operations | |
|---|---|
| Senior manager | $61,000 |
| Manager | 50,500 |
| Lead operator | 35,000 |

| Specialists | |
|---|---|
| ERP analyst | $80,000+ |
| CASE tools | 61,000 |
| Systems programmer | 54,000 |
| Lotus Notes developer | 52,500 |
| Q/A specialist | 49,000 |
| Webmaster | 47,000 |

**FIGURE 13.4**
INTERNATIONALIZATION

In the past few years, U.S. firms have turned to using programmers in other nations. For example, U.S. programmers are paid almost 12 times as much as Indian programmers. Hence, even though programmers are scarce in India (salary is 13 times the common labor salary versus 2 times for the United States), it is cheaper for U.S. firms to use these programmers.

| | SYSTEMS ANALYST | | COMPUTER PROGRAMMER | | TEXTILE WORKER | |
|---|---|---|---|---|---|---|
| | SALARY | BENEFITS | SALARY | BENEFITS | PER HOUR | BENEFITS |
| United States | 46,757 | 14,443 | 36,022 | 10,578 | 8.74 | 2.87 |
| Japan | 51,938 | 12,581 | 42,316 | 9,415 | 14.12 | 9.53 |
| Germany | 49,286 | 15,821 | 40,124 | 13,951 | 13.12 | 7.38 |
| France | 44,050 | 27,113 | 26,311 | 19,210 | 9.73 | 6.76 |
| Britain | 41,808 | 9,680 | 25,529 | 5,718 | 8.23 | 2.04 |
| India | 2,248 | 3,196 | 1,769 | 2,206 | 0.41 | 0.15 |
| Mexico | 20,794 | 15,057 | 14,917 | 11,161 | 1.68 | 1.25 |
| Hong Kong | 51,277 | 12,185 | 28,211 | 6,404 | 3.33 | 0.52 |

Data in U.S. dollars.

SOURCES: Towers Perrin, Werner International, American Textile Manufacturers' Institute. Differences can be affected by other factors, such as cost of living, productivity, access to equipment, and transportation and communication costs.

the Internet became more important to companies, all of the workers were trained in Web development, so there was less need for specialists.

Every year, *Computerworld* surveys workers in the industry and publishes average salaries. Job placement firms such as Robert Half also collect data on salaries. This data can be useful to you if you are searching for a job or thinking about a career in MIS. As a business manager, the numbers will give you an indication of the costs entailed in building and maintaining information systems. Basic averages are listed in Figure 13.3. As indicated by Figure 13.4, costs vary enormously by nation, which is leading some U.S. companies to use programmers from India, Scotland, and Russia.

**FIGURE 13.5**
MIS SKILLS
IN DEMAND
First column is percent
of companies reporting
great difficulty in filling
positions. Second
column is premiums
paid to workers with
those skills. Third
column is 1994 job ads
for positions.

| SKILL | 1998 COMPANIES (%) | 1998 SALARY PREMIUM (%) | 1994 JOB ADS (%) |
|---|---|---|---|
| Enterprise resource planning | | 17 | |
| Oracle (DMBS) | 15 | 13 | |
| Groupware tools | | 14 | |
| UNIX | 13 | | 22 |
| Networking | 12 | 11 | 40 |
| Cobol | 11 | 12 | 19 |
| Database management skills | 10 | 13 | 28 |
| Microsoft NT server | 9 | 11 | |
| AS/400 | 6 | | |
| Internet experience/skills | 6 | 11 | |
| Visual Basic | 6 | | 20 |
| Project management | 6 | 11 | |

SOURCE: *Computerworld,* November 16, 1998, and Arnett and Litecky, *Journal of Systems Management,* February 1994.

One way to see the changes occurring in MIS is to look at the types of skills that businesses are looking for in MIS applicants. Figure 13.5 shows the skills demanded in 1998/1999 compared to those in 1994. Notice the high demand in new categories (ERP, groupware, and Internet skills). Also note the increased importance of Cobol because of the year 2000 rewrites. The demand for ERP skills is also high because of the larger number of companies implementing new systems to minimize year 2000 problems.

## CENTRALIZATION AND DECENTRALIZATION

One of the most pressing questions facing businesses today is the issue of centralization. Interestingly, many of the discussions apply to the entire firm, not just to the information systems. Large companies that grew up as monolithic centralized corporations are considering breaking into smaller units with more decentralized control.

Almost none of the issues of centralization and decentralization are new—politicians, economists, and organizational theorists have debated them for hundreds of years. The basic argument for centralization revolves around the need to coordinate activities and efficiencies that can be gained from large-scale operations. Proponents of **decentralization** argue that moving control to smaller units produces a more flexible system that can respond faster to market changes and encourage individual differences, and innovate.

As with many arguments, there are different answers for different circumstances, and it is rare that the extreme choices are best. Wise managers will attempt to gain the advantages of both approaches. With information systems, four basic areas are subject to centralization or decentralization: hardware, software, data, and staffing. Determining the best way to organize information resources requires that managers understand the advantages and disadvantages for each of these areas.

### Hardware

Hardware resources are often a strong cause of changes in MIS. In particular, today's move toward decentralization is being driven by one important factor: the cost of hardware. Typical estimates of the cost of large central computers indicate that they cost

## The Cost of Computers

The cost of a computer consists of much more than hardware. The costs include even more than the software and data. In 1995, Forrester Research, Inc., estimated that large companies spend $3,830 annually to maintain each personal computer. Improved technology and standards are expected to cause costs to drop by 50 percent. The largest expense is providing one support person for every 50 personal computer users, which amounts to $1,420 per user. Breakdowns amount to about six days of lost time a year, adding up to $1,350 per personal computer.

**FIGURE 13.6**
COMPLETE
CENTRALIZATION

For many years, computers were expensive and there were few communication networks. Consequently, hardware, data, software, and MIS personnel were centrally located. Data was sent to the computer for processing and printed reports were distributed throughout the company. Users only dealt indirectly with MIS.

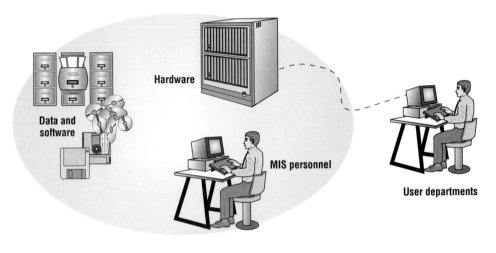

around $50,000 per million instructions per second (MIPS). The cost of personal computers is somewhere around $50 per MIPS. Although it is difficult to compare the features between the two types of machines, it is hard to ignore a computer that costs a thousand times less. Virtually all of the new computing power installed in companies in the last few years has been in the form of personal computers.

### Centralization

The biggest advantage of centralized IS hardware is that it is easier to share hardware, software, and data with multiple users. Complete centralization is shown in Figure 13.6. Consider a simple example. If a company installs an expensive printer in one user's office, it will be difficult for other users to get access to the printer. On the other hand, with only one central computer, all of the hardware, software, and data will be located in one place. All users can be given equal access to these facilities. By keeping all hardware, software, and personnel in one location, it is easier to avoid duplication and keep costs down.

Along the same lines, centralized hardware also makes it easier to control user access to the information system. By storing all data on one machine, it is easy to monitor all usage of the data. In a sense, all user access to data must first be approved by the MIS department. Any data alteration or transfer is much easier to control if it takes place on one machine.

There are also some cost advantages to maintaining centralized hardware. First, there is less duplication and more efficient use of the hardware. How often is a personal computer used? When a user is working on some other task, the machine usually sits idle on the desk. On the other hand, if one user stops processing jobs on a central computer, the additional resources (memory, disk space, processing time) are automatically allocated to other jobs.

**FIGURE 13.7**
While sales of all computers have increased, there is no question that personal computer sales have increased faster than any other computer.
SOURCES: Gartner Group and Dataquest.

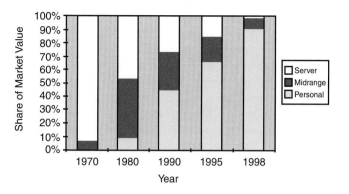

Centralized purchasing can also be used to save money. It is easier to standardize equipment if it is not spread throughout the company. It is generally possible to obtain discounts from vendors by buying larger quantities. Centralized purchases also make it easier to keep track of the amount of money spent on information technology. When user departments are responsible for all IT purchases, the lack of centralized control can lead to duplication of hardware.

### Decentralization

Decentralization of hardware carries its own advantages. First, there is less chance of a total breakdown. If your computer breaks, everyone else can continue working. You might even be able to borrow someone else's machine.

With decentralization, users can obtain personalized equipment. Perhaps a financial analyst needs an extremely fast machine to process complex equations. Or maybe a marketing representative needs a portable computer to collect data from clients. An advertising specialist could use special high-resolution graphics to help design promotions. In each case, the company saves money by buying each user exactly what he or she needs, and not forcing everyone to use one standardized product.

Currently, the third advantage is the most important: price. Any slight cost advantage from using centralized computers is destroyed by the enormous price advantage of personal computers. Of course, some of today's high-performance personal computers can be used as a central computer. Even so, users need some device to access that computer, and it does not cost much to give the devices the additional capabilities of separate personal computers. As observed by the Gartner Group, notice the trend in worldwide sales of computer systems displayed in Figure 13.7. The percentage of value spent on micros (defined as machines with a cost less than $25,000) has been steadily increasing since 1980. This trend is likely to continue or accelerate. Note that the total value of sales of virtually all types of computers has increased. For example, the Internet has encouraged firms to spend increasing amounts of money on large servers. However, the expenditure on personal computers overwhelms the other costs.

### Software and Data

Wherever there is hardware, it is also necessary to provide software. Nonetheless, it is possible to centralize some aspects of software, even though there are decentralized computers. The goal is to capture the advantages of both methods at the same time. Data files are similar to software files, but there are some additional features to consider when choosing where to store the data.

### Software Centralization

If software is standardized and purchased centrally, it is possible to negotiate lower prices from software vendors. In many cases, it is not necessary to purchase a separate copy of software for each user. Instead, a license is purchased that allows a specific number of people to use the software at one time. Because it is unlikely that every user will need the same software at the same time, this method can save a considerable amount of money. Additionally, if everyone uses the same basic software, there are fewer compatibility problems and it is easy for users to exchange data with co-workers. Similarly, upgrades, training, and assistance are much simpler if there are a limited number of packages to support. Imagine the time and effort involved if the company needs to upgrade a spreadsheet on 5,000 separate machines. Some companies have reported that by the time they managed to upgrade the entire company, an even newer version was released.

One difficulty with centralized software is that loading and running software across a network can be slower than if it is installed on each machine. Even with high-speed networks and fast file servers, users will notice that the applications load and run slower across the network. The problem is exacerbated when several users request the same application at the same time.

### Software Decentralization

Forcing users to choose identical packages can lead to major arguments between users and the MIS department. Many times users have different requirements or perhaps they simply have different preferences. If one group of users prefers the software that is different from the corporate standard, why should everyone in the company be forced to use the same tools? Cost becomes less of an issue as software prices drop. Support might be a problem, but major software packages today are similar. Data incompatibilities often can be resolved with conversion software.

To some extent, users should have the ability to customize their software to match their preferences. Today, most software packages enable users to choose colors, mouse or keyboard responsiveness, and locations to store personal files. If this software is moved to a centralized environment, you have to be careful to preserve this ability. One of the strengths of Windows 2000 is its ability to store individual user profiles on the server. Then from any machine, the desktop settings and preferences are retrieved from the server.

---

**Reality Bytes      13–2   Decentralization Is Hard**

According to Tom Peters, co-author of *In Search of Excellence,* decentralization in business took a great leap in the automobile industry of the 1920s. Ford and Sloan were battling for market share. Ford pioneered mass production to drive down the price of a car so that everyone could own one—but all of the cars were identical, down to the color. Sloan decided to organize his company (General Motors) into divisions (Chevrolet, Buick, etc.). Each division was responsible for its own profits, and each targeted a different consumer market. By the start of World War II, GM sales were accelerating past Ford's. The gains from decentralization can be important—if managers are able and willing to accept the flexibility and loose control required. For true decentralization means enabling the division managers to set their own directions and take responsibility for their own actions. Many companies have trouble accepting this structure and diversity.

One complication with enabling users to choose different software is that it can be difficult to determine the configurations of each machine. If a user has a problem, the MIS support person needs to know what software is installed on the machine. When installing new hardware and software, the support team needs to know what software exists on each target machine. Managers also need to track software usage when they purchase upgrades and to verify compliance with software licenses. Several software tools exist to help the MIS department track software usage and report on the configuration of each computer. A small file is installed on each computer that reports on the software, hardware, and configuration of each machine.

### Data Centralization

The most important feature of centralized data is the ability to share it with other users. Large central computers and minicomputers were designed from the ground up to share data. They were designed to solve the problems of allowing concurrent access and to protect the integrity of the data. Similarly, they have security facilities that enable owners of the data to specify which users can and cannot have access to the data. Centralized systems also monitor access and usage of the data to prevent problems.

Another important feature of centralized data is the ease of making backups. When all databases are stored on one machine, a single operator can be hired to maintain daily backups. If data files are lost, it is easy to restore them from the backups. With the data on one machine, it is easy to ensure that all files are regularly backed up. Contrast this situation with distributed personal computers, where users are generally responsible for making their own backup copies. How often do you personally make backups? Every night?

### Data Decentralization

The strongest advantage to decentralizing data is that it gives users better access to the data. Storing data where it is used provides faster access because it minimizes transmission time. Similarly, many people find it easier to access data when it is stored on their own personal computers—they know how the files are organized. Users also have complete control of the data and can prevent anyone else from even knowing that it exists. For data that does not need to be shared, this control presents no problems. However, scattered control of data can interfere with other users when many people need access to the data. An example of complete decentralization—including data, hardware and personnel is displayed in Figure 13.8.

**FIGURE 13.8**
COMPLETE DECENTRALIZATION
Each department maintains its own hardware, software, and data. Corporate standards and a network enable workers to utilize data across the company. MIS personnel are members of the user departments and support tasks within that department.

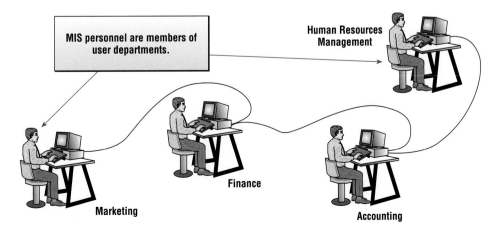

MIS personnel are members of user departments.

Human Resources Management

Marketing

Finance

Accounting

Data replication is sometimes used to provide the advantages of decentralized data—and still provide companywide access. With replication, the database is copied to multiple servers throughout the company. Users work on their local copies, which provide fast access to the data. The changes are copied to the other servers at regular intervals, so everyone has access to the latest data. This technique is often used with groupware products to distribute spreadsheets and word-processed documents.

## Personnel

When most users think about decentralization, they often forget about the information systems personnel. Traditionally, the MIS roles have been performed by centralized MIS staffs. However, as hardware becomes more decentralized there are increasing pressures to decentralize the personnel by having them report directly to user departments.

### Centralization

Most of the advantages of a centralized MIS staff accrue to the MIS workers. For example, MIS workers often feel more comfortable with other MIS specialists. Centralization creates a group of homogeneous workers who share the same education and experiences. Moving MIS workers to user departments places them in a minority position.

One implication of this situation is seen by looking at the career path of an MIS worker. In a centralized environment, workers are typically hired as programmers. They eventually become systems analysts. Some move on to become team or project leaders, and a few can look forward to becoming managers of IS departments and perhaps a CIO someday. If programmers are moved to user departments (say human resources), what career path do they have? Maybe they could become team leader or manager of the HRM department, but they would be competing with HRM specialists for those positions.

Centralization also makes it easier for the company to provide additional training to MIS staffers. Because hardware and software changes occur constantly, MIS employees need to continually learn new tools and techniques. If they are all located in a central facility, it is easy to set up training classes and informal meetings to discuss new technologies.

Centralization also gives the firm the ability to hire MIS specialists. If there are 50 positions available, two or three can be set aside for workers specializing in areas such as database administration or local area networks. If all workers are distributed to user areas, the individual departments will be less willing to pay for specialists.

Lastly, when the entire MIS staff is centralized, it is easier to see how much MIS is costing the firm. If the MIS functions are dispersed to user departments, they may be performed on a part-time basis by various employees. It is difficult to control the costs and evaluate alternatives when you don't know how much is being spent.

### Decentralization

The primary advantage to decentralized MIS staffing is that the support is closer to the users. As a result, they receive faster responses to questions and problems. More importantly, as the MIS staffers spend more time with the users, they gain a better understanding of the problems facing the users' department. Communication improves and problems are easier to identify and correct. These are powerful advantages to the individual departments and have the potential to create much better development and use of information systems.

### The Help Desk

One issue with decentralized MIS support is that it can be expensive to place MIS personnel in each department. Many companies compromise by creating a help desk that is staffed by MIS employees who specialize in helping business managers. When business managers have questions, workers at the help desk provide answers. Typical problems involve personal computers, networks, and access to corporate databases. One advantage for business managers is that they do not have to search for answers—they simply call one number. This system can also cut costs and ensure consistent support. The knowledge of the support workers is easily shared throughout the company. It is also easier to train and evaluate the workers.

To provide more decentralized support, some companies are using their networks to provide more detailed help to business departments. They set up a special program in the background on each personal computer. When someone calls for help, the microcomputer specialist can see the user's screen and take control of the user's machine. This method simplifies communication between the user and the specialist, making it easier to solve problems and make changes immediately. Of course, it also raises several security issues, because the help desk personnel could monitor any machine at any time.

**CLIENT-SERVER SOLUTIONS**

Centralization and decentralization are also strongly affected by the cost of telecommunications. With high transmission costs and slow speeds, companies formerly had few choices in determining the layout or architecture of the information technology. Most companies relied on clusters of separate data centers. Owing to recent changes in telecommunications (declining costs, increased bandwidth, and increased reliability), firms have moved to more flexible arrangements that use technology distributed throughout the company.

Figure 13.9 summarizes the benefits of centralization and decentralization. However, in practice, no company is completely centralized or completely decentralized. Each firm must find a point that balances the benefits and costs of each method. In order to investigate this process, it helps to look at the extreme situations first. Figure 13.6 illustrates how many of the MIS departments were organized in the days of central computers. The hardware, software, data, and personnel were all situated in one location. Data was typically collected manually from the business, reports were printed at the computer, and copies were distributed to the users. Data sharing existed, but only among applications on the central computer.

Many small businesses began with a different MIS organization. These businesses were unable to afford large central computers, so they relied on personal computers. Although they rarely have the money to pay for MIS workers, the MIS functions still have to be performed. The roles are typically filled on a part-time basis by other employees.

## Business Trends: Decentralization

One of the key trends in business in the 1990s has been the move toward decentralized management. The objective is to empower the managers who are close to the customers, enabling them to provide better service. However, if the overall management becomes more decentralized, features of the information system must also be decentralized. Serious problems arise when the information system does not match the organizational structure.

In MIS, the move toward decentralization is complicated by the fact that the information system must also support centralized goals. For instance, consolidated reports are produced for accounting, employee records, and environmental summaries. As a result, managers have to search for creative solutions that provide decentralized control yet produce the needed centralized information.

**FIGURE 13.9**
SUMMARY OF
BENEFITS OF
CENTRALIZATION AND
DECENTRALIZATION
There are advantages
to both centralization
and decentralization of
the MIS resources. The
ultimate objective is
to design an MIS
organization to benefit
from as many of the
advantages as possible
by combining both
centralization and
decentralization.

| | CENTRALIZATION | DECENTRALIZATION |
|---|---|---|
| **Hardware** | Share data | Less chance of breakdown |
| | Share expensive hardware | Users get personalized machines |
| | Control purchases | Microcomputers are cheaper |
| | Control usage | |
| | Less duplication | |
| | Efficient use of resources | |
| **Software** | Compatibility | Different user preferences |
| | Bulk buying discounts | Easier access |
| | Easier training | Customization |
| | Ease of maintenance | |
| **Data** | Easy backup | Not all data needs to be shared |
| | Easier to share | Easier and faster access |
| | Less duplication | Control and politics |
| | Security control & monitoring | |
| **Personnel** | Similar worker backgrounds | Faster response to users |
| | Easier training | More time with users |
| | Straightforward career path | Better understanding and communication |
| | Specialized staff | Different career path |
| | Easier to see and control costs | |

Today, many of these businesses have installed LANs that provide some capabilities to share data. However, data and software are often stored on many different computers. Figure 13.8 illustrates the configuration of a highly decentralized information system.

Although these two extremes have their uses, an intermediate position can do a better job of providing advantages offered by both methods. There are many possibilities: consider the various arrangements of hardware, software, data, and personnel. There are also many ways to decentralize or centralize each component. One common intermediate method is known as the client-server approach.

The **client-server model** separates all of the components into two categories: servers or clients. The functions associated with the server tend to be centralized, whereas the client components and tasks are dispersed among the users. The terms *client* and *server* deliberately imply a relationship between the two types of machines. Servers tend to be larger, faster computers with operating systems designed for multi-user access and control. Clients are typically microcomputers that are set up for use by one person at a time. Figure 13.10 shows a version of a client-server approach. To see the usefulness of this approach, examine the four components: hardware, software, data, and personnel.

## Hardware

The arrangement of the hardware is the most distinctive feature of the client-server model. It consists of one or more computers designated as servers. Managers and workers use client microcomputers that are attached to the servers through a local area network.

**FIGURE 13.10**
CLIENT-SERVER ORGANIZATION
Some hardware and a few MIS personnel are located in user departments. Most corporate data is maintained in a few centralized locations. The central MIS staff is responsible for transaction processing, standard reports, maintaining the shared databases, and supporting the corporate network. Individual departments create their own applications with the help of the MIS support staff.

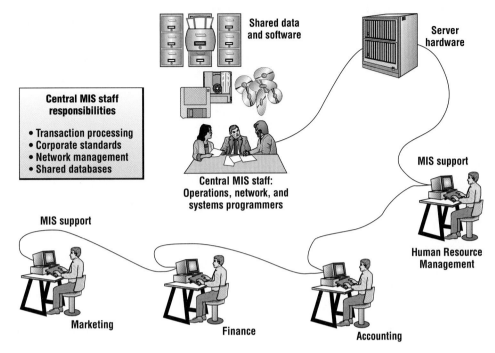

Shared data and software

Server hardware

**Central MIS staff responsibilities**

- Transaction processing
- Corporate standards
- Network management
- Shared databases

**Central MIS staff:** Operations, network, and systems programmers

**MIS support**

**Human Resource Management**

**MIS support**

**Marketing**

**Finance**

**Accounting**

The servers are typically centrally located. They might be high-end microcomputers, midrange computers, or mainframes. These servers and the network are selected and maintained by the MIS staff. They provide all of the necessary concurrency and security controls to grant multiple users access to data at the same time.

The client computers are generally personal computers designed for the use of a single person. They can be purchased by the individual users or departments (decentralized), or the company might set up a bulk purchase agreement with vendors. Oftentimes companies set up help desks or information centers that help users select standard hardware, configure it, install it, and handle repairs. Users gain the advantage of decentralized choice, and the company gains the advantages of having standardized machines.

Printers and other peripherals can be located with the servers, at individual client computers, or in departmental offices. Departmental printers are relatively popular because they can be monitored by a few key employees, yet still provide convenient access by most employees. Through the network, print jobs can be sent to any of the available printers. If one printer breaks down, the job can be routed to another printer.

In many ways, web sites represent a client-server approach to computing. The web sites tend to be run on servers, and they provide data that will be shared. They also provide a standard file format and a standard user interface. Individual client computers run browsers that enable users to retrieve files they need and perform any calculations on their machines. The one catch is that most web sites work one way: It can be difficult to transfer data up to the server.

## Software and Data

One of the primary goals of a client-server system is to provide the advantages of centralized control of software and data. Commercial software that is used by several users is

In 1996, Pacific Gas & Electric (PG&E) Company started a project with IBM to handle customer billing along with other routine operations. By 1998, deregulation of the electric industry had made the task so complicated that the system project was dropped, despite the companies having spent tens of millions of dollars.

A 1996 study by the Standish group research firm showed that 42 percent of corporate information systems were abandoned before completion. Large projects were particularly prone to failure, leading many executives to consider implementing smaller, less feature-laden projects. For example, Chrysler's financial division discarded a 100-percent computerized solution in favor of having clerks call dealers over the phone. Chrysler's Paul Knauss observed, "By adding some people into the equation, we could get 95 percent of what we needed," building the system in 90 days instead of a year and spending millions of dollars for a computerized solution.

Similarly, PG&E decided to stick with their 30-year-old technology and use a smaller project, with fewer features, to provide the basic information faster and cheaper. For example, instead of a modern Windows interface, the system will rely on plain text and keywords.

**FIGURE 13.11
CLIENT-SERVER BENEFITS**

The client-server approach provides benefits from two perspectives. Because it provides more support, more hardware, and better access to data, users gain increased participation and better use of IS resources. Through standardization and data centralization, the company achieves better integration and use of data.

| Immediate<br>1 to 2 Years<br>Users | Near-Term<br>3 to 5 Years<br>System Integration | Long-Term<br>6 to 10 Years<br>IT Efficiency |
|---|---|---|
| • Better access to data<br>• Increased participation<br>• Improved productivity | • Tighter integration across the company<br>• Faster IT responses<br>• Business process re-engineering | • Resource utilization<br>• New technology<br>• Adaptive systems |

stored on the servers. Only one copy of the software is needed, reducing the amount of storage space needed and making it easier to provide updates. The server keeps track of the number of people currently using the software to make sure it stays below the number authorized by the purchase license. The basic advantages of the client-server approach are summarized in Figure 13.11.

Data that will be shared with colleagues is also stored on the server—typically with a database management system. Transaction-processing systems can collect data and produce the traditional reports. These reports and the underlying data are stored on the server and can be accessed from the client computers.

Mail messages, data, and reports can be sent to other users. They are first stored on the server and forwarded to the users. In the case of multiple servers, the network operating system keeps track of the users and routes the messages to the appropriate servers, and then on to the user's client machine.

The network can also be used to provide data backup for each personal computer. With the appropriate software installed on each machine, data is automatically forwarded to the server for backup. As long as the personal computer is not turned off, the process is automatic and invisible to the user, making it easy to provide daily (even hourly) backup of all the data in the company.

## Personnel

The issue of centralized MIS personnel is perhaps the most complicated. With a local area network, it is easy to move hardware, software, and data around the company. It is not as easy to move people. However, the network can be used by MIS personnel to provide assistance to users. For example, say you are using a spreadsheet to build a marketing decision support model and you encounter a problem trying to create a graph. If your system was set up for network support, you simply call the MIS help desk. An MIS applications programmer can access your computer across the network, correct the problems, and set up your graph, all without leaving the office.

The MIS department maintains responsibility for the company's transaction-processing systems, which provide the bulk of the shared data in the firm. They also set up the servers and maintain the network. In order to ensure that everyone has access, the MIS department defines the databases and sets standards for hardware and software.

Some MIS personnel can be moved to user departments. In addition to helping with day-to-day problems, they can work on prototyping more complex applications. With their knowledge of the user requirements, they can serve as liaisons to the SDLC development team when major projects are designed.

## Peer-to-Peer Systems

Client-server systems are not the only way to achieve a balance between centralization and decentralization. In fact, in many ways they represent an intermediate step toward a more distributed system. Remember that firms still need to support the legacy systems that were created through the 1970s and 1980s. These centralized systems were designed to capture and process the transaction data of the companies. It is not easy to throw them away, especially since it takes time to build replacement systems. As a result, it is easiest to leave the central data on these machines and make them servers. The clients are typically personal computers that are connected to the servers over a local area network. Because most personal computers were designed for single users, they tend to work best when dealing with one user at a time. They are acceptable as clients, but early personal computers were limited in their ability to deal with many users simultaneously. As personal computer hardware, operating systems, and software improve, it becomes easier to connect personal computers directly to each other instead of relying on centralized servers. In a peer-to-peer system, any computer can be a server, a client, or both. This type of system allows greater flexibility in terms of storing and accessing data. However, many problems need to be resolved, such as security controls. Additionally, by scattering data across hundreds or thousands of computers, it becomes difficult for users to find the data they need. The basic issues in decentralizing control and distributing information system resources are summarized in Figure 13.12.

The Windows 2000 operating system is designed to facilitate peer-to-peer networking. Increasingly, the primary sharing mechanism is for each manager to set up a personal web site on his or her machine. This way, each person can choose what data to share on the intranet and set security permissions to provide limited access to the data. By keeping a corporate search engine, other workers in the company can quickly search for the data they need. Of course, this decentralized approach is more likely to lead to duplication of files. Since drive space is cheap, storage costs are not an issue, but there can be problems with identifying the most up-to-date version of a file.

**OBJECT ORIENTATION**

The use of decentralized or distributed computing has two conflicting effects on the use of objects. First, it increases the need for an object-oriented approach. However, it is much harder to manage objects in a distributed environment.

Almost all of the object-oriented development has occurred in the workstation worlds of UNIX and personal computers. To date, little object development takes place in centralized transaction processing. There are two reasons for the use of objects on workstations. First, the development of graphical user interfaces is greatly simplified by using an object approach. Second, it is easier for users to find and manipulate data scattered throughout a distributed system if the data is stored as objects. If objects are defined consistently across the organization, once managers learn the properties and uses of an object (e.g., customer data), they will be able to access that object anywhere it is used in the company.

The problem with objects in a distributed environment is easily spotted by the "If" statement in the last paragraph. With one or two centralized computers, it is relatively easy to ensure that all object definitions are the same and that everyone can get access to them. As hardware, data, and software get distributed throughout the company, it becomes increasingly difficult to maintain standards.

Consider a situation that will become increasingly common. A manager in one department creates a report using object tools and linking data from a variety of sources. The report works well—as long as it remains on the machine that created it. Problems arise when the report is passed electronically to managers using other machines in different locations. The objects in the report might not be accessible to the other managers, or they might be reached through different access paths. Similarly, managers in other locations probably use different software and hardware, and they might not be compatible with the objects on the report.

**FIGURE 13.12 DECENTRALIZATION SUMMARY**

Some organizations are moving toward a completely distributed environment, where each subunit becomes independent but connected. Each division is responsible for its own profits and costs. Information systems are the responsibility of each department. Communication systems are used to share data with other units and to improve transaction processing.

| DECENTRALIZATION ISSUES | | |
|---|---|---|
| **ORGANIZATIONAL IMPACT** | **STRENGTHS** | **WEAKNESSES** |
| Are operations interdependent? | End users gain control | Possible short-term bias in decision making |
| • Planning <br> • Development | Supports workgroups | Might not be optimal use of resources for corporation |
| • Physical resources <br> • Operations | Enables new organizational structures | Corporatewide interests can be lost |
| Can subunits relate solely through information and messages? | Increased organizational flexibility | IS staff might lose cohesiveness and support |
| Does corporate culture support decentralization? | | |

The industry is beginning to work on this problem, but it could be several years before the details are ironed out. One project is known as the **Common Object Request Broker Architecture (CORBA).** This model was largely developed in the UNIX community to enable objects to communicate with each other across networks. In 1994, Microsoft announced that its own *Object Linking and Embedding (OLE)* protocol would eventually incorporate the CORBA standards. Eventually, products based on these systems will be able to locate and share objects across networks. In the meantime, control of objects is a management issue that will require company standards, careful supervision, and considerable training and support.

**CHANGE AND OUTSOURCING**

In theory, the client-server approach offers many advantages, and many organizations have adopted or are considering variations of it. The only problem is that it can be difficult to change a company from its existing organization to a client-server approach. Existing systems that keep the company running were built and modified throughout decades. Most of the hardware and software were designed to be stand-alone systems; they were not intended to function as servers that exchange data with client computers. Firms have millions of dollars and millions of lines of code tied up in these systems; they cannot simply be discarded.

Second, even if a company decides to go with a client-server approach, there are still hundreds of alternatives. Some of these decisions are risky because some hardware and software choices will not survive the vagaries of the marketplace. The transition from existing systems to a new approach is complicated by the need to maintain the current system while exploring risky alternatives. Consider the problem from the standpoint of a firm in 1995. The existing mainframe systems are getting older, and the company needs to consider transferring to a client-server approach. The catch is that it is too hard to choose the appropriate technology. The best guess is that within a couple of years, the technology will stabilize, but what should the company do in the meantime? Purchasing new mainframes is an expensive proposition, especially if they will be discarded when the company switches to a client-server system. Yet, the firm is unwilling to risk a transfer to immature technology.

Partly because of changes, partly because of the distributed nature of the client-server approach, many firms have seen an increase in support costs when they convert to a client-server approach. In some cases, the support costs exceed the cost savings from using lower-cost machines. On the other hand, the increased costs often arise because of increased computer usage by managers.

One approach to this dilemma that some companies have taken is known as **outsourcing.** With outsourcing, the company sells its central computers and transfers portions of the MIS staff to a service company such as Electronic Data Systems (EDS) or Global Services, the IBM subsidiary. The company signs an agreement to use the services of the outsourcing firm for a fixed number of years. Depending on the agreement, the outsourcing firm can be responsible for anything from machine operation and maintenance, to development of new systems, to telecommunication services. The leading outsourcing companies are listed in Figure 13.13. Note the huge growth in outsourcing in the 1990s. This trend was partly due to the desire to cut costs, the inability to hire IT workers, the increasing standardization of IT services, and the need to focus on core business management. In 1998, *Computerworld* reported that an average of 20 percent of IS budgets was spent on outsourcing.

Outsourcing has primarily been used to decrease operating costs or to get the initial money from the sale of the machines. In particular, the company gains an infusion of

**FIGURE 13.13**
OUTSOURCING
REVENUE IN BILLIONS
OF DOLLARS
In the first half of
the 1990s, many
companies chose to
hire outside firms
to run their MIS
departments.

| COMPANY | 1991 | 1995 | 1996 | 1997 | 2000 (EST.) |
|---|---|---|---|---|---|
| IBM Global Services | 0.4 | 17.7 | 20.9 | 24.6 | 37 |
| EDS | 1.2 | 12.4 | 14.4 | 15.2 | 23 |
| CSC | 0.4 | 4.2 | 5.6 | 6.6 | 9 |
| Andersen Consulting | 0.5 | 4.2 | 5.3 | 6.6 | 9 |
| Affiliated Computer | 0.16 | 0.4 | 0.6 | 1.2 | 2 |
| Fiserv | 0.23 | 0.7 | 0.8 | 1.0 | 1 |
| Perot Systems | 0.16 | 0.3 | 0.6 | 0.8 | 1 |
| Total (est.) | 5.5 | 21.3 | 40.0 | 55.0 | 82 |

Data is taken from annual reports and company web sites.

## Reality Bytes    13–4    Outsourcing Benefits

On examining several companies, the benefits and costs of outsourcing are not always clear. For example, outsourcing does not automatically reduce costs. In some cases, it has led to increased costs. Staff flexibility is an important gain—particularly in businesses that experience fluctuations in demand for employees. Outsourcing also provides access to specialized skills and services—particularly useful in government organizations. Outsourcing also provides access to a larger pool of equipment. A large specialty firm (like EDS) can afford to purchase up-to-date equipment because it can be intensively managed. An important trade-off if a firm does outsource a service is the potential loss of innovation. With proper encouragement and management, internal employees have more incentive to propose and implement new ideas.

cash through the sale of the machines. Some firms have stated that they chose outsourcing because it enabled them to focus on their core business and not worry about maintaining computers and designing systems. Figure 13.14 illustrates conditions under which it is useful to consider outsourcing. As you move away from the center of the diagram, outsourcing becomes less useful. The most common uses of outsourcing are for straightforward applications of technology, including personal computer installation and servicing, legacy system maintenance, and routine application development.

On the other hand, situations that are unique or require advanced uses of information technology are best handled internally. For example, complex markets that benefit from strategic applications require the knowledge and experience of employees who work for the company. Likewise, situations that require tight security are easier to control if they remain in-house. Another reason to avoid outsourcing is when the outsourcing firm will have to pay the same costs that you face—because they will charge for an additional profit margin, the final cost can be higher. Examples include applications with high fixed costs or that require high levels of expensive state-of-the-art equipment or specialized MIS talent.

Competitive pressures are also leading many managers to consider outsourcing their information systems. As technology continues to change, it becomes increasingly difficult for general business managers to keep up with the technology. Each change brings requests for new hardware and software, and the need to reevaluate the use of technology within the firm. Changing technology also requires continual retraining of the information systems staff. At the same time, middle-level management positions are being cut, and managers are asked to take on more tasks. In these circumstances, Figure 13.15

Telecommunication networks require continual monitoring. The size of the network and the traffic volume make the job more difficult. The need to hold down costs results in a high use of technology with few workers.

**FIGURE 13.14**
OUTSOURCING EVALUATION

Outsourcing entails many trade-offs. It means transferring control of a crucial resource to an outside company. If you are really interested in development of strategic applications and leading-edge applications, it is usually better to use an internal development team. If you are dealing with older technology used mostly for transaction processing, it can be cheaper to hire an outside firm to maintain your applications.

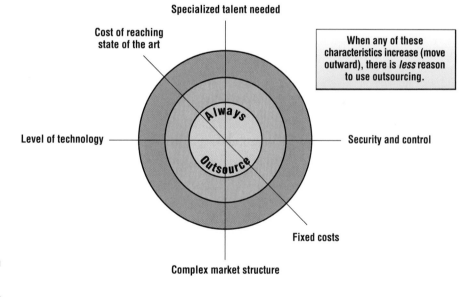

shows that it is easy to see why companies decide to transfer IS management to an expert through outsourcing.

There are drawbacks to outsourcing. First, there might be a slight increase in security risk because the MIS employees have weaker ties to the original company. On the other hand, outsourcing providers are likely to have stricter security provisions than an average firm does. A bigger question is the issue of who is responsible for identifying solutions and new uses of technology for the firm. If MIS workers are employed by an external firm, will it be their job to search for new applications? If not, who will?

**FIGURE 13.15**
OUTSOURCING
FORCES

Firms are being pushed
to cut margins. Many
are focusing on their
core competencies,
leaving little time
for wrestling with
technology. At the
same time, as the large
outsourcing firms gain
customers, their
efficiency improves and
they can offer more
services and more
specialists at better
rates.

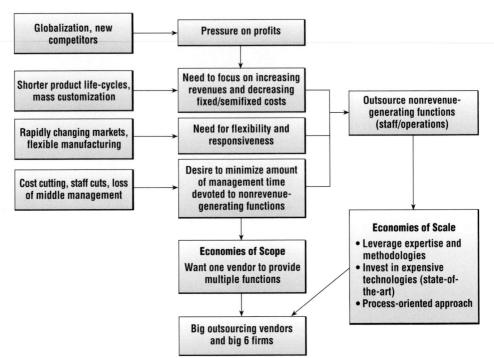

## SUMMARY

One of the more difficult problems facing MIS departments and company executives is the conflict between centralization and decentralization. These issues were involved in many decisions during the last 5 to 10 years, from politics to corporate organizations, to the way in which MIS fits into the organization. Although there is no single answer that applies to all situations, there has been a distinct trend during the last few years toward decentralization. In larger organizations, this propensity has been hampered by the highly centralized organizations and computer systems that have been in place for the last 30 years.

Decentralization of MIS can occur in any of four areas: hardware, software, data, and MIS personnel. Economics is driving the decentralization of hardware—because of tremendous price performance values in personal computers. The challenge is to accommodate this decentralization without losing the benefits of centralization. One option would be a completely decentralized information system, where each user and department is responsible for its own information. A more flexible option being pursued by many companies is an intermediate strategy involving the client-server approach. The goal of this approach is to capture the benefits of both decentralization and centralization.

Benefits to centralized hardware include economies of scale, easier maintenance, and better prices through negotiation strength. The primary benefit of decentralized hardware is the ability of users to acquire and control exactly the components they need. There are also substantial price advantages to personal computers at this point in time.

### A MANAGER'S VIEW

Identifying problems, making decisions, and building systems are not enough to keep a company running. Most organizations have an MIS department to build, maintain, and evaluate information technology. As a general business manager, you need to be aware of the various ways of organizing MIS resources: hardware, software, data, and personnel. The MIS resources must support the needs and organization of the business. When the MIS organization differs from the business system, there will be conflicts. You need to watch for these problems and adjust the organization or MIS as needed. The client-server approach is often used to attain the benefits of centralization and decentralization at the same time.

Benefits of centralized software management include easier upgrades and control over purchases and access, along with compatibility across the organization. The primary benefit to decentralization is increased flexibility and control gained by users. Similarly, the main benefit to centralized data is increased control over access, providing scheduled backups, and making it easier to share data. On the other hand, decentralization gives users a stronger ownership role, easier access (to their own data), and personal control.

Benefits to centralized MIS personnel accrue mainly to the MIS staff: It is easier to support training, MIS workers offer support to each other, and it is easier to hire specialists. The primary advantage of decentralization is better communication with users and faster response to user problems.

Some companies find it profitable to sell portions of their computer facilities to outside organizations such as IBM and EDS, in a transaction known as outsourcing. Outsourcing provides a short-term increase in cash for the company, access to computer specialists, and the ability to concentrate on the company's primary business. However, firms requiring specialized talent, high security and control, high levels of recent technology, new state-of-the-art information technology, or complex market structures should avoid outsourcing and retain in-house management of the information function.

## KEY WORDS

advocacy role, 553

centralization, 545

client-server model, 562

Common Object Request Broker
   Architecture (CORBA), 567

data integrity, 552

database administrator (DBA), 552

decentralization, 555

outsourcing, 567

standards, 551

systems analyst, 553

## WEB SITE REFERENCES

### Job Boards

| | |
|---|---|
| America's Job Bank | www.ajb.dni.us |
| Excite List | www.excite.com/careers/job_listings |
| Free Job | www.freejob.com |
| Monster | www.monster.com |
| Riley Guide | www.dbm.com/jobguide |
| U.S. Government | www.usajobs.opm.gov |
| Wall Street Journal | Careers.wsj.com |

## REVIEW QUESTIONS

1. What are the basic roles of the MIS department?
2. What types of MIS jobs are available?
3. What are the advantages of centralizing computer hardware? What are the advantages of decentralization?
4. What are the advantages of centralizing computer software? What are the advantages of decentralization?
5. What are the advantages of centralizing computer data? What are the advantages of decentralization?

6. What are the advantages of centralizing computer personnel? What are the advantages of decentralization?
7. How does the client server approach combine benefits of centralization and decentralization in terms of hardware, software, and personnel?
8. What are the potential advantages of outsourcing computer facilities? What are the drawbacks?

## EXERCISES

1. Interview computer users and managers in a local firm (or your university) and determine the degree of decentralization in their information system organization. Talk to several users and see whether their perceptions agree. Are they receiving all of the advantages of centralization and decentralization? If not, how could the system be modified to gain these benefits without significantly increasing the drawbacks? Be sure to analyze hardware, software, data, and personnel.

2. Interview some computer science majors to determine what types of jobs they are looking for. Also, interview some business-oriented MIS majors and compare the responses. Ask the subjects whether they would prefer working for a centralized IS department or within a decentralized department. What reasons do they give? Do they have a minor in a business discipline? (Team approach: Each team member should interview a different person, then combine the results and look for similarities and differences.)

3. Using salary surveys and local advertisements, find typical salaries for various MIS jobs in your area.

4. Make a list of symptoms you would expect to see in a company that has centralized databases and MIS personnel, but has just decentralized its departments and users have just bought hundreds of new personal computers in the last three years.

5. Make a list of symptoms you expect to see in a company that is "too decentralized." That is, company users are free to choose any hardware and software, and databases are maintained by each department. Data is shared through reports that are printed in each department and forwarded to other departments on paper. There is no central MIS staff and no CIO. Treat it as a company that started small using personal computers and grew but did not come up with a centralized information system approach.

## Rolling Thunder Database

6. Describe the organization of the existing information system. What changes would enable the system to run better? If the company doubles in size in three years, what organizational changes do you recommend for the information system?

7. How should the company handle typical information system tasks such as data backup, creating employee accounts, maintaining hardware, selecting new hardware and software, and so on?

8. Would you recommend a centralized or decentralized approach to information systems at the Rolling Thunder Bicycle company? Who is currently in charge of the major components? What problems can we anticipate if we continue with the existing structure?

## ADDITIONAL READING

Arnett, Kirk P., and C. R. Litecky, "Career Path Development for the Most Wanted Skills in the MIS Job Market," *Journal of Systems Management,* February 1994, pp. 6–10. [Job skills]

Fryer, Bronwyn. "Difficult at Best," *Computerworld,* January 4, 1999, p. 38. [High demand for staff with ERP skills]

"How Much Is that Ant in the Window?" *The Economist,* July 30, 1994, p. 63. [Labor costs for programmers and analysts in various nations]

"Managing Unruly Desktop Computers Costs Businesses Dearly," *The Wall Street Journal,* February 16, 1995, p. A1. [Maintenance costs of personal computers]

York, Thomas. "Shift in IT Roles Ahead: Changes in Business and Technology Will Alter IT Careers," *Infoworld,* January 18, 1999, p. 75. [Predicting the future of IT jobs is hard, but useful]

# CASES   *Financial Services*

The financial services industry is typically divided into banking and nonbanking organizations. Yet today, services overlap between these divisions in many different ways. Some of the services offered in this industry include, but are not limited to:

- Consumer loans such as home mortgages, home equity loans, and auto loans
- Personal and business lines of credit, especially profitable "sub-prime" credit risks
- Credit card and related credit (card) life insurance
- Purchase warranties and service guarantees generally offered with appliances and home electronics
- Equipment leases
- Investment management services
- Mutual fund management
- Multiple-line insurance
- Financial planning, including tax preparation and related services

## Financial Analysis

The financial services industry has witnessed a stunning 18.8 percent median sales growth over the last five years. The year 1996 ended with an 18.4 percent increase over 1995.

For the financial-service sector, profitability figures for 1996 reflected a median return on equity of 21.6 percent, compared to the overall U.S. industry of 13.0 percent. Median net income for 1996 amounted to $265 million per company. The U.S. industry overall amounted to $86 million per firm.

Handsome returns for the industry in 1996 were due to a steady interest rate environment, low inflation, and respectable gains in personal income. Also, lending spreads to sub-prime customers increased, increasing income.

Though credit card delinquencies and bankruptcies have been rising, many finance companies have witnessed a 50 percent increase in credit loans. Typically, sub-prime loans offer stronger growth opportunities and are more profitable than traditional loans or mortgages. Disposable income increases ranging between 4 to 6 percent annually have definitely helped the industry.

Personal bankruptcies have reached more than 1 million annually, but reserves have been increased industrywide. Though delinquent credit cards have reached as high as 3.66 percent, industry insiders expect this to come down with better management of credit card portfolios.

## Stock/Investment Outlook

The financial services industry has outperformed broad market averages for the last eight years, with the last two years being their most stellar. For 1996, EPS grew by 21.5 percent, compared to the entire U.S. industry of 6.4 percent.

Although trailing price to earnings ratios are average at about 15, industry analysts cannot find anything to be skeptical about as long as the economy remains robust, propelled by a strong loan growth. Also in 1996, eight consumer finance companies have gone public and their stock prices rose an average of 40 percent.

This industry tends to have many high-risk firms. Beta coefficients are higher than market averages. It is certainly a risk if lower creditworthy borrowers fall on hard times. In a sinking economy, financial firms, especially those specializing in noncollateralized loans, such as credit cards and personal lines of credit, may suffer.

If the economic downturn of the late 1980s in the real estate market is any indicator, highly leveraged finance companies could also be crippled by any extreme housing slump.

## Potential/Prospective for Growth

As previously mentioned, the favorable interest rate environment as well as low inflationary pressures has positioned the financial services industry well for the next few years. Although credit concerns could hurt some highly leveraged companies such as mortgage or credit card specialists, sizable spreads built into such sub-prime businesses make disastrous losses less likely.

Additionally, this industry is known for consistently developing innovative products. In a crowded market, the GM card quickly became successful by offering rebates on the purchase of GM cars based on levels of credit card use.

## Competitive Structure

The financial services industry is highly fragmented and competitive. Recently, there has been significant bank merger activity. Consolidation is a means of increasing efficiency, service levels, and product depth. It is also a means of spreading back-office costs over a larger product base. Not only do the money center banks compete with the growing super-regional and other large commercial banks, they compete with nonbank institutions providing financial services as well.

The industry's innovations have threatened traditional banks, yet banks are far from relinquishing their market share to finance companies. With the banking industry whittling away at the Glass-Stegall Act, banks will soon be muscling into industries such as brokerage and insurance. Some banks already sell insurance with certain restrictions. Additionally, banks are increasing their focus on credit card affiliations with airlines and other high-profile industries.

### Role of Research and Development

Research in the financial services industry is focused on product innovation and marketing. By researching new ways to market products, credit card issuers attempt to increase market share and develop new market niches. Many retail stores entering into the credit card business are utilizing cobranding to help increase market share. Cobranding strategies may allow smaller issuers to team up with larger organizations and obtain a competitive advantage.

Another marketing technique for the future involves utilizing the Internet. Due to the high costs of current mass marketing campaigns, Internet marketing will become a higher profile medium for advertising and financial services marketing. The challenge in this new distribution channel is to be innovative, effective, and targeted.

### Technological Investment and Analysis

Strategic advances in this customer-service oriented industry are propelled by technological innovation. Technological improvements have aided banks in their efforts to control expenses while providing better customer service. Electronic banking through phone lines, automated teller machines (ATMs), and personal computers give customers improved levels of service by offering 24-hour banking at convenient locations.

Many financial services firms have utilized enormous phone banks to provide customer service. The customer service representatives often have instantaneous access to large customer databases with the ability to give credit approval, status, and balances, as well as account maintenance.

Generally, financial institutions have concentrated the technology on transactions—particularly aimed at cutting costs. Bank managers are constantly reminded that their wealthier customers tend to be older and resistant to change.

### Recommendation for the Future

To get ahead in the competitive financial services industry, players must focus on leveraging technology and seizing opportunities that arise from regulation changes. It will also be important to consider strategies for a global market and for the consolidation and integration going on in the industry.

There is no doubt that the financial services industry will continue to outperform other industries. The ones that strive to reduce their administrative costs will be the most successful.

Technological and regulatory forces are moving the industry toward greater consolidation and product integration. Critical to financial firms' success will be their level of investment in technology and its ability to achieve cost savings. Increasingly finance is becoming a global rather than a national industry. The reliability of instantaneous telecommunications and the converging of economies around the world increases the importance of a global focus for successful financial services firms.

## CASE  *Fidelity Investments*

The headlines from throughout the year passed through his head again and again. "Magellan Had Near $1 Billion Outflow in July." "Lagging Fidelity Investments Launches Customer-Service Tour." "Fidelity after the Earthquake." "The $400 Billion Behemoth from Boston has Started to Slip: Can Ned Johnson's Famous Money Machine Get Back into High Gear?" In a banner year for the stock market, Fidelity's funds had consistently underperformed. There was, of course, the public relations problem with former Magellan manager Jeffrey Vinik, who had been accused of manipulating stock prices. Not to mention competition from hungrier, more agile competitors making a bid for the number-one spot. 1997 had not been a stellar year at Fidelity.

As Ned made his way to the office, he began to think practically. What were the issues facing Fidelity over the long term? Observers were correct to remark that "Johnson is . . . 'a sucker for a good idea.' Fidelity's hottest one was to leverage its massive technology infrastructure" (Collins, 1996), or "He adores technology and understands it as few CEOs do" (Allis, 1996). These authors focused more on the smoke than the fire.

Johnson's primary goal was to serve the customer, through high returns on their investment, quick access to information, and efficient administration of their accounts. Technology was an important tool, perhaps the tool, for establishing a service edge over the competition. It was not an end in itself. As the president of Fidelity Systems, Albert Aiello, set forth, "System objectives must flow from business objectives" (Rao, 1995).

Ned quietly entered 82 Devonshire, flashing a forced smile to fund managers as he made his way to his office in the corner of the top floor. He passed rooms full of young analysts and continuous streams of stock quotes, thinking about the weak performance for the past year. Ned was reminded of the unpredictability of investments. There was no widget-making flowchart that could guarantee Fidelity a good product in the investment sense. For Ned, the essential question became, how can we satisfy and grow our customer base in the face of the volatility of financial markets?

## Technological Investment and Analysis

In the span of a few months, during 1997, Fidelity completely revamped its Internet service, moving from being a confusing information provider to a place where "actionable solutions" are taking place. Today Fidelity's web page has become remarkably simplified; yet it seems to provide more information at the same time. Most importantly, investors can now trade online.

From the user's perspective, online trading is relatively simple. First, assuming one is already a Fidelity customer, one obtains a PIN number through a toll-free call. Second, customers must have suitable software, which means a browser that supports 128-bit encryption. This software is available online directly from Fidelity. The company has quickly progressed from having a token presence on the Net to operating a viable information and trading tool.

One piece of Fidelity's Internet service is real-time access to funds prices, a service also available over the telephone. The $9 million client-server system that provides this service takes a significant step beyond its predecessor. Until 1993, Fidelity used a system that now seems very involved.

A Fidelity customer service representative would answer a customer's phone call and pull up the customer's account on a personal terminal. If the customer asked for a quote on the price of a fund or stock, representatives would wait their turn to use a lazy-Susan-like terminal shared by five representatives. Often representatives would have to wait five minutes or more. Once the representative had the use of the terminal, he or she then needed to translate the name of the fund or stock into its abbreviated code through a paper list of codes. Other financial information was halfway across the room.

Fidelity's "Maxxess" system, which replaced the old technology, is considered to be the most sophisticated customer service approach in the industry (Collins, 1996). According to Fidelity Investment Systems Senior Vice-President Don Sundue, "If we went out and bought someone else's system off the shelf, we could get a reasonable facsimile of what we do here. But we wouldn't get to control our own destiny" (Bresnahan, 1997).

Based upon Microsoft Word, the system corrects the deficiencies of the former system. Integration is the key. Phone representatives can access all the information they need through one terminal. The system integrates information on a retail basis from diverse sources, including stock markets, news services, and analysts. This data is integrated with the customer's individual portfolio infor-

mation. Technologically, levels of servers feed seamlessly into the representatives' terminals. The local and regional servers maintain only the most requested information for that area. When unusual data is requested, the representative is automatically transferred to the national server.

Maxxess has saved Fidelity $20.5 million that formerly went to a third party. Maxxess is actually generating new revenue since the program is now being sold to outsiders who need real-time price quotes. Viewed as an investment, Fidelity delivered a 62.8 percent return on its technology expenditure investment from 1992 to 1997. In doing so, Fidelity has looked beyond a temporary fix, employing a long-term technology strategy that directly and quickly benefits the company while adding value for the customers and distinguishing Fidelity from its competitors.

While Fidelity has improved access to phone representatives, it has ironically made efforts to phase them out. Actual speaking calls, numbering 70,000 to 90,000 daily, represent only a quarter of total phone-ins. The rest are answered by Touch-Tone systems; this is a huge savings for Fidelity. The cost per speaking call is $11. Each phone interaction with a computer, on the other hand, costs Fidelity $0.70 (Bresnahan, 1997).

Another aspect of Fidelity's customer service and technological dominance is its Covington, Kentucky, mail distribution center. Unlike its rivals, Fidelity treats the mundane activity of processing mail as a core part of its business. It gives "every ounce of its energy" to bettering rivals in this service-oriented end of the business. This investment is made because, "consistent operations can help comfort customers amid volatile market swings, or, recently at Fidelity, mediocre investment results" (Hirsch, 1996). Fidelity is attempting to add as much predictability and efficiency as possible to its necessarily volatile business environment. High investment returns cannot be achieved every year, but sending out a prospectus or a statement on time is possible.

Fidelity's commitment to consistent service has not been cheap. The Kentucky operation cost $100 million, including a self-imposed testament to Fidelity's good corporate citizenship. The construction of the rural plant caused significant excavation, requiring Fidelity to rebuild hills surrounding their buildings to blend the 24-hour operation into the countryside. For instance, "a bundle was spent on an earth-tone, multistory garage, sloped to fit into the countryside so parking lots full of cars wouldn't sully the bucolic views" (Hirsch, 1996). This innovative facility broke new ground in mail distribution plants. It incorporated ideas like the heavy use of robotics from manufacturing. Suppliers such as Bell & Howell and Cisco-Eagle collaborated with Fidelity to develop sophisticated materials moving and sorting products.

The attention to detail in the mailing process says much about Fidelity's concern for customer service. The center ships over 140 million pieces of mail a year, in about 3,000 separate formats or "kits." These include prospectuses, promotional material, and personal statements. One extreme example of Fidelity's passion for detail is the type of paper on which the statements are printed.

Prior to construction of the new facility, Fidelity was plagued with paper that retained high amounts of moisture. This caused statements to curl and smudge easily. In consultation with paper producers, Fidelity experimented with drying the paper before printing, fine-tuning their method until the answer was discovered. The paper was dried in a 70-degree F room for two days, with humidity levels between 45 and 55 percent. This supports Director of Operations Christopher D. Cramer's claim that "paper and print are a strategic advantage" (Hirsch, 1996).

The Covington, Kentucky, center incorporates a sophisticated system in which "conveyor belts and rotating carousels, run by software unique to Fidelity, haul materials through cavernous, concrete rooms. Computers coordinate movements through nonstop gabfests with each other." This all occurs under one 256,000-square-foot roof. The automated storage and retrieval system (AS/RS) designed by ESKAY Corporation enables Fidelity to claim that when a customer makes a request for information, it will be in the mail the next day.

Customer names and addresses are pulled from a database and printed directly on the paper materials, which are then metered, bar coded, and sent across the country without seeing the inside of a U.S. postal facility. A least-cost-routing system ensures that the lowest priced shipping company is used for larger orders. Fidelity has even integrated this new plant with a "massively parallel" system from AT&T Global Information Solutions that quickly analyzes and sorts a customer database to determine which product offerings should be advertised by mail. This makes printing and mailing initiatives even more cost effective (Goldberg, 1995). Competitors see shipping as a necessary but uninteresting side note to the investments business. Fidelity puts customer service front and center, even in the shipping details.

Another area in which Fidelity is distinguishing itself is with 401(k) plans. Fidelity has distinguished itself not by its returns but because of its technological service. "The critical characteristic of a successful 401(k) or any financial service provider is technology. This is a factor Fidelity has historically emphasized" (Rohrer, 1994).

Previously, Fidelity's 401(k) operations were spread throughout the company. In 1989, Fidelity formed Fidelity Institutional Retirement Services to focus the energies of the disorganized, unwieldy department. The objectives of FIRSCo as a business were to "set the industry standard in customer service, sustaining double-digit annual growth, and continuing to achieve profitability in all segments of the business" (McColgan, 1997).

Today, when a FIRS employee walks into the office, "they have one mission, and that mission is 401(k)" (Rohrer, 1994).

To accomplish this change Fidelity Retirement has spent 20 percent of their $2 billion revenue on technology. When one of the 2 million customers calls, they reach a telephone representative whose computer accesses the online, continually updated portfolio of the caller. The integration of the departments has enabled it to branch out to every conceivable product distribution network, with only half of all revenues coming from direct marketing from Fidelity. The rest are sold through banks or other financial institutions.

Essentially, Fidelity views 401(k)s as a "record-keeping business." They plan to maintain the best-kept records in the business. While other companies may possess the same technology as Fidelity, no one has made such a long-standing commitment to continual change. Additionally, Fidelity plans to organize all benefits administration around the same 800 number. This will provide a one-stop shopping center for defined contributions, defined benefit plans, and health plans.

Fidelity notes that it puts employee first to maintain its outstanding service for customers. This is based upon the assumption that "staff of loyal, satisfied employees drives customer satisfaction and loyalty" which in turn drives profit and growth" (McColgan, 1997). Fidelity's Institutional Retirement Services Company has developed a well-organized, sequential program named Service Delivery University to ensure that employees have opportunities for professional growth and development.

### Recommendation for the Future

Although it processes paper better than anyone else in the business, the need to process paper in the future may not be so important. The plant in Covington, Kentucky, is very high-tech but possibly obsolete. Fidelity has applied technology in an area that may only be relevant in the short term. The ability to use the Internet to download prospectuses and other information about the company is already possible. Customers may also soon choose to see their accounts electronically. Thus, sending paper information may become less important.

Fidelity's Internet presence, although impressive, is similar to other Internet discount brokers. There is a low barrier to entry for an Internet presence. It remains to be seen whether Internet discount brokers will present a threat to larger, more established companies.

When Edward Johnson II was at the helm, Fidelity was a successful but undistinguished mutual fund company. When Ned III took over, Fidelity made its name in customer service and technology. It became known as an investment powerhouse with a culture that bred brash, risk-taking managers whose investments always seemed to show the best returns. Today, Fidelity is undergoing significant change. Although growth has been dramatic over the past few years, returns have faltered.

SOURCES: Sam Allis, "A Quiet Passion for Performance" in Time. September 30, 1996. 148:53. Article A 18701196. Business and Company ASAP (online).
Jennifer Breshahan, "Semper Fidelity" in CIO. February 1, 1997. 10:8 (62–6).
James Collins, "The Money Machine" in Time. September 30, 1996. 148:46. Article A18701195. Business and Company ASAP (online).
Michael Goldberg, "Powerful Processing," in Computerworld. July 3, 1995. 29:27(28).
James S Hirsch, "Stamp of Approval: A High-Tech System for Sending the Mail Unfolds at Fidelity; Robots at 'Kentucky Farm' Boost Output, Invigorate Back-Office Operations; Roling Hills of Red Balloons" in The Wall Street Journal. March 20, 1996. A1+.
James S. Hirsch, "Magellan's Stansky Put More Money in Stocks" in The Wall Street Journal, November 13, 1996. C1+.
Ellyn A McColgan, "How Fidelity Invests in Service Professionals" in Harvard Business Review. Jan–Feb 1997. 137–43.
Srikumar S Rao, "Network Asset Value: The Fine Art of Continually Upgrading Aging Computer Systems at Fidelity" in Financial World. December 5, 1995. 75–77.
Julie Rohrer, "The Fidelity Factor: Technology has Helped Fidelity Leap so Far Ahead of the 401(k) Pack that it's Doubtful Anyone can Catch Up" in Institutional Investor. October 1994. 227–8.

## QUESTIONS

1. What forces are driving the strategic direction for Fidelity Investments?
2. What has been the catalyst for change at Fidelity Investments?
3. Upon what technologies has Fidelity Investments relied?
4. What caused Fidelity to adopt such an extensive use of technology?
5. How successful has the implementation of technology been for Fidelity?
6. What does Fidelity's web page present about its business directives?
7. What challenges and opportunities is the industry facing?
8. How will technology impact the investment industry?
9. How will the capture and maintenance of customer data impact the corporation's future?

## ADDITIONAL READING

Ambrosio, Johanna. "Fidelity Posts 'Net Services," Computerworld, August 25, 1997, p. 45.

"Fidelity Emphasizes Web," Computerworld, August 18, 1997, p. 8.

"Fidelity Investments (one million online customers)," Wall Street & Technology, July 1998, p. 30.

"Fidelity Unit Outsources Corporate Actions Data," Wall Street & Technology, August 1998, p. 17.

Gillin, Paul. "Schwab Impresses," Computerworld, October 20, 1997, pp. 49–50.

Menagh, Melanie. "We're in the Money," Computerworld, November 23, 1998.

"Online Brokerage Arena to Explode with Services," PC Week, November 3, 1997, p. 90.

Schwartz, Jeffrey. "Fidelity's War Room—Brokerage Makes Sure It's the First to Know About Site Problems," InternetWeek, October 19, 1998, p. 1.

Thyfault, Mary E. "Speech Recognition for Stock Trading," InformationWeek, November 2, 1998, p. 40.

## CASE *Charles Schwab & Co.*

The days of ticker tape are over. Today, anyone with a personal computer terminal and a modem can get a stock quote, conduct company research, place a trade, or check the status of their portfolio. There is no need to speak with a stockbroker. In 1996, it was estimated that 14 percent of computer users who had Internet access obtained investment information or traded securities online.

Firms that offer order execution for low prices, known generally as discount brokers, have benefited greatly from technological innovation. These firms are gaining market share, currently receiving 13.6 percent of all retail commission revenues, up from 10.4 percent in 1990 and 5.4 percent in 1985. The growth in discount brokerage, the breadth of new financial products, and the increasing numbers of personal computers in homes are changing today's retail brokerage industry.

### Technological Investment and Analysis

Schwab utilization of technology can be viewed as foreshadowing the future. A recent survey by accounting and consulting firm, Ernst & Young, reported in the June 6, 1997, edition of *Financial Times,* indicates that the number of financial service firms using the Internet was ready to spiral upward. Internationally, the information technology budgets of financial services firms grew 4 to 6 percent from 1995 to 1996.

In 1992, Schwab was one of three industry members that revolutionized the mutual fund industry by utilizing information technology to offer a new distribution channel for mutual funds. Schwab called its mutual fund supermarket: OneSource. At the time it was introduced, OneSource provided a single point of purchase for more than 350 no-load mutual funds in 50 different fund families, allowing investors to switch between funds without a sales charge.

Today, OneSource collects approximately 600 mutual funds from 70 fund families in one product, making Schwab one of the top three mutual fund distributors. Development of this product was innovative, breaking what was then an industry standard. OneSource developers Tom Seip and John Coghlan claimed to have invented the mutual fund supermarket for themselves. Seip stated earlier, "We knew that this was how we wanted to buy mutual funds, and we figured there were millions of other people who did, too."

Until 1992, each mutual fund company serviced its own accounts. It was difficult for consumers to achieve both diversification and high performance in a single fund family. The result was consumers dealing with different firms, different statements, different rules, and different sales representatives. OneSource, through the use of technology, united Schwab with mutual fund providers to expand and diversify Schwab's product line.

OneSource changed the mutual fund business by providing consumers with a choice of funds from a variety of fund providers, summarized in a single account with one monthly statement to track all their funds. No transaction fees are incurred on OneSource accounts, allowing customers to shift money to different fund families without charge. Schwab is remunerated for OneSource directly by the funds, receiving between 0.25 and 0.40 percent for every $100 of fund shares held in the supermarket accounts.

OneSource could only be implemented with information technology. The consolidation of funds and a single summary statement of client fund holdings are possible only due to sophisticated technology and software applications. In 1994, two years after OneSource was started, Charles Schwab commented, "Technology is at the core of OneSource. The forces of technology have allowed us to introduce to the public a far-flung set of funds in one package, and it's only because of this [technology] that we are able to integrate all of these funds together into OneSource."

Schwab's sentiments were echoed by John Philip Coghlan, executive vice-president of Schwab Institutional, who commented, "We are very much a technology company. Before, we had a fairly monolithic system that would have made this approach into these different markets impossible." To implement OneSource, Schwab revamped their technology to a client-server platform. This system provides clients with the ability to download information on a daily basis for portfolio valuation.

Technology also provides the Schwab customers with a variety of methods in which to conduct OneSource business: via a broker on an 800 line available 24 hours per day or without human contact via a Touch-Tone phone or computer keyboard.

The impact of the OneSource innovation is reflected in Schwab's sales. In the first half of 1996, Schwab's sales of mutual funds through OneSource increased 70 percent from sales during the last half of 1995: a considerably faster rate than the industry's growth rate. OneSource has proven to be a forceful asset-gathering tool for Schwab, accumulating $60 billion in customer accounts in 1996.

OneSource's impact on the industry is also reflected in the fact that full service broker-dealers have amended their policies regarding brokers selling outside funds. Firms such as Smith Barney now offer investors a wide range of fund choices, partly in response to the competition posed by fund supermarkets such as OneSource and partly to demonstrate to customers that they want to provide the best products for each investor.

The success of OneSource is further underscored by Schwab's recent policy of charging new funds $12,000 to join the network. Schwab now collects fees from each fund ranging from 0.25 to 0.40 percent for shares held in the supermarket account *plus* a "membership fee" collected directly from the fund to allow the fund to be distributed through OneSource. Fee generation on the $60 billion Schwab held in account in 1996, at a minimum, totaled $150 million.

Schwab will undoubtedly continue to provide services it believes customers desire in OneSource, just as it did in January 1997 when it launched a dedicated web site for the mutual fund marketplace (www.schwab.com/funds).

In 1994, the Internet was not discussed at the Securities Industry Association's annual technology show. In 1995, the topic received substantial interest. In 1996, the annual show had an entire section devoted to the Internet. Such developments are reflective of the manner in which the Internet grew from an interesting new addition in the technology market to a primary channel of distribution for the investment industry. A 1996 study by Business Communications Company identified that the U.S. electronic trading market in 1995 was almost $1.4 billion and was expected to grow at an 11.9 percent average annual growth rate and reach a level of $2.3 billion by 2000.

Schwab was the first major brokerage to permit online trading via the World Wide Web. Schwab built its reputation as a discount broker as an aggressive user of new technology to cut costs, passing savings on to clients, so it was not surprising that it was the first major security industry member to implement Internet trading. What was noteworthy was that Schwab considered the Web sufficiently secure to risk putting customer accounts online.

At the beginning of 1996, Schwab estimated that 15 percent of its customers were trading online through the firm's computer network. After determining that the Web provided sufficient security to allow trading, Schwab initiated a pilot program for Web-based online trading in March 1996. Schwab's Internet trading commenced a mere year after the firm first established its Web homepage (www.schwab.com). Members of the pilot group who executed trades via the e.Schwab system were charged $39.00 per trade while non-e.Schwab customers received a 10 percent discount off the firm's regular commission schedule.

The success realized from the Internet pilot program resulted in Schwab offering Internet trading to all customers in May 1996. In addition, the cost savings Schwab realized from the increased percentage of trades executed electronically were passed on to its customers. Effective July 9, 1996, Schwab reduced its flat fee on all stock transactions up to 1,000 shares executed via e.Schwab to $29.95 and $0.03 for each additional share, a 23 percent reduction from the $39.00 fee imposed in March of the same year. This $29.95 rate is compared with Schwab's $70 rate for phone trades.

Schwab's advance into the Internet underscores its belief that online investing is the future of the brokerage business. Beth Sawi, vice-president with Schwab, commented: "All investors will be managing their investments through their PC." Sawi advised that prior to launching its online service, Schwab explored whether it would be taking away business from its existing market. The result of this research, Schwab determined that if it did not provide an Internet distribution channel, someone else would.

The technology Schwab implemented for its Internet trading was developed in-house. Schwab believed the knowledge it had gained from other trading software such as StreetSmart and e.Schwab, provided it with the ability to built a system with Internet-based transaction capabilities. Schwab provided Internet trading by linking its web site to its proprietary mainframe system. The system was enhanced with a custom code for menu-driven customer options.

Schwab utilized Netscape's Secure Sockets Layer technology, which includes encryption and is considered the industry standard for security technology. In offering online trading via the Internet, Schwab implied that the Net is secure ground for transmitting customer account information. Schwab extended security measures by prohibiting customers from changing an address, withdrawing money, or liquidating an account via the Internet.

Development of Schwab's Web-based trading is notable in that it was built in only eight weeks. This quick

| DATE | # OF ACCOUNTS | BILLION $ |
|---|---|---|
| December 1995 | 336,600 | 23.3 |
| June 1996 | 467,000 | 31.5 |
| December 1996 | 617,000 | 41.7 |
| January 1997 | 669,000 | 46.5 |
| February 1997 | 712,000 | 50.0 |

response is credited to several factors, which include planning ahead, working with small development teams, using internal staff, sticking to a short development cycle, and, while being concerned about security, not letting security concerns cripple development. Schwab successfully balanced results with the need to build an infrastructure.

Schwab has realized great success from its Internet experience. Trading via the Net provides Schwab clients with fast trades, easy access to real-time information (including portfolio accounting services, electronic news, and quote services), and cheaper brokerage commission. In March 1997, Schwab reported reaching $50 billion in online customer assets (both Internet traded and other online trading venues) in 700,000 active accounts. These figures reflect continued growth in Schwab's online business.

Through online accounts, individuals manage approximately $100 billion in assets. That figure was expected to jump to $525 billion by 2000. If Schwab's market share remains at 47 percent, it would have access to nearly $247 billion dollars of investment assets in the year 2000. Whatever the percent of online traded assets Schwab ultimately administers for its clients, online trading, to include Internet trading, will add up to a powerful asset-gathering tool.

Schwab does not intend to forsake its retail office or telecommunications presence. Randy Goldman, vice-president of electronic brokerage marketing at Schwab, commented in 1996, "In the world of electronics, when you really don't know who's on the other side of a trade, its nice to have the Schwab name out there."

Schwab's decision not to sacrifice its retail office operations is sound; a recent study by SRI Consulting estimates that in the next three to five years no more than 8 percent of all U.S. households will regularly use online brokerage services. However, that 8 percent of households represents 15 percent of all investors. Additional research identifies these users as prime customers who are financially competent and well informed: the type of client that financial institutions would want to attract.

## Technological Innovations

### Network

Schwab has implemented a customized Web-based analysis reporting application that helps the company locate and fix trading errors. It also helps identify market trends and track changes in tax law and other regulations. The application is code-named Schwab Metric and Analysis Reporting Tool (SMART).

SMART generates significant payback by automatically collecting information for audits on Schwab's finance controls and risk-assessment systems in one-sixth of the time previously required. It will also let Schwab capture trading errors proactively instead of reactively, reducing the time required for a correction from days to hours. SMART helps ICAD users be more productive, informed.

### Data

Schwab has an intranet, called the Schweb, being used to help marketers better understand customer trends by using data. If a customer opens an account with $10,000, Schwab wants to know if that customer also has significant additional funds available to invest. To get this information Schwab has installed Epiphany's Clarity, a Web package that can extract information from numerous sources, both legacy systems and external repositories.

Steve Blank, Epiphany's founder and executive vice-president of marketing, said Schwab had two choices: install an online analytical processing (OLAP) server and a variety of data extraction and mining tools along with a Web application server; or go with a shrink-wrapped product. Schwab chose Ephiphany's product.

### Recommendation for the Future

The financial services industry is being transformed by information technology, whether by development of value-added services for customers or new channels of distribution for its products. Technology has enabled the financial services industry to move from Ticker Tape to Cyberspace.

For a firm like Charles Schwab Corporation the changes occurring in the financial industry are an opportunity. The firm will have to continue its policy of determining its business goals and determining how it will best achieve these targets. Technology has been an important part of Schwab's success, enabling product innovations and new channels of distribution such as One-Source and Internet trading.

These technology-enabled products have helped Schwab achieve its business goals, but did not drive the firm's business decisions. To remain successful, Schwab will have to plan and prepare to address the changing landscape of the investment industry. Schwab must be ready to move on several issues or risk losing its market share.

First, Schwab needs to be attuned to the fact that its credibility is on the line for every trade it makes. If unable to maintain its credibility, customers will conduct business with Schwab's competitors. The firm must address the system capacity issues that it has been experiencing. Schwab's technology systems have to be prepared to handle unexpected high capacity trading.

Second, Schwab must continue to be an innovator in implementing technology in the investment service industry. Schwab has been successful due to its ability to address consumers' needs and product demands in a quick and cost-efficient manner. It is too early to tell if Internet Trading or VoiceBroker will have the same effect on the firm's bottom line as OneSource had. Regardless, Schwab must continue pursuing excellence in providing products and distribution channels that address client's needs. Technology has been a partner in Schwab's success and can be expected to continue being an ally in the firm reaching its future business goals.

The investment services industry is growing, thanks in part to aging baby boomers that are investing more and building up savings. Schwab is in position to seize this opportunity. With continued planning and preparation, Schwab will succeed in its business objectives of asset gathering, increased sales, and increased net income. Technology will continue to be an important component of this success.

### QUESTIONS

1. What is the catalyst for change at Charles Schwab?
2. What have become the critical success factors and core competencies for this industry?
3. How has the technological change been implemented at Schwab?
4. How successful has the technological change been at Schwab?
5. How does the corporation evaluate its financial ability to embark on a major technological program of advancement?
6. What does Schwab's web page present about its business?
7. How has technology impacted the industry?
8. How important is data to the Schwab's continued success?

### ADDITIONAL READING

"Charles Schwab to Market U.S. Stocks via Internet in Japan," *Newsbytes,* December 7, 1998.

Colkin, Eileen. "Surfin' Seniors," *InformationWeek,* October 26, 1998, p. 16.

Fletcher-MacDonald, Trina. "No. 7—Charles Schwab Extra Extranet Bonus," *InfoWorld,* October 5, 1998, p. 90.

Helenius, Tanya. "Acuity Delivers Real-Time, Online Interaction for Schwab," *Wall Street & Technology,* November 1998, p. 58.

Musich, Paula. "How to Keep (E-) Business Humming," *PC Week,* September 28, 1998, p. 1.

"Reining in Stock Frenzy," *PC Magazine,* March 9, 1999, p. 10.

Schwartz, Jeffrey, and Richard Karpinski, "The Price of Success—Commerce Sites Scramble to Meet Unexpected Demand," *InternetWeek,* February 8, 1999, p. 1.

Schwartz, Jeffrey. "Full Portfolios Managed," *InternetWeek,* December 7, 1998, p. 21.

———. "A Marketing Epiphany—Start-up's Data Analysis Package Powers Schwab Intranet," *InternetWeek,* August 3, 1998, p. 9.

Smith, Laura B. "Schwab Puts Stock in Voice Recognition," *PC Week,* June 22, 1998, p. 95.

Sullivan, Kristina B. "WAN Probes Broker Capacity," *PC Week,* January 11, 1999, p. 81.

Wilson, Beth. "Vital Signs," *PC/Computing,* March 1999, p. 14.

## DISCUSSION ISSUE

### *Outsourcing*

Outsourcing is a new term for an old concept in MIS. Rather than own the computers and hire a large MIS staff, a company may choose to let a specialized firm run the entire computer operations. Two of the largest firms specializing in running computer operations for other companies are EDS and IBM. For a fee, these companies will provide the main computers, communication links, software, and even software development and maintenance. The current debate over outsourcing began when Kodak decided to let IBM run its main computer operations. Part of the decision most likely was caused by the expenses incurred by Kodak when it lost a patent infringement suit to Polaroid, but there are many other issues involved and several other large firms have chosen not to run their own computer operations. Listen to Paul (vice-president of finance) and Corie (vice-president of MIS) of the fictional MegaPark Corporation, as they try to decide whether their firm should switch to outsourcing.

Paul:     Look at the charts. If we sell off our old computers and transfer the MIS staff to EDS, we can save $5 million a year.

Corie:     But what about the employees? Some of them have been with us for 15 years. What if they don't want to move? What if they don't like

EDS management? What about their seniority and pensions and . . .

Paul:     Who cares? We need to cut costs. At least they'll have jobs.

Corie:     Well, let's look at those costs. What happens when the outside firm raises its prices? We're at their mercy.

Paul:     Wait a minute. Now you're worried about increasing costs? You've been in here every year begging for more money! At least with outsourcing we get a set price schedule. You always overspend your budget. In the last five years, your budget has increased three times as fast as the rest of the company, and you still want more.

Corie:     Ouch. Well, what about service and responsibility to the users? As long as MIS is located here, I can deal with user problems immediately. We get together with them for lunch and play softball with the users. Because we see them all the time, we know what they want.

Paul:     EDS didn't say anything about a softball team, but your people spend most of the time on the phone anyway. With all of the communication networks they have, what difference does it make where the MIS team is located? Besides, EDS said they have more than 200 people with experience working in our industry, plus immediate access to thousands of others. And they are hiring most of our people as well.

Corie:     But can EDS be as responsive as we can? We've worked hard to reduce our MIS decision-making process and to involve users in all decisions. If a user department needs something, we can decide in a couple of weeks whether to commit resources to it. EDS personnel would take months to go through their decision-making process. We know the industry, and we know the people who work here.

Paul:     One of our competitors, Grand Consolidated, Limited, has used outsourcing for three years. The company increased its market share by 11 percent, mostly at our expense. Maybe the outsourcing didn't help, but it surely didn't hurt!

Corie:     All right. What about security? I'll bet you forgot that one. When all of our customer data is stored on our machines in our building, I know how to protect it. Now you're going to put all of this important information in someone else's computer. Even worse, EDS already handles one of our competitors. How do we know Grand Consolidated won't get access to our information?

Paul:    Get real, Corie. We sell pet rocks. We don't have any secret data.

Corie:    Of course we do. What about our employee evaluations? What about our plans for future products? What about our sales data concerning which products do well with which types of customers? What about our evaluations of our competitors? Of course, there's also our evaluations of environmental pollution legislation and which legislators might be sympathetic to our positions. Then, there's . . .

Paul:    All right, all right. I get the idea. We'll have to get EDS to establish some encryption system or something to protect our data. EDS must be doing something like that for the other companies it supports. I'm sure there are ways to protect our data.

Corie:    What about our new ad campaign? That was all computer generated. Same thing with the designs for next year's models. Which reminds me—we had to get some special equipment for those projects. How will we do that in the future?

Paul:    EDS says it can get us any equipment we need. And the managers there said with their company's size they can get it at better prices. Plus, we don't have to buy the hardware, so we don't get stuck with expensive, obsolete equipment. EDS always has the newest hardware.

Corie:    How about strategic uses of MIS? I've been thinking about some ways we can tie in to our suppliers' computers and improve our quality control. And I've been talking with some of our distributors so that we can get access to their computers and get better information on sales. Who is going to think up these ideas? Who will nail down the details? Who . . .

Paul:    You will, Corie. You're not going anywhere. Besides, since you no longer have to worry about the day-to-day details, you'll have more time to work on these big projects. You've raised some good points, and I really want to ask EDS about its security provisions and get our lawyers to look things over, but I've made up my mind.

Corie:    I'm not happy about it, but it might work out. Those computers were getting old. I wanted to replace them but I figured that within five years we'd switch to PC networks, so it would be a waste of money to buy new central computers today. Maybe the outsourcing will work until we're ready to switch to PC networks. If we outsource, will we ever be able to move MIS back in house?

## DISCUSSION QUESTIONS

1. What are the reasons a company might wish to outsource its information management?
2. What are the possible dangers of outsourcing?
3. How should a company evaluate the success or failure of its move to outsourcing?
4. If a company chooses to outsource its information management, how much of the MIS functions should the company keep in-house?
5. If you were an employee of an MIS department and your company decided to outsource, what would be your considerations in deciding whether to take a job with the company hired to do the information management?

# *Project Management*

Whether you work in information systems or any other discipline, project management is an important component of your job. Projects arise in many areas, examples include developing software, designing buildings, moving your operations to a larger building, developing a new advertising campaign, and organizing a fund-raising event.

Projects are defined in terms of a goal, the scope, a schedule, and the resources involved. Projects with precisely defined goals have a far better chance of succeeding. For example, a project goal of implementing a new general ledger system is easy to understand; a goal of "providing the best information to our employees" is next to impossible to understand, much less achieve. Well-defined goals have the advantage of keeping the project focused. For example, the 1960s U.S. goal of putting a man on the moon was a huge project, but the clearly defined goal made it easier to keep the project moving in the right direction. The 1980s and 1990s never-achieved goal of improving the IRS had little chance for success because no one knew what the end result should look like.

Scope is an issue of size and complexity, typically measured in terms of the number of tasks and the time frame involved. Projects can range anywhere from small to large. With only a few tasks and one or two people, you can afford to use informal project management techniques. As the project becomes larger or the tasks more complex, you will need a system to help you track the progress of each component. Be careful to match the management techniques to the scope of the project. Do not try to use informal techniques for large, complex projects, and do not try to impose rigid controls on short, simple projects.

A project ultimately must be divided into individual tasks. Some of the tasks depend on others. For example, when building a house you cannot paint the walls before they are constructed. A schedule shows the tasks, the time required to complete them (duration), and how they depend on other tasks.

Tasks are not accomplished by magic. They require resources. Generally, the most important resource consists of workers. Keeping costs under control is an important aspect of project management, so you need to assign workers to tasks. Sometimes you also need to schedule other resources, such as workrooms or machinery.

## PROJECT MANAGEMENT STEPS

Project management involves four primary steps: (1) define the project, (2) create the plan, (3) track and manage the project as it proceeds, and (4) close the project when the goal is achieved or the project is cancelled.

The project definition includes establishing the goal and identifying the major tasks. You must also identify your primary resources available and the major constraints. Finally, you should establish an initial timetable, including the final completion date and some of the major intermediate milestones.

The project plan is an important tool in managing the project. It outlines all of the tasks and the resources required to complete them. At the planning stage, you get time and resource estimates from the people who will perform the work on that stage. You must also identify the dependencies among the tasks. Which tasks can be performed independently? Which ones must wait for other tasks to finish?

Once the project is started, you need to monitor the progress and compare it to the plan. If some tasks take longer to complete, you must adjust the schedule. If some resources are overworked, you can decide if you want to add resources or accept the delays in the tasks. By constantly updating the project plan, you can identify potential problems and provide updated estimates of the completion date.

When the project is finished, review the original project plan and summarize the project. Were the original estimates accurate? What unexpected problems did you encounter? Were there sufficient resources for the project, or did you need to add more as the project evolved? These questions will help you generate better estimates on the next project.

## MICROSOFT PROJECT

It is impossible to memorize all the details involved in a project. You need to keep notes, and you need a system to track the progress, comparing actual values to the original estimates. Several project management tools exist to organize and help you analyze the data. The easiest way to use these tools is with an automated system like Microsoft Project.

In many ways, Microsoft Project is a specialized database. You enter data about the project, which is stored in a central database. The system then provides you with specialized views that help you see the relationships among the tasks, resources, and goals. By building on a DBMS, the system also allows you to retrieve data and create additional reports.

The Gantt and PERT charts are standard project planning tools for displaying and organizing tasks. The two provide similar types of information but in different formats. Some people prefer one method, other managers use both. The Tracking Gantt chart is used to compare estimates to the actual values while the project is in progress. The resource views provide details on how resources (e.g., workers) are assigned to tasks. The different views simply report the data from various perspectives (time, the resource, or tasks).

## SAMPLE PROJECT

The Rolling Thunder Bicycle company wants to raise its visibility by organizing a bicycle ride. Rides of 25, 50, and 100 miles will set up with rest stops, sag vehicles, and mechanical support. For a $20 fee, riders will also get a commemorative shirt. Profits from the ride will go to local charitable organizations. The date and general location of the ride have already been chosen. The ride will be called the Spring Forward Century. Organizing the ride requires several tasks. Volunteers from local bicycle clubs will help with some of the early tasks, and they will handle most of the tasks on the day of the ride.

Two projects have been set up to handle this example. The first project concentrates on tasks required to organize the ride. The tasks are grouped into the categories shown in Figure 13.1A. A few finishing tasks are required after the ride, such as sending thank-you notes, verifying the clean up, and writing final project notes. A second project is set up to handle day-of-the-ride tasks. These tasks involve more people and have a different time frame (hours instead of days), so it is easier to create separate projects.

It is possible to handle the planning using paper notes, but there are several advantages to using a tool like Microsoft Project to organize the preparations. One significant advantage is the ease of changing key factors and letting the system instantly display the new relationships. The first step in creating the project is to enter the finishing date (April 2, 2000) and tell the system to schedule backward from that date. The next step is to enter the task information. It is easiest to work with the Gantt chart view. A Gantt chart displays tasks down the left column and dates across the top of the screen. You enter each task by giving it a name and duration (length of time it requires). The Gantt chart displays the task as a horizontal bar, beginning on a certain date and extending for the specified duration. Initially, you do not care about the starting date. As you enter the tasks, you can group related tasks. Each of the groups in Figure 13.1A has a set of detailed tasks beneath it. You specify this hierarchical relationship by indenting ($\rightarrow$) the detailed tasks. You

- Choose starting point
- Legal paperwork
- Establish routes
- Create databases
- Create promotional materials
- Create commemorative shirts
- Register riders
- Organize volunteer groups
- Advertise ride
- Plan rest stops
- Plan registration

**FIGURE 13.1A**
PRIMARY TASKS FOR ORGANIZING THE SPRING FORWARD CENTURY RIDE
Each of these categories contains several detailed tasks.

can have multiple levels of groups, and the Gantt chart shows a summary bar for each group. If you want, you can roll up and hide the detail, enabling you to focus on the major groups.

Showing relationships among tasks is a critical step in project management. In particular, you need to link tasks that depend on each other. For example, the following tasks must be performed in order: create advertising poster, copy posters, distribute posters. We must complete the first task before beginning the next one. These relationships are created as links. In Microsoft Project, select two tasks and click the Link Tasks button (shown as a chain link). The Gantt chart will automatically move the earlier task to the left and connect the two with an arrow. You need to identify the relationships among all the tasks. Figure 13.2A shows that setting the dependencies establishes the main schedule of the tasks.

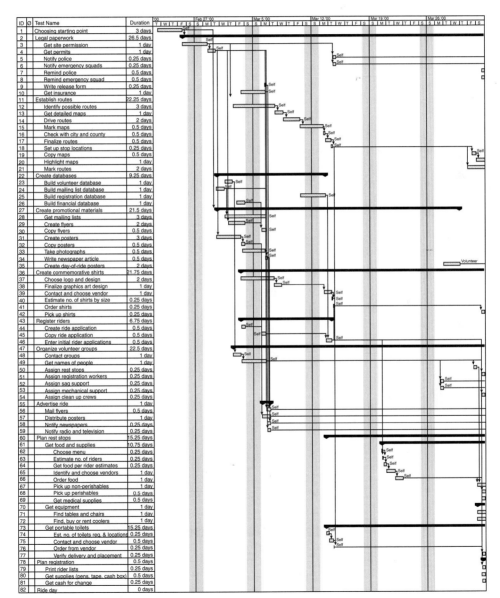

**FIGURE 13.2A**

GANTT CHART FOR SPRING FORWARD CENTURY RIDE

Dependence among the tasks is shown as lines. These links force some tasks to be completed first, which establishes the primary schedule.

## RESOURCE USAGE

You should also enter a list of resources, in this case the workers available for the project (yourself and a few volunteers). You can then assign workers to each task. The Resource graph shows you if the resources are over allocated (meaning that you either need to perform tasks earlier or find more resources). Microsoft Project has a tool for leveling the resources that will help arrange the tasks to allocate the resources better. However, you generally have to make adjustments to the schedule yourself.

Figure 13.3A shows the resource graphs for yourself and for the volunteers. The graph for the volunteers shows that they will not be able to complete all of the tasks scheduled for the Saturday before the ride. You will either have to get more volunteers or have them complete some of the tasks earlier. On examining the task list, you find several tasks that can be completed earlier; so you choose that solution.

Figure 13.3A also indicates two major time periods when you will be unable to complete the tasks assigned to you. Again, you either have to get volunteers to do more of the work, or you will have to

perform some of the tasks earlier. The answer will depend on which is easier: finding more workers or taking more time off your normal job so you can begin earlier. The third possibility is to find a way to complete the tasks faster. However, you will already have to rely heavily on this prospect during most of the month of March. Most days are already allocated at 200 to 300 percent of your time. You can survive by being more efficient and working nights and weekends. However, you still have to find a way to handle the two major peaks.

## MONITORING THE PROGRESS

Once you have established the detailed design, you should save a baseline of the project. The baseline is a saved version at a fixed point in time that you can keep for later reference. As each task is completed, you can mark its progress within the system. You can also track actual resource usage and costs by entering them into the appropriate worksheets. Then you can view charts or worksheets that compare the estimated (baseline) values to the actual data.

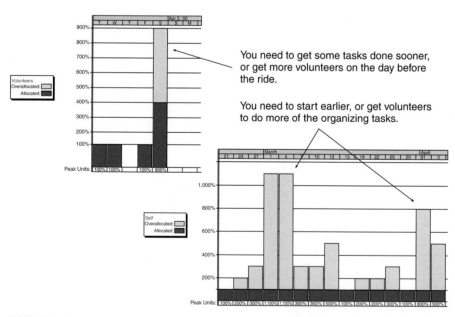

You need to get some tasks done sooner, or get more volunteers on the day before the ride.

You need to start earlier, or get volunteers to do more of the organizing tasks.

**FIGURE 13.3A**

RESOURCE NEEDS FOR ORGANIZING THE RIDE

You can probably solve the volunteer shortage by moving some of their tasks to Thursday and Friday. However, you will need additional volunteers to help with your two major peaks—or you will have to begin much earlier.

Additionally, if some tasks take longer than expected, you can enter the new data and the system will adjust the remaining tasks to show you the new completion times and resource requirements. If possible, you can add resources to put the project back on track. However, remember that adding more people to a complex project can just as easily cause more problems because it is harder to manage the larger staff.

## DAY OF THE RIDE

Figure 13.4A shows the Gantt chart for the day of the ride. Notice that tasks are scheduled by hours. Also notice that because of the advance planning, the day

of the ride is relatively straightforward. Few of the tasks are linked, which makes it easier to adjust if something goes wrong. However, with more volunteers to coordinate, communication will be an important factor. Many ride organizers use cellular phones to stay in touch with the volunteer drivers and rest-stop workers.

One useful feature of this Gantt chart is that it highlights the number of volunteers that will be needed. For example, you will need only four SAG drivers since they can loop the routes. The chart also shows that the driver from the 25-mile route can help out on the last sweep of the 100-mile route if there are delays or problems.

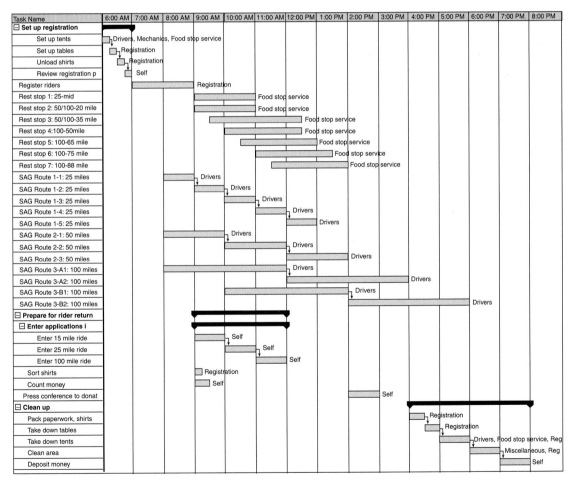

## FIGURE 13.4A
### GANTT CHART FOR THE DAY OF THE RIDE
Most of the tasks are relatively independent, which makes it easier to adjust for problems. However, many tasks take place at the same time, requiring more workers and good communication.

Likewise, you can get by with only five actual rest stops since that is the most needed at one time. When the riders clear out from the first stops on the 25- and 50-mile routes, the workers can be moved to the ending stops of the 100-mile route.

When you enter the tasks for registration, rest stops, and SAG drivers, you should check the advanced options and set the task duration as fixed. These tasks will always take the same amount of time regardless of the amount of resources you assign to them. You should also assign two workers to each rest stop. One of them could be a mechanic, but you need two people at a stop so that one can run for refills if needed.

## SUMMARY

Overall, the project planning system makes it easy to enter your tasks. By defining the dependencies among the tasks, most of your schedule is automatically set. The schedule also helps you determine the resources needed. The system can display a variety of views, including resource lists and a calendar. Microsoft Project can also automatically generate reminder entries for your calendar system, or it can e-mail notices to various people involved in the project. Finally, by tracking actual time, resources, and costs, the system makes it easier to estimate and plan for the next project.

## EXERCISES

1. Download a trial copy of Microsoft Project (if it is not available) and create the Bicycle Ride project. Print the Gantt chart.

| NAME | DURATION | DEPENDS ON | RESOURCES |
|---|---|---|---|
| 1 Set up registration | 1 hr | | |
| 2 Set up tents | 0.25 hrs | | Drivers, Mechanics, Food stop service |
| 3 Set up tables | 0.25 hrs | 2 | Registration |
| 4 Unload shirts | 0.25 hrs | 3 | Registration |
| 5 Review registration procedures | 0.25 hrs | 4 | Self |
| 6 Register riders | 2 hrs | | Registration [400%] |
| 7 Rest stop 1: 25-mid | 2 hrs | | Food stop service [200%] |
| 8 Rest stop 2: 50/100-20 mile | 2 hrs | | Food stop service [200%] |
| 9 Rest stop 3: 50/100-35 mile | 3 hrs | | Food stop service [200%] |
| 10 Rest stop 4: 100-50 mile | 2.5 hrs | | Food stop service [200%] |
| 11 Rest stop 5: 100-65 mile | 2.5 hrs | | Food stop service [200%] |
| 12 Rest stop 6: 100-75 mile | 2.5 hrs | | Food stop service [200%] |
| 13 Rest stop 7: 100-88 mile | 2.5 hrs | | Food stop service [200%] |
| 14 SAG Route 1-1: 25 miles | 1 hr | | Drivers |
| 15 SAG Route 1-2: 25 miles | 1 hr | 14 | Drivers |
| 16 SAG Route 1-3: 25 miles | 1 hr | 15 | Drivers |
| 17 SAG Route 1-4: 25 miles | 1 hr | 16 | Drivers |
| 18 SAG Route 1-5: 25 miles | 1 hr | 17 | Drivers |
| 19 SAG Route 2-1: 50 miles | 2 hrs | | Drivers |
| 20 SAG Route 2-2: 50 miles | 2 hrs | 19 | Drivers |
| 21 SAG Route 2-3: 50 miles | 2 hrs | 20 | Drivers |
| 22 SAG Route 3-A1: 100 miles | 4 hrs | | Drivers |
| 23 SAG Route 3-A2: 100 miles | 4 hrs | 22 | Drivers |
| 24 SAG Route 3-B1: 100 miles | 4 hrs | | Drivers |
| 25 SAG Route 3-B2: 100 miles | 4 hrs | 24 | Drivers |
| 26 Prepare for rider return | 3 hrs | | |
| 27 Enter applications in database | 3 hrs | | |
| 28 Enter 15 mile riders | 1hr | | Self |
| 29 Enter 25 mile riders | 1hr | 28 | Self |
| 30 Enter 100 mile riders | 1hr | 29 | Self |
| 31 Sort shirts | 0.25 hrs | | Registration |
| 32 Count money | 0.5 hrs | | Self |
| 33 Press conference to donate money | 1 hr | | Self |
| 34 Clean up | 3.5 hrs | | |
| 35 Pack paperwork, shirts, and material | 0.5 hrs | | Registration |
| 36 Take down tables | 0.5 hrs | 35 | Registration |
| 37 Take down tents | 1 hr | 36 | Drivers, Food stop service, Registration, Miscellaneous |
| 38 Clean area | 1 hr | 37 | Miscellaneous, Registration, Food stop service |
| 39 Deposit money | 0.5 hrs | 38 | Self |

2. By hand, draw a Gantt chart for the following project.

| Name | Duration | Depends on | Resources |
|---|---|---|---|
| 1 Feasibility statement | 5 days | | |
| 2 Get hardware list and costs | 1 day | | Analyst |
| 3 Count forms and reports | 1 day | | Analyst |
| 4 Estimate development time | 1 day | | Analyst |
| 5 Get benefits from user | 1 day | | Analyst |
| 6 Create statement | 1 day | 2, 3, 4, 5 | Analyst |
| 7 Management approval | 1 day | 1 | |
| 8 Analysis | 17 days | 7 | |
| 9 Interview users | 7 days | | Analyst |
| 10 Evaluate competition | 3 days | | Analyst |
| 11 Search for existing software | 3 days | | Analyst |
| 12 Evaluate options | 4 days | 9, 10, 11 | Analyst |
| 13 Management approval | 1 day | 8 | |
| 14 Design | 15 days | 13 | |
| 15 Design and create database | 2 days | | Analyst |
| 16 Build forms | 8 days | 15 | Programmer |
| 17 Create reports | 4 days | 15 | Programmer |
| 18 Design application | 3 days | | Programmer |
| 19 User approval | 1 day | 14 | |
| 20 Management approval | 1 day | 19 | |
| 21 Implementation | 10 days | 20 | |
| 22 Purchase hardware | 2 days | | Analyst |
| 23 Transfer data | 3 days | 22 | Programmer |
| 24 Integration test | 4 days | 23 | Programmer |
| 25 Train users | 1 day | | Trainer |
| 26 Write procedures | 1 day | | Analyst |
| 27 Transfer operations | 1 day | 24 | Analyst, Programmer |
| 28 Review | 1 day | | Analyst, Programmer |

3. Create the Gantt chart for exercise 2 using Microsoft Project. Assign resources at 100 percent as indicated and use resource leveling to determine the time it will take to complete the project.

4. For the project described in exercise 2, identify methods to reduce the overall project time.

5. For Rolling Thunder Bicycles, create a project analysis that describes the sequences and constraints of building a bicycle (from order through shipping).

# CHAPTER 14

# *Information Management and Society*

Drug companies form an increasingly important share of health care dollars. Patents for designer drugs enable them to fund new research, but competition requires them to watch costs and use information technology.

## ELI LILLY

Eli Lilly fared well during the early 1990s. This was in large part due to the success of its best-selling drug, Prozac. People suffering from depression have a chronic condition requiring a daily regiment of maintenance therapy. Often the therapy prescribed is Prozac. Prozac is the world's most widely prescribed brand name of antidepressant. It is used by more than 24 million people worldwide.

Competition has come from a direct competitor, SmithKline Beecham's Paxil, and from the Canadian government, where due to an expired patent, the government forced a price cut of 42 percent. The threat of this competition, which is, in effect, a threat to the company's cash flow, has forced Lilly to position itself strategically for a future without patent-protected profits from sales of Prozac. Lilly's strategic positioning has involved two major steps: increasing its presence in rapidly growing new markets and aggressively introducing new drugs.

**OVERVIEW**     The other chapters show how to use information systems to help perform business jobs, from personal tasks to helping the company gain a competitive edge. They also show that information technology is altering jobs and companies. As illustrated by Figure 14.1, companies do not exist in a vacuum, so technology is also affecting the "environment," or society.

How would you work if you suddenly lost all of your data or if your computers could not run? How long could a modern company survive without technology? There are a variety of threats to information and technology. Managers need to evaluate those possibilities and make contingency plans. Although technology may increase our vulnerability, it also provides tools to protect data. You need to understand how basic security systems work and how they are used to protect information.

**INTRODUCTION**     If nothing else, history has shown that technological change is inevitable. Competitive economics virtually guarantees that the search for new products, new manufacturing techniques, and other ways to gain competitive advantage will continue.

**FIGURE 14.1**
INFORMATION
MANAGEMENT
AND SOCIETY

Every organization and individual exists in a social environment. Changes in the firm and changes in technology affect the environment. Changes in the environment can affect the firm. An understanding of these interactions will make you a better manager.

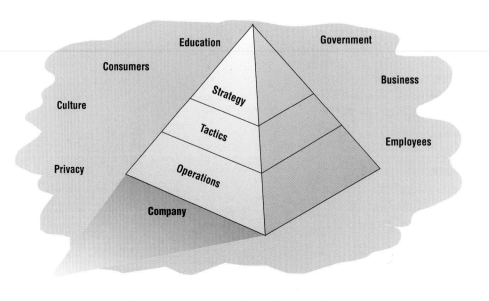

## Trends

The industrial revolution in the late 18th century caused many changes to society. Before the revolution, workers were predominantly employed as craftsmen, farmers, or lesser-skilled laborers. Mechanization brought standardization and assembly lines, for which jobs were reduced to simple, repetitive tasks.

As transportation improved, people moved from farms to cities, and cities spread to suburbs. Communication systems improved and linked the populations back together. Better product distribution mechanisms changed the way products are sold. Companies (such as Sears, through its catalogues)

began to distribute products nationally instead of relying on small local stores. National and international markets developed with every change in the communication and transportation systems.

These changes were so strong that philosophers and writers began to take note of how technological changes can affect society. From the bleak pictures painted by Dickens, Marx, and Orwell, to the fantastic voyages of Verne, Heinlein, and Asimov, we can read thousands of opinions and predictions about how technology might affect the political, economic, and social environments.

Changes in technology often affect society. Technology can change individuals, jobs, education, governments, and social interactions. As components of society, each group has rights and responsibilities to others, such as a "right" to **privacy** and obligations regarding ethics. As Figure 14.2 indicates, companies and governments collect data about many aspects of our lives.

Effects on individuals can be beneficial or detrimental. Often, a change in technology can help one set of individuals and harm another group. Typical problems include loss of privacy, depersonalization, and changing incentives or motivations. Advantages include lower prices and better products and service.

The effect on jobs is hard to predict, but most observers conclude that workers will require more education and training. Most authorities think that increases in technology in the past generally led to an increase in the number of jobs. Now, however, many of the new jobs require higher levels of education, and the workers displaced by technol-

**FIGURE 14.2**

Privacy? Many different records are kept on our lives. Some are maintained by governmental organizations, some by private companies. Some records are protected by privacy regulations; most are not.

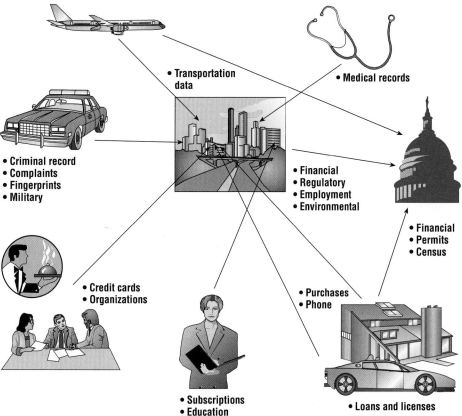

• **Transportation data**

• **Medical records**

• **Criminal record**
• **Complaints**
• **Fingerprints**
• **Military**

• **Financial**
• **Regulatory**
• **Employment**
• **Environmental**

• **Financial**
• **Permits**
• **Census**

• **Credit cards**
• **Organizations**

• **Purchases**
• **Phone**

• **Subscriptions**
• **Education**

• **Loans and licenses**

ogy rarely have the qualifications needed for the new jobs. Technology also has an effect on crime. As illustrated by Security Pacific, computers can be used to steal millions of dollars.

In addition to the increased demand, technology has provided new teaching methods. Although there is considerable debate over the costs and benefits of technology in education, there is usually a place for technology, even if only as a specialized technique. However, most educators remember the early claims of how television was going to revolutionize education. Fifty years later, television is beginning to play a role in education, but it is still hampered by the limited availability of two-way links.

Governments attempt to control these impacts of technology by creating laws, but laws often bring their own problems. Also, in times of rapid change, laws rarely keep up to the changes in technology. Governments are also directly affected by improved communication facilities. For example, technology makes it possible for governments to better understand the needs of the citizens and provide more avenues for communication.

Technology can alter any number of social interactions. Social groups can gain or lose power, and types or methods of criminals are altered. Additionally, society can become dependent on technology, which is not necessarily bad, but it causes problems if the technology is removed or substantially altered.

**INDIVIDUALS**      Information technology plays an important role in the lives of most individuals. Many jobs are directly involved in the collection, processing, and evaluation of data. Performance of many workers is continually monitored by computers. As consumers, virtually our entire lives are recorded and analyzed. Governments maintain massive files on all public aspects of our lives.

Although data has been collected on citizens for many years, recent improvements in technology raise greater concerns about privacy. As computer capabilities increase, it becomes possible to collect, integrate, and analyze the huge volume of data. Using publicly available data, it is possible to collect an amazing amount of data on any person.

## Privacy

Recall the use of technology to improve marketing discussed in Chapter 9. Marketing and sales can be improved by maintaining databases of consumer information and tracking sales and preferences at the customer level. Combining government statistics and data from market research firms with geographical data can provide a precise picture of consumer demands. It also might represent an invasion of privacy for individuals. With databases available even to small companies, it is easy to acquire basic data on any individual. For instance, phone numbers and addresses for approximately 80 million U.S. households can be obtained for around $100 on CD-ROMs. Voter registration, motor vehicle, and property records are routinely sold by state and local governments. However, the omnibus crime bill of 1994 placed restrictions on the sales of some governmental data, especially to individuals.

It is easy to obtain lists from universities, clubs and social organizations, magazine subscriptions, and mail-order firms. Statistical data can be purchased from the U.S. government. Although most U.S. agencies are forbidden from releasing specific individual observations until 50 years after the collection date, statistical averages can be highly accurate. By combining the statistical averages with your address, your actual income might be estimated to within a few thousand dollars. Also, there have been problems in the past with law enforcement and government employees selling personal data to private investigators. In 1991, 18 people were accused of selling social security information, including six government employees (*Government Computer News,* January 6, 1992, p. 58).

### Internationalization: Privacy

Different countries have different laws regarding protection of consumer data. In particular, some European nations have stricter controls than does the United States. There has been some discussion among these nations (notably France), that firms should be forced to keep consumer data within the originating country; that way it is still subject to the local laws. If a U.S. firm transmits its local French database back to the United States, the data can no longer be controlled by French law. Although such restrictions would be difficult to enforce, companies have an ethical obligation to support the laws of the nation in which they operate.

The United Kingdom has a requirement that all databases involving personal data must be registered with the data protection agency.

The European Union in general has a restriction on trading data that states that personal data can only be transferred to another country if the nation supports "adequate" protection of personal data. According to *Network World,* the EU is considering a requirement that all businesses register databases containing personal data. Additionally, businesses would be required to obtain individuals' permission to collect or process the data. They would also have to notify the individual each time the data is reused or sold.

In the United States, there are few laws or regulations regarding data held by private organizations. However, several federal laws control the use of data collected by government agencies. For example, federal agencies are restricted from sharing databases except in specific situations. In most cases, the FBI cannot access the IRS data without special permits. In terms of collection and use of data by private companies, there are few restrictions. Contrary to popular belief, there is no "right to privacy" specified in federal law. However, an element of privacy is contained in a few scattered federal laws and some state laws. For example, one federal law prohibits movie rental stores (and libraries) from disclosing lists of items rented by individuals.

Because most people prefer to maintain their privacy, companies have an ethical (and sometimes legal) obligation to respect their wishes. Individuals can always ask companies not to distribute personal data. Companies should give consumers the option of protecting personal data by building the option into their databases and informing consumers whenever companies collect data.

The Internet elevates the issue of privacy. It is relatively easy for a web site to track individual actions. Many sites closely track individual purchases. For instance, Amazon.com uses your prior purchases to suggest related books that might interest you. As of 1999, the U.S. government decided to allow the private sector to develop its own rules for dealing with privacy. However, several legislators have strongly suggested that at a minimum web sites should contain privacy statements so that visitors know how the company plans to use any personal data.

### Employee Privacy

Computers have created other problems with respect to individual privacy. They are sometimes used to monitor employees. Computers can automatically track all of the work done by each person. Some employers post this data on public bulletin boards to encourage employees to work harder. Some software available for local area networks enables managers to see exactly what every employee is doing—without the employees knowing they are being watched. Some employers read their employees' electronic-mail messages. Currently, all of these activities are legal in the United States. However, they can be intimidating to employees and seem to have little managerial value.

### Protecting Your Privacy

Despite the shortage of laws, you can take several actions to protect your privacy and restrict access to personal data. First, it is your responsibility to notify employers and companies you deal with to not distribute your personal data. You can also ask them why they need personal data and whether it is optional or required. In particular, all federal agencies are required to explain why they need data from you and the purposes for which it will be used. You can also write to direct marketing associations and file a request that your name not be included in general mailings or unsolicited phone calls. By using variations of your name or address, such as changing your middle initial, you can keep track of which organizations are selling personal data. In some cases, you can refuse to give out personal data (such as a social security or taxpayer identification number). If a private company insists, simply stop doing business with it. In a world where firms increasingly rely on a single number for identification, it is important that you protect that number.

With most government agencies and with banks, creditors, and credit-reporting agencies, you have the ability to check any data that refers to you. You have the right to disagree with any inaccurate data and request that it be changed. You can also file letters of explanation that are reported with the original data. In 1994, Congress updated the Fair Credit Reporting Act of 1970. The new version requires credit bureaus to verify disputed information within 30 days or delete it. Businesses that provide data to the credit agencies would also be required to investigate claims of incorrect information. The bill also limits who can have access to the data stored by the credit agencies and controls how it can be used in direct-marketing campaigns. In 1994, according to the Associated Press, the bureaus processed 450 million files, selling 1.5 million records a day and handling almost 2 billion pieces of data every month.

## Dehumanization

Companies should also be aware that many people find technology to be dehumanizing. Several years ago, Citicorp, a large bank based in New York, exhibited this **dehumanization** when it attempted to force people with small accounts to use automated teller machines instead of human tellers. The attempt lasted about a week and irritated many customers because they preferred to deal with humans. Similarly, many people feel they should be recognized by their name, and not have to rely on a number for identification. Companies can often minimize problems by using numbers only for internal identification and rely on a combination of name and address or phone number when they deal with customers.

---

### Reality Bytes    14–1    Problems with Social Security Numbers

Computer systems have the potential to cause serious problems for people. Most governmental computer systems use numbers to identify people. For instance, the federal government issues social security numbers (SSN), and states issue license numbers for drivers. The problem is that people tend to believe that these numbers are always correct—especially if they are stored in a computer. Peter Neumann provides these examples:

- After Terry Dean Rogan lost his wallet with driver's license and credit cards, someone impersonating Rogan committed two murders and two robberies, which resulted in a warrant being placed in the National Crime Information Center (NCIC) database. Rogan was arrested five times in 14 months, despite trying to get the NCIC records corrected on discovering the problem after his first arrest. (He eventually sued and won $55,000 from the Los Angeles police.)
- Martin Lee Dement spent two years in Los Angeles County jail because of botched use of the

then-new California Automated Latent Print System; a manual check of another suspect's fingerprints finally cleared him.
- A masquerader parlayed a bogus "duplicate" driver's license for Teresa Stover into $30,000 in credit card charges. The same department of motor vehicles branch in Bailey's Crossroads, Virginia, issued thousands of bogus licenses, allegedly for only a nominal bribe.
- A front-page article by Yasmin Anwar in the *San Francisco Chronicle* (August 30, 1991) noted that felonies for stealing, selling, or otherwise misusing SSNs are on the rise in the United States. For example, someone discovered 12 people were fraudulently using her SSN; another person found that someone using her SSN had obtained 16 credit cards in her name and charged $10,000; and a third discovered that her unemployment benefits had already been collected by five other people!

## Loss of Jobs

**JOBS** There is no question that technology causes some workers to lose their jobs. In the 19th century, Luddites reacted to textile automation by destroying machines. Information technology is no exception. Norbert Weiner, a computer pioneer in the 1940s, predicted a major depression would result from computers replacing workers. Despite these predictions, during the last 100 years, technology has increased the number of jobs and raised the standard of living of most workers. Since the introduction of computers in the 1950s, the world's economies have grown and incomes have increased. However, individual workers can lose jobs in the short run. Even in the long run, lower-skilled workers experience greater difficulty in finding new jobs. Figure 14.3 shows the changes in jobs for the next few years that are anticipated by the Bureau of Labor Statistics.

Most experts believe that technology increases the total number of jobs. New technology creates demand for designers, manufacturing firms to produce it, and people to maintain and repair it. Computer hardware also creates demands for software programmers. Additionally, technology can cause the economy to grow, creating more jobs in all sectors. By most indications, new jobs created by technology tend to be higher paying, physically safer, and less repetitive than those replaced by technology. Information technology can also reduce product prices, raising the standard of living by enabling people to buy more goods.

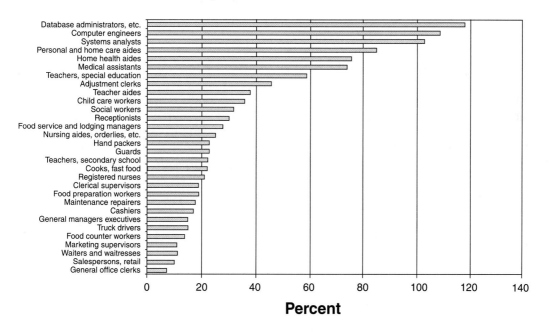

**Projected Job Growth 1998–**

**FIGURE 14.3**
**FUTURE JOBS**
Today there is no guarantee that your job will continue to exist. Demand for specialists changes constantly. Jobs that are well defined and require little innovation or thought can usually be performed easily by computers.

On the other hand, technology typically causes some workers to lose their jobs. Unfortunately, many of these displaced workers cannot be retrained for the new jobs created by the technology. Similarly, the new jobs might not pay as much money, have lower status, or might be less desirable work environments.

Governments have created several programs to provide benefits of money, retraining, and relocation to workers who lose their jobs. As managers, we need to understand the effects on employees when we introduce new technology. Many corporations provide ongoing educational payments and training classes to help workers improve their skills. Others provide out-placement services to help unemployed workers in their job search.

As individuals, we need to remember that changing technology can eliminate virtually any job. One of the best plans is to continue your education and learn new skills. Remember that technology continually changes. Some of the skills you learn today will be obsolete in a couple of years. We must all continually learn new skills and adapt to changes. Applying these skills in your current job adds experience that will help you find a new job. It also benefits your current employer and might help you keep your job or stay with the company if new technology makes your current job obsolete.

The concept of continually acquiring new skills sounds straightforward. However, many times you will have to choose among multiple technologies. Guessing wrong can lead you to invest time and money in a technology or skill that fades away. As you become more involved with technology, you will increasingly find it necessary to "predict" the future. Identifying trends and deciphering fact from rumor are important skills to learn.

## Physical Disabilities

Technology offers many possibilities to provide jobs for workers with physical disabilities. In fact, in 1992, the U.S. Congress passed the Americans with Disabilities Act, stating that companies are not allowed to discriminate against disabled employees. Common uses of technology include the use of scanners and speech synthesizers for visually impaired workers; voice input devices and graphics displays for workers who cannot use keyboards; and telecommuting for those who work from home.

Most Windows-based software contains features to facilitate usage by people with various physical challenges. In some cases, additional accessibility tools can be downloaded or purchased to provide more features. Speech recognition packages are useful for many applications.

Web sites still present accessibility problems, particularly for those with visual impairments. Many sites rely on color and graphics, which are difficult for the accessibility tools to interpret. These issues are being discussed by many vendors. Check Microsoft's accessibility site for more details.

## Telecommuting

The fact that about 70 percent of U.S. jobs are service-based jobs raises interesting possibilities for workers. Many services like accounting, legal advice, education, insurance, investments, data analysis, computer programming, and consulting are not tied to a physical location. As a service provider, you could be located anywhere and still perform your job—as long as you have the appropriate telecommunications system. As communication improves to include video links and faster document transfer, even more jobs can be performed from remote locations.

Some companies are experimenting with home-based workers, especially in cities such as Los Angeles and New York with long commute times. Some workers like the concept; others try it for a few months and return to a traditional workplace job. Several advantages and complications arise from the perspective of the worker, the firm, and society.

## Reality Bytes    14–2    Privacy Versus Anonymity at AOL

Six days after the bombing of the federal building in Oklahoma City in 1995, life took a nasty turn for Kenneth Zeran in Seattle. An unknown prankster posted an anonymous message on an American Online (AOL) bulletin board offering to sell "Naughty Oklahoma T-Shirts" with tasteless, offensive statements regarding the bombing. Interested purchasers were instructed to call Ken and given Mr. Zeran's home telephone number. After receiving a threatening phone call about every two minutes, Mr. Zeran called AOL. AOL authorities agreed to remove the message but would not issue a retraction.

Another, more tasteless message was posted the next day. Life got worse on May 1, when an Oklahoma City radio station read the first AOL posting over the air. Seattle police were called to provide a protective stakeout for Mr. Zeran because of the violent threats he was receiving.

Mr. Zeran sued the radio station in January 1996 and sued AOL in May 1996. The federal judge threw out the lawsuit against AOL because federal law (the Communications Decency Act of 1996 that became effective in February 1996) provides immunity from liability to computer service providers like AOL. Mr. Zeran eventually lost all of his appeals, including one to the U.S. Supreme Court in 1998. AOL did close the account from which the messages were posted. The court records indicate that Zeran never filed a claim against the individual prankster, but he claims that AOL made it impossible to identify the original party by failing to maintain adequate records of its users.

Telecommuting sounds appealing to those who spend hours in traffic commuting to work. Most knowledgeable workers can easily purchase the computer equipment needed to work at home. It is more difficult to provide the self-motivation and organization to be an effective worker. On the other hand, there are fewer interruptions from co-workers.

If a substantial number of workers choose to work from home, the firm gains two main advantages: (1) decreased costs through smaller offices, and (2) flexibility in hiring additional workers on a contract basis. Some people have predicted that companies might also gain from increased use of part-time workers, thus avoiding the cost of insurance and other benefits. The greatest complication to the firm is evaluating and managing employees. Without daily personal contact, including conversations, it is harder to spot problems and make informal suggestions as corrections.

To the worker, the most obvious benefit lies in reducing the time and expense of commuting to work. The biggest drawback lies in the loss of personal contact and daily ritual of a typical work schedule. Depending on your home environment, there can be substantially more interruptions and distractions at home. It is also more difficult to "get away" from your job. Working from home on a flexible schedule requires strong motivation and organization. Before you choose to work at home, talk to someone with experience.

A few firms have experimented with intermediate telecommuting options. As indicated in Figure 14.4, the firm leases smaller offices in city suburbs and workers operate from these satellite offices instead of one central location. The offices are linked by high-capacity telecommunication lines. Workers keep a traditional office environment but cut their commuting costs. Businesses maintain traditional management control but do not save as much money.

A few people have speculated about the effects on society if there is a large shift to telecommuting. At this point, there is not much evidence to support any of the hypotheses, but many of them focus on negative aspects. People could become isolated. Jobs could become highly competitive and short-term. Firms could list projects on the network and workers would compete for every job. Workers would essentially become independent contractors and bear the responsibilities and costs of insurance, retirement, and other benefits, with little or no job security. They would also have no loyalty to any particular firm. Firms could become loose coalitions of workers and teams that are constantly changing, with little control over future directions. It is hard to predict what will really happen, but by understanding the negative effects, they become easier to avoid.

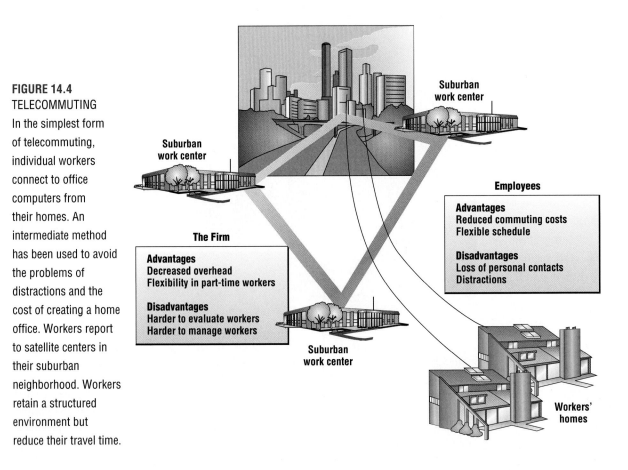

**FIGURE 14.4**
TELECOMMUTING
In the simplest form of telecommuting, individual workers connect to office computers from their homes. An intermediate method has been used to avoid the problems of distractions and the cost of creating a home office. Workers report to satellite centers in their suburban neighborhood. Workers retain a structured environment but reduce their travel time.

Suburban work center

Suburban work center

Suburban work center

**Employees**
Advantages
Reduced commuting costs
Flexible schedule

Disadvantages
Loss of personal contacts
Distractions

**The Firm**
Advantages
Decreased overhead
Flexibility in part-time workers

Disadvantages
Harder to evaluate workers
Harder to manage workers

Workers' homes

**EDUCATION AND TRAINING**

For hundreds of years, the principles and techniques of education have changed only slightly. As new technologies are introduced, people have often declared that the world of education would change markedly. Yet, few technologies have had a lasting impact on education. Television is a classic example. Although movies and news reports are sometimes used for teaching purposes, the role of television in formal education is minimal. However, it is used for informal education and for training, especially with the availability of videotapes for teaching specific tasks.

One of the drawbacks to video education is the lack of interaction and feedback. Multimedia tools that combine video, sound, and computer interaction represent one attempt to surmount this limitation. However, three basic problems arise when applying technology to education. First, technology is often expensive, especially compared to traditional methods. Second, it is time consuming to create lessons that generally are difficult to change. Third, there is little conclusive evidence that the techniques are equal to or superior to existing techniques. Especially in light of the first two problems, it is difficult to test the new technologies. In many cases, by the time prices have fallen and lessons are created, an even newer technology emerges.

Despite these obstacles, technological innovations are often used for specialized teaching purposes. For instance, interactive and multimedia computer tools can be used to provide more in-depth study for advanced students or to handle repetitive drills for those students needing extra work. Increasingly available two-way video links are used to connect teachers and students in remote locations.

New technologies are also used in business settings for retraining classes, partly to reduce the cost of hiring instructors and partly because the lessons are available to workers at any time, and can be studied at whatever speed the student desires.

The Internet is increasingly being pushed as a means to expand the reach of higher education. Several universities are experimenting with offering individual courses over the Internet. The early examples often consisted of simple e-mail-based systems where students worked on their own and occasionally sent messages to the instructor. A few organizations, such as the University of the South, currently offer complete programs over the Internet. Eventually, these programs will evolve—particularly as Internet transmission speeds improve to offer more interactive communication. Additionally, the educational tools will evolve to become more computer-based and interactive.

**GOVERNMENT**

Governments can be slow to adopt new technologies. Typically, government agencies have limited budgets, long procurement cycles, and requirements for special allocations to acquire new technology. They tend to have smaller IS staffs, who also receive less pay than their counterparts in private business. Additionally, government projects tend to be

---

**Reality Bytes    14–3    Employee Surveillance**

The American Management Association observes that 35 percent of companies monitor their employees' phone calls, e-mail messages, computer files, or videotape them. Of course, companies sometimes have a legitimate need to monitor employee performance. Likewise, theft and security issues may encourage a company to increase its surveillance. For example, employees of the Colgate-

Palmolive Company were experiencing thefts in the employee fitness center. When the company proposed installing hidden cameras, the union appealed to the National Labor Relations Board, which ordered that the company must negotiate with the union before installing the cameras. Note that California state law prohibits the use of cameras in sensitive areas such as restrooms and locker rooms.

large and involve thousands of people, which makes them expensive, harder to create, and more difficult to implement.

Nonetheless, governments are definitely affected by changes in technology. For example, many people believe that the fall of the centralized Eastern European governments was hastened by the improved communication facilities provided by computer networks and facsimile machines.

In the United States, the federal government has begun to provide information and responses to questions via the Internet. It is even possible to send electronic mail to the president—although the mail is actually read and answered by assistants. Almost all federal data is available in computer form. There are computerized indexes to help you locate data produced by the government. Even municipal governments are beginning to post notices and data on the Internet.

Technology is also used by politicians campaigning for office. For many years government officials have used databases to track letters and comments, solicit contributions, and tailor speeches to specific audiences. More direct use of technology occurred during the 1992 and 1996 presidential campaigns, during which some of the candidates used technology to create what they called "electronic town meetings," where citizens could call in questions and watch the candidate respond over television.

Several people have mentioned the possibility of creating electronic voting systems to provide faster tallies of votes. Potential problems exist in identifying the voters and preventing them from voting more than once. However, in 1994, several states implemented limited technology-based voting systems. Using these systems, voters can now vote anytime within a two-week period instead of standing in line on one particular day.

**SOCIAL INTERACTIONS**  As any good science fiction book illustrates, advances in technology can alter society in many different ways. Sometimes the responses are hard to predict, and they often occur gradually, so it can be difficult to spot patterns. At the moment, three patterns appear to be important: crime, social group power, and equal access to technology. The issue of crime is more complicated, so it is covered in its own section.

## Social Group Legitimacy

One interesting feature of technology is that it has substantially lowered communication costs, including the costs of producing and distributing information to large public groups. For example, desktop publishing systems enable groups to create professional-quality documents at low cost. Additionally, video production facilities are easily affordable by any group, and access to mass markets is provided free through *public-access channels* on cable television. Web sites can be created by anyone. These technologies enable small groups to reach a wider audience for minimal cost.

There is nothing wrong with the concept of *social group legitimacy;* in fact it is loosely protected by the "freedom of speech" provisions of the U.S. Constitution. Just remember that even "free" speech has many restrictions, including those related to defamation. The only catch is that with growing professionalism of small-group productions, it becomes harder to distinguish fact from fiction, and it is harder for the public to tell the difference between mainstream, professional commentary and radical extremists. For example, do you believe stories that are printed in the *New York Times?* What about stories printed in supermarket tabloids, that sport such titles as: "Space Alien Eats Movie Star"?

Now consider the Internet, and run some searches on medical questions. You will find hundreds of web sites and comments. Which ones do you believe? Web sites present the strongest challenge ever to trust and reliability issues. Literally anyone can create a site and say anything. Nonsensical comments will be found by the search engines and displayed along with accurate statements.

This issue has some interesting effects. For example, in several instances, disgruntled customers have created sites criticizing companies. If you search for a particular company, you are likely to encounter several of these sites. The Web makes it easy for people to criticize anyone—and the entire world can see the results. Of course, traditional defamation laws still apply, but in situations where there is an element of truth, companies will find it difficult to stop these activities.

The same issues can be applied to television broadcasts, except that for the moment, the high costs of broadcasts restrict this option to a few participants. With his "War of the Worlds" broadcast, Orson Welles shocked many listeners because they had come to accept radio broadcasts as fact. With existing technology, it is possible to create realistic-looking fictional broadcasts. It is not even necessary to resort to tricks such as hidden explosive charges. It is possible to create computer-generated images that exceed the quality of broadcast signals, so they appear to be realistic. Advertisers have made heavy use of these techniques. Every time you watch a commercial, you should remind yourself that a portion of what you are seeing is probably a computer-generated image. Now, imagine what would happen if an extremist organization used this same technology to create newscasts with altered pictures.

## Access to Technology

Picture a world in which financial instruments are traded electronically, goods are purchased through computer-television systems, libraries are converted to electronic media, and businesses require suppliers to exchange data over computer links. Large portions of the United States and Europe are getting closer to this scenario every day. Now, what happens to the individuals in poorer nations who can barely afford to eat, much less invest in personal and national information systems? If the means of production are based

---

**Reality Bytes     14–4    Recovering Evidence on Computers**

In the early to mid-1900s, the FBI revolutionized the investigation of crimes. By improving technology, standardization, and establishing training programs, the FBI and its national crime labs are able to solve relatively complex and difficult crimes. As crimes and investigations move into the computer arena, new techniques and training programs are needed. A firm called New Technologies, Inc. (www.forensics-intl.com) is one of the leaders in training investigators. New Technologies' students consist largely of security investigators in large firms. Michael Anderson at NTI developed a similar course for the FBI and other law-enforcement agencies. The National White Collar Crimes Center (www.iir.com/nwccc/nwccc.htm) and the International Association of Computer Investiga-tive Specialists (iacis.com) also offer courses in electronic sleuthing.

Most of these organizations, including (www.ontrack.com) also offer their services to companies that need help with investigations. The courses often focus on recovering data form computers. Deleting files on a computer does not really remove the data. Utility programs exist to help investigators search for, identify, and rebuild these pieces of data. Recovering data is not the only step. Other useful abilities include: tracing information sent on the Internet, verifying the accuracy of recovered data, and testifying in court. Accounting firms are also interested in the training, because they are increasingly being called on to identify and prevent computer fraud.

on technology and certain groups do not have access, the gap between the **haves** and **have-nots** will widen. Although some groups will be content to live without technology, some will become upset at the imbalance.

Some companies have worked to give others access to technology. A few recycle older computers to libraries and citizen centers. On the international front, businesses can donate older personal computers to organizations for shipment to other countries. After three to five years, the technology is often out of date in the United States, but even old technology is better than nothing in some countries. For many years (during the Cold War), the United States strictly controlled the export of technology. In 1995, the United States finally relaxed most of the restrictions but retained limitations on the export of some software and encryption products. It is wise to check with a lawyer or customs agent before attempting to export current technology.

## E-mail Freedom

Some organizations have observed an interesting feature when they first replaced paper mail with electronic-mail systems. The first people to use the technology are generally younger, more likely to take risks, and bolder than the typical employee. If the top management levels accept and respond to electronic messages, they are likely to get a different perspective on the organization, its problems, and potential solutions. E-mail systems provide a means for employees (and sometimes customers) at the lower levels to bypass the hierarchy of middle management. A few directed comments and words of encouragement can enhance this effect, which is useful if managers are searching for new approaches to solving problems.

## Liability and Control of Data

Virtually all of our legal structures and interpretations were created before the advent of a computerized society. Although federal and state governments have passed a few laws specifically to address problems with computer interaction, most legal systems still rely on laws and definitions created for a paper-based world. Sometimes these concepts do not fit well in a computerized environment. For example, how would you classify the operator of a web site? Is that person a publisher of information, like a newspaper? Or is the operator merely a vendor offering disk space to anonymous writers? In particular, are the owners of web sites responsible for the content of messages posted on their systems? To date, the court systems have tended to make the decision based on whether the owners exercise "editorial control." In 1995, the New York supreme court ruled that Prodigy could be sued for libel. An anonymous writer posted a message that was highly critical of the financial status of a certain firm. The firm claimed that the comments were false and sued Prodigy for publishing false information. Since its inception, Prodigy maintained a policy of forbidding people to post "profane" messages. The Prodigy staff used software to scan messages. The court noted that these actions constituted editorial control, so Prodigy could be treated as any other publisher of information (like a newspaper).

## Transactions and Money

In an electronic world where there is no physical exchange of items, how can people make payments? It is possible to purchase software, data, pictures, music, and other data over electronic networks. Four basic elements must exist for transactions to be acceptable: (1) The vendor must be able to verify the payment. (2) The buyer must be able to verify the receipt of goods or services. (3) The buyer must be able to limit and verify the amount paid. (4) No one should be able to intercept or reuse the financial data. In some situations, the two parties also need to be able to verify the identity of the other entity. All these factors are more complicated when they cross international boundaries with different legal environments.

The most common payment mechanism is the traditional credit card. With encryption, the fourth condition is relatively easy to meet, although the vendor must either delete the credit card data or take steps to prevent criminals from stealing the data after the transaction is complete. The vendor is protected because the credit card company is responsible for paying the vendor. Likewise, many credit card companies protect the buyer by canceling charges if the products are not received. In the United States, the buyer is protected from fraudulent charges by federal laws that place the responsibility onto the credit card company. The two drawbacks to credit card transactions are that the transaction cost is relatively high, and the buyer cannot be anonymous.

Several companies have proposed alternative payment mechanisms. As illustrated in Figure 14.5, most involve the use of a trusted third party (like a bank). **Digital cash** is an example, where buyers can make anonymous purchases on a network, and sellers are assured of receiving payment. Consumers transfer "real money" to the third party and receive one-time-use digital cash numbers. These numbers can be given to a vendor, who returns them to the third party for an account credit. Other methods, like the NetBill system, use the third party to verify the authenticity of the buyer and seller. The third party completes the transaction by transferring the money between accounts and forwarding a decryption key to the buyer.

**FIGURE 14.5**
ELECTRONIC TRANSACTIONS
One difficulty with electronic transactions is the need for electronic payments. Large payments or monthly payments can be made through most banks in the form of "real" money in checking accounts. These methods can be cumbersome and expensive for small transactions. Several companies have proposed standards for the creation of "digital cash." The goal is to create an electronic form of money that can be verified, is inexpensive to use, can support anonymity, and cannot be easily counterfeited.

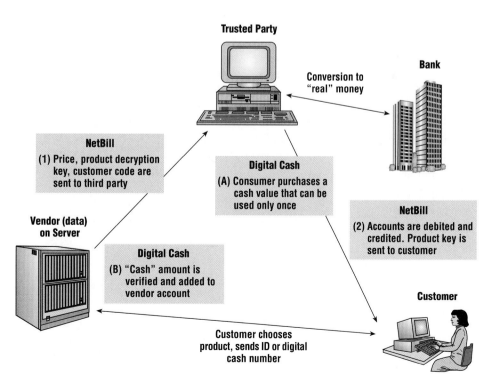

**Trusted Party**

**Bank**

Conversion to "real" money

**NetBill**
(1) Price, product decryption key, customer code are sent to third party

**Digital Cash**
(A) Consumer purchases a cash value that can be used only once

**NetBill**
(2) Accounts are debited and credited. Product key is sent to customer

**Vendor (data) on Server**

**Digital Cash**
(B) "Cash" amount is verified and added to vendor account

**Customer**

Customer chooses product, sends ID or digital cash number

**THREATS TO INFORMATION**

There are many potential threats to information systems and the data they hold. The complicated aspect is that the biggest *information threat* is from legitimate users and developers. Purely by accident, a user might enter incorrect data or delete important information. A designer might misunderstand an important function, and the system will produce erroneous results. An innocent programming mistake could result in incorrect or destroyed data. Minor changes to a frail system could result in a cascading failure of the entire system.

We can detect and prevent some of these problems through careful design, testing, training, and backup provisions. However, modern information systems are extremely complex. We cannot guarantee they will work "correctly" all of the time. Plus, the world poses physical threats that cannot be avoided: hurricanes, earthquakes, floods, and so on. Often, the best we can do is build contingency plans that enable the company to recover as fast as possible. The most important aspect of any disaster plan is to maintain adequate backup copies. With careful planning, organization, and enough money, firms are able to provide virtually continuous information system support.

A second set of problems arises from the fact that as technology changes, so do criminals. Today, only a desperate person would rob a bank with a gun. The probability of being caught is high and the amount of money stolen is low. Not that we wish to encourage anyone to become a thief, but the computer offers much easier ways to steal larger amounts of money. Consider the example of some thieves in West Hartford, Connecticut. In 1993, they stole an ATM from a warehouse and installed it at a shopping mall. They put a small amount of money in the machine and disabled the existing machine to encourage people to use theirs. When customers entered their personal identification numbers (PINs) to withdraw money, the ATM recorded the numbers. The thieves used the numbers to create their own ATM cards, which they used to withdraw thousands of dollars from ATMs along the east coast.

It is important to determine the potential threats to computer security described by Figure 14.6. For example, there were several well-publicized cases in the 1980s involving computer security. Most of these problems arose from **hackers** who used modems and personal computers to break into company computers. Similar publicity arose in the mid-1990s with respect to Internet hackers. Because these cases received so much attention, many people thought that their biggest problem was wild teenagers with cheap personal

**FIGURE 14.6**
THREATS TO INFORMATION
By far, the most serious threats are from "insiders": employees, mistakes, consultants, and partnerships. Businesses have to trust insiders to stay in operation, but you need to put limits on the access to data. It is possible for outsiders to break into most computer systems, but it is fairly difficult and often relies on the support of a person inside the company. Viruses can be a serious problem in terms of the time required to clean them out. You must constantly back up your work to keep it safe.

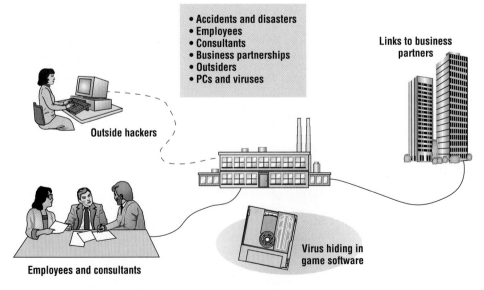

- Accidents and disasters
- Employees
- Consultants
- Business partnerships
- Outsiders
- PCs and viruses

Links to business partners

Outside hackers

Employees and consultants

Virus hiding in game software

computers. If you were to spend most of your computer security budget to combat this threat, it would be a waste of money. In practice, most computer crimes are committed by people inside the company.

## Employees

Employees are the heart of any company. Companies function and succeed by trusting their employees. Although almost all employees are honest and diligent, there is always the chance that one employee will use the company's knowledge, experience, and trust to misappropriate resources.

It can be difficult to identify people who might cause damage to the firm. Many companies today use psychological tests, background checks, and random drug tests to indicate potential problems. Most companies are wary of employees whose employment has been terminated. Businesses follow specific steps when employees leave, being particularly careful to remove the employees' access to company computers.

A more complicated problem arises with MIS employees. Programmers and analysts have to be trusted. Without them, there would be no software. However, it is generally best if the programmers are not the users of the program. Companies enforce a separation of duties among staff programmers and users. Think about what might happen if a bank teller was also responsible for writing the computer program used by tellers. It would be easy to use the computer to steal money from different accounts. Auditing transaction-processing systems is an important task for auditors.

Unscrupulous programmers have also been known to include "time bombs" in their software. Whenever the software runs, it checks a hidden file for a secret word. If the programmer leaves the company, the secret word does not get changed. When the program does not find the correct word, it starts deleting files. On large projects, these bombs can be impossible to spot (until they go off). The damage can usually be minimized by keeping good backups. Another danger area is that programmers might include a trap door or secret password that allows them to gain access to the software even if they leave the company. Sometimes these trap doors are installed innocently to enable programmers to make corrections faster. The important point is to make sure they are removed when the system is permanently installed.

An interesting class of threats to securing your data arises from negligence instead of deliberate actions by the users. For instance, employees might accidentally delete data. Or, carrying disks, tapes, or even laptop computers past magnetic fields can sometimes damage the files. In these cases, the best bet is to have backups readily available. More complicated problems arise when laptop computers are lost or even stolen. In addition to

## Reality Bytes    14–5    Computer Crime Statistics

Computer crime is notoriously difficult to measure. Companies are often afraid to report the crime because they fear additional attacks and they do not want to worry investors. In 1998, the Computer Security Institute and the FBI estimated that U.S. businesses lost $138 million to computer crime. In a different study, PricewaterhouseCoopers and

*Information Week* found that almost three-fourths of the companies experienced security problems. Of these attacks, 58 percent were from authorized employees, 24 percent from unauthorized employees, and 13 percent from former employees. Only 13 percent were from outside hackers, and 3 percent from competitors.

the data stored on the machines, the files often hold passwords for corporate computers. Many laptops provide passwords and encrypt the data to minimize these problems. One other problem that falls into this category is a warning to be careful about how you dispose of old tapes, disks, and computer equipment. In 1990, the U.S. Department of Justice sold some out-of-date equipment and tapes to a broker in Kentucky for $45. Unfortunately, the DOJ did not erase all of the data from the tapes. It turned out to be a serious problem; the tapes contained names and addresses of people in the Justice Department's witness protection program. Businesses run similar risks when they send computer equipment out for repairs.

In general, the best way to minimize problems from employees stems from typical management techniques. Hire workers carefully, treat employees fairly, have separation of jobs, use teamwork, and maintain constant checks on their work.

## Consultants

Consultants present the same potential problems as employees. However, consultants tend to be hired for a short time, so the firm knows even less about them than about regular employees. Consultants are generally used for specialized jobs, so there may not be any internal employees who can adequately monitor their work.

## Business Partnerships

As computers spread throughout every aspect of business, many companies share their data. For example, General Motors asks its suppliers to provide all information electronically. This electronic data interchange (EDI) means that business information is processed faster and with fewer errors. The problem is that in many cases, it means GM gives other companies considerable access to GM's computer and vice versa. For instance, if GM is thinking about increasing production, the managers might want to check supplier production schedules to make sure the suppliers could provide enough parts. To do it electronically, GM needs access to the suppliers' computers. To participate in business today, you must trust your partners. However, you have limited ability to evaluate all of their employees.

## Outsiders

There is some threat from outsiders who might dial up your computer and guess a password. Most of these threats can be minimized by using some common sense. For example, in the 1980s, some groups gained access to computers because the operators never changed the default password that was shipped with the computer! The Internet causes additional problems because it was designed to give other people access to your machines. The key lies to providing people with just the level of access they need.

## Personal Computers and Viruses

Personal computers represent a major point of vulnerability to companies today. Most microcomputer operating systems have limited security capabilities. Most do not have passwords, they cannot prevent files from being changed, and they do not keep track of usage and changes. Because many of them are connected to networks and to larger computers, they can be dangerous to computer security. If someone gets access to a microcomputer, he or she generally can gain access to the other computer systems in the company.

**FIGURE 14.7**

VIRUS ACTIVITY

Once a virus is loaded on your computer, you will need an antivirus software package to remove the virus. Several versions are available at low cost. A virus can come from any software that supports executable code. Because most packages use macro programming languages, even documents can contain viruses.

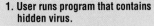

1. User runs program that contains hidden virus.
2. Virus copies itself into other programs on the computer.
3. Virus spreads until a certain date, then it deletes files, changes data, etc.

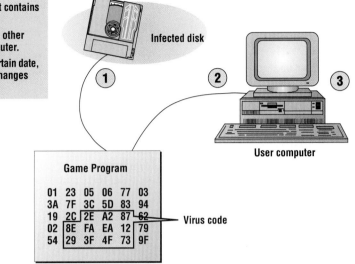

Infected disk

User computer

Game Program

| 01 | 23 | 05 | 06 | 77 | 03 |
| 3A | 7F | 3C | 5D | 83 | 94 |
| 19 | 2C | 2E | A2 | 87 | 62 |
| 02 | 8E | FA | EA | 12 | 79 |
| 54 | 29 | 3F | 4F | 73 | 9F |

Virus code

One particularly dangerous threat to personal computers comes in the form of a software program called a **virus.** As illustrated in Figure 14.7, a computer virus is a small program that hides inside another program. Someone might write a game and give it to you to play. If you like the game, you will pass it around to friends. Hiding inside the game, however, is a small piece of code, and every time you run the game, this piece of code copies itself to other files on your computer. Even if you stop playing the game, the virus will still be on your computer, hiding in the other software. A virus can quickly infect every computer in a company. Finally, at some point in time (perhaps a Friday the 13th or Michelangelo's birthday), the virus becomes active. It might display a harmless message or it might destroy all the files on your computer. A trickier virus might search for computer passwords stored on your personal computer and send them to a competitor.

A virus can be picked up from many sources. Antivirus software will search your computer for known viruses. Even so, firms continue to experience problems with viruses. Typical problems are listed in Figure 14.8. Until microcomputers gain additional levels of security, viruses will remain a problem. Again, the first rule of safety is to *always* have backups of your data and software. Even the backups might become infected, but if a virus destroys the files on your computer, at least you can recover the data. Because of the expanding capabilities of software, it is now possible to pick up a virus just by "reading" a document or spreadsheet file. Current software contains an internal programming language that can be used to carry and spread a virus. So far, these viruses are relatively easy to identify and to eliminate. Most software packages have a technique to disable programs (macros) when you open the document, for example, hold down the SHIFT key when you open the document.

**COMPUTER SECURITY**

Transaction and accounting data is clearly valuable to a company and needs to be protected. There are three major security issues: (1) unauthorized disclosure of information, (2) unauthorized modification, and (3) unauthorized withholding of information. As an example of the first problem, you would not want your competitor to get access to your new marketing plans. An example of the second problem would be if employees could modify their payroll records to change their pay rates. The third problem is less obvious,

**FIGURE 14.8**

VIRUS DAMAGE

Computer viruses can be expensive. It takes time to clean up all infected computers. Over one-third of the firms reported that it cost them more than $2,000 per incident to recover from a virus attack. While antivirus software helps, many people do not use it. Also, new viruses can sneak in before antivirus software is modified to spot them. Hence, in early 1996, 49 percent of the reported virus problems stemmed from the introduction of the Word.concept macro virus.

| DAMAGE | PERCENT OF FIRMS REPORTING PROBLEM IN 1991 | PERCENT OF FIRMS REPORTING PROBLEM IN 1996 |
|---|---|---|
| Loss of productivity | 62 | 81 |
| Message and lockup | 41 | 62 |
| Corrupted files | 38 | 59 |
| Lost data | 30 | 39 |
| Unreliable applications | 24 | 35 |
| System crash | 23 | 30 |

SOURCES: "Infection Risk Not Spurring Use of Antivirus Software," by Michael Alexander, *Computerworld,* December 16, 1991, p. 49 and by Computerworld, Inc., Framingham, MA 01701— Reprinted from *Computerworld.* "Old, New Viruses Swarm PC Users," by Gary H. Anthes, *Computerworld,* May 6, 1996, p. 55.

but just as important. Imagine what would happen if you needed to look at the latest inventory to decide how much to reorder, but the computer refused to give you access.

## Manual and Electronic Information

Protection of information is a topic that has existed forever. Not surprisingly, the strongest developments in security have come from the military. The armed services lead the way both in manual and electronic security. Military funding has paid for much of the development of computer security. Because manual security precautions existed long before computers, the initial work in computer security focused on applying these older techniques. Nevertheless, there are some major differences that arise from storing information electronically. To see the complications added by electronic storage of information, consider a hypothetical case of two spies looking for a letter. Juan has gained access to a personal computer, but Mike is in a musty basement library full of paper files.

Mike is not even sure he is in the right place. There are thousands of documents in the basement, and the letter might even be stored in some other building. The computer that Juan is searching is large enough to hold all of the company's information, so he only has to look in one place. For his search, Juan just uses the computer database. In seconds, he finds what he wants. He copies the letter to a disk, turns off the machine, and walks out the door. Mike is still walking up and down aisles in the basement trying to read file tags with his flashlight. When he finally finds the letter, he uses his trusty spy camera to take pictures of the letter, hoping they will be legible. Now he has to put the letter back exactly as he found it so no one can tell he copied it.

Obviously it is much easier to locate and copy data stored on computers. Even more importantly, it is easier to change the data. In many cases, data on computers can be changed without anyone knowing that the file was altered. It is even theoretically possible for a person to break into a computer by using the phone system or a computer network. The intruder does not have to physically enter the building.

## Backup Protection

One of the most important steps in protecting the information assets of the company is the use of backups. Data needs to be backed up on a regular basis. For some firms, that means making backup copies every night. In other cases, it means that sensitive data sets

SunGard is a premier provider of computer backup facilities and disaster planning services. Its fleet of Mobile Data Centers can be outfitted with a variety of distributed systems hardware and delivered to a disaster site within 48 hours.

have to be duplicated as soon as they are created. With centralized computers, it is relatively easy to have the machines automatically make copies of data that was changed during the day. In a completely decentralized environment, it is more difficult to make the copies. In many cases, users have to be responsible for making their own backups. Unfortunately, most users are reluctant to take the time to make daily backups of their work. That is where local area networks come in handy. Properly designed networks allow the MIS staff to connect to individual user machines and make the backups automatically. Of course, backup tapes have to be stored in a safe location. Also, you must be careful when you discard old data tapes to make sure they have been erased.

Along with the data, it is useful to make arrangements for backing up the computer hardware. What happens to a company if a disaster such as a flood, fire, or hurricane strikes the computer center? How long can a company survive without the management information system? Today, there are many ways to plan for and recover from disasters. Some companies make arrangements with similar firms in other locations. If one company experiences problems, it would move the processing to the data center of the other company. Of course, each company needs to have sufficient computer capabilities to support both operations.

A more common approach today is to contract with a disaster recovery services provider. Service providers like SunGard provide access to their commercial recovery facilities and provide several levels of support for various fees. One common level of support, called a **hot site,** consists of a fully configured computer center. Specific computer equipment is already installed and ready for immediate use. When the MIS staff declares a disaster, they install the backup tapes on the hot-site computers and use telecommunication lines to run the day-to-day operations. Another alternative is to contract for a **cold site,** which provides fully functional computer room space, without the computer equipment. If a disaster occurs, either the company or the disaster recovery services provider can arrange for the necessary equipment to be shipped to the cold site. There can be a delay of several days before the new data center will be operational.

SunGard Recovery Services Inc. has been a leading provider of total business recovery solutions since 1978. The company founded the industry and offers recovery services throughout North America. In addition to providing backup facilities, the company provides business continuity planning software and consulting services through its subsidiary, SunGard Planning Solutions Inc.

SunGard's Comprehensive Business Recovery^SM services include: computer hot-sites and cold-sites, electronic vaulting for data backup, network recovery, remote testing and recovery, and work group recovery services for voice, data, and LAN systems. Services are delivered through SunGard's network of MegaCenters®, and MetroCenters® as well as its fleet of Mobile Data Centers stationed at strategic points nationwide.

SunGard's Mobile Data Centers (shown in picture), are custom-designed units that can be outfitted with a variety of distributed systems hardware configured to replace any designated system when disaster strikes. Mobile Data Centers can arrive at the site of a disaster within 48 hours of notification. On making the appropriate network connections, the Mobile Data Center enables a company to quickly and easily restore operations from any parking lot near the original data facility.

For computer operations that absolutely must never be interrupted, some firms utilize a backup computer that is continuously running to maintain a complete copy of the daily operations. All data is maintained simultaneously at both locations. If problems arise with one machine, the second one takes over automatically. Specialty firms are now offering these **data mirroring** facilities. The outside firm is sent copies of all of your data as it is generated. The firm makes backup copies and provides virtually instantaneous renewal of service if something interferes with your main computer.

Although several options are available for central computers, there are fewer disaster plan alternatives for personal computers. Of course, the first step is to provide regular backups of the data and software. But, if a disaster wipes out the company's personal computer, what options are available? If you need only 20 or 30 machines, you might be able to buy them from a local vendor, but they often maintain small inventories to keep their costs down. Even large manufacturers like IBM and Compaq experience backlogs and might not be able to meet your needs. One useful alternative is to encourage your employees to buy computers for their use at home. If a disaster strikes, they can use modems and work out of their homes until you have time to set up new facilities and new hardware. Many companies provide generous computer purchase plans for their employees to encourage them to buy their own computers.

Along the same lines, if you want to keep your computer running—particularly servers—you need to install an **uninterruptable power supply (UPS).** A UPS is basically a large battery that is constantly recharged from the power outlet. The computer always runs off the battery, so if power fails, the computer keeps running. A UPS provides only a few minutes of power, but it protects the server during typical brownouts and short outages. If the power outage is extended, you will have time to shut down the machine safely or switch to auxiliary generators.

## User Identification

One difficulty with providing computer security lies in identifying the user. In a manual security system, a guard can be used to physically identify each person by asking to see identification. There are few vision systems available for computers and they are expensive. The most common method of identifying users to computers is with a password.

---

**Reality Bytes**    **14–7**    **Hot Site Keeps Canadian Firm Running**

QL Systems in Kingston, Ontario, maintains online legal databases with judgments from all court levels throughout Canada, as well as many administrative tribunals and legal news databases. On January 7,1998, a major ice storm wiped out power to large sections of Ontario—including QL Systems. Since their entire business depends on providing computer access, QL Systems was prepared for power outages. The immediate response was to switch to the uninterruptible power system (UPS), which lasted for three hours. Then the system was switched to the diesel backup generators. However, after 24 hours, the company contact IBM, its hot site provider. Because of the size of the storm, five of IBM's customers and 40 of IBM's division also declared emergencies. Nonetheless, by the time QL Systems had picked up the off-site storage tapes and driven to Toronto, the IBM hot site was ready for them.

---

**Reality Bytes**    **14–8**    **Anonymity**

To transmit data on the Internet requires that both parties know the address of the other computer. That means whenever you go to a web site or post a message, the administrator can store and track your Internet address. A few years ago, some Internet sites promised anonymity by serving as an intermediary. Your final destination saw only the intermediate site address. However, the intermediate machines still stored your address, and there were a few cases where the operators released that data.

In 1999, a new company called Zero-Knowledge (www.zks.net) offered a new anonymity service based on encrypted data. Located in Canada, the company is not subject to U.S. export restrictions on encryption. Austin Hill, president of the company, observed, "Even if we are subpoenaed for information about a customer, our answer would have to be [that] we don't know." Customers can subscribe for $10 a year. The current marketing focus is on social interaction issues, where people may wish to enter religious, social, or health discussions, without having to reveal their identity. However, the system could also be useful for managers who wish to examine their competitors' web sites.

---

### Passwords

Each user is given an account name and a password that are known only to the computer and the user. If someone correctly enters both the name and the password, the computer assumes it must be the user. This method is cheap, fast, and does not require too much effort by the user. However, there are problems. The biggest difficulty is that users are afraid of forgetting their password, so they choose words that are easy to remember. Unfortunately, passwords that are easy to remember tend to be obvious to other people. For instance, *never* use the words *password* or *secret* as a password. Similarly, do not use the names of relatives, pets, or celebrities. Most of these can be obtained by looking in a phonebook or asking someone you know. In fact, you should not use any actual words. Most people use only a couple thousand words in typical conversation. The goal is to make it hard for someone to guess the password. You need to choose passwords from the largest possible set of characters and numbers. There are two other rules about passwords: Change them often and never write them down. If you forget a password, the system administrator will let you create a new one. For additional security, many computer systems require users to change their passwords on a regular basis, such as every 30 or 60 days.

One drawback to passwords is that we need too many of them. Everything from ATM cards to phone calls to computer accounts uses passwords or *personal identification numbers (PINs)*. It is difficult to remember several different passwords, especially if you choose random letters and numbers and change them often. With so many passwords, it is tempting to write them down, which defeats their purpose. Some computer network security systems use a security server. Users log in once and the security server gives them access to all of the authorized servers. The system is most useful on large networks.

Passwords are not a perfect solution to identifying users. No matter how well they are chosen or how often they are changed, there is always a chance that someone could guess the password. They are so risky that U.S. government top-secret information is stored on computers that cannot be connected to phone lines. By physically preventing outsiders from using the computers, there is a smaller chance that the information could be compromised.

### Password Generators

Password generators are small electronic cards that users carry that generate new passwords every minute. The same system is embedded on the main computer. When you want to log in, you simply enter the number on the card. Since the password is changed every minute, you do not have to worry about anyone guessing it or intercepting it. On the other hand, you have to carry around the card.

### Biometrics

**Biometrics** is a field of study that attempts to identify people based on biological characteristics. The most promising devices are fingerprint and handprint readers. As shown in Figure 14.9, there is even a device that "reads" a thermal pattern of the user's face. Some work has been done on retina scanners that read the blood-vessel pattern at the back of the eye, or iris scanners that use a photograph of the eye to match a user. Most of these devices can be connected to terminals or personal computers, or used as door locks to identify and verify authorized users. Currently, the biggest drawbacks to these methods are (1) cost, (2) lack of standards, and (3) recognition errors.

**FIGURE 14.9**
BIOMETRIC DEVICES
Several methods exist to identify a person based on biological characteristics. Common techniques include fingerprint and handprint readers and retinal scanners. More exotic devices include body shape sensors and this thermal facial reader from Technology Recognition Systems, which uses infrared imaging to identify the user.

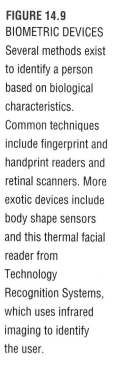
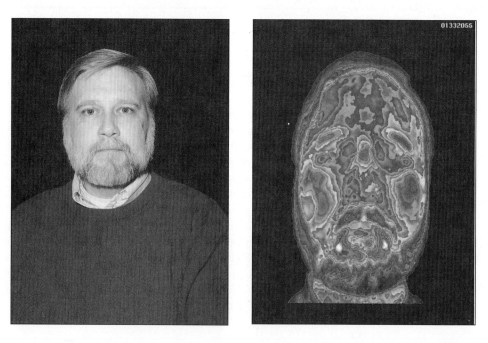

The first two problems are related. Although fingerprint readers are available for around $100, not many have been installed. Hence, they are affordable for a few individual machines, but they are not widespread enough for general use yet. When examining biometrics devices, you must always determine the level of Type I error rate. That is, what is the probability that the device will fail to recognize a legitimate user? Some systems are better than others. For example, some systems were based on voice recognition, but their accuracy is too low. Think about what happens if you have a cold. You would not be allowed to use your computer.

Biometric security devices have some important advantages. The user does not have to remember anything or carry keys around. They are reasonably accurate and difficult to fool by an unauthorized person. However, remember that no computer security system is perfect. Pretend you are writing a spy novel. How would a cold-blooded spy get around a fingerprint reader?

## Access Control

The importance of identifying the user is that as long as the computer can identify each user, you can control access to any piece of data. As manager of the marketing department, you could allow other managers to read the sales data but not change it. Similarly, the accounting department could allow managers to see the accounts payable data, but only the accounting department would be able to modify the data and write new checks. With a good security system, it is possible for the human resources manager to allow employees to look up work phone numbers in the corporate database but not to see salaries or other confidential information.

The common access controls available are read, write, execute, and delete. With these security features, the owner of the information can give other users exactly the type of access they need.

As a creator of data, it is your responsibility to set the appropriate access permissions. Today, most of your files will be shared through a web site. You can set aside different directories for each group of users and assign permissions to each directory. To avoid accidents, you generally do not give anyone delete permissions. Your main choice is which users should be able to read the data and which ones need to be able to change it. Of course, if multiple people have permission to change a document, you should set the document to track changes so you can see who made each change.

## Alternative Security Measures

### Audits

Accountants have long known that in order to maintain security over data, it is necessary to perform audits. There are too many ways for unscrupulous people to make changes to stored information. Audits are used to locate mistakes and to prevent fraud. Existing criminology practice states that in many cases, the threat of getting caught (by an audit) will convince most people to be more careful and to avoid fraudulent behavior. The same principles extend to security audits. By monitoring computer activity, auditing financial records, and periodically checking to see whether everyone is obeying security regulations, users are encouraged to follow the security guidelines of the company.

Of course, audits cost money and they interfere with the daily operations of the firm. As a result, it is important to schedule audits carefully and to keep an eye on the costs as well as the potential benefits. There are several professional organizations (such as the EDP Auditors Association) designed to help security employees learn more about the latest technologies and to teach them what to look for in audits. The American Institute of

Certified Public Accountants (AICPA) also provides standards and audit guidelines that are useful at combating fraud.

### Physical Access

Because it is so difficult to provide logical security to a computer, other mechanisms have been developed. Many of them rely on controlling physical access to the computer. For instance, computers and terminals should be kept in controlled areas. They must certainly be kept away from visitors and delivery people. Many types of locks and keys can be used to protect terminals and personal computers. Similarly, all documents should be controlled. Paper copies of important reports should be shredded.

### Monitoring

Another effective security provision is to monitor access to all of the data. Most computers can keep track of every change to every file. They can keep a log of who accesses each file. They track every time someone incorrectly enters a password. An audit trail of every file change can be provided to management. That means it is possible to find out who changed the salary data, what time it was changed, and from which terminal. All financial data is routinely audited by both internal and external auditors. Sometimes hidden control data is used to make sure procedures are followed.

### Hiring and Employee Evaluation

Because "insiders cause many problems" it makes sense to be careful when you hire employees. Employers should always check candidates' references. In more extreme situations, employers can check employee backgrounds for criminal records. There are several instances of disgruntled employees causing security problems. In many cases, the best security solution is to establish close relationships with your employees and encourage teamwork. Employees who work closely together can defuse potential problems and informally monitor the work of other employees.

## Encryption

Remember that personal computers were originally designed for only one user at a time, so most of them have minimal security provisions. Not until Windows NT (now Windows 2000) did secure operating systems become commonplace on desktops. So, what if you have a spreadsheet file that you need to protect so that others cannot read it? Or what if your corporate strategy files are stored on your laptop, and the laptop is stolen? Similarly, what if you need to send a disk to a subsidiary in another country? How can you protect the data from being read in these cases?

**Encryption** is a method of modifying the original information according to some code, so that it can only be read if the user knows the decryption key. Encryption can be used to transmit information from one computer to another. Information stored on a computer also can be encrypted. Even if someone guesses a password and gains access to the computer, the files will be gibberish without the encryption key—just like a scrambled cable TV signal.

There are two basic types of encryption. Most methods use a single key to both encrypt and decrypt a message. For example, the **Data Encryption Standard (DES)** method uses a single key. Although DES is a U.S. standard, versions of it are available throughout the world. A second method uses a **private key** and a **public key.** Whichever key is used to encrypt the message, the other key must be used to decrypt it. The **Rivest-Shamir-Adelman (RSA) algorithm** is an example of a method that uses two keys. RSA

## Reality Bytes    14–9    Outlaws and Police in Cyberspace

The Wild West had outlaws, followed by vigilantes, and legendary lawmen like Wyatt Earp. Sometimes it was hard to tell the difference between them. In many ways, the Internet is the new frontier—both for criminals and for law enforcement. Pete Hampton, who founded and runs the private InterGov organization, works on the side of law enforcement. His operations run three private agencies: WebPolice, ScamWatch, and Lost Child. They receive hundreds of complaints a day about Internet crime. Many are related to pornographic sites, but some involve e-mail threats, online stalking, and kidnapping attempts.

Hampton founded the WebPolice agency in 1986 when his daughter was harassed through e-mail by a co-worker. InterGov has a staff of 250, but has 800,000 volunteers available to help analyze and react to these threats. Hampton and his organization sometimes break into e-mail accounts and track criminals online—generally to try and identify the source of the threat. Hampton notes that "We don't go around beating people up. We just try to get them to cooperate with us, and if that doesn't work, we contact local law enforcement officials. But when I tell them, 'leave the little girl alone or else I'll rip your heart out through your nose,' they usually leave the little girl alone." His agencies have helped investigate more than 65,000 cases, sometimes after being called in by police, the FBI, or even Interpol. One of his more dramatic cases involved online threats against a girl in New Orleans. After her grandmother called WebPolice, Hampton notified the FBI, who used a police officer posing as the girl. The criminal was arrested for kidnapping as he was dragging the officer out of the house.

protection is available on a wide variety of computers. For example, PGP (pretty good privacy) is available worldwide, and most Internet browsers use a version of RSA to encrypt transmissions when they connect to a secure server.

Methods that use two keys have some interesting uses. They work because everyone knows your public key, but only you know the private key. Consider the example shown in Figure 14.10, in which Makiko and Takao want to send messages to each other using electronic mail. Makiko first types a letter. Then she encrypts the message with Takao's public key. This message can only be decrypted and read when Takao uses his private key. No one else can decrypt the message to read or change it. However, someone might be able to destroy the message before Takao gets it.

There is a second use of dual key systems called **authentication.** Let's say that Takao wants to send a message to Makiko. To make sure that only she can read it, he encrypts it with her public key. However, he is worried that someone has been sending false messages to Makiko using his name. Takao wants to make sure that Makiko knows the message came from him. If Takao also encrypts the message with his private key, it can only be decrypted with Takao's public key. When Makiko receives the message, she applies her private key and Takao's public key. If the message is readable, then Takao must have sent it. This situation is displayed in Figure 14.11.

Encryption should be seriously considered for any communications that are sent between computers. Without encryption, it is relatively easy for unauthorized people to deliberately or accidentally read the messages. Encryption is available with many personal computer software packages. Almost all spreadsheets and word processors permit you to encrypt your file when you save it. To read it back, you have to enter the correct password. You also can buy utility packages that will encrypt your entire disk drive, which can be useful for users who travel with their laptop computers. To retrieve any data on the disk drive, you have to enter the correct key value.

**FIGURE 14.10**
DUAL-KEY
ENCRYPTION
Makiko sends a
message that only Takao
can read. With a dual-
key system, one key
encrypts the message,
the other decrypts it.
Once Takao's public
key is applied to the
message, only Takao's
private key will retrieve
the message. Keys are
usually very large prime
numbers.

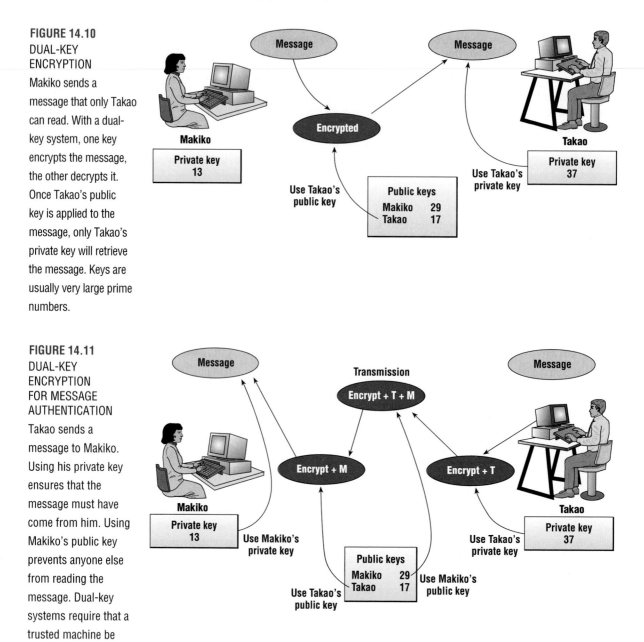

**FIGURE 14.11**
DUAL-KEY
ENCRYPTION
FOR MESSAGE
AUTHENTICATION
Takao sends a
message to Makiko.
Using his private key
ensures that the
message must have
come from him. Using
Makiko's public key
prevents anyone else
from reading the
message. Dual-key
systems require that a
trusted machine be
available to hold the
public keys.

## Encryption, Privacy, and Public Needs

It is easy to find situations for which firms and consumers need encryption to protect transactions and verify the identity of the participants. The demand increases as more transactions are moved online with little or no physical documentation. When phone conversations move to radio networks (cellular phones), we need to worry more about industrial espionage. Even simple messages deserve protection from a nosy co-worker. With faster hardware and improved software, it is easy to encrypt virtually any transaction, message, or phone call.

However, it is just as easy for drug dealers to encrypt their messages and lock their spreadsheets. Unethical government officials and lobbyists can just as easily prevent anyone else from reading their communications. Criminals of all types can use public net-

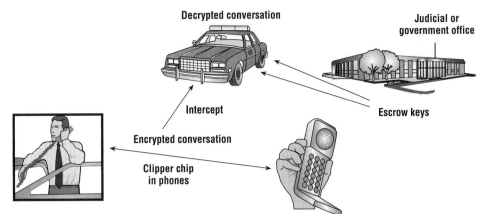

**FIGURE 14.12**

THE CLIPPER CHIP

The U.S. government is concerned that citizens and foreigners will use encryption for "undesirable" purposes, such as spying and committing crimes. The National Security Agency created a secret method of encrypting messages, including digital phone transmissions. Every encryption device can be broken with two special keys (numbers) that are held in escrow by judicial or governmental agencies. On receiving court permission, police would be able to decrypt any message or conversation.

works for their own communications, knowing that no one can decipher their messages. Likewise, foreign governments could use technology to hide their actions from public scrutiny.

Various law enforcement agencies and departments in the U.S. government believe that the widespread use of encryption will hinder their ability to identify and prosecute criminals. They are also concerned about making this technology available worldwide. In response to these problems, the U.S. government has taken three basic actions: (1) Export of strong encryption is denied—products using strong encryption are currently classified as "munitions" and prohibited from export. Despite several lawsuits and the widespread availability of strong encryption, the government has only slightly relaxed these restraints. (2) Various branches of the government, notably the top-secret National Security Agency (NSA) are rumored to have several supercomputers for code-breaking. (3) The U.S. government has created a secret encryption method that is being sold as the *Clipper chip.* It is primarily designed for use in oral communications (on phones) but can be used in any digital transmission. As Figure 14.12 illustrates, the Clipper chip has a unique feature: it uses two special **escrow keys.** Every chip has a unique number and two special key numbers. The plan is that these escrow keys will be filed with two governmental agencies. If the government suspects criminal activity, an official will obtain a judicial warrant to retrieve the keys. With these keys, the official can instantly decrypt any message using that specific chip. Following complaints by people concerned about privacy, the government chose to make use of the Clipper chip optional. However, it is required for use by (nonmilitary) governmental agencies. The government is hoping that official demand for products using the Clipper chip will drive prices down far enough to encourage use by private companies.

## Users

**RESPONSIBILITY AND ETHICS**

Computer users have certain responsibilities in terms of computer security and privacy. First, they have an obligation to obey the laws that pertain to computers. The U.S. government and some states, along with other nations, have laws against computer crimes. Other laws regarding stealing have also been applied to computer crimes. One law that has received much attention is the copyright law. European and U.S. copyright laws prohibit the copying of software except for necessary backup. It is the responsibility of users to keep up with the changes in the laws and to abide by them. In the last few years, software publishers have increased their efforts to stop illegal copying of software, called **software piracy.**

Although it might seem to be trivial, making illegal copies of software (or videotapes or other copyrighted works) can cause several problems. First, it takes money away from the legal owners of the software, which reduces their incentive to create new products. Second, you run the risk of hurting your employer. If employees illegally copy company-purchased software, the owners of the copyright can sue the employer. Third, copying software provides an illegal advantage over your competitors. A small design firm might decide to copy a $20,000 CAD design system instead of buying it. Consequently, honest firms are hurt because the original firm will be able to make lower bids on jobs because their costs are lower. Fourth, as an individual, you have a reputation to defend. If your friends, colleagues, or employers learn that you are willing to break the law by copying software, they can easily believe that you are willing to break other laws.

Users of computer systems also have an obligation as part of **computer ethics** to customers and clients. Most information in computer databases is confidential information. It should not be revealed to anyone except authorized employees. Some nations have laws to protect this privacy. If you find a company violating these laws, it is your responsibility to question the practice.

Users have an obligation to use the information provided by computer applications appropriately. When a user sets up calculations in a spreadsheet, the user must realize that those calculations might be wrong. The calculations must be tested and the information produced should always be checked for reasonableness. You should not believe information solely because it comes from a computer. All data should be verified.

## Programmers and Developers

Programmers would never get jobs if they could not be trusted. This trust is one of the most crucial requirements to being a programmer. As a programmer or developer, not only do you have to be honest, you must also avoid any appearance of dishonesty. For example, practical jokes involving security violations can be dangerous to your career.

Programmers have more responsibilities than many other employees. Software is used in many critical areas. If a programmer attempts a job that is beyond his or her capabilities, crucial errors can be introduced. For example, consider what might happen if an underqualified person took a job programming medical life support systems. If he or she made a mistake, a person might die. Although mistakes can be made by anyone, they are more likely to arise when a programmer attempts too difficult of a job.

Along the same lines, programmers have an obligation to test everything they do. It also means that companies have the responsibility to provide adequate time for programmers to perform the tests. The important step is to identify components that are critical and to build in safeguards.

There have been enormous increases in the demand for software in the last decade. At the same time, new tools allow programmers to create much more complex applications. But our ability to create this new software has far outstripped our ability to ensure that it is error free. Even commercial programs, such as word processors and spreadsheets, still have errors that can cause problems. In spite of the best efforts of conscientious, talented people, software used appropriately can produce erroneous information.

Liability for erroneous information produced by software has not been fully established yet. Laws and court decisions during the next few years should settle many aspects of who is responsible when software makes mistakes or fails. A related issue is the extent to which the user is responsible for correctly entering information needed by the program and for using the information produced by the program appropriately.

**Reality Bytes      14–10   Selling Your Life**

A company called *Nationwide Electronic Tracking (NET)* advertised that it had

"instant access" to a wide range of "confidential" computer data. For fees ranging from $5 to $175, NET promised, it could provide customers with data on virtually anyone in the country—private credit reports, business histories, driver's license records, even personal social security records and criminal history backgrounds.

This type of information could be valuable to a businessperson. For example, you could check out employees, customers, or even competitors. The catch is that most of this information is confidential.

Last week, NET was identified by the FBI as one player in a nationwide network of brokers and pri-

vate investigators who allegedly were pilfering confidential personal data from U.S. government computers and then selling them for a fee to lawyers, insurance companies, private employers, and other customers.

Police officers in various cities have been charged with selling information obtained from computer searches of local and federal databases. Besides the invasion of privacy issue, there is another serious problem with these databases:

The security of the FBI's database has long been a concern to civil libertarians, because roughly half of its arrest records are incomplete, failing to record whether charges were dropped or even whether a suspect was ultimately acquitted.

## Companies

Every company has obligations to society, customers, employees, and business partners. In terms of society, a firm must obey all relevant laws. For customers, firms must ensure privacy of data. That means companies will collect only the data that they truly need. The data must be safeguarded so that only those who need it for their job have access. If customer information is sold or distributed for other purposes, customers should be notified. Consumers must be allowed to remove their names from any distribution lists.

For employees, a company must provide training and monitoring (compliance programs) to ensure they understand the laws and are following them. Firms must provide sufficient funds to allow the employees to meet their individual responsibilities. Companies must provide enough time and money to test software adequately. Firms have an obligation to allow their employees a certain amount of privacy. For instance, companies have no reason to routinely monitor and read employees' electronic mail messages.

Companies are required to abide by all partnership agreements. In terms of computers, they must safeguard all data acquired from partners. They must not use the data in a manner that would injure the firms involved.

## Governments

Federal, state, and local governments have obligations to establish laws that provide a means for those unfairly injured to allow them to gain compensation from those who did the damage. Until the 1980s, relatively few laws at any level were specifically directed at computer usage. Instead, laws intended for other purposes were stretched to cover computer crimes. Frequently, citing mail fraud laws was the only recourse. Some criminals were not convicted because the crime was considered "victimless" by the jury, or the injured corporation declined to prosecute.

Starting in the mid-1980s, the federal government and nearly every state passed new laws concerning computer crime. The 1984 Computer Fraud and Abuse Act outlawed unauthorized access to data stored in federal government computers. In 1986, the Computer Fraud and Abuse Act and the Electronic Communications Privacy Act were enacted. The Computer Fraud and Abuse Act makes it a federal crime to alter, copy, view, or damage data stored in computers subject to federal law. The law provides fines of up to $100,000 and up to 20 years in prison. The Computer Abuse Amendments Act of 1994 expanded the original definitions to include transmission of harmful code such as viruses. It also distinguishes between actions taken "with reckless disregard" for potential damages (misdemeanor) and intentionally harmful acts (felony). It also modified the language so that crimes causing damages of more than $1,000 or involving medical records are within federal jurisdiction. Additionally, it placed controls on states in terms of selling drivers' license records.

Most states have enacted similar laws for the few computers that might not be subject to federal law. European countries have been ahead of the United States in developing legislation to deal with computer crime.

Legislation, enforcement, and judicial interpretation have not kept up with changes in technology. A major question that is unresolved is the extent to which copyright law applies to the "look and feel" of software. For example, Lotus Corporation sued Borland because Borland's Quattro Pro spreadsheet used menu titles similar to those used by the Lotus 123 spreadsheet. Some people are calling for legislation making it illegal to *write* a computer virus program, although there is some question that such a law might be an unnecessary restriction on freedom of speech or freedom of the press. In fact, there is considerable discussion over whether electronic mail and web site operators should be treated as members of the press and receive first amendment protections.

In terms of enforcement, most federal, state, and local agencies have few, if any, officers devoted to solving computer crimes. In fact, many software piracy cases have been pursued by U.S. Secret Service agents. One complication is that most law enforcement agencies lack proper training in computer usage and investigation of computer crimes.

## SUMMARY

Technological change and increasingly aggressive use of information systems by businesses have several consequences. Technology affects individuals, their jobs, educational systems, governments, and society as a whole. Businesses have to be careful to protect the privacy of consumers and workers. Security provisions, disclosure policies, and audits are used to ensure that data is only used for authorized purposes. To ensure accuracy, it is crucial to allow customers (and workers) to examine relevant data and make changes.

Technology is generally believed to increase the total number of jobs available. However, the workers displaced by the introduction of technology are rarely qualified for the new jobs. Businesses and governments need to provide retraining and relocation to help those workers who lose their jobs. Sometimes technology allows physically disabled people to work in jobs they might not otherwise be able to perform.

Improved communication networks, huge databases, and multimedia tools provide possibilities for education and training in the public and business sectors. However, because of high development costs, technology tends to be used for specialized training.

### A MANAGER'S VIEW

As a manager, you need to understand how businesses, technology, and society interact. Dealing with changes in privacy and security threats will become increasingly important to managing a company. Evaluating changes in society will also give you an advantage in the marketplace; it is important to know your customers. As a citizen, you need to be aware of the negative and positive effects of technology. In particular, changes in technology often lead to changes in political power and control. As a manager and a citizen, you are obligated to make ethical decisions and to understand the consequences of your actions.

Governments have long been involved in data collection, and technology enables them to work more efficiently. Of course, many political observers would argue that perhaps governments should not be *too* efficient. For example, it would be difficult for businesses to operate in an environment where the laws were changed every day. Technology also has the potential to improve communication between citizens and their representatives.

There are other interactions between technology and society. One feature is that lower prices, improved capabilities, and ease-of-use have made improved communication available to virtually any size group—providing a wider audience for small extremist groups. The new technologies also offer the ability to alter pictures, sound, and video, making it difficult to determine the difference between fact and fiction. Another important social issue is providing access to technology for everyone. It would be easy to create a world or nation consisting of *haves* and *have-nots* in terms of access to information. Those with information would be able to grow and earn more money, while those lacking the data continually lose ground.

Increasing dependence on technology brings with it new threats to the security of the firm. Managers need to recognize and evaluate these threats and understand some of the techniques used to minimize them. The most common threats come from inside the company, in terms of workers, consultants, and business partnerships. These threats are difficult to control, because firms have to trust these individuals to do their jobs. Training, oversight, audits, and separation of duties are common means to minimize threats. Depending on the communication systems used, there are threats from outsiders and viruses that can access computers with modems, over networks, or by intercepting communications. Dial-back modems, access controls, encryption, and antivirus software are common techniques to combat these threats.

Working in today's business environment means more than just doing your job. Each individual and firm has ethical obligations to consumers, workers, other companies, and society. In addition to obeying the laws, it is important for workers and companies to remember that the data in information systems refers to real people. The lives of people can be adversely affected by inaccurate data, poorly designed information systems, or abuse of the information.

## KEY WORDS

authentication, 619

biometrics, 616

cold site, 613

computer ethics, 622

Data Encryption Standard (DES), 618

data mirroring, 614

dehumanization, 598

digital cash, 607

encryption, 618

escrow key, 621

hackers, 608

haves and have-nots, 606

hot site, 613

privacy, 594

private key, 618

public key, 618

Rivest-Shamir-Adelman (RSA) algorithm, 618

software piracy, 621

uninterruptable power supply (UPS), 614

virus, 611

## WEB SITE REFERENCES

| | |
|---|---|
| **Comics** | |
| Cartoon Syndicate | www.unitedmedia.com |
| Dilbert Zone | www.dilbert.com |
| Doonesbury | www.doonesbury.com |
| **Time** | |
| NIST | www.bldrdoc.gov/timefreq/javaclck.htm |
| **Maps** | |
| GeoSystems | www.geosys.com |
| MapQuest | www.mapquest.com |
| **Jokes** | |
| Humor Space | www.humorspace.com |
| The Laffatorium | www.laffnow.com |
| **Animation** | |
| Hot Wired Animation | www.hotwired.com/animation |

| **Web Cameras** | |
|---|---|
| Digital Camera Network | www.dcn.com |
| Earth Cam Network | www.earthcam.net |
| Surf Lounge International | www.thegrid.net/fleming/cams.html |
| Web Cam Network | www.webcam.net/WebCams/WebCams.html |
| **Digital Books** | |
| Project Gutenberg | www.promo.net/pg |
| **Privacy and Fraud** | |
| National Fraud Information | www.fraud.org |
| Privacy Rights | www.privacyrights.org |

## REVIEW QUESTIONS

1. What privacy problems are individuals likely to experience as the use of computers and availability of data increase?
2. Do employees need to worry about the data collected by their employers?
3. Do you think increasing use of computers causes a loss of jobs? What about in the past or in the future?
4. How are computers helping disabled people to perform jobs?
5. How can computers be used in education and training?
6. Do you think state, local, and federal governments are making efficient use of computers? What privacy controls exist? Should there be additional controls?
7. In what ways have computers affected society and organizations? Will these patterns continue? Are there other important patterns that might arise?

8. What are the basic threats to information systems?
9. Why is computer security different from security for paper information?
10. How do computers recognize individual users?
11. What types of access control are typically available to restrict access to your data?
12. What alternative security measures can be used to minimize security risks?
13. How can data encryption be used to verify the author of a document or sales order?
14. What are the ethical responsibilities of users in terms of information systems?

## EXERCISES

1. If you have access to a local area network or a multiuser system that allows sharing of data, create a word-processed document and assign the proper security rights so that someone else in your class (or your instructor) can read the file but cannot alter it. As a team project, grant access only to your team members.
2. Team project: All team members should create a short spreadsheet. Protect each one with a password. Now, swap files and see whether a team member can guess your password. You must be able to restore your file without writing down your password. As an experiment, one team member should choose a password that is easy to guess.
3. Team project: Split into two groups. Individuals in each group will type a page of text into a word processor (pick any full page from the textbook). To

start, everyone will work on the project independently, but there is a deadline of no more than two days. Second, team members will pair up and type the document a second time. This time, while one person types the document, the other one will time his or her performance and count mistakes at the end. The goal is to find the team member who is fastest and makes the fewest mistakes. The trick is that each person's work will be monitored at all times. Now, when all members of the team have completed their tasks, get the team back together and answer the following questions: Was there more pressure while you were being watched? Were you nervous? More attentive? Were you faster the second time? Did you make more mistakes? Would you object to working under these conditions on a daily basis?

4. Obtain a copy of antivirus software (most universities have a site license for one) and check all of your disks for viruses. Did the program find any? How long did it take to check all of your disks? Do you often use disks on different computer systems? Do you know whether these systems are tested on a regular basis?

5. As a manager, you have an opening for a new employee. While checking the background of one applicant, you learn that two years ago he or she was fired from a job for deliberately accessing computer files of other employees and destroying data. One of your colleagues suggested that the incident means the person must know a lot about computers, which would be useful in your department. Are you willing to hire this person? Why or why not? If you are somewhat willing to hire the applicant, what questions would you ask in an interview, or what additional information would you want to see?

6. Imagine that a company develops a device that can drive a car, unassisted, on any major road. After the system is in use for two years, someone is killed in a car accident where one of the vehicles uses this new system. Should the injured people be allowed to sue the company that sells the system? What about the programmers who created it? What if the company knows that there is a 1 percent chance that an accident will occur while the system is being used? However, without the system, there is a 10 percent chance that you will be involved in an accident. Do these statistics change your answer? Do you think a system of this type should be required to have a 0 percent chance of error? Is such a level possible? Would you buy and use a system if these probabilities were true?

7. Do you think governmental agencies should share data about citizens? For example, should the FBI be able to access IRS records to locate suspected criminals? Should the FBI be allowed to access files from state and local governments? For instance, should all arrest records be automatically relayed to a central database? Should medical records be accessible to law enforcement agencies? Say that it is technically possible for the FBI to build a national database that contains DNA records for all citizens. If all medical records (from accidents, blood tests, and medical treatment) were computerized and automatically forwarded to the FBI, the agents could easily locate virtually any criminal.

### Rolling Thunder Database

8. What privacy problems might exist at Rolling Thunder? What rules or procedures should we enact to avoid problems?

9. What data access controls should we implement? Examine each data table and the input forms. Determine who should have "ownership" rights and decide which groups should have read or modify privileges.

10. What threats (physical and logical) exist to our information system? What steps should we take to minimize these threats and minimize problems?

11. What employee procedures and background checks should we perform to protect our information systems?

12. If Rolling Thunder Bicycles adds an Internet site to order bicycles and deal with customers, what security procedures should be implemented to protect the data?

## ADDITIONAL READING

Bequai, August. *Technocrimes.* Lexington, MA: Lexington Books, 1989. [Security Pacific and other cases]

Daragahi, Borzou. "States Must Do More to Stop Online Fraud," *Money Magazine,* February 12, 1999. [Investigations of security fraud]

Parker, Donn B. *Crime by Computer.* New York: Scribner, 1976. [Early cases of computer fraud and abuse]

Stoll, Clifford. *The Cuckoo's Egg: Tracking a Spy Through a Maze of Computer Espionage.* New York: Doubleday, 1989. [Fascinating story of a spy searching U.S. networks]

Whiteside, Thomas. *Computer Capers: Tales of Electronic Thievery, Embezzlement and Fraud.* New York: Crowell, 1978. [Early cases of computer fraud and abuse]

# CASES *Health Care*

The United States is a recognized global leader in the production of medical equipment and supplies. In 1996, the United States had 47 percent of the $130 billion global market for medical devices. The health care business is mature but also constantly changing. It is not subject to economic cycles to the same degree as other industries.

The health care industry consists of public, private, and nonprofit institutions. These institutions are hospitals; offices and clinics of medical doctors; nursing homes; other specialized health care facilities; managed care consisting of prepaid plans such as health care facilities; managed care consisting of prepaid plans such as health maintenance organizations (HMOs), preferred provider organizations (PPOs), and independent practice associations (IPAs).

Health care is different from other consumer purchases. We often do not know when we will need health care and most of the time consumers have very little say about what type of services they receive. America's complex health care system is a leader in the use of sophisticated and expensive technology.

Pressure for changes in this industry stems from large employers, intermediaries, managed care companies, and individual payers who are looking to cut health care cost. These customers are demanding more efficient, more responsive, and lower cost alternatives. This demand has led to the virtual restructuring of the health care industry, which has shifted its focus to a managed care model.

According to one survey, some form of managed care accounts for 74 percent of private-sector medical insurance. Medicaid enrollment in managed care has also continued to grow rapidly, with further plans underway in several states. Medicare enrollments also increased, although the pace remained well below that for Medicaid or private coverage.

## Financial Analysis

The health care industry in the United States is very large. In 1989, 12 percent of the U.S. GNP was spent on health care. This totaled $670 billion, compared to $4 billion in 1940. At this rate, health care expenditures will be $1.5 trillion by the year 2000.

The cost of the nation's health care rose about 19 percent in 1996 to reach an estimated $1,360 billion, or about $4,600 per capita. As health care expenditures have risen, their composition has changed. Public-sector spending on health care has risen faster than private-sector spending. Private-sector health care expenditures represented about 52 percent of total health care spending in 1995, down from 59 percent in 1980. Medicaid programs accounted for most of the 6 percent increase in public-sector spending.

Despite the 1.2 percent decline in the U.S. economy from 1990 to 1991, the Census Bureau estimated health care services revenue rose 9.5 percent from $521.7 billion to $571.3 billion. The highest revenue growth areas occurred in home health care services (19.2 percent), specialty outpatient facilities (17.4 percent), and nursing and personal care facilities (15.7 percent). Hospitals realized a 10.8 percent increase, while offices and clinics grew 7.2 percent during that period. Hospitals accounted for 58 percent of all revenues for the health services industries in 1995. In comparison, in 1997, European Union nations spent about 8 percent of GDP on healthcare (*Ethos,* 1998), Japan about 7 percent, Germany 9 percent, Canada 10 percent, and China 1 percent (Price-Waterhouse-Coopers web site).

| YEAR | PER CAPITA ($) | PERCENT OF GNP | TOTAL (BILLIONS$) |
|------|----------------|----------------|-------------------|
| 1950 | 80 | 4.4 | 12.7 |
| 1955 | 101 | 4.4 | 17.7 |
| 1960 | 142 | 5.2 | 26.9 |
| 1965 | 205 | 5.9 | 41.9 |
| 1970 | 349 | 7.4 | 75.0 |
| 1975 | 591 | 8.3 | 132.7 |
| 1980 | 1054 | 9.1 | 248.1 |
| 1985 | 1710 | 10.6 | 422.6 |
| 1987 | 1973 | 11.2 | 497.0 |

U.S. health care expenditure trend.

Medical products company margins are in the 25 to 30 percent range. Net profit margins of medical products producers in 1996 were 11.3 percent, for drug makers 17.8 percent, and for the Standard and Poor's 500 as a whole 5.7 percent.

### Stock/Investment Outlook

During the late 1980s large amounts of money were invested in the health care industry. The industry's profits and stocks were doing well. Health care costs rose and the prospect of aging baby-boomers increased expectations of future profits in the industry.

The outlook for health care stocks looks bright. Going into the new century, there will be improved pricing conditions, greater penetration of developing overseas markets, and rising contributions from new drugs and medical products. It was only in 1992 that talk of national price controls weighed heavily on the pharmaceutical industry. Wall Street's worries were not realized. The ten biggest U.S. pharmaceutical companies posted close to $22 billion in profits on $127 billion in sales for 1997, up 51 percent and 31 percent respectively, from 1994.

Drug makers are selling many new products. Warner-Lambert's cholesterol-lowering Lipitor is a big hit, with $450 million in sales in its first year. Eli Lilly's schizophrenia drug Zyprexa is useful, but also expensive; a one-year prescription costs about $2,150.

Improved regulatory conditions for both pharmaceutical and medical device industries have also helped stocks. Under political pressure the FDA has made its new drug device review procedures more efficient and approval times are now faster than they have been in years. Many new drug therapies for life-threatening conditions such as AIDS have recently been approved.

Rapid growth of HMOs and other managed care organizations is also viewed as a positive for the industry. Despite substantial discounts extended to these providers, they tend to be heavily reliant on cost-effective pharmaceuticals and other medical products that might prevent illness. The growing influence of managed care, which now represents over 50 percent of the medical products market, is expected to continue to spur the growth in sales of drugs and cost savings of medical products in the years ahead.

### Potential/Prospective for Growth

As the number of older Americans increases so does the prospect for growth in this industry. Almost 80 percent of people over the age of 65 have at least one form of chronic illness. This creates demand. Additionally, drug firms are constantly developing new products and therapies.

Health care organizations are reexamining their business practices. Virtually every health care organization in the country today is implementing, or at least contemplating, some form of change or reengineering process designed to make it more flexible and competitive.

The annual cost of health care for a family in the United States may reach $14,000 by the end of the decade. In 1992, average per capita spending for health care in the United States totaled $3,160 a year, up from $1,000 in 1980. The United States spends twice as much on health care as the average for the 24 industrialized countries in Europe and North America. There is speculation that the economic drain on the U.S. economy posed by rising health care costs threatens to jeopardize the United State's competitive position in international trade.

### Competitive Structure

Competition occurs throughout the health care system. The intensity of the competition varies in different sectors of the market. Many companies play a role, including pharmaceutical companies, product supply companies insurance companies, and HMOs. Medicaid and Medicare are two federal programs that are not immune to market forces but also are not quick to adapt and be cost effective.

### Role of Research and Development

Telemedicine began more than 30 years ago with development of two-way closed circuit television. It is now becoming workable as a new technology with potential for cost savings. Forty percent of existing telemedicine programs were started after 1996. It can be very useful for practitioners in places far from major medical centers.

Some of the benefits of telemedicine are realized in the monitoring of cardiac and kidney dialysis patients. There is also a growing acceptance in the fields of psychiatry, dermatology, and education.

### Technological Investment and Analysis

Millions of dollars are spent each year in new health technology and procedures. Along with the advances in technology, comes better diagnosis, more accurate EKGs, and more accurate laser surgery.

Technology growth that emphasizes quality improvement may seem to increase costs. Other improvements to productivity may decrease costs. The continued shift in insurance coverage to lower cost forms of managed care, primarily HMOs, will exert downward pressure on health care expenditures by enhancing cost-containment efforts.

### Recommendation for the Future

Managed care is having a major impact on the market for health care. It may be the reason for very low price inflation for many health care products in recent years. Certainly the federal government's threat to regulate health care has also kept medical price inflation lower that it might have otherwise been. To achieve low cost health care delivery, different systems and organizations should continue to be examined.

SOURCES: *PC Magazine*, Feb. 10, 1998 v17 n3 p40(1). Better your browser. (Ethos Software's Ethosware, 2.5, and the NetLaunch 3.13a and Auto WinNet98 4.1 browser utilities) (Software Review) (Brief Article) (Evaluation) Doug Beizer.

## CASE   *Eli Lilly*

How does a company increase its presence in the explosive pharmaceuticals-by-mail (PBM) market? If the company were paying attention to industry trends the answer would be through acquisition, of course. Increased presence is exactly what Eli Lilly achieved after purchasing the nation's largest PBM, PCS Health Systems. The subsequent purchase of IMS further strengthened the position by combining the resources of an information system provider with the services of a PBM.

This combination of resources has enabled Lilly to create an interactive information system networking physicians' offices to PCS offices and providing online drug benefit management services. The network specializes in areas for which Lilly has products. Therefore, not only have these acquisitions provided Lilly with a low-margin, highly profitable subsidiary, it has also created a brand-loyal consumer base for its products.

### Technological Investment and Analysis

"Elvis is alive and well," reads a Lilly press release regarding the deployment of a new corporate intranet. Eli Lilly Virtual Information Service, ELVIS for short, has seemingly transformed the Internet from a novelty into a critical resource for Lilly's 25,000 plus employees. The information system is an intranet run on Microsoft Windows 2000 servers and Netscape Communications servers running on Silicon Graphics computers. The system is accessed and utilized through the Netscape Navigator Web browser that was installed on every corporate desktop during 1996.

ELVIS provides employees access to corporate news bulletins, job postings, stock prices, and daily news on the pharmaceutical industry. Senior management is provided with an executive tracking system that maintains schedules (akin to a Web-based version of Microsoft Project) and an executive corporate information database. The most valuable features, however, are provided to the brand marketing teams and individual sales representatives. The intranet provides these employees with a means of accessing updated product information, market research, competitive analysis, customer lists, and sales leads from any location in the world, at any time, day or night. This feature further serves to synchronize sales information and pricing worldwide.

Portions of ELVIS are interactive, form-based pages. For example, a number of these pages allow users to order promotional material online directly from third-party distributors while still allowing Lilly to track the orders. Since the intranet's inception, it has been undergoing almost constant updates and modifications.

The second major investment made by Lilly in the area of computer-related technology is the purchase of two software products from BBN Domain Corporation. These products are intended to aid Lilly's R&D staff by automating and standardizing the data collection and regulatory reporting associated with new drug discovery.

This first of the two BBN Domain's products is Clintrace. Clintrace is used to simplify the process of adverse events reporting during the testing of new drugs and Clintrial is used to standardize the process of clinical trial data collection. Clintrial is intended to accelerate a new product's time to market by collecting, organizing, and managing data within regulatory guidelines. The software will be run on a client-server architecture networked to offices in more than 30 countries, which was constructed by Lilly specifically for this purpose. By utilizing these two products in this manner, Lilly foresees gaining a competitive advantage by standardizing clinical trial data collection and management procedures throughout its worldwide facilities and, as a result, getting new medicines to market more quickly.

Clearly these two expenditures on technology represent different directions. On the one hand, ELVIS provides an information link and forum for employees and creates a virtual corporate culture. On the other hand, the BBN Domain products provide a mechanism to enhance R&D productivity. These products, therefore, have the potential to give Lilly greater productivity.

### Technological Innovations

#### Data

"One of the most important things for us is the whole notion of helping discovery researchers cope with more data—and more complex data—than they've ever had before," says Thomas Trainer, Eli Lilly's VP and CIO. The alliance between the Indianapolis company's IT staff and researchers is so important that in 1997 the two groups set up shop down the hall from each other. "Lilly Research Laboratories and IT are literally hand-in-hand," says Tom Bumol, executive director of research technology and proteins.

Eli Lilly is focusing on the emerging field of bioinformatics, which uses specialized algorithms and databases to analyze the structure of genes. The analysis helps identify proteins that cause disease.

Bioinformatics is accelerating the pharmaceuticals industry beyond what technology does for businesses in general. At Eli Lilly, the IS staff and researchers are correlating data in several databases into a single relational database structure.

Lilly subscribes to a database of gene-sequencing information from Incyte Pharmaceuticals, Inc. They co-own a database generated by Millennium BioTherapeutics, Inc., and they generate their own gene sequencing information internally. In addition, the company downloads information nightly from public databases on the Internet, such as the federal government's Human Genome Project. All the data is stored in Oracle databases that run on Sun Microsystems servers.

## QUESTIONS

1. What is the source of the highest margin growth at Eli Lilly?
2. What has caused a change in the use of technology at Lilly?
3. Has technology improved productivity at Eli Lilly?
4. How successful has the technological change been?
5. How does Eli Lilly evaluate its financial ability to embark on a major technological program of advancement?
6. What role does data play in the future of Lilly?

## ADDITIONAL READING

Bicknell, David. "Gilding the Lilly" *Computer Weekly,* October 1, 1998, p. 34.

Caldwell, Bruce. "Desktop Control," *InformationWeek,* August 25, 1997, p. 119.

Cox, John. "Elvis Lives at Eli Lilly (ELVIS intranet information system)," *Network World,* December 23, 1996, p. 72.

Duffy, Jim. "Eli Lilly Cures IP Ills," *Network World,* November 25, 1996, p. 19.

Fusaro, Roberta. "Rating Intangibles No Easy Task," *Computerworld,* November 30, 1998, p. 8.

Gambon, Jill. "Lilly's $4B Health-Net Gamble," *InformationWeek,* September 16, 1996, p. 93.

Haber, Lynn. "Corporate Giants Test the Waters," *CommunicationsWeek,* March 18, 1996, p. S22.

Hoffman, Thomas. "Y2K: Who's Ready to Pitch In?" *Computerworld,* August 24, 1998, p. 39.

Kay, Emily. "LAN Managers Grab Control of the Net," *LAN Times,* June 17, 1996, p. 7.

King, Julia. "Lilly Finds Rx for Help Desk," *Computerworld,* May 20, 1996, p. 73.

McGee, Marianne Kolbasuk, and Gregory Dalton, "Lilly Outsources to EDS," *InformationWeek,* February 23, 1998, p. 34.

Paul, Laura Gibbons. "Getting the Best of Both Worlds," *PC Week,* June 17, 1996, p. 63.

Vijayan, Jaikumar. "Lilly Looks to Tighten Outsource Circle," *Computerworld,* August 25, 1997, p. 39.

Wilkinson, Stephanie. "Integrated Messaging 'Cons'," *PC Week,* March 11, 1996, p. 18.

## CASE  *Owens & Minor, Inc.*

It costs money every time an item in business is handled, so Owens & Minor (O&M) developed many ways to simplify the receipt and storage of materials, and to exploit state-of-the-art technology every step of the way. Many times, put-away means replenishing supplies directly to the point of use, bypassing the customer's warehouse or storeroom, and the attendant paperwork, altogether.

### Technological Story

O&M relies heavily on computer technology in warehouses and gets big rewards in terms of efficiency. The newest warehouse management system is a distributed network that provides each customer with the most flexible, custom-tailored information services to date. It helps to make sure the item is where it's supposed to be when it's supposed to be, even if it's off-site.

### Technological Investment and Analysis

O&M, like Baxter International and other medical supplies companies, understands the importance of information technology as the primary method of achieving cost savings. Some of the value-added services O&M can now offer customers include inventory management, electronic data interchange, logistical support, and an on-line order-entry system.

These services save customers money and time by allowing the customers direct access to O&M databases. The customer can check O&M's inventory levels and scheduling for deliveries directly. This information was proprietary a short time ago.

Another example of O&M's utilization of information technology was an upgrade to its warehouse computer system. Warehouse operations were consolidated at a cost of $25 million. By centralizing warehouse operations, O&M will have more control over inventory and scheduling, hopefully making the ordering and delivery process more efficient. Again, through technology upgrades, O&M continues to actively cut costs and deliver savings to the balance sheet and to customers.

## Recommendations for the Future

Despite the cost-consciousness of providers of medical care, and the threat of cuts in Medicare (which represents approximately two-fifths of hospital industry revenues), medical suppliers should experience an acceleration of both revenues and earnings in the years to come. In addition to increased cost and time efficiencies experienced by the exploitation of computerization, the industry will be driven by factors such as the graying of the baby–boomers (now 50 years old), an increase in foreign market demand, and a continuous flow of innovative diagnostic and therapeutic products.

Owens & Minor needs to continue to invest in technology in order to stay competitive in this fast-paced, highly unpredictable industry. With many products having become commodities, the pressure for companies to differentiate themselves is greater than ever.

## QUESTIONS

1. What forces are driving the strategic direction for Owens & Minor?
2. What has been the catalyst for change at Owens & Minor?
3. Upon which technologies have Owens & Minor relied?
4. What has caused a change in the use of technology at O&M?
5. How has the technological change been implemented?
6. Is Owens & Minor financially able to continue to embark on a major technological program of advancement?
7. What does Owens & Minor's web page present about its business directives?
8. What type of Web does the company have (promotional/transactional/informative)?

## ADDITIONAL READING

Condon, Bernard. "Mark Unhealthy Prognosis," *Forbes,* August 12, 1996, p. 20.

Karon, Paul. "Mark Owens & Minor Chain Management in Stable Condition," *InfoWorld,* September 9, 1996, p. 82.

"Mark Owens & Minor Inc.," *Defense Daily,* November 25, 1997, p. 8.

"Tenet Awards Owens and Minor $2 Billion Contract," *The New York Times,* October 29, 1998, p. C4.

Weston, Rusty. "Mark Growing Pains," *PC Week,* February 5, 1996, p. E1.

## DISCUSSION ISSUE

### *Security Limits?*

In many ways, it is impossible to provide complete security to any data. The ultimate protection would be to hide or destroy data so that no one could ever see it. Of course, no one could use the data. Problems arise because some people need to use data, but the organization also needs to control who can see and use certain information. One of the most difficult aspects of computer security is controlling access without interfering with the business and employee privacy.

Jenny has been working for a large company for the last three years. Axel was hired two months ago—he is a little more enthusiastic in his use of computers. Axel also has little faith in central administrators and rules.

*(Office, 9:15 A.M.)*

Axel:  Hey Jenny, check out these silly new rules. These guys have gone too far this time. It says here that certain employees can only access these accounts during working hours!

Jenny:  Really? Did you see the new PCs that MIS just delivered? They have warning stickers and special screws. We're not even allowed to open the cases.

Axel:  What are they worried about anyway? There's nothing in there to steal. Besides, it wouldn't take 30 seconds to get that screw out.

Jenny:  I don't know. I guess they're worried about us altering the machines. Or maybe they're afraid we'll do something to the network interface card to break security on the network.

Axel:  Well, too bad. I need to install my CD-ROM, and I'm not going to sit around and wait for tech support to get here. These rules are getting ridiculous.

*(Security center, 7:02 P.M.)*

Billy:  Hey Taggert, check out this report from the computer activity monitor. It says that Jenny down in finance is still logged in.

Taggert:  So, I've seen her work late some nights. She's on the authorized list, isn't she?

Billy:  Yeah, but I swear I passed her in the hall when I got back from dinner. Hang on, let's check the security logs . . . Yeah. There it is. She checked out at 6:32 P.M. Let's see . . . Yeah, the parking garage gate records show she drove out at 6:38 P.M. That doesn't give her time to get home and call in.

Taggert: Okay, then let's see who's logged on . . . The network monitor says the activity is coming from a machine in her office area. Run a quick personnel scan and see who hasn't checked out from that area yet. I'll start the logs so we can record everything.

Billy: The only one left is that new guy: Axel. His security background check came up negative, but there's not a lot of information about him. No suspicious associations, just a typical college graduate . . .

Taggert: Well, do a quick financial scan on him. The computer logs show Jenny's machine going online right about when his machine was switched off. I'm getting some weird feedback from his machine. Remind me to check out the security card in his computer later.

Billy: Well, there's nothing unusual in this credit analysis. Just the usual: He was late with a couple rent payments, some heavy credit card purchases, . . . wait, he did just buy a new car. Think it means anything?

Taggert: Maybe. Hang on, let's bring up the machine he's using . . . There. Now we can see everything he's doing.

Billy: Sure, but it doesn't make much sense to me. Looks like he's running some sort of statistical analysis . . . That's a report writer and a word processor running in the background. How do we know it's Axel? Maybe Jenny forgot and left her machine running?

Taggert: Hang on a second, wait until we get some keyboard activity. OK, there we go. Now, bring up the security camera over here . . . Yeah, there he is . . .

Billy: What's that on the side? Looks like a dismantled PC . . .

Taggert: Yeah, that's probably why I had trouble earlier. Well, I don't know what he's doing, but we've got him on at least two major security violations. The access one is a felony. That's enough for me. Send a termination notice to human resources, and let's go get him out of here. I'm locking up his computer now.

*(Office, 8:18 P.M.)*

Billy: Okay, Axel, hold it right there.

Axel: What the . . .? Who are you guys?

Taggert: Corporate security. Come with us . . .

Axel: What? Look, if it's about the computer, I can explain, mine broke, and . . .

Taggert: We don't want to hear it. You can confess tomorrow. Your boss can decide if we call in the police. Either way, you're out of here. Billy, escort him out. Then follow him home. Make sure he's here by 8:00 tomorrow morning. If he tries to leave, call the police and have him arrested.

## QUESTIONS

1. Do you think Axel is guilty of violating computer security laws? Is there enough evidence to prove it? Even if no laws were broken, should he lose his job for violating company procedures?
2. Assuming Axel really is guilty, what additional evidence might you try to collect? What risks does the company face if it lets him continue while security people look for more evidence?
3. Are these security capabilities available today? As an executive, would you create a security system like this one? Would you tell the employees about its capabilities or keep it a secret?
4. As a worker, how would you feel about working for a company with this type of security system? Would you want the company to tell you about all of its security capabilities?
5. Assume that you are in Axel's position (and that you are innocent). Your boss tells you that you must have a major report finished by 8:00 A.M. tomorrow. After she leaves, your computer breaks down. You try to fix it but don't succeed. You remember that your boss's computer has the same capabilities as yours and automatically connects to the network when you turn it on (the password is supplied by her startup program). What would you do? If you knew about all of the security features, what would you do?

# Computer-Related Laws

Laws form the foundation of society. They provide the structure that enables businesses to exist. As society changes the laws must also be changed. Hence, as the use of computers grows, we can expect to see more laws governing their use. Existing laws will be extended, and new ones created. To date, computer laws have been concerned with three primary areas: property rights, privacy, and crime. These areas overlap, and they cannot cover all possible issues. As information technology and robotics become entwined into all our activities, virtually any law can be applied or interpreted to the situation.

Laws continually change and new interpretations and applications regularly arise. You will generally need a lawyer to help you understand and apply the current laws. This short appendix can only provide you with a limited background. You can find additional information in many places on the Web. This information will help you identify problems and generally enable you to obey the laws. However, a lawyer is still the best source of information, particularly if you anticipate problems or conflicts.

## PROPERTY RIGHTS

A property right gives you ownership and control over an object. While the term originated with physical property, the more important issues now involve intellectual property. If you write a book, a song, or a computer program, you should be able to receive money from sales of that item. Copyright, patent, trademark, and trade secret laws provide definitions of ownership and control transfer of these rights. They provide you with the opportunity to prevent others from using or stealing your work. Each of the four types of property right laws applies to different material.

Copyrights are used for books, songs, and computer software. The laws apply to the specific item—such as a book. You cannot copyright a general concept. For example, you can obtain a copyright for a specific word-processing application. But other people are free to write similar applications, as long as they do not utilize your specific code or text. Copyrights generally last for 50 years after the death of the writer. In the case of a work produced by a group of workers in a company, the copyright lasts for 75 years after the publication of the work. After that time, the work falls into the public domain, where anyone can use or copy it with no restraints.

Patents were originally designed for mechanical devices although today you can receive a patent for any device that is innovative and useful. For many years, computer software applications could not receive patents because "laws of nature" including mathematical algorithms were specifically excluded. In the last few years, the U.S. Patent Office has changed this interpretation and now grants patents for computer software. A U.S. patent right exists for 20 years from the date the application was filed. The strength of a patent is that it prevents other people from creating a similar product even if they do not directly copy your work. Consequently, a patent is much more difficult to obtain than a copyright.

Trademarks are used to create a unique name. Once you find and trademark a name (or logo), no one else can use that name without your permission. It is relatively easy to obtain a trademark, except that you must find a name that no one else has already chosen.

Trade secret laws provide you with the ability to seek damages if someone steals your secret information. The catch is that you are responsible for protecting the information. The laws are generally used to enforce a nondisclosure agreement (NDA). If a company wants to work with another company or a consultant, it is a good idea to have the outsiders sign an NDA, in which they agree not to reveal any information you share. If you forget to have them sign an NDA and they release your "secret" information, you will have few options. It is your responsibility to protect the data.

These four basic protections have different purposes and different strengths and weaknesses. Copyrights and trademarks are relatively easy and inexpensive to obtain. You simply fill out a form, submit the material, and wait a few months for the agency to process the request. Actually, a copyright exists as soon as you create the material. You do not need to file the registration form. However, there are some legal and monetary advantages to registering the copyright. Patents require considerable documentation and a formal review to identify prior and related patents, and to determine the legitimacy of the innovation. They usually require the help of a specialized law firm, take at least a year to obtain, and will probably cost about $10,000 in legal and processing fees. Trade secret protection requires no registration with the government but requires you to create and enforce a security policy to ensure that your information is adequately protected.

In a digital age, copyright law is the most challenging to apply and to enforce. The first question is identifying ownership. Who owns a particular item? If you write a book on your own time with your own resources, then generally you own the rights. If you write a computer program for your employer as part of your job, the employer owns the copyright. Interestingly, if you are an outside contractor and create a program for a company, it is more likely that you own the copyright, unless you agree to transfer the rights.

There is an interesting exception to copyright law: mere collections of data cannot be copyrighted. Consider the example of *Feist Publications v. Rural Telephone Service* [499 U.S. 340 (1991)]. Feist wanted to publish a telephone directory, but Rural would not provide the data. So Feist copied much of the data from Rural's printed directory. The U.S. Supreme Court eventually ruled that Feist's action was not a copyright infringement because the directory contained only data, which is not sufficiently original to obtain a copyright. Now consider the case of *ProCD, Inc. v. Zeidenberg* [86 F3d 1447 (7th Cir. 1996)]. ProCD collects and publishes a CD-based list of phone numbers and addresses, which they generally obtain from printed phone directories. Zeidenberg purchased a copy of the CDs and transferred them to his web site. He then charged people to access the site. ProCD sued for violating the copyright laws. Based on the Feist case, Zeidenberg was found innocent of copyright in-

fringement. However, he was guilty of violating the shrink-wrap license agreement. Note that the data collection argument probably applies to most data collected by federal and state agencies.

Copyright protection gives you the ability to stop others from profiting from your work. There are a few minor exceptions—such as parody, excerpting short quotations, and educational "fair use," which allows educational institutions very limited provisions to make a limited number of copies for teaching purposes. A more interesting, unanticipated exception involves money. Consider the 1994 case of *U.S. v. LaMacchia,* who was a student running a bulletin board system on university computers. He routinely placed commercial software on the site and allowed people to download (steal) the software for their own use. The catch is that he did not charge access to the system and made no money from the process. Without this profit motive, the court ruled that LaMacchia could not be convicted on charges of criminal violation of the copyright laws. Of course, the commercial software vendors could sue him on civil grounds, but unless he was an unusually wealthy student, there would be little gain. On the other hand, the university could throw him out for violating university policy. Congress has proposed a law to modify the copyright provisions to cover this situation in the future.

Copying becomes a more serious problem every day. As more works are created and distributed in digital form, it becomes more difficult to protect them. Even though you might have a legal right to prevent copying, it becomes increasingly difficult to prevent the distribution of your work, particularly if individual ethics are weak. For example, say that you write a story and sell it through your web site. Once the first few people have read the story, they could copy it and e-mail it to their friends. What are you going to do? Arrest and sue your customers who first read the story? On the other hand, if a publisher took your story, printed it, and sold it, you clearly have the legal authority and monetary incentive to seek compensation. Consider a similar example. You build a web site and create some interesting graphics and sound effects. Over time, other people routinely download your objects and use them on their own sites. Have they violated copyright laws? Can you stop them? Can you even find them? Would it be economically worthwhile to pursue them?

It is unlikely that individual motivations and ethics will improve. That is, despite the laws, many people will still copy anything they can (software, art, text, photos, video clips, and so on). Whatever technology might be applied, it is unlikely to be economically feasible to pursue them. Yet, without incentive why should you create and distribute new works? One possible outcome is that large, expensive content will disappear. Why should you write and distribute an entire book in one piece, when most people would steal it instead of paying $20 a copy? Instead, you could sell the book a section at a time, for a few cents per section. By releasing the sections over time, people would have to pay to receive the most recent (and organized) sections. Yes, some people might wait and have a friend pay for the section and e-mail it, but it is a question of economics. If the price is low enough, more people will opt to get the data earlier and directly from the source.

The federal white paper ("Intellectual Property and the National Information Infrastructure") contains an extended discussion of copyright issues and possible federal solutions. It is available online from the Information Infrastructure Task Force (IITF) bulletin board. You should also read Pamela Samuelson's criticism of the white paper proposal, which points out that the discussion strongly favors copyright holders as opposed to the public, particularly since the primary author (Bruce Lehman) was a lobbyist for the copyright industry.

## PRIVACY

Privacy is an intriguing concept. Humans are a social group: We can accomplish far more by living in communities and sharing our talents. Yet, individuals have a desire to keep some things private. More to the point, we have a desire to control what information we wish to share. For example, you might not want everyone to know exactly how old you are or how many times you were sick last year, but it is okay if your mother knows these things, and possibly essential that your doctor knows them.

Society has a vested interest in knowing some things about you and your life. For example, communities need to know how much you paid for your car and your house so they can fairly assess taxes. Society needs to track criminal behavior to help identify antisocial people who might harm us. Medical researchers need to track diseases to identify trends, causes, and potential solutions.

Businesses have an incentive to obtain considerable amounts of data on groups and individuals. And individuals have an incentive to provide some information to businesses. Whenever you make a purchase, you need information, and businesses are generally happy to provide you that information. The problem is how do you find the business or company that best matches your needs? Conversely, how can a company identify its potential customers? With no information, companies might resort to mass e-mail (spam) that clogs networks and irritates people who have no use for the services advertised.

The catch is that we do need to share information about ourselves, with government agencies, researchers in various disciplines, and with businesses. Yet, there is no reason that everyone in the world should be able to obtain every detail of our lives. The difficulty lies in determining where to draw this line. It is further complicated by the fact that every person (and social group) has different preferences.

First, it is important to realize that there is no constitutionally defined "right to privacy," especially with respect to data. A few laws have been enacted in the United States to provide minimal restrictions on the use and sharing of personal data. The most notable are the following:

- Freedom of Information Act,
- Family Educational Rights and Privacy Act,
- Fair Credit Reporting Act,
- Privacy Act of 1974,
- Privacy Protection Act of 1980,
- Electronic Communications Privacy Act of 1986,
- Video Privacy Act of 1988,
- Driver's Privacy Protection Act of 1994.

The Freedom of Information Act generally provides people with the ability to obtain information held by governmental agencies. There are limits for national security and on the release of data relating to individual personal data. For example, you cannot ask the IRS for personal information about your neighbor.

The most important feature of the Family Educational Rights and Privacy Act is that it limits the release of educational data. Institutions can release basic information such as the names of students (commonly sold to businesses), but they cannot release grades without the students' express written permission.

The primary purpose of the Electronic Communications Privacy Act was to extend traditional wiretap provisions to "electronic communication," which includes cellular phone and e-mail transmissions. Essentially, the law makes it illegal for individuals to intercept these conversations, and requires law enforcement agencies to obtain court permission to intercept and record the conversations. On the other hand, it is specifically legal for an individual to record his or her transmissions (although a few states limit this right). Consequently, employers generally have the legal right (since they own the equipment) to monitor most communications by employees. Note that there may be some exceptions and an honest employer will always notify employees first.

The Fair Credit Reporting Act primarily gives consumers the right to inspect credit records—and it gives them the right to correct errors. The Driver's Privacy Act limits the use and release of state motor vehicle data. Its primary purpose was to prevent release of specific data to individual requesters. However, it has generous exceptions for insurance companies, research, and business use. The Video Privacy Act was created to limit the release of rental records from video stores and libraries.

The Privacy Protection Act of 1980 is primarily concerned with law enforcement investigations. It provides some definitions for when police searches are legitimate and when they are an invasion of privacy. The act predates the advances in information technology, so it is generally silent on the issue of privacy in terms of electronic data.

On the other hand, the Privacy Act of 1974 deals more directly with the collection and dissemination of information by the federal government. It specifically limits the collection of data by an agency to information that is relevant to its work. It provides citizens with the ability to examine and contest the data. The act initially limited agencies from sharing and matching data with other agencies, but most of these restraints have been removed by subsequent amendments. For example, the postal service is generally not permitted to disclose data on individual addresses. However, it does release data to a few large commercial service bureaus. Companies can submit address lists to these bureaus for correction of their mailing lists.

The bottom line is that this piecemeal approach to privacy means that it is difficult for consumers to determine their rights and for businesses to identify their responsibilities. Consequently, except for the few specific limitations (e.g., credit and educational records, most businesses are free to collect and share informa-

tion). On the other hand, you can improve relationships with customers by always asking them for permission to use and share personal data.

## INFORMATION ERA CRIMES

As commerce moves to digital form, existing crime laws need to be extended and new ones need to be created. The biggest concerns are fraud, theft, and destruction of property. To understand the complications, consider what happens if someone steals your car. Why is that bad? Largely because you no longer have the use of the car. Now, what if someone steals your company's marketing plan? Why is that bad? You still have the use of the plan. Similarly, what if someone deleted your computerized customer database? Assuming that you are smart enough to keep a backup, what have you lost? The point of these questions is to show you that our traditional views on crime may not apply to crime-related information. Additionally, computers create the prospect of new types of crime. For instance, what happens if someone writes a program that prevents you from obtaining access to your financial records? The alleged criminal did not steal or destroy anything, so what crime has been committed?

The Computer Fraud and Abuse Act of 1986 provides answers to many of the questions regarding crime in the digital realm. In particular, it outlaws (1) access to computers without authorization, (2) damage to computers, networks, data, and so on, (3) actions that lead to denial of service, and (4) interference with medical care. Interestingly, the act charged the U.S. Secret Service with enforcement.

Enforcement of the act has been challenging. It has been difficult to find qualified law enforcement personnel, including prosecutors. Additionally, many businesses are reluctant to prosecute cases because they do not want competitors or shareholders to learn the details. On the other hand, sometimes companies and the Secret Service are too enthusiastic in their pursuit of alleged criminals. For example, one of the first cases supported by the Electronic Frontier Foundation (EFF) involved a BBS that supplied a document obtained from the telephone company that detailed information about the 911 system. The phone company complained that the document was stolen and that hackers might use it to break into its system. The Secret Service confiscated the BBS computer equipment and arrested the teenage owner. In court, with the help of the EFF, it was shown the document could be purchased from the phone company for a few dollars.

If we examine crime historically, we see the same problems in preventing more traditional crime and enforcing the laws. In the United States, it was the introduction of the FBI and their professional investigative techniques that improved the detection and enforcement of various crimes. In the digital arena, until we gain more experience and improve training of police, attorneys, and judges, we will face the same problems of weak laws, difficulty in prosecution, and variable enforcement.

## ONLINE RESOURCES

http://fedlaw.gsa.gov/
Good overall links, but too much reliance on outside providers.

http://law.house.gov/
Searchable listings of the U.S. Code and Code of Federal Regulations.

http://www.lawcircle.com/observer/
Professional commentary on various issues in computer law.

http://lcweb.loc.gov/copyright/
U.S. copyright office.

http://www.uspto.gov/
U.S. patent office.

http://www.copyright.com/
U.S. copyright clearinghouse. You can pay here to make legal copies of documents for distribution within your company or school.

http://www.eff.org/
The Electronic Frontier Foundation. A private organization to influence legislation related to computers. Largely created by Mitch Kapor who founded Lotus.

http://www.epic.org/
Electronic privacy information center.

http://www.uspto.gov/web/offices/com/doc/ipnii/
The IITF white paper and proposal for copyright law modifications.

http://www.wired.com
The Copyright Grab, Pamela Samuelson, issue 4(1). A lawyers' perspective on the IITF white paper.

## EXERCISES

1. Explain what you would do if your employer asks you to use illegally copied software.
2. What laws does your state have that apply specifically to computer-related crimes?
3. You downloaded some data from a federal agency. Is it legal to sell that data as part of a software package you wrote?
4. How should U.S. police forces prepare for a probable increase in computer crimes?
5. Should new privacy laws be enacted to handle Internet and Web data? What aspects should they cover?

# *Glossary*

**10Base-T:** A system of connecting computers on a LAN using twisted-pair cable. The method relies on compression to increase raw transfer rates to 10 megabits per second.

**Access speed:** A measure of disk drive speed. Loosely, the time it takes a disk drive to move to a particular piece of data.

**Accounting journal:** Raw financial transaction data are collected by the accounting department and stored in a journal. Modern accounting requires the use of a double-entry system to ensure accurate data.

**Activity-based costing (ABC):** ABC allocates costs by examining a detailed breakdown of the production activities. The cost of each process is computed for each different product. The detail provides a better picture of the production cost for each item.

**Advocacy role:** Someone in MIS, usually the chief information officer, who bears responsibility for exploring and presenting new applications and uses of MIS within the company.

**Agent:** An object-oriented program designed for networks that is written to perform specific tasks in response to user requests. Agents are designed to automatically communicate with other agents to search for data and make decisions.

**American National Standards Institute (ANSI):** An organization responsible for defining many standards, including several useful information technology standards.

**American Standard Code for Information Interchange (ASCII):** A common method of numbering characters so they can be processed. For instance, the letter *A* is number 65. It is slowly being replaced by the ANSI character set table and the use of international code pages that can display foreign characters.

**Antitrust laws:** A variety of laws that make it illegal to use monopoly power. Some basic (economic) actions to achieve a competitive advantage are illegal. Strategic plans must be evaluated carefully to avoid violating these laws.

**Artificial intelligence (AI):** An attempt to build machines that can think like humans. Techniques evolved from this research help solve more complex problems. Useful techniques include expert systems, neural networks, massively parallel computers, and robotics.

**Assumptions:** Models are simplifications of real life, so they require assumptions about various events or conditions.

**Asynchronous Transfer Mode (ATM):** A packet-based network system that uses high-speed transmission lines (150 megabits and over) and routers to maximize network efficiency and throughput.

**Attributes:** Descriptions of an object or entity. For example, a customer object would at least have attributes for name, phone number, and address.

**Audit trail:** The ability to trace any transaction back to its source. In accounting, transaction values are accumulated on the general ledger and used to create reports. An audit trail is a set of marks or records to point back to the original transaction.

**Authentication:** The ability to verify the source of a message. Dual-key systems are a useful technique. The sender uses a private key to encrypt the message. The recipient applies the sender's public key. If the decrypted message is readable, it had to have come from the alleged sender, because the keys always work in pairs.

**Backbone:** A high-speed communication line that links multiple subnetworks. It is usually a fiber-optic line.

**Backward chaining:** In an expert system, the user enters a "conclusion" and asks to see whether the rules support that conclusion.

**Barriers to entry:** Anything that makes it more difficult for new firms to enter an industry. Several possibilities would violate antitrust laws. An acceptable barrier is the increased use of information systems, which raises the cost of entering an industry because a rival would have to spend additional money on information technology.

**Beginners All-purpose Symbolic Instruction Code (BASIC):** An early computer programming language designed to be easy to program and to teach. Visual Basic is a current version for Windows programming.

**Benchmark:** A set of routines or actions used to evaluate computer performance. By performing the same basic tasks on several machines, you can compare their relative speeds. Benchmarks are especially useful when the machines use different processors and different input and output devices.

**Binary data:** A collection of ones and zeros called bits. Computer processors operate only on binary data. All data forms are first converted to binary.

**Biometrics:** A field of study that is trying to determine how to identify people based on biological characteristics. The most common devices are fingerprint and handprint readers.

**Bit:** The smallest unit of data in a computer. All data is converted to bits or binary data. Each bit can be in one of two states: on or off. Bits are generally aggregated into collections called a byte.

**Bitmap:** A method of storing images. The picture is converted to individual dots that are stored as bits. Once a picture is stored in bitmap form, it is difficult to resize. However, bitmaps are good for displaying photographic images with subtle color shading.

**Board of directors:** A group of people paid to oversee and evaluate the decisions of the company. Technically the CEO reports to the board of directors, but they are charged more with reviewing the CEO's decisions. Most boards have the authority to remove a CEO, but many board members are selected by the CEO.

**Boolean search:** Searching for data by using the logic operators AND, OR, and NOT conditions in a WHERE statement, for example, find a list of customers where city = "Detroit" and age > 50 and do not own a car.

**Bottom-up development:** An approach to designing and building systems in which workers build system components to solve each problem as it arises. Eventually the pieces are combined to create an integrated system. The method relies on standards and controls to facilitate cooperation and integration. *See also* Top-down development.

**Brainstorming:** A group technique in which each individual is asked to come up with possible suggestions to a problem. Any ideas are useful, regardless of how wild they are. Even fanciful ideas could stimulate someone else to improve it or to explore a related area.

**Broadcasts:** A technique of transmitting messages using radio, micro, or infrared waves. Broadcast messages are sent to all devices in a certain area. Others in the vicinity can also receive the messages.

**Browser:** A software tool that converts World Wide Web data into a graphical page with hypertext links. Using standard (HTML) commands, companies can offer data and additional links to users. Users simply click on individual words and pictures to retrieve additional data and move to other network sites.

**Bulletin board system (BBS):** Similar to a typical bulletin board, except that people access it from computers. The BBS enables users to store comments, pictures, and files for other people to retrieve. Bulletin boards are usually organized by topics and can be searched for specific phrases or comments. They are a useful way to disseminate information that is of interest to many different people.

**Bus:** Most computers have special slots called a bus to provide high-speed connections to other devices. Various manufacturers make boards that fit into these slots. The processor can exchange data with these other devices, but performance is sometimes constrained by the design of the bus.

**Bus network:** A network organizing scheme in which each computer is attached to a common transmission medium. Protocols are needed to determine when a machine can transmit and to recover from collisions.

**Byte:** A collection of bits. Traditionally, 8 bits make up one byte. From binary arithmetic, an 8-bit byte can hold 2 to the 8th power, or 256, possible numbers. In many systems a byte is used to hold one character.

**C:** A powerful programming language that is flexible and creates efficient code. A language commonly used to build complex applications, and to create commercial software products.

**C++:** An object-oriented extension of the C programming language. It is commonly used to build commercial software. It produces efficient code and supports the development of reusable objects.

**Cable modem:** An Internet connection device that translates local area network protocols to turn over a television cable line. It can provide transmission speeds around 3 Mpbs. But the communication line is shared with other users.

**Cache:** A buffer between the processor and a slower device such as a printer, disk drive, or memory chips. The cache generally consists of high-speed memory. Data is transferred in bulk to the cache. It is then pulled out as it is needed, freeing up the processor to work on other jobs instead of waiting for the slower device to finish.

**Carrier-Sense, Multiple-Access/Collision Detection (CSMA/CD):** A communications protocol that determines how computers will behave on a shared-medium network. Ethernet protocols rely on CSMA/CD. Other alternatives are Token Ring and packet switching.

**Case-based reasoning:** An expert system approach that records information in the form of situations and cases. Users search for cases similar to their current problem and adapt the original solution.

**CD-ROM:** Compact disk-read only memory. Data is stored and retrieved with a laser. A special machine is required to create data on a CD-ROM. Used to hold data that does not change very often. Useful for multimedia applications because a disk can hold about 650 megabytes of data. The format used to store music CDs.

**Centralization:** A business scheme for performing most operations and making management decisions from one location in an organization. MIS organization can be examined in four areas: hardware, software, data, and personnel. *See also* Decentralization.

**Change agents:** Objects or people who cause or facilitate changes. Sometimes the change agent might be a new employee who brings fresh ideas, other times change can be mandated by top-level management. Sometimes an outside event such as a competitor or a hurricane forces an organization to change.

**Change drivers:** Concepts or products that have altered the way businesses operate. Classic examples include: bar-code scanners in retail stores, handheld miniterminals or notebooks by delivery firms and salespeople, and reservation systems by travel and entertainment industries.

**Charge-back system:** A scheme for charging other internal departments for services. For example, some firms charge departments a fee based on how often they use the central computer. The goal was to ration a limited resource by avoiding free use.

**Chart of accounts:** A listing of all of the accounts and subaccounts in the general ledger. It must be defined ahead of time for each business.

**Chief executive officer (CEO):** The head of a company. The person ultimately responsible for setting the direction and policies of the firm. Usually the CEO is also the chairperson of the board of directors.

**Chief information officer (CIO):** The person who is in charge of the MIS organization within a firm, charged with overseeing operations, setting MIS priorities, and being a top-level advocate for MIS. Also develops and supports strategy for the firm.

**Circular reference:** In a spreadsheet, a set of cells that eventually refer to each other. In the simplest example, cell A1 would use values stored in cell A2, but cell A2 uses the value stored in A1. This technique is sometimes used to create an iterative solution to a model.

**Classes:** Base descriptions of objects. Technically, classes describe generic attributes and methods. Objects are a specific instance of a class.

**Client-server network:** A network configuration in which a few machines are used as file servers and the others (clients) are independent workstations. Shared data is first sent to a file server where it can be examined or transferred by another client.

**Client-server organization:** A method of organizing the MIS function so that some operations are centralized while others are decentralized. The client-server model separates all of the components into two categories: servers or clients. The functions associated with the server tend to be centralized, whereas the client components and tasks are dispersed among the users.

**Clip art:** Artwork created and sold to be used by nonartists. Hundreds of collections are available of people, places, buildings, and other objects. Clip art images are often used to create presentations and illustrate reports.

**Clipboard:** The method used to transfer data between software packages in windows-oriented operating environments. All objects that are cut or copied are placed onto the clipboard, ready to be pasted to another location or another package. Clipboard viewers exist to show the current contents of the clipboard. Some software systems allow a clipboard to hold several cuttings. Many automatically delete the older cuts— keeping only the most recent.

**Clipper chip:** An encryption method created by the U.S. top-secret National Security Agency (NSA). It uses a secret algorithm to encrypt and decrypt digital messages. It was particularly designed for digital voice communication. Its key feature is the use of two escrow keys assigned to each chip. If the police decide they want to listen to a conversation between two suspects, they can get a court order, collect the escrow keys and instantly decrypt the call.

**Closed loop:** A system or piece of computer code in which every step in a control mechanism is contained inside the system, and does not utilize external input. *See also* Feedback.

**Closed system:** A system that is entirely self-contained and does not respond to changes in the environment. Most closed systems eventually fail due to entropy.

**Coaxial cable:** A cable used to transmit data. Cable television is a widespread application. The inner cable is surrounded by a plastic insulator, which is surrounded by a wire mesh conductor and an outer casing. The wire mesh insulates the internal signal wire from external interference.

**Cold site:** A facility that can be leased from a disaster backup specialist. A cold site contains power and telecommunication lines but no computer. In the event of a disaster, a company calls the computer vendor and begs for the first available machine to be sent to the cold site.

**Collision:** In networks, a collision arises when two computers attempt to broadcast messages at the same time. The network protocols need to identify the situation and determine which machine will go first.

**Column:** A vertical part of a table that holds data for one attribute of an entity in a database or spreadsheet. For example, a table to describe automobiles will have columns for make, model, and color.

**Command-line interface:** A method of controlling the computer by typing commands. The user must generally memorize specific commands. Older machines still use them because GUI systems require too much overhead. Some people prefer command lines, because it is faster to type one or two commands than to manipulate an image on the screen.

**Common Business-Oriented Language (COBOL):** An early programming language designed to handle typical transaction processing tasks. Its death has been predicted for years, but it is hard to throw away billions of lines of code.

**Common Object Request Broker Architecture (CORBA):** A model largely developed in the UNIX community that will enable objects to communicate with each other across networks. In particular, it is designed to enable users to combine different data types from various software vendors into a single compound document. The data could reside on any server on the network.

**Competitive advantage:** Something that makes your company better or stronger than your rivals. Examples include lower costs, higher quality, strong ties to loyal customers, and control over distribution channels.

**Compound document:** A document that incorporates different types of data: text, graphics, sound, and video. The different objects might be transmitted across a network to be included in a final document.

**Computer-aided design (CAD):** Programs that are used to create engineering drawings. CAD programs make it easy to modify drawings. They also make it easier to keep track of material specifications. They can perform spatial and engineering estimates on the designs, such as surface or volume calculations.

**Computer-aided software engineering (CASE):** Computer programs that are designed to support the analysis and development of computer systems. They make it easier to create, store, and share diagrams and data definitions. Some versions even generate code. There are two categories of CASE tools: software development and maintenance of existing systems.

**Computer ethics:** The concept that all of us have an obligation with respect to data. For example, managers have a responsibility to customers to protect personal data, to collect only data that is truly needed, and to give customers the ability to correct errors in personal data.

**Computer information system (CIS):** *See* Management information system (MIS).

**Computer-integrated manufacturing (CIM):** Using a computer to control most of the production equipment in a manufacturing environment. The computer can monitor the production statistics. It is also used to set individual machine controls.

**Concatenated key:** In relational databases, a key that consists of more than one column. The columns are combined to yield a unique primary key.

**Concurrency:** A situation that arises when applications attempt to modify the same piece of data at the same time. If two people are allowed to make changes to the same piece of data, the computer system must control the order in which it processes the two requests. Mixing the two tasks will result in the wrong data being stored in the computer.

**Context diagram:** The top level of a data flow diagram that acts as a title page and displays the boundaries of the system and displays the external entities that interact with the system.

**Converge:** The ability of an iterative model to stabilize on a fixed solution. The alternative is that values continually increase and never reach a solution.

**Critical success factors:** A limited number of concrete goals that must be met for the organization to be successful. Identifying these key factors helps determine the strategic directions and highlights the areas that can benefit from improved information systems.

**Cut, copy, paste:** A common mechanism used to transfer and link data between different software packages. The data to be transferred is marked. When it is cut or copied, it is placed on the clipboard. Switching to the second package, the object is pasted into the appropriate location. Dynamic and static links are specified through options in the "paste special" menu. With the cut option, the original object is deleted. With copy, the original is unchanged.

**Data:** Data consists of factual elements (or opinions or comments) that describe some object or event. Data can be thought of as raw numbers.

**Data administrator:** MIS manager who is charged with overseeing all of the data definitions and data standards for the company to ensure that applications can share data throughout the company.

**Data dictionary:** Contains all of the information to explain the terms used to define a system. Often includes report descriptions, business rules, and security considerations.

**Data encryption standard (DES):** An older method of encrypting data that was commonly used by financial institutions. With current computer capabilities that can break a DES-encrypted message, DES is no longer considered a secure encryption system.

**Data flow diagram (DFD):** A diagramming technique used to analyze and design systems. It shows how a system is divided into subsystems and highlights the flow of data between the processes and subsystems. It displays processes, external entities, files, data flows, and control flows.

**Data independence:** Separating programs from their data definition and storage. The main advantage is that it is possible to change the data without having to change the programs.

**Data integrity:** (1) A concept that implies data is as accurate as possible. It means the database contains few errors. (2) Keeping data accurate and correct as it is gathered and stored in the computer system.

**Data store:** A file or place where data is stored. In a realistic setting, a data store could be a computer file, file cabinet, or even a reference book.

**Data types:** To humans, there are four basic types of data: text and numbers, images, sound, and video. Each data type must be converted to binary form for computer processing.

**Data warehouse:** A single consolidation point for enterprise data from diverse production systems. The data is typically stored in one large file server or a central computer. Because legacy systems are difficult to replace, some data is copied into a data warehouse, where it is available for management queries and analysis.

**Database:** A collection of related data that can be retrieved easily and processed by computers. A collection of data tables.

**Database administrator (DBA):** (1) A person appointed to manage the databases for the firm. The DBA needs to know the technical details of the DBMS and the computer system. The DBA also needs to understand the business operations of the firm. (2) A management person in the MIS department charged with defining and maintaining the corporate databases. Maintaining data integrity is a key component of the job.

**Database management system (DBMS):** Software that defines a database, stores the data, supports a query language, produces reports, and creates data-entry screens.

**Decentralization:** Moving the major operations and decisions out to lower levels within the firm. In MIS, decentralization has largely been led by the declining cost and improved capabilities of personal computers. *See also* Centralization.

**Decision biases:** Without models and careful analysis, decisions made by people tend to be biased. There are several biases in each of the four systems categories: data acquisition, processing, output, and feedback.

**Decision support system (DSS):** Systems to use data collected by transaction processing systems to evaluate business models and assist managers to make tactical decisions. They have three major components: data collection, analysis of models, and presentation.

**Decision tree:** A graphical representation of logic rules. Each possible answer to a question or situation leads to a new branch of the tree.

**Default value:** A value that is automatically displayed by the computer. Users can often override the default by deleting the old value and entering a new one. The goal is to choose a value that will almost always be entered, so the user can skip that item.

**Dehumanization:** Some people feel that technology isolates people and decreases our contact with other members of society. Treating people as identification numbers and summary statistics can lead managers to forget the human consequences of their decisions.

**Descriptive model:** A model that is defined in words and perhaps pictures. Relationships between objects and variables tend to be subjective. Useful for an initial understanding of a system but difficult to evaluate by computer.

**Desktop Publishing (DTP):** The art of creating professional documents with personal computers and small laser printers. Beyond basic word processing, DTP software provides controls to standardize pages, improve the page layout, and establish styles.

**Detail section:** The section in a report that is repeated for every row in the associated tables. It is often used for itemized values, whereas group and page footers are used for subtotals.

**Diagnostic situations:** Spotting problems, searching for the cause, and implementing corrections. Examples include responding to exception reports to identify problems and potential solutions, and determining why the latest marketing approach did not perform as well as expected.

**Dial-back modem:** A special modem placed on a central computer. When a user attempts to log in, the dial-back modem breaks the connection and calls back a predefined phone number. Its use minimizes the threat of outsiders gaining access to the central computer.

**Digital cash:** An electronic version of money that is provided and verified by a trusted third party. It consists of an encrypted number for a specified value that can only be used one time. It provides for verifiable and anonymous purchases using networks.

**Digital subscriber line (DSL):** A special phone service connection available to customers within 3 miles of the phone company's switch. It provides about 1 Mbps transmission speed for Internet connections.

**Digital video disk (DVD):** A digital format primarily used for storing video and movies. However, it can also hold audio and traditional computer data. One side of the disk can hold over 3 gigabytes of data.

**Distribution channel:** Products are rarely distributed directly from the manufacturer to the final customer. There are layers of distributors in between. If a producer can gain control over this means of getting the product to consumers, the producer can prevent new rivals from entering the industry. Improved communication systems offer the possibility of eroding control over some distribution channels.

**Diverge:** The property of an iterative model where successive computations keep leading to larger values (in magnitude). The model never reaches a stable solution. Generally due to insufficient or incorrect feedback mechanisms.

**Documentation:** Descriptions of a system, its components, the data, and records of changes made to the system.

**Domain name server (DNS):** A computer on the Internet that converts mnemonic names into numeric Internet addresses. The names are easier for humans to remember, but the computers rely on the numeric addresses.

**Download:** To transfer files from a remote computer to a local computer (usually a personal computer). *See also* Upload.

**Drill down:** To use an information system to get increasingly detailed data about a company. In an enterprise information system, the ability to look at overall company data, then select breakdowns by regions, departments, or smaller levels.

**Dual-key encryption:** A method of encrypting a message that requires two keys: one to encrypt and one to decrypt. One of the keys is a public key that is available to anyone. The other key is private and must never be revealed to other people. RSA is a popular dual-key encryption system. Dual-key systems can also be used to authenticate the users.

**Dynamic data exchange:** An early method of linking data from multiple sources with the Windows operating system. The software packages literally send messages to other software packages, which enables them to combine and update data. *See also* dynamic integration and Object Linking and Embedding (OLE).

**Dynamic integration:** A means of linking data from multiple documents. One compound document (or container) can hold data objects created by other software. As the original data is changed, it is automatically updated in the container document. *See also* Static integration.

**E-mail:** Electronic mail, or messages that are transmitted from one computer user to another. Networks transfer messages between the computers. Users can send or retrieve messages at any time. The computer holds the message until the recipient checks in.

**EBCDIC:** Extended Binary Coded Decimal Interchange Code. A method of numbering characters so they can be processed by machines. Used exclusively by large IBM and compatible computers. *See also* ASCII.

**Electronic data interchange (EDI):** Exchanging transaction data with entities outside the control of your firm. Private connections can be established directly between two firms. Public networks are also being formed where one provider collects data and routes it to the appropriate client.

**Encryption:** A method of modifying the original information according to some code, so that it can only be read if the user knows the decryption key. It is used to safely transmit data between computers.

**End-user development:** Managers and workers are to develop their own small systems using database management systems, spreadsheets, and other high-level tools.

**Enterprise network:** A network that connects multiple subnetworks across an entire firm. Often, the networks use different protocols and different computer types, which complicates transmitting messages.

**Enterprise Resource Planning (ERP):** An integrated computer system running on top of a DBMS. It is designed to collect and organize data from all operations in an organization. Existing systems are strong in accounting, purchasing, and HRM.

**Ergonomics:** The study of how machines can be made to fit humans better. One of the main conclusions of this research in the computer area is that individuals need to be able to adjust input (and output) devices to their own preferences.

**Escrow key:** In an encryption system, it is a special key that can be used by government officials to decrypt a secret conversation. The Clipper chip uses escrow keys.

**Ethernet:** A network communications protocol that specifies how machines will exchange data. It uses a broadcast system in which one machine transmits its message on the communication medium. The other machines listen for messages directed to them.

**Event-driven approach:** (1) A user-interface approach where the user controls the sequence or operations and the software responds to these events. Events can range from a simple key-press to a voice command. (2) Modern, window-based software does not follow a sequential process. Instead, actions by users generate events. The programs respond to these events and alter data or offer additional choices. Typical events include mouse clicks pointing to items on the screen, keystrokes, changes to values, or transmissions from other systems.

**Exception report:** Report that is triggered by some event to signify a condition that is unusual and needs to be handled immediately.

**Executive information system (EIS):** A type of decision support system that collects, analyzes, and presents data in a format that is easy to use by top executives. To achieve this objective, the EIS is based on a model of the entire company. In most cases the model is presented graphically and the executives retrieve information by pointing to objects on the screen.

**Exhaustive testing:** Testing every possible combination of inputs to search for errors. Generally not a feasible option, so most computer systems will always contain errors.

**Expert system (ES):** The goal of an expert system is to help a novice achieve the same results as an expert. They can handle ill-structured and missing data. Current expert systems can only be applied to narrowly defined problems. Diagnostic problems are common applications for expert systems.

**Expert system shell:** A program that provides a way to collect data, enter rules, talk to users, present results, and evaluate the rules for an expert system.

**Export:** An older method of exchanging data among various software packages. One package exports the data by storing it in a format that can be read by other software. Object Linking and Embedding is a more powerful way to exchange data.

**External agents:** Entities that are outside the direct control of your company. Typical external agents are customers, suppliers, rivals, and governments. Competitive advantages can be found by producing better-quality items or services at a lower cost than your rivals. Also, many firms have strengthened their positions by building closer ties with their suppliers and customers.

**External entity:** Objects outside the boundary of a system that communicate with the system. Common business examples include suppliers, customers, government agencies, and management.

**Facsimile (Fax):** A combination scanner, transmitter, and receiver that digitizes an image, compresses it, and transmits it over phone lines to another facsimile machine.

**Fault-tolerant computer:** A computer or a system that is designed to continue functioning properly even if some of the components fail. Fault-tolerant machines rely on duplication of subsystems with continuous monitoring and automatic maintenance calls.

**Feasibility study:** A quick examination of the problems, goals, and expected costs of a proposed system. The objective is to determine whether the problem can reasonably be solved with a computer system.

**Feedback:** Well-designed systems have controls that monitor how well they meet their goal. The information measuring the goals and providing control to the system is known as feedback.

**Fiber-optic cable:** A thin glass or plastic cable that is internally reflective. It carries a light wave for extended distances and around corners.

**File server:** Computer on a network that is used to hold data and program files for users to share. To be effective, it should use a multitasking operating system.

**File Transfer Protocol (FTP):** A standard method of transferring files on the Internet. If you control a computer, you can give other users access to specific files on your computer without having to provide an account and password for every possible user.

**Five forces model:** Michael Porter's model used to search for competitive advantage. The five forces are: rivals, customers, suppliers, potential competitors, and substitute products.

**Flow chart:** An old pictorial method for describing the logic of a computer program. It has largely been replaced by pseudocode.

**Font size:** An important characteristic of text is its size. Size of type is typically measured in points. For reference, a capital letter in a 72-point font will be approximately 1 inch high.

**Forward chaining:** In an expert system, the ES traces your rules from the data entry to a recommendation. Forward chaining is used to display questions, perform calculations, and apply rules.

**Frame:** A related set of information that humans group together. Sometimes groupings can be arbitrary. A concept used in discussing AI applications and human cognition.

**Frame relay:** A network communication system that uses variable-length packets. It is useful for high-speed, large bursts of data. It is being used for long-distance network communications.

**Franchise:** A means of organizing companies. Independent operators pay a franchise fee to use the company name. They receive training and benefit from the name and advertising of the parent company. They purchase supplies from the parent company and follow the franchise rules.

**Front-end processor:** A simple communications device for large central computers that accepted all of the terminal wires and then assigned each user to an open communications port on the computer. This device decreased the number of physical access ports required on the computer.

**Functions:** *See* Methods.

**Fuzzy logic:** A way of presenting and analyzing logic problems that is designed to handle subjective descriptions (e.g., hot and cold).

**General ledger:** A collection of accounts that break financial data into specific categories. Common categories include accounts receivable, accounts payable, inventory, and cash.

**Geographic information system (GIS):** Designed to identify and display relationships among business data and locations. Used to display geographical relationships. Also used to plot delivery routes and create maps.

**Gigabyte:** Approximately 1 billion bytes of data. Technically, 1,024 to the third power (or 2 to the thirtieth), which is 1,073,741,824. The next highest increment is the terabyte.

**Global positioning system (GPS):** A system of 24 satellites created by the U.S. Department of Defense. The civilian receivers will identify a location to within about 50 feet. Used for navigation, tracking vehicles, and plotting delivery routes.

**Graphical User Interface (GUI):** A GUI system is based on a graphics screen instead of simple text, and users perform tasks by clicking a mouse button on or manipulating objects on the screen. For example, copies are made by dragging an item from one location on the screen to another. Pronounced as "gooey."

**Group breaks:** Reports are often broken into subsections so that data in each section is grouped together by some common feature. For example, a sales report might group items by department, with subtotals for each department.

**Group decision support system (GDSS):** A type of groupware that is designed to facilitate meetings and help groups reach a decision. Each participant uses a networked computer to enter ideas and comments. Votes can be recorded and analyzed instantly. Comments and discussion are automatically saved for further study.

**Groupware:** Software designed to assist teams of workers. There are four basic types: communication, workflow, meeting, and scheduling. The most common is communication software that supports messages, bulletin boards, and data file transfers and sharing.

**Hacker:** Primarily used to indicate a person who devotes a great deal of time trying to break into computer systems.

**Hardware:** Hardware consists of the physical equipment used in computing.

**High-Definition Television (HDTV):** Transmission of television signals in digital form. It provides clearer reception. It also supports encrypted transmissions so broadcasters can control who receives the images. HDTV also supports compression, so more data (better pictures or more channels) can be transmitted in the same frequency space.

**Hot links:** *See* Dynamic integration.

**Hot site:** A facility that can be leased from a disaster backup specialist. A hot site contains all the power, telecommunication facilities, and computers necessary to run a company. In the event of a disaster, a company collects its backup data tapes, notifies workers, and moves operations to the hot site.

**Hub:** A network device used to connect several computers to a network. Commonly used in a twisted-pair LAN. A cable runs from each computer's NIC to the hub. The hub is often connected to a router.

**Hypertext markup language (HTML):** The standard formatting system used to display pages on the Internet. Special tags (commands inside angle braces, e.g., <HTML>) provide formatting capabilities. Several software packages automatically store text in this format, so users do not have to memorize the tags.

**Icon:** A small picture on a computer screen that is used to represent some object or indicate a command. A classic example is the trash can used to delete files on the Apple Macintosh.

**Image:** A graphic representation that can be described by its resolution and the number of colors. They can be stored as bit-mapped or vector images.

**Import:** An older method of exchanging data among various software packages. Most software (e.g., a database management system) can export or store data in a text file format. Another software package (e.g., a spreadsheet) can import or retrieve this data. Object Linking and Embedding is a more powerful way to exchange data.

**Inference engine:** Within an expert system, the inference engine applies new observations to the knowledge base and analyzes the rules to reach a conclusion.

**Information:** Information represents data that has been processed, organized, and integrated to provide insight. The distinction between data and information is that information carries meaning and is used to make decisions.

**Information center:** An MIS group responsible for supporting end users. It typically provides a help desk to answer questions, programmers who provide access to corporate databases, training classes, and network support people to install and maintain networks.

**Information system:** A collection of hardware, software, data, and people designed to collect, process, and distribute data throughout an organization.

**Information threats:** There are two classes of threats to information: (1) physical, in the form of disasters; and (2) logical, which consists of unauthorized disclosure, unauthorized modification, and unauthorized withholding of data. The primary source of danger lies with insiders: employees, ex-employees, partners, or consultants.

**Inheritance:** Classes of objects are created or derived from other object classes. Each derived class inherits the attributes and methods of the prior class. For example, a savings account object can be derived from an account object. The savings account object will automatically have the same attributes and methods. Attributes and methods specific to the savings account can be added.

**Input devices:** People do not deal very well with binary data, so all data forms must be converted into binary form for the computer. Input devices—for example, keyboards, microphones, and bar-code readers—make the conversion.

**Input-Process-Output:** A shorthand description of a subsystem. Each subsystem receives inputs and performs some process. The output is passed to another subsystem.

**Integrated data:** The practice of combining data from many sources to make a decision. Data can come from different departments throughout the business, and it can come in many different forms. Networks, groupware, and products that support dynamic linking are all useful tools to integrate data to make better decisions.

**Integrated Services Digital Network (ISDN):** A set of services, and a transmission and control system, offered by telephone companies. It uses complete digital transmission of signals to improve transmission speed and quality.

**Internet:** A collection of computers loosely connected to exchange information worldwide. Owners of the computers make files and information available to other users. Common tools on the Internet include e-mail, ftp, telnet, and the World Wide Web.

**Internet service provider (ISP):** A private company that provides connections to the Internet. Individuals pay a fee to the ISP. The ISP pays a fee to a higher-level provider (e.g., NSP) to pass all communications onto the Internet.

**Intranet:** A network within an organization that utilizes standard Internet protocols and services. Essentially, this includes web sites that are accessible only for internal use.

**Iterative solution:** Building a model and evaluating it until the parameter values converge to a fixed solution. Sometimes an iterative model will diverge and never reach an acceptable solution. *See also* Circular reference.

**Joint application design (JAD):** A method to reduce design time by putting everyone in development sessions until the system is designed. Users, managers, and systems analysts participate in a series of intense meetings to design the inputs (data and screens), and outputs (reports) needed by the new system.

**Just-in-time (JIT) inventory:** A production system that relies on suppliers delivering components just as they are needed in production, instead of relying on inventory stocks. JIT requires close communication between manufacturers and suppliers.

**Kilobyte:** Approximately one thousand bytes of data. Technically it is 2 to the tenth, or 1,024.

**Knowledge:** Knowledge represents a higher level of understanding, including rules, patterns, and decisions. Knowledge-based systems are built to automatically analyze data, identify patterns, and recommend decisions.

**Knowledge base:** Within an expert system, the knowledge base consists of basic data and a set of rules.

**Knowledge engineer:** A person who helps build an expert system by organizing the data, devising the rules, and entering the criteria into the expert system shell. Trained to deal with experts to derive the rules needed to create an expert system. The engineer also converts the data and rules into the format needed by the expert system.

**Legacy systems:** Information systems that were created over several years and are now crucial to operating the company. They probably use older technology, and the software is difficult to modify. However, replacing them is difficult and likely to interfere with day-to-day operations. Any changes or new systems must be able to work with the older components.

**Local area network (LAN):** A collection of personal computers within a small geographical area, connected by a network. All of the components are owned or controlled by one company.

**Magnetic hard drives:** Magnetic hard drives (or disk drives) consist of rigid platters that store data with magnetic particles. Data is accessed by spinning the platters and moving a drive head across the platters to access various tracks.

**Magnetic ink character recognition (MICR):** A special typeface printed with ink containing magnetic particles. It can be read rapidly and reliably by computers. Banks are the primary users of MICR. Checks are imprinted with MICR routing numbers. MICR readers are more accurate than straight OCR because they pick up a stronger signal from magnetic particles in the ink.

**Mail filters:** Programs that automatically read e-mail and sort the messages according to whatever criteria the manager prefers. Junk mail can be discarded automatically.

**Management information system (MIS):** An MIS consists of five related components: hardware, software, people, procedures, and databases. The goal of management information systems is to enable managers to make better decisions by providing quality information.

**Manufacturing Resource Planning (MRP II):** An integrated approach to manufacturing. Beginning with the desired production levels, we work backward to determine the processing time, materials, and labor needed at each step. These results generate schedules and inventory needs. Sometimes known as a demand-pull system.

**Mass customization:** The ability to modify the production line often enough to produce more variations of the main product. The goal is to cover virtually all of the niche markets.

**Materials requirements planning (MRP):** An early production system, where at each stage of production, we evaluate the usage of materials to determine the optimal inventory levels.

**Mathematical model:** A model that is defined by mathematical equations. This format is easy to use for forecasts and for simulation analyses on the computer. Be careful not to confuse precision with accuracy. A model might forecast some value with great precision (e.g., 15.9371), but the accuracy could be quite less (e.g., actual values between 12 and 18).

**Media:** For the means of transmissions, connecting computers in a network. Common methods include twisted-pair and coaxial cable; fiber-optic lines; and radio, micro, and infrared waves.

**Megabyte:** Loosely, 1 million bytes of data. Technically, it is 1,048,576 bytes of data, which is 2 raised to the 20th power.

**Megaflops:** Millions of floating-point operations per second. A measure of the processor speed, it counts the number of common arithmetical operations that can be performed in one second.

**Megahertz:** One million cycles per second, a measure of the clock chip in a computer, which establishes how fast a processor can operate.

**Menu tree:** A graphical depiction of the menu choices available to users in a system.

**Metadata:** Describes the source data, and the transformation and integration steps, and defines the way the database or data warehouse is organized.

**Methods:** Descriptions of actions that an object can perform. For example, an employee object could be hired, promoted, or released. Each of these functions would necessitate changes in the employee attributes and in other objects. The methods carry out these changes.

**Microsecond:** One-millionth of a second. Few computer components are measured in microseconds, but some electrical devices and controllers operate in that range. One microsecond compared to one second is the same as comparing one second to 11.6 days.

**Million instructions per second (MIPS):** A measure of computer processor speed. Higher numbers represent a faster processor. However, different brands of processors use different instruction sets, so numbers are not always comparable.

**Millisecond:** One-thousandth of a second. Disk drives and some other input and output devices perform operations measured in milliseconds. One millisecond compared to one second is the same as comparing 1 second to 16.7 minutes.

**Mirror drive:** A backup system where data is automatically written to a second disk drive. If the primary drive fails, operations can be switched instantaneously to the mirror drive.

**Model:** A simplified, abstract representation of some real-world system. Some models can be written as mathematical equations or graphs, others are subjective descriptions. Models help managers visualize physical objects and business processes. Information systems help you build models, evaluate them, and organize and display the output.

**Modem:** Modulator-demodulator. A device that converts computer signals into sounds that can be transmitted (and received) across phone lines.

**Morphing:** Digital conversion of one image into another. The term is an abbreviation of *metamorphosis*. True morphing is done with digital video sequences, where the computer modifies each frame until the image converts to a new form.

**Multimedia:** The combination of the four basic data types: text, sound, video, and images (animation). In its broadest definition, multimedia encompasses virtually any combination of data types. Today, it typically refers to the use of sound, text, and video clips in digitized form that are controlled by the computer user.

**Multitasking:** A feature of operating systems that enables you to run more than one task or application at the same time. Technically, they do not run at exactly the same time. The processor divides its time and works on several tasks at once.

**Musical Instrument Data Interchange (MIDI):** A collection of standards that define how musical instruments communicate with each other. Sounds are stored by musical notation and are re-created by synthesizers that play the notes.

**Nanosecond:** One-billionth of a second. Computer processors and memory chips operate at times measured in nanoseconds. One nanosecond compared to 1 second is the same as comparing 1 second to 31.7 years.

**Natural language:** A human language used for communication with other humans, as opposed to a computer programming language or some other artificial language created for limited communication.

**Network interface card (NIC):** The communication card that plugs into a computer and attaches to the network communication medium. It translates computer commands into network messages and server commands.

**Network operating system (NOS):** A special operating system installed on a file server, with portions loaded to the client machines. It enables the machines to communicate and share files.

**Network service provider (NSP):** A high-level Internet service provider offering connections to ISPs. The NSP leases high-speed, high-capacity lines to handle the communication traffic from hundreds of ISPs.

**Neural network:** A collection of artificial neurons loosely designed to mimic the way the human brain operates. Especially useful for tasks that involve pattern recognition.

**Neuron:** The fundamental cell of human brains and nerves. Each of these cells is relatively simple, but there are approximately 100 million of them.

**News groups:** A set of electronic bulletin boards available on the Internet. Postings are continuously circulated around the network as people add comments.

**Normalization:** A set of rules for creating tables in a relational database. The primary rules are that there can be no repeating elements and every nonkey column must depend on the whole key and nothing but the key. Roughly, it means that each table should refer to only one object or concept.

**Numbers:** One of the basic data types, similar to text on input and output. Attributes include precision and a scaling factor that defines the true size or dimension of the number.

**Object:** A software description of some entity. It consists of attributes that describe the object, and functions (or methods) that describe the actions that can be taken by the object. Objects are generally related to other objects through an object hierarchy.

**Object hierarchy:** Objects are defined from other base objects. The new objects inherit the properties and functions of the prior objects.

**Object Linking and Embedding (OLE):** A standard created by Microsoft for its Windows operating system to create compound documents and dynamically link data objects from multiple software packages. You begin with a compound document or container that holds data from other software packages. These data objects can be edited directly (embedded). Most OLE software also supports dynamic linking.

**Object orientation:** An approach to systems and programming that classifies data as various objects. Objects have attributes or properties that can be set by the programmer or by users. Objects also have methods or functions that define the actions they can take. Objects can be defined from other objects, so most are derived from the four basic data types.

**Object-oriented development:** The ultimate goal of the object-oriented approach is to build a set of reusable objects and procedures. The idea is that eventually, it should be possible to create new systems or modify old ones simply by plugging in a new module or modifying an existing object.

**One-to-many relationship:** Some object or task that can be repeated. For instance, a customer can place many orders. In database normalization, we search for one-to-many relationships and split them into two tables.

**Open operating system:** An operating system that is supposed to be vendor neutral. It should run on hardware from several different vendors. When a buyer upgrades to a new machine, the operating system and software should function the same as before.

**Open system:** An open system learns by altering itself as the environment changes.

**Operating system:** A basic collection of software that handles jobs common to all users and programmers. It is responsible for connecting the hardware devices, such as terminals, disk drives, and printers. It also provides the environment for other software, as well as the user interface that affects how people use the machine.

**Operations level:** Day-to-day operations and decisions. In a manufacturing firm, machine settings, worker schedules, and maintenance requirements would represent management decisions at the operations level. Information systems are used at this level to collect data and perform well-defined computations.

**Optical character recognition (OCR):** The ability to convert images of characters (bitmaps) into computer text that can be stored, searched, and edited. Software examines a picture and looks for text. The software checks each line, deciphers one character at a time, and stores the result as text.

**Optimization:** The use of models to search for the best solutions: minimizing costs, improving efficiency, or increasing profits.

**Output devices:** Data stored in binary form on the computer must be converted to a format people understand. Output devices—for example, display screens, printers, and synthesizers—make the conversion.

**Outsourcing:** The act of transferring ownership or management of MIS resources (hardware, software and personnel) to an outside MIS specialist.

**Packets:** Network messages are split into packets for transmission. Each packet contains a destination and source address as well as a portion of the message.

**Packet switching network:** A communications protocol in which each message is placed into smaller packets. These packets contain a destination and source address. The packets are switched (or routed) to the appropriate computer. With high-speed switches, this protocol offers speeds in excess of 150 megabits per second.

**Page footer:** Data that are placed at the bottom of each page in a report. Common items include page totals and page numbers.

**Page header:** Data that is placed at the top of every page in a report. Common items include the report title, date, and column labels.

**Parallel processing:** Using several processors in the same computer. Each processor can be assigned different tasks, or jobs can be split into separate pieces and given to each processor. There are a few massively parallel machines that utilize several thousand processors.

**Parameter:** Variables in a model that can be controlled or set by managers. They are used to examine different situations or to tailor the model to fit a specific problem.

**Peer-to-peer network:** A network configuration in which each machine is considered to be an equal. Messages and data are shared directly between individual computers. Each machine continuously operates as both a client and a server.

**Photo-CD:** A standardized system created by Kodak to convert photographs to digital (bitmap) form and store them on optical disks.

**Pivot table:** A tool within Microsoft Excel used to extract and organize data. It enables users to examine aggregated data and quickly see the accompanying detail.

**Pixel:** Picture element, or a single dot on an image or video screen.

**Point-of-sale (POS) system:** A means of collecting data immediately when items are sold. Cash registers are actually data terminals that look up prices and instantly transmit sales data to a central computer.

**Polymorphism:** In an object design, different objects can have methods that have the same name but operate slightly differently. For example, a checking account object and a savings account object could each have a method called pay interest. The checking account might

pay interest monthly, whereas the savings account pays it quarterly.

**Portable document format (PDF):** A file format often used on the Internet. It can display documents with detailed precision, including special fonts and shading. Defined by Adobe, readers are freely available for many machines. Special software must be purchased to create the files.

**Precision (numeric):** In computers, numeric precision represents the number of digits stored to the right of the decimal point. So, 10.1234 is more precise than 10.12, however, it is not necessarily more accurate. The original value might not have been measured beyond two digits.

**Prediction:** Model parameters can be estimated from prior data. Sample data is used to forecast future changes based on the model.

**Primary key:** A column or set of columns that contains data to uniquely identify each row in a relational database table. For example, each customer must have a unique identifier, possibly a phone number or an internally generated customer number.

**Privacy:** (1) The concept that people should be able to go about their lives without constant surveillance, that personal information about people should not be shared without their permission. (2) Collecting personal data only when you have a legitimate use for it, allowing customers to correct and remove personal data. Protecting confidential data so that it is not released to anyone. Giving customers to option so you do not sell or lease their personal data.

**Private key:** In a dual-key encryption system, the key that is protected by the owner and never revealed. It is generally a very large number.

**Problem boundary:** The line that identifies the primary components of the system that are creating a specific problem. Subsystems inside the boundary can be modified to solve the problem or enhance the system. Subsystems outside the boundary cannot be altered at this time.

**Procedures:** Procedures are instructions that help people use the systems. They include items such as user manuals, documentation, and procedures to ensure that backups are made regularly.

**Process:** An activity that is part of a data flow diagram. Systems can be built to process goods or to process data. Most information system work focuses on processes that alter data.

**Process control:** The use of computers to monitor and control the production machines and robots. Production lines generally use many different machines, each requiring several adjustments or settings. Computer control simplifies and speeds the setup.

**Process control system:** A computerized system that monitors and controls a production line. Some systems are completely linked so that a central computer can set up machines on an entire assembly line.

**Process innovation:** Evaluating the entire firm to improve individual processes, and to search for integrated solutions that will reduce costs, improve quality, or boost sales to gain a competitive advantage. *See also* Re-engineering.

**Processor:** The processor is the heart of a computer. It carries out the instructions of the operating system and the application programs.

**Product differentiation:** The ability to make your products appear different from those of your rivals, thus attracting more customers. Information systems have been used to alter products and provide new services.

**Properties:** *See* Attributes.

**Protocols:** A set of definitions and standards that establish the communication links on a network. Networks are often classified by their choice of protocol. Common protocols include Ethernet, Token Ring, and TCP/IP.

**Prototyping:** An iterative system design technique that takes advantage of high-level tools to rapidly create working systems. The main objective of prototyping is to create a working version of the system as quickly as possible, even if some components are not included in the early versions.

**Pseudocode:** A loosely structured method to describe the logic of a program or outline a system. It uses basic programming techniques but ignores issues of syntax and relies on verbal descriptions.

**Public key:** In a dual-key encryption system, the key that is given to the public. Each person wishing to use dual-key encryption must have a different public key. The key works only in tandem with the user's private key.

**Query by example (QBE):** A visual method of examining data stored in a relational database. You ask questions and examine the data by pointing to tables on the screen and filling in templates.

**Random access memory (RAM):** High-speed memory chips that hold data for immediate processing. On most computers, data held in RAM is lost when the power is removed, so data must be moved to secondary storage.

**Rapid application development (RAD):** The goal of building a system much faster than with traditional SDLC methods. Using powerful tools (database management system, high-level languages, graphical toolkits, and objects), highly trained programmers can build systems in a matter of weeks or months. Using workgroups,

communication networks, and CASE tools, small teams can speed up the development and design steps.

**Read Only Memory (ROM):** A type of memory on which data can be stored only one time. It can be read as often as needed but cannot be changed. ROM keeps its data when power is removed, so it is used to hold certain core programs and system data that is rarely changed.

**Reduced instruction set computer (RISC):** When designing a RISC processor, the manufacturer deliberately limits the number of circuits and instructions on the chip. The goal is to create a processor that performs a few simple tasks very fast. More complex problems are solved in software. Because RISC processors require fewer circuits, they are easier to produce.

**Redundant Array of Independent Disks (RAID):** Instead of containing one large drive, a RAID system consists of several smaller drives. Large files are split into pieces stored on several different physical drives. The data pieces can be duplicated and stored in more than one location for backup. RAID systems also provide faster access to the data, because each of the drives can be searching through their part of the file at the same time.

**Re-engineering:** A complete reorganization of a company. Beginning from scratch, you identify goals along with the most efficient means of attaining those goals, and create new processes that change the company to meet the new goals. The term *re-engineering* and its current usage were made popular in 1990 by management consultants James Champy and Michael Hammer.

**Relational database:** A database in which all data is stored in flat tables that meet the normalization rules. Tables are logically connected by matching columns of data. System data, such as access rights, descriptions, and data definitions are also stored in tables.

**Repetitive stress injury (RSI):** An injury that occurs from repeating a stressful action. For instance, several people have complained that constant typing damages their wrists. Ergonomic design, adjusting your workspace, and taking breaks are common recommendations to avoid repetitive stress.

**Report:** A printed summary or screen display that is produced on a regular basis by a database management system. The main sections of a report are: report header, page header, group/break header, detail, group/break footer, page footer, and report footer.

**Request for proposal (RFP):** A list of specifications and questions sent to vendors asking them to propose (sell) a product that might fill those needs.

**Resolution:** The number of dots or pixels displayed per inch of horizontal or vertical space. Input and output devices, as well as images and video, are measured by their resolution. Higher values of dots-per-inch yield more detailed images.

**Reverse engineering:** The process of taking older software and rewriting it to modernize it and make it easier to modify and enhance. Reverse engineering tools consist of software that reads the program code from the original software and converts it to a form that is easier to modify.

**Rivals:** Any group of firms that are competing for customers and sales. Similar to competitors, but "competition" carries an economic definition involving many firms. Even an industry with two firms can experience rivalry.

**Rivest-Shamir-Adelman (RSA):** Three mathematicians who developed and patented a dual-key encryption system. The term often refers to the encryption technique. It is based on the computational difficulty of factoring very large numbers into their prime components.

**Rocket scientists:** Mathematically trained financial analysts who build complex mathematical models of the stock market and help create and price new securities.

**Router:** A communication device that connects subnetworks together. Local messages remain within each subnetwork. Messages between subnetworks are sent to the proper location through the router.

**Row:** A horizontal element that contains all of the data to describe an entity or object in a relational database or spreadsheet.

**Rules:** A set of conditions that describe a problem or a potential response. Generally expressed as "If . . . Then" conditions. Used by expert systems to analyze new problems and suggest alternatives.

**Sampler:** An input device that reads electrical signals from a microphone and stores the sound as a collection of numbers. It measures the frequency and amplitude of the sound waves thousands of times per second.

**Scalability:** The ability to buy a faster computer as needed and transfer all software and data without modification. True scalability enables users to buy a smaller computer today and upgrade later without incurring huge conversion costs.

**Scrolling region:** On a data entry form, a subform or section that is designed to collect multiple rows of data. Much like a spreadsheet, the user can move back and forth to alter or examine prior entries.

**Secondary storage:** Data storage devices that hold data even if they lose power. Typically cheaper than RAM, but slower. Disk drives are common secondary storage devices.

**Serifs:** The small lines, curlicues, and ornamentation on many typefaces. They generally make it easier for people to read words and sentences on printed output. Sans serif

typefaces have more white space between characters and are often used for signs and displays that must be read from a longer distance.

**Sign-off:** In a systems development life-cycle approach, the approval that managers must give to forms, reports, and computations at various stages of the development. This approval is given when they sign the appropriate documents.

**Simulation:** Models are used to examine what might happen if we decide to make changes to the process, to see how the system will react to external events, or to examine relationships in more detail.

**Social legitimacy:** At one time, mainstream organizations were identified by the quality of their presentation and their image. Large firms spend millions of dollars on graphic artists, professional designers, and professional printing. The decreasing cost of computers enables even small organizations to create an image that is hard to distinguish from large organizations.

**Software:** A collection of computer programs that are algorithms or logical statements that control the hardware.

**Software maintenance:** The act of fixing problems, altering reports, or extending an existing system to improve it. It refers to changes in the software, not to hardware tasks such as cleaning printers.

**Software piracy:** The act of copying software without paying the copyright owner. With few exceptions (e.g., backup), copying software is illegal. Companies and individuals who are caught have to pay thousands of dollars in penalties and risk going to jail. It is commonly accepted that piracy takes money away from the development of improved software.

**Software suites:** Collections of software packages that are designed to operate together. Theoretically, data from each package can be easily shared with data from the others. So word processors can incorporate graphics, and spreadsheets can retrieve data from the database management system. Suites are often sold at a substantial discount compared to buying each package separately.

**Sound:** One of the basic data types. There are two methods to describe sound: samples or MIDI. Digitized (sampled) sound is based on a specified sampling and playback rate, and fits into frequency and amplitude (volume) ranges.

**Speech recognition:** The ability of a computer to capture spoken words, convert them into text, and then take some action based on the command.

**SQL:** A structured query language supported by most major database management systems. The most common command is of the form: SELECT *column list* FROM *table list* JOIN *how tables are related* WHERE *condition* ORDER BY *columns*.

**Standard operating procedures:** A set of procedures that define how employees and managers should deal with certain situations.

**Standards:** An agreement that specifies certain technical definitions. Standards can be established by committees or evolve over time through market pressures. As technology changes, new standards are created.

**Static integration:** A means of combining data from two documents. A copy of the original is placed into the new document. Because it is static, changes made to the original document are not automatically updated. *See also* Dynamic integration.

**Statistical quality control (SQC):** The statistical analysis of measurement data to improve quality. Several statistical calculations and graphs are used to determine whether fluctuations are purely random or represent major changes that need to be corrected.

**Strategic decisions:** Strategic decisions involve changing the overall structure of the firm. They are long-term decisions and are unstructured. They represent an attempt to gain a competitive advantage over your rivals. They are usually difficult and risky decisions. MIS support for strategic decisions typically consists of gathering, analyzing, and presenting data on rivals, customers, and suppliers.

**Structured decisions:** Decisions that can be defined by a set of rules or procedures. They can be highly detailed, but they are defined without resorting to vague definitions.

**Structured walkthrough:** A review process in which the objective is to reveal problems, inaccuracies, ambiguities, and omissions in the systems design before the program code is finalized. The users are presented with a prototype or mockup of the proposed system.

**Switch:** A network device used to connect machines. Unlike a router, a switch creates a virtual circuit that is used by a single machine at a time.

**Switching costs:** The costs incurred in creating a similar information system when a customer switches to a rival firm. Information technology creates switching costs because customers would have to convert data, re-create reports, and retrain users.

**Synthesizer:** An electronic device to convert electrical signals into sound. One basic technique is FM synthesis, which generates and combines fixed waves to achieve the desired sound. A newer method combines short digitized samples of various instruments with waveforms to create more realistic sounds.

**Sysop:** System operator. Person in charge of an electronic bulletin board who organizes files and controls access and privileges.

**System:** A collection of interrelated objects that work toward some goal.

**Systems analysis and design:** A refinement of the scientific method that is used to analyze and build information systems.

**Systems analyst:** A common job in MIS. The analyst is responsible for designing new systems. Analysts must understand the business application and be able to communicate with users. Analysts must also understand technical specifications and programming details.

**Systems development life cycle (SDLC):** A formal method of designing and building information systems. There are five basic phases:(1) feasibility and planning, (2) systems analysis, (3) systems design, (4) implementation, and (5) maintenance and review.

**T1, T3:** An older communication link provided by phone companies. Used to carry digitized analog signals, it is being replaced with ISDN links. T1 refers to a group of 24 voice-grade lines and can carry 1.544 megabits per second (Mbps). A T2 trunk line is equivalent to 96 voice circuits providing 6.312 Mbps. T3 provides 44.736 Mbps, and T4 can carry 139,264 Mbps. Services can be leased at any of these levels, where greater bandwidth carries higher costs.

**Table:** A method of storing data in a relational database. Tables contain data for one entity or object. The columns represent attributes, and data for each item is stored in a single row. Each table must have a primary key.

**Tactical decisions:** Tactical decisions typically involve time frames of less than a year. They usually result in making relatively major changes to operations but staying within the existing structure of the organization. MIS support consists of databases, networks, integration, decision support systems, and expert systems.

**Telnet:** A method supported on the Internet that enables users of one computer to log on to a different computer. Once logged on to the new system, the user is treated as any other user on the system.

**Terabyte:** Approximately 1 trillion bytes of data. Technically, it is 2 to the 40th power.

**Text:** The simplest of the four basic data types, it also includes numbers. In its most basic form, text is made up of individual characters, which are stored in the computer as numbers. More sophisticated text is described by its typeface, font size, color, and orientation (rotation).

**Token Ring:** A communications protocol that describes when each machine can send messages. A machine can only transmit when it receives a special message called a token. When the message is finished or a time limit is reached, the token is passed to the next machine.

**Top-down development:** An approach to designing and building systems that begins with an analysis of the entire company and works down to increasing detail. A complete top-down approach is usually impossible because it takes too long to analyze everything. *See also* Bottom-up development.

**Total quality management (TQM):** A management doctrine that states that quality must be built into every process and item. Every step and each person must be dedicated to producing quality products and services.

**Transaction-processing system:** Transactions are exchanges between two parties. Transaction-processing systems record and collect this data for the organization. This data forms the foundation for all other information system capabilities. MIS support typically consists of databases, communication networks, and security controls.

**Transborder data flow (TBDF):** The transfer of data across national boundaries. Some countries place restrictions on the transfer of data, especially data that relates to citizens (and of course, data related to "national security"). Some people have discussed taxing the flow of data.

**Triggered rule:** In an expert system, if a rule is used in an application, it is said to have been triggered or fired.

**Trojan horse:** A special program that hides inside another program. Eventually, when the main program is run, the Trojan horse program might delete files, display a message, or copy data to an external computer.

**True color:** Humans can distinguish about 16 million colors. Devices that can display that many colors are said to display true color. It requires the device to use 3 bytes (24 bits) for each pixel.

**Turing test:** A test proposed by Alan Turing in which a machine would be judged "intelligent" if the software could use conversation to fool a human into thinking it was talking with a person instead of a machine.

**Twisted-pair cable:** Common dual-line wire. Often packaged as three or four pairs of wires. The cable can be run for only a limited distance, and the signal is subject to interference.

**Typeface:** A defined way to draw a set of text characters. Several thousand typefaces have been created to meet different artistic and communication needs. A common characterization is serif and sans serif typefaces.

**Unicode:** An international standard that defines character sets for every modern (living) language, and many extinct languages (e.g., Latin).

**Uninterruptable power supply (UPS):** A large battery and special circuitry that provides a buffer between the computer and the power supply. It protects the computer from spikes and brownouts.

**UNIX:** A popular operating system created by Bell Labs. It is designed to operate the same on hardware from several different vendors. Unfortunately, there are several varieties of UNIX, and software that operates on one version often must be modified to function on other machines.

**Unstable model:** A model that cannot be solved for a single solution. The solution might continually diverge, or it could oscillate between several alternatives. Generally due to insufficient or incorrect feedback mechanisms.

**Upload:** To transfer files from a local computer (usually a personal computer) to a distant computer. *See also* Download.

**Usenet:** *See* News groups.

**User resistance:** People often resist change. Implementation of a new system highlights this resistance. Managers and developers must prepare for this resistance and encourage users to change. Education and training are common techniques.

**Value chain:** A description of the many steps involved in creating a product or service. Each step adds value to the product or service. Managers need to evaluate the chain to find opportunities to expand the firm and gain more sales and profits.

**Vector image:** A stored collection of mathematical equations, representing lines, circles, and points. These equations can be rescaled to fit any output device or to any desired size. Users deal with the base objects, not the mathematical definitions.

**Version control:** Software that tracks changes made to other documents. Often used in software development to enable developers to go back to prior version.

**Vid$eo:** One of the basic data types. Video combines the attributes of images and sound. An important attribute is the frames-per-second definition. U.S. standard video operates at 30 frames-per-second, movie films run at 24 frames-per-second. Digitizing video requires capturing and playing back the frames at the appropriate speed.

**View:** A stored query. If you have a complex query that you have to run every week, you (or a database specialist) could create the query and save it as a view with its own name. It is then treated much like a simple table.

**Virtual reality (VR):** Virtual reality describes computer displays and techniques that are designed to provide a realistic image to user senses, including three-dimensional video, three-dimensional sound, and sensors that detect user movement that is translated to on-screen action.

**Virus:** A malicious program that hides inside another program. As the main program runs, the virus copies itself into other programs. At some point, the virus displays a message, shuts down the machine, or deletes all of the files.

**Visual BASIC:** A modern variation of the BASIC programming language created by Microsoft for application programming in Windows. A variation resides inside many of the Microsoft applications, enabling programmers to manipulate and exchange data among the database, spreadsheet, and word processor.

**Visual table of contents:** A graphical design method that shows how modules of a system are related. Versions of the technique are also used to display menu trees.

**Voice mail:** A messaging system similar to telephone answering machines but with additional features like message store and forward. You can use your computer to send messages to co-workers. There are tools that will read e-mail and fax messages over the phone, so managers can stay in touch while they are away from the computer.

**Voice recognition:** The ability of a computer to capture spoken words and convert them into text.

**Webmaster:** Specialized IS worker who is responsible for creating, maintaining, and revising a company's World Wide Web site. Webmasters use technical and artistic skills to create sites that attract browsers.

**Wide area network (WAN):** A network that is spread across a larger geographic area. In most cases, parts of the network are outside the control of a single firm. Long-distance connections often use public carriers.

**Window:** A portion of the computer screen. You can move each window or change its size. Windows enable you to display and use several applications on the screen at one time.

**Wisdom:** A level above knowledge. Wisdom represents intelligence, or the ability to analyze, learn, adapt to changing conditions, and create knowledge.

**Workflow software:** A type of groupware that is designed to automate forms handling and the flow of data in a company. Forms and reports are automatically routed to a list of users on the network. When each person adds comments or makes changes, it is routed to the next process.

**Workstations:** Computers attached to a network, designed for individual use. Typically, personal computers.

**World Wide Web (WWW):** A first attempt to set up an international database of information. Web browsers display graphical pages of information, including pictures. Hypertext connections enable you to get related information by clicking highlighted words.

**WORM (Write Once, Read Many) disk:** Similar to a CD-ROM, but it is easier to store data. Once data is written on the disk, it cannot be changed. Early WORM drives were superseded by lower-cost drives that can store data in standard CD-ROM format.

**WYSIWYG:** What you see is what you get. With a true WYSIWYG system, documents will look exactly the same on the screen as they do when printed. In addition to format, it means that the printer must have the same typefaces as the video display. Color printers use a system to match the colors on the monitor.

# Organization Index

# Subject Index

# *Photo Credits*